CASES AND MATERIALS

THE INTERNATIONAL LEGAL SYSTEM

SIXTH EDITION

by

MARY ELLEN O'CONNELL
Robert and Marion Short Chair in Law
and Research Professor of
International Dispute Resolution—Kroc Institute
University of Notre Dame

RICHARD F. SCOTT
Distinguished Professor of International Law
Thomas Jefferson School of Law
Professor of International Law Emeritus
The American University of Paris

NAOMI ROHT-ARRIAZA
Professor of Law
University of California
Hastings College of the Law

FOUNDATION PRESS
2010

THOMSON REUTERS

© 1971, 1981, 1988, 1995, 2001 FOUNDATION PRESS

© 2010 By THOMSON REUTERS/FOUNDATION PRESS

      195 Broadway, 9th Floor

      New York, NY 10007

      Phone Toll Free 1–877–888–1330

      Fax (212) 367–6799

      foundation–press.com

Printed in the United States of America

ISBN 978–1–59941–183–5

Mat #40510345

Dedicated to
The Rev. Theodore M. Hesburgh, C.S.C.,
and Peter, with love,

Lorraine, Karen, Jeffrey and Holly, with love,

and
Helen Roht, pioneer internationalist,
and Gilberto, Laura and Rafa, with love

PREFACE TO THE SIXTH EDITION

With each new edition of this casebook, its authors have reflected on the dramatic expansion and refinement of international law since the previous edition. This has certainly been true of international law since the 5th edition was published in 2001. Indeed, the whole history of international law is a history of dramatic expansion from its origins in Europe in the 17th century as a law for peaceful co-existence of states to today where it extends geographically to all parts of the globe and to most dimensions of international life. International law provides functional support to the international system and to humanity's aspirations for a more just, secure, and peaceful world.

More specifically, the functions of this body of law include the very creation and preservation of the international system, the provision of substantive rules of law to govern the relations of states among themselves and with international organizations, together with the fundamental rights of states, individuals and organizations in the system. These law-making functions are designed to "do justice" in those relations, to keep peace in the system, and to provide the durable means of facilitating the smooth conduct of international relations. The international legal system as we know it could not exist in any acceptable form without these applications of the rule of law.

Our view of the "international legal system" includes not only the traditional and evolving body of international law in the public sector but also the surrounding areas of the national law that bear on a state's conduct of foreign relations: the domestic constitutional systems' treatment of international law together with the domestic legislative and regulatory measures employed to implement international law. The domestic law feature of the system is the focus of Chapter 11 on "International Law in National and Regional Legal Systems", with material from the UK, France, U.S., Argentina, the European Union, and South Africa, but the topic appears throughout the casebook. We employ national and regional cases and legislation alongside international decisions and agreements to demonstrate both the complexity of the system and its uniqueness.

Material from other systems underscores that international law is very different from the domestic law of states. The casebook is designed to introduce students to this very different system with its unique means for law creation, application, and enforcement. We aim to introduce a whole legal curriculum in a book designed for a one semester course. The original authors of this casebook said the following in the preface to the first edition:

> We have done our best to make this book a teaching tool. It may be useful also to practitioners and even to scholars—at least at some

points. But what we have wanted most to do is to get the attention of today's law students, those men and women who, for better or worse, will have so much influence on how the world will go.[1]

The authors of the current edition have much the same aim. We have retained the first edition's goal of giving students a working knowledge of international law. Even in the first edition, however, the authors hoped only to build "trails toward the various advanced courses" in international law. That is all the more true of the current authors. In the intervening four decades international law has expanded exponentially. We very much encourage students to take additional courses in international law to build on the basic introduction found in this book. As international law has expanded, so have the opportunities for students to expand and deepen their knowledge of the system.

Nevertheless, while we encourage students to take more courses, it also our sincere belief that there is no substitute for a general introductory course, despite the inevitable constraint that many topics must be presented in abbreviated form. A general course provides students with knowledge of the foundations underlying the system as a whole—regardless of topic area. More importantly, a general course provides an understanding of the inter-connectedness of the system and the links between international law and other legal systems.

The current edition of the casebook was designed for just such a general course. It begins in Chapter 1 with a brief introduction to international law, its history, basic components, and some discussion of the nature of the world in which international law operates. Chapter 2 introduces the sources of international law and the basic processes of international law-making. Chapter 3 discusses the primary subjects of international law: states, individuals, and organizations of all kinds operating internationally. Chapter 4 reviews the scope of international law in terms of jurisdiction and immunity. Chapter 5 introduces human rights and Chapter 6 the law governing the world's environment and shared spaces. Chapter 7 is on the international economy. Chapter 8 concerns how responsibility for international legal wrongs is determined. Chapter 9 looks at dispute resolution, how claims are made and resolved at the international level. Chapter 10 sets out the basic rules for the lawful use of force, such as in self-defense. Chapter 11 introduces the place of international law in a variety of legal systems. Chapter 12 takes up a new question with this edition: has international law evolved from being primarily the law of an inter-state system to the law of a community? Some legal theorists suggest that as a body of law becomes more sophisticated, it fosters greater integration among the governed. Is international law having this impact on our world? Does this impact account for the concern registered by some about international law and their wish to limit its impact? In the world of today with its

---

1. JOSEPH MODESTE SWEENEY, COVEY T. OLIVER, & NOYES E. LEECH, CASES AND MATERIALS ON THE INTERNATIONAL LEGAL SYSTEM (1973).

extraordinary global challenges is it possible to limit international law? And if it were, what would be the cost of doing so? These are questions to consider as you pursue the materials in this casebook, and, perhaps, a career in international law.

We have made many changes to the last edition to meet these goals for the new edition. Nevertheless, we are very much indebted to all of our predecessors, but especially, Christopher Blakesly, Edwin Firmage, and Sharon Williams, authors of the fifth edition.

MARY ELLEN O'CONNELL
RICHARD F. SCOTT
NAOMI ROHT-ARRIAZA

January 2010

ACKNOWLEDGMENTS

We would like to thank Layla Krog of the Notre Dame Law School for exceptional office assistance. We would also like to thank our research assistants: Erin Watkins, Patrick Carrier, Rochelle Krebs, Kyle Sommer, Nino Guruli, Menaka Fernando, Sarah Newby, and Cara Hughes. At the Thomas Jefferson School of Law we would like to thank Professors Aaron Schwabach and Kenneth Vandevelde for comments on part of the draft manuscript, and the library staff, including Professor Karla Castetter, Patrick Meyer, Dorothy Hampton, Norma Dunn, June Macleod, Jane Larrington and Leigh Inman. Thanks also to Patti Ogden and Mary Cowsert of the Kresge Law Library of the Notre Dame Law School.

We would like to acknowledge our indebtedness to the following authors, publishers and organizations for giving us permission to reprint excerpts from the books, periodicals and other documents indicated below:

Oxford University Press, excerpt from, Mary Ellen O'Connell, The Power and Purpose of International Law, 3–13 (2008).

Routledge/Taylor & Francis Group, excerpt from, Richard W. Mansbach and Kirsten L. Rafferty, Introduction to Global Politics, 6–9 (2008).

Transaction Publishers, excerpt from, Hans Maull, On the Concept of International Order, in Challenges of Globalization, 93–108 (2005).

Addis, Adeno. Imagining the International Community: The Constitutive Dimension of Universal Jurisdiction. Human Rights Quarterly 31:1 (2009), 145–150. © 2009 The Johns Hopkins University Press. Reprinted with permission of The Johns Hopkins University Press.

University of Pennsylvania Press, excerpt from, Naomi Roht–Arriaza, The Pinochet Effect, vii–xii (2005).

Oxford University Press, excerpt from, Ian Brownlie, Principles of Public International Law, 6–12 (2008).

Oxford University Press, excerpt from, Robert Jennings and Arthur Watts, Oppenheim's International Law, 146 (1996).

Oxford University Press, excerpt from, Brad Roth, Governmental Illegitimacy in International Law, 253ff (1999).

Columbia Law School, excerpt from, Mary Ellen O'Connell, "Enhancing the Status of Non–State Actors," in Columbia J. of Transnat'l L., 437–440 (2005).

Oxford University Press, excerpt from, Thomas Schultz, "Carving up the Internet: Jurisdiction, Legal Orders, and the Private/Public International Law Interface," in European Journal of International Law (2008).

South Dakota Law Review, excerpt from, Arthur J. Goldberg, "The Shoot–Out at the Libyan Self–Styled People's Bureau," 30 S.D. L. Rev. 1 (1984).

Cambridge University Press, excerpt from, Naomi Roht–Arriaza, The New Landscape of Transitional Justice, Transitional Justice in the Twenty–First Century: Beyond Truth versus Justice (Naomi Roht–Arriaza & Javier Mariezcurrena eds., 2006).

Center for Human Rights & Humanitarian Law, excerpt from, Fiona McKay, Victim Participation in Proceedings before the International Criminal Court, 15 No. 3 Human Rights Brief 1 (2008).

Stanford Environmental Law Journal, excerpt from, Harro van Asselt and Joyeeta Gupta, Stretching Too Far? Developing Countries and the Role of Flexibility Mechanisms Beyond Kyoto, 28 Stanford Environmental Law Journal 311, 331 (2009).

Virginia Environmental Law Journal, Harry Schreiber, Ocean Governance and the Marine Fisheries Crisis: Two Decades of Innovation and Frustration, 20 Virginia Environmental Law Journal 119 (2001).

George Washington International Law Review, excerpt from, David Freestone, A Decade of the Law of the Sea Convention: Is it a Success?, 39 George Washington International Law Review 499 (2007).

The American Society of International Law, excerpt from, Peter L. Lallas, Current Development: The Stockholm Convention on Persistent Organic Pollutants, 95 American Journal International Law 692 (2001).

Ecology Law Quarterly, excerpt from, John S. Applegate, Synthesizing TSCA and REACH: Practical Principles for Chemical Regulation Reform, 35 Ecology Law Quarterly 721 (2008).

Yale Center for Environmental Law and Policy, excerpt from, Daniel C. Esty and Maria H. Ivanova, Making International Environmental Efforts Work: The Case for a Global Environmental Organization, Yale Center for Environmental Law and Policy (2001).

Foundation Press, excerpt from, David Hunter, James Salzman and Durwood Zaelke, International Environmental Law and Policy, 1239–1243 (Foundation Press 3d ed. 2007).

American Society of International Law, excerpt from, Jose Alvarez, "The Emerging Foreign Direct Investment Regime," in Proceedings of the Annual Meeting, 2 (2005).

American Society of International Law, excerpt from, Brice Clagget, "Title III of the Helms–Burton," in Am. J. of Int'l L., 2 (1996).

American Society of International Law, excerpt from, Thomas Franck, "Proportionality," in Am. J. of Int'l L., 742–752 (2008).

American Society of International Law, excerpt from, David D. Caron, "The Nature of the Iran–United States Claims Tribunal and the Evolving

Structure of International Dispute Resolution," in Am. J. of Int'l L., 104 (1990).

American Society of International Law, excerpt from, Sir Robert Y. Jennings, "The Proliferation of Adjudicatory Bodies: Dangers and Possible Answers," in Vol. 9 of the ASIL Bulletin, 2–7 (1995).

American Society of International Law, excerpt from, Jack M. Beard, "The Shortcomings of Indeterminacy in Arms Control Regimes: The Case of the Biological Weapons Convention," in Am. J. of Int'l L., 271–275 (2007).

Oxford University Press, excerpt from, Nout van Woudenberg, "The Long and Winding Road Towards an Instrument on Cluster Munitions," in J. of Conflict and Security L. (2007).

Columbia Journal of Transnational Law, Janet Koven Levit, The Constitutionalization of Human Rights in Argentina: Problem or Promise?, 37 Columbia Journal of Transnational Law 281 (1999).

Oxford University Press, excerpt from, Alexander Orakhelashvili, "The Idea of European International Law," in European J. of Int'l L. (2006).

American Society of International Law, excerpt from, Makau Mutua, "What is TWAIL?," in Proceedings of the Annual Meeting, 31–34 (2000).

Chicago Journal of International Law, excerpt from, David P. Fidler, "The Return of the Standard of Civilization," 2 Chi. J. Int'l L. 137 (2001).

Columbia Human Rights Law Review, excerpt from Dianne Otto, "Rethinking the Universality of Human Rights Law," Columbia Hum. Rights L. Rev., 1–4, 31 (1997).

American Society of International Law, excerpt from, Detlev F. Vagts, "Hegemonic International Law," in Am. J. of Int'l L., 843–846 (2001).

Springer, excerpt from, W. Michael Reisman, "The Democratization of Contemporary International Law–Making Processes and the Differentiation of Their Application," in Developments of International Law in Treaty Making, Rüdiger Wolfrum and Volker Röben, eds., 21–24 (2005).

Koninklijke BRILL NV, excerpt from, C.G. Weeramantry, Universalising International Law (2004).

Council of Europe, excerpt from "Council of Europe at a Glance" (2007).

Organization for Economic Cooperation and Development, excerpts from "Overview of the OECD: What Is It? History? Who Does What? Structure of the Organization? What is it?" (2007).

International Energy Agency, excerpts from "About the IEA (International Energy Agency" (2007).

International Energy Agency, excerpt from Richard Scott, "The History of the International Energy Agency," Vol 1, 61 (2007).

Journal of World Investment and Trade, excerpt from Kaj Hober, "The Energy Charter Treaty, an Overview," 323 (2007).

American Law Institute, Restatement of the Law (Third) "The Foreign Relations Law of the United States," 492 (1987).

Organization for Economic Cooperation and Development, excerpts from "Open Markets Matter: The Benefits of Trade and Investment Liberalization," Policy Briefs No. 8, 1, 4 (1998).

World Trade Organization, excerpts from "What is the World Trade Organization?" (1999).

Organization for Economic Cooperation and Development, excerpts from "Resolution of the Council on the Draft Convention on the Protection of Foreign Property," 3, 23 (1967).

American Society of International Law, "European Union: Demarches Protesting the Cuban Liberty and Democratic Solidarity (Libertad) Act," in International Legal Materials, 397 (1996).

American Society of International Law, excerpts from "Organization of American States: Inter-American Juridical Committee Opinion Examining the U.S. Helms-Burton Act", in International Legal Materials, 1322 (1996).

American Society of International Law, excerpts from "Mexico: Act to Protect Trade and Investment From Foreign Norms That Contravene International Law," in International Legal Materials 133 (1996).

Oxford University Press, excerpt from, Robert Jennings and Arthur Watts, Oppenheim's International Law, 127, 146, 341ff (9th ed., 1996).

SUMMARY OF CONTENTS

TABLE OF CONTENTS

TABLE OF CASES

Principal cases are in bold type. Non-principal cases are in roman type. References are to Pages.

CASES AND MATERIALS

THE INTERNATIONAL LEGAL SYSTEM

CHAPTER 1

INTRODUCTION TO THE INTERNATIONAL LEGAL SYSTEM

International law is the world's law. It emerged long before the rise of the modern state system in Europe in the 17th century. Early international law scholars conceived of law as having universal application and importance to people everywhere. As the state system developed, international law developed along with it to serve the needs of states. National leaders looked to international law to find the very definition of a "state" and the answers to such essential questions as the extent of land and maritime boundaries, the making of international agreements, and the appropriate means for settling disputes peacefully. By the time the first edition of this book was published in 1973, it was possible for the authors to describe international law as a "legal system." They stressed that an important feature of the system was the inter-connection between international law and national legal systems, making both more effective for the work they do.

In this edition of the book, the authors still see international law as a system of law that is deeply inter-connected with national legal systems, but we also see significant changes in international law and the state system since 1973. While states dominated consideration in the first edition, that dominance is no longer warranted. Individuals, organizations, and the international community itself are playing ever-larger roles in the making, application, and enforcement of international law. These actors other than states are increasingly the focus of international law. Throughout this edition, therefore, as we discuss the purpose, structure and content

1

of the international legal system, we will also consider how international law is evolving as a consequence of change in the world.

In the first section below we introduce the international legal system. The section begins with the problem of piracy—individuals perpetrating crimes beyond the boundaries of any one state. This problem demonstrates why the world needs international law. Piracy is a challenge that pre-dates the rise of the state system and persists to this day. It may be a particularly dramatic example of a problem requiring a response at the international level, but it is hardly unique. The excerpt by Mary Ellen O'Connell surveys the major categories of global challenges for which international law is especially suited to provide responses. Problems of war and peace, human rights, the economy, and the environment require a coordinated answer through international and national law.

Despite what appears to be the self-evident need for international law, there are skeptics who deny that international law is really law or deny that it is really law for powerful states. O'Connell responds to these skeptics. She accepts that international law differs from national law, but argues that it is characterized by the same core features essential to any system of law. International law, like most national law, is recognized as law by the community it governs. Moreover, international law is not sealed off from national or regional legal systems. The systems interact, providing—theoretically at least—for comprehensive law, without gaps, between the diverse communities in which we live. The various categories of law mutually reinforce the authority of the other.

After considering the basic features of international law and arguments as to its claim to be law, the chapter moves on to consider the world in which international law operates. In Section B we provide an overview of international relations today. The section focuses particularly on indications of future trends. Ultimately, law provides for order today by forecasting where future regulation is needed. Having some idea of where the world may be heading should provide context for assessing current international law and thinking prospectively about how it should continue to develop. The authors see the shift from a system where states predominate to one where the international community is the more accurate descriptive concept to be highly significant for understanding international law. In excerpts from judicial decisions and the writings of authors, we present indications of the emergence of a community at the international level. Some of the readings describe international law as one of the driving forces toward community. In another excerpt, Naomi Roht–Arriaza describes the dramatic events that led to holding an individual, the former dictator of Chile, General Augusto Pinochet, accountable in one state for crimes committed in another. This was a notable step on the road to community. Yet, it invites the question, how far did we go with that step?

Awareness of how the world is developing fosters understanding of the system of international law today as well as the direction of future trends. The discussion of the world of international law is also intended to encourage thinking about how international law can be improved.

Throughout the book, we raise the question how can international law work better? To respond to this question it is essential to know what international law is and how the world is evolving. Indeed, the book follows three themes throughout: what is international law, what is the nature of the world we live in, and how can international law be developed to meet the needs of our world more effectively? In this chapter we introduce these themes.

A.   THE NATURE OF THE INTERNATIONAL LEGAL SYSTEM

This section provides a concise introduction to the nature of international law, a topic that is explored throughout the book. It uses as a working definition that international law is the system of rules, principles, and processes intended to govern relations at the interstate level, including the relations among states, organizations, and individuals.* The section begins by looking at a problem that is quintessentially the type of problem that is the focus of international legal regulation, namely, piracy. Because pirates generally commit their crimes on the high seas beyond the jurisdiction of states, the suppression of piracy requires law that is applicable beyond national jurisdiction. Despite the existence of many such problems—indeed, more all the time—some of the giants of political and legal theory have raised doubts over the centuries about the proper classification of international law as law. We take up those doubts in Part 2 of this section. Part 3 considers briefly the relationship of international law and national law. It is worth noting that despite skepticism about international law as law discussed in Part 2, national legal systems invariably have legal principles clarifying the inter-relationship of the national legal system with the international one, providing additional evidence of the acceptance that international law is, indeed, law. We explore the international law—national law relationship in more detail in Chapter 11.

1.   PIRACY AND OTHER CHALLENGES ON THE INTERNATIONAL LAW AGENDA

Robbery and acts of violence on the high seas were problems known to the ancient Greeks, Romans, Chinese, and others. They remain problems

---

* A note on terminology: This section and the book generally discuss "public" international law, law of concern to governments and other "public" actors. An earlier term for this law was the "law of nations." Jeremy Bentham (1748–1832) coined the term "international law" and it has now replaced "law of nations." Public international law is typically distinguished from "private" international law, law governing the interactions of private parties that cross international boundaries. Private international law is sometimes referred to as "conflicts of law" because it includes rules for selecting the applicable national rules from among a number of possibilities. "Transnational" law refers to both public and private international law, often when both types of law are relevant. "Comparative" law is a method of legal analysis that compares one jurisdiction's law on a subject with another's. Foreign law is the law of another jurisdiction other than one's own. Foreign law may sometimes be the applicable law in one's national court under rules of conflicts of law, as may international law.

today. Piracy is the very sort of problem that demonstrates why we need international law. Piracy also indicates the long heritage of international law and the interconnections between international law and national legal systems. Piracy requires a coordinated international response given the ability of these criminals to move beyond any one state's jurisdiction. The United States Constitution of 1789 refers to the "crime of piracy, as defined by the law of nations." In the case excerpted below we see a national court—the U.S. Supreme Court—enforcing the international law on piracy against an individual of unstated nationality for acts against a Spanish ship at sea beyond U.S. jurisdiction. The Supreme Court uses an earlier term for international law, "the law of nations", but it is clearly talking about the same body of rules that the United Nations Security Council invoked 200 years later as seen in the second excerpt, a resolution addressing the problem of piracy.

U.S. v. Smith

Supreme Court of the United States
5 Wheat. 153, 18 U.S. 153, 5 L.Ed. 57 (1820)

February 25, 1820.

THIS was an indictment for piracy against the prisoner Thomas Smith, before the Circuit Court of Virginia, on the act of Congress, of the 3d of March, 1819, c. 76.

The jury found a special verdict as follows: "We, of the jury, find, that the prisoner, Thomas Smith, in the month of March, 1819, and others, were part of the crew of a private armed vessel, called the Creollo, (commissioned by the government of Buenos Ayres, a colony then at war with Spain,) and lying in the port of Margaritta; that in the month of March, 1819, the said prisoner and others of the crew mutinied, confined their officer, left the vessel, and in the said port of Margaritta, seized by violence a vessel called the Irresistible, a private armed vessel, lying in that port, commissioned by the government of Artigas, who was also at war with Spain; that the said prisoner and others, having so possessed themselves of the said vessel, the Irresistible, appointed their officers, proceeded to sea on a cruize, without any documents or commission whatever; and while on that cruize, in the month of April, 1819, on the high seas, committed the offence charged in the indictment, by the plunder and robbery of the Spanish vessel therein mentioned. If the plunder and robbery aforesaid be piracy under the act of the Congress of the United States, entitled, 'An act to protect the commerce of the United States, and punish the crime of piracy,' then we find the said prisoner guilty; if the plunder and robbery, above stated, be not piracy under the said act of Congress, then we find him, not guilty."

The Circuit Court divided on the question, whether this be piracy as defined by the law of nations, so as to be punishable under the act of Congress, of the 3d of March, 1819, and thereupon the question was certified to this Court for its decision.

Feb. 21st.

The Attorney General, for the United States, contended, that Congress, by referring to the law of nations for a definition of the crime of piracy, had duly exercised the power given them by the constitution, "to define and punish piracies and felonies committed on the high seas, and offences against the law of nations." By this reference they adopt the definition of the offence given by the writers on public law. All these writers concur in defining it to be, depredation on the seas, without the authority of a commission, or beyond its authority. If there be any defect of precision or slight uncertainty in the definitions of the crime of piracy given by different writers on the law of nations, it is no more than what is to be found in common law writers on the crime of murder. Yet we are constantly referred by the legislature to the common law for the definition of murder and other felonies which are mentioned in statutory provisions. But there is no defect in the definition of piracy by the authorities to which we are referred by this act. The definition given by them is certain, consistent, and unanimous; and pirates being hostes humani generis, are punishable in the tribunals of all nations. All nations are engaged in a league against them for the mutual defence and safety of all. This renders it the more fit and proper that there should be a uniform rule as to the definition of the crime, which can only be drawn from the law of nations, as the only code universally known and recognized by the people of all countries.

Mr. Webster, contra, argued, that the special verdict did not contain sufficient facts to enable the Court to pronounce the prisoner guilty of the offence charged. The facts found, do not necessarily infer his guilt, but, on the contrary, are consistent with his innocence; inasmuch as it appears that he was one of the crew of a vessel belonging to Buenos Ayres, although not acting at the time when the supposed offence was committed under the commission of that colony, but acting as a non-commissioned captor, and as such, seizing the property of Spanish subjects on the high seas. But even supposing the offence to be well found by the special verdict, it cannot be punished under this act, because the law is not a constitutional exercise of the power of Congress to define the crime of piracy. Congress is bound to define it in terms, and is not at liberty to leave it to be ascertained by judicial interpretation. To refer to the law of nations for a definition of the crime, is not a definition; for the very thing to be ascertained by the definition, is the law of nations on the subject. The constitution evidently presupposes that this crime, and other offences committed on the high seas, were not defined with sufficient precision by the law of nations, or any other law, to form a rule of conduct; or it would merely have given Congress the power of punishing these offences, without also imposing upon it the duty of defining them. The writers on public law do not define the crime of piracy with precision and certainty. It was this very defect which rendered it necessary that Congress should define, in terms, before it proceeded to exercise the power of punishing the offence. Congress must define it as the constitution has defined treason, not by referring to the law of nations in one case, or to the common law in the other, but by giving a distinct, intelligible explanation of the nature of the offence in the act itself.

Feb. 25th.

■ MR. JUSTICE STORY delivered the opinion of the court.

The act of Congress upon which this indictment is founded provides, "that if any person or persons whatsoever, shall, upon the high seas, commit the crime of piracy, as defined by the law of nations, and such offender or offenders shall be brought into, or found in the United States, every such offender or offenders shall, upon conviction thereof, &c. be punished with death."

The first point made at the bar is, whether this enactment be a constitutional exercise of the authority delegated to Congress upon the subject of piracies. The constitution declares, that Congress shall have power "to define and punish piracies and felonies committed on the high seas, and offences against the law of nations." The argument which has been urged in behalf of the prisoner is, that Congress is bound to define, in terms, the offence of piracy, and is not at liberty to leave it to be ascertained by judicial interpretation. * * *

In our judgment, the construction contended for proceeds upon too narrow a view of the language of the constitution. The power given to Congress is not merely "to define and punish piracies;" if it were, the words "to define," would seem almost superfluous, since the power to punish piracies would be held to include the power of ascertaining and fixing the definition of the crime. And it has been very justly observed, in a celebrated commentary, that the definition of piracies might have been left without inconvenience to the law of nations, though a legislative definition of them is to be found in most municipal codes. But the power is also given "to define and punish felonies on the high seas, and offences against the law of nations." The term "felonies," has been supposed in the same work, not to have a very exact and determinate meaning in relation to offences at the common law committed within the body of a county. However this may be, in relation to offences on the high seas, it is necessarily somewhat indeterminate, since the term is not used in the criminal jurisprudence of the admiralty in the technical sense of the common law. Offences, too, against the law of nations, cannot, with any accuracy, be said to be completely ascertained and defined in any public code recognised by the common consent of nations. In respect, therefore, as well to felonies on the high seas as to offences against the law of nations, there is a peculiar fitness in giving the power to define as well as to punish; and there is not the slightest reason to doubt that this consideration had very great weight in producing the phraseology in question.

But supposing Congress were bound in all the cases included in the clause under consideration to define the offence, still there is nothing which restricts it to a mere logical enumeration in detail of all the facts constituting the offence. Congress may as well define by using a term of a known and determinate meaning, as by an express enumeration of all the particulars included in that term. That is certain which is by necessary reference made certain. When the act of 1790 declares, that any person who shall commit the crime of robbery, or murder, on the high seas, shall be deemed a pirate, the crime is not less clearly ascertained than it would be by using the definitions of these terms as they are found in our treatises of the common law. In fact, by such a reference, the definitions are necessarily included, as much as if they stood in the text of the act. In respect to murder, where "malice aforethought" is of the essence of the offence, even if the common law definition were quoted in express terms, we should still be driven to deny that the definition was perfect, since the meaning of "malice aforethought" would remain to be gathered from the common law. There would then be no end to our difficulties, or our definitions, for each would involve some terms which might still require some new explanation. Such a construction of the constitution is, therefore, wholly inadmissible. To define piracies, in the sense of the constitution, is merely to enumerate the crimes which shall constitute piracy; and this may be done either by a reference to crimes having a technical name, and determinate extent, or by enumerating the acts in detail, upon which the punishment is inflicted.

It is next to be considered, whether the crime of piracy is defined by the law of nations with reasonable certainty. What the law of nations on this subject is, may be ascertained by consulting the works of jurists, writing professedly on public law; or by the general usage and practice of nations; or by judicial decisions recognising and enforcing that law. There is scarcely a writer on the law of nations, who does not allude to piracy as a crime of a settled and determinate nature; and whatever may be the diversity of definitions, in other respects all writers concur, in holding, that robbery, or forcible depredations upon the sea, animo furandi, is piracy. The same doctrine is held by all the great writers on maritime law, in terms that admit of no reasonable doubt. The common law, too, recognises and punishes piracy as an offence, not against its own municipal code, but as an offence against the law of nations, (which is part of the common law,) as an offence against the universal law of society, a pirate being deemed an enemy of the human race. Indeed, until the statute of 28th of Henry VIII. ch. 15. piracy was punishable in England only in the admiralty as a civil law offence; and that statute, in changing the jurisdiction, has been universally admitted not to have changed the nature of the offence. Sir Charles Hedges, in his charge at the Admiralty sessions, in the case of Rex v. Dawson, (5 State Trials,) declared in emphatic terms, that "piracy is only a sea term for robbery, piracy being a robbery committed within the jurisdiction of the admiralty." Sir Leoline Jenkins, too, on a like occasion, declared that "a robbery, when committed upon the sea, is what we call piracy;" and he cited the civil law writers, in proof. And it is manifest from the language of Sir William Blackstone, in his comments on piracy, that he considered the common law definition as distinguishable in no essential respect from that of the law of nations. So that, whether we advert to writers on the common law, or the maritime law, or the law of nations, we shall find that they universally treat of piracy as an offence against the law of nations, and that its true definition by that law is robbery upon the sea. And the general practice of all nations in punishing all persons, whether natives or foreigners, who have committed this offence against any persons whatsoever, with whom they are in amity, is a conclusive proof that the offence is supposed to depend, not upon the particular provisions of any municipal code, but upon the law of nations, both for its definition and punishment. We have, therefore, no hesitation in declaring, that piracy, by the law of nations, is robbery upon the sea, and that it is sufficiently and constitutionally defined by the fifth section of the act of 1819.

Another point has been made in this case, which is, that the special verdict does not contain sufficient facts upon which the Court can pronounce that the prisoner is guilty of piracy. We are of a different opinion. The special verdict finds that the prisoner is guilty of the plunder and robbery charged in the indictment; and finds certain additional facts from which it is most manifest that he and his associates were, at the time of committing the offence, freebooters upon the sea, not under the acknowledged authority, or deriving protection from the flag or commission of any government. If, under such circumstances, the offence be not piracy, it is difficult to conceive any which would more completely fit the definition.

It is to be certified to the Circuit Court, that upon the facts stated, the case is piracy, as defined by the law of nations, so as to be punishable under the act of Congress of the 3d of March, 1819.

■ MR. JUSTICE LIVINGSTON dissented.

United Nations   **S**/RES/1851 (2008)

 Security Council   Distr.: General
                                        16 December 2008

Resolution 1851 (2008)
Adopted by the Security Council at its 6046th meeting, on
16 December 2008

The Security Council,

Recalling its previous resolutions concerning the situation in Somalia, especially resolutions 1814 (2008), 1816 (2008), 1838 (2008), 1844 (2008), and 1846 (2008),

Continuing to be gravely concerned by the dramatic increase in the incidents of piracy and armed robbery at sea off the coast of Somalia in the last six months, and by the threat that piracy and armed robbery at sea against vessels pose to the prompt, safe and effective delivery of humanitarian aid to Somalia, and *noting* that pirate attacks off the coast of Somalia have become more sophisticated and daring and have expanded in their geographic scope, notably evidenced by the hijacking of the M/V Sirius Star 500 nautical miles off the coast of Kenya and subsequent unsuccessful attempts well east of Tanzania,

Reaffirming its respect for the sovereignty, territorial integrity, political independence and unity of Somalia, including Somalia's rights with respect to offshore natural resources, including fisheries, in accordance with international law,

Further reaffirming that international law, as reflected in the United Nations Convention on the Law of the Sea of 10 December 1982 (UNC-LOS), sets out the legal framework applicable to combating piracy and armed robbery at sea, as well as other ocean activities,

Again taking into account the crisis situation in Somalia, and the lack of capacity of the Transitional Federal Government (TFG) to interdict, or upon interdiction to prosecute pirates or to patrol and secure the waters off the coast of Somalia, including the international sea lanes and Somalia's territorial waters,

Noting the several requests from the TFG for international assistance to counter piracy off its coast, including the letter of 9 December 2008 from the President of Somalia requesting the international community to assist the TFG in taking all necessary measures to interdict those who use Somali territory and airspace to plan, facilitate or undertake acts of piracy and armed robbery at sea, and the 1 September 2008 letter from the President of Somalia to the Secretary–General of the UN expressing the appreciation of the TFG to the Security Council for its assistance and expressing the TFG's willingness to consider working with other States and regional organizations to combat piracy and armed robbery off the coast of Somalia,

Welcoming the launching of the EU operation Atalanta to combat piracy off the coast of Somalia and to protect vulnerable ships bound for Somalia, as well as the efforts by the North Atlantic Treaty Organization, and other States acting in a national capacity in cooperation with the TFG to suppress piracy off the coast of Somalia,

Also welcoming the recent initiatives of the Governments of Egypt, Kenya, and the Secretary–General's Special Representative for Somalia, and the United Nations Office on Drugs and Crime (UNODC) to achieve effective measures to remedy the causes, capabilities, and incidents of piracy and armed robbery off the coast of Somalia, and *emphasizing* the need for current and future counter-piracy operations to effectively coordinate their activities,

Noting with concern that the lack of capacity, domestic legislation, and clarity about how to dispose of pirates after their capture, has hindered more robust international action against the pirates off the coast of Somalia and in some cases led to pirates being released without facing justice, and *reiterating* that the 1988 Convention for the Suppression of Unlawful Acts Against the Safety of Maritime Navigation ("SUA Convention") provides for parties to create criminal offences, establish jurisdiction, and accept delivery of persons responsible for or suspected of seizing or exercising control over a ship by force or threat thereof or any other form of intimidation,

Welcoming the report of the Monitoring Group on Somalia of 20 November 2008 (S/2008/769), and *noting* the role piracy may play in financing embargo violations by armed groups,

Determining that the incidents of piracy and armed robbery at sea in the waters off the coast of Somalia exacerbate the situation in Somalia which continues to constitute a threat to international peace and security in the region,

Acting under Chapter VII of the Charter of the United Nations,

1. *Reiterates* that it condemns and deplores all acts of piracy and armed robbery against vessels in waters off the coast of Somalia;

2. *Calls* upon States, regional and international organizations that have the capacity to do so, to take part actively in the fight against piracy and armed robbery at sea off the coast of Somalia, in particular, consistent with this resolution, resolution 1846 (2008), and international law, by deploying naval vessels and military aircraft and through seizure and disposition of boats, vessels, arms and other related equipment used in the commission of piracy and armed robbery at sea off the coast of Somalia, or for which there are reasonable grounds for suspecting such use;

3. *Invites* all States and regional organizations fighting piracy off the coast of Somalia to conclude special agreements or arrangements with countries willing to take custody of pirates in order to embark law enforcement officials ("shipriders") from the latter countries, in particular countries in the region, to facilitate the investigation and prosecution of persons detained as a result of operations conducted under this resolution for acts of piracy and armed robbery at sea off the coast of Somalia, provided that the advance consent of the TFG is obtained for the exercise of third state jurisdiction by shipriders in Somali territorial waters and that such agreements or arrangements do not prejudice the effective implementation of the SUA Convention;

4. *Encourages* all States and regional organizations fighting piracy and armed robbery at sea off the coast of Somalia to establish an international cooperation mechanism to act as a common point of contact between and among states, regional and international organizations on all aspects of combating piracy and armed robbery at sea off Somalia's coast; and *recalls* that future recommendations on ways to ensure the long-term security of international navigation off the coast of Somalia, including the long-term security of WFP maritime deliveries to Somalia and a possible coordination and leadership role for the United Nations in this regard to rally Member States and regional organizations to counter piracy and armed robbery at sea off the coast of Somalia are to be detailed in a report by the Secretary–General no later than three months after the adoption of resolution 1846;

5. *Further encourages* all states and regional organizations fighting piracy and armed robbery at sea off the coast of Somalia to consider creating a centre in the region to coordinate information relevant to piracy and armed robbery at sea off the coast of Somalia, to increase regional capacity with assistance of UNODC to arrange effective shiprider agreements or arrangements consistent with UNCLOS and to implement the SUA Convention, the United Nations Convention against Transnational Organized Crime and other relevant instruments to which States in the

region are party, in order to effectively investigate and prosecute piracy and armed robbery at sea offences;

6. In response to the letter from the TFG of 9 December 2008, *encourages* Member States to continue to cooperate with the TFG in the fight against piracy and armed robbery at sea, *notes* the primary role of the TFG in rooting out piracy and armed robbery at sea, and *decides* that for a period of twelve months from the date of adoption of resolution 1846, States and regional organizations cooperating in the fight against piracy and armed robbery at sea off the coast of Somalia for which advance notification has been provided by the TFG to the Secretary–General may undertake all necessary measures that are appropriate in Somalia, for the purpose of suppressing acts of piracy and armed robbery at sea, pursuant to the request of the TFG, provided, however, that any measures undertaken pursuant to the authority of this paragraph shall be undertaken consistent with applicable international humanitarian and human rights law;

7. *Calls on* Member States to assist the TFG, at its request and with notification to the Secretary–General, to strengthen its operational capacity to bring to justice those who are using Somali territory to plan, facilitate or undertake criminal acts of piracy and armed robbery at sea, and *stresses* that any measures undertaken pursuant to this paragraph shall be consistent with applicable international human rights law;

8. *Welcomes* the communiqué issued by the International Conference on Piracy around Somalia held in Nairobi, Kenya, on 11 December 2008 and *encourages* Member States to work to enhance the capacity of relevant states in the region to combat piracy, including judicial capacity;

9. *Notes* with concern the findings contained in the 20 November 2008 Report of the Monitoring Group on Somalia that escalating ransom payments are fueling the growth of piracy in waters off the coast of Somalia, and that the lack of enforcement of the arms embargo established by resolution 733 (1992) has permitted ready access to the arms and ammunition used by the pirates and driven in part the phenomenal growth in piracy;

10. *Affirms* that the authorization provided in this resolution apply only with respect to the situation in Somalia and shall not affect the rights or obligations or responsibilities of Member States under international law, including any rights or obligations under UNCLOS, with respect to any other situation, and underscores in particular that this resolution shall not be considered as establishing customary international law, and *affirms further* that such authorizations have been provided only following the receipt of the 9 December 2008 letter conveying the consent of the TFG;

11. *Affirms* that the measures imposed by paragraph 5 of resolution 733 (1992) and further elaborated upon by paragraphs 1 and 2 or resolution 1425 (2002) shall not apply to weapons and military equipment destined for the sole use of Member States and regional organizations undertaking measures in accordance with paragraph 6 above;

12.   *Urges* States in collaboration with the shipping and insurance industries, and the IMO to continue to develop avoidance, evasion, and defensive best practices and advisories to take when under attack or when sailing in waters off the coast of Somalia, and *further urges* States to make their citizens and vessels available for forensic investigation as appropriate at the first port of call immediately following an act or attempted act of piracy or armed robbery at sea or release from captivity;

13.   *Decides* to remain seized of the matter.

NOTES AND QUESTIONS

1.   What is it about the crime of piracy that requires an international response? What role did international law play in the United States' response to piracy off the coast of Argentina in the early 1800s? Was that role different in significant ways to the response by a larger group of states to piracy off the coast of Somalia in the early 2000s? Could the international law being referenced by the Security Council still be described as Justice Story did, "as the only code universally known and recognized by the people of all countries"?

Can you think of other challenges to the international community that, like piracy, require an international response, guided by international law?

2.   Sharon Otterman, *Pirate Suspect Arrives in New York to Face Charges*

N.Y. TIMES, April 22, 2009

A Somali teenager is due to appear in a New York courtroom on Tuesday for arraignment on charges that he was one of a group of pirates who hijacked a United States-flagged cargo ship and held its American captain hostage for days in a lifeboat on the Indian Ocean.

The suspected pirate, who has been identified in press reports as Abduhl Wali-i-Musi, arrived in New York late Monday to face what are believed to be the first piracy charges in the United States in more than a century. . . .

New York is a logical site for the trial because the federal prosecutor's office in Manhattan has developed great expertise in trying crimes that occur outside the United States, including cases in Africa involving terrorism against Americans, such as the Al Qaeda bombings of two U.S. embassies in East Africa in 1998.

Under international law, any country can prosecute acts of piracy committed in international waters, but in practice, not all nations have incorporated anti-piracy statutes into their domestic legislation, said Roger Middleton, an expert on piracy at Chatham House, a research organization based in London.

Here is an excerpt from the U.S. Code with the provision relevant to Mr. Musi's prosecution. Does it look familiar?

U.S. Code: Piracy

Title 18. Crimes and Criminal Procedure

Part I. Crimes

Chapter 81. Piracy and Privateering

§ 1651.   Piracy under law of nations

Whoever, on the high seas, commits the crime of piracy as defined by the law of nations, and is afterwards brought into or found in the United States, shall be imprisoned for life.

§ 1652.   Citizens as pirates

Whoever, being a citizen of the United States, commits any murder or robbery, or any act of hostility against the United States, or against any citizen thereof, on the high seas, under color of any commission from any foreign prince, or state, or on pretense of authority from any person, is a pirate, and shall be imprisoned for life.

§ 1653.   Aliens as pirates

Whoever, being a citizen or subject of any foreign state, is found and taken on the sea making war upon the United States, or cruising against the vessels and property thereof, or of the citizens of the same, contrary to the provisions of any treaty existing between the United States and the state of which the offender is a citizen or subject, when by such treaty such acts are declared to be piracy, is a pirate, and shall be imprisoned for life.

3.   The Supreme Court justified Congress' mere reference to the law of nations for the definition of piracy as not unlike a reference to the common law in defining murder. The UN Security Council referred several times to definitions and rules in the 1982 UN Convention on the Law of the Sea. (UNCLOS is discussed in detail in Chapter 5.) The Supreme Court found the crime of piracy in customary international law; the Security Council in a treaty (also called, as in this instance, a convention.) These two primary sources of international law, along with the third primary source, the general principles of law, and several secondary sources are restated in the Statute of the International Court of Justice (ICJ) at Article 38. Article 38 is set out at the beginning of the book's chapter on sources, Chapter 2 *infra*.

4.   Note the various actors and the wide range of interests mentioned by both the Supreme Court and the Security Council in the two cases of piracy. We discuss the actors or subjects of international law in Chapter 3. Many of the interests impacted by the problem of piracy are the topic of later chapters, including human rights (Chapter 5), common spaces (Chapter 6), international economic issues (Chapter 7), and the use of force (Chapter 10). For more on the contemporary problem of piracy, see, JOHN S. BURNETT, DANGEROUS WATERS, MODERN PIRACY AND TERROR ON THE HIGH SEAS (2002).

2.   INTERNATIONAL LAW AS LAW

The challenges on the international law agenda from piracy to world financial markets demonstrate the ancient origins and contemporary importance of international law. Nevertheless, international law has been the focus of critique since the rise of the state system. The criticism in essence concerns the proper categorization of international law as a legal system as opposed to a system of morality or a non-binding code of conduct. The international system plainly lacks the sort of institutions typical of national legal systems. As you saw in the previous section, however, despite the lack of institutions, international law gets made, applied, and enforced. This indirect evidence that international law is law is supplemented by the next excerpt, which discusses directly the question of international law as law.

Mary Ellen O'Connell, The Power and Purpose of International Law

pp. 3–13 (2008)*

Hugo Grotius, the seventeenth-century Dutch scholar and diplomat credited with founding modern international law, responded vigorously to the theory presented by Machiavelli that sovereigns are above the law. In the Grotian worldview, law is as present and important for the rulers of nations in their relations as for individuals within nations. Law for nations was a moral necessity for Grotius: "[T]he hall-mark of wisdom for a ruler is to take account not only of the good of the nation committed to his care, but of the whole human race."[14] It was also a practical matter: "Such, in his opinion, is the impact of economic interdependence or of military security that there is no state so powerful that it can dispense with the help of others."

To deflect the compelling insights of Grotius and his followers, later scholars relied on the theory of the 19th Century British legal scholar, John Austin, who opined that international law is only a type of positive morality and not law because its rules are not the commands of a sovereign backed by sanctions.

* * *

[Another form of attack on international law came from Hans Morgenthau who considered international law a form of law, not morality, but found it too weak a form to win the compliance of powerful states in important matters.] Morgenthau was the highly influential German–American theorist of international law and relations, who spent 1943 to 1971 * * * teaching at the University of Chicago. * * * He thought the United States should comply with international law in the day-to-day aspects of international relations, such as transportation, diplomacy, and treaty making, but in questions relating to the pursuit of national (military) power, U.S. leaders must not consider themselves bound. Morgenthau had a narrow view of human nature. He believed human beings were compelled by that nature to pursue power and that such a pursuit overrides other

---

* Some footnotes omitted.

14. Hersch Lauterpacht, *The Grotian Tradition in International Law*, 23 BRIT. Y.B. INT'L L. 1, 31 (1946).

pursuits. Morgenthau stressed that as international law lacks effective sanctions to coerce compliance, and, therefore, imposed no real price for non-compliance, American leaders could and should pursue power free of concern about international law.

* * *

Morgenthau's attack on international law came not long after the end of the Second World War when the ideas of Hersch Lauterpacht and Hans Kelsen were in the ascendant. In 1946, Lauterpacht wrote the important article *The Grotian Tradition in International Law*. In it he contrasted the narrow view of human nature held by Machiavelli and Hobbes with that of the great founder of international law, the 17th century scholar and diplomat, Hugo Grotius. "For Machiavelli and Hobbes man is essentially selfish, anti-social, and unable to learn from experience. . . . [T]he basis of political obligation is interest pure and simple. . . . This is the typical realistic approach of contempt towards the 'little breed' of man. On that line of reasoning there is no salvation for humanity but irrevocable subjection to an order of effective force. . . ."

By contrast, Lauterpacht writes of Grotius's understanding of what impels human action. It is "the desire for society—not for society of any sort, but for peaceful and organized life according to the measure of his intelligence." "In fact, much of the appeal and potentialities of the Grotian tradition lies in the lesson which can be drawn from his conception of the social nature and constitution of man as a rational being in whom the element of moral obligation and foresight asserts itself triumphantly over unbridled selfishness and passion, both within the state and in the relations of states."

Kelsen, too, revived concepts associated with Hugo Grotius, who first wrote comprehensively of international law as law superior to the various national communities and enforced through the sanctions of war and reprisals. For Kelsen, as for Grotius, law's authority to bind even sovereign states is grounded in our belief in the authority of law. The sanction signals the rule and works at the margin to support law compliance. Kelsen presented himself as a positivist, but in his basic understanding of the nature of law, Lauterpacht rightly points out that he, like international law scholars in general, incorporates natural law explanations as to the authority and aspirations of international law.

* * *

As Kelsen taught, war and reprisals (coercive measures short of war) are international law's primary enforcement tools: the sanctions of international law. Other measures have been added over time in the form of coercive measures imposed by international organizations, courts and tribunals. Every rule of international law is in fact backed by a sanction, if not a specific one based in a treaty, then a general-purpose countermeasure. Austin was mistaken about the lack of sanctions in international law. What international law lacks is a compulsory system of dispute resolution so that neutral decision-makers play a role in the application of sanctions. International law enforcement still functions to a large extent through self-judging and self-help by victims of law violations, although this is declining.

Those critics who recognize that international law does have sanctions but still dismiss it because the sanctions are weak, in fact have no empirical basis for their view. Goldsmith and Posner, for example, while assuming that international law's sanctions are weaker than domestic law, acknowledge that domestic (presumably U.S.) traffic laws, tax laws, and drug laws are not well enforced. They omit U.S. immigration law, murder laws, domestic violence laws, rape laws, and the vast numbers of other laws that also are only rarely effectively enforced. Nor do they seem to recognize that regardless of the efficiency with which law is enforced, people will still recognize the binding quality of rules. Americans believe that the tax laws, the murder laws, and even the traffic laws are binding. They do so for reasons other than the sure knowledge that a policeman will arrest them if they violate these rules. Legal theorists have assured us for decades that sanctions are not the major reason why we obey the law. As Hart explained in response to Austin, the quality of a rule as a legal rule does not require proof that the rules are always and effectively enforced but rather that each legal rule is in fact backed by a sanction. International law's rules have such sanctions.

* * *

As Grotius, Kelsen, Henkin, Franck and others indicate, there is much about international law that transcends the material, positive acts such as consent. International law's claim to be law is based ultimately in belief. It contains peremptory norms, *jus cogens* principles, that cannot be altered by positive acts, including the norms against genocide, apartheid, extra-judicial killing, slavery, and torture. The third primary source of international law rules after customary international law and treaties is the general principles of law. These principles are typically derived from Roman law and were developed by the great Roman jurists on the basis of reason inspired by the natural order of things. General principles from this category, such as necessity, proportionality, and good faith, play an important role in regulating enforcement measures. While much in international law is based on positive acts of consent, ultimately the ontology and legitimacy of international law is based on more than consent, just as it is more than sanctions.

Nevertheless, consent and sanctions are vital aspects of international law, providing important evidence that the community believes in the system. While it is true that "[t]he essence of a legal system is the inherent fact, based on various psychological factors, that law is accepted by the community as a whole as binding, and the element of sanction is not an essential, or perhaps even an important, element in the functioning of the system,"[42] one of the ways that the international community demonstrates

---

42.   M.D.A. FREEMAN, LLOYD'S INTRODUCTION TO JURISPRUDENCE 215 (7th ed. 2001).

acceptance or belief that international law is law is through the system for sanctioning violations.

The violation of any rule of international law may be subject to a coercive sanction. These sanctions do not ensure complete compliance with the law, as some would like, but they do play at least three other significant roles in the establishment of international law as real law: they play a formal role in identifying legally binding rules; they coerce at least some violators into compliance; and, because of the first two roles, sanctions play a role in "internalizing" respect for international legal rules, thereby decreasing the need for coercive enforcement. Thus, sanctions are an essential part of international law, like any legal system, but not in the unsophisticated manner of simple police enforcement.

A community-created right to sanction non-compliance through forceful means is a key indicator that a rule is regarded as a legal rule and not a moral, social, or other type of rule. To allow coercive enforcement of anything short of a legal rule would be to allow the use of force outside the confines of law. It is to prevent just such unconstrained use of force that law came to be instituted in human communities.

Further, and related to the first two points, some international law violators will in fact be sanctioned. This actual application of the sanction will coerce some violators into compliance or into providing a remedy for non-compliance. The application of sanctions reminds others that sanctions exist, which in turn, supports more voluntary law compliance. Thus, sanctions, in a variety of ways help to ensure that international law compliance is occurring on a level sufficient to consider it effective law. Penalties or sanctions are

> required not as the normal motive for obedience, but as the *guarantee* that those who would voluntarily obey shall not be sacrificed to those who would not. To obey, without this, would be to risk going to the wall. Given this standing danger, what reason demands is *voluntary* cooperation in a *coercive* system.[50]

The majority in society must voluntarily comply with the rules for a legal system to be maintained. Without this majority compliance it would not be possible to claim that the community believes in the authority of the law.

Thus, general compliance, which is connected to the existence of sanctions for law violation, is important evidence that international law is accepted as law. Further evidence is found in the formal processes of law making, which, again, are related to the existence of sanctions. As mentioned above, the sources of international law are positivist—treaty, customary international law, and to some extent general principles or naturalist—general principles and peremptory norms. Rules emanating from these sources are binding and law violators may be sanctioned for non-compliance. Non-binding principles are sometimes called "soft law" to indicate some expectation of compliance but no right of sanction. The term is

---

50.   H.L.A. HART, THE CONCEPT OF LAW 193 (1961).

perhaps misleading in that without the sanction, principles are not "law" at all, soft or otherwise.

Because of the existence of naturalist elements in international law, courts and tribunals play an important role in interpreting these elements, but they are, arguably, just as vital in applying the rules emerging from the positive sources. Some form of adjudicative process has been part of international law since it began with the end of the Thirty Years' War in Europe in 1648. The treaties that ended that war, the Peace of Westphalia, contained elements that still comprise fundamental components of the international legal system, including the obligation to settle disputes through legal discourse not armed conflict. Grotius extolled the use of arbitration as an alternative to armed conflict in his 1625 book, *On the Law of War and Peace*. Several of the Spanish Scholastics, Grotius's predecessors, had suggested arbitration as a process to fill the gap in intercommunal relations left by the declining earthly authority of the Pope and Holy Roman Emperor. From these early ideas, courts have grown steadily in importance in both the theory and practice of international law. Not only do courts today adjudicate the existence and meaning of rules, they are playing a larger role in the proper application of sanctions. For sanctions to be legal sanctions, not just self-help actions of reprisal or revenge, Hans Kelsen and Hersch Lauterpacht explained the importance of courts in adjudicating both the wrong and the remedy. In addition to courts resolving disputes among states, Kelsen was an early advocate of courts for the purpose of holding individuals accountable for violations of international law. Individual accountability was in line with his view that states are led by real people, and people exercise their will, not the state itself.

Today, courts are generally available for both the interstate resolution of disputes and individual accountability. Thanks in particular to the World Trade Organization's dispute settlement body, ever-more sophisticated principles for the application of sanctions are being developed and applied. International criminal courts are now active in several places in the world.

* * *

International law has deficits, yet it persists as the single, generally accepted means to solve the world's problems.[60] It is not religion or ideology that the world has in common, but international law. Through international law, diverse cultures can reach consensus about the moral norms that we will commonly live by. As a result, international law is uniquely suited to mitigate the problems of armed conflict, terrorism, human rights abuse, poverty, disease and the destruction of the natural environment. It is the closest thing we have to a neutral vehicle for taking on the world's most complex issues and pressing problems.

---

60.   C.G. WEERAMANTRY, UNIVERSALISING INTERNATIONAL LAW 1–3 (2004).

In 1968, Louis Henkin first published some of the most famous words about international law of all time: "Almost all nations observe almost all of the principles of international law and almost all of their obligations almost all of the time." (Louis Henkin, *How Nations Behave* 47, 2d ed., 1979.) The excerpt by O'Connell discusses the roles of sanctions, consent, acceptance, internalization, idealism, and pragmatism for why international law exists and why states comply with it. Harold Koh offers similar reasons, but emphasizes the importance of national law in supporting compliance with international law.

Harold Koh, Why Obey International Law? Theories for Managing Conflicts with Municipal Law

Panel Discussion, 97 ASIL PROC. 111 (2003)

For the last decade, most of my work as a lawyer, as a scholar, and in the government has been devoted to the three questions that are the subject of this panel. First, why do nations obey international law? Second, why should they obey international law? Third, how do we manage any conflicts between applications of international and domestic law? In a 1997 Yale Law Journal article [*Review Essay: Why Do Nations Obey International Law?*, 106 YALE L.J. 2599], I offered five cumulative answers to the first question: "Why do nations obey international law?" I call these for short-hand purposes (1) reasons of power and coercion, (2) reasons of self-interest, (3) reasons of liberal theory, both rule legitimacy and political identity, (4) communitarian reasons, and (5) legal process reasons.

To clarify a very long hypothesis in a very short time-frame, how do we persuade scofflaws to obey the law in a domestic setting? In exactly the same ways. With persistent litterers or traffic violators, you first threaten them with coercion—reasons of power. Second, you tell them that it is in their long-term self-interest to obey the law—reasons of self-interest. Third, you say that they should obey because of the liberal Kantian ideas that the rules are fair (rule legitimacy) and that they should obey because they are law-abiding individuals (political identity). Fourth, you make appeals to community. By telling them, "we're part of a community," you ask them not to act purely in their narrow self-interest. Finally—the reasons lawyers understand best—reasons of process. We try to enmesh violators in processes, institutions, and regimes that internalize the norms into their own internal value sets.

———————

Koh particularly advocates bringing international law issues into domestic legal process. He argues, for example, for enforcing international law before domestic courts as the way to advance internalization of international law norms in national communities. The process goes the other way as well, as important rules of international law are influenced by national practices and as we seek to use international processes to, for example, ensure accountability of national leaders. The inter-relationship between the international legal system and national systems is briefly addressed in the next section, but is the central focus of Chapter 11.

NOTES AND QUESTIONS

1.   In your view, what is law? What purpose does it serve in any community? How do we ensure that it serves its purpose? In addition to international law and the law of states, can you identify other categories of "law"? What is it about international law that makes it difficult for some to accept that it is law? Must it be law to serve the goals of the international community?

2.   For more on international law theory, see, THE METHODS OF INTERNATIONAL LAW (Steven R. Ratner and Anne–Marie Slaughter eds., 2004); PHILIP ALLOTT, THE HEALTH OF NATIONS, SOCIETY AND LAW BEYOND THE STATE (2002); MARTTI KOSKENNIEMI, THE GENTLE CIVILIZER OF NATIONS, THE RISE AND FALL OF INTERNATIONAL LAW (1870–1960) (2001); MICHAEL BYERS, CUSTOM, POWER AND THE POWER OF RULES (1999); THOMAS FRANCK, THE POWER OF LEGITIMACY AMONG NATIONS (1990); THE STRUCTURE AND PROCESS OF INTERNATIONAL LAW: ESSAYS IN LEGAL PHILOSOPHY, DOCTRINE AND THEORY (R. St.J. Macdonald and Douglas M. Johnston eds., 1986). (In this collection see, especially, the essay by Covey T. Oliver for a sense of the theory underlying the first edition of this book: *The Future of Idealism in International Law: Structuralism, Humanism, and Survivialism*); CHARLES DE VISSCHER, THEORY AND REALITY IN PUBLIC INTERNATIONAL LAW (P.E. Corbett trans., 1968); PHILIP C. JESSUP, TRANSNATIONAL LAW (1956). *See also* Chapter 12 on the future of international law, *infra.*

3.   INTERNATIONAL LAW AND NATIONAL LEGAL SYSTEMS*

As *U.S. v. Smith* and Security Council Resolution 1851 indicate, the international legal system, regional systems, and national systems are very much interconnected. Increasing numbers of issues that arise within national legal systems have an international aspect. While some may prefer to seal the systems off from each other that simply cannot be achieved in today's world. It would require breaking off international trade, travel, diplomacy, enclosing the natural environment, and other impossible feats. Nevertheless, we do have principles for guiding us in cases of "conflicts of law." It may be that international law, regional and national law are both relevant to a particular issue. International law has its own principles for how to proceed if the rules cannot be harmonized.

I D.P. O'Connell, International Law
p. 38 (2d ed. 1970)

The Theory of the Relationship: Monism and Dualism

Almost every case in a municipal court in which a rule of international law is asserted to govern the decision raises the problem of the relationship

---

* Note on terminology: "national law" is also referred to as "domestic" law or "municipal" law. All three terms refer to the law created through national law-making processes.

of international law and municipal law; and in many cases before international tribunals it must also be disposed of when deciding the jurisdictional competence of a State to affect alien interests through its own internal legal order.

There are four possible attitudes towards the question:

(a) That international law has primacy over municipal law in both international and municipal decisions. This is the *monist* theory.

(b) That international law has primacy over municipal law in international decisions, and municipal law has primacy over international law in municipal decisions. This is the *dualist* theory.

(c) That municipal law has primacy over international law in both international and municipal decisions. This is a species of monism in reverse.

(d) That there should be no supposition of conflict between international law and municipal law.

(a) Monism

The monist position is an emanation of Kantian philosophy which favours a unitary conception of law. According to this view, since the capacities of States derive from the idea of law, the jurisdiction to exercise these capacities is granted by the law. It follows that the law to which jurisdictional reference must be made is independent of sovereignty and determinative of its limits. If a State exceeds the limits, its acts are invalid. This argument concedes to international law a broader and more fundamental competence than to municipal law. However, it tends to sidestep the point made by the dualists, namely, that a municipal court may be instructed to apply municipal law and not international law, and hence has no jurisdiction (using the term as descriptive of the capacity in municipal law to decide a case) to declare the relevant municipal law invalid. Hence, the characterization of the jurisdictional excess as "invalid," or even merely "illegal" (if there is any difference between the terms), is of no meaning internally within the municipal law of the acting State. To this objection, the monist has only one answer, that this conflict of duties, owing to a defect in organization, has been wrongly resolved.

* * *

(b) Dualism

The dualist position is associated with Hegelianism and has governed the judicial attitudes of States where this philosophy has prevailed. The common starting point is the proposition that law is an act of sovereign will, municipal law being differentiated from international law in that it is a manifestation of this will internally directed, as distinct from participation in a collective act of will by which the sovereign undertakes obligations with respect to other sovereigns. This results in a dualism of legal origin, of subjects and of subject matters. International law and municipal law are two quite different spheres of legal action, and theoretically there should be no point of conflict between them. Municipal law addresses itself to the subjects of sovereigns, international law to the sovereigns themselves. If the sovereign by an act of municipal law exceeds his competence in international law it does not follow that municipal law is void; it merely follows that the sovereign has violated international law. Anzilotti has explained the relationship between the dualist thesis and the alleged incapacity of the individual in international law as follows:

> A rule of international law is by its very nature absolutely unable to bind individuals, i.e., to confer upon them rights and duties. It is created by the collective will of States with the view of regulating their mutual relations; obviously it cannot therefore refer to an altogether different sphere of relations. If several States were to attempt the creation of rules regulating private relations, such an attempt, by the very nature of things, would not be a rule of international law, but a rule of uniform municipal law common to several States.

(c) Inverted monism

The theory that municipal law is in its nature superior to international law has never found favour in international tribunals, and is no more than an abstract possibility. It is associated with Bergbohm, whose almost pathological resentment against natural law led to an exaggerated emphasis on the State will. Unlike Austin, who would deny even the term "law" to international law and thereby avoid a potential collision of two systems, Bergbohm allows for international law as a manifestation of the "auto limitation" of the sovereign will. The State is superior to and antecedent to the international community, and remains the only law-making entity. Unlike Triepel, who would distinguish the State will as internally manifested from the State will as externally manifested, Bergbohm allows for only one manifestation, and international law is thus a derivation from municipal law.

(d) The theory of harmonization

According to this view, neither the monist nor the dualist position can be accepted as sound. Each attempts to provide an answer, derived from a single theoretical premise, to two quite different questions. The first question is whether international law is "law" in the same sense as municipal law, i.e., whether both systems are concordant expressions of a unique metaphysical reality. The second question is whether a given tribunal is required by its constitution to apply a rule of international law or municipal law, or vice versa, or authorized to accord primacy to the one over the other. The resemblance between the two questions is only apparent; the lack of jurisdiction in a given tribunal to accord primacy to international law in the event of a conflict between it and municipal law has no relevance to the question whether municipal law does or does not derive its competence from the same basic juridical reality as international law. In some federal systems of law, a State court may be required to apply state legislation which a federal court would declare unconstitutional. The norms of reference are different but the systems are concordant.

The starting point in any legal order is man himself, considered in relation to his fellow man. Law, it has often been said, is life, and life is law. The individual does not live his life exclusively in the legal order of the State any more than he lives it exclusively in the international order. He falls within both jurisdictions because his life is lived in both. Here again, the comparison with a federal system is instructive. It follows that a monistic solution to the problem of the relationship of international law and municipal law fails because it would treat the one system as a derivation of the other, ignoring the physical, metaphysical and social realities which in fact detach them. The world has not yet reached that state of organization where there is only one civitas maxima delegating specific jurisdiction to regional administrations.

But a dualist solution is equally deficient because it ignores the all-prevailing reality of the universum of human experience. States are the formal instruments of will for the crystallization of law, but the impulse to the law derives from human behavior and has a human goal. Positive international law is not pure whim, but an expression of needs and convictions. If it were otherwise, international law and municipal law would be competitive regimes ill-suited to the solution of human problems. The correct position is that international law and municipal law are concordant bodies of doctrine, each autonomous in the sense that it is directed to a specific, and, to some extent, an exclusive area of human conduct, but harmonious in that in their totality the several rules aim at a basic human good.

Administration des Douanes v. Société Cafés Jacques Vabre

France, Cour de Cassation (Chambres Reunies)
2 Common Market Law Reports (1975).

[The facts. The plaintiffs imported from Holland soluble coffee and mixtures of soluble coffee and chicory for resale on the French market. The French Customs Administration imposed a consumption tax on imports at a rate higher than the one used for soluble coffees manufactured and sold in France. The rate applicable to the imports was established by ministerial orders which were issued in 1967 on the basis of legislative authority incorporated in the Customs Code in 1966.

In their suit against the Customs Administration, the plaintiffs argued that the discriminatory tax on their imports was in violation of Article 95 of the Rome Treaty of 1957, establishing the European Economic Community, now Article 90 under the Consolidated Version adopted by the Treaty of Amsterdam of 1999. Article 95 provided in part:

> No Member State shall impose, directly or indirectly, on the products of other Member States any internal taxation of any kind in excess of that imposed directly or indirectly on similar domestic products.

The Customs Administration defended that the legislation of 1966, being later in time, prevailed. Both the Tribunal d'Instance and the Cour d'Appel de Paris held that the treaty prevailed by virtue of Article 55 of the French Constitution according to which treaties "have an authority superior to that of laws." The Customs Administration appealed to the supreme court of France, the Cour de Casssation, contending that the term "laws" did not include legislation enacted subsequent to the treaty.

The Cour de Cassation gives very great weight to the views of the procureur général, although it does not always agree with him. But, in accordance with tradition, it gives its judgments in terms so terse they are nearly delphic. As a result, the only sensible way to evaluate the judgment is to read it together with the text of the "submissions", i.e. the oral pleading delivered by the procureur général at the hearing before the court. Indeed, it is for this reason that his pleading—often a long one—is published by the French reporters together with the judgment of the court.]

Submissions of the Procureur Général
(M. Adolphe Touffait)

[The procureur général first argued that the term "laws" in Article 55 of the French Constitution covered legislation enacted subsequent to the treaty. A portion of his argument on this point follows.]

* * *

The relations between international law and internal law have been constructed, thought out and set out in the framework of systems classified under the headings of dualism and monism, each of these being the expression of a measure of historical truth, according to the dominant ideas on the national level and the evolution of international society.

* * *

The idea emerges irresistibly that there can be no international relations if the diplomatic agreements can be put in balk by unilateral decisions of the contracting powers, and the duty of the State to respect its international obligations becomes a fundamental principle, and on the morrow of the liberation politicians who were often lawyers realised that their ideas which might fall under the weight of legal and judicial tradition—would have to be incorporated solemnly in the Constitution if they were to triumph. That is how for the first time in France the Constitution of 27 October 1946, in its Articles 26 and 28, expressly and in general form incorporated the principle of the primacy of international treaties over internal laws.

Article 26 relates to laws prior to the Treaty. *Article 28 relates to laws subsequent to the Treaty.*

The fact that the equivalent of these two Articles of the 1946 Constitution is a single Article 55 in that of 1958 does not represent a change in will in the constitution-makers.

* * *

Besides, how is one to understand Article 55 otherwise? The concept of superiority only has sense with regard to subsequent laws.

If Article 55 had been intended to refer only to laws prior to the treaty it would have been sufficient for it to provide that "a treaty has statutory force", since it is an absolute principle that subsequent statute prevails over a prior statute.

An analysis of the texts, in accord with the international ethic intended by the makers of the Constitutions of 1946 and 1958, thus ineluctably leads to the consideration that the concept of superiority of treaties over statutes only has sense with regard to statutes subsequent to the treaty, as it is clear that the international legal order can only be realised and developed if the States loyally apply the treaties they have signed, ratified and published. (at 360–362)

[The procureur général went on to suggest the court should not rely on Article 55 in the French Constitution in holding that the treaty prevailed over the subsequent statute. He argued as follows.]

It would be possible for you to give precedence to the application of Article 95 of the Rome Treaty over the subsequent statute by relying on Article 55 of our Constitution, but personally I would ask you not to mention it and instead base your reasoning on the very nature of the legal order instituted by the Rome treaty.

Indeed, in so far as you restricted yourselves to deriving from Article 55 of our Constitution the primacy in the French internal system of Community law over national law you would be explaining and justifying that action as regards our country, but such reasoning would let it be accepted that it is on our Constitution and on it alone that depends the ranking of Community law in our internal legal system.

In doing so you would impliedly be supplying a far from negligible argument to the courts of the Member States which, lacking any affirmation in their constitutions of the primacy of the Treaty, would be tempted to deduce therefrom the opposite solution, as the Italian Constitutional court did in 1962 when it claimed that it was for internal constitutional law to fix the ranking of Community law in the internal order of each Member State.

Those are the reasons, Gentlemen, why I ask you not to base your reasoning on Article 55 of our Constitution; you will thus recognise that the transfer made by the States from their internal legal order to the Community legal order, within the limits of the rights and obligations corresponding to the provisions of the Treaty, involves a definitive limitation of their sovereign rights against which a subsequent unilateral act which is incompatible with the notion of Community cannot prevail.

* * *

In this great but difficult and delicate task of building Europe, *difficult* because it often comes up against national economic differences which have to be eliminated, *delicate* because all the institutions of the country are involved, Parliament, Government, Conseil Constitutionnel, Conseil d'Etat, Cour de Cassation, it is indispensable that all the decisions of these various organs should be compatible with the objectives of the Community, as it is necessary that the finalities of the Rome Treaty should inspire the interpretative law of all the Member States. [The Court then examines the history of these questions in the other Member States.]

* * *

This panoramic survey of the case law of the Member States of the European Economic Community suffices to demonstrate that after some years of groping and hesitation there has been created under the guidance of the Court of Justice of the European Communities, that attentive guardian of the will of the authors of the Treaty, by demonstrating, but avoiding the reefs of government by the judiciary—a European legal consciousness within all the national courts concerned to recognise the primacy of Community law without which there could not be created that Unity of the market which is desired by the signatory governments and approved by their national sovereignty, reaffirmed at the conferences in The Hague on 2 December 1969 and Paris on 20–21 October 1972; and it is for all these reasons that I conclude very firmly that the second ground of appeal should be dismissed. (at 363–367)

Judgment (of the Cour de Cassation)

[The court summarized the opposite contentions very briefly, including the position of the Customs Administration that the relevant section of the Customs Code had "the absolute authority which belongs to legislative provisions and which are binding on all French courts." It then went on to say:]

But the treaty 25 March 1957, which by virtue of the above mentioned Article of, the Constitution has an authority greater than that of statutes, institutes a separate legal order integrated with that of the Member States. Because of that separateness, the legal order which it has created is directly applicable to the nationals of those States and is binding on their courts. Therefore, the Cour d'Appel was correct and did not exceed its powers in deciding that Article 95 of the Treaty was to be applied in the instant case, and not section 265 of the Customs Code, even though the latter was later in date. Whence it follows that the ground [of appeal] must be dismissed. (at 369)

The headquarters building of the United Nations is in New York City. As a matter of geography, the UN is within the United States, but plainly the UN needs a certain amount of autonomy from the United States. The United States promised this in a treaty known as the Headquarters Agreement. The case below concerns U.S. legislation that the UN felt conflicted with the Headquarters Agreement, and, thus, with international law. The UN wished to allow a non-state actor organization, the Palestine

Liberation Organization, to have a permanent office near the UN to take advantage of its status as a permanent observer to the UN. The U.S. Congress classified the PLO as a terrorist organization that should not be allowed to have offices in the U.S. In the first case below, the International Court of Justice (ICJ) emphasizes the priority of international law in a case where national law and international law conflict. The next case considers how U.S. courts confront the same problem as the one just reviewed from France, namely, what to do when later legislation conflicts with a treaty. (For more on international organizations and international dispute resolution, see, *infra* Chapters 3 and 9, respectively.)

Applicability of the Obligation to Arbitrate Under Section 21 of the United Nations Headquarters Agreement of 26 June 1947

International Court of Justice
1988 I.C.J. Rep. 12 (Advisory Opinion of April 26) see p. 835

* * *

7. The question upon which the opinion of the Court has been requested is whether the United States of America (hereafter referred to as "the United States"), as a party to the United Nations Headquarters Agreement, is under an obligation to enter into arbitration. The Headquarters Agreement of 26 June 1947 came into force in accordance with its terms on 21 November 1947 by exchange of letters between the Secretary–General and the United States Permanent Representative. The Agreement was registered the same day with the United Nations Secretariat, in accordance with Article 102 of the Charter. In section 21, paragraph *(a)*, it provides as follows:

> "Any dispute between the United Nations and the United States concerning the interpretation or application of this agreement or of any supplemental agreement, which is not settled by negotiation or other agreed mode of settlement, shall be referred for final decision to a tribunal of three arbitrators, one to be named by the Secretary–General, one to be named by the Secretary of State of the United States, and the third to be chosen by the two, or, if they should fail to agree upon a third, then by the President of the International Court of Justice."

There is no question but that the Headquarters Agreement is a treaty in force binding the parties thereto. What the Court has therefore to determine, in order to answer the question put to it, is whether there exists a dispute between the United Nations and the United States of the kind contemplated by section 21 of the Agreement. * * *

* * *

8. The events in question centred round the Permanent Observer Mission of the Palestine Liberation Organization (referred to hereafter as

"the PLO") to the United Nations in New York. The PLO has enjoyed in relation to the United Nations the status of an observer since 1974, the Organization was invited to "participate in the sessions and the work of the General Assembly in the capacity of observer". Following this invitation, the PLO established an Observer Mission in 1974, and maintains an office, entitled office of the PLO Observer Mission at 115 East 65th Street, in New York City, outside the United Nations Headquarters District. Recognized observers are listed as such in official United Nations publications: the PLO appears in such publications in a category of "organizations which have received a standing invitation from the General Assembly to participate in the sessions and the work of the General Assembly as observers".

* * *

* * * Section 11 of the Headquarters Agreement provides that "The federal, state or local authorities of the United States shall not impose any impediments to transit to or from the headquarters district of: (1) representatives of Members * * * or the families of such representatives * * *; * * * (5) other persons invited to the headquarters district by the United Nations * * * on official business * * *."

Section 12 provides that, "[T]he provisions of section 11 shall be applicable irrespective of the relations existing between the Governments of the persons referred to in that section and the Government of the United States."

Section 13 provides *(inter alia)* that, "[L]aws and regulations in force in the United States regarding the entry of aliens shall not be applied in such manner as to interfere with the privileges referred to in section 11."

* * *

24. On 11 March 1988 the Acting Permanent Representative of the United States to the United Nations wrote to the Secretary–General, referring to General Assembly resolutions 42/229A and 42/229B and stating as follows:

"I wish to inform you that the Attorney General of the United States has determined that he is required by the Anti–Terrorism Act of 1987 to close the office of the Palestine Liberation Organization Observer Mission to the United Nations in New York, irrespective of any obligations the United States may have under the Agreement between the United Nations and the United States regarding the Headquarters of the United Nations. If the PLO does not comply with the Act, the Attorney General will initiate legal action to close the PLO Observer Mission on or about March 21, 1988, the effective date of the Act. This course of action will allow the orderly enforcement of the Act."

* * *

This letter was delivered by hand to the Secretary–General by the Acting Permanent Representative of the United States. * * * On receiving the letter, the Secretary–General protested to the Acting Permanent Representative and stated that the decision taken by the United States Government as outlined in the letter was a clear violation of the Headquarters Agreement between the United Nations and the United States.

* * *

[The Court examined the requirements of Section 21 and found that they were satisfied.]

57. The Court must therefore conclude that the United States is bound to respect the obligation to have recourse to arbitration under section 21 of the Headquarters Agreement. The fact remains however that, as the Court has already observed, the United States has declared (letter from the Permanent Representative, 11 March 1988) that its measures against the PLO Observer Mission were taken "irrespective of any obligations the United States may have under the [Headquarters] Agreement". If it were necessary to interpret that statement as intended to refer not only to the substantive obligations laid down in, for example, sections 11, 12 and 13, but also to the obligation to arbitrate provided for in section 21, this conclusion would remain intact. It would be sufficient to recall the fundamental principle of international law that international law prevails over domestic law. This principle was endorsed by judicial decision as long ago as the arbitral award of 14 September 1872 in the *Alabama* case between Great Britain and the United States, and has frequently been recalled since, for example in the case concerning the *Greco–Bulgarian "Communities"* in which the Permanent Court of International Justice laid it down that

> "it is a generally accepted principle of international law that in the relations between Powers who are contracting Parties to a treaty, the provisions of municipal law cannot prevail over those of the treaty"
>
> *(P.C.I.J., Series B, No.* 17, p. 32).

* * *

58. For these reasons,

THE COURT,

Unanimously,

Is of the opinion that the United States of America, as a party to the Agreement between the United Nations and the United States of America regarding the Headquarters of the United Nations of 26 June 1947, is under an obligation, in accordance with section 21 of that Agreement, to enter into arbitration for the settlement of the dispute between itself and the United Nations.

United States v. Palestine Liberation Organization

United States District Court, Southern District of New York
695 F.Supp. 1456 (1988)

■ PALMIERI, DISTRICT JUDGE.

The Anti-terrorism Act of 1987 (the "ATA"), is the focal point of this lawsuit. At the center of controversy is the right of the Palestine Liberation Organization (the "PLO") to maintain its office in conjunction with its work as a Permanent Observer to the United Nations. The case comes before the court on the government's motion for an injunction closing this office and on the defendants' motions to dismiss.

I
Background

The United Nations' Headquarters in New York were established as an international enclave by the Agreement Between the United States and the United Nations Regarding the Headquarters of the United Nations (the "Headquarters Agreement"). This agreement followed an invitation extended to the United Nations by the United States, one of its principal founders, to establish its seat within the United States.

As a meeting place and forum for all nations, the United Nations, according to its charter, was formed to:

> maintain international peace and security ...; to develop friendly relations among nations, based on the principle of equal rights and self-determination of peoples ...; to achieve international cooperation in solving international problems of an economic, social, cultural or humanitarian character ...; and be a centre for harmonizing the actions of nations in the attainment of these common ends. UN. Charter art. 1. Today, 159 of the United Nations' members maintain missions to the UN. in New York. UN. Protocol and Liaison Service, Permanent Missions to the United Nations No. 262 3–4 (1988) (hereinafter "Permanent Missions No. 262"). In addition, the United Nations has, from its incipiency, welcomed various non-member observers to participate in its proceedings. See Permanent Missions to the United Nations: Report of the Secretary–General, 4 UN. GAOR C.6 Annex (Agenda Item 50) 16, 17¶ 14, UN. Doc. A/939/Rev.1 (1949) (hereinafter Permanent Missions: Report of the Secretary–General). Of these, several non-member nations, intergovernmental organizations, and other organizations currently maintain "Permanent Observer Missions" in New York.

The PLO falls into the last of these categories and is present at the United Nations as its invitee. See Headquarters Agreement, § 11, 61 Stat. at 761 (22 U.S.C. § 287 note).

The PLO has none of the usual attributes of sovereignty. It is not accredited to the United States and does not have the benefits of diplomatic immunity. There is no recognized state it claims to govern. It purports to serve as the sole political representative of the Palestinian people. See generally Kassim, The Palestine Liberation Organization Claim to Status: A Juridical Analysis Under International Law, 9 Den.J.International L. & Policy 1 (1980). The PLO nevertheless considers itself to be the representative of a state, entitled to recognition in its relations with other governments, and is said to have diplomatic relations with approximately one hundred countries throughout the world. *Id.* at 19.

* * *

It is important to note for the purposes of this case that a primary goal of the United Nations is to provide a forum where peaceful discussions may displace violence as a means of resolving disputed issues. At times our responsibility to the United Nations may require us to issue visas to persons who are objectionable to certain segments of our society. *Id.,* transcript at 37, partially excerpted in Department of State, 1974 Digest of United States Practice in International Law, 27, 28.

Since 1974, the PLO has continued to function without interruption as a permanent observer and has maintained its Mission to the United Nations without trammel, largely because of the Headquarters Agreement, which we discuss below.

II
The Anti–Terrorism Act

In October 1986, members of Congress requested the United States Department of State to close the PLO offices located in the United States. That request proved unsuccessful, and proponents of the request introduced legislation with the explicit purpose of doing so.

The result was the ATA, 22 U.S.C. §§ 5201–5203. It is of a unique nature. We have been unable to find any comparable statute in the long history of Congressional enactments. The PLO is stated to be "a terrorist organization and a threat to the interests of the United States, its allies, and to international law and should not benefit from operating in the United States." 22 U.S.C. § 5201(b). The ATA was added, without committee hearings, as a rider to the Foreign Relations Authorization Act for Fiscal Years 1988–89, which provided funds for the operation of the State Department, including the operation of the United States Mission to the United Nations. Pub.L. 100–204 § 101, 101 Stat. 1331, 1335. The bill also authorized payments to the United Nations for maintenance and operation. *Id.* § 102(a)(1), 101 Stat. at 1336; see also *id.* § 143, 101 Stat. at 1386.

The ATA, which became effective on March 21, 1988, forbids the establishment or maintenance of "an office, headquarters, premises, or other facilities or establishments within the jurisdiction of the United States at the behest or direction of, or with funds provided by" the PLO, if the purpose is to further the PLO's interests. 22 U.S.C. § 5202(3). The ATA also forbids spending the PLO's funds or receiving anything of value except informational material from the PLO, with the same *mens rea* requirement. *Id.* §§ 5202(1) and (2).

Ten days before the effective date, the Attorney General wrote the Chief of the PLO Observer Mission to the United Nations that "maintaining a PLO Observer Mission to the United Nations will be unlawful," and advised him that upon failure of compliance, the Department of Justice would take action in federal court. This letter is reproduced in the record as item 28 of the Compendium prepared at the outset of this litigation pursuant to the court's April 21, 1988 request to counsel (attached as Appendix B). It is entitled "Compendium of the Legislative History of the Anti–Terrorism Act of 1987, Related Legislation, and Official Statements of the Department of Justice and the Department of State Regarding This Legislation." The documents in the compendium are of great interest.

The United States commenced this lawsuit the day the ATA took effect, seeking injunctive relief to accomplish the closure of the Mission. The United States Attorney for this District has personally represented that no action would be taken to enforce the ATA pending resolution of the litigation in this court.

* * *

IV
The Duty to Arbitrate

Counsel for the PLO and for the United Nations and the Association of the Bar of the City of New York, as *amici curiae*, have suggested that the court defer to an advisory opinion of the International Court of Justice. *Applicability of the Obligation to Arbitrate Under Section 21 of the United Nations Headquarters Agreement of 26 June 1947*, 1988 I.C.J. No. 77 (April 26, 1988) (*U.N. v. U.S.*). That decision holds that the United States is bound by Section 21 of the Headquarters Agreement to submit to binding arbitration of a dispute precipitated by the passage of the ATA. Indeed, it is the PLO's position that this alleged duty to arbitrate deprives the court of subject matter jurisdiction over this litigation.

In June 1947, the United States subscribed to the Headquarters Agreement, defining the privileges and immunities of the United Nations' Headquarters in New York City, thereby becoming the "Host Country"—a descriptive title that has followed it through many United Nations proceedings. The Headquarters Agreement was brought into effect under United States law, with an annex, by a Joint Resolution of Congress approved by the President on August 4, 1947. The PLO rests its argument, as do the *amici*, on Section 21(a) of the Headquarters Agreement, which provides for arbitration in the case of any dispute between the United Nations and the United States concerning the interpretation or application of the Headquarters Agreement. Because interpretation of the ATA requires an interpretation of the Headquarters Agreement, they argue, this court must await the decision of an arbitral tribunal yet to be appointed before making its decision.

Section 21(a) of the Headquarters Agreement provides, in part:

"Any dispute *between the United Nations and the United States* concerning the interpretation or application of this agreement or of any supplemental agreement, which is not settled by negotiation or other agreed mode of settlement, shall be referred for final decision to a tribunal of three arbitrators...." 61 Stat. at 764 (22 U.S.C. § 287 note) (emphasis supplied).

Because these proceedings are not in any way directed to settling any dispute, ripe or not, between the United Nations and the United States, Section 21, is, by its terms, inapplicable. The fact that the Headquarters Agreement was adopted by a majority of both Houses of Congress and approved by the President, see 61 Stat. at 768, might lead to the conclusion that it provides a rule of decision requiring arbitration any time the interpretation of the Headquarters Agreement is at issue in the United States Courts. That conclusion would be wrong for two reasons.

First, this court cannot direct the United States to submit to arbitration without exceeding the scope of its Article III powers. What sets this case apart from the usual situation in which two parties have agreed to binding arbitration for the settlement of any future disputes, requiring the court to stay its proceedings, cf. 9 U.S.C. § 3 (1982), is that we are here involved with matters of international policy. This is an area in which the courts are generally unable to participate. These questions do not lend themselves to resolution by adjudication under our jurisprudence. *See generally Baker v. Carr, 369* U.S. 186, 211–13, 82 S.Ct. 691, 707–08, 7 L.Ed.2d 663 (1962). The restrictions imposed upon the courts forbidding them to resolve such questions (often termed "political questions") derive not only from the limitations which inhere in the judicial process but also from those imposed by Article III of the Constitution. *Marbury v. Madison,* 5 U.S. (1 Cranch) 137, 170, 2 L.Ed. 60 (1803) (Marshall, C.J.) ("The province of the court is, solely, to decide on the right of individuals, not to inquire how the executive, or executive officers, perform duties in which they have a discretion. Questions in their nature political, or which are, by the constitution and laws, submitted to the executive can never be made in this Court."). The decision in Marbury has never been disturbed.

The conduct of the foreign relations of our Government is committed by the Constitution to the executive and legislative—the "political"—departments of the government. As the Supreme Court noted in *Baker v. Carr,* supra, 369 U.S. at 211, 82 S.Ct. at 707, not all questions touching upon international relations are automatically political questions. Nonetheless, were the court to order the United States to submit to arbitration, it would violate several of the tenets to which the Supreme Court gave voice in *Baker v. Carr, supra,* 369 U.S. at 217, 82 S.Ct. at 710. Resolution of the question whether the United States will arbitrate requires "an initial policy determination of a kind clearly for nonjudicial discretion;" deciding whether the United States will or ought to submit to arbitration, in the face of a determination not to do so by the executive, would be impossible without the court "expressing lack of the respect due coordinate branches of government;" and such a decision would raise not only the "potentiality" but the reality of "embarrassment from multifarious pronouncements by various departments on one question." It is for these reasons that the ultimate decision as to how the United States should honor its treaty obligations with the international community is one which has, for at least one hundred years, been left to the executive to decide. *Goldwater v. Carter,* 444 U.S. 996, 996–97, 100 S.Ct. 533, 533, 62 L.Ed.2d 428 (1979) (vacating, with instructions to dismiss, an attack on the President's action in terminating a treaty with Taiwan)....

The task of the court in this case is to interpret the ATA in resolving this dispute between numerous parties and the United States. Interpretation of the ATA, as a matter of domestic law, falls to the United States courts. In interpreting the ATA, the effect of the United States' international obligations—the United Nations Charter and the Headquarters Agreement in particular—must be considered. As a matter of domestic law, the interpretation of these international obligations and their reconciliation, if possible, with the ATA is for the courts....

V
The Anti–Terrorism Act and the Headquarters Agreement

If the ATA were construed as the government suggests, it would be tantamount to a direction to the PLO Observer Mission at the United Nations that it close its doors and cease its operations instanter. Such an interpretation would fly in the face of the Headquarters Agreement, a prior treaty between the United Nations and the United States, and would abruptly terminate the functions the Mission has performed for many years.

This conflict requires the court to seek out a reconciliation between the two.

Under our constitutional system, statutes and treaties are both the supreme law of the land, and the Constitution sets forth no order of precedence to differentiate between them. U.S. Const. art. VI, cl. 2. Wherever possible, both are to be given effect. *E.g. Trans World Airlines, Inc. v. Franklin Mint Corp.,* 466 U.S. 243, 252, 104 S.Ct. 1776, 1783, 80 L.Ed.2d 273 (1984)....

* * *

B.   Reconciliation of the ATA and the Headquarters Agreement.

The lengths to which our courts have sometimes gone in construing domestic statutes so as to avoid conflict with international agreements are suggested by a passage from Justice Field's dissent in *Chew Heong, supra,* 112 U.S. at 560, 560–61, 67 S.Ct. at 267, 267 (1884):

> I am unable to agree with my associates in their construction of the act ... restricting the immigration into this country of Chinese laborers. That construction appears to me to be in conflict with the language of that act, and to require the elimination of entire clauses and the interpolation of new ones. It renders nugatory whole provisions which were inserted with sedulous care. The change thus produced in the operation of the act is justified on the theory that to give it any other construction would bring it into conflict with the treaty; and that we are not at liberty to suppose that Congress intended by its legislation to disregard any treaty stipulations.

Chew Heong concerned the interplay of legislation regarding Chinese laborers with treaties on the same subject. During the passage of the statute at issue in *Chew Heong,* "it was objected to the legislation sought that the treaty of 1868 stood in the way, and that while it remained unmodified, such legislation would be a breach of faith to China...." *Id.* at 569, 67 S.Ct. at 272. In spite of that, and over Justice Field's dissent, the Court, in Justice Field's words, "narrow[ed] the meaning of the act so as measurably to frustrate its intended operation." Four years after the decision in *Chew Heong,* Congress amended the act in question to nullify that decision. Ch. 1064, 25 Stat. 504. With the amended statute, there could be no question as to Congress' intent to supersede the treaties, and it was the later enacted statute which took precedence. *The Chinese Exclusion Case, supra,* 130 U.S. at 598–99, 9 S.Ct. at 627 (1889).

* * *

Congress' failure to speak with one clear voice on this subject requires us to interpret the ATA as inapplicable to the Headquarters Agreement. This is so, in short, for the reasons which follow.

First, neither the Mission nor the Headquarters Agreement is mentioned in the ATA itself. Such an inclusion would have left no doubt as to Congress' intent on a matter which had been raised repeatedly with respect to this act, and its absence here reflects equivocation and avoidance, leaving the court without clear interpretive guidance in the language of the act. Second, while the section of the ATA prohibiting the maintenance of an office applies "notwithstanding any provision of law to the contrary," 22 U.S.C. § 5202(3), it does not purport to apply notwithstanding any *treaty.* The absence of that interpretive instruction is especially relevant because elsewhere in the same legislation Congress expressly referred to "United States law (including any treaty)." 101 Stat. at 1343. Thus Congress failed, in the text of the ATA, to provide guidance for the interpretation of the act, where it became repeatedly apparent before its passage that the prospect of an interpretive problem was inevitable. Third, no member of Congress expressed a clear and unequivocal intent to supersede the Headquarters Agreement by passage of the ATA. In contrast, most who addressed the subject of conflict denied that there would be a conflict: in their view, the Headquarters Agreement did not provide the PLO with any right to maintain an office. Here again, Congress provided no guidance for the interpretation of the ATA in the event of a conflict which was clearly foreseeable. And Senator Claiborne Pell, Chairman of the Senate Foreign Relations Committee, who voted for the bill, raised the possibility that the Headquarters Agreement would take precedence over the ATA in the event of a conflict between the two. His suggestion was neither opposed nor debated, even though it came in the final minutes before passage of the ATA.

A more complete explanation begins, of course, with the statute's language. The ATA reads, in part:

It shall be unlawful, if the purpose be to further the interests of the PLO * * *.

(3) notwithstanding any provision of law to the contrary, to establish or maintain an office, headquarters, premises, or other facilities or establishments within the jurisdiction of the United States at the behest or direction of, or with funds provided by the PLO....

22 U.S.C. § 5202(3).

The Permanent Observer Mission to the United Nations is nowhere mentioned *in haec verba* in this act, as we have already observed. It is nevertheless contended by the United States that the foregoing provision requires the closing of the Mission, and this in spite of possibly inconsistent international obligations. According to the government, the act is so clear that this possibility is nonexistent. The government argues that its position is supported by the provision that the ATA would take effect "notwithstanding any provision of law to the contrary," 22 U.S.C. § 5202(3), suggesting that Congress thereby swept away any inconsistent international obligations of the United States. In effect, the government urges literal application of the maxim that in the event of conflict between two laws, the one of later date will prevail: *leges posteriores priores contrarias abrogant.*

We cannot agree. The proponents of the ATA were, at an early stage and throughout its consideration, forewarned that the ATA would present a potential conflict with the Headquarters Agreement. It was especially important in those circumstances for Congress to give clear, indeed unequivocal guidance, as to how an interpreter of the ATA was to resolve the conflict. Yet there was no reference to the Mission in the text of the ATA, despite extensive discussion of the Mission in the floor debates. Nor was there reference to the Headquarters Agreement, or to any treaty, in the ATA or in its "notwithstanding" clause, despite the textual expression of intent to supersede treaty obligations in other sections of the Foreign Relations Authorization Act, of which the ATA formed a part. Thus Congress failed to provide unequivocal interpretive guidance in the text of the ATA, leaving open the possibility that the ATA could be viewed as a law of general application and enforced as such, without encroaching on the position of the Mission at the United Nations.

The interpretation would present no inconsistency with what little legislative history exists. There were conflicting voices both in Congress and in the executive branch before the enactment of the ATA. Indeed, there is only one matter with respect to which there was unanimity—the condemnation of terrorism. This, however, is extraneous to the legal issues involved here. At oral argument, the United States Attorney conceded that there was no evidence before the court that the Mission had misused its position at the United Nations or engaged in any covert actions in furtherance of terrorism. If the PLO is benefiting from operating in the United States, as the ATA implies, the enforcement of its provisions outside the context of the United Nations can effectively curtail that benefit.

The record contains voices of congressmen and senators forceful in their condemnation of terrorism and of the PLO and supporting the notion that the legislation would close the mission. There are other voices, less certain of the validity of the proposed congressional action and preoccupied by problems of constitutional dimension. And there are voices of Congressmen uncertain of the legal issues presented but desirous nonetheless of making a "political statement." During the discussions which preceded and followed the passage of the ATA, the Secretary of State and the Legal Adviser to the Department of State a former member of this Court, voiced their opinions to the effect that the ATA presented a conflict with the Headquarters Agreement.

Yet no member of Congress, at any point, explicitly stated that the ATA was intended to override any international obligation of the United States.

The only debate on this issue focused not on whether the ATA would do so, but on whether the United States in fact had an obligation to provide access to the PLO. Indeed, every proponent of the ATA who spoke to the matter argued that the United States did not have such an obligation. For instance, Senator Grassley, after arguing that the United States had no obligation relating to the PLO Mission under the Headquarters Agreement, noted in passing that Congress had the *power* to modify treaty obligations. But even there, Senator Grassley did not argue that the ATA would supersede the Headquarters Agreement in the event of a conflict. 133 Cong. Rec. S 15,621–22 (daily ed. November 3, 1987). This disinclination to face the prospect of an actual conflict was again manifest two weeks later, when Senator Grassley explained, "as I detailed earlier . . ., the United States has *no international legal obligation* that would preclude it from closing the PLO Observer Mission." 133 Cong. Rec. S 16,505 (daily ed. November 20, 1987) (emphasis supplied). As the Congressional Record reveals, at the time of the ATA's passage (on December 15 in the House and December 16 in the Senate), its proponents were operating under a misapprehension of what the United States' treaty obligation entailed. 133 Cong. Rec. S 18,190 (daily ed. December 16, 1987) (statement of Sen. Helms) (closing the Mission would be "entirely within our Nation's obligations under international law"); 133 Cong. Rec. H 11,425 (daily ed. December 15, 1988) (statement of Rep. Burton) (observer missions have "no—zero—rights in the Headquarters Agreement.")

In sum, the language of the Headquarters Agreement, the longstanding practice under it, and the interpretation given it by the parties to it leave no doubt that it places an obligation upon the United States to refrain from impairing the function of the PLO Observer Mission to the United Nations. The ATA and its legislative history do not manifest Congress' intent to abrogate this obligation. We are therefore constrained to interpret the ATA as failing to supersede the Headquarters Agreement and inapplicable to the Mission.

Concerns over conflicting national and international law arise in a variety of forums. The Organization of Economic Cooperation and Development (OECD) is, like the UN, an international organization comprised of sovereign states. It has its headquarters in Paris and is devoted to economic and commercial issues. (The OECD is discussed in greater detail in Chapter 3.) In 1989, the OECD's Committee on Fiscal Affairs made a report on the subject of national legislation overriding tax treaties. The Committee made its Report to the Council of the OECD, where 24 member states from the traditional market economy countries of North America, Western Europe and the Far East were represented. In acting on the Committee's Report, the OECD Council acting by consensus on October 2, 1989, its 717th Session, recommended Member Countries:

1. To undertake promptly bilateral or multilateral consultations to address problems connected with tax treaty provisions, whether arising in their own country or raised by countries with which they have tax treaties:

2. To avoid enacting legislation which is intended to have effects in clear contradiction to international treaty obligations.

NOTES AND QUESTIONS

1. The OECD Council recommends that states "avoid" enacting national legislation that conflicts with treaties. Can states, however, avoid all conflicts between national law and international law? Think about why conflicts occur. Consider the analogous case of a federal legal system like the United States. Can U.S. States always avoid conflicts with Federal law? How are such conflicts handled within the U.S. system? How can they generally be avoided?

2. What is the international law rule as enunciated by the ICJ in the *Headquarters* case as to cases of national law—international law conflicts? Could the international legal system have a different rule?

3. Compare the approach of the French court in *Vabres* and the U.S. court in the *PLO Mission* case. In both cases, a treaty was found to prevail over later-in-time legislation but the reasoning is very different. Are the values underlying the decisions also significantly different? Can you tell from these decisions whether the U.S. and France are monist or dualist? For more on international law and national legal systems, see Chapter 11.

4. In addition to being introduced to the purpose and sources of international law, you have also been introduced to many of the relevant actors. Consider the categories of actors that have already appeared in the chapter. We will consider them again in the next section and in detail in the next chapter.

B. THE WORLD OF THE INTERNATIONAL LEGAL SYSTEM

1. INTERNATIONAL CHALLENGES AND THE ROLE OF LAW

As the authors included in this section explain, the world is a place of change but also continuity. It is a place where globalization is occurring while at the same time, people seek stronger association with local communities. In other words, modern communications and transportation are creating a more homogenized, interconnected world, and people search for identity and distinctiveness through culture, religion, and language. The world today is characterized by cross-cutting trends. The challenges indicated in Section A above in part result from the impact of conflicting trends. International law is a tool for responding to global challenges in a way that minimizes violence and unjust outcomes. It aims to create greater order and predictability in our complex world.

Richard Mansbach and Kirsten Rafferty, History and Global Politics: Change and Continuity

pp. 6–9, Introduction to Global Politics (2008)

Global politics reflects both change and continuity. By change we mean *the transformation of key structures and processes that has a major impact on the nature of global politics*. Where there is significant and rapid change, there are discontinuities between past and present with features of the present not recognizable in the past. For example, the shift from the medieval European order of overlapping rights, privileges, and ownership based on a feudal agrarian economy to a world of sovereign states enjoying exclusive legal authority over internal affairs constituted a major transformation in global politics. So, too, was the shift in security and military strategy that was brought about by the introduction of nuclear weapons after World War II. More recently, the end of the Cold War produced a dramatically different world: the United States emerged as the world's only superpower; Russia, China, and the countries of Eastern Europe joined the global economic system; globalization linked the fates of people around the world as never before; and suicidal fanaticism produced an unprecedented security problem. None of these developments was predicted, and, therefore, there was little planning to deal with them.

The other side of change is continuity *which refers to the gradual evolution of structures or processes such that the present retains key features of the past*. Although global politics is constantly changing—with new events and new actors (countries and other groups whose behavior is relevant to global politics) emerging all the time—there is nonetheless much to be learned from the past experiences of states and other global actors. For example, terrorism is not new, even though certain features of contemporary terrorism are novel. In fact, few events—however unexpected—come from out of the blue. Much that seems novel actually has roots in the past, and familiarity with history makes the present more understandable, helps us to plan for the future, and allows us to avoid making the same mistakes over again. Although some aspects of every event are unique, history provides important analogies and vital experience.

An acquaintance with history is necessary for identifying change and continuity. * * *

Change is part of the natural rhythm of our lives, but when it accelerates to the point where we are "strangers in a strange land," as many people all over the world felt in the aftermath of September 11th, people become fearful, anxious, mistrustful, and disoriented. Sometimes, as in this case, change is genuinely threatening and really does imperil the safety and well-being of individuals and society. Suicide bombers, who look forward to martyrdom and paradise, are particularly menacing, as threats of retaliation cannot prevent them from acting. However, at other times change is frightening, but does not have the same disastrous consequence. For instance, for over 300 years the territorial state has been the fulcrum of global politics. Thus the field became known as international politics or international relations because it focused exclusively on relations among (*inter*) sovereign states. Such a focus is called "state-centric." But some observers point to the gradual proliferation of important actors other than states such as giant transnational corporations like IBM and ExxonMobil, international organizations like the United Nations and the World Bank, and nongovernmental groups like Greenpeace and Al Qaeda as evidence that sovereign states no longer enjoy unchallenged primacy—and control—in global politics (a term that allows us to speak of a wider galaxy of actors than states alone). In the state-centric world, governments make most authoritative decisions, but in the expanded world of global politics, authoritative decisions are also made by numerous domestic, transnational, and international institutions and groups, both formal and informal, creating a complex universe of what is termed global governance in which the governments of nation-states represent only one type of global authority.

Also, rapid economic change creates fears of future poverty and social dislocation. Workers in U.S. industries like textiles will almost certainly lose their jobs in coming years owing to the growth of similar industries in Asia and South America, where production costs are lower than in America. The American economy will have to restructure and former textile workers will have to seek training and employment in other sectors. Likewise, rapid political change, such as the collapse of the Soviet Empire in the late 1980s and early 1990s, raises anxiety about reduced status, loss of freedom, or even threats of war and violence.

But whether or not we fear changes matters less than how we react to them. Dramatic change can lead to either conflict or cooperation among global actors. Some leaders genuinely learn from novel events, while others ignore them and keep on in the same old ways. * * *

[T]he world is changing in complex ways, and knowledge of history does not tell us how change takes place. Is change a random or stochastic process—a product of mere chance—or is it determined by the past? Is history linear and progressive, or does it take the form of long cycles? Such questions remain unanswered. However, political, economic, social, and cultural systems are becoming more interconnected as people, things, and ideas move freely across state frontiers. This process, known as globalization, erodes state borders, challenges the control states exercise over their populations, reduces the importance of territory, creates dangerous new forms of violence, and encourages globe-girdling economic and cultural forces.

Yet, not everything is new. War, for example, has been central to global politics for millennia. If we understood its causes, we would eliminate them to prevent the horrifying levels of death and destruction that accompany armed conflict. Instead, even as wars among states grow less frequent, wars involving terrorists, ethnic minorities, and other groups become more frequent, with the potential to become even more deadly. Notwithstanding numerous efforts to explain war, we still quote from ancient philosophers and writers like Thucydides, a Greek historian from the fifth century BC, to understand and explain them. Thucydides sought to identify the causes and consequences of war "for eternity." His great work, *The History of the Peloponnesian War*, told the story of a great war that pitted Athens and its allies against Sparta and its allies, culminating in the destruction of Athens, the birthplace of democracy. His claim that the relative power of the city-states provided an important explanation of why war erupted tells us that we should pay careful attention to rapid changes in power, for example, China's rapid increase in military and economic capabilities. However, rapid change in the distribution of power is only one possible cause of war. Even today, we still cannot explain the outbreak of war with certainty. The Greek city-states of Thucydides' world gave way over the centuries to larger, more powerful, and more dangerous political communities, territorial states, which dominated global politics for over three centuries and which continue to play a major role in today's world.

Hanns Maull, On the Concept of "International Order"

pp. 93–108, CHALLENGES OF GLOBALIZATION (Pfaller and Lerch eds., 2005)

We first need to recognize that, while "international order" is not a Western concept, its present shape and prevailing notions about international order *are* Western in a rather deep sense: at present, international order and the debate about it is the product of what the historian William H. McNeill has called "The Rise of the West"—the ascendance of the European world through the dynamics of modernization, of which globalization represents but the most recent and most advanced stage.

Western notions of international order, however, are ambivalent. The present international order, as expressed, e.g., in the Charter of the United Nations, is built around several core norms: the norms of nonviolent conflict resolution, of states rights (sovereignty) and of human rights. The latter two clearly are in tension with each other, and the UN Charter is profoundly ambivalent as to whose international order it establishes—is it an order of and for states, or of and for individuals? This tension is further accentuated by the fact that states are both indispensable sources of protection and massive violation of human rights. How then, should "international order" be conceived in the struggle against terrorism with global reach? Does "international order" concern only states, or ultimately all human beings? And is international order a static or a dynamic concept? Does it discourage or promote change?

International Order—for Whom?

Traditionally, concepts of international order have settled on states as their constituency, and have accepted war as an evil to be exorcised or at least tamed. Consequently, one widespread notion of "international order" equates order with international stability, that is, stable, predictable and controlled relations between states, in which turbulence, chaos and violence are largely (though not necessarily completely) absent. This notion of order focuses on interstate relations, and more specifically on relations between the major powers.

By and large, international order over the last half century has been successfully secured in the sense of this definition. A major conflagration between the powers was avoided, and generally the incidence of interstate war has been declining. States indeed have been the principal beneficiaries of this order, as suggested by the fact that their number has increased very substantially since 1945.

Yet even before September 11, it was already clear that this rather narrow definition of international order was no longer very useful, for several reasons:

- First, this perspective neglects the realities of transnational and international interdependence. The state no longer resembles the billiard ball with which traditional models of international relations had played. Societies and states have become dependent on, and vulnerable to developments elsewhere. With the oil shocks of the 1970s, economic security joined traditional national security as a key concern of security policy makers; with the Chernobyl incident, environmental destruction and cross-border pollution were added. Now, international terrorism has been highlighted as a new security concern emanating from non-state actors, rather than from other states. In short, the sources of threats to security have broadened to include both states and non-state actors, and as the former have been successfully reigned in, sources of threats have tended to come from the latter.

- Second, the concept of security in international relations has undergone subtle but important changes. Individual and social security concerns have come to assume greater salience in national security policies, while the traditional emphasis on territorial integrity and political autonomy has receded at least in the OECD world. During the Cold War, societies had been taken hostage by military security strategies of Mutual Assured Destruction. With the disappearance of this threat new risks to individual and collective security have assumed greater importance. Thus, the "new" security agenda of proliferation, organized crime, drugs, environmental destruction and, of course, international terrorism began to crystallize and make its ways into official security policy documents and policies.

- With the terrorist attacks of September 11, the concept of security has undergone a further mutation. Hitherto, it was assumed that international terrorism would pursue specific demands and hence be amenable to negotiation, and that it would respect certain thresholds: terrorists, it was argued, were interested in maximum media exposure but not in maximum casualties and wanton destruction for its own sake. With the rise of religiously motivated terrorism, this logic has looked increasingly shaky, terrorist attacks may now be justified in very broad, vague and non-negotiable terms and aimed at maximum destruction and loss of lives. Moreover, the sources of the terrorist threat may well lie within our own societies, both in the form of organizational nodes of transnational terrorist networks such as al Qaeda and through terrorists from our own societies (as seems to be the case with the anthrax attacks in the United States). While it is arguable whether globalization really should be considered as one—or even *the*—cause for the terrorist attacks of September 11, it is clear that the attacks represent globalization in action: al Qaeda has perfectly understood and exploited the opportunities for networked terrorist operations in the age of globalization. In sum, a notion of international order which abstracts from conditions within states and interdependencies between societies no longer is meaningful. What is needed is a concept which covers both intra- and interstate relations, both state and society. This has increasingly been recognized by the international community itself, as indicated by the shift in international law and international practice towards "humanitarian intervention".

Defense of the Status Quo or Alliance for Progress?

A second Western definition of "international order" tends to equate it with the prevailing international status quo. This definition is both broader and more narrow than the previous one. It is broader because it includes domestic political arrangements within states, at least to the extent they are important for sustaining existing arrangements of international governance. But it is more narrow because it is more resistant to change than the first definition, which does allow for changes in international governance, as long as the system's essential structure remains intact.

This definition, too, has obvious flaws. Although the West in general, and the United States in particular, have been dominant in and beneficiaries of the present international order, they are only in part upholders of the status quo. America, in particular, is also an anti-status quo power. First, American foreign policy is profoundly value-oriented: the promotion of democracy and human rights, for example, has had—for all the political pragmatism and business acumen which undeniably has always loomed large in U.S. foreign policy—significant and important international repercussions against the political status quo. The demise of the Soviet empire, the Iranian revolution or the political changes in the Philippines from President Ferdinand Marcos to Corazon Aquino and in Indonesia (from President Suharto to Presidents Habibie and Wahid) illustrate this point.

Secondly, America constantly challenges the status quo through its espousal of capitalist market economics. As a form of economic organization, capitalism is highly dynamic, highly creative and highly destructive. America has long been the lead power in global capitalism and its most powerful proponent. America, and the West in general, therefore will not only try to uphold but also constantly challenge the status quo, in search of a wealthier and better world.

International Order Equals Rules–Based International Relations

In the final analysis, then, the Western concept of international order therefore is geared towards change, to accommodate the dynamics of capitalism and the values of democracy. It tries to integrate domestic, democratic politics, the vulnerabilities of interdependence and the realities of globalization in the notion of rules-based international relations. The "rules" for international order are those which inform our own political and economic systems. In the OECD world of Western industrialized democracies, problems of war and civil strife have been successfully contained: the West enjoys the "democratic peace" of Immanuel Kant—in political relations within states, but also between them. This historical experience of Western societies in "civilizing" the management of social conflicts through self-restraint and the establishment of effective monopolies of force has been analyzed most cogently by the German sociologist Norbert Elias. Elias' model, which originally aimed at explaining the progress of "civilized" politics within states, can also be transposed, through processes of gradual "enlargement", onto other political contexts above the nation-state, regionally (e.g., in the European Union) and even globally. The model can be summarized in six major objectives which Dieter Senghaas has called the "civilizational hexagon". Those six objectives are interdependent; taken together, they describe a complex program for enhancing international order. The six objectives are:

- constraining and eventually monopolizing the use of force,
- developing a non-violent culture of conflict management,
- fostering the rule of law,
- building institutions,
- providing for participation in decision-making by those affected by the decisions, and
- providing for social equity and fairness.

In sum, the Western concept of international order prescribes a process of controlled, peaceful and evolutionary change towards a more civilized world in the sense of the civilizational hexagon. "Change" makes clear that this concept transcends the status quo, both domestically and internationally; "evolutionary" recognizes that the realization of this utopian project can only be done step by step; "peaceful" emphasizes constraints on the use of force in this process; and "controlled" suggests that, as change ought to go in certain directions, it needs to be politically controlled—we are therefore talking about a process in which politics is in charge. In this concept of international order, states are pivotal: they constitute the foundations on which international order rests by ensuring rules-based behavior and non-violent conflict management within their domain, but also between them. Together, they shape the evolving rules and institutions of international order by providing for the negotiation, legitimation and implementation of international agreements; and they provide the critical building blocks of international order through their support for such arrangements by supplying the political, financial and human resources and the political will needed to make those arrangements and their institutions effective. Their importance for international order can, therefore, hardly been overstated.

But if the state is pivotal to international order, it also continues to be its nemesis. For the state to be able to play its crucial role constructively, it will need to conform to the standards of a just order set by the civilizational hexagon. From this perspective, the task of ordering international relations concerns not just inter-state and transnational, but also intrastate relations; in fact, it implies a convergence and eventual fusion of principles of domestic and international order, as economic, social, political and cultural interdependencies between states and societies continue to thicken. Failure to promote and enhance international order, on the other hand, would lead to the degradation of domestic order through corrosive influences of international anarchy. The ultimate consequence of deficient global governance thus would be the advance of violence within states.

* * *

* * * At the core of the supply/demand gap in international governance caused by globalization, and hence of the precariousness and fragility of international order, lies an overburdened state. Effective international governance requires functioning states as a necessary (though not a sufficient) condition; in reality, however, states often seem overburdened and overstretched even in the successful "first world" and deeply deficient, if not completely defunct, in much of the world beyond. Only functioning states can provide the building blocks for a vibrant international order; yet there are preciously few strong states around.

NOTES AND QUESTIONS

1.   Mansbach and Rafferty comment that "One can view global politics from any of several perspectives or levels of analysis. The core question here is whether the most powerful explanation for key events is to be found in the characteristics of individuals, states, or the global system as a whole." What is your view? How might your answer impact your analysis of international law?

2.   Can you tell which category of actors Maull finds most important in the on-going evolution toward or away from order in the world? Which of his conceptions of order do you find most compelling? What is the role of international law in achieving order in international relations? What other tools do we have that can contribute to order other than law? While we

may grant that anarchy is antithetical to human flourishing, what are the disadvantages of the other extreme?

3. Are there indications in either excerpt of an international community in addition to the system of states? Are you surprised to find how important Maull finds states to be? It has been far more fashionable in recent decades to argue for reducing the power of states and replacing them with something else.

Maull argues that the UN Charter is ambivalent to the tension between the state and the individual. Is the focus on the state in international law a means to an end or an end in itself? Do you see the dangers or problems of having a global system built on individual rights and responsibilities alone? See Chapter 3 *Subjects of International Law*.

4. What do international lawyers need to know from international relations scholars? What should international relations scholars learn from international lawyers? For a collection of essays that brings the two disciplines together, see, FOUNDATIONS OF INTERNATIONAL LAW AND POLITICS (Oona A. Hathaway and Harold Hongju Koh eds., 2005).

Since the 1960s, international relations scholars have devoted more attention to arguing that international law is not law or is not important in the system of international relations than to understanding the actual role of international law in the system. Maull is a real exception and there are others, but why do you suppose they are exceptions? *See* MARY ELLEN O'CONNELL, THE POWER AND PURPOSE OF INTERNATIONAL LAW 57–68 (2008).

5. For more on the world of international law and how it may be developing, see PETER CALVOCORESSI, WORLD POLITICS SINCE 1945 (9TH ED. 2009); NATIONAL INTELLIGENCE COUNCIL, GLOBAL TRENDS 2025: A TRANSFORMED WORLD (2008); JAMES N. ROSENAU, ALONG THE DOMESTIC–FOREIGN FRONTIER, EXPLORING GOVERNANCE IN A TURBULENT WORLD (1997).

2.   THE ROLE OF LAW IN SHAPING THE INTERNATIONAL SYSTEM

The excerpts above provide forward-looking assessments of the nature of the international system. Consider the view of Addis Adeno in the excerpt below that international law helps shape our concepts of the world. His references to universal jurisdiction are exemplified in the pivotal case of Augusto Pinochet, whose actions allegedly in violation of international law in Chile were considered before the national courts of Spain and the United Kingdom.

Addis Adeno, Imagining the International Community*

pp. 145–50, 31 HUM. RTS. Q. (2009)

Jurisdictional norms, perhaps more than other norms, play an important role in defining communities. They define what a nation, a state, or a

---

* Footnotes omitted.

city is. To prescribe jurisdictional rules is, therefore, to constitute an identity—to assert that for certain purposes we deem the particular territorial entity as being a community of interests. Traditional international prescriptive jurisdictions define the authority of every state vis-à-vis other states, and consequently they define the very nature of the territorial community we call the state. Universal jurisdiction, on the other hand, can be seen as one process through which we imagine the international community as a community of interest.

It is important to note that the phrase "imagined communities" is not used to suggest that the international community, as constituted by universal jurisdiction, is false or fabricated. Benedict Anderson, who coined the phrase "imagined community" to describe the nation, observes that "all communities larger than primordial villages of face-to-face contact (and perhaps even these) are imagined." They are *imagined* because members of those communities "will never know their fellow-members, meet them, or even hear of them, yet in the minds of each lives the image of their communion." Communities are imagined or constituted in several ways. As Anderson notes, "Communities are to be distinguished, not by their falsity/genuineness, but by the style in which they are imagined." Universal jurisdiction is one way through which the international community is imagined. The process of imagining here is of two kinds: universal jurisdiction assumes the existence of a community as it simultaneously constitutes that community. What is the nature of the international community that is imagined (assumed and constituted) through the provision and exercise of universal jurisdictions?

A. Diverse Community

Hannah Arendt argued that the salient characteristic of the human condition is the potential for and the reality of diversity. For Arendt, what made the Nazi crime an attack on the human condition was that it was "an attack upon human diversity as such, that is, upon a characteristic of the 'human status' without which the very words 'mankind' or 'humanity' would be devoid of meaning." Genocide is a good example of an attack on diversity, one designed to cure humanity of its salient characteristic, its "infinite plurality." Genocide is an attack on the very nature of what makes an international community, a community of diverse peoples. How is an attack on human diversity an attack on the international community? The attempt to "cure" this or that community of diversity deprives all of us of various possibilities of being. It diminishes us in the literal as well as in the metaphoric sense.

Genocide and crimes against humanity transgress more than the Kantian categorical imperative of treating humans as ends rather than as means to ends. Rather than merely robbing them of their dignity, these crimes make humans "superfluous" qua humans, to use an Arendtian description. In some sense, slavery, another crime subject to universal jurisdiction, fits this category. Slavery does not simply use humans as means, but it denies the slave's very humanity. Slavery is social death, not simply an infringement on human dignity. Thus, to some extent slavery is also about curing us of diversity by denominating a class of people as not fully human and thus not part of us. While genocide is physical extermination of a group, slavery is social extermination of a group on the basis of some characteristics that are taken as indicators of the less than human nature of the particular group. Each—physical and social decimations—tries to define humanity in a way that excludes a portion of humankind. It is in that sense that one could argue that crimes such as genocide, slavery, and crimes against humanity diminish all of us.

In the current global condition, the threat of physical extermination of groups and forms of being, because they are different or look different, is rather high. Likewise, the concern of the international community to prevent or minimize that risk is proper. This is both because most nation-states are multiethnic and multinational and because weapons of mass destruction are becoming more widely available. Consequently, crimes such as genocide and crimes against humanity have emerged as serious threats to the diverse international community we call humankind.

So, one aspect of the international community that is imagined through the provision of universal jurisdiction is a community of diverse peoples and diverse ways of being. This diversity defines not only the international community (the community of communities) but the constituent communities (nation-states) as well. An act that attempts to diminish that diversity diminishes all of us, both literally and metaphorically. Consequently, offenses that are intended to cure us of diversity—such as genocide and crimes against humanity—are the concern of all of us.

The protection of the constitutive norms could come in one of two ways—by recognizing the particular norm as custom or by codifying it in a treaty. Nothing prevents the international community from codifying a customary norm in a treaty and requiring that member states prosecute or extradite while at the same time recognizing the right of all members of the international community to exercise universal jurisdiction over those offenses under customary international law. * * * [I]n a strict sense, universal jurisdiction is customary in nature, for only then can it be available to all constituent units of the international community. A treaty binds those and only those who become parties to it.

B. A Vulnerable Community

Another defining feature of the current international community is its vulnerability. One could say that the international community consists of communities of equal vulnerability. Globalization and new technologies have increasingly given substance to the body of an international community while at the same time making that community much more vulnerable to destructive threats. The very processes that have made the world a community of communication have also made it an easier target of destructive attacks. Some of the *jus cogens* norms could be understood as directed at protecting the community from these vulnerabilities.

Clearly many threats endanger the well-being and survival of the international community as a whole, but the most immediate source of vulnerability is the threat from terrorism. Every nation—from India to Ethiopia, from Sri Lanka to Russia, from Pakistan to the United States—is vulnerable to terrorist attacks. Although terrorism has been with us for a very long time, the wide-scale threat it poses and the magnitude of the damage it is capable of inflicting are qualitatively different now. It would make sense, then, to recognize universal jurisdiction over offenses—such as terrorism—that are viewed as potential threats to all. Indeed, in some ways the idea of equal vulnerability could explain the recognition of piracy in an earlier era as an international crime subject to universal jurisdiction. One could reasonably argue that piracy only threatened the seafaring powers and their citizens, rather than the international community as a whole, as terrorism appears to do.

Two lessons may be drawn from the comparison between piracy and terrorism. First, if the common vulnerability posed to the international community (the community of commerce and navigation) was the main justification for subjecting piracy to universal jurisdiction, then clearly terrorism should also be subject to universal jurisdiction. The challenge from terrorism is more global than the historical challenge of piracy. Second, the comparison between terrorism and piracy suggests that a self-defined international community perceives its vulnerabilities as a matter of specific historical conditions. During the seventeenth, eighteenth, nineteenth, and early twentieth centuries, for all practical purposes the sea powers saw themselves as the international community. Thus, vulnerability to their commerce and navigation was seen as vulnerability to the entire community. To the extent that communities are constructed of social meanings and that "[s]ocial meanings are historical in character," it follows that communities are historical in character. The international community, like any other community, is a creature of specific historical conditions. In that sense, universal jurisdiction is a marker of the international community at a given historical time.

Although terrorism is a candidate for universal jurisdiction because it threatens all nations in the same way that piracy did (and in some sense still does), there is good reason for national courts to continue to be suspicious about treating terrorism as a universal crime under customary international law; there is no agreed upon international definition of terrorism. To be sure, there are movements toward such a definition. The Terrorism Financing Convention of 1999, Security Council Resolution 1566, and the Report of the High–Level Panel suggest definitions that are more or less similar and could provide the basis for an agreeable account of what constitutes terrorism for the purpose of universal jurisdiction. Despite these challenges, there are specific acts—such as airplane hijacking and bombing—that are regarded as terrorist acts and to which most states are vulnerable. Terrorism of this nature can truly be said to lead to an international community of equal vulnerability. Not surprisingly, states have acted as a community to protect themselves from the common threats posed by these acts.

Naomi Roht–Arriaza, The Pinochet Effect

pp. vii–xii (2005)

The arrest of Augusto Pinochet in London in October 1998 electrified the world. Pinochet was, after all, a symbol of the dictatorships that had plagued much of the world during the 1970s and 1980s. All that had gone wrong in that era, in Chile and elsewhere, was captured in a photograph. A stern group of officers flanks General Pinochet, in dark glasses and uniform, arms crossed, who stares implacably into the camera, daring anyone to challenge him. That image, flashed across the world, became the dark symbol of a dark era. Maybe that's why, a quarter-century later, it retains its potency. The story of the general's downfall has the same end-of-an-era resonance.

* * * Salvador Allende, a doctor and a Socialist, was elected president of Chile in 1970. His experiment creating democratic socialism came to a bloody end in September 1973. After months of plotting the military staged a coup, supported by opposition political parties, the United States, the business sector and a good part of the Chilean middle class. Allende killed himself as the presidential palace was strafed by the Air Force; Congress was dissolved, the Constitution was suspended, and a military junta ruled by decree. The Junta soon came to be dominated by General Augusto Pinochet, whom Allende had appointed as army chief. Pinochet centralized control, created a separate secret police under his personal jurisdiction, and eventually had himself named President and head of the Armed Forces. Under his dictatorship, some five thousand people were killed, over a thousand detained and disappeared, tens of thousands were imprisoned and tortured or forced into exile. After the first years of dictatorship, the crimes became more selective. Requests to the courts for writs of habeas corpus routinely went unanswered. Families were told that their loved ones had no doubt left the country, taken new lovers, been mowed down in military confrontations or internecine squabbles of the left. Fear clamped down on Chile. Those who were killed, it was said, had deserved what they got; their families were shunned, neighbors divided, the press silenced. It lasted, in all, seventeen years.

Many of those who fled the Allende debacle found refuge, at first, in neighboring Argentina. But soon, and especially after 1975, the Argentine military took power and began its own campaign of terror. Not content to crush the country's armed insurgencies, they too struck at a broad swath of Argentine Society, including left-wing supporters of ex-president Juan Perón, students, professionals, exiles from other Latin American regimes, and anyone who seemed to get in the way. In the end, over 30,000 died, most of them taken away to secret detention centers and camps, tortured, tossed still alive from airplanes into the sea or shot and buried in unmarked graves. Pregnant women gave birth manacled and blindfolded, and were then killed and their babies given to military families. Jews were marked for especially sadistic treatment. The terror eventually engulfed the entire Southern Cone of Latin America, as the militarized regimes of Chile, Argentina, Uruguay, Paraguay, Bolivia, and Brazil coordinated their efforts to find and destroy opponents through Operation Condor, sending dissi-dents found in one country to another to disappear. Operation Condor was led by Manuel Contreras, Pinochet's secret police chief.

Argentina and Chile eventually reverted to civilian rule, in 1986 and 1990 respectively. The Raúl Alfonsín government in Argentina commis-sioned a group of notables headed by writer Ernesto Sábato (also known as CONADEP) to report on the fate of the disappeared. Their report, *Nunca Más (Never Again)* established the existence of more than three hundred death camps, the names of the disappeared and the geography of terror. It was a best-seller in Argentina. Alfonsín turned to the military courts, believing that the armed forces could purge their own, but after a year of stonewalling the civilian courts took over cases against the military brass. Nine members of the ruling juntas were tried for crimes including torture and murder. Efforts to reach further down into the military ranks ran into threats of mutiny from disgruntled officers. So Alfonsín, afraid of jeopardiz-ing a fragile transition, backed off. He passed laws limiting the time within which prosecutions could be brought. When those laws didn't sufficiently placate a restive military, he followed up with a "due obedience" law that made it practically impossible to indict any but a handful of top officers. The final insult came when his successor, Carlos Menem, in 1990 pardoned the junta leaders along with the few others who were still subject to prosecution.

In Chile, before leaving government the military had exacted a consti-tutional scheme that reserved a key role for them. The arrangement reserved a percentage of foreign exchange for the military, retained Pino-chet as armed forces chief until 1997, and then made him a senator for life along with other nonelected senators. The incoming Aylwin government did not even try prosecutions. Chastened by the Argentine experience, Patricio Aylwin promised the truth, "and as much justice as possible." His Truth and Reconciliation Commission published a three-volume report that in-cluded the names of known victims of the dictatorship along with what could be discovered about their fate. But the report named no names of those responsible, and the Commission got little help from the military in finding out what had happened. Although Aylwin encouraged the courts to make use of information passed on to them by the Commission or from other sources, he did not try to overturn a military self-amnesty that immunized them from prosecution for crimes committed before 1978—the bulk of the military's crimes. Rather, he focused on reparations payments to victims, and took the then unparalleled step of publicly apologizing, in the name of the Chilean state, for the crimes committed in its name.

By the mid–1990s, both countries' governments were anxious to move on. Both saw continuing concerns about the disappeared and their children, and about justice for the victimizers, as distractions from the beckoning issues of economic growth and global integration. The human rights movements that had sustained family members and social activists through years of dictatorship were at a loss, reduced in numbers, unable to impose their agenda, and unsure how to combine demands about an accounting of the past with attention to current injustice. The international community, for whom Chile and Argentina were the poster children of repressive regimes during the 1970s, called off its scrutiny and reestablished the flow of loans and trade. The Chilean "economic miracle" was held up as a model for the developing world. No suggestion of ad hoc UN Criminal Tribunals here. A controlled and limited transition from dictatorship to democracy, based on pacts among elites, partial truths, and very partial justice, seemed to have become the template for other Latin American countries, and even for other continents. End of story.

Or was it?

* * *

On October 16, 1998, Scotland Yard detectives arrested General Pinochet at the London Clinic, where he was recovering from back surgery. Pinochet would spend the next eighteen months fighting his extradition to Spain, where a judge had charged him with genocide, terrorism, and torture, all committed in Chile two decades before. When he was finally released, ostensibly on grounds of ill health, he would return to a different country, in a different world.

Never again could dictators find refuge in their official position to excuse them from charges of torturing and killing their own people. The venerable British House of Lords, in two separate decisions, found that Pinochet could be extradited to Spain to stand trial for his crimes. A 1984 treaty committed all the countries involved to either prosecute alleged torturers or turn them over to someone who would; this was the first time it had been used to extradite a suspect to a country other than his own to stand trial. With the *Pinochet* precedent, human rights treaties like the 1984 Convention Against Torture took on new teeth. Long seen as well-intentioned but hollow declarations, they became *real*, able, at least for a time, to put people behind bars for heinous crimes of state. By 2001, there were at least half a dozen proceedings pending in different national courts against current or former heads of state, and more against various torturers and *génocidaires*.

Regina v. Bartle and the Commissioner of Police for the Metropolis and Others, Ex Parte Pinochet

House of Lords (On Appeal from a Divisional Court of the Queen's Bench Division) Session 1998–99

Lord Browne–Wilkinson

The facts

On 11 September 1973 a right-wing coup evicted the left-wing regime of President Allende. The coup was led by a military junta, of whom

Senator (then General) Pinochet was the leader. At some stage he became head of state. The Pinochet regime remained in power until 11 March 1990 when Senator Pinochet resigned.

There is no real dispute that during the period of the Senator Pinochet regime appalling acts of barbarism were committed in Chile and elsewhere in the world: torture, murder and the unexplained disappearance of individuals, all on a large scale. Although it is not alleged that Senator Pinochet himself committed any of those acts, it is alleged that they were done in pursuance of a conspiracy to which he was a party, at his instigation and with his knowledge. He denies these allegations. None of the conduct alleged was committed by or against citizens of the United Kingdom or in the United Kingdom.

In 1998 Senator Pinochet came to the United Kingdom for medical treatment. The judicial authorities in Spain sought to extradite him in order to stand trial in Spain on a large number of charges. Some of those charges had links with Spain. But most of the charges had no connection with Spain. The background to the case is that to those of left-wing political convictions Senator Pinochet is seen as an arch-devil: to those of right-wing persuasions he is seen as the saviour of Chile. It may well be thought that the trial of Senator Pinochet in Spain for offences all of which related to the state of Chile and most of which occurred in Chile is not calculated to achieve the best justice. But I cannot emphasise too strongly that that is no concern of your Lordships. Although others perceive our task as being to choose between the two sides on the grounds of personal preference or political inclination, that is an entire misconception. Our job is to decide two questions of law: are there any extradition crimes and, if so, is Senator Pinochet immune from trial for committing those crimes. If, as a matter of law, there are no extradition crimes or he is entitled to immunity in relation to whichever crimes there are, then there is no legal right to extradite Senator Pinochet to Spain or, indeed, to stand in the way of his return to Chile. If, on the other hand, there are extradition crimes in relation to which Senator Pinochet is not entitled to state immunity then it will be open to the Home Secretary to extradite him. The task of this House is only to decide those points of law.

On 16 October 1998 an international warrant for the arrest of Senator Pinochet was issued in Spain. On the same day, a magistrate in London issued a provisional warrant ("the first warrant") under section 8 of the Extradition Act 1989. He was arrested in a London hospital on 17 October 1998. On 18 October the Spanish authorities issued a second international warrant. A further provisional warrant ("the second warrant") was issued by the magistrate at Bow Street Magistrates Court on 22 October 1998 accusing Senator Pinochet of:

"(1) Between 1 January 1988 and December 1992 being a public official intentionally inflicted severe pain or suffering on another in the performance or purported performance of his official duties;

(2) Between the first day of January 1988 and 31 December 1992 being a public official, conspired with persons unknown to intention-

ly inflict severe pain or suffering on another in the performance or purported performance of his official duties;

(3) Between the first day of January 1982 and 31 January 1992 he detained other persons (the hostages) and in order to compel such persons to do or to abstain from doing any act threatened to kill, injure or continue to detain the hostages;

(4) Between the first day of January 1982 and 31 January 1992 conspired with persons unknown to detain other persons (the hostages) and in order to compel such persons to do or to abstain from doing any act, threatened to kill, injure or continue to detain the hostages;

(5) Between January 1976 and December 1992 conspired together with persons unknown to commit murder in a Convention country."

Senator Pinochet started proceedings for habeas corpus and for leave to move for judicial review of both the first and the second provisional warrants. Those proceedings came before the Divisional Court (Lord Bingham of Cornhill C.J., Collins and Richards JJ.) which on 28 October 1998 quashed both warrants. Nothing turns on the first warrant which was quashed since no appeal was brought to this House. The grounds on which the Divisional Court quashed the second warrant were that Senator Pinochet (as former head of state) was entitled to state immunity in respect of the acts with which he was charged. However, it had also been argued before the Divisional Court that certain of the crimes alleged in the second warrant were not "extradition crimes" within the meaning of the Act of 1989 because they were not crimes under U.K. law at the date they were committed. Whilst not determining this point directly, the Lord Chief Justice held that, in order to be an extradition crime, it was not necessary that the conduct should be criminal at the date of the conduct relied upon but only at the date of request for extradition.

* * *

The appeal first came on for hearing before this House between 4 and 12 November 1998. The Committee heard submissions by counsel for the Crown Prosecution Service as appellants (on behalf of the Government of Spain), Senator Pinochet, Amnesty International as interveners and an independent amicus curiae. Written submissions were also entertained from Human Rights Watch. That Committee entertained argument based on the extended scope of the case as put forward in the Request for Extradition. It is not entirely clear to what extent the Committee heard submissions as to whether all or some of those charges constituted "extradition crimes". There is some suggestion in the judgments that the point was conceded. Certainly, if the matter was argued at all it played a very minor role in that first hearing. Judgment was given on 25 November 1998 (see [1998] 3 W.L.R. 1456). The appeal was allowed by a majority (Lord Nicholls of Birkenhead, Lord Steyn and Lord Hoffmann, Lord Slynn of Hadley and Lord Lloyd of Berwick dissenting) on the grounds that Senator Pinochet was not entitled to immunity in relation to crimes under international law. On 15 January 1999 that judgment of the House was set aside

on the grounds that the Committee was not properly constituted: see
[1999] 2 W.L.R. 272. The appeal came on again for rehearing on 18 January
1999 before your Lordships. * * *

* * *

It is therefore quite clear from the words I have emphasised that under
the Act of 1870 the double criminality rule required the conduct to be
criminal under English law at the conduct date not at the request date.
Paragraph 20 of Schedule 1 to the Act of 1989 provides:

> " 'extradition crime', in relation to any foreign state, is to be construed
> by reference to the Order in Council under section 2 of the Extradition
> Act 1870 applying to that state as it had effect immediately before the
> coming into force of this Act and to any amendments thereafter made
> to that Order;"

Therefore in this class of case regulated by Schedule 1 to the Act of 1989
the same position applies as it formerly did under the Act of 1870, i.e. the
conduct has to be a crime under English law at the conduct date.

* * *

Torture

Apart from the law of piracy, the concept of personal liability under
international law for international crimes is of comparatively modern
growth. The traditional subjects of international law are states not human
beings. But consequent upon the war crime trials after the 1939–45 World
War, the international community came to recognise that there could be
criminal liability under international law for a class of crimes such as war
crimes and crimes against humanity. Although there may be legitimate
doubts as to the legality of the Charter of the Nuremberg Tribunal, in my
judgment those doubts were stilled by the Affirmation of the Principles of
International Law recognised by the Charter of Nuremberg Tribunal
adopted by the United Nations General Assembly on 11 December 1946.
That Affirmation affirmed the principles of international law recognised by
the Charter of the Nuremberg Tribunal and the judgment of the Tribunal
and directed the Committee on the codification of international law to treat
as a matter of primary importance plans for the formulation of the
principles recognised in the Charter of the Nuremberg Tribunal. At least
from that date onwards the concept of personal liability for a crime in
international law must have been part of international law. In the early
years state torture was one of the elements of a war crime. In consequence
torture, and various other crimes against humanity, were linked to war or
at least to hostilities of some kind. But in the course of time this linkage
with war fell away and torture, divorced from war or hostilities, became an
international crime on its own: see *Oppenheim's International Law* (Jennings and Watts edition) vol. 1, 996; note 6 to Article 18 of the *I.L.C. Draft
Code of Crimes Against Peace*; *Prosecutor v. Furundžija* Tribunal for
Former Yugoslavia, Case No. 17–95–17/1–T. Ever since 1945, torture on a
large scale has featured as one of the crimes against humanity: see, for

example, U.N. General Assembly Resolutions 3059, 3452 and 3453 passed in 1973 and 1975; Statutes of the International Criminal Tribunals for former Yugoslavia (Article 5) and Rwanda (Article 3).

Moreover, the Republic of Chile accepted before your Lordships that the international law prohibiting torture has the character of jus cogens or a peremptory norm, i.e. one of those rules of international law which have a particular status. In *Furundžija (supra)* at para. 153, the Tribunal said:

> "Because of the importance of the values it protects, [the prohibition of torture] has evolved into a peremptory norm or jus cogens, that is, a norm that enjoys a higher rank in the international hierarchy than treaty law and even 'ordinary' customary rules. The most conspicuous consequence of this higher rank is that the principle at issue cannot be derogated from by states through international treaties or local or special customs or even general customary rules not endowed with the same normative force.... Clearly, the jus cogens nature of the prohibition against torture articulates the notion that the prohibition has now become one of the most fundamental standards of the international community. Furthermore, this prohibition is designed to produce a deterrent effect, in that it signals to all members of the international community and the individuals over whom they wield authority that the prohibition of torture is an absolute value from which nobody must deviate." * * *

The *jus cogens* nature of the international crime of torture justifies states in taking universal jurisdiction over torture wherever committed. International law provides that offences *jus cogens* may be punished by any state because the offenders are "common enemies of all mankind and all nations have an equal interest in their apprehension and prosecution": *Demjanjuk v. Petrovsky* (1985) 603 F.Supp. 1468; 776 F.2d 571.

It was suggested by Miss Montgomery, for Senator Pinochet, that although torture was contrary to international law it was not strictly an international crime in the highest sense. In the light of the authorities to which I have referred (and there are many others) I have no doubt that long before the Torture Convention of 1984 state torture was an international crime in the highest sense.

NOTES AND QUESTIONS

1.   The issues featured in this chapter, including piracy, terrorism, trade, and torture, all demonstrate overlapping competence between national and international law. Can you think of issues that fall solely within the realm of international law or solely within national law? Consider the most important legal issues of today—what are they and do they tend to be national, international or mixed?

2.   What concept do you think best describes the world of today: state system, international society, international community, or something else? Consider the definition of community offered by Adeno. Note the seeming contradiction in his view that the international "community" is defined by

its diversity. Is it possible to have law in the midst of so much diversity. Is not "law" dependent on a common culture with common values? We will return to this subject in Chapter 12, but it is worth keeping in mind throughout the book.

3. Consider also what the *Pinochet* case tells you. Is the type of litigation that occurred in the case a way to build a community? Did it show that we have a common set of values we are willing to enforce through criminal litigation? Or was it an exceptional case that actually exposed how little we do to uphold international law? For more on human rights and accountability, see Chapter 5, *infra*.

4. Does international law play a role in shaping the world or is it merely reflective of a world shaped by other influences? What are the important influences on the world a student of international law should keep in mind while studying international law?

5. What do we citizens of the world hope international law can accomplish for us? As you read further in this book consider the strengths and weaknesses you see in the system of international law for fulfilling the purposes you understand it to have. One weakness traditionally cited is lack of a police force to enforce international law. (See Section A.2 above.) Is a police force essential to law? What is essential?

6. In this excerpt by Andreas Paulus, he seems to prefer the concept "international society" to "international community" and considers whether the world is moving toward community or away from it. Indeed, as a result of the diversity and complexity of the world, we may have moved beyond traditional topics of concern to international law, such as enforcement (discussed in Section A.2) and conflicts with national law (discussed in A.3.) Today, we face the challenge of growing specialization and even fragmentation of the law. According to Paulus,

> Any comprehensive vision of the international community will have to respond to the objection that the diversity of international society cannot be captured by one single concept. Indeed, it appears that in view of the diversity of contemporary international law, fragmentation rather than community has become the key term to describe contemporary international society (Koskenniemi 2006b; Koskenniemi and Leino 2002). Whereas some lament—or try to re-establish (Dupuy 2002)—the lost unity, others embrace the shift "from territoriality to functionality," from a world of sovereign territorial states to a world of functional institutions limited to specific issue areas (Luhmann 1995b: 571, 1997: 158–60). More radical representatives of this view claim that the different systems lack minimal commonality to maintain any coherent overarching system of general international law (Fischer–Lescano and Teubner 2004: 10004–16). * * * [T]he perception of an increasing autonomy of the subsystems does not[, however,] lead to a complete substitution of general international law. On the contrary, in a fragmented international legal order, some sort of bond between the different parts is necessary. The use of the concept of the international

community is an expression of the need for such an overarching conception of the "whole" of international law. * * *

ANDREAS PAULUS, *International Law and International Community*, ROUTLEDGE HANDBOOK OF INTERNATIONAL LAW 50 (David Armstrong ed., 2009).

7.   What role does the Internet play in developing an international community? What will national boundaries mean to the next generation? For more on the Internet and international law, see Chapter 4 (jurisdiction) and Chapter 10 (cyberattacks).

8.   For more on international law in general, see, IAN BROWNLIE, PRINCIPLES OF PUBLIC INTERNATIONAL LAW (7th ed. 2008); MALCOLM N. SHAW, INTERNATIONAL LAW (6th ed. 2008); A. V. LOWE, INTERNATIONAL LAW (2007); PETER MALANCZUK, AKEHURST'S MODERN INTRODUCTION TO INTERNATIONAL LAW (7th rev'd ed. 1997); OSCAR SCHACHTER, INTERNATIONAL LAW IN THEORY AND PRACTICE (1995).

See also the many volumes in the Library of Essays in International Law, Robert McCorquodale, general editor, and for background on important judicial decisions you will find in this book see INTERNATIONAL LAW STORIES (John Noyes, et al. eds., 2007).

9.   On the history of international law see DOUGLAS JOHNSTON, THE HISTORICAL FOUNDATIONS OF WORLD ORDER: THE TOWER AND THE ARENA (2008); WILHELM G. GREWE, THE EPOCHS OF INTERNATIONAL LAW 108–111 (trans. & rev'd, Michael Byers 2000); ARTHUR NUSSBAUM, A CONCISE HISTORY OF THE LAW OF NATIONS 35 (rev'd ed. 1962).

CHAPTER 2

THE SOURCES AND EVIDENCE OF INTERNATIONAL LAW

Section A. **Treaties.**
      1. Formation.
      2. Interpretation.
      3. Performance.
Section B. **Customary International Law.**
Section C. **General Principles and Equity.**
      1. General Principles.
      2. Equity.
Section D. **Subsidiary Sources and Evidence.**
Section E. **Peremptory Norms (*Jus Cogens*).**

As discussed in Chapter 1, the international legal system does not have a legislature or parliament, as such, for the making of international law. Yet the law gets made. Indeed, so much gets made that, as was also mentioned in Chapter 1, some scholars are concerned about international law fragmenting into so many specialties. This seems unlikely, however, given important unifying features of the system. One of the most important is the doctrine of sources. For something to be a rule of international law, it must be traced to one of the recognized sources regardless of whether the topic is human rights, the environment, the economy, international organizations or other major areas of specialization. The doctrine of sources holds that international law has three primary and several secondary sources of rules. The sources are restated in the Statute of the International Court of Justice:

*Article 38 of the Statute of the International Court of Justice**

1. The Court, whose function is to decide in accordance with international law such disputes as are submitted to it, shall apply:

a. international conventions, whether general or particular, establishing rules expressly recognized by the contesting states;

---

* For this and other documents relevant to the International Court of Justice see the Website of the International Court: http://www.icj-cij.org.

b.   international custom, as evidence of a general practice accepted as law;

c.   the general principles of law recognized by civilized nations;

d.   subject to the provisions of Article 59, judicial decisions and the teachings of the most highly qualified publicists of the various nations, as subsidiary means for the determination of rules of law.

2.   This provision shall not prejudice the power of the Court to decide a case *ex aequo et bono*, if the parties agree thereto.

* * *

Article 38 also gives an indication of what evidence we look to in assessing rules of international law. In this chapter, we will focus on the primary sources but will also consider secondary sources as well as evidence and one further category of international law that is not mentioned in Article 38, peremptory norms, also called *jus cogens* norms. For more on the sources of international law in general, see SOURCES OF INTERNATIONAL LAW (Martti Koskenniemi ed. 2000) (Library of Essays in International Law).

A.   TREATIES

Article 38 refers first to "[i]nternational conventions, whether general or particular, establishing rules expressly recognized by the contesting states * * * " Not only are treaties a basic source of international law, they are *the* key vehicle by which the international system changes most rapidly. Treaties provide the mechanism for the various subjects of international law to arrange their relations, indeed, to make their own law. This aspect of treaties is similar to domestic contract law. What one calls a treaty is not important; they may be called conventions, *concordats,* charters, agreements, articles of agreement, pacts, protocols, accords, and memoranda of understanding, among other designations. On the other hand, differences are important between multilateral and bilateral treaties and other agreements in which reservations or other special rules are allowed.

The authoritative source for most rules with respect to treaties is, not surprisingly, a treaty. In 1969, the United Nations International Law Commission (ILC), a body of elected specialists in international law with the mandate to work on progressive development of the law, completed the drafting of the Vienna Convention on the Law of Treaties (VCLT or Vienna Convention). The Vienna Convention is in general considered binding even on non-parties, as customary international law.* By its terms it is limited to written treaties between sovereign states (Articles 1, 2) but, in fact, its provisions are relied on for guidance in the making, interpretation and

---

* With respect to the United States, *see* Marian L. Nash, *Contemporary Practice of the United States Relating to International Law*, 75 AM. J. INT'L L. 142, 147 (1981) and ARTHUR ROVINE, DIGEST OF U.S. PRACTICE IN INTERNATIONAL LAW 1973, 307, 482–83 (1974).

fulfillment of unwritten agreements and agreements between states and international organizations, as well as between organizations.*

The doctrine of sources does not indicate any hierarchy among the three primary sources. In theory, treaty rules, rules of customary international law, and general principles are of equal stature. Only peremptory norms have a status superior to other categories of rules. Nevertheless, treaties have certain characteristics that give them advantages over the other sources: they are often in written form making treaty rules precise and verifiable; treaties can be designed for specific purposes, and do not necessarily require a long period of time to come into force. Perhaps the greatest disadvantage of treaties compared with the other sources is that they require express consent to bind. While express consent may mean in some cases parties to treaties are more likely to comply with their treaty obligations, it is also true that states and other subjects of international law may avoid being bound by important rules of the international community simply by withholding consent. In this respect, other sources have the advantage over treaties from the perspective of the community as opposed, perhaps, to individual states. Consent also distinguishes law-making in the international system and in national systems. Most legislation in national systems is generally binding without the consent of the governed.

International agreements cover a wide range of interests. The spectrum extends from those that are in effect conveyances of real estate (treaties of lease, cession and measurement of boundaries), through mutual promises to pursue common lines of action (military alliances, mutual defense, safety at sea), to organic arrangements that function much as constitutions (the U.N. Charter). Some international agreements are regarded as executed internationally as between the parties when made (boundary treaties). Others are executory, such as the mutual promises of the members of NATO to consider an attack on one an attack on all and to respond effectively. Still others may require implementing legislation.

International agreements have given the international legal system almost all the rules that exist on international economic law. In the more traditional political areas, international agreements may alter, expand, or restate customary international law. Treaties may have a "common-law"-like, customary law-creating characteristic. A series of treaties, or even one widely adopted, may create customary international law. This possibility is discussed in the next section, customary international law. Treaties also may "codify" rules of customary international law. Finally, given the lack so far of an effective international parallel to national legislatures or judiciaries, multilateral agreements are used to make new law, such as those relating to pollution of the high seas, uses of the moon, Antarctica,

---

* The ILC did draft a treaty on the law of treaties for international organizations. It has not entered into force. Many provisions are similar to the Vienna Convention. See the 1986 Vienna Convention of the Law of Treaties between States and International Organizations or between International Organizations, http://untreaty.un.org/ilc/texts/instruments/english/con ventions/1_2_1986.pdf.

aerial hijacking, protection of human rights, or the creation of an international criminal court. Treaties that have legislative characteristics are sometimes called law-making treaties (*traité-lois*). They establish a series of legislation-like rules among nations. UNCLOS, introduced in Chapter 1, is well-known as a law-making treaty. Other treaties take the form of more simple conracts (*traités contrats*). America's purchase of a vast tract of territory from France in 1803, known as the Louisiana Purchase, was a *traités contrat*. As may already be plain, practitioners in every area of law deal regularly with treaties and need to know the law of treaties.

1.   FORMATION

Legal Status of Eastern Greenland

Denmark v. Norway
Permanent Court of International Justice, 1933
P.C.I.J., Ser. A/B, No. 53 (April 5)

* * *

By an Application instituting proceedings, filed with the Registry of the Court on July 12th, 1931, in accordance with Article 40 of the Statute and Article 35 of the Rules of Court, the Danish Government, relying on the optional clause of Article 36, paragraph 2, of the Statute, brought before the Permanent Court of International Justice a suit against the Norwegian Government on the ground that the latter had, on July 10th, 1931, published a proclamation declaring that it had proceeded to occupy certain territories in Eastern Greenland, which, in the contention of the Danish Government, were subject to the sovereignty of the Crown of Denmark. The Application, after thus indicating the subject of the dispute, proceeds to formulate the claim by asking the Court for judgment to the effect that "the promulgation of the above-mentioned declaration of occupation and any steps taken in this respect by the Norwegian Government constitute a violation of the existing legal situation and are accordingly unlawful and invalid."

The Danish submission in the written pleading, that the Norwegian occupation of July 10th, 1931, is invalid, is founded upon the contention that the area occupied was at the time of the occupation subject to Danish sovereignty; that the area is part of Greenland, and at the time of the occupation Danish sovereignty existed over all Greenland; consequently it could not be occupied by another Power. In support of this contention, the Danish Government advances two propositions. First, that the sovereignty which Denmark now enjoys over Greenland has existed for a long time, has been continuously and peacefully exercised and, until the present dispute, has not been contested by any Power. This proposition Denmark sets out to establish as a fact. Second, that Norway has by treaty or otherwise herself recognized Danish sovereignty over Greenland as a whole and therefore cannot now dispute it.

* * *

The Court will now consider the second Danish proposition that Norway had given certain undertakings which recognized Danish sovereignty over all Greenland. These undertakings have been fully discussed by the two Parties, and in three cases the Court considers that undertakings were given.

* * *

In addition to the [above] engagements, the Ihlen declaration, viz. the reply given by M. Ihlen, the Norwegian Minister for Foreign Affairs, to the Danish Minister on July 22nd, 1919, must also be considered.

* * *

* * * [T]he point is whether the Ihlen declaration—even if not constituting a definitive recognition of Danish sovereignty—did not constitute an engagement obliging Norway to refrain from occupying any part of Greenland. The Danish request and M. Ihlen's reply were recorded by him in a minute . . . [:]

* * *

II.   Today I informed the Danish Minister that the Norwegian Government would not make any difficulties in the settlement of this question. 22/7–19Ih.

The incident has reference, first to the attitude to be observed by Denmark before the Committee of the Peace Conference at Paris in regard to Spitzbergen, this attitude being that Denmark would not "oppose the wishes of Norway in regard to the settlement of this question"; as is known, these wishes related to the sovereignty over Spitzbergen. Secondly, the request showed that "the Danish Government was confident that the Norwegian Government would not make any difficulty" in the settlement of the Greenland question; the aims that Denmark had in view in regard to the last-named island were to secure the "recognition by all the Powers concerned of Danish sovereignty over the whole of Greenland," and that there should be no opposition "to the Danish Government extending their political and economic interests to the whole of Greenland." It is clear from the relevant Danish documents which preceded the Danish Minister's démarche at Christiania on July 14th, 1919, that the Danish attitude in the Spitzbergen question and the Norwegian attitude in the Greenland question were regarded in Denmark as interdependent, and this interdependence appears to be reflected also in M. Ihlen's minutes of the interview. Even if this interdependence—which, in view of the affirmative reply of the Norwegian Government, in whose name the Minister for Foreign Affairs was speaking, would have created a bilateral engagement—is not held to have been established, it can hardly be denied that what Denmark was asking of Norway ("not to make any difficulties in the settlement of the [Greenland] question") was equivalent to * * * indicating her readiness to concede in the Spitzbergen question (to refrain from opposing "the wishes of Norway in regard to the settlement of this question"). What Denmark desired to obtain from Norway was that the latter should do nothing to obstruct the Danish plans [for] Greenland. The declaration which the

Minister * * * gave on July 22nd, 1919, on behalf of the Norwegian Government, was definitely affirmative: "I told the Danish Minister today that the Norwegian Government would not make any difficulty in the settlement of this question."

The Court considers it beyond all dispute that a reply of this nature given by the Minister for Foreign Affairs on behalf of his Government in response to a request by the diplomatic representative of a foreign Power, in regard to a question falling within his province, *is binding upon the country to which the Minister belongs.* (emphasis added).

* * *

It follows that, as a result of the undertaking involved in the Ihlen declaration of July 22nd, 1919, Norway is under an obligation to refrain from contesting Danish sovereignty over Greenland as a whole, and a fortiori to refrain from occupying a part of Greenland.

* * *

For these reasons, the court, by twelve votes to two, (1) decides that the declaration of occupation promulgated by the Norwegian Government on July 10th, 1931, and any steps taken in this respect by that Government, constitute a violation of the existing legal situation and are accordingly unlawful and invalid;

* * *

■ Dissenting Opinion of MR. ANZILOTTI:

* * *

The question whether the so-called Ihlen declaration was merely a provisional indication (Norwegian contention) or a definitive undertaking (Danish contention) has been debated at length.

* * *

The outcome of all this is therefore an agreement, concluded between the Danish Minister, on behalf of the Danish Government, and the Norwegian Minister for Foreign Affairs, on behalf of the Norwegian Government, by means of purely verbal declarations. The validity of this agreement has been questioned, having regard, in the first place, to its verbal form, and to the competence of the Minister for Foreign Affairs. As regards the form, it should be noted that as both Parties are agreed as to the existence and tenor of these declarations, the question of proof does not arise. Moreover, there does not seem to be any rule of international law requiring that agreements of this kind must necessarily be in writing, in order to be valid. The question of the competence of the Minister for Foreign Affairs is closely connected with the contents of the agreement in question; and these have already been determined.

No arbitral or judicial decision relating to the international competence of a Minister for Foreign Affairs has been brought to the knowledge of the Court; nor has this question been exhaustively treated by legal authorities. In my opinion, it must be recognized that the constant and general practice of States has been to invest the Minister for Foreign Affairs—the direct agent of the chief of the State—with authority to make statements on current affairs to foreign diplomatic representatives, and in particular to inform them as to the attitude which the government, in whose name he speaks, will adopt in a given question. Declarations of this kind are binding upon the State.

As regards the question whether Norwegian constitutional law authorized the Minister for Foreign Affairs to make the declaration, that is a point which, in my opinion, does not concern the Danish Government: it was M. Ihlen's duty to refrain from giving his reply until he had obtained any assent that might be requisite under the Norwegian laws. * * *

[Observations and another dissenting opinion Omitted.]

NOTES AND QUESTIONS

1.   Judge Anzilotti was one of the outstanding judges of Permanent Court of International Justice, a court that preceded the International Court of Justice. (See Chapter 9, *infra*.) Anzilotti agreed with the majority on the issues of oral treaties and the binding effect internationally of a foreign minister's commitment in excess of his constitutional authority. (Cf. Articles 27, 46, and 47 of the Vienna Convention.) How and why was the Ihlen declaration sufficient to bind Norway? Did the majority opinion, and especially the dissent, accept agency principles as part of international law? If so, by what authority? What are the boundaries of this "agency" that the Court and international law recognize? *See,* Vienna Convention article 7(i)(b): "[if it] appears from the practice of the states concerned or from other circumstances that their intention was to consider that person as representing the state for such purposes and to dispense with full powers * * *." See also Article 47.

2.   The VCLT defines a treaty for purposes of the Convention in Article 2(1) as follows:

(a) "treaty" means an international agreement concluded between States in written form and governed by international law, whether embodied in a single instrument or in two or more related instruments and whatever its particular designation.

For general purposes and in light of *Eastern Greenland*, how would you amend this definition? *See also* VCLT Article 3.

This book and the Document Supplement are full of examples that are unquestionably treaties, such as the United Nations Charter to which every state in the world is a party as of 2009. The following documents are also found in the Document Supplement (and online):

Exchange of Letters between the European Union and the Government of Kenya on the conditions and modalities for the transfer of persons suspected of having committed acts of piracy and detained by the European Union-led naval force (EUNAVFOR), and seized property in the possession of EUNAVFOR, from EUNAVFOR to Kenya and for their treatment after such transfer [December 2008].

Is this exchange of letters a treaty? What if the parties expressly state at the time of the exchange that they do not intend it to be a treaty? States have for centuries produced such things as "gentlemen's agreements" and other non-binding arrangements. Their purpose is to procure a certain course of conduct without the ability to take enforcement action in the case of non-compliance. Does contract law have an analog? What is the advantage of entering into non-binding agreements? See the discussion of "soft law", *infra*, p. 159.

3. The VCLT provides default provisions for the conclusion, consent to, and entry into force of treaties. See Articles 6–18. Typically, the parties to a multinational treaty will sign the treaty after it is drafted to indicate agreement with the text and intent to take further steps to be bound. The treaty itself usually indicates what those steps are, such as depositing an instrument of ratification with a despositary. The Secretary General of the United Nations is most often designated as the despositary for multilateral treaties. National law will specify any additional steps an individual state must take to join a treaty. In the United States, the Constitution specifies that the Senate must give its advice and consent to treaties by a two-thirds vote before the president may ratify them. U.S. Constitution, Article II, Section 2 (see Chapter 11, *infra*.)

4. For further reading on treaties, see, ANTHONY AUST, MODERN TREATY LAW AND PRACTICE (2000); LORD McNAIR, THE LAW OF TREATIES (1986); SIR IAN SINCLAIR, THE VIENNA CONVENTION ON THE LAW OF TREATIES (2d ed. 1984).

a. RESERVATIONS

A state or international organization may wish to join a treaty, but be unwilling or unable to accept certain aspects of it. Some treaties, especially those aiming at wide adherence, may permit parties to make reservations. The VCLT Article 2(1)(d) defines a *reservation* as "a unilateral statement, however phrased or named, made by a State, when signing, ratifying, accepting, approving or acceding to a treaty, whereby it purports to exclude or to modify the legal effect of certain provisions of the treaty in their application to that state." At one time, it was thought that any reservation to a multilateral treaty required the express consent of all parties before the reserving party could join the treaty. (This is still the rule for obvious reasons in bilateral treaties.) The law changed as is discussed in the *Genocide Convention* case below. Permitting reservations without the express consent of all will allow more parties to join a treaty, but it may also lead to undermining the integrity of the treaty as parties attempt to make reservations incompatible with treaties, the problem in the second excerpt below, *Belilos v. Switzerland*. *See* VCLT Articles 19–23. It should be noted that many important multilateral treaties forbid reservations to avoid the problems they raise. UNCLOS is an example.

Reservations to the Convention on Genocide

International Court of Justice
1951 I.C.J. Rep. 15 (Advisory Opinion of May 28)

[On November 16th, 1950, the General Assembly requested the Court to respond to the following questions concerning the Genocide Convention:] I.

Can the reserving State be regarded as being a party to the Convention while still maintaining its reservation if the reservation is objected to by one or more of the parties to the Convention but not by others? II. If the answer to Question I is in the affirmative, what is the effect of the reservation as between the reserving State and: (a) The parties which object to the reservation? (b) Those which accept it? III. What would be the legal effect as regards the answer to Question I if an objection to a reservation is made: (a) By a signatory which has not yet ratified? (b) By a State entitled to sign or accede but which has not yet done so?

* * *

The Court observes that the three questions referred to it for an Opinion have certain common characteristics. All three questions are expressly limited by the terms of the Resolution of the General Assembly to the Convention on the Prevention and Punishment of the Crime of Genocide * * *[. T]he replies which the Court is called upon to give to them are necessarily and strictly limited to that Convention. The Court will seek these replies in the rules of law relating to the effect to be given to the intention of the parties to multilateral conventions. The * * * questions are purely abstract in character. They refer neither to the reservations which have, in fact, been made to the Convention by certain States, nor to the objections which have been made to such reservations by other States. They do not even refer to the reservations which may in future be made in respect of any particular article; nor do they refer to the objections to which these reservations might give rise. * * *

The Court observes that this question [1] refers, not to the possibility of making reservations to the Genocide Convention, but solely to the question whether a contracting State which has made a reservation can, while still maintaining it, be regarded as being a party to the Convention, when there is a divergence of views between the contracting parties concerning this reservation, some accepting the reservation, others refusing to accept it.

* * *

The Court recognizes that an understanding was reached within the General Assembly on the faculty to make reservations to the Genocide Convention and that it is permitted to conclude therefrom that States becoming parties to the Convention gave their assent thereto. It must now determine what kind of reservations may be made and what kind of objections may be taken to them.

The solution of these problems must be found in the special characteristics of the Genocide Convention. * * * The origins of the Convention show that it was the intention of the United Nations to condemn and punish genocide as "a crime under international law" involving a denial of the right of existence of entire human groups, a denial which shocks the conscience of mankind and results in great losses to humanity, and which is contrary to moral law and to the spirit and aims of the United Nations (Resolution 96(1) of the General Assembly, December 11th 1946). The first consequence arising from this conception is that the principles underlying the Convention are principles which are recognized by civilized nations as binding on States, even without any conventional obligation. A second consequence is the universal character both of the condemnation of genocide and of the co-operation required "in order to liberate mankind from such an odious scourge" (Preamble to the Convention). The Genocide Convention was therefore intended by the General Assembly and by the contracting parties to be definitely universal in scope. It was in fact approved on December 9th, 1948, by a resolution which was unanimously adopted by fifty-six States.

The objects of such a convention must also be considered. The Convention was manifestly adopted for a purely humanitarian and civilizing purpose. It is indeed difficult to imagine a convention that might have this dual character to a greater degree, since its object on the one hand is to safeguard the very existence of certain human groups and on the other to confirm and endorse the most elementary principles of morality. In such a convention the contracting States do not have any interests of their own; they merely have, one and all, a common interest, namely, the accomplishment of those high purposes which are the raison d'etre of the convention. Consequently, in a convention of this type one cannot speak of individual advantages or disadvantages to States, or of the maintenance of a perfect contractual balance between rights and duties. The high ideals which inspired the Convention provide, by virtue of the common will of the parties, the foundation and measure of all its provisions.

* * *

The object and purpose of the Genocide Convention imply that it was the intention of the General Assembly and of the States which adopted it that as many States as possible should participate. The complete exclusion from the Convention of one or more States would not only restrict the scope of its application, but would detract from the authority of the moral and humanitarian principles which are its basis. It is inconceivable that the contracting parties readily contemplated that an objection to a minor reservation should produce such a result. But even less could the contracting parties have intended to sacrifice the very object of the Convention in favour of a vain desire to secure as many participants as possible. The object and purpose of the Convention thus limit both the freedom of making reservations and that of objecting to them. It follows that it is the compatibility of a reservation with the object and purpose of the Convention that must furnish the criterion for the attitude of a State in making the reservation on accession as well as for the appraisal by a State in objecting to the reservation. Such is the rule of conduct which must guide every State in the appraisal which it must make, individually and from its own standpoint, of the admissibility of any reservation.

Any other view would lead either to the acceptance of reservations which frustrate the purposes which the General Assembly and the contracting parties had in mind, or to recognition that the parties to the Convention have the power of excluding from it the author of a reservation, even a minor one, which may be quite compatible with those purposes. It has nevertheless been argued that any State entitled to become a party to the Genocide Convention may do so while making any reservation it chooses by virtue of its sovereignty. The Court cannot share this view. It is obvious that so extreme an application of the idea of State sovereignty could lead to a complete disregard of the object and purpose of the Convention.

On the other hand, it has been argued that there exists a rule of international law subjecting the effect of a reservation to the express or tacit assent of all the contracting parties. This theory rests essentially on a contractual conception of the absolute integrity of the convention as adopted. This view, however, cannot prevail if, having regard to the character of the convention, its purpose and its mode of adoption, it can be established that the parties intended to derogate from that rule by admitting the faculty to make reservations thereto.

It does not appear, moreover, that the conception of the absolute integrity of a convention has been transformed into a rule of international law. The considerable part which tacit assent has always played in estimating the effect which is to be given to reservations scarcely permits one to state that such a rule exists, determining with sufficient precision the effect of objections made to reservations. In fact, the examples of objections made to reservations appear to be too rare in international practice to have given rise to such a rule. It cannot be recognized that the report which was adopted on the subject by the Council of the League of Nations on June 17th, 1927, has had this effect. At best, the recommendation made on that date by the council constitutes the point of departure of an administrative practice which, after being observed by the Secretariat of the League of Nations, imposed itself, so to speak, in the ordinary course of things on the Secretary–General of the United Nations in his capacity of depositary of conventions concluded under the auspices of the League. But it cannot be concluded that the legal problem of the effect of objections to reservations has in this way been solved. * * *

It may, however, be asked whether the General Assembly of the United Nations, in approving the Genocide Convention, had in mind the practice according to which the Secretary–General, in exercising his functions as a depositary, did not regard a reservation as definitively accepted until it had been established that none of the other contracting States objected to it. If this were the case, it might be argued that the implied intention of the contracting parties was to make the effectiveness of any reservation to the Genocide Convention conditional on the assent of all the parties. The Court does not consider that this view corresponds to reality. It must be pointed out, first of all, that the existence of an administrative practice does not in itself constitute a decisive factor in ascertaining what views the contracting States to the Genocide Convention may have had concerning the rights and duties resulting therefrom. It must also be pointed out that there existed among the American States members both of the United Nations and of the Organization of American States, a different practice which goes so far as to permit a reserving State to become a party irrespective of the nature of the reservations or of the objections raised by other contracting States. The preparatory work of the Convention contains nothing to justify the statement that the contracting States implicitly had any definite practice in mind. Nor is there any such indication in the subsequent attitude of the contracting States: neither the reservations made by certain States nor the position adopted by other States towards those reservations permit the conclusion that assent to one or the other of these practices had been given. Finally, * * * the debate on reservations to multilateral treaties which took place in the Sixth Committee at the fifth session of the General Assembly reveals a profound divergence of views, some delegations being attached to the idea of the absolute integrity of the Convention, others favoring a more flexible practice which would bring about the participation of as many States as possible. It results from the foregoing considerations that Question I, on account of its abstract character, cannot be given an absolute answer. The appraisal of a reservation and the effect of objections that might be made to it depend upon the particular circumstances of each individual case.

[Portions of the opinion setting forth the Court's reasoning as to Questions II and III omitted.]

The COURT is of the opinion,

In so far as concerns the Convention on the Prevention and Punishment of the Crime of Genocide, in the event of a State ratifying or acceding to the Convention subject to a reservation made either on ratification or on accession, or on signature followed by ratification:

On Question I: by seven votes to five that a State which has made and maintained a reservation which has been objected to by one or more of the parties to the Convention but not by others, can be regarded as being a party to the Convention if the reservation is compatible with the object and purpose of the Convention; otherwise, that State cannot be regarded as being a party to the Convention.

On Question II: by seven votes to five (a) that if a party to the Convention objects to a reservation which it considers to be incompatible with the object and purpose of the Convention it can in fact consider that the reserving State is not a party to the Convention; (b) that if, on the other hand, a party accepts the reservation as being compatible with the object and purpose of the Convention, it can in fact consider that the reserving State is a party to the Convention. * * * That an objection to a reservation made by a State which is entitled to sign or accede but which has not yet done so, is without legal effect. * * * [Dissenting opinions omitted.]

Vienna Convention on the Law of Treaties

1155 U.N.T.S. 331 (1969).

Article 19
Formulation of reservations

A State may, when signing, ratifying, accepting, approving or acceding to a treaty, formulate a reservation unless:

(a) the reservation is prohibited by the treaty;

(b) the treaty provides that only specified reservations, which do not include the reservation in question, may be made; or

(c) in cases not failing under subparagraphs *(a)* and *(b)*, the reservation is compatible with the object and purpose of the treaty.

Article 20
Acceptance of and objection to reservations

1.   A reservation expressly authorized by a treaty does not require any subsequent acceptance by the other contracting States unless the treaty so provides.

2.   When it appears from the limited number of the negotiating States and the object and purpose of a treaty that the application of the treaty in its entirety between all the parties is an essential condition of the consent of each one to be bound by the treaty, a reservation requires acceptance by all the parties.

3.   When a treaty is a constituent instrument of an international organization and unless it otherwise provides, a reservation requires the acceptance of the competent organ of that organization.

4.   In cases not falling under the preceding paragraphs and unless the treaty otherwise provides:

(a) acceptance by another contracting State of a reservation constitutes the reserving State a party to the treaty in relation to that other State if or when the treaty is in force for those States;

(b) an objection by another contracting State to a reservation does not preclude the entry into force of the treaty as between the objecting and reserving States unless a contrary intention is definitely expressed by the objecting State;

(c) an act expressing a State's consent to be bound by the treaty and containing a reservation is effective as soon as at least one other contracting State has accepted the reservation.

5.   For the purposes of paragraphs 2 and 4 and unless the treaty otherwise provides, a reservation is considered to have been accepted by a State if it shall have raised no objection to the reservation by the end of a period of twelve months after it was notified of the reservation or by the date on which it expressed its consent to be bound by the treaty, whichever is later.

Article 21
Legal effects of reservations and of objections to reservations

1.   A reservation with regard to another party in accordance with articles 19, 20, and 23:

(a) modifies for the reserving State in its relations with that other party the provisions of the treaty to which the reservation relates to the extent of the reservation; and

(b) modifies those provisions to the same extent for that other party in its relations with the reserving State.

2.   The reservation does not modify the provisions of the treaty for the other parties to the treaty *inter se*.

3.   When a State objecting to a reservation has not opposed the entry into force of the treaty between itself and the reserving State, the provisions to which the reservation relates do not apply as between the two States to the extent of the reservation.

Belilos v. Switzerland

European Court of Human Rights, April 29, 1988
10 E.H.R.R. 466, 479–83

[Marlène Belilos was accused of taking part in a demonstration in Lausanne without the necessary permit. She was found guilty by a police board in absentia and fined. She maintained that she had not demonstrated and sought to appeal the fine. At the time of the case, Switzerland did not allow for appeals for fines levied by municipal courts. Belilos took this case to the European Court of Human Rights claiming her right to a fair trial under Article 6(1) of the European Convention on Human Rights. Switzerland defended on the basis of a "declaration" it made at the time of entering into the ECHR.]

Judgment

I.   The Government's preliminary objection

38.   By way of a preliminary objection, the Government argued that Mrs. Belilos's application was incompatible with the international undertakings entered into by Switzerland under Article 6(1) of the Convention. It relied on the interpretative declaration made when the instrument of ratification was deposited [in November 1974], which is worded as follows:

> "The Swiss Federal Council considers that the guarantee of fair trial in Article 6(1) of the Convention, in the determination of civil rights and obligations or any criminal charge against the person in question is intended solely to ensure ultimate control by the judiciary over the acts or decisions of the public authorities relating to such rights or obligations or the determinations of such a charge."

39.   The Court will examine the nature of the declaration in issue and then, if appropriate, its validity for the purposes of Article 64 of the Convention, which reads as follows:

> "1.   Any State may, when signing the Convention or when depositing its instrument of ratification, make a reservation in respect of any particular provision of the Convention to the extent that any law then in force in its territory is not in conformity with the provision. Reservations of a general character shall not be permitted under this Article.

2. Any reservation made under this Article shall contain a brief statement of the law concerned."

40. The applicant contended that the declaration could not be equated with a reservation. When ratifying the Convention, Switzerland had made two "reservations" and two "interpretative declarations"; in so doing, it had adopted a terminology that had been chosen quite deliberately. A reservation resulted in the Convention's being inapplicable in respect of a particular point, whereas a declaration on the other hand was only provisional in nature, pending a decision of the Strasbourg organs. * * *

41. The Commission likewise reached the conclusion that the declaration was a mere interpretative declaration which did not have the effect of a reservation; it based its view both on the wording of the declaration and on the preparatory work. The latter showed that Switzerland's intention had been to deal with the situation arising as a result of the Court's judgment of 16 July 1971 in the *Ringeisen* case, i.e. in respect of administrative proceedings relating to civil rights; it did not, on the other hand, provide any indication of how the declaration might be applied as a reservation in the case of criminal proceedings. More generally, the Commission considered that if a State made both reservations and interpretative declarations at the same time, the latter could only exceptionally be equated with the former.

42. In the Government's submission, on the other hand, the declaration was a "qualified" interpretative declaration. It consequently was in the nature of a reservation within the meaning of Article 2(1)(d) of the *Vienna Convention on the Law of Treaties* of 23 May 1969, which provides:

> "Reservation" means a unilateral statement, however phrased or named, made by a State, when signing, ratifying, accepting, approving or acceding to a treaty, whereby it purports to exclude or to modify the legal effect of certain provisions of the treaty in their application to that State.

43. The first of the considerations relied on by the Government was the purpose of the declaration. It claimed that it was to preserve proceedings which, while coming within the "civil" or "criminal" ambit of Article 6(1), initially took place before administrative authorities, in such a way that the court or courts to which appeal lay did not—or did not fully— review the facts. The declaration thus reflected the wish to respect the cantons' distinctive features recognised in the Federal Constitution, with regard to procedure and the administration of justice. * * *

47. The Court acknowledges that the wording of the original French text of the declaration, though not altogether clear, can be understood as constituting a reservation.

* * *

The Government derived an additional argument from the fact that there had been no reaction from the Secretary General of the Council of Europe or from the States Parties to the Convention.

The Secretary General had made no comment when he notified the Council of Europe member States of the reservations and interpretative declarations contained in Switzerland's instrument of ratification. Yet, so the Government maintained, it was open to him as the depositary, who had important prerogatives, to ask for clarifications and to make observations on the instruments he received, as he had shown in the case of the declaration made under Article 25 by the Turkish Government on 28 January 1987. As far as the reservations and interpretative declarations of Switzerland were concerned, it had, when they were in the process of formulation, made extensive enquiries of the Council of Europe's Legal Affairs Directorate so as to ensure that there was no objection from the Secretary General.

As to the States Parties, they did not deem it necessary to ask Switzerland for explanations regarding the declaration in question and had therefore considered it acceptable as a reservation under Article 64 or under general international law. The Swiss Government inferred that it could in good faith take the declaration as having been tacitly accepted for the purposes of Article 64.

The Court does not agree with that analysis. The silence of the depositary and the Contracting States does not deprive the Convention institutions of the power to make their own assessment.

* * *

[The Court went on to assess the declaration under the Convention's provision on reservations, Article 64:]

55.   The Court [concludes:] By "reservation of a general character" in Article 64 is meant in particular a reservation couched in terms that are too vague or broad for it to be possible to determine their exact meaning and scope. While the preparatory work and the Government's explanations clearly show what the respondent State's concern was at the time of ratification, they cannot obscure the objective reality of the actual wording of the declaration. The words "ultimate control by the judiciary over the acts or decision of the public authorities relating to [civil] rights or obligations or the determination of [a criminal] charge" do not make it possible for the scope of the undertaking by Switzerland to be ascertained exactly, in particular as to which categories of dispute are included and as to whether or not the "ultimate control by the judiciary" takes in the facts of the case. They can therefore be interpreted in different ways, whereas Article 64(1) requires precision and clarity. In short, they fall foul of the rule that reservations must not be of a general character.

[The Court also finds that Switzerland's reservation did not comply with Article 64(2) since it did not contain "a brief statement of the law concerned."]

C.   Conclusion

60.   In short, the declaration in question does not satisfy two of the requirements of Article 64 of the Convention, with the result that it must

be held to be invalid. At the same time, it is beyond doubt that Switzerland is, and regards itself as, bound by the Convention irrespective of the validity of the declaration. Moreover, the Swiss Government recognized the Court's competence to determine the latter issue, which they argued before it. The Government's preliminary objection must therefore be rejected.

* * *

Like the Commission and the Government, the Court recognises that it is necessary to ascertain the original intention of those who drafted the declaration. In its view, the documents show that Switzerland originally contemplated making a formal reservation but subsequently opted for the term "declaration". Although the documents do not make the reasons for the change of nomenclature entirely clear, they do show that the Federal Council has always been concerned to avoid the consequences which a broad view of the right of access to the courts—a view taken in the *Ringeisen* judgment—would have for the system of public administration and of justice in the cantons and consequently to put forward the declaration as qualifying Switzerland's consent to be bound by the Convention.

49.   The question whether a declaration described as "interpretative" must be regarded as a "reservation" is a difficult one, particularly—in the instant case—because the Swiss Government has made both "reservations" and "interpretative declarations" in the same instrument of ratification. More generally, the Court recognises the great importance, rightly emphasised by the Government, of the legal rules applicable to reservations and interpretative declarations made by States Parties to the Convention. Only reservations are mentioned in the Convention, but several States have also (or only) made interpretative declarations, without always making a clear distinction between the two.

In order to establish the legal character of such a declaration, one must look behind the title given to it and seek to determine the substantive content. In the present case, it appears that Switzerland meant to remove certain categories of proceedings from the ambit of Article 6(1) and to secure itself against an interpretation of that Article which it considered to be too broad. However, the Court must see to it that the obligations arising under the Convention are not subject to restrictions which would not satisfy the requirements of Article 64 as regards reservations. Accordingly, it will examine the validity of the interpretative declaration in question, as in the case of a reservation, in the context of this provision.

* * *

b.   AMENDMENT AND MODIFICATION

VCLT Articles 39–41 provide for the amendment and modification of treaties. Reservations, amendments, modifications, as well as additions to treaties in the form of protocols and successive treaties on the same subject, may result in parties having different obligations to different parties on the same subject. Many of today's multilateral treaties are perhaps best described as sets of bilateral treaties. Lawyers must carefully assess what any particular party has agreed to and be certain this knowledge is up-to-date. With online resources this is now relatively simple to do.

NOTES AND QUESTIONS

1.   Reservations have been a particular problem with respect to human rights treaties. This may be due to the fact that such treaties are fundamentally promises to the state's own nationals and not to other states. In other words, they are not reciprocal in nature as the GATT or UNCLOS are. Do you see why reciprocal treaties tend not to allow reservations or to have fewer of them? In addition, human rights treaties affect well-developed areas of national law as was seen in the *Belilos* case. The United States is a party to the Convention Against Torture but has applied two reservations, nine declarations and one understanding to its instrument of ratification, including the following reservation:

> (1) That the United States considers itself bound by the obligation under article 16 to prevent "cruel, inhuman or degrading treatment or punishment", only insofar as the term "cruel, inhuman or degrading treatment or punishment" means the cruel, unusual and inhumane treatment or punishment prohibited by the Fifth, Eighth, and/or Fourteenth Amendments to the Constitution of the United States.

See,   http://treaties.un.org/Pages/ViewDetails.aspx?src=TREATY&mtdsg_no=IV–9&chapter=4&lang=en. Is this a permissible reservation? Following the *Belilos* case, should other states object to this reservation (if they do) or simply accept that the United States will be held to the obligations of the CAT regardless of the treaty? For more on U.S. reservations to human rights treaties, see Chapter 5.

2.   A number of treaty regimes have begun to develop methods of amendment or modification that require less than express consent of states. Some treaties have the possibility for new provisions that states must expressly opt-out of to prevent being bound. Other treaty regimes draft new provisions that are not put to the vote but are used in the form of "soft" law. Treaties are also effectively modified through subsequent practice or interpretation. (See the next section on treaty interpretation.) On these newer means of law-making, see, Christian Tomuschat, *Obligations Arising for States Without or Against Their Will*, *in* 241 Recueil des Cours 241 (1993). Do you think such developments are an improvement in international law? Does it depend on the subject? Should states be bound automatically to meet new safety standards for maritime vessels but not be bound to meet new human rights standards without express consent?

2.   INTERPRETATION

Older systemic scholarship sometimes presented canons for interpretation of treaties. While these appear to have fallen into disuse for a time, courts may be returning to them as predictable and stable guides to interpretation. Understanding how a judge is likely to interpret a treaty is fairer to subjects of the law than the eclectic approaches developed in the 1960s–1990s drawing on anthropology, sociology, psychology, linguistics, and literary criticism. Nevertheless, judges have developed more sophisticated approaches to the traditional rules of interpretation through the benefit of research from a variety of disciplines.

The Vienna Convention restates the core rule of interpretation: start with the text and the ordinary meaning of the text. That ordinary meaning should be understood in context and in light of the treaty's object and purpose.

Article 31
General rule of interpretation

1.   A treaty shall be interpreted in good faith in accordance with the ordinary meaning to be given to the terms of the treaty in their context and in the light of its object and purpose.

2.   The context for the purpose of the interpretation of a treaty shall comprise, in addition to the text, including its preamble and annexes:

(a) any agreement relating to the treaty which was made between all the parties in connection with the conclusion of the treaty;

(b) any instrument which was made by one or more parties in connection with the conclusion of the treaty and accepted by the other parties as an instrument related to the treaty.

* * *

Article 32
Supplementary means of interpretation

Recourse may be had to supplementary means of interpretation, including the preparatory work of the treaty and the circumstances of its conclusion, in order to confirm the meaning resulting from the application of article 31, or to determine the meaning when the interpretation according to article 31:

(a) leaves the meaning ambiguous or obscure; or

(b) leads to a result which is manifestly absurd or unreasonable.

In Chapter 7, we introduce international economic law. The World Trade Organization (WTO) is the primary institution relevant to international economic law. A large number of treaties have been concluded under its auspices regulating everything from trade in goods to trade in intellectual property. At the heart of these agreements is the General Agreement on Tariffs and Trade (GATT). This treaty was originally agreed to in 1947 but was updated when the WTO was formed in 1994. The primary purpose of the GATT is to promote free trade. The WTO has a sophisticated dispute settlement system that some have called a world court for trade. One of the first disputes to be heard by the WTO's Dispute Settlement Body (DSB) concerned an attempt by the United States to save endangered sea turtles worldwide by limiting the importation of shrimp from countries where shrimpers did little or nothing to protect turtles in the course of harvesting shrimp. This excerpt from the appellate decision in the case demonstrates how the DSB uses the VCLT to interpret WTO agreements. The outcome of the case is discussed in Chapter 7.

Import Prohibition of Certain Shrimp and Shrimp Products*

World Trade Organization Appellate Body
WT/DS58/AB/R (Oct. 12, 1998)

I.   Introduction: Statement of the Appeal

1.   This is an appeal by the United States from certain issues of law and legal interpretations in the Panel Report, *United States–Import Prohibition of Certain Shrimp and Shrimp Products*.[1] Following a joint request for consultations by India, Malaysia, Pakistan and Thailand on 8 October 1996,[2] Malaysia and Thailand requested in a communication dated 9 January 1997,[3] and Pakistan asked in a communication dated 30 January 1997[4], that the Dispute Settlement Body (the "DSB") establish a panel to examine their complaint regarding a prohibition imposed by the United States on the importation of certain shrimp and shrimp products by Section 609 of Public Law 101–162[5] ("Section 609") and associated regulations and judicial rulings. On 25 February 1997, the DSB established two panels in accordance with these requests and agreed that these panels would be consolidated into a single Panel, pursuant to Article 9 of the *Understanding on Rules and Procedures Governing the Settlement of Disputes* (the "DSU")⁻ * * *.

2.   The relevant factual and regulatory aspects of this dispute are set out in the Panel Report, in particular at paragraphs 2.1–2.16. Here, we outline the United States measure at stake before the Panel and in these appellate proceedings. The United States issued regulations in 1987 pursuant to the Endangered Species Act of 1973 requiring all United States shrimp trawl vessels to use approved Turtle Excluder Devices ("TEDs") or tow-time restrictions in specified areas where there was a significant mortality of sea turtles in shrimp harvesting. These regulations, which became fully effective in 1990, were modified so as to require the use of approved TEDs at all times and in all areas where there is a likelihood that

---

* Some footnotes omitted.

1.   WT/DS58/R, 15 May 1998.

2.   WT/DS58/1, 14 October 1996.

3.   WT/DS58/6, 10 January 1997.

4.   WT/DS58/7, 7 February 1997.

5.   16 United States Code (U.S.C.) § 1537.

shrimp trawling will interact with sea turtles, with certain limited exceptions.

3. Section 609 was enacted on 21 November 1989. Section 609(a) calls upon the United States Secretary of State, in consultation with the Secretary of Commerce, *inter alia*, to "initiate negotiations as soon as possible for the development of bilateral or multilateral agreements with other nations for the protection and conservation of ... sea turtles" and to "initiate negotiations as soon as possible with all foreign governments which are engaged in, or which have persons or companies engaged in, commercial fishing operations which, as determined by the Secretary of Commerce, may affect adversely such species of sea turtles, for the purpose of entering into bilateral and multilateral treaties with such countries to protect such species of sea turtles; ...." Section 609(b)(1) imposed, not later than 1 May 1991, an import ban on shrimp harvested with commercial fishing technology which may adversely affect sea turtles. * * *

4. Second, certification shall be granted to harvesting nations that provide documentary evidence of the adoption of a regulatory program governing the incidental taking of sea turtles in the course of shrimp trawling that is comparable to the United States program *and* where the average rate of incidental taking of sea turtles by their vessels is comparable to that of United States vessels.[14] According to the 1996 Guidelines, the Department of State assesses the regulatory program of the harvesting nation and certification shall be made if the program includes: (i) the required use of TEDs that are "comparable in effectiveness to those used in the United States. Any exceptions to this requirement must be comparable to those of the United States program ..."; and (ii) "a credible enforcement effort that includes monitoring for compliance and appropriate sanctions."[15] The regulatory program may be in the form of regulations, or may, in certain circumstances, take the form of a voluntary arrangement between industry and government. Other measures that the harvesting nation undertakes for the protection of sea turtles will also be taken into account in making the comparability determination. The average incidental take rate "will be deemed comparable if the harvesting nation requires the use of TEDs in a manner comparable to that of the U.S. program...."

5. The 1996 Guidelines provide that all shrimp imported into the United States must be accompanied by a Shrimp Exporter's Declaration form attesting that the shrimp was harvested either in the waters of a nation currently certified under Section 609 or "under conditions that do not adversely affect sea turtles", * * *. A 25 November 1996 ruling of the United States Court of International Trade clarified that shrimp harvested by manual methods which did not harm sea turtles could still be imported from non-certified countries.[21] On 4 June 1998, the United States Court of Appeals for the Federal Circuit vacated the decisions of the United States

---

14. Section 609(b)(2)(A) and (B).

15. 1996 Guidelines, p. 17344.

21. *Earth Island Institute v. Warren Christopher*, 948 Fed. Supp. 1062 (CIT 1996).

Court of International Trade of 8 October and 25 November 1996.[22] In practice, however, exemption from the import ban for TED-caught shrimp from non-certified countries remained unavailable while this dispute was before the Panel and before us.

6.   The 1991 Guidelines limited the geographical scope of the import ban imposed by Section 609 to countries in the wider Caribbean/western Atlantic region, and granted these countries a three-year phase-in period. The 1993 Guidelines maintained this geographical limitation. On 29 December 1995, the United States Court of International Trade held that the 1991 and 1993 Guidelines violated Section 609 by limiting its geographical scope to shrimp harvested in the wider Caribbean/western Atlantic region, and directed the Department of State to extend the ban worldwide not later than 1 May 1996.[25] On 10 April 1996, the United States Court of International Trade refused a subsequent request by the Department of State to postpone the 1 May 1996 deadline. On 19 April 1996, the United States issued the 1996 Guidelines, extending Section 609 to shrimp harvested in *all* foreign countries effective 1 May 1996.

7.   In the Panel Report, the Panel reached the following conclusions:

In the light of the findings above, we conclude that the import ban on shrimp and shrimp products as applied by the United States on the basis of Section 609 of Public Law 101–162 is not consistent with Article XI:1 of GATT 1994, and cannot be justified under Article XX of GATT 1994.[27]

* * *

113.   Article XX of the GATT 1994 reads, in its relevant parts:

Article XX
General Exceptions

Subject to the requirement that such measures are not applied in a manner which would constitute a means of arbitrary or unjustifiable discrimination between countries where the same conditions prevail, or a disguised restriction on international trade, nothing in this Agreement shall be construed to prevent the adoption or enforcement by any Member of measures:

. . .

(*b*) necessary to protect human, animal or plant life or health;

. . .

(*g*) relating to the conservation of exhaustible natural resources if such measures are made effective in conjunction with restrictions on domestic production or consumption;

---

22.   1998 U.S. App. Lexis 11789.

25.   *Earth Island Institute v. Warren Christopher*, 913 Fed. Supp. 559 (CIT 1995).

27.   Panel Report, para. 8.1.

114. The Panel did not follow all of the steps of applying the "customary rules of interpretation of public international law" as required by Article 3.2 of the DSU. As we have emphasized numerous times, these rules call for an examination of the ordinary meaning of the words of a treaty, read in their context, and in the light of the object and purpose of the treaty involved. A treaty interpreter must begin with, and focus upon, the text of the particular provision to be interpreted. It is in the words constituting that provision, read in their context, that the object and purpose of the states parties to the treaty must first be sought. Where the meaning imparted by the text itself is equivocal or inconclusive, or where confirmation of the correctness of the reading of the text itself is desired, light from the object and purpose of the treaty as a whole may usefully be sought.[83]

115. In the present case, the Panel did not expressly examine the ordinary meaning of the words of Article XX. The Panel disregarded the fact that the introductory clauses of Article XX speak of the "manner" in which measures sought to be justified are "applied". In *United States— Gasoline*, we pointed out that the chapeau of Article XX "by its express terms addresses, not so much the questioned measure or its specific contents as such, *but rather the manner in which that measure is applied*."[84] (emphasis added) The Panel did not inquire specifically into how the *application* of Section 609 constitutes "a means of arbitrary or unjustifiable discrimination between countries where the same conditions prevail, or a disguised restriction on international trade." What the Panel did, in purporting to examine the consistency of the measure with the chapeau of Article XX, was to focus repeatedly on the *design of the measure itself*. For instance, the Panel stressed that it was addressing "a particular situation where a Member has taken unilateral measures which, *by their nature*, could put the multilateral trading system at risk."[85] (emphasis added)

116. The general design of a measure, as distinguished from its application, is, however, to be examined in the course of determining whether that measure falls within one or another of the paragraphs of Article XX following the chapeau. The Panel failed to scrutinize the *immediate* context of the chapeau: i.e., paragraphs (a) to (j) of Article XX. Moreover, the Panel did not look into the object and purpose of the *chapeau of Article XX*. Rather, the Panel looked into the object and purpose of the *whole of the GATT 1994 and the WTO Agreement*, which object and

---

83. I. Sinclair, *The Vienna Convention on the Law of Treaties*, 2nd ed. (Manchester University Press, 1984), pp. 130–131.

84. Adopted 20 May 1996, WT/DS2/AB/R, p. 22.

85. Panel Report, para. 7.60. The Panel also stated, in paras. 7.33–7.34 of the Panel Report:

... Pursuant to the chapeau of Article XX, a measure may discriminate, but not in an "arbitrary" or "unjustifiable" manner.

We therefore move to consider *whether the U.S. measure* conditioning market access on the adoption of certain conservation policies by the exporting Member *could be considered as "unjustifiable" discrimination* . . . . (emphasis added)

purpose it described in an overly broad manner. Thus, the Panel arrived at the very broad formulation that measures which "undermine the WTO multilateral trading system" must be regarded as "not within the scope of measures permitted under the chapeau of Article XX." Maintaining, rather than undermining, the multilateral trading system is necessarily a fundamental and pervasive premise underlying the *WTO Agreement*; but it is not a right or an obligation, nor is it an interpretative rule which can be employed in the appraisal of a given measure under the chapeau of Article XX. In *United States—Gasoline*, we stated that it is "important to underscore that the purpose and object of the introductory clauses of Article XX is generally the prevention of *'abuse of the exceptions of* [*Article XX*]*'*." (emphasis added) The Panel did not attempt to inquire into how the measure at stake was being *applied in such a manner* as to constitute *abuse or misuse of a given kind of exception.*

117.   The above flaws in the Panel's analysis and findings flow almost naturally from the fact that the Panel disregarded the sequence of steps essential for carrying out such an analysis. The Panel defined its approach as first "determin[ing] whether the measure at issue satisfies the conditions contained in the chapeau." If the Panel found that to be the case, it said that it "shall then examine whether the U.S. measure is covered by the terms of Article XX(b) or (g)." The Panel attempted to justify its interpretative approach in the following manner:

> As mentioned by the Appellate Body in its report in the *Gasoline* case, in order for the justification of Article XX to be extended to a given measure, it must not only come under one or another of the particular exceptions—paragraphs (a) to (j)—listed under Article XX; it must also satisfy the requirements imposed by the opening clause of Article XX. We note that panels have in the past considered the specific paragraphs of Article XX before reviewing the applicability of the conditions contained in the chapeau. However, *as the conditions contained in the introductory provision apply to any of the paragraphs of Article XX, it seems equally appropriate to analyse first the introductory provision of Article XX.* (emphasis added)

* * *

118.   In *United States—Gasoline*, we enunciated the appropriate method for applying Article XX of the GATT 1994:

> In order that the justifying protection of Article XX may be extended to it, the measure at issue must not only come under one or another of the particular exceptions—paragraphs (a) to (j)—listed under Article XX; it must also satisfy the requirements imposed by the opening clauses of Article XX. *The analysis is,* in other words, *two-tiered: first, provisional justification by reason of characterization of the measure under XX(g); second, further appraisal of the same measure under the introductory clauses of Article XX.*[92] (emphasis added)

---

92.   Adopted 20 May 1996, WT/DS2/AB/R, p. 22.

119. The sequence of steps indicated above in the analysis of a claim of justification under Article XX reflects, not inadvertence or random choice, but rather the fundamental structure and logic of Article XX. The Panel appears to suggest, albeit indirectly, that following the indicated sequence of steps, or the inverse thereof, does not make any difference. To the Panel, reversing the sequence set out in *United States—Gasoline* "seems equally appropriate."[93] We do not agree.

120. The task of interpreting the chapeau so as to prevent the abuse or misuse of the specific exemptions provided for in Article XX is rendered very difficult, if indeed it remains possible at all, where the interpreter (like the Panel in this case) has not first identified and examined the specific exception threatened with abuse. The standards established in the chapeau are, moreover, necessarily broad in scope and reach: the prohibition of the *application* of a measure "in a manner which would constitute a means of *arbitrary* or *unjustifiable discrimination* between countries where the same conditions prevail" or "a *disguised restriction* on international trade."(emphasis added) When applied in a particular case, the actual contours and contents of these standards will vary as the kind of measure under examination varies. What is appropriately characterizable as "arbitrary discrimination" or "unjustifiable discrimination", or as a "disguised restriction on international trade" in respect of one category of measures, need not be so with respect to another group or type of measures. The standard of "arbitrary discrimination", for example, under the chapeau may be different for a measure that purports to be necessary to protect public morals than for one relating to the products of prison labour.

121. The consequences of the interpretative approach adopted by the Panel are apparent in its findings. The Panel formulated a broad standard and a test for appraising measures sought to be justified under the chapeau; it is a standard or a test that finds no basis either in the text of the chapeau or in that of either of the two specific exceptions claimed by the United States. The Panel, in effect, constructed an *a priori* test that purports to define a category of measures which, *ratione materiae*, fall outside the justifying protection of Article XX's chapeau.[94] In the present case, the Panel found that the United States measure at stake fell within that class of excluded measures because Section 609 conditions access to the domestic shrimp market of the United States on the adoption by exporting countries of certain conservation policies prescribed by the United States. It appears to us, however, that conditioning access to a Member's domestic market on whether exporting Members comply with, or adopt, a policy or policies unilaterally prescribed by the importing Member may, to some degree, be a common aspect of measures falling within the scope of one or another of the exceptions (a) to (j) of Article XX. Paragraphs (a) to (j) comprise measures that are recognized as *exceptions to substantive obligations* established in the GATT 1994, because the domestic policies embodied in such measures have been recognized as important and legiti-

---

93. Panel Report, para. 7.28.

94. See, for example, Panel Report, para. 7.50.

mate in character. It is not necessary to assume that requiring from exporting countries compliance with, or adoption of, certain policies (although covered in principle by one or another of the exceptions) prescribed by the importing country, renders a measure *a priori* incapable of justification under Article XX. Such an interpretation renders most, if not all, of the specific exceptions of Article XX inutile, a result abhorrent to the principles of interpretation we are bound to apply.

122.   We hold that the findings of the Panel quoted in paragraph 112 above, and the interpretative analysis embodied therein, constitute error in legal interpretation and accordingly reverse them.

———————

For a further discussion of the case and the Appellate Body's decision respecting the U.S.'s sea turtle program, see Chapter 7.

LaGrand

Germany v. U.S.
International Court of Justice
2001 I.C.J. Rep. 466 (Judgment of June 27)

1.   On 2 March 1999 the Federal Republic of Germany (hereinafter referred to as "Germany") filed in the Registry of the Court an Application instituting proceedings against the United States of America (hereinafter referred to as the "United States") for "violations of the Vienna Convention on Consular Relations [of 24 April 1963]" (hereinafter referred to as the "Vienna Convention").

In its Application, Germany based the jurisdiction of the Court on Article 36, paragraph 1, of the Statute of the Court and on Article I of the Optional Protocol concerning the Compulsory Settlement of Disputes, which accompanies the Vienna Convention (hereinafter referred to as the "Optional Protocol").

2.   Pursuant to Article 40, paragraph 2, of the Statute, the Application was forthwith communicated to the Government of the United States; and, in accordance with paragraph 3 of that Article, all States entitled to appear before the Court were notified of the Application.

3.   On 2 March 1999, the day on which the Application was filed, the German Government also filed in the Registry of the Court a request for the indication of provisional measures based on Article 41 of the Statute and Articles 73, 74 and 75 of the Rules of Court.

By a letter dated 2 March 1999, the Vice–President of the Court, acting President in the case, addressed the Government of the United States in the following terms:

"Exercising the functions of the presidency in terms of Articles 13 and 32 of the Rules of Court, and acting in conformity with Article 74, paragraph 4, of the said Rules, I hereby draw the attention of [the]

Government [of the United States] to the need to act in such a way as to enable any Order the Court will make on the request for provisional measures to have its appropriate effects.''

By an Order of 3 March 1999, the Court indicated certain provisional measures (see paragraph 32 below).

* * *

65.   Germany's first submission requests the Court to adjudge and declare:

> "that the United States, by not informing Karl and Walter LaGrand without delay following their arrest of their rights under Article 36 subparagraph 1*(b)* of the Vienna Convention on Consular Relations, and by depriving Germany of the possibility of rendering consular assistance, which ultimately resulted in the execution of Karl and Walter LaGrand, violated its international legal obligations to Germany, in its own right and in its right of diplomatic protection of its nationals, under Articles 5 and 36 paragraph 1 of the said Convention''.

* * *

74.   Article 36, paragraph 1, establishes an interrelated regime designed to facilitate the implementation of the system of consular protection. It begins with the basic principle governing consular protection: the right of communication and access (Art. 36, para. 1*(a)*.) This clause is followed by the provision which spells out the modalities of consular notification (Art. 36, para. 1*(b)*.) Finally Article 36, paragraph 1*(c),* sets out the measures consular officers may take in rendering consular assistance to their nationals in the custody of the receiving State. It follows that when the sending State is unaware of the detention of its nationals due to the failure of the receiving State to provide the requisite consular notification without delay, which was true in the present case during the period between 1982 and 1992, the sending State has been prevented for all practical purposes from exercising its rights under Article 36, paragraph 1. It is immaterial for the purposes of the present case whether the LaGrands would have sought consular assistance from Germany, whether Germany would have rendered such assistance, or whether a different verdict would have been rendered. It is sufficient that the Convention conferred these rights, and that Germany and the LaGrands were in effect prevented by the breach of the United States from exercising them, had they so chosen.

* * *

92.   The Court will now consider Germany's third submission in which it asks the Court to adjudge and declare:

> "that the United States, by failing to take all measures at its disposal to ensure that Walter LaGrand was not executed pending the final decision of the International Court of Justice on the matter violated its international legal obligation to comply with the Order on Provisional

Measures issued by the Court on 3 March 1999, and to refrain from any action which might interfere with the subject matter of a dispute while judicial proceedings are pending".

* * *

94.   Germany claims that the United States committed a threefold violation of the Court's Order of 3 March 1999:

"(1) Immediately after the International Court of Justice had rendered its Order on Provisional Measures. Germany appealed to the U.S. Supreme Court in order to reach a stay of the execution of Walter LaGrand in accordance with the International Court's Order to the same effect. In the course of these proceedings—and in full knowledge of the Order of the International Court—the Office of the Solicitor General, a section of the U.S. Department of Justice—in a letter to the Supreme Court argued once again that: 'an order of the International Court of Justice indicating provisional measures is not binding and does not furnish a basis for judicial relief'.

This statement of a high-ranking official of the Federal Government . . . had a direct influence on the decision of the Supreme Court.

(2) In the following, the U.S. Supreme Court—an agency of the United States—refused by a majority vote to order that the execution be stayed. In doing so, it rejected the German arguments based essentially on the Order of the International Court of Justice on Provisional Measures . . .

(3) Finally, the Governor of Arizona did not order a stay of the execution of Walter LaGrand although she was vested with the right to do so by the laws of the State of Arizona. Moreover, in the present case, the Arizona Executive Board of Clemency—for the first time in the history of this institution—had issued a recommendation for a temporary stay, not least in light of the international legal issues involved in the case . . ."

* * *

98.   Neither the Permanent Court of International Justice, nor the present Court to date, has been called upon to determine the legal effects of orders made under Article 41 of the Statute. As Germany's third submission refers expressly to an international legal obligation "to comply with the Order on Provisional Measures issued by the Court on 3 March 1999", and as the United States disputes the existence of such an obligation, the Court is now called upon to rule expressly on this question.

99.   The dispute which exists between the Parties with regard to this point essentially concerns the interpretation of Article 41, which is worded in identical terms in the Statute of each Court (apart from the respective references to the Council of the League of Nations and the Security Council). This interpretation has been the subject of extensive controversy in the literature. The Court will therefore now proceed to the interpretation of Article 41 of the Statute. It will do so in accordance with customary

international law, reflected in Article 31 of the 1969 Vienna Convention on the Law of Treaties. According to paragraph 1 of Article 31, a treaty must be interpreted in good faith in accordance with the ordinary meaning to be given to its terms in their context and in the light of the treaty's object and purpose.

100.   The French text of Article 41 reads as follows:

"1.   La Cour a le pouvoir *d'indiquer,* si elle estime que les circonstances l'exigent, quelles mesures conservatoires due droit de chacun *doivent* être prises à titre provisoire.

2.   En attendant l'arrêt définitif, *l'indication* de ces mesures est immédiatement notifiée aux parties et au Conseil de sécurité." (Emphasis added.)

In this text, the terms "indiquer" and "l'indication" may be deemed to be neutral as to the mandatory character of the measure concerned; by contrast the words "doivent être prises" have an imperative character.

For its part, the English version of Article 41 reads as follows:

1.   The Court shall have the power to *indicate,* if it considers that circumstances so require, any provisional measures which *ought* to be taken to preserve the respective rights of either party.

2.   Pending the final decision, notice of the measures *suggested* shall forthwith be given to the parties and to the Security Council. (Emphasis added.)

According to the United States, the use in the English version of "indicate" instead of "order", of "ought" instead of "must" or "shall", and of "suggested" instead of "ordered", is to be understood as implying that decisions under Article 41 lack mandatory effect. It might however be argued, having regard to the fact that in 1920 the French text was the original version, that such terms as "indicate" and "ought" have a meaning equivalent to "order" and "must" or "shall".

101.   Finding itself faced with two texts which are not in total harmony, the Court will first of all note that according to Article 92 of the Charter, the Statute "forms an integral part of the present Charter". Under Article 111 of the Charter, the French and English texts of the latter are "equally authentic". The same is equally true of the Statute.

In cases of divergence between the equally authentic versions of the Statute, neither it nor the Charter indicates how to proceed. In the absence of agreement between the parties in this respect, it is appropriate to refer to paragraph 4 of Article 33 of the Vienna Convention on the Law of Treaties, which in the view of the Court again reflects customary international law. This provision reads "when a comparison of the authentic texts discloses a difference of meaning which the application of Articles 31 and 32 does not remove the meaning which best reconciles the texts, having regard to the object and purpose of the treaty, shall be adopted".

The Court will therefore now consider the object and purpose of the Statute together with the context of Article 41.

102. The object and purpose of the Statute is to enable the Court to fulfil the functions provided for therein, and in particular, the basic function of judicial settlement of international disputes by binding decisions in accordance with Article 59 of the Statute. The context in which Article 41 has to be seen within the Statute is to prevent the Court from being hampered in the exercise of its functions because the respective rights of the parties to a dispute before the Court are not preserved. It follows from the object and purpose of the Statute, as well as from the terms of Article 41 when read in their context, that the power to indicate provisional measures entails that such measures should be binding, inasmuch as the power in question is based on the necessity, when the circumstances call for it, to safeguard, and to avoid prejudice to, the rights of the parties as determined by the final judgment of the Court. The contention that provisional measures indicated under Article 41 might not be binding would be contrary to the object and purpose of that Article.

103. A related reason which points to the binding character of orders made under Article 41 and to which the Court attaches importance, is the existence of a principle which has already been recognized by the Permanent Court of International Justice when it spoke of:

> "the principle universally accepted by international tribunals and likewise laid down in many conventions ... to the effect that the parties to a case must abstain from any measure capable of exercising a prejudicial effect in regard to the execution of the decision to be given, and, in general, not allow any step of any kind to be taken which might aggravate or extend the dispute" *(Electricity Company of Sofia and Bulgaria, Order of 5 December* 1939. *P.C.I.J. Series A/B. No. 79,* p. 199).

Furthermore measures designed to avoid aggravating or extending disputes have frequently been indicated by the Court. They were indicated with the purpose of being implemented (citations omitted).

104. Given the conclusions reached by the Court above in interpreting the text of Article 41 of the Statute in the light of its object and purpose, it does not consider it necessary to resort to the preparatory work in order to determine the meaning of that Article. The Court would nevertheless point out that the preparatory work of the Statute does not preclude the conclusion that orders under Article 41 have binding force.

105. The initial preliminary draft of the Statute of the Permanent Court of International Justice, as prepared by the Committee of Jurists established by the Council of the League of Nations, made no mention of provisional measures. A provision to this effect was inserted only at a later stage in the draft prepared by the Committee, following a proposal from the Brazilian jurist Raul Fernandes.

Basing himself on the Bryan Treaty of 13 October 1914 between the United States and Sweden, Raul Fernandes had submitted the following text:

> "Dans le cas où la cause due différend consiste en actes déterminés déjà effectués ou sur le point de l'être, la Cour pourra ordonner, dans le plus bref délai, à titre provisoire, des mesures conservatoires adéquates, en attendant le jugement définitif." (Comité consultatif de juristes, *Procès-verbaux des séances due comité,* 16 juin–24 juillet 1920 (avec annexes), La Haye, 1920, p. 609.)

In its English translation this text read as follows:

> "In case the cause of the dispute should consist of certain acts already committed or about to be committed, the Court may, provisionally and with the least possible delay, order adequate protective measures to be taken, pending the final judgment of the Court." (Advisory Committee of Jurists, *Procés-verbaux of the Proceedings of the Committee,* 16 June–24 July 1920 (with Annexes), The Hague, 1920, p. 609.)

The Drafting Committee prepared a new version of this text, to which two main amendments were made: on the one hand, the words "la Cour pourra ordonner" ("the Court may . . . order") were replaced by "la Cour a le pouvoir d'indiquer" ("the Court shall have the power to suggest"), while, on the other, a second paragraph was added providing for notice to be given to the parties and to the Council of the "measures suggested" by the Court. The draft Article *2bis* as submitted by the Drafting Committee thus read as follows:

> "Dans le cas où la cause due différend consiste en un acte effectué ou sur le point de l'être la Cour a le pouvoir d'indiquer, si elle estime que les circonstances l'exigent, quelles mesures conservatoires du droit de chacun doivent être prises à titre provisoire.
>
> "En attendant son arrêt, cette suggestion de la Cour est immédiatement transmise aux parties et au Conseil." (Comité consultatif de juristes; *Procès-verbaux des séances due comité,* 16 juin–24 juillet 1920 (avec annexes), La Haye, 1920, p. 567–568.)

The English version read:

> "If the dispute arises out of an act which has already taken place or which is imminent, the Court shall have the power to suggest, if it considers that circumstances so require, the provisional measures that should be taken to preserve the respective rights of either party.
>
> Pending the final decision, notice of the measures suggested shall forthwith be given to the parties and the Council." (Advisory Committee of Jurists, *Procés-verbaux of the Proceedings of the Committee,* 16 June–24 July 1920 (with Annexes), The Hague, 1920, pp. 567–568.)

The Committee of Jurists eventually adopted a draft Article 39, which amended the former Article *2bis* only in its French version: in the second paragraph, the words *"cette suggestion"* were replaced in French by the words *"l'indication"*.

106.   When the draft Article 39 was examined by the Sub–Committee of the Third Committee of the first Assembly of the League of Nations, a number of amendments were considered. Raul Fernandes suggested again to use the word "ordonner" in the French version. The Sub–Committee decided to stay with the word "indiquer", the Chairman of the Sub–Committee observing that the Court lacked the means to execute its decisions. The language of the first paragraph of the English version was then made to conform to the French text: thus the word "suggest" was replaced by "indicate", and "should" by "ought to". However, in the second paragraph of the English version, the phrase "measures suggested" remained unchanged.

The provision thus amended in French and in English by the Sub–Committee was adopted as Article 41 of the Statute of the Permanent Court of International Justice. It passed as such into the Statute of the present Court without any discussion in 1945.

107.   The preparatory work of Article 41 shows that the preference given in the French text to *"indiquer"* over *"ordonner"* was motivated by the consideration that the Court did not have the means to assure the execution of its decisions. However, the lack of means of execution and the lack of binding force are two different matters. Hence, the fact that the Court does not itself have the means to ensure the execution of orders made pursuant to Article 41 is not an argument against the binding nature of such orders.

108.   The Court finally needs to consider whether Article 94 of the United Nations Charter precludes attributing binding effect to orders indicating provisional measures. That Article reads as follows:

"1. Each Member of the United Nations undertakes to comply with the decision of the International Court of Justice in any case to which it is a party.

2.   If any party to a case fails to perform the obligations incumbent upon it under a judgment rendered by the Court, the other party may have recourse to the Security Council, which may, if it deems necessary, make recommendations or decide upon measures to be taken to give effect to the judgment."

The question arises as to the meaning to be attributed to the words "the decision of the International Court of Justice" in paragraph 1 of this Article. This wording could be understood as referring not merely to the Court's judgments but to any decision rendered by it, thus including orders indicating provisional measures. It could also be interpreted to mean only judgments rendered by the Court as provided in paragraph 2 of Article 94. In this regard, the fact that in Articles 56 to 60 of the Court's Statute, both the word "decision" and the word "judgment" are used does little to clarify the matter.

Under the first interpretation of paragraph 1 of Article 94, the text of the paragraph would confirm the binding nature of provisional measures; whereas the second interpretation would in no way preclude their being accorded binding force under Article 41 of the Statute. The Court accordingly concludes that Article 94 of the Charter does not prevent orders made under Article 41 from having a binding character.

109.   In short, it is clear that none of the sources of interpretation referred to in the relevant Articles of the Vienna Convention on the Law of Treaties, including the preparatory work, contradict the conclusions drawn from the terms of Article 41 read in their context and in the light of the object and purpose of the Statute. Thus, the Court has reached the conclusion that orders on provisional measures under Article 41 have binding effect.

NOTES AND QUESTIONS

1. In a case decided in July 2009, the International Court of Justice tackled the challenging interpretation issue of the changing meaning of words over time. The court was called upon to interpret a Spanish phrase (*con objetos de comercio*) in a treaty between Nicaragua and Costa Rica of 1858. *Dispute Regarding Navigational and Related Rights* (Costa Rica v. Nicaragua) 2009 I.C.J. Rep. (July 13). The Court said this on the issue:

> 63.   * * * It is true that the terms used in a treaty must be interpreted in light of what is determined to have been the parties' common intention, which is, by definition, contemporaneous with the treaty's conclusion. That may lead a court seised of a dispute, or the parties themselves, when they seek to determine the meaning of a treaty for purposes of good-faith compliance with it, to ascertain the meaning a term had when the treaty was drafted, since doing so can shed light on the parties' common intention. The Court has so proceeded in certain cases requiring it to interpret a term whose meaning had evolved since the conclusion of the treaty at issue, and in those cases the Court adhered to the original meaning (to this effect, see, for example, the Judgment of 27 August 1952 in the case concerning *Rights of Nationals of the United States of America in Morocco (France v. United States of America) (I.C.J. Reports 1952,* p. 176), on the question of the meaning of "dispute" in the context of a treaty concluded in 1836, the Court having determined the meaning of this term in Morocco when the treaty was concluded; the Judgment of 13 December 1999 in the case concerning *Kasikili/Sedudu Island (Botswana/Namibia) (I.C.J. Reports 1999 (II), p. 1062, para. 25)* in respect of the meaning of "centre of the main channel" and "thalweg" when the Anglo–German Agreement of 1890 was concluded).

> 64.   This does not however signify that, where a term's meaning is no longer the same as it was at the date of conclusion, no account should ever be taken of its meaning at the time when the treaty is to be interpreted for purposes of applying it.

On the one hand, the subsequent practice of the parties, within the meaning of Article 31(3)*(b)* of the Vienna Convention, can result in a departure from the original intent on the basis of a tacit agreement between the parties. On the other hand, there are situations in which the parties' intent upon conclusion of the treaty was, or may be presumed to have been, to give the terms used—or some of them—a meaning or content capable of evolving, not one fixed once and for all, so as to make allowance for, among other things, developments in international law. In such instances it is indeed in order to respect the parties' common intention at the time the treaty was concluded, not to depart from it, that account should be taken of the meaning acquired by the terms in question upon each occasion on which the treaty is to be applied.

Does the court's "evolutionary interpretation" sound like the opposite of U.S. Supreme Court Justice Antonin Scalia's "originalism"? Justice Scalia argues that when he reads the words of the U.S.'s Constitution, drafted in 1789, he seeks to apply the meaning of the words as the drafters would have understood them. Is there a more attractive middle ground between "originalism" and "evolutionary interpretation" for dealing with the problem of the changing meaning of words over time?

2.   For further reading on treaty interpretation, see, RICHARD K. GARDINER, TREATY INTERPRETATION (2008) and DAVID J. BEDERMAN, CLASSICAL CANONS: RHETORIC CLASSICISM AND TREATY INTERPRETATION (2001).

3.   PERFORMANCE

Once parties have formed a treaty and understand their obligations under it, all that remains is to fulfill the obligations. The Vienna Convention states as the bases of performance in Article 26:

> Every treaty in force is binding upon the parties to it and must be performed by them in good faith.

The rule that a treaty undertaking should be performed in good faith certainly preceded the Vienna Convention, but some authorities contended prior to the adoption of the VCLT that the proper standard, at least for some types of treaties, was utmost fidelity (*uberrima fides*). The concept is similar to that of fiduciary obligation in Anglo–American law. Article 26 of the Vienna Convention adopts the good faith standard for all treaties. Judge Lauterpacht's separate opinion in the *Norwegian Loans Case* (1957) noted that "[u]nquestionably, the obligation to act in accordance with good faith, being a general principle of law, is also part of international law." Norwegian Loans (France v. Norway) 1957 I.C.J. Rep. 9, 53.

When a party does not perform its treaty obligations, it may have an excuse releasing it from performance or it may be in breach, in which case it owes a remedy to other parties. The law of state responsibility is the set of rules determining when a state has violated an international legal obligation and the consequences of violation. It is the subject of Chapter 8 below. Here, by way of introduction to that chapter and to review the rules of performance and breach with respect to treaties, we consider a case involving performance under a bilateral treaty between Hungary and Slovakia.

The Gabčíkovo–Nagymaros Project

Hungary/Slovakia
International Court of Justice
1997 I.C.J. Rep. 7 (Judgment of Sept. 25)

15.   The present case arose out of the signature, on 16 September 1977, by the Hungarian People's Republic and the Czechoslovak People's Republic, of a treaty "concerning the construction and operation of the Gabčíkovo–Nagymaros System of Locks" (hereinafter called the "1977 Treaty"). The names of the two contracting States have varied over the years: hereinafter they will be referred to as Hungary and Czechoslovakia. The 1977 Treaty entered into force on 30 June 1978.

It provides for the construction and operation of a System of Locks by the parties as a "joint investment". According to its Preamble, the barrage system was designed to attain

> "the broad utilization of the natural resources of the Bratislava–Budapest section of the Danube river for the development of water resources, energy, transport, agriculture and other sectors of the national economy of the Contracting Parties".

The joint investment was thus essentially aimed at the production of hydroelectricity, the improvement of navigation on the relevant section of the Danube and the protection of the areas along the banks against flooding. At the same time, by the terms of the Treaty, the contracting parties undertook to ensure that the quality of water in the Danube was not impaired as a result of the Project, and that compliance with the obligations for the protection of nature arising in connection with the construction and operation of the System of Locks would be observed.

16.   The Danube is the second longest river in Europe, flowing along or across the borders of nine countries in its 2,860–kilometre course from the Black Forest eastwards to the Black Sea. For 142 kilometres, it forms the boundary between Slovakia and Hungary.

* * *

18.   Article 1, paragraph 1, of the 1977 Treaty describes the principal works to be constructed in pursuance of the Project. It provided for the building of two series of locks, one at Gabčíkovo (in Czechoslovak territory) and the other at Nagymaros (in Hungarian territory), to constitute "a single and indivisible operational system of works". * * *

According to Article 14,

> "The discharge specified in the water balance of the approved joint contractual plan shall be ensured in the bed of the Danube [between

Dunakiliti and Sap] unless natural conditions or other circumstances temporarily require a greater or smaller discharge."

Paragraph 3 of that Article was worded as follows:

"In the event that the withdrawal of water in the Hungarian–Czecho-slovak section of the Danube exceeds the quantities of water specified in the water balance of the approved joint contractual plan and the excess withdrawal results in a decrease in the output of electric power, the share of electric power of the Contracting Party benefiting from the excess withdrawal shall be correspondingly reduced."

Article 15 specified that the contracting parties

"shall ensure, by the means specified in the joint contractual plan, that the quality of the water in the Danube is not impaired as a result of the construction and operation of the System of Locks".

* * *

It was stipulated in Article 19 that:

"The Contracting Parties shall, through the means specified in the joint contractual plan, ensure compliance with the obligations for the protection of nature arising in connection with the construction and operation of the System of Locks."

Article 20 provided for the contracting parties to take appropriate measures, within the framework of their national investments, for the protection of fishing interests in conformity with the Convention concerning Fishing in the Waters of the Danube, signed at Bucharest on 29 January 1958.

* * *

Finally a dispute settlement provision was contained in Article 27, worded as follows:

"1. The settlement of disputes in matters relating to the realization and operation of the System of Locks shall be a function of the government delegates.

2. If the government delegates are unable to reach agreement on the matters in dispute, they shall refer them to the Governments of the Contracting Parties for decision."

* * *

Work on the Project started in 1978. On Hungary's initiative, the two parties first agreed, by two Protocols signed on 10 October 1983 (one amending Article 4, paragraph 4, of the 1977 Treaty and the other the Agreement on mutual assistance), to slow the work down and to postpone putting into operation the power plants, and then, by a Protocol signed on 6 February 1989 (which amended the Agreement on mutual assistance), to accelerate the Project.

22.   As a result of intense criticism which the Project had generated in Hungary, the Hungarian Government decided on 13 May 1989 to suspend the works at Nagymaros pending the completion of various studies which the competent authorities were to finish before 31 July 1989. On 21 July 1989, the Hungarian Government extended the suspension of the works at Nagymaros until 31 October 1989, and, in addition, suspended the works at Dunakiliti until the same date. Lastly, on 27 October 1989, Hungary decided to abandon the works at Nagymaros and to maintain the status quo at Dunakiliti.

23.   During this period, negotiations were being held between the parties. Czechoslovakia also started investigating alternative solutions. One of them, subsequently known as * * * Variant C included the construction at Cunovo of an overflow dam and a levee linking that dam to the south bank of the bypass canal. The corresponding reservoir was to have a smaller surface area and provide approximately 30 per cent less storage than the reservoir initially contemplated. * * *

On 23 July 1991, the Slovak Government decided "to begin, in September 1991, construction to put the Gabčíkovo Project into operation by the provisional solution". That decision was endorsed by the Federal Czechoslovak Government on 25 July. Work on Variant C began in November 1991. Discussions continued between the two parties but to no avail, and, on 19 May 1992, the Hungarian Government transmitted to the Czechoslovak Government a Note Verbale terminating the 1977 Treaty with effect from 25 May 1992. On 15 October 1992, Czechoslovakia began work to enable the Danube to be closed and, starting on 23 October, proceeded to the damming of the river.

* * *

89.   By the terms of Article 2, paragraph 1(c), of the Special Agreement, the Court is asked, thirdly, to determine "what are the legal effects of the notification, on 19 May 1992, of the termination of the Treaty by the Republic of Hungary".

* * *

90.   The Court will recall that, by early 1992, the respective parties to the 1977 Treaty had made clear their positions with regard to the recourse by Czechoslovakia to Variant C. Hungary in a Note Verbale of 14 February 1992 had made clear its view that Variant C was a contravention of the 1977 Treaty * * *; Czechoslovakia insisted on the implementation of Variant C as a condition for further negotiation. On 26 February 1992, in a letter to his Czechoslovak counterpart, the Prime Minister of Hungary described the impending diversion of the Danube as "a serious breach of international law" and stated that, unless work was suspended while further enquiries took place, "the Hungarian Government [would] have no choice but to respond to this situation of necessity by terminating the 1977 inter-State Treaty". In a Note Verbale dated 18 March 1992, Czechoslovakia reaffirmed that, while it was prepared to continue negotiations "on

every level", it could not agree "to stop all work on the provisional solution".

On 24 March 1992, the Hungarian Parliament passed a resolution authorizing the Government to terminate the 1977 Treaty if Czechoslovakia did not stop the works by 30 April 1992. On 13 April 1992, the Vice–President of the Commission of the European Communities wrote to both parties confirming the willingness of the Commission to chair a committee of independent experts including representatives of the two countries, in order to assist the two Governments in identifying a mutually acceptable solution. Commission involvement would depend on each Government not taking "any steps . . . which would prejudice possible actions to be undertaken on the basis of the report's findings". The Czechoslovak Prime Minister stated in a letter to the Hungarian Prime Minister dated 23 April 1992, that his Government continued to be interested in the establishment of the proposed committee "without any preliminary conditions"; criticizing Hungary's approach, he refused to suspend work on the provisional solution, but added, "in my opinion, there is still time, until the damming of the Danube (i.e., until October 31, 1992), for resolving disputed questions on the basis of agreement of both States".

On 7 May 1992, Hungary, in the very resolution in which it decided on the termination of the Treaty, made a proposal, this time to the Slovak Prime Minister, for a six-month suspension of work on Variant C. The Slovak Prime Minister replied that the Slovak Government remained ready to negotiate, but considered preconditions "inappropriate".

91.   On 19 May 1992, the Hungarian Government transmitted to the Czechoslovak Government a Declaration notifying it of the termination by Hungary of the 1977 Treaty as of 25 May 1992. In a letter of the same date from the Hungarian Prime Minister to the Czechoslovak Prime Minster, the immediate cause for termination was specified to be Czechoslovakia's refusal, expressed in its letter of 23 April 1992, to suspend the work on Variant C during mediation efforts of the Commission of the European Communities. In its Declaration, Hungary stated that it could not accept the deleterious effects for the environment and the conservation of nature of the implementation of Variant C which would be practically equivalent to the dangers caused by the realization of the original Project. It added that Variant C infringed numerous international agreements and violated the territorial integrity of the Hungarian State by diverting the natural course of the Danube.

* * *

92.   During the proceedings, Hungary presented five arguments in support of the lawfulness, and thus the effectiveness, of its notification of termination. These were the existence of a state of necessity; the impossibility of performance of the Treaty; the occurrence of a fundamental change of circumstances; the material breach of the Treaty by Czechoslovakia; and, finally, the development of new norms of international environmental law. Slovakia contested each of these grounds.

93. On the first point, Hungary stated that, as Czechoslovakia had "remained inflexible" and continued with its implementation of Variant C, "a temporary state of necessity eventually became permanent, justifying termination of the 1977 Treaty".

Slovakia, for its part, denied that a state of necessity existed on the basis of what it saw as the scientific facts; and argued that even if such a state of necessity had existed, this would not give rise to a right to terminate the Treaty under the Vienna Convention of 1969 on the Law of Treaties.

94. Hungary's second argument relied on the terms of Article 61 of the Vienna Convention, which is worded as follows:

Article 61
Supervening Impossibility of Performance

1. A party may invoke the impossibility of performing a treaty as a ground for terminating or withdrawing from it if the impossibility results from the permanent disappearance or destruction of an object indispensable for the execution of the treaty. If the impossibility is temporary, it may be invoked only as a ground for suspending the operation of the treaty.

2. Impossibility of performance may not be invoked by a party as a ground for terminating, withdrawing from or suspending the operation of a treaty if the impossibility is the result of a breach by that party either of an obligation under the treaty or of any other international obligation owed to any other party to the treaty.

Hungary declared that it could not be "obliged to fulfil a practically impossible task, namely to construct a barrage system on its own territory that would cause irreparable environmental damage". It concluded that "By May 1992 the essential object of the Treaty—an economic joint investment which was consistent with environmental protection and which was operated by the two parties jointly—had permanently disappeared, and the Treaty had thus become impossible to perform."

In Hungary's view, the "object indispensable for the execution of the treaty", whose disappearance or destruction was required by Article 61 of the Vienna Convention, did not have to be a physical object, but could also include, in the words of the International Law Commission, "a legal situation which was the raison détre of the rights and obligations".

Slovakia claimed that Article 61 was the only basis for invoking impossibility of performance as a ground for termination, that paragraph 1 of that Article clearly contemplated physical "disappearance or destruction" of the object in question, and that, in any event, paragraph 2 precluded the invocation of impossibility "if the impossibility is the result of a breach by that party . . . of an obligation under the treaty".

95. As to "fundamental change of circumstances", Hungary relied on Article 62 of the Vienna Convention on the Law of Treaties which states as follows:

Article 62
Fundamental Change of Circumstances

1.   A fundamental change of circumstances which has occurred with regard to those existing at the time of the conclusion of a treaty, and which was not foreseen by the parties, may not be invoked as a ground for terminating or withdrawing from the treaty unless:

   (a) the existence of those circumstances constituted an essential basis of the consent of the parties to be bound by the treaty; and

   (b) the effect of the change is radically to transform the extent of obligations still to be performed under the treaty.

2.   A fundamental change of circumstances may not be invoked as a ground for terminating or withdrawing from a treaty:

   (a) if the treaty establishes a boundary; or

   (b) if the fundamental change is the result of a breach by the party invoking it either of an obligation under the treaty or of any other international obligation owed to any other party to the treaty.

3.   If, under the foregoing paragraphs, a party may invoke a fundamental change of circumstances as a ground for terminating or withdrawing from a treaty it may also invoke the change as a ground for suspending the operation of the treaty.

Hungary identified a number of "substantive elements" present at the conclusion of the 1977 Treaty which it said had changed fundamentally by the date of notification of termination. These included the notion of "socialist integration", for which the Treaty had originally been a "vehicle", but which subsequently disappeared; the "single and indivisible operational system", which was to be replaced by a unilateral scheme; the fact that the basis of the planned joint investment had been overturned by the sudden emergence of both States into a market economy; the attitude of Czechoslovakia which had turned the "framework treaty" into an "immutable norm"; and, finally, the transformation of a treaty consistent with environmental protection into "a prescription for environmental disaster".

Slovakia, for its part, contended that the changes identified by Hungary had not altered the nature of the obligations under the Treaty from those originally undertaken, so that no entitlement to terminate it arose from them.

96.   Hungary further argued that termination of the Treaty was justified by Czechoslovakia's material breaches of the Treaty, and in this regard it invoked Article 60 of the Vienna Convention on the Law of Treaties, which provides:

Article 60
Termination or Suspension of the Operation of a Treaty as a
Consequence of its Breach

1.   A material breach of a bilateral treaty by one of the parties entitles the other to invoke the breach as a ground for terminating the treaty or suspending its operation in whole or in part.

2. A material breach of a multilateral treaty by one of the parties entitles:

(a) the other parties by unanimous agreement to suspend the operation of the treaty in whole or in part or to terminate it either:

(i) in the relations between themselves and the defaulting State, or

(ii) as between all the parties;

(b) a party specially affected by the breach to invoke it as a ground for suspending the operation of the treaty in whole or in part in the relations between itself and the defaulting State;

(c) any party other than the defaulting State to invoke the breach as a ground for suspending the operation of the treaty in whole or in part with respect to itself if the treaty is of such a character that a material breach of its provisions by one party radically changes the position of every party with respect to the further performance of its obligations under the treaty.

3. A material breach of a treaty, for the purposes of this article, consists in

(a) a repudiation of the treaty not sanctioned by the present Convention; or

(b) the violation of a provision essential to the accomplishment of the object or purpose of the treaty.

4. The foregoing paragraphs are without prejudice to any provision in the treaty applicable in the event of a breach.

5. Paragraphs 1 to 3 do not apply to provisions relating to the protection of the human person contained in treaties of a humanitarian character, in particular to provisions prohibiting any form of reprisals against persons protected by such treaties.

Hungary claimed in particular that Czechoslovakia violated the 1977 Treaty by proceeding to the construction and putting into operation of Variant C, as well as failing to comply with its obligations under Articles 15 and 19 of the Treaty. Hungary further maintained that Czechoslovakia had breached other international conventions (among them the Convention of 31 May 1976 on the Regulation of Water Management Issues of Boundary Waters) and general international law.

Slovakia denied that there had been, on the part of Czechoslovakia or on its part, any material breach of the obligations to protect water quality and nature, and claimed that Variant C, far from being a breach, was devised as "the best possible approximate application" of the Treaty. It furthermore denied that Czechoslovakia had acted in breach of other international conventions or general international law.

97. Finally, Hungary argued that subsequently imposed requirements of international law in relation to the protection of the environment precluded performance of the Treaty. The previously existing obligation not

to cause substantive damage to the territory of another State had, Hungary claimed, evolved into an erga omnes obligation of prevention of damage pursuant to the "precautionary principle". On this basis, Hungary argued, its termination was "forced by the other party's refusal to suspend work on Variant C".

Slovakia argued, in reply, that none of the intervening developments in environmental law gave rise to norms of *jus cogens* that would override the Treaty. Further, it contended that the claim by Hungary to be entitled to take action could not in any event serve as legal justification for termination of the Treaty under the law of treaties, but belonged rather "to the language of self-help or reprisals".

* * *

98.   The question, as formulated in Article 2, paragraph 1(c), of the Special Agreement, deals with treaty law since the Court is asked to determine what the legal effects are of the notification of termination of the Treaty. The question is whether Hungary's notification of 19 May 1992 brought the 1977 Treaty to an end, or whether it did not meet the requirements of international law, with the consequence that it did not terminate the Treaty.

99.   The Court has referred earlier to the question of the applicability to the present case of the Vienna Convention of 1969 on the Law of Treaties. The Vienna Convention is not directly applicable to the 1977 Treaty inasmuch as both States ratified that Convention only after the Treaty's conclusion. Consequently only those rules which are declaratory of customary law are applicable to the 1977 Treaty. As the Court has already stated above (see paragraph 46), this is the case, in many respects, with Articles 60 to 62 of the Vienna Convention, relating to termination or suspension of the operation of a treaty. On this, the Parties, too, were broadly in agreement.

100.   The 1977 Treaty does not contain any provision regarding its termination. Nor is there any indication that the parties intend to admit the possibility of denunciation or withdrawal. On the contrary, the Treaty establishes a long-standing and durable regime of joint investment and joint operation. Consequently, the parties not having agreed otherwise, the Treaty could be terminated only on the limited grounds enumerated in the Vienna Convention.

* * *

101.   The Court will now turn to the first ground advanced by Hungary, that of the state of necessity. In this respect, the Court will merely observe that, even if a state of necessity is found to exist, it is not a ground for the termination of a treaty. It may only be invoked to exonerate from its responsibility a State which has failed to implement a treaty. Even if found justified, it does not terminate a Treaty; the Treaty may be ineffective as long as the condition of necessity continues to exist; it may in fact be dormant, but—unless the parties by mutual agreement terminate

the Treaty—it continues to exist. As soon as the state of necessity ceases to exist, the duty to comply with treaty obligations revives.

* * *

102. Hungary also relied on the principle of the impossibility of performance as reflected in Article 61 of the Vienna Convention on the Law of Treaties. Hungary's interpretation of the wording of Article 61 is, however, not in conformity with the terms of that Article, nor with the intentions of the Diplomatic Conference which adopted the Convention. Article 61, paragraph 1, requires the "permanent disappearance or destruction of an object indispensable for the execution" of the treaty to justify the termination of a treaty on grounds of impossibility of performance. During the conference, a proposal was made to extend the scope of the article by including in it cases such as the impossibility to make certain payments because of serious financial difficulties * * *. Although it was recognized that such situations could lead to a preclusion of the wrongfulness of non-performance by a party of its treaty obligations, the participating States were not prepared to consider such situations to be a ground for terminating or spending a treaty, and preferred to limit themselves to a narrower concept.

103. Hungary contended that the essential object of the Treaty—an economic joint investment which was consistent with environmental protection and which was operated by the two contracting parties jointly—had permanently disappeared and that the Treaty had thus become impossible to perform. It is not necessary for the Court to determine whether the term "object" in Article 61 can also be understood to embrace a legal regime as in any event, even if that were the case, it would have to conclude that in this instance that regime had not definitively ceased to exist. The 1977 Treaty—and in particular its Articles 15, 19 and 20—actually made available to the parties the necessary means to proceed at any time, by negotiation, to the required readjustments between economic imperatives and ecological imperatives. The Court would add that, if the joint exploitation of the investment was no longer possible, this was originally because Hungary did not carry out most of the works for which it was responsible under the 1977 Treaty; Article 61, paragraph 2, of the Vienna Convention expressly provides that impossibility of performance may not be invoked for the termination of a treaty by a party to that treaty when it results from that party's own breach of an obligation flowing from that treaty.

* * *

104. Hungary further argued that it was entitled to invoke a number of events which, cumulatively, would have constituted a fundamental change of circumstances. In this respect it specified profound changes of a political nature, the Project's diminishing economic viability, the progress of environmental knowledge and the development of new norms and prescriptions of international environmental law (see paragraph 95 above).

The Court recalls that, in the *Fisheries Jurisdiction* case (*I.C.J. Reports 1973*, p. 63, para. 36), it stated that, "Article 62 of the Vienna

Convention on the Law of Treaties, ... may in many respects be considered as a codification of existing customary law on the subject of the termination of a treaty relationship on account of change of circumstances".

The prevailing political situation was certainly relevant for the conclusion of the 1977 Treaty. But the Court will recall that the Treaty provided for a joint investment programme for the production of energy, the control of floods and the improvement of navigation on the Danube. In the Court's view, the prevalent political conditions were thus not so closely linked to the object and purpose of the Treaty that they constituted an essential basis of the consent of the parties and, in changing, radically altered the extent of the obligations still to be performed. The same holds good for the economic system in force at the time of the conclusion of the 1977 Treaty. Besides, even though the estimated profitability of the Project might have appeared less in 1992 than in 1977, it does not appear from the record before the Court that it was bound to diminish to such an extent that the treaty obligations of the parties would have been radically transformed as a result.

The Court does not consider that new developments in the state of environmental knowledge and of environmental law can be said to have been completely unforeseen. What is more, the formulation of Articles 15, 19 and 20, designed to accommodate change, made it possible for the parties to take account of such developments and to apply them when implementing those treaty provisions.

The changed circumstances advanced by Hungary are, in the Court's view, not of such a nature, either individually or collectively, that their effect would radically transform the extent of the obligations still to be performed in order to accomplish the Project. A fundamental change of circumstances must have been unforeseen; the existence of the circumstances at the time of the Treaty's conclusion must have constituted an essential basis, of the consent of the parties to be bound by the Treaty. The negative and conditional wording of Article 62 of the Vienna Convention on the Law of Treaties is a clear indication moreover that the stability of treaty relations requires that the plea of fundamental change of circumstances be applied only in exceptional cases.

* * *

105.   The Court will now examine Hungary's argument that it was entitled to terminate the 1977 Treaty on the ground that Czechoslovakia had violated its Articles 15, 19 and 20 (as well as a number of other conventions and rules of general international law); and that the planning, construction and putting into operation of Variant C also amounted to a material breach of the 1977 Treaty.

106.   As to that part of Hungary's argument which was based on other treaties and general rules of international law, the Court is of the view that it is only a material breach of the treaty itself, by a State party to that treaty, which entitles the other party to rely on it as a ground for terminating the treaty. The violation of other treaty rules or of rules of

general international law may justify the taking of certain measures, including countermeasures, by the injured State, but it does not constitute a ground for termination under the law of treaties.

107.   Hungary contended that Czechoslovakia had violated Articles 15, 19 and 20 of the Treaty by refusing to enter into negotiations with Hungary in order to adapt the Joint Contractual Plan to new scientific and legal developments regarding the environment. Articles 15, 19 and 20 oblige the parties jointly to take, on a continuous basis, appropriate measures necessary for the protection of water quality, of nature and of fishing interests.

Articles 15 and 19 expressly provide that the obligations they contain shall be implemented by the means specified in the Joint Contractual Plan. The failure of the parties to agree on those means cannot, on the basis of the record before the Court, be attributed solely to one party. The Court has not found sufficient evidence to conclude that Czechoslovakia had consistently refused to consult with Hungary about the desirability or necessity of measures for the preservation of the environment. The record rather shows that, while both parties indicated, in principle, a willingness to undertake further studies, in practice Czechoslovakia refused to countenance a suspension of the works at Dunakiliti and, later, on Variant C, while Hungary required suspension as a prior condition of environmental investigation because it claimed continuation of the work would prejudice the outcome of negotiations. In this regard it cannot be left out of consideration that Hungary itself, by suspending the works at Nagymaros and Dunakiliti, contributed to the creation of a situation which was not conducive to the conduct of fruitful negotiations.

108.   Hungary's main argument for invoking a material breach of the Treaty was the construction and putting into operation of Variant C. As the Court has found in paragraph 79 above, Czechoslovakia violated the Treaty only when it diverted the waters of the Danube into the bypass canal in October 1992. In constructing the works which would lead to the putting into operation of Variant C, Czechoslovakia did not act unlawfully.

In the Court's view, therefore the notification of termination by Hungary on 19 May 1992 was premature. No breach of the Treaty by Czechoslovakia had yet taken place and consequently Hungary was not entitled to invoke any such breach of the Treaty as a ground for terminating it when it did.

109.   In this regard, it should be noted that, according to Hungary's Declaration of 19 May 1992, the termination of the 1977 Treaty was to take effect as from 25 May 1992, that is only six days later. Both Parties agree that Articles 65 to 67 of the Vienna Convention on the Law of Treaties, if not codifying customary law, at least generally reflect customary international law and contain certain procedural principles which are based on an obligation to act in good faith. As the Court stated in its Advisory Opinion on the *Interpretation of the Agreement of 25 March 1951 between the WHO and Egypt* (in which case the Vienna Convention did not apply): "Precisely what periods of time may be involved in the observance of the duties to

consult and negotiate; and what period of notice of termination should be given, are matters which necessarily vary according to the requirements of the particular case. In principle, therefore, it is for the parties in each case to determine the length of those periods by consultation and negotiation in good faith." (I.C.J. Reports 1980, p. 96, para. 49.)

The termination of the Treaty by Hungary was to take effect six days after its notification. On neither of these dates had Hungary suffered injury resulting from acts of Czechoslovakia. The Court must therefore confirm its conclusion that Hungary's termination of the Treaty was premature.

110.   Nor can the Court overlook that Czechoslovakia committed the internationally wrongful act of putting into operation Variant C as a result of Hungary's own prior wrongful conduct. As was stated by the Permanent Court of International Justice: "It is, moreover, a principle generally accepted in the jurisprudence of international arbitration, as well as by municipal courts, that one Party cannot avail himself of the fact that the other has not fulfilled some obligation or has not had recourse to some means of redress, if the former Party has, by some illegal act, prevented the latter from fulfilling the obligation in question, or from having recourse to the tribunal which would have been open, to him." (*Factory at Chorzów, Jurisdiction, Judgment No. 8, 1927, P.C.I.J., Series A, No. 9*, p. 31.) Hungary, by its own conduct, had prejudiced its right to terminate the Treaty; this would still have been the case even if Czechoslovakia, by the time of the purported termination, had violated a provision essential to the accomplishment of the object or purpose of the Treaty.

* * *

111.   Finally, the Court will address Hungary's claim that it was entitled to terminate the 1977 Treaty because new requirements of international law for the protection of the environment precluded performance of the Treaty.

112.   Neither of the Parties contended that new peremptory norms of environmental law had emerged since the conclusion of the 1977 Treaty, and the Court will consequently not be required to examine the scope of Article 64 of the Vienna Convention on the Law of Treaties. On the other hand, the Court wishes to point out that newly developed norms of environmental law are relevant for the implementation of the Treaty and that the parties could, by agreement, incorporate them through the application of Articles 15, 19 and 20 of the Treaty. These articles do not contain specific obligations of performance but require the parties, in carrying out their obligations to ensure that the quality of water in the Danube is not impaired and that nature is protected, to take new environmental norms into consideration when agreeing upon the means to be specified in the Joint Contractual Plan.

By inserting these evolving provisions in the Treaty, the parties recognized the potential necessity to adapt the Project. Consequently, the Treaty is not static, and is open to adapt to emerging norms of international law. By means of Articles 15 and 19, new environmental norms can be incorporated in the Joint Contractual Plan.

The responsibility to do this was a joint responsibility. The obligations contained in Articles 15, 19 and 20 are, by definition, general and have to be transformed into specific obligations of performance through a process of consultation and negotiation. Their implementation thus requires a mutual willingness to discuss in good faith actual and potential environmental risks.

It is all the more important to do this because as the Court recalled in its Advisory Opinion on the *Legality of the Threat or Use of Nuclear Weapons*, "the environment is not an abstraction but represents the living space, the quality of life and the very health of human beings, including generations unborn" *(I.C.J. Reports 1996*, para. 29; see also paragraph 53 above).

The awareness of the vulnerability of the environment and the recognition that environmental risks have to be assessed on a continuous basis have become much stronger in the years since the Treaty's conclusion. These new concerns have enhanced the relevance of Articles 15, 19 and 20.

113. The Court recognizes that both Parties agree on the need to take environmental concerns seriously and to take the required precautionary measures, but they fundamentally disagree on the consequences this has for the joint Project. In such a case, third-party involvement may be helpful and instrumental in finding a solution, provided each of the Parties is flexible in its position.

114. Finally, Hungary maintained that by their conduct both parties had repudiated the Treaty and that a bilateral treaty repudiated by both parties cannot survive. The Court is of the view, however, that although it has found that both Hungary and Czechoslovakia failed to comply with their obligations under the 1977 Treaty, this reciprocal wrongful conduct did not bring the Treaty to an end nor justify its termination. The Court would set a precedent with disturbing implications for treaty relations and the integrity of the rule *pacta sunt servanda* if it were to conclude that a treaty in force between States, which the parties have implemented in considerable measure and at great cost over a period of years, might be unilaterally set aside on grounds of reciprocal non-compliance. It would be otherwise, of course, if the parties decided to terminate the Treaty by mutual consent. But in this case, while Hungary purported to terminate the Treaty, Czechoslovakia consistently resisted this act and declared it to be without legal effect.

* * *

115. In the light of the conclusions it has reached above, the Court, in reply to the question put to it in Article 2, paragraph 1(c), of the Special Agreement (see paragraph 89), finds that the notification of termination by Hungary of 19 May 1992 did not have the legal effect of terminating the 1977 Treaty and related instruments.

* * *

NOTES AND QUESTIONS

1. In addition to the obligation on treaty parties to comply with their treaty obligations in good faith, the VCLT also includes an article setting forth obligations prior to becoming a party:

Article 18
Obligation not to defeat the object and purpose of a treaty prior
to its entry into force

A State is obliged to refrain from acts which would defeat the object and purpose of a treaty when:

(*a*) it has signed the treaty or has exchanged instruments constituting the treaty subject to ratification, acceptance or approval, until it shall have made its intention clear not to become a party to the treaty; or

(*b*) it has expressed its consent to be bound by the treaty, pending the entry into force of the treaty and provided that such entry into force is not unduly delayed.

The United States may have been the first state to remove a signature from a treaty to avoid having the obligation not to defeat the object and purpose of a treaty. In 2002, John Bolton, an under-secretary in the U.S. State Department sent a letter to Secretary General Kofi Annan informing him that "the United States does not intend to become a party" to the Rome Statute of the International Criminal Court. "Accordingly, the United States has no legal obligations arising from its signature on December 31, 2000." Press Statement, International Criminal Court: Letter to UN Secretary General Kofi Annan, (May 2, 2002). The ICC will be discussed again in Chapters 5 and 9.

2. International agreements may be for fixed time periods, ending automatically at the expiration of the time set. Others provide for automatic renewal if nothing is done at the end of the period. If no time period is fixed, an international agreement continues until legally terminated. Treaties may declare that they continue in perpetuity, but some, such as the 1903 canal treaty between the United States and Panama or the lease agreement between China and the United Kingdom for the island of Hong Kong have not so continued.

The Vienna Convention provides a default provision for the termination of treaties where one is not agreed by the parties:

Article 54
Termination of or withdrawal from a treaty under its provisions
or by consent of the parties

The termination of a treaty or the withdrawal of a party may take place:

(a) in conformity with the provisions of the treaty; or

(b) at any time by consent of all the parties after consultation with the other contracting States. * * *

Article 56
Denunciation of or withdrawal from a treaty containing no
provision regarding termination, denunciation or withdrawal

1. A treaty which contains no provision regarding its termination and which does not provide for denunciation or withdrawal is not subject to denunciation or withdrawal unless:

(a) it is established that the parties intended to admit the possibility of denunciation or withdrawal; or

(b) a right of denunciation or withdrawal may be implied by the nature of the treaty.

2. A party shall give not less than twelve months' notice of its intention to denounce or withdraw from a treaty under paragraph 1.

Should the provisions on withdrawal apply to withdrawing a signature to avoid Article 18 obligations?

A few international agreements that fix no time period are considered to be of perpetual duration, such as those creating the European Union or the United Nations. Many treaties that create international organizations (often called constitutive treaties) provide procedures for amendment (e.g., the U.N. Charter, articles 108 and 109.) Typically such treaties do not provide for withdrawal but withdrawals have taken place nevertheless. In the case of the United Nations, Indonesia withdrew for a period but returned.

The VCLT provides that treaties will become void if they conflict with an emerging rule of *jus cogens*. They are void *ab initio* if they conflict with an existing norm. VCLT Articles 53 and 64. See the discussion of *jus cogens* in Section E. below.

3. International agreements are all equally durable in a strict legal sense, but actual practice indicates that some are more durable than others. In international relations practice treaties, bipartite and multipartite, that create territorial rights (said to be executory treaties) are usually stable. So are treaties that deal with a common problem or need shared by the parties. Bilateral treaties that are or become out of balance as to mutuality of interests are susceptible to unilateral termination. Where, in the past, war has either terminated or suspended international agreements, peace treaties may clarify the situation by stipulating the pre-war bilateral treaties that the parties deem still to be in force and by stating for the negotiating history of the peace treaty that multipartite treaties remain in force, unless specific counter-stipulation is made. The peace treaties negotiated with Italy, Finland, Hungary, Romania and Bulgaria at Paris in 1946 followed the method just described. When the issue is whether an international agreement has an internal legal effect, a national court looks to the element of the national government that has charge of international relations for guidance as to whether the agreement is still in effect. In some states subsequent inconsistent national law may affect the internal legal standing of the international agreement, although internationally it has not been legally ended. Various cases in Chapter 11 illustrate this problem in

United States law. See the reports of the International Law Commission on the affect of armed conflict on treaties. Report of the International Law Commission, 58th session, GA Sup. No. 10 (A/61/10) (2006).

4.   States and international organizations have a tendency to change over time. They grow, split-up and cease to exist. This fact of life has resulted in rules governing succession to treaties. The topic grew in importance after World War II with the break up of the European colonial empires, but it resurfaced at the end of the Cold War with the break-up of the Soviet Union and Yugoslavia.

Certain types of treaties, as just mentioned, generally continue in force even after the break-up of a state, in particular, boundary treaties. Other treaties must be negotiated newly, such as membership of a new entity in the United Nations. Sir Francis Vallat, Succession of States in Respect of Treaties, 2 U.N.Y.B. INT'L L. COMM'N 1 (1974).

Boundary treaties that do not change with the change of states, in a sense, provide rights to third states. Treaties providing for areas such as outer space and Antarctica not only provide rights to third states but place obligations on them as well. These treaties set up what are called "objective" regimes. See the VCLT, Articles 34–38, and Chapter 6.

5.   VCLT Article 27 restates a rule of international law familiar to you by now:

Article 27
Internal law and observance of treaties

A party may not invoke the provisions of its internal law as justification for its failure to perform a treaty. This rule is without prejudice to article 46.

6.   For further reading on various aspects of performance, see, MAKING TREATIES WORK: HUMAN RIGHTS, ENVIRONMENT AND ARMS CONTROL (Geir Ulfstein ed., 2007).

B.   CUSTOMARY INTERNATIONAL LAW

Ian Brownlie, Principles of Public International Law*

pp. 6–12 (7th ed., 2008)

DEFINITION

Article 38 refers to "international custom, as evidence of a general practice accepted as law", and Brierly remarks that "what is sought for is a general recognition among States of a certain practice as obligatory". Although occasionally the terms are used interchangeably, "custom" and "usage" are terms of art and have different meanings. A usage is a general

---

* Footnotes omitted.

practice which does not reflect a legal obligation, and examples are ceremonial salutes at sea and the practice of exempting diplomatic vehicles from parking prohibitions.

EVIDENCE

The material sources of custom are very numerous and include the following: diplomatic correspondence, policy statements, press releases, the opinions of official legal advisers, official manuals on legal questions, e.g. manuals of military law, executive decisions and practices, orders to naval forces etc., comments by governments on drafts produced by the International Law Commission, state legislation, international and national judicial decisions, recitals in treaties and other international instruments, a pattern of treaties in the same form, the practice of international organs, and resolutions relating to legal questions in the United Nations General Assembly. Obviously the value of these sources varies and much depends on the circumstances.

THE ELEMENTS OF CUSTOM

(a) Duration

Provided the consistency and generality of a practice are proved, no particular duration is required: the passage of time will of course be a part of the evidence of generality and consistency. A long (and, much less, an immemorial) practice is not necessary, and rules relating to airspace and the continental shelf have emerged from fairly quick maturing of practice. The International Court does not emphasize the time element as such in its practice.

(b) Uniformity, consistency of the practice

This is very much a matter of appreciation and a tribunal will have considerable freedom of determination in many cases. Complete uniformity is not required, but substantial uniformity is, and thus in the *Fisheries* case the Court refused to accept the existence of a 10–mile rule for bays.

The leading pronouncements by the Court appear in the Judgment in the *Asylum* case [Colombia/Peru, 1950 I.C.J. Rep. 266, 276–7]:

> The party which relies on a custom . . . must prove that this custom is established in such a manner that it has become binding on the other party . . . that the rule invoked . . . is in accordance with a constant and uniform usage practised by the States in question, and that this usage is the expression of a right appertaining to the State granting asylum and a duty incumbent on the territorial State. This follows from Article 38 of the Statute of the Court, which refers to international custom "as evidence of a general practice accepted as law".

> The facts brought to the knowledge of the Court disclose so much uncertainty and contradiction, so much fluctuation and discrepancy in the exercise of diplomatic asylum and in the official views expressed on different occasions; there has been so much inconsistency in the rapid

succession of conventions on asylum, ratified by some States and rejected by others, and the practice has been so much influenced by considerations of political expediency in the various cases, that it is not possible to discern in all this any constant and uniform usage, accepted as law. . . .

(c) Generality of the practice

This is an aspect which complements that of consistency. Certainly universality is not required, but the real problem is to determine the value of abstention from protest by a substantial number of states in face of a practice followed by some others. Silence may denote either tacit agreement or a simple lack of interest in the issue. It may be that the Court in the *Lotus* case misjudged the consequences of absence of protest and also the significance of fairly general abstention from prosecutions by states other than the flag state. In the *Fisheries Jurisdiction Case (United Kingdom* v. *Iceland)* the International Court referred to the extension of a fishery zone up to a 12–mile limit "which appears now to be generally accepted" and to "an increasing and widespread acceptance of the concept of preferential rights for coastal states" in a situation of special dependence on coastal fisheries.

(d) *Opinio juris et necessitatis*

The Statute of the International Court refers to "a general practice *accepted as law*". Brierly speaks of recognition by states of a certain practice "as obligatory", and Hudson requires a "conception that the practice is required by, or consistent with, prevailing international law". Some writers do not consider this psychological element to be a requirement for the formation of custom, but it is in fact a necessary ingredient. The sense of legal obligation, as opposed to motives of courtesy, fairness, or morality, is real enough, and the practice of states recognizes a distinction between obligation and usage. The essential problem is surely one of proof, and especially the incidence of the burden of proof.

In terms of the practice of the International Court of Justice—which provides a general guide to the nature of the problem—there are two methods of approach. In many cases the Court is willing to assume the existence of an *opinio juris* on the bases of evidence of a general practice, or a consensus in the literature, or the previous determinations of the Court or other international tribunals. However, in a significant minority of cases the Court has adopted a more rigorous approach and has called for more positive evidence of the recognition of the validity of the rules in question in the practice of states. The choice of approach appears to depend upon the nature of the issues (that is, the state of the law may be a primary point in contention), and the discretion of the Court.

Three cases have involved the more exacting second method of approach, of which the first was the *Lotus* [P.C.I.J. *France v. Turkey*, Ser. A, no. 10], in which the Permanent Court said;

> Even if the rarity of the judicial decisions to be found among the reported cases were sufficient to prove in point of fact the circumstances alleged by the Agent for the French Government, it would merely show that States had often, in practice, abstained from instituting criminal proceedings, and not that they recognized themselves as being obliged to do so; for only if such abstention were based on their being conscious of a duty to abstain would it be possible to speak of an international custom. The alleged fact does not allow one to infer that States have been conscious of having such a duty; on the other hand ... there are other circumstances calculated to show that the contrary is true.

Presumably the same principles should apply to both positive conduct and abstention, yet in the *Lotus* the Court was not ready to accept continuous conduct as prima facie evidence of a legal duty and required a high standard of proof of the issue of *opinio juris*.

In the *North Sea Continental Shelf Cases* [*infra*] the International Court was also strict in requiring proof of the *opinio juris*. The Court did not presume the existence of *opinio juris* either in the context of the argument that the equidistance-special circumstances basis of delimiting the continental shelf had become a part of general or customary law at the date of the Geneva Convention of 1958, or in relation to the proposition that the *subsequent* practice of states based upon the Convention had produced a customary rule. However, it is incorrect to regard the precise findings as in all respects incompatible with the view that the existence of a general practice raises a presumption of *opinio juris*. In regard to the position *before* the Convention concerning the equidistance principle, there was little "practice" apart from the records of the International Law Commission, which revealed the experimental aspect of the principle prior to 1958. Considering the argument that practice *based upon* the Convention had produced a customary rule the Court made it clear that its unfavourable reception to the argument rested primarily upon two factors: *(a)* the peculiar form of the equidistance principle in Article 6 of the Convention was such that the rules were not of a norm-creating character; *(b)* the Convention had only been in force for less than three years when the proceedings were brought and consequently:

> Although the passage of only a short period of time is not necessarily, or of itself, a bar to the formation of a new rule of customary international law on the basis of what was originally a purely conventional rule, an indispensable requirement would be that within the period in question, short though it might be, State practice, including that of States whose interests are specially affected, should have been both extensive and virtually uniform in the sense of the provision invoked;—and should moreover have occurred in such a way as to show a general recognition that a rule of law or legal obligation is involved.

Nevertheless, the general tenor of the Judgment is hostile to the presumption as to *opinio juris* and the Court quoted the passage from the *Lotus* case set out above.

A broadly similar approach was adopted by the Judgment of the Court in the *Case of Nicaragua* v. *United States* (Merits) [*infra*], and the Court expressly referred to the *North Sea Cases:*

> In considering the instances of the conduct above described, the Court has to emphasize that, as was observed in the *North Sea Continental Shelf* cases, for a new customary rule to be formed, not only must the acts concerned "amount to a settled practice", but they must be accompanied by the *opinio juris sive necessitatis*. Either the States taking such action or other States in a position to react to it, must have behaved so that their conduct is "evidence of a belief that this practice is rendered obligatory by the existence of a rule of law requiring it. The need for such a belief, i.e. the existence of a subjective element, is implicit in the very notion of the *opinio juris sive necessitatis*". *(ICJ Reports* (1969), 44, para. 77.)

BILATERAL RELATIONS AND LOCAL CUSTOMS

In the case concerning *U.S. Nationals in Morocco* the Court quoted the first of the passages from the *Asylum* case quoted earlier and continued: "In the present case there has not been sufficient evidence to enable the Court to reach a conclusion that a right to exercise consular jurisdiction founded upon custom or usage has been established *in such a manner that it has become binding on Morocco*".

In this case the Court may seem to have confused the question of law-making and the question of opposability, i.e. the specific relations of the United States and Morocco. The fact is that general formulae concerning custom do not necessarily help in penetrating the complexities of the particular case. The case concerning a *Right of Passage over Indian Territory* raised an issue of bilateral relations, the existence of a local custom in favour of Portugal in respect of territorial enclaves inland from the port of Daman (Damão). In this type of case the general law is to be varied and the proponent of the special right has to give affirmative proof of a sense of obligation on the part of the territorial sovereign: *opinio juris* is here not to be presumed on the basis of continuous practice and the notion of *opinio juris* merges into the principle of acquiescence.

THE PERSISTENT OBJECTOR

The way in which, as a matter of practice, custom resolves itself into a question of special relations is illustrated further by the rule that a state may contract out of a custom in the process of formation. Evidence of objection must be clear and there is probably a presumption of acceptance which is to be rebutted. Whatever the theoretical underpinnings of the principle, it is well recognized by international tribunals, and in the practice of states. Given the majoritarian tendency of international relations the principle is likely to have increased prominence.

THE SUBSEQUENT OBJECTOR

In the *Fisheries* case part of the Norwegian argument was that certain rules were not rules of general international law, and, even if they were, they did not bind Norway, which had "consistently and unequivocally manifested a refusal to accept them". The United Kingdom admitted the general principle of the Norwegian argument here while denying that, as a matter of fact, Norway had consistently and unequivocally manifested a refusal to accept the rules. Thus the United Kingdom regarded the question as one of persistent objection. The Court did not deal with the issue in this way, however, and the *ratio* in this respect was that Norway had departed from the alleged rules, if they existed, *and other states had acquiesced* in this practice. But the Court is not too explicit about the role of acquiescence in validating a subsequent contracting out of rules. Here one has to face the problem of change in a customary regime. Presumably, if a substantial number of states assert a new rule, the momentum of increased defection, complemented by acquiescence, may result in a new rule, as in the case of the law on the continental shelf. If the process is slow and neither the new rule nor the old have a majority of adherents then the consequence is a network of special relations based on opposability, acquiescence, and historic title.

PROOF OF CUSTOM

In principle a court is presumed to know the law and may apply a custom even if it has not been expressly pleaded. In practice the proponent of a custom has a burden of proof the nature of which will vary according to the subject-matter and the form of the pleadings. Thus in the *Lotus* case the Court spoke of the plaintiff's burden in respect of a general custom. Where a local or regional custom is alleged, the proponent "must prove that this custom is established in such a manner that it has become binding on the other Party".

The Paquete Habana
The Lola

United States Supreme Court
175 U.S. 677, 20 S.Ct. 290, 44 L.Ed. 320 (1900)

■ MR. JUSTICE GRAY delivered the opinion of the court.

These are two appeals from decrees of the District Court of the United States for the Southern District of Florida, condemning two fishing vessels and their cargoes as prize of war.

Each vessel was a fishing smack, running in and out of Havana, and regularly engaged in fishing on the coast of Cuba; sailed under the Spanish flag; was owned by a Spanish subject of Cuban birth; living in the city of Havana; was commanded by a subject of Spain, also residing in Havana; and her master and crew had no interest in the vessel, but were entitled to shares, amounting in all to two thirds, of her catch, the other third belonging to her owner. Her cargo consisted of fresh fish, caught by her crew from the sea, put on board as they were caught, and kept and sold alive. Until stopped by the blockading squadron, she had no knowledge of the existence of the war, or of any blockade. She had no arms or ammunition on board, and made no attempt to run the blockade after she knew of its existence, nor any resistance at the time of the capture.

The Paquete Habana was a sloop, 43 feet long on the keel, and of 25 tons burden, and had a crew of three Cubans, including the master, who had a fishing license from the Spanish Government, and no other commission or license. She left Havana March 25, 1898; sailed along the coast of Cuba to Cape San Antonio at the western end of the island, and there fished for twenty-five days, lying between the reefs off the cape, within the territorial waters of Spain; and then started back for Havana, with a cargo of about 40 quintals of live fish. On April 25, 1898, about two miles off Mariel, and eleven miles from Havana, she was captured by the United States gunboat Castine.

The Lola was a schooner, 51 feet long on the keel, and of 35 tons burden, and had a crew of six Cubans, including the master, and no commission or license. She left Havana April 11, 1898, and proceeded to Campeachy Sound off Yucatan, fished there eight days, and started back for Havana with a cargo of about 10,000 pounds of live fish. On April 26, 1898, near Havana, she was stopped by the United States steamship Cincinnati, and was warned not to go into Havana, but was told that she would be allowed to land at Bahia Honda. She then changed her course, and put for Bahia Honda, but on the next morning, when near that port, was captured by the United States steamship Dolphin.

Both the fishing vessels were brought by their captors into Key West. A libel for the condemnation of each vessel and her cargo as prize of war was there filed on April 27, 1898; a claim was interposed by her master, on behalf of himself and the other members of the crew, and of her owner; evidence was taken, showing the facts above stated; and on May 30, 1898, a final decree of condemnation and sale was entered, "the court not being satisfied that as a matter of law, without any ordinance, treaty or proclamation, fishing vessels of this class are exempt from seizure."

Each vessel was thereupon sold by auction; the Paquete Habana for the sum of $490; and the Lola for the sum of $800. There was no other evidence in the record of the value of either vessel or of her cargo.

* * *

We are then brought to the consideration of the question whether, upon the facts appearing in these records, the fishing smacks were subject to capture by the armed vessels of the United States during the recent war with Spain.

By an ancient usage among civilized nations, beginning centuries ago, and gradually ripening into a rule of international law, coast fishing vessels, pursuing their vocation of catching and bringing in fresh fish, have been recognized as exempt, with their cargoes and crews, from capture as prize of war.

This doctrine, however, has been earnestly contested at the bar; and no complete collection of the instances illustrating it is to be found, so far as we are aware, in a single published work, although many are referred to and discussed by the writers on international law, notably in 2 Ortolan, Règles Internationales et Diplomatie de la Mer, (4th ed.) lib. 3, c. 2, pp. 51–56; in 4 Calvo, Droit International, (5th ed.) §§ 2367–2373; in De Boeck, Propriété Priéé Ennemie sous Pavilion Ennemi, § 191–196; and in Hall, International Law, (4th ed.) § 148. It is therefore worth the while to trace the history of the rule, from the earliest accessible sources, through the increasing recognition of it, with occasional setbacks, to what we may now justly consider as its final establishment in our own country and generally throughout the civilized world.

The earliest acts of any government on the subject, mentioned in the books, either emanated from, or were approved by, a King of England.

In 1403 and 1406, Henry IV issued orders to his admirals and other officers, entitled "Concerning Safety for Fishermen—*De Securitate pro Piscatoribus.*" By an order of October 26, 1403, reciting that it was made pursuant to a treaty between himself and the King of France; and for the greater safety of the fishermen of either country, and so that they could be, and carry on their industry, the more safely on the sea, and deal with each other in peace; and that the French King had consented that English fishermen should be treated likewise; it was ordained that French fishermen might, during the then pending season for the herring fishery, safely fish for herrings and all other fish * * *.

The treaty made October 2, 1521, between the Emperor Charles V and Francis I of France, through their ambassadors, recited that a great and fierce war had arisen between them, because of which there had been, both by land and by sea, frequent depredations and incursions on either side, to the grave detriment and intolerable injury of the innocent subjects of each; and that a suitable time for the herring fishery was at hand, and, by reason of the sea being beset by the enemy, the fishermen did not dare to go out, whereby the subject of their industry, bestowed by heaven to allay the hunger of the poor, would wholly fail for the year, unless it were otherwise provided. * * * And it was therefore agreed that the subjects of each sovereign, fishing in the sea, or exercising the calling of fishermen, could and might, until the end of the next January, without incurring any attack, depredation, molestation, trouble or hindrance soever, safely and freely, everywhere in the sea, take herrings and every other kind of fish, the existing war by land and sea notwithstanding; and further that, during the time aforesaid, no subject of either sovereign should commit, or attempt or presume to commit, any depredation, force, violence, molestation or vexation, to or upon such fishermen, or their vessels, supplies, equipments, nets and fish, or other goods soever truly appertaining to fishing. The treaty was made at Calais, then an English possession. It recites that the ambassadors of the two sovereigns met there at the earnest request of Henry VIII, and with his countenance, and in the presence of Cardinal Wolsey, his chancellor and representative. And towards the end of the treaty it is agreed that the said King and his said representative, "by whose means the treaty stands concluded, shall be conservators of the agreements therein, as if thereto by both parties elected and chosen." 4 Dumont, Corps Diplomatique, pt. 1, pp. 352, 353.

The herring fishery was permitted, in time of war, by French and Dutch edicts in 1536. Bynkershoek, Quæstiones Juris Publicæ, lib. 1, c. 3; 1 Emerigon des Assurances, c. 4, sect. 9; c. 12, sect. 19, § 8.

France, from remote times, set the example of alleviating the evils of war in favor of all coast fishermen. In the compilation entitled Us et Coutumes de la Mer, published by Cleirac in 1661, and in the third part thereof, containing "Maritime or Admiralty Jurisdiction—*la Jurisdiction de la Marine ou d'Admirauté*—as well in time of peace as in time of war," article 80 is as follows: "The admiral may in time of war accord fishing truces—tresves pescheresses—to the enemy and to his subjects; provided that the enemy will likewise accord them to Frenchmen." Cleirac, 544. * * *

The same custom would seem to have prevailed in France until towards the end of the seventeenth century.

* * *

The doctrine which exempts coast fishermen with their vessels and cargoes from capture as prize of war has been familiar to the United States from the time of the War of Independence.

* * *

* * * England, as well as France, during the American Revolutionary War, abstained from interfering with the coast fisheries. *The Young Jacob and Johanna,* 1 C. Rob. 20; 2 Ortolan, 53; Hall, § 148.

In the treaty of 1785 between the United States and Prussia, article 23, (which was proposed by the American Commissioners, John Adams, Benjamin Franklin and Thomas Jefferson, and is said to have been drawn up by Franklin,) provided that, if war should arise between the contracting parties, "all women and children, scholars of every faculty, cultivators of the earth, artisans, manufacturers and fishermen, unarmed and inhabiting unfortified towns, villages or places, and in general all others whose occupations are for the common subsistence and benefit of mankind, shall be allowed to continue their respective employments, and shall not be molested in their persons; nor shall their houses or goods be burnt or otherwise destroyed, nor their fields wasted, by the armed force of the enemy, into whose power, by the events of war, they may happen to fall; but if anything is necessary to be taken from them for the use of such armed force, the same shall be paid for at a reasonable price." 8 Stat. 96; 1 Kent Com. 91 note; Wheaton's History of the Law of Nations, 306, 308. Here was the clearest exemption from hostile molestation or seizure of the persons, occupations, houses and goods of unarmed fishermen inhabiting unfortified places. The article was repeated in the later treaties * * *.

Since the United States became a nation, the only serious interruptions, so far as we are informed, of the general recognition of the exemption of coast fishing vessels from hostile capture, arose out of the mutual suspicions and recriminations of England and France during the wars of the French Revolution.

In the first years of those wars, England having authorized the capture of French fishermen, a decree of the French National Convention of October 2, 1793, directed the executive power "to protest against this conduct, theretofore without example; to reclaim the fishing boats seized; and, in case of refusal, to resort to reprisals." But in July, 1796, the Committee of Public Safety ordered the release of English fishermen seized under the former decree, "not considering them as prisoners of war." *La Nostra Segnora de la Piedad,* (1801) cited below; 2 De Cussy, Droit Maritime, 164, 165; 1 Massé, Droit Commercial, (2d ed.) 266, 267.

On January 24, 1798, the English Government, by express order, instructed the commanders of its ships to seize French and Dutch fishermen with their boats. 6 Martens, Recueil des Traités, (2d ed.) 505; 6 Schoell, Histoire des Traités, 119; 2 Ortolan, 53. After the promulgation of that order, Lord Stowell (then Sir William Scott) in the High Court of Admiralty of England condemned small Dutch fishing vessels as prize of war. In one case, the capture was in April, 1798, and the decree was made November 13, 1798. *The Young Jacob and Johanna,* 1 C. Rob. 20. In another case, the decree was made August 23, 1799. *The Noydt Gedacht,* 2 C. Rob. 137, note.

For the year 1800, the orders of the English and French governments and the correspondence between them may be found in books already referred to. 6 Martens, 503–512; 6 Schoell, 118–120; 2 Ortolan, 53, 54. The doings for that year may be summed up as follows: On March 27, 1800, the French government, unwilling to resort to reprisals, reenacted the orders given by Louis XVI in 1780, above mentioned, prohibiting any seizure by the French ships of English fishermen, unless armed, or proved to have made signals to the enemy. On May 30, 1800, the English government, having received notice of that action of the French government, revoked its order of January 24, 1798. But, soon afterwards, the English government complained that French fishing boats had been made into fireboats at Flushing, as well as that the French government had impressed, and had sent to Brest, to serve in its flotilla, French fishermen and their boats, even those whom the English had released on condition of their not serving; and on January 21, 1801, summarily revoked its last order, and again put in force its order of January 24, 1798. On February 16, 1801, Napoleon Bonaparte, then First Consul, directed the French commissioner at London to return at once to France, first declaring to the English government that its conduct, "contrary to all the usages of civilized nations, and to the common law which governs them, even in time of war, gave to the existing war a character of rage and bitterness which destroyed even the relations usual in a loyal war," and "tended only to exasperate the two nations, and to put off the term of peace;" and that the French government, having always made it "a maxim to alleviate as much as possible the evils of war, could not think, on its part, of rendering wretched fishermen victims of a prolongation of hostilities, and would abstain from all reprisals."

On March 16, 1801, the Addington Ministry, having come into power in England, revoked the orders of its predecessors against the French fishermen; maintaining, however, that "the freedom of fishing was nowise founded upon an agreement, but upon a simple concession;" that "this concession would be always subordinate to the convenience of the moment," and that "it was never extended to the great fishery, or to commerce in oysters or in fish." And the freedom of the coast fisheries was again allowed on both sides. 6 Martens, 514; 6 Schoell, 121; 2 Ortolan, 54; Manning, Law of Nations, (Amos ed.) 206.

* * *

Wheaton, in his Digest of the Law of Maritime Captures and Prizes, published in 1815, wrote: "It has been usual in maritime wars to exempt from capture fishing boats and their cargoes, both from views of mutual accommodation between neighboring countries, and from tenderness to a poor and industrious order of people. This custom, so honorable to the humanity of civilized nations, has fallen into disuse; and it is remarkable that both France and England mutually reproach each other with that breach of good faith which has finally abolished it." Wheaton on Captures, c. 2, § 18.

This statement clearly exhibits Wheaton's opinion that the custom had been a general one, as well as that it ought to remain so. His assumption that it had been abolished by the differences between France and England at the close of the last century was hardly justified by the state of things when he wrote, and has not since been borne out.

During the wars of the French Empire, as both French and English writers agree, the coast fisheries were left in peace. 2 Ortolan, 54; De Boeck, § 193; Hall, § 148. De Boeck quaintly and truly adds, "and the incidents of 1800 and of 1801 had no morrow—*n'eurent pas de lendemain.*"

In the war with Mexico in 1846, the United States recognized the exemption of coast fishing boats from capture. In proof of this, counsel have referred to records of the Navy Department, which this court is clearly authorized to consult upon such a question.

* * *

France, in the Crimean War in 1854, and in her wars with Austria in 1859 and with Germany in 1870, by general orders, forbade her cruisers to trouble the coast fisheries, or to seize any vessel or boat engaged therein, unless naval or military operations should make it necessary. Calvo, § 2372; Hall, § 148; 2 Ortolan, (4th ed.) 449; 10 Revue de Droit International, (1878) 399.

* * *

Since the English orders in council of 1806 and 1810, before quoted, in favor of fishing vessels employed in catching and bringing to market fresh fish, no instance has been found in which the exemption from capture of private coast fishing vessels, honestly pursuing their peaceful industry, has been denied by England, or by any other nation. And the Empire of Japan, (the last State admitted into the rank of civilized nations,) by an ordinance promulgated at the beginning of its war with China in August, 1894, established prize courts, and ordained that "the following enemy's vessels are exempt from detention," including in the exemption "boats engaged in coast fisheries," as well as "ships engaged exclusively on a voyage of scientific discovery, philanthropy or religious mission." Takahashi, International Law, 11, 178.

International law is part of our law, and must be ascertained and administered by the courts of justice of appropriate jurisdiction, as often as questions of right depending upon it are duly presented for their determination. For this purpose, where there is no treaty, and no controlling executive or legislative act or judicial decision, resort must be had to the customs and usages of civilized nations; and, as evidence of these, to the works of jurists and commentators, who by years of labor, research and experience, have made themselves peculiarly well acquainted with the subjects of which they treat. Such works are resorted to by judicial tribunals, not for the speculations of their authors concerning what the law ought to be, but for trustworthy evidence of what the law really is. *Hilton v. Guyot,* 159 U.S. 113, 163, 164, 214, 215.

* * *

The Paquete Habana, as the record shows, was a fishing sloop of 25 tons burden, sailing under the Spanish flag, running in and out of Havana, and regularly engaged in fishing on the coast of Cuba. Her crew consisted of but three men, including the master; and, according to a common usage in coast fisheries, had no interest in the vessel, but were entitled to two thirds of her catch, the other third belonging to her Spanish owner, who, as well as the crew, resided in Havana. On her last voyage, she sailed from Havana along the coast of Cuba, about two hundred miles, and fished for twenty-five days off the cape at the west end of the island, within the territorial waters of Spain; and was going back to Havana, with her cargo of live fish, when she was captured by one of the blockading squadron, on April 25, 1898. She had no arms or ammunition on board; she had no knowledge of the blockade, or even of the war, until she was stopped by a blockading vessel; she made no attempt to run the blockade, and no resistance at the time of the capture; nor was there any evidence whatever of likelihood that she or her crew would aid the enemy.

In the case of the Lola, the only differences in the facts were that she was a schooner of 35 tons burden, and had a crew of six men, including the master; that after leaving Havana, and proceeding some two hundred miles along the coast of Cuba, she went on, about a hundred miles farther, to the coast of Yucatan, and there fished for eight days; and that, on her return, when near Bahia Honda, on the coast of Cuba, she was captured, with her cargo of live fish, on April 27, 1898. These differences afford no ground for distinguishing the two cases.

Each vessel was of a moderate size, such as is not unusual in coast fishing smacks, and was regularly engaged in fishing on the coast of Cuba. The crew of each were few in number, had no interest in the vessel, and received, in return for their toil and enterprise, two thirds of her catch, the other third going to her owner by way of compensation for her use. Each vessel went out from Havana to her fishing ground, and was captured when returning along the coast of Cuba. The cargo of each consisted of fresh fish, caught by her crew from the sea, and kept alive on board. Although one of the vessels extended her fishing trip across the Yucatan Channel and fished on the coast of Yucatan, we cannot doubt that each was engaged in the coast fishery, and not in a commercial adventure, within the rule of international law.

The two vessels and their cargoes were condemned by the District Court as prize of war; the vessels were sold under its decrees; and it does not appear what became of the fresh fish of which their cargoes consisted.

Upon the facts proved in either case, it is the duty of this court, sitting as the highest prize court of the United States, and administering the law of nations, to declare and adjudge that the capture was unlawful, and without probable cause; and it is therefore, in each case,

Ordered, that the decree of the District Court be reversed, and the proceeds of the sale of the vessel, together with the proceeds of any sale of her cargo, be restored to the claimant, with damages and costs.

North Sea Continental Shelf Cases

Germany/Denmark, Germany/The Netherlands
International Court of Justice
1969 I.C.J. Rep. 3 (Judgment of Feb. 20)

1. By the two Special Agreements respectively concluded between the Kingdom of Denmark and the Federal Republic of Germany, and between the Federal Republic and the Kingdom of the Netherlands, the Parties have submitted to the Court certain differences concerning "the delimitation as between the Parties of the areas of the continental shelf in the North Sea which appertain to each of them."

* * *

[T]he Court is requested to decide what are the applicable "principles and rules of international law". The Court is not asked actually to delimit

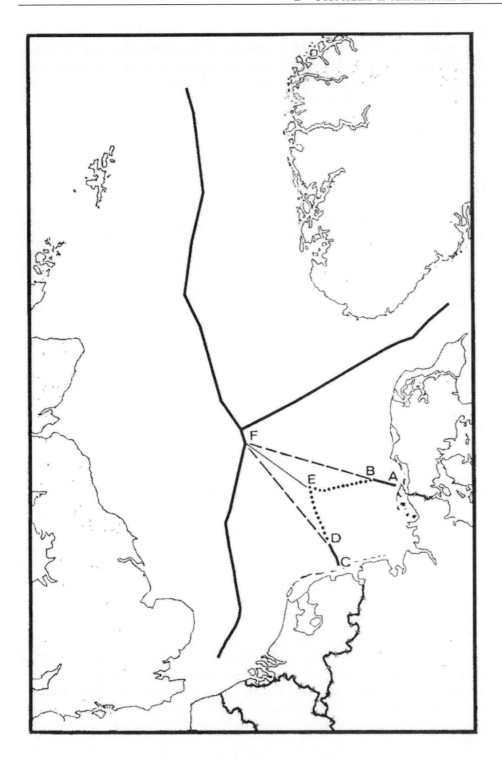

the further boundaries which will be involved, this task being reserved by the Special Agreements to the Parties, which undertake to effect such a delimitation "by agreement in pursuance of the decision requested from the . . . Court"—that is to say on the basis of, and in accordance with, the principles and rules of international law found by the Court to be applicable.

* * *

[T]he Parties have taken up fundamentally different positions. On behalf of the Kingdoms of Denmark and the Netherlands it is contended that the whole matter is governed by a mandatory rule of law which, reflecting the language of Article 6 of the Convention on the Continental Shelf concluded at Geneva on 29 April 1958, was designated by them as the "equidistance-special circumstances" rule. According to this contention, "equidistance" is not merely a method of the cartographical construction of a boundary line, but the essential element in a rule of law which may be stated as follows,—namely that in the absence of agreement by the Parties to employ another method or to proceed to a delimitation on an ad hoc basis, all continental shelf boundaries must be drawn by means of an equidistance line, unless, or except to the extent to which, "special circumstances" are recognized to exist,—an equidistance line being, it will be recalled, a line every point on which is the same distance away from whatever point is nearest to it on the coast of each of the countries concerned—or rather, strictly, on the baseline of the territorial sea along that coast. [See lines A–E and C–E on the figure, *supra*.] As regards what constitutes "special circumstances", all that need be said at this stage is that according to the view put forward on behalf of Denmark and the Netherlands, the configuration of the German North Sea coast, its recessive character, and the fact that it makes nearly a right-angled bend in mid-course, would not of itself constitute, for either of the two boundary lines concerned, a special circumstance calling for or warranting a departure from the equidistance method of delimitation: only the presence of some special feature, minor in itself—such as an islet or small protuberance—but so placed as to produce a disproportionately distorting effect on an otherwise acceptable boundary line would, so it was claimed, possess this character.

14.   These various contentions, together with the view that a rule of equidistance-special circumstances is binding on the Federal Republic, are founded by Denmark and the Netherlands partly on the 1958 Geneva Convention on the Continental Shelf * * *, and partly on general considerations of law relating to the continental shelf, lying outside this Convention. * * *

15.   The Federal Republic, for its part, while recognizing the utility of equidistance as a method of delimitation, and that this method can in

many cases be employed appropriately and with advantage, denies its obligatory character for States not parties to the Geneva Convention, and contends that the correct rule to be applied, at any rate in such circumstances as those of the North Sea, is one according to which each of the States concerned should have a "just and equitable share" of the available continental shelf, in proportion to the length of its coastline or sea-frontage. It was also contended on behalf of the Federal Republic that in a sea shaped as is the North Sea, the whole bed of which, except for the Norwegian Trough, consists of continental shelf at a depth of less than 200 metres, and where the situation of the circumjacent States causes a natural convergence of their respective continental shelf areas, towards a central point situated on the median line of the whole seabed—or at any rate in those localities where this is the case—each of the States concerned is entitled to a continental shelf area extending up to this central point [point F in the figure *supra*] (in effect a sector), or at least extending to the median line at some point or other. In this way the "cut-off" effect, of which the Federal Republic complains, caused * * * by the drawing of equidistance lines at the two ends of an inward curving or recessed coast, would be avoided. * * *

16.   Alternatively, the Federal Republic claimed that if, contrary to its main contention, the equidistance method was held to be applicable, then the configuration of the German North Sea coast constituted a "special circumstance" such as to justify a departure from that method of delimitation in this particular case.

* * *

25.   The Court now turns to the legal position regarding the equidistance method. The first question to be considered is whether the 1958 Geneva Convention on the Continental Shelf is binding for all the Parties in this case—that is to say whether, as contended by Denmark and the Netherlands, the use of this method is rendered obligatory for the present delimitations by virtue of the delimitations provision (Article 6) of that instrument, according to the conditions laid down in it. * * *

26.   The relevant provisions of Article 6 of the Geneva Convention, paragraph 2 of which Denmark and the Netherlands contend not only to be applicable as a conventional rule, but also to represent the accepted rule of general international law on the subject of continental shelf delimitation as it exists independently of the Convention, read as follows:

"1.   Where the same continental shelf is adjacent to the territories of two or more States whose coasts are opposite each other, the boundary of the continental shelf appertaining to such States shall be determined by agreement between them. In the absence of agreement, and unless another boundary line is justified by special circumstances, the boundary is the median line, every point of which is equidistant from the nearest point of the baselines from which the breadth of the territorial sea of each State is measured.

    2.   Where the same continental shelf is adjacent to the territories of two adjacent States, the boundary of the continental shelf shall be determined by agreement between them. In the absence of agreement, and unless another boundary line is justified by special circumstances, the boundary shall be determined by application of the principle of equidistance from the nearest points of the baselines from which the breadth of the territorial sea of each State is measured.''

The Convention received 46 signatures and, up-to-date, there have been 39 ratifications or accessions. It came into force on 10 June 1964, having received the 22 ratifications or accessions required for that purpose (Article 11), and was therefore in force at the time when the various delimitations of continental shelf boundaries described earlier (paragraphs 1 and 5) took place between the Parties. But, under the formal provisions of the Convention, it is in force for any individual State only in so far as, having signed it within the time-limit provided for that purpose, that State has also subsequently ratified it; or, not having signed within that time-limit, has subsequently acceded to the Convention. Denmark and the Netherlands have both signed and ratified the Convention, and are parties to it, the former since 10 June 1964, the latter since 20 March 1966. The Federal Republic was one of the signatories of the Convention, but has never ratified it, and is consequently not a party.

* * *

    37.   It is maintained by Denmark and the Netherlands that the Federal Republic, whatever its position may be in relation to the Geneva Convention, considered as such, is in any event bound to accept delimitation on an equidistance-special circumstances basis, because the use of this method is not in the nature of a merely conventional obligation, but is, or must now be regarded as involving, a rule that is part of the corpus of general international law;—and, like other rules of general or customary international law, is binding on the Federal Republic automatically and independently of any specific assent, direct or indirect, given by the latter. This contention has both a positive law and a more fundamentalist aspect. As a matter of positive law, it is based on the work done in this field by international legal bodies, on State practice and on the influence attributed to the Geneva Convention itself,—the claim being that these various factors have cumulatively evidenced or been creative of the *opinio juris sive necessitatis*, requisite for the formation of new rules of customary international law.

* * *

    47.   A review of the genesis and development of the equidistance method of delimitation * * * may appropriately start with the instrument, generally known as the "Truman Proclamation", issued by the Government of the United States on 28 September 1945. Although this instrument

was not the first or only one to have appeared, it has in the opinion of the Court a special status. Previously, various theories as to the nature and extent of the rights relative to or exercisable over the continental shelf had been advanced by jurists, publicists and technicians. The Truman Proclamation however, soon came to be regarded as the starting point of the positive law on the subject, and the chief doctrine it enunciated, namely that of the coastal State as having an original, natural, and exclusive (in short a vested) right to the continental shelf off its shores, came to prevail over all others, being now reflected in Article 2 of the 1958 Geneva Convention on the Continental Shelf. With regard to the delimitation of lateral boundaries between the continental shelves of adjacent States, a matter which had given rise to some consideration on the technical, but very little on the juristic level, the Truman Proclamation stated that such boundaries "shall be determined by the United States and the State concerned in accordance with equitable principles". These two concepts, of delimitation by mutual agreement and delimitation in accordance with equitable principles, have underlain all the subsequent history of the subject. They were reflected in various other State proclamations of the period, and after, and in the later work on the subject.

48.   It was in the International Law Commission of the United Nations that the question of delimitation as between adjacent States was first taken up seriously as part of a general juridical project; for outside the ranks of the hydrographers and cartographers, questions of delimitation were not much thought about in earlier continental shelf doctrine. Juridical interest and speculation was focussed mainly on such questions as what was the legal basis on which any rights at all in respect of the continental shelf could be claimed, and what was the nature of those rights. As regards boundaries, the main issue was not that of boundaries between States but of the seaward limit of the area in respect of which the coastal State could claim exclusive rights of exploitation. As was pointed out in the course of the written proceedings, States in most cases had not found it necessary to conclude treaties or legislate about their lateral sea boundaries with adjacent States before the question of exploiting the natural resources of the seabed and subsoil arose;—practice was therefore sparse.

49.   In the records of the International Law Commission, which had the matter under consideration from 1950 to 1956, there is no indication at all that any of its members supposed that it was incumbent on the Commission to adopt a rule of equidistance because this gave expression to, and translated into linear terms, a principle of proximity inherent in the basic concept of the continental shelf, causing every part of the shelf to appertain to the nearest coastal State and to no other, and because such a rule must therefore be mandatory as a matter of customary international law. Such an idea does not seem ever to have been propounded. Had it been, and had it had the self-evident character contended for by Denmark and the Netherlands, the Commission would have had no alternative but to adopt it, and its long continued hesitations over this matter would be incomprehensible.

50.   It is moreover, in the present context, a striking feature of the Commission's discussions that during the early and middle stages, not only was the notion of equidistance never considered from the standpoint of its having *a priori* a character of inherent necessity: it was never given any special prominence at all, and certainly no priority.

* * *

60.   The conclusions so far reached leave open, and still to be considered, the question whether on some basis other than that of an *a priori* logical necessity, i.e., through positive law processes, the equidistance principle has come to be regarded as a rule of customary international law, so that it would be obligatory for the Federal Republic in that way, even though Article 6 of the Geneva Convention is not, as such, opposable to it. For this purpose it is necessary to examine the status of the principle as it stood when the Convention was drawn up, as it resulted from the effect of the Convention, and in the light of State practice subsequent to the Convention; but it should be clearly understood that in the pronouncements the Court makes on these matters it has in view solely the delimitation provisions (Article 6) of the Convention, not other parts of it, nor the Convention as such.

61.   The first of these questions can conveniently be considered in the form suggested on behalf of Denmark and the Netherlands themselves in the course of the oral hearing, when it was stated that they had not in fact contended that the delimitation article (Article 6) of the Convention "embodied already received rules of customary law in the sense that the Convention was merely declaratory of existing rules". Their contention was, rather, that although prior to the Conference, continental shelf law was only in the formative stage, and State practice lacked uniformity, yet "the process of the definition and consolidation of the emerging customary law took place through the work of the International Law Commission, the reaction of governments to that work and the proceedings of the Geneva Conference"; and this emerging customary law became "crystallized in the adoption of the Continental Shelf Convention by the Conference".

62.   Whatever validity this contention may have in respect of at least certain parts of the Convention, the Court cannot accept it as regards the delimitation provision (Article 6), the relevant parts of which were adopted almost unchanged from the draft of the International Law Commission that formed the basis of discussion at the Conference. The status of the rule in the Convention therefore depends mainly on the processes that led the Commission to propose it. These processes have already been reviewed in connection with the Danish–Netherlands contention of an *a priori* necessity for equidistance, and the Court considers this review sufficient for present purposes also, in order to show that the principle of equidistance, as it now figures in Article 6 of the Convention, was proposed by the Commission with considerable hesitation, somewhat on an experimental basis, at most *de lege ferenda*, and not at all *de lege lata* or as an emerging rule of customary international law. This is clearly not the sort of founda-

tion on which Article 6 of the Convention could be said to have reflected or crystallized such a rule.

63.   The foregoing conclusion receives significant confirmation from the fact that Article 6 is one of those in respect of which, under the reservations article of the Convention (Article 12) reservations may be made by any State on signing, ratifying or acceding—for, speaking generally, it is a characteristic of purely conventional rules and obligations that, in regard to them, some faculty of making unilateral reservations may, within certain limits, be admitted;—whereas this cannot be so in the case of general or customary law rules and obligations which, by their very nature, must have equal force for all members of the international community, and cannot therefore be the subject of any right of unilateral exclusion exercisable at will by any one of them in its own favour. Consequently, it is to be expected that when, for whatever reason, rules or obligations of this order are embodied, or are intended to be reflected in certain provisions of a convention, such provisions will figure amongst those in respect of which a right of unilateral reservation is not conferred, or is excluded. This expectation is, in principle, fulfilled by Article 12 of the Geneva Continental Shelf Convention, which permits reservations to be made to all the articles of the Convention "other than to Articles 1 to 3 inclusive"—these three Articles being the ones which, it is clear, were then regarded as reflecting, or as crystallizing, received or at least emergent rules of customary international law relative to the continental shelf, amongst them the question of the seaward extent of the shelf; the juridical character of the coastal State's entitlement; the nature of the rights exercisable; the kind of natural resources to which these relate; and the preservation intact of the legal status as high seas of the waters over the shelf, and the legal status of the superjacent air-space.

64.   The normal inference would therefore be that any articles that do not figure among those excluded from the faculty of reservation under Article 12, were not regarded as declaratory of previously existing or emergent rules of law; and this is the inference the Court in fact draws in respect of Article 6 (delimitation), having regard also to the attitude of the International Law Commission to this provision, as already described in general terms. Naturally this would not of itself prevent this provision from eventually passing into the general corpus of customary international law by one of the processes considered in paragraphs 70–81 below. But that is not here the issue. What is now under consideration is whether it originally figured in the Convention as such a rule.

65.   It has however been suggested that the inference drawn at the beginning of the preceding paragraph is not necessarily warranted, seeing that there are certain other provisions of the Convention, also not excluded from the faculty of reservation, but which do undoubtedly in principle relate to matters that lie within the field of received customary law, such as the obligation not to impede the laying or maintenance of submarine cables or pipelines on the continental shelf seabed (Article 4), and the general obligation not unjustifiably to interfere with freedom of navigation, fishing,

and so on (Article 5, paragraphs 1 and 6). These matters however, all relate to or are consequential upon principles or rules of general maritime law, very considerably ante-dating the Convention, and not directly connected with but only incidental to continental shelf rights as such. They were mentioned in the Convention, not in order to declare or confirm their existence, which was not necessary, but simply to ensure that they were not prejudiced by the exercise of continental shelf rights as provided for in the Convention. Another method of drafting might have clarified the point, but this cannot alter the fact that no reservation could release the reserving party from obligations of general maritime law existing outside and independently of the Convention, and especially obligations formalized in Article 2 of the contemporaneous Convention on the High Seas, expressed by its preamble to be declaratory of established principles of international law.

* * *

69.   In the light of these various considerations, the Court reaches the conclusion that the Geneva Convention did not embody or crystallize any pre-existing or emergent rule of customary law, according to which the delimitation of continental shelf areas between adjacent States must, unless the Parties otherwise agree, be carried out on all equidistance-special circumstances basis. A rule was of course embodied in Article 6 of the Convention, but as a purely conventional rule. Whether it has since acquired a broader basis remains to be seen: *qua* conventional rule however, as has already been concluded, it is not opposable to the Federal Republic.

70.   The Court must now proceed to the last stage in the argument put forward on behalf of Denmark and the Netherlands. This is to the effect that even if there was at the date of the Geneva Convention no rule of customary international law in favour of the equidistance principle, and no such rule was crystallized in Article 6 of the Convention, nevertheless such a rule has come into being since the Convention, partly because of its own impact, partly on the basis of subsequent State practice,—and that this rule, being now a rule of customary international law binding on all States, including therefore the Federal Republic, should be declared applicable to the delimitation of the boundaries between the Parties' respective continental shelf areas in the North Sea.

71.   In so far as this contention is based on the view that Article 6 of the Convention has had the influence, and has produced the effect, described. it clearly involves treating that Article as a norm-creating provision which has constituted the foundation or, or has generated a rule which, while only conventional or contractual in its origin, has since passed into the general corpus of international law, and is now accepted as such by the *opinio juris*, so as to have become binding even for countries which have never, and do not, become parties to the Convention. There is no doubt that this process is a perfectly possible one and does from time to time occur: it constitutes indeed one of the recognized methods by which new

rules of customary international law may be formed. At the same time this result is not lightly to be regarded as having been attained.

72.   It would in the first place be necessary that the provision concerned should, at all events potentially, be of a fundamentally norm-creating character such as could be regarded as forming the basis of a general rule of law. Considered *in abstracto* the equidistance principle might be said to fulfil this requirement. Yet in the particular form in which it is embodied in Article 6 of the Geneva Convention, and having regard to the relationship of that Article to other provisions of the Convention, this must be open to some doubt. In the first place, Article 6 is so framed as to put second the obligation to make use of the equidistance method, causing it to come after a primary obligation to effect delimitation by agreement. Such a primary obligation constitutes an unusual preface to what is claimed to be a potential general rule of law. Without attempting to enter into, still less pronounce upon any question of *jus cogens*, it is well understood that, in practice, rules of international law can, by agreement, be derogated from in particular cases, or as between particular parties,—but this is not normally the subject of any express provision, as it is in Article 6 of the Geneva Convention. Secondly the part played by the notion of special circumstances relative to the principle of equidistance as embodied in Article 6, and the very considerable, still unresolved controversies as to the exact meaning and scope of this notion, must raise further doubts as to the potentially norm-creating character of the rule. Finally, the faculty of making reservations to Article 6, while it might not of itself prevent the equidistance principle being eventually received as general law, does add considerably to the difficulty of regarding this result as having been brought about (or being potentially possible) on the basis of the Convention: for so long as this faculty continues to exist, and is not the subject of any revision brought about in consequence of a request made under Article 13 of the Convention—of which there is at present no official indication—it is the Convention itself which would, for the reasons already indicated, seem to deny to the provisions of Article 6 the same norm-creating character as, for instance, Articles 1 and 2 possess.

73.   With respect to the other elements usually regarded as necessary before a conventional rule can be considered to have become a general rule of international law, it might be that, even without the passage of any considerable period of time, a very widespread and representative participation in the convention might suffice of itself, provided it included that of States whose interests were specially affected. In the present case however, the Court notes that, even if allowance is made for the existence of a number of States to whom participation in the Geneva Convention is not open, or which, by reason for instance of being land-locked States, would have no interest in becoming parties to it, the number of ratifications and accessions so far secured is, though respectable, hardly sufficient. That non-ratification may sometimes be due to factors other than active disapproval of the convention concerned can hardly constitute a basis on which positive acceptance of its principles can be implied: the reasons are speculative, but the facts remain.

74.   As regards the time element, the Court notes that it is over ten years since the Convention was signed, but that it is even now less than five since it came into force in June 1964, and that when the present proceedings were brought it was less than three years, while less than one had elapsed at the time when the respective negotiations between the Federal Republic and the other two Parties for a complete delimitation broke down on the question of the application of the equidistance principle. Although the passage of only a short period of time is not necessarily, or of itself, a bar to the formation of a new rule of customary international law on the basis of what was originally a purely conventional rule, an indispensable requirement would be that within the period in question, short though it might be, State practice, including that of States whose interests are specially affected, should have been both extensive and virtually uniform in the sense of the provision invoked;—and should moreover have occurred in such a way as to show a general recognition that a rule of law or legal obligation is involved.

75.   The Court must now consider whether State practice in the matter of continental shelf delimitation has, subsequent to the Geneva Convention, been of such a kind as to satisfy this requirement. Leaving aside cases which, for various reasons, the Court does not consider to be reliable guides as precedents, such as delimitations effected between the present Parties themselves, or not relating to international boundaries, some fifteen cases have been cited in the course of the present proceedings, occurring mostly since the signature of the 1958 Geneva Convention, in which continental shelf boundaries have been delimited according to the equidistance principle—in the majority of the cases by agreement, in a few others unilaterally—or else the delimitation was foreshadowed but has not yet been carried out. Amongst these fifteen are the four North Sea delimitations United Kingdom/Norway–Denmark–Netherlands, and Norway/Denmark already mentioned in paragraph 4 of this Judgment. But even if these various cases constituted more than a very small proportion of those potentially calling for delimitation in the world as a whole, the Court would not think it necessary to enumerate or evaluate them separately, since there are, *a priori*, several grounds which deprive them of weight as precedents in the present context.

76.   To begin with, over half the States concerned, whether acting unilaterally or conjointly, were or shortly became parties to the Geneva Convention, and were therefore presumably, so far as they were concerned, acting actually or potentially in the application of the Convention. From their action no inference could legitimately be drawn as to the existence of a rule of customary international law in favour of the equidistance principle. As regards those States, on the other hand, which were not, and have not become parties to the Convention, the basis of their action can only be problematical and must remain entirely speculative. Clearly, they were not applying the Convention. But from that no inference could justifiably be drawn that they believed themselves to be applying a mandatory rule of customary international law. There is not a shred of evidence that they did and, as has been seen (paragraphs 22 and 23), there is no lack of other

reasons for using the equidistance method, so that acting, or agreeing to act in a certain way, does not of itself demonstrate anything of a juridical nature.

77.   The essential point in this connection—and it seems necessary to stress it—is that even if these instances of action by non-parties to the Convention were much more numerous than they in fact are, they would not, even in the aggregate, suffice in themselves to constitute the *opinio juris*;—for, in order to achieve this result, two conditions must be fulfilled. Not only must the acts concerned amount to a settled practice, but they must also be such, or be carried out in such a way, as to be evidence of a belief that this practice is rendered obligatory by the existence of a rule of law requiring it. The need for such a belief, i.e., the existence of a subjective element, is implicit in the very notion of the *opinio juris sive necessitatis*. The States concerned must therefore feel that they are conforming to what amounts to a legal obligation. The frequency, or even habitual character of the acts is not in itself enough. There are many international acts, e.g., in the field of ceremonial and protocol, which are performed almost invariably, but which are motivated only by considerations of courtesy, convenience or tradition, and not by any sense of legal duty.

78.   In this respect the Court follows the view adopted by the Permanent Court of International Justice in the *Lotus* case, as stated in the following passage, the principle of which is, by analogy, applicable almost word for word, *mutatis mutandis*, to the present case (P.C.I.J., Series A, No. 10, 1927, at p. 28):

> "Even if the rarity of the judicial decisions to be found ... were sufficient to prove ... the circumstance alleged ..., it would merely show that States had often, in practice, abstained from instituting criminal proceedings, and not that they recognized themselves as being obliged to do so; for only if such abstention were based on their being conscious of having a duty to abstain would it be possible to speak of an international custom. The alleged fact does not allow one to infer that States have been conscious of having such a duty; on the other hand, ... there are other circumstances calculated to show that the contrary is true."

Applying this dictum to the present case, the position is simply that in certain cases—not a great number—the States concerned agreed to draw or did draw the boundaries concerned according to the principle of equidistance. There is no evidence that they so acted because they felt legally compelled to draw them in this way by reason of a rule of customary law obliging them to do so—especially considering that they might have been motivated by other obvious factors.

79.   Finally, it appears that in almost all of the cases cited, the delimitations concerned were median-line delimitations between opposite States, not lateral delimitations between adjacent States. For reasons which have already been given * * * the Court regards the case of median-line delimitations between opposite States as different in various respects, and as being sufficiently distinct not to constitute a precedent for the delimita-

tion of lateral boundaries. In only one situation discussed by the Parties does there appear to have been a geographical configuration which to some extent resembles the present one, in the sense that a number of States on the same coastline are grouped around a sharp curve or bend of it. No complete delimitation in this area has however yet been carried out. But the Court is not concerned to deny to this case, or any other of those cited, all evidential value in favour of the thesis of Denmark and the Netherlands. It simply considers that they are inconclusive, and insufficient to bear the weight sought to be put upon them as evidence of such a settled practice, manifested in such circumstances, as would justify the inference that delimitation according to the principle of equidistance amounts to a mandatory rule of customary international law,—more particularly where lateral delimitations are concerned.

* * *

81.   The Court accordingly concludes that if the Geneva Convention was not in its origins or inception declaratory of a mandatory rule of customary international law enjoining the use of the equidistance principle for the delimitation of continental shelf areas between adjacent States, neither has its subsequent effect been constitutive of such a rule; and that State practice up-to-date has equally been insufficient for the purpose.

[The case continues below at p. 150.]

Military and Paramilitary Activities In and Against Nicaragua

Nicaragua v. United States
International Court of Justice
1986 I.C.J. Rep. 14 (Judgment of June 27)

[In 1984, Nicaragua brought a case against the United States to the International Court of Justice for mining its harbors, overflight of its territory and aid to the Contra rebels seeking the overthrow of Nicaragua's government. The U.S. defended its actions as measures of collective self-defense of El Salvador. The U.S. argued Nicaragua was aiding rebels seeking the overthrow of El Salvador's government. The U.S. had accepted by treaty to go the ICJ in respect of disputes to which other states had made the same acceptance. (The ICJ will be discussed in detail in Chapter 9.) The United States, however, attached a reservation to its acceptance that any case involving a multilateral treaty had to involve other affected states. Since Nicaragua was alleging the U.S. had violated the UN Charter, among other treaties, the U.S. argued that the ICJ could not proceed in light of the reservation and the several affected states not participating in the case. The ICJ, however, found it had jurisdiction on the basis of violations of customary international law.]

172.   The Court has now to turn its attention to the question of the law applicable to the present dispute. In formulating its view on the significance of the United States multilateral treaty reservation, the Court

has reached the conclusion that it must refrain from applying the multilateral treaties invoked by Nicaragua in support of its claims, without prejudice either to other treaties or to the other sources of law enumerated in Article 38 of the Statute. The first stage in its determination of the law actually to be applied to this dispute is to ascertain the consequences of the exclusion of the applicability of thc multilateral treaties for the definition of the content of the customary international law which remains applicable.

* * *

175.   The Court does not consider that, in the areas of law relevant to the present dispute, it can be claimed that all the customary rules which may be invoked have a content exactly identical to that of the rules contained in the treaties which cannot be applied by virtue of the United States reservation. On a number of points, the areas governed by the two sources of law do not exactly overlap, and the substantive rules in which they are framed are not identical in content. But in addition, even if a treaty norm and a customary norm relevant to the present dispute were to have exactly the same content, this would not be a reason for the Court to take the view that the operation of the treaty process must necessarily deprive the customary norm of its separate applicability. Nor can the multilateral treaty reservation be interpreted as meaning that, once applicable to a given dispute, it would exclude the application of any rule of customary international law the content of which was the same as, or analogous to, that of the treaty-law rule which had caused the reservation to become effective.

176.   As regards the suggestion that the areas covered by the two sources of law are identical, the Court observes that the United Nations Charter, the convention to which most of the United States argument is directed, by no means covers the whole area of the regulation of the use of force in international relations. On one essential point, this treaty itself refers to pre-existing customary international law; this reference to customary law is contained in the actual text of Article 51, which mentions the "inherent right" (in the French text the "droit naturel") of individual or collective self-defence, which "nothing in the present Charter shall impair" and which applies in the event of an armed attack. The Court therefore finds that Article 51 of the Charter is only meaningful on the basis that there is a "natural" or "inherent" right of self-defence, and it is hard to see how this can be other than of a customary nature, even if its present content has been confirmed and influenced by the Charter. Moreover the Charter, having itself recognized the existence of this right, does not go on to regulate directly all aspects of its content. For example, it does not contain any specific rule whereby self-defence would warrant only measures which are proportional to the armed attack and necessary to respond to it, a rule well established in customary international law. Moreover, a definition of the "armed attack" which, if found to exist, authorizes the exercise of the "inherent right" of self-defence, is not provided in the Charter, and is not part of treaty law. It cannot therefore be held that Article 51 is a provision which "subsumes and supervenes" customary international law.

It rather demonstrates that in the field in question, the importance of which for the present dispute need hardly be stressed customary international law continues to exist alongside treaty law. The areas governed by the two sources of law thus do not overlap exactly, and the rules do not have the same content. This could also be demonstrated for other subjects, in particular for the principle of non-intervention.

177.   But as observed above (paragraph 175), even if the customary norm and the treaty norm were to have exactly the same content, this would not be a reason for the Court to hold that the incorporation of the customary norm into treaty-law must deprive the customary norm of its applicability as distinct from that of the treaty norm. The existence of identical rules in international treaty law and customary law has been clearly recognized by the Court in the North Sea Continental Shelf cases. To a large extent, those cases turned on the question whether a rule enshrined in a treaty also existed as a customary rule, either because the treaty had merely codified the custom, or caused it to "crystallize", or because it had influenced its subsequent adoption. The Court found that this identity of content in treaty law and in customary international law did not exist in the case of the rule invoked, which appeared in one article of the treaty, but did not suggest that such identity was debarred as a matter of principle: on the contrary, it considered it to be clear that certain other articles of the treaty in question "were ... regarded as reflecting, or as crystallizing, received or at least emergent rules of customary international law" (I.C.J. Reports 1969, p. 39, para. 63). More generally, there are no grounds for holding that when customary international law is comprised of rules identical to those of treaty law, the latter "supervenes" the former, so that the customary international law has no further existence of its own.

178.   There are a number of reasons for considering that, even if two norms belonging to two sources of international law appear identical in content, and even if the States in question are bound by these rules both on the level of treaty-law and on that of customary international law, these norms retain a separate existence. This is so from the standpoint of their applicability. In a legal dispute affecting two States, one of them may argue that the applicability of a treaty rule to its own conduct depends on the other State's conduct in respect of the application of other rules, on other subjects, also included in the same treaty. For example, if a State exercises its right to terminate or suspend the operation of a treaty on the ground of the violation by the other party of a "provision essential to the accomplishment of the object or purpose of the treaty" (in the words of Art. 60, para. 3 (b), of the Vienna Convention on the Law of Treaties), it is exempted, vis-à-vis the other State. from a rule of treaty-law because of the breach by that other State of a different rule of treaty-law. But if the two rules in question also exist as rules of customary international law, the failure of the one State to apply the one rule does not justify the other State in declining to apply the other rule. Rules which are identical in treaty law and in customary international law are also distinguishable by reference to the methods of interpretation and application. A State may accept a rule contained in a treaty not simply because it favours the application of the

rule itself, but also because the treaty establishes what that State regards as desirable institutions or mechanisms to ensure implementation of the rule. Thus, if that rule parallels a rule of customary international law, two rules of the same content are subject to separate treatment as regards the organs competent to verify their implementation, depending on whether they are customary rules or treaty rules. The present dispute illustrates this point.

* * *

182. The Court concludes that it should exercise the jurisdiction conferred upon it by the United States declaration of acceptance under Article 36, paragraph 2, of the Statute, to determine the claims of Nicaragua based upon customary international law notwithstanding the exclusion from its jurisdiction of disputes "arising under" the United Nations and Organization of American States Charters.

183. In view of this conclusion, the Court has next to consider what are the rules of customary international law applicable to the present dispute. For this purpose, it has to direct its attention to the practice and *opinio juris* of States; as the Court recently observed, "It is of course axiomatic that the material of customary international law is to be looked for primarily in the actual practice and *opinion juris* of States, even though multilateral conventions may have an important role to play in recording and defining rules deriving from custom, or indeed in developing them." *(Continental Shelf (Libyan Arab Jamahiriyu/Malta), I.C.J. Reports 1985,* pp. 29–30, para. 27.) * * *

184. The Court notes that there is in fact evidence, to be examined below, of a considerable degree of agreement between the Parties as to the content of the customary international law relating to the non-use of force and non-intervention. This concurrence of their views does not however dispense the Court from having itself to ascertain what rules of customary international law are applicable. The mere fact that States declare their recognition of certain rules is not sufficient for the Court to consider these as being part of customary international law, and as applicable as such to those States. Bound as it is by Article 38 of its Statute to apply, *inter alia,* international custom "as evidence of a general practice accepted as law", the Court may not disregard the essential role played by general practice.

Where two States agree to incorporate a particular rule in a treaty, their agreement suffices to make that rule a legal one, binding upon them; but in the field of customary international law, the shared view of the Parties as to the content of what they regard as the rule is not enough. The Court must satisfy itself that the existence of the rule in the opinio juris of States is confirmed by practice.

185. In the present dispute, the Court, while exercising its jurisdiction only in respect of the application of the customary rules of non-use of force and non-intervention, cannot disregard the fact that the Parties are bound by these rules as a matter of treaty law and of customary international law. Furthermore, in the present case, apart from the treaty commit-

ments binding the Parties to the rules in question, there are various instances of their having expressed recognition of the validity thereof as customary international law in other ways. It is therefore in the light of this "subjective element"—the expression used by the Court in its 1969 Judgment in the North Sea Continental Shelf cases (I.C.J. Reports 1969, p. 44)—that the Court has to appraise the relevant practice.

186. It is not to be expected that in the practice of States the application of the rules in question should have been perfect, in the sense that States should have refrained, with complete consistency, from the use of force or from intervention in each other's internal affairs. The Court does not consider that, for a rule to be established as customary, the corresponding practice must be in absolutely rigorous conformity with the rule. In order to deduce the existence of customary rules, the Court deems it sufficient that the conduct of States should, in general, be consistent with such rules, and that instances of State conduct inconsistent with a given rule should generally have been treated as breaches of that rule, not as indications of the recognition of a new rule. If a State acts in a way prima facie incompatible with a recognized rule, but defends its conduct by appealing to exceptions or justifications contained within the rule itself, then whether or not the State's conduct is in fact justifiable on that basis, the significance of that attitude is to confirm rather than to weaken the rule.

* * *

187. The Court must therefore determine, first, the substance of the customary rules relating to the use of force in international relations, applicable to the dispute submitted to it. The United States has argued that, on this crucial question of the lawfulness of the use of force in inter-State relations, the rules of general and customary international law, and those of the United Nations Charter, are in fact identical. In its view this identity is so complete that, as explained above * * * it constitutes an argument to prevent the Court from applying this customary law, because it is indistinguishable from the multilateral treaty law which it may not apply. In its Counter–Memorial on jurisdiction and admissibility the United States asserts that "Article 2(4) of the Charter *is* customary and general international law". It quotes with approval an observation by the International Law Commission to the effect that

> "the great majority of international lawyers today unhesitatingly hold that Article 2, paragraph 4, together with other provisions of the Charter, authoritatively declares the modern customary law regarding the threat or use of force" (ILC *Yearbook,* 1966, Vol. II, p. 247).

The United States points out that Nicaragua has endorsed this view, since one of its counsel asserted that "indeed it is generally considered by publicists that Article 2 paragraph 4, of the United Nations Charter is in this respect an embodiment of existing general principles of international law". And the United States concludes:

"In sum the provisions of Article 2(4) with respect to the lawfulness of the use of force *are* 'modern customary law' (International Law Commission. *toc. cit.*) and the 'embodiment of general principles of international law' (counsel for Nicaragua, Hearing of 25 April 1984, morning, *loc. cit.*). There is no other 'customary and general international law' on which Nicaragua can rest its claims."

"It is, in short, inconceivable that this Court could consider the lawfulness of an alleged use of armed force without referring to the principal source of the relevant international law—Article 2(4) of the United Nations Charter."

As for Nicaragua, the only noteworthy shade of difference in its view lies in Nicaragua's belief that

"in certain cases the rule of customary law will not necessarily be identical in content and mode of application to the conventional rule".

188.   The Court thus finds that both Parties take the view that the principles as to the use of force incorporated in the United Nations Charter correspond, in essentials, to those found in customary international law. The Parties thus both take the view that the fundamental principle in this area is expressed in the terms employed in Article 2, paragraph 4, of the United Nations Charter. They therefore accept a treaty-law obligation to refrain in their international relations from the threat or use of force against the territorial integrity or political independence of any State, or in any other manner inconsistent with the purposes of the United Nations.

The Court has however to be satisfied that there exists in customary international law an *opinio juris* as to the binding character of such abstention. This *opinio juris* may, though with all due caution, be deduced from, inter alia, the attitude of the Parties and the attitude of States towards certain General Assembly resolutions, and particularly resolution 2625 (XXV) entitled "Declaration on Principles of International Law concerning Friendly Relations and Co-operation among States in accordance with the Charter of the United Nations". The effect of consent to the text of such resolutions cannot be understood as merely that of a "reiteration or elucidation" of the treaty commitment undertaken in the Charter. On the contrary, it may be understood as an acceptance of the validity of the rule or set of rules declared by the resolution by themselves. The principle of non-use of force, for example, may thus be regarded as a principle of customary international law, not as such conditioned by provisions relating to collective security, or to the facilities or armed contingents to be provided under Article 43 of the Charter. It would therefore seem apparent that the attitude referred to expresses an opinion juris respecting such rule (or set of rules), to be thenceforth treated separately from the provisions, especially those of an institutional kind, to which it is subject on the treaty-law plane of the Charter.

189.   As regards the United States in particular, the weight of an expression of opinion juris can similarly be attached to its support of the resolution of the Sixth International Conference of American States con-

demning aggression (18 February 1928) and ratification of the Montevideo Convention on Rights and Duties of States (26 December 1933). Article 11 of which imposes the obligation not to recognize territorial acquisitions or special advantages which have been obtained by force. Also significant is United States acceptance of the principle of the prohibition of the use of force which is contained in the declaration on principles governing the mutual relations of States participating in the Conference on Security and Co-operation in Europe (Helsinki, 1 August 1975), whereby the participating States undertake to "refrain in their mutual relations, as well as in their international relations in general," (emphasis added) from the threat or use of force. Acceptance of a text in these terms confirms the existence of an opinio juris of the participating States prohibiting the use of force in international relations.

190. A further confirmation of the validity as customary international law of the principle of the prohibition of the use of force expressed in Article 2, paragraph 4, of the Charter of the United Nations may be found in the fact that it is frequently referred to in statements by State representatives as being not only a principle of customary international law but also a fundamental or cardinal principle of such law. The International Law Commission, in the course of its work on the codification of the law of treaties, expressed the view that "the law of the Charter concerning the prohibition of the use of force in itself constitutes a conspicuous example of a rule in international law having the character of *jus cogens*" (paragraph (1) of the commentary of the Commission to Article 50 of its draft Articles on the Law of Treaties, *ILC* Yearbook, 1966–11, p. 247). Nicaragua in its Memorial on the Merits submitted in the present case states that the principle prohibiting the use of force embodied in Article 2, paragraph 4, of the Charter of the United Nations "has come to be recognized as *jus cogens*". The United States, in its Counter–Memorial on the questions of jurisdiction and admissibility, found it material to quote the views of scholars that this principle is a "universal norm", a "universal international law", a "universally recognized principle of international law", and a "principle of *jus cogens*".

[The case continues in Chapter 10.]

NOTES AND QUESTIONS

1. What advantages does custom offer as a source compared with treaties? Why might some scholars, nevertheless, question the legitimacy of customary rules? How does a rule of customary international law change or terminate? See THE NATURE OF CUSTOMARY LAW (Amanda Perreau–Saussine and James Bernard Murphy eds., 2007).

2. Note that Justice Gray in the *Paquette Habana* case not only sets out in exemplary fashion evidence of a rule of custom, he also describes international legal process—the making of treaties, claims, counter-claims, protests, and the like that result in a rule of custom remaining viable or not.

3. As the court points out in both the *North Sea Continental Shelf* case and the *Nicaragua* case, it is possible for a treaty rule to develop into a rule

of customary international law. The United States has with respect to a number of treaties declared that certain provisions are part of customary international law and binding on states generally but certain other provisions are not binding on non-parties, including the United States. The U.S. has taken this position with respect to the following treaties:

- law of the sea, *see* Statement on United States Oceans Policy, 1 PUB. PAPERS 378, 378–79 (Mar. 10, 1983);

- law of treaties, *see* Marian L. Nash, *Contemporary Practice of the United States Relating to International Law*, 75 AM. J. INT'L L. 142, 147 (1981);

- 1977 Additional Protocol I to the 1949 Geneva Conventions, *see* Michael Matheson, *Session One: The United States Position on the Relation of Customary International Law to the 1977 Protocols Additional to the 1949 Geneva Conventions*, 2 AM. U. J. INT'L L. & POL'Y 419–31 (1987);

- Rules regulating the protection of cultural property during armed conflict, *see* Department of Defense, January 1993 Report of the Department of Defense, United States of America to Congress on International Policies and Procedures regarding the Protection of Natural and Cultural Resources During Times of War. Reprinted as Appendix VII *in* Patrick J. Boylan, *Review of the Convention for the Protection of Cultural Property in the Event of Armed Conflict (The Hague Convention of 1954)* 202 (1993) *available at* http://unesdoc. unesco.org/images/0010/001001/100159eo.pdf;

- Rules relating to resort to force, *see* Case Concerning Military and Paramilitary Activities in and Against Nicaragau (Nic. v. U.S.) 1986 ICJ para. 189 (June 27) (referencing the U.S.'s memorials in the case).

Is there not a problem for the international community if states can pick and choose the provisions they like from multilateral treaties that might have taken years to negotiate (UNCLOS took ten years) but exclude the rest? Treaties are often the result of compromise. A party gives up something respecting one provision to get something in exchange. Is there, however, any remedy so long as treaties require express consent and custom develops as it does? *See* MARK E. VILLIGER, CUSTOMARY INTERNATIONAL LAW AND TREATIES: A MANUAL ON THE THEORY AND PRACTICE OF THE INTERRELATION OF SOURCES (2d ed. 1997).

4. How did the ICJ handle the problem of "negative custom" in the *Nicaragua* case? "Negative custom" refers to examples of practice contrary to the rule. The common law has a similar challenge in distinguishing between violations of a rule and practice forming a new or different custom. Did the ICJ adopt the right approach for the international community?

5. In the *Paquete Habana*, the U.S. Supreme Court explained famously that international law is part of the law of the United States. The following excerpt by Linda Carter and others provides an overview of the place of customary international law in national legal systems:

In common law states, courts usually justify their application of customary international law by stating that international law is part of the law of the land. * * *

National constitutions may provide a specific legal basis for the application of rules of customary international law. Among those a number of modest formulations provide (or contain language to the effect) that "The State shall endeavour to . . . foster respect for international law and treaty obligations in the dealings of organized peoples with one another." Article 5l(c), the 1950 Constitution of India. Comparable provisions are found in the constitutions of a number of countries, including Bulgaria Article 24(1), Nepal Article 26(15), Namibia Article 96(d), the Netherlands Article 90, and Romania, Article 10.

Some constitutions provide a basis for courts to apply rules of customary international law by declaring specifically that international law is part of the law of the land, including the following examples. The Austrian Constitution of 1928 states in Article 9(1): "[t]he generally recognized principles of International Law are integral parts of the Federal Law." Article 2(2) of the 1987 Philippine Constitution states: "The Philippines . . . adopts the generally accepted principles of international law as part of the law of the land." Article 15 of the Russian Constitution of 1993 states that: "[T]he commonly recognized principles and norms of international law and the international treaties of the Russian Federation shall be a component part of its legal system." Article 25 of the 1949 German Constitution, as amended, provides: "The general rules of public international law constitute an integral part of federal law. They take precedence over statutes and directly create rights and duties for the inhabitants of the federal territory." * * *

Stronger terms of acceptance of international law are found in other national constitutions, including Article 29(3) of the Constitution of Ireland (text of 1990), which provides that: "Ireland accepts the generally recognized principles of international law as its rule of conduct in its relations with other States." Article 98(2) of the Japanese Constitution of 1946 provides that "the . . . established laws of nations shall be faithfully observed". The Hungarian Constitution of 1949, as amended in 1997, is exceptional in providing, in Ch. 1, sec. 7, that: "[t]he legal system of the Republic of Hungary accepts the generally recognized principles of international law, and shall harmonize the country's domestic law with the obligations assumed under international law."

LINDA CARTER et al., GLOBAL ISSUES IN CRIMINAL LAW 19–20 (2008). *See also*, Chapter 11, *infra*.

6.   The ICJ found in *Dispute Regarding Navigational and Related Rights* (Costa Rica v. Nicaragua) 2009 I.C.J. Rep. (July 13) a bilateral custom between Nicaragua and Costa Rica.

141. The Court recalls that the Parties are agreed that all that is in dispute is fishing by Costa Rican riparians for subsistence purposes. There is no question of commercial or sport fishing. The Court also notes that the Parties have not attempted to define subsistence fishing (except by those exclusions) nor have they asked the Court to provide a definition. Subsistence fishing has without doubt occurred over a very long period. Leaving aside for the moment the issue of fishing in the river from boats, a point to which the Court will return, the Parties agree that the practice of subsistence fishing is long established. They disagree however whether the practice has become binding on Nicaragua thereby entitling the riparians as a matter of customary right to engage in subsistence fishing from the bank. The Court observes that the practice, by its very nature, especially given the remoteness of the area and the small, thinly spread population, is not likely to be documented in any formal way in any official record. For the Court, the failure of Nicaragua to deny the existence of a right arising from the practice which had continued undisturbed and unquestioned over a very long period, is particularly significant. The Court accordingly concludes that Costa Rica has a customary right. That right would be subject to any Nicaraguan regulatory measures relating to fishing adopted for proper purposes, particularly for the protection of resources and the environment.

This is the ICJ's entire treatment of the issue. Does it appear that the court left something out of the analysis? Do bilateral customs fit the definition of customary rules?

What about regional customs? In the *Asylum* case the ICJ implied their existence but did not find one. See the *Asylum Case* (Colombia/Peru) 1950 I.C.J. Rep. 266 (Judgment of Nov. 20).

7. For further reading on customary international law, see, ALAN BOYLE AND CHRISTINE CHINKIN, THE MAKING OF INTERNATIONAL LAW (2007); ANTHONY D'AMATO, INTERNATIONAL LAW TODAY: A HAND BOOK (2006), PETER MALACZUK, AKEHURST'S MODERN INTRODUCTION TO INTERNATIONAL LAW (8th rev. ed. 2002); and G.M. DANILENKO, LAW MAKING IN THE INTERNATIONAL COMMUNITY (1993).

C. GENERAL PRINCIPLES AND EQUITY

Courts and scholars have said far less about general principles than treaties or customary international law, despite the equal status of general principles in Article 38. It seems to us that general principles deserve that equal status. They play a vital role in international law. In particular, general principles guide international law processes, assuring fairness and equity. Indeed, fairness and equity *are* general principles of law. You have already encountered the principle of good faith that governs the process of treaty formation and performance. The excerpt below from the ICJ's decision in *Barcelona Traction* mentions the obligation of courts to apply the law reasonably. Such principles may be thought of as inherent in legal systems and are the result of reasoning about what the law requires to fulfill the purposes of promoting order, justice, and peaceful dispute resolution, and are, therefore, not so much a development of positive law making as natural law. The ICJ also identifies a second category of general principles in *Barcelona Traction*: principles common to legal systems. These principles, such as the nationality of corporations, tend to be part of the positive law of national systems and part of international law through the source of general principles.

Equity plays a dual role in international law, which explains the inclusion of equity in this section. Rules and processes should be "equitable". The division of shared resources should be equitable, which does not necessarily mean proportionate shares. More about the principle of equity, especially respecting maritime boundaries, is provided below in another excerpt from the *North Sea Continental Shelf* case. It is possible for the ICJ to also decide cases irrespective of legal rules and principles, simply on the basis of what the judges think is a good outcome. The court has the power "to decide a case *ex aequo et bono*, if the parties agree thereto." (Article 38(2)). The ICJ has not done so, but the possibility is there and the need to distinguish the general principle of equity from decisions based on achieving a good result exists, too.

1.   GENERAL PRINCIPLES

South West Africa Cases

Liberia and Ethiopia v. South Africa
International Court of Justice
1966 I.C.J. Rep. 6 (July 18) (Second Phase)

■ Dissenting Opinion of JUDGE TANAKA

If a law exists independently of the will of the State and, accordingly, cannot be abolished or modified even by its constitution, because it is deeply rooted in the conscience of mankind and of any reasonable man, it may be called "natural law" in contrast to "positive law".

Provisions of the constitutions of some countries characterize fundamental human rights and freedoms as "inalienable", "sacred", "eternal", "inviolate", etc. Therefore, the guarantee of fundamental human rights and freedoms possesses a super-constitutional significance.

If we can introduce in the international field a category of law, namely *jus cogens*, recently examined by the International Law Commission, a kind of imperative law which constitutes the contrast to the *jus dispositivum*, capable of being changed by way of agreement between States, surely the law concerning the protection of human rights may be considered to belong to the *jus cogens*.

As an interpretation of Article 38, paragraph 1(c), we consider that the concept of human rights and of their protection is included in the general principles mentioned in that Article.

Such an interpretation would necessarily be open to the criticism of falling into the error of natural law dogma. But it is undeniable that in Article 38, paragraph 1(c), some natural law elements are inherent. It extends the concept of the source of international law beyond the limit of legal positivism according to which, the States being bound only by their own will, international law is nothing but the law of the consent and auto-limitation of the State. But this viewpoint, we believe, was clearly overruled by Article 38, paragraph 1(c), by the fact that this provision does not require the consent of States as a condition of the recognition of the general principles. States which do not recognize this principle or even deny its validity are nevertheless subject to its rule. From this kind of source international law could have the foundation of its validity extended beyond the will of States, that is to say, into the sphere of natural law and assume an aspect of its supra-national and supra-positive character.

The above-mentioned character of Article 38, paragraph 1(c), of the Statute is proved by the process of the drafting of this article by the Committee of Jurists. The original proposal made by Baron Descamps referred to "*la conscience juridique des peuples civilisés*", a concept which clearly indicated an idea originating in natural law. This proposal met with the opposition of the positivist members of the Committee, represented by Mr. Root. The final draft, namely Article 38, paragraph 1(c), is the product of a compromise between two schools, naturalist and positivist, and therefore the fact that the natural law idea became incorporated therein is not difficult to discover (see particularly Jean Spiropoulos, *Die Allgemeine Rechtsgrundsätze im Völkerrecht*, 1928, pp. 60 ff.; Bin Cheng, op. cit., pp. 24–26).

Furthermore, an important role which can be played by Article 38, paragraph 1(c), in filling in gaps in the positive sources in order to avoid *non liquet* decisions, can only be derived from the natural law character of this provision. Professor Brierly puts it, "its inclusion is important as a rejection of the positivistic doctrine, according to which international law consists solely of rules to which States have given their consent" (J. L. Brierly, *The Law of Nations*, 6th ed., p. 63). Mr. Rosenne comments on the general principles of law as follows:

> "Having independent existence, their validity as legal norms does not derive from the consent of the parties as such ... The Statute places this element on a footing of formal equality with two positivist elements of custom and treaty, and thus is positivist recognitions of the Grotian concept of the co-existence implying no subjugation of positive law and so-called natural law of nations in the Grotian sense." (Shabtai Rosenne, *The International Court of Justice*, 1965, Vol. II, p. 610.)

Now the question is whether the alleged norm of non-discrimination and non-separation as a kind of protection of human rights can be considered as recognized by civilized nations and included in the general principles of law.

First the recognition of a principle by civilized nations, as indicated above, does not mean recognition by all civilized nations, nor does it mean recognition by an official act such as a legislative act; therefore the recognition is of a very elastic nature. The principle of equality before the law, however, is stipulated in the list of human rights recognized by the municipal system of virtually every State no matter whether the form of government be republican or monarchical and in spite of any differences in the degree of precision of the relevant provisions. This principle has become an integral part of the constitutions of most of the civilized countries in the world. Common-law countries must be included. (According to *Constitutions of Nations*, 2nd ed., by Amos J. Peaslee, 1956, Vol. 1, p. 7, about 73 per cent. of the national constitutions contain clauses respecting equality.)

The manifestation of the recognition of this principle does not need to be limited to the act of legislation as indicated above; it may include the attitude of delegations of member States in cases of participation in resolutions, declarations, etc., against racial discrimination adopted by the organs of the League of Nations, the United Nations and other organizations which, as we have seen above, constitute an important element in the generation of customary international law.

From what we have seen above, the alleged norm of non-discrimination and non-separation, being based on the United Nations Charter, particularly Articles 55*(c)*, 56, and on numerous resolutions and declarations of the General Assembly and other organs of the United Nations, and owing to its nature as a general principle, can be regarded as a source of international law according to the provisions of Article 38, paragraph 1*(a)–(c)*. In this case three kinds of sources are cumulatively functioning to defend the above-mentioned norm: (1) international convention, (2) international custom and (3) the general principles of law.

Practically the justification of any one of these is enough, but theoretically there may be a difference in the degree of importance among the three. From a positivistic, voluntaristic viewpoint, first the convention, and next the custom, is considered important, and general principles occupy merely a supplementary position. On the contrary, if we take the supranational objective viewpoint, the general principles would come first and the two others would follow them. If we accept the fact that convention and custom are generally the manifestation and concretization of already existing general principles, we are inclined to attribute to this third source of international law the primary position vis-à-vis the other two.

To sum up, the principle of the protection of human rights has received recognition as a legal norm under three main sources of international law, namely (1) international conventions, (2) international custom and (3) the general principles of law. Now, the principle of equality before the law or equal protection by the law presents itself as a kind of human rights norm. Therefore, what has been said on human rights in general can be applied to the principle of equality. (Cf. Wilfred Jenks, *The Common Law of Mankind*, 1958, p. 121. The author recognizes the principle of respect for human rights including equality before the law as a general principle of law.)

Barcelona Traction, Light and Power Company, Limited

Belgium v. Spain
International Court of Justice
1970 I.C.J. Rep. 3 (Feb. 5) (Second Phase)

37.   In seeking to determine the law applicable to this case, the Court has to bear in mind the continuous evolution of international law. Diplomatic protection deals with a very sensitive area of international relations, since the interest of a foreign State in the protection of its nationals confronts the rights of the territorial sovereign, a fact of which the general law on the subject has had to take cognizance in order to prevent abuses and friction. From its origins closely linked with international commerce, diplomatic protection has sustained a particular impact from the growth of international economic relations, and at the same time from the profound transformations which have taken place in the economic life of nations. These latter changes have given birth to municipal institutions, which have transcended frontiers and have begun to exercise considerable influence on international relations. One of these phenomena which has a particular bearing on the present case is the corporate entity.

38.   In this field international law is called upon to recognize institutions of municipal law that have an important and extensive role in the international field. This does not necessarily imply drawing any analogy between its own institutions and those of municipal law, nor does it amount to making rules of international law dependent upon categories of municipal law. All it means is that international law has had to recognize the corporate entity as an institution created by States in a domain essentially within their domestic jurisdiction. This in turn requires that, whenever legal issues arise concerning the rights of States with regard to the treatment of companies and shareholders, as to which rights international law has not established its own rules, it has to refer to the relevant rules of municipal law. Consequently, in view of the relevance to the present case of the rights of the corporate entity and its shareholders under municipal law, the Court must devote attention to the nature and interrelation of those rights.

* * *

39.   Seen in historical perspective, the corporate personality represents a development brought about by new and expanding requirements in the economic field, an entity which in particular allows of operation in circumstances which exceed the normal capacity of individuals. As such it has become a powerful factor in the economic life of nations. Of this, municipal law has had to take due account, whence the increasing volume of rules governing the creation and operation of corporate entities, endowed with a specific status. These entities have rights and obligations peculiar to themselves.

40.   There is, however, no need to investigate the many different forms of legal entity provided for by the municipal laws of States, because

the Court is concerned only with that exemplified by the company involved in the present case: Barcelona Traction—a limited liability company whose capital is represented by shares. There are, indeed, other associations, whatever the name attached to them by municipal legal systems, that do not enjoy independent corporate personality. The legal difference between the two kinds of entity is that for the limited liability company it is the overriding tie of legal personality which is determinant; for the other associations, the continuing autonomy of the several members.

41.   Municipal law determines the legal situation not only of such limited liability companies but also of those persons who hold shares in them. Separated from the company by numerous barriers, the shareholder cannot be identified with it. The concept and structure of the company are founded on and determined by a firm distinction between the separate entity of the company and that of the shareholder, each with a distinct set of rights. The separation of property rights as between company and shareholder is an important manifestation of this distinction. So long as the company is in existence the shareholder has no right to the corporate assets.

42.   It is a basic characteristic of the corporate structure that the company alone, through its directors or management acting in its name, can take action in respect of matters that are of a corporate character. The underlying justification for this is that, in seeking to serve its own best interests, the company will serve those of the shareholder too. Ordinarily, no individual shareholder can take legal steps, either in the name of the company or in his own name. If the shareholders disagree with the decisions taken on behalf of the company they may, in accordance with its articles or the relevant provisions of the law, change them or replace its officers, or take such action as is provided by law. Thus to protect the company against abuse by its management or the majority of shareholders, several municipal legal systems have vested in shareholders (sometimes a particular number is specified) the right to bring an action for the defence of the company, and conferred upon the minority of shareholders certain rights to guard against decisions affecting the rights of the company vis-à-vis its management or controlling shareholders. Nonetheless the shareholders' rights in relation to the company and its assets remain limited, this being, moreover, a corollary of the limited nature of their liability.

43.   At this point the Court would recall that in forming a company, its promoters are guided by all the various factors involved, the advantages and disadvantages of which they take into account. So equally does a shareholder, whether he is an original subscriber of capital or a subsequent purchaser of the company's shares from another shareholder. He may be seeking safety of investment, high dividends or capital appreciation—or a combination of two or more of these. Whichever it is, it does not alter the legal status of the corporate entity or affect the rights of the shareholder. In any event he is bound to take account of the risk of reduced dividends, capital depreciation or even loss, resulting from ordinary commercial haz-

ards or from prejudice caused to the company by illegal treatment of some kind.

* * *

44.   Notwithstanding the separate corporate personality, a wrong done to the company frequently causes prejudice to its shareholders. But the mere fact that damage is sustained by both company and shareholder does not imply that both are entitled to claim compensation. Thus no legal conclusion can be drawn from the fact that the same event caused damage simultaneously affecting several natural or juristic persons. Creditors do not have any right to claim compensation from a person who, by wronging their debtor, causes them loss. In such cases, no doubt, the interests of the aggrieved are affected, but not their rights. Thus whenever a shareholder's interests are harmed by an act done to the company, it is to the latter that he must look to institute appropriate action; for although two separate entities may have suffered from the same wrong, it is only one entity whose rights have been infringed.

45.   However, it has been argued in the present case that a company represents purely a means of achieving the economic purpose of its members, namely the shareholders, while they themselves constitute in fact the reality behind it. It has furthermore been repeatedly emphasized that there exists between a company and its shareholders a relationship describable as a community of destiny. The alleged acts may have been directed at the company and not the shareholders, but only in a formal sense: in reality, company and shareholders are so closely interconnected that prejudicial acts committed against the former necessarily wrong the latter; hence any acts directed against a company can be conceived as directed against its shareholders, because both can be considered in substance, i.e., from the economic viewpoint, identical. Yet even if a company is no more than a means for its shareholders to achieve their economic purpose, so long as it is *in esse* it enjoys an independent existence. Therefore the interests of the shareholders are both separable and indeed separated from those of the company, so that the possibility of their diverging cannot be denied.

46.   It has also been contended that the measures complained of, although taken with respect to Barcelona Traction and causing it direct damage, constituted an unlawful act vis-à-vis Belgium, because they also, though indirectly, caused damage to the Belgian shareholders in Barcelona Traction. This again is merely a different way of presenting the distinction between injury in respect of a right and injury to a simple interest. But, as the Court has indicated, evidence that damage was suffered does not *ipso facto* justify a diplomatic claim. Persons suffer damage or harm in most varied circumstances. This in itself does not involve the obligation to make reparation. Not a mere interest affected, but solely a right infringed involves responsibility, so that an act directed against and infringing only the company's rights does not involve responsibility towards the shareholders, even if their interests are affected.

47.   The situation is different if the act complained of is aimed at the direct rights of the shareholder as such. It is well known that there are

rights which municipal law confers upon the latter distinct from those of the company, including the right to any declared dividend, the right to attend and vote at general meetings, the right to share in the residual assets of the company on liquidation. Whenever one of his direct rights is infringed, the shareholder has an independent right of action. On this there is no disagreement between the Parties. But a distinction must be drawn between a direct infringement of the shareholder's rights, and difficulties or financial losses to which he may be exposed as the result of the situation of the company.

48.   The Belgian Government claims that shareholders of Belgian nationality suffered damage in consequence of unlawful acts of the Spanish authorities and, in particular, that the Barcelona Traction shares, though they did not cease to exist, were emptied of all real economic content. It accordingly contends that the shareholders had an independent right to redress, notwithstanding the fact that the acts complained of were directed against the company as such. Thus the legal issue is reducible to the question of whether it is legitimate to identify an attack on company rights, resulting in damage to shareholders, with the violation of their direct rights.

49.   The Court has noted from the Application, and from the reply given by Counsel on 8 July 1969, that the Belgian Government did not base its claim on an infringement of the direct rights of the shareholders. Thus it is not open to the Court to go beyond the claim as formulated by the Belgian Government and it will not pursue its examination of this point any further.

* * *

50.   In turning now to the international legal aspects of the case, the Court must, as already indicated, start from the fact that the present case essentially involves factors derived from municipal law—the distinction and the community between the company and the shareholder—which the Parties, however widely their interpretations may differ, each take as the point of departure of their reasoning. If the Court were to decide the case in disregard of the relevant institutions of municipal law it would, without justification, invite serious legal difficulties. It would lose touch with reality, for there are no corresponding institutions of international law to which the Court could resort. Thus the Court has, as indicated, not only to take cognizance of municipal law but also to refer to it. It is to rules generally accepted by municipal legal systems which recognize the limited company whose capital is represented by shares, and not to the municipal law of a particular State, that international law refers. In referring to such rules, the Court cannot modify, still less deform them.

51.   On the international plane, the Belgian Government has advanced the proposition that it is inadmissible to deny the shareholders' national State a right of diplomatic protection merely on the ground that another State possesses a corresponding right in respect of the company itself. In strict logic and law this formulation of the Belgian claim to *jus standi* assumes the existence of the very right that requires demonstration. In fact the Belgian Government has repeatedly stressed that there exists no

rule of international law which would deny the national State of the shareholders the right of diplomatic protection for the purpose of seeking redress pursuant to unlawful acts committed by another State against the company in which they hold shares. This, by emphasizing the absence of any express denial of the right, conversely implies the admission that there is no rule of international law which expressly confers such a right on the shareholders' national State.

52.   International law may not, in some fields, provide specific rules in particular cases. In the concrete situation, the company against which allegedly unlawful acts were directed is expressly vested with a right, whereas no such right is specifically provided for the shareholder in respect of those acts. Thus the position of the company rests on a positive rule of both municipal and international law. As to the shareholder, while he has certain rights expressly provided for him by municipal law as referred to in paragraph 42 above, appeal can, in the circumstances of the present case, only be made to the silence of international law. Such silence scarcely admits of interpretation in favour of the shareholder.

* * *

92.   Since the general rule on the subject does not entitle the Belgian Government to put forward a claim in this case, the question remains to be considered whether nonetheless, as the Belgian Government has contended during the proceedings, considerations of equity do not require that it be held to possess a right of protection. It is quite true that it has been maintained that, for reasons of equity, a State should be able, in certain cases, to take up the protection of its nationals, shareholders in a company which has been the victim of a violation of international law. Thus a theory has been developed to the effect that the State of the shareholders has a right of diplomatic protection when the State whose responsibility is invoked is the national State of the company. Whatever the validity of this theory may be, it is certainly not applicable to the present case, since Spain is not the national State of Barcelona Traction.

93.   On the other hand, the Court considers that, in the field of diplomatic protection as in all other fields of international law, it is necessary that the law be applied reasonably. It has been suggested that if in a given case it is not possible to apply the general rule that the right of diplomatic protection of a company belongs to its national State, considerations of equity might call for the possibility of protection of the shareholders in question by their own national State. This hypothesis does not correspond to the circumstances of the present case.

94.   In view, however, of the discretionary nature of diplomatic protection, considerations of equity cannot require more than the possibility for some protector State to intervene, whether it be the national State of the company, by virtue of the general rule mentioned above, or, in a secondary capacity, the national State of the shareholders who claim protection. In this connection, account should also be taken of the practical effects of deducing from considerations of equity any broader right of protection for the national State of the shareholders. It must first of all be observed that it would be difficult on an equitable basis to make distinctions according to

any quantitative test: it would seem that the owner of 1 per cent. and the owner of 90 per cent. of the share-capital should have the same possibility of enjoying the benefit of diplomatic protection. The protector State may, of course, be disinclined to take up the case of the single small shareholder, but it could scarcely be denied the right to do so in the name of equitable considerations. In that field, protection by the national state of the shareholders can hardly be graduated according to the absolute or relative size of the shareholding involved.

95.   The Belgian Government, it is true, has also contended that as high a proportion as 88 per cent. of the shares in Barcelona Traction belonged to natural or juristic persons of Belgian nationality, and it has used this as an argument for the purpose not only of determining the amount of the damages which it claims, but also of establishing its right of action on behalf of the Belgian shareholders. Nevertheless, this does not alter the Belgian Government's position, as expounded in the course of the proceedings, which implies, in the last analysis, that it might be sufficient for one single share to belong to a national of a given State for the latter to be entitled to exercise its diplomatic protection.

96.   The Court considers that the adoption of the theory of diplomatic protection of shareholders as such, by opening the door to competing diplomatic claims, could create an atmosphere of confusion and insecurity in international economic relations. The danger would be all the greater inasmuch as the shares of companies whose activity is international are widely scattered and frequently change hands. It might perhaps be claimed that, if the right of protection belonging to the national States of the shareholders were considered as only secondary to that of the national State of the company, there would be less danger of difficulties of the kind contemplated. However, the Court must state that the essence of a secondary right is that it only comes into existence at the time when the original right ceases to exist. As the right of protection vested in the national State of the company cannot be regarded as extinguished because it is not exercised, it is not possible to accept the proposition that in case of its non-exercise the national States of the shareholders have a right of protection secondary to that of the national State of the company.

* * *

101.   For the above reasons, the Court is not of the opinion that, in the particular circumstances of the present case, *jus standi* is conferred on the Belgian Government by considerations of equity.

2.   EQUITY

North Sea Continental Shelf Cases

Germany/Denmark, Germany/The Netherlands
International Court of Justice
1969 I.C.J. Rep. 3 (Judgment of Feb. 20)

88.   The Court comes next to the rule of equity. The legal basis of that rule in the particular case of the delimitation of the continental shelf as

between adjoining States has already been stated. It must however be noted that the rule rests also on a broader basis. Whatever the legal reasoning of a court of justice, its decisions must by definition be just, and therefore in that sense equitable. Nevertheless, when mention is made of a court dispensing justice or declaring the law, what is meant is that the decision finds its objective justification in considerations lying not outside but within the rules, and in this field it is precisely a rule of law that calls for the application of equitable principles. There is consequently no question in this case of any decision *ex aequo et bono,* such as would only be possible under the conditions prescribed by Article 38, paragraph 2, of the Court's Statute. Nor would this be the first time that the Court has adopted such an attitude, as is shown by the following passage from the Advisory Opinion given in the case of *Judgments of the Administrative Tribunal of the I.L.O. upon Complaints Made against Unesco (I.C.J. Reports 1956,* at p. 100):

> "In view of this the Court need not examine the allegation that the validity of the judgments of the Tribunal is vitiated by excess of jurisdiction on the ground that it awarded compensation *ex aequo et bono*. It will confine itself to stating that, in the reasons given by the Tribunal in support of its decision on the merits, the Tribunal said: 'That redress will be ensured *ex aequo et bono* by the granting to the complainant of the sum set forth below.' It does not appear from the context of the judgment that the Tribunal thereby intended to depart from principles of law. The apparent intention was to say that, as the precise determination of the actual amount to be awarded could not be based on any specific rule of law, the Tribunal fixed what the Court, in other circumstances, has described as the true measure of compensation and the reasonable figure of such compensation *(Corfu Channel* case, Judgment of December 15th, 1949, *I.C.J. Reports* 1949, p. 249)."

89. It must next be observed that, in certain geographical circumstances which are quite frequently met with, the equidistance method, despite its known advantages, leads unquestionably to inequity, in the following sense:

(a) The slightest irregularity in a coastline is automatically magnified by the equidistance line as regards the consequences for the delimitation of the continental shelf. Thus it has been seen in the case of concave or convex coastlines that if the equidistance method is employed, then the greater the irregularity and the further from the coastline the area to be delimited, the more unreasonable are the results produced. So great an exaggeration of the consequences of a natural geographical feature must be remedied or compensated for as far as possible, being of itself creative of inequity.

(b) In the case of the North Sea in particular, where there is no outer boundary to the continental shelf, it happens that the claims of several States converge, meet and intercross in localities where, despite their distance from the coast, the bed of the sea still unquestionably consists of continental shelf. A study of these convergences, as revealed by the

maps, shows how inequitable would be the apparent simplification brought about by a delimitation which, ignoring such geographical circumstances, was based solely on the equidistance method.

90.   If for the above reasons equity excludes the use of the equidistance method in the present instance, as the sole method of delimitation, the question arises whether there is any necessity to employ only one method for the purposes of a given delimitation. There is no logical basis for this, and no objection need be felt to the idea of effecting a delimitation of adjoining continental shelf areas by the concurrent use of various methods. The Court has already stated why it considers that the international law of continental shelf delimitation does not involve any imperative rule and permits resort to various principles or methods, as may be appropriate, or a combination of them, provided that, by the application of equitable principles, a reasonable result is arrived at.

91.   Equity does not necessarily imply equality. There can never be any question of completely refashioning nature, and equity does not require that a State without access to the sea should be allotted an area of continental shelf, any more than there could be a question of rendering the situation of a State with an extensive coastline similar to that of a State with a restricted coastline. Equality is to be reckoned within the same plane, and it is not such natural inequalities as these that equity could remedy. But in the present case there are three States whose North Sea coastlines are in fact comparable in length and which, therefore, have been given broadly equal treatment by nature except that the configuration of one of the coastlines would, if the equidistance method is used, deny to one of these States treatment equal or comparable to that given the other two. Here indeed is a case where, in a theoretical situation of equality within the same order, an inequity is created. What is unacceptable in this instance is that a State should enjoy continental shelf rights considerably different from those of its neighbours merely because in the one case the coastline is roughly convex in form and in the other it is markedly concave, although those coastlines are comparable in length. It is therefore not a question of totally refashioning geography whatever the facts of the situation but, given a geographical situation of quasi-equality as between a number of States, of abating the effects of an incidental special feature from which an unjustifiable difference of treatment could result.

92.   It has however been maintained that no one method of delimitation can prevent such results and that all can lead to relative injustices. This argument has in effect already been dealt with. It can only strengthen the view that it is necessary to seek not one method of delimitation but one goal. It is in this spirit that the Court must examine the question of how the continental shelf can be delimited when it is in fact the case that the equidistance principle does not provide an equitable solution. As the operation of delimiting is a matter of determining areas appertaining to different jurisdictions, it is a truism to say that the determination must be equitable; rather is the problem above all one of defining the means whereby the delimitation can be carried out in such a way as to be

recognized as equitable. Although the Parties have made it known that they intend to reserve for themselves the application of the principles and rules laid down by the Court, it would, even so, be insufficient simply to rely on the rule of equity without giving some degree of indication as to the possible ways in which it might be applied in the present case, it being understood that the Parties will be free to agree upon one method rather than another, or different methods if they so prefer.

93.   In fact, there is no legal limit to the considerations which States may take account of for the purpose of making sure that they apply equitable procedures, and more often than not it is the balancing-up of all such considerations that will produce this result rather than reliance on one to the exclusion of all others. The problem of the relative weight to be accorded to different considerations naturally varies with the circumstances of the case.

94.   In balancing the factors in question it would appear that various aspects must be taken into account. Some are related to the geological, others to the geographical aspect of the situation, others again to the idea of the unity of any deposits. These criteria, though not entirely precise, can provide adequate bases for decision adapted to the factual situation.

* * *

98.   A final factor to be taken account of is the element of a reasonable degree of proportionality which a delimitation effected according to equitable principles ought to bring about between the extent of the continental shelf appertaining to the States concerned and the lengths of their respective coastlines,—these being measured according to their general direction in order to establish the necessary balance between States with straight, and those with markedly concave or convex coasts, or to reduce very irregular coastlines to their truer proportions. The choice and application of the appropriate technical methods would be a matter for the parties. One method discussed in the course of the proceedings, under the name of the principle of the coastal front, consists in drawing a straight baseline between the extreme points at either end of the Coast concerned, or in some cases a series of such lines. Where the parties wish to employ in particular the equidistance method of delimitation, the establishment of one or more baselines of this kind can play a useful part in eliminating or diminishing the distortions that might result from the use of that method.

99.   In a sea with the particular configuration of the North Sea, and in view of the particular geographical situation of the Parties' coastlines upon that sea, the methods chosen by them for the purpose of fixing the delimitation of their respective areas may happen in certain localities to lead to an overlapping of the areas appertaining to them. The Court considers that such a situation must be accepted as a given fact and resolved either by an agreed, or failing that by an equal division of the overlapping areas, or by agreements for joint exploitation, the latter solution appearing particularly appropriate when it is a question of preserving the unity of a deposit.

Diversion of Water from the Meuse

The Netherlands v. Belgium
Permanent Court of International Justice, 1937
P.C.I.J. Ser. A/B, No. 70, p. 73 (June 28)

■ Individual Opinion of Judge Hudson

While I concur in the judgment of the Court, I should prefer a fuller statement of the reasons for the result reached in regard to one point in this case, and it seems incumbent upon me to add the following observations.

The Netherlands Government has asked the Court to say that the alimentation of certain canals by the Neerhaeren Lock with water taken from the Meuse elsewhere than at Maestricht is contrary to the Treaty of 1863, and to order that Belgium should discontinue that alimentation. On the other hand, the Belgian Government has asked the Court to say that the alimentation of these canals has not become contrary to the Treaty of 1863 by reason of the fact that lock-water discharged by the *bona fide* operation for the passage of boats of the Neerhaeren Lock, which cannot be treated more unfavourably than the Bosscheveld Lock, is confused with water of the Meuse taken by the *prise d'eau* at Maestricht. In its submissions the Belgian Government does not ask the Court to say that the operation of the Bosscheveld Lock results in an alimentation of the canals which constitutes a violation of the Treaty; but the Belgian Agent contends (Counter–Memorial, p. 17) that if the Court should decide that the functioning of the Belgian lock at Neerhaeren is in opposition to the Treaty of 1863, it ought to admit *a fortiori* that the functioning of the Netherlands lock of Bosscheveld is not more regular *(n'est pas non plus regulier).* A further submission of the Belgian Government, offered alternatively *(tres subsidiairement),* asks the Court to say that by the construction of works contrary to the provisions of the Treaty the Netherlands has lost the right to invoke the Treaty against Belgium.

On this presentation of the case, the Court must consider the functioning of the Bosscheveld Lock in connection with that of the Neerhaeren Lock. The first question is, therefore, whether the two locks are to be placed on the same footing.

The Bosscheveld Lock is situated in a short canal which may be referred to as the Bosscheveld canal. This canal leads from the Meuse, at a point below Maestricht and one hundred metres below the *prise d'eau* constructed in execution of Article I of the Treaty of 1863, into the Zuid–Willemsvaart Canal. It is entirely in Netherlands territory. It was opened for the passage of boats in 1931, without any previous agreement with the Belgian Government. As the level of the Zuid–Willemsvaart is lower than that of the Meuse, the Bosscheveld Canal contains [a lock].

* * *

What are widely known as principles of equity have long been considered to constitute a part of international law, and as such they have often been applied by international tribunals. Mérignhac, *Traité théorique et pratique de l'Arbitrage international* (1895), p. 295; Ralston, *Law and Procedure of International Tribunals* (new ed., 1926), pp. 53–57. A sharp division between law and equity, such as prevails in the administration of justice in some States, should find no place in international jurisprudence; even in some national legal systems, there has been a strong tendency towards the fusion of law and equity. Some international tribunals are expressly directed by the *compromise* which control them to apply "law and equity". See the Cayuga Indians Case, Nielsen's Report of the United States–British Claims Arbitration (1926), p. 307. Of such a provision, a special tribunal of the Permanent Court of Arbitration said in 1922 that "the majority of international lawyers seem to agree that these words are to be understood to mean general principles of justice as distinguished from any particular systems of jurisprudence". Proceedings of the United States–Norwegian Tribunal (1922), p. 141. Numerous arbitration treaties have been concluded in recent years which apply to differences "which are justiciable in their nature by reason of being susceptible of decision by the application of the principles of law or equity". Whether the reference in an arbitration treaty is to the application of "law and equity" or to justiciability dependent on the possibility of applying "law or equity", it would seem to envisage equity as a part of law.

The Court has not been expressly authorized by its Statute to apply equity as distinguished from law. Nor, indeed, does the Statute expressly direct its application of international law, though as has been said on several occasions the Court is "a tribunal of international law". Series A, No.7, p. 19; Series A, Nos. 20/21, p. 124. Article 38 of the Statute expressly directs the application of "general principles of law recognized by civilized nations", and in more than one nation principles of equity have an established place in the legal system. The Court's recognition of equity as a part of international law is in no way restricted by the special power conferred upon it "to decide a case *ex aqua et bono,* if the parties agree thereto". Anzilotti, *Corso di Diritto internazionale* (3rd ed., 1928), p. 108; Habicht, *Power of the International Judge to give a Decision* ex aequo et bono (1935), pp. 61 *et seq.*; Lauterpacht, *Private Law Sources and Analogies of International Law* (1927), pp. 63 *et seq.* Cf., Monskhéli, "L'équité en droit international moderne", *40 Revue générale de Droit international public* (1933), p. 347; Strupp, "Le droit du juge international de statuer selon l'équité", 33 *Recueil des Cours* (1930), pp. 357 *et seq.* It must be concluded, therefore, that under Article 38 of the Statute, if not independently of that Article, the Court has some freedom to consider principles of equity as part of the international law which it must apply.

It would seem to be an important principle of equity that where two parties have assumed an identical or a reciprocal obligation, one party which is engaged in a continuing nonperformance of that obligation should not be permitted to take advantage of a similar non-performance of that obligation by the other party. The principle finds expression in the so-called maxims of. equity which exercised great influence in the creative period of the development of the Anglo–American law. Some of these maxims are, "Equality is equity"; "He who seeks equity must do equity". It is in line with such maxims that "a court of equity refuses relief to a plaintiff whose conduct in regard to the subject-matter of the litigation has been improper". 13 Halsbury's *Laws 01 England* (2nd ed., 1934), p. 87. A very similar principle was received into Roman Law. The obligations of a vendor and a vendee being concurrent, "neither could compel the other to 'perform unless he had done, or tendered' his own part". Buckland, *Text Book 01 Roman Law* (2nd ed., 1932), p. 493. The *exceptio non adimpleti contractus* required a claimant to prove that he had performed or offered to perform his obligation. Girard, *Droit romain* (8th ed., 1929), p. 567; Saleilles, in 6 *Annales de Droit commercial,* (1892), p. 287, and 7 *id.* (1893), pp. 24, 97 and 175. This conception was the basis of Articles 320 and 322 of the German Civil Code, and even where a code is silent on the point Planiol states the general principle that "dans tout rapport synallagmatique, chacune des deux parties ne peut exiger la prestation qui lui est due que si elle offre elle-même d'exécuter son obligation". Planiol, *Droit civil,* Vol. 2 (6th ed., 1912), p. 230.

The general principle is one of which an international tribunal should make a very sparing application. It is certainly not to be thought that a complete fulfilment of all its obligations under a treaty must be proved as a condition precedent to a State's appearing before an international tribunal to seek an interpretation of that treaty. Yet, in a proper case, and with scrupulous regard for the limitations which are necessary, a tribunal bound by international law ought not to shrink from applying a principle of such obvious fairness.

On the assumption that the alimentation of canals by the functioning of the Neerhaeren Lock and the Bosscheveld Lock is contrary to the Treaty of 1863, is this a case in which the Court ought to apply the principle referred to? Here the Parties are not before the Court under a special agreement in which they have mutually agreed to seek the Court's interpretation of the Treaty of 1863. This proceeding was instituted by the Netherlands. The jurisdiction of the Court rests on the declarations made by the Parties under paragraph 2 of Article 36 of the Statute. It is the Court's obligatory jurisdiction which is invoked, without challenge by Belgium. If it is important that this jurisdiction should not be attenuated by the action of the Court itself, it is no less important that it be exercised within the limitations which equity imposes. As the moving Party, the Netherlands asks that the Belgian action with respect to the operation of the Neerhaeren Lock be declared contrary to the Treaty of 1863, and that Belgium be ordered to discontinue that action. Yet, in its operation of the Bosscheveld Lock, the Netherlands itself is now engaged in taking precisely similar action, similar in fact and similar in law. This seems to call for an application of the principle of equity stated above.

One result of applying the principle will be that even if the Court should be of the opinion that the Belgian action with regard to the functioning of the Neerhaeren Lock is contrary to the Treaty of 1863, it should nevertheless refuse in this case to order Belgium to discontinue that action. In equity, the Netherlands is not in a position to have such relief decreed to her. Belgium cannot be ordered to discontinue the operation of the Neerhaeren Lock when the Netherlands is left free to continue the operation of the Bosscheveld Lock. The general principle is a sound one that reparation is "the corollary of the violation of the obligations resulting from an engagement between States"; and "it is a principle of international law, and even a general conception of law, that any breach of an engagement involves an obligation to make reparation". Series A, No. 17, pp. 27, 29. Yet, in a particular case in which it is asked to enforce the obligation to make reparation, a court of international law cannot ignore special circumstances which may call for the consideration of equitable principles. Here the Netherlands asks, not for reparation for a past violation of the Treaty of 1863, but for protection against a continuance of that violation in the future. The Court is asked to decree a kind of specific performance of a reciprocal obligation which the demandant itself is not performing. It must clearly refuse to do so.

NOTES AND QUESTIONS

1.   Why do you think the ICJ does not actually identify the source of its rule for the nationality of corporations or the source of its rule that the law must be applied reasonably? Indeed, although general principles may be identified in the decisions of many international courts and tribunals, they are rarely linked to the third primary source of Article 38. Why?

2.   The discussion here has largely ignored the words "recognized by civilized states." While references to "civilized states" is generally a holdover from colonial times when some populations viewed themselves as more "civilized" than others, a few international law scholars insist on retaining the reference to support the position that if a general principle cannot be found in the positive law of a state, it is not a general principle. As Judge Tanaka reveals, however, the drafters of Article 38 disagreed about whether general principles had to be grounded in positive law. Some general principles of importance to the international legal system, such as the equality of states before the law, may not be found in national law and are not demonstrable through customary international law. Can you think of examples of such principles beyond those already mentioned?

3.   Why do you think states do not ask for decisions *ex aequo et bono*?

4.   For further reading on general principles and equity, see, BIN CHENG, GENERAL PRINCIPLES OF LAW AS APPLIED BY INTERNATIONAL COURTS AND TRIBUNALS (1953). See also Chapter 9 for a discussion of international dispute settlement processes and the principles relied upon to ensure fair procedure.

D.   SUBSIDIARY SOURCES AND EVIDENCE

Article 38 of the ICJ Statute refers to three primary sources and equity but also in paragraph (1)(d): "judicial decisions and the teachings of the most highly qualified publicists of the various nations, as subsidiary means for the determination of rules of law." Note that Article 38 does not refer to judicial decisions and writers as "sources" but as means for determining the law emanating from the primary sources. Still, the practice is to call these "subsidiary sources" and in reality we often rely on judges and scholars to identify rules. We cite their opinions and writings and not the underlying evidence of the rule. This is especially true of rules of customary international law and general principles.

Until the middle of the 20th century writers were perhaps more influential than judges in the international system. Justice Gray extols writers in *Paquete Habana* (*supra*):

> [R]esort must be had to the customs and usages of civilized nations; and, as evidence of these, to the works of jurists and commentators, who by years of labor, research and experience, have made themselves peculiarly well acquainted with the subjects of which they treat. Such works are resorted to by judicial tribunals, not for the speculations of their authors concerning what the law ought to be, but for trustworthy evidence of what the law really is.

After making this statement, he goes on to review the work of writers for almost ten pages. Note, however, how Gray refers to the proper use of writers, not as a source of the law but as giving reliable evidence. The Supreme Court in *Paquete Habana* used the works of scholars to confirm the conclusions it drew from assessing evidence first hand. Consider what it looked to to determine state practice and *opinio juris*. Consider, too, the type of evidence used in the interpretation of treaties. How did Tanaka determine that equality before the law was a general principle?

Today the international legal system has a large number of international courts. Judges today in applying international law are more likely to refer to the evidence offered by prior judicial decisions than writers. Indeed, while the ICJ does not have a formal rule of *stare decisis*, its practice is to remain faithful to its prior decisions and to cite them frequently in subsequent decisions.

The one organization in the world where all states may come together and discuss their views on almost any question is the United Nations. The General Assembly brings states together on the basis of equality (each state has one vote). The General Assembly adopts resolutions after debate and by a vote. Votes condemning terrorism, torture, or piracy provide an indication of the legal opinion of many states in the world on a particular subject. For example, well before the 1984 Convention Against Torture was adopted, the General Assembly adopted a Declaration on the Protection of All Persons from Being Subjected to Torture and Other Cruel, Inhuman or Degrading Treatment or Punishment (the "Torture Declaration") by the General Assembly on 9 December 1975 (resolution 3452 (XXX)). This resolution was sometimes cited as the source of a ban on torture. Yet, under the Charter, General Assembly resolutions are not binding except as to internal matters. (See Chapter 3 *infra*.) Under the doctrine of the sources of international law, therefore, when a state joins a resolution, it is engaging in a state practice. Some types of resolutions indicate the official legal opinion of the state as well—such as in the resolution condemning torture.

The ICJ relied on General Assembly resolutions in the *Nicaragua* case as evidence of state practice and *opinio juris*—the elements of rules of custom. We saw the process of analyzing such evidence in the *Paquete Habana* case and the *North Sea Continental Shelf* cases. Some scholars argue that even before a rule of custom "crystallizes" as customary international law, the principle in the making has some binding status— perhaps not unlike the non-binding "gentleman's" agreements discussed above. These scholars use the term "soft law" for such non-binding norms. "Soft law" may emerge from less formal sources than treaty and custom. In this age of global, instant communication, a new norm or principle that is supported all around the world by civil society may not have a place in Article 38, but the need to respect such norms is evident. "Soft law" has been discussed particularly with respect to human rights (*see infra* Chapter 5) and the environment (*see infra* Chapter 6). It may be misleading to refer to non-binding norms as "soft *law*", as one of the essential characteristics of a rule of law is that it may be enforced. Jan Klabbers, *The Redundancy of Soft Law*, 65 Nordic J. Int'l L. 167 (1996). Nevertheless, we have in the world rules in the making, respected guidelines, codes of conduct, resolutions, and the like that play an important role in support of the international community's purposes. Commitment and Compliance, The Role of Non-Binding Norms in the International Legal System (Dinah Shelton ed., 2000).

NOTE AND QUESTIONS

The discussion in this section concerns the evidence looked to prove that a rule meets the test for a treaty, rule of customary international law, or general principle. Most of the discussion focused on rules of customary international law. Courts accept a wide variety of evidence to show the development of state practice and *opinio juris* needed to prove a rule of custom. The judicial decisions excerpted here do not discuss the standard being applied to the evidence. Presumably courts must apply a formal standard to evidence such as the rule that a preponderance of the evidence favors the finding of a customary rule or that the facts must be proven by clear and convincing evidence. In fact, the ICJ has no established rules respecting the evidence it uses:

> Despite over one hundred years of international adjudication, and sixty years of Security Council fact-finding, we cannot point to any well-established set of rules governing evidence in international law * * *. According to Lobel:
>
>> Questions involving the standards and mechanisms for assessing complicated factual inquiries are generally not accorded the same treatment given by the legal academy to the more abstract issues involved in defining relevant international law standards. Unfortunately, international incidents generally involve disputed issues of fact, and in the absence of an international judicial or other

centralized fact-finding mechanism, the ad hoc manner in which nations evaluate factual claims is often decisive.

* * *

The International Court of Justice has no established rules of evidence according to Highet:

> The court's function in establishing the facts consists in its assessing the weight of the evidence produced in so far as is necessary for the determination of the concrete issue which it finds to be the one which it has to decide. For this reason, there is little to be found in the way of rules of evidence, and a striking feature of the jurisprudence is the ability of the Court frequently to base its decision on undisputed facts, and in reducing voluminous evidence to manageable proportions. Generally, in application of the principle *actori incumbit probatio* the court will formally require the party putting forward a claim to establish the elements of facts and of law on which the decision in its favour might be given.

> In the *Nicaragua* case, the International Court of Justice (ICJ) did not enunciate a standard of evidence but did refer to the need for "sufficient proof." By implication this is a standard of convincing evidence. The judgment certainly does not reveal that the ICJ required proof beyond a reasonable doubt. On the other hand, in rejecting some of Nicaragua's claims, the Court appeared to require more than a mere preponderance of the evidence. The United States did not contest the case on the merits. Nicaragua still put in evidence with respect to all its claims; presumably it had a preponderance. Nevertheless, the court felt some of the claims failed. The court held some claims did not meet the requirement that the case be "well founded in fact and law" as required by article 53 of the Court's Statute, governing cases where one party fails to defend.

Mary Ellen O'Connell, *Evidence of Terror*, 7 J. OF CON. & SEC. L. 21, 22–24 (2002) (footnotes omitted). *See also infra* Chapter 9 and the discussion of the operation of international courts and tribunals.

What evidence standard should be associated with the sources of international law? Is it acceptable to rely on subsidiary sources as we do?

E.   PEREMPTORY NORMS (*JUS COGENS*)

The final section of this chapter concerns a category of international legal principles not mentioned in Article 38 of the ICJ Statute. Peremptory norms are the higher norms of international law that may not be changed by treaty. They are perhaps best explained by natural law theory as argued in the excerpt by O'Connell in Chapter 1.

Free Zones of Upper Savoy and the District of Gex

France v. Switzerland
Permanent Court of International Justice, 1932
P.C.I.J., Ser. A/B, No. 46

[France contended that the Treaty of Versailles (1919) abrogated certain tariff-free areas within France, on the border with Switzerland in the region of Geneva. Switzerland claimed that her rights in these areas had been provided in the post-Napoleonic settlement of Europe, by various treaties stemming from the Congress of Vienna, in the years 1814–15. The court found that Switzerland had sufficiently participated in the earlier arrangements as to have acquired rights as to the free zones. It also decided that the Treaty of Versailles was not intended to abrogate these rights. Nevertheless, the court expressed a viewpoint on the question whether the rights that Switzerland might have acquired as a non-party to the 1814–15 treaties could have been taken away by France and other parties to the Versailles treaty, to which Switzerland was not a party. On third party rights the court made a statement which a common law lawyer would call *obiter dictum*. It appears below.]

It cannot be lightly presumed that stipulations favourable to a third State have been adopted with the object of creating an actual right in its favour. There is however nothing to prevent the will of sovereign States from having this object and this effect. The question of the existence of a right acquired under an instrument drawn between other States is therefore one to be decided in each particular case: it must be ascertained whether the States which have stipulated in favour of a third State meant to create for that State an actual right *which the latter has accepted as such*. [Emphasis supplied.]

* * *

Egon Schwelb, Some Aspects of International *Jus Cogens* as Formulated by the International Law Commission

61 Am. J. Int'l L. 946, 949 (1967)

Jurisprudence on International *Jus cogens*.

* * *

In the case of the S.S. Wimbledon the question whether Germany, as a neutral in the Polish–Russian war, was in 1921 under the obligation to permit contraband destined for Poland to pass through the Kiel Canal. The Court decided that Article 380 of the Peace Treaty of Versailles applied, under which the Canal was to be maintained open to the vessels of all nations at peace with Germany. Mr. Schücking, the German national judge, dissented. One of his arguments was the consideration that, by permitting the passage of the ship carrying contraband, Germany would have violated the duties of a neutral. It cannot have been the intention of the victorious states, he said, to bind Germany to commit offenses against third states. It would have been impossible to give effect to such an intention because it is impossible to undertake by treaty a valid obligation to perform acts which would violate the rights of third parties.

Richard D. Kearney and Robert E. Dalton, The Treaty on Treaties

64 AM. J. INT'L L. 495, 535 (1970)

* * * The committee of the whole moved immediately to one of the most controversial articles produced by the Commission—Article 53 on treaties conflicting with a peremptory norm of international law or, as it is customarily described, the *Jus Cogens* Doctrine. The Commission [proposed]: "A treaty is void if it conflicts with a peremptory norm of general international law from which no derogation is permitted and which can be modified only by a subsequent norm of general international law having the same character." Although the principle that there are fundamental requirements of international behavior that cannot be set aside by treaty is considered a fairly recent development, it has been incorporated into Section 116 of the Restatement [of American Foreign Relations Law] in the following terms: "An international agreement may be made with respect to any matter except to the extent that the agreement conflicts with, a) the rules of international law incorporating basic standards of international conduct. * * * " Both the Commission's article and the *Restatement*, however, present the same difficulty: they leave open the question what is a peremptory norm or what is a basic standard of international conduct.

* * *

In his second report Waldock had proposed three categories of *jus cogens*: (a) the use or threat of force in contravention of the principles of the United Nations Charter; (b) international crimes so characterized by international law; (c) acts or omissions whose suppression is required by international law. The discussion in the Commission indicated such varying viewpoints on what constituted *jus cogens* that the categories were dropped. A comment regarding the resulting draft is pertinent: "Mr. Bartos explained that the drafting committee had been compelled to refrain from giving any definition of *jus cogens* whatever, because two-thirds of the Commission had been opposed to each formula proposed." The position in the conference reflected the position in the Commission. There was no substantial attack made upon the concept of *jus cogens*. Indeed, it would be very difficult to make a sustainable case that two states are free to make a treaty in which they agree to attack and carve up a third state or to sell some of their residents to each other as slaves. But as Minagawa points out, "examples such as the treaty permitting piracy or re-establishing slavery appear to concern merely '*une pure hypothèse d'école*'." The real problem was how to define the test for recognizing a rule of *jus cogens*.

* * *

The Austrian jurist, Hanspeter Neuhold, gives in his analysis of the 1968 session a lively account of the conclusion of debate:

> After five meetings had been devoted to discussing the various problems of *jus cogens*, the scene was set for the final showdown at a night meeting which lasted almost till midnight. It was fought with all the weapons which the arsenal of the rules of procedure offered the delegates. Thus, the representative of the USA introduced a motion to defer the vote on article [53] and to refer all amendments to the Drafting Committee with a view to working out a more acceptable text. This proposal was endorsed by the United Kingdom and France. Conversely, the Ghanaian delegate, who was supported by the representatives of India and the USSR, moved to take a vote immediately, since the various delegations had made their positions sufficiently clear. Motions to adjourn the debate and to close the discussion were defeated. Other motions requesting a division of the original United States proposal caused considerable confusion. At last, a roll call was taken on the motion submitted by the USA to defer voting on article [53] and the amendments thereto, which failed to obtain the necessary majority by the narrowest margin possible: 42 votes were cast in favour, the same number against, with 7 abstentions. Ironically enough, if a request by Ghana for priority of her motion to vote at once had been adopted and the votes cast in the same way, the United States motion would have prevailed indirectly * * *. Reference to recognition of *jus cogens* by the national and regional legal systems of the world was rejected. * * *

A dispute then arose as to the meaning of that vote and whether the principle of *jus cogens* had been adopted. The chairman settled the matter by ruling that the *jus cogens* principle had been adopted and that the drafting committee was to see if the text could be made clearer. * * * A peremptory norm was defined as "a norm accepted and recognized by the international community of States as a whole * * *."

Siderman v. Republic of Argentina

United States Court of Appeals, Ninth Circuit
965 F.2d 699 (1992)

■ FLETCHER, CIRCUIT JUDGE:

FACTS

The factual record, which consists only of the Sidermans' complaint and numerous declarations they submitted in support of their claims, tells a horrifying tale of the violent and brutal excesses of an anti-Semitic military junta that ruled Argentina. On March 24, 1976, the Argentine military overthrew the government of President Maria Estela Peron and seized the reins of power for itself, installing military leaders of the central government and the provincial governments of Argentina. That night, ten masked men carrying machine guns forcibly entered the home of Jose and

Lea Siderman, husband and wife, in Tucuman Province, Argentina. The men, who were acting under the direction of the military governor of Tucuman, ransacked the home and locked Lea in the bathroom. They then blindfolded and shackled 65–year old Jose, dragged him out of his home, tossed him into a waiting car, and drove off to an unknown building. For seven days the men beat and tortured Jose. Among their tools of torture was an electric cattle prod, which they used to shock Jose until he fainted. As they tortured him, the men repeatedly shouted anti-Semitic epithets * * *. They inflicted all of these cruelties upon Jose Siderman because of his Jewish faith.

At the end of this nightmarish week, his body badly bruised and his ribs broken, Jose was taken out of the building and driven to an isolated area, where the masked men tossed him out of the car. The men told Jose that if he and his family did not leave Tucuman and Argentina immediately, they would be killed. On the day of Jose's release, he and Lea fled to Buenos Aires in fear for their lives. Their son Carlos followed shortly thereafter, and the night Carlos left Tucuman, military authorities ransacked his home. In June 1976, Jose, Lea, and Carlos left Argentina for the United States, where they joined Susana Siderman de Blake. She is the daughter of Jose and Lea and is a United States citizen.

Before the hasty flight from Tucuman to Buenos Aires, Jose was forced to raise cash by selling at a steep discount part of his interest in 127,000 acres of land. Prior to their departure for the United States, the Sidermans also made arrangements for someone to oversee their family business, Inmobiliaria del No–Oeste, S.A. ("INOSA"), an Argentine corporation. Susana Siderman de Blake, Carlos Siderman and Lea Siderman each owned 33% of INOSA and Jose owned the remaining one percent. Its assets comprised numerous real estate holdings including a large hotel in Tucuman, the Hotel Gran Corona. The Sidermans granted management powers over INOSA to a certified public accountant in Argentina.

After the Sidermans left Argentina for the United States, Argentine military officers renewed their persecution of Jose. They altered real property records in Tucuman to show that he had owned not 127,000, but 127, acres of land in the province. They then initiated a criminal action against him in Argentina, claiming that since he owned only 127 acres he had sold land that did not belong to him. Argentina sought the assistance of our courts in obtaining jurisdiction over his person, requesting via a letter rogatory that the Los Angeles Superior Court serve him with documents relating to the action. The court, unaware of Argentina's motives, complied with the request.

Soon thereafter, while he was travelling in Italy, Jose was arrested pursuant to an extradition request from Argentina to the Italian government. Argentina charged that Jose had fraudulently obtained the travel documents enabling him to leave Argentina in 1976. Jose was not permitted to leave Cremora, Italy, for seven months, and actually was imprisoned for 27 days, before an Italian Appeals Court finally held that Argentina's extradition request would not be honored, as it was politically motivated and founded on pretextual charges.

The Argentine military also pursued INOSA with vigor. In April 1977, INOSA was seized through a sham "judicial intervention," a proceeding in which property is put into receivership. The purported reasons for the intervention were that INOSA lacked a representative in Argentina and that INOSA had obtained excessive funds from a Tucuman provincial bank. Though these reasons were pretexts for persecuting the Sidermans because of their religion and profiting from their economic success, the Sidermans were unable to oppose the intervention because Argentine officials had imprisoned and killed the accountant to whom they had granted management powers over INOSA. In 1978, the Sidermans retained an attorney in Argentina and brought a derivative action in a Tucuman court in an effort to end the intervention. The court ordered that the intervention cease, and the order was upheld by the Supreme Court of Tucuman, but the order remains unenforced and the intervention has continued. Argentine military officials and INOSA's appointed receivers have extracted funds from INOSA, purchased various assets owned by INOSA at sharply discounted prices, and diverted INOSA's profits and revenues to themselves.

In 1982, Jose, Lea, and Carlos, who by then had become permanent residents of the United States, and Susana, a United States citizen since 1967, turned to federal court for relief. They filed a complaint asserting eighteen causes of action based on the torture and harassment of Jose by Argentine officials and the expropriation of their property in Argentina. Named defendants included the Republic of Argentina, the Province of Tucuman, INOSA, and numerous individual defendants who participated in the wrongdoing. In December 1982, the Sidermans properly served Argentina and Tucuman with the Summons and Complaint. The Argentine Embassy subsequently sought assistance from the U.S. State Department, which informed Argentina that it would have to appear and present any defenses it wished to assert to the district court, including the defense of sovereign immunity, or risk a default judgment. The State Department also provided a directory of lawyer referral services. Despite receiving this information, Argentina did not enter an appearance, and the Sidermans filed a motion for default judgment.

On March 12, 1984, the district court dismissed the Sidermans' expropriation claims *sua sponte* on the basis of the act of state doctrine and ordered a hearing for the Sidermans to prove up their damages on the torture claims. The Sidermans moved for reconsideration of the court's dismissal of the expropriation claims. On September 28, 1984, the court denied the motion for reconsideration and entered a default judgment on the torture claims, awarding Jose damages and expenses totalling $2.6 million for his torture claims and awarding Lea $100,000 for her loss of consortium claim.

The damages award finally elicited a response from Argentina, which filed a motion for relief from judgment on the ground that it was immune from suit under the FSIA [Foreign Sovereign Immunity Act, see Chapter 4] and that the district court therefore lacked both subject matter and personal jurisdiction. The United States filed a suggestion of interest, asking the court to consider the issue of foreign sovereign immunity but indicating no view of the merits. On March 7, 1985, the district court vacated the default judgment and dismissed the Sidermans' action on the ground of Argentina's immunity under the FSIA. The Sidermans filed a timely notice of appeal. We have jurisdiction over the appeal pursuant to 28 U.S.C. § 1291. * * *

II.   Torture Claims

The question of Argentina's immunity from the Sidermans' torture claims is squarely presented, without the procedural complications surrounding the district court's treatment of the expropriation claims. The district court dismissed the torture claims on the ground that they fell within no exception to immunity under the FSIA. In defending the district court's decision on appeal, Argentina argues that the Sidermans' claims are foreclosed by the Supreme Court's opinion in *Argentine Republic v. Amerada Hess*.

* * *

A.   *Jus Cogens*

The Sidermans contend that Argentina does not enjoy sovereign immunity with respect to its violation of the *jus cogens* norm of international law condemning official torture. While we agree with the Sidermans that official acts of torture of the sort they allege Argentina to have committed constitute a *jus cogens* violation, we conclude that *Amerada Hess* forecloses their attempt to posit a basis for jurisdiction not expressly countenanced by the FSIA.

As defined in the Vienna Convention on the Law of Treaties, a *jus cogens* norm, also known as a "peremptory norm" of international law, "is a norm accepted and recognized by the international community of states as a whole as a norm from which no derogation is permitted and which can be modified only by a subsequent norm of general international law having the same character." Vienna Convention on the Law of Treaties, art. 53, May 23, 1969, *[hereinafter "Vienna Convention"]; see also* Restatement § 102 Reporter's Note 6. *Jus cogens* is related to customary international law (the direct descendant of the law of nations), which the Restatement defines as the "general and consistent practice of states followed by them from a sense of legal obligation." Restatement § 102(2). Courts ascertain customary international law "by consulting the works of jurists, writing professedly on public law; or by the general usage and practice of nations; or by judicial decisions recognizing and enforcing that law." *U.S. v. Smith,* * * * (Story, J.); *see also The Paquete Habana* * * * (in ascertaining and administering customary international law, courts should resort "to the customs and usages of civilized nations, and, as evidence of these, to the works of jurists and commentators"); *Filartiga v. Pena–Irala* * * * Courts seeking to determine whether a norm of customary international law has attained the status of *jus cogens* look to the same sources, but must also determine whether the international community recognizes the norm as one "from which no derogation is permitted." *Committee of U.S. Citizens Living in Nicaragua v. Reagan* * * * [hereinafter "CUSCLIN"] (quoting Vienna Convention, art. 53). In CUSCLIN, the only reported federal decision to give extended treatment to *jus cogens*, the court described *jus cogens* as an elite subset of the norms recognized as customary international law.

While *jus cogens* and customary international law are related, they differ in one important respect. Customary international law, like international law defined by treaties and other international agreements, rests on the consent of states. A state that persistently objects to a norm of customary international law that other states accept is not bound by that norm, see Restatement § 102 Comment d. just as a state that is not party to an international agreement is not bound by the terms of that agreement. International agreements and customary international law create norms known as *jus dispositivum*, the category of international law that "consists of norms derived from the consent of states" and that is founded "on the self-interest of the participating states * * *." *Jus dispositivum* binds only "those states consenting to be governed by it."

In contrast, *jus cogens* "embraces customary laws considered binding on all nations," * * * and "is derived from values taken to be fundamental by the international community, rather than from the fortuitous or self-interested choices of nations." * * * Whereas customary international law derives solely from the consent of states, the fundamental and universal norms constituting *jus cogens* transcend such consent, as exemplified by the theories underlying the judgments of the Nuremberg tribunals following World War II * * *. The legitimacy of the Nuremberg prosecutions rested not on the consent of the Axis Powers and individual defendants, but on the nature of the acts they committed: acts that the laws of all civilized nations define as criminal * * *. The universal and fundamental rights of human beings identified by Nuremberg-rights against genocide, enslavement, and other inhumane acts * * * are the direct ancestors of the universal and fundamental norms recognized as *jus cogens*. In the words of the International Court of Justice, these norms, which include "principles and rules concerning the basic rights of the human person," are the concern of all states; "they are obligations erga omnes." *The Barcelona Traction* (Belgium v. Spain), 1970 I.C.J. 3, 32.

Because *jus cogens* norms do not depend solely on the consent of states for their binding force, they "enjoy the highest status within international law." COSCLIN. For example, a treaty that contravenes *jus cogens* is considered under international law to be void ab initio. See Vienna Convention, art. 53; Restatement § 102 Comment k. Indeed, the supremacy of *jus cogens* extends over all rules of international law; norms that have attained the status of *jus cogens* "prevail over and invalidate international agreements and other rules of international law in conflict with them." Restatement § 102 Comment k. A *jus cogens* norm is subject to modification or derogation only by a subsequent *jus cogens* norm. *Id.*

The Sidermans claim that the prohibition against official torture has attained the status of a *jus cogens* norm. There is no doubt that the prohibition against official torture is a norm of customary international law, as the Second Circuit recognized more than ten years ago in the landmark case of *Filartiga v. Pena–Irala* * * *. Dr. Filartiga and his daughter, citizens of Paraguay, sued Paraguayan officials who had tortured Dr. Filartiga's son to death. They alleged jurisdiction under the Alien Tort Statute, which grants the district courts "original jurisdiction of any civil action by an alien for a tort only, committed in violation of the law of nations or a treaty of the United States' " 28 U.S.C. § 1350. Dr. Filartiga claimed that the defendants' torture of his son, perpetrated under color of official authority, violated a norm of customary international law prohibiting official torture, and the court agreed. Judge Kaufman, writing for the court, explained that "there are few, if any, issues in international law today on which opinion seems to be so united as the limitations on a state's power to torture persons held in its custody." * * * Judge Kaufman catalogued the evidence in support of this view, citing several declarations of the General Assembly and human rights conventions prohibiting torture, modern municipal law to the same effect, and the works of jurists, and finally concluded "that official torture is now prohibited by the law of nations."

Other authorities have also recognized that official torture is prohibited by customary international law. In *Forti v. Suarez–Mason*, a suit predicated on atrocities committed by the same Argentine military government alleged to be responsible for the torture of Jose Siderman, the district court held that "official torture constitutes a cognizable violation of the law of nations," and described the prohibition against official torture as "universal, obligatory, and definable." Similarly, in *Tel–Oren v. Libyan Arab Republic*, (opinion of Edwards, J.) which involved an action against the Palestine Liberation Organization for its acts of terrorism, Judge Edwards identified torture as a violation of customary international law. Judge Bork, although raising considerable opposition to the application of customary international law in U.S. courts, see *id.* (opinion of Bork, J.), at the same time conceded that the international law prohibition against torture is not disputed. *Id.* The Restatement of Foreign Relations also holds to the view that customary international law prohibits official torture. Restatement § 702(d). Finally, the world now has an international agreement focused specifically on the prohibition against torture: The Convention Against Torture and Other Cruel, Inhuman or Degrading Treatment or Punishment, 39 U.N. GAOR Supp. (No. 51), 23 I.L.M. 1027 (1984) [hereinafter "Torture Convention"], which entered into force on June 26, 1987. The United States signed the Torture Convention in April 1988, the United States Senate gave its advice and consent in October 1988, see 136 Cong. Rec. S 17486–92 (daily ed. October 27, 1990), and it now awaits the President's filing of the instrument of ratification with the Secretary–General of the United Nations.

In light of the unanimous view of these authoritative voices, it would be unthinkable to conclude other than that acts of official torture violate customary international law. And while not all customary international law carries with it the force of a *jus cogens* norm, the prohibition against official torture has attained that status. In CUSCLIN, the D.C. Circuit announced that torture is one of a handful of acts that constitute violations of *jus cogens*. In *Filartiga*, though the court was not explicitly considering *jus cogens*, Judge Kaufman's survey of the universal condemnation of torture provides much support for the view that torture violates *jus cogens*. In Judge Kaufman's words, "[a]mong the rights universally proclaimed by all nations, as we have noted, is the right to be free of physical torture." Supporting this case law is the Restatement, which recognizes the prohibition against official torture, as one of only a few *jus cogens* norms. Restatement § 702 Comment n (also identifying *jus cogens* norms prohibiting genocide, slavery, murder or causing disappearance of individuals, prolonged arbitrary detention, and systematic racial discrimination). Finally, there is widespread agreement among scholars that the prohibition against official torture has achieved the status of a *jus cogens* norm * * *.

Given this extraordinary consensus, we conclude that the right to be free from official torture is fundamental and universal, a right deserving of the highest status under international law, a norm of *jus cogens*. The crack of the whip, the damp of the thumb screw, the crush of the iron maiden, and, in these more efficient modern times, the shock of the electric cattle prod are forms of torture that the international order will not tolerate. To subject a person to such horrors is to commit one of the most egregious violations of the personal security and dignity * * *. That states engage in official torture cannot be doubted, but all states believe it is wrong, all that engage in torture deny it, and no state claims a sovereign right to torture its own citizens. See *Filartiga*, * * * (noting that no contemporary state asserts "a right to torture its own or another nation's citizens"); at n. 15 ("The fact that the prohibition against torture is often honored in the breach does not diminish its binding effect as a norm of international law."). Under international law, any state that engages in official torture violates *jus cogens*.

The question in the present case is what flows from the allegation that Argentina tortured Jose Siderman and thereby violated a *jus cogens* norm. The Sidermans contend that when a foreign state's act violates *jus cogens*, the state is not entitled to sovereign immunity with respect to that act. This argument begins from the principle that *jus cogens* norms "enjoy the highest status within international law," CUSCLIN, [*supra*] and thus "prevail over and invalidate * * * other rules of international law in conflict with them," Restatement § 102 Comment k. The Sidermans argue that since sovereign immunity itself is a principle of international law, it is trumped by *jus cogens*. In short, they argue that when a state violates *jus cogens*, the cloak of immunity provided by international law falls away, leaving the state amenable to suit. *[For the sovereign immunity discussion in Siderman, see Chapter 4, infra].*

* * *

* * * [W]e conclude that if violations of *jus cogens* committed outside the United States are to be exceptions to immunity, Congress must make them so. The fact that there has been a violation of *jus cogens* does not confer jurisdiction under the FSIA.

* * *

The district court erred in dismissing the Sidermans' torture claims.

CONCLUSION

The Sidermans' complaint and the evidence they have presented in support of their allegations paint a horrifying portrait of anti-Semitic, government-sponsored tyranny. The record that so far has been developed in this case reveals no ground for shielding Argentina from the Sidermans' claims that their family business was stolen from them by the military junta that took over the Argentine government in 1976. It further suggests that Argentina has implicitly waived its sovereign immunity with respect to the Sidermans' claims for torture.

We REVERSE and REMAND.

Barcelona Traction, Light and Power Company, Limited

Belgium v. Spain
International Court of Justice
1970 I.C.J. Rep. 3 (Second Phase) (Judgment of Feb. 5)

32.   In these circumstances it is logical that the Court should first address itself to what was originally presented as the subject-matter of the third preliminary objection: namely the question of the right of Belgium to exercise diplomatic protection of Belgian shareholders in a company which is a juristic entity incorporated in Canada, the measures complained of having been taken in relation not to any Belgian national but to the company itself.

33.   When a State admits into its territory foreign investments or foreign nationals, whether natural or juristic persons, it is bound to extend to them the protection of the law and assumes obligations concerning the treatment to be afforded them. These obligations, however, are neither absolute nor unqualified. In particular, an essential distinction should be drawn between the obligations of a State towards the international community as a whole, and those arising vis-à-vis another State in the field of diplomatic protection. By their very nature the former are the concern of all States. In view of the importance of the rights involved, all States can be held to have a legal interest in their protection; they are obligations *erga omnes*.

34.   Such obligations derive, for example, in contemporary international law, from the outlawing of acts of aggression, and of genocide, as also from the principles and rules concerning the basic rights of the human person, including protection from slavery and racial discrimination. Some

of the corresponding rights of protection have entered into the body of general international law *(Reservations to the Convention on the Prevention and Punishment of the Crime of Genocide, Advisory Opinion, I.C.J. Reports 1951,* p. 23); others are conferred by international instruments of a universal or quasi-universal character.

35.   Obligations the performance of which is the subject of diplomatic protection are not of the same category. It cannot be held, when one such obligation in particular is in question, in a specific case, that all States have a legal interest in its observance. In order to bring a claim in respect of the breach of such an obligation, a State must first establish its right to do so, for the rules on the subject rest on two suppositions:

> "The first is that the defendant State has broken an obligation towards the national State in respect of its nationals. The second is that only the party to whom an international obligation is due can bring a claim in respect of its breach." *(Reparation for Injuries Suffered in the Service of the United Nations, Advisory Opinion, I.C.J. Reports 1949,* pp. 181–182.)

In the present case it is therefore essential to establish whether the losses allegedly suffered by Belgian shareholders in Barcelona Traction were the consequence of the violation of obligations of which they were the beneficiaries. In other words: has a right of Belgium been violated on account of its nationals' having suffered infringement of their rights as shareholders in a Company not of Belgian nationality?

36.   Thus it is the existence or absence of a right, belonging to Belgium and recognized as such by international law, which is decisive for the problem of Belgium's capacity.

> "This right is necessarily limited to intervention [by a State] on behalf of its own nationals because, in the absence of a special agreement, it is the bond of nationality between the State and the individual which alone confers upon the State the right of diplomatic protection, and it is as a part of the function of diplomatic protection that the right to take up a claim and to ensure respect for the rules of international law must be envisaged." *(Panevezys–Saldutiskis Railway, Judgment, 1939, P.C.I. J., Series A/B, No. 76,* p. 16.)

It follows that the same question is determinant in respect of Spain's responsibility towards Belgium. Responsibility is the necessary corollary of a right. In the absence of any treaty on the subject between the Parties, this essential issue has to be decided in the light of the general rules of diplomatic protection.

NOTES AND QUESTIONS

1. *Siderman* was settled generously in Siderman's favor just before trial. *See* N.Y. TIMES, Sept. 14, 1996 and N.Y. TIMES, Sept. 2, 1996. In *Committee of U.S. Citizens Living in Nicaragua v. Reagan,* 859 F.2d 929, 940 (D.C. Cir. 1988) The Court said: "*Jus cogens* describes peremptory norms of law,

which are nonderogable and form the highest level of international law." The case is discussed further in Chapters 9 and 11.

2. The ICJ in *Barcelona Traction* never mentions *jus cogens*. Could the norms it refers to as being subject to *erga omnes* claims (the prohibitions on aggression, genocide, slavery, and racism) come from an Article 38 source? What is the problem with trying to derive such norms from the sources listed in Article 38? The ICJ does mention *jus cogens* in the *Nicaragua* case but only to indicate the U.S. sees UN Charter Article 2(4) prohibiting force as a *jus cogens* norm. Does this reference offer at least tacit support by the court for this category of legal principles?

3. See Paul Tavernier, *L'identification des règles fondamentales, un probléme résolu?* and Stefan Kadelbach, *Jus cogens, Obligations* Erga Omnes *and other Rules—The Identification of Fundamental Norms in* THE FUNDAMENTAL RULES OF THE INTERNATIONAL LEGAL ORDER, *JUS COGENS* AND *ERGA OMNES* 1, 21 (Christian Tomuschat and Jean–Marc Thouvenin eds., 2006). Both authors take the view that while there is widespread acceptance of *jus cogens*, the international legal community lacks consensus on many aspects of the category. Tavernier concludes optimistically that the indeterminacy surrounding *jus cogens* may in fact be a help, not a hindrance to future development.

4. Greek courts have faced the issue posed in *Siderman* and found that states responsible for committing *jus cogens* violations do not enjoy immunity from national court jurisdiction. See Case No. 11/2000. Aerios Pagos (Hellenic Supreme Court), May 4, 2000. *See also* Bernard H. Oxman, Maria Gavouneli & Ilias Bantekas, *Sovereign Immunity—Tort Exception—Jus cogens Violations—World War II Reparations—International Humanitarian Law,* 95 AM. J. INT'L L. 198 (2001). Italian courts agreed with this Greek finding and sought to enforce awards against Germany for international crimes committed during the Second World War. Germany has sought a decision of the International Court of Justice on the question. *See Jurisdictional Immunities of the State* (Germany v. Italy), 2008 I.C.J. Rep. (Application of Germany) (Dec. 23).

The Inter–American Commission on Human Rights has found a *jus cogens* norm prohibiting the use of the death penalty to punish crimes committed by juveniles. The Michael Domingues Case: Report of the Inter–American Commission on Human Rights (Report No. 62/02, Merits, Case 12.285, Michael Domingues/United States, Oct. 22, 2002).

The International Criminal Tribunal for Yugoslavia held that a *jus cogens* norm against torture was superior to national law. Prosecutor v. Furundžija, Case IT–95–17/1 (Appeals Chamber, International Tribunal for the Former Yugoslavia 2002).

And in an advisory opinion on the rights of migrant workers, Judge Antonio A. Cançado Trindade explained that the juridical foundation of his concurring opinion was the natural law. He invoked the fathers of international law, Vitoria, Suarez, and Grotius, all of whom recognized international law's central concern with the human being and law's authority based in the natural law: "To Grotius, natural law derives from human reason, is a 'dictate of the *recta ratio*', and imposes limits to the 'unrestricted conduct of the rule of the States. The States are subjected to Law, and International Law has an objective, independent foundation, and above the will of the States." Inter–American Court of Human Rights, Advisory Opinion on the *Judicial Condition and Rights of the Undocumented Migrants,* Concurring Opinion of Judge A.A. Cançado Trindade at 3, citing E. Jimenez de Arechaga, "El Legado de Grocio y el Concepto de un Orden Internacional Justo", in I PENSAMIENTO JURIDICIO Y SOCIEDAD INTERNACIONAL–LIBRO-HOMENAJE AL PROFESOR A. TRUYOL Y SERRA 608, 612–613, 617 (Universidad Complutense de Madrid 1986).

5.   Can you tell from the readings and notes why *jus cogens* and natural law theory in general are heavily contested? Who should decide what a *jus cogens* norm is? What is a theory for their change and development? Is there sufficient evidence of the category? What role does such a category of principles play in a legal system?

6.   For further reading on *jus cogens,* see Alexander Orakhelashvili, Peremptory Norms in International Law (2006) and Lauri Hannikainen, Peremptory Norms (Jus Cogens) in International Law, Historical Development, Criteria, Present Status (1988).

CHAPTER 3

SUBJECTS OF INTERNATIONAL LAW

Section A. States.
    1. Rights and Duties of States.
    2. Elements of Statehood.
    3. Recognition.
    4. Self–Determination.
Section B. Non-state Actors.
    1. Individuals.
    2. Communities and Groups.
    3. Corporations, Vessels, and Vehicles.
Section C. International Organizations.
    1. Creation and Attributes of International Organizations.
    2. Law–Making by International Organizations.
    3. Responsibility and Control of International Organizations.

By now you have seen that international law touches all possible actors subject to the law—states, individuals, groups, and organizations of all kinds. Some traditionalists will insist that international law began with and retained a narrow focus on states until the second half of the 20th century when human rights law became a major subfield. Any perusal of Grotius's writing, however, gives a different impression. As Judge Cançado Trindade observed on the previous page, Grotius makes plain that the purpose of supra-national rules is the welfare of human beings and communities. *See also*, Mark W. Janis, *Individuals as Subjects of International Law*, 17 CORNELL INT'L L. J. 61 (1984). With the rise of the state system in the 17th century and the birth of theories of state sovereignty in the 18th century, some scholars did lose sight of the human beings for whose welfare all law exists. By the middle of the 20th century, however, individuals, groups, and other non-state actors were again at center stage, along with states. Non-state actors are also generally subject to national law as well as international law. This fact can and does lead to conflicts of law and the need for coordination among the international, regional, and national legal systems. This chapter will look at the three major categories of actors subject to international law, but the main focus will be on states and inter-governmental organizations—how international law defines them and what their primary rights and duties are. Chapters 5 and 7 will look more closely at the rights and duties of non-state actors. Chapter 4 looks at the international legal principles for avoiding conflicts.

A. STATES

Louis Henkin, International Law: Politics, Values and Functions*

pp. 29–30 (1990)

Who is a State?

A system of States implies that a "State" can be defined, or, at least, that the system knows a State when it sees one. Princes needed no definition; they knew each other. When Statehood gradually succeeded princehood, there was no need to define a State: in the early days of the modern system, the original members—nations governed by princes—were in place and remained (unless swallowed up by conquest or agreement). Later entries into the system resulted from fission or fusion: by breaking away from existing States and establishing independence (e.g., the United States in 1776, and other countries in Europe and Latin America in the nineteenth and early twentieth centuries); by forming a State out of several States or of non-States (as with unifications in Italy and Germany or the Austro–Hungarian Empire); or, later, by coming into the system from the outside (usually from Asia or Africa).

Both in the day of nations governed by princes and later in the age of States, one might have described—defined—the entities composing the system by their obvious characteristics. Scholars developed such a definition, and, since what *is,* often becomes what *ought to be,* the description acquired normative character. Half a century ago, a number of American States adopted such a descriptive-normative definition by international agreement:

> "The State as a person of international law should possess the following qualifications: *(a)* a permanent population; *(b)* a defined territory; *(c)* a Government; and *(d)* capacity to enter into relations with the other States."

The first three elements—population, territory, and Government—seem to be not requisite qualifications, but descriptions of States as we know them. Capacity to conduct foreign relations is an inter-State addition for inter-State purposes. That definition with minor variations is accepted as law. The definition of a State is ordinarily not important; it acquires significance when definition is invoked to influence events. For example, a part of a State seeking to secede and desiring acceptance by the international system will assert its Statehood by pointing to its population and its territory, its Government and its capacity to enter into relations with other

---

* Footnotes omitted.

States; the State resisting secession may deny the qualifications of the entity aspiring to Statehood; other States may resort to the definition to support their acceptance of (or their refusal to accept) the secession. Or, States, having created an organization—such as the United Nations—in which they saw fit to limit membership to States only, may resort to the definition in debatable cases, with States supporting the admission of an entity to membership as well as States resisting such admission invoking the definition to support their position.

Emerich de Vattel, The Law of Nations or the Principles of Natural Law

pp. 3–6, 11 (Charles G. Fenwick, trans. of the 1758 ed. (1916))

Idea and General Principles of the Law of Nations.

Nations or States are political bodies, societies of men who have united together and combined their forces, in order to procure their mutual welfare and security.

Such a society has its own affairs and interests; it deliberates and takes resolutions in common, and it thus becomes a moral person having an understanding and a will peculiar to itself, and susceptible at once of obligations and of rights.

The object of this work is to establish on a firm basis the obligations and the rights of Nations. The *Law of Nations* is *the science of the rights which exist between Nations or States, and of the obligations corresponding to these rights.*

It will be seen from this treatise how States, as such, ought to regulate their actions. We shall examine the obligations of a Nation towards itself as well as towards other Nations, and in this way we shall determine the rights resulting from those obligations; for since a right is nothing else but the power of doing what is morally possible, that is to say, what is good in itself and conformable to duty, it is clear that right is derived from duty, or passive obligation, from the obligation of acting in this or that manner. A Nation must therefore understand the nature of its obligations, not only to avoid acting contrary to its duty, but also to obtain therefrom a clear knowledge of its rights, of what it can lawfully exact from other Nations.

Since Nations are composed of men who are by nature free and independent, and who before the establishment of civil society lived together in the state of nature, such Nations or sovereign States must be regarded as so many free persons living together in the state of nature.

Proof can be had from works on the *natural law* that liberty and independence belong to man by his very nature, and that they can not be taken from him without his consent. Citizens of a State, having yielded them in part to the sovereign, do not enjoy them to their full and absolute extent. But the whole body of the Nation, the State, so long as it has not voluntarily submitted to other men or other Nations, remains absolutely free and independent.

As men are subject to the laws of nature, and as their union in civil society can not exempt them from the obligation of observing those laws, since in that union they remain none the less men, the whole Nation, whose common will is but the outcome of the united wills of the citizens, remains subject to the laws of nature and is bound to respect them in all its undertakings. And since *right* is derived from *obligation,* as we have just remarked, a Nation has the same rights that nature gives to men for the fulfillment of their duties.

We must therefore apply to nations the rules of the natural law to discover what are their obligations and their rights; hence the *Law of Nations* is in its origin merely the *Law of Nature applied to Nations.* Now the just and reasonable application of a rule requires that the application be made in a manner suited to the nature of the subject; but we must not conclude that the Law of Nations is everywhere and at all points the same as the natural law, except for a difference of subjects, so that no other change need be made than to substitute Nations for individuals. A civil society, or a State, is a very different subject from an individual person, and therefore, by virtue of the natural law, very different obligations and rights belong to it in most cases. The same general rule, when applied to two different subjects, can not result in similar principles, nor can a particular rule, however just for one subject, be applicable to a second of a totally different nature. Hence there are many cases in which the natural law does not regulate the relations of States as it would those of individuals. We must know how to apply it conformably to its subjects; and the art of so applying it, with a precision founded upon right reason, constitutes of the Law of Nations a distinct science.

We use the term *necessary Law of Nations* for that law which results from applying the natural law to Nations. It is *necessary,* because Nations are absolutely bound to observe it. It contains those precepts which the natural law dictates to States, and it is no less binding upon them than it is upon individuals. For States are composed of men, their policies are determined by men, and these men are subject to the natural law under whatever capacity they act. This same law is called by Grotius and his followers the *internal Law of Nations,* inasmuch as it is binding upon the conscience of Nations. Several writers call it the *natural Law of Nations.*

Since, therefore, the necessary Law of Nations consists in applying the natural law to states, and since the natural law is not subject to change, being founded on the nature of things and particularly upon the nature of man, it follows that the necessary Law of Nations is not subject to change.

Since this law is not subject to change and the obligations which it imposes are necessary and indispensable, Nations can not alter it by agreement, nor individually or mutually release themselves from it.

It is by the application of this principle that a distinction can be made between lawful and unlawful treaties or conventions and between customs which are innocent and reasonable and those which are unjust and deserving of condemnation.

Things which are just in themselves and permitted by the necessary Law of Nations may form the subject of an agreement by Nations or may be given sacredness and force through practice and custom. Indifferent affairs may be settled either by treaty, if Nations so please, or by the introduction of some suitable custom or usage. But all treaties and customs contrary to the dictates of the necessary Law of Nations are unlawful. We shall see, however, that they are not always conformable to the *inner* law of conscience, and yet, for reasons to be given in their proper place, such conventions and treaties are often valid by the *external* law. Owing to the freedom and independence of Nations, the conduct of one Nation may be unlawful and censurable according to the laws of conscience, and yet other Nations must put up with it so long as it does not infringe upon their perfect rights. The liberty of a Nation would not remain complete if other Nations presumed to inspect and control its conduct; a presumption which would be contrary to the natural law, which declares every Nation free and independent of all other Nations.

Such is man's nature that he is not sufficient unto himself and necessarily stands in need of the assistance and intercourse of his fellows, whether to preserve his life or to perfect himself and live as befits a rational animal. Experience shows this clearly enough. We know of men brought up among bears, having neither the use of speech nor of reason, and limited like beasts to the use of the sensitive faculties. We observe, moreover, that nature has denied man the strength and the natural weapons with which it has provided other animals, and has given him instead the use of speech and of reason, or at least the ability to acquire them by intercourse with other men. Language is a means of communication, of mutual assistance, and of perfecting man's reason and knowledge; and, having thus become intelligent, he finds a thousand means of caring for his life and its wants. Moreover, every man realizes that he could not live happily or improve his condition without the help of intercourse with other men. Therefore, since nature has constituted men thus, it is a clear proof that it means them to live together and mutually to aid and assist one another.

From this source we deduce a natural society existing among all men. The general law of this society is that each member should assist the others in all their needs, as far as he can do so without neglecting his duties to himself—a law which all men must obey if they are to live conformably to their nature and to the designs of their common Creator; a law which our own welfare, our happiness, and our best interests should render sacred to each one of us. Such is the general obligation we are under of performing our duties; let us fulfill them with care if we would work wisely for our greatest good.

It is easy to see how happy the world would be if all men were willing to follow the rule we have just laid down. On the other hand, if each man thinks of himself first and foremost, if he does nothing for others, all will be alike miserable. Let us labor for the good of all men; they in turn will labor for ours, and we shall build our happiness upon the firmest foundations.

Since the universal society of the human race is an institution of nature itself, that is, a necessary result of man's nature, all men of whatever condition are bound to advance its interests and to fulfill its duties. No convention or special agreement can release them from the obligation. When, therefore, men unite in civil society and form a separate State or Nation they may, indeed, make particular agreements with others of the same State, but their duties towards the rest of the human race remain unchanged; but with this difference, that when men have agreed to act in common, and have given up their rights and submitted their will to the whole body as far as concerns their common good, it devolves thenceforth upon that body, the State, and upon its rulers, to fulfill the duties of humanity towards outsiders in all matters in which individuals are no longer at liberty to act, and it peculiarly rests with the State to fulfill these duties towards other States. * * * [T]hat men, when united in society, remain subject to the obligations of the Law of Nature. This society may be regarded as a moral person, since it has an understanding, a will, and a power peculiar to itself; and it is therefore obliged to live with other societies or States according to the laws of the natural society of the human race, just as individual men before the establishment of civil society lived according to them; with such exceptions, however, as are due to the difference of the subjects.

The end of the natural society established among men in general is that they should mutually assist one another to advance their own perfection and that of their condition; and Nations, too, since they may be regarded as so many free persons living together in a state of nature, are bound mutually to advance this human society. Hence the end of the great society established by nature among all nations is likewise that of mutual assistance in order to perfect themselves and their condition.

* * *

Nations or Sovereign States.

A Nation or a State, as we have already said in the introduction, is a political body, a society of men who have united together and combined their forces in order to procure their mutual welfare and security.

From the fact that this group of men forms a society in which they have common interests and must act in concert it is necessary that a public authority be set up, which shall regulate and prescribe the duties of each member with respect to the object of the association. This public authority constitutes the *sovereignty;* and he, or they, in whom it is vested is the *sovereign.*

We observe that by the act of civil or political association each citizen subjects himself to the authority of the whole body in all that relates to the common good. This authority is therefore an essential characteristic of the political body or State, but its exercise may be intrusted to different hands, as the society may prescribe.

If the body of the people reserve to itself the sovereign authority or the right to rule, the government is a popular one, a *democracy*; if it intrust this power to a certain number of citizens, to a Senate, it constitutes itself as an *aristocratic* republic; lastly, if it vest the sovereign authority in one individual, the State becomes a *monarchy*.

These three kinds of government can be variously combined and modified. We shall not enter into details here, for that is the province of *general public law*. It will answer for the purposes of this work: to lay down the general principles required to decide questions which may arise between Nations.

Every Nation which governs itself, under whatever form, and which does not depend on any other Nation, is a *sovereign State*. Its rights are, in the natural order, the same as those of every other State. Such is the character of the moral persons who live together in a society established by nature and subject to the Law of Nations. To give a Nation the right to a definite position in this great society, it need only be truly sovereign and independent; it must govern itself by its own authority and its own laws.

1. RIGHTS AND DUTIES OF STATES

United Nations   A/RES/25/2625

 General Assembly   Distr: General
                                                         24 October 1970

Twenty-fifth session
Agenda item 85
Resolutions adopted by the General Assembly
[Adopted on a Report from the Sixth Committee (A/8082)]
2625 (XXV). Declaration on Principles of International Law concerning Friendly Relations and Co-operation among States in accordance with the Charter of the United Nations

* * *

The General Assembly,

Reaffirming in the terms of the Charter of the United Nations that the maintenance of international peace and security and the development of friendly relations and co-operation between nations are among the fundamental purposes of the United Nations,

Recalling that the peoples of the United Nations are determined to practise tolerance and live together in peace with one another as good neighbours,

Bearing in mind the importance of maintaining and strengthening international peace founded upon freedom, equality, justice and respect for fundamental human rights and of developing friendly relations among nations irrespective of their political, economic and social systems or the levels of their development,

Bearing in mind also the paramount importance of the Charter of the United Nations in the promotion of the rule of law among nations,

Considering that the faithful observance of the principles of international law concerning friendly relations and co-operation among States and the fulfillment in good faith of the obligations assumed by States, in accordance with the Charter, is of the greatest importance for the maintenance of international peace and security and for the implementation of the other purposes of the United Nations,

* * *

1.   Solemnly proclaims the following principles:

The principle that States shall refrain in their international relations from the threat or use of force against the territorial integrity or political independence of any State or in any other manner inconsistent with the purposes of the United Nations

Every State has the duty to refrain in its international relations from the threat or use of force against the territorial integrity or political independence of any State, or in any other manner inconsistent with the purposes of the United Nations. Such a threat or use of force constitutes a violation of international law and the Charter of the United Nations and shall never be employed as a means of settling international issues.

A war of aggression constitutes a crime against the peace, for which there is responsibility under international law.

In accordance with the purposes and principles of the United Nations, States have the duty to refrain from propaganda for wars of aggression.

Every State has the duty to refrain from the threat or use of force to violate the existing international boundaries of another State or as a means of solving international disputes, including territorial disputes and problems concerning frontiers of States.

Every State likewise has the duty to refrain from the threat or use of force to violate international lines of demarcation, such as armistice lines, established by or pursuant to an international agreement to which it is a party or which it is otherwise bound to respect. Nothing in the foregoing shall be construed as prejudicing the positions of the parties concerned with regard to the status and effects of such lines under their special regimes or as affecting their temporary character.

States have a duty to refrain from acts of reprisal involving the use of force.

Every State has the duty to refrain from any forcible action which deprives peoples referred to in the elaboration of the principle of equal rights and self-determination of their right to self-determination and freedom and independence.

Every State has the duty to refrain from organizing or encouraging the organization of irregular forces or armed bands including mercenaries, for incursion into the territory of another State.

Every State has the duty to refrain from organizing, instigating, assisting or participating in acts of civil strife or terrorist acts in another State or acquiescing in organized activities within its territory directed towards the commission of such acts, when the acts referred to in the present paragraph involve a threat or use of force.

The territory of a State shall not be the object of military occupation resulting from the use of force in contravention of the provisions of the Charter. The territory of a State shall not be the object of acquisition by another State resulting from the threat or use of force. No territorial acquisition resulting from the threat or use of force shall be recognized as legal. Nothing in the foregoing shall be construed as affecting:

a.   Provisions of the Charter or any international agreement prior to the Charter regime and valid under international law; or

b.   The powers of the Security Council under the Charter.

All States shall pursue in good faith negotiations for the early conclusion of a universal treaty on general and complete disarmament under effective international control and strive to adopt appropriate measures to reduce international tensions and strengthen confidence among States.

All States shall comply in good faith with their obligations under the generally recognized principles and rules of international law with respect to the maintenance of international peace and security, and shall endeavour to make the United Nations security system based on the Charter more effective.

Nothing in the foregoing paragraphs shall be construed as enlarging or diminishing in any way the scope of the provisions of the Charter concerning cases in which the use of force is lawful.

The principle that States shall settle their international disputes by peaceful means in such a manner that international peace and security and justice are not endangered

Every State shall settle its international disputes with other States by peaceful means in such a manner that international peace and security and justice are not endangered.

States shall accordingly seek early and just settlement of their international disputes by negotiation, inquiry, mediation, conciliation, arbitration, judicial settlement, resort to regional agencies or arrangements or other peaceful means of their choice. In seeking such a settlement the parties shall agree upon such peaceful means as may be appropriate to the circumstances and nature of the dispute.

The parties to a dispute have the duty, in the event of failure to reach a solution by any one of the above peaceful means, to continue to seek a settlement of the dispute by other peaceful means agreed upon by them.

States parties to an international dispute, as well as other States shall refrain from any action which may aggravate the Situation so as to endanger the maintenance of international peace and security, and shall act in accordance with the purposes and principles of the United Nations.

International disputes shall be settled on the basis of the Sovereign equality of States and in accordance with the Principle of free choice of means. Recourse to, or acceptance of, a settlement procedure freely agreed to by States with regard to existing or future disputes to which they are parties shall not be regarded as incompatible with sovereign equality.

Nothing in the foregoing paragraphs prejudices or derogates from the applicable provisions of the Charter, in particular those relating to the pacific settlement of international disputes.

The principle concerning the duty not to intervene in matters within the domestic jurisdiction of any State, in accordance with the Charter

No State or group of States has the right to intervene, directly or indirectly, for any reason whatever, in the internal or external affairs of any other State. Consequently, armed intervention and all other forms of interference or attempted threats against the personality of the State or against its political, economic and cultural elements, are in violation of international law.

No State may use or encourage the use of economic political or any other type of measures to coerce another State in order to obtain from it the subordination of the exercise of its sovereign rights and to secure from it advantages of any kind. Also, no State shall organize, assist, foment, finance, incite or tolerate subversive, terrorist or armed activities directed towards the violent overthrow of the regime of another State, or interfere in civil strife in another State.

The use of force to deprive peoples of their national identity constitutes a violation of their inalienable rights and of the principle of non-intervention.

Every State has an inalienable right to choose its political, economic, social and cultural systems, without interference in any form by another State.

Nothing in the foregoing paragraphs shall be construed as reflecting the relevant provisions of the Charter relating to the maintenance of international peace and security.

The duty of States to co-operate with one another in accordance with the Charter

States have the duty to co-operate with one another, irrespective of the differences in their political, economic and social systems, in the various spheres of international relations, in order to maintain international peace and security and to promote international economic stability and progress, the general welfare of nations and international co-operation free from discrimination based on such differences.

* * *

States should co-operate in the economic, social and cultural fields as well as in the field of science and technology and for the promotion of international cultural and educational progress. States should co-operate in the promotion of economic growth throughout the world, especially that of the developing countries.

The principle of equal rights and self-determination of peoples

By virtue of the principle of equal rights and self-determination of peoples enshrined in the Charter of the United Nations, all peoples have the right freely to determine, without external interference, their political status and to pursue their economic, social and cultural development, and every State has the duty to respect this right in accordance with the provisions of the Charter.

Every State has the duty to promote, through joint and separate action, realization of the principle of equal rights and self-determination of peoples, in accordance with the provisions of the Charter, and to render assistance to the United Nations in carrying out the responsibilities entrusted to it by the Charter regarding the implementation of the principle * * *.

Every State has the duty to promote through joint and separate action universal respect for and observance of human rights and fundamental freedoms in accordance with the Charter.

The establishment of a sovereign and independent State, the free association or integration with an independent State or the emergence into any other political status freely determined by a people constitute modes of implementing the right of self-determination by that people.

Every State has the duty to refrain from any forcible action which deprives peoples referred to above in the elaboration of the present principle of their right to self-determination and freedom and independence. In their actions against, and resistance to, such forcible action in pursuit of the exercise of their right to self-determination, such peoples are entitled to seek and to receive support in accordance with the purposes and principles of the Charter.

The territory of a colony or other Non–Self–Governing Territory has, under the Charter, a status separate and distinct from the territory of the State administering it; and such separate and distinct status under the Charter shall exist until the people of the colony or Non–Self–Governing Territory have exercised their right of self-determination in accordance with the Charter, and particularly its purposes and principles.

Nothing in the foregoing paragraphs shall be construed as authorizing or encouraging any action which would dismember or impair, totally or in part, the territorial integrity or political unity of sovereign and independent States conducting themselves in compliance with the principle of equal rights and self-determination of peoples as described above and thus possessed of a government representing the whole people belonging to the territory without distinction as to race, creed or colour.

Every State shall refrain from any action aimed at the partial or total disruption of the national unity and territorial integrity of any other State or country.

The principle of sovereign equality of States

All States enjoy sovereign equality. They have equal rights and duties and are equal members of the international community, notwithstanding differences of an economic, social, political or other nature.

In particular, sovereign equality includes the following elements:

a.   States are judicially equal;

b.   Each State enjoys the rights inherent in full sovereignty;

c.   Each State has the duty to respect the personality of other States;

d.   The territorial integrity and political independence of the State are inviolable;

e.   Each State has the right freely to choose and develop its political, social, economic and cultural systems;

f.   Each State has the duty to comply fully and in good faith with its international obligations and to live in peace with other States.

The principle that States shall fulfil in good faith the obligations assumed by them in accordance with the Charter

Every State has the duty to fulfil in good faith the obligations assumed by it in accordance with the Charter of the United Nations.

Every State has the duty to fulfil in good faith its obligations under the generally recognized principles and rules of international law.

Every State has the duty to fulfil in good faith its obligations under international agreements valid under the generally recognized principles and rules of international law.

Where obligations arising under international agreements are in conflict with the obligations of Members of the United Nations under the Charter of the United Nations, the obligations under the Charter shall prevail.

* * *

2.   ELEMENTS OF STATEHOOD

There is general agreement that only those entities with certain characteristics including territory, population, and a government with capacity to enter into international relations qualify as states. These characteristics are often referred to as the "Montevideo" factors in reference to a treaty that never entered into force on the definition of statehood.

Montevideo Convention on the Rights and Duties of States

December 26, 1933

* * *

ARTICLE 1

The state as a person of international law should possess the following qualifications: a) a permanent population; b) a defined territory; c) government; and d) capacity to enter into relations with the other states.

ARTICLE 2

The federal state shall constitute a sole person in the eyes of international law.

ARTICLE 3

The political existence of the state is independent of recognition by the other states. Even before recognition the state has the right to defend its integrity and independence, to provide for its conservation and prosperity, and consequently to organize itself as it sees fit, to legislate upon its interests, administer its services, and to define the jurisdiction and competence of its courts.

The exercise of these rights has no other limitation than the exercise of the rights of other states according to international law.

ARTICLE 4

States are juridically equal, enjoy the same rights, and have equal capacity in their exercise. The rights of each one do not depend upon the power which it possesses to assure its exercise, but upon the simple fact of its existence as a person under international law.

ARTICLE 5

The fundamental rights of states are not susceptible of being affected in any manner whatsoever.

ARTICLE 6

The recognition of a state merely signifies that the state which recognizes it accepts the personality of the other with all the rights and duties determined by international law. Recognition is unconditional and irrevocable.

ARTICLE 7

The recognition of a state may be express or tacit. The latter results from any act which implies the intention of recognizing the new state.

ARTICLE 8

No state has the right to intervene in the internal or external affairs of another.

ARTICLE 9

The jurisdiction of states within the limits of national territory applies to all the inhabitants.

Nationals and foreigners are under the same protection of the law and the national authorities and the foreigners may not claim rights other or more extensive than those of the nationals.

ARTICLE 10

The primary interest of states is the conservation of peace. Differences of any nature which arise between them should be settled by recognized pacific methods.

[Articles 11–16 omitted.]

* * *

The Montevideo Convention embodies the "declaratory theory." Under this theory the factors are enough for an entity to qualify as a state. Recognition by other states is only "declaratory" of a fact established in international law. By contrast, the "constitutive theory" holds that recognition is what constitutes an entity a state. The preference by the international community for one theory or the other has changed over time. Today the clearest proof of statehood is membership in the United Nations. All members are characterized by the Montevideo factors, but they have also been voted into membership into the United Nations, which only admits states. Today, one can be sure that all members of the United Nations are states.

United Nations Charter

Article 3

The original Members of the United Nations shall be the states which, having participated in the United Nations Conference on International Organization at San Francisco, or having previously signed the Declaration by United Nations of 1 January 1942, sign the present Charter and ratify it in accordance with Article 110.

Article 4

1. Membership in the United Nations is open to all other peace-loving states which accept the obligations contained in the present Charter and, in the judgment of the Organization, are able and willing to carry out these obligations.

2. The admission of any such state to membership in the United Nations will be effected by a decision of the General Assembly upon the recommendation of the Security Council.

Charter of the Organization of American States

Article 9

States are juridically equal, enjoy equal rights and equal capacity to exercise these rights, and have equal duties. The rights of each State depend not upon its power to ensure the exercise thereof, but upon the mere fact of its existence as a person under international law.

Statute of the International Court of Justice

Article 34(1)

Only states may be parties in cases before the Court.

———————

There are many entities that have all the factors of statehood but are plainly not states, at least not ones that will become members of the United Nations—the subunits of a federation for example, such as the 50 U.S. States, Bavaria in the Federal Republic of Germany or Victoria in Australia. The European Union (EU) is not a member of the United Nations. Most would agree it is not a state, but it is also more than an international organization. We briefly introduce the EU below in the discussion of international organizations because that is how it began its existence. It is probably safest to say in 2009 that the EU is a *sui generis* entity. Then there are entities that wish to become states, but other states are opposed to allowing membership in the UN, this was the case in 2009 of, for example, Taiwan, Palestine, and Kosovo. Other entities plainly do not have all the criteria to be states and likely never will, but they have some indicia of statehood that gives them more status than entities with fewer or no indicia of statehood. The Holy See and Andorra are two examples. The next case reveals the importance of recognition in the attainment of statehood. Just artificially creating the Montevideo factors should not be sufficient.

In re Citizenship of X

Federal Republic of Germany, Administrative Court of Cologne, 1978
Report by Stefan Riesenfeld 77 Am. J. Int'l L. 160 (1983)

Plaintiff, a German citizen by birth, obtained a document, issued on August 26, 1975, conferring upon him citizenship of the "Duchy of Sealand." The so-called Duchy consists of a former anti-aircraft platform, erected by the United Kingdom approximately 8 nautical miles off its southern coast, outside its [then] territorial waters. The platform rests on strong pillars connecting it with the seabed, and it has an area of approximately 1,300 square meters. The British forces abandoned the installation after the end of World War II, and in 1967 a British army officer, Major R.B., took possession and proclaimed it the Duchy of Sealand. Major R.B. issued a constitution for his territory, assuming the title of Roy of Sealand.

At present, 106 persons are citizens of the Duchy of Sealand, and 40 persons reside on it. Plaintiff occupies the office of Minister of Foreign Affairs and President of the State Council.

Plaintiff instituted proceedings for a declaratory judgment establishing loss of his German nationality by virtue of his having acquired the citizenship of a foreign nation. The court dismissed the action for the reason that the Duchy of Sealand did not qualify as a foreign state under international law and therefore could not confer foreign nationality so as to warrant loss of German citizenship in accordance with the German Law on Nationality of 1913.

The court held that to constitute a state under international law three essential attributes had to be present, territory, population, and government. The Duchy of Sealand lacked at least two of these. First, territory must consist of a naturally created portion of the earth's surface and not of a man-made island. Second, population denotes a group of persons leading a common life and forming a living-community, a bond that did not exist among the citizens of the Duchy of Sealand, not even among the 40 persons staying on the platform.

This case is another unsuccessful attempt to establish a new state on an artificial island in order to escape the laws of the coastal state. Similar efforts in Italy and the United States have also failed.

----

a. THE TERRITORIAL ELEMENT IN STATEHOOD

The existence of a state is conditioned upon its occupation of a defined area. Territory often correlates with the other organic requirements for statehood: the requirement of a defined population and the requirement of a government in control of it.

Acquisition of land territory. Historically, competition for the acquisition of land territory has been a main feature of international relations and the source of bitter and violent conflicts as well. Conquest was a common and legally recognized form of acquisition of title to territory. This method has been unlawful since the adoption of the UN Charter in 1945, and the conquest of one state by another has come to an end since then. In 1991, Iraq tried to conquer Kuwait but was repulsed by a combined military effort, involving almost the entire international community. Today, the use of force is still used to try to enforce boundary claims or to secede. It cannot be said, therefore, that the use of force has been entirely excluded from state control of territory. It has, however, ended for the purpose of conquest. Similarly, territory occupied in warfare is not subject to acquisition. (These rules on the use of force are discussed in detail in Chapter 10.) The current prohibition on conquest does not mean, however, that the many states that exist today as a result of conquest must find some way to re-establish title to territory. International law incorporates a principle known as "intertemporal law." Vaughan Lowe explains it in the context of territory:

The Legal effect of conduct is to be determined in accordance with the law as it was at the time of the conduct. For example, since the outlawing in the mid-twentieth century of the use of force in international relations it has been unlawful to gain territory by the use of force (even force used in self-defence). But large areas of the globe were incorporated into the States of which they are now part as a result of use of force. According to the doctrine, however, if territory could lawfully be gained by force at the time that those areas were acquired by force, the State had and still has good title to them.

VAUGHAN LOWE, INTERNATIONAL LAW 140 (2007). Do you think the ICJ's new concept of evolutionary interpretation (mentioned in Chapter 2 above) affects intertemporal law when it comes to acquisition of territory?

Another important change in this area is the frequent use by states of the International Court of Justice and arbitral tribunals to resolve boundary disputes. One brief look at the Website of the ICJ reveals that boundary disputes are the most common category of case that reaches the court (www.icj-cij.org.) Judicial settlement of boundary disputes is an effective and rational way to clarify title to territory and is in keeping with the obligation to settle disputes peacefully. Many boundary disputes and title questions are, of course, also settled by negotiated agreement. Some of these settlements feature voluntary relinquishment of territory or relinquishment in exchange for payment, including in-kind payment in the form of land swaps.

Discovery, once a major means of land acquisition, is no longer possible for lack of land to discover. All known land is owned by one state or another, except for the Antarctic continent. Antarctica, once subject to various claims, including discovery and sectorial longitudinal projections, is immunized from national territorial claims by an "internationalizing" agreement, the Antarctic Treaty of December 1, 1959, 12 U.S.T. 794, 402 U.N.T.S. 71. The Arctic is not land, but, as it is said in Russian, "the Northern Frozen Ocean." Areas beyond national jurisdiction, including Antarctica, the Arctic, the oceans, outer space and celestial bodies will be considered in Chapter 6, *infra*.

While the "age of discovery" and acquisition of territory by discovery is over, that period has left the world with many undefined boundaries. European explorers "discovered" lands outside Europe, claimed them for their national states, proceeded to establish colonies, and to administer them. Few places in the world are any longer formally designated "colonies." In 2009, the United Nations was monitoring about 16 "non-self-governing territories." See also the discussion below of the right of self-determination. For those states that emerged from colonialism, determining boundaries and title to territory has been a common challenge. The ICJ has resolved many such disputes and now has a well-developed jurisprudence on the determination of post-colonial boundaries. For Central American boundaries it began applying the principle *uti posseditis juris*, which is explained in the case below. Similar principles are evident in the settlement of African boundary disputes, see *Kasikili/Sedudu Island* (Botswana/Namibia) 1999 I.C.J. Rep. 1045 and in Asian disputes, see *Sovereignty over Pulau Ligitan and Pulau Sipadan* (Indonesia/Malaysia) 2002 I.C.J. Rep. 625.

In addition to land territory states also have title and rights to certain maritime and air space appurtenant to the land. These areas are also discussed in Chapter 6. For a detailed discussion of how states have come into existence, see JAMES CRAWFORD, THE CREATION OF STATES IN INTERNATIONAL LAW (2d ed. 2006).

The Island of Palmas Case (or Miangas)
United States of America v. The Netherlands
Award of the Tribunal, The Hague, 4 April 1928

[Under the peace treaty that ended the Spanish–American War of 1898, the Treaty of Paris, Spain handed over to the U.S. most of its remaining overseas possessions. The Netherlands protested the inclusion of one island near the Philippines, however, claiming it belonged to the Netherlands. The U.S. and the Netherlands agreed to resolve the conflicting claims through arbitration before a sole arbitrator.]

* * *

The *title alleged by the United States of America* as constituting the immediate foundation of its claim is that of cession, brought about by the Treaty of Paris, which cession transferred all rights of sovereignty which Spain may have possessed in the region indicated in Article III of the said Treaty and therefore also those concerning the Island of Palmas (or Miangas).

It is evident that Spain could not transfer more rights than she herself possessed. This principle of law is expressly recognized in a letter dated April 7th, 1900, from the Secretary of State of the United States to the Spanish Minister at Washington concerning a divergence of opinion which arose about the question whether two islands claimed by Spain as Spanish territory and lying just outside the limits traced by the Treaty of Paris were to be considered as included in, or excluded from the cession. This letter * * * contains the following passage: "The metes and bounds defined in the treaty were not understood by either party to limit or extend Spain's right of cession. Were any island within those described bounds ascertained to belong in fact to Japan, China, Great Britain or Holland, the United States could derive no valid title from its ostensible inclusion in the Spanish cession. The compact upon which the United States negotiators insisted was that all Spanish title to the archipelago known as the Philippine Islands should pass to the United States—no less or more than Spain's actual holdings therein, but all. This Government must consequently hold that the only competent and equitable test of fact by which the title to a disputed cession in that quarter may be determined is simply this: 'Was it Spain's to give? If valid title belonged to Spain, it passed; if Spain had no valid title, she could convey none.'"

Whilst there existed a divergence of views as to the extension of the cession to certain Spanish islands outside the treaty limits, it would seem that the cessionary Power never envisaged that the cession * * * should comprise territories on which Spain had not a valid title, though falling within the limits traced by the Treaty. It is evident that whatever may be the right construction of a treaty, it cannot be interpreted as disposing of the rights of independent third Powers.

* * *

The essential point is therefore whether the Island of Palmas (or Miangas) at the moment of the conclusion and coming into force of the Treaty of Paris formed a part of the Spanish or Netherlands territory. The United States declares that Palmas (or Miangas) was Spanish territory and denies the existence of Dutch sovereignty; the Netherlands maintain the existence of their sovereignty and deny that of Spain.

* * *

It is admitted by both sides that international law underwent profound modifications between the end of the Middle–Ages and the end of the 19th century, as regards the rights of discovery and acquisition of uninhabited regions or regions inhabited by * * * semi-civilised peoples. Both Parties are also agreed that a juridical fact must be appreciated in the light of the law contemporary with it, and not of the law in force at the time when a dispute in regard to it arises or falls to be settled. The effect of discovery by Spain is therefore to be determined by the rules of international law in force in the first half of the 16th century—or (to take the earliest date) in the first quarter of it, i.e. at the time when the Portuguese or Spaniards made their appearance in the Sea of Celebes.

If the view most favourable to the American arguments is adopted— with every reservation as to the soundness of such view—that is to say, if we consider as positive law at the period in question the rule that discovery as such, i.e. the mere fact of seeing land, without any act, even symbolical, of taking possession, involved *ipso jure* territorial sovereignty and not merely an "inchoate title", a *jus ad rem*, to be completed eventually by an actual and durable taking of possession within a reasonable time, the question arises whether sovereignty yet existed at the critical date, i.e. the moment of conclusion and coming into force of the Treaty of Paris.

As regards the question which of different legal systems prevailing at successive periods is to be applied in a particular case (the so-called intertemporal law), a distinction must be made between the creation of rights and the existence of rights. The same principle which subjects the act creative of a right to the law in force at the time the right arises, demands that the existence of the right, in other words its continued manifestation, shall follow the conditions required by the evolution of law. International law in the 19th century, having regard to the fact that most parts of the globe were under the sovereignty of States members of the community of nations, and that territories without a master had become relatively few, took account of a tendency already existing and especially developed since the middle of the 18th century, and laid down the principle that occupation, to constitute a claim to territorial sovereignty, must be effective, that is, offer certain guarantees to other States and their nationals. It seems therefore incompatible with this rule of positive law that there should be regions which are neither under the effective sovereignty of a State, nor without a master, but which are reserved for the exclusive influence of one State, in virtue solely of a title of acquisition which is no longer recognized by existing law, even if such a title ever conferred territorial sovereignty. For these reasons, discovery alone, without any subsequent act, cannot at the present time suffice to prove sovereignty over the Island of Palmas (or Miangas); and in so far as there is no sovereignty, the question of an abandonment properly speaking of sovereignty by one State in order that the sovereignty of another may take its place does not arise.

If on the other hand the view is adopted that discovery does not create a definitive title of sovereignty, but only an "inchoate" title, such a title exists, it is true, without external manifestation. However, according to the view that has prevailed at any rate since the 19th century, an inchoate title of discovery must be completed within a reasonable period by the effective occupation of the region claimed to be discovered. This principle must be applied in the present case, for the reasons given above in regard to the rules determining which of successive legal systems is to be applied (the so-called intertemporal law). Now, no act of occupation nor, except as to a recent period, any exercise of sovereignty at Palmas by Spain has been alleged. But even admitting that the Spanish title still existed as inchoate in 1898 and must be considered as included in the cession under Article III of the Treaty of Paris, an inchoate title could not prevail over the continuous and peaceful display of authority by another State; for such display may prevail even over a prior, definitive title put forward by another State.

* * *

FOR THESE REASONS the Arbitrator, in conformity with Article I of the Special Agreement of January 23rd, 1925, DECIDES that:

THE ISLAND OF PALMAS (or MIANGAS) forms in its entirety a part of Netherlands territory.

Done at The Hague, this fourth day of April 1928.

MAX HUBER, Arbitrator.

Land, Island and Maritime Frontier Dispute

El Salvador/Honduras; Nicaragua intervening
International Court of Justice
1992 I.C.J. Rep. 350 (Judgment of Sept. 11)

GENERAL INTRODUCTION

27.   * * * [T]he dispute brought before the present Chamber [of five judges] * * * is composed of three main elements: the dispute over the land

boundary; the dispute over the legal situation of the islands; and the dispute over the legal situation of the maritime spaces. * * *

28.   The two Parties (and the intervening State) are States which came into existence with the break-up of the Spanish Empire in Central America, and their territories correspond to administrative sub-divisions of that empire. While it was from the outset accepted that the new international boundaries should be determined by the application of the principle generally accepted in Spanish America of the *uti possidetis juris,* whereby the boundaries were to follow the colonial administrative boundaries, the problem, as in the case of many other boundaries in the region, was to determine where those boundaries actually lay. In the words of the 1933 Award of the Arbitral Tribunal presided over by Chief Justice Charles Evans Hughes in the case concerning the border between Guatemala and Honduras, in which the task of the arbitrator was to determine the "juridical line" of the "*uti possidetis* of 1821":

> "It must be noted that particular difficulties are encountered in drawing the line of '*uti possidetis* of 1821', by reason of the lack of trustworthy information during colonial times with respect to a large part of the territory in dispute. Much of this territory was unexplored. Other parts which had occasionally been visited were but vaguely known. In consequence, not only had boundaries of jurisdiction not been fixed with precision by the Crown, but there were great areas in which there had been no effort to assert any semblance of administrative authority." (United Nations, *Reports of International Arbitral Awards,* Vol. II, p. 1325.)

29.   The independence of Central America from the Spanish Crown was proclaimed on 15 September 1821. Thereafter until 1839, Honduras and El Salvador made up, together with Costa Rica, Guatemala and Nicaragua, the Federal Republic of Central America, which broadly corresponded to what had formerly been the Spanish Captaincy–General of Guatemala, or Kingdom of Guatemala. On the disintegration of the Federal Republic, El Salvador and Honduras, along with the other component States, became, and have since remained, separate States.

30.   It was in respect of the islands of the Gulf of Fonseca, all of which had been under Spanish sovereignty, that a dispute first became manifest. In 1854 there was a proposal that the Consul of the United States of America might purchase from Honduras land on the island of El Tigre. El Salvador, by a diplomatic Note of 12 October 1854, referred to this proposal, to which it objected, and made a clear claim to the islands * * *, where certain survey operations by Honduras had come to its notice. No response by Honduras to this communication has been produced, but no sale of islands was proceeded with.

31.   Seven years later, on 14 May 1861, the El Salvador Minister for Foreign Relations addressed a Note to the Government of Honduras proposing that negotiations be entered into to demarcate the lands of [certain villages in El Salvador and Honduras] * * *. This may be taken to mark the inception of the dispute over the land boundary, which subse-

quently expanded to extend to practically the whole land frontier at different dates between 1880 and 1972. The tripoint between the territories of Guatemala, Honduras and El Salvador, from which the boundary between the latter two States runs to the Gulf of Fonseca, was finally agreed only in 1935, after the arbitration of Chief Justice Hughes already referred to * * *.

32.   The maritime dispute was slower to come to light. An attempt was made in 1884 to delimit the waters of the Gulf [of Fonseca] between El Salvador and Honduras, by the inclusion of such a delimitation in a boundary convention, the Cruz–Letona Convention of 1884, which was however not ratified by Honduras, but the negotiation of this Convention enabled both Parties to indicate the nature of their claims. A delimitation of part of the waters of the Gulf was concluded between Nicaragua and Honduras in 1900 * * *. In 1916 proceedings were brought by El Salvador against Nicaragua before the Central American Court of Justice, which raised the question of the status of the waters of the Gulf. Subsequently with the development of the law of the sea, each Party modified its maritime legislation so as to indicate claims as to the legal régime of the waters outside the Gulf.

33.   The dispute—particularly the land boundary dispute—has over the years been the subject of a number of direct negotiations between the Parties in conferences, starting with the El Mono Conference in July 1861 * * * [The Chamber goes on to detail the many attempts at a negotiated settlement.]

35.   In 1969 a series of border incidents occurred, which gave rise to tension between the two countries, the suspension of diplomatic and consular relations and, finally, armed conflict, which lasted from 14 to 18 July 1969. After one hundred hours of hostilities, the Organization of American States succeeded in bringing about a cease-fire and the withdrawal of troops; nevertheless the formal state of war between the two States was to persist for more than ten years. * * *

36.   * * * On 6 October 1976 there was concluded in Washington a "Convention for the Adoption of a Mediation Procedure between the Republics of El Salvador and Honduras", under the auspices of the Organization of American States, and the former President of the International Court of Justice, José Luis Bustamante y Rivero, was chosen as Mediator, the procedure of mediation to be conducted in Lima, Peru. The mediation process began on 18 January 1978 and led to the conclusion of a General Treaty of Peace, signed on 30 October 1980 in Lima, which was ratified by El Salvador on 21 November 1980 and by Honduras on 8 December 1980. [The General Treaty of Peace contained provisions that eventually resulted in a Chamber of the ICJ being asked to resolve the remaining land, island and maritime disputes between El Salvador and Honduras.]

THE LAND BOUNDARY: INTRODUCTION

40.   Both Parties are agreed that the primary principle to be applied for the determination of the land frontier is the *uti possidetis juris* * * *.

For Honduras the norm of international law applicable to the dispute is simply the *uti possidetis juris*; El Salvador, relying on the terms of Article 26 of the General Treaty of Peace, strongly contests that this is the sole law applicable, and invokes, as well as the *uti possidetis juris*, what have been variously called "arguments of a human nature" or "*effectivités*", to be examined further on in this Judgment.

41.   There can be no doubt about the importance of the *uti possidetis juris* principle as one which has, in general, resulted in certain and stable frontiers throughout most of Central and South America, or about the applicability of that principle to the land boundary between the Parties in the present case. Nevertheless these certain and stable frontiers are not the ones that find their way before international tribunals for decision. These latter frontiers are almost invariably the ones in respect of which *uti possidetis juris* speaks for once with an uncertain voice. It can indeed almost be assumed that boundaries which, like the ones in this case, have remained unsettled since independence, are ones for which the *uti possidetis juris* arguments are themselves the subject of dispute. It is not a matter of surprise, therefore, that the Chamber has not found these land-frontier questions easy to determine; and it may be useful briefly to indicate some of the considerations that have tended to be common to the sectors submitted to the Chamber.

42.   The meaning of the principle of *uti possidetis juris* is authoritatively stated in the Judgment of the Chamber in the *Frontier Dispute* case:

> "The essence of the principle lies in its primary aim of securing respect for the territorial boundaries at the moment when independence is achieved. Such territorial boundaries might be no more than delimitations between different administrative divisions or colonies all subject to the same sovereign. In that case, the application of the principle of *uti possidetis* resulted in administrative boundaries being transformed into international frontiers in the full sense of the term." (*I.C.J. Reports* 1986, p. 566, para. 23.)

* * * Thus the principle of *uti possidetis juris* is concerned as much with title to territory as with the location of boundaries; certainly a key aspect of the principle is the denial of the possibility of *terra nullius*.

* * *

44.   Neither Party has * * * produced any legislative or similar material indicating specifically, with the authority of the Spanish Crown, the extent of the territories and the location of the boundaries of the relevant provinces in each area of the land boundary. Both Parties have instead laid before the Chamber numerous documents, of different kinds, some of which, referred to collectively as "titles" *(titulos),* concern grants of land in the areas concerned by the Spanish Crown, from which, it is claimed, the provincial boundaries can be deduced. Some of these actually record that a particular landmark or natural feature marked the boundary of the provinces at the time of the grant; but for the most part this is not so, and the

Chamber is asked, in effect, to conclude, in the absence of other evidence of the position of a provincial boundary, that where a boundary can be identified between the lands granted by the authorities of one province and those granted by the authorities of the neighbouring province, this boundary may be taken to have been the provincial boundary and thus the line of the *uti possidetis juris*. Thus it was the territorial aspect of that principle rather than its boundary aspect that was the one mainly employed by both Parties in their arguments before the Chamber. The location of boundaries seemed often, in the arguments of the Parties, to be incidental to some "claim", or "title", or "grant", respecting a parcel of territory, within circumambient boundaries only portions of which are now claimed to form an international boundary. It is rather as if the disputed boundaries must be constructed like a jig-saw puzzle from certain already cut pieces so that the extent and location of the resulting boundary depend upon the size and shape of the fitting piece.

* * *

46. The six disputed sectors of the land boundary are merely breaks in the continuity of the boundary of which seven sectors were agreed in the General Peace Treaty of 1980 * * *. Nevertheless, no argument was addressed to the Chamber by either Party concerning the compatibility of a claimed boundary with that already agreed in the General Treaty of Peace and to which each sector of the claimed boundary must be joined at one or both ends. Moreover, no information has been vouchsafed to the Chamber about the particular reasons which determined those parts of the common boundary which were agreed in the General Treaty of Peace, and which are to be continued by the claimed boundary. In the circumstances the Chamber is entitled to assume that the agreed boundary was arrived at applying principles and processes similar to those urged upon the Chamber by the Parties for the non-agreed sectors. In this connection the Chamber also observes the predominance of local features, particularly rivers, in the definition of the agreed sectors, and considers that given the task of delimitation, it is entitled and bound to have an eye to the topography of each land sector. When therefore the very many instruments cited, even after minute examination, are found to give no clear and unambiguous indication, the Chamber has felt it right similarly to take some account of the suitability of certain topographical features to provide an identifiable and convenient boundary. The Chamber is here appealing not so much to any concept of "natural frontiers", but rather to a presumption underlying the boundaries on which the *uti possidetis juris* operates. Considerations of this kind have been a factor in boundary-making everywhere, and accordingly are likely, in cases otherwise dubious, to have been a factor also with those who made the provincial boundaries previous to 1821.

47. The 1980 General Treaty of Peace does not specify the criteria employed for the determination of the sectors of the land boundary which were recorded in it as already agreed. There is however a link between the task of the Chamber and the task of the Joint Frontier Commission initially entrusted by the General Treaty of Peace with the delimitation of

the non-agreed sectors; this link is provided by the reference in Article 5 of the Special Agreement itself to the provisions of that Peace Treaty. That Article provides:

> "In accordance with the provisions of the first paragraph of Article 38 of the Statute of the International Court of Justice, the Chamber, when delivering its Judgment, will take into account the rules of international law applicable between the Parties, including, where pertinent, the provisions of the General Treaty of Peace."

This reference to the rules of international law and to the "first paragraph" of Article 38 obviously excludes the possibility of any decision *ex aequo et bono*. The reference to the General Treaty of Peace which, as a treaty between the Parties, would in any event have to be applied by the Chamber by reason of Article 38 of the Court's Statute is presumably intended to make it clear to the Chamber that it should also apply, "where pertinent", even those Articles which in the Treaty are addressed specifically to the Joint Frontier Commission. The treaty provision that has played the greatest part in the pleadings before the Chamber is Article 26. It reads:

* * *

[Translation]

> "For the delimitation of the frontier line in areas subject to controversy, the Joint Frontier Commission shall take as a basis the documents which were issued by the Spanish Crown or by any other Spanish authority, whether secular or ecclesiastical, during the colonial period, and which indicate the jurisdictions or limits of territories or settlements. It shall also take account of other evidence and arguments of a legal, historical, human or any other kind, brought before it by the Parties and admitted under international law."

48.   * * * [I]t seems to the Chamber to be doubtful whether any list of priorities of one kind of evidence over another can properly be read into this very general provision. It is very clear, however, that the kind of evidence first referred to in Article 26, namely documents indicating the jurisdictions or limits of territories or settlements, is directed to establishing the boundaries according to the *uti possidetis juris* of 1821; even though that principle is not expressly mentioned in either the Special Agreement or the General Treaty of peace.

* * *

57.   As already mentioned above, El Salvador contends that the *uti possidetis juris* principle is the primary, but not the only, legal element to be taken into consideration for the determination of the land boundary. It has put forward in addition in that respect a body of arguments referred to either as "arguments of a human nature" or as arguments based on *"effectivités"*. In terms of the governing texts, the justification for invoking these human arguments or *effectivités* is the second part of Article 26 of the 1980 General Treaty of Peace, already quoted above, which provides that

the Joint Frontier Commission "shall also take into account other evidence and arguments of a legal, historical, human or any other kind, brought before it by the Parties and admitted under international law". Honduras also recognizes a certain confirmatory role for *effectivités,* and has submitted evidence of acts of administration of its own for that purpose, or to show that its own *effectivités* in the areas concerned were stronger than those of El Salvador; but at this stage of the Chamber's analysis, it will be convenient to examine in particular certain arguments of El Salvador.

58. The factual considerations which El Salvador has brought to the attention of the Chamber fall into two categories. On the one hand, there are arguments and material relating to demographic pressures in El Salvador creating a need for territory, as compared with the relatively sparsely populated Honduras; and on the other the superior natural resources (e.g., water for agriculture and hydroelectric power) said to be enjoyed by Honduras. On the first point, El Salvador apparently does not claim that a frontier deriving from the principle of the *uti possidetis juris* could be adjusted subsequently (except by agreement) on the grounds of unequal population density, and this is clearly right. It will be recalled that the Chamber in the *Frontier Dispute* case emphasized that even equity *infra legem,* a recognized concept of international law, could not be resorted to in order to modify an established frontier inherited from colonization, whatever its deficiencies (see *I.C.J. Reports 1986,* p. 633, para. 149). El Salvador claims that such an inequality existed even before independence, and that its ancient possession of the territories in dispute, "based on historic titles, is also based on reasons of crucial human necessity". The Chamber will not lose sight of this dimension of the matter; but it is one without direct legal incidence. For the *uti possidetis juris,* the question is not whether the colonial province needed wide boundaries to accommodate its population, but where those boundaries actually were; and post-independence *effectivités,* where relevant, have to be assessed in terms of actual events, not their social origins. As to the argument of inequality of natural resources, the Court, in the case concerning the *Continental Shelf (Tunisia/Libyan Arab Jamahiriya),* took the view that economic considerations of this kind could not be taken into account for the delimitation of the continental shelf areas appertaining to two States *(I.C.J. Reports 1982,* p. 77, para. 107); still less can they be relevant for the determination of a land frontier which came into existence on independence.

59. A further category of considerations urged by El Salvador relates to the alleged occupation of the disputed areas by Salvadorian citizens, their ownership of land in those areas, the supply of public services there by the Government of El Salvador, and its exercise there of judicial, administrative and political competences, and military jurisdiction. * * * These claims by El Salvador relate both to areas which it asserts appertain to it on the basis of the *uti possidetis juris* boundary derived from consideration of *titulos ejidales,* and to areas lying outside the lands comprised in those *titulos.* It appears however that El Salvador no longer maintains the far-reaching reliance on administrative control and *effectivités* presented in its Reply and quoted in the preceding paragraph; at the

hearings, its counsel contended only that *effectivités* could be taken into account to confirm the *titulos ejidales,* or independently of them, in some marginal areas of limited size, where there is no such applicable title.

60.   Honduras rejects the applicability of any argument of "effective control"; it suggests that that concept only refers, in the terms of the Arbitral Award in the Guatemala/Honduras arbitration * * *, to administrative control during the period prior to independence, based on the will of the Crown of Spain, and that El Salvador's theory of "administrative control" is anachronistic. So far as acts of administrative control subsequent to independence are concerned, Honduras considers that, at least since 1884, no acts of sovereignty in the disputed areas can be relied on in view of the duty to respect the status quo in an area of dispute. It has however presented considerable material (as an Annex to its Reply) to show that Honduras also can rely on arguments of a human kind, that there are "human settlements" of Honduran nationals in the disputed areas in all six sectors, and that various judicial and other authorities of Honduras have exercised and are exercising their functions in those areas. This material has been presented under such headings as: criminal proceedings; police or security; appointment of Deputy Mayors; public education; payment of salaries of employees and remuneration to public officials; land concessions; transfer or sale of immovable property; registration of births; registration of deaths; and miscellaneous, including parish baptismal records.

61.   Both Parties have invoked, in relation to this claim of El Salvador, the analysis in the Judgment of the Chamber of the Court in the *Frontier Dispute* case of the relationship between "titles" and "*effectivités*" *(I.C.J. Reports 1986,* pp. 586–587, para. 63). As already noted above, the Chamber in that case was dealing with the "colonial effectivités", i.e., the conduct of the administrative authorities during the colonial period, whereas the acts relied on by El Salvador in the present case occurred after the independence of the two States, and in some cases in very recent years. The Chamber in the *Frontier Dispute* case referred also (*inter alia*) to the hypothesis of administration of a disputed territory by a State (not a colonial sub-division) other than the one possessing legal title (loc. Cit., p. 587); it may be taken to have had post-colonial *effectivités* also in mind. The passage in question reads as follows:

> " * * * Where the act corresponds exactly to law, where effective administration is additional to the *uti possidetis juris,* the only role of effectivité is to confirm the exercise of the right derived from a legal title. Where the act does not correspond to the law, where the territory which is the subject of the dispute is effectively administered by a State other than the one possessing the legal title, preference should be given to the holder of the title. In the event that the *effectivité* does not co-exist with any legal title, it must invariably be taken into consideration. Finally, there are cases where the legal title is not capable of showing exactly the territorial expanse to which it relates. The effectivités can then play an essential role in showing how the title is

interpreted in practice." (*I.C.J. Reports 1986,* pp. 586–587, para. 63.)
* * *

* * *

66.   The Chamber will examine in relation to each disputed sector of the land boundary the evidence of post-independence *effectivités* presented by each Party. It cannot be excluded, however, that even when such claims of *effectivités* are given their due weight, the situation may arise in some areas whereby a number of the nationals of the one Party will, following the delimitation of the disputed sectors, find themselves living in the territory of the other, and property rights apparently established under the laws of the one Party will be found to have been granted over land which is part of the territory of the other. The Chamber has every confidence that such measures as may be necessary to take account of this situation will be framed and carried out by both Parties, in full respect for acquired rights, and in a humane and orderly manner. In this regard, the Chamber notes with satisfaction the recognition, in a joint declaration made by the Presidents of the two Parties in San Salvador on 31 July 1986, of the need to set up * * * "a Special Commission to study and propose solutions for the human, civil and economic problems which may affect their compatriots, once the frontier problem has been resolved . . ."

* * *

67.   There has also been some argument between the Parties about the "critical date" in relation to this dispute. The principle of *uti possidetis juris* is sometimes stated in almost absolute terms, suggesting that the position at the date of independence is always determinative; in short, that no other critical date can arise. As appears from the discussion above, this cannot be so. A later critical date clearly may arise, for example, either from adjudication or from a boundary treaty. Thus, in the previous Latin American boundary arbitrations it is the award that is now determinative, even though it be based upon a view of the *uti possidetis juris* position. The award's view of the *uti possidetis juris* position prevails and cannot now be questioned juridically, even if it could be questioned historically. So for such a boundary the date of the award has become a new and later critical date. Likewise there can be no question that the parts of the El Salvador/Honduras boundary fixed by the General Treaty of Peace of 1980 now constitute the boundary and 1980 is now the critical date. If the *uti possidetis juris* position can be qualified by adjudication and by treaty, the question then arises whether it can be qualified in other ways, for example, by acquiescence or recognition. There seems to be no reason in principle why these factors should not operate, where there is sufficient evidence to show that the parties have in effect clearly accepted a variation, or at least an interpretation, of the *uti possidetis juris* position.

* * *

[The Chamber then proceeded to apply these principles to each of the disputed sectors to complete the land boundary. The discussion of the title to the islands and maritime areas is omitted. Maritime boundaries are generally discussed in Chapter 6 *infra*.]

NOTES AND QUESTIONS

1. El Salvador was not happy with the court's decision respecting all sectors of the land boundary. It requested a revision of the Judgment, arguing in part that a river along the border had jumped its bank in an evident avulsion that should not have affected the course of the boundary. The ICJ found that if any avulsion had occurred, it was before the critical date. *See Application for Revision of the Judgment of 11 September 1992* (El Salvador v. Honduras, Nicaragua intervening) 2003 I.C.J. Rep. 392 (Judgment of Dec. 18).

For purposes of determining the affect of an avulsion in the case, what is the critical date?

2. In *Land, Island* the court and the parties all agreed that the colonial administrative boundaries should become the international boundaries. This is the general conclusion reached by the ICJ in other post-colonial boundary cases. Is there something contradictory about retaining the boundaries imposed by an imperial power when a colony has won its independence? Why do you think that so many post-colonial states appear to accept this outcome? Note also that the court says the colonial boundaries prevail even where that may divide communities. Recall the discussion of boundary treaties in Chapter 2. The general principle is that boundary treaties should be particularly stable, but what about self-determination? *See infra*, p. 220.

3. In those parts of the boundary where the colonial boundary was unclear, the court looked to actual administration. Is this the same concept as that referred to by Huber in the *Island of Palmas* case above? And what are *effectivités*? *See also* Temple of Preah Vihear (Cambodia v. Thailand) 1962 I.C.J. Rep. 6 (Judgment of June 15) (prescription, estoppel and acquiescence.)

Note also that unclear boundaries are not fatal to statehood. Indeed, many states in the world have some undefined boundaries. International law requires some clarity with regard to the state's territory but is flexible respecting the final determination of all boundaries.

4. International law also provides for a change in boundaries through the slow natural movement of a river or other body of water, known as accretion. Boundaries will not be altered, however, if the change is sudden, which is known as avulsion. *See The Chamizal Case* (Mexico/U.S.) (June 15, 1911) XI R.I.A.A. 309.

5. The court in *Land, Island* uses the term *res nullius* (also *terra nullius*), meaning thing or land belonging to no one. In the area of acquisition of territory, this refers to territory open for acquisition because no one owns it. The ICJ gave an advisory opinion in the *Western Sahara* case in which it made clear that territory where organized communities lived was not *terra*

nullius, even if the community was not organized as a contemporary state is today. 1975 I.C.J. Rep. 12 (Advisory Opinion of Oct. 16).

6. *Rights over Territory Short of Title.* A state may cede to another a portion of its territory, just as a person may pass title to his property in private law. Also, just as rights in property short of title may be created in private law, so it is in international law with respect to the territory of a state. A state may lease to another a portion of its territory for a term of years. The convention between the United States and Panama of November 18, 1903, granted to the United States in perpetuity the use, occupation and control of a ten-mile strip of Panamanian territory for the purpose of constructing and operating a ship canal, and in this zone the United States exercised all the rights it "would possess and exercise if it were the sovereign of the territory" to the entire exclusion of the exercise by Panama of any such sovereign rights.

7. The Duchy of Sealand did not have "territory" because it did not have natural territory. Nor did it have a population because in a sense it did not have a natural population, a community, as opposed to a group commonly using the address to avoid taxes. The court did not mention that the population was also very small. Should that make a difference? Is 40 too few for a state? Nauru, a South Pacific Island nation, has a population of under 14,000 in 2009. Is that too small? Can a state be too big?

8. For further reading on territorial acquisition under international law, see, SUZANNE LALONDE, DETERMINING BOUNDARIES IN A CONFLICTED WORLD: THE ROLE OF UTI POSSEDITIS (2002) and JOSHUA CASTELLINO, INTERNATIONAL LAW AND SELF-DETERMINATION: THE INTERPLAY OF THE POLITICS OF TERRITORIAL POSSESSION WITH FORMULATIONS OF POST-COLONIAL NATIONAL IDENTITY (2002).

b. THE ELEMENT OF GOVERNMENT

The Tinoco Claims

Great Britain v. Costa Rica,
Case no. 15 (Oct. 18, 1923)*

■ TAFT, Sole Arbitrator

THE FACTS.—This arbitration was concerned with claims by Great Britain against Costa Rica arising out of acts by the Government of President Tinoco in respect of (*a*) certain banking transactions in which the Royal Bank of Canada was concerned, and (*b*) a petroleum concession granted to a British company.

In January, 1917, the Government of Costa Rica was overthrown by Frederico Tinoco, the Secretary for War. Tinoco, after having assumed power, called an election and set up a new Constitution in June, 1917. In August, 1919, Tinoco retired and left the country. In September his Government fell. A new election was then held and the old Constitution restored.

---

* Footnotes omitted.

The Bank Transactions.—On 29 June, 1919, shortly before the fall of Tinoco, the Banco Internacional de Costa Rica was authorised by law to issue currency notes for 15,000,000 colones. On 10 July this Law was amended, and by an Order of the President of the same date a provisional issue of bonds of 1000 colones each to a total amount of 2,500,000 colones was authorised; these bonds were to be treated as bills of the Banco Internacional and were to be realised by the Treasury. On 16 July a cheque drawn by the Finance Minister on the Banco Internacional for 1,000,000 colones was paid in to the credit of the Government with the Royal Bank of Canada. On presentation of the cheque the Royal Bank received from the Banco Internacional a thousand "bills" in the form last mentioned. It was arranged between the Finance Minister and the Bank that these "bills" should be withheld from circulation and be replaced by current issues of notes. Subsequently the Government, as alleged by the Bank, drew cheques against these "bills" and the cheques were honoured by the Bank. All the "bills" except two were still held by the Bank.

The Concessions.—On 26 June, 1918, the Chamber of Deputies of the Tinoco Government approved a concession, in the form of a contract, between Aguilar, Minister of Public Works, authorised by the President of the Republic, and the attorney of John M. Amory, of New York. Apparently (see Case No. 95, Facts) the latter acted as the agent of a British company known as the British Petroleum Oil Fields Ltd., which owned all the stock of the Central Costa Rica Petroleum Co. Ltd. in whose name the concession at the time of submission to arbitration stood. The concession related to petroleum, hydrocarbons and allied substances.

On 22 August, 1922, the Constitutional Congress of the restored Costa Rican Government by a law entitled "Law of Nullities No. 41" invalidated the legislation of 29 June, 1919, and 8 July, 1919, the presidential Order of the latter date and all transactions between the State and the holders of the "bills" issued thereunder, and also the petroleum concession.

The Tinoco Government was recognised by twenty States. It was not recognised by the United States of America, Great Britain, France or Italy. The Department of State of the United States made a number of pronouncements in which non-recognition of the Tinoco Government was explained by reference to the policy of the United States to refuse recognition to Governments established by revolutionary means unless it is clearly proven that it is elected by legal and constitutional means. In the arbitration Great Britain contended that the Government of Costa Rica and the Banco Internacional were bound to recognise the validity of the "bills" held by the Royal Bank and make them good, or, alternatively, to pay the money spent by the Bank in honouring the cheques drawn for Government purposes. Great Britain also contended that the concession must be recognised and given effect to by the Costa Rican Government.

It was contended on behalf of Costa Rica, in opposition to the British claim, that the Tinoco Government was not a *de facto* or a *de jure* Government according to rules of international law, and that it could not therefore bind by its acts the subsequent Costa Rican Governments; that the contracts and obligations of the Tinoco Government were void as contrary to the Constitution of Costa Rica abolished by that Government; that as Great Britain refused to recognise the Tinoco Government during its tenure of power she was now estopped from claiming that that Government could confer rights in a manner binding upon its predecessor; and that the British subjects, on whose behalf the claims were put forward, were bound either by the law of Costa Rica or by the contracts in question to pursue their remedies before the courts of Costa Rica and not to have recourse to diplomatic protection of their home State.

Held: (*a*) *Continuity of States and Obligations of Governments*—citing Moore, Borchard, and others: That it was a general principle of international law that a change of Government has no effect upon the international obligations of a State.

(*b*) *Status of the Tinoco Government*: That that Government was an actual sovereign Government. There was no substantial evidence showing that Tinoco was not in actual and peaceful administration without resistance by any one until a few months before the time when he retired and resigned. It was impossible to accept the argument that the Tinoco Government could not be considered a *de facto* Government because it was not established and maintained in accordance with the Constitution of Costa Rica. "To hold that a government which establishes itself and maintains a peaceful administration with the acquiescence of the people for a substantial period of time does not become a *de facto* government unless it conforms to a previous constitution would be to hold that within the rules of international law a revolution contrary to the fundamental law of the existing government cannot establish a new government. This cannot be, and is not, true. The change by revolution upsets the rule of the authorities in power under the then existing fundamental law, and sets aside the fundamental law in so far as the change of rule makes it necessary. To speak of a revolution creating a *de facto* government which conforms to the limitations of the old constitution, is to use a contradiction in terms. The same government continues internationally, but not the internal law of its being. The issue is not whether the new government assumes power or conducts its administration under constitutional limitations established by the people during the incumbency of the government it has overthrown. The question is, has it really established itself in such a way that all within its influence recognize its control, and that there is no opposing force assuming to be a government in its place? Is it discharging its functions as a government usually does, respected within its own jurisdiction?" (at p. 154).

(*c*) *Effects of Non–Recognition* (*in particular Non–Recognition as the Result of the Revolutionary Origin of the de facto Government*): That non-recognition by other nations is usually appropriate evidence that a Government has not attained the independence and control entitling it by international law to be regarded as a Government. But the granting or withholding of recognition, if it is to constitute evidence of this nature, must be determined by an enquiry into the actual sovereignty and control and not by one into the legitimacy or regularity of the Government claiming recognition. The latter reasons were the cause of non-recognition by the United States and, following its example, by the principal Allied Powers. But non-recognition on the ground of illegitimacy of origin was not a postulate of international law and did not secure general acquiescence. The fact that Costa Rica was a party to a treaty concluded in 1907 between the five Central American republics and binding the parties not to recognise in the future Governments of revolutionary origin prior to the re-establishment of constitutional forms as the result of free elections could not affect the rights of subjects of a Government which was not a party to that convention or amend or change rules of international law on the matter of recognition.

(*d*) *The Contention that a State Refusing Recognition to a Government is Estopped from Urging Claims Based upon the Acts of that Government*: That international law did not recognise an estoppel of this nature. There were no elements of equitable estoppel in the argument advanced by Costa Rica. "The failure to recognize the *de facto* government did not lead the succeeding government to change its position in any way upon the faith of it. Non-recognition may have aided the succeeding government to come into power; but subsequent presentation of claims based on the *de facto* existence of the previous government and its dealings does not work an injury to the succeeding government in the nature of a fraud or breach of faith. An equitable estoppel to prove the truth must rest on previous conduct of the person to be estopped, which has led the person claiming the estoppel into a position in which the truth will injure him. There is no such case here.

"There are other estoppels recognized in municipal law than those which rest on equitable considerations. They are based on public policy. It may be urged that it would be in the interest of the stability of governments and the orderly adjustment of international relations, and so a proper rule of international law, that a government in recognizing or refusing to recognize a government claiming admission to the society of nations should thereafter be held to an attitude consistent with its deliberate conclusion on this issue. Arguments for and against such a rule occur to me; but it suffices to say that I have not been cited to text writers of authority or to decisions of significance indicating a general acquiescence of nations in such a rule. Without this, it cannot be applied here as a principle of international law."

The argument that municipal courts are as a rule bound to follow the attitude of the executive department in respect of recognition of foreign Governments is not relevant to the issue. Great Britain, although she refused to recognise the Tinoco Government, was entitled to change her position and to maintain that that Government could create rights in British subjects. The failure to recognise the Tinoco Government may be used against Great Britain as evidence to disprove the actual existence of that Government, but this does not prevent her from changing her position. "Should a case arise in one of its own courts after it has changed its position, doubtless that court would feel it incumbent upon it to note the change in its further rulings."

Neither was it possible to admit the argument that as the British subjects in question knew of the refusal of their Government to recognise the Tinoco Government they could not now rely on the protection of Great Britain. This was entirely a question between Great Britain and her subjects. Unlike the United States, Great Britain had not warned her subjects that she would not protect diplomatically persons entering into relations with the Tinoco Government.

(e) *As to the Argument that the Claimants in Question were Bound to Refrain from Invoking the Aid of their Government*: That any such obligation did not bind the Governments in question. (See Case No. 96.)

(f) *As to the Merits of the Claim*: That the Law of Nullities did not either in respect of the banking transactions or the concessions work an injury of which Great Britain was entitled to complain. (See Case No. 95.)

* * *

Entities appear to need a government to become states but if governments become ineffective or disappear entirely, statehood is not lost. Somalia lost effective government in the late 1980s and has yet to reacquire it as of 2009, but the state of Somalia remains a member of the United Nations. Should this be the case?

3. RECOGNITION

I Robert Jennings and Arthur Watts, Oppenheim's International Law

p. 127 (9th ed., 1996)

In a broad sense recognition involves the acceptance by a state of any fact or situation occurring in its relations with other states. In the context of recognition of states and governments, however, recognition is of particular significance. It is of great importance, both as a device of international law and as a political act of the state granting recognition. Because of its important legal and political consequences, recognition in this particular sense must be distinguished from a looser use of the term conveying mere acknowledgement or cognisance of an existing situation.

Recognition is accorded to a particular body in a particular capacity. Thus usually a community is recognised as a sovereign state, or an administration is recognised as the government of such a state. But circumstances may call for recognition only in some special capacity: for example, a regime may be recognised only as the government of that part of the territory of the state which it controls, or a community may be recognised as something else than a sovereign state.

The grant of recognition is an act on the international plane, affecting the mutual rights and obligations of states, and their status or legal capacity in general. Recognition also has consequences at the national level, as where the application of rules of municipal law is affected by a decision to recognise a new state or government. Furthermore, the rules of international law relating to recognition are rules of customary international law, and their application in particular circumstances may be modified by treaty obligations.

a.   RECOGNITION OF STATES

I Robert Jennings and Arthur Watts, Oppenheim's International Law

p. 127 (9th ed., 1996)

The international community is composed primarily of states. Any changes in the composition of the international community are of immediate concern to existing states, whether those changes involve members of that community (usually states) or the authorities (usually governments) through which they act. The matter is of legal importance because it is when an entity becomes a member of the international community that it thereupon becomes bound by the obligations, and a beneficiary of the rights, prescribed by international law for states and their governments.

There is, however, no settled view whether recognition is the only means through which a new state becomes part of the international community. On the one view if a new state comes into existence as a matter of fact, it thereupon enters into the international community and becomes of right an international person regardless of whether it has been recognised.

Although in practice recognition is necessary to enable every new state to enter into official intercourse with other states, theoretically every new state becomes, according to this view, a member of the international community *ipso facto* by its rising into existence: recognition is thus viewed as purely declaratory or confirmatory in nature, supplying only the necessary evidence of the fact of a state's existence.

The opposed view is that it is a rule of international law that no new state has a right as against other states to be recognised by them; that no state has a duty to recognise a new state; that a new state before its recognition cannot claim any right which a member of the international community has as against other members; and that it is recognition which constitutes the new state as a member the international community.

The problem is largely theoretical because state practice is inconclusive and may be rationalised either way. The international community is still largely decentralised. The extent to which a new state is able to participate in the international community is in practice largely determined by the extent of its bilateral relationships with other states, which in turn depends primarily on its recognition by them. Only by being granted recognition is a new state fully admitted by an existing state into its circle of bilateral relationships within the framework of international law; this is precisely what the existing state intends when granting recognition, and what it knows it is preventing when withholding recognition. The grant of recognition by a state is a unilateral act affecting essentially bilateral relations, and neither constitutes nor declares the recognised state to be a member of the international community as a whole. Recognition of a new state by only one state will make it an international person to the limited extent of its relations with that state, but such limited personality cannot realistically be regarded as membership of the international community in general. That is the result of recognition by a significant number of existing states, for example by a sufficient majority to secure admission to the major multilateral organisations. Such a degree of recognition is usually present when, but is unlikely to be present unless, the new state is in effective existence in fact.

The overwhelming practice of states does not accept that the mere claim of a community to be an independent state automatically gives it a right to be so regarded, or that an existing state is justified in recognising or refusing to recognise a new community as a state in disregard of whether it fulfils the factual requirements of statehood. While the grant of recognition is within the discretion of states, it is not a matter of arbitrary will or political concession, but is given or refused in accordance with legal principle. That principle, which applies alike to recognition of states, governments, belligerents, or insurgents, is that, when certain conditions of fact (not in themselves contrary to international law) are shown to exist, recognition is permissible and is consistent with international law in that it cannot (as may recognition accorded before those facts are clearly established) be considered to constitute intervention; and that, while recognition is accordingly declaratory of those facts, it is also constitutive of the rights and duties of the recognised community in its relations with the recognising state.

* * *

Although not always consistent, the bulk of state practice probably supports the view that governments do not deem themselves free to grant or refuse recognition to new states in an arbitrary manner, by exclusive reference to their own political interests, and regardless of legal principle. Undoubtedly, quite apart from the element of discretion left to states in assessing the facts concerning the existence of a new state and in determining the timing of an act of recognition, it is unavoidable that political considerations from time to time influence the grant or refusal of recognition; some states, indeed, go further and assert that recognition is essentially a matter within their political discretion. It may be, however, that it is largely a matter of degree, since there probably are no states which do not allow some role to considerations of policy, while those states which treat recognition as a matter of policy do not usually in practice disregard the imperatives to which a new state's effective existence gives rise. These variations do not affect the essential legal nature of the process of recognition. Recognition, while declaratory of an existing fact, is constitutive in its nature, at least so far as concerns relations with the recognising state. It marks the beginning of the effective enjoyment of the international rights and duties of the recognized community.

European Community: Declaration on Yugoslavia and on the Guidelines on the Recognition of New States

December 16, 1991, 31 I.L.M. 1485 (1992)

DECLARATION ON YUGOSLAVIA

(Extraordinary EPC Ministerial Meeting, Brussels, 16 December 1991)

The European Community and its member States discussed the situation in Yugoslavia in the light of their guidelines on the recognition of new states in Eastern Europe and in the Soviet Union. They adopted a common position with regard to the recognition of Yugoslav Republics. In this connection they concluded the following:

The Community and its member States agree to recognise the independence of all the Yugoslav Republics fulfilling all the conditions set out below. The implementation of this decision will take place on January 15, 1992.

They are therefore inviting all Yugoslav Republics to state by 23 December whether:

—they wish to be recognised as independent States;

—they accept the commitments contained in the above-mentioned guidelines;

—they accept the provisions laid down in the draft Convention—especially those in Chapter II on human rights and rights of national or ethnic groups—under consideration by the Conference on Yugoslavia;

—they continue to support the efforts of the Secretary General and the Security Council of the United Nations; and

—the continuation of the Conference on Yugoslavia.

The applications of those Republics which reply positively will be submitted through the Chair of the Conference to the Arbitration Commission for advice before the implementation date.

In the meantime, the Community and its member States request the UN Secretary General and the UN Security Council to continue their efforts to establish an effective cease-fire and promote a peaceful and negotiated outcome to the conflict. They continue to attach the greatest importance to the early deployment of a UN peace-keeping force referred to in UN Security Council Resolution 724.

The Community and its member States also require a Yugoslav Republic to commit itself, prior to recognition, to adopt constitutional and political guarantees ensuring that it has no territorial claims towards a neighbouring Community State and that it will conduct no hostile propaganda activities versus a neighbouring Community State, including the use of a denomination which implies territorial claims.

b. RECOGNITION OF GOVERNMENTS

I Robert Jennings and Arthur Watts, Oppenheim's International Law
p. 146 (9th ed., 1996)*

Recognition of a change in the headship of a state, or in its government, or in the title of an old state, are matters of importance. But such recognition must not be confused with recognition of the state itself. If a foreign state refuses to recognise a new Head of State or a change in the government of an old state, the latter does not thereby lose its recognition as an international person, although no formal official intercourse is possible between the two states as long as recognition is not given either expressly or tacitly. Recognition of a government as the government of a state presupposes, and will normally imply, recognition of a state. If no state is recognised, the "government" cannot be recognised as the government of a state, although it may be recognised in some other capacity.

* * *

§ 43 *When coming into power normally and constitutionally* On the accession of a new Head of State, other states are as a rule notified and usually recognise the new head of State by some formal act such as a message of congratulations; in the case of a normal constitutional change of government there is usually no such formal notification or recognition. In practice, when a new Head of State has come into his position in a normal and constitutional manner, such as succession to the throne on the death of the reigning monarch or at a presidential election, recognition is a matter of course; as it also is where a state changes its constitutional form from, for instance, a monarchy to a republic, in a constitutional manner and without anything in the nature of a revolution. Nor would there be any question of withholding recognition of the new government after a change in the government following elections. In such cases recognition causes no difficulties and often takes place informally and by implication from a continuation of normal bilateral diplomatic dealings in such a way as to leave no doubt as to the intention to continue recognition.

§ 44 *When coming into power abnormally and in a revolutionary manner* When, however, the new Head of State or government comes into power not in a constitutional manner but after a *coup d'état,* a revolution (which need not involve bloodshed), or any other event involving a break in legal continuity, the determination by other states of the attitude to be adopted towards the new Head of State or government is often difficult.

---

* Some italics added.

They are called upon to decide whether the new authority can be properly regarded as representing the state in question.

Such a decision is unavoidable, since states act through their governments and most if not all aspects of international relations depend upon acceptance of a government's right to act and speak for the state. The decision that a new government may properly represent the state concerned is not, however, one which needs to be formally or publicly announced, and a number of states, including since 1980 the United Kingdom, now follow the policy of not doing so. Instead, the nature of their relations with an authority claiming to be the government of a state is determined by and deduced from the circumstances of each case: recognition will be more a matter of implication than of express declaration. In deciding whether formally to recognise a new government, or whether the circumstances are such that relations with it should be those which are normal between governments, the recognising state exercises a discretion which, although necessarily wide, is not arbitrary.

* * *

§ 45   *Criteria for recognition of governments*   As with recognition of new states, so also with recognition of governments the decision is not one determined solely by political considerations on the part of the recognising state. A government which is in fact in control of the country and which enjoys the habitual obedience of the bulk of the population with a reasonable expectancy of permanence, can be said to represent the state in question and as such to be deserving of recognition. The preponderant practice of states, in particular that of the United Kingdom, in the recognition of governments has been based on the principle of effectiveness thus conceived.

* * *

States granting recognition often distinguish between *de jure* and *de facto* recognition. These terms are convenient but elliptical: the terms *de jure* or *de facto* qualify the state or government recognised rather than the act of recognition itself. Those terms are in this context probably not capable of literal analysis, particularly in terms of the *ius* to which recognition *de jure* refers. The distinction between *de jure* and *de facto* recognition is in essence that the former is the fullest kind of recognition while the latter is a lesser degree of recognition, taking account on a provisional basis of present realities. Thus *de facto* recognition takes place when, in the view of the recognising state, the new authority, although actually independent and wielding effective power in the territory under its control, has not acquired sufficient stability or does not as yet offer prospects of complying with other requirements of recognition.

Thus after the First World War, the governments of various new states, such as Finland, Latvia and Estonia, which formerly constituted part of the Russian Empire, were recognised in the first instance as *de facto* governments pending the final territorial settlement in that part of the world. The Government of the Soviet Union, although, to all appearances, firmly and effectively established, was recognised for a number of years after its establishment by many states *de facto* only on the ground that, in their view, it was unwilling to fulfil its international obligations in such matters as compensation for the confiscated property of foreign subjects and acknowledgement of liability for financial obligations incurred by its predecessors. Recognition of a government de facto may be limited to such areas as are actually under its control. Such recognition will often in time be replaced by the grant of *de jure* recognition. While *de facto* recognition usually falls to be considered in the context of new states or governments, it may also be relevant in other circumstances such as the extension of a state's territory or its absorption of another previously independent state.

* * *

Brad Roth, Governmental Illegitimacy in International Law

p. 253ff (1999)

* * *

Apart from the special circumstances of "colonial, alien, or racist domination", the international community has made every effort to avoid judgments regarding the legitimacy of member state governments. Officially, it has no process for conferring collective recognition on governments. Recognition and non-recognition continue to be spoken of as political acts within the sovereign discretion of individual states, and a regime's legal capacity to assert rights, incur obligations and authorize acts on behalf of state is subject to no systematic process of authoritative determination. Yet international bodies cannot evade the responsibility of collective legal recognition; where rival ruling apparatuses purport to act in the name of the political community, the question of a putative government's legal capacities thrusts itself upon the international community.

* * *

Collective bodies must, inevitably, assess the legitimacy of rival ruling apparatuses in determining (1) whether to accept state delegation credentials issued by a putative government; and (2) whether to condemn foreign military assistance rendered to a putative government. The two questions, both occasioned by conditions of internal armed conflict, are frequently very closely connected: the putative government that gains the seat is poised to establish which foreign military assistance is duly "invited", and which constitutes unlawful intervention. Notwithstanding the disclaimers rendered by its participants, the credentials process serves as a process of collective legal recognition.

In its first 45 Years, the U.N. General Assembly was the site of eight major credentials contests. One case, South Africa, * * * and another controversy, concerning Israel, turned on matters of external behavior (and, implicitly, the legitimacy of the political community itself) rather than on the capacity of the ruling apparatus to represent the political community. The other cases were: China (Nationalists v. Communists, 1949–71); Hungary (Soviet-installed Kadar Government, 1956–63); Congo–Leopoldville (President Kasavubu v. ousted Prime Minister Lumumba, 1960); Yemen (Egyptian-backed Republic v. ousted monarchy, 1962); Cambodia I (Lon Nol Government v. Royalist-backed Khmer Rouge insurgency, 1973–74); and Cambodia II (Vietnamese-installed "People's Republic" v. "Democratic Kampuchea" resistance, 1979–90).

Regional bodies have faced analogous contests with implications for the admissibility of foreign involvement in internal armed conflict. In January 1976, the Organization of African Unity faced the choice of admitting the People's Republic of Angola, thereby recognizing the MPLA government at the expense of the rival "Democratic People's Republic of Angola", both of which were backed by foreign troops. In June 1979, the Organization of American States faced the choice of "prematurely" withdrawing recognition of Nicaragua's Somoza government in favor of the Sandinista-led Provisional government, which was being assisted by neighboring states.

* * *

A.   U.N. Credentials and Collective Legal Recognition

1.   The U.N. Credentials Process

. . . From the standpoint of legal theory, the linkage of representation in an international organization and recognition of a government is a confusion of two institutions which have superficial similarities but are essentially different.

The recognition of a new State, or of a new government of an existing State, is a unilateral act which the recognizing government can grant or withhold. . . .

. . . On the other hand, membership of a State in the United Nations and representation of a State in organs is clearly determined by a collective act of the appropriate organ.

So noted a U.N. Legal Memorandum in 1950, as it sought to grapple with problem of Chinese representation, the first of the U.N. credentials controversies. It is the General Assembly's practice to accept delegation credentials where they have been properly issued by the head of state, head of government or foreign minister of a member state; where delegations present credentials issued by officials of rival ruling apparatuses, the General Assembly is forced to choose which ruling apparatus shall represent the state in that body. In emphasizing that the credentials process is not a form of collective recognition, the quoted Legal Memorandum sought to reassure the wary that U.N. representation is without prejudice to member states' political disapproval—expressed by a denial of recognition—of the government that the seated delegation represents.

The Memorandum sidestepped the larger issue: the need to establish with clarity for the international community which of two contestants is the bearer of the state's rights, powers and responsibilities at international law. If the credentials decision is a collective process, whereas the recognition decision is a matter of individual state prerogative, the need for coherence in the international legal system clearly argues for the former to be preferred as the arbiter of legal capacity.

* * *

The United Nations Charter nowhere expressly grants the General Assembly the capacity to make so weighty a determination, whether declaratory or constitutive, regarding the legal legitimacy of governments. The Charter's drafters apparently understood that [i]n the course of the operations from day to day of the various organs of the Organization, it is inevitable that each organ will interpret such parts of the Charter as are applicable to its function. Since, as one expert has put it, "the General Assembly's exercise of authority in [this area] is based not on a grant of authority in the Charter but on necessity, the scope of such authority is defined by and is coextensive with the necessity that gave rise to it". * * *

More generally, a General Assembly vote on credentials gauges the balance of legal opinion in the international community on the question of which contestant apparatus is entitled to represent the state in deliberations on international problems. Where the vote goes overwhelmingly in favor of one of the contestants, the collective *opinio juris* has far-reaching implications: it is either constitutive of a putative government's *de jure* status or persuasively declaratory of the presence of underlying facts sufficient to establish that status.

Thus, a General Assembly vote on credentials cannot be dissociated from the matter of legal recognition, notwithstanding that a simple majority decision on a delegation's credentials may be insufficient to resolve the issue of the putative government's legal capacity to assert rights, incur obligations and authorize acts on behalf of the state. (By contrast, a joint decision of the General Assembly and Security Council to admit a putative state to the United Nations establishes clearly the entity's legal entitlement to the protections of the international system, as the discourse on Bosnia–Herzegovina reflects). There is thus ample basis to take credentials decisions seriously.

* * *

NOTES AND QUESTIONS

1. In the summer of 2009 the president of Honduras was removed from office in unusual circumstances. According to Douglass Cassel:

> In the early morning hours of Sunday, June 28, 2009, acting on a judicial warrant to arrest President Zelaya for alleged crimes, the nation's military stormed the presidential palace, and arrested the chief executive in his pajamas. Then, exceeding its warrant, and in violation of an express provision of the Honduran Constitution, the military put the pajama-clad president on a plane to Costa Rica. With Zelaya involuntarily exiled, the Honduran Congress met that afternoon, listened to a reading of a supposed letter of resignation from him, and promptly accepted it. The Congress then issued a decree

purporting to depose Zelaya on other grounds, and to replace him by the president of the Congress, Rigoberto Micheletti. President Zelaya's removal and replacement were swiftly denounced as a *coup d'état* by governments throughout the region, including by U.S. President Obama, and by the United Nations General Assembly, the Inter–American Commission on Human Rights, and the General Assembly of the Organization of American States (OAS). Invoking the Inter–American Democratic Charter, the OAS General Assembly termed the coup an "unconstitutional alteration of the democratic order," thus triggering the suspension of Honduras from participation in the OAS.

Although the United States joined in the 33–0 OAS vote, the Obama Administration stopped short of deeming Zelaya's ouster a "military coup," which would trigger a statutorily mandated suspension of U.S. intergovernmental foreign assistance to Honduras. Nonetheless, the Administration suspended military and inter-governmental development aid as a matter of policy. At least one witness at a congressional hearing went further, calling Zelaya's removal a "military coup" requiring an aid suspension.

By contrast, the removal and replacement of Zelaya were vigorously defended by a broad, if not unanimous, array of Honduran civil authorities—including all 15 members of the Supreme Court, the chief prosecutor, an overwhelming majority of Congress, and the new, *de facto* government. In written communiqués, they insisted that his ouster was a lawful and constitutional action to defend Honduran democracy and the rule of law from a president who had defied both courts and Constitution, and who was maneuvering to amend the Constitution to allow him to run for a second term. Similar views have been expressed by a number of members of the U.S. Congress.

On the day he was deposed, President Zelaya, in violation of a court order, was attempting to conduct a referendum on whether to call a constitutional convention. His arrest that morning was pursuant to a judicial warrant from a civilian court, for alleged crimes against the form of government, treason, abuse of authority and usurpation of functions.

Honduras: Coup d'Etat in Constitutional Clothing, 13 ASIL INSIGHT (Issue 9) July 29, 2009.

Was the Obama Administration right to avoid characterizing the situation as a "military coup"? Was it a coup at all? If not, then have the U.S. and other members of the OAS acted in violation of the very pro-democracy principles they were seeking to defend?

Do populations have a right to democratic government today? Consider the next case in light of this question, *Re Seccession of Quebec*.

2.   Legal issues concerning recognition and non-recognition have arisen in domestic courts. The classic issue has been: in the absence of diplomatic recognition of a state or of a regime by the pertinent department or branch of the forum state government, may such entity or regime be treated by

domestic courts as having juridical existence? The courts of a forum state may be incapable of acting at all. Or, the courts might feel that the characterizations of parties as state entities or as governments should be made by the diplomatic branch. The courts, however, might make such decisions for themselves. If so, what law would they apply? International? Principles of law common to the world's major legal systems? Judicial notice? Analogies to the private law of entities such as corporations?

Access to courts was denied to the non-recognized Soviet government in a number of states. *See, R.S.F.S.R. v. Cibrario,* 235 N.V. 255, 139 N.E. 259 (1923). The non-recognized Soviet government was refused the right to sue in *Soviet Government v. Ericsson,* Sweden, Supreme Court, 1921, [1919–1922] Ann.Dig. 54 (No. 30). The outcome was the same in *Societe Despa v. USSR,* Belgium, Court of Appeal of Liege, 1931, Pasicrisie II, 108 (1931). In *USSR v. Luxembourg and Saar Company,* Luxembourg, Tribunal of Commerce of Luxembourg, 1935, Sirey, IV, 26 (1936), the USSR was allowed to sue but on the ground it had been impliedly recognized by Luxembourg and hence the bar against bringing the suit had been removed. In some states, however, the unrecognized regime has been allowed to sue. *Commercial Representation of the USSR v. Levant Red Sea Coal Co.,* Egypt, Tribunal of Alexandria, 1933, 62 J.Dr. Int'l 199 (1935); *Republic of the South Moluccas v. Netherlands New Guinea,* Netherlands, District Court of the Hague, 1954, 21 Int'l L.Rep. 48 (1957). The policy to deny an unrecognized government access to courts does not extend to a corporation or its assignee owned by the unrecognized government. *See* 1987 *Restatement,* Comment *a* to Section 205 and Reporters' Note 1 to that section setting forth United States cases in point.

3.   The lawmaking authority of unrecognized governments was discussed in *Am Luther Co. v. James Sagor & Co.,* [1921] 3 K.B. 532, 539:

> BANKES, L.J. The action was brought to establish the plaintiff company's right to a quantity of veneer or plywood which had been imported by the defendants from Russia. The plaintiffs' case was that they are a Russia company having a factory or mill at Staraja in Russia for the manufacture of veneer or plywood, and that in the year 1919 the so-called Republican Government of Russia without any right or title to do so seized all the stock at their mill and subsequently purported to sell the quantity in dispute in this action to the defendants. The plaintiffs contended that the so-called Republican Government had no existence as a government, that it had never been recognized by His Majesty's Government, and that the seizure of their goods was pure robbery. As an alternative they contended that the decree of the so-called government nationalizing all factories, as a result of which their goods were seized, is not a decree which the Courts of this country would recognize.

> The answer of the defendants was two-fold. In the first place they contended that the Republican Government which had passed the decree nationalizing all factories was the de facto Government of Russia at the time, and had been recognized by His Majesty's Govern-

ment as such, and that the decree was one to which the Courts of this country could not refuse recognition. Secondly they contended that the plaintiff company was an Estonian and not a Russian company * * *. Roche, J. decided the two main points in the plaintiffs' favour. Upon the evidence which was before the * * * judge I think that his decision was quite right. As the case was presented in the Court below the appellants relied on certain letters from the Foreign Office as establishing that His Majesty's Government had recognized the Soviet Government as the de facto Government of Russia. The principal letters are referred to by the learned judge in his judgment. He took the view that the letters relied on did not establish the appellants' contention. * * * I entirely agree.

In this Court the appellants asked leave to adduce further evidence, and as the respondents raised no objection, the evidence was given. It consisted of two letters from the Foreign Office dated respectively April 20 and 22, 1921. The first is in reply to a letter dated April 12, which the appellants' solicitors wrote to the Under Secretary of State for Foreign Affairs, asking for a "Certificate for production to the Court of Appeal that the Government of the Russian Socialist Federal Soviet Republic is recognized by His Majesty's Government as the de facto Government of Russia." To this request a reply was received dated April 20, 1921, in these terms: "I am directed by Earl Curzon of Kedleston to refer to your letter of April 12, asking for information as to the relations between His Majesty's Government and the Soviet Government of Russia. (2.) I am to inform you that His Majesty's Government recognize the Soviet Government as the de facto Government of Russia." The letter of April 22 is in reply to a request for information whether His Majesty's Government recognized the Provisional Government of Russia, and as to the period of its duration, and the extent of its jurisdiction. The answer contains (inter alia) the statement that the Provisional Government came into power on March 14, 1917, that it was recognized by His Majesty's Government as the then existing Government of Russia, and that the Constituent Assembly remained in session until December 13, 1917, when it was dispersed by the Soviet authorities. The statement contained in the letter of April 20 is accepted by the respondents' counsel as the proper and sufficient proof of the recognition of the Soviet Government as the de facto Government of Russia.

* * *

* * * [U]pon the construction which I place upon the communication of the Foreign Office to which I have referred, this Court must treat the Soviet Government, which the Government of this country has now recognized as the de facto Government of Russia, as having commenced its existence at a date anterior to any date material to the dispute between the parties to this appeal.

An attempt was made by the respondents' counsel to draw a distinction between the effect of a recognition of a government as a de facto government and the effect of a recognition of a government as a government de jure, and to say that the latter form of recognition might relate back to acts of state of a date earlier than the date of recognition, whereas the former could not. Wheaton quoting from Mountague Bernard states the distinction between a de jure and a de facto government thus (1): "A de jure government is one which, in the opinion of the person using the phrase, ought to possess the powers of sovereignty, though at the time it may be deprived of them. A de facto government is one which is really in possession of them, although the possession may be wrongful or precarious." For some purposes no doubt a distinction can be drawn between the effect of the recognition by a sovereign state of the one form of government or of the other, but for the present purpose in my opinion no distinction can be drawn. The Government of this country having, to use the language just quoted, recognized the Soviet Government as the Government really in possession of the powers of sovereignty in Russia, the acts of that Government must be treated by the Courts of this country with all the respect due to the acts of a duly recognized foreign sovereign state.

* * *

4. *The Problem of One China or Two.* In 1949, at the close of the civil war in China between the Nationalist authority of Chiang kai-shek and the communists led by Mao Zedong, the defeated Nationalists repaired to Taiwan and the communists established on the mainland the Peoples Republic of China (PRC). Until 1979 the United States continued to recognize only the Taiwan regime as "China". At the United Nations the Taiwan authorities continued to represent "China" as a member of that organization. This could not, of course, continue forever, and eventually consideration was given to the recognition of the PRC and its communist government. Part of that problem was: what to do about Taiwan as "China".

Richard M. Nixon established political relations with the People's Republic of China, having begun to indicate a shift in the United States position early in his first administration. Diplomatic relations between the United States and Beijing were formally established by the *Joint Communique on the Establishment of Diplomatic Relations between the United States of America and the People's Republic of China,* January 1, 1979, U.S. Dept. of State Bull., January 1979, pp. 25–26, in which each of the parties agreed to recognize the other, a formula that the People's Republic had insisted upon with other well-recognized states, such as the United Kingdom and France, when these, some years earlier, shifted relations from Taiwan to Beijing. Agreements were concluded—and became effective at signature on January 31, 1979,—concerning: Consular Relations, 30 U.S.T. 17; Cultural Relations, 30 U.S.T. 26; and Scientific Cooperation, 30 U.S.T. 35.

In view of the unofficial relations maintained with Taiwan by so many states, should it be considered to be a state, although perhaps a state a bit different from the usual? Why should that not be possible? In fact, it appears that the American Institute of Taiwan functions like an embassy and actually all U.S. relations with Taiwan are much like those with any state or government. Are there not entities, such as the Holy See, which do not meet the requirements expected of a state in the traditional sense? According to Reporters' Note 8 to Section 201 of the 1987 *Restatement,* the authorities on Taiwan do not even claim that it is a state. See *International Agreements and U.S.–Taiwan Relations,* 22 Harv. I.L.J. 451 (1981). On July 9, 1999, Taiwan President Lee Teng-hui made a suggestion that Taiwan–Chinese relations should be reclassified as "special state-to-state" ties, but Beijing responded with hostile rhetoric and threats of the use of force to prevent the "independence" of Taiwan, notwithstanding that Taiwan continues to function in most respects as a fully independent state. *(See* N.Y.TIMES, July 13, 1999, p. A1, col. 1.)

4.   SELF-DETERMINATION

Despite much discussion of the decline of the state, many communities around the world are currently seeking independent statehood. In today's world this means separating or seceding from another state. Where the state agrees to this, there is no obstacle in international law. Where agreement is lacking, some claim international law will still support secession in circumstances where a right of self-determination has been denied. This right is discussed in the following case.

Re: Secession of Quebec

Supreme Court of Canada
August 2, 1998, 37 I.L.M. 1340 (1998)

[The Governor in Council of Canada referred to the Supreme Court questions concerning the right of Quebec to secede from Canada. After giving a negative response to the first question (Can Quebec secede unilaterally under Canada's constitution?), the Court turned to the second question: (Can Quebec unilaterally secede under international law?)]

B.   *Question 2*

Does international law give the National Assembly, legislature or government of Quebec the right to effect the secession of Quebec from Canada unilaterally? In this regard, is there a right to self-determination under international law that would give the National Assembly, legislature or government of Quebec the right to effect the secession of Quebec from Canada unilaterally?

109   For reasons already discussed, the Court does not accept the contention that Question 2 raises a question of "pure" international law which this Court has no jurisdiction to address. Question 2 is posed in the context of a Reference to address the existence or non-existence of a right of unilateral secession by a province of Canada. The amicus curiae argues that this question ultimately falls to be determined under international law. In addressing this issue, the Court does not purport to act as an arbiter between sovereign states or more generally within the international

community. The Court is engaged in rendering an advisory opinion on certain legal aspects of the continued existence of the Canadian federation. International law has been invoked as a consideration and it must therefore be addressed.

110   The argument before the Court on Question 2 has focused largely on determining whether, under international law, a positive legal right to unilateral secession exists in the factual circumstances assumed for the purpose of our response to Question 1. Arguments were also advanced to the effect that, regardless of the existence or non-existence of a positive right to unilateral secession, international law will in the end recognize effective political realities—including the emergence of a new state—as facts. While our response to Question 2 will address considerations raised by this alternative argument of "effectivity", it should first be noted that the existence of a positive legal entitlement is quite different from a prediction that the law will respond after the fact to a then existing political reality. These two concepts examine different points in time. The questions posed to the Court address legal rights in advance of a unilateral act of purported secession. While we touch below on the practice governing the international recognition of emerging states, the Court is as wary of entertaining speculation about the possible future conduct of sovereign states on the international level as it was under Question 1 to speculate about the possible future course of political negotiations among the participants in the Canadian federation. In both cases, the Reference questions are directed only to the legal framework within which the political actors discharge their various mandates.

(1) *Secession at International Law*

[The Supreme Court's Summary of conclusions are set forth below. In reaching these conclusions, the Court's citations of authority included the following: R. Y. Jennings, *The Acquisition of Territory in International Law* (1963) at pp. 8–9; A. Cassese, *Self–Determination of Peoples: A legal reappraisal* (1995) at pp. 171–72; K, Doehring, *"Self–Determination" in B. Simma, ed., The Charter of the United Nations: A Commentary* (1994) at pp. 60, 70; United Nations Charter, Articles 1 and 55; Article 1 of the International Covenant on Civil and Political Rights, 999 U.N.T.S. 171 and the International Covenant on Economic, Social and Cultural Rights, 993 U.N.T.S. 3; the Declaration on Principles of International law Concerning Friendly Relations and Co-operation Among States in Accordance with the Charter of the United Nations, GA Res. 2625 (XXV), 24 October 1970; the Vienna Declaration and Programme of Action, adopted by the U.N. World Conference on Human Rights, NConf. 157/24, 25 June 1993; the Declaration on the Occasion of the Fiftieth Anniversary of the United Nations, GA RES 50/6, 9 November 1995; the Final Act of the Conference on Security and Co-operation in Europe, 14 LL.M. 1292 (1972) (Part VIII); H.W.R. Wade, *The Basis of Legal Sovereignty* [1955] Camb. L.J. 172, 196; the *European Community Declaration on the Guidelines on the Recognition of New States in Eastern Europe and in the Soviet Union,* 31 LL.M. 1485 (1992) p. 1487; S.A. de Smith, *Constitutional Lawyers in Revolutionary*

Situations [1968] 7 West. Ont.L. Rev. 93, 96, and Reference re Manitoba Language Rights, [1985] 1 S.C.R. 721, 753.]

* * *

IV. *Summary of Conclusions*

* * *

154   We have also considered whether a positive legal entitlement to secession exists under international law in the factual circumstances contemplated by Question 1, i.e., a clear democratic expression of support on a clear question for Quebec secession. Some of those who supported an affirmative answer to this question did so on the basis of the recognized right to self-determination that belongs to all "peoples". Although much of the Quebec population certainly shares many of the characteristics of a people, it is not necessary to decide the "people" issue because, whatever may be the correct determination of this issue in the context of Quebec, a right to secession only arises under the principle of self-determination of peoples at international law where "a people" is governed as part of a colonial empire; where "a people" is subject to alien subjugation, domination or exploitation; and possibly where "a people" is denied any meaningful exercise of its right to self-determination within the state of which it forms a part. In other circumstances, peoples are expected to achieve self-determination within the framework of their existing state. A state whose government represents the whole of the people or peoples resident within its territory, on a basis of equality and without discrimination, and respects the principles of self-determination in its internal arrangements, is entitled to maintain its territorial integrity under international law and to have that territorial integrity recognized by other states. Quebec does not meet the threshold of a colonial people or an oppressed people, nor can it be suggested that Quebecers have been denied meaningful access to government to pursue their political, economic, cultural and social development. In the circumstances, the National Assembly, the legislature or the government of Quebec do not enjoy a right at international law to effect the secession of Quebec from Canada unilaterally.

155   Although there is no right, under the Constitution or at international law, to unilateral secession, that is secession without negotiation on the basis just discussed, this does not rule out the possibility of an unconstitutional declaration of secession leading to a de facto secession. The ultimate success of such a secession would be dependent on recognition by the international community, which is likely to consider the legality and legitimacy of secession having regard to, amongst other facts, the conduct of Quebec and Canada, in determining whether to grant or withhold recognition. Such recognition, even if granted, would not, however, provide any retroactive justification for the act of secession, either under the Constitution of Canada or at international law.

156   The reference questions are answered accordingly.

Judgment accordingly.

NOTES AND QUESTIONS

1.   Following World War I, the representatives to the Paris Peace conference sponsored plebiscites or referendums throughout Europe to determine
whether populations wished to remain within their current state boundaries, become part of different states or become independent. Poland and
Czechoslovakia emerged as a result of the vote. The Aaland Islands had
been associated with Finland but wished to be part of Sweden because of
language and other cultural ties. The case was not resolved by a plebiscite
because of geo-political concerns over the growing power of the Soviet
Union, so the League of Nations took up the question upon its establishment. The League appointed a Commission of Inquiry that eventually
reported that the Aaland Islands should remain part of Finland. The
Commission found that the "agitation" for separating from Finland arose
in the Aaland Islands during a period when Finland was in a state of
political turmoil. With that over and Finnish sovereignty established, the
Commission found that the Aaland Islands could have their concerns
alleviated by an autonomy arrangement with certain rights given to Sweden for oversight. The autonomy arrangement was considered sufficient to
satisfy the Islanders' right of self-determination. *See, Report of the International Commission of Jurists on the Legal Aspects of the Aaland Islands
Question*, LEAGUE OF NATIONS OFFICIAL JOURNAL, spec. supp. no. 3 (1920).

   Does the outcome of this case sound consistent with the Canadian
Supreme Court's decision *Re Succession of Quebec*? If populations do not
have extensive rights of self-government or autonomy, do they then have a
right to secede? May they take up arms to accomplish this?

2.   In the former Yugoslavia, Kosovo was a province of Serbia. Its largely
Albanian ethnic population, however, enjoyed a good deal of autonomy, but
that was taken away by Slobodan Milosevic, the leader of Serbia, as
Yugoslavia began to disintegrate. Ibrahim Rugova, a leader of the Albanian
population, tried through non-violent resistance to regain autonomy. Milosevic responded with repression. Other Kosovo Albanians grew impatient
and formed the Kosovo Liberation Army that began to engage Serb forces
in Kosovo. By 1998, the U.S. and several European states grew alarmed by
the mounting violence and began to fear that atrocities would be committed
such as those that occurred as Croatia and Bosnia–Herzegovina established their independence. In March 1999, the North Atlantic Treaty
Organization (NATO), a collective self-defense organization consisting of
European states, the U.S., and Canada, bombed Serbia for 78 days. This
use of force conflicted with the terms of the UN Charter on the use of force
and resulted in an on-going debate about the appropriateness of "humanitarian intervention." (The international law on the use of force is the
subject of Chapter 10 *infra*.) NATO hoped in this case that the bombing
would pressure Milosevic into pulling Serb forces out of Kosovo. When
Milosevic did finally remove his troops they were replaced by an international coalition of forces and eventually a United Nations force. In the 10
years that followed, the Serb population of Kosovo either fled or were killed
so that by 2009, only 10% remained of the pre–1999 population. The Serb
people removed Milosevic from power and sent him to the International

Criminal Tribunal for the former Yugoslavia in The Hague to stand trial for genocide, war crimes, and crimes against humanity. The new leaders of Serbia offered Kosovo autonomy.

In 2008, the leader of the Kosovo Albanians rejected the autonomy offer and declared Kosovo an independent state. The U.S. and several other states quickly extended recognition. By 2009, 60 had done so, but twice that number did not follow suit. Rather, they requested an advisory opinion of the International Court of Justice as to whether Kosovo's unilateral declaration of independence was consistent with international law. The ICJ press release respecting the case begins as follows:

> THE HAGUE, 10 October 2008. On 8 October 2008 the General Assembly of the United Nations adopted resolution A/RES/63/3 in which, referring to Article 65 of the Statute of the Court, it requested the International Court of Justice to "render an advisory opinion on the following question: Is the unilateral declaration of independence by the Provisional Institutions of Self–Government of Kosovo in accordance with international law?"

3.   By contrast to Kosovo, the Dalai Lama, the spiritual leader of many Tibetans, has called autonomy for within China rather than outright independence for Tibet. See *Dalai Lama: Growing Support in China for Tibetans*, http://www.dalailama.com/news.407.htm (Aug. 4, 2009). Why do you think the Dalai Lama would be content with autonomy for Tibet? Could there be reasons other than the evident one that he believes convincing China to give Tibet independence is hopeless? The Dalai Lama is one of the world's leading proponents of non-violence. Might this fact play a role in his position? Why do you suppose China resists giving autonomy to Tibet? How might Tibetans persuade China using non-violent means?

4.   When a state such as Yugoslavia breaks up, a number of succession issues arise. Succession with respect to treaties was discussed in Chapter 2. Other succession issues concern membership in international organizations and the division of assets and debts. *See,* TAI-HENG CHENG, STATE SUCCESSION AND COMMERCIAL OBLIGATIONS (2006).

5.   Who is the "self" in self-determination? In other words, who should have a right of self-determination, whether for statehood, autonomy or other status in international relations? Can you tell from the *Secession of Quebec* case or the *Aaland Islands* case? See the discussion of communities and indigenous people *infra*.

6.   For more on self-determination, see, EDWARD McWHINNEY, SELF–DETERMINATION OF PEOPLES AND PLURAL-ETHNIC STATES IN CONTEMPORARY INTERNATIONAL LAW: FAILED STATES, NATION-BUILDING AND THE ALTERNATIVE, FEDERAL OPTION (2007) and KAREN KNOP, DIVERSITY AND SELF-DETERMINATION IN INTERNATIONAL LAW (2002).

B.   NON–STATE ACTORS

The previous section ended with a discussion of certain communities that have many of the attributes of statehood but have not achieved that status. International law, nevertheless, contains a growing body of rights and duties for such communities depending on certain factors. Grotius discusses whether non-self-governing communities ever have the right to rebel, but for much of the 19th and the first half of the 20th Century, communities that had not achieved statehood had few rights beyond those of individuals. This section will begin with a brief discussion of major principles of international law with respect individuals—human beings, "natural individuals." The more detailed discussion of their rights and duties is found in Chapter 5. The law that applies to groups of individuals, whether communities, non-governmental organizations or criminal groups, is provided next. The final section briefly introduces legal persons such as corporations but also vessels and some other subjects of international of a similar type. The detailed discussion of international economic law, of great relevance to major corporations today, is found in Chapter 7.

1. Individuals

As you saw in the *LaGrand* case in Chapter 1, and the Tinoco Claims arbitration above, individuals can receive protection from their state of nationality when living or traveling in other states. This is just one of the many reasons why it is important for individuals to have a nationality—a tie to a sovereign state, the most privileged of international law's subjects. International law provides principles governing the extension of nationality to individuals. This section first discusses the grant of nationality, then the situation of persons in the world without a nationality, "stateless persons."

a. NATIONALITY

The Notteböhm Case

Liechtenstein v. Guatemala
International Court of Justice
1955 I.C.J. Rep. 4 (Judgment of April 6)

* * *

By the Application filed, the Government of Liechtenstein instituted proceedings before the Court in which it claimed restitution and compensation on the ground that the Government of Guatemala had "acted towards the person and property of Mr. Friedric Notteböhm, a citizen of Liechtenstein, in a manner contrary to international law". In its Counter–Memorial, the Government of Guatemala contended that this claim was inadmissible on a number of grounds, and one of its objections to the admissibility of the claim related to the nationality of the person for whose protection Liechtenstein had seised the Court.

It appears to the Court that this plea in bar is of fundamental importance and that it is therefore desirable to consider it at the outset. Guatemala has referred to a well-established principle of international law, which it expressed in [its] Counter–Memorial, where it is stated that "it is the bond of nationality between the State and the individual which alone confers upon the State the right of diplomatic protection''. * * *

Liechtenstein considers itself to be acting in conformity with this principle and contends that Notteböhm is its national by virtue of the naturalization conferred upon him. Notteböhm was born at Hamburg [in] 1881. He was German by birth, and still possessed German nationality when, in October 1939, he applied for naturalization in Liechtenstein.

In 1905 he went to Guatemala. He took up residence there and made that country the headquarters of his business activities, which increased and prospered; these activities developed in the field of commerce, banking and plantations. Having been an employee in the firm of Notteböhm Hermanos, which had been founded by his brothers Juan and Arturo, he became their partner in 1912 and later, in 1937, he was made head of the firm. After 1905 he sometimes went to Germany on business and to other countries for holidays. He continued to have business connections in Germany. He paid a few visits to a brother who had lived in Liechtenstein since 1931. Some of his other brothers, relatives and friends were in Germany, others in Guatemala. He himself continued to have his fixed abode in Guatemala until 1943, until the occurrence of the events which constitute the basis of the present dispute.

In 1939, after having provided for the safeguarding of his interests in Guatemala by a power of attorney given to the firm of Notteböhm Hermanos on March 22nd, he left that country at a date fixed by Counsel for Liechtenstein as at approximately the end of March or the beginning of April, when he seems to have gone to Hamburg, and later to have paid a few brief visits to Vaduz where he was at the beginning of October 1939. It was then, on October 9th, a little more than a month after the opening of the second World War marked by Germany's attack on Poland, that his attorney, Dr. Marxer, submitted an application for naturalization on behalf of Notteböhm.

The Liechtenstein Law of January 4th, 1934, lays down the conditions for the naturalization of foreigners, specifies the supporting documents to be submitted and the undertakings to be given and defines the competent organs for giving a decision and the procedure to be followed. The Law specifies certain mandatory requirements, namely, that the applicant for naturalization should prove: (1) "that the acceptance into the Home Corporation (Heimatverband) of a Liechtenstein commune has been promised to him in case of acquisition of the nationality of the State"; (2) that he will lose his former nationality as a result of naturalization, although this requirement may be waived under stated conditions. It further makes naturalization conditional upon compliance with the requirement of residence for at least three years in the territory of the Principality, although it is provided that "this requirement can be dispensed with in circumstances deserving special consideration and by way of exception". In addition, the applicant for naturalization is required to submit a number of documents, such as evidence of his residence in the territory of the Principality, a certificate of good conduct issued by the competent authority of the place of residence, documents relating to his property and income and, if he is not a resident in the Principality, proof that he has concluded an agreement with the Revenue authorities, "subsequent to the revenue commission of the presumptive home commune having been heard". The Law further provides for the payment by the applicant of a naturalization fee, which is fixed by the Princely Government and amounts to at least one half of the sum payable by the applicant for reception into the Home Corporation of a Liechtenstein commune, the promise of such reception constituting a condition under the Law for the grant of naturalization.

* * *

As to the consideration of the application by the competent organs and the procedure to be followed by them, the Law provides that the Government, after having examined the application and the documents pertaining thereto, and after having obtained satisfactory information concerning the applicant, shall submit the application to the Diet. If the latter approves the application, the Government shall submit the requisite request to the Prince, who alone is entitled to confer nationality of the Principality.

* * *

This was the legal position with regard to applications for naturalization at the time when Notteböhm's application was submitted.

On October 9th, 1939, Notteböhm, "resident in Guatemala since 1905 (at present residing as a visitor with his brother, Hermann Notteböhm, in Vaduz)", applied for admission as a national of Liechtenstein and, at the same time, for the previous conferment of citizenship in the Commune of Mauren. He sought dispensation from the condition of three years' residence as prescribed by law, without indicating the special circumstances warranting such waiver. He submitted a statement of the Credit Suisse in Zurich concerning his assets, and undertook to pay 25,000 Swiss francs to the Commune of Mauren, 12,500 Swiss francs to the State, to which was to be added the payment of dues in connection with the proceedings. He further stated that he had made "arrangements with the Revenue Authorities of the Government of Liechtenstein for the conclusion of a formal agreement to the effect that he will pay an annual tax of naturalization amounting to Swiss francs 1,000, of which Swiss francs 600 are payable to the Commune of Mauren and Swiss francs 400 are payable to the Principality of Liechtenstein, subject to the proviso that the payments of these taxes will be set off against ordinary taxes which will fall due if the applicant takes up residence in one of the Communes of the Principality". He further undertook to deposit as security a sum of 30,000 Swiss francs. He also gave certain general information as to his financial position and indicated that he would never become a burden to the Commune whose citizenship he was seeking.

* * *

A document dated October 15th, 1939, certifies that on that date the Commune of Mauren conferred the privilege of its citizenship upon Mr. Notteböhm and requested the Government to transmit it to the Diet for approval. A certificate of October 17th, 1939, evidences the payment of the taxes required to be paid by Mr. Notteböhm. On October 20th, 1939, Mr. Notteböhm took the oath of allegiance and a final arrangement concerning liability to taxation was concluded on October 23rd. This was the procedure followed in the case of the naturalization of Notteböhm. A certificate of nationality has also been produced, signed on behalf of the Government of the Principality and dated October 20th, 1939, to the effect that Notteböhm was naturalized by Supreme Resolution of the Reigning Prince dated October 13th, 1939.

Having obtained a Liechtenstein passport, Notteböhm had it visaed by the Consul General of Guatemala in Zurich on December 1st, 1939, and returned to Guatemala at the beginning of 1940, where he resumed his former business activities and in particular the management of the firm of Notteböhm Hermanos.

* * * Liechtenstein requests the Court to find and declare, first, "that the naturalization of Mr. Notteböhm in Liechtenstein on October 13th, 1939, was not contrary to international law", and, secondly, "that Liechtenstein's claim on behalf of Mr. Notteböhm as a national of Liechtenstein is admissible before the Court".

The Final Conclusions of Guatemala, on the other hand, request the Court "to declare that the claim of the Principality of Liechtenstein is inadmissible", and set forth a number of grounds relating to the nationality of Liechtenstein granted to Notteböhm by naturalization.

Thus, the real issue before the Court is the admissibility of the claim of Liechtenstein in respect of Notteböhm. Liechtenstein's first submission referred to above is a reason advanced for a decision by the Court in favour of Liechtenstein, while the several grounds given by Guatemala on the question of nationality are intended as reasons for the inadmissibility of Liechtenstein's claim. The present task of the Court is limited to adjudicating upon the admissibility of the claim of Liechtenstein in respect of Notteböhm on the basis of such reasons as it may itself consider relevant and proper.

To decide upon the admissibility of the Application, the Court must ascertain whether the nationality conferred on Notteböhm by Liechtenstein by means of a naturalization which took place in the circumstances which have been described, can be validly invoked as against Guatemala, whether it bestows upon Liechtenstein a sufficient title to the exercise of protection in respect of Notteböhm as against Guatemala and therefore entitles it to seise the Court of a claim relating to him. In this connection, Counsel for Liechtenstein said: "the essential question is whether Mr. Notteböhm, having acquired the nationality of Liechtenstein, that acquisition of nationality is one which must be recognized by other States". This formulation is accurate, subject to the twofold reservation that, in the first place, what is involved is not recognition for all purposes but merely for the purposes of the admissibility of the Application, and, secondly, that what is involved is not recognition by all States but only by Guatemala.

The Court does not propose to go beyond the limited scope of the question which it has to decide, namely whether the nationality conferred on Notteböhm can be relied upon as against Guatemala in justification of the proceedings instituted before the Court. It must decide this question on the basis of international law; to do so is consistent with the nature of the question and with the nature of the Court's own function.

* * *

Since no proof has been adduced that Guatemala has recognized the title to the exercise of protection relied upon by Liechtenstein as being derived from the naturalization which it granted to Notteböhm, the Court must consider whether such an act of granting nationality by Liechtenstein directly entails an obligation on the part of Guatemala to recognize its effect, namely, Liechtenstein's right to exercise its protection. In other words, it must be determined whether that unilateral act by Liechtenstein is one which can be relied upon against Guatemala in regard to the exercise of protection. The Court will deal with this question without considering that of the validity of Notteböhm's naturalization according to the law of Liechtenstein.

It is for Liechtenstein, as it is for every sovereign State, to settle by its own legislation the rules relating to the acquisition of its nationality, and to confer that nationality by naturalization granted by its own organs in accordance with that legislation. It is not necessary to determine whether international law imposes any limitations on its freedom of decision in this domain. Furthermore, nationality has its most immediate, its most far-reaching and, for most people, its only effects within the legal system of the State conferring it. Nationality serves above all to determine that the person upon whom it is conferred enjoys the rights and is bound by the obligations which the law of the State in question grants to or imposes on its nationals. This is implied in the wider concept that nationality is within the domestic jurisdiction of the State.

But the issue which the Court must decide is not one which pertains to the legal system of Liechtenstein. It does not depend on the law or on the decision of Liechtenstein whether that State is entitled to exercise its protection, in the case under consideration. To exercise protection, to apply to the Court, is to place oneself on the plane of international law. It is international law which determines whether a State is entitled to exercise protection and to seise the Court. The naturalization of Notteböhm was an act performed by Liechtenstein in the exercise of its domestic jurisdiction. The question to be decided is whether that act has the international effect here under consideration.

* * *

* * * International arbitrators, having before them allegations of nationality by the applicant State which were contested by the respondent State, have sought to ascertain whether nationality had been conferred by the applicant State in circumstances such as to give rise to an obligation on the part of the respondent State to recognize the effect of that nationality.

To decide this question arbitrators have evolved certain principles for determining whether full international effect was to be attributed to the nationality invoked. The same issue is now before the Court: it must be resolved by applying the same principles.

The courts of third States, when confronted by a similar situation, have dealt with it in the same way. * * *

International arbitrators have decided in the same way numerous cases of dual nationality, where the question arose with regard to the exercise of protection. They have given their preference to the real and effective nationality, that which accorded with the facts, that based on stronger factual ties between the person concerned and one of the States whose nationality is involved. Different factors are taken into consideration, and their importance will vary from one case to the next: the habitual residence of the individual concerned is an important factor, but there are other factors such as the centre of his interests, his family ties, his participation in public life, attachment shown by him for a given country and inculcated in his children, etc.

Similarly, the courts of third States, when they have before them an individual whom two other States hold to be their national, seek to resolve the conflict by having recourse to international criteria and their prevailing tendency is to prefer the real and effective nationality.

The same tendency prevails in the writings of publicists and in practice. This notion is inherent in the provisions of Article 3, paragraph 2, of the Statute of the Court. National laws reflect this tendency.

* * *

The practice of certain States which refrain from exercising protection in favour of a naturalized person when the latter has in fact, by his prolonged absence, severed his links with what is no longer for him anything but his nominal country, manifests the view of these States that, in order to be capable of being invoked against another State, nationality must correspond with the factual situation. * * *

The character thus recognized on the international level as pertaining to nationality is in no way inconsistent with the fact that international law leaves it to each State to lay down the rules governing the grant of its own nationality. The reason for this is that the diversity of demographic conditions has thus far made it impossible for any general agreement to be reached on the rules relating to nationality, although the latter by its very nature affects international relations. It has been considered that the best way of making such rules accord with the varying demographic conditions in different countries is to leave the fixing of such rules to the competence of each State. On the other hand, a State cannot claim that the rules it has thus laid down are entitled to recognition by another State unless it has acted in conformity with this general aim of making the legal bond of nationality accord with the individual's genuine connection with the State which assumes the defence of its citizens by means of protection as against other States.

* * *

According to the practice of States, to arbitral and judicial decisions and to the opinions of writers, nationality is a legal bond having as its basis a social fact of attachment, a genuine connection of existence, interests and sentiments, together with the existence of reciprocal rights and duties. It may be said to constitute the juridical expression of the fact that the individual upon whom it is conferred, either directly by the law or as the result of an act of the authorities, is in fact more closely connected with the population of the State conferring nationality than with that of any other State. Conferred by a State, it only entitles that State to exercise protection vis-à-vis another State, if it constitutes a translation into juridical terms of the individual's connection with the State which has made him its national.

Diplomatic protection and protection by means of international judicial proceedings constitute measures for the defence of the rights of the State.

* * *

Since this is the character which nationality must present when it is invoked to furnish the State which has granted it with a title to the exercise of protection and to the institution of international judicial proceedings, the Court must ascertain whether the nationality granted to Notteböhm by means of naturalization is of this character or, in other words, whether the factual connection between Notteböhm and Liechtenstein in the period preceding, contemporaneous with and following his naturalization appears to be sufficiently close, so preponderant in relation to any connection which may have existed between him and any other State, that it is possible to regard the nationality conferred upon him as real and effective, as the exact juridical expression of a social fact of a connection which existed previously or came into existence thereafter.

Naturalization is not a matter to be taken lightly. * * *

To appraise its international effect, it is impossible to disregard the circumstances in which it was conferred, the serious character which attaches to it, the real and effective, and not merely the verbal preference of the individual seeking it for the country which grants it to him.

At the time of his naturalization does Notteböhm appear to have been more closely attached by his tradition, his establishment, his interests, his activities, his family ties, his intentions for the near future to Liechtenstein than to any other State? * * *

* * *

The essential facts are as follows: At the date when he applied for naturalization Notteböhm had been a German national from the time of his birth. He had always retained his connections with members of his family who had remained in Germany and he had always had business connections with that country. His country had been at war for more than a month, and there is nothing to indicate that the application for naturalization then made by Notteböhm was motivated by any desire to dissociate himself from the Government of his country.

He had been settled in Guatemala for 34 years. He had carried on his activities there. It was the main seat of his interests. He returned there shortly after his naturalization, and it remained the centre of his interests and of his business activities. He stayed there until his removal as a result of war measures in 1943. He subsequently attempted to return there, and he now complains of Guatemala's refusal to admit him. There, too, were several members of his family who sought to safeguard his interests.

In contrast, his actual connections with Liechtenstein were extremely tenuous. No settled abode, no prolonged residence in that country at the time of his application for naturalization: the application indicates that he was paying a visit there and confirms the transient character of this visit by its request that the naturalization proceedings should be initiated and concluded without delay. No intention of settling there was shown at that time or realized in the ensuing weeks, months or years—on the contrary, he returned to Guatemala very shortly after his naturalization and showed every intention of remaining there. If Notteböhm went to Liechtenstein in 1946, this was because of the refusal of Guatemala to admit him. No indication is given of the grounds warranting the waiver of the condition of residence, required by the 1934 Nationality Law, which waiver was implicitly granted to him. There is no allegation of any economic interests or of any activities exercised or to be exercised in Liechtenstein, and no manifestation of any intention whatsoever to transfer all or some of his interests and his business activities to Liechtenstein. It is unnecessary in this connection to attribute much importance to the promise to pay the taxes levied at the time of his naturalization. The only links to be discovered between the Principality and Notteböhm are the short sojourns already referred to and the presence in Vaduz of one of his brothers: but his brother's presence is referred to in his application for naturalization only as a reference to his good conduct. Furthermore, other members of his family have asserted Notteböhm's desire to spend his old age in Guatemala.

These facts establish, on the one hand, the absence of any bond of attachment between Notteböhm and Liechtenstein and, on the other hand, the existence of a long-standing and close connection between him and Guatemala, a link which his naturalization in no way weakened. That naturalization was not based on any real prior connection with Liechtenstein, nor did it in any way alter the manner of life of the person upon whom it was conferred in exceptional circumstances of speed and accommodation. In both respects, it was lacking in the genuineness requisite to an act of such importance, if it is to be entitled to be respected by a State in the position of Guatemala. It was granted without regard to the concept of nationality. * * *

Naturalization was asked for not so much for the purpose of obtaining a legal recognition of Notteböhm's membership in fact in the population of Liechtenstein, as it was to enable him to substitute for his status as a national of a belligerent State that of a national of a neutral State, with the sole aim of thus coming within the protection of Liechtenstein but not of becoming wedded to its traditions, its interests, its way of life or of assuming the obligations—other than fiscal obligations—and exercising the rights pertaining to the status thus acquired. Guatemala is under no obligation to recognize a nationality granted in such circumstances. Liechtenstein consequently is not entitled to extend its protection to Notteböhm vis-à-vis Guatemala and its claim must, for this reason, be held to be inadmissible.

The Court is not therefore called upon to deal with the other pleas in bar put forward by Guatemala or the Conclusions of the Parties other than those on which it is adjudicating in accordance with the reasons indicated above. For these reasons, The COURT, by eleven votes to three, Holds that the claim submitted by the Government of the Principality of Liechtenstein is inadmissible. * * *

NOTES AND QUESTIONS

1.   In its *Advisory Opinion on Nationality Decrees in Tunis and Morocco* (France and Great Britain), 1923, P.C.I.J., Ser. B, No. 4, the court was asked whether a dispute between France and Great Britain as to nationality decrees in Tunis and Morocco was or was not, by international law, solely a matter of domestic jurisdiction under Article 15, paragraph 8, of the Covenant of the League of Nations (compare U.N. Charter Article 2(7) which now governs the question of domestic jurisdiction). Apparently on the ground that the relations between France and Great Britain and their protectorates were determined by international agreements and that "it will be necessary to resort to international law in order to decide what the value of an agreement of this kind may be as regards third States," the court expressed the opinion that the dispute was not, by international law, solely a matter of domestic jurisdiction. But for the existence of the agreements, however, the court presumably would not have taken jurisdiction: "The question whether a certain matter is or is not solely within the jurisdiction of a State is an essentially relative question; it depends upon the development of international relations. Thus, in the present state of international law, questions of nationality are, in the opinion of the Court, in principle within this reserved domain." However, the evolution of customary and treaty law, particularly in the field of human rights, raises the question whether the International Court of Justice should be expected to reach the same conclusion today.

2.   How far does *Notteböhm* reach? Liechtenstein's claim was asserted against another state, Guatemala, with which Notteböhm had, in the language of the court, "a long-standing and close connection," a "link" which his naturalization in no way weakened. Notteböhm had been sent by Guatemala to the United States for internment during World War II. Suppose that the United States had injured Notteböhm by seizing and retaining, without compensation, property that he had removed to a bank in the United States. Suppose that Liechtenstein brought an action against the United States in the International Court of Justice on behalf of

Notteböhm. Suppose also that the United States asked the Court to declare the claim inadmissible on the ground that Liechtenstein has no standing. How should the court rule? *See Flegenheimer Case,* 14 Rep. of Int'l Arb. Awards 327 (Italian–United States Conciliation Commission, 1958). The International Law Commission (I.L.C.), in its *Report on Diplomatic Protection,* 52nd Session, May 1–June 9th and 10th–August, 2000, UNGAOR Fifty-fifth Session, Supp. No. 10 *(N55/10),* 141, 158–164 (2000), discussed this issue and the view of the special rapporteur was that based on doubts about the legality of Liechtenstein's conferral of nationality on *Notteböhm* and his closer ties to Guatemala than with Liechtenstein that the International Court of Justice "had not purported to pronounce on the status of Notteböhm's nationality vis-à-vis all States." Note that in the *Barcelona Traction case,* 1970 I.C.J. Rep. 3, that the International Court of Justice held that in the case of severe human rights abuses, which are viewed as being severe enough that all states have an obligation *erga omnes* not to participate in them, *any state may intervene.*

3. If a stateless person persuaded *any* state to espouse his claim against a state that wrongfully harmed him, but with which he previously had no link, should the requested state be permitted to make the claim before the Court?

4. *Dual or Multiple Nationality.* The traditional rule codified in the 1930 Hague Convention on Conflict of Nationality Laws, 179 L.N.T.S. 89, article 4 provides that a state "may not afford diplomatic protection to one of its nationals against a state whose nationality such a person also possesses." *See The Canevaro Case (Italy v. Peru)* 11 R.I.A.A. 397 (1912). However, in *Iran–U.S. Case No. A/18 (Iran–U.S. Claims Tribunal),* 5 Iran–U.S.C.T. 251 (1984), it was held that this rule did not apply where the dual national brought an individual claim. Furthermore, the Tribunal cast doubt on the present day validity of the 1930 Hague Convention and held that the rule should be that of dominant or effective nationality. Today, it is common for states to permit multiple nationalities. Is there any danger in this? *See also,* the United Nations Compensation (1991–2007) for claims against Iraq http://www.uncc.ch/.

5. For further reading on nationality and citizenship, *see,* PETER SPIRO, BEYOND CITIZENSHIP: AMERICAN IDENTITY AFTER GLOBALIZATION (2008) and RANDALL HANSEN AND PATRICK WEIL, DUAL NATIONALITY, SOCIAL RIGHTS, AND FEDERAL CITIZENSHIPS IN THE U.S. AND EUROPE: THE REINVENTION OF CITIZENSHIP (2002).

b. STATELESSNESS

Re Immigration Act and Hanna

Canada, Supreme Court of British Columbia, 1957
21 Western Weekly Rep. 400

■ SULLIVAN, J. This is a "hard case" of the kind of which it is said that bad law is made. The applicant George Christian Hanna, whom I shall refer to as "Hanna" in these reasons for judgment, is a young man without a country—one of those unfortunate "stateless" persons of the world whose status is a matter of concern to humanitarians and has prompted men and women of good will of all countries to seek relief for such persons through the agency of the Economic and Social Council of the United Nations. A convention was adopted by that council in September 1954, to which, however, Canada is not a signatory.

The matter comes before me by way of habeas corpus with certiorari in aid. Hanna seeks a judicial declaration that his detention under a deportation order made by F. Wragg, an immigration officer (acting as a special inquiry officer) dated January 18, 1957, and confirmed on appeal to an immigration appeal board duly constituted under the provisions of the Immigration Act, RSC, 1952, ch. 325, is illegal: (1) Because the deportation order is defective, incomplete, impossible of interpretation or enforcement and beyond the statutory authority of Mr. Wragg to make; and (2) Because the immigration appeal board improperly denied Hanna the right to be heard, either in person or by counsel, at the appeal proceedings before such board.

The issues thus presented for my determination are strictly legal in nature and narrow in their scope. I have no right to reflect upon and must guard against the danger that the strictly legal opinion which I am required to express should be influenced in any degree by considerations of human sympathy for this unfortunate (23–year–old) young applicant in the frustrating dilemma with which fate seems to have confronted him throughout his lifetime prior to his last arrival in Canada as ship-bound prisoner aboard a tramp motor-ship in her ceaseless meanderings from port to port throughout the world. The deportation order in question is in the words and figures following:

Department of Citizenship and Immigration Deportation Order Against

Christian George Hanna of Djibouti, French Somaliland

under section 28 of the Immigration Act. On the basis of the evidence adduced at an inquiry held at the Immigration Building, Vancouver, B.C., on January 18, 1957 I have reached the decision that you may not come into or remain in Canada as of right and that you are a member of the prohibited class described in paragraph (t) of Section 5 of the Immigration Act, in that you do not fulfil or comply with the conditions or requirements of Subsection (1), Subsection (3) and Subsection (8) of Section 18 of the Immigration Regulations.

I hereby order you to be detained and to be deported to the place whence you came to Canada, or to the country of which you are a national or citizen, or to the country of your birth, or to such country as may be approved by the minister.

Date 18 January 1957, [Sgd.] F. WRAGG, Special Inquiry Officer [Sgd.] C.G. HANNA.

Subsecs. (1), (3) and (8) of sec. 18 of the regulations to which said deportation order refers require that an immigrant possess a passport and visa; and that his passport or other travel document bear a medical certificate in approved form.

It should be stated at the outset that no Canadian court has power to assist Hanna in his plea that he be given right of residence in Canada. That is a decision for immigration officials, and for them alone, to make. Similarly all right of exercise of discretionary power to exempt from strict compliance with the requirements of the Immigration Act or regulations made thereunder is vested in and is the prerogative of only the minister, deputy minister, director, or such other persons as may be authorized to act for the director. * * *

* * *

It may be helpful to outline Hanna's history and background as it is disclosed by the scanty material before me. Most of such material consists of Hanna's sworn testimony, given in the English language, when he was before Mr. Wragg on January 18, 1957, at which time his knowledge and proficiency in the use of our language was not as great as it may be now. He says that he was born at sea and that no known record of his birth is extant. The name of the vessel aboard which he was born, and particulars of her nationality or port of registry are unknown. His father was named George Hanna and supposedly travelled to French Somaliland from Liberia, a small republic situate on the west coast of Africa. His mother's maiden name was Marian Marika and she was a native of Ethiopia (or Abyssinia)— a country whose status either as empire or vassal of Italy at any given time can be determined only by reference to historical data bearing upon Emperor Haile Selassie's struggles in warfare with the late Benito Mussolini. Hanna understands that his parents met and were married at Djibouti, the capital city of French Somaliland. The accuracy of his information in this respect should be easy to check. French Somaliland is a very small country. It has been a French colony for about 80 years. * * * Hanna was the only child born of his parents' marriage and both of his parents are dead. Continuing the narrative according to Hanna's understanding of events, his father left his mother to seek employment in Liberia. Subsequently his mother, being pregnant at the time, and seeking to rejoin her husband, took passage on a ship sailing out of Djibouti. She became ill and gave birth to Hanna when the ship was one day at sea, and because of her illness the ship was put about and returned to Djibouti where she and her newborn child were placed in a hospital or home for women. Thereafter Hanna was cared for by his mother who worked at various times at Addis Ababa and Dire Wawa (both in Ethiopia) and at Djibouti in French Somaliland, until Hanna was six years of age. She then died and thereafter Hanna more or less "raised himself" as he puts it, with some assistance from a kindly old Turkish gentleman at Djibouti and others, including a Japanese gentleman at Dire Wawa in Ethiopia.

During his years of infancy and adolescence Hanna seems to have crossed and recrossed the international boundaries of Ethiopia, French

Somaliland, British Somaliland and Eritrea (formerly an Italian colony but now a province of Ethiopia by virtue of the recommendation of a United Nations' committee adopted by the General Assembly in 1952) without encountering difficulty with the immigration officials of those countries. I suppose that youth was in his favour at the outset, and I suppose, too, that the international boundaries referred to were not too well defined at that time. That still seems to be the case. I understand that the accurate fixation of the international borders convergent upon the small area of French Somaliland is a problem which presently engages the attention of the United Nations' General Assembly.

In this way Hanna lived and worked from time to time (inter alia) in the ports of Zeila and Berbera in British Somaliland where he picked up a smattering of English. He says that his mother spoke English and, although he never saw his father, it is his understanding that his parents conversed in English. This would be consistent with Hanna's theory that his father was a native of Liberia—a republic which most people look upon as a virtual protectorate of the United States of America, and where English is spoken.

As he grew older Hanna seems to have encountered and had difficulty with the immigration officers of these adjacent countries, in none of which he could claim right of residence. He thereby learned that possession of a birth certificate is an indispensable requirement of modern society. He learned "the hard way" that some of the fundamental human rights with which all men are endowed by their Creator at birth were not his to enjoy without the intervention and benevolent assistance of some temporal power—a power to be exercised in many cases according to the whim or opinion of immigration officers whose numbers are legion in most sovereign states. That is not to say, of course, that he or anyone else possesses an inherent right to enter or remain in Canada unless born here. The late Right Honorable W.L. Mackenzie King, Prime Minister of Canada, said in the House of Commons on May 1, 1947, that "It is not a 'fundamental human right' of an alien to enter Canada. It is a privilege. It is a matter of domestic policy."

* * *

Almost three years ago, when he was in the port of Massaua, Eritrea, Hanna stowed away in an Italian tramp steamer in the hope of being carried in her to some country which would grant him asylum and right of residence. His plan met with frustration because upon arrival of such ship at any port he was immediately locked up and denied permission to land. After a year or more of such aimless wandering and imprisonment, Hanna escaped from the Italian vessel when she called at Beirut in the republic of Lebanon, and concealed himself in the hold of the Norwegian motor-ship "Gudveig." As a stowaway in such latter vessel he fared no better than before. He was held prisoner aboard "The Gudveig" for more than 16 months and made three or more trips to Canada in her until his release under writ of habeas corpus in these proceedings. He first came before Clyne, J., upon return of a show cause summons on January 18, 1957, wherein he challenged the legality of his detention by the master of "The Gudveig." My learned brother there held (correctly, in my respectful opinion) that the master's detention of Hanna was not illegal since the master was subject to and bound by the regulations applicable to "stowaways" as passed pursuant to the provisions of the Immigration Act. Thereafter Hanna made application to enter Canada and his status was thereby changed from that of "stowaway" to that of "immigrant." An immigrant is defined by sec. 2(i) of the Immigration Act as follows: (i) "immigrant" means a person who seeks admission to Canada for permanent residence.

* * * And so, at a time when it had become a widely publicized matter of general public knowledge or repute that Hanna possessed no proof of birth nor documents of any kind, he was granted the privilege of appearing before three separate departmental tribunals for the purpose of proving—if he could—that he did in fact possess such documents. Of course, he was unable to discharge that onus, and the deportation order followed which is now under attack in these proceedings.

[Now to] that deportation order. Was it an order which the special inquiry officer had legal authority to make in all of the circumstances existing at the time of its making? It contains four separate directives which are stated in the alternative and, presumably, in the order of their importance.

The most important directive is, No. 1, that Hanna be deported to the place whence he came to Canada. The next directive is, No. 2, that he be deported to the country of which he is a national or citizen. The next is, No. 3, that he be deported to the country of his birth. The final alternative is, No. 4, that he be deported to such country as may be approved by the minister.

The No. 4 directive is meaningless in the absence of anything to show a possibility of the minister ever finding a country which would be willing to admit this young man in the face of Canada's refusal to admit him. It cannot be assumed that travel documents are of less significance in other countries than here. The thing goes further than that, however, because sec. 40(2) of our Act makes the minister's power of designation and approval of "such country" conditional upon the owners of the M.S. "Gudveig" first making request for such ministerial approval. Even then, as I interpret the statute, the approval of the minister could have no effect unless after finding "a country that is willing to receive him," Hanna were to indicate that such country is "acceptable" to him.

Directives No. 2 and No. 3 referring, respectively, to country of nationality or citizenship and country of birth, may be discussed together. Neither of these directives could possibly be complied with. In the absence of satisfactory evidence of nationality of a legitimate father and lack of any evidence as to the nationality or registry of the ship aboard which Hanna was born, these directives of the deportation order are meaningless. The inescapable fact is that Hanna is a "stateless person," and the efforts of the department to prove otherwise have not been impressive. I was presented with evidence (consisting of affidavits by lawyers in Oslo, Norway, and a Canadian immigration officer) in support of the submission that Hanna is not "stateless" and that the words of the directive "country of your birth," therefore, are not meaningless. The trouble is that whilst the affidavit of the immigration officer fixes Hanna's birthplace as Djibouti in French Somaliland, the Norwegian lawyers suggest that he is an Egyptian who was born at Alexandria. None of this conflicting evidence is credible. It is all based on hearsay and, perhaps, the least said about it, the better.

[Now for] consideration of directive No. 1—that Hanna be deported to the place whence he came to Canada. What does it mean?

The department's position, as I understand it, is that it could mean a number of things which it leaves to other people to determine for themselves. The place whence Hanna came to Canada might be the port of Beirut in the republic of Lebanon since that is the place where he first stowed away in the M.S. "Gudveig." Perhaps that interpretation is favoured by the department since it has presented certain material tending to show that if Lebanese authorities can be satisfied that Hanna stowed away at Beirut, they might permit him to land in their country—a country, incidentally, which is quite as foreign to Hanna as it is to me. Then again the department seems to suggest that the place whence Hanna came to Canada could be the United Kingdom and an affidavit is presented for the purpose of showing that "The Gudveig" sailed non-stop from the United Kingdom to Vancouver on her last voyage with Hanna aboard. Perhaps the place whence Hanna came to Canada could be the port of Massaua in Eritrea, since that was the starting point of his aimless wanderings as a stowaway in search of a country which would give him right of residence. Other interpretations are possible, but it seems to me that the matter of correct interpretation is of comparative unimportance here. The thing of importance, is that the special inquiry officer delegated to the master or owners of "The Gudveig" the responsibility for saying what his deportation order means; and, apart from the circumstances that he himself does not seem to know what it means, I am of opinion that he has not that power of delegation under the Act. I have had reference to the authorities cited by counsel wherein it was held that deportation orders made (as this one was) in form approved by the minister were valid and enforceable notwithstanding their multiplicity of alternative directives, but in none of such cases were the facts comparable to the extraordinary facts of this amazing case. In each of such cases the meaning of the deportation order in the form used was clearly apparent to everyone concerned or affected by it. In no case did the deportation order require subsequent inquiry or investigation by anyone for determination of its meaning. In none was there a necessarily incidental delegation of his authority by the special inquiry officer who made the order for deportation. These are some of the things which distinguish Hanna's case from all others.

From whatever angle one views it, so far as Hanna is concerned, this deportation order amounted to a sentence of imprisonment aboard "The

Gudveig" for an indefinite term, and in my opinion and finding, no immigration officer has the legal right to exercise such drastic power.

* * *

For the reasons previously expressed, there will be judgment for Hanna in these proceedings, with costs. That does not mean that he has established any legal right to enter or remain in Canada. As previously stated, it is for immigration officials and for them alone to grant or withhold that privilege. This judgment does not mean that Hanna may not be deported legally from Canada by further proceedings properly instituted and conducted in accordance with the provisions and intent of the Immigration Act. It means only that the present deportation order is illegal and that Hanna is entitled to be released from detention thereunder; and I so order.

* * *

NOTES AND QUESTIONS

1.   What happens to Hanna now? In *Staniszewski v. Watkins*, 80 F.Supp. 132 (S.D.N.Y.1948), a stateless seaman was released after being detained at Ellis Island for about seven months. The court observed that the government was "willing that he go back to the ship, but if he were sent back aboard ship and sailed to the port * * * from which he last sailed to the United States, he would probably be denied permission to land." The court said, "There is no other country that would take him, without proper documents." The court sustained the seaman's writ of habeas corpus and ordered his release: "He will be required to inform the immigration officials at Ellis Island by mail on the 15th of each month, stating where he is employed and where he can be reached. If the government does succeed in arranging for petitioner's deportation to a country that will be ready to receive him as a resident, it may then advise the petitioner to that effect and arrange for his deportation in the manner provided by law."

Similarly, in *Public Prosecutor v. Zinger,* France, Tribunal of the Seine, 1936, [1935–37] Ann.Dig. 307 (No. 138), the court ordered the release of a stateless person who had been imprisoned for failure to obey expulsion orders. The court weighed the alternatives of releasing the man or imprisoning him "at the cost of the French taxpayer" for an offence which he could not help committing, since he was unable to leave French territory. The court concluded: "release is the best solution."

2.   Three more recent cases led to favorable results for the detained aliens. In *Zadvydas v. Davis* and *Ashcroft v. Kim Ho Ma,* 28 June, 2001, the U.S. Supreme Court applied an implicit reasonableness limitation of detention and presumptive reasonableness duration of six months in cases where they were detained by U.S. immigration authorities beyond the 90 day removal period under U.S. law (69 USLW 4581 and 4626). The third case had a belated but happy ending under administrative action. In September 1999, at the Charles de Gaulle Airport near Paris, French authorities finally allowed Marham Karimi Nasseri to leave the airport where he had been

living in the passenger area for 11 years because, on account of unlawful entry, authorities would not permit him to enter France, and because other countries would not accept him. New York Times, 27 September 1999, p. A4, Col. 1.

2.   Communities and Groups

a.   COMMUNITIES

United Nations Declaration on the Rights of Indigenous Peoples

September 13, 2007
UN General Assembly Res. 61/295

* * *

Article 1

Indigenous peoples have the right to the full enjoyment, as a collective or as individuals, of all human rights and fundamental freedoms as recognized in the Charter of the United Nations, the Universal Declaration of Human Rights and international human rights law.

Article 2

Indigenous peoples and individuals are free and equal to all other peoples and individuals and have the right to be free from any kind of discrimination, in the exercise of their rights, in particular that based on their indigenous origin or identity.

Article 3

Indigenous peoples have the right to self-determination. By virtue of that right they freely determine their political status and freely pursue their economic, social and cultural development.

Article 4

Indigenous peoples, in exercising their right to self-determination, have the right to autonomy or self-government in matters relating to their internal and local affairs, as well as ways and means for financing their autonomous functions.

Article 5

Indigenous peoples have the right to maintain and strengthen their distinct political, legal, economic, social and cultural institutions, while retaining their right to participate fully, if they so choose, in the political, economic, social and cultural life of the State.

Article 6

Every indigenous individual has the right to a nationality.

Article 7

1.   Indigenous individuals have the rights to life, physical and mental integrity, liberty and security of person.

2.   Indigenous peoples have the collective right to live in freedom, peace and security as distinct peoples and shall not be subjected to any act of genocide or any other act of violence, including forcibly removing children of the group to another group.

Article 8

1.   Indigenous peoples and individuals have the right not to be subjected to forced assimilation or destruction of their culture.

* * *

NOTES AND QUESTIONS

1.   The complete declaration may be found in the documents book and online. Review the complete document. Do you know to whom the declaration applies? Who are "indigenous people?"

2.   The declaration refers to the right of "self-determination" of indigenous people. Is that a different right than the one discussed in the previous section and claimed by the people of Quebec and Kosovo?

3.   In addition to indigenous people and ethnic groups claiming self-determination, what other communities can you identify that should have protection for their community status under international law? Members of religions? Ideological groups? What is a "community"?

4.   For more on indigenous peoples and international law, see, FREDERICO LENZERINI, REPARATONS FOR INDIGENOUS PEOPLES: INTERNATIONAL AND COMPARATIVE PERSPECTIVES (2008) and S. JAMES ANAYA, INDIGENOUS PEOPLES IN INTERNATIONAL LAW (1996).

b.   GROUPS

Mary Ellen O'Connell, Enhancing the Status of Non–State Actors

43 COL. J. OF TRANS 'L 437–440 (2005)*

The Evolution of Non–State Actors under International Law

These days, when we hear "non-state actor," we tend to think "terrorist organization." As a technical matter, however, non-state actors can be any actor on the international plane other than a sovereign state. Conveniently, most sovereign states are identifiable by their membership in the United Nations. Non-state actors, therefore, are those actors on the international plane that are not members of the United Nations. Inter-governmental organizations,[2] non-governmental organizations (NGOs), and indi-

---

* Most footnotes omitted.

    2. "Intergovernmental organization" may be defined as "an association of States established by and based upon a treaty, which pursues common aims and which has its own special

viduals—natural and juridical—can all be classified as non-state actors. We will focus here on those international non-state actors that consist of groups of human beings rather than groups of sovereign states. The law-abiding non-state actors such as Amnesty International, Greenpeace, Doctors Without Borders, CARE, and Human Rights Watch are typically designated "NGOs."[3] Across the legal divide we find organized crime and terrorist groups such as the Mafia, the Colombian drug cartel, the Irish Republican Army, Hamas, Abu Sayyef, and Al–Qaeda.

NGOs traditionally have had the legal status of individuals, and consequently, like most individuals, they generally exist under national law—the law of the place where they are created as well as the law of the places where they are active. Little, if any, case law exists describing the parameters of this status. The International Court of Justice (ICJ) decided in *Barcelona Traction* that corporations have the nationality of the place of incorporation. By analogy, the same can be said of those non-state actors that are formed under the law of a particular state, usually as a non-profit or charitable organization. Individual members of any type of non-state actor group enjoy basic human rights wherever they are. NGOs as organizations may, like corporations, claim treatment by a foreign government at the "minimal international standard." Among other things, NGO property may not be nationalized without compensation. Like corporations, NGOs must comply with both the law of the state of nationality as well as the law of the state where they are active. Still, NGOs, through the 1990s, gained greater rights and duties directly from international law. NGOs, supported by some governments, steadily pressed for greater rights of access—to state territory and to law-making fora. A certain amount of progress was made. This progress, however, was often thought to be at the cost of the nation-state's own status on the international plane.

By contrast, international criminal groups remained almost entirely subject to national criminal law. During the Nuremberg trials, the Nazi SS and other organizations were declared criminal entities under international law. But apparently no one was prosecuted for mere membership in these organizations. A variety of treaties today mandate that governments prohibit, through national criminal law, the existence of such groups and/or the right of such groups to carry out certain specified acts. Some limited principles of international law, therefore, are relevant. For the most part, however, non-state actors, especially criminal groups, are regulated under national law and have only limited status or "personality" on the international plane.

Nevertheless, commentators have also suggested that the preeminence of the state is challenged by criminal organizations. Professor Schachter

---

organs to fulfill particular functions within the organization...." Rudolf L. Bindschedler, *International Organizations, General Aspects, in* 2 ENCYCLOPEDIA OF INTERNATIONAL LAW 1289–90 (Rudolf Bernhardt ed., 1992).

3. According to Steve Charnovitz, the term "NGO" originated with the United Nations Charter. Steve Charnovitz, *Two Centuries of Participation: NGOs and International Governance,* 18 MICH. J. INT'L L. 183, 186 (1997). * * *

identified the impact on the state of "uncivil" society or criminal organizations:

> Criminal activity, of course, has always challenged state authority, but from the standpoint of international law a new dimension has been added. States and the international community are now threatened by transnational crime on an unprecedented scale. Some of the ... causes of globalization as well as the new communication networks have also increased the power of lawless groups. The scale of illegal drug traffic dwarfs the gross national product of many states and appears to be beyond the effective control of individual states or even the world community as a whole. The illegal arms trade also flourishes ostensibly beyond state control. International money laundering has expanded into a huge business. Terrorist activities, while mainly political in aim, also belong in the category of international criminal activity. All of these activities dramatically underscore the weakness of nation-states and of the international legal system.

Since 1990, however, counter-trends are evident respecting the prominence of non-state actors and their challenge to the state. * * * [T]he premier NGOs—the international humanitarian assistance organizations * * * have made the most progress toward enhanced status, owing to their enjoyment of international legal rights ensured in treaties and to their willingness to accept international legal duties that accompany those rights. * * * [S]ome cases indicat[e] a slowed pace toward greater international personality for NGOs. On the other hand, for groups at the opposite end of the non-state actor spectrum—international criminal organizations that use violence to achieve their goals—the United States [after 9/11] reversed its long-held position that terrorists and other criminal organizations receive no legal recognition as international actors.

* * *

2009 Annual Report of the International Committee of the Red Cross

May 25, 2009
www.icrc.org

The work of the ICRC is based on the four Geneva Conventions of 1949, their two Additional Protocols of 1977 and Additional Protocol III of 2005, the Statutes of the International Red Cross and Red Crescent Movement, and the resolutions of the International Conferences of the Red Cross and Red Crescent.

The ICRC's mission is to provide the victims of armed conflict with protection and assistance. To that end, the ICRC takes direct and immediate action in response to emergency situations, while at the same time promoting preventive measures, such as the dissemination and national implementation of IHL. It was on the ICRC's initiative that States adopted the original Geneva Convention of 1864. Since then, the ICRC, with the support of the entire Red Cross and Red Crescent Movement, has put constant pressure on governments to adapt IHL to changing circumstances, in particular to modern developments in the means and methods of warfare, so as to provide more effective protection and assistance for conflict victims. Today, all States are bound by the four Geneva Conventions of 1949, which, in times of armed conflict, protect wounded, sick and shipwrecked members of the armed forces, prisoners of war and civilians. Over three-quarters of all States are currently party to the 1977 Protocols additional to the Geneva Conventions. Protocol I protects the victims of international armed conflicts, while Protocol II protects the victims of non-international armed conflicts. These instruments have in particular codified the rules protecting the civilian population against the effects of hostilities. The legal bases of any action undertaken by the ICRC may be summed up as follows:

the four Geneva Conventions and Additional Protocol I confer on the ICRC a specific mandate to act in the event of international armed conflict. In particular, the ICRC has the right to visit prisoners of war and civilian internees. The Conventions also give the ICRC a broad right of initiative

in situations of armed conflict that are not international in character, the ICRC enjoys a right of humanitarian initiative recognized by the international community and enshrined in Article 3 common to the four Geneva Conventions

in the event of internal disturbances and tensions, and in any other situation that warrants humanitarian action, the ICRC also enjoys a right of initiative, which is affirmed and recognized in the Statutes of the International Red Cross and Red Crescent Movement. Thus, wherever IHL does not apply, the ICRC may offer its services to governments without that offer constituting interference in the internal affairs of the State concerned

Gabor Rona, The ICRC's Status: In a Class of Its Own

Feb. 17, 2004
www.icrc.org

The ICRC is sometimes referred to as a "non-governmental organization", or NGO. In fact, it's not—but neither is it an international or intergovernmental organization. So, what is its status?

* * *

The ICRC has a hybrid nature. As a private association formed under the Swiss Civil Code, its existence is not in itself mandated by governments. And yet its functions and activities—to provide protection and assistance to victims of conflict—are mandated by the international community of States and are founded on international law, specifically the Geneva Conventions, which are among the most widely ratified treaties in the world. Because of this the ICRC, like any intergovernmental organization, is recognized as having an "international legal personality" or status of its own. It enjoys working facilities (privileges and immunities) comparable to those of the United Nations, its agencies, and other intergovernmental organizations. Examples of these facilities include exemption from taxes and customs duties, inviolability of premises and documents, and immunity from judicial process.

Why does it matter? The ICRC can only do its job of providing protection and assistance to conflict victims if its working principles of impartiality, independence and neutrality are respected. It is through recognition of the ICRC's privileges and immunities that States and international organizations acknowledge their respect for those principles. Thus, in line with its international legal mandate, the ICRC's privileges and immunities are widely recognized by governments, by the United Nations and by other organizations. This means that the ICRC is not treated as a private entity or an NGO, but as an intergovernmental organization for the work it does under its international mandate. The legal basis for the ICRC's essential privileges and immunities are recognized in various ways, including:

Headquarters Agreements between the ICRC and governments, or state legislation. In the nearly 80 countries in which the ICRC carries out significant operations, its international legal personality, judicial immunity and testimonial privilege (right not to be called as a witness) is recognized either by treaty or by legislation

Judicial decisions. Several domestic and international tribunals have ruled on the ICRC's judicial immunity and testimonial privileges. Recently, the International Criminal Tribunal for the former Yugoslavia (ICTY) distinguished the ICRC from NGOs by citing its international legal mandate and status, including its right to decline to testify. The rules of procedure and evidence of the newly established International Criminal Court also reflect the position of the more than one hundred states that drafted the document, that the ICRC enjoys testimonial immunity.

The United Nations and other international organizations. The ICRC has been granted observer status at the UN General Assembly and enjoys similar status with other international, intergovernmental organizations.

NOTES AND QUESTIONS

1. You have probably heard of national Red Cross organizations such as the American Red Cross, the British Red Cross, etc. These are linked to the ICRC but are separate entities with distinctive missions, and a legal status within states. The 1999 Annual Report of the ICRC, explained:

> The International Red Cross and Red Crescent Movement is made up of the National Societies, the ICRC and the International Federation of Red Cross and Red Crescent Societies. Although each of the Movement's components engages in different activities, they are all united by the same Fundamental Principles: humanity, impartiality, neutrality, independence, voluntary service, unity and universality.

As its founding institution, the ICRC has certain statutory responsibilities towards the Movement. In particular, it is responsible for ensuring respect for and promoting knowledge of the Fundamental Principles, recognizing new National Red Cross or Red Crescent Societies which meet the Current conditions for recognition, and discharging the mandates entrusted to it by the International Conference of the Red Cross and Red Crescent. The ICRC takes an active part in the Movement's statutory meetings, which it often organizes jointly with the Federation.

2. A professor of criminal justice has observed: "Piracy is and always has been a crime of universal jurisdiction * * * The definition involves non-state actors threatening harm to innocent persons. In the case of terrorists, the motive is political. In the case of pirates, the motive is profit. The motive strikes me as a distinction that does not create a difference." Does motive make a difference respecting status in international law? Should it? Do you see other differences between terrorists groups and pirates?

Would it be more accurate to compare terrorists with participants in armed conflict (combatants) rather than criminals such as pirates or drug cartels? The United States seemed to be making this argument when it declared after the attacks of September 11, 2001, a "global war on terrorism." Might there be a reason for comparing terrorists to combatants not criminals, other than the accuracy of the comparison? See Chapter 10. *See also*, CHRISTOPHER L. BLAKESLEY, TERRORISM AND ANTI-TERRORISM: A NORMATIVE AND PRACTICAL ASSESSMENT (2006).

3. *Networks*. Anne–Marie Slaughter has written about something she calls "networks." These are loose associations of people across international boundaries that have no formal organization, such as judges or bankers. Should they have a formal status in international law? Would a formal status of any kind eliminate them from the category of "network"? If they do deserve a status, do social networks deserve one, too? *See* ANNE–MARIE SLAUGHTER, THE NEW WORLD ORDER (2004).

3. CORPORATIONS, VESSELS, AND VEHICLES

a. CORPORATIONS

The leading judicial decision on the nationality of corporations is the *Barcelona Traction Case* (1970) excerpted above. Its basic holding is that a corporation may be protected diplomatically only by the state in which it is incorporated. Belgium lost its case, brought before the ICJ against Spain on behalf of the Belgian shareholders, because the corporation was chartered in Canada, and thus had the nationality of that country. This is the prevailing rule; *see*, 1987 RESTATEMENT § 213, especially Reporters' Notes 1–9. "Civil law" countries have been said to ascribe nationality on the basis of the locus of corporate activity (*siege social*), but the Restatement takes the position that this is an additional, not a different, requirement; *see*, Reporters' Note 6. What does this mean? What if a corporation organized in Canada has its *siege social* in France? American corporation law tends to permit "piercing the veil" between a corporation and its shareholders when the court finds police-power public interest. Would this make a difference? Transnational and international decisions do not seem to have accepted this U.S. practice, although European Community law has adopted it for antitrust actions. At a time when the United Kingdom was not a Community member, *Imperial Chemicals Industries, Ltd.,* a British parent corporation, was held subject to (then) EEC (now EU) prosecution as a member of the dye-stuffs cartel, because it was "present" within the EEC through subsidiaries. *See, Imperial Chemical Industries Ltd. v. Commission,* Case, 11 COM.MKT.L.R. 557 (1972). Would the then EEC countries have accepted a British claim to assert diplomatic protection as to ICI on the "present-through-subsidiary" principle, if the subsidiary, but not ICI, had a *siege social* in an EEC country? What if the subsidiary, organized in an EU country were entirely managed by a non-EU parent corporation operating in that country, say Norway? *Consider, Elettronica Sicula* S.p.A. (ELSI Case) (U.S. v. Italy) 1989 I.C.J. Rep. 15.

Judge Jessup discussed the general requirement of effective nationality in a separate opinion in the *Barcelona Traction* case:

Bacelona Traction, Light and Power Company, Limited

Belgium v. Spain
International Court of Justice
1970 I.C.J. Rep. 3 (Judgment of Feb. 5) (Second Phase)

38.   There is no question that, under international law, a State has in general a right to extend its diplomatic protection to a corporation which has its nationality, or national character as it is more properly called. The proposition raises two questions:

(1) What are the tests to determine the national character of a corporation?

(2) Assuming the appropriate tests are met, must that national character be "real and effective" as shown by the "link" between the corporation and the State, just as, in the Notteböhm case, this Court decided that a certain claim to nationality is not enough in all situations to justify a State in extending its diplomatic protection to a natural person?

39.   There are two standard tests of the "nationality" of a corporation. The place of incorporation is the test generally favoured in the legal systems of the common law, while the siege social is more generally accepted in the civil law systems. There is respectable authority for requiring that both tests be met.

It is not possible to speak of a single rule for all purposes. The tests used in private international law have their own character.

Commercial treaties and claims conventions often contain their own definitions of which companies shall be considered to have the nationality of a State for purposes of the treaty. The tests used for such purposes may be quite different—even in the practice of the same State—from the tests used for other purposes. For example, the "control" test was widely used to determine the enemy character of property during war, but it is not established in international law as a general test of the nationality of a corporation. On the other hand, control may constitute the essential link which, when joined to nationality, gives the State the right to extend diplomatic protection to the corporation. It is a familiar fact that the laws of certain States provide favourable conditions for companies incorporating therein, especially in relation to taxation. Canada is one such State, Liechtenstein is another. In the United States, many companies find it advantageous, for various reasons, to incorporate in Delaware or New Jersey. Charters secured for such reasons may be called "charters of convenience".

40.   The Judgment of the Court of Notteböhm, Second Phase, in 1955, has been widely discussed in the subsequent literature of international law particularly with reference to the so-called "link theory" by which the effectiveness of nationality may be tested. It has been argued that the doctrine is equally applicable in the case of ships flying "flags of convenience" and in relation to the diplomatic protection of corporations. I have maintained the view that it should apply in both those situations.

* * *

43.   It has also been argued that the Court should not pass judgment on the question whether there existed the necessary link between Canada and Barcelona Traction without hearing argument on behalf of Canada. Canada might have sought to intervene in the instant case under Article 62 of the Statute, but it did not do so. It is said that after judgment is pronounced in this case of Belgium v. Spain, Canada might find some jurisdictional ground to found an application to institute a case of Canada v. Spain. It is known that no such jurisdictional ground now exists. It seems quite unreal to suppose that Spain would now agree with Canada upon a compromise submitting to the Court a Canadian claim on behalf of Barcelona Traction, thus exposing Spain to the new hazard of being required to pay some two hundred millions of dollars of damages. But if the Court were properly seised of an application by Canada, it would have to take cognizance of the fact that following Article 59 of the Statute, "The decision of the Court has no binding force except between the parties and in respect of that particular case". Had the Court endorsed the application of the link principle to juristic persons, in its present decision in Belgium v. Spain, Canada could have argued against that conclusion in the hypothetical case of Canada v. Spain, or might have relied on Spanish admissions that Canada was entitled to protect the company.

44.   It seems to be widely thought that the "link" concept in connection with the nationality of claims, originated in the International Court of Justice's Judgment in Notteböhm. I do not agree that in that instance the Court created a new rule of law. Indeed the underlying principle was already well established in connection with diplomatic claims on behalf of corporations. To look for the link between a corporation and a State is

merely another example of what is now the familiar practice of "lifting the veil". The practice of such States as the United States and Switzerland had already given weight to the proposition that a corporation would not be protected solely because it was incorporated in the State, i.e., had the State's nationality; some other link was required and that link usually was related to the ownership of shares. Such abstention, being as it were "against interest", has special probative value.

Three years after the decision in Notteböhm, the Italian–United States Conciliation Commission, under the presidency of the late Professor Sauser Hall, in the Flegenheimer case stated:

The right of challenge of the international court, authorizing it to determine whether, behind the nationality certificate or the acts of naturalization produced, the right to citizenship was regularly acquired, is in *conformity with the very broad rule* of *effectivity* which dominates the law of nationals entirely and allows the court to fulfill its legal function and remove the inconveniences specified. (Emphasis supplied.)

b.   VEHICLES AND VESSELS

United Nations Convention on the Law of the Sea

December 10, 1982
21 I.L.M. 1261 (1982)

Article 91

Nationality of ships

1.   Every State shall fix the conditions for the grant of its nationality to ships, for the registration of ships in its territory, and for the right to fly its flag. Ships have the nationality of the State whose flag they are entitled to fly. There must exist a genuine link between the State and the ship.

2.   Every State shall issue to ships to which it has granted the right to fly its flag documents to that effect.

Article 92

Status of ships

1.   Ships shall sail under the flag of one State only and, save in exceptional cases expressly provided for in international treaties or in this Convention, shall be subject to its exclusive jurisdiction on the high seas. A ship may not change its flag during a voyage or while in a port of call, save in the case of a real transfer of ownership or change of registry.

2.   A ship which sails under the flags of two or more States, using them according to convenience, may not claim any of the nationalities in question with respect to any other State, and may be assimilated to a ship without nationality.

Article 93

Ships flying the flag of the United Nations, its specialized agencies and the International Atomic Energy Agency

The preceding articles do not prejudice the question of ships employed on the official service of the United Nations, its specialized agencies or the International Atomic Energy Agency, flying the flag of the organization.

Article 94

Duties of the flag State

1.   Every State shall effectively exercise its jurisdiction and control in administrative, technical and social matters over ships flying its flag.

2.   In particular every State shall:

(a) maintain a register of ships containing the names and particulars of ships flying its flag, except those which are excluded from generally accepted international regulations on account of their small size; and

(b) assume jurisdiction under its internal law over each ship flying its flag and its master, officers and crew in respect of administrative, technical and social matters concerning the ship.

3.   Every State shall take such measures for ships flying its flag as are necessary to ensure safety at sea with regard, inter alia, to:

(a) the construction, equipment and seaworthiness of ships;

(b) the manning of ships, labour conditions and the training of crews, taking into account the applicable international instruments;

(c) the use of signals, the maintenance of communications and the prevention of collisions.

* * *

The M/V "Saiga" (No. 2) Case (Saint Vincent and the Grenadines v. Guinea)

International Tribunal for the Law of the Sea, 1 July 1999
38 I.L.M. 1323 (1999)

[Saint Vincent and Grenadines commenced this proceeding seeking damages for losses arising out of the actions of Guinea described below. The Tribunal took jurisdiction by agreement of the parties. Guinea interposed a number of preliminary objections, including the three Challenges to admissibility concerning Registration of the Saiga, Genuine Link, and Nationality of Claims, discussed in the following excerpts from the Judgment of the Tribunal.]

31.   The Saiga is an oil tanker. At the time of its arrest on 28 October 1997, it was owned by Tabona Shipping Company Ltd. of Nicosia, Cyprus, and managed by Seascot Shipmanagement Ltd. of Glasgow, Scotland. The ship was chartered to Lemania Shipping Group Ltd. of Geneva, Switzer-

land. The Saiga was provisionally registered in Saint Vincent and the Grenadines on 12 March 1997. The Master and crew of the ship were all of Ukrainian nationality. There were also three Senegalese nationals who were employed as painters. The Saiga was engaged in selling gas oil as bunker and occasionally water to fishing and other vessels off the coast of West Africa. The owner of the cargo of gas oil on board was Addax BV of Geneva, Switzerland.

32. Under the command of Captain Orlov, the Saiga left Dakar, Senegal, on 24 October 1997 fully laden with approximately 5,400 metric tons of gas oil. On 27 October 1997, between 0400 and 1400 hours [at an identified point], the Saiga supplied gas oil to three fishing vessels, the Giuseppe Primo and the Kriti, both flying the flag of Senegal, and the Eleni S, flying the flag of Greece. The point was approximately 22 nautical miles from Guinea's island of Alcatraz. All three fishing vessels were licensed by Guinea to fish in its exclusive economic zone. The Saiga then sailed in a southerly direction to supply gas oil to other fishing vessels at a prearranged place. Upon instructions from the owner of the cargo in Geneva, it later changed course and sailed towards another location beyond the southern border of the exclusive economic zone of Guinea.

33. At 0800 hours on 28 October 1997, the Saiga, according to its log book, was at [another identified point] * * *. It had been drifting since 0420 hours while awaiting the arrival of fishing vessels to which it was to supply gas oil. This point was south of the southern limit of the exclusive economic zone of Guinea. At about 0900 hours the Saiga was attacked by a Guinean patrol boat (P35). Officers from that boat and another Guinean patrol boat (P328) subsequently boarded the ship and arrested it. On the same day, the ship and its crew were brought to Conakry, Guinea, where its Master was detained. * * * The travel documents of the members of the crew were taken from them by the authorities of Guinea and armed guards were placed on board the ship. On 1 November 1997, two injured persons from the Saiga, Mr. Sergey Klyuyev and Mr. Djibril Niasse, were permitted to leave Conakry for Dakar for medical treatment. Between 10 and 12 November 1997, the cargo of gas oil on board the ship, amounting to 4,941.322 metric tons, was discharged on the orders of the Guinean authorities. Seven members of the crew and two painters left Conakry on 17 November 1997, one crew member left on 14 December 1997 and six on 12 January 1998. The Master and six crew members remained in Conakry until the ship was released on 28 February 1998.

* * *

Challenges to admissibility
Registration of the Saiga

55. The first objection raised by Guinea to the admissibility of the claims set out in the application is that Saint Vincent and the Grenadines does not have legal standing to bring claims in connection with the measures taken by Guinea against the Saiga. The reason given by Guinea for its contention is that on the day of its arrest the ship was "not validly registered under the flag of Saint Vincent and the Grenadines" and that,

consequently, Saint Vincent and the Grenadines is not legally competent to present claims either on its behalf or in respect of the ship, its Master and the other members of the crew, its owners or its operators.

* * *

57. The facts relating to the registration of the Saiga, as they emerge from the evidence adduced before the Tribunal, are as follows:

(a) The Saiga was registered provisionally on 12 March 1997 as a Saint Vincent and the Grenadines ship under section 36 of the Merchant Shipping Act of 1982 of Saint Vincent and the Grenadines (hereinafter "the Merchant Shipping Act"), The Provisional Certificate of Registration issued to the ship on 14 April 1997 stated that it was issued by the commissioner for Maritime Affairs of Saint Vincent and the Grenadines on behalf of the Government of Saint Vincent and the Grenadines under the terms of the Merchant Shipping Act. The Certificate stated: "This Certificate expires on 12 September 1997."

(b) The registration of the ship was recorded in the Registry Book of Saint Vincent and the Grenadines on 26 March 1997. The entry stated: "Valid thru: 12/09/1997".

(c) A Permanent Certificate of Registration was issued on 28 November 1997 by the Commissioner for Maritime Affairs of Saint Vincent and the Grenadines on behalf of that State. The Certificate stated: "This Certificate is permanent."

58. Guinea contends that the ship was unregistered between 12 September 1997 and 28 November 1997 because the Provisional Certificate of Registration expired on 12 September 1997 and the Permanent Certificate of Registration was issued on 28 November 1997. From this Guinea concludes: "It is thus very clear that the M/V 'SAIGA was not validly registered' in the time period between 12 September 1997 and 28 November 1997. For this reason, the M/V 'SAIGA' may [be] qualified to be a ship without nationality at the time of its attack." Guinea also questioned whether the ship had been deleted from the Maltese Register where it was previously registered.

60. * * * With regard to the question raised by Guinea concerning the previous registration of the ship, Saint Vincent and the Grenadines stated that its authorities had received from the owner of the ship "satisfactory evidence that the ship's registration in the country of last registration had been closed" as required by section 37 of the Merchant Shipping Act.

62. The question for consideration is whether the Saiga had the nationality of Saint Vincent and the Grenadines at the time of its arrest. The relevant provision of the Convention is article 91, * * * * [see text above].

63. Article 91 leaves to each State exclusive jurisdiction over the granting of its nationality to ships. In this respect, article 91 codifies a well-established rule of general international law. Under this article, it is for

Saint Vincent and the Grenadines to fix the conditions for the grant of its nationality to ships, for the registration of ships in its territory and for the right to fly its flag. These matters are regulated by a State in its domestic law. Pursuant to article 91, paragraph 2, Saint Vincent and the Grenadines is under an obligation to issue to ships to which it has granted the right to fly its flag documents to that effect. The issue of such documents is regulated by domestic law.

64.   International law recognizes several modalities for the grant of nationality to different types of ships. In the case of merchant ships, the normal procedure used by States to grant nationality is registration in accordance with domestic legislation adopted for that purpose. This procedure is adopted by Saint Vincent and the Grenadines in the Merchant Shipping Act.

65.   Determination of the criteria and establishment of the procedures for granting and withdrawing nationality to ships are matters within the exclusive jurisdiction of the flag State. Nevertheless, disputes concerning such matters may be subject to the procedures under Part XV of the Convention, especially in cases where issues of interpretation or application of provisions of the Convention are involved.

66.   The Tribunal considers that the nationality of a ship is a question of fact to be determined, like other facts in dispute before it, on the basis of evidence adduced by the parties.

67.   Saint Vincent and the Grenadines has produced evidence before the Tribunal to support its assertion that the Saiga was a ship entitled to fly its flag at the time of the incident giving rise to the dispute. In addition to making references to the relevant provisions of the Merchant Shipping Act, Saint Vincent and the Grenadines has drawn attention to several indications of Vincentian nationality on the ship or carried on board. These include the inscription of "Kingstown" as the port of registry on the stern of the vessel, the documents on board and the ship's seal which contained the words "SAIGA Kingstown" and the then current charter-party which recorded the flag of the vessel as "Saint Vincent and the Grenadines".

68.   The evidence adduced by Saint Vincent and the Grenadines has been reinforced by its conduct. Saint Vincent and the Grenadines has at all times material to the dispute operated on the basis that the Saiga was a ship of its nationality. It has acted as the flag State of the ship during all phases of the proceedings. It was in that capacity that it invoked the jurisdiction of the Tribunal in its Application for the prompt release of the Saiga and its crew under article 292 of the Convention and in its Request for the prescription of provisional measures under article 290 of the Convention.

69.   As far as Guinea is concerned, the Tribunal cannot fail to note that it did not challenge or raise any doubts about the registration or nationality of the ship at any time until the submission of its Counter-Memorial in October 1998. Prior to this, it was open to Guinea to make

inquiries regarding the registration of the Saiga or documentation relating to it. * * *

70.   With regard to the previous registration of the Saiga, the Tribunal notes the statement made by Saint Vincent and the Grenadines in paragraph 60. It considers this statement to be sufficient.

71.   The Tribunal recalls that, in its Judgment of 4 December 1997 and in its Order of 11 March 1998, the Saiga is described as a ship flying the flag of Saint Vincent and the Grenadines.

72.   On the basis of the evidence before it, the Tribunal finds that Saint Vincent and the Grenadines has discharged the initial burden of establishing that the Saiga had Vincentian nationality at the time it was arrested by Guinea. Guinea had therefore to prove its contention that the ship was not registered in or did not have the nationality of Saint Vincent and the Grenadines at that time. The Tribunal considers that the burden has not been discharged and that it has not been established that the Saiga was not registered in or did not have the nationality of Saint Vincent and the Grenadines at the time of the arrest.

73.   The Tribunal concludes:

(a) it has not been established that the Vincentian registration or nationality of the Saiga was extinguished in the period between the date on which the Provisional Certificate of Registration was stated to expire and the date of issue of the Permanent Certificate of Registration;

(b) in the particular circumstances of this case, the consistent conduct of Saint Vincent and the Grenadines provides sufficient support for the conclusion that the Saiga retained the registration and nationality of Saint Vincent and the Grenadines at all times material to the dispute;

(c) in view of Guinea's failure to question the assertion of Saint Vincent and the Grenadines that it is the flag State of the Saiga when it had every reasonable opportunity to do so and its other conduct in the case, Guinea cannot successfully challenge the registration and nationality of the Saiga at this stage;

(d) in the particular circumstances of this case, it would not be consistent with justice if the Tribunal were to decline to deal with the merits of the dispute.

74.   For the above reasons, the Tribunal rejects Guinea's objection to the admissibility of the claims of Saint Vincent and the Grenadines based on the ground that the Saiga was not registered in Saint Vincent and the Grenadines at the time of its arrest and that, consequently, the Saiga did not have Vincentian nationality at that time.

Genuine link

75.   The next objection to admissibility raised by Guinea is that there was no genuine link between the Saiga and Saint Vincent and the Grenadines. Guinea contends that "without a genuine link between Saint Vincent and the Grenadines and the M/V 'Saiga', Saint Vincent and the Grenadines' claim concerning a violation of its right of navigation and the

status of the ship is not admissible before the Tribunal vis-à-vis Guinea, because Guinea is not bound to recognise the Vincentian nationality of the M/V 'Saiga', which forms a prerequisite for the mentioned claim in international law''.

79. Article 91, paragraph 1, of the Convention provides: "There must exist a genuine link between the State and the ship." Two questions need to be addressed in this connection. The first is whether the absence of a genuine link between a flag State and a ship entitles another State to refuse to recognize the nationality of the ship. The second question is whether or not a genuine link existed between the Saiga and Saint Vincent and the Grenadines at the time of the incident.

80. With regard to the first question, the Tribunal notes that the provision in article 91, paragraph 1, of the Convention, requiring a genuine link between the State and the ship, does not provide the answer. Nor do articles 92 and 94 of the Convention, which together with article 91 constitute the context of the provision, provide the answer. The Tribunal, however, recalls that the International Law Commission, in article 29 of the Draft Articles on the Law of the Sea adopted by it in 1956, proposed the concept of a "genuine link" as a criterion not only for the attribution of nationality to a ship but also for the recognition by other States of such nationality. After providing that "ships have the nationality of the State whose flag they are entitled to fly", the draft article continued: "Nevertheless, for purposes of recognition of the national character of the ship by other States, there must exist a genuine link between the State and the ship". This sentence was not included in article 5, paragraph 1, of the Convention on the High Seas of 29 April 1958 (hereinafter "the 1958 Convention"), which reads, in part, as follows:

> There must exist a genuine link between the State and the ship; in particular, the State must effectively exercise its jurisdiction and control in administrative, technical and social matters over ships flying its flag.

Thus, while the obligation regarding a genuine link was maintained in the 1958 Convention, the proposal that the existence of a genuine link should be a basis for the recognition of nationality was not adopted.

81. The Convention follows the approach of the 1958 Convention. Article 91 retains the part of the third sentence of article 5, paragraph 1, of the 1958 Convention which provides that there must be a genuine link between the State and the ship. The other part of that sentence, stating that the flag State shall effectively exercise its jurisdiction and control in administrative, technical and social matters over ships flying its flag, is reflected in article 94 of the Convention, dealing with the duties of the flag State.

82. Paragraphs 2 to 5 of article 94 of the Convention outline the measures that a flag State is required to take to exercise effective jurisdiction as envisaged in paragraph 1. Paragraph 6 sets out the procedure to be followed where another State has "clear grounds to believe that proper

jurisdiction and control with respect to a ship have not been exercised". That State is entitled to report the facts to the flag State which is then obliged to "investigate the matter and, if appropriate, take any action necessary to remedy the situation". There is nothing in article 94 to permit a State which discovers evidence indicating the absence of proper jurisdiction and control by a flag State over a ship to refuse to recognize the right of the ship to fly the flag of the flag State.

83.   The conclusion of the Tribunal is that the purpose of the provisions of the Convention on the need for a genuine link between a ship and its flag State is to secure more effective implementation of the duties of the flag State, and not to establish criteria by reference to which the validity of the registration of ships in a flag State may be challenged by other States.

84.   This conclusion is not put into question by the United Nations Convention on Conditions for Registration of Ships of 7 February 1986 invoked by Guinea. This Convention (which is not in force) sets out as one of its principal objectives the strengthening of "the genuine link between a State and ships flying its flag". In any case, the Tribunal observes that Guinea has not cited any provision in that Convention which lends support to its contention that "a basic condition for the registration of a ship is that also the owner or operator of the ship is under the jurisdiction of the flag State".

85.   The conclusion is further strengthened by the Agreement for the Implementation of the Provisions of the United Nations Convention on the Law of the Sea of 10 December 1982 Relating to the Conservation and Management of Straddling Fish Stocks and Highly Migratory Fish Stocks opened for signature on 4 December 1995 and the Agreement to Promote Compliance with International Conservation and Management Measures by Fishing Vessels on the High Seas of 24 November 1993. These Agreements, neither of which is in force, set out, inter alia, detailed obligations to be discharged by the flag States of fishing vessels but do not deal with the conditions to be satisfied for the registration of fishing vessels.

86.   In the light of the above considerations, the Tribunal concludes that there is no legal basis for the claim of Guinea that it can refuse to recognize the right of the Saiga to fly the flag of Saint Vincent and the Grenadines on the ground that there was no genuine link between the ship and Saint Vincent and the Grenadines.

Nationality of claims

103.   In its last objection to admissibility, Guinea argues that certain claims of Saint Vincent and the Grenadines cannot be entertained by the Tribunal because they relate to violations of the rights of persons who are not nationals of Saint Vincent and the Grenadines. According to Guinea, the claims of Saint Vincent and the Grenadines in respect of loss or damage sustained by the ship, its owners, the Master and other members of the crew and other persons, including the owners of the cargo, are clearly claims of diplomatic protection. In its view, Saint Vincent and the Grenadines is not competent to institute these claims on behalf of the persons

concerned since none of them is a national of Saint Vincent and the Grenadines. During the oral proceedings, Guinea withdrew its objection as far as it relates to the shipowners, but maintained it in respect of the other persons.

104. In opposing this objection, Saint Vincent and the Grenadines maintains that the rule of international law that a State is entitled to claim protection only for its nationals does not apply to claims in respect of persons and things on board a ship flying its flag. In such cases, the flag State has the right to bring claims in respect of violations against the ship and all persons on board or interested in its operation. Saint Vincent and the Grenadines, therefore, asserts that it has the right to protect the ship flying its flag and those who serve on board, irrespective of their nationality.

105. In dealing with this question, the Tribunal finds sufficient guidance in the Convention. The Convention contains detailed provisions concerning the duties of flag States regarding ships flying their flag. Articles 94 and 217, in particular, set out the obligations of the flag State which can be discharged only through the exercise of appropriate jurisdiction and control over natural and juridical persons such as the Master and other members of the crew, the owners or operators and other persons involved in the activities of the ship. No distinction is made in these provisions between nationals and non-nationals of a flag State. Additionally, articles 106, 110, paragraph 3, and 111, paragraph 8, of the Convention contain provisions applicable to cases in which measures have been taken by a State against a foreign ship. These measures are, respectively, seizure of a ship on suspicion of piracy, exercise of the right of visit on board the ship, and arrest of a ship in exercise of the right of hot pursuit. In these cases, the Convention provides that, if the measures are found not to be justified, the State taking the measures shall be obliged to pay compensation "for any loss or damage" sustained. In these cases, the Convention does not relate the right to compensation to the nationality of persons suffering loss or damage. Furthermore, in relation to proceedings for prompt release under article 292 of the Convention, no significance is attached to the nationalities of persons involved in the operations of an arrested ship.

106. The provisions referred to in the preceding paragraph indicate that the Convention considers a ship as a unit, as regards the obligations of the flag State with respect to the ship and the right of a flag State to seek reparation for loss or damage caused to the ship by acts of other States and to institute proceedings under article 292 of the Convention. Thus the ship, every thing on it, and every person involved or interested in its operations are treated as an entity linked to the flag State. The nationalities of these persons are not relevant.

107. The Tribunal must also call attention to an aspect of the matter which is not without significance in this case. This relates to two basic characteristics of modern maritime transport: the transient and multinational composition of ships' crews and the multiplicity of interests that may

be involved in the cargo on board a single ship. A container vessel carries a large number of containers, and the persons with interests in them may be of many different nationalities. This may also be true in relation to cargo on board a break-bulk carrier. Any of these ships could have a crew comprising persons of several nationalities. If each person sustaining damage were obliged to look for protection from the State of which such person is a national, undue hardship would ensue.

108.   The Tribunal is, therefore, unable to accept Guinea's contention that Saint Vincent and the Grenadines is not entitled to present claims for damages in respect of natural and juridical persons who are not nationals of Saint Vincent and the Grenadines.

109.   In the light of the above considerations, the Tribunal rejects the objection to admissibility based on nationality of claims.

Brownlie, Principles of Public International Law

pp. 425–426, 427 (7th ed. 2008)*

The Convention for the Regulation of Aerial Navigation of 1919, and later the Chicago Convention of 1944, provided that the nationality of aircraft is governed by the state of registration. The former stipulated that registration could only take place in the state of which the owners were nationals, while the latter merely forbids dual registration. Neither Convention applied in time of war, and the latter Convention does not apply to state aircraft, i.e. aircraft used in military, customs and police services. The Tokyo Convention on Offenses Committed on Board Aircraft provides that the state of registration has jurisdiction over offenses and acts committed on board. * * * Obviously the *Nottebohm* principle ought to apply to aircraft as it does to ships. It must surely apply at the least to discover to which state non-civil aircraft belong, but it is probable that even where the Chicago Convention applies, issues of diplomatic protection are not precluded by registration. In bilateral treaties the United States has reserved the right to refuse a carrier permit to an airline designated by the other contracting party "in the event substantial ownership and effective control of such airlines are not vested in nationals of the other contracting party".

* * *

The Space Treaty of 1967 does not employ the concept of nationality in relation to objects launched into outer space. Article VIII of the Treaty provides in part that the state of registration shall retain jurisdiction and control over such object, and over any personnel thereof, while in outer space or on a celestial body. In the [1975] Convention on Registration of Objects Launched into Outer Space it is provided that the launching state shall maintain a register of space objects. Each state of registry has a duty

---

* Footnotes omitted.

to furnish certain information to the Secretary–General of the United Nations.

––––––––––

For more on international law relevant to air space and outer space, *see,* BRIAN F. HAVEL, BEYOND OPEN SKIES: A NEW REGIME FOR INTERNATIONAL AVIATION (2009) and DETLER WOLTER, COMMON SECURITY IN OUTER SPACE AND INTERNATIONAL LAW (2006).

C.   INTERNATIONAL ORGANIZATIONS

International organizations are sometimes referred to as *public international organizations* or *intergovernmental organizations* (IOs) to distinguish them from *Nongovernmental Organizations (NGOs)* which are also important actors in the international system as you saw in the previous section. NGOs are typically established under and are governed by a *national legal system* rather than international law. However, the international organizations considered in this section are established under and pursuant to *international law,* in most cases by a treaty, to which the Vienna Convention on the Law of Treaties applies:

Article 5
Treaties constituting international organizations and treaties adopted within an international organization

The present Convention applies to any treaty which is the constituent instrument of an international organization and to any treaty adopted within an international organization without prejudice to any relevant rules of the organization.

International organizations are not "states", of course, under the criteria for statehood taken up in above. IOs have no territory as such but hold private titles of ownership or rights under leases to the real property they occupy at their headquarters or other locations. Organizations also lack populations in the sense that states are populated with individual human beings and various forms of domestic entities made subject to the states' clearly sovereign powers. Organizations, however, do have constituent states as members and do exercise certain powers with respect to them. They also have secretariats which correspond broadly to national civil services and are subject to institutional command. Organizations do enjoy international legal personality as required for the full and effective exercise of their functions.

The comparison becomes more blurred, however, when we look at the statehood criterion of a "government" exercising independent (or "sovereign") control over its territory and "population" and having effective power to engage in foreign relations. Some institutional elements analogous to a government are present in international organizations, and they do carry out "foreign relations" in the regular use of the diplomatic process forms and in entering into legally binding treaty relations. In the UN system (as well as in other organizations), there are internal bodies fulfilling some legislative-like functions, notably the UN Security Council and the General Assembly, but they are subject to the extensive limitations set forth in the United Nations Charter. There is an "executive" type function exercised by the Secretary–General and the Secretariat, again with limited although potentially far reaching powers. There is also a judicial "branch", in the form of the International Court of Justice, the Law of the Sea Tribunal, the International Criminal Court, the European Court of Justice and other courts and tribunals, but with limitations on jurisdiction provided in the constituent instrument of each. Are the elements of statehood present here in more than merely a formal or theoretical legal sense?

Although the keystone of the international system in operation remains the "sovereign" state, seen close-up in Section B above, possible competitors over the past hundred years or so have been visible on or over the horizon. Has the development and recent integration of the United Nations system and some 300 other intergovernmental organizations caused the disintegration of sovereignty? Have competitors to state sovereignty arrived? If not, do they have a reasonable prospect of arriving in the foreseeable future? To consider those questions, you need to look at some of the defining legal characteristics of international organizations, especially those which have a generally worldwide or "universal" membership of states and which exercise a number of specified powers and functions more or less in parallel to those of states, including the European Union which exercises carefully defined and limited but nonetheless "sovereign" powers in the economic sector. Bear in mind that the U.N. Charter refers in Article 2 to the principle of "sovereign equality" of "Members" (i.e., states) and is totally silent about "sovereignty of international organizations".

We first focus on the threshold questions of creation and legal personality of IOs before turning briefly to the structure and role of the United Nations and its sixteen other organizations qualified under Article 57 of the Charter as UN Specialized Agencies. We also look at the European Union and a representative number of regional and functional organizations, followed by an introduction to three of the key legal problems of organizations: law making, responsibility, and control.

1. CREATION AND ATTRIBUTES OF INTERNATIONAL ORGANIZATIONS

a. CONSTITUENT INSTRUMENT

Philippe Sands and Pierre Klein, Bowett's Law of International Institutions

p. 442 (2001)

The constituent instrument of an international Organisation is almost always a treaty, although in some exceptional cases an international

Organisation may be created by act of one or more existing international organisations. The constituent instrument will provide for the functions and objects of the Organisation, and indicate how they are to be achieved. It will also provide for the framework against which secondary acts of the Organisation may be adopted and its other practice developed, even if such practise sometimes departs from the original object of a particular provision of the constituent instrument. On occasion the constituent instrument might also indicate the relationship between the Organisation and other rules of international law, as well as any applicable or relevant rules of national law.

As a treaty the constituent instrument will be governed by the rules, reflected in the 1969 Vienna Convention on the Law of Treaties (as well as those of the 1986 Vienna Convention*) which are expressly stated to apply' "to any treaty which is the constituent instrument of an international Organisation and to any treaty adopted within an international Organisation without prejudice to any relevant rules of the Organisation" (Article 5(3)). The last part of this provision indicates the primacy which is to be given to "any relevant rules of the Organisation", whilst recognising that where the instrument is silent on such rules the 1969 Convention could play a decisive role. The rules of the 1969 Convention which are most relevant to the life of international institutions are generally recognised to reflect customary law. In this way the law governing the activities of international institutions is subjected to the principles of the 1969 Vienna Convention, including in relation to such matters as the circumstances governing the conclusion of the treaty, reservations, the rules governing the relationship between the constituent instrument and other treaties, interpretation, * * * and withdrawal and termination.

b. LEGAL PERSONALITY

A question of major interest is whether the U.N. enjoys the capacity to act as an institution in its own name through the device of international legal personality, as states do. For the U.N., functional legal personality is provided clearly in Articles 104 and 105.1 of the Charter as follows:

Article 104

> The Organization shall enjoy in the territory of each of its Members such legal capacity as may be necessary for the exercise of its functions and the fulfilment of its purposes.

Article 105.1

> The Organization shall enjoy in the territory of each of its Members such privileges and immunities as are necessary for the fulfilment of its purposes.

---

* Vienna Convention on the Law of Treaties Between States and International Organizations or Between International Organizations, www.un.org

While these provision are developed in later agreements discussed below, the Charter is silent about legal personality in the territory of non-Members and sheds little direct light on the question of the U.N.'s capacity to pursue international claims as states may do on behalf of themselves and their nationals. In 1949 these questions were addressed in one of the earlicst advisory cases brought to the International Court of Justice. In reaching its conclusions favorable to United Nations powers, the Court considered some of the broader issues of the function and nature of the United Nations.

Reparation for Injuries Suffered in the Service of the United Nations

International Court of Justice
1949 I.C.J. Rep. 174 (Advisory Opinion of April 11)

[The General Assembly submitted the following legal question to the Court for an advisory opinion:

Question I: In the event of an agent of the United Nations in the performance of his duties suffering injury in circumstances involving the responsibility of a State, has the United Nations, as an Organization, the capacity to bring an international claim against the responsible de jure or de facto government with a view to obtaining the reparation due in respect of the damage caused (a) to the United Nations, (b) to the victim or to persons entitled through him? (Question II is omitted)].

THE COURT:

* * *

Competence to bring an international claim is, for those possessing it, the capacity to resort to the customary methods recognized by international law for the establishment, the presentation and the settlement of claims. Among these methods may be mentioned protest, request for an enquiry, negotiation, and request for submission to an arbitral tribunal or to the Court in so far as this may be authorized by the Statute.

This capacity certainly belongs to the State; a State can bring an international claim against another State. Such a claim takes the form of a claim between two political entities, equal in law, similar in form, and both the direct subjects of international law. It is dealt with by means of negotiation, and cannot, in the present state of the law as to international jurisdiction, be submitted to a tribunal, except with the consent of the States concerned.

When the Organization brings a claim against one of its Members, this claim will be presented in the same manner, and regulated by the same procedure. It may, when necessary, be supported by the political means at the disposal of the Organization. In these ways the Organization would find a method for securing the observance of its rights by the Member against which it has a claim.

But, in the international sphere, has the Organization such a nature as involves the capacity to bring an international claim? In order to answer this question, the Court must first enquire whether the Charter has given the Organization such a position that it possesses, in regard to its Members, rights which it is entitled to ask them to respect. In other words, does the Organization possess international personality? This is no doubt a doctrinal expression, which has sometimes given rise to controversy. But it will be used here to mean that if the Organization is recognized as having that personality, it is an entity capable of availing itself of obligations incumbent upon its Members.

To answer this question, which is not settled by the actual terms of the Charter, we must consider what characteristics it was intended thereby to give to the Organization.

* * *

The Charter has not been content to make the Organization created by it merely a centre "for harmonizing the actions of nations in the attainment of these common ends" (Article I, para. 4). It has equipped that centre with organs, and has given it special tasks. It has defined the position of the Members in relation to the Organization by requiring them to give it every assistance in any action undertaken by it (Article 2, para. 5), and to accept and carry out the decisions of the Security Council; by authorizing the General Assembly to make recommendations to the Members; by giving the Organization legal capacity and privileges and immunities in the territory of each of its Members; and by providing for the conclusion of agreements between the Organization and its Members. Practice—in particular the conclusion of conventions to which the Organization is a party—has confirmed this character of the Organization, which occupies a position in certain respects in detachment from its Members
* * *

In the opinion of the Court, the Organization was intended to exercise and enjoy, and is in fact exercising and enjoying, functions and rights which can only be explained on the basis of the possession of a large measure of international personality and the capacity to operate upon an international plane. It is at present the supreme type of international organization, and it could not carry out the intentions of its founders if it was devoid of international personality. It must be acknowledged that its Members, by entrusting certain functions to it, with the attendant duties and responsibilities, have clothed it with the competence required to enable those functions to be effectively discharged.

Accordingly, the Court has come to the conclusion that the Organization is an international person. That is not the same thing as saying that it is a State, which it certainly is not, or that its legal personality and rights and duties are the same as those of a State. Still less is it the same thing as saying that it is "a super-State", whatever that expression may mean. It does not even imply that all its rights and duties must be upon the international plane, any more than all the rights and duties of a State must be upon that plane. What it does mean is that it is a subject of international law and capable of possessing international rights and duties, and that it has capacity to maintain its rights by bringing international claims.

The next question is whether the sum of the international rights of the Organization comprises the right to bring the kind of international claim described in the Request for this Opinion. That is a claim against a State to obtain reparation in respect of the damage caused by the injury of an agent of the Organization in the course of the performance of his duties. Whereas a State possesses the totality of international rights and duties recognized by international law, the rights and duties of an entity such as the Organization must depend upon its purposes and functions as specified or implied in its constituent documents and developed in practice. The functions of the Organization are of such a character that they could not be effectively discharged if they involved the concurrent action, on the international plane, of fifty-eight or more Foreign Offices, and the Court concludes that the Members have endowed the Organization with capacity to bring international claims when necessitated by the discharge of its functions.

* * *

The Charter does not expressly confer upon the Organization the capacity to include, in its claim for reparation, damage caused to the victim or to persons entitled through him. The Court must therefore begin by enquiring whether the provisions of the Charter concerning the functions of the Organization, and the part played by its agents in the performance of those functions, imply for the Organization power to afford its agents the limited protection that would consist in the bringing of a claim on their behalf for reparation for damage suffered in such circumstances. Under international law, the Organization must be deemed to have those powers which, though not expressly provided in the Charter, are conferred upon it by necessary implication as being essential to the performance of its duties. This principle of law was applied by the Permanent Court of International Justice to the International Labour Organization in its Advisory Opinion No. 13 of July 23rd, 1926 (Series B., No. 13, p. 18), and must be applied to the United Nations.

Having regard to its purposes and functions already referred to, the Organization may find it necessary, and has in fact found it necessary, to entrust its agents with important missions to be performed in disturbed parts of the world. Many missions, from their very nature, involve the agents in unusual dangers to which ordinary persons are not exposed. For the same reason, the injuries suffered by its agents in these circumstances will sometimes have occurred in such a manner that their national State would not be justified in bringing a claim for reparation on the ground of diplomatic protection, or, at any rate, would not feel disposed to do so. Both to ensure the efficient and independent performance of these missions and to afford effective support to its agents, the Organization must provide them with adequate protection.

* * *

The obligations entered into by States to enable the agents of the Organization to perform their duties are undertaken not in the interest of the agents, but in that of the Organization. When it claims redress for a breach of these obligations, the Organization is invoking its own right, the right that the obligations due to it should be respected. On this ground, it asks for reparation of the injury suffered, for "it is a principle of international law that the breach of an engagement involves an obligation to make reparation in an adequate form"; as was stated by the Permanent Court in its Judgment No. 8 of July 26th, 1927 (Series A, No. 9, p. 21). In claiming reparation based on the injury suffered by its agent, the Organization does not represent the agent, but is asserting its own right, the right to secure respect for undertakings entered into towards the Organization.

* * *

[The Court Answered Question I(a) and I(b) in the affirmative.]

NOTE

In addition to Articles 104 and 105 quoted above, the U.N's juridical capacity was spelled out in the Convention on the Privileges and Immunities of the United Nations, 1 U.N.T.S. 15 (1946). Article 1, Section 1 as follows:

The United Nations shall possess juridical personality.

It shall have capacity:

(a) to contract;

(b) to acquire and dispose of movable and immovable property;

(c) to institute legal proceedings.

A parallel text was adopted for the UN Specialized Agencies, 33 U.N.T.S. 261 covering 16 organizations in the United Nations system (listed below). More or less parallel rules have also been adopted for other international organizations. See for example the Treaty Establishing the European Economic Community, Articles 281 and 282, and the World Trade Organization Agreement, Article VIII. Legal personality provisions are commonly contained in the treaty establishing the organization, in the two UN system Conventions cited above, in a Headquarters Agreement between the organization and the host Member State, or a combination of these instruments. Although they rarely give rise to serious controversy, one case is worthy of note. While the EU's operational need for legal personality has been fully satisfied by the EEC texts cited above, the 2004 Draft Treaty Establishing a Constitution for Europe would have adopted for the European Union in Article I–7 the following simple text: "The Union shall have legal personality", but this became a political issue between states favoring stronger Union, which supported this text, versus those opposed, which did not, and was considered to be one of the causes of the failure of the Draft Constitution. In the end, the draft Reform Treaty (Lisbon Treaty) developed late in 2007 confers legal personality on the

European Union, essentially retaining the legal effect of the failed Draft Constitution on this question.

Ian Brownlie, Principles of Public International Law
p. 677 (7th ed. 2008)

The criteria of legal personality in organizations may be summarized as follows:

1.   a permanent association of states, with lawful objects, equipped with organs;

2.   a distinction, in terms of legal powers and purposes, between the organization and its member states;

3.   the existence of legal powers exercisable on the international plane and not solely within the national systems of one or more states.

These criteria relate to delicate issues of law and fact and are not always easy to apply. * * *

[T]he really difficult questions concern the particular capacities of the organization as a legal person and its relations to members, third states, and other organizations. Before these questions are considered it may give more point to the criteria summarized above if certain distinctions are drawn. Thus an organization may exist but lack the organs and objects necessary for legal personality: the British Commonwealth is an association of this kind. * * * Joint agencies of states, for example an arbitral tribunal or river commission, may have restricted capacities and limited independence, with the executive and jurisdictional powers, and legal personality is only a matter of degree. * * * If an organization has considerable independence and power to intervene in the affairs of member states, the latter may come to have a status akin to that of membership in a federal union. It may be noted also that, while an organization with legal personality is normally established by treaty, this is by no means necessary and the source could equally be the resolution of a conference of states or a uniform practice. The constitutional basis of the United Nations Conference on Trade and Development (UNCTAD) and of the United Nations Industrial Development Organization (UNIDO) must be found in resolutions of the General Assembly.

c.   SCOPE AND ROLES OF SELECTED ORGANIZATIONS: SUMMARIES

This material looks at a representative sampling of public international organizations with references to typical or other features of general interest. The United Nations is taken up first as the foremost organization with the assignment of the most comprehensive roles in war and peace and general issues of international relations, world-wide membership, and structures which have influenced many other organizations, including the U.N's specialized agencies. The WTO appears next in view of its world wide membership and a number of unusual features, followed by the European

Union which can be classified not only as a co-operative organization like the others, but also as a "regional economic integration organization" with sovereign powers in limited areas of competence, making it *sui generis*. They are followed by four "regional organizations" of particular interest: the North Atlantic Treaty Organization (NATO), the Council of Europe (COE), the Organization of American States (OAS) and the African Union (AU). In addition there are organizations commonly known as "functional organizations" in view of their specialized and limited competences, including the Organization for Economic Co-operation and Development (OECD), the Organization of Petroleum Exporting Countries (OPEC), the International Energy Agency (IEA) and the Energy Charter Treaty (ECT) taken up in this discussion. While these and other classifications are employed for easy reference, the classifications are only indicative and many organizations could be readily included in more than one of them.

1.) *The United Nations System*

If the international legal system has a formal constitution or something approaching it, the governing legal instrument would be the United Nations Charter which created the United Nations in 1945 after the close of hostilities in World War II. The U.N is the first international organization with all but universal, world wide membership, charged with the responsibility for maintaining international peace and security, developing friendly relations among nations, achieving international co-operation in solving international problems of an economic, social, cultural, or humanitarian nature, and in promoting and encouraging respect for human rights and fundamental freedoms. The Organization functions as a center for harmonizing the actions of nations in the attainment of these common ends. (Article 1). With all of it strengths and weaknesses, the United Nations continues today to rank as the foremost international organization.

In addition, the Charter codifies some of the basic principles of the international system stated in legally binding terms in international law. These include the sovereign equality of all its Members, fulfillment in good faith of their obligations under the Charter, settlement of their disputes by peaceful means, refraining in their international relations from the threat or use of force, and giving the United Nations assistance in any action it takes in accordance with the Charter. The organization is to ensure that states which are not Members of the U.N. shall act in accordance with these principle so far as may be necessary for the maintenance of international peace and security. A final principle declares that nothing in the Charter shall authorize the U.N to intervene in matters which are essentially within the domestic jurisdiction any state or to submit such matters to pacific settlement under the Charter, with the exceptions of enforcement measures. (Article 2).

The Charter also establishes the principle organs of the U.N. system together with a number of rules governing them. Some of the essential features of these organs are taken up briefly below.

The UN in Brief—

http://www.un.org/Overview/uninbrief/contents.html*

The General Assembly.

All U.N. Member States are represented in the General Assembly—a "parliament of nations", although it does not normally legislate in the way parliaments do. The Assembly meets regularly and in special sessions to consider the world's most pressing international problems within the competence of the Assembly. Each of the UN's 191 Member States has one vote. Decisions on such key issues as international peace and security, admitting new members and the UN budget are decided by two-thirds majority. Other matters are decided by simple majority. In recent years, a special effort has been made to reach decisions through consensus, rather than by taking a formal vote.

The Assembly is empowered to adopt recommendations to Members or to the Security Council on most matters within the scope of the Charter, but not legally binding decisions in most situations. Although the Assembly cannot force action by any State, its recommendations are an important indication of world opinion and represent the moral authority of the community of nations. They can have far-reaching legal consequences, for example, in influencing customary international law and in leading to preparation and adoption of new treaties, as in the work of the International Law Commission discussed below. Among the Assembly's responsibilities is the encouragement of "the progressive development of international law and its codification." [See Articles 9–22].

* * *

The Security Council

The UN Charter gives the Security Council primary responsibility for maintaining international peace and security. The Council may convene at any time, whenever peace is threatened. Under the Charter, all Member States are obligated to carry out the Council's decisions.

There are 15 Council Members. Five of these—China, France, the Russian Federation, the United Kingdom and the United States—are permanent members. The other 10 are elected by the General Assembly for two-year terms. Member States continue to discuss changes in Council membership and working methods to reflect today's political and economic realities.

Decisions of the Council require nine "yes" votes. Except in votes on procedural questions, a decision cannot be taken if there is a "no" vote, or veto, by a permanent member.

When the Council considers a threat to international peace, it first explores ways to settle the dispute peacefully. It may suggest principles for a settlement or undertake mediation. In the event of fighting, the Council tries to secure a ceasefire. It may send a peacekeeping mission to help the parties maintain the truce and to keep opposing forces apart.

---

* Last accessed July 2009.

The Council can take measures to enforce its decisions. It can impose economic sanctions or order an arms embargo. On rare occasions, the Council has authorized Member States to use "all necessary means," including collective military action, to see that its decisions are carried out.

The Council also makes recommendations to the General Assembly on the appointment of a new Secretary–General and on the admission of new Members to the UN. [See Articles 23–32]

International Court of Justice

The International Court of Justice, also known as the World Court, is the main judicial organ of the UN. Its 15 judges are elected by the General Assembly and the Security Council, voting independently and concurrently. The Court decides disputes between countries, based on the voluntary participation of the States concerned. If a State agrees to participate in a proceeding, it is obligated to comply with the Court's decision. The Court also gives advisory opinions to the United Nations and its specialized agencies. [See Articles 92–96] Additional authorities on the ICJ may be found in Chapter 9 *infra*.

Secretariat

The Secretariat carries out the substantive and administrative work of the United Nations as directed by the General Assembly, the Security Council and the other organs. At its head is the Secretary–General, who provides overall policy and administrative guidance. The Secretary–General is appointed by the General Assembly upon the recommendation of the Security Council and serves as the chief administrative officer of the Organization.

The Secretariat consists of departments and offices with a total staff of about 7,500 under the regular budget, drawn from some 170 countries. Duty stations include UN Headquarters in New York, as well as UN offices in Geneva, Vienna, Nairobi and other locations.

See Charter Articles 97–101, and Simon Chesterton, SECRETARY OR GENERAL?—THE SECRETARY-GENERAL IN WORLD POLITICS (2007).

United Nations, The International Law Commission

http://www.un.org/law/ilc/

The Governments participating in the drafting of the Charter of the United Nations were overwhelmingly opposed to conferring on the United Nations legislative power to enact binding rules of international law. As a corollary, they also rejected proposals to confer on the General Assembly the power to impose certain general conventions on States by some form of majority vote. There was, however, strong support for conferring on the General Assembly the more limited powers of study and recommendation, which led to the adoption of the following provision in Article 13, paragraph 1:

   1.   The General Assembly shall initiate studies and make recommendations for the purpose of:

      a.   encouraging the progressive development of international law and its codification.

The Commission was established by the UN General Assembly in 1947, and meets in Geneva for up to three months each summer (May–July). It is composed of 34 experts representing the world's principal legal systems, each elected for a term of five years by the UN General Assembly to serve in their personal capacity rather than as representatives of governments.

Over the years the Commission has considered a large number of the most important areas of international law, leading in many cases to the successful development of treaties, such as the Vienna Convention on Diplomatic Relations of 1961, the Vienna Convention on Consular Relations of 1963, the Vienna Convention on the Law of Treaties of 1969, the United Nations Convention on the Law of the Sea of 1982, the Vienna Convention on the Law of Treaties between States and International Organizations, or Between Two or more International Organizations of 1986, the Rome Statute of the International Criminal Court of 1998, and the United Nations Convention on Jurisdictional Immunities of States and Their Property of 2004. References to all of these authoritative treaties will be found in the chapters that follow.

Agencies in the United Nations System In addition to the United Nations itself, the United Nations system includes 16 "Specialized Agencies" recognized pursuant to Charter Article 57 and linked to the UN through co-operative agreements. Article 57(1) provides: "The various specialized agencies, established by intergovernmental agreement and having wide international responsibilities, as defined in their basic instruments, in economic, social, cultural, educational, health, and related fields, shall be brought into relationship with the United Nations in accordance with the provisions of Article 63." These agencies are autonomous international organizations created by their own intergovernmental agreements or other legal instruments, have their own internal policy and management structures, secretariats and budgets. Some of them, like the International Labour Organization and the Universal Postal Union, are older than the UN itself. Many have international legal rules developed in their constituent instruments, their own legal personality, privileges and immunities arrangements, and develop separate law-making conventions and other instruments. They are qualified to submit requests for advisory opinions to the International Court of Justice.

As identified in *The U.N in Brief* cited above, these agencies are:

- FAO (Food and Agricultural Organization of the UN). Works to improve agricultural productivity and food security, and to better the living standards of rural populations.

- IAEA (International Atomic Energy Agency). An autonomous intergovernmental organization under the aegis of the UN, it works for the safe and peaceful uses of atomic energy.

- ICAO (International Civil Aviation Organization). Sets international standards for the safety, security and efficiency of air transport, and serves as the coordinator for international cooperation in all areas of civil aviation.

- IFAD (International Fund for Agricultural Development). Mobilizes financial resources to raise food production and nutrition levels among the poor in developing countries.

- ILO (International Labour Organization). Formulates policies and programmes to improve working conditions and employment opportunities, and sets labour standards used by countries around the world.

- IMF (International Monetary Fund). Facilitates international monetary cooperation and financial stability and provides a permanent forum for consultation, advice and assistance on financial issues. See also Chapter 7 below.

- IMO (International Maritime Organization). See also Chapter 6 below. Works to improve international shipping procedures, raise standards in marine safety and reduce marine pollution by ships.

- ITU (International Telecommunications Union). Fosters international cooperation to improve telecommunications of all kinds, coordinates usage of radio and TV frequencies, promotes safety measures and conducts research.

- UNESCO (UN Educational, Scientific and Cultural Organization). Promotes education for all, cultural development, protection of the world's natural and cultural heritage, international cooperation in science, press freedom and communication.

- UNIDO (UN Industrial Development Organization). See also Chapter 7 below. Promotes the industrial advancement of developing countries through technical assistance, advisory services and training.

- UPU (Universal Postal Union). Establishes international regulations for postal services, provides technical assistance and promotes cooperation in postal matters.

- WHO (World Health Organization). Coordinates programmes aimed at solving health problems and the attainment by all people of the highest possible level of health. It works in such areas as immunization, health education and the provision of essential drugs.

- WIPO (World Intellectual Property Organization). Promotes international protection of intellectual property and fosters cooperation on copyrights, trademarks, industrial designs and patents.

- (World Bank Group). Provides loans and technical assistance to developing countries to reduce poverty and advance sustainable economic growth. See Chapter 7 below.
- WMO (World Meteorological Organization). Promotes scientific research on the Earth's atmosphere and on climate change, and facilitates the global exchange of meteorological data.
- WTO (World Tourism Organization). Serves as a global forum for tourism policy issues and a practical source of tourism know-how.

In addition, a number of UN offices, programmes and funds—such as the Office of the UN High Commissioner for Human Rights, Office of the UN High Commissioner for Refugees (UNHCR), the UN Development Programme (UNDP) and the UN Children's Fund (UNICEF)—work to improve the economic and social condition of people around the world. They report to the General Assembly or the Economic and Social Council.

Funding The General Assembly voting rule providing one vote for each Member State applies, with the two-thirds rule applicable to budgetary questions; thus the funding decisions are binding on all Members, even those casting a negative vote. Article 17 provides:

1. The General Assembly shall consider and approve the budget of the Organization.

2. The expenses of the Organization shall be borne by the Members as apportioned by the General Assembly.

3. The General Assembly shall consider and approve any financial and budgetary arrangements with specialized agencies referred to in Article 57 and shall examine the administrative budgets of such specialized agencies with a view to making recommendations to the agencies concerned.

2.) *The World Trade Organization (WTO)*

The WTO operates outside of the U.N. system, as do all of the other organizations discussed below. The WTO was introduced in Chapter 2 and will be taken up again in Chapter 7.

3.) *The European Union and Other Regional Economic Integration Organizations (REIOs)*

The European Union is regarded by many as the most far-reaching and innovative international organization in developing legal principles and structures in recent times. The EU now presents amply developed institutions of economic integration reaching well beyond other international organizations in scope and depth, and the EU experience has influenced other regions to consider or to establish regional integration organizations.

European Union, Guide for Americans

http://www.eurunion.org/infores/euguide/euguide2007.pdf

The European Union is not a federation like the United States. Nor is it simply an organization for cooperation between governments, like the United Nations. Neither is it a State intended to replace existing states, but it *is* much more than any other international organization. The EU is, in fact, unique. Never before have countries voluntarily agreed to set up common institutions to which they delegate some of their sovereignty so that decisions on specific matters of joint interest can be made democratically at a higher, in this case European, level. All EU decisions and procedures are based on the treaties agreed to by all EU countries, under which sovereignty is shared in specified areas. The result is a union of 27 Member States covering 1.6 million square miles with roughly half a billion people producing almost a third of the world's gross national product and speaking more than 23 languages, bound together by a desire to promote peace, democracy, prosperity, stability, and the rule of law.

The EU embraces the fundamental values shared by its Member States across a multitude of cultures, languages, and traditions. The Member States agree that democracy is the best form of government. They believe in societies that encourage pluralistic political thought and endorse freedom of speech and religion. They support free market economies—where economic development and growth are driven by the private sector and facilitated by governments. They believe prosperous countries have an obligation to help poorer and less developed regions and nations. And they value living together in peace as well as promoting these principles globally.

The EU sets high standards for membership. Candidate states must have stable democratic governments; respect for the rule of law, minorities, and human rights; a functioning market economy; and the ability to take on the obligations of EU membership. That is, prospective members must have the capacity to adopt and implement the body of EU laws and regulations that ensures cooperation in a multitude of areas in addition to trade and the economy, including citizens' rights, freedom, security, and justice, job creation, regional development, environmental protection, and making globalization work for everyone. * * *

The Treaties That Built the Union

The European Union has been built through a series of treaties that represent binding commitments by the Member States. Treaties are negotiated by Member States through intergovernmental conferences, or ''IGCs,'' that culminate in a summit chaired by the Member State holding the Council presidency. This process began with three separate treaties dating from the 1950s: the European Coal and Steel Community Treaty (ECSC), the European Atomic Energy Community Treaty (EURATOM), and the

European Economic Community Treaty (EEC). In 1967, the ECSC, the EAEC, and the EEC collectively became known as the European Communities. * * *

The Treaty on European Union, signed in Maastricht, Netherlands ("the Maastricht Treaty"), and in effect since November 1993, was a major overhaul of the founding treaties. Maastricht provided a blueprint to achieve Economic and Monetary Union (EMU), further developed the Union's inherent political dimension through the new Common Foreign and Security Policy (CFSP), and expanded cooperation in judicial and policing matters. * * *

[The Treaty of Lisbon, in 2007 becomes the next treaty in this series, displacing the Constitution Treaty. Some of the objectives of the Treaty of Lisbon are taken up below.]

How is the EU Run? A Unique Governing System

The European Union is governed by several institutions that reflect the EU's unique, dual supranational and intergovernmental character. The EU has the power to enact laws that are directly binding on citizens from many countries, a fact that distinguishes the Union from any other government or international organization. [See Chapter 11 material on the EU.]

Member States have relinquished part of their national sovereignty to EU institutions, leading to descriptions of the Union as a supranational entity, with many decisions made and final authority residing at the EU level. In specified areas, the Member States work together in their collective interest through EU institutions to administer sovereign powers jointly. The EU's decision-making process involves three main institutions, all set up in the 1950s under the EU's founding treaties.

The European Commission proposes new legislation while the Council of the European Union and European Parliament adopt the laws. This institutional triangle produces policies and laws that apply throughout the EU. Two other institutions also play a vital role: the European Court of Justice upholds the rule of European law, and the Court of Auditors checks the financing of Union activities.

Other institutions and bodies also play important roles.

Governing Institutions

[More detailed information on the European Commission, the Council of the European Union and the European Parliament can be found in the Guide for Americans cited above.]

The European Court of Justice

The European Court of Justice (ECJ) of the European Communities was set up under the ECSC Treaty in 1952. Based in Luxembourg, it acts as the European Union's Supreme Court.

The ECJ ensures that EU legislation is interpreted and applied uniformly in all EU countries. The Court has the power to settle legal disputes between EU Member States, EU institutions, businesses, and individuals. Its rulings are binding. The Court is composed of one judge per Member State, appointed by joint agreement between the governments of the EU Member States for a renewable term of six years. For the sake of efficiency, however, the Court usually sits as a Grand Chamber of just 13 judges, or in chambers of three or five judges.

The Court is assisted by eight advocates-general who present reasoned opinions on the cases brought before the Court, publicly and impartially.

To help the Court of Justice cope with a large caseload and to afford citizens better legal protection, a Court of First Instance [CFI] was created in 1989. This court (which is attached to the Court of Justice) is responsible for certain kinds of cases, particularly actions brought by private individuals, companies, and some organizations, as well as cases relating to competition law. * * *

P.S.R.F. Mathijsen, A Guide to European Law

p. 26, 50 (9th ed. 2007)

Community Acts

For those who are subject to Community law, the main question with regard to the acts is to be able to determine whether or not they are "binding" on them. According to the Court [European Court of Justice], an act is binding when it "brings about a distinctive change in the legal position of a party" * * *. [That consists of regulations, directives and decisions.]

Sources of Community Law

Some 50 years ago, I drafted an article to be inserted in the Chapter of the ECSC Treaty concerning the Court of Justice, which would indicate the sources of law to be applied. Although different words would be used today, its basic indications still seem to be applicable:

"1. The Court whose function it is to ensure the rule of law in the execution of this Treaty, shall apply:

    (a) the provisions of this Treaty and of the judicial acts issued by the institutions;

    (b) the conventions to which the Community is a party or which are undertaken on its behalf;

    (c) the customary law of the Community;

    (d) the general principles of the law of the Community;

    (e) the municipal law of the Member States in case of explicit or tacit reference

2.   In case of reference to international law, the Court shall apply Article 38, paragraph 1, of the Statute of the International Court of justice.

* * *

4.   As auxiliary means for the determination of the applicable law, the Court shall apply the decisions of international tribunals, those of the Community and the doctrine". * * *

The Reform Treaty ("Lisbon Treaty")

The Treaty of Lisbon, The Treaty at a Glance
http://europa.eu/lisbon_treaty/glance/index_en.htm

On 13 December 2007, EU leaders signed the Treaty of Lisbon [not yet in force in 2009], thus bringing to an end several years of negotiation about institutional issues.

The Treaty of Lisbon amends the current EU and EC treaties, without replacing them. It will provide the Union with the legal framework and tools necessary to meet future challenges and to respond to citizens' demands.

1.   A more democratic and transparent Europe, with a strengthened role for the European Parliament and national parliaments, more opportunities for citizens to have their voices heard and a clearer sense of who does what at European and national level.

2.   A more efficient Europe, with simplified working methods and voting rules, streamlined and modern institutions for a EU of 27 members and an improved ability to act in areas of major priority for today's Union.

3.   A Europe of rights and values, freedom, solidarity and security, promoting the Union's values, introducing the Charter of Fundamental Rights into European primary law, providing for new solidarity mechanisms and ensuring better protection of European citizens.

4.   Europe as an actor on the global stage will be achieved by bringing together Europe's external policy tools, both when developing and deciding new policies. The Treaty of Lisbon will give Europe a clear voice in relations with its partners worldwide. It will harness Europe's economic, humanitarian, political and diplomatic strengths to promote European interests and values worldwide, while respecting the particular interests of the Member States in Foreign Affairs.

NOTE

The European Union experience with regional economic integration has influenced states in other regions to consider their own regional developments. One of the most advanced of these may be Mercosur, the Southern Market, composed of Argentina, Paraguay, Uruguay and Brazil. The objectives of Mercosur include the free transit of production goods and of services, between the member states, the elimination of tariffs and other trade restrictions, the establishment of a common tariff, co-ordination of economic policies and the harmonization of legislation in relevant areas to strengthen the economic process. (See the 1991 Treaty establishing a Common Market, 30 I.L.M. 1041 (1991), and http://www.mercosur.int/). For Africa, there is the Treaty Establishing the African Economic Community (AEC)—1991: commonly known as the Abuja Treaty, in operation since 1994, http://www.africa-union.org/. Economic integration aspirations and activity are also seen in the 1972 Caribbean Community (CARICOM) www.caricom.org, the Association of Southeast Asian Nations (ASEAN) www.aseansec.org, and in the Asia Pacific Economic Co-operation of 1989, www.apecsec.org.

4.) Regional Organizations

North Atlantic Treaty Organization (NATO)

What is NATO?
http://www/nato.int/nato-welcome/index.html 2007

The North Atlantic Treaty Organization (NATO) is an alliance of 28 countries from North America and Europe committed to fulfilling the goals of the North Atlantic Treaty signed on 4 April 1949. In accordance with the Treaty, the fundamental role of NATO is to safeguard the freedom and security of its member countries by political and military means. NATO safeguards the Allies' common values of democracy, individual liberty, the rule of law and the peaceful resolution of disputes, and promotes these values throughout the Euro-Atlantic area.

NATO provides a forum in which the United States, Canada and European countries can consult together on security issues of common concern and take joint action in addressing them. NATO is committed to defending its member states against aggression or the threat of aggression and to the principle that an attack against one or several members would be considered an attack against all.

* * *

NATO is an intergovernmental organization. The 28 member countries retain their full sovereignty. All NATO decisions are taken jointly by the member countries on the basis of consensus. The North Atlantic Council is the principal decision-making body within NATO. It brings together high-level representatives of each member country to discuss policy or operational questions requiring collective decisions.

* * * Decisions are agreed upon on the basis of unanimity and common accord. There is no voting or decision by majority. This means that policies decided upon by the North Atlantic Council (NAC) are supported by and are the expression of the collective will of all the sovereign states that are members of the Alliance and are accepted by all of them.

Speaking about NATO's performance and future, Zbigniew Brzezinski wrote:

> In assessing NATOs evolving role, one has to take into account the historical fact that in the course of its 60 years the alliance has institutionalized three truly monumental transformations in world affairs: first, the end of the centuries-long "civil war" within the West for transoceanic and European supremacy; second, the United States' post-World War II commitment to the defense of Europe against Soviet domination (resulting from either a political upheaval or even World War III); and third, the peaceful termination of the Cold War, which ended the geopolitical division of Europe and created the preconditions for a larger democratic European Union.
>
> * * *
>
> NATO, however, has the experience, the institutions, and the means to eventually become the hub of a globe-spanning web of various regional cooperative-security undertakings among states with the growing power to act. The resulting security web would fill a need that the United Nations by itself cannot meet but from which the UN system would actually benefit. In pursuing that strategic mission, NATO would not only be preserving transatlantic political unity; it would also be responding to the twenty-first century's novel and increasingly urgent security agenda.
>
> *An Agenda for NATO—Toward a Global Security Web,* 88 Foreign Affairs 2, 20 (no. 5, 2009).

Not everyone is as optimistic about NATO's future as Brzezinksi. Can you think why? What will happen to NATO should the EU develop its own military forces? For more on the international law governing the use of force by NATO, see UN Charter, Chapter VIII and Chapter 10 below.

The Council of Europe at a Glance

http://www.coe.int/T/E/Com/About_Coe/Brochures/At_a_glance.asp 2007

Origins and membership

Set up in 1949, the Council of Europe is a political intergovernmental organisation. Its permanent headquarters are in Strasbourg, France. It represents 47 European pluralist democracies, with 5 observers (Canada, the Holy See, Japan, Mexico and the United States of America).

Aims

—to protect human rights and the rule of law in all member states; to consolidate democratic stability in Europe by backing political, legal and

—constitutional reform nationally, regionally and locally;

—to seek solutions to social problems such as discrimination against minorities, xenophobia, intolerance, bioethics and cloning, terrorism, trafficking in human beings,

—organised crime and corruption, cybercrime, violence against children;

—to promote social cohesion and social rights.

Structure

● The Committee of Ministers, the decision-making body, comprising the Foreign Ministers of the 47 member states or their permanent diplomatic representatives;

● The Parliamentary Assembly, the deliberative body, grouping 318 members (and 318 substitutes) from the 47 national parliaments and delegations from non-member states;

● The Congress of Local and Regional Authorities of the Council of Europe—two chambers, one for local and one for regional authorities;

● The European Court of Human Rights, based in Strasbourg, permanently in session and dealing with all procedures from admissibility to final judgment. The Parliamentary Assembly elects judges for a six-year term.

* * *

Major activities

Human rights for everyone

The 1950 European Convention on Human Rights establishes a single, permanent system to control and protect human rights: the European Court of Human Rights. Anyone who claims that his or her rights have been infringed may lodge a complaint if no further legal remedies are available in the national courts. [For more on human rights, see Chapter 5.]

In a political climate which encourages interdependence between states, international law is constantly developing, and is increasingly becoming a key factor in the organisation of inter-state relations. The Council of Europe is accordingly working to co-ordinate its member states' activities in this field.

The Council of Europe does it through its Committee of Legal Advisers on Public International Law (CAHDI), an intergovernmental committee which brings together the legal advisers of the Ministries for foreign affairs of the member States of the Council of Europe as well as of a significant number of observer States and Organisations.

The Council of Europe has an extensive program of work in European and international law, described on the COE website—www.coe.org—under the heading of "Building Europe together on the Rule of Law".

The Organization of American States, Who We Are

www.oas.org

The Organization of American States (OAS) is the world's oldest regional organization, dating back to the First International Conference of

American States, held in Washington, D.C., from October 1889 to April 1890. At that meeting the establishment of the International Union of American Republics was approved. The Charter of the OAS was signed in Bogotá in 1948 and entered into force in December 1951. The Charter was subsequently amended by the Protocol of Buenos Aires, signed in 1967, which entered into force in February 1970; by the Protocol of Cartagena de Indias, signed in 1985, which entered into force in November 1988; by the Protocol of Managua, signed in 1993, which entered into force on January 29, 1996; and by the Protocol of Washington, signed in 1992, which entered into force on September 25, 1997. The OAS currently has 35 member states. In addition, the Organization has granted permanent observer status to 62 states, as well as to the European Union.

The Organization of American States (OAS) is an international organization established in 1948 to achieve among its member states, as Article 1 of its Charter indicates, "an order of peace and justice, to promote their solidarity, to strengthen their collaboration, and to defend their sovereignty, their territorial integrity, and their independence." Today it comprises the 35 independent States of the Americas and constitutes the principal political, juridical, and social governmental forum in the Hemisphere.

However, the establishment of the international organization that today brings together all the States of the Americas and the Caribbean marked one stage of a long process that dates back to 1889, when, in and around the Conferences of American States, a web of provisions and institutions was being woven that came to be known as the "inter-American system," the oldest of the international institutional systems.

[The Inter–American human rights system is introduced in Chapter 5.]

The African Union in a Nutshell

http://www.africa-union.org/root/au/AboutAu/au_in_a_nutshell_en.htm#intro

Introduction

The advent of the African Union (AU) can be described as an event of great magnitude in the institutional evolution of the continent. On 9.9.1999, the Heads of State and Government of the Organisation of African Unity issued a Declaration (the Sirte Declaration) calling for the establishment of an African Union, with a view, inter alia, to accelerating the process of integration in the continent to enable it play its rightful role in the global economy while addressing multifaceted social, economic and political problems compounded as they are by certain negative aspects of globalisation.

The main objectives of the OAU were, inter alia, to rid the continent of the remaining vestiges of colonization and apartheid; to promote unity and solidarity among African States; to coordinate and intensify cooperation for development; to safeguard the sovereignty and territorial integrity of Member States and to promote international cooperation within the framework of the United Nations. Indeed, as a continental organization the OAU provided an effective forum that enabled all Member States to adopt coordinated positions on matters of common concern to the continent in international fora and defend the interests of Africa effectively.

Through the OAU Coordinating Committee for the Liberation of Africa, the Continent worked and spoke as one with undivided determination in forging an international consensus in support of the liberation struggle and the fight against apartheid.

Advent of the AU

The OAU initiatives paved the way for the birth of the AU. In July 1999, the Assembly decided to convene an extraordinary session to expedite the process of economic and political integration in the continent. Since then, four Summits have been held leading to the official launching of the African Union * * *

The Vision of the AU

The AU is Africa's premier institution and principal organization for the promotion of accelerated socio-economic integration of the continent, which will lead to greater unity and solidarity between African countries and peoples.

The AU is based on the common vision of a united and strong Africa and on the need to build a partnership between governments and all segments of civil society, in particular women, youth and the private sector, in order to strengthen solidarity and cohesion amongst the peoples of Africa.

As a continental organization it focuses on the promotion of peace, security and stability on the continent as a prerequisite for the implementation of the development and integration agenda of the Union.

The Organs of the AU

The Assembly Composed of Heads of State and Government or their duly accredited representatives. The Assembly of Heads of State and Government is the supreme organ of the Union. *The Executive Council* Composed of Ministers or Authorities designated by the Governments of Members States. The Executive Council is responsible to the Assembly.

The Commission Composed of the Chairperson, the Deputy Chairperson, eight Commissioners and Staff members; Each Commissioner shall be responsible for a portfolio. *The Permanent Representatives' Committee* Composed of Permanent Representatives of Member States accredited to the Union. The Permanent Representatives Committee is charged with the responsibility of preparing the work of the Executive Council. *Peace and Security Council (PSC)* By decision AHG/Dec 160 (xxxvii) of the Summit of Lusaka, July 2001, a decision was made for the creation within the African Union of the Peace and Security Council. The Protocol establishing the PSC is in the process of ratification. *Pan–African Parliament* A Pan–African Parliament, an organ to ensure the full participation of African peoples in governance, development and economic integration of the Continent. * * * *ECOSOCC* The Economic, Social and Cultural Council, an advisory organ composed of different social and professional groups of the Member States of the Union. * * * *The Court of Justice* A Court of Justice of the Union shall be established. * * * *The Specialized Technical Committees* The following Specialized Technical Committees are meant to address sectoral issues and are at Ministerial Level:

The Committee on Rural Economy and Agricultural Matters;

The Committee on Monetary and Financial Affairs;

The Committee on Trade, Customs and Immigration Matters;

The Committee on Industry, Science and Technology, Energy, Natural Resources and Environment;

The Committee on Transport, Communications and Tourism;

The Committee on Health, Labour and Social Affairs; and

The Committee on Education, Culture and Human Resources.

The Financial Institutions

The African Central Bank

The African Monetary Fund

The African Investment Bank

5.) *Functional Organizations*

Functional international organizations represent another category which is open to some interpretation, for regional and other organizations noted above may also boast a specified functional dimension, and might fall as well into this category. NATO for one, and the multilateral development banks (See Chapter 7D below) could fit both categories. The U.N. Specialized Agencies tend to universality in membership and are functional in purpose. The functional organizations would include the World Trade Organization, which is discussed in Section 7B. This leaves principally the OECD, OPEC and IEA to be taken up here.

Overview of the OECD: What is it? History? Who does what? Structure of the Organisation?

www.oecd.org 2007

The Organisation for Economic Co-operation and Development has been called a think tank, a monitoring agency, a rich man's club and an unacademic university. It has elements of all, but none of these descriptions captures the essence of the OECD.

The OECD groups 30 member countries in a unique forum to discuss, develop and refine economic and social policies. They compare experiences, seek answers to common problems and work to co-ordinate domestic and international policies to help members and non-members deal with an increasingly globalised world. Their exchanges may lead to agreements to act in a formal way for example by establishing legally binding agreements to crack down on bribery, or codes for free flow of capital and services. The OECD is also known for "soft law"—non-binding instruments on difficult issues such as its Guidelines for multinational enterprises. Beyond agreements, the discussions at the OECD make for better-informed work within member countries' own governments across the broad spectrum of public policy and help clarify the impact of national policies on the international community.

The OECD is a group of like-minded countries. Essentially membership is limited only by a country's commitment to a market economy and a pluralistic democracy. It is rich, in that its 30 members produce two thirds of the world's goods and services, but it is by no means exclusive. The core of original European and North American members has expanded to include Japan, Australia, New Zealand, Finland, Mexico, Korea and four former communist states in Europe: the Czech Republic, Hungary, Poland and the Slovak Republic. Non-members are invited to subscribe to OECD agreements and treaties, and the Organisation now involves in its work some 70 non-member countries from Brazil, China and Russia to least developed countries in Africa and elsewhere.

* * *

The Council

Decision-making power is vested in the OECD Council. It is made up of one representative per member country, plus a representative of the European Commission. * * * The work mandated by the Council is carried out by the OECD secretariat.

* * *

Peer reviews

Mutual examination by governments, multilateral surveillance and a peer review process through which the performance of individual countries is monitored by their peers, all carried out at committee-level, are at the heart of our effectiveness. An example of the peer review process at work is to be found in the Working Group on Bribery, which monitors the implementation by signatory countries of the OECD Convention on Combating Bribery of Foreign Officials in International Business Transactions.

Agreements, standards and recommendations

Discussions at OECD committee-level sometimes evolve into negotiations where OECD countries agree on rules of the game for international co-operation. They can culminate in formal agreements by countries, for example on combating bribery, on arrangements for export credits, or on the treatment of capital movements. They may produce standards and models, for example in the application of bilateral treaties on taxation, or recommendations, for example on cross-border co-operation in enforcing laws against spam. They may also result in guidelines, for example on corporate governance or environmental practices.

Organization of Petroleum Exporting Countries, (OPEC), OPEC History and Functions

http://www.opec.org/

The Organization of the Petroleum Exporting Countries (OPEC) is a permanent, intergovernmental Organization, created at the Baghdad Conference on September 10–14, 1960, by Iran, Iraq, Kuwait, Saudi Arabia and Venezuela. The five Founding Members were later joined by nine other Members: Qatar (1961); Indonesia (1962); Socialist Peoples Libyan Arab Jamahiriya (1962); United Arab Emirates (1967); Algeria (1969); Nigeria (1971); Ecuador (1973–1992, [and 2007]); Gabon (1975–1994) and Angola (2007). * * *

OPEC's objective is to co-ordinate and unify petroleum policies among Member Countries, in order to secure fair and stable prices for petroleum producers; an efficient, economic and regular supply of petroleum to consuming nations; and a fair return on capital to those investing in the industry.

OPEC rose to international prominence during [the 1970s] * * *, as its Member Countries took control of their domestic petroleum industries and acquired a major say in the pricing of crude oil on world markets. There were two oil pricing crises, triggered by the Arab oil embargo in 1973 and the outbreak of the Iranian Revolution in 1979, but fed by fundamental imbalances in the market; both resulted in oil prices rising steeply. * * *

The OPEC Member Countries coordinate their oil production policies in order to help stabilise the oil market and to help oil producers achieve a reasonable rate of return on their investments. This policy is also designed to ensure that oil consumers continue to receive stable supplies of oil.

About the IEA (International Energy Agency)

www.iea.org (2007)

The International Energy Agency is the energy forum for 26 industrialised countries. IEA member governments are committed to taking joint measures to meet oil supply emergencies. They also have agreed to share energy information, to co-ordinate their energy policies and to co-operate in the development of rational energy programmes that ensure energy security, encourage economic growth and protect the environment. These provisions are embodied in the Agreement on an International Energy Programme, the treaty pursuant to which the Agency was established in 1974. * * *

The oil crisis of 1973–1974 shocked the nations of the industrialized world into taking action to ensure that they would never again be so vulnerable to a major disruption in oil supplies. The result was the creation in 1974 of the International Energy Agency (IEA), a co-opeative grouping of most of the countries of the OECD, committed to responding swiftly and effectively to future oil emergencies and to reducing their dependence on oil. To attain these objectives, member countries agreed to establish emergency oil stocks, reduce consumption—and if necessary—share supplies. They also committed to increase the efficiency of their use of energy, to conserve this valuable resource and to diversify their energy supplies through development of alternatives to oil.

* * *

Richard Scott, The History of the International Energy Agency

Vol. 1, p. 61 (1994) www.iea.org (2007)

The Agreement on an International Energy Program, signed on behalf of the initial sixteen Member states on 18 November 1974 [28 in 2009], reflected the founders' conviction that the Program should be established in an international treaty rather than in an instrument of lesser juridical standing. The most compelling reason for the treaty approach was the need to establish the Agency's Emergency Sharing System, set out in the first five Chapters of the Agreement, in absolutely binding terms from a legal standpoint. In situations of oil supply disruptions presenting high economic and political stakes, it could not be excluded that states might be drawn into action which did not entirely conform to the interests of the group as a whole. Internal as well as external forces acting on the states might have disruptive effects in the course of a crisis, particularly a deep and prolonged crisis bringing severe suffering to their constituencies. At times the costs of compliance with a system of oil sharing might be high. The short term interests of a country could run counter to respect for the interests of the group as a whole. In some situations there could be pressures by oil producers on selected Members. Or compliance might jeopardize other political objectives, leading industrial countries toward "beggar-my-neighbor" rather than co-operative sharing actions. * * *

The founders concluded that the best way to *minimize* these problems was to use legally binding provisions on the *key elements* of the system and to embody those provisions in an international treaty, thus making the commitments as formal, visible and convincing as possible. A treaty could be expected to assist Members with their own constituencies in times of crisis. The adoption of legal undertakings would have the advantage of placing them within the international legal system and subjecting them to incentives for compliance. Monitoring and administration would also be greatly facilitated, particularly with the advantage of the IEA reporting, reviewing and performance assessment capabilities. In that context, since the incentives for implementation would then become readily apparent, the Program would be much more effective than it might have been if established on political formulations with less formal standing than the legal arrangements which were adopted in the treaty.

Kaj Hober, The Energy Charter Treaty, An Overview

8 J. of World Investment and Trade 323 (2007)

In the early 1990s, various ideas were discussed on how to develop energy cooperation between Eastern and Western Europe. Russia and many of its neighbouring countries were rich in energy but in great need of investment to reconstruct their economies. At the same time, Western European countries were trying to diversify their sources of energy supplies to decrease their potential dependence on other parts of the world. There was, therefore, a recognized need to set up a commonly accepted foundation for energy cooperation between the states of the Eurasian continent. It was out of this need that the Energy Charter Process was born.

The first formal step in the Energy Charter process was the adoption and signing of the European Energy Charter (the "EEC") in December 1991. The EEC was not a binding international treaty, but rather a political declaration of Principles which the signatories declared themselves intent on pursuing. However, the EEC contained guidelines for the negotiation of what was later to become the Energy Charter Treaty (the "ECT") and a set of protocols.

The ECT and the Energy Charter Protocol on Energy Efficiency and Related Environmental Aspects were signed in December 1994 and entered into force in April 1998. As of today, the ECT has been signed by 51 states and the European Union. The treaty has been ratified by 45 states and the European Union. It is noteworthy that the Russian Federation has signed but not ratified the treaty. The Russian Federation has, however, accepted provisional application of the treaty.

* * *

2.2 INVESTMENT PROMOTION AND PROTECTION

The provisions of the ECT regarding foreign investments are considered to be the cornerstone of the treaty. The aim of the foreign investment regime is to create a *"level playing field"* for investments in the energy sector and to minimize the non-commercial risks associated with such investments. Under the ECT, a distinction is made between the pre-investment phase of making an investment and the post-investment phase relating to investments already made. While the provisions concerning the pre-investment phase primarily set up a "soft" regime of "best endeavour" obligations, the ECT creates a "hard" regime for the post-investment phase with binding obligations for the contracting states similar to the investment protection provisions of the North American Free Trade Agreement (NAFTA) and bilateral investment treaties (BITs).

* * *

2.4 TRADE

The ECT'S trade provisions, based on the trading regime of the GATT and the Trade Amendment to the ECT of 1998 (bringing the ECT into line with WTO rules and practises) are founded on the principles of non-discrimination, transparency and a commitment to the progressive liberalisation of international trade.

Thus, the ECT introduces the trade provisions of GATT/WTO to the energy sector. The importance of this is that when the ECT entered into force in 1998, 19 of its members were not parties to the WTO. In 2006, 9 members were still non-parties to the WTO.

For more on trade and investment, see Chapter 7 below.

2.   LAW-MAKING BY INTERNATIONAL ORGANIZATIONS

Various Roles

While international organizations have not reached the legislative summit of law-making in the manner of modern well-developed democratic states, they do exercise legislative functions of very great importance within their respective fields of subject-matter jurisdiction. Of course, states still carry the main legislative role in developing customary international law and in becoming parties to international treaties as foreseen in Article 38 of the Statute of the ICJ. However, international organizations may be empowered to adopt legally binding rules and do influence international law in various ways, as will be seen below in this Section and throughout this volume.

The very process of establishing IOs may lead to law-making in the form of negotiation and agreement on substantive rules of international law and in adopting the institutional structure of the organization, as in Article 2 of the UN Charter. Moreover, many IOs have established bodies which are empowered to adopt rules legally binding on their members (for example, the UN under Chapter VII, the EU, OECD, OPEC) and even on non-members (UN under Article 2(6) and Chapter VII). The EU doubtless holds the record for the sheer volume of legislation it has adopted through bodies established under the EU treaties. Much of the internal law of all IOs is also adopted by that internal procedure.

More often organizations adopt declarations and recommendations which normally do not have direct legislative effect. However, these instruments may approach legal effect in cases of declarations made in a legal context authorized by the IO's treaty to establish an obligation or in containing a clear statement of legal rules. Recommendations with legal content may be seen as establishing, interpreting or modifying customary international rules, and thus may evolve into official statements of law.

Organizations may enter into legally binding international agreements with states or other organizations, and the practice of IOs may be accepted as evidence of state practice, since these organization consist of states.

An obvious law-making function is achieved in the judgments of international courts which are themselves international IOs, such as the

ICJ, the *ad hoc* international criminal courts, the International Criminal Court, the International Tribunal for the Law of the Sea, the European Court of Justice and the Human Rights Tribunals among others. This is true even for "advisory opinions" which do not directly apply as contentious judgments do, but state rules and are often cited by governments and international courts as authoritative.

The law-making function of IOs is perhaps most far-reaching in the cases of the Security Council decisions creating the ad hoc international criminal courts and in special situations requiring UN administration or governance. Examples are the Security Council Resolution 687 adopted at the close of the first Gulf war and in the administration of Kosovo and East–Timor.

Matthias Ruffert, The Administration of Kosovo and East–Timor By the International Community

50 I.C.L.Q. 613, 622 (2001)

Since their inception the institutions of the UN-administration in Kosovo and East–Timor have developed a comprehensive activity in legislative matters and have enacted various "Regulations" in areas such as economic law, taxation and court procedure. * * * [T]he legislation promulgated by the UN-administrations in Kosovo and East–Timor is United Nations law derived from the powers of that Organisation. The administrative institutions were established by Resolutions 1244 (1999) and 1272 (1999) by the Security Council, and the Special Representatives * * *. In the beginning of their missions, both Special Representatives issued Regulations relying on the respective Resolutions which contain basic, "constitutional" rules. According to these Regulations, all powers—legislative, executive and judiciary—are vested in UNMIK and UNTAET and have to be exercised by the Special Representative. Further, they proclaim adherence of the UN-administration to human rights as laid down in a series of universal and regional declarations and treaties * * * The same category of superior regulations comprises those on the structure and the composition of administrative panels and authorities, on official journals and, in a certain sense, on political parties and co-operation with non-governmental organisations. * * *

Thus, there is a hierarchy of norms, from the UN–Charter at the top, through Security Council Resolutions and the "constitutional" Regulations, down to regulations on specific matters or even single administrative directions. From this perspective, the legal system as described is part of the UN legal system, but with reference to specific territory. This legal system has to be in conformity with the UN–Charter, and the subsidiary organs of the UN are committing themselves in the "constitutional" Regulations to adhere to human rights treaties membership of which is limited to States.

* * *

José Alvarez, International Organizations as Law-Makers

p. 588 (2005)

10.1 IOs and the Traditional Sources of Law

Political scientists and economists have told us why IOs have become what many of these organizations, such as the ILO, were explicitly intended to be: effective treaty machines. Even those organizations not explicitly designed to become venues for treaty-making, such as ICAO, have become useful venues for multilateral treaty negotiations. * * * More generally, IOs are effective treaty-makers for the same reasons many of them are effective sites for other forms of standard-setting: because they encourage iterated cooperation; promote pooling of information, expertise, and resources; reduce transaction costs, uncertainty, and free riders; and facilitate path dependencies.

Constructivists would also suggest a more radical notion: the existence of IOs has itself helped to change the felt needs of states and has helped to convince states that they need some treaties. The argument, difficult to prove empirically but plausible, is that at least some modern multilateral treaties are not the product of pre-determined state interests but result, at least in part, from the actions of relevant epistemic communities—from the promotional and information gathering efforts of groups such as international civil servants and transnational networks of government regulators—whose very existence and tactics are inextricably linked to IOs. Leading candidates of treaties evincing this characteristic include the Rome Statute for the International Criminal Court—a treaty that probably would not exist but for the Security Council's establishment of ad hoc war crimes tribunals, many years of efforts by the ILC, as well as the peculiarities of established procedures within UN negotiating conferences; * * *

Whether or not IOs are given whole or partial credit for these or other treaties, there is no doubt that IOs have changed how multilateral treaties are concluded.

R. (on the application of Al–Jedda (FC) Appellant) v. Secretary of State (Respondent)

United Kingdom, House of Lords Judgments
[2007] UKHL 58

[Appellant al-Jedda, a UK and Iraqi national, was detained by British forces in Iraq for having participated in various terrorist activities. He was not formally charged with any offenses and was not brought before any tribunal. He challenged his detention on the basis of Article 5(1) of the European Convention on Human Rights, to which the UK was a party. Excerpts below from the Lord Bingham of Cornhill's opinion examine the question of the relationship between Article 5(1) of the Convention and Article 103 of the U.N Charter. If Article 5(1) were applicable, al-Jedda would prevail in this case. If the resolutions of the Security Council legally enabled the UK to carry out this detention and if Article 103 of the Charter were applicable, the protection of the European Convention would be trumped by the Security Council Resolutions and his case would fail. In the end the Law Lords panel ruled unanimously in favor of the latter alternative.]

Lord Bingham of Cornhill

26.   As already indicated, this issue turns on the relationship between article 5(1) of the European Convention and article 103 of the UN Charter. The central questions to be resolved are whether, on the facts of this case, the UK became subject to an obligation (within the meaning of article 103) to detain the appellant and, if so, whether and to what extent such obligation displaced or qualified the appellant's rights under article 5(1).

27.   Article 5(1) protects one of the rights and freedoms which state parties to the European Convention have bound themselves to secure to everyone within their jurisdiction. It has been recognised as a right of paramount importance. It is one to which, by virtue of the Human Rights Act 1998, UK courts must give effect. Its terms are familiar: "Everyone has the right to liberty and security of person. No one shall be deprived of his liberty save in the following cases and in accordance with a procedure prescribed by law: ..." There follows a list of situations in which a person may, in accordance with a procedure prescribed by law, be deprived of his liberty. It is unnecessary to recite the details of these situations, since none of them is said to apply to the appellant. In the absence of some exonerating condition, the detention of the appellant would plainly infringe his right under article 5(1).

30.   It remains to take note of article 103, a miscellaneous provision contained in Chapter XVI. It provides:

"In the event of a conflict between the obligations of the Members of the United Nations under the present Charter and their obligations under any other international agreement, their obligations under the present Charter shall prevail".

This provision lies at the heart of the controversy between the parties. For while the Secretary of State contends that the Charter, and UNSCRs 1511 (2003), 1546 (2004), 1637 (2005) and 1723 (2006), impose an obligation on the UK to detain the appellant which prevails over the appellant's conflicting right under article 5(1) of the European Convention, the appellant insists that the UNSCRs referred to, read in the light of the Charter, at most authorise the UK to take action to detain him but do not oblige it to do so, with the result that no conflict arises and article 103 is not engaged.

31.   There is an obvious attraction in the appellant's argument since, as appears from the summaries of UNSCRs 1511 and 1546 given above in paras. 12 and 15, the resolutions use the language of authorisation, not

obligation, and the same usage is found in UNSCRs 1637 (2005) and 1723 (2006). In ordinary speech to authorise is to permit or allow or license, not to require or oblige. I am, however, persuaded that the appellant's argument is not sound, for three main reasons.

[On the issue of the UK having been authorized in various Security Council resolutions to act under UN auspices but not having been ordered to do so, the opinion (paragraphs 32–33) recognized the obligation of the UK to take security measures as an occupying power under humanitarian law of war and academic writing, and this applies to actions taken under U.N. auspices, as in the present case.]

34.   I am further of the opinion * * * that in a situation such as the present "obligations" in article 103 should not in any event be given a narrow, contract-based, meaning. The importance of maintaining peace and security in the world can scarcely be exaggerated, and that (as evident from the articles of the Charter quoted above) is the mission of the UN. Its involvement in Iraq was directed to that end, following repeated determinations that the situation in Iraq continued to constitute a threat to international peace and security. As is well known, a large majority of states chose not to contribute to the multinational force, but those which did (including the UK) became bound by articles 2 and 25 to carry out the decisions of the Security Council in accordance with the Charter so as to achieve its lawful objectives. It is of course true that the UK did not become specifically bound to detain the appellant in particular. But it was, I think, bound to exercise its power of detention where this was necessary for imperative reasons of security. It could not be said to be giving effect to the decisions of the Security Council if, in such a situation, it neglected to take steps which were open to it.

35.   Emphasis has often been laid on the special character of the European Convention as a human rights instrument. But the reference in article 103 to "any other international agreement" leaves no room for any excepted category, and such appears to be the consensus of learned opinion. The decisions of the International Court of Justice (*Case Concerning Questions of Interpretation and Application of the 1971 Montreal Convention Arising From the Aerial Incident at Lockerbie* [1992] ICJ Rep. 3, para. 39; *Case Concerning Application of the Convention on the Prevention and Punishment of the Crime of Genocide* [1993] ICJ Rep. 325, per Judge ad hoc Lauterpacht, pp. 439–440, paras. 99–100) give no warrant for drawing any distinction save where an obligation is *jus cogens* and according to Judge Bernhardt it now seems to be generally recognised in practice that binding Security Council decisions taken under Chapter VII supersede all other treaty commitments (Simma (ed.), *The Charter of the United Nations: A Commentary,* 2nd ed. (2002), pp. 1299–1300).

36.   I do not think that the European Court, if the appellant's article 5(1) claim were before it as an application, would ignore the significance of article 103 of the Charter in international law. The court has on repeated

occasions taken account of provisions of international law, invoking the interpretative principle laid down in article 31(3)(c) of the Vienna Convention on the Law of Treaties, acknowledging that the Convention cannot be interpreted and applied in a vacuum and recognising that the responsibility of states must be determined in conformity and harmony with the governing principles of international law: see, for instance, *Loizidou v. Turkey* (1996) 23 EHRR 513, paras. 42–43, 52; *Bankovic v. Belgium* (2001) 11 BHRC 435, para. 57; *Fogarty v. United Kingdom* (2001) 34 EHRR 302, para. 34; *Al–Adsani v. United Kingdom* (2001) 34 EHRR 273, paras. 54–55; *Behrami and Saramati*, above, para. 122. In the latter case, in para. 149, the court made the strong statement quoted in para. 21 above.

37.   The appellant is, however, entitled to submit, as he does, that while maintenance of international peace and security is a fundamental purpose of the UN, so too is the promotion of respect for human rights. On repeated occasions in recent years the UN and other international bodies have stressed the need for effective action against the scourge of terrorism but have, in the same breath, stressed the imperative need for such action to be consistent with international human rights standards such as those which the Convention exists to protect. He submits that it would be anomalous and offensive to principle that the authority of the UN should itself serve as a defence of human rights abuses. This line of thinking is reflected in the judgment of the European Court in *Waite and Kennedy v. Germany* (1999) 30 EHRR 261, para. 67, where the court said:

> "67. The court is of the opinion that where states establish international organisations in order to pursue or strengthen their co-operation in certain fields of activities, and where they attribute to these organisations certain competences and accord them immunities, there may be implications as to the protection of fundamental rights. It would be incompatible with the purpose and object of the Convention, however, if the contracting states were thereby absolved from their responsibility under the Convention in relation to the field of activity covered by such attribution. It should be recalled that the Convention is intended to guarantee not theoretical or illusory rights, but rights that are practical and effective . . ."

The problem in a case such as the present is acute, since it is difficult to see how any exercise of the power to detain, however necessary for imperative reasons of security, and however strong the safeguards afforded to the detainee, could do otherwise than breach the detainee's rights under article 5(1).

39.   Thus there is a clash between on the one hand a power or duty to detain exercisable on the express authority of the Security Council and, on the other, a fundamental human right which the UK has undertaken to secure to those (like the appellant) within its jurisdiction. How are these to be reconciled? There is in my opinion only one way in which they can be reconciled: by ruling that the UK may lawfully, where it is necessary for

imperative reasons of security, exercise the power to detain authorised by UNSCR 1546 and successive resolutions, but must ensure that the detainee's rights under article 5 are not infringed to any greater extent than is inherent in such detention. I would resolve the second issue in this sense.

3. RESPONSIBILITY AND CONTROL OF INTERNATIONAL ORGANIZATIONS

Jan Klabbers, An Introduction to International Institutional Law

p. 300 (2002)

It is one of the more settled principles of international law, as authoritatively formulated by the Permanent Court of International justice in the classic *Chorzow Factory* case, that a violation of international law entails responsibility and the obligation to make reparation in one form or another. When it concerns the activities of states, the basic rule is, all sorts of difficulties notwithstanding, relatively straightforward: states are responsible for internationally wrongful acts that can be attributed to them.

With international organizations, however, the question is whether the organization can be held responsible for internationally wrongful acts and, if so, whose acts qualify and upon whom does responsibility eventually come to rest. While states can by and large be treated, for purposes of international law, as unitary actors, the same is not self-evident when it comes to international organizations, which are, after all, the creations of states. Here, once again, the layered nature of international organizations becomes visible: behind the "organizational veil" the contours of the organization's member-states can be discerned.

* * *

Notwithstanding the uncertainty expressed above by Professor Klabbers, the general principle of responsibility of international organizations under the rules of international law has become quite clear. As early as 1980 the International Court of Justice stated in an Advisory opinion that "International organizations are subjects of international law and, as such, are bound by any obligations incumbent upon them under general rules of international law, under their constitutions or under international agreements to which they are parties." *Interpretation of the Agreement of March 25, 1951 between the WHO and Egypt*, 1980 I.C.J. Rep. 73, para. 37 (Advisory Opinion of Dec. 20). For systematic development of this principle, we now turn to the International Law Commission's authoritative views on this subject.

Draft Articles on the Responsibility of International Organizations

International Law Commission
http://untreaty.un.org/ilc/reports/2005/2005report.htm

Article 1

Scope of the present draft articles

1. The present draft articles apply to the international responsibility of an international organization for an act that is wrongful under international law.

2. The present draft articles also apply to the international responsibility of a State for the internationally wrongful act of an international organization.

Article 3

General principles

1. Every internationally wrongful act of an international organization entails the international responsibility of the international organization.

2. There is an internationally wrongful act of an international organization when conduct consisting of an action or omission:

(a) Is attributable to the international organization under international law; and

(b) Constitutes a breach of an international obligation of that international organization.

Article 4

General rule on attribution of conduct to an international organization

1. The conduct of an organ or agent of an international organization in the performance of functions of that organ or agent shall be considered as an act of that organization under international law whatever position the organ or agent holds in respect of the organization.

2. For the purposes of paragraph 1, the term "agent" includes officials and other persons or entities through whom the organization acts.

3. Rules of the organization shall apply to the determination of the functions of its organs and agents.

4. For the purpose of the present draft article, "rules of the organization" means, in particular: the constituent instruments; decisions, resolutions and other acts taken by the organization in accordance with those instruments; and established practice of the organization.

Article 5

Conduct of organs or agents placed at the disposal of an international organization by a State or another international organization

The conduct of an organ of a State or an organ or agent of an international organization that is placed at the disposal of another international organization shall be considered under international law an act of the latter organization if the organization exercises effective control over that conduct.

Article 6

Excess of authority or contravention of instructions

The conduct of an organ or an agent of an international organization shall be considered an act of that organization under international law if the organ or agent acts in that capacity, even though the conduct exceeds the authority of that organ or agent or contravenes instructions.

Article 7

Conduct acknowledged and adopted by an international organization as its own

Conduct which is not attributable to an international organization under the preceding draft article shall nevertheless be considered an act of that international Organization under international law if and to the extent that the organization acknowledges and adopts the conduct in question as its own.

NOTES

The establishment of the principles of responsibility of international organizations represents a major step forward in the international legal system, even when these principles are stated as rather abstract formulations. But there is a practical side of the story. With the principles comes the problem of the corresponding appropriate means of redress and remedies which may be found in the internal institutions of organizations, in the pacific settlement of disputes systems in international law, and in national procedures, much of which appears in other chapters of this volume. This subject is taken up comprehensibly in Karel Wellens, *Remedies against International Organizations* (2002).

See also in Chapter 4 below, the opinion of the Netherlands' District Court in *The Association of Citizens Mothers of Srebrenica v. The State of the Netherlands and the United Nations,* on the immunity of the United Nations and Chapter 9 on the obligation of the World Health Organization (WHO) to negotiate with Egypt.

Government of Austria and NYU, The UN Security Council and the Rule of Law

Final Report and Recommendations, 2004–2008 Executive Summary (2008)

(iv) The Council is a creature of law but there is no formal process for reviewing its decisions; the ultimate sanctions on its authority are political. These include challenges to the Council's authority through the General Assembly, or individual or collective refusal to comply with its decisions. It is in no one's interest to push these political limits. For its part, the Council should limit itself to using its extraordinary powers for extraordinary purposes. When it is necessary to pass resolutions of a legislative character, respect for them will be enhanced by a process that ensures transparency, participation, and accountability. When the Council contemplates judicial functions, it should draw on existing institutions of international law.

(v) Sanctions targeted at individuals have presented a challenge to the authority of the Council: legal proceedings have been commenced in various jurisdictions and there is evidence that sanctions are not always applied rigorously. The Council should be proactive in further improving "fair and clear procedures" to protect the rights of individuals affected by its decisions, complying with minimum standards and providing on its own for periodic review.

(vi) The Security Council is most legitimate and most effective when it submits itself to the rule of law. Though the Council does not operate free of legal limits, the most important limit on the Council is self-restraint. Member States' preparedness to recognize the authority of the Council depends in significant part on how responsible and accountable it is—and is seen to be—in the use of its extraordinary powers. All Member States and the Security Council itself thus have an interest in promoting the rule of law and strengthening a rules-based international system.

Questions of Interpretation and Application of the 1971 Montreal Convention arising from the Aerial Incident at Lockerbie

(Libyan Arab Jamahiriya v. United States of America)
International Court of Justice
1998 I.C.J. Rep. 115 (Judgment of Feb. 27)

[This case involves questions of criminal jurisdiction of national courts in cases arising out of the destruction of Pan Am Flight 103 over Lockerbie Scotland in 1988 with the loss of 270 lives. Two Libyan nationals were indicted in Scotland and the U.S. for having caused this loss by placing a bomb on board the aircraft. Libya claimed jurisdiction on the basis of the Montreal Convention which provided in such cases for a state in which an alleged offender is found to prosecute in its courts or to extradite him. The UN Security Council adopted several binding resolutions requiring Libya to surrender the accused individuals for trial outside of Libya. In its preliminary objections to the Libyan action in the ICJ, the U.S. claimed that the UN Security Council resolutions had an overriding effect on the Convention and that the two accused individuals should accordingly be surrendered for trial outside of Libya. In it opinion on the U.S. preliminary objections, the ICJ in effect deferred decision of this issue by joining it with consideration of the merits of the case to be taken up at a later time. Excerpts from the strong dissenting opinion of I.C.J. President Schwebel appear below.]

DISSENTING OPINION OF PRESIDENT SCHWEBEL

[Joining the preliminary objections to the merits] will prolong a challenge to the integrity and authority of the Security Council. It may be taken as providing excuse for continued defiance of the Council's binding resolutions. It may be seen as prejudicing an important contemporary aspect of the Council's efforts to maintain international peace and security by combating State-sponsored international terrorism. Justice for the victims of an appalling atrocity may be further delayed and denied. The Court may have opened itself, not only in this but in future cases, to appearing to offer to recalcitrant States a means to parry and frustrate decisions of the Security Council by way of appeal to the Court.

Judicial Review

That last spectre raises the question of whether the Court is empowered to exercise judicial review of the decisions of the Security Council, a question as to which I think it right to express my current views. The Court is not generally so empowered, and it is particularly without power to overrule or undercut decisions of the Security Council made by it in pursuance of its authority under Articles 39, 41 and 42 of the Charter to determine the existence of any threat to the peace, breach of the peace, or act of aggression and to decide upon responsive measures to be taken to maintain or restore international peace and security. * * *

The texts of the Charter of the United Nations and of the Statute of the Court furnish no shred of support for a conclusion that the Court possesses a power of judicial review in general, or a power to supervene the decisions of the Security Council in particular. On the contrary, by the absence of any such provision, and by according the Security Council "primary responsibility for the maintenance of international peace and security", the Charter and the Statute import the contrary. So extraordinary a power as that of judicial review is not ordinarily to be implied and never has been on the international plane. If the Court were to generate such a power, the Security Council would no longer be primary in its assigned responsibilities, because if the Court could overrule, negate, modify—or, as in this case, hold as proposed that decisions of the Security Council are not "opposable" to the principal object State of those decisions and to the object of its sanctions—it would be the Court and not the Council that would exercise, or purport to exercise, the dispositive and hence primary authority. * * *

It does not follow from the facts that the decisions of the Security Council must be in accordance with the Charter, and that the International Court of Justice is the principal judicial organ of the United Nations, that the Court is empowered to ensure that the Council's decisions do accord with the Charter. To hold that it does so follow is a monumental *non sequitur*, which overlooks the truth that, in many legal systems, national and international, the subjection of the acts of an organ to law by no means entails subjection of the legality of its actions to judicial review. In many cases, the system relies not upon judicial review but on self-censorship by the organ concerned or by its members or on review by another political organ.

Judicial review could have been provided for at San Francisco, in full or lesser measure, directly or indirectly, but both directly and indirectly it was not in any measure contemplated or enacted. Not only was the Court not authorized to be the ultimate interpreter of the Charter, as the Court acknowledged in the case concerning *Certain Expenses of the United Nations*. Proposals which in restricted measure would have accorded the Court a degree of authority, by way of advisory proceedings, to pass upon the legality of proposed resolutions of the Security Council in the sphere of peaceful settlement—what came to be Chapter VI of the Charter—were not accepted. What was never proposed, considered, or, so far as the records reveal, even imagined, was that the International Court of Justice would be entrusted with, or would develop, a power of judicial review at large, or a power to supervene, modify, negate or confine the applicability of resolutions of the Security Council whether directly or in the guise of interpretation. * * *

The conclusions to which the travaux préparatoires [preparatory work] and text of the Charter lead are that the Court was not and was not meant to be invested with a power of judicial review of the legality or effects of decisions of the Security Council. Only the Security Council can determine what is a threat to or breach of the peace or act of aggression under Article 39, and under Article 39 only it can "decide what measures shall be taken . . . to maintain or restore international peace and security". Two States at variance in the interpretation of the Charter may submit a dispute to the Court, but that facility does not empower the Court to set aside or second-guess the determinations of the Security Council under Article 39. Contentious cases may come before the Court that call for its passing upon questions of law raised by Council decisions and for interpreting pertinent Council resolutions. But that power cannot be equated with an authority to review and confute the decisions of the Security Council.

It may of course be maintained that the Charter is a living instrument; that the present-day interpreters of the Charter are not bound by the intentions of its drafters of 50 years ago; that the Court has interpreted the powers of the United Nations constructively in other respects, and could take a constructive view of its own powers in respect of judicial review or some variation of it. The difficulty with this approach is that for the Court to engraft upon the Charter régime a power to review, and revise the reach of, resolutions of the Security Council would not be evolutionary but revolutionary. It would be not a development but a departure, and a great and grave departure. It would not be a development even arguably derived from the terms or structure of the Charter and Statute. It would not be a development arising out of customary international law, which has no principle of or provision for judicial review. It would not be a development drawn from the general principles of law. Judicial review, in varying forms, is found in a number of democratic polities, most famously that of the United States, where it was developed by the Supreme Court itself. But it is by no means a universal or even general principle of government or law. It is hardly found outside the democratic world and is not uniformly found in it. Where it exists internationally, as in the European Union, it is expressly provided for by treaty in specific terms. The United Nations is far from being a government, or an international organization comparable in its integration to the European Union, and it is not democratic.

The conclusion that the Court cannot judicially review or revise the resolutions of the Security Council is buttressed by the fact that only States may be parties in cases before the Court. The Security Council cannot be a party. For the Court to adjudge the legality of the Council's decisions in a proceeding brought by one State against another would be for the Court to adjudicate the Council's rights without giving the Council a hearing, which would run counter to fundamental judicial principles. * * * Any such judgment could not bind the Council, because, by the terms of Article 59 of the Statute, the decision of the Court has no binding force except between the parties and in respect of that particular case.

At the same time, a judgment of the Court which held resolutions of the Security Council adopted under Chapter VII of the Charter not to bind or to be "opposable" to a State, despite the terms of Article 25* of the Charter, would seriously prejudice the effectiveness of the Council's resolutions and subvert the integrity of the Charter. Such a holding would be tantamount to a judgment that the resolutions of the Security Council were ultra vires, at any rate in relation to that State. That could set the stage for an extraordinary confrontation between the Court and the Security Council. It could give rise to the question, is a holding by the Court that the Council has acted *ultra vires* a holding which of itself is *ultra vires*?

* * *

Yassin Abdullah Kadi v. Council of the European Union and Commission of the European Communities

European Court of Justice
Joined Cases C–402/05 and C–415 P, September 3, 2008

[See the background of this case and excerpts from the Judgment provided in Chapter 11, Section D, below. The UN Security Council had adopted resolutions directed against certain terrorist activities, a decision including provision for the freezing of funds and other financial assets of the Taliban and others. The Security Council's Sanctions Committee designated Mr. Kadi among others whose funds and financial assets were to be frozen but made no provision for the fundamental rights of such persons to be heard and to have their property rights respected. The EU Council adopted a parallel implementing act in the form of a regulation for the EU, applicable to Mr. Kadi but again without recognition of these fundamental rights under EU law. One of the issues before the ECJ was the juridical relationship between the decision of the Security Council and the EU regulation in apparent conflict. In its judgment annulling the EU Council

---

* Article 25 states that: "The Members of the United Nations agree to accept and carry out the decisions of the Security Council in accordance with the present Charter."

regulation, the European Court of Justice made the following statement on this issue.]

286   In this regard it must be emphasised that, in circumstances such as those of these cases, the review of lawfulness thus to be ensured by the Community judicature applies to the Community act intended to give effect to the international agreement at issue, and not to the latter as such.

287   With more particular regard to a Community act which, like the contested regulation, is intended to give effect to a resolution adopted by the Security Council under Chapter VII of the Charter of the United Nations, it is not, therefore, for the Community judicature, under the exclusive jurisdiction provided for by Article 220 EC, to review the lawfulness of such a resolution adopted by an international body, even if that review were to be limited to examination of the compatibility of that resolution with jus cogens.

288   However, any judgment given by the Community judicature deciding that a Community measure intended to give effect to such a resolution is contrary to a higher rule of law in the Community legal order would not entail any challenge to the primacy of that resolution in international law.

NOTES AND QUESTIONS

1.   Could you envisage the world in the 21st Century without international organizations? What would distinguish the world with IOs from one without them? Consider the differences in orderly legal management of international relations in the 19th Century compared to the 21st. Is it anarchy versus world government or something in between? How would you characterize the 21st Century system of management? Is a weakening or disintegration of state sovereignty taking place?

2.   How would you compare the leading legal elements of the United Nations to those of the European Union?

3.   ICJ President Schwebel stated in his Dissent in the *Montreal Convention* case that:

> "The United Nations is far from being a government, or an international organization comparable in its integration to the European Union, and it is not democratic."

Do you agree with this assessment? Why?

4.   If you were asked to draft a modern version of ICJ Statute Article 38 on the sources of international law, what role if any would you attribute to the UN and other IOs under current practice? How would you formulate the amendment to Article 38?

5.   Do you consider that the ICJ should have authority to review, approve or disapprove actions taken by IOs? Would you distinguish between various organizations, or various organs such as the Security Council the General Assembly and subsidiary bodies in the case of the UN? Should human

rights issues be considered with high standing? For more on the inter-relationship of IOs and courts, see Chapter 4 below.

6.   For further reading: SIMON CHESTERMAN, SECRETARY OR GENERAL—THE UN SECRETARY-GENERAL IN WORLD POLITICS (2007); THOMAS FRANK, SIMON CHESTERMAN AND DAVID MALONE, LAW AND PRACTICE OF THE UNITED NATIONS (2007); HENRY G. SCHEMERS & NIELS M. BLOKKER, INTERNATIONAL INSTITUTIONAL LAW (2003); STEPHEN C. SCHLESINGER, ACT OF CREATION: THE FOUNDING OF THE UNITED NATIONS, A STORY OF SUPERPOWERS, SECRET AGENTS, WARTIME ALLIES AND ENEMIES, AND THEIR QUEST FOR A PEACEFUL WORLD (2004); JAN KLABBERS, AN INTRODUCTION TO INTERNATIONAL INSTITUTIONAL LAW (2002); PHILIPPE SANDS AND PIERRE KLEIN, BOWETT'S LAW OF INTERNATIONAL INSTITUTIONS (2001).

CHAPTER 4

JURISDICTION AND IMMUNITIES

A.   JURISDICTION

Jurisdiction is surely the international law favorite of governments, for the rules which have evolved in this sector provide them with legal authority for the basic, every day actions of governments over their respective territories and at times beyond the limits of these territories. International law thus grants jurisdiction (or we might also say authority or competence) for the state to establish governmental structures, to legislate, to adjudicate disputes, to enforce the law, to tax, to control and exploit national resources, to control immigration and to carry out the whole array of familiar powers of governments and statehood. As one international lawyer notes, this explains why governments may be said "to love international law."* In a sovereign state system such as ours, governments simply could not function without it.

Yet the term "jurisdiction" is encountered in many other contexts, including of course in the internal organization of states and in the field of international organizations. The jurisdiction of the domestic courts of states or their subdivisions falls for the most part outside of our subject in

---

* Philip Trimble, *International Law, World Order and Critical Legal Studies*, 42 STANFORD L. REV. 811, 833 (1990).

this chapter, although we will work with these courts and their jurisdiction in some detail below in Section B on immunity of states and in Section C on diplomatic immunities. The jurisdiction of international organizations is taken up in Chapter 3 *supra*.

So long as state action is confined wholly within state borders without affecting neighboring or distant states, (or their companies and persons), international jurisdictional issues would normally not arise, for the acting state in that case would be operating within its established sovereignty and jurisdiction. Note that the classic territorial rule of jurisdiction was stated in severe terms by Chief Justice John Marshall in *The Schooner Exchange v. McFaddon*, 11 U.S. (7 Cranch) 116, 3 L.Ed. 287 (1812) as follows:

> The jurisdiction of the nation within its own territory is necessarily exclusive and absolute. It is susceptible of no limitation not imposed by itself. Any restriction upon it, deriving validity from an external source, would imply a diminution of its sovereignty to the extent of the restriction * * *.

Since Chief Justice Marshall's time, the international law of jurisdiction has evolved to accommodate cases where many states have found occasion to legislate (prescribe), adjudicate and enforce national law beyond the territory (extraterritorially), at times despite strong legal objections of other states affected. After the last two hundred years of growing globalization, the international movement of people, firms, financing, goods and services, technology and communication, the state's legal interests have also migrated abroad to bring about conflicts with the interests of other states seeking to protect their own sovereign prerogatives and expectations. Many of the basic contours and principles of the modern international law of jurisdiction are now well situated in the international legal system and are laid out in the following Canadian Supreme Court opinion.

R. v. Hape

Supreme Court of Canada
[2007] 2 S.C.R. 292, 2007 SCC 26

■ LEBEL, J.—

1   At issue in this appeal is whether the *Canadian Charter of Rights and Freedoms* applies to extraterritorial searches and seizures by Canadian police officers. The appellant, Lawrence Richard Hape, is a Canadian businessman. He was convicted of two counts of money laundering contrary to s. 9 of the *Controlled Drugs and Substances Act*, S.C. 1996, c. 19. At his trial, the Crown adduced documentary evidence that the police had gathered from the records of the appellant's investment company while searching its premises in the Turks and Caicos Islands. [West Indian islands under United Kingdom sovereignty]. The appellant sought to have that evidence excluded, pursuant to s. 24(2) of the *Charter*, on the basis that the *Charter* applies to the actions of the Canadian police officers who conducted

the searches and seizures and that the evidence was obtained in violation of his right under s. 8 of the *Charter* to be secure against unreasonable search and seizure. For the reasons that follow, I would affirm the convictions and dismiss the appeal.

25 The appellant argues that the *Charter* applies to the actions of the RCMP [Canadian police officers] in the course of their searches and seizures at the BWIT's office [Appellant's investment company], notwithstanding that those actions took place outside Canada. He submits that Canadian authorities are subject to the *Charter* even when operating outside the territorial boundaries of Canada and that it can be seen from the evidence in the case at bar that the searches and seizures were the product of and were integral to an investigation that was completely planned by the RCMP. * * *

35 As I will explain, certain fundamental rules of customary international law govern what actions a state may legitimately take outside its territory. Those rules are important interpretive aids for determining the jurisdictional scope of s. 32(1) of the *Charter*. The use of customary international law to assist in the interpretation of the *Charter* requires an examination of the Canadian approach to the domestic reception of international law.

36 The English tradition follows an adoptionist approach to the reception of customary international law. Prohibitive rules of international custom may be incorporated directly into domestic law through the common law, without the need for legislative action. According to the doctrine of adoption, the courts may adopt rules of customary international law as common law rules in order to base their decisions upon them, provided there is no valid legislation that clearly conflicts with the customary rule: I. Brownlie, *Principles of Public International Law* (6th ed. 2003), at p. 41. Although it has long been recognized in English common law, the doctrine received its strongest endorsement in the landmark case of *Trendtex Trading Corp. v. Central Bank of Nigeria*, [1977] 1 Q.B. 529 (C.A.). Lord Denning considered both the doctrine of adoption and the doctrine of transformation, according to which international law rules must be implemented by Parliament before they can be applied by domestic courts. In his opinion, the doctrine of adoption represents the correct approach in English law. Rules of international law are incorporated automatically, as they evolve, unless they conflict with legislation. He wrote, at p. 554:

It is certain that international law does change. I would use of international law the words which Galileo used of the earth: "But it does move." International law does change and the courts have applied the changes without the aid of any Act of Parliament. . . .

. . . Seeing that the rules of international law have changed—and do change—and that the courts have given effect to the changes without any Act of Parliament, it follows to my mind inexorably that the rules of international law, as existing from time to time, do form part of our English law. It follows, too, that a decision of this court—as to what was the ruling of international law 50 or 60 years ago—is not binding on this court today. International law knows no rule of *stare decisis*. If this court today is satisfied that the rule of international law on a subject has changed from what it was 50 or 60 years ago, it can give effect to that change—and apply the change in our English law—without waiting for the House of Lords to do it.

39   * * * In my view, following the common law tradition, it appears that the doctrine of adoption [of international law] operates in Canada such that prohibitive rules of customary international law should be incorporated into domestic law in the absence of conflicting legislation. The automatic incorporation of such rules is justified on the basis that international custom, as the law of nations, is also the law of Canada unless, in a valid exercise of its sovereignty, Canada declares that its law is to the contrary. Parliamentary sovereignty dictates that a legislature may violate international law, but that it must do so expressly. Absent an express derogation, the courts may look to prohibitive rules of customary international law to aid in the interpretation of Canadian law and the development of the common law.

40   One of the key customary principles of international law, and one that is central to the legitimacy of claims to extraterritorial jurisdiction, is respect for the sovereignty of foreign states. That respect is dictated by the maxim, lying at the heart of the international legal structure, that all states are sovereign and equal. Article 2(1) of the *Charter of the United Nations*, Can. T.S. 1945 No. 7, recognizes as one of that organization's principles the "sovereign equality of all its Members." The importance and centrality of the principle of sovereign equality was reaffirmed by the General Assembly in the 1970 *Declaration on Principles of International Law concerning Friendly Relations and Co-operation among States in accordance with the Charter of the United Nations*, GA Res. 2625 (XXV), 24 October 1970, which expanded the scope of application of the principle to include non-U.N. member states. A renowned international law jurist, Antonio Cassese, writes that of the various principles recognized in the U.N. Charter and the 1970 Declaration:

[T]his is unquestionably the only one on which there is unqualified agreement and which has the support of all groups of States, regardless of ideologies, political leanings, and circumstances. It is safe to conclude that sovereign equality constitutes the linchpin of the whole body of international legal standards, the fundamental premise on which all international relations rest.

See A. Cassese, *International Law* (2nd ed. 2005), at p. 48.

41   The principle of sovereign equality comprises two distinct but complementary concepts: sovereignty and equality. "Sovereignty" refers to the various powers, rights and duties that accompany statehood under international law. Jurisdiction—the power to exercise authority over persons, conduct and events—is one aspect of state sovereignty. Although the two are not coterminous, jurisdiction may be seen as the quintessential feature of sovereignty. Other powers and rights that fall under the umbrella of sovereignty include the power to use and dispose of the state's

territory, the right to state immunity from the jurisdiction of foreign courts and the right to diplomatic immunity. In his individual opinion in *Customs Régime between Germany and Austria* (1931), P.C.I.J. Ser. A/B, No. 41, at p. 57, Judge Anzilotti defined sovereignty as follows: "Independence ... is really no more than the normal condition of States according to international law; it may also be described as *sovereignty* (*suprema potestas*), or *external sovereignty*, by which is meant that the State has over it no other authority than that of international law." (Emphasis in original)

45   In order to preserve sovereignty and equality, the rights and powers of all states carry correlative duties, at the apex of which sits the principle of non-intervention. Each state's exercise of sovereignty within its territory is dependent on the right to be free from intrusion by other states in its affairs and the duty of every other state to refrain from interference. This principle of non-intervention is inseparable from the concept of sovereign equality and from the right of each state to operate in its territory with no restrictions other than those existing under international law. (For a discussion of these principles, see the comments of Arbitrator Huber in the *Island of Palmas Case* (*Netherlands v. United States*) (1928), 2 R.I.A.A. 829, at pp. 838–39.)

46   Sovereign equality remains a cornerstone of the international legal system. Its foundational principles—including non-intervention and respect for the territorial sovereignty of foreign states—cannot be regarded as anything less than firmly established rules of customary international law, as the International Court of Justice held when it recognized non-intervention as a customary principle in the *Case concerning Military and Paramilitary Activities In and Against Nicaragua (Nicaragua v. United States of America)*, [1986] I.C.J. Rep. 14, at pp. 106. As the International Court of Justice noted on that occasion, the status of these principles as international customs is supported by both state practice and *opinio juris*, the two necessary elements of customary international law. Every principle of customary international law is binding on all states unless superseded by another custom or by a rule set out in an international treaty. As a result, the principles of non-intervention and territorial sovereignty may be adopted into the common law of Canada in the absence of conflicting legislation. These principles must also be drawn upon in determining the scope of extraterritorial application of the *Charter*.

47   Related to the principle of sovereign equality is the concept of comity of nations. Comity refers to informal acts performed and rules observed by states in their mutual relations out of politeness, convenience and goodwill, rather than strict legal obligation: *Oppenheim's International Law*, at pp. 50–51. When cited by the courts, comity is more a principle of interpretation than a rule of law, because it does not arise from formal obligations. * * *

50   The nature and limitations of comity need to be clearly understood. International law is a positive legal order, whereas comity, which is of the nature of a principle of interpretation, is based on a desire for states to act courteously towards one another. Nonetheless, many rules of inter-

national law promote mutual respect and, conversely, courtesy among states requires that certain legal rules be followed. In this way, "courtesy and international law lend reciprocal support to one another": M. Akehurst, "Jurisdiction in International Law" (1972–1973), 46 *Brit. Y.B. Int'l L.* 145, at p. 215. The principle of comity reinforces sovereign equality and contributes to the functioning of the international legal system. Acts of comity are justified on the basis that they facilitate interstate relations and global cooperation; however, comity ceases to be appropriate where it would undermine peaceable interstate relations and the international order.

52   In an era characterized by transnational criminal activity and by the ease and speed with which people and goods now cross borders, the principle of comity encourages states to cooperate with one another in the investigation of transborder crimes even where no treaty legally compels them to do so. At the same time, states seeking assistance must approach such requests with comity and respect for sovereignty. Mutuality of legal assistance stands on these two pillars. Comity means that when one state looks to another for help in criminal matters, it must respect the way in which the other state chooses to provide the assistance within its borders. That deference ends where clear violations of international law and fundamental human rights begin. If no such violations are in issue, courts in Canada should interpret Canadian law, and approach assertions of foreign law, in a manner respectful of the spirit of international cooperation and the comity of nations.

53   One final general principle bears on the resolution of the legal issues in this appeal. It is a well-established principle of statutory interpretation that legislation will be presumed to conform to international law. The presumption of conformity is based on the rule of judicial policy that, as a matter of law, courts will strive to avoid constructions of domestic law pursuant to which the state would be in violation of its international obligations, unless the wording of the statute clearly compels that result.
* * *

(1) International Law Principles of Jurisdiction

58   Jurisdiction takes various forms, and the distinctions between them are germane to the issue raised in this appeal. Prescriptive jurisdiction (also called legislative or substantive jurisdiction) is the power to make rules, issue commands or grant authorizations that are binding upon persons and entities. The legislature exercises prescriptive jurisdiction in enacting legislation. Enforcement jurisdiction is the power to use coercive means to ensure that rules are followed, commands are executed or entitlements are upheld. As stated by S. Coughlan et al. in "Global Reach, Local Grasp: Constructing Extraterritorial Jurisdiction in the Age of Globalization" (2007), 6 *C.J.L.T.* 29, at p. 32, "enforcement or executive jurisdiction refers to the state's ability to act in such a manner as to give effect to its laws (including the ability of police or other government actors to investigate a matter, which might be referred to as *investigative jurisdiction*)" (emphasis in original). Adjudicative jurisdiction is the power of a

state's courts to resolve disputes or interpret the law through decisions that carry binding force. See Cassese, at p. 49; Brownlie, at p. 297.

59 International law—and in particular the overarching customary principle of sovereign equality—sets the limits of state jurisdiction, while domestic law determines how and to what extent a state will assert its jurisdiction within those limits. Under international law, states may assert jurisdiction in its various forms on several recognized grounds. The primary basis for jurisdiction is territoriality: *Libman*, at p. 183. It is as a result of its territorial sovereignty that a state has plenary authority to exercise prescriptive, enforcement and adjudicative jurisdiction over matters arising and people residing within its borders, and this authority is limited only by the dictates of customary and conventional international law. The principle of territoriality extends to two related bases for jurisdiction, the objective territorial principle and the subjective territorial principle. According to the objective territorial principle, a state may claim jurisdiction over a criminal act that commences or occurs outside the state if it is completed, or if a constituent element takes place, within the state, thus connecting the event to the territory of the state through a sufficiently strong link: Brownlie, at p. 299. See also *Libman*, at pp. 212–13. Subjective territoriality refers to the exercise of jurisdiction over an act that occurs or has begun within a state's territory even though it has consequences in another state.

60 Territoriality is not the only legitimate basis for jurisdiction, however. * * * [D]isputes and events commonly have implications for more than one state, and competing claims for jurisdiction can arise on grounds other than territoriality, which are, of course, extraterritorial in nature. Of those bases for jurisdiction, the most common is the nationality principle. States may assert jurisdiction over acts occurring within the territory of a foreign state on the basis that their nationals are involved. For example, a state may seek to try and punish one of its nationals for a crime committed in another state. The nationality principle is not necessarily problematic as a justification for asserting prescriptive or adjudicative jurisdiction in order to attach domestic consequences to events that occurred abroad, but it does give rise to difficulties in respect of the extraterritorial exercise of enforcement jurisdiction. Under international law, a state may regulate and adjudicate regarding actions committed by its nationals in other countries, provided enforcement of the rules takes place when those nationals are within the state's own borders. When a state's nationals are physically located in the territory of another state, its authority over them is strictly limited. I will discuss this below.

61 There are other bases of extraterritorial jurisdiction that, although less widely recognized, are nonetheless cited from time to time as justifications for a state's assertion of jurisdiction. One example is the principle of universal jurisdiction, pursuant to which jurisdiction may be asserted over acts committed, in other countries, by foreigners against other foreigners. Assertions of universal jurisdiction are not based on any link of territoriality or nationality between the crime or the perpetrator and the state: L.

Reydams, *Universal Jurisdiction: International and Municipal Legal Perspectives* (2003), at p. 5. For that reason, universal jurisdiction is confined to the most serious crimes and includes crimes under international law. Any state that obtains custody of accused persons may try and punish those who have committed crimes under international law: Brownlie, at p. 303.

62   The interplay between the various forms and bases of jurisdiction is central to the issue of whether an extraterritorial exercise of jurisdiction is permissible. At the outset, it must be borne in mind, first, that the exercise of jurisdiction by one state cannot infringe on the sovereignty of other states and, second, that states may have valid concurrent claims to jurisdiction. Even if a state can legally exercise extraterritorial jurisdiction, whether the exercise of such jurisdiction is proper and desirable is another question: Coughlan et al., at p. 31. Where two or more states have a legal claim to jurisdiction, comity dictates that a state ought to assume jurisdiction only if it has a real and substantial link to the event. As La Forest J. noted in *Libman*, at p. 213, what constitutes a "real and substantial link" justifying jurisdiction may be "coterminous with the requirements of international comity".

63   In the classic example, Parliament might pass legislation making it a criminal offence for Canadian nationals to smoke in the streets of Paris, thereby exercising extraterritorial prescriptive jurisdiction on the basis of nationality. If France chooses to contest this, it may have a legitimate claim of interference with its territorial sovereignty, since Canada's link to smoking on the Champs-Élysées is less real and substantial than that of France. France's territorial jurisdiction collides with Canada's concurrent claim of nationality jurisdiction. The mere presence of the prohibition in the *Criminal Code* of Canada might be relatively benign from France's perspective. However, France's outrage might be greater if Canadian courts tried a Canadian national in Canada for violating the prohibition while on vacation in Paris. It would be greater still if Canadian police officers marched into Paris and began arresting Canadian smokers or if Canadian judges established a court in Paris to try offenders.

64   This example demonstrates the nuances of extraterritorial jurisdiction. It is not uncommon for states to pass legislation with extraterritorial effects or, in other words, to exercise extraterritorial prescriptive jurisdiction. This is usually done only where a real and substantial link with the state is evident. Similarly, comity is not necessarily offended where a state's courts assume jurisdiction over a dispute that occurred abroad (extraterritorial adjudicative jurisdiction), provided that the enforcement measures are carried out within the state's own territory. The most contentious claims for jurisdiction are those involving extraterritorial *enforcement* of a state's laws, even where they are being enforced only against the state's own nationals, but in another country. The fact that a state has exercised extraterritorial prescriptive jurisdiction by enacting legislation in respect of a foreign event is necessary, but not in itself sufficient, to justify the state's exercise of enforcement jurisdiction outside its borders: F.A. Mann, "The Doctrine of International Jurisdiction Revisited After Twenty

Years", in W. M. Reisman, ed., *Jurisdiction in International Law* (1999), 139, at p. 154.

65   The Permanent Court of International Justice stated in the *Lotus* case, at pp. 18–19, that jurisdiction "cannot be exercised by a State outside its territory except by virtue of a permissive rule derived from international custom or from a convention". See also *Cook*, at para. 131. According to the decision in the *Lotus* case, extraterritorial jurisdiction is governed by international law rather than being at the absolute discretion of individual states. While extraterritorial jurisdiction—prescriptive, enforcement or adjudicative—exists under international law, it is subject to strict limits under international law that are based on sovereign equality, non-intervention and the territoriality principle. According to the principle of non-intervention, states must refrain from exercising extraterritorial enforcement jurisdiction over matters in respect of which another state has, by virtue of territorial sovereignty, the authority to decide freely and autonomously (see the opinion of the International Court of Justice in the *Military and Paramilitary Activities* case, at p. 108). Consequently, it is a well-established principle that a state cannot act to enforce its laws within the territory of another state absent either the consent of the other state or, in exceptional cases, some other basis under international law. See Brownlie, at p. 306; *Oppenheim's International Law*, at p. 463. This principle of consent is central to assertions of extraterritorial enforcement jurisdiction.

104   Although, on the basis of nationality, Canada has some jurisdiction over Canadian agents acting abroad, that jurisdiction is subject to the caveat that the matter must be within the authority of Parliament or the provincial legislatures. Consequently, Canada's jurisdiction is circumscribed by the territorial jurisdiction of the state in which its agents are operating. For example, Canadian consular officials operating abroad have some immunity from local laws on the basis of nationality jurisdiction, but that does not mean they have the power to abide by Canadian laws and only Canadian laws when in the host state. Bastarache J. correctly noted in *Cook* that a Canadian police officer is not stripped of his or her status as such on crossing the border into the U.S., but the officer's authority to exercise state powers is necessarily curtailed. Canada does not have authority over all matters respecting what the officer may or may not do in the foreign state. Where Canada's authority is limited, so too is the application of the *Charter*.

105   Neither Parliament nor the provincial legislatures have the power to authorize the enforcement of Canada's laws over matters in the exclusive territorial jurisdiction of another state. Canada can no more dictate what procedures are followed in a criminal investigation abroad than it can impose a taxation scheme in another state's territory. Criminal investigations implicate enforcement jurisdiction, which, pursuant to the principles of international law discussed above, cannot be exercised in another country absent the consent of the foreign state or the application of another rule of international law under which it can so be exercised. While concurrent jurisdiction over prosecutions of crimes linked with more

than one country is recognized under international law, the same is not true of investigations, which are governed by and carried out pursuant to territorial jurisdiction as a matter inherent in state sovereignty. Any attempt to dictate how those activities are to be performed in a foreign state's territory without that state's consent would infringe the principle of non-intervention. And, as mentioned above, without enforcement, the *Charter* cannot apply.

117   The appellant took issue in this appeal with the trial judge's finding that the RCMP and Turks and Caicos officers were engaged in a "co-operative investigation". There is no magic in the words co-operative investigation, because the issue relates not to who participated in the investigation but to the fact that it occurred on foreign soil and that consent was not given for the exercise of extraterritorial jurisdiction by Canada. When investigations are carried out within another country's borders, that country's law will apply. A cooperative effort involving police from different countries "does not make the law of one country applicable in the other country": *Terry*, at para. 18.

118   In short, although Canadian state actors were involved, the searches and seizures took place in Turks and Caicos and so were not matters within the authority of Parliament. The *Charter* does not apply.

* * *

1.   Territoriality

The S.S. Lotus

France v. Turkey
Permanent Court of International Justice, 1927
P.C.I.J., Ser. A, No. 10

* * * By a special agreement signed at Geneva on October 12th, 1926, between the Governments of * * * [France and Turkey], [who] have submitted to the Permanent Court of International Justice the question of jurisdiction which has arisen between them following upon the collision which occurred on August 2nd, 1926, between the steamships Boz–Kourt and Lotus.

According to the special agreement, the Court has to decide the following questions:

(1) Has Turkey, contrary to Article 15 of the Convention of Lausanne of July 24th, 1923, respecting conditions of residence and business and jurisdiction, acted in conflict with the principles of international law—and if so, what principles?—by instituting, following the collision which occurred on August 2nd, 1926, on the high seas between the French steamer Lotus and the Turkish steamer Boz–Kourt and upon the arrival of the French steamer at Constantinople—as well as against the captain of the Turkish steamship—joint criminal proceedings in pursuance of Turkish law against M. Demons, officer of the watch on board the Lotus at the time of the

collision, in consequence of the loss of the Boz–Kourt having involved the death of eight Turkish sailors and passengers?

* * *

On August 2nd, 1926, just before midnight, a collision occurred between the French mail steamer Lotus, proceeding to Constantinople, and the Turkish collier Boz–Kourt, between five and six nautical miles to the north of Cape Sigri (Mitylene). The Boz–Kourt, which was cut in two, sank, and eight Turkish nationals who were on board perished. After having done everything possible to succour the shipwrecked persons, of whom ten were able to be saved, the Lotus continued on its course to Constantinople, where it arrived on August 3rd.

At the time of the collision, the officer of the watch on board the Lotus was M. Demons, a French citizen, lieutenant in the merchant service and first officer of the ship, whilst the movements of the Boz–Kourt were directed by its captain, Hassan Bey, who was one of those saved * * *

* * *

On August 5th, Lieutenant Demons was requested by the Turkish authorities to go ashore to give evidence. The examination * * * led to the * * * [arrest] of Lieutenant Demons—without previous notice being given to the French Consul–General—and Hassan Bey, amongst others. This arrest, which has been characterized by the Turkish Agent as arrest pending trial (arrestation préventive), was effected in order to ensure that the criminal prosecution instituted against the two officers, on a charge of manslaughter, by the Public Prosecutor of Stamboul, on the complaint of the families of the victims of the collision, should follow its normal course.

The case was first heard by the Criminal Court of Stamboul on August 28th. * * * Lieutenant Demons submitted that the Turkish Courts had no jurisdiction; the Court, however, overruled his objection. * * *

* * * [T]he Criminal Court delivered its judgment, the terms of which have not been communicated to the Court by the Parties. It is, however, common ground, that it sentenced Lieutenant Demons to eighty days' imprisonment and a fine of twenty-two pounds, Hassan Bey being sentenced to a slightly more severe penalty.

Before approaching the consideration of the principles of international law contrary to which Turkey is alleged to have acted—thereby infringing the terms of Article 15 of the Convention of Lausanne of July 24th, 1923, respecting conditions of residence and business and jurisdiction—, it is necessary to define, in the light of the written and oral proceedings, the position resulting from the special agreement. * * *

* * *

1.   The collision which occurred * * *, between the S.S. Lotus, flying the French flag, and the S.S. Boz–Kourt, flying the Turkish flag, took place on the high seas: the territorial jurisdiction of any State other than France and Turkey therefore does not enter into account.

2.   The violation, if any, of the principles of international law would have consisted in the taking of criminal proceedings against Lieutenant Demons. It is not therefore a question relating to any particular step in these proceedings—such as his being put to trial, his arrest, his detention pending trial or the judgment given by the Criminal Court of Stamboul— but of the very fact of the Turkish Courts exercising criminal jurisdiction. That is why the arguments put forward by the Parties in both phases of the proceedings relate exclusively to the question whether Turkey has or has not, according to the principles of international law, jurisdiction to prosecute in this case.

The discussions have borne exclusively upon the question whether criminal jurisdiction does or does not exist in this case.

3.   The prosecution was instituted because the loss of the Boz–Kourt involved the death of eight Turkish sailors and passengers. * * * It is * * * a case of prosecution for involuntary manslaughter. * * * There is no doubt that [the death of the victims] may be regarded as the direct outcome of the collision, and the French Government has not contended that this relation of cause and effect cannot exist.

* * *

5.   The prosecution was instituted in pursuance of Turkish legislation. * * * Article 6 of the Turkish Penal Code, * * * runs as follows:

> [Translation] Any foreigner who, apart from the cases contemplated by Article 4, commits an offence abroad to the prejudice of Turkey or of a Turkish subject, for which offence Turkish law prescribes a penalty involving loss of freedom for a minimum period of not less than one year, shall be punished in accordance with the Turkish Penal Code provided that he is arrested in Turkey. * * *

* * *

Even if the Court must hold that the Turkish authorities had seen fit to base the prosecution of Lieutenant Demons upon the above-mentioned Article 6, the question submitted to the Court is not whether that article is compatible with the principles of international law; it is more general. The Court is asked to state whether or not the principles of international law prevent Turkey from instituting criminal proceedings against Lieutenant Demons under Turkish law. Neither the conformity of Article 6 in itself with the principles of international law nor the application of that article by the Turkish authorities constitutes the point at issue; it is the very fact of the institution of proceedings which is held by France to be contrary to those principles. * * *

II

Having determined the position resulting from the terms of the special agreement, the Court must now ascertain which were the principles of international law that the prosecution of Lieutenant Demons could conceivably be said to contravene.

It is Article 15 of the Convention of Lausanne of July 24th, 1923, respecting conditions of residence and business and jurisdiction, which refers the contracting Parties to the principles of international law as regards the delimitation of their respective jurisdiction. [The clause reads]:

Subject to the provisions of Article 16, all questions of jurisdiction shall, as between Turkey and the other contracting Powers, be decided in accordance with the principles of international law.

* * * In these circumstances it is impossible—except in pursuance of a definite stipulation—to construe the expression "principles of international law" otherwise than as meaning the principles which are in force between all independent nations and which therefore apply equally to all the contracting Parties.

* * *

III

* * * The French Government contends that the Turkish Courts, * * * to have jurisdiction, should be able to point to some title to jurisdiction recognized by international law in favour of Turkey. * * * The Turkish Government takes the view that Article 15 allows Turkey jurisdiction whenever such jurisdiction does not * * * conflict with a principle of international law.

* * *

International law governs relations between independent States. The rules of law binding upon States therefore emanate from their own free will as expressed in conventions or by usages generally accepted as expressing principles of law and established in order to regulate the relations between these co-existing independent communities or with a view to the achievement of common aims. Restrictions upon the independence of States cannot therefore be presumed.

Now the first and foremost restriction imposed by international law upon a State is that—failing the existence of a permissive rule to the contrary—it may not exercise its power in any form in the territory of another State. In this sense jurisdiction is certainly territorial; it cannot be exercised by a State outside its territory except by virtue of a permissive rule derived from international custom or from a convention.

It does not, however, follow that international law prohibits a State from exercising jurisdiction in its own territory, in respect of any case which relates to acts which have taken place abroad, and in which it cannot rely on some permissive rule of international law. Such a view would only be tenable if international law contained a general prohibition to States to extend the application of their laws and the jurisdiction of their courts to persons, property and acts outside their territory, and if, as an exception to this general prohibition, it allowed States to do so in certain specific cases. But this is certainly not the case under [current] international law. Far from laying down a general prohibition ... that States may not extend the application of their laws and the jurisdiction of their courts to persons, property and acts outside their territory, it leaves them in this respect a wide measure of discretion which is only limited ... by prohibitive rules; as regards other cases, every State remains free to adopt the principles which it regards as ... most suitable.

This discretion left to States by international law explains the great variety of rules which they have been able to adopt without objections or complaints on the part of other States; it is * * * to remedy the difficulties resulting from such variety that efforts have been made for many years past, both in Europe and America, to prepare conventions the effect of which would be precisely to limit the discretion at present left to States in this respect by international law, thus making good the existing lacunae in respect of jurisdiction or removing the conflicting jurisdictions arising from the diversity of the principles * * * [in] various States.

In these circumstances, all that can be required of a State is that it should not overstep the limits which international law places upon its jurisdiction; within these limits, its title to exercise jurisdiction rests in its sovereignty. It follows from the foregoing that the contention of the French Government to the effect that Turkey must in each case be able to cite a rule of international law authorizing her to exercise jurisdiction, is opposed to the generally accepted international law to which Article 15 of the Convention of Lausanne refers. * * *

* * *

[We] therefore must * * * ascertain whether * * * there exists a rule of international law limiting the freedom of States to extend the criminal jurisdiction [under the] circumstances of the present case.

IV

The Court will now proceed to ascertain whether general international law, to which Article 15 of the Convention of Lausanne refers, contains a rule prohibiting Turkey from prosecuting Lieutenant Demons.

For this purpose, it will in the first place examine the value of the arguments advanced by the French Government, without however omitting to take into account other possible aspects of the problem, which might show the existence of a restrictive rule applicable in this case.

The arguments advanced by the French Government [include]:

(1) International law does not allow a State to take proceedings with regard to offences committed by foreigners abroad, simply by reason of the nationality of the victim; and such is the situation in the present case because the offence must be regarded as having been committed on board the French vessel.

* * *

As regards the first argument, the Court * * * [recalls] that its examination is strictly confined to the specific situation in the present case, [based on the *compromis* submitting to jurisdiction].

* * * The characteristic features of the situation of fact are as follows: there has been a collision on the high seas between two vessels flying different flags, on one of which was one of the persons alleged to be guilty of the offence, whilst the victims were on board the other.

This being so, the Court does not think it necessary to consider the contention that a State cannot punish offences committed abroad by a foreigner simply by reason of the nationality of the victim. For this contention only relates to the case where the nationality of the victim is the only criterion on which the criminal jurisdiction of the State is based. Even if that argument were correct generally speaking—and in regard to this the Court reserves its opinion—it could only be used in the present case if international law forbade Turkey to take into consideration the fact that the offence produced its effects on the Turkish vessel and consequently in a place assimilated to Turkish territory in which the application of Turkish criminal law cannot be challenged, even in regard to offences committed there by foreigners. But no such rule of international law exists. No argument has come to the knowledge of the Court from which it could be deduced that States recognize themselves to be under an obligation towards each other only to have regard to the place where the author of the offence happens to be at the time of the offence. On the contrary, it is certain that the courts of many countries, even of countries which have given their criminal legislation a strictly territorial character, interpret criminal law in the sense that offences, the authors of which at the moment of commission are in the territory of another State, are nevertheless to be regarded as having been committed in the national territory, if one of the constituent elements of the offence, and more especially its effects, have taken place there. French courts have, in regard to a variety of situations, given decisions sanctioning this way of interpreting the territorial principle. Again, the Court does not know of any cases in which governments have protested against the fact that the criminal law of some country contained a rule to this effect or that the courts of a country construed their criminal law in this sense. Consequently, once it is admitted that the effects of the offence were produced on the Turkish vessel, it becomes impossible to hold that there is a rule of international law which prohibits Turkey from prosecuting Lieutenant Demons because of the fact that the author of the offence was on board the French ship. Since, as has already been observed, the special agreement does not deal with the provision of Turkish law under which the prosecution was instituted, but only with the question whether the prosecution should be regarded as contrary to the principles of international law, there is no reason preventing the Court from confining itself to observing that, in this case, a prosecution may also be justified from the point of view of the so-called territorial principle.

* * * The fact that the judicial authorities may have committed an error in their choice of the legal provision applicable to the particular case and compatible with international law only concerns municipal law and can only affect international law in so far as a treaty provision enters into account, or the possibility of a denial of justice arises.

* * *

The offence for which Lieutenant Demons appears to have been prosecuted was an act—of negligence or imprudence—having its origin on board the Lotus, whilst its effects made themselves felt on board the Boz–Kourt. These two elements are, legally, entirely inseparable, so much so that their separation renders the offence nonexistent. Neither the exclusive jurisdiction of either State, nor the limitations of the jurisdiction of either State, nor the limitations of the jurisdiction of each to the occurrences which took place on the respective ships would appear calculated to satisfy the requirements of justice and effectively to protect the interests of the two States. It is only natural that each should be able to exercise jurisdiction and to do so in respect of the incident as a whole. It is therefore a case of concurrent jurisdiction.

* * *

For These Reasons, the COURT, having heard both Parties, gives, by the President's casting vote—the votes being equally divided—, judgment to the effect

. . . that, following the collision which occurred on August 2nd, 1926, on the high seas between the French steamship Lotus and the Turkish steamship Boz–Kourt, and upon the arrival of the French ship at Stamboul, and in consequence of the loss of the Boz–Kourt having involved the death of eight Turkish nationals, Turkey, by instituting criminal proceedings in pursuance of Turkish law against Lieutenant Demons, officer of the watch on board the Lotus at the time of the collision, has not acted in conflict with the principles of international law, contrary to Article 15 of the Convention of Lausanne of July 24th, 1923, * * *;

* * * [Separate and dissenting opinions omitted.]

NOTES AND QUESTIONS

1.   The *Lotus* case is the most important decision of an international court regarding jurisdiction. It establishes that international law has few outright restrictions on jurisdiction. The limits on enforcement jurisdiction seen in *Hape* are the most important. The *Lotus* case is also well known for establishing the rule of extraterritoriality where acts are committed beyond the territory of the forum state, but the effects of those acts are felt within the forum state. Can you identify these elements in the PCIJ's decision?

2.   Is the following comment by the PCIJ still true today? "[T]he rules of law binding upon States therefore emanate from their own free will as expressed in conventions or by usages generally accepted as expressing principles of law and established in order to regulate the relations between these co-existing independent communities or with a view to the achievement of common aims. Restrictions upon the independence of States cannot therefore be presumed . . ."

3.   In the 1996 *Nuclear Weapons* case, the International Court of Justice took the opportunity to consider the scope of the *Lotus* decision. (*Legality of the Threat or Use of Nuclear Weapons* 1996 I.C.J. 226 [at p. 237]). . . . The use of the word 'permitted' in the question put by the General

Assembly was criticized before the Court by certain States on the ground that this [the use of the term 'permitted'] implied that the threat or the use of nuclear weapons would only be permissible if authorization could be found in a treaty provision or in customary international law." * * * Such a starting point, those states submitted, was incompatible with the very basis of international law, which rests upon the principles of sovereignty and consent; accordingly, and contrary to what was implied by use of the word "permitted", states are free to threaten or use nuclear weapons unless it can be shown that they are bound not to do so by reference to a prohibition in either treaty law or custom. . . .

Have you found so far that the rules of international law are formulated as *prohibitions* as indicated in the *Lotus* opinion or are they formulated as *permissions. Or both?*

4.   Jurisdiction over maritime zones are regulated by UNCLOS introduced in Chapter 1. See also the *Land, Island, and Maritime* case, *supra* Chapter 3. This topic will be discussed in detail in Chapter 6 *infra*.

5.   Note that the *Lotus* collision was said to occur between 5 and 6 nautical miles off shore, a location then on the high seas. Consider UNCLOS Article 97 which provides in part:

In the event of a collision * * * concerning a ship on the high seas, involving the penal or disciplinary responsibility of the master or of any person in the service of the ship, no penal or disciplinary proceedings may be instituted against such persons except before the judicial or administrative authorities either of the flag state or of the state of which such person is a national.

What effect would Article 97 have on the jurisdiction question? We might assume that the location of the collision would now fall within the Turkish territorial sea (up to 12 miles seaward of the baseline). Would that change the jurisdiction question for Turkey? UNCLOS 27.1 provides that coastal states jurisdiction should not be exercised on board a foreign ship in the territorial sea for arrest or investigations of criminal cases, subject to a number of exceptions, including "(a) if the consequences of the crime extend to the coastal State." Does this provision adopt the "effects" theory? Would a collision and deaths make an *a fortiori* case for coastal state jurisdiction? What weight should be given to Article 2.1 that provides "The sovereignty of a coastal state extends, beyond its land territory and internal waters * * * to an adjacent belt of sea, described as the territorial sea"?

6.   The bulk of legislation in all countries would appear to apply only to the territory of the legislating state, and in fact is so applied. Thus it is a natural assumption that statutes do not apply extraterritorially unless a clear intention to that effect is disclosed in the legislation or in its background history. This assumption has ripened into a legal formulation as stated by the U.S. Supreme Court in *Equal Employment Opportunity Commission v. Arabian American Oil Co.,* 499 U.S. 244, 248, 111 S.Ct. 1227, 113 L.Ed.2d 274 (1991) in the following:

It is a longstanding principle of American law "that legislation of Congress, unless a contrary intent appears, is meant to apply only within the territorial jurisdiction of the United States." *Foley Bros., 336 U.S., at 285, 69 S.Ct., at 577.* This "canon of construction . . . is a valid approach whereby unexpressed congressional intent may be ascertained." *Ibid.* It serves to protect against unintended clashes between our laws and those of other nations which could result in international discord. See *McCulloch v. Sociedad Nacional de Marineros de Honduras,* 372 U.S. 10, 20–22, 83 S.Ct. 671, 677–678, 9 L.Ed.2d 547 (1963).

This useful presumption, seen also below in Justice Scalia's dissent in the *Hartford Fire Ins. Co* case, clearly applies in cases where the extraterritorial effect would be felt in another sovereign state, but should it apply in territory which is *not* part of a state, like Antarctica? That problem arose in *Environmental Defense Fund, Inc. v. Walter E. Massey in his official Capacity as Director, National Science Foundation, and National Science Foundation,* 986 F.2d 528 (D.C. Cir.1993) where the plaintiff sought to compel the preparation of a environmental impact statement before authorities proceeded with plans to incinerate food wastes in Antarctica. The Court held that the presumption against extraterritoriality of the applicable statute did not apply in this case because the environmental impact statement action would be carried out entirely within the United States, even thought the effects that might be expected to arise in the Antarctic, and in this case there was sufficient U.S. interest and authority to support that action. There was of course no other sovereign involved.

7.   In 2008, the U.S. Supreme Court held in *Boumediene v. Bush,* 553 U.S. ___, 128 S.Ct. 2229, 171 L.Ed.2d 41 (2008) that persons held in U.S. custody outside the United States had the right in certain circumstances under the U.S. Constitution to apply for a writ of habeas corpus in U.S. courts. See more on this case in Chapter 10. Compare *Boumediene* with *Hape* above.

a.   APPLICATIONS OF THE EFFECTS DOCTRINE

National legislation on economic matters has figured prominently in the development of jurisdiction rules. Where the legislation is intended to apply only within the territory of the legislating state, international jurisdiction questions normally do not arise. Where that intent is not clear or where legislation specifically refers to the regulation of activities wholly outside of the territory, conflicts with legislation or expectations of other states do arise, and international jurisdiction rules may come into play. For these reasons, the U.S. antitrust and EC competition law governing transactions entered into in one state but producing economic damage in other states have contributed to the lore and law of our jurisdiction cases, particularly the effects doctrine stated in *Lotus* as the means for obtaining extraterritorial jurisdiction.

One of the earliest of these U.S. cases is *American Banana v. United Fruit Co.,* 213 U.S. 347, 29 S.Ct. 511, 53 L.Ed. 826 (1909) where these two

U.S. companies competed with each other in Panama and Costa Rica in the banana trade. In this case the defendant engaged in a number of activities to monopolize that trade and to maintain unreasonable prices to the detriment of the defendant. In affirming the dismissal of the complaint for not stating a cause of action, Justice Holmes wrote for the Court:

> * * * It is obvious that, however stated, the plaintiff's case depends on several rather startling propositions. In the first place the acts causing the damage were done, so far as appears, outside the jurisdiction of the United States and within that of other states. It is surprising to hear it argued that they were governed by the act of Congress.
>
> * * *
>
> The general and almost universal rule is that the character of an act as lawful or unlawful must be determined wholly by the law of the country where the act is done. * * *
>
> For another jurisdiction, if it should happen to lay hold of the actor, to treat him according to its own notions rather than those of the place where he did the acts, not only would be unjust, but would be an interference with the authority of another sovereign, contrary to the comity of nations, which the other state concerned justly might resent. * * *
>
> * * *
>
> The foregoing considerations would lead in case of doubt to a construction of any statute as intended to be confined in its operation and effect to the territorial limits over which the lawmaker has general and legitimate power. "All legislation is prima facie territorial." * * * Words having universal scope, such as "Every contract in restraint of trade," "Every person who shall monopolize," etc., will be taken as a matter of course to mean only every one subject to such legislation, not all that the legislator subsequently may be able to catch. In the case of the present statute the improbability of the United States attempting to make acts done in Panama or Costa Rica criminal is obvious, yet the law begins by making criminal the acts for which it gives a right to sue. We think it entirely plain that what the defendant did in Panama or Costa Rica is not within the scope of the statute so far as the present suit is concerned. * * *

The classic case which did find jurisdiction in an antitrust case attaching liability for conduct of non-nationals outside of the United States is *United States v. Aluminum Co. of America*, 148 F.2d 416 (2d Cir.1945) a prosecution under the Sherman Antitrust Act. In this conspiracy case known as the *Alcoa* case, shareholders of French, German, Swiss and British corporations established a separate Swiss corporation to operate a cartel to carry out two agreements among them to fix prices and engage in related restrictive practices concerning aluminum trade in the U.S. and other markets. In his landmark opinion, Justice Learned Hand stated [pp. 443–4] that:

* * * we are concerned only with whether Congress chose to attach liability to the conduct outside the United States of persons not in allegiance to it. That being so, the only question open is whether Congress intended to impose the liability, and whether our own Constitution permitted it to do so: as a court of the United States, we cannot look beyond our own law. Nevertheless, it is quite true that we are not to read general words, such as those in this Act, without regard to the limitations customarily observed by nations upon the exercise of their powers; limitations which generally correspond to those fixed by the "Conflict of Laws." We should not impute to Congress an intent to punish all whom its courts can catch, for conduct which has no consequences within the United States. * * * Both agreements would clearly have been unlawful, had they been made within the United States; and it follows from what we have just said that both were unlawful, though made abroad, if they were intended to affect imports and did affect them.

Hartford Fire Ins. Co. v. California

United States Supreme Court
509 U.S. 764, 113 S.Ct. 2891, 125 L.Ed.2d 612 (1993)

■ Justice Souter[.] * * *

I.   The two petitions before us stem from consolidated litigation comprising the complaints of 19 States and many private plaintiffs alleging that the defendants, members of the insurance industry, conspired in violation of § 1 of the Sherman Act to restrict the terms of coverage of commercial general liability (CGL) insurance available in the United States. Because the cases come to us on motions to dismiss, we take the allegations of the complaints as true.

A.   According to the complaints, the object of the conspiracies was to force certain primary insurers (insurers who sell insurance directly to consumers) to change the terms of their standard CGL insurance policies to conform with the policies the defendant insurers wanted to sell * * * [The complaints alleged a violation of § 1 of the Sherman Act by certain London reinsurers who conspired to: (a) coerce primary insurers in the United States to offer CGL coverage on a claims-made basis, thereby making "occurrence CGL coverage on a claims-made basis unavailable in the State of California for many risks;" (b) limit coverage of pollution risks in North America, thereby rendering "pollution liability coverage ... almost entirely unavailable for the vast majority of casualty insurance purchasers in the State of California;" and (c) limit coverage of seepage, pollution, and property contamination risks in North America, "thereby eliminating such coverage in the State of California."]

III.   * * * At the outset, we note that the District Court undoubtedly had jurisdiction of these Sherman Act claims, as the London reinsurers apparently concede. ("Our position is not that the Sherman Act does not apply in the sense that a minimal basis for the exercise of jurisdiction doesn't exist here. Our position is that there are certain circumstances, and that this is one of them, in which the interests of another State are sufficient that the exercise of that jurisdiction should be restrained"). Although the proposition was perhaps not always free from doubt, see American Banana Co. v. United Fruit Co., 213 U.S. 347 (1909), it is well established by now that the Sherman Act applies to foreign conduct that was meant to produce and did in fact produce some substantial effect in the United States. [cit.] Such is the conduct alleged here: that the London reinsurers engaged in unlawful conspiracies to affect the market for insurance in the United States and that their conduct in fact produced substantial effect.

According to the London reinsurers, the District Court should have declined to exercise such jurisdiction under the principle of international comity The Court of Appeals agreed that courts should look to that principle in deciding whether to exercise jurisdiction under the Sherman Act. This availed the London reinsurers nothing, however. To be sure, the Court of Appeals believed that "application of [American] antitrust laws to the London reinsurance market 'would lead to significant conflict with English law and policy,'" and that "[s]uch a conflict, unless outweighed by other factors, would by itself be reason to decline exercise of jurisdiction." (citation omitted). But other factors, in the court's view, including the London reinsurers' express purpose to affect U.S. commerce and the substantial nature of the effect produced, outweighed the supposed conflict and required the exercise of jurisdiction in this litigation.

* * *

The only substantial question in this litigation is whether "there is in fact a true conflict between domestic and foreign law." Societe Nationale Industrielle Aerospatiale v. U.S. Dist. Court for Southern Dist. of Iowa, 482 U.S. 522, 555 (1987) (Blackmun, J., concurring in part and dissenting in part). The London reinsurers contend that applying the Act to their conduct would conflict significantly with British law, and the British Government, appearing before us as amicus curiae, concurs. [cit.] They assert that Parliament has established a comprehensive regulatory regime over the London reinsurance market and that the conduct alleged here was perfectly consistent with British law and policy. But this is not to state a conflict. "[T]he fact that conduct is lawful in the state in which it took place will not, of itself, bar application of the United States antitrust laws," even where the foreign state has a strong policy to permit or encourage such conduct. Restatement (Third) Foreign Relations Law § 415, Comment j; [cit.] No conflict exists, for these purposes, "where a person subject to regulation by two states can comply with the laws of both." Restatement (Third) Foreign Relations Law § 403, Comment e. Since the London reinsurers do not argue that British law requires them to act in some fashion prohibited by the law of the United States, [cit.], or claim that their compliance with the laws of both countries is otherwise impossible, we see no conflict with British law. See Restatement (Third) Foreign Relations Law § 403, Comment e, § 415, Comment j. We have no need in this litigation to address other considerations that might inform a decision to refrain from the exercise of jurisdiction on grounds of international comity.

IV. The judgment of the Court of Appeals is affirmed * * * and the cases are remanded for further proceedings consistent with this opinion. It is so ordered.

Justice Scalia[.] * * * I dissent from the Court's ruling concerning the extraterritorial application of the Sherman Act. * * *

The Petitioners * * *, various British corporations and other British subjects, argue that certain of the claims against them constitute an inappropriate extraterritorial application of the Sherman Act. It is important to distinguish two distinct questions raised by this petition: whether the District Court had jurisdiction, and whether the Sherman Act reaches the extraterritorial conduct alleged here. On the first question, I believe that the District Court had subject-matter jurisdiction over the Sherman Act claims against all the defendants (personal jurisdiction is not contested). Respondents asserted nonfrivolous claims under the Sherman Act, and 28 U.S.C. § 1331 vests district courts with subject-matter jurisdiction over cases "arising under" federal statutes. * * * [T]hat is sufficient to establish the District Courts jurisdiction over these claims. * * *

* * *

Two canons of statutory construction are relevant in this inquiry. The first is the "longstanding principle of American law 'that legislation of Congress, unless a contrary intent appears, is meant to apply only within the territorial jurisdiction of the United States.'"

* * *

But if the presumption against extraterritoriality has been overcome or is otherwise inapplicable, a second canon of statutory construction becomes relevant: "[A]n act of congress ought never to be construed to violate the law of nations if any other possible construction remains." Murray v. Schooner Charming Betsy, 2 Cranch 64, 118 (1804) (Marshall, C.J.).

* * *

More recent lower court precedent has also tempered the extraterritorial application of the Sherman Act with considerations of "international comity." [cit.] The "comity" they refer to is not the comity of courts, whereby judges decline to exercise jurisdiction over matters more appropriately adjudged elsewhere, but rather what might be termed "prescriptive comity": the respect sovereign nations afford each other by limiting the reach of their laws. That comity is exercised by legislatures when they enact laws, and courts assume it has been exercised when they come to interpreting the scope of laws their legislatures have enacted. It is a traditional component of choice-of-law theory. * * *

Under the Restatement, a nation having some "basis" for jurisdiction to prescribe law should nonetheless refrain from exercising that jurisdiction "with respect to a person or activity having connections with another state when the exercise of such jurisdiction is unreasonable." Restatement

(Third) § 403(1). The "reasonableness" inquiry turns on a number of factors including, but not limited to: "the extent to which the activity takes place within the territory [of the regulating state]," id., § 403(2)(a); "the connections, such as nationality, residence, or economic activity, between the regulating state and the person principally responsible for the activity to be regulated," id., § 403(2)(b); "the character of the activity to be regulated, the importance of regulation to the regulating state, the extent to which other states regulate such activities, and the degree to which the desirability of such regulation is generally accepted," id., § 403(2)(c); "the extent to which another state may have an interest in regulating the activity," id., § 403(2)(g); and "the likelihood of conflict with regulation by another state," id., § 403(2)(h). Rarely would these factors point more clearly against application of United States law. The activity relevant to the counts at issue here took place primarily in the United Kingdom, and the defendants in these counts are British corporations and British subjects having their principal place of business or residence outside the United States. Great Britain has established a comprehensive regulatory scheme governing the London reinsurance markets, and clearly has a heavy "interest in regulating the activity," id., § 403(2)(g). [cit.] * * * Considering these factors, I think it unimaginable that an assertion of legislative jurisdiction by the United States would be considered reasonable, and therefore it is inappropriate to assume, in the absence of statutory indication to the contrary, that Congress has made such an assertion.

F. Hoffmann La Roche Ltd. v. Empagran S.A. et al.

United States Supreme Court
542 U.S. 155, 124 S.Ct. 2359, 159 L.Ed.2d 226 (2004)

■ JUSTICE BREYER delivered the opinion of the Court.

The Foreign Trade Antitrust Improvements Act of 1982 (FTAIA) excludes from the Sherman Act's reach much anticompetitive conduct that causes only foreign injury. It does so by setting forth a general rule stating that the Sherman Act "shall not apply to conduct involving trade or commerce ... with foreign nations." 96 Stat. 1246, 15 U.S.C. § 6a. It then creates exceptions to the general rule, applicable where (roughly speaking) that conduct significantly harms imports, domestic commerce, or American exporters.

We here focus upon anticompetitive price-fixing activity that is in significant part foreign, that causes some domestic antitrust injury, and that independently causes separate foreign injury. We ask two questions about the price-fixing conduct and the foreign injury that it causes. First, does that conduct fall within the FTAIA's general rule excluding the Sherman Act's application? That is to say, does the price-fixing activity constitute "conduct involving trade or commerce ... with foreign nations"? We conclude that it does.

Second, we ask whether the conduct nonetheless falls within a domestic-injury exception to the general rule, an exception that applies (and makes the Sherman Act nonetheless applicable) where the conduct (1) has a "direct, substantial, and reasonably foreseeable effect" on domestic commerce, and (2) "such effect gives rise to a [Sherman Act] claim." §§ 6a(1)(A), (2). We conclude that the exception does not apply where the plaintiff's claim rests solely on the independent foreign harm.

To clarify: The issue before us concerns (1) significant foreign anticompetitive conduct with (2) an adverse domestic effect and (3) an independent foreign effect giving rise to the claim. In more concrete terms, this case involves vitamin sellers around the world that agreed to fix prices, leading to higher vitamin prices in the United States and independently leading to higher vitamin prices in other countries such as Ecuador. We conclude that, in this scenario, a purchaser in the United States could bring a Sherman Act claim under the FTAIA based on domestic injury, but a purchaser in Ecuador could not bring a Sherman Act claim based on foreign harm.

* * * We turn now to the basic question presented, that of the exception's application. Because the underlying antitrust action is complex, potentially raising questions not directly at issue here, we reemphasize that we base our decision upon the following: The price-fixing conduct significantly and adversely affects both customers outside the United States and customers within the United States, but the adverse foreign effect is independent of any adverse domestic effect. In these circumstances, we find that the FTAIA exception does not apply (and thus the Sherman Act does not apply) for two main reasons.

This rule of statutory construction cautions courts to assume that legislators take account of the legitimate sovereign interests of other nations when they write American laws. It thereby helps the potentially conflicting laws of different nations work together in harmony—a harmony particularly needed in today's highly interdependent commercial world.

No one denies that America's antitrust laws, when applied to foreign conduct, can interfere with a foreign nation's ability independently to regulate its own commercial affairs. But our courts have long held that application of our antitrust laws to foreign anticompetitive conduct is nonetheless reasonable, and hence consistent with principles of prescriptive comity, insofar as they reflect a legislative effort to redress *domestic* antitrust injury that foreign anticompetitive conduct has caused.

Damien Geradin, Marc Reysen and David Henry, Extraterritoriality, Comity and Cooperation in EC Competition Law

http://ssrn.com/abstract=1175003 (2008)

The antitrust set up within the EC is based on a two-tier system whereby the Commission and Member State national competition authorities ("NCAs") have parallel competence to apply Articles 81 and 82 EC in a particular case. Article 81(1) EC prohibits agreements between undertakings, decisions by associations of undertakings and concerted practices which restrict or distort competition and which may affect trade between Member States. * * * Article 82 EC prohibits the abuse by one or more undertakings of a dominant position within the common market or in a substantial part of it insofar as it may affect trade between Member States. An abuse is characterized by the exploitation of customers and/or the exclusion of competitors.

* * *

III. EC COMPETITION LAW AND EXTRATERRITORIALITY

Articles 81 and 82 EC are silent as to whether they apply extraterritorially as a result of which their extraterritorial application has been developed by Commission decisional practice and a Court created corpus of case law. Indeed, it is now established that Articles 81 and 82 EC apply no matter where an undertaking has its headquarters or where the agreement has been concluded. In assessing whether the long jurisdictional arm of Articles 81 and 82 EC applies to undertakings located outside the Community three legal theories have been propounded. The first is the "economic entity" doctrine which has as its underpinnings the nationality principle (A). The second is the "implementation" doctrine which is based on the territoriality principle (B), and the third is the "effects doctrine" which extends subject-matter jurisdiction to all situations where the economic effects in the EU of anti-competitive actions taken abroad are immediate, reasonably foreseeable and substantial (C).

(A) The "economic entity" doctrine

Dyestuffs represents the seminal EC case as far as the economic entity doctrine is concerned. On the basis of the nationality principle, jurisdiction was asserted over non-EC parent undertakings by attributing liability to them for the illegal price fixing of dyestuffs by their subsidiaries located in the EC over which the non-EC parent undertaking exercised control. The ECJ held that the fact that a subsidiary has separate legal personality is not sufficient to exclude the possibility of imputing its conduct to the parent company. The ECJ went further by holding that such may be the case in particular where the subsidiary, although having separate legal personality, does not decide independently upon its own conduct on the market but carries out in all material respects the instructions given to it by the parent company. Similar reasoning is to be found in the ECJ's *Continental Can* judgment.

According to the *Dyestuffs* line of case law, therefore, the nub of the issue is to check the extent to which a non-EC parent undertaking controls its subsidiaries located in the EC in order to establish a single economic entity. In the eyes of the ECJ control is to be assessed against, *inter alia*, the shareholding of the parent undertaking in the subsidiary. A finding that there is a single economic entity brings a non-EC undertaking within the scope of the EC competition law provisions. Though the effects of the relevant practices were briefly alluded to, a response on the application of the "effects doctrine" was shied away from, preference being accorded to handing down a judgment based on the established doctrine of a single economic entity. The ECJ's coy stance vis-à-vis the effects doctrine, however, could be attributed to the fact that Europe's political elite at that time vociferously criticized the doctrine when employed by the U.S. antitrust authorities.

(B) The "implementation doctrine"

The implementation doctrine represents an alternative legal construct as far as the extraterritorial application of EC competition law is concerned, its advent reflecting the inherent limitations of the economic entity doctrine in that it could not be stretched to catch purely non-European players. Pursuant to this doctrine, which is based on the territoriality principle, agreements and practices fall within the purview of Articles 81 and 82 EC irrespective of where they find their geographic origin, the decisive factor being whether they are *implemented* within the European Community and trade between Member States is affected. According to the ECJ in its *Woodpulp* judgment:

> "It should be observed that an infringement of Article [81], such as the conclusion of an agreement which has had the effect of restricting competition within the common market, consists of conduct made up of two elements, the *formation* of the agreement, decision or concerted practice and the *implementation* thereof. If the applicability of prohibitions laid down under competition law were made to depend on the place where the agreement, decision or concerted practice was formed, the result would obviously be to give undertakings an easy means of evading those prohibitions. The decisive factor is therefore the place where it is implemented. The producers in this case implemented their pricing agreement within the common market. It is immaterial in that respect whether or not they had recourse to subsidiaries, agents, sub-agents, or branches within the Community in order to make their contacts with purchasers within the Community. Accordingly the Community's jurisdiction to apply its competition rules to such conduct is covered by the territoriality principle as universally recognized in public international law".

According to *Woodpulp*, therefore, the criterion as to the implementation of an agreement is satisfied by mere sale within the Community, no matter the location of the sources of supply and the production plant and where the anti-competitive arrangement was entered into. A corollary of this is that Community jurisdiction is triggered by the simple fact that products are directly sold to Community purchasers. One commentator has indeed argued that the triggering of Community jurisdiction on the basis of direct sales to Community purchasers sits uneasily with public international law as "it does not constitute a sufficiently close and relevant link with the regulating State that is compelling enough to justify jurisdiction on its part". Despite such misgivings, however, the Commission recently made explicit reference to the *Woodpulp* judgment in order to assert jurisdiction over a global price-fixing cartel for lysine involving undertakings from third countries.

(C) The "effects doctrine"

A third triggering doctrine for the purposes of asserting extraterritorial jurisdiction is based on the economic effects felt within the Community. Though the effects doctrine has been recognized and accepted by the Commission, testimony of which is borne by dicta in various Commission decisions and in Commission Notices, the ECJ has never handed down a judgment explicitly affirming the doctrine, preferring to rely on the more politically uncontroversial economic entity and implementation doctrines. In *Wood Pulp*, for example, the Commission held that the relevant pulp producers and trade associations had infringed Article 81(1) EC all of which had their registered offices outside the Community with only few having some kind of representation, such as a subsidiary, within the EC. The Commission explicitly made reference to the effect of the agreements and practices on prices announced and/or charged to customers and on resale of pulp within the EC in order to assert jurisdiction.

On appeal, Advocate–General Darmon espoused the effects doctrine reflecting a belief among several Advocate–Generals that the doctrine should become an established concept of EC law. In particular, he opined that "there is no rule of international law which is capable of being relied upon against the criterion of the direct, substantial and foreseeable effect". Despite the Advocate–General's fervent view that the effects doctrine should become a cornerstone of EC competition law when applying it extraterritorially, the ECJ subsequently relied on the implementation doctrine (see above) to assert jurisdiction over undertakings located outside the Community.

* * *

In the vast majority of cases, however, the fact that the "effects doctrine" has not been formally recognized by the ECJ will have no bearing on the ability to assert jurisdiction extraterritorially. The economic entity and implementation doctrines should be more than sufficient. In this regard, whether one applies the implementation doctrine or the effects doctrine similar outcomes should normally be reached, although it is arguable that the latter doctrine is wider in scope. The fact, however, that the ECJ has thus far fudged on handing down an unequivocal ruling on the effects doctrine as such means that the effects doctrine as a concept of Community law remains unresolved.

* * *

NOTES AND QUESTIONS

1. In the *Hartford* and *Hoffmann* cases, do you find that the balancing of interests required by the comity principles to be "reasonable" under the circumstances?

2. The effects doctrine reaches far beyond the U.S anti-trust and EU competition sectors. In the trade and investment fields, for example, the "effects" doctrine had been employed to justify the extraterritorial application of the Helms Burton Act which created a cause of action for "traffick-

ers" in uncompensated assets of U.S. citizens expropriated by Castro's Cuba, including such assets sold to non-citizens of the U.S. or Cuba. See Chapter 7, Section 4 below, in particular the selection from Clagget's article in the AJIL. Note that Helms–Burton attracted strong protests and blocking legislation in a number of countries that might be affected.

3.   The EU's rejection of the "effects" doctrine, at least in name, in favor of the "implementation": doctrine might reflect strong views held in the UK in opposition to the "effects" doctrine. The EU has complained for years about the U.S. applications of extraterritoriality. See e.g. EU, *U.S. Barriers to Trade and Investment Report for 2007, ch.3.1 on extraterritoriality, at* http://www.eurunion.org/eu/. How do you think the EU would respond to a cartel case like *Wood Pulp*, if the entire transaction were made outside of the EU, including passage of title and with delivery of product assured by EU buyers' agents acting outside of the EU rather than sellers agents or subsidiaries within the EU? Would the "implementation" doctrine work in those circumstances against the North American cartel members? What if all of these arrangements were made by transactions on the Internet, to which we now turn?

b.   INTERNET PROBLEMS

Thomas Schultz, Carving Up the Internet: Jurisdiction, Legal Orders, and the Private/Public/International Law Interface

19 EJIL 799, 802 (2008)

I.   Conventional Wisdom about the Internet

The Internet used to be conceived of as a place that was free from regulation. It was thought that everything on the Internet would be free. Free not in the sense of obtaining something for free, but in the sense of being unrestricted. To use Lawrence Lessigs' words, it was not " 'free' as in 'free beer', but 'free' as in 'free speech' 'free markets,' 'free trade,' 'free enterprise,' 'free will and free elections' ". It was thought that this inability to regulate was an inherent characteristic of the online world. The famous *Declaration of the Independence of Cyberspace*, comes to mind:

> Governments of the Industrial world . . . you have no sovereignty where we gather. . . . I declare the global social space we are building to be naturally independent of the tyrannies you seek to impose on us. Cyberspace does not lie within your borders. Do not think that you can build it. It is an act of nature.[11]

Today those words sound odd, but they were taken very seriously for many years, If they were shocking at the time, it was because people believed they were shown this new creature, this rearm of freedom that would challenge the social and political order that the modern nation-state

---

11.   Barlow, 'A Declaration of the Independence of Cyberspace' (1996), available at www. eff.org/~Barlow/Declaration–Final.html

had achieved. The spectre of the state of nature was looming. But the words of the *Declaration* did not shock people in the sense that what it said was shockingly wrong. This inherent liberty on the Internet was taken for granted; it was used as a postulate until it was clearly demonstrated that what we can do on the Internet depends on the laws of technology just as our non-electronic actions depend on the laws of nature. Technology allows us to do or prevents us from doing all the things we can or cannot do on the Internet, and technology can be shaped so as to enshrine values of liberty or values of control. The proof of concept had been established. It had been shown that the Internet could be a place of exquisite control just as it used to be a place of exquisite liberty. Thus, the first inherent characteristic' claim had been repealed.

But another claim largely remained, and is still very much prevalent today. It is the idea that the Internet is necessarily global. The word "cyberspace" at least partly sprang from there, and it shaped a great part of the meaning it subsequently acquired. The entire *lex electronic movement* is built on that assumption. Most writings on the regulation of the Internet insist on the idea that what marks it as different is that it is global. Such "illusions of a borderless world" remain very strongly anchored in our collective imagination. But the reality appears to be that the Internet is being carved up into discrete legal spheres.

Yahoo! Inc. v. La Ligue Contre Le Racisme

United States Court of Appeals, Ninth Circuit
433 F.3d 1199 (2006)

■ W. FLETCHER, CIRCUIT JUDGE, * * *

Yahoo!, an American Internet service provider, brought suit in federal district court in diversity against La Ligue Contre Le Racisme et L'Antisemitisme ("LICRA") and L'Union des Etudiants Juifs de France ("UEJF") seeking a declaratory judgment that two interim orders by a French court are unrecognizable and unenforceable. The district court held that * * * the French orders are not enforceable in the United States because such enforcement would violate the First Amendment. * * *

I.   Background

Yahoo! is a Delaware corporation with its principal place of business in California. Through its United States-based website yahoo.com, Yahoo! makes available a variety of Internet services, including a search engine, e-mail, web page hosting, instant messaging, auctions, and chat rooms. While some of these services rely on content created by Yahoo!, others are forums and platforms for user-generated content.

Yahoo! users can, for example, design their own web pages, share opinions on social and political message boards, play fantasy baseball games, and post items to be auctioned for sale. Yahoo! does not monitor such user-created content before it is posted on the web through Yahoo! sites.

Yahoo!'s United States website is written in English. It targets users in the United States and relies on servers located in California. Yahoo!'s foreign subsidiaries, such as Yahoo! France, Yahoo! U.K., and Yahoo! India, have comparable websites for their respective countries. The Internet addresses of these foreign-based websites contain their two-letter country designations, such as fr.yahoo.com, uk.yahoo.com, and in.yahoo.com. Yahoo!'s foreign subsidiaries' sites provide content in the local language, target local citizens, and adopt policies that comply with local law and customs. In actual practice, however, national boundaries are highly permeable. For example, any user in the United States can type www.fr.yahoo.com into his or her web browser and thereby reach Yahoo! France's website. Conversely, any user in France can type www.yahoo.com into his or her browser, or click the link to Yahoo.com on the Yahoo! France home page, and thereby reach yahoo.com.

Sometime in early April 2000, LICRA's chairman sent by mail and fax a cease and desist letter, dated April 5, 2000, to Yahoo!'s headquarters in Santa Clara, California. The letter, written in English, stated in part:

> [W]e are particularly choked [sic] to see that your Company keeps on presenting every day hundreds of nazi symbols or objects for sale on the Web.

> This practice is illegal according to French legislation and it is incumbent upon you to stop it, at least on the French Territory.

> Unless you cease presenting nazi objects for sale within 8 days, we shall size [sic] the competent jurisdiction to force your company to abide by the law.

On April 10, * * * LICRA filed suit against Yahoo! and Yahoo! France in the Tribunal de Grande Instance de Paris. On April 20, UEJF joined LICRA's suit in the French court. LICRA and UEJF used United States Marshals to serve process on Yahoo! in California.

After a hearing on May 15, 2000, the French court issued an "interim" order on May 22 requiring Yahoo! to *"take all necessary measures to dissuade and render impossible"* any access [from French territory] via Yahoo.com to the Nazi artifact auction service and to any other site or service that may be construed as constituting an apology for Nazism or a contesting of Nazi crimes" (emphasis added). Among other things, the French court required Yahoo! to take particular specified actions "[b]y way of interim precautionary measures." Yahoo! was required "to cease all hosting and availability in the territory of [France] from the 'Yahoo.com' site ... of messages, images and text relating to Nazi objects, relics, insignia, emblems and flags, or which evoke Nazism," and of "Web pages displaying text, extracts, or quotes from 'Mein Kampf' and the '[Protocols of the Elders of Zion]'" at two specified Internet addresses. Yahoo! was further required to remove from "all browser directories accessible in the territory of the French Republic" the "index heading entitled 'negationists' and any link "bringing together, equating, or presenting directly or indirectly as equivalent'' sites about the Holocaust and sites by Holocaust deniers.

The May 22 interim order required Yahoo! France (as distinct from Yahoo!) to remove the "negationists" index heading and the link to negationist sites, described above, from fr.yahoo.com. The order further required Yahoo! France to post a warning on fr.yahoo.com stating to any user of that website that, in the event the user accessed prohibited material through a search on Yahoo.com, he or she must "desist from viewing the site concerned[,] subject to imposition of the penalties provided in French legislation or the bringing of legal action against him."

The order stated that both Yahoo! and Yahoo! France were subject to a penalty of 100,000 Euros per day of delay or per confirmed violation, and stated that the "possibility of liquidation of the penalties thus pronounced" was "reserve[d]." * * *

Yahoo! objected to the May 22 order. It contended, among other things, that "there was no technical solution which would enable it *to comply fully* with the terms of the court order." (Emphasis added.) In response, the French court obtained a written report from three experts. The report concluded that under current conditions approximately 70% of Yahoo! users operating from computer sites in France could be identified. The report specifically noted that Yahoo! already used such identification of French users to display advertising banners in French. The 70% number applied irrespective of whether a Yahoo! user sought access to an auction site, or to a site denying the existence of the Holocaust or constituting an apology for Nazism.

* * *

In a second interim order, issued on November 20, 2000, the French court reaffirmed its May 22 order and directed Yahoo! to comply within three months, "subject to a penalty of 100,000 Francs per day of delay effective from the first day following expiry of the 3 month period." (The May 22 order had specified a penalty of 100,000 Euros rather than 100,000 Francs.) The court "reserve[d] the possible liquidation of the penalty" against Yahoo!. The French court's November 20 order required Yahoo! France (as distinct from Yahoo!) to display "a warning to surfers even before they have made use of the link to Yahoo.com, to be brought into effect within 2 months following notification of the present order." However, the French court found "that YAHOO FRANCE has complied *in large measure* with the spirit and letter of the order of 22nd May 2000[.]" (Emphasis added.)

In early 2001, after both interim orders had been entered by the French court, and after Yahoo! had filed suit in federal district court, Yahoo! adopted a new policy prohibiting use of auctions or classified advertisements on Yahoo.com "to offer or trade in items that are associated with or could be used to promote or glorify groups that are known principally for hateful and violent positions directed at others based on race or similar factors." Yahoo! has represented, in this court and elsewhere, that its new policy has not been adopted in response to the French court's orders, but rather for independent reasons. Yahoo's new policy eliminates much of the conduct prohibited by the French orders. However, after conducting its own Internet research on yahoo.com, the district court found that even after this policy change, Yahoo! "appear[s]" not to have fully complied with the orders with respect to its auction site. 169 F.Supp.2d at 1185. For example, the district court found that Yahoo! continued to allow the sale of items such as a copy of *Mein Kampf* and stamps and coins from the Nazi period on which the swastika is depicted. *Id.* The district court also found that access was available through yahoo.com to various sites in response to searches such as "Holocaust/5 did not happen." *Id.*

* * *

1.   Enforceability of the Monetary Penalty

Yahoo! contends that the threat of a monetary penalty hangs like the sword of Damocles. However, it is exceedingly unlikely that the sword will ever fall. We may say with some confidence that, for reasons entirely independent of the First Amendment, the French court's orders are not likely to result in the enforcement of a monetary penalty in the United States. * * * Further, LICRA and UEJF have represented that they have no intention of seeking a monetary penalty by the French court so long as Yahoo! does not revert to its "old ways."

More important, even if the French court were to impose a monetary penalty against Yahoo!, it is exceedingly unlikely that any court in California—or indeed elsewhere in the United States—would enforce it. California's Uniform Act does not authorize enforcement of "fines or other penalties." Cal.Civ.Proc.Code § 1713.1(2). The Act includes a savings clause, *see* Cal.Civ.Proc.Code § 1713.7, but the fine is equally unenforceable under California common law doctrine.

California courts follow the generally-observed rule that, " '[u]nless required to do so by treaty, no state [*i.e.,* country] enforces the penal judgments of other states [*i.e.,* countries].' " * * *

2.   First Amendment

Yahoo! argues that any restriction on speech and speech-related activities resulting from the French court's orders is a substantial harm under the First Amendment. We are acutely aware that this case implicates the First Amendment, and we are particularly sensitive to the harm that may result from chilling effects on protected speech or expressive conduct. In this case, however, the harm to First Amendment interests—if such harm exists at all—may be nowhere near as great as Yahoo! would have us believe. * * * Any restraint on such activities is entirely voluntary and self-imposed.

The only potential First Amendment violation comes from the restriction imposed by the interim orders—if indeed they impose any restrictions—on the speech-related activities in which Yahoo! is now engaged, and which might be restricted if further compliance with the French court's orders is required. For example, Yahoo! continues to allow auctions of copies of *Mein Kampf,* and it maintains that the French court's orders prohibit it from doing so. The French court might find that Yahoo! has not yet complied "in large measure" with its orders, and that Yahoo! is prohibited by its orders from allowing auctions of copies of *Mein Kampf.*

Even if the French court took this step, Yahoo!'s claim to First Amendment protection would be limited. We emphasize that the French court's interim orders do not by their terms require Yahoo! to restrict access by Internet users in the United States. They only require it to restrict access by users located in France. That is, with respect to the *Mein Kampf* example, the French court's orders—even if further compliance is required—would by their terms only prohibit Yahoo! from allowing auctions of copies of *Mein Kampf* to users in France.

The core of Yahoo!'s hardship argument may thus be that it has a First Amendment interest in allowing access by users in France. Yet under French criminal law, Internet service providers are forbidden to permit French users to have access to the materials specified in the French court's orders. French users, for their part, are criminally forbidden to obtain such access. In other words, as to the French users, Yahoo! is necessarily arguing that it has a First Amendment right to violate French criminal law and to facilitate the violation of French criminal law by others. As we indicated above, the extent—indeed the very existence—of such an extraterritorial right under the First Amendment is uncertain.

Dow Jones and Company Inc. v. Gutnick

High Court of Australia
[2002] HCA 56

1. GLEESON CJ, McHUGH, GUMMOW AND HAYNE JJ. The appellant, Dow Jones & Company Inc. ("Dow Jones"), prints and publishes the *Wall Street Journal* newspaper and *Barron's* magazine. Since 1996, Dow Jones has operated WSJ.com, a subscription news site on the World Wide Web.

2. The edition of *Barron's Online* for 28 October 2000 (and the equivalent edition of the magazine which bore the date 30 October 2000) contained an article entitled "Unholy Gains" in which several references were made to the respondent, Mr. Joseph Gutnick. Mr. Gutnick contends that part of the article defamed him. He has brought an action in the Supreme Court of Victoria against Dow Jones claiming damages for defamation. Mr. Gutnick lives in Victoria. He has his business headquarters there * * * and much of his social and business life could be said to be focused in Victoria.

* * *

4. The principal issue debated in the appeal to this Court was where was the material of which Mr. Gutnick complained published? Was it published in Victoria? The answer to these questions was said to affect,

even determine, whether proceedings in the Supreme Court of Victoria should, as Dow Jones contended, be stayed on the ground that that Court was a clearly inappropriate forum for determination of the action * * *

5.   Dow Jones entered a conditional appearance to the process served upon it. It applied to a Judge of the Supreme Court of Victoria (Hedigan J) for an order that service of the writ and statement of claim be set aside or an order that further proceedings in the matter be permanently stayed.

* * *

7.   A deal of evidence was led before the primary judge seeking to establish the way in which, and the place at which, information found at a website like WSJ.com is published. It will be necessary to say something more about what that evidence revealed. His Honour concluded that the statements of which Mr. Gutnick sought to complain were "published in the State of Victoria when downloaded by Dow Jones subscribers who had met Dow Jones's payment and performance conditions and by the use of their passwords". He rejected Dow Jones's contention that the publication of the article in *Barron's Online* occurred at the servers maintained by Dow Jones in New Jersey in the United States. Being therefore of the opinion that the defamation of which Mr. Gutnick complained had occurred in Victoria, Hedigan J. concluded that Victoria was not a clearly inappropriate forum for trial of the proceeding and dismissed Dow Jones's application.

* * *

17.   Dow Jones has its editorial offices for *Barron's*, *Barron's Online* and WSJ.com in the city of New York. Material for publication in *Barron's* or *Barron's Online*, once prepared by its author, is transferred to a computer located in the editorial offices in New York city. From there it is transferred either directly to computers at Dow Jones's premises at South Brunswick, New Jersey, or via an intermediate site operated by Dow Jones at Harborside, New Jersey. It is then loaded onto six servers maintained by Dow Jones at its South Brunswick premises.

18.   The principal burden of the argument advanced by Dow Jones on the hearing of the appeal in this Court was that articles published on *Barron's Online* were published in South Brunswick, New Jersey, when they became available on the servers which it maintained at that place.

* * *

20.   Dow Jones submitted that it was preferable that the publisher of material on the World Wide Web be able to govern its conduct according only to the law of the place where it maintained its web servers, unless that place was merely adventitious or opportunistic. Those who, by leave, intervened in support of Dow Jones generally supported this contention. The alternative, so the argument went, was that a publisher would be bound to take account of the law of every country on earth, for there were no boundaries which a publisher could effectively draw to prevent anyone, anywhere, downloading the information it put on its web server.

23.   It is necessary to begin by making the obvious point that the law of defamation seeks to strike a balance between, on the one hand, society's interest in freedom of speech and the free exchange of information and ideas (whether or not that information and those ideas find favour with any particular part of society) and, on the other hand, an individual's interest in maintaining his or her reputation in society free from unwarranted slur or damage. The way in which those interests are balanced differs from society to society. * * *

* * *

35.   For present purposes, what it is important to notice is that what began as a term describing a rule that all causes of action for widely circulated defamation should be litigated in one trial, and that each publication need not be separately pleaded and proved, came to be understood as affecting, even determining, the choice of law to be applied in deciding the action. To reason in that way confuses two separate questions: one about how to prevent multiplicity of suits and vexation of parties, and the other about what law must be applied to determine substantive questions arising in an action in which there are foreign elements.

* * *

38.   In the course of argument much emphasis was given to the fact that the advent of the World Wide Web is a considerable technological advance. So it is. But the problem of widely disseminated communications is much older than the Internet and the World Wide Web. The law has had to grapple with such cases ever since newspapers and magazines came to be distributed to large numbers of people over wide geographic areas. Radio and television presented the same kind of problem as was presented by widespread dissemination of printed material, although international transmission of material was made easier by the advent of electronic means of communication.

44.   * * * In the case of material on the World Wide Web, it is not available in comprehensible form until downloaded on to the computer of a person who has used a web browser to pull the material from the web server. It is where that person downloads the material that the damage to reputation may be done. Ordinarily then, that will be the place where the tort of defamation is committed.

48.   As has been noted earlier, Mr. Gutnick has sought to confine his claim in the Supreme Court of Victoria to the damage he alleges was caused to his reputation *in Victoria* as a consequence of the publication that occurred *in that State*. The place of commission of the tort for which Mr. Gutnick sues is then readily located as Victoria. That is where the damage to his reputation of which he complains in this action is alleged to have occurred, for it is there that the publications of which he complains were comprehensible by readers. It is his reputation in *that State*, and only that State, which he seeks to vindicate. It follows, of course, that substantive issues arising in the action would fall to be determined according to the law of Victoria. But it also follows that Mr. Gutnick's claim was thereafter a

claim for damages for a tort committed in Victoria, not a claim for damages for a tort committed outside the jurisdiction. There is no reason to conclude that the primary judge erred in the exercise of his discretion to refuse to stay the proceeding.

Actions for publications in several places

49.   More difficult questions may arise if complaint were to be made for an injury to reputation which is said to have occurred as a result of publications of defamatory material in a number of places. For the reasons given earlier, in resolving those difficulties, it may be necessary to distinguish between cases where the complaint is confined to publications made in Australia, but in different States and Territories, and cases where publication is alleged to have occurred outside Australia, either with or without publication within Australia. * * *

54.   * * * [T]he spectre which Dow Jones sought to conjure up in the present appeal, of a publisher forced to consider every article it publishes on the World Wide Web against the defamation laws of every country from Afghanistan to Zimbabwe is seen to be unreal when it is recalled that in all except the most unusual of cases, identifying the person about whom material is to be published will readily identify the defamation law to which that person may resort.

55.   The appeal should be dismissed with costs.

56.   GAUDRON J. I agree with Gleeson CJ, * * * I would wish to add some comments of my own.

* * *

115.   *Effectiveness of remedies*: Any suggestion that there can be no effective remedy for the tort of defamation (or other civil wrongs) committed by the use of the Internet (or that such wrongs must simply be tolerated as the price to be paid for the advantages of the medium) is self-evidently unacceptable. Instruments of international human rights law recognise the right of "[e]veryone . . . to hold opinions without interference" and to enjoy "the right to freedom of expression . . . [including] freedom to seek, receive and impart information and ideas of all kinds, regardless of frontiers . . . through any . . . media of his choice". However, such instruments also recognise that those rights carry "duties and responsibilities". They may therefore "be subject to certain restrictions, but these shall only be such as are provided by law and are necessary . . . [f]or respect of the rights or reputations of others".

116.   The International Covenant of Civil and Political Rights also provides that "[n]o one shall be subjected to arbitrary or unlawful interference with his privacy, family, home or correspondence, nor to unlawful attacks on his honour and reputation". And that "[e]veryone has the right to the protection of the law against such interference or attacks". Accordingly, any development of the common law of Australia, consistent with such principles should provide effective legal protection for the honour, reputation and personal privacy of individuals. To the extent that our law

does not do so, Australia, like other nations so obliged, is rendered accountable to the relevant treaty body for such default.

* * *

118.   *A new rule for a unique technology*: In response to the suggestion that similar questions have existed at least since telegraph and international shortwave radio and that such potential liability is a commonplace in the world of global television distributed by satellite, the appellant pointed to the peculiarities of Internet publication. Viewed in one way, the Internet is not simply an extension of past communications technology. It is a new means of creating continuous relationships in a manner that could not previously have been contemplated. According to this view, the Internet is too flexible a structure to be controlled by a myriad of national laws, purportedly applied with no more justification than is provided by the content of such laws, usually devised long before the Internet arrived. For stored information, accessible in cyberspace, the new technology was said to demand a new approach. This would be true as much for the law of taxation, commercial transactions and other areas, as for the law of defamation.

119.   *The urgency of a new rule*: To wait for legislatures or multilateral international agreement to provide solutions to the legal problems presented by the Internet would abandon those problems to "agonizingly slow" processes of lawmaking. Accordingly, courts throughout the world are urged to address the immediate need to piece together gradually a coherent transnational law appropriate to the "digital millennium". The alternative, in practice, could be an institutional failure to provide effective laws in harmony, as the Internet itself is, with contemporary civil society— national and international. The new laws would need to respect the entitlement of each legal regime not to enforce foreign legal rules contrary to binding local law or important elements of local public policy. But within such constraints, the common law would adapt itself to the central features of the Internet, namely its global, ubiquitous and reactive characteristics. In the face of such characteristics, simply to apply old rules, created on the assumptions of geographical boundaries, would encourage an inappropriate and usually ineffective grab for extra-territorial jurisdiction.

NOTES AND QUESTIONS

1.   Although the *Yahoo* cases in France and in the United States had not been brought to final conclusions by 2009, they are widely considered as the leading cases on Internet law. What are the elements of those cases that might explain this importance? Do you find that they might represent a major step away from full freedom of expression in the Internet? Explain. Would that also be true of *Gutnick*?

2.   In *Gutnick*, Gleesen, C.J. seems to rely principally on the common law of defamation in much the same way as one might judge a local publication arising wholly in Victoria, while Gaudron J., in his concurring opinion gives greater weight to possible international law considerations and development. Would you agree with either or would you have a different approach?

Why? What if Mr. Gutnick should seek to enforce a favorable judgment in the United States? Would the first Amendment present an issue? See *Bachchan v. India Abroad Publications Inc.,* 154 Misc.2d 228, 585 N.Y.S.2d 661 (1991).

3. You have probably noticed that this Internet world is moving rapidly. Since the two cases above were decided, the scope, content and importance of the Internet have enlarged dramatically, and this is expected to continue. Also changing rapidly are the technology for delivering Internet content and the ability of Internet service providers to target particular regions and countries and to block access to Internet material and actions. The range of subjects of controversy has enlarged beyond Internet auctions and defamation problems to include data theft, intellectual property violations, data tampering, file-sharing, online fraud, identity theft, illegal adoptions, gambling, hate speech, domestic political influence, Internet viruses and the like, pornography, privacy invasion, war-like attacks on government functions and Internet disruption, and other illegal or inappropriate actions, The Internet portals thus find themselves making judgments in myriads of cases about the legality, illegality, or appropriateness in those cases, where offending actions are taken on the Internet by others throughout the world with the aid of the portals, but with little if any prior control by them.

4. The Internet is no longer a *sui generis* free world of communication and other actions. The growing appearance of borders along national lines has raised questions of international law of jurisdiction and management by the international community. Some of the jurisdiction issues are seen in the *Yahoo* and *Gutnick* cases, but without full consideration of such practical matters as how to enforce the law if the portal does not maintain assets on the local scene. In *Yahoo,* on account of Yahoos adjustments, the enforcement stage was not formally reached; in *Gutnick,* Dow Jones agreed to pay Mr. Gutnick substantial amounts in settlement.

5. The international policy questions of Internet management have progressed over the years but remain largely unresolved. There is management by the technicians or others privately involved in Internet service provider companies and organizations. There is also the Internet Corporation for Assigned Names and Numbers (known as ICANN), which is a system grounded on the active presence and responsibility of a major government, in this case the United States, with governments participating in an advisory Internet Governance Forum (IGF) convened by the U.N. Secretary General, and with the private sector carrying the main operational burden. Another possibility would turn responsibility over to an intergovernmental organization which would be established under a treaty with legally binding rules and which would be dominated by the member governments. Building on the work of intergovernmental organizations already active in this field, the new organization would enable governments, when necessary to organize the system, set policies and rules and make the decisions.

6. The record of intergovernmental organizations in this sector has been a mixed one to date, as seen in the following examples. The Council of

Europe adopted in 2001 the Convention on Cybercrime (www.coe.org), the first of its kind, "to pursue a common criminal policy aimed at the protection of society against cybercrime, especially by adopting appropriate legislation and fostering international co-operation." This Convention in 2009 had been ratified by 23 parties (22 Council of Europe Member States and the United States). In the international trade field, the World Trade Organization Appellate Body has ruled on U.S. anti-web gambling legislation (www.wto.org/), and favorably so in part. In 1995 the European Parliament and the EU Council adopted Directive 95/46/EC on the protection and free movement of individuals' personal data. Considered in the aggregate, the role of international organizations has been productive but limited in its scope and function.

7.   For further information on Internet governance, consult Jeffrey Rosen, *Google's Gatekeepers*, New York Times Magazine, November 28, 2008, p. 50, nytimes.com; *Marching off to Cyberwar*, The Economist Technology Quarterly, December 6, 2008, p. 20; and Jack Goldsmith and Tim Wu, Who Controls the Internet?, Illusions of a Borderless World (2008).

2.   Nationality: Active and Passive

The active personality principle provides jurisdiction over a *state's* nationals. The passive personality principle provides jurisdiction over those who *injure* a state's nationals. Ascribed nationality is where a state's nationality is ascribed to a legal person such as a corporation, a ship or an aircraft. The basis for extending nationality to natural and legal persons is discussed in Chapter 3. These principles emphasize the role of the state's duty to protect its sovereignty, dignity and security, which are infringed when a national commits a crime or is the victim of a crime. Indeed, sovereignty is considered to a degree to be based on a state's ability to control and protect its nationals.

a.   ACTIVE PERSONALITY

The nationality principle stems from the Roman Law that a citizen carried his law on his back. For many *"Civil Law"* nations this is a very important, almost sacrosanct (often constitutional), basis of jurisdiction which permits a state to prescribe rules of conduct for nationals even when they are outside its territory. On the French approach, for example, see Dominique Carreau, *Droit International*, para. 883 (2007). The rationale is that national sovereign pride and honor are tainted when a national commits an offense abroad. It is considered necessary that the state have authority to control its nationals to ensure that its laws, policy, reputation, and sovereignty are respected. Another aspect of this principle is that it assumes that the national's own system of justice is the more appropriate and fair one to apply to nationals. Thus, they refuse to extradite them. *See generally*, Michael Plachta, *(Non)–Extradition of Nationals: A Neverending Story?*, 13 Emory Intl L.Rev. 77 (1999). Although the application and use of nationality jurisdiction is not as pronounced in Anglo–American systems as it is on the Continent or in Latin America, it is not uncommon. Unlike most European and Latin American counterparts, however, the U.S. does not refuse to extradite its nationals.

United States v. Clark

United States Court of Appeals, Ninth Circuit
435 F.3d 1100 (2006)

■ McKEOWN, CIRCUIT JUDGE.

* * * At issue is whether Congress exceeded its authority to regulate Commerce with foreign Nations, U.S. Const. art. I, § 8, cl. 3, in enacting a statute that makes it a felony for any U.S. citizen who travels in "foreign commerce," i.e. to a foreign country, to then engage in an illegal commercial sex act with a minor. 18 U.S.C. § 2423(c). We hold that Congress acted within the bounds of its constitutional authority.

* * * Clark was indicted under the provisions of the newly-enacted Prosecutorial Remedies and Other Tools to End the Exploitation of Children Today Act of 2003 ("PROTECT Act"), Pub.L. No. 108–21, 117 Stat. 650 (2003). He pled guilty to two counts under 18 U.S.C. § 2423(c) and (e) but reserved the right to appeal his pre-trial motion to dismiss based on constitutional, jurisdictional, and statutory construction grounds. *See United States v. Clark,* 315 F.Supp.2d 1127 (W.D.Wash.2004) (order denying Clark's motion to dismiss). [Discussion of the constitutional issues omitted]

I.   SECTION 2423(c) COMPORTS WITH THE PRINCIPLES OF INTERNATIONAL LAW

We start with Clark's argument that extraterritorial application of § 2423(c) violates principles of international law. On de novo review, *United States v. Felix–Gutierrez,* 940 F.2d 1200, 1203–04 (9th Cir.1991), we hold that extraterritorial application is proper based on the nationality principle.

The legal presumption that Congress ordinarily intends federal statutes to have only domestic application, *see Small v. United States,* 544 U.S. 385, 125 S.Ct. 1752, 1755, 161 L.Ed.2d 651 (2005), is easily overcome in Clark's case because the text of § 2423(c) is explicit as to its application outside the United States. *See* 18 U.S.C. § 2423(c) (titled "Engaging in illicit sexual conduct in foreign places" and reaching people "who travel[ ] in foreign commerce"); *see also Sale v. Haitian Ctrs. Council, Inc.,* 509 U.S. 155, 176, 113 S.Ct. 2549, 125 L.Ed.2d 128 (1993) (explaining that there must be "affirmative evidence of intended extraterritorial application"). By its terms, the provision is exclusively targeted at extraterritorial conduct.

Having addressed this threshold issue, we ask whether the exercise of extraterritorial jurisdiction in this case comports with principles of international law. *See United States v. Vasquez–Velasco,* 15 F.3d 833, 839 (9th Cir.1994) ("In determining whether a statute applies extraterritorially, we also presume that Congress does not intend to violate principles of international law.") (citing *McCulloch v. Sociedad Nacional de Marineros de Honduras,* 372 U.S. 10, 21–22, 83 S.Ct. 671, 9 L.Ed.2d 547 (1963)); *see also*

United States v. Neil, 312 F.3d 419, 421 (9th Cir.2002). Of the five general principles that permit extraterritorial criminal jurisdiction, the nationality principle most clearly applies to Clark's case. The nationality principle "permits a country to apply its statutes to extraterritorial acts of its own nationals." *United States v. Hill,* 279 F.3d 731, 740 (9th Cir.2002). Jurisdiction based solely on the defendant's status as a U.S. citizen is firmly established by our precedent. *See, e.g., United States v. Walczak,* 783 F.2d 852, 854 (9th Cir.1986) (holding that jurisdiction over a U.S. citizen who violated a federal statute while in Canada was proper under the nationality principle); *McKeel v. Islamic Repub. of Iran,* 722 F.2d 582, 588 (9th Cir.1983) (noting that nationality principle permits states to punish the wrongful conduct of its citizens); *United States v. King,* 552 F.2d 833, 851 (9th Cir.1976) (commenting that nationality principle would apply to U.S. citizen defendants). Clark's U.S. citizenship is uncontested. Accordingly, extraterritorial application of § 2423(c) to Clark's conduct is proper based on the nationality principle.

Clark also seeks to invalidate the statute because, in his view, extraterritorial application is unreasonable. *See* Restatement (Third) of Foreign Relations Law of the United States § 403 (1987); *Vasquez–Velasco,* 15 F.3d at 840–41 (holding that extraterritorial application of U.S. statute to violent crimes associated with drug trafficking was reasonable under international law). The record provides no support for this argument. Clark cites no precedent in which extraterritorial application was found unreasonable in a similar situation. Cambodia consented to the United States taking jurisdiction and nothing suggests that Cambodia objected in any way to Clark's extradition and trial under U.S. law. Clark himself stated to a U.S. official in Cambodia that he "wanted to return to the United States" because he saw people dying in the Cambodian prison "and was very much afraid that if [he] stayed in that prison, [he] would not survive." Having been saved from immediate prosecution in Cambodia, it is somewhat ironic that he now challenges the law in a United States court.

* * *

AFFIRMED.

b. PASSIVE PERSONALITY

The Cutting Case Letter, Secretary of State to United States Ambassador to Mexico

Foreign Relations of the United States 751 (1888)
Department of State, Washington, November 1, 1887

SIR: On the 19th of July 1886, the minister of the United States at the City of Mexico was instructed to demand ... the Mexican Government [to] release ... A.K. Cutting, a [U.S.] citizen ..., then imprisoned at Paso del Norte since, on a charge of libel alleged to have been published by him in Texas.

The case was first brought to the notice of the Department by Mr. Brigham, consul of the United States at Paso del Norte, who ... reported that Mr. Cutting had been arrested and imprisoned ... for the publication in Texas ... of an alleged libel against a citizen of Mexico * * *

* * * It is sufficient here to state, ... that the ground upon which Mr. Cutting's release was demanded was that the judicial tribunals of Mexico were not competent under the rules of international law to try a [U.S.] citizen ... for an offense committed and consummated in his own country, merely because the person offended happened to be a Mexican. * * *

* * * Not only was this claim, which is defined in Article 186 of the Mexican penal code, defended and enforced by [Trial] Judge Zubia, ... whose decision was affirmed by the supreme court of Chihuahua * * *, but the claim was defended and justified by the Mexican Government. * * *

But, however this may be, this Government is still compelled to deny what it denied on the 19th of July, 1886, and what the Mexican Government has since executively and judicially maintained, that a citizen of the United States can be held under the rules of international law to answer in Mexico for an offense committed in the United States, simply because the object of that offense happens to be a citizen of Mexico. * * *

* * *

As to the question of international law, I am unable to discover any principle upon which the assumption of jurisdiction made in Article 186 of the Mexican penal code can be justified. There is no principle better settled than that the penal laws of a country have no extraterritorial force. Each state may, it is true, provide for the punishment of its own citizens for acts committed by them outside of its territory; but this makes the penal law a personal statute, and while it may give rise to inconvenience and injustice in many cases, it is a matter in which no other Government has the right to interfere. To say, however, that the penal laws of a country can bind foreigners and regulate their conduct, either in their own or any other foreign country, is to assert a jurisdiction over such countries and to impair their independence. Such is the consensus of opinion of the leading authorities on international law at the present day * * *. There being then no principle of international law which justifies such a pretension, any assertion of it must rest, as an exception to the rule, either upon the general concurrence of nations or upon express conventions. Such a concurrence in respect to the claim made in Article 186 of the Mexican penal code can not be found in the legislation of the present day. Though formerly asserted by a number of minor states, it has now been generally abandoned, and may be regarded as almost obsolete.

* * *

It has constantly been laid down in the United States as a rule of action, that citizens of the United States cannot be held answerable in foreign countries for offenses which were wholly committed and consummated either in their own country or in other countries not subject to the jurisdiction of the punishing state. When a citizen of the United States commits in his own country a violation of its laws, it is his right to be tried under and in accordance with those laws, and in accordance with the fundamental guaranties of the Federal Constitution in respect to criminal trials in every part of the United States.

To say that he may be tried in another country for his offense, simply because its object happens to be a citizen of that country, would be to assert that foreigners coming to the United States bring hither the penal laws of the country from which they come, and thus subject citizens of the United States in their own country to an indefinite criminal responsibility. Such a pretension can never be admitted. * * *

* * *

You are therefore instructed to say to the Mexican Government, not only that an indemnity should be paid to Mr. Cutting for his arrest and detention in Mexico on the charge of publishing a libel in the United States against a Mexican, but also, in the interests of good neighborhood and future amity, that the statute proposing to confer such extraterritorial jurisdiction should, as containing a claim invasive of the independent sovereignty of a neighboring and friendly state, be repealed. * * *

* * *

T.F. BAYARD.

United States v. Yunis

United States Court of Appeals, District of Columbia Circuit
924 F.2d 1086 (1991)

■ MIKVA, CHIEF JUDGE:

I. Background

On June 11, 1985, appellant and four other men boarded Royal Jordanian Airlines Flight 402 ("Flight 402") shortly before its scheduled departure from Beirut, Lebanon. They wore civilian clothes and carried military assault rifles, ammunition bandoleers, and hand grenades. Appellant took control of the cockpit and forced the pilot to take off immediately. The remaining hijackers tied up Jordanian air marshals assigned to the flight and held the civilian passengers, including two American citizens, captive in their seats. The hijackers explained to the crew and passengers that they wanted the plane to fly to Tunis, where a conference of the Arab League was under way. The hijackers further explained that they wanted a meeting with delegates to the conference and that their ultimate goal was removal of all Palestinians from Lebanon.

* * *

An American investigation identified Yunis as the probable leader of the hijackers and prompted U.S. civilian and military agencies, led by the Federal Bureau of Investigation (FBI), to plan Yunis' arrest. After obtaining an arrest warrant, the FBI put "Operation Goldenrod" into effect in

September 1987. Undercover FBI agents lured Yunis onto a yacht in the eastern Mediterranean Sea with promises of a drug deal, and arrested him once the vessel entered international waters. The agents transferred Yunis to a United States Navy munitions ship and interrogated him for several days as the vessel steamed toward a second rendezvous, this time with a Navy aircraft carrier. Yunis was flown to Andrews Air Force Base from the aircraft carrier, and taken from there to Washington, D.C. In Washington, Yunis was arraigned on an original indictment charging him with conspiracy, hostage taking, and aircraft damage. A grand jury subsequently returned a superseding indictment adding additional aircraft damage counts and a charge of air piracy.

* * *

A.   Jurisdictional Claims

Yunis appeals first of all from the district court's denial of his motion to dismiss for lack of subject matter and personal jurisdiction. *See United States v. Yunis,* 681 F.Supp. 896 (D.D.C.1988). Appellant's principal claim is that, as a matter of domestic law, the federal hostage taking and air piracy statutes do not authorize assertion of federal jurisdiction over him. Yunis also suggests that a contrary construction of these statutes would conflict with established principles of international law, and so should be avoided by this court. * * *

* * *

Appellant's argument that we should read the Hostage Taking Act * * * to avoid tension with international law falls flat. Yunis points to no treaty obligations of the United States that give us pause. Indeed, Congress intended through the Hostage Taking Act to execute the International Convention Against the Taking of Hostages, which authorizes any signatory state to exercise jurisdiction over persons who take its nationals hostage "if that State considers it appropriate." International Convention Against the Taking of Hostages, *opened for signature* Dec. 18, 1979, art. 5, para. 1, 34 U.N. GAOR Supp. (No. 39), 18 I.L.M. 1456, 1458. *See* H.R. CONF. REP. No. 1159, 98th Cong., 2d Sess. * * * 134, 418 (1984), *reprinted in* 1984 U.S.Code Cong. & Admin.News 3182, 3710, 3714.

Nor is jurisdiction precluded by norms of customary international law. The district court concluded that two jurisdictional theories of international law, the "universal principle" and the "passive personal principle," supported assertion of U.S. jurisdiction to prosecute Yunis on hijacking and hostage-taking charges. *See Yunis,* 681 F.Supp. at 899–903. * * * Under the passive personal principle, a state may punish non-nationals for crimes committed against its nationals outside of its territory, at least where the state has a particularly strong interest in the crime. *See id.* at § 402 comment g; *United States v. Benitez,* 741 F.2d 1312, 1316 (11th Cir.1984) (passive personal principle invoked to approve prosecution of Colombian citizen convicted of shooting U.S. drug agents in Colombia), *cert. denied,* 471 U.S. 1137, 105 S.Ct. 2679, 86 L.Ed.2d 698 (1985).

Relying primarily on the Restatement, Yunis argues that hostage taking has not been recognized as a universal crime and that the passive personal principle authorizes assertion of jurisdiction over alleged hostage takers only where the victims were seized because they were nationals of the prosecuting state. Whatever merit appellant's claims may have as a matter of international law, they cannot prevail before this court. Yunis seeks to portray international law as a self-executing code that trumps domestic law whenever the two conflict. That effort misconceives the role of judges as appliers of international law and as participants in the federal system. Our duty is to enforce the Constitution, laws, and treaties of the United States, not to conform the law of the land to norms of customary international law. *See* U.S. CONST. art. VI. As we said in *Committee of U.S. Citizens Living in Nicaragua v. Reagan,* 859 F.2d 929 (D.C.Cir.1988): "Statutes inconsistent with principles of customary international law may well lead to international law violations. But within the domestic legal realm, that inconsistent statute simply modifies or supersedes customary international law to the extent of the inconsistency." *Id.* at 938. *See also Federal Trade Comm'n v. Compagnie de Saint–Gobain–Pont–a–Mousson,* 636 F.2d 1300, 1323 (D.C.Cir.1980) (U.S. courts "obligated to give effect to an unambiguous exercise by Congress of its jurisdiction to prescribe even if such an exercise would exceed the limitations imposed by international law").

To be sure, courts should hesitate to give penal statutes extraterritorial effect absent a clear congressional directive. *See Foley Bros. v. Filardo,* 336 U.S. 281, 285, 69 S.Ct. 575, 577, 93 L.Ed. 680 (1949); *United States v. Bowman,* 260 U.S. 94, 98, 43 S.Ct. 39, 41, 67 L.Ed. 149 (1922). Similarly, courts will not blind themselves to potential violations of international law where legislative intent is ambiguous. *See Murray v. The Schooner Charming Betsy,* 6 U.S. (2 Cranch) 64, 118, 2 L.Ed. 208 (1804) ("[A]n act of congress ought never to be construed to violate the law of nations, if any other possible construction remains...."). But the statute in question reflects an unmistakable congressional intent, consistent with treaty obligations of the United States, to authorize prosecution of those who take Americans hostage abroad no matter where the offense occurs or where the offender is found. Our inquiry can go no further.

* * *

NOTES AND QUESTIONS

1. The passive personality theory has traditionally been anathema to U.S. law and practice. Its rationale is that, because criminal law has as its essential object to protect public and private interests (the private ones implicating the public), the victim's national system has the better appreciation of what protection should be afforded. But the passive theory raises questions of fairness, since jurisdiction and levels of penalties may vary from state to state depending on the nationality of the victim, without reference to the place where the offense occurs. While the offender could reasonably be deemed to foresee penalties at the place of the offense, the

offender might not know the nationality of the victims, much less the law of the victims' countries.

2. In the *Lotus case, supra*, France argued before the Permanent Court of International Justice that "international law does not allow a State to [proceed against] offences committed by foreigners abroad, simply by reason of the nationality of the victim," but the court did not reach a clear decision on that precise issue. If the issue should appear now before the ICJ on facts like those in *Lotus*, how do you think the Court should decide the issue? Why? What if the issue arose in a land based terrorist attack?

3. In *Dresser Industries and the Siberian Pipeline,* 549 F.Supp. 108 (D.D.C.1982), a U.S. federal court approved, in 1982, a Commerce Department plan to penalize *Dresser Industries,* a U.S. Company, for supplying equipment to the Siberian pipeline in defiance of Reagan Administration sanctions (*Export Administration Act of 1979*). *Dresser France*, a wholly owned French subsidiary operating in France, was required by French law to supply the equipment. *Dresser France* argued that complying with the U.S. order would subject it to penalties in France. Dresser U.S. had refused to order its French subsidiary to defy a French Government order to deliver. The press reported that both companies could face criminal sanctions in the U.S. and that *Dresser France* would be placed on a "denial list," which would prevent it from having any commercial dealings with the U.S. Does the U.S. or the French government have the right to control the conduct of Dresser France? Was it appropriate for the U.S. Government to sanction a wholly owned foreign subsidiary of a U.S. company for complying with its own government's orders? The U.S. Department of Justice refused to concede that the French order was "valid under French law." European Governments registered protests against such expansive extraterritorial jurisdiction. Do you agree with the Justice Department official, who argued that France could not validly exercise jurisdiction over Dresser France? Does the U.S. have authority under U.S. law to order Dresser France not to ship the equipment, or to punish them for doing so? Under international law? If the answer differs in each, which is the better rule? Compare the ease by which the EU Court of Justice pierced the corporate veil of subsidiaries of the *Woodpulp* cartel members in determining its EC competition jurisdiction, discussed above in Section 2.a.

4. See U.S. legislation on nationality and terrorism reproduced in the document supplement.

3. THE PROTECTIVE PRINCIPLE: EXTRATERRITORIAL CONDUCT AFFECTING IMPORTANT STATE INTERESTS

United States v. Pizzarusso

United States Court of Appeals, Second Circuit
388 F.2d 8 (1968)

■ MEDINA, CIRCUIT JUDGE. This case ... brings before this Court for the first time the question of the jurisdiction of the District Court to indict and convict a foreign citizen of the crime of knowingly making a false statement under oath in a visa application to an American consular official located in a foreign country, in violation of 18 U.S.C. Section 1546 [on fraud, misuse of visas, permits, and other entry documents]. Supreme Court cases give some guidance but none of them passes on this question directly.

The indictment charges that Pizzarusso wilfully made under oath a number of false statements in her "Application for Immigrant Visa And Alien Registration" at the American Consulate, Montreal, Canada. * * * Although at all times pertinent to this case she was a citizen of Canada, she was taken into custody in the Southern District of New York. * * *

Upon the issuance of the visa and by its use Mrs. Pizzarusso immediately entered [U.S. territory], but this fact is not [relevant or] . . . material, as we find the crime was complete when the false statements were made to an American consular official in Montreal. * * *

The evidence to sustain the charge is so overwhelming that we shall not pause to discuss it. Indeed, the only contention made on this appeal is that the District Court lacked jurisdiction to indict appellant and convict her of the crime alleged. As we find no lack of jurisdiction, we affirm the judgment. Our reasons follow.

* * *

International law has recognized, in varying degrees, five bases of jurisdiction with respect to the enforcement of the criminal law. * * * Thus both the territoriality and nationality principles, under which jurisdiction is determined by either the situs of the crime or the nationality of the accused, are universally accepted. The third basis, the protective principle, covers the instant case. By virtue of this theory a state "has jurisdiction to prescribe a rule of law attaching legal consequences to conduct outside its territory that threatens its security as a state or the operation of its governmental functions, provided the conduct is generally recognized as a crime under the law of states that have reasonably developed legal systems" Restatement (Second), Foreign Relations, Section 33 (1965). See also Harvard Research Section 7.

Traditionally, the United States has relied primarily upon the territoriality and nationality principles, * * * and judges have often been reluctant to ascribe extraterritorial effect to statutes. * * * Our courts have developed what has come to be termed the objective territorial principle as a means of expanding the power to control activities detrimental to the state. This principle has been aptly defined by Mr. Justice Holmes in Strassheim v. Daily. "Acts done outside a jurisdiction, but intended to produce and producing detrimental effects within it, justify a state in punishing the cause of the harm as if he had been present at the effect * * *." * * * Underlying this principle is the theory that the "detrimental effects" constitute an element of the offense and since they occur within the country, jurisdiction is properly invoked under the territorial principle. * * *

However, the objective territorial principle is quite distinct from the protective theory. Under the latter, all the elements of the crime occur in the foreign country and jurisdiction exists because these actions have a "potentially adverse effect" upon security or governmental functions, and there need not be any actual effect in the country as would be required under the objective territorial principle. Courts have often failed to perceive this distinction. * * * A violation of 18 U.S.C.A. Section 1546 is complete at the time the alien perjures himself in the foreign country. It may be possible that the particular criminal sanctions of Section 1546 will never be enforced unless the defendant enters the country, but entry is not an element of the statutory offense. Were the statute re-drafted and entry made a part of the crime we would then be presented with a clear case of jurisdiction under the objective territorial principle.

Affirmed.

4. UNIVERSAL JURISDICTION

Regina v. Bartle and the Commissioner of Police for the Metropolis and Others Ex Parte Pinochet

United Kingdom, House of Lords, 24 March 1999
Pinochet III, [1999] 2 All ER 97, 170, 2 WLR 827, 38 I.L.M.581, 644 (1999)

■ LORD MILLETT

* * * In my opinion, crimes prohibited by international law attract universal jurisdiction under customary international law if two criteria are satisfied. First, they must be contrary to a peremptory norm of international law so as to infringe a jus cogens. Secondly, they must be so serious and on such a scale that they can justly be regarded as an attack on the international legal order. Isolated offences, even if committed by public officials, would not satisfy these criteria. The first criterion is well attested in the authorities and text books: for a recent example, see the judgment of the international tribunal for the territory of the former Yugoslavia in *Prosecutor v. Anto Furundzija* given on 10 December 1998, where the court stated:

> "at the individual level, that is, of criminal liability, it would seem that one of the consequences of the jus cogens character bestowed by the international community upon the prohibition of torture is that every state is entitled to investigate, prosecute, and punish or extradite individuals accused of torture who are present in a territory under its jurisdiction."

The second requirement is implicit in the original restriction to war crimes and crimes against peace, the reasoning of the court in *Eichmann,* and the definitions used in the more recent Conventions establishing ad hoc international tribunals for the former Yugoslavia and Rwanda.

Every state has jurisdiction under customary international law to exercise extra-territorial jurisdiction in respect of international crimes which satisfy the relevant criteria. Whether its courts have extra-territorial jurisdiction under its internal domestic law depends, of course, on its constitutional arrangements and the relationship between customary international law and the jurisdiction of its criminal courts. The jurisdiction of the English criminal courts is usually statutory, but it is supplemented by the common law. Customary international law is part of the common law, and accordingly I consider that the English courts have and always have had extra-territorial criminal jurisdiction in respect of crimes of universal jurisdiction under customary international law.

* * *

In my opinion, the systematic use of torture on a large scale and as an instrument of state policy had joined piracy, war crimes and crimes against peace as an international crime of universal jurisdiction * * * I would hold that the courts of this country already possessed extra-territorial jurisdiction in respect of torture and conspiracy to torture on the scale of the charges in the present case and did not require the authority of statute to exercise it. I understand, however, that your Lordships take a different view, and consider that statutory authority is required before our courts can exercise extra-territorial criminal jurisdiction even in respect of crimes of universal jurisdiction. Such authority was conferred for the first time by section 134 of the Criminal Justice Act 1988, but the section was not retrospective. I shall accordingly proceed to consider the case on the footing that Senator Pinochet cannot be extradited for any acts of torture committed prior to the coming into force of the section.

The Torture Convention did not create a new international crime. But it redefined it. Whereas the international community had condemned the widespread and systematic use of torture as an instrument of state policy, the Convention extended the offence to cover isolated and individual instances of torture provided that they were committed by a public official. I do not consider that offences of this kind were previously regarded as international crimes attracting universal jurisdiction. The charges against Senator Pinochet, however, are plainly of the requisite character. The Convention thus affirmed and extended an existing international crime and imposed obligations on the parties to the Convention to take measures to prevent it and to punish those guilty of it. As Burgers and Danielus[*] explained, its main purpose was to introduce an institutional mechanism to enable this to be achieved. Whereas previously states were entitled to take jurisdiction in respect of the offence wherever it was committed, they were now placed under an obligation to do so. Any state party in whose territory a person alleged to have committed the offence was found was bound to offer to extradite him or to initiate proceedings to prosecute him. * * *

United States v. Yousef

United States Court of Appeals, Second Circuit
327 F.3d 56 (2003)

[In this airline bombing case, Ramzi Yousef, a non-U.S citizen or resident, developed with others an elaborate plan to bomb a dozen U.S. flag

---

[*] *See* J. HERMAN BURGERS AND HANS DANIELUS, HANDBOOK ON THE CONVENTION ON TORTURE (1988).

airliners. Most of these aircraft were bound from South Eastern Asia locations for U.S. destinations. The bombs were to be placed aboard the aircraft en route. Yousef took various preparatory actions outside of the U.S. but before the plan itself could be carried out, Yousef was arrested in Pakistan, delivered to FBI agents, and transported to the United States where he was tried and convicted of various crimes relating to conspiracy to bomb United States airliners in Southeast Asia and of other offenses.]

■ Before: WALKER, CHIEF JUDGE, WINTER and CABRANES, CIRCUIT JUDGES.

In Count Nineteen, Yousef alone was charged with violating 18 U.S.C. § 32(b)(3) for placing a bomb on a civil aircraft registered in another country. Specifically, Yousef was charged with planting a bomb on board a Philippine Airlines flight traveling from the Philippines to Japan on December 11, 1994. The aircraft was a civil aircraft registered in the Philippines.

There is no dispute that Congress intended § 32(b) to apply to attacks on non-United States-flag aircraft. The statute applies expressly to placing a bomb on aircraft registered in other countries while in flight, no matter where the attack is committed, and provides for jurisdiction over such extraterritorial crimes whenever, *inter alia,* "an offender is afterwards found in the United States." 18 U.S.C. § 32(b).

* * *

iii. The Universality Principle Provides for Jurisdiction over Only a Limited Set of Acts Violating the Law of Nations

The District Court erred in holding that the universality principle provides a basis for jurisdiction over Yousef for the acts charged in Count Nineteen because the universality principle permits jurisdiction over only a limited set of crimes that cannot be expanded judicially, as discussed in full below. The District Court's reliance on the qualified language in *Yunis* that aircraft-related crime *"may well be"* one of the few crimes supporting universal jurisdiction, *Yousef,* 927 F.Supp. at 681 (quoting *Yunis,* 924 F.2d at 1092) (emphasis added), is facially at odds with this requirement because such language reflects that these crimes are not unequivocally condemned by all States.

* * *

The universality principle permits a State to prosecute an offender of any nationality for an offense committed outside of that State and without contacts to that State, but only for the few, near-unique offenses uniformly recognized by the "civilized nations" as an offense against the "Law of Nations." The strictly limited set of crimes subject to universal jurisdiction cannot be expanded by drawing an analogy between some new crime such as placing a bomb on board an airplane and universal jurisdiction's traditional subjects. Nor, as discussed above in our consideration of the use of sources in international law, can universal jurisdiction be created by reliance on treatises or other scholarly works consisting of aspirational propositions that are not themselves good evidence of customary international law, much less primary sources of customary international law. *See Yousef,* 927 F.Supp. at 681.

* * *

The class of crimes subject to universal jurisdiction traditionally included only piracy. * * * In modern times, the class of crimes over which States can exercise universal jurisdiction has been extended to include war crimes and acts identified after the Second World War as "crimes against humanity." *See, e.g., Demjanjuk v. Petrovsky,* 776 F.2d 571, 582–83 (6th Cir.1985), *vacated on other grounds,* 10 F.3d 338 (6th Cir.1993).

* * *

Universal jurisdiction over violations of the laws of war was not suggested until the Second World War. *See* Theodor Meron, *International Criminalization of Internal Atrocities,* 89 Am. J. Int'l L. 554, 572 (1995) (citing Hersch Lauterpacht, *The Law of Nations and the Punishment of War Crimes,* 2 Brit. Y.B. Int'l L. 58, 65 (1944), as the first to propose universal jurisdiction over war criminals). Following the Second World War, the United States and other nations recognized "war crimes" and "crimes against humanity," including "genocide as crimes for which international law permits the exercise of universal jurisdiction." *Demjanjuk,* 776 F.2d at 582.

A commentator of the time explained that war crimes are "similar to piratical acts" because "[i]n both situations there is . . . a lack of any adequate judicial system operating on the spot where the crime takes place—in the case of piracy it is because the acts are on the high seas and in the case of war crimes because of a chaotic condition or irresponsible leadership in time of war." Willard B. Cowles, *Universality of Jurisdiction Over War Crimes,* 33 Cal. L. Rev. 177, 194 (1945).

The historical restriction of universal jurisdiction to piracy, war crimes, and crimes against humanity demonstrates that universal jurisdiction arises under customary international law only where crimes (1) are universally condemned by the community of nations, and (2) by their nature occur either outside of a State or where there is no State capable of punishing, or competent to punish, the crime (as in a time of war).

Unlike those offenses supporting universal jurisdiction under customary international law—that is, piracy, war crimes, and crimes against humanity—that now have fairly precise definitions and that have achieved universal condemnation, "terrorism" is a term as loosely deployed as it is powerfully charged * * *

We regrettably are no closer now * * * to an international consensus on the definition of terrorism or even its proscription. The mere existence of the phrase "state-sponsored terrorism" proves the absence of agreement on basic terms among a large number of States that terrorism violates public international law. Moreover, there continues to be strenuous disagreement among States about what actions do or do not constitute terrorism, nor have we shaken ourselves free of the cliché that "one man's terrorist is another man's freedom fighter." We thus conclude that * * *

terrorism—unlike piracy, war crimes, and crimes against humanity—does not provide a basis for universal jurisdiction.

Terrorism is defined variously by the perpetrators' motives, methods, targets, and victims. Motive-based definitions suffer from confusion because of the attempt to carve out an exception for assertedly legitimate armed struggle in pursuit of self-determination. For example, under one of the various United Nations resolutions addressing terrorism, armed and violent acts do not constitute "terrorism" if committed by peoples seeking self-determination in opposition to a violently enforced occupation. *See, e.g.,* Declaration on Principles of International Law Concerning Friendly Relations Among Co-operating States in Accordance with the Charter of the United Nations, Oct. 24, 1970, G.A. Res. 2625, 25 U.N. GAOR Supp. (No. 28) at 21, U.N. Doc. A/8028 (1971), reprinted in 9 I.L.M. 1292 (1970). This attempt to distinguish "terrorists" from "freedom fighters" potentially could legitimate as non-terrorist certain groups nearly universally recognized as terrorist, including the Irish Republican Army, Hezbollah, and Hamas. [citations omitted]

* * *

b. Jurisdiction Is Proper Under United States Laws Giving Effect to Its Obligations Under the Montreal Convention

In Count Nineteen, Yousef was charged with, and convicted of, violating 18 U.S.C. § 32(b)(3). Title 18 U.S.C. § 32 was enacted as part of the Aircraft Sabotage Act of 1984, Pub. L. No. 98–473, 98 Stat. 1837, 2187–88, which, as discussed above, implements the Montreal Convention. Section 32(a) proscribes offenses, and attempts and conspiracies to commit offenses, against United States-flag aircraft; Section 32(b) proscribes the same offenses when committed against the aircraft of all other nations. Absent § 32(b)'s extension of jurisdiction over perpetrators of offenses against non-United States-flag aircraft, the statute would not effectuate the purpose of the Convention—to forbid all States parties to the Convention from affording aircraft terrorists a safe haven by requiring each party to the Convention to extradite offenders to another party State or to prosecute the offender * * *

In sum, even though Yousef's prosecution under Count Nineteen did not comport with the universality principle, jurisdiction was properly predicated on the Montreal Convention and the United States' own statutes giving effect to the Convention.

Deena R. Hurwitz, Universal Jurisdiction and the Dilemmas of International Criminal Justice: The Sabra and Shatila Case in Belgium

HUMAN RIGHTS ADVOCACY STORIES (Deena Hurwitz et al. eds., 2009)

* * *

Universal Jurisdiction in Practice: The Belgian Legal Context.

The government first drafted a bill in 1989 to implement the Geneva Conventions, which it had ratified in 1952. The bill was submitted to Parliament in 1991, and debated while the atrocities in the former Yugoslavia raged. In May 1993, the U.N. Security Council passed a Resolution establishing the International Criminal Tribunal for the Former Yugoslavia, with jurisdiction to prosecute grave breaches of the 1949 Geneva Conventions, violations of the laws or customs of war, genocide, and crimes against humanity. The debates in the Belgian Parliament reflected concern over the grave violations of humanitarian law witnessed in the Iraq–Kuwait war, the former Yugoslavia and Somalia. A Senate proposal to include violations of Protocol II to the Geneva Conventions was easily accepted, criminalizing war crimes and torture. The Act was passed unanimously in June 1993.

Between the passage of the Act in 1993 and its amendment in 1999, nine other European countries passed universal jurisdiction laws. Six completed trials resulted in four convictions and two acquittals.

*   *   *

By 2000, some twenty-four states had universal jurisdiction laws of various form, (including incidentally, Israel), but Belgium's was the most far-reaching. As amended in 1999, the Belgian Law was a model of pure universal jurisdiction, covering genocide, war crimes and crimes against humanity and requiring no nexus whatsoever between the acts, the accused and the state of Belgium. Inspired by the Pinochet ruling in the British House of Lords, the 1999 Law also included the principle that "immunity attaching to the official capacity of a person" should not be a bar to prosecution. Under Belgian law an individual charged with committing such violations of international law could be indicted, investigated, and tried *in absentia*, without ever setting foot on Belgian soil.

*   *   *

[On June 12, 2003], at a press conference following the NATO defense ministers meeting in Brussels, U.S. Defense Secretary Donald Rumsfeld threatened that American officials might stop attending NATO meetings in Belgium "because of a law that allows 'spurious' suits accusing American leaders of war crimes. Rumsfeld said the United States would withhold any further funding for a new NATO headquarters building until the matter is resolved."

Within a month, the Belgian political parties negotiating a new government coalition agreed to withdraw the Law. The final version of the Law adopted August 5, 2003 annulled the 1993/1999 universal jurisdiction statute. As amended, it could more accurately be called an international crimes law, with certain limited possibilities for "universal" extraterritorial jurisdiction. Among its provisions: (1) Belgian authorities have extraterritorial ("universal") jurisdiction over a narrow set of crimes (genocide, crimes against humanity, and war crimes) where required by treaty or customary international law; and (2) the accused or the victim is a Belgian national or resident for at least three years (determined from the date proceedings commence for the defendant, and by the date of the crime for the victim). (3) Where the victim alone has the requisite links to Belgium, only the federal prosecutor may initiate the case, even in *absentia*. He is not required to involve an investigating judge if there was no nexus to Belgium, and his decision may not be appealed. Further, the *constitution partie civile* is eliminated for these crimes. The August 2003 Law further recognized functional immunity for heads of state and incumbent ministers, consistent with the ICJ *Arrest Warrant* judgment. [The full text of the 2003 Belgian law is available at 42 I.L.M. 1258 (2003)].

NOTES AND QUESTIONS

1.   U.S. officials have been under scrutiny since revelations beginning in 2004 of abuse of persons detained after 9/11. Accusations have arisen of torture and secret detention. According to Alan Weiner:

> Finally, apart from the question of state responsibility on the part of the United States, it is possible that individual interrogators or lawyers may be subject to criminal prosecution outside the United States. Torture is an offense subject to universal jurisdiction, and under the Torture Convention, any state party may potentially prosecute acts of torture no matter where they have occurred. A decision not to prosecute in the United States—whether based on the availability of strong defenses under domestic law or on or policy considerations—does not preclude other states from exercising criminal jurisdiction. We have already seen the initiation of a criminal investigation in Spain of six U.S. Government officials—including two OLC lawyers—for torture that allegedly took place at the U.S. military facility at Guantanamo Bay, Cuba. Individuals involved in either the design or execution of the enhanced interrogation program are accordingly vulnerable to arrest and prosecution if they travel outside the United States.

See ASIL Insight, Vol. 13. Issue 6, May 15, 2009, available on the ASIL website.

2.   See also, *Center for Constitutional Rights et al. v. Donald Rumsfeld et al.*, Germany, Federal Court of Justice: Decision of the General Federal Prosecutor, February 10, 2005, 45 I.L.M. 119 (2006). According to Christopher L. Blakesley & Dan E. Stigall:

> Terrorism is quickly becoming a crime of universal jurisdiction. Treaties and domestic criminal laws define "terrorism" to include several separate universally condemned offenses—including abducting people and intentional or wanton violence against innocent civilians. * * *
>
> Recently, many multilateral treaties have condemned various international offenses that could be characterized as terrorism under this broad definition. International conventions proscribing genocide, apartheid, and hostage-taking provide examples of a type of universal jurisdiction established among states-parties that either reflects or has developed into customary international law. For example, the Hague

Convention grants all contracting parties jurisdiction over unlawful seizures of control of aircraft and obligates the party obtaining custody of the alleged hijackers to prosecute or extradite them, and the Montreal Convention extends the Hague Convention to include acts of sabotage. The obligations in these treaties have likely become customary international law, as virtually all nations consider themselves legally obliged to abide by their rules. When this occurs, they become truly universal crimes. * * *

But it is not always easy to determine the point at which customary international law and the application of true universal jurisdiction is created. The International Court of Justice, in the *Arrest Warrant Case (Democratic Republic of The Congo v. Belgium* [separate opinion of Judge Guillaume]) noted that although the "purpose of multilateral treaties is to assure universal punishment of the offences in question by denying perpetrators refuge in all States, it is incorrect to denominate this jurisdiction as true universal jurisdiction." * * * Thus, such multilateral treaties, unless they rest upon customary international law, "oblige contracting States to enact domestic (or 'municipal') laws that proscribe certain conduct." *The Myopia of U.S. v. Martinelli: Extraterritorial Jurisdiction in the 21st Century*, 39 GEO. WASH. INT'L L. REV. 1, 28 (2007).

How do you think the *Yousef* court might consider this issue?

3. Note the following analysis in NAOMI ROHT-ARRIAZA, THE PINOCHET EFFECT: TRANSNATIONAL JUSTICE IN THE AGE OF HUMAN RIGHTS 193–4 (2005):

Territorial and Transnational Prosecutions

The relationship of the transnational forum to the domestic one is complex. First are the concerns, previously mentioned, about unfair trials and double standards between strong and weak countries. More fundamentally, does universal jurisdiction only come into play as a backstop when national courts cannot or will not act? Even if you agree with the general premise that, where possible, domestic courts are better at judging questions of mass crimes on their own territory— they have more knowledge of the situation, access to the evidence, ability to change local perceptions and power balances—that still leaves open the thorny questions of capacity. Everyone agrees that under some circumstances, the local courts cannot do the job, especially where the suspects—are still powerful or the courts compromised. How should one court decide whether another country's judiciary is unable or unwilling to act, or adequately criminalizes the acts and provides due process?

4. Such prosecution in national courts is not the sole legal procedure for bringing to justice persons charged with these serious international crimes. What other procedures might be appropriate? Certainly the International Criminal Court and the ad hoc international criminal tribunals taken up in Chapter 5—would be available in cases falling within their respective jurisdictions. What advantages and disadvantages would you see for each?

Would you consider national or international tribunals to provide the most appropriate procedure? Why?

5. What effect would you expect the availability of these international tribunals (as well as others in the future) to have on the need for universal jurisdiction in the international system? How does the German General Prosecutor's decision mentioned above affect this assessment?

6. Forward looking concluding thoughts on the universal jurisdiction process are stated by Judges Higgins, Kooijmans and Buergenthal in their Joint Separate Opinion paragraph 75 in the I.C.J. *Case Concerning the Arrest Warrant of 11 April 2000,* [2002] ICJ Reports, p. 3; 41 I.L.M. 536 (2002). Speaking of a balance of interests, they said:

> * * * On the one scale, we find the interest of the community of mankind to prevent and stop impunity for perpetrators of grave crimes against its members; on the other, there is the interest of the community of States to allow them to act freely on the inter-State level without unwarranted interference. A balance therefore must be struck between two sets of functions which are both valued by the international community. Reflecting these concerns, what is regarded as a permissible jurisdiction and what is regarded as the law on immunity are in constant evolution. The weights on the two scales are not set for all perpetuity. Moreover, a trend is discernible that in a world which increasingly rejects impunity for the most repugnant offences, the attribution of responsibility and accountability is becoming firmer, the possibility for the assertion of jurisdiction wider and the availability of immunity as a shield more limited. * * *

This case continues below in the discussion of immunity of state officials.

5. ENFORCEMENT

The Eichmann Case in the Security Council and in Israel

Israel charged Adolf Eichmann in the District court with having committed crimes against the Jewish people, crimes against humanity and war crimes in his service as a high-ranking officer in Hitlerian German government, responsible for implementing German policy toward Jews and for coordinating the transport of victims of the Holocaust. Avoiding arrest and prosecution by Allied and German authorities, Eichmann escaped from Germany and established himself secretly in Argentina during the post-World War II period. In May, 1960, Israel obtained physical custody of Eichmann when Israel intelligence agents kidnapped him in Argentina and removed him by force to Israel. This was done without the consent or knowledge of Argentina, which protested vigorously against this violation of Argentine sovereignty and complained to the U.N. Security Council.

On June 23, 1960, the Security Council adopted the following Resolution S/4349, 8 votes to none, with 2 abstentions (Poland and the USSR).

The Security Council,

"*Having examined* the complaint that the transfer of Adolf Eichmann to the territory of Israel constitutes a violation of the sovereignty of the Argentine Republic,

"*Considering* that the violation of the sovereignty of a Member State is incompatible with the Charter of the United Nations,

"*Having regard* to the fact that reciprocal respect for and the mutual protection of the sovereign rights of States are an essential condition for their harmonious coexistence,

"*Noting* that the repetition of acts such as that giving rise to this situation would involve a breach of the principles upon which international order is founded, creating an atmosphere of insecurity and distrust incompatible with the preservation of peace,

"*Mindful* of the universal condemnation of the persecution of the Jews under the Nazis and of the concern of people in all countries that Eichmann should be brought to appropriate justice for the crimes of which he is accused,

"*Noting* at the same time that this resolution should in no way be interpreted as condoning the odious crimes of which Eichmann is accused,

"1. *Declares* that acts such as that under consideration, which affect the sovereignty of a Member State and therefore cause international friction, may, if repeated, endanger international peace and security;

"2. *Requests* the Government of Israel to make appropriate reparation in accordance with the Charter of the United Nations and the rules of international law;

"3. *Expresses* the hope that the traditionally friendly relations between Argentina and Israel will be advanced."

Shortly thereafter the dispute between the two states was settled, but the proceedings against Eichmann continued, resulting in a guilty verdict and a sentence of death. On appeal, the Israeli Supreme Court, noted that it agreed entirely with the reasoning of the District Court, which had stated in paragraph 41 of its Judgment:

'41.   It is an established rule of law that a person being tried for an offence against the laws of a State may not oppose his trial by reason of the illegality of his arrest or of the means whereby he was brought within the jurisdiction of that State. The courts in England, the United States and Israel have constantly held that the circumstances of the arrest and the mode of bringing of the accused into the territory of the State have no relevance to his trial, and they have consistently refused in all instances to enter upon an examination of these circumstances.

The Supreme Court also stated:

Counsel for the appellant also argued that in the Resolution of the United Nations Security Council dated June 23, 1960, the Government of Israel was requested to make appropriate reparation to Argentina for the violation to her sovereignty; hence it may be, inferred that the matter involves a violation of international law and in these circumstances it is not conceivable that the Court should refuse to examine the factual question of whether the Government of Israel was a party to the abduction of the appellant.

We cannot accept this argument * * * it clearly transpires that all that the Security Council sought to do was to help towards a settlement of the dispute which had arisen between the two countries in consequence of Argentina's complaint of the violation of her sovereignty. As the District Court has shown, in so far as there was any such violation by the Government of Israel the appellant cannot benefit by it, and therefore what was said in the resolution regarding the settlement of the dispute between the two countries cannot avail the appellant or accord him any rights, especially as the dispute has meanwhile been settled.

See *Attorney–General (Israel) v. Adolf Eichmann,* Judgment of the District Court, *December 12, 1961,*and the Supreme Court, May 29, 1962, 36 I.L.R. 5, 277.

United States v. Alvarez–Machain

United States Supreme Court
504 U.S. 655, 112 S.Ct. 2188, 119 L.Ed.2d 441 (1992)

■ CHIEF JUSTICE REHNQUIST delivered the opinion of the Court.

The issue in this case is whether a criminal defendant, abducted to the United States from a nation with which it has an extradition treaty, thereby acquires a defense to the jurisdiction of this country's courts. We hold that he does not, and that he may be tried in federal district court for violations of the criminal law of the United States.

Respondent, Humberto Alvarez–Machain, is a citizen and resident of Mexico. He was indicted for participating in the kidnap and murder of United States Drug Enforcement Administration (DEA) special agent Enrique Camarena–Salazar and a Mexican pilot working with Camarena, Alfredo Zavala–Avelar. The DEA believes that respondent, a medical doctor, participated in the murder by prolonging Agent Camarena's life so that others could further torture and interrogate him. On April 2, 1990, respondent was forcibly kidnaped from his medical office in Guadalajara, Mexico, to be flown by private plane to El Paso, Texas, where he was arrested by DEA officials. The District Court concluded that DEA agents were responsible for respondent's abduction, although they were not personally involved in it. *United States v. Caro–Quintero,* 745 F.Supp. 599, 602–604, 609 (CD Cal.1990).

* * *

Respondent moved to dismiss the indictment, claiming that his abduction constituted outrageous governmental conduct, and that the District Court lacked jurisdiction to try him because he was abducted in violation of the extradition treaty between the United States and Mexico. Extradition Treaty, May 4, 1978, [1979] United States–United Mexican States, 31 U.S.T. 5059, T.I.A.S. No. 9656 (Extradition Treaty or Treaty). The District Court rejected the outrageous governmental conduct claim, but held that it lacked jurisdiction to try respondent because his abduction violated the Extradition Treaty. The District Court discharged respondent and ordered that he be repatriated to Mexico. 745 F.Supp., at 614.

* * *

In the instant case, the Court of Appeals affirmed the District Court's finding that the United States had authorized the abduction of respondent, and that letters from the Mexican Government to the United States Government served as an official protest of the Treaty violation. Therefore, the Court of Appeals ordered that the indictment against respondent be dismissed and that respondent be repatriated to Mexico. 946 F.2d, at 1467. We granted certiorari, 502 U.S. 1024, 112 S.Ct. 857, 116 L.Ed.2d 766 (1992), and now reverse.

[Discussion of the extradition treaty issues omitted]

* * *

In *Ker v. Illinois,* 119 U.S. 436, 7 S.Ct. 225, 30 L.Ed. 421 (1886), * * * we addressed the issue of a defendant brought before the court by way of a forcible abduction. Frederick Ker had been tried and convicted in an Illinois court for larceny; his presence before the court was procured by means of forcible abduction from Peru. A messenger was sent to Lima with the proper warrant to demand Ker by virtue of the extradition treaty between Peru and the United States. The messenger, however, disdained reliance on the treaty processes, and instead forcibly kidnaped Ker and brought him to the United States. We distinguished Ker's case from *Rauscher,* on the basis that Ker was not brought into the United States by virtue of the extradition treaty between the United States and Peru, and rejected Ker's argument that he had a right under the extradition treaty to be returned to this country only in accordance with its terms. We rejected Ker's due process argument more broadly, holding in line with "the highest authorities" that "such forcible abduction is no sufficient reason why the party should not answer when brought within the jurisdiction of the court which has the right to try him for such an offence, and presents no valid objection to his trial in such court." *Ker, supra,* at 444, 7 S.Ct., at 229.

* * *

[T]he language of the Treaty, in the context of its history, does not support the proposition that the Treaty prohibits abductions outside of its terms. The remaining question, therefore, is whether the Treaty should be interpreted so as to include an implied term prohibiting prosecution where the defendant's presence is obtained by means other than those established by the Treaty. See *Valentine,* 299 U.S., at 17, 57 S.Ct., at 106 ("Strictly the question is not whether there had been a uniform practical construction denying the power, but whether the power had been so clearly recognized that the grant should be implied").

* * *

Respondent and his *amici* may be correct that respondent's abduction was "shocking," Tr. of Oral Arg. 40, and that it may be in violation of general international law principles. Mexico has protested the abduction of respondent through diplomatic notes, App. 33–38, and the decision of whether respondent should be returned to Mexico, as a matter outside of the Treaty, is a matter for the Executive Branch. We conclude, however, that respondent's abduction was not in violation of the Extradition Treaty between the United States and Mexico, and therefore the rule of *Ker v. Illinois* is fully applicable to this case. The fact of respondent's forcible abduction does not therefore prohibit his trial in a court in the United States for violations of the criminal laws of the United States.

The judgment of the Court of Appeals is therefore reversed, and the case is remanded for further proceedings consistent with this opinion.

So ordered.

■ JUSTICE STEVENS, with whom JUSTICE BLACKMUN and JUSTICE O'CONNOR join, dissenting.

The Court correctly observes that this case raises a question of first impression. * * * The case is unique for several reasons. It does not involve an ordinary abduction by a private kidnaper, or bounty hunter, as in *Ker v. Illinois,* 119 U.S. 436, 7 S.Ct. 225, 30 L.Ed. 421 (1886); nor does it involve the apprehension of an American fugitive who committed a crime in one State and sought asylum in another, as in *Frisbie v. Collins,* 342 U.S. 519, 72 S.Ct. 509, 96 L.Ed. 541 (1952). Rather, it involves this country's abduction of another country's citizen; it also involves a violation of the territorial integrity of that other country, with which this country has signed an extradition treaty.

A Mexican citizen was kidnapped in Mexico and charged with a crime committed in Mexico; his offense allegedly violated both Mexican and American law. Mexico has formally demanded on at least two separate occasions that he be returned to Mexico and has represented that he will be prosecuted and, if convicted, punished for his offense. It is clear that Mexico's demand must be honored if this official abduction violated the 1978 Extradition Treaty between the United States and Mexico. In my opinion, a fair reading of the treaty in light of our decision in *United States v. Rauscher,* 119 U.S. 407, 7 S.Ct. 234, 30 L.Ed. 425 (1886), and applicable principles of international law, leads inexorably to the conclusion that the District Court, *United States v. Caro–Quintero,* 745 F.Supp. 599 (CD Cal.1990), and the Court of Appeals for the Ninth Circuit, 946 F.2d 1466 (1991) (*per curiam*), correctly construed that instrument.

* * *

It is true, as the Court notes, that there is no express promise by either party to refrain from forcible abductions in the territory of the other nation. * * * Relying on that omission, the Court, in effect, concludes that the Treaty merely creates an optional method of obtaining jurisdiction over alleged offenders, and that the parties silently reserved the right to resort to self-help whenever they deem force more expeditious than legal process. If the United States, for example, thought it more expedient to torture or simply to execute a person rather than to attempt extradition, these options would be equally available because they, too, were not explicitly prohibited by the Treaty. That, however, is a highly improbable interpretation of a consensual agreement, which on its face appears to have been intended to set forth comprehensive and exclusive rules concerning the subject of extradition. In my opinion, "the manifest scope and object of the treaty itself," *Rauscher,* 119 U.S., at 422, 7 S.Ct., at 242, plainly imply a mutual undertaking to respect the territorial integrity of the other contracting party. That opinion is confirmed by a consideration of the "legal context" in which the Treaty was negotiated. *Cannon v. University of Chicago,* 441 U.S. 677, 699, 99 S.Ct. 1946, 1958, 60 L.Ed.2d 560 (1979).

* * *

Although the Court's conclusion in *Rauscher* was supported by a number of judicial precedents, the holdings in these cases were not nearly as uniform as the consensus of international opinion that condemns one Nation's violation of the territorial integrity of a friendly neighbor.[4] It is shocking that a party to an extradition treaty might believe that it has secretly reserved the right to make seizures of citizens in the other party's territory.[5] Justice Story found it shocking enough that the United States would attempt to justify an American seizure of a foreign vessel in a Spanish port:

> "But, even supposing, for a moment, that our laws had required an entry of The Apollon, in her transit, does it follow that the power to arrest her was meant to be given, after she had passed into the exclusive territory of a foreign nation? We think not. *It would be monstrous* to suppose that our revenue officers were authorized to

---

4. This principle is embodied in Article 17 of the Charter of the Organization of American States, Apr. 30, 1948, 2 U.S.T. 2394, T.I.A.S. No. 2361, as amended by the Protocol of Buenos Aires, Feb. 27, 1967, 21 U.S.T. 607, T.I.A.S. No. 6847, as well as numerous provisions of the United Nations Charter, June 26, 1945, 59 Stat. 1031, T.S. No. 993 (to which both the United States and Mexico are signatories). See generally Mann, Reflections on the Prosecution of Persons Abducted in Breach of International Law, in International Law at a Time of Perplexity 407 (Y. Dinstein & M. Tabory eds. 1989).

5. When Abraham Sofaer, Legal Adviser of the State Department, was questioned at a congressional hearing, he resisted the notion that such seizures were acceptable: " 'Can you imagine us going into Paris and seizing some person we regard as a terrorist ...? [H]ow would we feel if some foreign nation—let us take the United Kingdom—came over here and seized some terrorist suspect in New York City, or Boston, or Philadelphia, ... because we refused through the normal channels of international, legal communications, to extradite that individual?' " Bill To Authorize Prosecution of Terrorists and Others Who Attack U.S. Government Employees and Citizens Abroad: Hearing before the Subcommittee on Security and Terrorism of the Senate Committee on the Judiciary, 99th Cong., 1st Sess., 63 (1985).

enter into foreign ports and territories, for the purpose of seizing vessels which had offended against our laws. It cannot be presumed that congress would voluntarily justify such a clear violation of the laws of nations." *The Apollon,* 9 Wheat. 362, 370–371, 6 L.Ed. 111 (1824) (emphasis added).[6]

The law of nations, as understood by Justice Story in 1824, has not changed. Thus, a leading treatise explains:

"A State must not perform acts of sovereignty in the territory of another State. It is ... a breach of International Law for a State to send its agents to the territory of another State to apprehend persons accused of having committed a crime. Apart from other satisfaction, the first duty of the offending State is to hand over the person in question to the State in whose territory he was apprehended." 1 Oppenheim's International Law 295, and n. 1 (H. Lauterpacht 8th ed. 1955).[7]

Commenting on the precise issue raised by this case, the chief reporter for the American Law Institute's Restatement of Foreign Relations used language reminiscent of Justice Story's characterization of an official seizure in a foreign jurisdiction as "monstrous":

"When done without consent of the foreign government, abducting a person from a foreign country is a gross violation of international law and gross disrespect for a norm high in the opinion of mankind. It is a blatant violation of the territorial integrity of another state; it eviscerates the extradition system (established by a comprehensive network of treaties involving virtually all states)."

III

A critical flaw pervades the Court's entire opinion. It fails to differentiate between the conduct of private citizens, which does not violate any treaty obligation, and conduct expressly authorized by the Executive Branch of the Government, which unquestionably constitutes a flagrant

---

6. Justice Story's opinion continued: "The arrest of the offending vessel must, therefore, be restrained to places where our jurisdiction is complete, to our own waters, or to the ocean, the common highway of all nations. It is said, that there is a revenue jurisdiction, which is distinct from the ordinary maritime jurisdiction over waters within the range of a common shot from our shores. And the provisions in the Collection Act of 1799, which authorize a visitation of vessels within four leagues of our coasts, are referred to in proof of the assertion. But where is that right of visitation to be exercised? In a foreign territory, in the exclusive jurisdiction of another sovereign? Certainly not; for the very terms of the act confine it to the ocean, where all nations have a common right, and exercise a common sovereignty. And over what vessels is this right of visitation to be exercised? By the very words of the act, over our own vessels, and over foreign vessels bound to our ports, and over no others. To have gone beyond this, would have been an usurpation of exclusive sovereignty on the ocean, and an exercise of an universal right of search, a right which has never yet been acknowledged by other nations, and would be resisted by none with more pertinacity than by the American." *The Apollon,* 9 Wheat., at 371–372.

7. See Restatement § 432, Comment *c* ("If the unauthorized action includes abduction of a person, the state from which the person was abducted may demand return of the person, and international law requires that he be returned").

violation of international law, and in my opinion, also constitutes a breach of our treaty obligations. Thus, at the outset of its opinion, the Court states the issue as "whether a criminal defendant, abducted to the United States from a nation with which it has an extradition treaty, thereby acquires a defense to the jurisdiction of this country's courts." * * * That, of course, is the question decided in *Ker v. Illinois,* 119 U.S. 436, 7 S.Ct. 225, 30 L.Ed. 421 (1886); it is not, however, the question presented for decision today.

* * *

The significance of this Court's precedents is illustrated by a recent decision of the Court of Appeal of the Republic of South Africa. Based largely on its understanding of the import of this Court's cases—including our decision in *Ker*—that court held that the prosecution of a defendant kidnaped by agents of South Africa in another country must be dismissed. *S v. Ebrahim,* S.Afr.L.Rep. (Apr.-June 1991). The Court of Appeal of South Africa—indeed, I suspect most courts throughout the civilized world—will be deeply disturbed by the "monstrous" decision the Court announces today. For every nation that has an interest in preserving the Rule of Law is affected, directly or indirectly, by a decision of this character. As Thomas Paine warned, an "avidity to punish is always dangerous to liberty" because it leads a nation "to stretch, to misinterpret, and to misapply even the best of laws." To counter that tendency, he reminds us:

> "He that would make his own liberty secure must guard even his enemy from oppression; for if he violates this duty he establishes a precedent that will reach to himself."

I respectfully dissent.

NOTES AND QUESTIONS

1. On August 12, 1992, the U.S. Department of Justice issued a memorandum, to all U.S. Attorneys concerning "Extraordinary Renditions and United States v. Alvarez–Machain," requesting that "they inform their staff that the Alvarez–Machain decision does not constitute a 'green light' for unrestricted efforts to secure custody over persons abroad without regard to international extradition treaties, or the laws of foreign states, international law, or coordination with the Department of Justice. It is the policy of the Department that all efforts to secure custody over persons outside the United States through the use of an Alvarez–Machain-type rendition must be approved in advance by the Department of Justice in Washington, where the proposal will be subject to any necessary inter-agency coordination." The Memorandum also requested that they "notice that the policy considerations just discussed also apply to efforts by state and local authorities to secure custody of persons located in foreign countries. Any state or local law enforcement official who participates in the abduction of a person from another country could be charged with kidnapping in that foreign country, and might even face extradition to that country upon its request." 32 I.L.M. 277 (1993).

2.   The Inter–American Juridical Committee adopted an opinion on the "international legality" of the Supreme Court's decision on August 15, 1992, at the request of the Permanent Council of the Organization of American States. The Legal Opinion (CJI/RES.II–15/92) was adopted nine votes in favor, with one abstention. The Committee indicated that "[t]his opinion, as requested, is confined to examining the decision of the United States Supreme Court from the standpoint of its conformity with public international law. The Committee 'considers ... that the abduction in question was a serious violation of [public] * * * international law since it was a transgression of the territorial sovereignty of Mexico.' Reparations should also be made, '[p]ursuant to the rules governing state responsibility in international law', in this case being the repatriation of Alvarez–Machain to Mexico" * * *. 32 I.L.M. 277 (1993).

3.   Following the Supreme Court decision, the *Alvarez–Machain* case went to trial in the District Court which led to a judgment of acquittal. After he was released and returned to Mexico, Alvarez–Machain commenced an action against the United States and others in the District Court seeking damages under the Federal Tort Claims Act and the Alien Torts Statute which was unsuccessful. *See Sosa v. Alvarez–Machain*, 542 U.S. 692, 124 S.Ct. 2739, 159 L.Ed.2d 718 (2004).

4.   The issue of unlawful abduction of the accused in the International Tribunal for the Former Yugolavia arose in *Prosecutor v. Dragan Nikolic* Appeals Chamber, ITCY (June 5, 2003), opinion available at http://www.un.org/icty/nikolic/appeal/decision-e/030605.pdf. Indicted for crimes against humanity and war crimes, the accused alleged that he was unlawfully abducted from Serbia and Montenegro to Bosnia and Herzegovina, a violation of sovereignty. He attributed responsibility for the abduction to the SFOR (the NATO led inter-governmental Stabilization Force) or to the OTP (Office of the Prosecutor of the Tribunal) for complicity, which should lead the Tribunal to set aside jurisdiction.

   The Tribunal found that precedents from national courts in France, Germany, Israel, South Africa, the United Kingdom and the United States were divided on the jurisdiction issue. However, of genocide, crimes against humanity and war crimes, because of their special character and seriousness, seemed to present a good reason for not setting aside jurisdiction. The Tribunal also found it easier for courts to assert their jurisdiction in the absence of complaint by the state whose sovereignty has been breached or where there is a diplomatic resolution between the states involved. Moreover, accountability for these crimes is "a necessary condition for the achievement of international justice", and that feature outweighs the damage to sovereignty of the state where the abduction took place, especially where there has been no complaint and the state has acquiesced in the Tribunal's jurisdiction. While human rights concerns might lead to a different outcome in cases where the accused is very seriously mistreated, maybe even subject to inhuman, cruel or degrading treatment or torture, the Appeals Chamber concluded that in this case there was no basis for declining jurisdiction.

5.   Professor Ian Brownlie summarizes broadly the public international law on the illegal seizure jurisdiction issue as follows:

> "While international responsibility may arise as a consequence of the illegal seizure of offenders, the violation of the law does not affect the validity of the subsequent exercise of jurisdiction over them". Ian Brownlie, *Principles of Public International Law* 7th Ed., 318 (2008).

Do you agree with that summary? Certainly the *Eichmann*, and *Alvarez–Machain* outcomes tend to support Brownlie. But do you see any reasons for a more cautious or nuanced legal judgement? For example, the Security Council resolution reproduced in the *Eichmann* opinion touches a number of issues. Does the Council assume that the kidnapping of Eichmann was a violation of international law? If so, what was the basis of the Council's own jurisdiction to make such a determination? What weight should be given to it? Why do you think the Council was silent on the issue of repatriation of Eichmann? In *Alvarez–Machain* the majority (6–3) adopts and applies the international rule of illegality of the violation of Mexican sovereignty. Should the majority opinion have weight as a precedent? What weight if any should be assigned to the minority opinion? In *Nikolic,* Judge Meron recognized the divided case law in national courts and retained jurisdiction because of the high value of the humanitarian law in that case, but might set jurisdiction aside in cases of serious human rights violations at the outset by public authorities in making the illegal seizure. Do these considerations suggest to you that Professor Brownlie's summary legal statement might be developed further? If so, how would you formulate it?

6.   How would you relate the issue in the *Hape* case at the beginning of this chapter with the *Alvarez–Machain* case above?

B.   Sovereign Immunity

In addition to the jurisdiction questions developed in Section A above, judicial proceedings involving a foreign state, government entity, or public official defendant, may present issues about entitlement of these parties to claim sovereign immunity in the forum state.

The venerable doctrines of foreign sovereign immunities are a product of constant evolution in customary international law, adjusted by twentieth century legislation, judicial decisions, and by the treaty process of codification. This section examines that process with respect to "state immunity" (also called "sovereign immunity") for states and state officials. Section C takes up the related topics of diplomatic and consular privileges and immunities as well as the privileges and immunities of international organizations, their property and persons connected with them.

As will be seen, the concrete international legal rules on jurisdictional immunity are still not wholly free from uncertainty and dispute, despite several centuries of judicial, legislative and diplomatic efforts to clarify and to unify them. The practice of states is now widespread and abundant, as seen in the International Law Commission background documents for the

United Nations Convention on Jurisdictional Immunities of States and Their Property (www.un.ilc.org), and in the Council of Europe's *State Practice Regarding State Immunities* (2006).

State immunities seek to shield a foreign sovereign from the exercise of jurisdiction, principally from the jurisdiction of foreign states' courts in cases where the sovereign has not given consent. Sovereign immunities serve the purposes of allowing a state to act in its best interest without fear that its actions will be disrupted by adjudication in another state, and also to ensure that the public property of the state remains available for public purposes, free from the constraints of the foreign forum's powers of attachment and execution. While diplomatic and consular immunities are largely codified in generally accepted Vienna Conventions, to protect their missions, property and personnel, sovereign immunities are established largely under customary international law, possibly in the process of codification under a United Nations Convention not yet in force. Immunities are strongest for states and for the diplomatic process, less so for the consular functions. More or less parallel immunities are afforded international organizations and their property and staffs under separate international agreements. These distinctions spring from history, from differing assessments of the need to protect the entities and officials subject to these rules, and all are in constant application and development, pointing in the general direction of a reduction in their scope of application.

One reason for the trend to reduce these immunities is, of course, the problem of doing justice. When immunity in any of the sectors mentioned above is applied, the public interest of the state or organization may well deserve and need protection from foreign courts, for various reasons we will see, but at the same time the immunity for the one side often produces an injustice for the other party invoking the judicial process. The policy of avoiding injustice has clearly been on the rise over the last century, manifested in the number of successful adjustments in immunity law in favor of the party potentially losing out to immunity. More progress in that direction may well be foreseen, and in each case there appear at least two tacit questions along the following lines. (1) What could be done in cases like this one to protect the losing party's right to be heard and to receive and enforce a judgment; that is, how could we do justice here? (2) In determining whether there should be immunity, how can the legal system effectively ensure accountability of the responsible states, public officials, diplomats, consular officers, international organizations and persons connected with them.

I Robert Jennings and Arthur Watts, Oppenheim's International Law

pp. 341ff (9th ed., 1996)

§ 109 Equality of states and immunity from jurisdiction. It is often said that a * * * consequence of state equality is that—according to the rule *par in parem non habet imperium*—no state can claim Jurisdiction over another. The jurisdictional immunity of foreign states has often also been variously—and often simultaneously—deduced not only from the principle of equality but also from the principles of independence and of dignity of states. It is doubtful whether any of these considerations supplies a satisfactory basis for the doctrine of immunity. There is no obvious impairment of the rights of equality, or independence, or dignity of a state if it is subjected to ordinary judicial processes within the territory of a foreign state—in particular if that state, as appears to be the tendency in countries under the rule of law, submits to the jurisdiction of its own courts in respect of claims brought against it. The grant of immunity from suit amounts in effect to a denial of a legal remedy in respect of what may be a valid legal claim; as such, immunity is open to objection.

However, the practice of states over a long period has established that foreign states enjoy a degree of immunity from the jurisdiction of the courts of another state. This practice has consisted primarily of the application of the internal laws of states by judicial decisions, taking into account, in some states, communications made to the courts by the executive branch of government. Consequently the decisions reached have varied in points of detail, and sometimes in substance, according to the laws of the different states concerned. Despite these variations, which are now fewer than they once were, state practice is sufficiently established and generally consistent to allow the conclusion that, whatever the doctrinal basis may be, customary international law admits a general rule, to which there are important exceptions, that foreign states cannot be sued.

The customary international law rule is now accompanied by legislation in a number of states, including in the United States the Foreign Sovereign Immunities Act of 1976 as amended (FSIA), in the United Kingdom and Canada by similar legislation, and by treaties, principally the United Nations Convention on Jurisdictional Immunities of States and Their Property of 2004, and the European Convention on State Immunity of 1972, taken up below. Since state immunity questions are often raised in national courts, Chapter 11 below on International Law in National and Regional Systems provides background that could be usefully perused at this point.

1.   THE IMMUNITY OF STATES

a.   ABSOLUTE AND RESTRICTIVE PRINCIPLES

Republic of Austria et al., Petitioners v. Altmann

United States Supreme Court
541 U.S. 677, 124 S.Ct. 2240, 159 L.Ed.2d 1 (2004)

[In this proceeding against the Austrian State and others, Maria Altmann sought to recover six highly valuable paintings by the distinguished painter Gustav Klimt. These paintings were in the collection of her uncle in Austria prior to World War II. The uncle donated one to the Austrian National Gallery. Nazis acquired the other five, which eventually came into the possession of the Austrian National Gallery as well. She and other heirs claimed to be the rightful owners of the paintings. For more on the case, see Mary Ellen O'Connell, *Beyond Wealth, Stories of Art, War, and Greed*, 59 ALA. L. R. (2008).

Altmann asserted jurisdiction of U.S. Federal courts under the FSIA Sec. 1605(a)(3) exception to state immunity of cases in which "rights in property taken in violation of international law are in issue". The petitioners claimed that the taking of the art works occurred prior to the adoption of the FSIA at a time when the United States applied a rule of absolute sovereign immunity in actions before U.S. courts against foreign sovereigns. On that issue the Court ruled in favor of Altmann, who later prevailed in an arbitration proceeding concerning her rights, and all of the paintings were ultimately delivered to her in the United States. In Justice Stevens' Opinion there appear the following passages on the historical background on foreign sovereign immunity law in the United States.]

III

Chief Justice Marshall's opinion in *Schooner Exchange v. McFaddon,* 7 Cranch 116, 3 L.Ed. 287 (1812), is generally viewed as the source of our foreign sovereign immunity jurisprudence. In that case, the libellants claimed to be the rightful owners of a French ship that had taken refuge in the port of Philadelphia. The Court first emphasized that the jurisdiction of the United States over persons and property within its territory "is susceptible of no limitation not imposed by itself," and thus foreign sovereigns have no right to immunity in our courts. *Id.,* at 136. Chief Justice Marshall went on to explain, however, that as a matter of comity, members of the international community had implicitly agreed to waive the exercise of jurisdiction over other sovereigns in certain classes of cases, such as those involving foreign ministers or the person of the sovereign. Accepting a suggestion advanced by the Executive Branch, see *id.,* at 134, the Chief Justice concluded that the implied waiver theory also served to exempt the *Schooner Exchange*—"a national armed vessel ... of the emperor of France"—from United States courts' jurisdiction. *Id.,* at 145–146.

In accordance with Chief Justice Marshall's observation that foreign sovereign immunity is a matter of grace and comity rather than a constitutional requirement, this Court has "consistently ... deferred to the decisions of the political branches—in particular, those of the Executive Branch—on whether to take jurisdiction" over particular actions against foreign sovereigns and their instrumentalities. *Verlinden B.V. v. Central Bank of Nigeria,* 461 U.S. 480, 486, 103 S.Ct. 1962, 76 L.Ed.2d 81 (1983) (citing *Ex parte Peru,* 318 U.S. 578, 586–590, 63 S.Ct. 793, 87 L.Ed. 1014 (1943); *Republic of Mexico v. Hoffman,* 324 U.S. 30, 33–36, 65 S.Ct. 530, 89 L.Ed. 729 (1945)). Until 1952 the Executive Branch followed a policy of requesting immunity in all actions against friendly sovereigns. 461 U.S., at 486, 103 S.Ct. 1962. In that year, however, the State Department concluded that "immunity should no longer be granted in certain types of cases."[8] App. A to Brief for Petitioners 1a. In a letter to the Acting Attorney General, the Acting Legal Adviser for the Secretary of State, Jack B. Tate, explained that the Department would thereafter apply the "restrictive theory" of sovereign immunity:

"A study of the law of sovereign immunity reveals the existence of two conflicting concepts of sovereign immunity, each widely held and firmly established. According to the classical or absolute theory of sovereign immunity, a sovereign cannot, without his consent, be made a respondent in the courts of another sovereign. According to the newer or restrictive theory of sovereign immunity, the immunity of the sovereign is recognized with regard to sovereign or public acts *(jure imperii)* of a state, but not with respect to private acts *(jure gestionis)*. . . . [I]t will hereafter be the Department's policy to follow the restrictive theory . . . in the consideration of requests of foreign governments for a grant of sovereign immunity." *Id.,* at 1a, 4a–5a.

As we explained in our unanimous opinion in *Verlinden,* the change in State Department policy wrought by the "Tate Letter" had little, if any, impact on federal courts' approach to immunity analyses: "As in the past, initial responsibility for deciding questions of sovereign immunity fell primarily upon the Executive acting through the State Department," and courts continued to "abid[e] by" that Department's " 'suggestions of immunity.' " 461 U.S., at 487, 103 S.Ct. 1962. The change did, however, throw immunity determinations into some disarray, as "foreign nations often placed diplomatic pressure on the State Department," and political considerations sometimes led the Department to file "suggestions of immunity in cases where immunity would not have been available under the restrictive theory." *Id.,* at 487–488, 103 S.Ct. 1962. Complicating matters further, when foreign nations failed to request immunity from the State Department:

"[T]he responsibility fell to the courts to determine whether sovereign immunity existed, generally by reference to prior State Department decisions. . . . Thus, sovereign immunity determinations were made in two different branches, subject to a variety of factors, sometimes including diplomatic considerations. Not surprisingly, the governing standards were neither clear nor uniformly applied." *Ibid.*

In 1976 Congress sought to remedy these problems by enacting the FSIA, a comprehensive statute containing a "set of legal standards governing claims of immunity in every civil action against a foreign state or its political subdivisions, agencies, or instrumentalities." *Id.,* at 488, 103 S.Ct. 1962. The Act "codifies, as a matter of federal law, the restrictive theory of

---

8. Letter from Jack B. Tate, Acting Legal Adviser, U.S. Dept. of State, to Acting U.S. Attorney General Philip B. Perlman (May 19, 1952), reprinted in 26 Dept. State Bull. 984–985 (1952), and in *Alfred Dunhill of London, Inc. v. Republic of Cuba,* 425 U.S. 682, 711–715, 96 S.Ct. 1854, 48 L.Ed.2d 301 (1976) (App. 2 to opinion of the Court).

sovereign immunity," *ibid.,* and transfers primary responsibility for immunity determinations from the Executive to the Judicial Branch. The preamble states that "henceforth" both federal and state courts should decide claims of sovereign immunity in conformity with the Act's principles. 28 U.S.C. § 1602.

The Act itself grants federal courts jurisdiction over civil actions against foreign states, § 1330(a) and over diversity actions in which a foreign state is the plaintiff, § 1332(a)(4); it contains venue and removal provisions, §§ 1391(f), 1441(d); it prescribes the procedures for obtaining personal jurisdiction over a foreign state, § 1330(b); and it governs the extent to which a state's property may be subject to attachment or execution, §§ 1609–1611. Finally, the Act carves out certain exceptions to its general grant of immunity, including the expropriation exception on which respondent's complaint relies. See *supra,* at 2245–2246, and n. 5. These exceptions are central to the Act's functioning: "At the threshold of every action in a district court against a foreign state, . . . the court must satisfy itself that one of the exceptions applies," as "subject-matter jurisdiction in any such action depends" on that application. *Verlinden,* 461 U.S., at 493–494, 103 S.Ct. 1962.

If the concerns about formal doctrines of equality, independence, dignity, and avoidance of embarrassment no longer carry their former weight, there remain other considerations which explain the durability of the sovereign immunity doctrine. The judicial branch may be, or at least may feel, constrained at hearing charges or claims against a sovereign, because of lack of expertise and potential intrusion into political issues. Judicial determinations rendered against a foreign state or its leading officials could interfere with the conduct of the forum state's foreign relations. Although this problem is sometimes exaggerated, serious problems can arise. For example, embarrassment and international conflict could occur if a court were to adopt a rule, apply a treaty interpretation or make a decision at variance with the views of the forum executive advanced in negotiations with another state. Protection of a foreign state from nuisance cases, from the abusive use of the courts as a negotiating tool or as a "public forum" for political advantage is another reason for sovereign immunity's continued viability. The case for immunity is strong when judicial action may interfere with the forum state's continuing or future foreign relations. Concerns about protecting governmental operations are particularly noteworthy in cases of attachment and execution affecting a foreign government's property situated in the forum state. The foregoing policy concerns have affected outcomes of decisions, resulting in the continuing uncertainty and at times inconsistency in the law. The materials below cover many of these situations.

In sum, the case for sovereign immunity, particularly in the traditional absolute sense, has become much less acceptable or perhaps obsolete. More erosion of the traditional doctrine of absolute immunity may be reasonably foreseen. See the discussion of *jus cogens* and sovereign immunity in Chapter 2 *supra*.

Absolute Theory of Immunity

Chief Justice Marshall articulated the principle of absolute immunity in the famous *Schooner Exchange* Case, quoted above. Absolute immunity was attacked in the early part of the 20th century, often in cases in which foreign state owned vessels were engaged in maritime commerce. In 1926, however, the United States Supreme Court refused to limit the scope of the immunity in an *in rem* proceeding to enforce a cargo damage claim against a merchant vessel owned and operated by Italy. The Court stated:

> We think the principles [of immunity] are applicable alike to all ships held and used by a government for a public purpose, and that when, for the purpose of advancing the trade of its people or providing revenue for its treasury, a government acquires, mans and operates ships in the carrying trade, they are public ships in the same sense that warships are. We know of no international usage which regards the maintenance and advancement of the economic welfare of a people in time of peace as any less a public purpose than the maintenance and training of a naval force. *Berizzi Bros. Co. v. S.S. Pesaro,* 271 U.S. 562 (1926).

In a pre-FSIA case, *Victory Transport Inc. v. Comisaria General*, 336 F.2d 354, 360 (2d Cir. 1964), the Court stated that it was disposed to deny a claim of immunity:

> * * * unless it is plain that the activity in question falls within one of the categories of strictly political or public acts about which sovereigns have traditionally been quite sensitive. Such acts are generally limited to the following categories:
>
> (1) internal administrative acts, such as expulsion of an alien.
>
> (2) legislative acts such as naturalization.
>
> (3) acts concerning the armed forces.
>
> (4) acts concerning diplomatic activity.
>
> (5) public loans.

The 1982 U.N. Convention on the Law of the Sea (UNCLOS)

Article 95
Immunity of warships on the high seas

Warships on the high seas have complete immunity from the jurisdiction of any State other than the flag State.

Article 96
Immunity of ships used only on government non-commercial service

Ships owned or operated by a State and used only on government non-commercial service shall, on the high seas, have complete immunity from jurisdiction of any State other than the flag State.

Exceptions Forum state policy considerations have traditionally led to a few exceptions to the absolute immunity principle, such as those relating to rights in immovable property (real property) situated in the forum state and rights in movable property in the forum state when acquired by succession or gift. Section 1605(4) of the U.S. Foreign Sovereign Immunities Act retained those exceptions. Article 7 of the Nürnberg Charter of 1945 provided in Article 7 that "The official position of defendants, whether as Heads of State of responsible officials in Government Departments, shall not be considered as freeing them from responsibility...". Similar principles appear in the statutes of the Former Yugoslavia and Rwanda Tribunals as well as the Rome Statute of the International Criminal Court. See Chapter 5 below.

The U.S. Foreign Sovereign Immunities Act of 1976

28 U.S.C. Secs. 1330, 1332, 1391(f), 1441(d), 1602–1611

This comprehensive legislation on state immunity went into effect in January 1977. Excerpts are contained in the Documentary Supplement. It clearly incorporates the restrictive theory. As the State Departments Legal Adviser put it in his testimony: "Under international law today, a foreign state is entitled to sovereign immunity only in the cases based on its 'public' acts. However, where a law suit is based on a commercial transaction or some other 'private' act of the foreign state, the foreign state is not entitled to sovereign immunity. The specific applications of this principle of international law are codified in * * * the proposed bill."

The *fundamental rule* is stated in Section 1604: "Subject to existing international agreements to which the United States is a party at the time of enactment of this Act a foreign state shall be immune from the jurisdiction of the courts of the United States and of the States except as provided in sections 1605 to 1607 of this chapter." In accordance with the terms of those sections, there are ten categories of exceptions to section 1604:

(1) waiver of immunity

(2) commercial activity

(3) rights in property taken in violation of international law

(4) rights in property in the United States acquired by succession or gift or right immovable property in the United States

(5) money damage tort actions for personal injuries or death or damage to or loss of property occurring in the United States

(6) enforcement of an arbitration agreement made by a foreign state with or for the benefit of a private party, in prescribed situations

(7) money damage actions for personal injuries or death caused by an act of torture, extrajudicial killing, aircraft sabotage, or hostage taking, or the provision of material support or resources for that act, where the foreign state is designated as a state sponsor of terrorism

(8) maritime liens against a vessel where the lien is based upon commercial activities and in certain other situations

(9) foreclosure of a preferred mortgage under the Ship Mortgage Act of 1920

(10) counterclaims.

In 1972 the United Kingdom became a signatory to the European Convention on State Immunity, discussed below. This Convention, found in 11 I.L.M. 470 (1972), incorporates the restrictive theory. To give effect to the Convention, the U.K. enacted the State Immunity Act of 1978, found in 17 I.L.M. 1123 (1978). Recent actions concerning the 1978 Act include *Jones v. Ministry of Interior Al–Mamlaka* below at Subsection 2. *See also* the more or less parallel Canadian State Immunity Act, R.S.C. 1885, c. S–18asam.

International Agreements Movement toward the "restrictive principle" is occurring as a function of a number of treaty provisions in force or under consideration as well as national legislation and judicial decisions. These sources may well be moving customary law in that direction by accretion. The first of these treaties is the Brussels Convention of 1926, with thirty-three ratifications (but not the United States), which applied the restrictive principle to government owned or operated vessels involved in trade. See Andrew Dickinson, Ray Lindsay, and James P. Loonam, *State Immunity* 1 (2004). The European Convention on State Immunity and Additional Protocol of May 16, 1972 adopted the restrictive principle on a broader basis, including the commercial exception as provided in Article 7.1, which reads:

> A Contracting state cannot claim immunity from the jurisdiction of a court of another Contracting State if it has on the territory of the State of the forum an office, agency, or other establishment through which it engages, in the same manner as a private person, in an industrial, commercial or financial activity, and the proceedings relate to that activity of the office, agency or establishment.

In 2009 there were 9 signatories to the European Convention (Austria, Belgium, Cyprus, Germany, Luxembourg, Netherlands, Portugal, Switzerland and the United Kingdom) and 7 countries which had given their consent to be bound. See http://conventions.coe.int.

Leading the way to a United Nations Convention, the International Law Commission adopted Draft Articles on Jurisdiction of States and Their Property (UN A/46/405, on 11 September, 1991; 30 I.L.M. 1554, 1565). Article 5 of the Draft Articles contains the following broad provision: "A State enjoys immunity, in respect of itself and its property, from the jurisdiction of the courts of another State subject to the provisions of the present articles," in more or less the same pattern as the U.S., U.K. and Canadian statutes, qualified in a substantial number of exceptions. Although the Draft Articles were never adopted as such in treaty form, they nevertheless influenced later decisions on state immunity, were considered by some as a reflection of the evolving customary international law on this subject, and led the way to the adoption of the United Nations Convention, which is the most recent and authoritative treaty on this subject.

United Nations Convention on Jurisdictional Immunities of States and Their Property

ASIL, International Law in Brief, May 9, 2005, www.asil.org

[The full text is annexed to UNGA Res. A/59/38, 2004, 44 I.L.M. 801 (2005) and selections are set forth in the Documentary Supplement. In 2009 there were 28 signatories and 6 ratifications of this Convention. It is not yet in force.]

The U.N. General Assembly adopted the U.N. Convention on Jurisdictional Immunities of States and Their Property on December 2, 2004. In doing so, the General Assembly stressed the importance of uniformity and clarity in the law of jurisdictional immunities of States and expressed its deep appreciation to the International Law Commission and the Ad Hoc Committee on Jurisdictional Immunities of States and Their Property.

The U.N. Convention on Jurisdictional Immunities of States and Their Property provides for a presumption of immunity, as supported by principles of customary international law.

Article 2 sets forth the definition of "State" as "(1) the State and its various organs of government; (ii) constituent units of a federal State or political subdivisions of the State, which are entitled to perform acts in the exercise of sovereign authority, and are acting in that capacity; (iii) agencies or instrumentalities of the State or other entities, to the extent that they are entitled to perform and are actually performing acts in the exercise of sovereign authority of the State."

Article 4 of the Convention entitled "Non-retroactivity of the present Convention" provides that "the present Convention shall not apply to any question of jurisdictional immunities of States or their property arising in a proceeding instituted against a State before a court of another State prior to the entry into force of the present Convention for the States concerned."

Article 10 provides that State immunity cannot be invoked for commercial transactions. Article 14 sets forth an exception for intellectual and industrial property, stating that States cannot invoke immunity in proceedings related to the determination of intellectual property rights, even if such rights are provisional in the forum State, or to an alleged infringement by the State in the territory of the forum State.

Unlike the U.S. Foreign Sovereign Immunities Act (FSIA), there is no exception to immunity for expropriation. Nor is there an exception for acts of state-sponsored terrorism, as appears in the FSIA.

Article 21 sets forth categories of property that shall not be considered as property intended for use by the State for other than government, non-commercial purposes. These categories include military property, property (including any bank account) intended to be used for diplomatic missions or missions to international organizations, property of the central bank or other monetary authority of the State, property forming part of the cultural heritage or scientific interest of the State.

Additional information on these and related questions can be found on the U.N. website. Detailed analysis of the Convention is found in David Stewart, *The UN Convention on Jurisdictional Immunities of States and Their Property*, 99 AM. J. INT'L L. 194 (2005) and in *Immunity and Accountability: Is the Balance Shifting?*, 99 ASIL PROC. 227 (2005).

Notwithstanding the progress of codification of state immunity law, the underlying rules of customary law continue to apply, of course, to states not parties to the treaties and to situations not covered by them. In the preamble to the Convention as adopted by the General Assembly the States Parties are: "*Affirming* that the rules of customary international law continue to govern matters not regulated by the provisions of the present Convention".

NOTES AND QUESTIONS

1. Immunity questions can appear in connection with the Security Council's management of peace and security responsibilities under Chapter VII of the U.N. Charter. The Council's immunity decisions under this chapter are legally binding on Member States and take precedence over obligations undertaken in other international agreements (see Chapters 3 *supra* and 10 *infra*). Immunity questions arose following the liberation of Kuwait in 1991 when the Security Council created a Compensation Fund and procedure for settling claims against Iraq in order to assist with the establishment of a democratic government and contribute to stability and security of that country. The Fund's resources included indigenous petroleum, petroleum products, and natural gas. The Council, for example, adopted S/Res/1483 of 22 May, 2003 to provide immunity for Iraqi assets intended to compensate for consequences of its invasion of Kuwait in 1991.

2.   Do you agree with the assertion that the trend has been to reduce the scope and application of sovereign immunity? What elements in the above readings support your conclusion? How would you formulate the theoretical basis for the retention of sovereign immunity?

3.   What advantages and disadvantages do you see in codification of state immunity law? Would you support this codification? The United States has not signed and at the time of writing is not expected to do so.

b.   THE MODERN GENERAL RULE OF IMMUNITY AND EXCEPTIONS

Argentine Republic v. Amerada Hess Shipping Corp.

United States Supreme Court
488 U.S. 428, 109 S.Ct. 683, 102 L.Ed.2d 818 (1989)

■ CHIEF JUSTICE REHNQUIST delivered the opinion of the Court.

Two Liberian corporations sued the Argentine Republic in a United States District Court to recover damages for a tort allegedly committed by its armed forces on the high seas in violation of international law. We hold that the District Court correctly dismissed the action, because the Foreign Sovereign Immunities Act of 1976 (FSIA), 28 U.S.C. § 1330 et seq., does not authorize jurisdiction over a foreign state in this situation.

Respondents alleged the following facts in their complaints. Respondent United Carriers, Inc., a Liberian corporation, chartered one of its oil tankers, the Hercules, to respondent Amerada Hess Shipping Corporation, also a Liberian corporation. The contract was executed in New York City. Amerada Hess used the Hercules to transport crude oil from the southern terminus of the Trans–Alaska Pipeline in Valdez, Alaska, around Cape Horn in South America, to the Hess refinery in the United States Virgin Islands. On May 25, 1982, the Hercules began a return voyage, without cargo but fully fueled, from the Virgin Islands to Alaska. At that time, Great Britain and petitioner Argentine Republic were at war over an archipelago of some 200 islands—the Falkland Islands to the British, and the Islas Malvinas to the Argentineans—in the South Atlantic off the Argentine coast. On June 3, United States officials informed the two belligerents of the location of United States vessels and Liberian tankers owned by United States interests then traversing the South Atlantic, including the Hercules, to avoid any attacks on neutral shipping.

By June 8, 1982, after a stop in Brazil, the Hercules was in international waters about 600 nautical miles from Argentina and 500 miles from the Falklands; she was outside the "war zones" designated by Britain and Argentina. At 12:15 Greenwich mean time, the ship's master made a routine report by radio to Argentine officials, providing the ship's name, international call sign, registry, position, course, speed, and voyage description. About 45 minutes later, an Argentine military aircraft began to circle the Hercules. The ship's master repeated his earlier message by radio to Argentine officials, who acknowledged receiving it. Six minutes later, without provocation, another Argentine military plane began to bomb the Hercules; the master immediately hoisted a white flag. A second bombing soon followed, and a third attack came about two hours later, when an Argentine jet struck the ship with an air-to-surface rocket. Disabled but not destroyed, the Hercules reversed course and sailed to Rio de Janeiro, the nearest safe port. At Rio de Janeiro, respondent United Carriers determined that the ship had suffered extensive deck and hull damage, and that an undetonated bomb remained lodged in her No. 2 tank. After an investigation by the Brazilian Navy, United Carriers decided that it would be too hazardous to remove the undetonated bomb, and on July 20, 1978, the Hercules was scuttled 250 miles off the Brazilian coast. * * *

* * * In the FSIA, Congress added a new chapter 97 to Title 28 of the United States Code, 28 U.S.C. §§ 1602–1611, which is entitled "Jurisdictional Immunities of Foreign States." Section 1604 provides that "[s]ubject to existing international agreements to which the United States [was] a party at the time of the enactment of this Act[,] a foreign state shall be immune from the jurisdiction of the courts of the United States and of the States except as provided in sections 1605 to 1607 of this chapter." The FSIA also added § 1330(a) to Title 28; it provides that "[t]he district courts shall have original jurisdiction without regard to amount in controversy of any nonjury civil action against a foreign state * * * as to any claim for relief in personam with respect to which the foreign state is not entitled to immunity under sections 1605–1607 of this title or under any applicable international agreement." § 1330(a).

We think that the text and structure of the FSIA demonstrate Congress' intention that the FSIA be the sole basis for obtaining jurisdiction over a foreign state in our courts. Section 1604 and § 1330(a) work in tandem: § 1604 bars federal and state courts from exercising jurisdiction when a foreign state is entitled to immunity, and § 1330(a) confers jurisdiction on district courts to hear suits brought by United States citizens and by aliens when a foreign state is not entitled to immunity. As we said in Verlinden, the FSIA "must be applied by the district courts in every action against a foreign sovereign, since subject-matter jurisdiction in any such action depends on the existence of one of the specified exceptions to foreign sovereign immunity." *Verlinden B.V. v. Central Bank of Nigeria*, 461 U.S. 480, 493 (1983).

* * *

Having determined that the FSIA provides the sole basis for obtaining jurisdiction over a foreign state in federal court, we turn to whether any of the exceptions enumerated in the Act apply here. These exceptions include cases involving the waiver of immunity, § 1605(a)(1), commercial activities occurring in the United States or causing a direct effect in this country, § 1605(a)(2), property expropriated in violation of international law, § 1605(a)(3), real estate, inherited, or gift property located in the United States, § 1605(a)(4), non-commercial torts occurring in the United States, § 1605(a)(5), and maritime liens, § 1605(b). We agree with the District Court that none of the FSIA's exceptions applies on these facts.

Respondents assert that the FSIA exception for noncommercial torts, § 1605(a)(5), is most in point. This provision denies immunity in a case "in which money damages are sought against a foreign state for personal injury or death, or damage to or loss of property, occurring in the United States and caused by the tortious act or omission of that foreign state or of any official or employee of that foreign state while acting within the scope of his office or employment." 28 U.S.C. § 1605(a)(5).

Section 1605(a)(5) is limited by its terms, however, to those cases in which the damage to or loss of property occurs in the United States. Congress' primary purpose in enacting § 1605(a)(5) was to eliminate a foreign state's immunity for traffic accidents and other torts committed in the United States, for which liability is imposed under domestic tort law. See H.R.Rep., at 14, 20–21. * * *

In this case, the injury to respondents' ship occurred on the high seas some 5,000 miles off the nearest shores of the United States * * *.

* * *

The result * * * is not altered by the fact that petitioner's alleged tort may have had effects in the United States. Respondents state, for example, that the Hercules was transporting oil intended for use in this country and that the loss of the ship disrupted contractual payments due in New York. Under the commercial activity exception to the FSIA, § 1605(a)(2), a foreign state may be liable for its commercial activities "outside the territory of the United States" having a "direct effect" inside the United States. But the noncommercial tort exception, § 1605(a)(5), upon which respondents rely, makes no mention of "territory outside the United States" or of "direct effects" in the United States. Congress' decision to use explicit language in § 1605(a)(2), and not to do so in § 1605(a)(5), indicates that the exception in § 1605(a)(5) covers only torts occurring within the territorial jurisdiction of the United States. Respondents do not claim that § 1605(a)(2) covers these facts.

We also disagree with respondents' claim that certain international agreements entered into by petitioner and by the United States create an exception to the FSIA here. * * * Nor do we see how a foreign state can waive its immunity under § 1605(a)(1) by signing an international agreement that contains no mention of a waiver of immunity to suit in United States courts or even the availability of a cause of action in the United States. * * *

We hold that the FSIA provides the sole basis for obtaining jurisdiction over a foreign state in the courts of this country, and that none of the enumerated exceptions to the Act applies to the facts of this case. The judgment of the Court of Appeals is therefore

REVERSED.

NOTES AND QUESTIONS

1. Were the U.S. contacts and interests in this case sufficiently strong for U.S. courts to take jurisdiction, compared, for example, to contacts and interests for the courts of the United Kingdom or Liberia?

2.   What harm might be done if U.S. courts were to take jurisdiction in such cases? Are there any benefits? Would a decision taking jurisdiction have carried the risk that U.S. courts might become a world judiciary in actions grounded on international law violations of foreign governments? Would this have been an exercise of universal jurisdiction as discussed above? Is there any obstacle in international law respecting a state adjudicating serious international law violations? See Mary Ellen OConnell, *National Judicial Measures*, in THE POWER AND PURPOSE OF INTERNATIONAL LAW, Chap. 9 (2008).

3.   What remedies remained for *Amerada Hess* after this proceeding was concluded against it?

1.) *Commercial Activities*

Republic of Argentina and Banco Central De La Republica Argentina, Petitioners v. Weltover, Inc.

United States Supreme Court
504 U.S. 607, 112 S.Ct. 2160, 119 L.Ed.2d 394 (1992)

■ JUSTICE SCALIA delivered the opinion of the Court.

This case requires us to decide whether the Republic of Argentina's default on certain bonds issued as part of a plan to stabilize its currency was an act taken "in connection with a commercial activity" that had a "direct effect in the United States" so as to subject Argentina to suit in an American court under the Foreign Sovereign Immunities Act of 1976, 28 U.S.C. §§ 1602 et seq.

* * * Argentina's currency is not one of the mediums of exchange accepted on the international market. Argentine businesses engaging in foreign transactions must pay in U.S. dollars or some other internationally accepted currency. [It has been] difficult for Argentine borrowers to obtain such funds, principally because of the instability of the Argentine currency. To address these problems, petitioners, the Republic of Argentina and its central bank, Banco Central (collectively Argentina), in 1981 instituted a foreign exchange insurance contract program (FEIC), under which Argentina effectively agreed to assume the risk of currency depreciation in cross-border transactions involving Argentine borrowers. This was accomplished by Argentina's agreeing to sell to domestic borrowers, in exchange for a contractually predetermined amount of local currency, the necessary U.S. dollars to repay their foreign debts when they matured, irrespective of intervening devaluations.

* * * Argentina did not possess sufficient reserves of U.S. dollars to cover the FEIC contracts as they became due in 1982. The Argentine government thereupon adopted certain emergency measures, including refinancing of the FEIC-backed debts by issuing to the creditors government bonds. These bonds, called "Bonods," provide for payment of interest

and principal in U.S. dollars; payment may be made through transfer on the London, Frankfurt, Zurich, or New York market, at the election of the creditor. [T]he foreign creditor had the option of either accepting the Bonods in satisfaction of the initial debt, thereby substituting the Argentine government for the private debtor, or maintaining the debtor/creditor relationship with the private borrower and accepting the Argentine government as guarantor.

When the Bonods began to mature in May 1986, Argentina concluded that it lacked sufficient foreign exchange to retire them. Pursuant to a Presidential Decree, Argentina unilaterally extended the time for payment, and offered bondholders substitute instruments as a means of rescheduling the debts. [Three creditors] refused to accept the rescheduling, and insisted on full payment, specifying New York as the place where payment should be made. Argentina did not pay, and respondents then brought this breach-of-contract action, * * * relying on the Foreign Sovereign Immunities Act of 1976 as the basis for jurisdiction. * * *

In the proceedings below, respondents relied only on the third clause of § 1605(a)(2) to establish jurisdiction and our analysis is therefore limited to considering whether this lawsuit is (1) "based * * * upon an act outside the territory of the United States; (2) that was taken in connection with a commercial activity" of Argentina outside this country; and (3) that "cause[d] a direct effect in the United States." The complaint in this case alleges only one cause of action on behalf of each of the respondents, viz., a breach-of-contract claim based on Argentina's attempt to refinance the Bonods rather than to pay them according to their terms. The fact that the cause of action is in compliance with the first of the three requirements—that it is "based upon an act outside the territory of the United States" (presumably Argentina's unilateral extension)—is uncontested. The dispute pertains to whether the unilateral refinancing of the Bonods was taken "in connection with a commercial activity" of Argentina, and whether it had a "direct effect in the United States." We address these issues in turn.

A

Respondents and their *amicus,* the United States, contend that Argentina's issuance of, and continued liability under, the Bonods constitute a "commercial activity" and that the extension of the payment schedules was taken "in connection with" that activity. The latter point is obvious enough, and Argentina does not contest it; the key question is whether the activity is "commercial" under the FSIA. The FSIA defines "commercial activity" to mean: "[E]ither a regular course of commercial conduct or a particular commercial transaction or act. The commercial character of an activity shall be determined by reference to the nature of the course of conduct or particular transaction or act, rather than by reference to its purpose." 28 U.S.C. § 1603(d).

This definition, however, leaves the critical term "commercial" largely undefined: The first sentence simply establishes that the commercial nature of an activity does *not* depend upon whether it is a single act or a regular course of conduct, and the second sentence merely specifies what element of the conduct determines commerciality (i.e., nature rather than purpose), but still without saying what "commercial" means.

* * *

* * * [W]e conclude that when a foreign government acts, not as regulator of a market, but in the manner of a private player within it, the foreign sovereign's actions are "commercial" within the meaning of the FSIA. Moreover, because the Act provides that the commercial character of an act is to be determined by reference to its "nature" rather than its "purpose", 28 U.S.C. § 1603(d), the question is not whether the foreign government is acting with a profit motive or instead with the aim of fulfilling uniquely sovereign objectives. Rather, the issue is whether the particular actions that the foreign state performs (whatever the motive behind them) are the *type* of actions by which a private party engages in "trade and traffic or commerce," Black's Law Dictionary 270 (6th ed. 1990). See, e.g., *Rush–Presbyterian–St. Luke's Medical Center v. Hellenic Republic*, 877 F.2d 574, 578 (CA7), cert. denied. Thus, a foreign government's issuance of regulations limiting foreign currency exchange is a sovereign activity, because such authoritative control of commerce cannot be exercised by a private party; whereas a contract to buy army boots or even bullets is a "commercial" activity, because private companies can similarly use sales contracts to acquire goods, see, e.g., *Stato di Rumania v. Trutta*, [1926] Foro It. I 584, 585–586, 589 (Corte di Cass. del Regno, Italy), translated and reprinted in part in 26 Am.J.Int'l L. 626–629 (Supp.1932).

Argentina contends that, although the FSIA bars consideration of "purpose," a court must nonetheless fully consider the *context* of a transaction in order to determine whether it is "commercial." Accordingly, Argentina claims that the Court of Appeals erred by defining the relevant conduct in what Argentina considers an overly generalized, a contextual manner and by essentially adopting a *per se* rule that all "issuance of debt instruments" is "commercial."

Argentina points to the fact that the transactions in which the Bonods were issued did not have the ordinary commercial consequence of raising capital or financing acquisitions. Assuming for the sake of argument that this is not an example of judging the commerciality of a transaction by its purpose, the ready answer is that private parties regularly issue bonds, not just to raise capital or to finance purchases, but also to refinance debt. * * * Engaging in a commercial act does not require the receipt of fair value, or even compliance with the common-law requirements of consideration.

* * *

However difficult it may be in some cases to separate "purpose" (i.e., the *reason* why the foreign state engages in the activity) from nature (i.e., the outward form of the conduct that the foreign state performs or agrees to perform), see *De Sanchez, supra*, at 1393, the statute unmistakably commands that to be done. 28 U.S.C. § 1603(d). We agree with the Court of

Appeals, see 941 F.2d, at 151, that it is irrelevant *why* Argentina participated in the bond market in the manner of a private actor; it matters only that it did so. We conclude that Argentina's issuance of the Bonods was a "commercial activity" under the FSIA.

B

The remaining question is whether Argentina's unilateral rescheduling of the Bonods had a "direct effect" in the United States, 28 U.S.C. § 1605(a)(2).

We * * * have little difficulty concluding that Argentina's unilateral rescheduling of the maturity dates on the Bonods had a "direct effect" in the United States. Respondents had designated their accounts in New York as the place of payment, and Argentina made some interest payments into those accounts before announcing that it was rescheduling the payments. Because New York was thus the place of performance for Argentina's ultimate contractual obligations, the rescheduling of those obligations necessarily had a "direct effect" in the United States: Money that was supposed to have been delivered to a New York bank for deposit was not forthcoming. We reject Argentina's suggestion that the "direct effect" requirement cannot be satisfied where the plaintiffs are all foreign corporations with no other connections to the United States. We expressly stated in *Verlinden* that the FSIA permits a foreign plaintiff to sue "a foreign sovereign in the courts of the United States, provided the substantive requirements of the Act are satisfied." * * *

NOTES AND QUESTIONS

1. Article 2.2 of the United Nations Convention provides that:

> 2. In determining whether a contract or transaction is a "commercial transaction" under paragraph 1(c), reference should be made primarily to the nature of the contract or transaction, but its purpose should also be taken into account if the parties to the contract or transaction have so agreed, or if, in the practice of the State of the forum, that purpose is relevant to determining the non-commercial character of the contract or transaction.

The corresponding FSIA text in Sec. 1603 (d) provides that:

> The commercial character of an activity shall be determined by reference to the nature of the course of conduct or particular transaction or act, rather than by reference to its purpose.

How would you define the differences in these two texts? If the United Nations Convention provision were applicable, do you think Justice Scalia would have reached the same result? Why? If the "context" of the transaction indicated potentially high public importance, would this be taken into account under the FSIA? Should it?

2. Plaintiff in *Saudi Arabia v. Nelson*, 507 U.S. 349, 113 S.Ct. 1471, 123 L.Ed.2d 47 (1993), alleged that he was detained and tortured by Saudi Arabian authorities. He had been hired in the United States to work as a

monitoring systems engineer at a Saudi Arabian (government) hospital. Nelson alleged that agents of the Saudi Government arrested him after he complained about safety defects in the hospital. He claimed that he was shackled, beaten, kept for days without food, tortured and confined in a rat infested overcrowded cell. In addition, he claimed that his wife was told by a government official that her husband's release could be arranged, if she provided sexual favors.

Nelson was released after 39 days of confinement. Upon his return, he brought an action in the Federal District Court for the Southern District of Florida, claiming that the Saudi conduct violated his human rights. He sought damages from the Saudi Government for, among other things, negligent failure to warn him of the dangers of working in a Saudi hospital, for various intentional torts, including "battery, unlawful detainment, wrongful arrest and imprisonment, false imprisonment, inhuman torture, disruption of normal family life, and infliction of mental anguish."

A majority of the Supreme Court held that the suit could not properly be maintained under the FSIA, because the conduct of which Nelson complained was not "based upon commercial activity," but "upon an abuse of sovereign power." It noted that the Act requires more than "mere connection with" or "relation to" commerce for conduct to be "based upon commercial activity." 28 U.S.C. § 1603(d). Justices White and Blackmun concurred, arguing that the conduct *was, indeed, based upon commercial activity,* "but went along with the decision, because they found that the activity was neither carried on in nor connected to the United States."

3. What should be the test for "commercial activity" under the FSIA: the overall character of the operation or the particular actions complained of? Is there an element of subjectivity in determinations of this kind? Is the definition of "commercial activity" in 28 U.S.C. § 1603(d) satisfactory? It seems to be largely circular. How much guidance can it give the Courts? The Supreme Court has looked at the precise conduct involved. Note the differences in the United States, United Kingdom, and Canadian legislation. The U.S. legislation applies the nature of the transaction test, rather than its "purpose." The U.K. legislation gives a list of activities that are considered "commercial." The Canadian legislation uses the "nature of the transaction" test. However, the Supreme Court of Canada in *The United States v. The Public Service Alliance of Canada*, 1992, 32 I.L.M. 1 (1993) held that this did not preclude consideration of its purpose. Does the codification in the United Nations Convention help?

2.) Terrorism, Human Rights and Jus Cogens

Rein v. Socialist People's Libyan Arab Jamahiriya

United States Court of Appeals, Second Circuit
162 F.3d 748 (1998)

■ CALABRESI, CIRCUIT JUDGE:

Defendants-appellants, collectively "Libya," appeal from the denial of their motion to dismiss. The plaintiffs, who are the survivors and representatives of persons killed aboard Pan Am 103 above Lockerbie, Scotland, brought suit against Libya alleging wrongful death, pain and suffering, and a variety of other injuries. * * *

In 1994, some of the present plaintiffs brought suit against some of the present defendants, claiming that Libya and its agents were responsible for destroying Pan Am 103. * * * When the previous litigation was brought in 1994, no provision of the FSIA deprived Libya of sovereign immunity in suits of this sort. Accordingly, the United States District Court for the Eastern District of New York (Platt, J.) dismissed the case for lack of subject matter jurisdiction. *Smith v. Socialist People's Libyan Arab Jamahiriya*, 886 F.Supp. 306 (E.D.N.Y.1995). We affirmed. *Smith v. Socialist People's Libyan Arab Jamahiriya*, 101 F.3d 239 (2d Cir.1996), cert. denied, 117 S.Ct. 1569 (1997).

In 1996, the Antiterrorism and Effective Death Penalty Act ("AEDPA") amended the FSIA by adding what is now 28 U.S.C. § 1605(a)(7). Under this new section, foreign states that have been designated as state sponsors of terrorism are denied immunity from damage actions for personal injury or death resulting from aircraft sabotage. Shortly after passage of the AEDPA, the present plaintiffs filed (against the present defendants) substantially the same claims that had been previously dismissed.

* * *

The decision to subject Libya to jurisdiction under § 1605(a)(7) was manifestly made by Congress itself rather than by the State Department. At the time that § 1605(a)(7) was passed, Libya was already on the list of state sponsors of terrorism. No decision whatsoever of the Secretary of State was needed to create jurisdiction over Libya for its alleged role in the destruction of Pan Am 103. That jurisdiction existed the moment that the AEDPA amendment became law.

* * *

The district court's determination that subject matter jurisdiction exists over the present action is affirmed. All other aspects of this interlocutory appeal are dismissed for want of appellate jurisdiction.

The issue of state immunity in terrorism related cases has produced considerable litigation in the United States and elsewhere. Summaries of these cases have appeared for some years in the "Contemporary Practice of the United States Relating to International Law" section of the American Journal of International Law.

In 2009, the state sponsors of terrorism as determined by the Department of State were: Cuba, Iran, Sudan, and Syria. Libya was removed from the list on June 30, 2006. http://www.state.gov/s/ct/c//14151.htm.

Note that in September, 1990 following Iraq's invasion of Kuwait, the United States formally designated Iraq as a state sponsor of terrorism. In 1996 Congress amended FSIA § 1605(a)(7) to withdraw sovereign immunity in money damage actions against a foreign state for actions taken while the state was so designated. Following the defeat of the main Iraqi forces and removal of Saddam Hussein from power, U.S. policy in Iraq turned to favoring development of that country under a new regime. There then being no reason to maintain the state supporter of terrorism designation of Iraq, Congress adopted in 2003 legislation empowering the President to make inapplicable to Iraq any legislation that applied to state supporters of terrorism, and the President exercised that authority fully. *Republic of Iraq v. Beaty et al.*, 556 U.S. ___ (2009), presented money damage claims against Iraq for alleged mistreatment by Iraqi officials during the 1991 Gulf War but the Supreme Court decided unanimously that:

> "When the President exercised his authority to make inapplicable to Iraq all provisions of law that apply to countries that have supported terrorism, the exception to foreign sovereign immunity for state sponsors of terrorism became inoperative as against Iraq. As a result, the courts below lacked jurisdiction . . ." (at p. 17).

See also the terrorism exception to immunity at 28 U.S.C. § 1605(A) in the document supplement.

———

Jones v. Ministry of Interior Al–Mamlaka Al–Arabiya AS Saudiya (the Kingdom of Saudi Arabia) and others

House of Lords
[2006] UKHL 26

LORD HOFFMANN

My Lords,

36. The question is whether the claimants, who allege that they were tortured by members of the Saudi Arabian police, can sue the responsible officers and the Kingdom of Saudi Arabia itself. The Court of Appeal held that they could sue the officers but that the Kingdom was protected by state immunity. In my opinion both are so protected.

37. Mr. Ronald Jones, who alleges that in 2001 he was held in solitary confinement and systematically tortured for 67 days, appeals against the decision of the Court of Appeal that the Kingdom is immune from suit. The language of section 1(1) of the State Immunity Act 1978 (hereafter "SIA") is unequivocal:

"A state is immune from the jurisdiction of the courts of the United Kingdom except as provided in the following provisions of this Part of this Act."

It is not suggested that this case falls within the terms of any other provision of the Act.

38.   In *Al–Adsani v. Government of Kuwait (No. 2)* (1996) 107 ILR 536, on similar facts, the Court of Appeal held that the State was immune. Ward LJ said (at p. 549) "the Act is as plain as plain can be." But Mr. Crystal QC, who appeared for Mr. Jones, submitted that section 1(1) should be read subject to an implied exception for claims which allege torture.

39.   The argument in support of this submission involves three steps. First, article 6 of the European Convention on Human Rights (hereafter "the Convention") guarantees a right of access to a court for the determination of civil claims and that right is prima facie infringed by according immunity to the Kingdom. Secondly, although the right is not absolute and its infringement by state immunity is ordinarily justified by mandatory rules of international law, no immunity is required in cases of torture. That is because the prohibition of torture is a peremptory norm or jus cogens which takes precedence over other rules of international law, including the rules of state immunity. Thirdly, section 3 of the Human Rights Act 1998 (hereafter "HRA") requires a court, so far as it is possible to do so, to read legislation in a way which is compatible with the Convention rights. This can be done by introducing an implied exception. I do not accept any of these steps in the argument but will postpone consideration of the first and third until I have discussed the second.

40.   The second and crucial step was rejected by the European Court of Human Rights in *Al–Adsani v. United Kingdom* (2001) 34 EHRR 273. The majority opinion said (at paragraph 56) that measures taken by a member state which "reflect generally recognised rules of public international law" could not in principle be regarded as imposing a disproportionate restriction on access to a court. State immunity was such a rule. As for the alleged exception for torture, the court said (at para. 61):

"Notwithstanding the special character of the prohibition of torture in international law, the court is unable to discern in the international instruments, judicial authorities or other materials before it any firm basis for concluding that, as a matter of international law, a state no longer enjoys immunity from civil suit in the courts of another state where acts of torture are alleged."

41.   Mr. Crystal [Counsel for Jones] submitted that the decision of the majority was wrong. The House should prefer the reasoning of the minority. But in my opinion the majority was right.

42.   A peremptory norm or jus cogens is defined in article 53 of the Vienna Convention of the Law of Treaties of 23 May 1969 (which provides that a treaty is void if, at the time of its conclusion, it conflicts with such a norm) as:

"a norm accepted and recognised by the international community of states as a whole as a norm from which no derogation is permitted".

43.   As the majority accepted, there is no doubt that the prohibition on torture is such a norm: for its recognition as such in this country, see *R v. Bow Street Metropolitan Stipendiary Magistrate, Ex p Pinochet Ugarte (No. 3)* [2000] 1 AC 147. Torture cannot be justified by any rule of domestic or international law. But the question is whether such a norm conflicts with a rule which accords state immunity. The syllogistic reasoning of the minority in *Al–Adsani* 34 EHRR 273, 298–299 simply assumes that it does:

"The acceptance therefore of the jus cogens nature of the prohibition of torture entails that a state allegedly violating it cannot invoke hierarchically lower rules (in this case, those on state immunity) to avoid the consequences of the illegality of its actions."

44.   The jus cogens is the prohibition on torture. But the United Kingdom, in according state immunity to the Kingdom, is not proposing to torture anyone. Nor is the Kingdom, in claiming immunity, justifying the use of torture. It is objecting in limine to the jurisdiction of the English court to decide whether it used torture or not. As Hazel Fox has said (*The Law of State Immunity* (2002), 525):

"State immunity is a procedural rule going to the jurisdiction of a national court. It does not go to substantive law; it does not contradict a prohibition contained in a jus cogens norm but merely diverts any breach of it to a different method of settlement. Arguably, then, there is no substantive content in the procedural plea of state immunity upon which a jus cogens mandate can bite."

45.   To produce a conflict with state immunity, it is therefore necessary to show that the prohibition on torture has generated an ancillary procedural rule which, by way of exception to state immunity, entitles or perhaps requires states to assume civil jurisdiction over other states in cases in which torture is alleged. Such a rule may be desirable and, since international law changes, may have developed. But, contrary to the assertion of the minority in *Al–Adsani*, it is not *entailed* by the prohibition of torture. (See also Swinton J. in *Bouzari v. Islamic Republic of Iran* (2002) 124 ILR 427, 443 at para. 62).

46.   Whether such an exception is now recognised by international law must be ascertained in the normal way from treaties, judicial decisions and the writings of reputed publicists. * * *

There is nothing in the Torture Convention which creates an exception to state immunity in civil proceedings. * * *

47.   The other relevant treaty is the United Nations Convention on Jurisdictional Immunities of States and Their Property (2004) (hereafter "the State Immunity Convention") which has been signed but not yet ratified by the United Kingdom and a number of other states. It is the result of many years work by the International Law Commission and codifies the law of statute immunity. Article 5, in terms similar to section 1(1) of SIA, provides that:

"A state enjoys immunity, in respect of itself and its property, from the jurisdiction of the courts of another state subject to the provisions of the present Convention."

There follows a number of exceptions but none for cases in which there is an allegation of torture.

48. The next source of international law is judicial decisions. I shall start with international tribunals. In *Democratic Republic of the Congo v. Belgium (Case concerning arrest warrant of 11 April 2000)* [2002] ICJ Rep. 3 ("the Arrest Warrant Case.") * * * [see excerpts below in subsection 4, especially paragraphs 48 and 58].

49. What this case shows is that the jus cogens nature of the rule alleged to have been infringed by the state or one of its officials does not provide an automatic answer to the question of whether another state has jurisdiction. It is necessary carefully to examine the sources of international law concerning the particular immunity claimed. Thus *Pinochet (No 3)* derived from the terms of the Torture Convention (and in particular, the definition of torture) the removal from torturers of an immunity from criminal prosecution which was based simply on the fact that they had acted or purported to act on behalf of the state. But the *Arrest Warrant* case confirms the opinion of the judges in the *Pinochet* case that General Pinochet would have enjoyed immunity, on a different basis, if he had still been Head of State.

50. In a separate concurring opinion, Judges Higgins, Kooijmans and Buergenthal speculated about possible future developments in international law. They said (at para. 48) that in civil matters they saw "the beginnings of a very broad form of extraterritorial jurisdiction." Such a jurisdiction had been exercised in torture cases by Federal Courts in the United States under the terms of the Alien Tort Claims Act (hereafter "ATCA"). I shall discuss some of these cases later, but the comment of the judges in the *Arrest Warrant* case was chilly:

"While this unilateral exercise of the function of guardian of international values has been much commented on, it has not attracted the approbation of states generally."(para. 48)

51. The judgment of the International Criminal Tribunal for the Former Yugoslavia in *Prosecutor v. Furundzija* (1998) 38 I.L.M. 317 contains an interesting discussion of the international law which prohibits torture. First (at p. 348) the prohibition covers potential breaches. That does not concern us here. Secondly (pp. 348–349), it imposes obligations erga omnes. That means that obligations are:

"owed towards all the other members of the international community, each of which then has a correlative right [which] gives rise to a claim for compliance accruing to each and every member, which then has the right to insist on fulfilment of the obligation or in any case to call for the breach to be discontinued."

52. This presumably means that a state whose national has been tortured by the agents of another state may claim redress before a tribunal

which has the necessary jurisdiction. But that says nothing about state immunity in domestic courts. * * *

53. Thirdly (pp. 349–350), the prohibition has acquired the status of jus cogens. As to this, the tribunal said:

"155. The fact that torture is prohibited by a peremptory norm of international law has other effects at the inter-state and individual levels. At the inter-state level, it serves to internationally de-legitimise any legislative, administrative or judicial act authorising torture. It would be senseless to argue, on the one hand, that on account of the jus cogens value of the prohibition against torture, treaties or customary rules providing for torture would be null and void ab initio, and then be unmindful of a state say, taking national measures authorising or condoning torture or absolving its perpetrators through an amnesty law. If such a situation were to arise, the national measures, violating the general principle and any relevant treaty provision, would produce the legal effects discussed above and in addition would not be accorded international legal recognition. Proceedings could be initiated by potential victims if they had locus standi before a competent international or national judicial body with a view to asking it to hold the national measure to be internationally unlawful; or the victim could bring a civil suit for damage in a foreign court, which would therefore be asked inter alia to disregard the legal value of the national authorising act."

54. The observations about the possibility of a civil suit for damages are not directed to the question of state immunity. They assume the existence of a "competent international or national judicial body" before which the claimant has locus standi and are concerned to emphasise that a national measure purporting to legitimate torture will be disregarded.

59. I turn next to the decisions of national courts. In *Siderman v. Republic of Argentina* (1992) 965 F. 2d 699 (9th Cir.) the U.S. Court of Appeals decided that Argentina was entitled to state immunity in an action alleging torture. The reasoning of the court (at p. 718) left open the possibility that there might be such an exception in customary international law, derived from the jus cogens nature of the prohibition on torture ("the ... argument carries much force") but held that the court was bound by the unequivocal terms of the FSIA. While *Siderman* turned upon the terms of national legislation, the legislation itself is evidence against a state practice of having an exception to state immunity in torture cases.

60. In *Bouzari v. Islamic Republic of Iran* 124 ILR 427 the question of whether customary international law recognised a torture exception to state immunity was specifically raised. In the Superior Court Swinton J examined the authorities, including the *Arrest Warrant* case [2002] ICJ Rep 3 and *Al–Adsani* 34 EHRR 273 and concluded (at para 73) that:

"the decisions of state courts, international tribunals and state legislation do not support the conclusion that there is a general state practice which provides an exception from state immunity for acts of torture committed outside the forum state.''

———————

However, the *Al–Adsani* case dissent warrants consideration, particularly in light of the general trend of international law in diminishing state immunity and in light of the evolution of the theoretical basis for immunity change seen above in the ICJ *Arrest Warrant* case, below in Sub Section 4.

Case of Al–Adsani v. The United Kingdom

European Court of Human Rights
(Application no. 35763/97)
Judgment, 21 November 2001

Joint Dissenting Opinion of Judges Rozakis and Caflisch Joined by Judges Wildhaber, Costa, Cabral Barreto and Vajić

We regret that we are unable to concur with the Court's majority in finding that, in the present case, there has not been a violation of Article 6 of the Convention [for the Protection of human Rights and Fundamental Freedoms] in so far as the right of access to a court is concerned. Unlike the majority, we consider that the applicant was unduly deprived of his right of access to English courts to entertain the merits of his claim against the State of Kuwait although that claim was linked to serious allegations of torture. To us the main reasoning of the majority—that the standards applicable in civil cases differ from those applying in criminal matters when a conflict arises between the peremptory norm of international law on the prohibition of torture and the rules on State immunity—raises fundamental questions, and we disagree for the following reasons.

* * *

By accepting that the rule on prohibition of torture is a rule of *jus cogens*, the majority recognise that it is hierarchically higher than any other rule of international law, be it general or particular, customary or conventional, with the exception, of course, of other *jus cogens* norms. For the basic characteristic of a *jus cogens* is that, as a source of law in the now vertical international legal system, it overrides any other rule which does not have the same status. In the event of a conflict between a *jus cogens* rule and any other rule of international law, the former prevails. The consequence of such prevalence is that the conflicting rule is null and void, or, in any event, does not produce legal effects which are in contradiction with the content of the peremptory rule.

4.   The majority, while accepting that the rule on the prohibition of torture is a *jus cogens* norm, refuse to draw the consequences of such acceptance. They contend that a distinction must be made between criminal proceedings, where apparently they accept that a *jus cogens* rule has the overriding force to deprive the rules of sovereign immunity from their

legal effects, and civil proceedings, where, in the absence of authority, they consider that the same conclusion cannot be drawn. * * *

[T]he distinction made by the majority between civil and criminal proceedings, concerning the effect of the rule of the prohibition of torture, is not consonant with the very essence of the operation of the *jus cogens* rules. It is not the nature of the proceedings which determines the effects that a *jus cogens* rule has upon another rule of international law, but the character of the rule as a peremptory norm and its interaction with a hierarchically lower rule. The prohibition of torture, being a rule of *jus cogens*, acts in the international sphere and deprives the rule of sovereign immunity of all its legal effects in that sphere. The criminal or civil nature of the domestic proceedings is immaterial. The jurisdictional bar is lifted by the very interaction of the international rules involved, and the national judge cannot admit a plea of immunity raised by the defendant State as an element preventing him from entering into the merits of the case and from dealing with the claim of the applicant for the alleged damages inflicted upon him.

* * *

Dissenting Opinion of Judge Ferrari Bravo

What a pity! The Court, whose task in this case was to rule whether there had been a violation of Article 6 § 1, had a golden opportunity to issue a clear and forceful condemnation of all acts of torture. To do so, it need only have upheld the thrust of the House of Lords' judgment in *Regina v. Bow Street Metropolitan Stipendiary and Others, ex parte Pinochet Ugarte (No. 3)* (judgment of 24 March 1999 [2000] Appeal Cases 147), to the effect that the prohibition of torture is now *jus cogens*, so that torture is a crime under international law. It follows that every State has a duty to *contribute* to the punishment of torture and cannot hide behind formalist arguments to avoid having to give judgment.

I say to "contribute" to punishment, and not, obviously, to punish, since it was clear that the acts of torture had not taken place in the United Kingdom but elsewhere, in a State over which the Court did not have jurisdiction.

But it is precisely one of those old formalist arguments which the Court endorsed when it said (in paragraph 61 of the judgment) that it was unable to discern any rules of international law requiring it not to apply the rule of immunity from civil suit where acts of torture were alleged. And the Court went further, notwithstanding its analysis of the cases mentioned in paragraphs 62 to 65, concluding sadly in paragraph 66 that the contrary rule was not *yet* accepted * * *!

There will be other such cases, but the Court has unfortunately missed a very good opportunity to deliver a courageous judgment.

NOTES AND QUESTIONS

1. See the discussion in Chapter 2 *supra* of Germany's case against Italy for failing to respect sovereign immunity in a case of a *jus cogens* violation.

Jurisdictional Immunities of the State (*Germany v. Italy*), International Court of Justice, Press Release, No. 2009/18, 4 May 2009, www.icj-cij.org. Do you find that any of the theories justifying sovereign immunity would be properly applied to human rights cases? Is there a case to be made for universal jurisdiction without sovereign immunity in cases of some or any such violations of international law? If immunity is applied, what other means of redress might be available?

2. Considering the text of FSIA Section 1605, reproduced in the *Rein* opinion, would you conclude that there is a general exception denying immunity in cases of terrorism?

3. In the *Pinochet* case, *supra* Lord Millet stated that

> International law cannot be supposed to have established a crime having the character of a jus cogens and at the same time to have provided an immunity which is co-extensive with the obligation it seeks to impose.

How would you apply this statement in reaching a conclusion on the problem in the *Al–Adasni* case above?

4. Compare the effect of *jus cogens* in civil cases by Lord Hoffman in the *Jones* case with the views of the minority in *As–Adsani*. Should jus cogens protect immunity in civil cases but not in criminal cases? Why?

5. Do you see any functional reason to retain immunity in such cases? Explain.

3.) *Rights in Immovable Property*

Permanent Mission of India to the United Nations et al. v. City of New York

United States Supreme Court
551 U.S. 193, 127 S.Ct. 2352, 168 L.Ed.2d 85 (2007)

■ JUSTICE THOMAS delivered the opinion of the Court.

The Foreign Sovereign Immunities Act of 1976 (FSIA), 28 U.S.C. § 1602 *et seq.*, governs federal courts' jurisdiction in lawsuits against foreign sovereigns. Today, we must decide whether the FSIA provides immunity to a foreign sovereign from a lawsuit to declare the validity of tax liens on property held by the sovereign for the purpose of housing its employees. We hold that the FSIA does not immunize a foreign sovereign from such a suit.

I

The Permanent Mission of India to the United Nations is located in a 26–floor building in New York City that is owned by the Government of India. Several floors are used for diplomatic offices, but approximately 20 floors contain residential units for diplomatic employees of the mission and their families. The employees—all of whom are below the rank of Head of

Mission or Ambassador—are Indian citizens who receive housing from the mission rent free.

* * *

Under New York law, real property owned by a foreign government is exempt from taxation if it is "used exclusively" for diplomatic offices or for the quarters of a diplomat "with the rank of ambassador or minister plenipotentiary" to the United Nations. N.Y. Real Prop. Tax Law Ann. *2355 § 418 (West 2000). But "[i]f a portion only of any lot or building . . . is used exclusively for the purposes herein described, then such portion only shall be exempt and the remainder shall be subject to taxation. . . ." *Ibid.*

For several years, the City of New York (City) has levied property taxes against petitioners for the portions of their buildings used to house lower level employees. Petitioners, however, refused to pay the taxes. By operation of New York law, the unpaid taxes eventually converted into tax liens held by the City against the two properties. As of February 1, 2003, the Indian Mission owed about $16.4 million in unpaid property taxes and interest * * *

* * *

As a threshold matter, property ownership is not an inherently sovereign function. See *Schooner Exchange v. McFaddon, 7 Cranch 116, 145, 3 L.Ed. 287* (1812) ("A prince, by acquiring private property in a foreign country, may possibly be considered as subjecting that property to the territorial jurisdiction, he may be considered as so far laying down the prince, and assuming the character of a private individual"). In addition, the FSIA was also meant "to codify . . . the pre-existing real property exception to sovereign immunity recognized by international practice." *Reclamantes, supra,* at 1521 (Scalia, J.). Therefore, it is useful to note that international practice at the time of the FSIA's enactment also supports the City's view that these sovereigns are not immune. The most recent restatement of foreign relations law at the time of the FSIA's enactment states that a foreign sovereign's immunity does not extend to "an action to obtain possession of or establish a property interest in immovable property located in the territory of the state exercising jurisdiction." Restatement (Second) of Foreign Relations Law of the United States § 68(b), p. 205 (1965). As stated above, because an action seeking the declaration of the validity of a tax lien on property is a suit to establish an interest in such property, such an action would be allowed under this rule.

* * *

In sum, the Vienna Convention does not unambiguously support either party on the jurisdictional question. In any event, nothing in the Vienna Convention deters us from our interpretation of the FSIA. Under the language of the FSIA's exception for immovable property, petitioners are not immune from the City's suits.

4.) Employment Issues

Barrondon v. United States of America

France, Court of Cassation, 1998
116 I.L.R. 622 (2000)

[In this action, Madame Barraondon sought damages against the United States following her dismissal as a nurse and medical secretary for the U.S. Embassy in Paris. The Court of Appeal of Versailles held that her action was inadmissible, in apparent recognition of the immunity of the U.S. for such actions. The Cour de Cassation stated that it "considered the principle of immunity from jurisdiction of foreign states", and in the end determined that immunity did not apply in her circumstances. In its analysis the Cour considered the Appeal Court's findings on Madame's Barrondon's tasks at the Embassy]:

> —First, the giving of assistance to American and non-American employees of the Embassy and associated agencies as well as to military personnel (first aid, various forms of care, contacts with doctors and hospitals, the organization of medical transfers, medical assistance to visitors . . .);

> Secondly, Madame Barrandon was required to provide a medical secretariat (medical translations, medical reports, information)

> Finally, she was to ensure the sterilization and maintenance of surgical instruments and dressings.

> It followed, according to the Court of Appeal, that Madame Barrandon performed her functions for the benefit of American and non-American civil and military personnel posted in Paris, as well as visitors to the Embassy, in the interests of the public service organized by the United States of America for the benefit of its agents, nationals and foreign citizens subject to its authority or for whom it was responsible.

> [This Court considers,] however, that it results from the findings of' the Court of Appeal that the tasks performed by Madame Barrandon did not give her any special responsibility for the performance of the public service of the Embassy, so that her dismissal constituted an ordinary act of administration (acte de gestion).

> It follows that the Court of Appeal did not draw the correct legal consequences from its findings and violated the above-mentioned principle.

NOTE

Article 11 of the United Nations Convention might or might not lead to a similar result. Immunity is barred in general, but there are a number of significant exceptions. Immunity is retained in Article 11(2), for example: if the employee has been recruited to perform functions in the exercise of governmental authority, the employee is a diplomatic agent or consular officer, the employee is a member of the diplomatic staff of a permanent mission to an international organization, the employee enjoys diplomatic immunity, or if "the subject matter of the proceeding is the recruitment, renewal or employment or reinstatement of an individual. Paragraph 2(e) denies immunity where the subject-matter of the proceeding is the dismissal or termination of employment of an individual, and as determined by the head of State, the head of Government or the Minister for Foreign Affairs of the employer State, such a proceeding would interfere with the security interests of that State." Paragraph (e) denies immunity for nationals and residents of the employer State and paragraph (f) covers the case where the employee and the employer State have otherwise agreed.

5.) Waiver

States may of course waive sovereign immunity. See Sampson v. Federal Republic of Germany, 250 F.3d 1145 (7th Cir. 2001), 2001 for a discussion concluding Germany did not waive its immunity from suit in the case.

2.   Immunity of State Officials: Head of State and Others

Modern international law on the subject of immunity for Head of State and other high officials of government began with Article 7 of the Charter of the International Military Tribunal establishing the Nuremberg war crime trials after World War II in precluding immunity of heads of state in those proceedings. The Security Council in S/RES/827 (1993) adopted a parallel exception incident to the creation of the International Tribunal to prosecute crimes in the former Yugoslavia. Article 7.2 of the Annex to that Resolution provides that: "The official position of any accused person, whether as Head of State or Government or as a responsible Government official, shall not relieve such person of criminal responsibility nor mitigate punishment". An identical provision was adopted for the Rwanda Tribunal (see Article 6.2 of that Tribunal's Statute, 33 I.L.M. 1598, 1604 (1994)) and another is provided more permanently in the Rome Statute of the International Criminal Court, 37 I.L.M. 999 (1998). Broader issues of immunity and impunity have arisen in the International Court of Justice and in national courts as seen in the cases that follow, beginning with the landmark *Pinochet* case. See Chapter 1.

Regina v. Bartle and the Commissioner of Police for the Metropolis and Others Ex Parte Pinochet

House of Lords, 24 March 1999
Pinochet III, [1999] 2 All ER 97, 170, 2 WLR 827, 38 I.L.M. 581, 644 (1999)

By a majority of six to one, the House of Lords denied immunity on the torture charges.

LORD BROWNE–WILKINSON

My Lords,

State immunity

This is the point around which most of the argument turned. It is of considerable general importance internationally since, if Senator Pinochet is not entitled to immunity in relation to the acts of torture alleged to have occurred after 29 September 1988, it will be the first time so far as counsel have discovered when a local domestic court has refused to afford immunity to a head of state or former head of state on the grounds that there can be no immunity against prosecution for certain international crimes.

Given the importance of the point, it is surprising how narrow is the area of dispute. There is general agreement between the parties as to the rules of statutory immunity and the rationale which underlies them. The issue is whether international law grants state immunity in relation to the international crime of torture and, if so, whether the Republic of Chile is entitled to claim such immunity even though Chile, Spain and the United Kingdom are all parties to the Torture Convention and therefore contractually bound to give effect to its provisions from 8 December 1988 at the latest.

* * * State immunity probably grew from the historical immunity of the person of the monarch. In any event, such personal immunity of the head of state persists to the present day: the head of state is entitled to the same immunity as the state itself The diplomatic representative of the foreign state in the forum state is also afforded the same immunity in recognition of the dignity of the state which he represents. This immunity enjoyed by a head of state in power and an ambassador in post is a complete immunity attaching to the person of the head of state or ambassador and rendering him immune from all actions or prosecutions whether or not they relate to matters done for the benefit of the state. Such immunity is said to be granted ratione personae.

What then when the ambassador leaves his post or the head of state is deposed? The position of the ambassador is covered by the Vienna Convention on Diplomatic Relations, 1961. After providing for immunity from arrest (Article 29) and from criminal and civil jurisdiction (Article 31), Article 39(1) provides that the ambassador's privileges shall be enjoyed from the moment he takes up post, and subsection (2) provides:

> "(2) When the functions of a person enjoying privileges and immunities have come to an end, such privileges and immunities shall normally cease at the moment when he leaves the country, or on expiry of a reasonable period in which to do so, but shall subsist until that time, even in case of armed conflict. However, with respect to acts performed by such a person in the exercise of his functions as a member of the mission, immunity shall continue to subsist."

The continuing partial immunity of the ambassador after leaving post is of a different kind from that enjoyed ratione personae while he was in post. Since he is no longer the representative of the foreign state he merits no particular privileges or immunities as a person. However in order to preserve the integrity of the activities of the foreign state during the period when he was ambassador, it is necessary to provide that immunity is afforded to his official acts during his tenure in post. If this were not done the sovereign immunity of the state could be evaded by calling in question acts done during the previous ambassador's time. Accordingly under Article 39(2) the ambassador, like any other official of the state, enjoys immunity in relation to his official acts done while he was an official. This limited immunity, ratione materiae, is to be contrasted with the former immunity ratione personae which gave complete immunity to all activities whether public or private.

In my judgment at common law a former head of state enjoys similar immunities, ratione materiae, once he ceases to be head of state. He too loses immunity ratione personae on ceasing to be head of state: see Watts *The Legal Position in International Law of Heads of States, Heads of Government and Foreign Ministers* p. 88 and the cases there cited. He can be sued on his private obligations: *Ex–King Farouk of Egypt v. Christian Dior* (I 957) 24 I.L.R. 228, *Jimenez v. Aristeguieta* (1962) 31 1 F. 2d 547. As ex head of state he cannot be sued in respect of acts performed whilst head of state in his public capacity: *Hatch v. Baez* [1876] 7 Hun. 596. Thus, at common law, the position of the former ambassador and the former head of state appears to be much the same: both enjoy immunity for acts done in performance of their respective functions whilst in office.

* * *

The question then which has to be answered is whether the alleged Organisation of state torture by Senator Pinochet (if proved) would constitute an act committed by Senator Pinochet as part of his official functions as head of state. It is not enough to say that it cannot be part of the functions of the head of state to commit a crime. Actions which are criminal under the local law can still have been done officially and therefore give rise to immunity ratione materiae. The case needs to be analyzed more closely.

Can it be said that the commission of a crime which is an international crime against humanity and *jus cogens* is an act done in an official capacity on behalf of the state? I believe there to be strong ground for saying that the implementation of torture as defined by the Torture Convention cannot be a state function. This is the view taken by Sir Arthur Watts (*supra*) who said * * * at p. 84 * * *:

> "It can no longer be doubted that as a matter of general customary international law a head of state will personally be liable to be called to account if there is sufficient evidence that he authorised or perpetrated such serious international crimes."

It can be objected that Sir Arthur was looking at those cases where the international community has established an international tribunal in relation to which the regulating document expressly makes the head of state subject to the tribunal's jurisdiction: see, for example, the Nuremberg Charter Article 7, the Statute of the International Tribunal for former Yugoslavia, the Statute of the International Tribunal for Rwanda and the Statute of the International Criminal Court. It is true that in these cases it is expressly said that the head of state or former head of state is subject to the court's jurisdiction. But those are cases in which a new court with no existing jurisdiction is being established. The jurisdiction being established by the Torture Convention and the Hostages Convention is one where existing domestic courts of all the countries are being authorised and required to take jurisdiction internationally. The question is whether, in this new type of jurisdiction, the only possible view is that those made subject to the jurisdiction of each of the state courts of the world in relation to torture are not entitled to claim immunity.

I have doubts whether, before the coming into force of the Torture Convention, the existence of the international crime of torture as *jus cogens* was enough to justify the conclusion that the organization of state torture could not rank for immunity purposes as performance of an official function. At that stage there was no international tribunal to punish torture and no general jurisdiction to permit or require its punishment in domestic courts. Not until there was some form of universal jurisdiction for the punishment of the crime of torture could it really be talked about as a fully constituted international crime. But in my judgment the Torture Convention did provide what was missing: a worldwide universal jurisdiction. Further, it required all member states to ban and outlaw torture: Article 2. How can it be for international law purposes an official function to do something which international law itself prohibits and criminalises? Thirdly, an essential feature of the international crime of torture is that it must be committed "by or with the acquiescence of a public official or other person acting in an official capacity." As a result all defendants in torture cases will be state officials. Yet, if the former head of state has immunity, the man most responsible will escape liability while his inferiors (the chiefs of police, junior army officers) who carried out his orders will be liable. I find it impossible to accept that this was the intention.

Finally, and to my mind decisively, if the implementation of a torture regime is a public function giving rise to immunity *ratione materiae*, this produces bizarre results. *Immunity ratione materiae* applies not only to ex-heads of state and ex-ambassadors but to all state officials who have been involved in carrying out the functions of the state. Such immunity is necessary in order to prevent state immunity being circumvented by prosecuting or suing the official who, for example, actually carried out the torture when a claim against the head of state would be precluded by the doctrine of immunity. If that applied to the present case, and if the implementation of the torture regime is to be treated as official business sufficient to found an immunity for the former head of state, it must also be official business sufficient to justify immunity for his inferiors who actually did the torturing. Under the Convention the international crime of torture can only be committed by an official or someone in an official capacity. They would all be entitled to immunity. It would follow that there can be no case outside Chile in which a successful prosecution for torture can be brought unless the State of Chile is prepared to waive its right to its officials' immunity. Therefore the whole elaborate structure of universal jurisdiction over torture committed by officials is rendered abortive and one of the main objectives of the Torture Convention—to provide a system under which there is no safe haven for torturers—will have been frustrated. In my judgment all these factors together demonstrate that the notion of continued immunity for ex-heads of state is inconsistent with the provisions of the Torture Convention.

For these reasons in my judgment if, as alleged, Senator Pinochet organised and authorised torture after 8 December 1988, he was not acting in any capacity which gives rise to immunity *ratione materiae* because such actions were contrary to international law, Chile had agreed to outlaw such conduct and Chile had agreed with the other parties to the Torture Convention that all signatory states should have jurisdiction to try official torture (as defined in the Convention) even if such torture were committed in Chile.

* * *

NOTES AND QUESTIONS

1.   Sovereign immunity or diplomatic immunity? The *Pinochet* opinion, like others in the readings above, raises at times the question whether the issue being decided is one of sovereign immunity or of diplomatic immunity. Or are both part and parcel of the same thing? Does it help to speak of the ratione materiae or ratione personae? Does Article 39(2) apply to persons who are not diplomatic agents? Lord Browne–Wilkinson spoke of the common law as the bridge. Is that an appropriate solution?

2.   The impact of Pinochet. *Pinochet* is theoretically quite far reaching if it applies broadly to violations of humanitarian law and serious war crimes, including international aggression committed by government officers, or to all subjects of universal jurisdiction under international law. Would this be a desirable outcome when the law of aggression, for example, may not yet be fully developed and free from ambiguity? Would cases like Senator Pinochet's be better heard by a multinational forum, like the International Criminal Court, rather than national courts? Why?

3.   How would you advise former heads of state to conduct themselves in the light of the Pinochet case?

4.   Should immunity apply to *serving* heads of state? That sensitive question was a key element in the *Gadaffi* Case in the highest competent court of France in 2001, which found it did not have jurisdiction over a serving head of state. *Gadaffi*, France, Court of Cassation, March 13, 2001, Judgment of the Court of Cassation 125 ILR 490, reproduced in part in Chapter 11. Would such immunity apply in cases before the International Criminal Court or the Ad Hoc international criminal Tribunals? See Chapter 5 *infra*.

Case Concerning the Arrest Warrant of 11 April 2000

Democratic Republic of the Congo v. Belgium
International Court of Justice
2002 I.C.J. Rep. 3 (Judgment of Feb. 14)

[In this first case on official immunity to come before the ICJ, a Belgian Magistrate issued "an international arrest warrant in absentia" against Mr. Abdulaye Yerodia Ndombasi, then serving as the Foreign Minister of the Democratic Republic of the Congo. Mr. Yerodia was charged with grave violations of the law of war, and Belgium claimed jurisdiction the basis of its legislation and the principle of "universal jurisdiction". The Congo commenced the present proceedings to have the Court annul the warrant on the ground, among others, that as Foreign Minister, Mr. Yerodia was entitled to immunity under international law. A divided Court developed what has been called a "functional" view of the theoretical basis for the immunity, that is, the immunity can be justified on the basis of the nature and importance of the function of the offending governmental body or official rather than the traditional principles of sovereign equality and independence of states. Portions of the Court's Judgment below take up the issue of immunity.]

51.   The Court would observe at the outset that in international law it is firmly established that, as also diplomatic and consular agents, certain holders of high-ranking office in a State, such as the Head of State, Head of Government and Minister for Foreign Affairs, enjoy immunities from jurisdiction in other States, both civil and criminal. For the purposes of the present case, it is only the immunity from criminal jurisdiction and the inviolability of an incumbent Minister for Foreign Affairs that fall for the Court to consider.

* * *

53.   In customary international law, the immunities accorded to Ministers for Foreign Affairs are not granted for their personal benefit, but to ensure the effective performance of their functions on behalf of their respective States. In order to determine the extent of these immunities, the Court must therefore first consider the nature of the functions exercised by a Minister for Foreign Affairs. He or she is in charge of his or her Government's diplomatic activities and generally acts as its representative in international negotiations and intergovernmental meetings. Ambassadors and other diplomatic agents carry out their duties under his or her authority. His or her acts may bind the State represented, and there is a presumption that a Minister for Foreign Affairs, simply by virtue of that office, has full powers to act on behalf of the State (see, e.g., Art. 7, para. 2(a), of the 1969 Vienna Convention on the Law of Treaties). In the performance of these functions, he or she is frequently required to travel internationally, and thus must be in a position freely to do so whenever the need should arise. He or she must also be in constant communication with the Government, and with its diplomatic missions around the world, and be capable at any time of communicating with representatives of other States. The Court further observes that a Minister for Foreign Affairs, responsible for the conduct of his or her State's relations with all other States, occupies a position such that, like the Head of State or the Head of Government, he or she is recognized under international law as representative of the State solely by virtue of his or her office. He or she does not have to present

letters of credence: to the contrary, it is generally the Minister who determines the authority to be conferred upon diplomatic agents and countersigns their letters of credence. Finally, it is to the Minister for Foreign Affairs that *chargés d'affaires* are accredited.

54.   The Court accordingly concludes that the functions of a Minister for Foreign Affairs are such that, throughout the duration of his or her office, he or she when abroad enjoys full immunity from criminal jurisdiction and inviolability. That immunity and that inviolability protect the individual concerned against any act of authority of another State which would hinder him or her in the performance of his or her duties.

55.   In this respect, no distinction can be drawn between acts performed by a Minister for Foreign Affairs in an "official" capacity, and those claimed to have been performed in a "private capacity", or, for that matter, between acts performed before the person concerned assumed office as Minister for Foreign Affairs and acts committed during the period of office. Thus, if a Minister for Foreign Affairs is arrested in another State on a criminal charge, he or she is clearly thereby prevented from exercising the functions of his or her office. The consequences of such impediment to the exercise of those official functions are equally serious, regardless of whether the Minister for Foreign Affairs was, at the time of arrest, present in the territory of the arresting State on an "official" visit or a "private" visit, regardless of whether the arrest relates to acts allegedly performed before the person became the Minister for Foreign Affairs or to acts performed while in office, and regardless of whether the arrest relates to alleged acts performed in an "official" capacity or a "private" capacity. Furthermore, even the mere risk that, by travelling to or transiting another State a Minister for Foreign Affairs might be exposing himself or herself to legal proceedings could deter the Minister from travelling internationally when required to do so for the purposes of the performance of his or her official functions.

* * *

56.   The Court will now address Belgium's argument that immunities accorded to incumbent Ministers for Foreign Affairs can in no case protect them where they are suspected of having committed war crimes or crimes against humanity. In support of this position, Belgium refers in its Counter–Memorial to various legal instruments creating international criminal tribunals, to examples from national legislation, and to the jurisprudence of national and international courts.

* * *

58.   The Court has carefully examined State practice, including national legislation and those few decisions of national higher courts, such as the House of Lords or the French Court of Cassation. It has been unable to deduce from this practice that there exists under customary international law any form of exception to the rule according immunity from criminal jurisdiction and inviolability to incumbent Ministers for Foreign Affairs, where they are suspected of having committed war crimes or crimes against humanity.

* * *

61. Accordingly, the immunities enjoyed under international law by an incumbent or former Minister for Foreign Affairs do not represent a bar to criminal prosecution in certain circumstances.

First, such persons enjoy no criminal immunity under international law in their own countries, and may thus be tried by those countries' courts in accordance with the relevant rules of domestic law.

Secondly, they will cease to enjoy immunity from foreign jurisdiction if the State which they represent or have represented decides to waive that immunity.

Thirdly, after a person ceases to hold the office of Minister for Foreign Affairs, he or she will no longer enjoy all of the immunities accorded by international law in other States. Provided that it has jurisdiction under international law, a court of one State may try a former Minister for Foreign Affairs of another State in respect of acts committed prior or subsequent to his or her period of office, as well as in respect of acts committed during that period of office in a private capacity.

Fourthly, an incumbent or former Minister for Foreign Affairs may be subject to criminal proceedings before certain international criminal courts, where they have jurisdiction. * * *

* * *

71. * * * As in the case of the warrant's issue, its international circulation from June 2000 by the Belgian authorities, given its nature and purpose, effectively infringed Mr. Yerodia's immunity as the Congo's incumbent Minister for Foreign Affairs and was furthermore liable to affect the Congo's conduct of its international relations. Since Mr. Yerodia was called upon in that capacity to undertake travel in the performance of his duties, the mere international circulation of the warrant, even in the absence of "further steps" by Belgium, could have resulted, in particular, in his arrest while abroad. The Court observes in this respect that Belgium itself cites information to the effect that Mr. Yerodia, "on applying for a visa to go to two countries, [apparently] learned that he ran the risk of being arrested as a result of the arrest warrant issued against him by Belgium", adding that "[t]his, moreover, is what the [Congo] . . . hints when it writes that the arrest warrant 'sometimes forced Minister Yerodia to travel by roundabout routes' ". Accordingly, the Court concludes that the circulation of the warrant, whether or not it significantly interfered with Mr. Yerodia's diplomatic activity, constituted a violation of an obligation of Belgium towards the Congo, in that it failed to respect the immunity of the incumbent Minister for Foreign Affairs of the Congo and, more particularly, infringed the immunity from criminal jurisdiction and the inviolability then enjoyed by him under international law.

NOTES AND QUESTIONS

1. Following the ICJ *Arrest Warrant* case, above, the Belgian Code of Criminal Procedure was modified by the insertion of the following text:

"Article 1bis, Paragraph 1. In accordance with international law, there shall be no prosecution with regard to:

—Heads of State, heads of government, and ministers of foreign affairs, during their terms of office, and any other person whose immunity is recognized by international law;

—Persons who have immunity, full or partial, based on a treaty by which Belgium is bound.

Paragraph 2. In accordance with international law, no act of coercion involving the bringing of criminal proceedings may be initiated during the time of their stay, against any person officially invited to stay in the territory of the Kingdom by the Belgian authorities or by an international organization established in Belgium and with which Belgium has concluded a headquarters agreement." (42 I.L.M. 1258 (2003))

2.   The Belgian Court of Cassation in *H.A. v. S.A.* and others ruled in favor of immunity against claims for genocide, crimes against humanity and war crimes for Ariel Sharon while serving as Prime Minister of Israel. (42 I.L.M. 596 (2003)). In the UK, a Senior District Judge recognized the immunity of Robert Mugabe while president and Head of State of Zimbabwe (see 53 ICLQ 770 (2004)), and the case of Israeli Defense minister General Mofaz led to a similar result as reported in 53 ICLQ 771 (2004).

3.   In recent years there has been substantial legislative and judicial interest in immunities for high officials. Under the terms of Section 14(1) of the UK State Immunity Act of 1978, immunities and privileges apply to the sovereign or other foreign head of state in his public capacity, to the government of that state and to any department of that government. Section 20 states that the Diplomatic Privileges Act 1964 shall apply to—(a) a sovereign or other head of state; (b) members of his family forming part of his household; and (c) his private servants. *See* Andrew Dickinson, Rae Lindsay and James P. Loonam, State Immunity, 397.

4.   Two provisions of the United Nations Convention discussed above have a bearing on the immunity of state officials. In Article 2(b) the definition of "State" includes "(iv) representatives of the State acting in that capacity", while Article 3(2) provides that: "The present Convention is without prejudice to privileges and immunities accorded under international law to heads of state ratione personae".

5.   *Status of Forces.* Many countries and the European have "Status of Forces Agreements" to address the status of their military forces while present in a foreign country. The U.S. is party to more than 100 of these agreements in various shapes and sizes. Background and analysis from a U.S. perspective on this subject are contained in Congressional Research Service, *Report to Congress: Status of Forces Agreement (SOFA): What Is It, and Might One Be Utilized in Iraq?* (June 16, 2008). It states generally (p. 7): "SOFA is the legal protection from prosecution that will be afforded U.S. personnel while present in a foreign country. The agreement establishes which party to the agreement is able to assert criminal and/or civil

jurisdiction. In other words, the agreement establishes how the domestic civil and criminal laws are applied to U.S. personnel while serving in a foreign country.''

6.   If national and international courts are declining to innovate in the immunities field, and the balancing theory invoked in the *Arrest Warrant* Case above seems appropriate, how would you advise on the question of procedures to bring about the necessary changes in the law of state immunity?

7.   In addition to the immunity of states' heads of state and high officials, there are questions of restraints on property in pre-judgment and post judgment enforcement measures in national courts, such as attachments and execution enforcement measures. These issues are governed by Part IV of the United Nations Convention, and for the U.S. in Sections 1610 and 1611 of the FSIA, where specific exceptions are provided. Texts of these authorities are reproduced in the Document Supplement.

Further Reading Hazel Fox, The Law of State Immunity, 2nd ed. (2008); Rosanne Van Alebeek, The Immunity of States and Their Officials in International Criminal Law and International Human Rights Law (2008).

C.   Diplomatic Immunity and Protections

The *Arrest Warrant* and other cases above discuss the need for diplomats and diplomatic immunity.

Legal protection of the diplomatic process in most of its manifestations developed as customary international law over the centuries to become one of the most venerable, vital, and well respected parts of the international legal system. The principal source of diplomatic law in recent times has been the Vienna Convention on the Law of Diplomatic Relations of 1961 in force in 2009 in 186 countries (see selections in the Documentary Supplement). This body of international law is so well codified in the Convention that most of the rules are now readily available in understandable and mostly in unambiguous form on jurisdictional immunity and on protection in accordance with the special duty of receiving states to protect diplomatic premises and personnel.

Reflecting several centuries of application and experience, modern diplomatic law enjoys all but universal acceptance as reliable and workable body of rules, despite the many violations such as those which appear in the readings to follow. The international rules protecting the diplomatic process are supported by internal legislation in most countries, and by the practical notion of reciprocity which carries the substantial risk that violation by one country is likely to lead to consideration of reciprocal counter-violations by others. The Vienna Convention also carries the promise of further adaptability and evolution through customary international law, as suggested in the last paragraph of its Preamble which affirms ''* * * that the rules of customary international law should continue to govern questions not expressly regulated by the provisions of the present Convention''.

The Preamble of the Convention serves as an excellent introduction to this subject. The Preamble correctly recognizes the status of diplomatic agents going back to "ancient times", and refers to such basic concepts as the doctrine of "sovereign equality of states", the "maintenance of international peace and security", and the "development of friendly relations among nations, irrespective of their differing constitutional and social systems", all reflecting United Nations formulations which have particular application in the diplomatic field. Privileges and immunities are conferred for the purpose "not to benefit the individuals but to ensure the efficient performance of the *functions* of diplomatic missions as representing states", a concept employed repeatedly by the authorities represented in this chapter.

Immunities in the diplomatic field are closely related to state immunities developed in Section B, where the underlying concepts are seen as evolving from "sovereign equality" and "national independence" toward protection for the state functions of the immunity holder. The question of "doing justice" to claimants losing out in litigation to the holders of immunities arises in the diplomatic immunities field just as it does in the state immunities field.

The functions of the diplomatic missions are authoritatively described in Article 3.1 of the Vienna Convention as follows:

(a) representing the sending State in the receiving State;

(b) protecting in the receiving State the interests of the sending State and of its nationals, within the limits permitted by international law;

(c) negotiating with the Government of the receiving State;

(d) ascertaining by all lawful means conditions and developments in the receiving State, and reporting thereon to the Government of the sending State;

(e) promoting friendly relations between the sending State and the receiving State, and developing their economic, cultural and scientific relations.

United States policy in this sector is established in the U.S. Foreign Missions Act set forth in the Document Supplement.

1. DIPLOMATS

a. INVIOLABILITY OF DIPLOMATIC PREMISES AND OTHER PROPERTY

Vienna Convention on Diplomatic Relations

http://www.un.int/usa/host_dip.htm

Article 22

1. The premises of the mission shall be inviolable. The agents of the receiving State may not enter them, except with the consent of the head of the mission.

2.   The receiving State is under a special duty to take all appropriate steps to protect the premises of the mission against any intrusion or damage and to prevent any disturbance of the peace of the mission or impairment of its dignity.

3.   The premises of the mission, their furnishings and other property thereon and the means of transport of the mission shall be immune from search, requisition, attachment or execution.

Article 24

The archives and documents of the mission shall be inviolable at any time and wherever they may be.

Article 29

The person of a diplomatic agent shall be inviolable. He shall not be liable to any form of arrest or detention. The receiving State shall treat him with due respect and shall take all appropriate steps to prevent any attack on his person, freedom or dignity.

Article 30

1.   The private residence of a diplomatic agent shall enjoy the same inviolability and protection as the premises of the mission.

2.   His papers, correspondence and, except as provided in paragraph 3 of article 31, his property, shall likewise enjoy inviolability.

---

767 Third Avenue Associates v. Permanent Mission of the Republic of Zaire

United States Court of Appeals, Second Circuit
988 F.2d 295 (1993)

■ CARDAMONE, CIRCUIT JUDGE:

This appeal emerges out of a landlord-tenant dispute. When the Zaire mission to the United Nations occupying leased space on the east side of midtown Manhattan repeatedly fell into arrears on its rent, it was sued by its landlord. The tenant's defense against being evicted was diplomatic immunity. A district court refused to credit this defense and instead granted summary judgment to the landlord for back rent and also awarded it possession of the premises, ordering United States Marshals to remove the Mission physically if it failed to vacate in a timely manner.

Enforcement of an owner's common law right to obtain possession of its premises upon the tenant's non-payment of rent may not override an established rule of international law. Nor under the guise of local concepts of fairness may a court upset international treaty provisions to which the United States is a party. The reason for this is not a blind adherence to a rule of law in an international treaty, uncaring of justice at home, but that by upsetting existing treaty relationships American diplomats abroad may well be denied lawful protection of their lives and property to which they would otherwise be entitled. That possibility weighs so heavily on the scales of justice that it militates against enforcement of the landlord's right to obtain possession of its property for rental arrears.

* * *

DISCUSSION

I   Inapplicability of Foreign Sovereign Immunities Act

The inviolability of a United Nations mission under international and U.S. law precludes the forcible eviction of the Mission. Applicable treaties, binding upon federal courts to the same extent as domestic statutes, *see Trans World Airlines, Inc. v. Franklin Mint Corp.*, 466 U.S. 243, 26061, 104 S.Ct. 1776, 1786–87, 80 L.Ed.2d 273 (1984); *United States v. Palestine Liberation Org.*, 695 F.Supp. 1456, 1464 (S.D.N.Y.1988) [see Excerpts in Chapter 1 above], establish that Zaire's Permanent Mission is inviolable. The district court erred in misinterpreting the applicable treaties and in carving out a judicial exception to the broad principle of mission inviolability incorporated in those agreements.

Although the United States' support for appellant is based solely on a number of relevant treaties, the district court rested its decision in part on an interpretation of the Foreign Sovereign Immunities Act, 28 U.S.C. §§ 1602–1611 (1988). That Act deserves brief discussion since the landlord continues to raise its provisions. While Sage Realty correctly asserts that Congress aimed to permit courts to make sovereign immunity determinations, see id. § 1602, plaintiffs give short shrift to the Act's explicit provision that it operates "[s]ubject to existing international agreements to which the United States is a party." *Id.* § 1609. Because of this provision the diplomatic and consular immunities of foreign states recognized under various treaties remain unaltered by the Act. *See Mashayekhi v. Iran*, 515 F.Supp. 41, 42 (D.D.C.1981) ("Under the FSIA ..., what were then 'existing international agreements' remain valid and superior to the FSIA wherever terms concerning immunity contained in the previous agreement conflict with the FSIA."); * * *

II   International Agreements

A.   Generally

The international agreements presented us and relied upon by the United States all pre-date the Foreign Sovereign Immunities Act. They include the United Nations Charter, 59 Stat. 1031 (1945), the Agreement Between the United Nations and the United States of America Regarding the Headquarters of the United Nations, June 26–Nov. 21 1947, 61 Stat. 754, 756 [hereafter the U.N. Headquarters Agreement], the Convention on the Privileges and Immunities of the United Nations, adopted Feb. 13, 1946, 21 U.S.T. 1418 [hereafter the U.N. Convention on Privileges and

Immunities], and the Vienna Convention on Diplomatic Relations, done Apr. 18, 1961, 23 U.S.T. 3227 [hereafter the Vienna Convention].

The first three of those treaties provide for various diplomatic protections and immunities without specific reference to mission premises. The U.N. Charter, for example, provides "[r]epresentatives of the Members of the United Nations and officials of the Organization shall similarly enjoy such privileges and immunities as are necessary for the independent exercise of their functions in connection with the Organization." U.N. Charter, supra, Art. 105(2). The U.N. Headquarters Agreement states that representatives of member states "shall, whether residing inside or outside the headquarters district, be entitled in the territory of the United States to the same privileges and immunities ... as it accords to diplomatic envoys accredited to it." U.N. Headquarters Agreement, supra, Art. V(4). The Convention on Privileges and Immunities of the United Nations recites in somewhat more detail that representatives of member states shall "enjoy the following privileges and immunities: (a) immunity from personal arrest or detention ...; (b) inviolability for all papers and documents; ... (g) such other privileges, immunities and facilities not inconsistent [with] the foregoing as diplomatic envoys enjoy...." U.N. Convention on Privileges and Immunities, supra, Art. IV, § 11.

B.   Vienna Convention

While these Treaty provisions standing alone shed little light on the immunities granted a permanent mission, the 1961 Vienna Convention speaks directly to the issue of mission premises. Article 22 of that Convention declares:

> 1.   The premises of the mission shall be inviolable. The agents of the receiving State may not enter them, except with the consent of the head of the mission.

> Article 22, section 2 of the Vienna Convention goes on to note a host state's "special duty" to protect "the premises of the mission" from "any intrusion or damage" and "prevent any disturbance of the peace of the mission or impairment of its dignity"; Article 22, section 3 further states that the premises of a mission shall be immune from "search, requisition, attachment or execution." Mission premises covered by the Convention include both owned and leased property. *See Report of the International Law Commission*, Diplomatic Intercourse and Immunities, U.N. GAOR, 13th Sess., Supp. 9, U.N. Doc. a/3859 (1958), reprinted in [1958] II Y.B. Int'l L. Comm'n 89, 95, U.N. Doc. a/CN.4/SER.A/1958/Add.1

* * *

As the United States correctly points out, the drafters of the Vienna Convention considered and rejected exceptions, opting instead for broad mission inviolability. For instance, one proposal in an early Convention draft offered an exception to the prohibition on any non-consensual entry by the receiving state. The exception posed was one to be strictly limited to emergencies presenting "grave and imminent risks" to life, property or national security. See *Diplomatic Intercourse and Immunities*, Projet de codification du droit relatif aux relations et immunités diplomatiques, U.N. Doc. a/CN.4/91, *reprinted in* [1955] II Y.B. Int'l L. Comm'n 9, 11, U.N. Doc. a/CN.4/SER.a./1955/Add.1. This proposed exception that would have altered the rule of mission inviolability then existing under customary international law, *id.* at 16, was not adopted. The 1957 draft of the article covering the subject of mission inviolability rejected the proposed exception, and this exception never resurfaced in later drafts. *See Report of the International Law Commission*, Diplomatic Intercourse and Immunities, U.N. GAOR, 12th Sess., Supp. 9, U.N. Doc. A/3223 (1957), *reprinted in* [1957] II Y.B. Int'l L. Comm'n 131, 136, U.N. Doc. a/CN.4/SER.a/1957/Add.1 [hereafter 1957 Report of Int'l Law Comm'n]. The commentary to the draft article that was ultimately adopted explicitly emphasized the lack of exceptions to inviolability, stating "the receiving State is obliged to prevent its agents from entering the premises for any official act whatsoever." *Id.* at 137. Nothing could be stated more plainly.

* * *

III   Inviolability Recognized Without Exception

A.   Under International Law

The fact that the Vienna Convention codified longstanding principles of customary international law with respect to diplomatic relations further supports the view that the Convention recognized no exceptions to mission inviolability. *See* Higgins, *Abuse of Diplomatic Privileges, supra*, at 642 (The Vienna Convention "is agreed to be largely confirmatory of existing customary law."); Secretariat Memorandum, *supra*, at 134. The Convention codified a wide range of diplomatic protections accorded foreign missions over the centuries, *see* Higgins, *Abuse of Diplomatic Privileges, supra*, at 641–42, and recognized the independence and sovereignty of mission premises that existed under customary international law.

* * *

The risk in creating an exception to mission inviolability in this country is of course that American missions abroad would be exposed to incursions that are legal under a foreign state's law. Foreign law might be vastly different from our own, and might provide few, if any, substantive or procedural protections for American diplomatic personnel. Were the United States to adopt exceptions to the inviolability of foreign missions here, it would be stripped of its most powerful defense, that is, that international law precludes the non-consensual entry of its missions abroad. Another related consideration is the frequent existence of a small band of American nationals residing in foreign countries, often business personnel. Recent history is unfortunately replete with examples demonstrating how fragile is the security for American diplomats and personnel in foreign countries; their safety is a matter of real and continuing concern. Potential exposure of American diplomats to harm while serving abroad and to American nationals living abroad is not "pure conjecture," as plaintiffs blithely assert.

* * *

Perhaps most telling, no support may be found for an interpretation of limited inviolability in either the commentary to the Vienna Convention or the scholarly literature concerning the convention and the customary international law principles it codified.

Plaintiffs' position is also refuted by what has occurred in practice. The United States has consistently respected the complete inviolability of missions and consulates. Even in extreme cases U.S. authorities will not enter protected premises without permission following, for example, bomb threats. Nor have local authorities been permitted to enter to conduct health and building safety inspections without the consent of the mission involved. *See, e.g.*, Eleanor C. McDowell, Digest of United States Practice in International Law 1976, 198–99 (1977). An affidavit from the counselor for Host Country Affairs for the United States Mission to the United Nations attests that after the Soviet mission to the U.N. was bombed in 1979, the FBI and local police officers were all refused entry to the mission until the Soviets consented to allow certain law enforcement officers to enter. Absent such consent, the United States tells us, government officials would not have attempted to enter the Soviet mission's premises.

* * *

Hence, that portion of the district court's order awarding Sage Realty immediate possession of the premises and directing U.S. Marshals to remove the mission, its effects, and its personnel physically from the premises must be reversed.

* * *

Congress is of course the branch of government best suited to address the full array of concerns involved in altering the Vienna Convention. Already, the legislature has enacted the Diplomatic Relations Act of 1978, 22 U.S.C. §§ 254a–e (1988), to counter some of the more flagrant abuses of diplomatic privilege observed in this country. That Act gives the President the power "on the basis of reciprocity" to establish privileges and immunities for missions and their members "which result in more favorable or less favorable treatment than is provided under the Vienna Convention." *Id.* § 254c. Although the act requires liability insurance coverage for diplomatic missions and their representatives and families to insure against negligence arising from the operation of motor vehicles, vessels or aircraft, *id.* § 254e, it contains no restrictions on mission inviolability. While Congress and the President—via the Diplomatic Relations Act—possess the power to limit mission inviolability, neither has chosen to exercise that power. Our sister branches of government may more appropriately initiate whatever revision, if any, of the Vienna Convention is deemed necessary.

Republic of Zaire v. Duclaux

The Netherlands, Court of Appeal of the Hague, 18 February 1988
94 Int'l L. Rep. 368 (1994)

Under Dutch law a declaration of bankruptcy is a very far-reaching measure. It constitutes judicial seizure of the entire assets of the debtor concerned with a view to their forced sale to enable the assets thus realized to be distributed among all the creditors. By virtue of being declared bankrupt the debtor also automatically, by law, forfeits control over and the use of the assets which form part of the bankrupt estate.

It cannot be denied that if a Dutch court were to declare a sovereign State (which has an embassy or diplomatic mission in the Netherlands) bankrupt, as the Court of first instance did to the Republic of Zaire, this would in no small measure impede the efficient performance of the functions of that State's official diplomatic representation in the Netherlands in view of the nature, effects and consequences of a bankruptcy under the Dutch Bankruptcy Act, which have been considered above. This would be particularly true if, as in the present case, the trustee in bankruptcy were also to be declared competent to open letters and telegrams addressed to the sovereign sending State.

Since such a bankruptcy would therefore entail a by no means insubstantial infringement of the independence of the sending State vis-à-vis the receiving State, given that, at the very minimum, the diplomatic mission would not be able to function properly, the sending State can, under the generally recognized rules of international law, invoke its immunity from execution in proceedings before a court in the receiving State asked to give judgment on a petition for the sending State to be declared bankrupt.

* * * The judgment appealed against must be quashed and the Court of Appeal, giving judgment again, must declare that the Court does not have jurisdiction on the grounds of exceptions recognized under international law.

NOTES AND QUESTIONS

1.   Law Applicable on Embassy Premises. In *Radwan v. Radwan,* England, Family Division, [1972] 3 W.L.R. 735, there was a claim that the Egyptian law of divorce by a simple declaration procedure should apply when carried out at the Egyptian consulate in London, essentially a claim of "extraterritoriality". Noting that this term has been in use for 250 years, the Court stated that three theories have been invoked to explain the admitted principles that diplomatic premises and property are inviolable by the agents of the receiving state:

> (a) The strict extraterritorial fiction. The premises are regarded by a legal fiction as outside the territory of the receiving state and as part of the territory of the sending state. (b) The representative theory. The premises are immune from entry without consent of the head of the mission, as the mission represents or personifies the sovereignty of the sending state. (c) The theory of functional necessity. The immunity is granted by the receiving state because it is necessary to enable the mission to carry out its functions.

The Court adopted the following observation of Mr. J.E.S. Fawcett, quoted in the opinion as follows:

But there are two popular myths about diplomats and their immunities which we must clear away; one is that an embassy is foreign territory * * * The premises of a mission are inviolable, and the local authorities may enter them only with the consent of the head of the mission. But this does not make the premises foreign territory or take them out of the reach of the local law for many purposes: for example, a commercial transaction in an embassy may be governed by the local law, particularly tax law; marriages may be celebrated there only if conditions laid down by the local law are met; and a child born in it will, unless his father has diplomatic status, acquire the local nationality. * * *

2.   Jurisdiction of sending state over crimes committed within diplomatic premises. *In United States v. Erdos*, 474 F.2d 157 (4th Cir.1973), the chargé d'affaires at the American Embassy in Equitorial Guinea was convicted of killing another Embassy employee within the Embassy compound. The Court construed 18 U.S.C. § 7(3), which deals with the special maritime and territorial jurisdiction of the United States, as embracing an Embassy in a foreign country.

In 1978, the former Ambassador of Austria to Yugoslavia was sentenced by an Austrian court to a heavy fine for accidentally killing the French Ambassador to Yugoslavia upon their return from a hunting trip. The court relied on Article 31(4) of the Vienna Convention which specifies that immunity from the jurisdiction of the receiving state does not exempt the diplomat from the jurisdiction of the sending state. 82 Revue Générale de Droit International Public 1086 (1978).

3.   Diplomatic asylum. Latin American states assert that a right to grant asylum in the diplomatic premises exists by virtue of a regional custom peculiar to them. The existence of such a right was tested and denied in the *Asylum Case* (Colombia v. Peru) [1950] I.C.J.Rep. 266. The holding of the court that the Colombian government had failed to prove the existence of a regional custom of asylum may have induced the adoption of a new convention on asylum by the Tenth Inter–American Conference at Caracas in 1954. 6 Whiteman *Digest of International Law* at 436 (1963–1973).

The United States Department of State has consistently maintained that a state does not have a right to grant asylum under international law. The granting of asylum to Cardinal Mindszenty by the American Embassy in Budapest in 1956 was explained as "exceptional." 6 Whiteman, Digest supra at 463–464. It lasted for 15 years.

Arthur Goldberg,* The Shoot–Out at the Libyan Self–Styled People's Bureau: A Case of State–Supported Terrorism

30 SOUTH DAKOTA L. REV. 1 (1984)

* * *

---

* The author, Arthur G. Goldberg, was formerly Associate Justice of the Supreme Court of the United States and Ambassador to the United Nations.

The facts of the shoot-out at the Libyan People's Bureau in London have been extensively reported. Two gunmen in the Libyan self-styled "People's Bureau" in London opened fire on a crowd of peaceful anti-Qaddafi demonstrators. These demonstrators were conducting their peaceful protest on a sidewalk adjacent to the Libyan People's Bureau, yet the gunmen inside chose to shoot at them, killing Constable Fletcher and wounding eleven demonstrators and bystanders. Ten days after this barbaric incident, the British Government provided the killers and their murder weapons with safe passage out of the country.

On the same day that British police escorted the murderers to Heathrow Airport, Constable Fletcher was buried. At the time of her funeral, the Home Secretary, Mr. Leon Brittan, stated that the British police were prevented under the terms of the Vienna Convention on Diplomatic Relations from storming the so-called People's Bureau to apprehend the killers and bring them to justice. Mr. Brittan asserted Her Majesty's government could not act because the murderers, the premises of the People's Bureau, and the bags within which the lethal weapons were concealed were all immune according to the Convention. Prime Minister Thatcher and the Foreign Secretary Howe, supported the Home Secretary's view in the debate in the House of Commons. With all respect, I disagree. The Vienna Convention, like all treaties, must be sensibly interpreted. In this unruly age of state-sponsored terrorism, the Vienna Convention must not be construed so as to be a suicide pact for civilized countries. Treaties must be read in their entirety, with some provisions necessarily modified by others. Nothing could be more foolish than to accept a simple-minded, literal reading of each of the Convention's articles. The privileges and immunities granted by the Convention are rights declared in words, but rights declared in words are not to be lost in reality.

* * *

[T]he Home Secretary * * * claimed the British police under the Vienna Convention could not storm the so-called Libyan People's Bureau to capture the killers and confiscate their weapons as material evidence. * * * I disagree. Colonel Qaddafi's People's Bureau in London scarcely qualifies as a *bona fide* embassy whose premises are inviolable under the Vienna Convention. * * * [T]he London People's Bureau, according to reliable evidence, has harbored assassination teams directed by Qaddafi against Libyan dissidents. Murder factories are not embassies, and therefore do not come within the scope of the Vienna Convention. That treaty is designed to grant immunity to a proper embassy devoted to diplomatic relations. Article 41, section 3 of the Convention states that the "premises of the mission must not be used in any manner incompatible with the functions of the mission as laid down in the * * * Convention or by other rules of general international law * * *." Harboring hit squads clearly does not come within the protection of that provision.

The People's Bureau in London therefore is not a *bona fide* embassy. It was, in my opinion, subject under established rules of international law to search and seizure by the British police after the brutal murder of Constable Fletcher and the wounding of others.

Warren Hoge, Britain Agrees to Restore Ties to Libya

INTERNATIONAL HERALD TRIBUNE, July 8 1999, p. 1

LONDON—Britain said Wednesday it was resuming diplomatic relations with Libya after 15 years because Tripoli had agreed to assist British police in the investigation of the fatal shooting of a London police officer outside the Libyan Embassy in London in 1984.

Foreign Secretary Robin Cook told the House of Commons that Libya had also agreed to pay compensation to the family of the slain constable and accepted "general responsibility," for the killing, which caused the severing of relations. The policewoman, Yvonne Fletcher, 25, died from a single wound in the back, and witnesses have said the shot came from a window of the embassy.

* * *

Britain cut off diplomatic relations with Tripoli immediately, and public outrage in Britain grew when the Libyan diplomats were given a heroes welcome on their return home. Mr. Cook said Wednesday's breakthrough would lead to the British Interests Section in Tripoli being upgraded to full embassy status and the appointment of an ambassador "as quickly as practical." He said a joint British–Libyan statement "accepts general responsibility for the actions of those in the Libyan People's Bureau at the time of the shooting." The Libyans "express deep regret to the family for what occurred and offer to pay compensation now to the family. Libya agrees to participate and cooperate with the continuing police investigation and to accept its outcome," he said.

The Fletcher family issued a statement welcoming Libya's new willingness to assist the investigation and said, "We hope that there can now be progress on identifying precisely who was responsible for Yvonne's death. The path to full justice is now open." In a statement, Scotland Yard called the move "a positive step."

NOTES AND QUESTIONS

1. Immunity for diplomatic property extends to immunity from execution to satisfy judgments. United Nations Convention on Jurisdictional Immunities of States and Their Property, UNGA Res. A/59/38, 2004, 44 I.L.M. 801 (2005). Articles 18 and 19 of the Convention provide immunity for property of a State with certain exceptions. One of those exceptions relates to post-judgment measures of restraint. State property in certain situations involving use or intended use for "other than government non-commercial purposes". Article 21 makes it clear that such diplomatic property is thus subject to immunity from measures of restraint:

Article 21
Specific categories of property

1.   The following categories, in particular, of property of a State shall not be considered as property specifically in use or intended for use by the State for other than government non-commercial purposes under article 19, subparagraph (c):

(a) property, including any bank account, which is used or intended for use in the performance of the functions of the diplomatic mission of the State or its consular posts, special missions, missions to international organizations or delegations to organs of international organizations or to international conferences;

See also, *Russian Federation v. Noga Import/Export Company*, France, Court of Appeal of Paris, 10 August 2000, 127 INT'L L. REP. 156 (2000).

b.   IMMUNITY AND INVIOLABILITY OF DIPLOMATIC AGENTS

Protection is provided in the Vienna Convention which entered into force for the U.S. on December 13, 1972. Previously the applicable U.S. legislation had dated from the eighteenth century (Act of 30 April 1790, ch. 9, § 25, 22 U.S.C. § 252) and conferred broad immunity from both criminal and civil jurisdiction upon ambassadors, their domestic servants, and other diplomatic personnel. However, the Vienna Convention granted a narrower measure of immunity to all diplomatic personnel. The Department of Justice took the position that the Convention did not repeal or supersede the greater measure of immunity provided by existing legislation. ARTHUR ROVINE, DIGEST OF UNITED STATES PRACTICE IN INTERNATIONAL LAW 1973, at 143. The Diplomatic Relations Act, repealing the previous legislation and giving effect to the Convention as controlling domestic law, was enacted on September 30, 1978. 22 U.S.C. §§ 254a–254e, 28 U.S.C. § 1364 and is summarized in 73 A.J.I.L. 129 (1979).

NOTES AND QUESTIONS

1.   *Protection Afforded.* Articles 29–44 of the Vienna Convention (see Articles reproduced in the Documentary Supplement) afford broad protection to diplomatic agents: including personal inviolability for himself and his personal residence, immunity from arrest or detention, immunity from the jurisdiction of local courts, from criminal, and (subject to certain exceptions) civil and administrative jurisdiction, immunity from certain local laws, from execution, from local dues and taxes (subject to exceptions such as indirect taxes included in the price of goods), immunity from customs duties, personal service (military and jury service) and social security requirements as well as immunity from the obligation to give evidence as a witness. The specific terms of these immunities and their exceptions are provided in the Convention articles cited above.

2.   *Rationale: Immunity of Diplomatic Agents.* Diplomatic immunity rests on two grounds: (1) it ensures the effective performance by the diplomatic agent; and (2) it protects the diplomatic agent's person and dignity. Before

the Vienna Convention, however, a number of states rejected the representational considerations, i.e., those pertaining to the personal dignity of diplomatic agents. They took the position that functional necessity was the sole basis of diplomatic immunity.

In the states adopting the rationale of functional necessity, the courts distinguished between the official acts and the private acts of a diplomatic representative, immunity being granted for the former, but not for the latter. The distinction had an obvious parallel in the distinction made by many courts in continental civil law states between the public acts of a foreign state (for which immunity is granted) and its private acts (for which no immunity is given).

Eileen Denza, Diplomatic Law

p. 460 (3d ed. 2008)

The Duty to Respect Laws and Regulations of the Receiving State

This is much the most important of the four general obligations of a diplomatic agent. "* * * In the older writers this duty was seen as a corollary of the duty on the part of the receiving State to accord privileges and immunities. Many of these writers saw the diplomat as being exempt as a matter of substance from the legal duties and liabilities prescribed by the laws of the receiving State, but having instead a moral duty, or a duty of courtesy to respect them. The duty to 'respect' the laws of the receiving State was something less than a legal duty to obey them. The modern theory, however, is that certainly in regard to his private acts and now even in regard to his official acts a diplomat is subject as a matter of legal substance to the laws of the receiving State except where these laws make a specific exception in his favour. Such exceptions may be made in order to give effect to an international rule (as in matters of tax and social security) or they may be made as a matter of domestic policy, perhaps for reasons of comity or of reciprocity. * * * [N]ational courts have emphasized that immunity is procedural in character and does not affect any underlying substantive liability, and this is now a well-established rule."

* * *

c. SPECIAL MISSIONS AND HEADS OF STATE OR PERSONS OF HIGH RANK

Diplomatic Missions and Embassy Property (U.S. Digest, Ch. 4, § 1)

The Department of State has observed that it is necessary and useful periodically to reiterate and clarify the standards for the accreditation of foreign diplomatic personnel assigned to the United States. By a circular note to the Chiefs of Mission at Washington, dated May 23, 1989, Secretary of State James A. Baker III reiterated the Department's requirement that, to be recognized as a diplomatic agent, a person must possess a recognized diplomatic title and must, as well, perform duties of a diplomatic nature. Secretary Baker reminded the Chiefs of Mission that the accreditation of diplomats was solely within the discretion of the Department of State and that requests for accreditation in diplomatic status of personnel performing duties of an administrative and technical nature were incompatible with both Department policy and the Vienna Convention on Diplomatic Relations (1961). Marian Nash Leach, *Contemporary Practice of the United States Relating to International Law*, 83 AM. J. INT'L L. 905, 910 (1989).I, a special mission is defined as a "temporary mission, representing the State, which is sent by one State to another State with the consent of the latter for the purpose of dealing with it on specific questions or of performing in relation to it a specific task."

Special missions. On December 8, 1969, the General Assembly of the United Nations adopted and opened for signature on December 16, 1969, a Convention on Special Missions. For its text, see, U.N. Document A/Res/ 2530(24) of December 8, 1969 and A/Res/2530(24), Corr. 1 of January 2, 1970. The Convention entered into force on June 21, 1985. As of 2009, 39 states were parties to the Convention; the United States was not. In Article

NOTES AND QUESTIONS

1. Waiver may provide a solution in some but perhaps not all cases. Some governments are reluctant to permit a waiver of immunity even in cases where the sending state's interest might be minimal, as in the automobile accident cases, especially if the sending state senses a risk of higher pressure being exerted upon it to waive immunity in future cases where the sending state might have superior interests it wished to protect. Nevertheless, waiver by the sending state (but not by the diplomatic agent) is clearly available under Article 32 of the Vienna Convention, subject to the rule that it "must always be express". For analysis of Article 32, see Eileen Denza, *Diplomatic Law* 330 (3d Ed., 2008) The Makharadze case in Washington provides a dramatic example.

> On January 3, 1997, a diplomat posted at the Embassy of Georgia in Washington, D.C., Gueorgui Makharadze, was speeding in his car when it crashed, causing a multicar collision that killed sixteen year old Joviane Waltrick and injured four other persons. * * *

> The U.S. Attorney's office for the District of Columbia informed the Department of State that its initial review of the evidence indicated that Makharadze could be charged with negligent homicide, involuntary manslaughter, or second-degree murder. Consequently, on January 9, the Department of State requested that the Georgian Embassy waive Makharadze's immunity from criminal prosecution. * * *

By diplomatic note dated February 14, the Embassy responded as follows:

> "The Government of Georgia has considered the request of the United States Department of State and according to Article 32 of the Vienna Convention on Diplomatic Relations has waived the diplomatic immunity for Mr. George Makharadze, so he can be prosecuted in the United States."

After welcoming this decision, State Department spokesman Nicholas Burns noted that it was "highly unusual in modem diplomacy for a head of state to take a step like this. But given the emotions in the United States, given the feelings of the family and the local community here in Washington, D.C., we think it's the appropriate step for the Government of Georgia to take." * * *

In October, Makharadze pleaded guilty. As part of a plea bargain, prosecutors agreed not to object to the diplomat's request to serve his sentence in a federal prison instead of in the District's Lorton Correctional Complex. He was sentenced to seven to twenty years in prison on December 19.

Waiver of Georgian Diplomat's Immunity From Criminal Prosecution, 93 AM. J. INT'L L.

On June 20, 2000, CNN reported that Mr. Makharadze had been removed from a federal prison in North Carolina and repatriated to finish serving his sentence in the Republic of Georgia. The government of Georgia requested the transfer of prisoner custody under Council of Europe Convention on the Transfer of Sentenced Persons Treaty, to which both countries are signatories. (http://archives.cnn.com/2000/US/06/30/georgia.diplomat/).

d. SANCTIONS AGAINST DIPLOMATS

During a * * * debate in the Parliamentary Standing Committee for Foreign Affairs, the Minister for Foreign Affairs made, inter alia, the following remarks: * * * a foreign diplomat cannot be prosecuted, unless his Government or he himself waives his right to immunity * * *.

Yet, there are some sanctions. First, expulsion from the host country, which goes further than recall. * * * Secondly, the person in question can be called to account through his ambassador * * * and one can ensure that civil liability, at least, be assumed. Thirdly, the foreign government does sometimes take this liability on itself. There have been cases of ordinary offences such as nonpayment of large amounts for the purchase of cars, food, etc. being committed; in these cases the nomination of a new ambassador was made conditional on previous settlement of those questions. * * * [I]t is a principle of public international law that the host country should put nothing in the way of a diplomat which would hinder him from complete freedom to exercise his functions and should remove any existing hindrances. [But there] are of course limits; for instance, when a diplomat obviously abuses his position. I am thinking of cases in which espionage activities lead to expulsion. Then there are local customs: one should behave according to local standards. One also oversteps the limit, therefore, by violating unwritten morals of a host country, by behaving in a provocative manner, by being drunk in a public place or, in countries where ladies go veiled, by insisting on seeing what is going on behind the veil. I just give a few examples that do not require the exercise of much imagination on the part of this illustrious assembly. In these cases of what I would call overstepping the limit, the diplomat concerned may be declared persona non grata * * *

Statement of the Minister for Foreign Affairs of the Netherlands, 2 Netherlands Yearbook of International Law 170 (1971).

See also *United States Diplomatic and Consular Staff In Tehran (United States v. Iran)*, 1980 I.C.J.REP. 3 in Chapter 8, *infra*.

2. CONSULS

The Vienna Convention on Consular Relations, which governs consular functions, was signed on April 24, 1963. The Convention entered into force on March 19, 1967; in 2009, there were 172 parties, including the United States in 1969. 21 U.S.T. 77, 596 U.N.T.S. 261. It largely reflects the underlying customary international law on this subject. The last paragraph of the preamble affirms that "the rules of customary international law continue to govern matters not expressly regulated by the provisions of the present Convention". Excerpts from the Convention are set forth in the Documentary Supplement.

Consular functions are provided broadly in Article 5 to include protection in the receiving state of the interests of the sending state and its nationals, furthering the development of commercial, economic, cultural and scientific relations with the receiving state, promotion of friendly relations, ascertaining by lawful means developments and conditions in the receiving state, helping nations of the receiving state in various ways, including issuance of passports visas, notary services and taking other administrative actions, as well as other actions set forth at some length in Article 5 and in accordance with its terms.

The rules for protection of consular officers, premises and property are not as strictly framed as the parallel rules governing embassies and diplomatic agents, and this is true for the rules of personal inviolability and jurisdictional immunity which provide:

Article 41
Personal inviolability of consular officers

1. Consular officers shall not be liable to arrest or detention pending trial, except in the case of grave crime and pursuant to a decision by the competent judicial authority.

2. Except in the case specified in paragraph 1 of this article, consular officers shall not be committed to prison or be liable to any other form of restriction on their personal freedom save in execution of a judicial decision of final effect.

3. If criminal proceedings are instituted against a consular officer, he must appear before the competent authorities. Nevertheless, the proceedings shall be conducted with the respect due to him by reason of his official

position and, except in the case specified in paragraph 1 of this article, in a manner which will hamper the exercise of consular functions as little as possible. When, in the circumstances mentioned in paragraph 1 of this article, it has become necessary to detain a consular officer, the proceedings against him shall be instituted with the minimum of delay.

Article 43
Immunity from jurisdiction

1.   Consular officers and consular employees shall not be amenable to the jurisdiction of the judicial or administrative authorities of the receiving State in respect of acts performed in the exercise of consular functions.

Re: Rissmann

Italy, Court of Genoa, 1970
1 ITALIAN YEARBOOK OF INTERNATIONAL LAW 254 (1975)

[Following divorce proceedings between the Italian mother and the German father Muller Werner, a Genoa Court awarded custody of their child Maria Luisa to the mother residing with the child in Italy. Maria Luisa had German as well as Italian nationality, and a German Court had awarded her custody to the father. The mother informed the German Consul General in Genoa and the Head of Police of her guardianship and her disapproval of the issuing to the child of a passport or other travel document, but the German Consul Dr. Rissmann at the father's request later issued the child a German passport and assisted with the child's arrangements for travel to Germany. In this criminal proceeding charging Dr. Rissmann with violations of Italian law, consular immunity was invoked by the German Embassy in Rome on behalf of Dr. Rissmann.]

* * *

Clearly, in view of the fact that, inter alia, the minor had been legally entrusted by the Italian judge to her mother, the Consul in issuing her with a passport as a German citizen and facilitating her return to Germany was certainly acting in conflict with the Italian legal system * * *

But it is necessary to clarify the question as to whether there exists in the present case the necessary conditions and circumstances for the application of consular immunity. According to agreed doctrine (developed from jurisprudence of the principal States) and to general international law, even prior to the last Convention on Consular Relations concluded in Vienna [in] 1963 * * * there existed functional immunity for Consuls: namely, exemption from local jurisdiction in civil and criminal matters in respect of acts performed in the exercise of their office.

* * *

We must now examine whether or not the action of the Consul Rissmann which gives rise to this case fell within the scope of his consular functions. As far as concerns the present judgment, suffice to observe that Art. 5 of the Convention includes among consular functions * * * respectively, the issuing of passports and travel documents to citizens of the State concerned and the giving of assistance to the same * * *. It is certain that Muller was a German citizen, [so] there can be no doubt that Rissmann, in issuing her with a German passport, was carrying out a true and proper official act as Consul, and this is because, in view of the fact that a minor was in question, he had not only the consent but even the express request on the part of the father, a German citizen, entitled to guardianship of her which entitlement had never lapsed * * *.

[W]e must * * * hold that proceedings cannot be brought against Rissmann in respect of the charges made against him, since, as a person who enjoys consular immunity, he is exempted from criminal action * * *.

Another major function of consuls is to send assistance when nationals are arrested or detained in a foreign country. The police in a number of countries often fail to notify consuls of the fact their nationals are in custody. This problem in the U.S. has led Germany, Paraguay, and Mexico to take the U.S. to the I.C.J. See the *LaGrand* Case, 2001 I.C.J.Rep. 466 and *supra* Chapter 2, *Avena and other Mexican Nationals (Mexico v. United States of America)*, International Court of Justice, March 31, 2004, http://www.icj-cij.org.

NOTES AND QUESTIONS

1. *Inviolability*. Do you agree with Justice Goldberg's views on the Constable Fletcher case? What would be the consequences of his views being applied? Or not being applied? How would the reciprocity principle be applied?

2. *Deterrence*. The sanctions discussed above should have sufficient adverse effects upon the diplomatic agent's career to provide a stronger deterrent than even the waiver of immunity. However, those sanctions do not respond to the need to do justice to third parties who are prevented by immunity from pursing just claims. Nor do they point to criminal penalties which might reflect strongly established policies of both the sending the receiving state. Does the international system provide solutions to these problems?

3. *Convention on the Prevention and Punishment of Crimes Against Internationally Protected Persons, including Diplomatic Agents.*

> The Convention, signed December 14, 1973, entered into force for the United States on October 26, 1976. 13 I.L.M. 41 (1974). By 2009, 171 states were parties. Article 1 of the convention provides that "internationally protected person" means:

> * * * (a) a Head of State, including any member of a collegial body performing the functions of a Head of State under the constitution of the State concerned, a Head of Government or a Minister for Foreign Affairs,

whenever any such person is in a foreign State, as well as members of his family who accompany him;

> (b) any representative of a State or any agent of an international organization of an intergovernmental character who, at the time when and in the place where a crime against him, his official premises, his private accommodation or his means of transport is committed, is entitled pursuant to international law to special protection from any attack on his person, freedom or dignity, as well as members of his family forming part of his household; * * *

The Convention is designed to deny safe haven to those who attack, kidnap or inflict grievous bodily harm upon diplomatic agents or other internationally protected persons. A main feature of the Convention is the requirement that a party in whose territory the offender is found must either prosecute or extradite the offender.

4. *Prosecution in the Sending State.* Vienna Convention Article 31 takes an important step in that direction in providing in para. 4: "The immunity of a diplomatic agent from the jurisdiction of the receiving state does not exempt him from the jurisdiction of the sending state". The active nationality principle could also help with jurisdiction of the sending state. What else might be required for this procedure to be effective?

5. *Civil Actions.* Another possibility of response is legal action by the claimant in the civil courts of the diplomat's home country. Even assuming the service of process could be effected, do you see any problems in this procedure? Another is for the claimant to enlist the assistance of its own government, not only to apply pressures as suggested in the readings, but ultimately also to lodge a formal diplomatic claim against the sending state, or even to take the case to the International Court of Justice. In what situations would that help?

6. *Self-Contained versus Open System.* Note that in paragraph 86 in the *Tehran Hostages* judgment above, the ICJ referred to diplomatic law as constituting a "self-contained system", which presumably means that sanctions for violation are limited to reciprocal types of actions described in the judgment. Nevertheless, the Court refers in the operational part of the judgment to an obligation of Iran to make reparation to the United States for the injury. Bruno Simma and Dirk Pulkowski, in *Of Planets and the Universe: Self-contained Regimes in International Law*, in 17 EUR. J. INT'L LAW 483, 512 (2006), found the self-contained regime notion to be an overstatement. While a counter-measure which "infringes the inviolability of diplomatic or consular agents, premises, archives and documents" is prohibited (Article 50c, Draft Articles on State Responsibility) (see Chapter 8 below), are all other remedies under general international law to be excluded? What are your views on this subject?

7. *Reform.* In all of these possibilities, the international system is still decentralized and fragmented. If you were devising a comprehensive reform of the system what elements would you consider? How would you take into

account the known sensitivities of governments about sovereignty, dignity, embarrassment and at times security?

8. *Scope of Immunities*. How would you describe the differences between diplomatic and consular immunity?

9. *Liability of Receiving States*. Do you do any impediments to proceedings against receiving states on failure to protect issues discussed in Section F above?

10.   Further Reading: CRAIG BARKER, THE PROTECTION OF DIPLOMATIC PERSONNEL (2006); EILEEN DENZA, DIPLOMATIC LAW (3d ed. 2008); LUKE T. LEE AND JOHN QUIGLEY, CONSULAR LAW AND PRACTICE (2d ed. 2008); JOHN SHAW, THE AMBASSADOR—THE LIFE OF A WORKING DIPLOMAT (2006).

3.   INTERNATIONAL ORGANIZATIONS

a.   FUNCTIONAL IMMUNITY OF THE ORGANIZATION

Restatement of the Law (Third) The Foreign Relations Law of the United States

p. 492 (1987)

Immunities of International Organizations

Introductory Note:

International organizations have achieved independent legal personality under international law largely since the Second World War. * * * Earlier, they were seen largely as "unincorporated" associations of individual states and sometimes claimed the immunities of one or all of their member states. When international organizations acquired legal personality by international agreement, they also acquired privileges and immunities in their own right.

The privileges and immunities of an international organization and its officials, and of member representatives, are generally established by the constitution of the organization, e.g., Article 105 of the United Nations Charter, and are often supplemented by special agreement. See, e.g., the Convention on Privileges and Immunities of the United Nations, 21 U.S.T., to which [in 2009, 157] states (including the United States) were party, and the Convention on Privileges and Immunities of the Specialized Agencies, 33 U.N.T.S. 261, to which [in 2009, 116] states were party (but not the United States). An international organization sometimes enjoys additional privileges and immunities by agreement with a particular state, for example, an agreement between the organization and the state that is the seat of its headquarters, such as the Headquarters Agreement between the United States and the United Nations. * * * Strictly, those agreements are binding only on states parties to them, but an organization may also enjoy basic privileges and immunities vis-à-vis non-member states under customary law. * * *

The privileges and immunities of international organizations are "functional," and, though modeled after those of states, differ from them in some measure, both in conception and content. Unlike states, international organizations are not "sovereign" and draw on no history of sovereignty and no tradition of sovereign immunity. State and diplomatic immunities apply equally and reciprocally between one state and another; the immunities of an international organization are claimed, without reciprocity, by an organization vis-à-vis a state, generally a member state. Most such claims, in fact, arise in the few particular states in whose territories the organizations have their headquarters or conduct their principal activities. * * *

United Nations Charter Article 105

1. The Organization shall enjoy in the territory of each of its Members such privileges and immunities as are necessary for the fulfilment of its purposes.

2. Representatives of the Members of the United Nations and officials of the Organization shall similarly enjoy such privileges and immunities as are necessary for the independent exercise of their functions in connexion with the Organization.

3. The General Assembly may make recommendations with a view to determining the details of the application of paragraphs 1 and 2 of this Article or may propose conventions to the Members of the United Nations for this purpose.

League of Arab States v. T

Belgium, Court of Cassation (2001)
127 ILR 94 (2002)

[The respondent T, an Egyptian citizen, commenced this action for wrongful discharge from his long employment as a chauffeur for the League of Arab States in Belgium. Following the widespread practice of other international organizations, the League had negotiated with Belgium the text of a Headquarters Agreement (such as the UN has with the United States and UNESCO has with France, and which typically provide for privileges and immunities of the Organization). However, in this case the Headquarters agreement had not entered into force at the time of the proceedings. T had prevailed below, and again in the Court of Cassation which dismissed the appeal.]

Pursuant to Article 167(2) of the Constitution, the King concludes treaties, with the exception of those that relate to those matters listed in paragraph 3 of the same Article, which fall within the competence of the Council of the Communities and the regions. Treaties concluded by the King only enter into force after having received the assent of the chambers of Parliament.

* * *

It results from the response of this Court to the first part of this ground of appeal that a treaty concluded by the King only enters into force after it has received the assent of the chambers of Parliament even if it covers in part matters relating to the competence of the councils of the communities and the regions. * * *

There is no general principle of public international law, within the meaning of Article 38(1)(c) of the Statute of the International Court of justice, signed in San Francisco on 26 June 1945 and approved by the Law [Belgian] of 14 December 1945, recognizing the jurisdictional immunity of international organizations in relation to the States which have created or recognized those organizations.

Broadbent v. Organization of American States

United States Court of Appeals, District of Columbia Circuit
628 F.2d 27 (1980)

■ LEVENTHAL, CIRCUIT JUDGE:

* * *

I. Background

The plaintiffs-appellants are seven former staff members of the General Secretariat of OAS. Before their termination, they had been employed at the permanent headquarters of the organization in Washington, D.C., for periods ranging from six to twenty-four years. They are all United States citizens or foreign nationals admitted to permanent residency in the United States.

The appellants were dismissed from the Secretariat on August 31, 1976, due to a reduction in force mandated by the OAS General Assembly. * * *

* * * [A]ppellants brought this action in the district court, alleging breach of contract and seeking damages totaling three million dollars. The OAS moved to quash service and dismiss the complaint, asserting that the district court lacked subject matter jurisdiction and that the OAS is immune from service of process * * *

II. Analysis

A. Jurisdiction

* * *

The International Organizations Immunities Act of 1945, 22 U.S.C. § 288a(b) (1979), grants to international organizations which are designated by the President* "the same immunity from suit and every form of

_____

* [Court's Note] By Executive Order 10533 (June 3, 1954), 19 Fed.Reg. 3289 (1954), President Eisenhower designated the OAS an international organization entitled to the privileges and immunities conferred by the IOIA.

judicial process as is enjoyed by foreign governments, except to the extent that such organizations may expressly waive their immunity for the purpose of any proceedings or by the terms of any contract." As of 1945, the statute granted absolute immunity to international organizations, for that was the immunity then enjoyed by foreign governments.

The Foreign Sovereign Immunities Act of 1976, 28 U.S.C. § 1602 et seq. (1979), codified what, in the period between 1946 and 1976, had come to be the immunity enjoyed by sovereign states—restrictive immunity. The central feature of restrictive immunity is the distinction between the governmental or sovereign activities of a state (acts jure imperii) and its commercial activities (acts jure gestionis). Foreign states may not be found liable for their governmental activities by American courts; but they enjoy no immunity from liability for their commercial activities.

Contention for restrictive immunity

Appellants—and the United States as amicus curiae—submit the following syllogism: the IOIA conferred on international organizations the same immunity enjoyed by foreign governments; the FSIA indicates that foreign governments now enjoy only restrictive immunity; therefore, international organizations enjoy only restrictive immunity. They are supported by the general doctrine that ordinarily, "[a] statute which refers to the law of a subject generally adopts the law on the subject as of the time the law was invoked * * * includ[ing] all the amendments and modifications of the law subsequent to the time the reference statute was enacted."

Contention for absolute immunity

The OAS and several other international organizations as amici curiae counter that Congress granted international organizations absolute immunity in the IOIA, and it has never modified that grant. They rely on three implications of a legislative intent *not* to apply to international organizations the post World War II evolutions in the doctrine of sovereign immunity.

[T]he FSIA is generally silent about international organizations. No reference to such organizations is made in the elaborate definition of "state" in § 1603, and only § 1611 even alludes to their existence.

* * *

We need not decide this difficult question of statutory construction. On *either* theory of immunity—absolute or restrictive—an immunity exists sufficient to shield the organization from lawsuit on the basis of acts involved here.

We hold that the relationship of an international organization with its internal administrative staff is noncommercial, and, absent waiver, activities defining or arising out of that relationship may not be the basis of an action against the organization—regardless of whether international organizations enjoy absolute or restrictive immunity.

The Association of Citizens Mothers of Srebrenica v. The State of the Netherlands and the United Nations*

The District Court in The Hague
Judgment in incidental proceedings, July 10, 2008, Rechspraak, Netherlands

In this case the Association and ten individual claimants sought compensation from the Netherlands and from the United Nations and for other relief on allegations that in July 1995 the worst genocide since World War II occurred in the East Bosnian enclave of Srebrenica. The Netherlands State and the UN were charged with responsibility for the fall of the enclave and the consequential murder by Bosnian Serbs of 8,000—10,000 citizens of Bosnia–Herzegovina who had taken refuge within the enclave. The State and the UN's acts (and omissions) in implementing various UN resolutions declaring the enclave Srebrenica a "Safe area" were alleged to be in wrongful violations of their undertakings to the surviving relatives of men murdered by Bosnian Serbs and to the Association representing the interests of the victims' relatives.

On the central legal issue of U.N. immunity, the Court stated:

5.13.   Point of departure is that the UN itself, according to its letter to the Dutch Permanent Representative to the UN, * * * dated August 17, 2007, expressly invokes its immunity. As far as the Court knows the UN to date has always invoked its immunity with regard to actions within the functional framework referred to just now, and no exceptions were ever made in practice. The Association et al. have not put forward anything from which the opposite follows. On the basis of this the Court concludes that in international-law practise the absolute immunity of the UN is the norm and is respected.

In its analysis of the legal issues, the Court rejected a number of challenges to the immunity of the United Nations, based upon the necessity rule of Article 105.1 of the U.N. Charter, the Genocide Convention, the prohibitions of the International Covenant on Civil and Political Rights and European Convention on Human Rights for the protection of Human Rights and Fundamental Freedoms, holding that the U.N. immunity rule was not impaired by these instruments. In the end, the Court declared that it has no jurisdiction to hear the action against the United Nations.

5.14.   The Court dismisses the argument by the Association et al. that the immunity of the UN only exists in those instances in which the domestic court addressed—in this case, a court in the Netherlands—actually considers the acts and omissions the UN is blamed for as "necessary" by virtue of the restrictive subordinate clause "as are necessary for the fulfilment of its purposes." In view of, inter alia, the manner in which the norm of article 105, subsection 1 of the UN Charter was detailed in the Convention, it is in principle not at the discretion of a national court to give its opinion on the "necessity" of the UN actions within the functional

---

* *See* Netherlands International Law Review, LV, 425ff for background, text and citations. Reported to have been appealed to the Netherland Court of Appeal, April 9, 2009. Srebrenica Generalized Blog, May 26, 2009.

framework described in 5.12. A testing on the merits or comprehensive testing is also contrary to the ratio of the immunity of the UN as enshrined in international law. The Court subscribes to the State's assertion that for this reason domestic courts should not assess the acts and omissions of UN bodies on missions such as the one in Bosnia–Herzegovina but with the greatest caution and restraint. It is very likely that more far-reaching testing will have huge consequences for the Security Council's decision-making on similar peace-keeping missions.

5.15.   Neither does the available, but scant, jurisprudence about the scope of the standard of article 105, subsection 1 of the UN Charter afford grounds for the conclusion that a national court, if and insofar as it has scope for testing, can proceed in any other way than with the utmost reticence. In its advisory opinion of April 29, 1999 on the immunity of a UN worker the International Court of Justice ruled that wrongful acts possibly committed by the UN are not open to assessment by national courts, but should take place in the context of specific dispute settlement as provided for in article VIII, paragraph 29 of the Convention (Difference Relating to Immunity from Legal Process of a Special Rapporteur of the Commission on Human Rights, Advisory Opinion, I.C.J. Reports 1999, p. 62, paragraph 66). * * *

5.16. Now that the interpretation of article 105 of the UN Charter does not offer grounds for restricting the immunity, the question arises whether other international-law standards—outside of the UN frame of reference—prompt a different opinion. This inquiry into conflicting standards is necessary because there are insufficient grounds for accepting a full and unconditional prevailing of international-law obligations of the State under the UN Charter over other international-law obligations of the State. The rule of article 103 of the UN Charter invoked by the State does not always and right away bring relief in the event of conflicting obligations of a peremptory nature (ius cogens) or conflicting human rights obligations of an international customary law nature.

5.17. According to the Association et al. article 105 subsection 1 of the UN Charter is incompatible with mandatory standards derived from, inter alia, international law on genocide (the Genocide Convention) and the articles 14 ICCPR and 6 ECHR.

5.18. The Genocide Convention comprises as principal rule the penalization of genocide. From article 1 of this Convention it is clear that the parties to the treaty, including the Netherlands, undertake to prevent genocide—and therefore not to commit the crime themselves—as well as to punish it.

5.19. Neither the text of the Genocide Convention or any other treaty, nor international customary law or the practice of states offer scope in this respect for the obligation of a Netherlands court to enforce the standards of the Genocide Convention by means of a civil action. * * *

5.20. In its judgment of November 21, 2001 the European Court for Human Rights ruled in the case of Al–Adsani v. the UK (no. 35763/97) that there is no scope for an infringement of the in principle existing immunity of a national state, in that case Kuwait, with regard to a civil action because of conflict with the prohibition on torture laid down in article 3 ECHR. As there is no evidence that later the European Court for Human Rights deviated from this line the Court concludes that there is no generally accepted standard in international-law practice on the basis of which current immunities allow exception within the framework of enforcement in civil law of the standards of ius cogens, like the prohibitions on genocide and torture. That the issue in this case was the relationship between state immunity and the prohibition on torture and not the relation between the immunity of international organizations and the prohibition on genocide does not lead to a different opinion in the present case. Just as little as there is any basis in law for a hierarchy between different types of immunity, there are no grounds for a hierarchy between different standards of ius cogens.

* * *

b. IMMUNITIES OF PERSONS CONNECTED WITH INTERNATIONAL ORGANIZATIONS

In addition to the organizations themselves, international immunities are extended to persons representing members of international organizations as well as officials and experts appointed by international organizations. Representatives of U.N. Members and officials of the organization "enjoy such privileges and immunities as are necessary for the independent exercise of their functions in connection with the Organization" pursuant to Article 105(2) of the U.N. Charter. For the U.N., the details of this status are provided in Article V of the 1946 General Convention on the Privileges and Immunities of the United Nations, and a separate but similar Convention covers the U.N. Specialized Agencies. Other organizations usually have comparable protection under independent arrangements in their constituent instruments or Protocols, or by Headquarters Agreements with the host states.

Tachiona v. United States

United States Court of Appeals, Second Circuit
386 F.3d 205 (2004)

[Tachiona's complaint sought redress against Mugabe and Mudenge (respectively President and Foreign Minister of Zimbabwe), against ZANU–PF, and others for alleged torture, assault, execution, and other acts of violence at the hands of ZANU–PF members and upon the orders of ZANU–PF officials, including Mugabe and Mudenge. In September 2000, Mugabe and Mudenge visited New York City as Zimbabwe delegates to the United Nations ("U.N.") Millennium Summit. During their visit, they were both served with the complaint in this action, one in his personal capacity and the other on behalf of ZANU–PF. The United States filed a "suggestion of immunity" pursuant to 28 U.S.C. § 517 in which it asserted that the claims against the two men should be dismissed on grounds of diplomatic and head-of-state immunity. The Government further argued that the claims against ZANU–PF should be dismissed because "under both the Head of state and diplomatic immunity doctrines, [Mugabe and Mudenge] had personal Inviolability and could not be served with legal process in any capacity, including on behalf of ZANU–PF." In the end the Court confirmed the dismissal judgment on those two defendants.

Review the *Case Concerning the Arrest Warrant of 11 April 2000 (Democratic Republic of the Congo v. Belgium)*, in Section B.4 above.]

■ JOHN M. WALKER, JR., CHIEF JUDGE.

A. *Diplomatic Immunity*

The district court dismissed plaintiffs' claims against Mugabe and Mudenge because, inter alia, it concluded that the two were entitled to diplomatic immunity under the U.N. Convention on Privileges and Immunities and the Vienna Convention. We affirm for substantially the same reasons articulated by the district court.

The immunities afforded temporary representatives like Mugabe and Mudenge who visit the United States for a U.N. conference are set forth in Article IV, section 11 of the U.N. Convention on Privileges and Immunities:

Representatives of Members to the principal and subsidiary organs of the United Nations and to conferences convened by the United Nations, shall, while exercising their functions and during their journey to and from the place of meeting, enjoy the following privileges and immunities:

a. immunity from personal arrest or detention and from seizure of their personal baggage, and, in respect of words spoken or written and all acts done by them in their capacity as representatives, immunity from legal process of every kind;

* * *

U.N. Convention on Privileges and Immunities, *supra,* 21 U.S.T. 1418, art. IV, § 11. The only part of this section that expressly addresses the immunity from legal process afforded temporary U.N. representatives is section 11(a). Standing alone, section 11(a) would not protect Mugabe and Mudenge from suit based on any acts of violence they perpetrated in Zimbabwe, because such acts are not "acts done by them in their capacity as representatives." Section 11(g), however, extends to temporary U.N. representatives "such other privileges, immunities and facilities not inconsistent with [sections 11(a) to (f)] as diplomatic envoys enjoy."

The Vienna Convention, which governs the privileges and immunities that are extended to diplomatic envoys, provides for a much more robust form of immunity from legal process than that afforded by section 11(a) of the U.N. Convention on Privileges and Immunities. With limited exceptions, it broadly immunizes diplomatic representatives from the civil jurisdiction of the United States courts.

* * *

First, the United States government officials who ratified the U.N. Convention on Privileges and Immunities plainly believed that it would afford full diplomatic immunity to temporary U.N. representatives. Two excerpts from a report of the Senate Committee on Foreign Relations, which was charged with considering whether the United States should ratify the U.N. Convention on Privileges and Immunities, are particularly relevant. *See generally* Comm. on Foreign Relations, *Convention on the Privileges and Immunities of the United Nations,* S. Exec. Rep. No. 91–17, at 3, 11–12 (1970) [hereinafter Senate Report]. The first is a statement by State Department Legal Advisor John R. Stevenson during hearings before the committee on March 9, 1970. He said:

At the present time resident representatives are already granted full diplomatic privileges and immunities under the headquarters agreement. Nonresident representatives, on the other hand, are only covered by the International Organizations Immunities Act and that grants them immunities relating to acts performed by them in their official capacity.

At the time of these hearings, the "headquarters agreement" between the United States and the U.N. governed immunity from suit for *resident* U.N. representatives. *See* Agreement respecting the headquarters of the United Nations, June 26, 1947, U.S.–U.N., 61 Stat. 3416, T.I.A.S. No. 1676 (entered into force Nov. 21, 1947). Article V, § 15 of the headquarters agreement provided that resident representatives "shall . . . be entitled in the territory of the United States to the same privileges and immunities, subject to corresponding conditions and obligations, as [the United States] accords to diplomatic envoys accredited to it." *Id.* at 3428. By contrast, *temporary* U.N. representatives were only "immune from suit and legal process relating to acts performed by them in their official capacity and falling within their functions as . . . representatives." 22 U.S.C. § 288d(b) (2001).

Under the [U.N. Convention on Privileges and Immunities], the nonresident representatives would also receive full diplomatic privileges and immunities. * * * [M]any of the nonresident representatives are distinguished parliamentarians who come to New York for very short periods of time and we believe they should be treated with the same respect as the permanent representatives. *Id.* app. at 11–12 (Stat. of Hon. John R. Stevenson, Legal Advisor, Dep't of State). * * *

With regard to representatives of members, currently only resident representatives of permanent missions to the U.N. have full diplomatic immunities. Nonresident representatives enjoy only functional immunities; that is, immunities with respect to their official acts. Under the [U.N. Convention on Privileges and Immunities], these nonresident representatives will also be entitled to full diplomatic immunities.

Since none of the * * * exceptions under Article 31(1) is relevant here, Mugabe and Mudenge are both entitled to diplomatic immunity from suit under the terms of the Vienna Convention and the U.N. Convention on Privileges and Immunities. Therefore, the claims filed against them individually were properly dismissed.

NOTES

1. *United States ex rel. Casanova v. Fitzpatrick*, 214 F.Supp. 425 (S.D.N.Y. 1963) involved the immunity status of an attaché and Resident Member of the Cuban Delegation to the United Nations. Detained under charges of conspiracy to commit sabotage and to violate the Federal Agents Registration Act, Casanova's defense on his petition for a writ of habeas corpus was grounded on Article 105(1) of the U.N. Charter, the Headquarters Agreement of the United States with the United Nations and the Law of Nations. The Court ruled that the Article 105 provision was unavailable to Casanova because it provides only for functional immunity and that "Conspiracy to commit sabotage against the Government of the United States is not a function of any mission or member of a mission to the United Nations." The Headquarters Agreement defense was also unavailing because the Agreement required the accord of the sending State, the United Nations and the host state before immunity would attach in a particular case, and in this case the United States had never given its accord. For the Law of Nations defense, the Court noted that the governing authorities on immunity are the Charter, the Headquarters Agreement and statutes which foreclosed application of the Law of Nations.

2. *The Vienna Convention on the Representation of States in Their Relations with International Organizations of a Universal Character.* This Convention was adopted by a United Nations conference in March 1975 and by 2009 had 34 parties but had not yet entered into force. The United States became a signatory but has not given its consent to be bound by the convention. The head of the United States delegation to the conference considered the Convention as needlessly expanding the obligations of host states. "Article 66, for example, is an expansion of current privileges and immunities for which no justification has been given. Administrative and technical staff, who have no representational functions, are accorded virtually the same privileges and immunities as would be accorded the ambassador to the host state." ELEANOR C. MCDOWELL, DIGEST OF UNITED STATES PRACTICE IN INTERNATIONAL LAW 1975, at 40 (1976).

3. See also *United States v. Palestine Liberation Organization*, 695 F.Supp. 1456 (S.D.N.Y. 1988), 27 I.L.M. 1055, discussed in Chapter 1 *supra*.

4. See also, the Convention on the Privileges and Immunities of the United Nations, *supra*, Article V, Officials:

> Section 17. The Secretary–General will specify the categories of officials to which the provisions of this article and article VII shall apply. He shall submit these categories to the General Assembly. Thereafter these categories shall be communicated to the Governments of all Members. The names of the officials included in these categories shall from time to time be made known to the Governments of Members.

> Section 18. Officials of the United Nations shall:

> (a) be immune from legal process in respect of words spoken or written and all acts performed by them in their official capacity; * * *

5. *Experts on Mission.* In 1994 The U.N. Economic and Social Council endorsed the decision of the Commission on Human Rights to appoint Mr. Dato' Param Cumaraswamy, a Malasian jurist, as Rapporteur to conduct an inquiry into the independence of judges, lawyers and court officials, and to identify and record attacks on them. The following year the Rapporteur gave an interview on this subject to International Commercial Litigation, a U.K. publication circulated in Malaysia, which resulted in the filing in Malaysia of defamation actions against the Rapporteur. Thereafter, U.N. Legal Counsel and the Secretary General informed the Malaysian authorities that the Rapporteur was entitled to immunity from legal process. The authorities were also requested to inform the Malaysian courts accordingly, but this was not done, even after repeated requests and efforts on the part of the United Nations. Indeed, the Malaysian authorities disputed this application of immunity. The Rapporteur's motion to quash the writ was denied by the Malaysian court which assessed him with costs in a significant amount. On August 5, 1998, ECOSOC requested the ICJ to give an advisory opinion on the immunity question. Selections from the ICJ's opinion on that request follow:

38. The Court will initially examine the first part of the question laid before the Court by the Council, which is:

"the legal question of the applicability of Article VI, Section 22, of the Convention on the Privileges and Immunities of the United Nations in the case of Cumaraswamy as Special Rapporteur of the Commission on Human Rights on the independence of judges and lawyers, taking into account the circumstances set out in paragraphs 1 to 15 of the note by the Secretary–General...."

41. The General Convention contains an Article VI entitled "Experts on Missions for the United Nations." It is comprised of two Sections (22 and 23). Section 22 provides:

"Experts (other than officials coming within the scope of Article V) performing missions for the United Nations shall be accorded such privileges and immunities as are necessary for the independent exercise of their functions during the period of their missions, including time spent on journeys in connection with their missions. In particular they shall be accorded:

* * *

(b) in respect of words spoken or written and acts done by them in the course of the performance of their mission, immunity from legal process of every kind. This immunity from legal process shall continue to be accorded notwithstanding that the persons concerned are no longer employed on missions for the United Nations."

42. In its Advisory Opinion of 14 December 1989 on the *Applicability of Article VI, Section 22, of the Convention on the Privileges and Immunities of the United Nations*, the Court examined the applicability of Section 22 *ratione personae, ratione temporis* and *ratione loci.*

In this context the Court stated:

"The purpose of Section 22 is * * * evident, namely, to enable the United Nations to entrust missions to persons who do not have the status of an official of the Organization, and to guarantee them 'such privileges and immunities as are necessary for the independent exercise of their functions' * * * The essence of the matter lies not in their administrative position but in the nature of their mission." *(I.C.J. Reports 1989, p. 194, para. 47.)*

In that same Advisory Opinion, the Court concluded that a Special Rapporteur who is appointed by the Sub–Commission on Prevention of Discrimination and Protection of Minorities and is entrusted with a research mission must be regarded as an expert on mission within the meaning of Article VI, Section 22, of the General Convention (*ibid.*, p. 197, para. 55).

43.   The same conclusion must be drawn with regard to Special Rapporteurs appointed by the Human Rights Commission, of which the Sub–Commission is a subsidiary organ. It may be observed that Special Rapporteurs of the Commission usually are entrusted not only with a research mission but also with the task of monitoring human rights violations and reporting on them. But what is decisive is that they have been entrusted with a mission by the United Nations and are therefore entitled to the privileges and immunities provided for in Article VI, Section 22, that safeguard the independent exercise of their functions.

* * *

Difference Relating to Immunity From Legal Process of a Special Rapporteur of the Commission on Human Rights, (Advisory Opinion), 1999 I.C.J. REP. 62.

6.   Explain the difference between "absolute immunity" and "functional immunity" as applied to international organizations. How do these concepts apply to the scope of immunities of the organizations as such, to representatives of Member States and to staff members and experts of organizations?

7.   Would you agree with the suggestion that only "limited immunities" should be available to organizations? If that is the case for states, is it not an *a fortiori* case for limited immunities of organizations? If so, how should they be limited? Why do you think they have not always been limited so far?

8.   Should human rights considerations trump organizations' treaty based immunities in this sector? As against states, national courts have been reluctant to deny sovereign immunity (see the *Jones* and *Al–Adsani* cases in Section B.3.b above; cf. *Barrondon* in Section B.3.d above.). Should organizations retain their immunity in the face of human rights violations? The highest courts of two states have come to negative conclusions on that issue. In *African Development Bank v. Mr. X,* ILDC 778, Reporter Yann Kerbrat (Fr. 2005), the French Cour de Cassation found in a employment

termination case that a treaty based immunity of the Bank could not be applied because of the Bank's failure to make available a tribunal competent to decide such cases, and that this failure was a denial of justice under the French concept of "l'ordre public international". In a similar case, *Drago A. v. International Genetic Resources Institute* (IPGRD, ILDC 827, Commentator Alessandro Chechi (IT 2007)), the Italian Court of Cassation declined to apply a treaty based immunity because the organization failed to respect its treaty commitment to provide an impartial judicial remedy for such disputes. The Court relied on the public act—private act distinction which in this case required the classification of employment issues as falling in the private act category for which immunity was not applicable.

9.   What are your views on functional immunities of organizations' staff members and experts? The United Nations has an interest not only to protect its staff members and experts on mission under the established immunity rules, but also to ensure where these individuals should not enjoy impunity when they have committed crimes falling outside of their functional immunity. Thus the General Assembly on January 8, 2008 adopted A/Res/62/63 whereby it

> 2.   *Strongly urges* States to take all appropriate measures to ensure that crimes by United Nations officials and experts on mission do not go unpunished and that the perpetrators of such crimes are brought to justice, without prejudice to the privileges and immunities of such persons and the United Nations under international law, and in accordance with international human rights standards, including due process;
>
> 3.   *Strongly urges* all States to consider establishing to the extent that they have not yet done so jurisdiction, particularly over crimes of a serious nature, as known in their existing domestic criminal laws, committed by their nationals while serving as United Nations officials or experts on mission, at least where the conduct as defined in the law of the State establishing jurisdiction also constitutes a crime under the laws of the host State;
>
> 9.   *Requests* the Secretary–General to bring credible allegations that reveal that a crime may have been committed by United Nations officials and experts on mission to the attention of the States against whose nationals such allegations are made, and to request from those States an indication of the status of their efforts to investigate and, as appropriate, prosecute crimes of a serious nature, as well as the types of appropriate assistance States may wish to receive from the Secretariat for the purposes of such investigations and prosecutions;

Note that this resolution does not appear to impair in any way the fundamental immunities of these categories of personnel or of the United Nation itself.

CHAPTER 5

HUMAN RIGHTS

A. HUMAN RIGHTS

In 1946, with Europe in ruins and with the memory of millions of dead fresh in their minds, a small group of negotiators met at the newly-formed United Nations to draft a compilation of those rights that were inherent to human dignity, and that had to be respected by all states, individuals and organs of society. They included men and women from France, China, Lebanon, Chile, the USSR and the United Kingdom, and were chaired by the U.S. delegate, Eleanor Roosevelt. The result was the Universal Declaration of Human Rights (UDHR), approved by the General Assembly of the United Nations on December 10, 1948.

Of course, 1948 was not the beginning of the concept of human rights. The Code of Hammurabi (1728–1686 B.C.), the writings of early Chinese philosophers Mencius and Hsun-tzu, the Magna Carta, the writings of early international law scholars Suarez, Las Casas, and Grotius, the Declaration of Independence, and the French Declaration of the Rights and Duties of Man all contain human rights concepts. States that claimed damages for injuries to their citizens while abroad argued for a minimum standard of justice to which all states must adhere, in arbitral proceedings during the 19th and early 20th centuries. The movement to stop the slave trade and abolish slavery in the 18th and 19th centuries had many of the characteristics of a modern human rights movement, including a combination of lawsuits, media campaigns, consumer boycotts and legislation. In the early 20th century, calls for the protection of workers' rights in capitalist societies led to the creation of the International Labor Organization in 1918. And the law of war, which dates back to antiquity, from the end of the 19th century on contained the "Martens clause," which established that: "populations and belligerents remain under the protection and empire of the principles of international law, as they result from the usages established between civilized nations, from the laws of humanity and the requirements of the public conscience." Thus, the "laws of humanity" applied even when no specific rule of warfare could be referenced. These long-standing norms were widely accepted as part of customary international law and general principles.

Most of the law of human rights has been codified in the period from 1948 until today. The United Nations Charter refers to human rights in Articles 55 and 56. Art. 55 reads: "the United Nations shall promote: . . . universal respect for, and observance of, human rights and fundamental freedoms for all without distinction as to race, sex, language or religion," while Article 56 affirms that "All Members pledge themselves to take joint and separate action in co-operation with the Organization for the achievement of the purposes set forth in Article 55."* The Universal Declaration contained a list of basic civil, political, economic, social and cultural rights, conceived of as a "common standard of achievement." As its name suggests, the UDHR is not a binding treaty. However, over time many of its substantive provisions (especially those regarding basic civil rights) have become widely recognized as reflective of customary international law, either as elaborations of the U.N. Charter provisions or due to their widespread incorporation into subsequent international instruments, national constitutions and jurisprudence the world over.

The next step was to convert those rights into legally binding treaties, a process that took the next twenty years and resulted in two treaties, the International Covenant on Civil and Political Rights (ICCPR) and the International Covenant on Economic, Social and Cultural Rights (ICESCR). Those treaties were followed by other global treaties, on the rights of women, children, migrant workers, the disabled, and the rights to be free from racial discrimination, torture and enforced disappearance. In addition to the global treaties, there are three well-developed regional human rights systems, in Europe, the Americas and (to a lesser extent) Africa, and incipient systems in the Middle East and Asia. In addition, there are a host of UN declarations, resolutions, guidelines, principles, standards, interpretative comments and decisions of quasi-judicial bodies, and other forms of "soft law" on human rights. The process of codification continues, although more slowly because many of the basic rights are already in treaty form.

In the late twentieth and early twenty-first centuries the emphasis shifted from codification to improved enforcement. Of course, as with other

---

* Charter of the United Nations, June 26, 1945, 59 Stat. 1031, T.S. NO. 993, 3 Bevans 1153, *entered into force* Oct. 24, 1945, Chapter IX, Art. 55–56.

areas of international law, the first and most important enforcement mechanism for human rights treaties is their incorporation into domestic law, so that they can be enforced by domestic means. These may include the use of administrative agencies, ombudsmen, government programs or support for private action as well as recourse to courts. On top of this is layered a set of international institutions. The major treaties all create expert bodies tasked with overseeing implementation. These treaty bodies receive periodic reports from states parties about compliance with their obligations, question government representatives and publish their conclusions. They also, in some cases, issue "general comments" setting out in greater detail the meaning of the treaty text, and in the case of seven of the treaties, they can also recommend action in the case of individual complaints, if the state is willing to allow it. Other instruments, for example in the torture context, set up systems of periodic visits to places of detention, in an effort to prevent torture. There is also a system of United Nations consideration of human rights problems outside the context of a specific treaty, considered below. Regional human rights bodies also issue reports and recommendations, conduct on-site visits, and otherwise try to influence state behavior. The regional human rights courts may issue damages awards and injunctive relief that are binding on states parties, in addition to creating a corpus of case law widely used by other international bodies and national courts.

As we have seen, much of international law consists of law between states to support the needs of states. The law of human rights is qualitatively different: this is law that requires states to limit themselves in their relationship with their inhabitants. The question of why states would agree to so limit themselves touches on the deep philosophical foundations of human rights, and the longstanding debate between positivists and natural law advocates as to the nature of rights generally. Natural lawyers see rights as arising from a Supreme Being, or from Nature or the intrinsic qualities of humans, but then cannot satisfactorily explain why different people have differing views as to which rights are necessary and how they are to be defined. Positivists, in contrast, see rights as arising from freely entered-into state commitments, reflected in treaties or customary law, that set out the definitions and limits of rights, but they have a hard time explaining how rights can then antecede, and be held in opposition to, a non rights-respecting state. To illustrate, if Nazi Germany makes it legal to persecute Jews and has signed no treaties prohibiting such acts, how can that still be a rights violation? Human rights draws from both traditions.

This quality of regulating states' obligations to other states that limits how they treat those living within their borders or under their jurisdiction gives international human rights law constitution-like dimensions that differ from other areas of international law. Treaties and other public declarations of law are not meant simply as contractual arrangements but as authoritative statements of global values, meant for the broadest possible consumption. Some international human rights norms are now considered so fundamental to the international system that they have attained the status of *jus cogens* norms, that is, norms that admit of no derogation by states. Other aspects of the specific character of international human rights obligations are explored below.

1. Finding Human Rights Law Obligations

Dolly M. E. Filartiga and Joel Filartiga v. Americo Norberto Peña–Irala

United States Court of Appeals, Second Circuit
630 F.2d 876 (1980)

The appellants, plaintiffs below, are citizens of the Republic of Paraguay. Dr. Joel Filartiga, a physician, describes himself as a longstanding opponent of the government of President Alfredo Stroessner, which has held power in Paraguay since 1954. His daughter, Dolly Filartiga, arrived in the United States in 1978 under a visitor's visa, and has since applied for permanent political asylum. The Filartigas brought this action in the Eastern District of New York against Americo Norberto Peña–Irala (Peña), also a citizen of Paraguay, for wrongfully causing the death of Dr. Filartiga's seventeen-year old son, Joelito. Because the district court dismissed the action for want of subject matter jurisdiction, we must accept as true the allegations contained in the Filartigas' complaint and affidavits for purposes of this appeal.

The appellants contend that on March 29, 1976, Joelito Filartiga was kidnapped and tortured to death by Peña, who was then Inspector General of Police in Asunción, Paraguay. Later that day, the police brought Dolly Filartiga to Peña's home where she was confronted with the body of her brother, which evidenced marks of severe torture. As she fled, horrified, from the house, Peña followed after her shouting, "Here you have what you have been looking for for so long and what you deserve. Now shut up." The Filartigas claim that Joelito was tortured and killed in retaliation for his father's political activities and beliefs.

Shortly thereafter, Dr. Filartiga commenced a criminal action in the Paraguayan courts against Peña and the police for the murder of his son. As a result, Dr. Filartiga's attorney was arrested and brought to police headquarters where, shackled to a wall, Peña threatened him with death. This attorney, it is alleged, has since been disbarred without just cause.

During the course of the Paraguayan criminal proceeding, which is apparently still pending after four years, another man, Hugo Duarte, confessed to the murder. Duarte, who was a member of the Peña household, claimed that he had discovered his wife and Joelito in flagrante delicto, and that the crime was one of passion. The Filartigas have submitted a photograph of Joelito's corpse showing injuries they believe refute this claim. Dolly Filartiga, moreover, has stated that she will offer evidence of three independent autopsies demonstrating that her brother's death "was the result of professional methods of torture." Despite his confession, Duarte, we are told, has never been convicted or sentenced in connection with the crime.

In July of 1978, Peña sold his house in Paraguay and entered the United States under a visitor's visa. He was accompanied by Juana Bautista Fernández Villalba, who had lived with him in Paraguay. The couple remained in the United States beyond the term of their visas, and were living in Brooklyn, New York, when Dolly Filartiga, who was then living in Washington, D. C., learned of their presence. Acting on information provided by Dolly the Immigration and Naturalization Service arrested Peña and his companion, both of whom were subsequently ordered deported on April 5, 1979 following a hearing. They had then resided in the United States for more than nine months.

Almost immediately, Dolly caused Peña to be served with a summons and civil complaint at the Brooklyn Navy Yard, where he was being held pending deportation. The complaint alleged that Peña had wrongfully caused Joelito's death by torture and sought compensatory and punitive damages of $10,000,000. The Filartigas also sought to enjoin Peña's deportation to ensure his availability for testimony at trial.

Appellants rest their principal argument in support of federal jurisdiction upon the Alien Tort Statute, 28 U.S.C. § 1350, which provides: "The district courts shall have original jurisdiction of any civil action by an alien for a tort only, committed in violation of the law of nations or a treaty of the United States." Since appellants do not contend that their action arises directly under a treaty of the United States, a threshold question on the jurisdictional issue is whether the conduct alleged violates the law of nations. In light of the universal condemnation of torture in numerous international agreements, and the renunciation of torture as an instrument of official policy by virtually all of the nations of the world (in principle if not in practice), we find that an act of torture committed by a state official against one held in detention violates established norms of the international law of human rights, and hence the law of nations.

[The Paquete] Habana is particularly instructive for present purposes, for it held that the traditional prohibition against seizure of an enemy's coastal fishing vessels during wartime, a standard that began as one of comity only, had ripened over the preceding century into "a settled rule of international law" by "the general assent of civilized nations." *Id*. at 694, 20 S.Ct. at 297; accord, *id*. at 686, 20 S.Ct. at 297. Thus it is clear that courts must interpret international law not as it was in 1789, but as it has evolved and exists among the nations of the world today. See *Ware v. Hylton*, 3 U.S. (3 Dall.) 198, 1 L.Ed. 568 (1796) (distinguishing between "ancient" and "modern" law of nations).

The requirement that a rule command the "general assent of civilized nations" to become binding upon them all is a stringent one. Were this not so, the courts of one nation might feel free to impose idiosyncratic legal rules upon others, in the name of applying international law. . . .

The United Nations Charter (a treaty of the United States, see 59 Stat. 1033 (1945)) makes it clear that in this modern age a state's treatment of its own citizens is a matter of international concern. It provides:

With a view to the creation of conditions of stability and well-being
which are necessary for peaceful and friendly relations among nations
. . . the United Nations shall promote . . . universal respect for, and
observance of, human rights and fundamental freedoms for all without
distinctions as to race, sex, language or religion.

Id. Art. 55. And further:

All members pledge themselves to take joint and separate action in
cooperation with the Organization for the achievement of the purposes
set forth in Article 55.

Id. Art. 56.

While this broad mandate has been held not to be wholly self-executing, *Hitai v. Immigration and Naturalization Service*, 343 F.2d 466, 468 (2d
Cir. 1965), this observation alone does not end our inquiry. For although
there is no universal agreement as to the precise extent of the "human
rights and fundamental freedoms" guaranteed to all by the Charter, there
is at present no dissent from the view that the guaranties include, at a bare
minimum, the right to be free from torture. This prohibition has become
part of customary international law, as evidenced and defined by the
Universal Declaration of Human Rights, General Assembly Resolution
217(III)(A) (Dec. 10, 1948) which states, in the plainest of terms, "no one
shall be subjected to torture."[10] The General Assembly has declared that
the Charter precepts embodied in this Universal Declaration "constitute
basic principles of international law." G.A.Res. 2625 (XXV) (Oct. 24, 1970).

Particularly relevant is the Declaration on the Protection of All Persons from Being Subjected to Torture, General Assembly Resolution 3452,
30 U.N. GAOR Supp. (No. 34) 91, U.N.Doc. A/1034 (1975), which is set out
in full in the margin. The Declaration expressly prohibits any state from
permitting the dastardly and totally inhuman act of torture. Torture, in
turn, is defined as "any act by which severe pain and suffering, whether
physical or mental, is intentionally inflicted by or at the instigation of a
public official on a person for such purposes as . . . intimidating him or
other persons." The Declaration goes on to provide that "(w)here it is
proved that an act of torture or other cruel, inhuman or degrading
treatment or punishment has been committed by or at the instigation of a
public official, the victim shall be afforded redress and compensation, in
accordance with national law." This Declaration, like the Declaration of
Human Rights before it, was adopted without dissent by the General
Assembly. Nayar, "Human Rights: The United Nations and United States
Foreign Policy," 19 Harv. Int'l L.J. 813, 816 n.18 (1978).

These U.N. declarations are significant because they specify with great
precision the obligations of member nations under the Charter. Since their
adoption, "(m)embers can no longer contend that they do not know what
human rights they promised in the Charter to promote." Sohn, "A Short

---

10.   Eighteen nations have incorporated the Universal Declaration into their own constitutions. 48 Revue Internationale de Droit Penal Nos. 3 & 4, at 211 (1977).

History of United Nations Documents on Human Rights," in The United Nations and Human Rights, 18th Report of the Commission (Commission to Study the Organization of Peace ed. 1968). Moreover, a U.N. Declaration is, according to one authoritative definition, "a formal and solemn instrument, suitable for rare occasions when principles of great and lasting importance are being enunciated." 34 U.N. ESCOR, Supp. (No. 8) 15, U.N. Doc. E/CN.4/1/610 (1962) (memorandum of Office of Legal Affairs, U.N. Secretariat). Accordingly, it has been observed that the Universal Declaration of Human Rights "no longer fits into the dichotomy of 'binding treaty' against 'non-binding pronouncement,' but is rather an authoritative statement of the international community." E. Schwelb, Human Rights and the International Community 70 (1964). Thus, a Declaration creates an expectation of adherence, and "insofar as the expectation is gradually justified by State practice, a declaration may by custom become recognized as laying down rules binding upon the States." 34 U.N. ESCOR, *supra*. Indeed, several commentators have concluded that the Universal Declaration has become, in toto, a part of binding, customary international law. Nayar, *supra*, at 816–17; Waldlock, "Human Rights in Contemporary International Law and the Significance of the European Convention," Int'l & Comp. L.Q., Supp. Publ. No. 11 at 15 (1965).

Turning to the act of torture, we have little difficulty discerning its universal renunciation in the modern usage and practice of nations. *Smith, supra*, 18 U.S. (5 Wheat.) at 160–61, 5 L.Ed. 57. The international consensus surrounding torture has found expression in numerous international treaties and accords. E.g., American Convention on Human Rights, Art. 5, OAS Treaty Series No. 36 at 1, OAS Off. Rec. OEA/Ser 4 v/II 23, doc. 21, rev. 2 (English ed., 1975) ("No one shall be subjected to torture or to cruel, inhuman or degrading punishment or treatment"); International Covenant on Civil and Political Rights, U.N. General Assembly Res. 2200 (XXI)A, U.N. Doc. A/6316 (Dec. 16, 1966) (identical language); European Convention for the Protection of Human Rights and Fundamental Freedoms, Art. 3, Council of Europe, European Treaty Series No. 5 (1968), 213 U.N.T.S. 211 (semble). The substance of these international agreements is reflected in modern municipal i.e. national law as well. Although torture was once a routine concomitant of criminal interrogations in many nations, during the modern and hopefully more enlightened era it has been universally renounced. According to one survey, torture is prohibited, expressly or implicitly, by the constitutions of over fifty-five nations, including both the United States and Paraguay. Our State Department reports a general recognition of this principle:

There now exists an international consensus that recognizes basic human rights and obligations owed by all governments to their citizens.... There is no doubt that these rights are often violated; but virtually all governments acknowledge their validity.

Department of State, Country Reports on Human Rights for 1979, published as Joint Comm. Print, House Comm. on Foreign Affairs, and Senate Comm. on Foreign Relations, 96th Cong. 2d Sess. (Feb. 4, 1980), Introduction at 1. We have been directed to no assertion by any contemporary state of a right to torture its own or another nation's citizens. Indeed,

United States diplomatic contacts confirm the universal abhorrence with which torture is viewed:

> In exchanges between United States embassies and all foreign states with which the United States maintains relations, it has been the Department of State's general experience that no government has asserted a right to torture its own nationals. Where reports of torture elicit some credence, a state usually responds by denial or, less frequently, by asserting that the conduct was unauthorized or constituted rough treatment short of torture.[15]

Memorandum of the United States as Amicus Curiae at 16 n.34.

Having examined the sources from which customary international law is derived the usage of nations, judicial opinions and the works of jurists[16] we conclude that official torture is now prohibited by the law of nations. The prohibition is clear and unambiguous, and admits of no distinction between treatment of aliens and citizens. Accordingly, we must conclude that the dictum in *Dreyfus v. von Finck, supra*, 534 F.2d at 31, to the effect that "violations of international law do not occur when the aggrieved parties are nationals of the acting state," is clearly out of tune with the current usage and practice of international law. The treaties and accords cited above, as well as the express foreign policy of our own government,[17] all make it clear that international law confers fundamental rights upon all people vis-a-vis their own governments. While the ultimate scope of those rights will be a subject for continuing refinement and elaboration, we hold that the right to be free from torture is now among them.

NOTES AND QUESTIONS

1. How does the *Filartiga* court marshall evidence of the existence of a customary international law norm? How does it use treaties? Does it matter

---

15. The fact that the prohibition of torture is often honored in the breach does not diminish its binding effect as a norm of international law. As one commentator has put it, "The best evidence for the existence of international law is that every actual State recognizes that it does exist and that it is itself under an obligation to observe it. States often violate international law, just as individuals often violate municipal law; but no more than individuals do States defend their violations by claiming that they are above the law." J. Brierly, *The Outlook for International Law* 4–5 (Oxford 1944).

16. See note 4, *supra*: see also *Ireland v. United Kingdom*, Judgment of Jan. 18, 1978 (European Court of Human Rights), summarized in (1978) Yearbook, European Convention on Human Rights 602 (Council of Europe) (holding that Britain's subjection of prisoners to sleep deprivation, hooding, exposure to hissing noise, reduced diet and standing against a wall for hours was "inhuman and degrading," but not "torture" within meaning of European Convention on Human Rights).

17. E.g., 22 U.S.C. § 2304(a)(2) ("Except under circumstances specified in this section, no security assistance may be provided to any country the government of which engages in a consistent pattern of gross violations of internationally recognized human rights."); 22 U.S.C. § 2151(a) ("The Congress finds that fundamental political, economic, and technological changes have resulted in the interdependence of nations. The Congress declares that the individual liberties, economic prosperity, and security of the people of the United States are best sustained and enhanced in a community of nations which respects individual civil and economic rights and freedoms").

that the treaties are for the most part unratified? What other sources of law does it use? How does it weigh the importance of these sources? Is this consistent with how we saw customary law defined in Chapter 2? Is it consistent with the International Court of Justice's decisions in the *North Sea Continental Shelf* cases and *Nicaragua* case, discussed in Chapter 2?

In its 2009 report, Amnesty International found that half the countries in the world use torture. How can the court assert that there is a customary law norm given this contrary state practice?

2. *The Alien Tort Statute.** The Filartigas brought suit under a 1789 U.S. law that gives jurisdiction in U.S. federal courts over a limited number of international law violations. In *Sosa v. Alvarez–Machain*, 542 U.S. 692, 124 S.Ct. 2739, 159 L.Ed.2d 718 (2004), the U.S. Supreme Court held that actionable violations had to "rest on a norm of international character accepted by the civilized world and defined with a specificity comparable to the features of the 18th-century paradigms we have recognized." These included attacks on ambassadors, piracy, and violation of safe-conducts. The Court also approved of cases, including *Filartiga,* involving torture and summary execution. Lower courts have also found actionable harms of slavery and slave-like practices (*Doe I v. Unocal Corp.*, 395 F.3d 932 (9th Cir. 2002), *vacated en banc*, 403 F.3d 708 (9th Cir. 2005); *Presbyterian Church of Sudan v. Talisman Energy, Inc.*, 2005 WL 2082847 (S.D.N.Y. 2005), *reversed on other grounds* 582 F.3d 244 (2d Cir. 2009); *Doe v. Islamic Salvation Front*, 993 F.Supp. 3 (D.D.C. 1998)); war crimes (*Kadic v. Karadžić*, 74 F.3d 377 (2d Cir. 1996)); crimes against humanity (*Cabello v. Fernandez–Larios*, 402 F.3d 1148 (11th Cir. 2005), *Mehinovic v. Vuckovic*, 198 F.Supp.2d 1322 (N.D.Ga. 2002)); genocide (*Kadic*); extrajudicial killing, *In re Estate of Marcos, Human Rights Litigation (Hilao v. Marcos)*, 25 F.3d 1467 (9th Cir. 1994)); systematic racial discrimination, *Tachiona v. Mugabe*, 234 F.Supp.2d 401 (S.D.N.Y. 2002) and forced disappearance (*Forti v. Suarez–Mason*, 694 F.Supp. 707, 709 (N.D. Cal. 1988), *Xuncax v. Gramajo*, 886 F.Supp. 162, 184–85 (D.Mass. 1995)). Courts have disagreed on whether cruel, inhuman and degrading treatment or punishment meets the standard, compare *Xuncax* (majority view) with *Forti v. Suarez–Mason*, 694 F.Supp. 707 (N.D.Cal. 1988). Most courts have not found environmental harms (*Flores v. Southern Peru Copper Corp.*, 414 F.3d 233 (2d Cir. 2003)) or short arbitrary detention (*Sosa*) to be actionable. Is this the right list of violations? Does a human rights violation have to also be an international crime to be actionable under the ATS, a statute providing for civil damages? Other states allow for a civil remedy in cases involving extraterritorial crimes, but only after a finding of criminal guilt, and usually based on a notion of universal jurisdiction or of jurisdiction based on the nationality of the victims. Should the ATS be subject to the same limitations? See Justice Breyer's concurrence in *Sosa*.

3. *Torture Defined.* What is the definition of torture the court uses? Where does it come from? At the time the case was decided, there was no specific treaty defining torture. The 1984 Convention Against Torture and

---

* 28 U.S.C.A. § 1350 (2008).

other Cruel, Inhuman or Degrading Treatment or Punishment defines torture in article 1 as:

> any act by which severe pain or suffering, whether physical or mental, is intentionally inflicted on a person for such purposes as obtaining from him or a third person information or a confession, punishing him for an act he or a third person has committed or is suspected of having committed, or intimidating or coercing him or a third person, or for any reason based on discrimination of any kind, when such pain or suffering is inflicted by or at the instigation of or with the consent or acquiescence of a public official or other person acting in an official capacity. It does not include pain or suffering arising only from, inherent in or incidental to lawful sanctions.

Do you see any potential problems with this definition? Could it cover the actions of (1) an off-duty policeman who is invited into a jail to "have some fun?" (2) a husband who beats his wife in their home for disobedience? (3) a prisoner stoned to death pursuant to duly enacted national law?

4. Note that the *Filartiga* court considers the prohibition on torture to be customary international law, but does not discuss its status as a norm of *jus cogens*. International Courts have found that the Prohibition on Torture is a *jus cogens* norm. In *Prosecutor v. Furundzija*, the International Criminal Tribunal for the Former Yugoslavia (ICTY) held that "[b]ecause of the importance of the values it protects, (the prohibition of torture) has evolved into a peremptory norm of *jus cogens*, that is a norm that enjoys a higher rank in the international hierarchy than treaty law and even 'ordinary' customary rules. Clearly, the *jus cogens* nature of the prohibition against torture articulates the notion that the prohibition has now become one of the most fundamental standards of the international community." Prosecutor v. Furundzija, Case No. ICTY–95–17/1–T, Judgment, 10 Dec. 1998, para. 153. U.S. courts have agreed. In *Committee of U.S. Citizens Living in Nicaragua v. Reagan*, 859 F.2d 929 (D.C. Cir. 1988), the Court found that compliance with a ICJ judgment was not a *jus cogens* norm, adding: "Our conclusion is strengthened when we consider those few norms that arguably do meet the stringent criteria for jus cogens. The recently revised Restatement acknowledges two categories of such norms: 'the principles of the United Nations Charter prohibiting the use of force,' Restatement Sec. 102 comment k, and fundamental human rights law that prohibits genocide, slavery, murder, torture, prolonged arbitrary detention, and racial discrimination."

The interpretation of human rights standards like those prohibiting torture, may also vary over time. The evolution of these standards will depend, in part, on the particular nature of human rights obligations as involving the underlying values of protection of individual rights.

Republic of Ireland v. The United Kingdom

European Court of Human Rights
25 Eur. Ct. H.R. (ser. A) (1978)

* * *

11. The tragic and lasting crisis in Northern Ireland lies at the root of the present case. In order to combat what the respondent Government

describes as "the longest and most violent terrorist campaign witnessed in either part of the island of Ireland", the authorities in Northern Ireland exercised from August 1971 until December 1975 a series of extrajudicial powers of arrest, detention and internment. The proceedings in this case concern the scope and the operation in practice of those measures as well as the alleged ill-treatment of persons thereby deprived of their liberty.

* * *

96.   Twelve persons arrested on 9 August 1971 and two persons arrested in October 1971 were singled out and taken to one or more unidentified centres. There, between 11 to 17 August and 11 to 18 October respectively, they were submitted to a form of "interrogation in depth" which involved the combined application of five particular techniques.

These methods, sometimes termed "disorientation" or "sensory deprivation" techniques, were not used in any cases other than the fourteen so indicated above. It emerges from the Commission's establishment of the facts that the techniques consisted of:

   (a) wall-standing: forcing the detainees to remain for periods of some hours in a "stress position", described by those who underwent it as being "spread eagled against the wall, with their fingers put high above the head against the wall, the legs spread apart and the feet back, causing them to stand on their toes with the weight of the body mainly on the fingers";

   (b) hooding: putting a black or navy coloured bag over the detainees' heads and, at least initially, keeping it there all the time except during interrogation;

   (c) subjection to noise: pending their interrogations, holding the detainees in a room where there was a continuous loud and hissing noise;

   (d) deprivation of sleep: pending their interrogations, depriving the detainees of sleep;

   (e) deprivation of food and drink: subjecting the detainees to a reduced diet during their stay at the centre and pending interrogations.

* * *

167.   The five techniques were applied in combination, with premeditation and for hours at a stretch; they caused, if not actual bodily injury, at least intense physical and mental suffering to the persons subjected thereto and also led to acute psychiatric disturbances during interrogation. They accordingly fell into the category of inhuman treatment within the meaning of Article 3. The techniques were also degrading since they were such as to arouse in their victims feelings of fear, anguish and inferiority capable of humiliating and debasing them and possibly breaking their physical or moral resistance.

[. . .] Although the five techniques, as applied in combination, undoubtedly amounted to inhuman and degrading treatment, although their object was the extraction of confessions, the naming of others and/or information and although they were used systematically, they did not occasion suffering of the particular intensity and cruelty implied by the word torture as so understood.

The issue of the boundary between torture and cruel, inhuman and degrading treatment or punishment (CIDTP) was revisited in the following case:

Selmouni v. France

European Court of Human Rights
App. No. 25803/94, 29 Eur. H.R. Rep. 403 (1999)

* * *

9.   On 25 November 1991 Mr. Selmouni was arrested following surveillance of a hotel in Paris. ... He denied any involvement in drug trafficking.

10.   Mr Selmouni was held in police custody from 8:30 p.m. on 25 November 1991 until 7 p.m. on 28 November 1991. He was questioned by police officers from the Seine–Saint–Denis Criminal Investigation Department ("SDPJ 93") in Bobigny.

* * *

70.   The applicant complained that the manner in which he had been treated while in police custody had given rise to a violation of Article 3 of the Convention, according to which:

"No one shall be subjected to torture or to inhuman or degrading treatment or punishment." * * *

96.   In order to determine whether a particular form of ill-treatment should be qualified as torture, the Court must have regard to the distinction, embodied in Article 3, between this notion and that of inhuman or degrading treatment. As the European Court has previously found, it appears that it was the intention that the Convention should, by means of this distinction, attach a special stigma to deliberate inhuman treatment causing very serious and cruel suffering (see the Ireland v. the United Kingdom judgment cited above, pp. 66–67, § 167).

100.   In other words, it remains to be established in the instant case whether the "pain or suffering" inflicted on Mr. Selmouni can be defined as "severe" within the meaning of Article 1 of the United Nations Convention. The Court considers that this "severity" is, like the "minimum severity" required for the application of Article 3, in the nature of things, relative; it depends on all the circumstances of the case, such as the

duration of the treatment, its physical or mental effects and, in some cases, the sex, age and state of health of the victim, etc.

101. ... However, having regard to the fact that the Convention is a "living instrument which must be interpreted in the light of present-day conditions", the Court considers that certain acts which were classified in the past as "inhuman and degrading treatment" as opposed to "torture" could be classified differently in future. It takes the view that the increasingly high standard being required in the area of the protection of human rights and fundamental liberties correspondingly and inevitably requires greater firmness in assessing breaches of the fundamental values of democratic societies. * * *

NOTES AND QUESTIONS

1. The European Court of Human Rights was established under the auspices of the Council of Europe, through the 1950 Convention on the Protection of Human Rights and Fundamental Freedoms. It has jurisdiction over 47 countries, including many former Soviet states and sits full time in Strasbourg, France. It receives communications from both individuals and states alleging violations by states of the rights guaranteed in the Convention. There have only been a handful of cases where one state has brought a case against another—the first was *Ireland v. UK*. Why might states be reluctant to bring cases against other states? Other human rights treaties also often provide for states to take action against other states, but these are rarely if ever used.

2. The European regional human rights system until 1998 had a two-tier structure of Commission and Court. Protocol 11 to the European Convention on Human Rights and Fundamental Freedoms (ECHRFF) replaces that system with a single Court composed of separate Chambers on Admissibility and Merits along with an Appeal Chamber. The number of cases before the Court has risen exponentially over the last two decades, from 1657 in 1990 to 39,850 in 2008. The caseload has strained the Court, leading to a new Protocol to streamline its operations. That Protocol, Number 14, as of 2009 was awaiting ratification by Russia in order to enter into force.

3. How does the court determine where the line lies between torture and cruel, inhuman and degrading treatment or punishment (CIDTP) lies? How should it consider what is adequate severity? Will severity be context-specific? Will the existence of CIDTP? Why does the court say that the line between the two will vary over time? *See Soering v. The United Kingdom*, 1/1989/161/217, Eur.Ct.H.R., 7 July 1989, (in which the court found that "[what] constitutes 'inhumane or degrading treatment or punishment' depends on all the circumstances of the case. Furthermore, inherent to the whole of the convention is a search for a fair balance between the demands of the general interest of the community and the requirements of protection of the individual's fundamental rights.") What should the court consider? *See Tyrer v. UK*, Eur.Ct.H.R. (Ser. A) at 26 (25 April 1978) ("birching" of minor by school authorities violates Article 3) (*A. v. U.K.*

(100/1997/884/1096), 23 September 1998); (caning by stepfather violates Art. 3); but see *Costello–Roberts v. UK*, Series A, No. 247C (23 March 1993) (whacks of soft-soled shoe on 7–year old does not violate Art. 3).

4.   None of the basic human rights treaties distinguishes between torture and CIDTP: the ICCPR, ECHRFF, American Convention on Human Rights (ACHR) and African Charter on Human and People's Rights (ACHPR) all contain absolute prohibitions on both. Why does it matter then whether the acts are construed as torture or as something else?

5.   The subsequent 1984 Convention Against Torture (CAT), on the other hand, does distinguish between the two in several significant ways. Article 4 of the Convention requires that torture be criminalized in national law, and Article 5 allows states to exercise jurisdiction over persons accused of torture when the crime was committed in their territory, against their nationals, by their nationals, or when the offender is found in their territory, even if the torture took place elsewhere. The Convention requires states to investigate acts of torture, extradite or prosecute torturers found on their soil, and provide redress to victims. The only obligations regarding CIDTP are found in Article 10, which requires training of law enforcement officers and inclusion of the prohibition on CITDP in the instructions regarding duties and functions of public officers. Why would the drafters of the Convention have made this distinction? Is it even sensible to try to draw these lines?

6.   In addition to severity, the difference between torture and CIDTP has turned on whether there is an adequate showing that one of the purposes listed in the Convention Against Torture—obtaining information, punishment, or discriminatory motive—is present. See Sir Nigel Rodley, *The Definition(s) of Torture in International Law*, 66 Current Legal Probs. 467–93 (2002).

7.   What is the requisite degree of "severity?" In a now-infamous 2002 memorandum from the Office of Legal Counsel (lawyers in the Department of Justice who provide general legal advice for all of the federal government) then-Deputy Assistant Attorney General John Yoo argued that to constitute torture, the pain caused must be "of an intensity akin to that which accompanies serious physical injury such as death or organ failure". Does that seem to comport with the international precedents defining torture? Yoo's opinion was withdrawn by the OLC in 2005. The OLC nevertheless continued to support the use of "waterboarding" as not amounting to torture.

8.   What difference did it make that the U.K. government was facing a significant threat from the Irish Republican Army, and that its actions were in response to that threat? Note that under all human rights treaties, the prohibition on torture is non-derogable, that is, there is no state of war or national emergency that can justify states in violating their obligations. In 1999, the Israeli Supreme Court decided a case involving the treatment of Palestinian militants in Israeli jails, who had been subjected to a number of similar techniques, including shaking, hooding, stress positions, sleep

deprivation and excessive tightening of handcuffs. The State argued that the techniques were necessary given the terrorist threat, especially the possibility of a "ticking bomb"—an attack that could be averted by their use. The Court found the techniques unlawful, holding that:

> the "necessity" defence, found in the Penal Law, cannot serve as a basis of authority for the use of these interrogation practices, or for the existence of directives pertaining to GSS investigators, allowing them to employ interrogation practices of this kind. Our decision does not negate the possibility that the "necessity" defence be available to GSS investigators, be within the discretion of the Attorney General, if he decides to prosecute, or if criminal charges are brought against them, as per the Court's discretion.

The Court concluded:

> ... This decision opens with a description of the difficult reality in which Israel finds herself security wise. We shall conclude this judgment by re-addressing that harsh reality. We are aware that this decision does not ease dealing with that reality. This is the destiny of democracy, as not all means are acceptable to it, and not all practices employed by its enemies are open before it. Although a democracy must often fight with one hand tied behind its back, it nonetheless has the upper hand. Preserving the Rule of Law and recognition of an individual's liberty constitutes an important component in its understanding of security. At the end of the day, they strengthen its spirit and its strength and allow it to overcome its difficulties. ...

Supreme Court of Israel, *Judgment Concerning the Legality of the General Security Services' Interrogation Methods*, November 1999, 38 I.L.M. 1471.

Are the same considerations relevant to the United States' "war" against Al–Qaeda and the Taliban?

2.   GLOBAL HUMAN RIGHTS TREATIES AND THE UN SYSTEM: RATIFICATION, MONITORING, AND COMPLIANCE

a.   RATIFICATION OF HUMAN RIGHTS TREATIES

Most states are parties to the major human rights treaties. The United States, along with China, has a relatively spotty record on ratification of treaties. It is one of only two nations (the other is Somalia) that have not ratified the Convention on the Rights of the Child (CRC). The U.S. is a party only to the International Covenant on Civil and Political Rights, the Convention on the Elimination of Racial Discrimination (CERD), and the Convention Against Torture (CAT). The Obama administration pledged to bring the Convention on the Elimination of Discrimination Against Women (CEDAW) to the Senate for a vote. (You can find information on treaty ratifications, reservations and the like at www.ohchr.org.)

However, even where treaties are widely ratified, they may be of limited effectiveness due to a host of reservations, understandings and declarations (RUDs) that limit states' commitments. Most human rights treaties are silent on the issue of which reservations are allowed; recall that under the Vienna Convention on the Law of Treaties (VCLT), if the treaty itself is silent, a reservation is invalid if it violates the object and purpose of the treaty. See the *Reservations* and *Belilos* cases, *supra*, Chapter 2. How can we determine whether a specific reservation meets this test? Say, for example, that Egypt files a reservation to the Convention on the Elimination of Discrimination Against Women, which reads: "Reservation to the text of article 16 concerning the equality of men and women in all matters relating to marriage and family relations during the marriage and upon its dissolution, without prejudice to the Islamic Sha'ria's provisions whereby women are accorded rights equivalent to those of their spouses so as to ensure a just balance between them." Assuming Sha'ria law treats men and women differently regarding divorce and custody, how would the VCLT determine whether this is an invalid reservation? What would be the effect if, say, Sweden, objected to the reservation on grounds that it violates the object and purpose of the treaty? Why might states fail to object to a reservation of this type even if they thought it violated the object and purpose of the treaty? Does a reciprocity regime even make sense when dealing with a multilateral treaty concerning the state's obligations to respect and protect the rights of its own inhabitants? What is the alternative?

The Human Rights Committee, an expert body charged with interpreting states' compliance with the ICCPR, has proposed that "the compatibility of a reservation with the object and purpose of the Covenant must be established objectively, by reference to legal principles." Human Rights Committee, General Comment 24 (52), *General comment on issues relating to reservations made upon ratification or accession to the Covenant or the Optional Protocols thereto, or in relation to declarations under article 41 of the Covenant*, U.N. Doc. CCPR/C/21/Rev.1/Add.6 (1994). Does an objective test make more sense? What would such an objective test be based on? The Committee has proposed looking at the non-derogable nature of the right, the capacity to undermine the supportive guarantees of the Covenant, or the existence of "widely formulated reservations which essentially render ineffective all Covenant rights which would require any change in national law." Who would decide? The Committee suggests that it should decide in the case of the ICCPR, since it needs to know exactly what the state's obligations are before it can evaluate compliance with them. Is this sensible? What if the state's joining the treaty regime depended on the existence of the reservation? Could the Committee override the state's intent and, in effect, "sever" the offending reservation? Or, if the reservation is considered an indispensable part of the state's ratification, does this mean the state is not actually a party to the treaty if the reservation is unacceptable? What effect would this have on the number of states signing treaties? Is broad acceptance of human rights treaty regimes more important than the strength of the obligations actually accepted? The International Law Commission has rejected the Committee's approach. *ILC Annual Report*, 1997, UN Doc. A/CN.4/SER. A/1997/Add. 1(Part II), Ch. V.

The U.S. Senate has imposed a host of RUDs to ratification of human rights treaties. These include specific reservations regarding issues like the death penalty for minors, separation of juveniles and adults in criminal proceedings, prohibition of propaganda for war and others. In addition, the Senate has declared that the substantive provisions of human rights treaties are not self-executing. For a discussion of the American concept of the "non-self executing" treaty, see Chapter 11 below. See also William Schabas, *Invalid Reservations to the International Covenant on Civil and Political Rights: Is the United States Still a Party?*, 21 BROOKLYN J. INT'L L. 277 (1995) and generally Louis Henkin, *U.S. Ratification of Human Rights Conventions: The Ghost of Senator Bricker*, 89 AM. J. INT'L L. 341, 341 (1995).

b.   MONITORING OF COMPLIANCE WITH TREATIES

The global treaties share a similar monitoring mechanism. All eight treaties: International Covenant on Civil and Political Rights (ICCPR); International Covenant on Economic, Social and Cultural Rights (ICESCR); International Convention on the Elimination of All Forms of Racial Discrimination (ICERD); Convention on the Elimination of All Forms of Discrimination against Women (CEDAW); Convention on the Rights of the Child (CRC); Convention against Torture and Other Cruel, Inhuman or Degrading Treatment or Punishment (CAT); Convention on the Protection of the Rights of all Migrant Workers and Members of their Families (CPMW); Convention on the Rights of Persons with Disabilities (CRPD); and International Convention on the Protection of All Persons from Forced Disappearance (ICPFD) set up a committee of experts, numbering between 7 and 21, to oversee state compliance with those treaties it has ratified. States agree, as part of their treaty obligations, to report on a periodic basis to the committees on their implementation of the treaty. These reports are to consider the measures that the state party has adopted to give effect to the provisions of the treaty, the progress made, and the factors and difficulties the state party has encountered that have affected fulfillment of its obligations under the treaty.

What do you think states are likely to report on their compliance with their own human rights obligations? Is there any way the expert committees can overcome the likely self-serving nature of state reports? All the treaty bodies now receive information from non-governmental organizations on the states whose reports they are considering. Is this enough of a check? What purposes could such mandatory reporting serve given the tendency for states to focus on formal laws and gloss over shortcomings? Is there any domestic data-gathering or discussion that might be generated by such a requirement? Under what conditions?

Over time, the committees have developed techniques to try to improve the state reporting system. These include question and answer sessions with state representatives, concluding remarks after consideration of the reports, and assigning committee members to follow up with respect to specific issues. The expert bodies have also begun to coordinate their work.

Nonetheless, according to the Office of the High Commissioner for Human Rights, as of 2007 there were 1472 overdue reports from states. The process of coordination and consolidation of the treaty bodies' work has been slow:

> Note by the Office of the United Nations High Commissioner for Human Rights, *Effective functioning of human rights mechanisms: treaty bodies*, Commission on Human Rights, U.N. Doc. E/CN.4/2003/126, 26 February 2003.
>
> 1. In its resolution 57/300, adopted at its fifty-seventh session, the General Assembly, having considered the report of the Secretary–General entitled "Strengthening of the United Nations: an agenda for further change" (A/57/387), encouraged States parties to the human rights treaties and the respective treaty bodies to review the reporting procedures of the treaty bodies with a view to developing a more coordinated approach and to streamlining the reporting requirements under these treaties. The resolution also requested the United Nations High Commissioner for Human Rights to support this exercise....
>
> 2. In chapter II, section B, of his report on strengthening of human rights, the Secretary–General emphasized the importance of continued efforts to modernize the human rights treaty system. Against the background of growing delayed reporting or non-reporting by States parties to human rights treaty bodies, as well as the difficult demands reporting to six committees imposes on States parties, the Secretary–General proposed (a) that the Committees craft a more coordinated approach to their activities; and (b) that they standardize their varied reporting requirements, and that each State be allowed to produce a single report summarizing its adherence to the full range of international human rights treaties to which it is a party (para. 51). The Secretary–General also requested the High Commissioner for Human Rights to consult with treaty bodies on new streamlined reporting procedures and submit his recommendations to him by September 2003....

As of 2009, this process is ongoing. What else could be done to improve state compliance with the reporting system? Should the treaty bodies have the power to expel states that do not carry out its recommendations? That do not report at all? Would a smaller, more demanding system be an improvement over widespread ratification combined with weak compliance? Why or why not?

c. INDIVIDUAL COMPLAINT MECHANISMS

In addition to considering state reports, the expert committees of all the major treaties except the CRC accept individual communications of treaty violations, but only under certain circumstances. Most importantly, the state must specially accept the committee's jurisdiction to hear individual complaints (there is also a provision for state against state complaints, but it has never been used). With respect to the Human Rights Committee that monitors compliance with the ICCPR, this is done by ratifying the First Optional Protocol to the Covenant; in the case of CEDAW and the ICESCR there is also an Optional Protocol; in other cases states declare that they specially accept a provision of the treaty providing for consideration of individual communications. In addition, complaints must relate to a specific violation of the treaty, must be brought within a certain time period, and complainants must exhaust domestic remedies. When an expert committee receives a complaint, it generally asks the state for a response. It then, perhaps after more briefing (but without a hearing or witness testimony) will decide whether the petition is admissible and, if so, whether there has been a violation. If the committee finds a violation, it will issue recommendations to the state as to how to remedy it. There is no right to damages. If the state does not comply, the committee will issue increasingly sharp reminders and may raise the issue during consideration of periodic reports. However, there are few real teeth to the process, aside from negative publicity, "naming and shaming" and whatever spillover effects on the state's reputation (like aid or trade restrictions) accrue from a finding of violations.

d. U.N. CHARTER–BASED MECHANISMS

The treaty bodies, as the name suggests, only monitor states that are parties to the relevant treaties. But what if a state has not ratified any treaties? Now what? All states parties to the UN Charter can be the subject of general United Nations human rights procedures, based on the provisions of the Universal Declaration and general human rights law. Until recently, those provisions were established and carried out by the Commission on Human Rights, but in 2006 the Commission was replaced by the Human Rights Council, composed of 47 states elected by regional blocs. Unlike the treaty-based committees, the Council is composed of diplomats, and its proceedings are highly political. It meets at least three times a year in Geneva, and can also meet in emergency session when necessary. The members of the Council agree to regularly subject themselves to a process called Universal Periodic Review, in which the Council reviews the human rights records of each of its members every two years. The idea was that notorious human rights violators should not be allowed to sit on the Council and pass judgment on the rights practices of others. In practice, to date the reviews have lasted at most a day, though typically only a few hours, and have been less searching than many advocates hoped.

The Council can take a number of actions in cases of human rights violations. It can pass resolutions expressing various degrees of concern about human rights situations, and can appoint a special rapporteur or representative to investigate the human rights situation in a country and report back to the Council. The situation must reflect a "consistent pattern of gross violations"—a single incident is not enough. Given the political nature of the Council, are there certain types of countries that are more likely to be subject to this procedure? Less likely?

As an advocate, how would you go about convincing states to pass a resolution condemning human rights violations in Myanmar in 2009 or in Tibet? You will have to worry about which state should carry the resolution, how to shore up support among different regional blocs, and also what to ask for—how will you keep the issue before the Council?

In addition to these public procedures, there is also a private one, known as the 1503 procedure after the UN Resolution establishing it. Individual violations may be submitted to the Sub-committee on Communications of the Council so long as domestic remedies have been exhausted, if they are part of a pattern of similar gross violations. Are there any advantages to a private procedure, compared to a public one? The sub-committee will ask the state about the violations, and if the complaint is found to have merit, it will be forwarded to another sub-committee, which will privately attempt to remedy the violation. The entire process takes more than a year, but has resulted in changes in state behavior, especially with respect to states where the necessary political will for public "naming and shaming" does not exist. See David Weissbrodt and Maria Luis Bartolomei, *The Effectiveness of International Human Rights Pressures: The Case of Argentina*, 1976–1983, 75 MINN. L. REV. 1009 (1991).

One of the most useful innovations of the U.N. system has been the creation of "thematic" rapporteurs or working groups who focus on specific violations or human rights problems, rather than countries. The first working group, on Enforced Disappearances, was formed in 1977, as a result of an Amnesty International proposal initially accepted by states because they thought a thematic mechanism would be less threatening because it would be less likely to point fingers at any one state. See IAN GUEST, BEHIND THE DISAPPEARANCES (Penn Press, 1990). The thematic mechanisms do not require any showing of a pattern and practice nor exhaustion of domestic remedies; however, the violation complained of must come within the mandate of the rapporteur. The thematic rapporteurs or working groups may engage in site visits, issue urgent action appeals to governments, request information, receive and compile information on violations, issue reports, and lobby for legal or policy changes. There are almost 30 such mechanisms, including rapporteurs on torture, summary execution, violence against women, and human rights obligations of corporations, among others.

e. THE INTER–AMERICAN SYSTEM

The Inter–American Commission on Human Rights was created by the Organization of American States in 1948. Its seven members are charged with monitoring the observance of human rights in the Americas. It carries out fact-finding missions on OAS member states' observance of human rights norms, serves as a treaty-drafting body, holds hearings on human rights-related issues, and hears individual communications from any person or organization that believes their rights have been violated and that meets certain requirements, chief among them exhaustion of domestic remedies. When the state involved is a party to the 1978 American Convention on

Human Rights (Pact of San José), the Commission applies the provisions of the Convention. When the state is not a party to the Convention (i.e. in cases involving the United States, Canada, or a few Caribbean states), the Commission applies the 1948 American Declaration on the Rights and Duties of Man. Although as the name suggests, the Declaration is not a binding treaty, the Commission asserts that the Charter of the OAS, as amended by the 1967 Protocol of Buenos Aires and the Statute and Regulations of the Commission give it the authority to rule on the human rights observance of all OAS member states. (Not surprisingly, the United States disagrees.) The Commission has considered and made recommendations on cases involving the U.S. dealing with the juvenile death penalty, the detentions at Guantánamo Bay, Native American rights to land, abortion, political representation for Washington, DC, and a number of other issues.

Only states that have both ratified the American Convention and also specially accepted its jurisdiction are subject to the rulings of the Inter–American Court of Human Rights. The Court, based in Costa Rica, has 7 judges appointed by the States Parties to the Convention (nations of any OAS state may be judges, however). Only the Commission or a State Party—not aggrieved individuals—may ask the Court to hear a case.

One of the most innovative aspects of the jurisprudence of the Inter–American Court has been its expansive view of remedies. Article 63 of the American Convention provides: the Inter–American Court can, if it finds a violation has occurred, rule "that the injured party be ensured the enjoyment of his right or freedom that was violated . . . that the consequences of the measure or situation that constituted the breach of such right or freedom be remedied and that fair compensation be paid to the injured party." American Convention on Human Rights, Art. 63. Damages have been awarded for lost earnings, for medical and other expenses, for moral damages, and for the loss of life's project, by which the court means the limitations and changes in life plans and prospects brought about by the violator's actions. Damages have also been awarded to family members, either on a showing of loss of support and companionship, or, in an increasing number of cases, based on a presumption that close family members suffered as a result of the violation. Punitive damages are generally not allowed. In the Inter–American system, damage awards have ranged from some $25,000 for massacre survivors, to over $200,000 for the families of executed or disappeared individuals. In the European human rights system, award levels have varied widely, with the greatest damages reserved for cases involving violations of property rights.

But remedies have gone far beyond money damages to encompass restitution of jobs or pensions, orders to find the remains of the disappeared (in one case by dredging a lake to do so), to investigate the violations and prosecute those responsible, and to modify laws, change government structures or institute new ones (on child protection, for example). The Court has also often ordered symbolic reparations including publication of its judgment in local papers, a public apology by the state, or naming streets, schools, or funded scholarships after the victim. It has also ordered collective reparations in cases of harm to communities, especially indigenous communities. These have included ordering the state to provide and staff health centers, schools, and other services, to maintain community monuments to the victims, and to create community development funds or other sources of livelihood, identification and demarcation of traditional indigenous territories and granting of such territories to indigenous communities. *Case of the Yakye Axa Indigenous Community v. Paraguay* Judgment of June 17, 2005. See generally Gabriella Citroni and Karla I. Quintana Osuna, Reparations for Indigenous Peoples in the Case Law of the Inter–American Court of Human Rights, in REPARATIONS FOR INDIGENOUS PEOPLES: INTERNATIONAL AND COMPARATIVE PERSPECTIVES (Federico Lenzerini, ed.) (2008).

3. THE NATURE OF STATE OBLIGATIONS

As we have seen, human rights law is enforced in part through treaty obligations on states to comply. But what exactly is the scope of those obligations? The following two cases, from two different regional systems for the protection of human rights, explore this issue.

Velásquez Rodríguez Case

Inter–Am.Ct.H.R. (Ser. C) No. 4 (1988)

1. The Inter–American Commission on Human Rights (hereinafter "the Commission") submitted the instant case to the Inter–American Court of Human Rights (hereinafter the "Court") on April 24, 1986. It originated in a petition (No. 7920) against the State of Honduras (hereinafter "Honduras" or "the Government"), which the Secretariat of the Commission received on October 7, 1981. * * *

3. According to the petition filed with the Commission, and the supplementary information received subsequently, Manfredo Velásquez, a student at the National Autonomous University of Honduras, "was violently detained without a warrant for his arrest by members of the National Office of Investigations (DNI) and G–2 of the Armed Forces of Honduras." The detention took place in Tegucigalpa on the afternoon of September 12, 1981. According to the petitioners, several eyewitnesses reported that Manfredo Velásquez and others were detained and taken to the cells of Public Security Forces Station No. 2 located in the Barrio El Manchen of Tegucigalpa, where he was "accused of alleged political crimes and subjected to harsh interrogation and cruel torture." The petition added that on September 17, 1981, Manfredo Velásquez was moved to the First Infantry Battalion, where the interrogation continued, but that the police and security forces denied that he had been detained.

4. After transmitting the relevant parts of the petition to the Government, the Commission, on various occasions, requested information on the matter. Since the Commission received no reply, it applied Article 42

(formerly 39) of its Regulations and presumed "as true the allegations contained in the communication of October 7, 1981, concerning the detention and disappearance of Angel Manfredo Velásquez Rodríguez in the Republic of Honduras" and pointed out to the Government "that such acts are most serious violations of the right to life (Art. 4) and the right to personal liberty (Art. 7) of the American Convention" (Resolution 30/83 of October 4, 1983). * * *

[Exhaustion of Domestic Remedies]

57.   Article 46(1)(a) of the Convention provides that, in order for a petition or communication lodged with the Commission in accordance with Articles 44 or 45 to be admissible, it is necessary

"that the remedies under domestic law have been pursued and exhausted in accordance with generally recognized principles of international law."

58.   The same article, in the second paragraph, provides that this requirement shall not be applicable when

"a.   the domestic legislation of the state concerned does not afford due process of law for the protection of the right or rights that have allegedly been violated;

b.   the party alleging violation of his rights has been denied access to the remedies under domestic law or has been prevented from exhausting them; or

c.   there has been unwarranted delay in rendering a final judgment under the aforementioned remedies."

59.   In its Judgment of June 26, 1987, the Court decided, inter alia, that "the State claiming non-exhaustion has an obligation to prove that domestic remedies remain to be exhausted and that they are effective" (Velásquez Rodríguez Case, Preliminary Objections, supra 23, para. 88).

60.   Concerning the burden of proof, the Court did not go beyond the conclusion cited in the preceding paragraph. The Court now affirms that if a State which alleges non-exhaustion proves the existence of specific domestic remedies that should have been utilized, the opposing party has the burden of showing that those remedies were exhausted or that the case comes within the exceptions of Article 46(2). It must not be rashly presumed that a State Party to the Convention has failed to comply with its obligation to provide effective domestic remedies.

61.   The rule of prior exhaustion of domestic remedies allows the State to resolve the problem under its internal law before being confronted with an international proceeding. This is particularly true in the international jurisdiction of human rights, because the latter reinforces or complements the domestic jurisdiction (American Convention, Preamble).

62.   It is a legal duty of the States to provide such remedies, as this Court indicated in its Judgment of June 26, 1987, when it stated:

"The rule of prior exhaustion of domestic remedies under the international law of human rights has certain implications that are present in the Convention. Under the Convention, States Parties have an obligation to provide effective judicial remedies to victims of human rights violations (Art. 25), remedies that must be substantiated in accordance with the rules of due process of law (Art. 8(1)), all in keeping with the general obligation of such States to guarantee the free and full exercise of the rights recognized by the Convention to all persons subject to their jurisdiction (Art. 1).

63. Article 46(1)(a) of the Convention speaks of "generally recognized principles of international law." Those principles refer not only to the formal existence of such remedies, but also to their adequacy and effectiveness, as shown by the exceptions set out in Article 46(2).

64. Adequate domestic remedies are those which are suitable to address an infringement of a legal right. A number of remedies exist in the legal system of every country, but not all are applicable in every circumstance. If a remedy is not adequate in a specific case, it obviously need not be exhausted. A norm is meant to have an effect and should not be interpreted in such a way as to negate its effect or lead to a result that is manifestly absurd or unreasonable. For example, a civil proceeding specifically cited by the Government, such as a presumptive finding of death based on disappearance, the purpose of which is to allow heirs to dispose of the estate of the person presumed deceased or to allow the spouse to remarry, is not an adequate remedy for finding a person or for obtaining his liberty.

65. Of the remedies cited by the Government, habeas corpus would be the normal means of finding a person presumably detained by the authorities, of ascertaining whether he is legally detained and, given the case, of obtaining his liberty. The other remedies cited by the Government are either for reviewing a decision within an inchoate proceeding (such as those of appeal or cassation) or are addressed to other objectives. If, however, as the Government has stated, the writ of habeas corpus requires the identification of the place of detention and the authority ordering the detention, it would not be adequate for finding a person clandestinely held by State officials, since in such cases there is only hearsay evidence of the detention, and the whereabouts of the victim is unknown.

66. A remedy must also be effective—that is, capable of producing the result for which it was designed. Procedural requirements can make the remedy of habeas corpus ineffective: if it is powerless to compel the authorities; if it presents a danger to those who invoke it; or if it is not impartially applied.

67. On the other hand, contrary to the Commission's argument, the mere fact that a domestic remedy does not produce a result favorable to the petitioner does not in and of itself demonstrate the inexistence or exhaustion of all effective domestic remedies. For example, the petitioner may not have invoked the appropriate remedy in a timely fashion.

68.   It is a different matter, however, when it is shown that remedies are denied for trivial reasons or without an examination of the merits, or if there is proof of the existence of a practice or policy ordered or tolerated by the government, the effect of which is to impede certain persons from invoking internal remedies that would normally be available to others. In such cases, resort to those remedies becomes a senseless formality. The exceptions of Article 46(2) would be fully applicable in those situations and would discharge the obligation to exhaust internal remedies since they cannot fulfill their objective in that case.

69.   [The record contained evidence that petitioners had brought three habeas corpus petitions, all of which were rejected, and two criminal complaints that were also unsuccessful.] In the Government's opinion, a writ of habeas corpus does not exhaust the remedies of the Honduran legal system because there are other remedies, both ordinary and extraordinary, such as appeal, cassation, and the extraordinary writ of *amparo*, as well as the civil remedy of a presumptive finding of death. In addition, in criminal procedures parties may use whatever evidence they choose. With respect to the cases of disappearances mentioned by the Commission, the Government stated that it had initiated some investigations and had opened others on the basis of complaints, and that the proceedings remain pending until those presumed responsible, either as principals or accomplices, are identified or apprehended. * * *

76.   The record ... contains testimony of members of the Legislative Assembly of Honduras, Honduran lawyers, persons who were at one time disappeared, and relatives of disappeared persons, which purports to show that in the period in which the events took place, the legal remedies in Honduras were ineffective in obtaining the liberty of victims of a practice of enforced or involuntary disappearances (hereinafter "disappearance" or "disappearances"), ordered or tolerated by the Government. The record also contains dozens of newspaper clippings which allude to the same practice. According to that evidence, from 1981 to 1984 more than one hundred persons were illegally detained, many of whom never reappeared, and, in general, the legal remedies which the Government claimed were available to the victims were ineffective.

77.   That evidence also shows that some individuals were captured and detained without due process and subsequently reappeared. However, in some of those cases, the reappearances were not the result of any of the legal remedies which, according to the Government, would have been effective, but rather the result of other circumstances, such as the intervention of diplomatic missions or actions of human rights organizations.

78.   The evidence offered shows that lawyers who filed writs of habeas corpus were intimidated, that those who were responsible for executing the writs were frequently prevented from entering or inspecting the places of detention, and that occasional criminal complaints against military or police officials were ineffective, either because certain procedural steps were not taken or because the complaints were dismissed without further proceedings. * * *

80.   The testimony and other evidence received and not refuted leads to the conclusion that, during the period under consideration, although there may have been legal remedies in Honduras that theoretically allowed a person detained by the authorities to be found, those remedies were ineffective in cases of disappearances because the imprisonment was clandestine; formal requirements made them inapplicable in practice; the authorities against whom they were brought simply ignored them, or because attorneys and judges were threatened and intimidated by those authorities.

81.   Aside from the question of whether between 1981 and 1984 there was a governmental policy of carrying out or tolerating the disappearance of certain persons, the Commission has shown that although writs of habeas corpus and criminal complaints were filed, they were ineffective or were mere formalities. The evidence offered by the Commission was not refuted and is sufficient to reject the Government's preliminary objection that the case is inadmissible because domestic remedies were not exhausted.

82.   The Commission presented testimony and documentary evidence to show that there were many kidnappings and disappearances in Honduras from 1981 to 1984 and that those acts were attributable to the Armed Forces of Honduras (hereinafter "Armed Forces"), which was able to rely at least on the tolerance of the Government. Three officers of the Armed Forces testified on this subject at the request of the Court. * * *

[The Nature of the State's Obligations]

159.   The Commission has asked the Court to find that Honduras has violated the rights guaranteed to Manfredo Velásquez by Articles 4, 5 and 7 of the Convention. The Government has denied the charges and seeks to be absolved.

160.   This requires the Court to examine the conditions under which a particular act, which violates one of the rights recognized by the Convention, can be imputed to a State Party thereby establishing its international responsibility.

161.   Article 1(1) of the Convention provides:

"Article 1. Obligation to Respect Rights

1.   The States Parties to this Convention undertake to respect the rights and freedoms recognized herein and to ensure to all persons subject to their jurisdiction the free and full exercise of those rights and freedoms, without any discrimination for reasons of race, color, sex, language, religion, political or other opinion, national or social origin, economic status, birth, or any other social condition."

162.   This article specifies the obligation assumed by the States Parties in relation to each of the rights protected. Each claim alleging that one of those rights has been infringed necessarily implies that Article 1(1) of the Convention has also been violated. * * *

164.   Article 1(1) is essential in determining whether a violation of the human rights recognized by the Convention can be imputed to a State Party. In effect, that article charges the States Parties with the fundamental duty to respect and guarantee the rights recognized in the Convention. Any impairment of those rights which can be attributed under the rules of international law to the action or omission of any public authority constitutes an act imputable to the State, which assumes responsibility in the terms provided by the Convention.

165.   The first obligation assumed by the States Parties under Article 1(1) is "to respect the rights and freedoms" recognized by the Convention....

166.   The second obligation of the States Parties is to "ensure" the free and full exercise of the rights recognized by the Convention to every person subject to its jurisdiction. This obligation implies the duty of the States Parties to organize the governmental apparatus and, in general, all the structures through which public power is exercised, so that they are capable of juridically ensuring the free and full enjoyment of human rights. As a consequence of this obligation, the States must prevent, investigate and punish any violation of the rights recognized by the Convention and, moreover, if possible attempt to restore the right violated and provide compensation as warranted for damages resulting from the violation.

167.   The obligation to ensure the free and full exercise of human rights is not fulfilled by the existence of a legal system designed to make it possible to comply with this obligation—it also requires the government to conduct itself so as to effectively ensure the free and full exercise of human rights.

168.   The obligation of the States is, thus, much more direct than that contained in Article 2, which reads:

Article 2. Domestic Legal Effects

"Where the exercise of any of the rights or freedoms referred to in Article 1 is not already ensured by legislative or other provisions, the States Parties undertake to adopt, in accordance with their constitutional processes and the provisions of this Convention, such legislative or other measures as may be necessary to give effect to those rights or freedoms."

169.   According to Article 1(1), any exercise of public power that violates the rights recognized by the Convention is illegal. Whenever a State organ, official or public entity violates one of those rights, this constitutes a failure of the duty to respect the rights and freedoms set forth in the Convention.

170.   This conclusion is independent of whether the organ or official has contravened provisions of internal law or overstepped the limits of his authority: under international law a State is responsible for the acts of its agents undertaken in their official capacity and for their omissions, even when those agents act outside the sphere of their authority or violate internal law.

171.   This principle suits perfectly the nature of the Convention, which is violated whenever public power is used to infringe the rights recognized therein. If acts of public power that exceed the State's authority or are illegal under its own laws were not considered to compromise that State's obligation under the treaty, the system of protection provided for in the Convention would be illusory.

172.   Thus, in principle, any violation of rights recognized by the Convention carried out by an act of public authority or by persons who use their position of authority is imputable to the State. However, this does not define all the circumstances in which a State is obligated to prevent, investigate and punish human rights violations, nor all the cases in which the State might be found responsible for an infringement of those rights. An illegal act which violates human rights and which is initially not directly imputable to a State (for example, because it is the act of a private person or because the person responsible has not been identified) can lead to international responsibility of the State, not because of the act itself, but because of the lack of due diligence to prevent the violation or to respond to it as required by the Convention.

173.   Violations of the Convention cannot be founded upon rules that take psychological factors into account in establishing individual culpability. For the purposes of analysis, the intent or motivation of the agent who has violated the rights recognized by the Convention is irrelevant—the violation can be established even if the identity of the individual perpetrator is unknown. What is decisive is whether a violation of the rights recognized by the Convention has occurred with the support or the acquiescence of the government, or whether the State has allowed the act to take place without taking measures to prevent it or to punish those responsible. Thus, the Court's task is to determine whether the violation is the result of a State's failure to fulfill its duty to respect and guarantee those rights, as required by Article 1(1) of the Convention.

174.   The State has a legal duty to take reasonable steps to prevent human rights violations and to use the means at its disposal to carry out a serious investigation of violations committed within its jurisdiction, to identify those responsible, to impose the appropriate punishment and to ensure the victim adequate compensation.

175.   This duty to prevent includes all those means of a legal, political, administrative and cultural nature that promote the protection of human rights and ensure that any violations are considered and treated as illegal acts, which, as such, may lead to the punishment of those responsible and the obligation to indemnify the victims for damages. It is not possible to make a detailed list of all such measures, since they vary with the law and the conditions of each State Party. Of course, while the State is obligated to prevent human rights abuses, the existence of a particular violation does not, in itself, prove the failure to take preventive measures. On the other hand, subjecting a person to official, repressive bodies that practice torture and assassination with impunity is itself a breach of the duty to prevent violations of the rights to life and physical integrity of the person, even if

that particular person is not tortured or assassinated, or if those facts cannot be proven in a concrete case.

176.   The State is obligated to investigate every situation involving a violation of the rights protected by the Convention. If the State apparatus acts in such a way that the violation goes unpunished and the victim's full enjoyment of such rights is not restored as soon as possible, the State has failed to comply with its duty to ensure the free and full exercise of those rights to the persons within its jurisdiction. The same is true when the State allows private persons or groups to act freely and with impunity to the detriment of the rights recognized by the Convention.

177.   In certain circumstances, it may be difficult to investigate acts that violate an individual's rights. The duty to investigate, like the duty to prevent, is not breached merely because the investigation does not produce a satisfactory result. Nevertheless, it must be undertaken in a serious manner and not as a mere formality preordained to be ineffective. An investigation must have an objective and be assumed by the State as its own legal duty, not as a step taken by private interests that depends upon the initiative of the victim or his family or upon their offer of proof, without an effective search for the truth by the government. This is true regardless of what agent is eventually found responsible for the violation. Where the acts of private parties that violate the Convention are not seriously investigated, those parties are aided in a sense by the government, thereby making the State responsible on the international plane.

178.   In the instant case, the evidence shows a complete inability of the procedures of the State of Honduras, which were theoretically adequate, to carry out an investigation into the disappearance of Manfredo Velásquez, and of the fulfillment of its duties to pay compensation and punish those responsible, as set out in Article 1(1) of the Convention.

179.   As the Court has verified above, the failure of the judicial system to act upon the writs brought before various tribunals in the instant case has been proven. Not one writ of habeas corpus was processed. No judge had access to the places where Manfredo Velásquez might have been detained. The criminal complaint was dismissed.

180.   Nor did the organs of the Executive Branch carry out a serious investigation to establish the fate of Manfredo Velásquez. There was no investigation of public allegations of a practice of disappearances nor a determination of whether Manfredo Velásquez had been a victim of that practice. The Commission's requests for information were ignored to the point that the Commission had to presume, under Article 42 of its Regulations, that the allegations were true. The offer of an investigation in accord with Resolution 30/83 of the Commission resulted in an investigation by the Armed Forces, the same body accused of direct responsibility for the disappearances. This raises grave questions regarding the seriousness of the investigation. The Government often resorted to asking relatives of the victims to present conclusive proof of their allegations even though those allegations, because they involved crimes against the person, should have been investigated on the Government's own initiative in fulfillment of the

State's duty to ensure public order. This is especially true when the allegations refer to a practice carried out within the Armed Forces, which, because of its nature, is not subject to private investigations. No proceeding was initiated to establish responsibility for the disappearance of Manfredo Velásquez and apply punishment under internal law. All of the above leads to the conclusion that the Honduran authorities did not take effective action to ensure respect for human rights within the jurisdiction of that State as required by Article 1(1) of the Convention.

181.   The duty to investigate facts of this type continues as long as there is uncertainty about the fate of the person who has disappeared. Even in the hypothetical case that those individually responsible for crimes of this type cannot be legally punished under certain circumstances, the State is obligated to use the means at its disposal to inform the relatives of the fate of the victims and, if they have been killed, the location of their remains.

182.   The Court is convinced, and has so found, that the disappearance of Manfredo Velásquez was carried out by agents who acted under cover of public authority. However, even had that fact not been proven, the failure of the State apparatus to act, which is clearly proven, is a failure on the part of Honduras to fulfill the duties it assumed under Article 1(1) of the Convention, which obligated it to ensure Manfredo Velásquez the free and full exercise of his human rights.

183.   The Court notes that the legal order of Honduras does not authorize such acts and that internal law defines them as crimes. The Court also recognizes that not all levels of the Government of Honduras were necessarily aware of those acts, nor is there any evidence that such acts were the result of official orders. Nevertheless, those circumstances are irrelevant for the purposes of establishing whether Honduras is responsible under international law for the violations of human rights perpetrated within the practice of disappearances.

184.   According to the principle of the continuity of the State in international law, responsibility exists both independently of changes of government over a period of time and continuously from the time of the act that creates responsibility to the time when the act is declared illegal. The foregoing is also valid in the area of human rights although, from an ethical or political point of view, the attitude of the new government may be much more respectful of those rights than that of the government in power when the violations occurred.

185.   The Court, therefore, concludes that the facts found in this proceeding show that the State of Honduras is responsible for the involuntary disappearance of Angel Manfredo Velásquez Rodríguez. Thus, Honduras has violated Articles 7, 5 and 4 of the Convention. * * *

NOTES AND QUESTIONS

1. *Exhaustion of Domestic Remedies.* In order to bring a complaint before an international human rights body, the petitioner typically must show she

has exhausted domestic remedies. Why would this be? According to the court, who bears the burden of proof on failure to exhaust? On specific remedies yet to be exhausted? What purpose(s) does an exhaustion requirement serve? Are there dangers in requiring exhaustion of all remedies, especially where the state is actively seeking to avoid outside review of its human rights policies? Do the exceptions in the American Convention on Human Rights, Art. 46(2) (above at paragraph 58) respond adequately to those dangers? Other human rights bodies also qualify the exhaustion requirement by requiring remedies to be effective, adequate, and not unreasonably prolonged. For more on the exhaustion of remedies rule, see Chapter 9.

2. *The Role of Pattern and Practice Evidence.* Why does the court discuss what has happened to lawyers in other cases and other people who have apparently suffered the same fate as Manfredo Veláquez? How is this evidence relevant to the question of exhaustion? To the proof that Veláquez' disappearance is attributable to the Honduran government?

3. *Veláquez–Rodríguez* was the first contentious case heard before the Inter–American Court of Human Rights. During the period from 1981–85, the court found, almost 150 people disappeared in Honduras. During roughly comparable periods in the late 1970s and early 1980s, between 10,000 and 30,000 people suffered the same fate in Argentina, up to 40,000 in Guatemala, and thousands more in Peru, Chile, Colombia and elsewhere. Why then would the Inter-American commission choose as its first case to bring to the court the relatively small number of disappearances in Honduras?

Part of the explanation may have to do with the quality of the evidence available to the court. Witnesses who testified included several people who had themselves been "disappeared people" but who, because of family connections or other reasons, managed to emerge alive from their secret detention. One of these people had been in the jail cell next to Velásquez, who identified himself and asked for help. The court also heard from a police officer who described his conversations with the military recruit who had arrested Velásquez, and from another soldier who took him out to be shot. Lawyers and human rights activists also discussed the fate of those who tried to discover the whereabouts of the disappeared. Do you think this kind of evidence is often available in disappearance cases?

4. *State Responsibility.* What is the Honduran state's argument about its responsibility for what happened to Manfredo Velásquez? If state officers were acting illegally, why should the state be responsible for their acts? What about if those responsible for Velásquez' fate are off-duty police and military officers? What if they are members of paramilitary groups aligned with, but not paid by, the government? What if Velásquez was in the middle of an acrimonious dispute with a vicious neighbor? Are there any limits to the state's responsibility? Should there be? Does it matter that what happened to Velásquez seems to be part of an overall pattern and practice? What if there was only a single disappearance, without the overall context? The court's broad holding on the scope and nature of the due

diligence obligation has been adopted by the European Court of Human Rights in cases like *E. and Others v. the United Kingdom*, No. 33218/96, judgment of 26 November 2002, para. 103 (failure of officials to investigate child sexual and physical abuse is a violation of the state's obligation to protect against inhuman and degrading treatment); *Kaya v. Turkey*, judgment of 19 February 1998, Reports of Judgments and Decisions 1998–I, p. 324 (failure of authorities to investigate the disappearance of a man known to be at high risk of attack by security forces); *Finucane v. the United Kingdom*, No. 29178/95, judgment of July 1 2003 (investigation into murder of solicitor conducted by members of the police force implicated in his killing constituted insufficient investigation under Article 2). For more on state responsibility, see Chapter 8.

5.   *Provisional Measures*. The Inter–American Court can order provisional measures when requested to safeguard witnesses or petitioners. During the course of the litigation here, Miguel Angel Pavon was killed shortly after testifying in the case. The police officer, Sergeant José Isaias Vilorio, was also killed in broad daylight just before giving his testimony. The lawyers for petitioners received death threats, and the petitioner, Velásquez' sister, had to leave the country. The Court directed the government to provide security assurances for all the witnesses, lawyers and families involved in the case, and the government agreed. What kinds of considerations about security do lawyers bringing these cases need to keep in mind? What can they do if the government does not comply with the Court's provisional measures order? The Inter–American Commission can also order precautionary measures in cases where life or other irreparable harm is at issue. See Chapter 9 for more on provisional measures and their enforcement.

Velásquez's sister eventually settled in the U.S., and brought a civil case under the Alien Tort Statute against one of the army officers responsible for her brothers' detention. She and five other plaintiffs won $47 million, but the defendant was deported to Honduras and never paid.

6.   What are the implications of the holding in *Velásquez* for cases involving domestic violence and other forms of violence against women? Does the due diligence standard enunciated in the case provide a yardstick with which to measure State responsibility for private acts more generally? See U.N. Declaration on the Elimination of Violence Against Women, General Assembly resolution 48/104 of 20 December 1993, U.N. Doc. A/RES/48/104, 23 February 1994 (due diligence standard in Article 4); Committee on the Elimination of Discrimination against Women (CEDAW) General Recommendation 19 ("States may also be responsible for private acts if they fail to act with due diligence"); Report of the Special Rapporteur on Violence Against Women, Its Causes and Consequences (Radhika Coomaraswamy), U.N. Doc. E/CN.4/1996/53, 6 Feb. 1996.

4.   State Obligations: Economic, Social and Cultural Rights

Scope. Velásquez and its progeny establish both affirmative and negative obligations for violations of fundamental civil and political rights like the right to life and to be free from torture and arbitrary detention. Should other kinds of rights be treated in the same way? One source of controversy has involved the enforcement of economic, social and cultural rights like those contained in the ICESCR.

Social and Economic Rights Action Center & the Center for Economic and Social Rights v. Nigeria*

African Commission on Human and People's Rights
Communication No. 155/96 (2001)

Summary of Facts:

1.   The Communication alleges that the military government of Nigeria has been directly involved in oil production through the State oil company, the Nigerian National Petroleum Company (NNPC), the majority shareholder in a consortium with Shell Petroleum Development Corporation (SPDC), and that these operations have caused environmental degradation and health problems resulting from the contamination of the environment among the Ogoni People.

2.   The Communication alleges that the oil consortium has exploited oil reserves in Ogoniland with no regard for the health or environment of the local communities, disposing toxic wastes into the environment and local waterways in violation of applicable international environmental standards. The consortium also neglected and/or failed to maintain its facilities causing numerous avoidable spills in the proximity of villages. The resulting contamination of water, soil and air has had serious short and long-term health impacts, including skin infections, gastrointestinal and respiratory ailments, and increased risk of cancers, and neurological and reproductive problems.

3.   The Communication alleges that the Nigerian Government has condoned and facilitated these violations by placing the legal and military powers of the State at the disposal of the oil companies. The Communication contains a memo from the Rivers State Internal Security Task Force, calling for "ruthless military operations".

4.   The Communication alleges that the Government has neither monitored operations of the oil companies nor required safety measures that are standard procedure within the industry. The Government has withheld from Ogoni Communities information on the dangers created by oil activities. Ogoni Communities have not been involved in the decisions affecting the development of Ogoniland.

5.   The Government has not required oil companies or its own agencies to produce basic health and environmental impact studies regarding hazardous operations and materials relating to oil production, despite the obvious health and environmental crisis in Ogoniland. The government has even refused to permit scientists and environmental organisations from

---

* Footnotes omitted.

entering Ogoniland to undertake such studies. The government has also ignored the concerns of Ogoni Communities regarding oil development, and has responded to protests with massive violence and executions of Ogoni leaders.

6.   The Communication alleges that the Nigerian government does not require oil companies to consult communities before beginning operations, even if the operations pose direct threats to community or individual lands.

9.   The Communication alleges that the Nigerian government has destroyed and threatened Ogoni food sources through a variety of means. The government has participated in irresponsible oil development that has poisoned much of the soil and water upon which Ogoni farming and fishing depended. In their raids on villages, Nigerian security forces have destroyed crops and killed farm animals. The security forces have created a state of terror and insecurity that has made it impossible for many Ogoni villagers to return to their fields and animals. The destruction of farmlands, rivers, crops and animals has created malnutrition and starvation among certain Ogoni Communities.

Complaint:

The communication alleges violations of Articles 2, 4, 14, 16, 18(1), 21, and 24 of the African Charter. . . .

44.   Internationally accepted ideas of the various obligations engendered by human rights indicate that all rights—both civil and political rights and social and economic—generate at least four levels of duties for a State that undertakes to adhere to a rights regime, namely the duty to respect, protect, promote, and fulfil these rights. These obligations universally apply to all rights and entail a combination of negative and positive duties. As a human rights instrument, the African Charter is not alien to these concepts and the order in which they are dealt with here is chosen as a matter of convenience and in no way should it imply the priority accorded to them. Each layer of obligation is equally relevant to the rights in question.

45.   At a primary level, the obligation to respect entails that the State should refrain from interfering in the enjoyment of all fundamental rights; it should respect right-holders, their freedoms, autonomy, resources, and liberty of their action. With respect to socio economic rights, this means that the State is obliged to respect the free use of resources owned or at the disposal of the individual alone or in any form of association with others, including the household or the family, for the purpose of rights-related needs. And with regard to a collective group, the resources belonging to it should be respected, as it has to use the same resources to satisfy its needs.

46.   At a secondary level, the State is obliged to protect right-holders against other subjects by legislation and provision of effective remedies. This obligation requires the State to take measures to protect beneficiaries of the protected rights against political, economic and social interferences. Protection generally entails the creation and maintenance of an atmo-

sphere or framework by an effective interplay of laws and regulations so that individuals will be able to freely realize their rights and freedoms. This is very much intertwined with the tertiary obligation of the State to promote the enjoyment of all human rights. The State should make sure that individuals are able to exercise their rights and freedoms, for example, by promoting tolerance, raising awareness, and even building infrastructures.

47. The last layer of obligation requires the State to fulfil the rights and freedoms it freely undertook under the various human rights regimes. It is more of a positive expectation on the part of the State to move its machinery towards the actual realisation of the rights. This is also very much intertwined with the duty to promote mentioned in the preceding paragraph. It could consist in the direct provision of basic needs such as food or resources that can be used for food (direct food aid or social security).

48. Thus States are generally burdened with the above set of duties when they commit themselves under human rights instruments. Emphasising the all embracing nature of their obligations, the International Covenant on Economic, Social, and Cultural Rights, for instance, under Article 2(1), stipulates exemplarily that States "undertake to take steps . . . by all appropriate means, including particularly the adoption of legislative measures." Depending on the type of rights under consideration, the level of emphasis in the application of these duties varies. But sometimes, the need to meaningfully enjoy some of the rights demands a concerted action from the State in terms of more than one of the said duties. Whether the government of Nigeria has, by its conduct, violated the provisions of the African Charter as claimed by the Complainants is examined here below.
* * *

50. The Complainants allege that the Nigerian government violated the right to health and the right to clean environment as recognized under Articles 16 and 24 of the African Charter by failing to fulfill the minimum duties required by these rights. This, the Complainants allege, the government has done by—:

—Directly participating in the contamination of air, water and soil and thereby harming the health of the Ogoni population,

—Failing to protect the Ogoni population from the harm caused by the NNPC Shell Consortium but instead using its security forces to facilitate the damage

—Failing to provide or permit studies of potential or actual environmental and health risks caused by the oil operations

Article 16 of the African Charter reads:

"(1) Every individual shall have the right to enjoy the best attainable state of physical and mental health.

(2) States Parties to the present Charter shall take the necessary measures to protect the health of their people and to ensure that they receive medical attention when they are sick."

Article 24 of the African Charter reads:

"All peoples shall have the right to a general satisfactory environment favourable to their development."

51.   These rights recognise the importance of a clean and safe environment that is closely linked to economic and social rights in so far as the environment affects the quality of life and safety of the individual. As has been rightly observed by Alexander Kiss, "an environment degraded by pollution and defaced by the destruction of all beauty and variety is as contrary to satisfactory living conditions and the development as the breakdown of the fundamental ecologic equilibria is harmful to physical and moral health."

52.   The right to a general satisfactory environment, as guaranteed under Article 24 of the African Charter or the right to a healthy environment, as it is widely known, therefore imposes clear obligations upon a government. It requires the State to take reasonable and other measures to prevent pollution and ecological degradation, to promote conservation, and to secure an ecologically sustainable development and use of natural resources. Article 12 of the International Covenant on Economic, Social and Cultural Rights (ICESCR), to which Nigeria is a party, requires governments to take necessary steps for the improvement of all aspects of environmental and industrial hygiene. The right to enjoy the best attainable state of physical and mental health enunciated in Article 16(1) of the African Charter and the right to a general satisfactory environment favourable to development (Article 16(3)) already noted obligate governments to desist from directly threatening the health and environment of their citizens. The State is under an obligation to respect the just noted rights and this entails largely non-interventionist conduct from the State for example, not from carrying out, sponsoring or tolerating any practice, policy or legal measures violating the integrity of the individual.

53.   Government compliance with the spirit of Articles 16 and 24 of the African Charter must also include ordering or at least permitting independent scientific monitoring of threatened environments, requiring and publicising environmental and social impact studies prior to any major industrial development, undertaking appropriate monitoring and providing information to those communities exposed to hazardous materials and activities and providing meaningful opportunities for individuals to be heard and to participate in the development decisions affecting their communities.

54.   We now examine the conduct of the government of Nigeria in relation to Articles 16 and 24 of the African Charter. Undoubtedly and admittedly, the government of Nigeria, through NNPC has the right to produce oil, the income from which will be used to fulfil the economic and social rights of Nigerians. But the care that should have been taken as

outlined in the preceding paragraph and which would have protected the rights of the victims of the violations complained of was not taken. To exacerbate the situation, the security forces of the government engaged in conduct in violation of the rights of the Ogonis by attacking, burning and destroying several Ogoni villages and homes.

55. The Complainants also allege a violation of Article 21 of the African Charter by the government of Nigeria. The Complainants allege that the Military government of Nigeria was involved in oil production and thus did not monitor or regulate the operations of the oil companies and in so doing paved a way for the Oil Consortiums to exploit oil reserves in Ogoniland. Furthermore, in all their dealings with the Oil Consortiums, the government did not involve the Ogoni Communities in the decisions that affected the development of Ogoniland. The destructive and selfish role-played by oil development in Ogoniland, closely tied with repressive tactics of the Nigerian Government, and the lack of material benefits accruing to the local population may well be said to constitute a violation of Article 21.

Article 21 provides:

''1. All peoples shall freely dispose of their wealth and natural resources. This right shall be exercised in the exclusive interest of the people. In no case shall a people be deprived of it.

2. In case of spoliation the dispossessed people shall have the right to the lawful recovery of its property as well as to an adequate compensation.

3. The free disposal of wealth and natural resources shall be exercised without prejudice to the obligation of promoting international economic co-operation based on mutual respect, equitable exchange and the principles of international law.

4. States parties to the present Charter shall individually and collectively exercise the right to free disposal of their wealth and natural resources with a view to strengthening African unity and solidarity.

5. States Parties to the present Charter shall undertake to eliminate all forms of foreign economic exploitation particularly that practised by international monopolies so as to enable their peoples to fully benefit from the advantages derived from their national resources.''

56. The origin of this provision may be traced to colonialism, during which the human and material resources of Africa were largely exploited for the benefit of outside powers, creating tragedy for Africans themselves, depriving them of their birthright and alienating them from the land. The aftermath of colonial exploitation has left Africa's precious resources and people still vulnerable to foreign misappropriation. The drafters of the Charter obviously wanted to remind African governments of the continent's painful legacy and restore co-operative economic development to its traditional place at the heart of African Society.

57. Governments have a duty to protect their citizens, not only through appropriate legislation and effective enforcement but also by protecting them from damaging acts that may be perpetrated by private

parties (See Union des Jeunes Avocats /Chad). This duty calls for positive action on the part of governments in fulfilling their obligation under human rights instruments. The practice before other tribunals also enhances this requirement as is evidenced in the case Velásquez Rodríguez v. Honduras. In this landmark judgment, the Inter–American Court of Human Rights held that when a State allows private persons or groups to act freely and with impunity to the detriment of the rights recognised, it would be in clear violation of its obligations to protect the human rights of its citizens. Similarly, this obligation of the State is further emphasised in the practice of the European Court of Human Rights, in X and Y v. Netherlands. In that case, the Court pronounced that there was an obligation on authorities to take steps to make sure that the enjoyment of the rights is not interfered with by any other private person.

58.   The Commission notes that in the present case, despite its obligation to protect persons against interferences in the enjoyment of their rights, the Government of Nigeria facilitated the destruction of the Ogoniland. Contrary to its Charter obligations and despite such internationally established principles, the Nigerian Government has given the green light to private actors, and the oil Companies in particular, to devastatingly affect the well-being of the Ogonis. By any measure of standards, its practice falls short of the minimum conduct expected of governments, and therefore, is in violation of Article 21 of the African Charter.

59.   The Complainants also assert that the Military government of Nigeria massively and systematically violated the right to adequate housing of members of the Ogoni community under Article 14 and implicitly recognised by Articles 16 and 18(1) of the African Charter.

Article 14 of the Charter reads:

"The right to property shall be guaranteed. It may only be encroached upon in the interest of public need or in the general interest of the community and in accordance with the provisions of appropriate laws."

Article 18(1) provides:

"The family shall be the natural unit and basis of society. It shall be protected by the State . . ."

60.   Although the right to housing or shelter is not explicitly provided for under the African Charter, the corollary of the combination of the provisions protecting the right to enjoy the best attainable state of mental and physical health, cited under Article 16 above, the right to property, and the protection accorded to the family forbids the wanton destruction of shelter because when housing is destroyed, property, health, and family life are adversely affected. It is thus noted that the combined effect of Articles 14, 16 and 18(1) reads into the Charter a right to shelter or housing which the Nigerian Government has apparently violated.

61.   At a very minimum, the right to shelter obliges the Nigerian government not to destroy the housing of its citizens and not to obstruct efforts by individuals or communities to rebuild lost homes. The State's obligation to respect housing rights requires it, and thereby all of its organs

and agents, to abstain from carrying out, sponsoring or tolerating any practice, policy or legal measure violating the integrity of the individual or infringing upon his or her freedom to use those material or other resources available to them in a way they find most appropriate to satisfy individual, family, household or community housing needs. Its obligations to protect obliges it to prevent the violation of any individual's right to housing by any other individual or non-state actors like landlords, property developers, and land owners, and where such infringements occur, it should act to preclude further deprivations as well as guaranteeing access to legal remedies. The right to shelter even goes further than a roof over ones head. It extends to embody the individual's right to be let alone and to live in peace—whether under a roof or not.

62.   The protection of the rights guaranteed in Articles 14, 16 and 18(1) leads to the same conclusion. As regards the earlier right, and in the case of the Ogoni People, the Government of Nigeria has failed to fulfil these two minimum obligations. The government has destroyed Ogoni houses and villages and then, through its security forces, obstructed, harassed, beaten and, in some cases, shot and killed innocent citizens who have attempted to return to rebuild their ruined homes. These actions constitute massive violations of the right to shelter, in violation of Articles 14, 16, and 18(1) of the African Charter.

63.   The particular violation by the Nigerian Government of the right to adequate housing as implicitly protected in the Charter also encompasses the right to protection against forced evictions. The African Commission draws inspiration from the definition of the term "forced evictions" by the Committee on Economic Social and Cultural Rights which defines this term as "the permanent removal against their will of individuals, families and/or communities from the homes and/or which they occupy, without the provision of, and access to, appropriate forms of legal or other protection". Wherever and whenever they occur, forced evictions are extremely traumatic. They cause physical, psychological and emotional distress; they entail losses of means of economic sustenance and increase impoverishment. They can also cause physical injury and in some cases sporadic deaths.... Evictions break up families and increase existing levels of homelessness. In this regard, General Comment No. 4 (1991) of the Committee on Economic, Social and Cultural Rights on the right to adequate housing states that "all persons should possess a degree of security of tenure which guarantees legal protection against forced eviction, harassment and other threats" (E/1992/23, annex III. Paragraph 8(a)). The conduct of the Nigerian government clearly demonstrates a violation of this right enjoyed by the Ogonis as a collective right.

64.   The Communication argues that the right to food is implicit in the African Charter, in such provisions as the right to life (Art. 4), the right to health (Art. 16) and the right to economic, social and cultural development (Art. 22). By its violation of these rights, the Nigerian Government trampled upon not only the explicitly protected rights but also upon the right to food implicitly guaranteed.

65.   The right to food is inseparably linked to the dignity of human beings and is therefore essential for the enjoyment and fulfilment of such other rights as health, education, work and political participation. The African Charter and international law require and bind Nigeria to protect and improve existing food sources and to ensure access to adequate food for all citizens. Without touching on the duty to improve food production and to guarantee access, the minimum core of the right to food requires that the Nigerian Government should not destroy or contaminate food sources. It should not allow private parties to destroy or contaminate food sources, and prevent peoples' efforts to feed themselves.

66.   The government's treatment of the Ogonis has violated all three minimum duties of the right to food. The government has destroyed food sources through its security forces and State Oil Company; has allowed private oil companies to destroy food sources; and, through terror, has created significant obstacles to Ogoni communities trying to feed themselves. The Nigerian government has again fallen short of what is expected of it as under the provisions of the African Charter and international human rights standards, and hence, is in violation of the right to food of the Ogonis.

67.   The Complainants also allege that the Nigerian Government has violated Article 4 of the Charter which guarantees the inviolability of human beings and everyone's right to life and integrity of the person respected. Given the wide spread violations perpetrated by the Government of Nigeria and by private actors (be it following its clear blessing or not), the most fundamental of all human rights, the right to life has been violated. The Security forces were given the green light to decisively deal with the Ogonis, which was illustrated by the wide spread terrorisations and killings. The pollution and environmental degradation to a level humanly unacceptable has made it living in the Ogoni land a nightmare. The survival of the Ogonis depended on their land and farms that were destroyed by the direct involvement of the Government. These and similar brutalities not only persecuted individuals in Ogoniland but also the whole of the Ogoni Community as a whole. They affected the life of the Ogoni Society as a whole. The Commission conducted a mission to Nigeria from the 7th–14th March 1997 and witnessed first hand the deplorable situation in Ogoni land including the environmental degradation.

68.   The uniqueness of the African situation and the special qualities of the African Charter on Human and Peoples' Rights imposes upon the African Commission an important task. International law and human rights must be responsive to African circumstances. Clearly, collective rights, environmental rights, and economic and social rights are essential elements of human rights in Africa. The African Commission will apply any of the diverse rights contained in the African Charter. It welcomes this opportunity to make clear that there is no right in the African Charter that cannot be made effective. As indicated in the preceding paragraphs, however, the Nigerian Government did not live up to the minimum expectations of the African Charter.

69.   The Commission does not wish to fault governments that are labouring under difficult circumstances to improve the lives of their people. The situation of the people of Ogoniland, however, requires, in the view of the Commission, a reconsideration of the Government's attitude to the allegations contained in the instant communication. The intervention of multinational corporations may be a potentially positive force for development if the State and the people concerned are ever mindful of the common good and the sacred rights of individuals and communities. The Commission however takes note of the efforts of the present civilian administration to redress the atrocities that were committed by the previous military administration as illustrated in the Note Verbale referred to in paragraph 30 of this decision.

For the above reasons, the Commission,

Finds the Federal Republic of Nigeria in violation of Articles 2, 4, 14, 16, 18(1), 21 and 24 of the African Charter on Human and Peoples' Rights;

Appeals to the government of the Federal Republic of Nigeria to ensure protection of the environment, health and livelihood of the people of Ogoniland by:

—Stopping all attacks on Ogoni communities and leaders by the Rivers State Internal Securities Task Force and permitting citizens and independent investigators free access to the territory;

—Conducting an investigation into the human rights violations described above and prosecuting officials of the security forces, NNPC and relevant agencies involved in human rights violations;

—Ensuring adequate compensation to victims of the human rights violations, including relief and resettlement assistance to victims of government sponsored raids, and undertaking a comprehensive cleanup of lands and rivers damaged by oil operations;

—Ensuring that appropriate environmental and social impact assessments are prepared for any future oil development and that the safe operation of any further oil development is guaranteed through effective and independent oversight bodies for the petroleum industry; and

—Providing information on health and environmental risks and meaningful access to regulatory and decision-making bodies to communities likely to be affected by oil operations.

Urges the government of the Federal Republic of Nigeria to keep the African Commission informed of the outcome of the work of:

—The Federal Ministry of Environment which was established to address environmental and environment related issues prevalent in Nigeria, and as a matter of priority, in the Niger Delta area including the Ogoni land;

—The Niger Delta Development Commission (NDDC) enacted into law to address the environmental and other social related problems in the Niger Delta area and other oil producing areas of Nigeria; and

—The Judicial Commission of Inquiry inaugurated to investigate the issues of human rights violations.

NOTES AND QUESTIONS

1. On what grounds does the African Commission find a violation of the African (Banjul) Charter? In particular, how does it find a violation of the right to shelter (para. 60) and the right to food (para. 64)? Are these rights explicitly in the Charter? How does the Court then know how to define them?

2. What duties does the State assume with respect to these rights? How are the different aspects (respect, protect, fulfill) different? What does each entail?

3. *The African system of human rights protection*: As the foregoing excerpts indicate, the African Charter on Human and Peoples Rights, completed in 1981, contained some innovations in human rights law. The provisions on the right to environment, to the free disposal of natural resources, and to development, as well as the inclusion of civil, political, economic, social and cultural rights within the same document are particularly noteworthy. In contrast, both the American and European Conventions cover only civil and political rights, with economic, social and cultural rights relegated to a separate Protocol or Charter with provisions less amenable to enforcement. The African Charter also contains a list of duties owed by individuals, including duties towards the family, society and the state, duties to respect and consider others without discrimination, and duties to preserve and strengthen national independence, African unity, and positive African cultural values. Should human rights treaties contain duties for individuals in addition to rights? Is there something in the history or culture of Africa that explains the differences in the African Charter?

4. The African Commission on Human and Peoples' Rights operated for many years without a corresponding human rights court. In 1998, a Protocol to the African Charter created an African Court of Human and Peoples' Rights, but the opening of the court was delayed when the court merged with another incipient regional court to become the African Court of Justice and Human Rights, based in Tanzania and composed of two chambers, one specifically on human rights. The Court's human rights chambers will eventually be able to hear cases involving violations of any human rights instrument that the state in question has ratified. However, as of 2009 few African states had accepted the competence of the new court to hear complaints from individuals or NGOs.

5. *Economic, Social and Cultural rights*: As mentioned at the beginning of the chapter, one of the two United Nations covenants that make up the International Bill of Rights focuses on economic, social and cultural rights. These include rights to work, to decent working conditions, to form and join trade unions, to social security, to protection of mothers and children, to an adequate standard of living including adequate food, clothing and housing, to the highest attainable standard of physical and mental health,

to education (including free and compulsory primary education), and to take part in cultural life. Compared to the rights to be free of torture, slavery, summary execution or arbitrary detention contained in the Covenant on Civil and Political Rights, do these rights present any particular difficulties of implementation?

Consider the following language of the Covenant on ESC Rights:

Art. 2(1) Each State Party to the present Covenant undertakes to take steps, individually and through international assistance and co-operation, especially economic and technical, to the maximum of its available resources, with a view to achieving progressively the full realization of the rights recognized in the present Covenant by all appropriate means, including particularly the adoption of legislative measures.

Compare this provision to the corresponding provision of the Covenant on Civil and Political Rights:

Art. 2(1): Each State Party to the present Covenant undertakes to respect and to ensure to all individuals within its territory and subject to its jurisdiction the rights recognized in the present Covenant, without distinction of any kind . . .

2(2). Where not already provided for by existing legislative or other measures, each State Party to the present Covenant undertakes to take the necessary steps, in accordance with its constitutional processes and with the provisions of the present Covenant, to adopt such laws or other measures as may be necessary to give effect to the rights recognized in the present Covenant.

Why are they different? What real obligations are contained in the ESC Covenant? Look at the provisions on discriminatory treatment. Do these require immediate application, or are they also subject to "progressive implementation"?

One distinction often drawn between the two Covenants is that the ICCPR covers negative rights, while the ICESCR is concerned with positive rights. Negative rights require states simply to refrain from action, as in "do not torture, do not prohibit freedom of expression." The right to an adequate standard of living, in contrast, is thought to require positive intervention—and expenditure—by the state to make it effective. Is there a clear alignment between political and civil rights and negative rights, on the one hand, and economic, social and cultural rights and positive rights, on the other? How would you define the positive aspects of the right to due process? The negative aspects of the right to housing? Does the African Commission's "respect-protect-fulfill" typology help resolve this problem?

As a mental exercise, try to define the respect-protect-fulfill aspects of the following:

—the right to adequate food

—the right to education

—the right of minorities to enjoy their own culture, religion and language

—the right to humane conditions of detention.

How different are the first two (ESC) rights from the latter two (CP) rights? Do they all require government expenditure? Do they all have potentially negative as well as positive aspects?

Another frequently-raised objection to including ESC rights as "real" human rights is the difficulty inherent in adjudicating such "programmatic" rights. What additional difficulties do positive rights entail for deciding whether a state has breached its obligations? Is it possible to determine how much a state should be spending on housing, or healthcare in order not to violate its treaty obligations? How different is this from deciding how much a state should be spending on its prison system, or on counsel for indigent defendants? How much is the "maximum of available resources"? What about a state's defense spending, or its ruler's fifteen luxury villas? Can courts decide these issues? Can Committees of human rights experts? See the Optional Protocol to the ICESCR, discussed above. *See UN Committee on Economic, Social and Cultural Rights (CESCR), General Comment No. 3: The Nature of States Parties' Obligations (Art. 2, Para. 1, of the Covenant)*, 14 December 1990, E/1991/23, available at: http://www.unhcr.org/refworld/docid/4538838e10.html.

The South African Constitutional Court has pioneered the judicial application of economic, social and cultural rights, which are included in the 1994 post-apartheid constitution. See, e.g. Grootboom v. South Africa, Case CCT 11/00, 4 Oct. 2000 (right to access to housing for squatters); Treatment Action Centre v. South Africa, Case CCT 08/02 (5 July 2002) (right to health—access to drugs to prevent mother-child transmission of HIV virus).

Are economic, social and cultural rights as rights necessarily socialist, or are they compatible with capitalism? Is there anything in the International Covenant on Economic, Social and Cultural Rights that specifies that the actual services—health, education, housing, work and the like—must be provided by the state? Can the state meet its obligations even if these services are provided by private enterprise, insurance, cooperatives, or public-private partnerships? How? What then is the exact nature of the state's role?

5. LIMITATIONS ON RIGHTS, THE MARGIN OF APPRECIATION, AND UNIVERSALITY

Some of the rights established in the major human rights treaties are absolute. These rights, also described as nonderogable, cannot be abrogated by states even in times of grave national emergency and war. For example, the ICCPR states that the right to life, to be free of slavery and torture and ill-treatment, freedom from *ex post facto* laws and sentencing, right to legal recognition as a person, and freedom of thought, conscience and religion and not to be imprisoned for debt are nonderogable. They are also not subject to any limitations, although there may be (and, as we have seen, have been) debates about the outer contours of the content of the rights. Of course, those norms that are considered *jus cogens* or peremptory are also applicable at all times. Other rights are absolute, but may be temporarily suspended under certain emergency circumstances. For example, the provisions of the ICCPR, fair trial procedure and conditions of detention may be suspended in cases of "public emergency" which threatens the life of the nation and the existence of which is officially proclaimed, so long as the states notify the existence of the emergency and the restrictions are no greater or longer than those required given the exigencies of the situation.

A third set of rights are defined as limited. For example, the rights to freedom of expression, freedom to manifest religion, freedom of association and peaceful assembly, and freedom of movement are subject to limitations. Consider Article 19 of the ICCPR, which provides:

> The exercise of the rights provided for in paragraph 2 of this article carries with it special duties and responsibilities. It may therefore be subject to certain restrictions, but these shall only be such as are provided by law and are necessary:
>
> (a) For respect of the rights or reputations of others;
>
> (b) For the protection of national security or of public order (ordre public), or of public health or morals.

———

The European Court has developed the most extensive jurisprudence on the meaning of these limitation or "clawback" clauses. Consider the following case involving the rights to freedom of religion and freedom from discrimination:

Case of Leyla Sahin v. Turkey

European Court of Human Rights
Application no. 44774/98 (2005)
41 Eur. H.R. Rep. 8

* * *

3. The applicant alleged that her rights and freedoms under Articles 8, 9, 10 and 14 of the Convention and Article 2 of Protocol No. 1 had been violated by regulations on wearing the Islamic headscarf in institutions of higher education. * * *

THE FACTS

I. THE CIRCUMSTANCES OF THE CASE

14. The applicant was born in 1973 and has lived in Vienna since 1999, when she left Istanbul to pursue her medical studies at the Faculty of Medicine at Vienna University. She comes from a traditional family of practising Muslims and considers it her religious duty to wear the Islamic headscarf.

15.   On 26 August 1997 the applicant, then in her fifth year at the Faculty of Medicine at Bursa University, enrolled at the Cerrahpasa Faculty of Medicine at Istanbul University. She says she wore the Islamic headscarf during the four years she spent studying medicine at the University of Bursa and continued to do so until February 1998.

16.   On 23 February 1998 the Vice–Chancellor of Istanbul University issued a circular, the relevant part of which provides:

"By virtue of the Constitution, the law and regulations, and in accordance with the case-law of the Supreme Administrative Court and the European Commission of Human Rights and the resolutions adopted by the university administrative boards, students whose 'heads are covered' (who wear the Islamic headscarf) and students (including overseas students) with beards must not be admitted to lectures, courses or tutorials. Consequently, the name and number of any student with a beard or wearing the Islamic headscarf must not be added to the lists of registered students. However, students who insist on attending tutorials and entering lecture theatres although their names and numbers are not on the lists must be advised of the position and, should they refuse to leave, their names and numbers must be taken and they must be informed that they are not entitled to attend lectures. If they refuse to leave the lecture theatre, the teacher shall record the incident in a report explaining why it was not possible to give the lecture and shall bring the incident to the attention of the university authorities as a matter of urgency so that disciplinary measures can be taken."

17.   On 12 March 1998, in accordance with the aforementioned circular, the applicant was denied access by invigilators to a written examination on oncology because she was wearing the Islamic headscarf. On 20 March 1998 the secretariat of the chair of orthopaedic traumatology refused to allow her to enroll because she was wearing a headscarf. On 16 April 1998 she was refused admission to a neurology lecture and on 10 June 1998 to a written examination on public health, again for the same reason. * * *

[The applicant appealed, and eventually the Constitutional Court denied her application.]

II.   RELEVANT LAW AND PRACTICE

* * *

B.   History and Background

1.   Religious dress and the principle of secularism

30.   The Turkish Republic was founded on the principle that the State should be secular (laik). Before and after the proclamation of the Republic on 29 October 1923, the public and religious spheres were separated through a series of revolutionary reforms: the abolition of the caliphate on 3 March 1923; the repeal of the constitutional provision declaring Islam the religion of the State on 10 April 1928; and, lastly, on 5 February 1937, a

constitutional amendment according constitutional status to the principle of secularism (see Article 2 of the Constitution of 1924 and Article 2 of the Constitutions of 1961 and 1982, as set out in paragraph 29 above).

31.   The principle of secularism was inspired by developments in Ottoman society in the period between the nineteenth century and the proclamation of the Republic. The idea of creating a modern public society in which equality was guaranteed to all citizens without distinction on grounds of religion, denomination or sex had already been mooted in the Ottoman debates of the nineteenth century. Significant advances in women's rights were made during this period (equality of treatment in education, the introduction of a ban on polygamy in 1914, the transfer of jurisdiction in matrimonial cases to the secular courts that had been established in the nineteenth century).

32.   The defining feature of the Republican ideal was the presence of women in public life and their active participation in society. Consequently, the ideas that women should be freed from religious constraints and that society should be modernised had a common origin. Thus, on 17 February 1926 the Civil Code was adopted, which provided for equality of the sexes in the enjoyment of civic rights, in particular with regard to divorce and succession. Subsequently, through a constitutional amendment of 5 December 1934 (Article 10 of the 1924 Constitution), women obtained equal political rights to men.

33.   The first legislation to regulate dress was the Headgear Act of 28 November 1925 (Law no. 671), which treated dress as a modernity issue. Similarly, a ban was imposed on wearing religious attire other than in places of worship or at religious ceremonies, irrespective of the religion or belief concerned, by the Dress (Regulations) Act of 3 December 1934 (Law no. 2596).

34.   Under the Education Services (Merger) Act of 3 March 1924 (Law no. 430), religious schools were closed and all schools came under the control of the Ministry of Education. The Act is one of the laws with constitutional status that are protected by Article 174 of the Turkish Constitution.

35.   In Turkey, wearing the Islamic headscarf to school and university is a recent phenomenon which only really began to emerge in the 1980s. There has been extensive discussion on the issue and it continues to be the subject of lively debate in Turkish society. Those in favour of the headscarf see wearing it as a duty and/or a form of expression linked to religious identity. However, the supporters of secularism, who draw a distinction between the başörtüsü (traditional Anatolian headscarf, worn loosely) and the türban (tight, knotted headscarf hiding the hair and the throat), see the Islamic headscarf as a symbol of a political Islam. As a result of the accession to power on 28 June 1996 of a coalition government comprising the Islamist Refah Partisi, and the centre-right Doğru Yol Partisi, the debate has taken on strong political overtones. The ambivalence displayed by the leaders of the Refah Partisi, including the then Prime Minister, over their attachment to democratic values, and their advocacy of a plurality of

legal systems functioning according to different religious rules for each religious community was perceived in Turkish society as a genuine threat to republican values and civil peace (see Refah Partisi (the Welfare Party) and Others v. Turkey [GC], nos. 41340/98, 41342/98, 41343/98 and 41344/98, ECHR 2003–II). * * *

D.   Comparative law

55.   For more than twenty years the place of the Islamic headscarf in State education has been the subject of debate across Europe. In most European countries, the debate has focused mainly on primary and secondary schools. However, in Turkey, Azerbaijan and Albania it has concerned not just the question of individual liberty, but also the political meaning of the Islamic headscarf. These are the only member States to have introduced regulations on wearing the Islamic headscarf in universities.

56.   In France, where secularism is regarded as one of the cornerstones of republican values, legislation was passed on 15 March 2004 regulating, in accordance with the principle of secularism, the wearing of signs or dress manifesting a religious affiliation in State primary and secondary schools. The legislation inserted a new Article L. 141–5–1 in the Education Code which provides: "In State primary and secondary schools, the wearing of signs or dress by which pupils overtly manifest a religious affiliation is prohibited. The school rules shall state that the institution of disciplinary proceedings shall be preceded by dialogue with the pupil."

The Act applies to all State schools and educational institutions, including post-baccalaureate courses (preparatory classes for entrance to the grandes écoles and vocational training courses). It does not apply to State universities. In addition, as a circular of 18 May 2004 makes clear, it only concerns "... signs, such as the Islamic headscarf, however named, the kippa or a cross that is manifestly oversized, which make the wearer's religious affiliation immediately identifiable".

57.   In Belgium there is no general ban on wearing religious signs at school. In the French Community a decree of 13 March 1994 stipulates that education shall be neutral within the Community. Pupils are in principle allowed to wear religious signs. However, they may do so only if human rights, the reputation of others, national security, public order, and public health and morals are protected and internal rules complied with. Further, teachers must not permit religious or philosophical proselytism under their authority or the organisation of political militancy by or on behalf of pupils. The decree stipulates that restrictions may be imposed by school rules. On 19 May 2004 the French Community issued a decree intended to institute equality of treatment. In the Flemish Community, there is no uniform policy among schools on whether to allow religious or philosophical signs to be worn. Some do, others do not. When pupils are permitted to wear such signs, restrictions may be imposed on grounds of hygiene or safety.

58.   In other countries (Austria, Germany, the Netherlands, Spain, Sweden, Switzerland and the United Kingdom), in some cases following a

protracted legal debate, the State education authorities permit Muslim pupils and students to wear the Islamic headscarf.

59.   In Germany, where the debate focused on whether teachers should be allowed to wear the Islamic headscarf, the Constitutional Court stated on 24 September 2003 in a case between a teacher and the Land of Baden–Württemberg that the lack of any express statutory prohibition meant that teachers were entitled to wear the headscarf. Consequently, it imposed a duty on the Länder to lay down rules on dress if they wished to prohibit the wearing of the Islamic headscarf in State schools.

60.   In Austria there is no special legislation governing the wearing of the headscarf, turban or kippa. In general, it is considered that a ban on wearing the headscarf will only be justified if it poses a health or safety hazard for pupils.

61.   In the United Kingdom a tolerant attitude is shown to pupils who wear religious signs. Difficulties with respect to the Islamic headscarf are rare. The issue has also been debated in the context of the elimination of racial discrimination in schools in order to preserve their multicultural character. . . .

In R. (On the application of Begum) v. Headteacher and Governors of Denbigh High School ([2004] EWHC 1389 (Admin)), the High Court had to decide a dispute between the school and a Muslim pupil wishing to wear the jilbab (a full-length gown). The school required pupils to wear a uniform, one of the possible options being the headscarf and the shalwar kameeze (long traditional garments from the Indian subcontinent). In June 2004 the High Court dismissed the pupil's application, holding that there had been no violation of her freedom of religion. However, that judgment was reversed in March 2005 by the Court of Appeal, which accepted that there had been interference with the pupil's freedom of religion, as a minority of Muslims in the United Kingdom considered that a religious duty to wear the jilbab from the age of puberty existed and the pupil was genuinely of that opinion. No justification for the interference had been provided by the school authorities, as the decision-making process was not compatible with freedom of religion.

62.   In Spain there is no express statutory prohibition on pupils' wearing religious head coverings in State schools. By virtue of two royal decrees of 26 January 1996, which are applicable in primary and secondary schools unless the competent authority—the autonomous community—has introduced specific measures, the school governors have power to issue school rules which may include provisions on dress. Generally speaking, State schools allow the headscarf to be worn.

63.   In Finland and Sweden the veil can be worn at school. However, a distinction is made between the burka (the term used to describe the full veil covering the whole of the body and the face) and the niqab (a veil covering all the upper body with the exception of the eyes). In Sweden mandatory directives were issued in 2003 by the National Education Agency. These allow schools to prohibit the burka and niqab, provided they

do so in a spirit of dialogue on the common values of equality of the sexes and respect for the democratic principle on which the education system is based.

64.   In the Netherlands, where the question of the Islamic headscarf is considered from the standpoint of discrimination rather than of freedom of religion, it is generally tolerated. In 2003 a non-binding directive was issued. Schools may require pupils to wear a uniform provided that the rules are not discriminatory and are included in the school prospectus and that the punishment for transgressions is not disproportionate. A ban on the burka is regarded as justified by the need to be able to identify and communicate with pupils. In addition, the Equal Treatment Commission ruled in 1997 that a ban on wearing the veil during physical education classes for safety reasons was not discriminatory.

65.   In a number of other countries (Russia, Romania, Hungary, Greece, the Czech Republic, Slovakia and Poland), the issue of the Islamic headscarf does not yet appear to have given rise to any detailed legal debate. * * *

THE LAW

I.   ALLEGED VIOLATION OF ARTICLE 9 OF THE CONVENTION

70.   The applicant submitted that the ban on wearing the Islamic headscarf in institutions of higher education constituted an unjustified interference with her right to freedom of religion, in particular, her right to manifest her religion.

She relied on Article 9 of the Convention, which provides:

"1.   Everyone has the right to freedom of thought, conscience and religion; this right includes freedom to change his religion or belief and freedom, either alone or in community with others and in public or private, to manifest his religion or belief, in worship, teaching, practice and observance.

2.   Freedom to manifest one's religion or beliefs shall be subject only to such limitations as are prescribed by law and are necessary in a democratic society in the interests of public safety, for the protection of public order, health or morals, or for the protection of the rights and freedoms of others."

A.   The Chamber judgment

71.   The Chamber found that the Istanbul University regulations restricting the right to wear the Islamic headscarf and the measures taken thereunder had interfered with the applicant's right to manifest her religion. It went on to find that the interference was prescribed by law and pursued one of the legitimate aims set out in the second paragraph of Article 9 of the Convention. It was justified in principle and proportionate to the aims pursued and could therefore be regarded as having been "necessary in a democratic society" (see paragraphs 66–116 of the Chamber judgment).

B.   The parties' submissions to the Grand Chamber

* * *

74.   The Government asked the Grand Chamber to endorse the Chamber's finding that there had been no violation of Article 9.

C.   The Court's assessment

75.   The Court must consider whether the applicant's right under Article 9 was interfered with and, if so, whether the interference was "prescribed by law", pursued a legitimate aim and was necessary in a democratic society within the meaning of Article 9 § 2 of the Convention.

1.   Whether there was interference

* * *

78.   As to whether there was interference, the Grand Chamber endorses the following findings of the Chamber (see paragraph 71 of the Chamber judgment):

> "The applicant said that, by wearing the headscarf, she was obeying a religious precept and thereby manifesting her desire to comply strictly with the duties imposed by the Islamic faith. Accordingly, her decision to wear the headscarf may be regarded as motivated or inspired by a religion or belief and, without deciding whether such decisions are in every case taken to fulfil a religious duty, the Court proceeds on the assumption that the regulations in issue, which placed restrictions of place and manner on the right to wear the Islamic headscarf in universities, constituted an interference with the applicant's right to manifest her religion."

2.   "Prescribed by law"

* * *

(b) The Court's assessment

84.   The Court reiterates its settled case-law that the expression "prescribed by law" requires firstly that the impugned measure should have a basis in domestic law. It also refers to the quality of the law in question, requiring that it be accessible to the persons concerned and formulated with sufficient precision to enable them—if need be, with appropriate advice—to foresee, to a degree that is reasonable in the circumstances, the consequences which a given action may entail and to regulate their conduct (see Gorzelik and Others v. Poland [GC], no. 44158/98, § 64, ECHR 2004–I). * * *

98.   In these circumstances, the Court finds that there was a legal basis for the interference in Turkish law, namely transitional section 17 of Law no. 2547 read in the light of the relevant case-law of the domestic courts. The law was also accessible and can be considered sufficiently precise in its terms to satisfy the requirement of foreseeability. It would have been clear to the applicant, from the moment she entered Istanbul University, that there were restrictions on wearing the Islamic headscarf

on the university premises and, from 23 February 1998, that she was liable to be refused access to lectures and examinations if she continued to do so.

3. Legitimate aim

99. Having regard to the circumstances of the case and the terms of the domestic courts' decisions, the Court is able to accept that the impugned interference primarily pursued the legitimate aims of protecting the rights and freedoms of others and of protecting public order, a point which is not in issue between the parties.

4. "Necessary in a democratic society"

* * *

(b) The Court's assessment

(i) General principles

104. The Court reiterates that, as enshrined in Article 9, freedom of thought, conscience and religion is one of the foundations of a "democratic society" within the meaning of the Convention. This freedom is, in its religious dimension, one of the most vital elements that go to make up the identity of believers and their conception of life, but it is also a precious asset for atheists, agnostics, sceptics and the unconcerned. The pluralism indissociable from a democratic society, which has been dearly won over the centuries, depends on it. That freedom entails, inter alia, freedom to hold or not to hold religious beliefs and to practise or not to practise a religion (see, among other authorities, Kokkinakis v. Greece, judgment of 25 May 1993, Series A no. 260–A, p. 17, § 31, and Buscarini and Others v. San Marino [GC], no. 24645/94, § 34, ECHR 1999–I).

105. While religious freedom is primarily a matter of individual conscience, it also implies, inter alia, freedom to manifest one's religion, alone and in private, or in community with others, in public and within the circle of those whose faith one shares. Article 9 lists the various forms which manifestation of one's religion or belief may take, namely worship, teaching, practice and observance (see, mutatis mutandis, Cha'are Shalom Ve Tsedek v. France [GC], no. 27417/95, § 73, ECHR 2000–VII).

Article 9 does not protect every act motivated or inspired by a religion or belief (see, among many other authorities, Kala v. Turkey, judgment of 1 July 1997, Reports of Judgments and Decisions 1997–IV, p. 1209, § 27; Arrowsmith v. the United Kingdom, no. 7050/75, Commission's report of 12 October 1978, Decisions and Reports (DR) 19, p. 5; C. v. the United Kingdom, no. 10358/83, Commission decision of 15 December 1983, DR 37, p. 142; and Tepeli and Others v. Turkey (dec.), no. 31876/96, 11 September 2001).

106. In democratic societies, in which several religions coexist within one and the same population, it may be necessary to place restrictions on freedom to manifest one's religion or belief in order to reconcile the interests of the various groups and ensure that everyone's beliefs are respected (see Kokkinakis, cited above, p. 18, § 33). This follows both from

paragraph 2 of Article 9 and the State's positive obligation under Article 1 of the Convention to secure to everyone within its jurisdiction the rights and freedoms defined therein.

107.   The Court has frequently emphasised the State's role as the neutral and impartial organiser of the exercise of various religions, faiths and beliefs, and stated that this role is conducive to public order, religious harmony and tolerance in a democratic society. It also considers that the State's duty of neutrality and impartiality is incompatible with any power on the State's part to assess the legitimacy of religious beliefs or the ways in which those beliefs are expressed (see Manoussakis and Others v. Greece, judgment of 26 September 1996, Reports 1996–IV, p. 1365, § 47; Hasan and Chaush v. Bulgaria [GC], no. 30985/96, § 78, ECHR 2000–XI; Refah Partisi (the Welfare Party) and Others v. Turkey [GC], nos. 41340/98, 41342/98, 41343/98 and 41344/98, § 91, ECHR 2003–II), and that it requires the State to ensure mutual tolerance between opposing groups (see United Communist Party of Turkey and Others v. Turkey, judgment of 30 January 1998, Reports 1998–I, p. 27, § 57). Accordingly, the role of the authorities in such circumstances is not to remove the cause of tension by eliminating pluralism, but to ensure that the competing groups tolerate each other (see Serif v. Greece, no. 38178/97, § 53, ECHR 1999–IX).

108.   Pluralism, tolerance and broadmindedness are hallmarks of a "democratic society". Although individual interests must on occasion be subordinated to those of a group, democracy does not simply mean that the views of a majority must always prevail: a balance must be achieved which ensures the fair and proper treatment of people from minorities and avoids any abuse of a dominant position (see, mutatis mutandis, Young, James and Webster v. the United Kingdom, judgment of 13 August 1981, Series A no. 44, p. 25, § 63, and Chassagnou and Others v. France [GC], nos. 25088/94, 28331/95 and 28443/95, § 112, ECHR 1999–III). Pluralism and democracy must also be based on dialogue and a spirit of compromise necessarily entailing various concessions on the part of individuals or groups of individuals which are justified in order to maintain and promote the ideals and values of a democratic society (see, mutatis mutandis, the United Communist Party of Turkey and Others, cited above, pp. 21–22, § 45, and Refah Partisi (the Welfare Party) and Others, cited above § 99). Where these "rights and freedoms" are themselves among those guaranteed by the Convention or its Protocols, it must be accepted that the need to protect them may lead States to restrict other rights or freedoms likewise set forth in the Convention. It is precisely this constant search for a balance between the fundamental rights of each individual which constitutes the foundation of a "democratic society" (see Chassagnou and Others, cited above, § 113).

109.   Where questions concerning the relationship between State and religions are at stake, on which opinion in a democratic society may reasonably differ widely, the role of the national decision-making body must be given special importance (see, mutatis mutandis, Cha'are Shalom Ve Tsedek, cited above, § 84, and Wingrove v. the United Kingdom,

judgment of 25 November 1996, Reports 1996–V, pp. 1957–58, § 58). This will notably be the case when it comes to regulating the wearing of religious symbols in educational institutions, especially (as the comparative-law materials illustrate—see paragraphs 55–65 above) in view of the diversity of the approaches taken by national authorities on the issue. It is not possible to discern throughout Europe a uniform conception of the significance of religion in society (see Otto–Preminger–Institut v. Austria, judgment of 20 September 1994, Series A no. 295–A, p. 19, § 50), and the meaning or impact of the public expression of a religious belief will differ according to time and context (see, among other authorities, Dahlab v. Switzerland (dec.), no. 42393/98, ECHR 2001–V). Rules in this sphere will consequently vary from one country to another according to national traditions and the requirements imposed by the need to protect the rights and freedoms of others and to maintain public order (see, mutatis mutandis, Wingrove, cited above, p. 1957, § 57). Accordingly, the choice of the extent and form such regulations should take must inevitably be left up to a point to the State concerned, as it will depend on the specific domestic context (see, mutatis mutandis, Gorzelik and Others, cited above, § 67, and Murphy v. Ireland, no. 44179/98, § 73, ECHR 2003–IX).

110.   This margin of appreciation goes hand in hand with a European supervision embracing both the law and the decisions applying it. The Court's task is to determine whether the measures taken at national level were justified in principle and proportionate (see Manoussakis and Others, cited above, p. 1364, § 44). In delimiting the extent of the margin of appreciation in the present case, the Court must have regard to what is at stake, namely the need to protect the rights and freedoms of others, to preserve public order and to secure civil peace and true religious pluralism, which is vital to the survival of a democratic society (see, mutatis mutandis, Kokkinakis, cited above, p. 17, § 31; Manoussakis and Others, cited above, p. 1364, § 44; and Casado Coca, cited above, p. 21, § 55).

111.   The Court also notes that in the decisions in Karaduman v. Turkey (no. 16278/90, Commission decision of 3 May 1993, DR 74, p. 93) and Dahlab (cited above) the Convention institutions found that in a democratic society the State was entitled to place restrictions on the wearing of the Islamic headscarf if it was incompatible with the pursued aim of protecting the rights and freedoms of others, public order and public safety. In Karaduman, measures taken in universities to prevent certain fundamentalist religious movements from exerting pressure on students who did not practise their religion or who belonged to another religion were not considered to constitute interference for the purposes of Article 9 of the Convention. Consequently, it is established that institutions of higher education may regulate the manifestation of the rites and symbols of a religion by imposing restrictions as to the place and manner of such manifestation with the aim of ensuring peaceful coexistence between students of various faiths and thus protecting public order and the beliefs of others (see, among other authorities, Refah Partisi (the Welfare Party) and Others, cited above, § 95). In Dahlab, which concerned the teacher of a class of small children, the Court stressed among other matters the

"powerful external symbol" which her wearing a headscarf represented and questioned whether it might have some kind of proselytising effect, seeing that it appeared to be imposed on women by a religious precept that was hard to reconcile with the principle of gender equality. It also noted that wearing the Islamic headscarf could not easily be reconciled with the message of tolerance, respect for others and, above all, equality and non-discrimination that all teachers in a democratic society should convey to their pupils.

(ii) Application of the foregoing principles to the present case

112.   The interference in issue caused by the circular of 23 February 1998 imposing restrictions as to place and manner on the rights of students such as Ms. Sahin to wear the Islamic headscarf on university premises was, according to the Turkish courts (see paragraphs 37, 39 and 41 above), based in particular on the two principles of secularism and equality.

113.   In its judgment of 7 March 1989, the Constitutional Court stated that secularism, as the guarantor of democratic values, was the meeting point of liberty and equality. The principle prevented the State from manifesting a preference for a particular religion or belief; it thereby guided the State in its role of impartial arbiter, and necessarily entailed freedom of religion and conscience. It also served to protect the individual not only against arbitrary interference by the State but from external pressure from extremist movements. The Constitutional Court added that freedom to manifest one's religion could be restricted in order to defend those values and principles (see paragraph 39 above).

114.   As the Chamber rightly stated (see paragraph 106 of its judgment), the Court considers this notion of secularism to be consistent with the values underpinning the Convention. It finds that upholding that principle, which is undoubtedly one of the fundamental principles of the Turkish State which are in harmony with the rule of law and respect for human rights, may be considered necessary to protect the democratic system in Turkey. An attitude which fails to respect that principle will not necessarily be accepted as being covered by the freedom to manifest one's religion and will not enjoy the protection of Article 9 of the Convention (see Refah Partisi (the Welfare Party) and Others, cited above, § 93).

115.   After examining the parties' submissions, the Grand Chamber sees no good reason to depart from the approach taken by the Chamber (see paragraphs 107–09 of the Chamber judgment) as follows:

"... The Court ... notes the emphasis placed in the Turkish constitutional system on the protection of the rights of women ... Gender equality—recognised by the European Court as one of the key principles underlying the Convention and a goal to be achieved by member States of the Council of Europe (see, among other authorities, Abdulaziz, Cabales and Balkandali v. the United Kingdom, judgment of 28 May 1985, Series A no. 94, pp. 37–38, § 78; Schuler–Zgraggen v. Switzerland, judgment of 24 June 1993, Series A no. 263, pp. 21–22, § 67; Burgharz v. Switzerland, judgment of 22 February 1994, Series A no.

280–B, p. 29, § 27; Van Raalte v. the Netherlands, judgment of 21 February 1997, Reports 1997–I, p. 186, § 39 in fine; and Petrovic v. Austria, judgment of 27 March 1998, Reports 1998–II, p. 587, § 37)— was also found by the Turkish Constitutional Court to be a principle implicit in the values underlying the Constitution ...

... In addition, like the Constitutional Court ..., the Court considers that, when examining the question of the Islamic headscarf in the Turkish context, it must be borne in mind the impact which wearing such a symbol, which is presented or perceived as a compulsory religious duty, may have on those who choose not to wear it. As has already been noted (see Karaduman, decision cited above, and Refah Partisi (the Welfare Party) and Others, cited above, § 95), the issues at stake include the protection of the 'rights and freedoms of others' and the 'maintenance of public order' in a country in which the majority of the population, while professing a strong attachment to the rights of women and a secular way of life, adhere to the Islamic faith. Imposing limitations on freedom in this sphere may, therefore, be regarded as meeting a pressing social need by seeking to achieve those two legitimate aims, especially since, as the Turkish courts stated ..., this religious symbol has taken on political significance in Turkey in recent years.

... The Court does not lose sight of the fact that there are extremist political movements in Turkey which seek to impose on society as a whole their religious symbols and conception of a society founded on religious precepts ... It has previously said that each Contracting State may, in accordance with the Convention provisions, take a stance against such political movements, based on its historical experience (see Refah Partisi (the Welfare Party) and Others, cited above, § 124). The regulations concerned have to be viewed in that context and constitute a measure intended to achieve the legitimate aims referred to above and thereby to preserve pluralism in the university.''

116. Having regard to the above background, it is the principle of secularism, as elucidated by the Constitutional Court (see paragraph 39 above), which is the paramount consideration underlying the ban on the wearing of religious symbols in universities. In such a context, where the values of pluralism, respect for the rights of others and, in particular, equality before the law of men and women are being taught and applied in practice, it is understandable that the relevant authorities should wish to preserve the secular nature of the institution concerned and so consider it contrary to such values to allow religious attire, including, as in the present case, the Islamic headscarf, to be worn.

117. The Court must now determine whether in the instant case there was a reasonable relationship of proportionality between the means employed and the legitimate objectives pursued by the interference.

118. Like the Chamber (see paragraph 111 of its judgment), the Grand Chamber notes at the outset that it is common ground that practising Muslim students in Turkish universities are free, within the

limits imposed by the constraints of educational organisation, to manifest their religion in accordance with habitual forms of Muslim observance. In addition, the resolution adopted by Istanbul University on 9 July 1998 shows that various other forms of religious attire are also forbidden on the university premises (see paragraph 47 above). * * *

120.   Furthermore, the process whereby the regulations that led to the decision of 9 July 1998 were implemented took several years and was accompanied by a wide debate within Turkish society and the teaching profession (see paragraph 35 above). The two highest courts, the Supreme Administrative Court and the Constitutional Court, have managed to establish settled case-law on this issue (see paragraphs 37, 39 and 41 above). It is quite clear that throughout that decision-making process the university authorities sought to adapt to the evolving situation in a way that would not bar access to the university to students wearing the veil, through continued dialogue with those concerned, while at the same time ensuring that order was maintained and in particular that the require-ments imposed by the nature of the course in question were complied with. * * *

122.   In the light of the foregoing and having regard to the Contract-ing States' margin of appreciation in this sphere, the Court finds that the interference in issue was justified in principle and proportionate to the aim pursued.

123.   Consequently, there has been no breach of Article 9 of the Convention.

DISSENTING OPINION OF JUDGE TULKENS

(Translation)

For a variety of mutually supporting reasons, I did not vote with the majority on the question of Article 9 of the Convention or of Article 2 of Protocol No. 1, which concerns the right to education. I do, however, fully agree with the Court's ruling that the scope of the latter provision extends to higher and university education.

A.   Freedom of religion

3.   I would perhaps have been able to follow the margin-of-apprecia-tion approach had two factors not drastically reduced its relevance in the instant case. The first concerns the argument the majority use to justify the width of the margin, namely the diversity of practice between the States on the issue of regulating the wearing of religious symbols in educational institutions and, thus, the lack of a European consensus in this sphere. The comparative-law materials do not allow of such a conclusion, as in none of the member States has the ban on wearing religious symbols extended to university education, which is intended for young adults, who are less amenable to pressure. The second factor concerns the European supervision that must accompany the margin of appreciation and which, even though less extensive than in cases in which the national authorities have no margin of appreciation, goes hand in hand with it. However, other

than in connection with Turkey's specific historical background, European supervision seems quite simply to be absent from the judgment. However, the issue raised in the application, whose significance to the right to freedom of religion guaranteed by the Convention is evident, is not merely a "local" issue, but one of importance to all the member States. European supervision cannot, therefore, be escaped simply by invoking the margin of appreciation.

4.   On what grounds was the interference with the applicant's right to freedom of religion through the ban on wearing the headscarf based? In the present case, relying exclusively on the reasons cited by the national authorities and courts, the majority put forward, in general and abstract terms, two main arguments: secularism and equality. While I fully and totally subscribe to each of these principles, I disagree with the manner in which they were applied here and to the way they were interpreted in relation to the practice of wearing the headscarf. In a democratic society, I believe that it is necessary to seek to harmonise the principles of secularism, equality and liberty, not to weigh one against the other.

5.   As regards, firstly, secularism, I would reiterate that I consider it an essential principle and one which, as the Constitutional Court stated in its judgment of 7 March 1989, is undoubtedly necessary for the protection of the democratic system in Turkey. Religious freedom is, however, also a founding principle of democratic societies. Accordingly, the fact that the Grand Chamber recognised the force of the principle of secularism did not release it from its obligation to establish that the ban on wearing the Islamic headscarf to which the applicant was subject was necessary to secure compliance with that principle and, therefore, met a "pressing social need". Only indisputable facts and reasons whose legitimacy is beyond doubt—not mere worries or fears—are capable of satisfying that requirement and justifying interference with a right guaranteed by the Convention. Moreover, where there has been interference with a fundamental right, the Court's case-law clearly establishes that mere affirmations do not suffice: they must be supported by concrete examples (see Smith and Grady v. the United Kingdom, nos. 33985/96 and 33986/96, § 89, ECHR 1999–VI). Such examples do not appear to have been forthcoming in the present case.
* * *

7.   ... The majority thus consider that wearing the headscarf contravenes the principle of secularism. In so doing, they take up position on an issue that has been the subject of much debate, namely the signification of wearing the headscarf and its relationship with the principle of secularism.

In the present case, a generalised assessment of that type gives rise to at least three difficulties. Firstly, the judgment does not address the applicant's argument—which the Government did not dispute—that she had no intention of calling the principle of secularism, a principle with which she agreed, into question. Secondly, there is no evidence to show that the applicant, through her attitude, conduct or acts, contravened that principle. This is a test the Court has always applied in its case-law (see Kokkinakis v. Greece, judgment of 25 May 1993, Series A no. 260–A, and

United Communist Party of Turkey and Others v. Turkey, judgment of 30 January 1998, Reports 1998–I). Lastly, the judgment makes no distinction between teachers and students, whereas in Dahlab (decision cited above), which concerned a teacher, the Court expressly noted the role-model aspect which the teacher's wearing the headscarf had. While the principle of secularism requires education to be provided without any manifestation of religion and while it has to be compulsory for teachers and all public servants, as they have voluntarily taken up posts in a neutral environment, the position of pupils and students seems to me to be different.

8.   Freedom to manifest a religion entails everyone being allowed to exercise that right, whether individually or collectively, in public or in private, subject to the dual condition that they do not infringe the rights and freedoms of others and do not prejudice public order (Article 9 § 2).

As regards the first condition, this could have not been satisfied if the headscarf the applicant wore as a religious symbol had been ostentatious or aggressive or was used to exert pressure, to provoke a reaction, to proselytise or to spread propaganda and undermined—or was liable to undermine—the convictions of others. However, the Government did not argue that this was the case and there was no evidence before the Court to suggest that Ms. Sahin had any such intention. As to the second condition, it has been neither suggested nor demonstrated that there was any disruption in teaching or in everyday life at the university, or any disorderly conduct, as a result of the applicant's wearing the headscarf. Indeed, no disciplinary proceedings were taken against her.

9.   The majority maintain, however, that, "when examining the question of the Islamic headscarf in the Turkish context, it must be borne in mind the impact which wearing such a symbol, which is presented or perceived as a compulsory religious duty, may have on those who choose not to wear it" (see paragraph 115 of the judgment).

Unless the level of protection of the right to freedom of religion is reduced to take account of the context, the possible effect which wearing the headscarf, which is presented as a symbol, may have on those who do not wear it does not appear to me, in the light of the Court's case-law, to satisfy the requirement of a pressing social need. Mutatis mutandis, in the sphere of freedom of expression (Article 10), the Court has never accepted that interference with the exercise of the right to freedom of expression can be justified by the fact that the ideas or views concerned are not shared by everyone and may even offend some people. . . .

10.   In fact, it is the threat posed by "extremist political movements" seeking to "impose on society as a whole their religious symbols and conception of a society founded on religious precepts" which, in the Court's view, serves to justify the regulations in issue, which constitute "a measure intended to . . . preserve pluralism in the university" (see paragraph 115 in fine of the judgment). The Court had already made this clear in Refah Partisi (the Welfare Party) and Others (cited above, § 95), when it stated: "In a country like Turkey, where the great majority of the population belong to a particular religion, measures taken in universities to prevent

certain fundamentalist religious movements from exerting pressure on students who do not practise that religion or on those who belong to another religion may be justified under Article 9 § 2 of the Convention.''

While everyone agrees on the need to prevent radical Islamism, a serious objection may nevertheless be made to such reasoning. Merely wearing the headscarf cannot be associated with fundamentalism and it is vital to distinguish between those who wear the headscarf and ''extremists'' who seek to impose the headscarf as they do other religious symbols. Not all women who wear the headscarf are fundamentalists and there is nothing to suggest that the applicant held fundamentalist views. She is a young adult woman and a university student, and might reasonably be expected to have a heightened capacity to resist pressure, it being noted in this connection that the judgment fails to provide any concrete example of the type of pressure concerned. The applicant's personal interest in exercising the right to freedom of religion and to manifest her religion by an external symbol cannot be wholly absorbed by the public interest in fighting extremism.

11. Turning to *equality*, the majority focus on the protection of women's rights and the principle of sexual equality (see paragraphs 115 and 116 of the judgment). Wearing the headscarf is considered on the contrary to be synonymous with the alienation of women. The ban on wearing the headscarf is therefore seen as promoting equality between men and women. However, what, in fact, is the connection between the ban and sexual equality? The judgment does not say. Indeed, what is the signification of wearing the headscarf? As the German Constitutional Court noted in its judgment of 24 September 2003,[f] wearing the headscarf has no single meaning; it is a practice that is engaged in for a variety of reasons. It does not necessarily symbolise the submission of women to men and there are those who maintain that, in certain cases, it can even be a means of emancipating women. What is lacking in this debate is the opinion of women, both those who wear the headscarf and those who choose not to.

12. On this issue, the Grand Chamber refers in its judgment to Dahlab (cited above), taking up what to my mind is the most questionable part of the reasoning in that decision, namely that wearing the headscarf represents a ''powerful external symbol'', which ''appeared to be imposed on women by a religious precept that was hard to reconcile with the principle of gender equality'' and that the practice could not easily be ''reconciled with the message of tolerance, respect for others and, above all, equality and non-discrimination that all teachers in a democratic society should convey to their pupils'' (see paragraph 111 in fine of the judgment).

It is not the Court's role to make an appraisal of this type—in this instance a unilateral and negative one—of a religion or religious practice, just as it is not its role to determine in a general and abstract way the signification of wearing the headscarf or to impose its viewpoint on the

---

f. Federal Constitutional Court of Germany, judgment of the Second Division of 24 September 2003, 2BvR 1436/042.

applicant. The applicant, a young adult university student, said—and there is nothing to suggest that she was not telling the truth—that she wore the headscarf of her own free will. In this connection, I fail to see how the principle of sexual equality can justify prohibiting a woman from following a practice which, in the absence of proof to the contrary, she must be taken to have freely adopted. Equality and non-discrimination are subjective rights which must remain under the control of those who are entitled to benefit from them. "Paternalism" of this sort runs counter to the case-law of the Court, which has developed a real right to personal autonomy on the basis of Article 8 (see Keenan v. the United Kingdom, no. 27229/95, § 92, ECHR 2001–III; Pretty v. the United Kingdom, no. 2346/02, §§ 65–67, ECHR 2002–III; and Christine Goodwin v. the United Kingdom [GC], no. 28957/95, § 90, ECHR 2002–VI). Finally, if wearing the headscarf really was contrary to the principle of equality between men and women in any event, the State would have a positive obligation to prohibit it in all places, whether public or private.

13.   Since, to my mind, the ban on wearing the Islamic headscarf on the university premises was not based on reasons that were relevant and sufficient, it cannot be considered to be interference that was "necessary in a democratic society" within the meaning of Article 9 § 2 of the Convention. In these circumstances, there has been a violation of the applicant's right to freedom of religion, as guaranteed by the Convention.

NOTES AND QUESTIONS

1.   *The margin of appreciation*: many cases involving restrictions on rights follow the mode of analysis in Şahin. See if you can sketch out the steps in that analysis. What is the right at issue in Şahin? What is the nature of the interference with that right? Is it according to law? Is it for a legitimate purpose? Which? How does the Court know it is legitimate? Even if legitimate, are there still limits on what rights limitations the state can impose? What does it mean to be "necessary in a democratic society"? Are the elements of appropriate, least restrictive and proportional separate elements or ways of expressing the same idea? How does the Court's balancing differ from constitutional balancing in your national legal system?

2.   Why does Judge Tulkens disagree? Is she persuasive? Note that she was the only female judge on the panel.

3.   Would the result here be different if the petitioners were high school students? Elementary school students? Orthodox Jewish young men wearing yarmulkes? What about religiously-mandated haircuts? See *Doglu v. France*, ECHR, Application No. 27058/05, 4 Dec. 2008. Does it matter what other European states do with respect to allowing or prohibiting headscarves or other religious symbols? Why? Should it matter? How is this consistent with a uniform application of a universal standard? See Eyal Benvenisti, *Margin of Appreciation, Consensus and Universal Standards*, 31 N. Y. U. J. of Int'l L. and Pol. (1998–99) 843.

4.   How does the Court know what the social consequences of enforcing a ban—or not enforcing it—will be? What do you think of the dissent's argument on this question? Is it clear what the effect of the ban will be on women? On Muslim schoolgirls? What if women themselves are divided on the proper state response?

5.   What role should cultural differences play in the definition and interpretation of rights? Should the content of rights differ from place to place, or are rights universal? Does your answer differ if you think human rights are basically a Western invention, or if you think they reflect certain values present, in one form or another, in all cultures? Does it depend on the nature of the right: that is, would you be more willing to accept an argument that freedom of expression is relative in a headscarf case than, for example, an argument that what constitutes torture varies from culture to culture? What about stoning or amputation under Sha'ria law? What about indefinite solitary confinement? Does the fact that most debates in which the cultural relativism argument is raised involve the rights of women affect your views? Is it even possible to speak of a static, immutable culture in the age of air travel and the Internet? See, for more discussion of this issue, JACK DONNELLEY, UNIVERSAL HUMAN RIGHTS IN THEORY AND PRACTICE (2002); ABDULLAHI AHMED AN-NAIM, HUMAN RIGHTS IN CROSS-CULTURAL PERSPECTIVES: A QUEST FOR CONSENSUS (1991).

6.   In addition to these limitations on rights, there are other limitations on the jurisdiction of the regional human rights bodies. One such limitation is geographic: violations by member states are not actionable unless the acts took place in the territory or under the jurisdiction of the state party. Thus, when NATO forces bombed the Serbian television stations during the Kosovo conflict, killing or injuring 32 civilians, the ECHR declared the suit inadmissable as the jurisdiction of the Convention was primarily territorial. *Bankovič and others v. Belgium and others* (Appl. No. 52207/99), Admissibility Decision of 12 December 2001, 11 B.H.R.C. 435. However, in 2007 the British House of Lords, applying the law of the ECHR, ruled that an Iraqi detained by UK troops in Iraq was subject to the protections of the European Convention, but that such protection does not extend to Iraqi civilians outside the troops' effective control. *Al–Skeini and Others v. Secretary of State for Defence* [2007] UKHL 26, United Kingdom: House of Lords, 13 June 2007, available at: http://www.unhcr.org/refworld/docid/4672880a2.html [accessed 2 July 2009].

B.   ACCOUNTABILITY FOR INTERNATIONAL CRIMES

The common sense of mankind demands that law shall not stop with the punishment of petty crimes by little people. It must also reach men who possess themselves of great power and make deliberate and concerted use of it to set in motion evils which leave no home in the world untouched.

—Justice Robert Jackson, Chief Prosecutor at Nuremberg, Opening Statement

Most of public international law concerns the relationships among states. Even where individual rights are concerned (see Part A) states are responsible for respecting, protecting and fulfilling the rights of their citizens, and if they don't, they are answerable as states. However, there have always been exceptions. Piracy, for example, has long been considered an international crime giving rise to individual responsibility. (See chapter 1). Over time, other crimes, many of which also constitute violations of international human rights law if carried out under state auspices, have been declared international crimes, which states either can or must prosecute. At the same time, ordinary crimes increasingly cross borders, as do ordinary (and extraordinary!) criminals, giving rise to a vastly expanded corpus of international criminal law concerned with extradition, mutual legal assistance, enforcement of sentences and the like.

This section considers these overlapping international legal regimes and issues. We start with an overview of the evolution of thinking about what states can, and should, do after mass atrocities have been committed, especially in the wake of large-scale repression or armed conflict. We then consider the international architecture that is emerging to prosecute war crimes, genocide and crimes against humanity. We look at some of the difficulties in both defining the crimes and in creating effective ways of dealing with them given the limits of state cooperation. In this context, we consider the work of the *ad hoc* International Criminal Tribunals for the Former Yugoslavia (ICTY) and Rwanda (ICTR) as well as the mixed or hybrid tribunals that combine international and national staff and crimes. We then go on to explore the structure and functioning of the International Criminal Court.

The following excerpt outlines the recent history and broad issues involved.

Naomi Roht–Arriaza, The New Landscape of Transitional Justice

TRANSITIONAL JUSTICE IN THE TWENTY-FIRST CENTURY: BEYOND TRUTH VERSUS JUSTICE (Naomi Roht–Arriaza and Javier Mariezcurrena eds., 2006)

Post conflict attempts at justice are not new: war crimes trials go back to the 14th century. In the wake of both World Wars there were trials, successful and not. Torturers were tried after the fall of the Greek dictatorship of the 1970s, while a consensus among elites postponed questions of justice and reparations in post-Franco Spain and in post-Salazar Portugal.[1] The decade that concluded with the fall of the Berlin Wall

---

1. See Bassiouni, *Post–Conflict Justice* (Transnational Press, 2002) for early efforts; for the 1970s see Alexandra Barahona de Brito, ed. *The Politics of Memory* (Oxford University

coincided with a wave of changes, negotiated or compelled, from military dictatorships to civilian governments in the Southern Cone of South America, the Philippines and in a number of African countries. The negotiated end of South Africa's apartheid regime, and ends to the civil wars of Central America, soon followed.

These events raised a lively debate regarding the proper strategy after a dictatorship falls or a civil conflict ends. Much of the debate was framed by the conditions of transition in Latin America and Eastern Europe [in the early 1980s]. In the former, the prior dictators and their military and civilian supporters still wielded a good deal of power, and could credibly threaten mayhem if their interests were not respected. Moreover, these transitions were largely negotiated between elites, not compelled by the military defeat of one side in a civil conflict or by popular uprising. Under these circumstances, diplomats, political scientists and also some human rights activists argued that it was shortsighted to overwhelm newly install-ed, fragile civilian governments with demands for criminal prosecutions. Thus, amnesties were an inevitable concession, trading justice for the past in exchange for justice in the future.

In Argentina and later in Chile, incoming civilian governments had commissioned broad-based commissions of notables to investigate and document the human rights violations of the prior regime. While both the Argentine Sábato Commission and Chile's Truth and Reconciliation Commission actually turned their findings over to the courts (and, in Argentina, members of the ruling juntas and a few other top security force officers were prosecuted), the model of a "truth commission" gained force as a "second-best" option where trials were deemed too destabilizing. Truth commissions seemed less confrontational while still not ignoring the violations and doing something for victims. Such commissions focus on a defined period in the past, exist for a limited period, are official, and are tasked with, at a minimum, compiling a narrative of the past violations and recommending ways to repair the damage and prevent its repetition.[2]

The emphasis on "truth" required a theory of why the truth was so important. In Latin America, the rationale was tied to the nature of the repression. For the most part, the military governments did not openly kill their opponents. Rather, large numbers of people were disappeared, picked up by official or unofficial security forces that then refused to acknowledge the detention. Almost all were killed, often after extended torture, and in many cases the bodies were never found. Even when the regimes' opponents were outright murdered, it was often by unofficial death squads who

---

Press, 2001), Juan Linz and Alfred Stepan, *Problems of Democratic Transition and Consolidation: Southern Europe, South America, and Post–Communist Europe* (Johns Hopkins University Press, 1996), John Herz, *From Dictatorship to Democracy: Coping with the Legacies of Authoritarianism and Totalitarianism* (Westport, CT: Greenwood Press, 1982); for Spain's efforts, starting in the early 2000s, to finally confront the legacy of Francoism, see Equipo Nizkor's website, www.derechos.org/nizkor/spain.

2. Priscilla Hayner, *Unspeakable Truths: Confronting State Terror and Atrocity*, (New York, NY: Routledge, 2001).

wore civilian clothes and provided a measure of deniability. The families of those who disappeared were ostracized as a climate of generalized terror set in.

In Eastern Europe, the period of massive killings had usually passed long before, but there was a pervasive sense of constant surveillance and arbitrary punishment handed down by a state that hid its true face. Opening up of state archives and historical commissions, and efforts to remove the offenders from public office, were the Eastern European responses. Truth was needed to reverse the silence and denial of the dictatorship years, to establish the extent, origin and nature of the crimes, which were not well known, and to know who had collaborated in an effort to limit their future influence. Even though the human rights violations in both places were usually common knowledge, there was a huge gap between knowledge and acknowledgement.[3] And in the post-cold war era, investigation of the past would not necessarily entail alignment with one superpower, or aid and comfort to the other.

Psychological research, especially with torture survivors, reinforced the notion that truth was important in itself. Survivors seemed to be helped by telling their story to a sympathetic listener and by seeing it within a larger social context. It seemed reasonable that, just as individuals need "closure" to leave trauma behind, whole traumatized societies would benefit from a public airing leading to closure. Religious leaders chimed in, arguing that knowing the truth would allow the victims to forgive without forgetting and the perpetrators to confess and atone, thus setting the stage for former enemies to live together. Human rights lawyers began to argue for a "right to truth" independent of criminal prosecution.[4]

The South African experience became the best known of these experiments. An amnesty law was required in the country's interim constitution, but the Parliament decided to tie amnesty to full disclosure of the crimes by any individual seeking amnesty. They grafted this amnesty-for-truth process onto a Truth and Reconciliation Commission aimed at hearing victims' stories, documenting the violations, and providing recommendations for change.

The backers of the South African TRC, did not argue merely that a truth commission was a second-best alternative where trials were unavailable. Rather, they insisted, a well-run commission could accomplish things no trial could provide. It could focus on the overall pattern of violations, rather than zeroing in on just those cases that happened to be brought to trial. It could keep the focus of testimony and discussion on the victims rather than the perpetrators, and allow victims to testify in a supportive setting more conducive to healing than the sometimes brutal cross-examination of a criminal or civil trial. By offering amnesty in exchange for

---

3. Thomas Nagel made this point at an early conference on transitional justice sponsored by the Aspen Institute.

4. See, for instance, *Carmen Aguiar de Lapacó v. Argentina*, Inter–American Commission Case 12.059, Report 21/00, OEA/Ser.L/V/II.106 Doc. 3 rev. at 340 (1999).

confession, it could elicit information from perpetrators that would be unlikely to emerge in a criminal trial where the burden of proof remained on the state. Moreover, non-judicial methods were better at dealing with the many shades of gray that characterize most conflicts. Trials divided the universe into a small group of guilty parties and an innocent majority, which was thereby cleansed of wrongdoing. In reality, however, large numbers of people supported those who committed the actual violations, and even larger numbers turned their faces away and were silent. Trials could not adequately engage with those nuances. A restorative justice approach, focusing on the victims and on reintegration of offenders rather than the retributive justice ascribed to the criminal law, was preferable.

Truth commissions became a staple of the transitional justice menu. [They were incorporated into U.N. sponsored peace accords in El Salvador, Guatemala, Haiti, Sierra Leone, Democratic Republic of Congo, Burundi and elsewhere]. Over time, critiques arose. Such commissions assumed there was a single "truth" to be molded from the disparate strands of interests and experience. They could contribute to a compiling of "factual" truth, but not necessarily to the creation of a common narrative or common understanding. They frustrated and at times even retraumatized victims who, having unearthed their pain, were left wondering to what end. The model of short-term catharsis as a basis for healing was disputed by therapists, and the empirical evidence showed that testifying in public was beneficial for some victims, but not others. They did nothing to affect local power relationships.

Moreover, the South African example, widely praised internationally, received a more critical reception at home. While it had many positive aspects, the TRC did not lead automatically to reconciliation either between blacks and whites or among blacks ("revealing is healing" turned out to only be true sometimes), almost no high-ranking officials of the apartheid government came forward to ask for amnesty, and the courts were largely unwilling to pursue cases, even well-founded ones, against those who distained the offer of amnesty for truth. Although other countries emerging from conflict adapted parts of the South African scheme, none adopted it wholesale.

The debate over what was helpful to victims exemplified a broadening of the thinking on transitional justice to a wider range of disciplines. No longer were lawyers, diplomats and political scientists the only practitioners involved. Forensic anthropologists and other scientists helped identify bodies and describe patterns of violence, providing evidence for UN reports, truth commission reports and ongoing judicial investigations, as well as facilitating the return of remains to bodies and communities. Their work has kept the issue of the disappeared before the public in Latin America and elsewhere. DNA analysis of missing children in Argentina has united families and led to new trials. Statisticians and epidemiologists assisted truth commissions and NGOs in the collection and analysis of data on the missing and other human rights abuses. Educators became involved in writing and revising history, museum curators and artists in memorialization, religious figures in defining the preconditions for reconciliation.

From country to country as well a process of diffusion of experiences and ideas followed. Chileans advised the South Africans on their TRC; the South Africans inspired the idea of confession and conditional amnesty in a number of places. The peace agreement drafters designed the Guatemalan Historical Clarification Commission to *not* mimic aspects of the earlier Salvadoran Truth Commission. But each place was also unique, influenced not only by international advisors and funders but by the strength of its own human rights movement, of opposing political forces and the nature and extent of the conflict.

While truth commissions became widely known, other elements of the transitional justice "toolbox" where used far less frequently. Vetting or cleansing of political leaders and security forces was a major component of efforts in the Czech Republic and elsewhere in Eastern and Central Europe, but was criticized for being overbroad and based on unreliable secret police records. Army officers were vetted in El Salvador; in Argentina, military promotions were contingent on human rights screening. Reparations programs were implemented in Argentina, Chile, and (eventually, on a scaled-down basis) South Africa, and are just now being carried out in Guatemala and Peru. Beyond these, reparations programs are scarce, although they are a frequent TC recommendation.

By the time of the South African TRC in 1995, a further set of considerations had to be added to the mix. In the early 1990s, a bloody ethnic conflict in the former Yugoslavia left 200,000 dead. Western powers dithered, but eventually agreed to try to deter ongoing atrocities by setting up an international criminal tribunal. In addition to deterrence, the tribunal was supposed to contribute to reconciliation through justice, to create a historical record, and to remove some of the worst offenders from positions of power. It was set up via Security Council resolution, which in theory at least ensured the cooperation of all U.N. members. A year later, in 1994, the slaughter of over three quarters of a million people, prompted the creation of a similar international criminal tribunal for Rwanda. Both tribunals were set up outside the situs of the conflicts, both because of security concerns and because it was felt that an outside court, staffed largely by outsiders, would have the advantages of impartiality, credibility and expertise that would be lacking in compromised or decimated national legal systems.

Criminal prosecution was seen as essential in these cases in part because the killings had been massive, open and notorious (indeed, broadcast on Rwandan radio) and so a "truth commission," by itself, was thought both inadequate and unnecessary.[6] Moreover, these were not cases where a rigid security force hierarchy under state control attacked perceived enemies of the state. Rather, they were much murkier, involving

---

6.   Aryeh Neier, *War Crime: Brutality, Genocide, Terror, and the Struggle for Justice* (New York: Times Books/Random House, 1998).

ethnic and resource-based as well as political conflict, looser chains of command, and the involvement of many more paramilitary groups, gangs of thugs, and ordinary citizens on all sides. Often, ethnically based conflicts set community against community, neighbor against neighbor. It seemed clear that in some cases at least, justice as well as truth were crucial. Only trials could provide for the confrontation of evidence and witnesses that would create an unimpeachable factual record, Moreover, only trials could adequately individualize responsibility, holding the guilty parties liable without stigmatizing entire ethnic or religious groups. This was important to avoid continuing bouts of violence as well as the temptation of private revenge.

The Tribunals were praised for reaffirming the principle that accountability was an important international concern. Their Statutes, Rules of Evidence and Procedure, and rulings were milestones in the development of international criminal law, and they served as training grounds for a corps of international investigators, lawyers and judges. They developed important jurisprudence on genocide, crimes against humanity and war crimes, among other issues. They contributed to creating an authoritative record of the origins and nature of the violence, incapacitated a number of offenders, allowed some victims to tell their story, and limited the ability of some local authorities to do further mischief. They established that heads of state were not immune from trial before an international tribunal, and pioneered techniques like the use of sealed indictments and plea bargains in the international criminal context. . . .

And yet, by the start of the new decade criticism mounted as well. The Tribunals were enormously expensive and time-consuming, and critics noted that the same resources might have been better spent on rebuilding the national legal systems. Their very distance, both literal and figurative, made them seem remote from the "target" societies, and it was doubtful whether the populations of the Balkans or Rwanda accepted the facts established in their rulings as authoritative.[f] It was unclear what their long-term legacy would be, as domestic courts seemed woefully unprepared to take up the cases the Tribunals lacked resources to pursue even as the Tribunals faced deadlines to wrap up their activities. There was very little outreach to the "target" communities, and little collaboration between the Tribunals and domestic courts in the Former Yugoslavia and Rwanda.

Two other events at the end of the 1990s raised the profile of international justice efforts: the creation of the International Criminal Court and the arrest of Augusto Pinochet. After a number of preparatory meetings, a conference convened in 1998 to create the International Criminal Court. The ICC has jurisdiction over genocide, crimes against humanity, and war crimes taking place after July 1, 2002. (A fourth crime, aggression, will be added once defined.) Unlike the Yugoslav and Rwanda Tribunals, the ICC's jurisdiction is complementary to that of national

---

f. Eric Stover and Harvey Weinstein, eds., *My Neighbor, My Enemy: Justice and Community in the Aftermath of Mass Atrocity* (Cambridge University Press, 2004).

courts: it can only prosecute when local courts prove unable or unwilling to do so. . . .

Scarcely three months after the signing of the Rome Statute, the former head of Chile's military government, Augusto Pinochet, was arrested in London under a provision of Spanish law providing jurisdiction in local courts for cases of genocide, terrorism and other international crimes under ratified treaties. The British House of Lords found that he had no immunity as a former head of state from charges of torture, and that torture constituted an "extradition crime". The highest Spanish criminal appeals court also upheld the prosecution under Spain's universal jurisdiction law. Eventually, Pinochet was found unfit for trial and sent home, but by that time the taboo on complaints against him had been broken. He was soon charged in a number of cases, his parliamentary immunity stripped, and as of this writing he is awaiting a ruling on whether trial can proceed*; many of his closest associates are in prison. Transnational prosecutions seemed a viable option as a complement to national or international ones, or at least as a way to avoid creating safe-havens for traveling dictators. They also seemed able, at least under some circumstances, to unblock or catalyze domestic legal processes. A rash of other transnational prosecutions followed.

These two major trends—the increasing use of investigative or "truth and reconciliation" commissions and the use of international and transnational trials—came together by the beginning of the new millennium. The debate about truth versus justice seemed to be resolving in favor of an approach that recognized the value of both approaches. Even those who had argued strenuously in favor of a non-prosecutorial, "truth-centered" approach recognized exceptions for crimes against humanity, while advocates of prosecution recognized that a truth-seeking and truth-telling exercise could serve as a valuable precursor or complement, even if not a substitute, for prosecutions. This mutual recognition combined with increasing attention at the international level to issues of reparations and structural reform. . . .

Moreover, each element affected the shape and possibilities of the others, in an "ecological model"[7] of social reconstruction or reclamation. "Truth-telling" followed by neither reparations nor prosecutions seemed to make victims' accounts meaningless, while reparations without public acknowledgement of the facts looked to many victims like "blood money" paid for their silence. Prosecutions without a forum where a larger narrative could emerge created a partial, fortuitous view of history (dependent on evidence and the ability to apprehend defendants), while a truth commission without a tie to judicial actions against perpetrators begged the question of what the consequences of truth should be. Only by interweaving, sequencing and accommodating multiple pathways to justice could some kind of larger justice in fact emerge.

---

* Pinochet died in 2006 before standing trial.

7. Laurel E. Fletcher and Harvey M. Weinstein, *Violence and Social Repair: Rethinking the Contribution of Justice to Reconciliation*, 24:3 Human Rights Quarterly 573 (2002).

NOTES AND QUESTIONS

1. The excerpt above includes a number of possible measures for dealing with past (and sometimes ongoing) conflict. What about the "do nothing" option? Is it better to "forgive and forget" rather than engage in trials, truth-seeking, reparations or other measures? Why or why not? Under any circumstances? What if such measures threaten to trigger military coups or renewed war? To what extent should that decision be based on popular or legislative sentiment and to what extent are these rights-based issues that cannot be decided through majority vote? To what extent are cultural variations relevant?

2. What is the role of international law in setting limits on what states can decide to do with respect to accountability? A number of treaties, and the increasing weight of international opinion, holds that some crimes are not subject to limits like amnesties or statutes of limitations. Is this an unwise rigidity that can complicate efforts at peace, or a necessary limit that keeps governments from delaying "positive peace" in the interest of short-term expediency? See Diane Orentlicher, *Settling Accounts: The Duty to Prosecute Human Rights Violations of a Prior Regime*, 100 YALE L.J. 2537 (1991); LOUISE MALLINDER, AMNESTY, HUMAN RIGHTS AND POLITICAL TRANSITIONS: BRIDGING THE PEACE AND JUSTICE DIVIDE (2008); NAOMI ROHT-ARRIAZA, IMPUNITY AND HUMAN RIGHTS IN INTERNATIONAL LAW AND PRACTICE (1995).

3. Reparations have, until recently, largely been a matter of state-to-state post-war reparations or reparations for injuries to aliens. In addition to the court-ordered reparations described above, governments have set up administrative reparations programs for widespread harms. These type of reparations largely date from the German reparations programs to Holocaust victims, slave laborers and others. In more recent years, the governments of Chile, Argentina, Guatemala, Peru, Colombia, Ghana, Morocco, Sierra Leone and others have embarked on individual reparations programs, which include some combination of individual awards, service packages, "collective reparations" to communities, and symbolic reparations. See ELAZAR BARKAN, THE GUILT OF NATIONS: RESTITUTION AND NEGOTIATING HISTORICAL INJUSTICES (2000); JOHN TORPEY, MAKING WHOLE WHAT HAS BEEN SMASHED: ON REPARATIONS POLITICS, (2006); WHEN SORRY ISN'T ENOUGH: THE CONTROVERSY OVER APOLOGIES AND REPARATIONS FOR HUMAN INJUSTICE (Roy L. Brooks, ed., 1999); THE HANDBOOK OF REPARATIONS (Pablo de Greiff, ed., 2006).

4. Another common problem in post-armed conflict or transitional societies is the need to reform the security forces and the public sector, weeding out human rights violators and the corrupt while not crippling public administration. Vetting processes in El Salvador involved individual evaluations of high-ranking military officers, while in Eastern Europe wholesale dismissals of former Communists were widely seen as unjust, especially since such dismissals were often based on suspect evidence from secret police files. In Iraq, an aggressive process of dismissing Ba'athist officials from their posts (including disbanding the army) was also considered a profound failure, creating a vacuum in administration and a corps of unemployed who were then easily recruited for violent militias. Expert

consensus holds that "vetting processes should ... be based on assessments of individual conduct," and can help not only to reform government, but to fill the impunity gap left by an inability to criminally prosecute all abusers. Office of the High Commissioner for Human Rights, Rule-of-Law Tools for Post–Conflict States: *Vetting: An Operational Framework* (2006) p. 3. See also the publications of the International Center for Transitional Justice on vetting, available at http://ictj.org/en/news/pubs/index.html.

1. INDIVIDUAL CRIMINAL ACCOUNTABILITY AND THE GROWTH OF INTERNATIONAL TRIBUNALS

The Second World War presented the Allies with the question of what to do with the defeated leaders of Nazi Germany. British Prime Minister Churchill was reportedly in favor of simply shooting them, while the Russian leaders wanted a show trial—and then shooting. The view finally prevailed that a real trial, based on due process, was necessary, as Justice Robert Jackson, Chief Prosecutor at Nuremberg, put it, to establish "undeniable proofs of incredible events." "That four great nations, flushed with victory and stung with injury stay the hand of vengeance and voluntarily submit their captive enemies to the judgment of the law is one of the most significant tributes that Power has ever paid to Reason," Jackson told the International Military Tribunal at Nuremberg. While most of the trials related to Nazi crimes were carried out by national courts (see below), the crimes of the top leadership were committed in more than one country, and thus only an international tribunal was considered adequate to try them.

The Charter of the IMT specified the crimes to be tried:

Article 6

The Tribunal established by the Agreement referred to in Article 1 hereof for the trial and punishment of the major war criminals of the European Axis countries shall have the power to try and punish persons who, acting in the interests of the European Axis countries, whether as individuals or as members of organizations, committed any of the following crimes.

The following acts, or any of them, are crimes coming within the jurisdiction of the Tribunal for which there shall be individual responsibility:

a. *Crimes against peace:* namely, planning, preparation, initiation or waging of a war of aggression, or a war in violation of international treaties, agreements or assurances, or participation in a common plan or conspiracy for the accomplishment of any of the foregoing;

b. *War crimes:* namely, violations of the laws or customs of war. Such violations shall include, but not be limited to, murder, ill-treatment or deportation to slave labour or for any other purpose of civilian population of or in occupied territory, murder or ill-treatment of prisoners of war or persons on the seas, killing of hostages, plunder of public or private property, wanton destruction of cities, towns or villages, or devastation not justified by military necessity;

c. *Crimes against humanity:* namely, murder, extermination, enslavement, deportation, and other inhumane acts committed against any civilian population, before or during the war; or persecutions on political, racial or religious grounds in execution of or in connection with any crime within the jurisdiction of the Tribunal, whether or not in violation of the domestic law of the country where perpetrated.

Leaders, organizers, instigators and accomplices participating in the formulation or execution of a common plan or conspiracy to commit any of the foregoing crimes are responsible for all acts performed by any persons in execution of such plan.

This broad view of individual criminal responsibility has been carried forward to the tribunals established in the 1990s.

In addition to specifying the crimes, the Charter made clear that official position would not shield a defendant, and that following orders was not a defense, although it could be used to mitigate punishment. In Article 16, the Charter specified that defendants were entitled to due process, including rights to obtain copies of documents attached to the indictment, choose defense counsel and cross-examine witnesses. However, formal rules of evidence were not followed. These innovations were also followed by later tribunals.

Nonetheless, the IMT process was criticized on a number of grounds. First, as "victor's justice": the victorious Allies sat in judgment on the acts of the defeated Nazi leadership, but the Tribunal ignored Allied depredations like the bombing of Dresden or the use of the atomic bomb. Jackson answered this objection thus: "The worldwide scope of the aggressions carried out by these men has left but few real neutrals. Either the victors must judge the vanquished or we must leave the defeated to judge themselves. After the first World War, we learned the futility of the latter course."*

Second, the defendants complained that they were being tried for crimes that had not been previously codified, especially on the count of "crimes against humanity." While making war in violation of treaties was recognized as a violation of international law and war crimes, as noted above, had been defined, it was not clear at the time whether individual criminal responsibility resulted from their commission. Crimes against humanity, while mentioned in general terms in prior treaties, had never been codified at all: the count was added to the London Charter to account for crimes, like the Holocaust, by Germans against Germans and other non-

---

* Jackson is referring to the requirement, in the Versailles Treaty ending WWI, that the Kaiser be tried for crimes against peace and war crimes. It never happened, because the Netherlands, where he had gone into exile, refused to hand him over for trial. See Gary Bass, *Stay the Hand of Vengeance: The Politics of War Crimes Tribunals*, (Princeton, Princeton University Press, 2000).

enemy peoples. This violated the prohibition on *ex post facto* prosecutions (also known as the principle of legality). Nonsense, replied the IMT's defenders: these crimes had long been violations of customary international law, and the defendants had knowledge that their actions were legally, as well as morally, wrong. One result of this debate was the inclusion in the major human rights treaties of an article prohibiting trial for acts that were not criminal *under national or international law* at the time committed.*

Finally, the Charter of the IMT allowed for a finding that defendants formed part of a criminal organization, like the SS. Subsequent tribunals have rejected this approach as involving "collective punishment," although recent discussions have raised the issue anew in the context of accounting for collective support and acquiescence in mass atrocity. See Fletcher and Weinstein, *Violence and Social Repair: Rethinking the Contribution of Justice to Reconciliation*, 31:1 Human Rights Quarterly 163–220 (February 2009); Jose Alvarez, *Crimes of State/Crimes of Hate: Lessons from Rwanda*, 24 Yale Journal of International Law 365 (1999); Mark Drumbl, *Atrocity, Punishment and International Law* (Cambridge: Cambridge University Press, 2007).

The IMT tried only 22 defendants. Hundreds more were tried in national courts set up by the Occupying Powers, especially the U.S. and the British. These trials were conducted under the law of Control Council Law No. 10. The definition of crimes against humanity was broader, including "murder, extermination, enslavement, deportation, imprisonment, torture, rape or other inhumane acts," and dropped the requirement of a nexus to the war. The UN General Assembly in 1950 reaffirmed the basic elements of the London Charter in the Principles of International Law Recognized in the Charter of the Nüremberg Tribunal and in the Judgment of the Tribunal, International Committee of the Red Cross, International Humanitarian Law, Treaties & Documents http://www.icrc.org/ihl.nsf/FULL/390 [last accessed July 14, 2009]. For a further discussion of crimes against the peace and war crimes, see Chapter 10.

In 1948, states negotiated the Convention on the Prevention and Punishment of the Crime of Genocide. Genocide, a term newly coined by Raphael Lempkin, was defined in Article 2 as specified acts "committed with the intent to destroy, in whole or in part, a national, ethnical, racial or religious group, as such." The treaty makes genocide a crime under international law, and requires that states criminalize genocide in their own law and to punish wrongdoers "whether they are constitutionally responsible rulers, public officials or private individuals." It also requires states to prevent genocide—although this obligation has been extremely difficult to implement. It contemplates prosecutions of individuals in either the territorial state or in an international criminal tribunal. However, the effort to create such tribunals was frozen by the Cold War. During this period, mass atrocities in places like Cambodia (1975–79; 1.8 million dead), Nigeria/Biafra (1966–70; 3 million dead), Guatemala (1960–85; 200,000

---

* For example, the ICCPR Art. 15, European Convention on Human Rights and Fundamental Freedoms Art. 7, American Convention on Human Rights, Art. 9.

dead), and Indonesia (1965–66; 500,000 dead) went unpunished and largely unremarked; efforts to investigate or try the crimes met with little success.

With the end of the Cold War, new possibilities opened up. Soon enough, the promise of a new, more just order was put to the test by the breakup of the former Yugoslavia and the outbreak of wars in the region that led to widespread displacement, "ethnic cleansing" and atrocities. Despite lofty promises of "never again," television viewers saw emaciated civilians in concentration camps in the heart of Europe. This was unacceptable, but no state was willing to take more than minimal steps to stop it. Under these conditions, in 1993, the UN Security Council decided to create an international criminal tribunal. The resolution creating the International Criminal Tribunal for the former Yugoslavia follows.

Security Council Resolution 827 (1993)

U.N. Doc. S/Res/827 (1993)

The Security Council . . .

Convinced that in the particular circumstances of the former Yugoslavia the establishment as an ad hoc measure by the Council of an international tribunal and the prosecution of persons responsible for serious violations of international humanitarian law would enable this aim to be achieved and would contribute to the restoration and maintenance of peace;

Believing that the establishment of an international tribunal and the prosecution of persons responsible for the above-mentioned violations of international humanitarian law will contribute to ensuring that such violations are halted and effectively redressed; . . .

Reaffirming in this regard its decision in resolution 808 (1993) that an international tribunal shall be established for the prosecution of persons responsible for serious violations of international humanitarian law committed in the territory of the former Yugoslavia since 1991;

Considering that, pending the appointment of the Prosecutor of the International Tribunal, the Commission of Experts established pursuant to resolution 780 (1992) should continue on an urgent basis the collection of information relating to evidence of grave breaches of the Geneva conventions and other violations of international humanitarian law as proposed in its interim report (S/25274);

Acting under Chapter VII of the Charter of the United Nations;

1. *Approves* the report of the Secretary General;

2. *Decides* hereby to establish an international tribunal for the sole purpose of prosecuting persons responsible for serious violations of international humanitarian law committed in the territory of the former Yugoslavia between 1 January 1991 and a date to be determined by the Security Council upon the restoration of peace and to this end to adopt the Statute of the International Tribunal annexed to the above-mentioned report;

3.   *Requests* the Secretary–General to submit to the judges of the International Tribunal, upon their election, any suggestions received from States for the rules of procedure and evidence called for in Article 15 of the Statute of the International Tribunal;

4.   *Decides* that all states shall cooperate fully with the International Tribunal and its organs in accordance with the present resolution and the Statute of the International Tribunal and that consequently all States shall take any measures necessary under their domestic law to implement the provisions of the present resolution and the Statute, including the obligation of States to comply with requests for assistance or orders issued by a Trial Chamber under Article 29 of the Statute;

5.   *Urges* States and intergovernmental and non-governmental organizations to contribute funds, equipment and services to the International Tribunal, including the offer of expert personnel;

6.   *Decides* that the determination of the seat of the International Tribunal is subject to the conclusion of appropriate arrangements between the United Nations and the Netherlands acceptable to the Council, and that the International Tribunal may sit elsewhere when it considers it necessary for the efficient exercise of its functions;

7.   *Decides* also that the work of the International Tribunal shall be carried out without prejudice to the right of the victims to seek, through appropriate means, compensation for damages incurred as a result of violations of international humanitarian law;

8.   *Requests* the Secretary–General to implement urgently the present resolution and in particular to make practical arrangements for the effective functioning of the International Tribunal at the earliest time and to report periodically to the Council;

9.   *Decides* to remain actively seized of the matter.

The ICTY was faced with a challenge to its institutional legitimacy in its first case, *Prosecutor* v. *Duško Tadić.*

The Prosecutor of the Tribunal v. Duško Tadić (Decision on the Defence Motion for Interlocutory Appeal on Jurisdiction)

International Criminal Tribunal for the Former Yugoslavia (ICTY), Case No. IT–94–1, Decision on the Defense Motion for Interlocutory Appeal on Jurisdiction, (Appeals Chamber, 2 Oct. 1995)

* * *

1.   Does The International Tribunal Have Jurisdiction?

* * *

14.   In its decision, the Trial Chamber declares:

"[I]t is one thing for the Security Council to have taken every care to ensure that a structure appropriate to the conduct of fair trials has been created; it is an entirely different thing in any way to infer from that careful structuring that it was intended that the International Tribunal be empowered to question the legality of the law which established it. The competence of the International Tribunal is precise and narrowly defined; as described in Article 1 of its Statute, it is to prosecute persons responsible for serious violations of international humanitarian law, subject to spatial and temporal limits, and to do so in accordance with the Statute. That is the full extent of the competence of the International Tribunal." (Decision at Trial, at para. 8.)

Both the first and the last sentences of this quotation need qualification. The first sentence assumes a subjective stance, considering that jurisdiction can be determined exclusively by reference to or inference from the intention of the Security Council, thus totally ignoring any residual powers which may derive from the requirements of the "judicial function" itself. That is also the qualification that needs to be added to the last sentence.... This power, known as the principle of *"Kompetenz–Kompetenz"* in German or *"la compétence de la compétence"* in French, is part, and indeed a major part, of the incidental or inherent jurisdiction of any judicial or arbitral tribunal, consisting of its "jurisdiction to determine its own jurisdiction." It is a necessary component in the exercise of the judicial function and does not need to be expressly provided for in the constitutive documents of those tribunals, although this is often done (see, e.g., Statute of the International Court of Justice, Art. 36, para. 6) ... the Appeals Chamber finds that the International Tribunal has jurisdiction to examine the plea against its jurisdiction based on the invalidity of its establishment by the Security Council.

These arguments raise a series of constitutional issues which all turn on the limits of the power of the Security Council under Chapter VII of the Charter of the United Nations and determining what action or measures can be taken under this Chapter, particularly the establishment of an international criminal tribunal. * * *

29. ... The situations justifying resort to the powers provided for in Chapter VII are a "threat to the peace", a "breach of the peace" or an "act of aggression." While the "act of aggression" is more amenable to a legal determination, the "threat to the peace" is more of a political concept. But the determination that there exists such a threat is not a totally unfettered discretion, as it has to remain, at the very least, within the limits of the Purposes and Principles of the Charter. * * *

32. ... Appellant has attacked the legality of this decision [n.b. to create the Tribunal] at different stages before the Trial Chamber as well as before this Chamber on at least three grounds:

a) that the establishment of such a tribunal was never contemplated by the framers of the Charter as one of the measures to be taken under Chapter VII; as witnessed by the fact that it figures nowhere in the provisions of that Chapter, and more particularly in Articles 41 and 42 which detail these measures;

b) that the Security Council is constitutionally or inherently incapable of creating a judicial organ, as it is conceived in the Charter as an executive organ, hence not possessed of judicial powers which can be exercised through a subsidiary organ;

c) that the establishment of the International Tribunal has neither promoted, nor was capable of promoting, international peace, as demonstrated by the current situation in the former Yugoslavia.

* * *

33.   The establishment of an international criminal tribunal is not expressly mentioned among the enforcement measures provided for in Chapter VII, and more particularly in Articles 41 and 42.

Obviously, the establishment of the International Tribunal is not a measure under Article 42, as these are measures of a military nature, implying the use of armed force. Nor can it be considered a "provisional measure" under Article 40. . . .

34.   *Prima facie*, the International Tribunal matches perfectly the description in Article 41 of "measures not involving the use of force." Appellant, however, has argued before both the Trial Chamber and this Appeals Chamber, that:

". . . [I]t is clear that the establishment of a war crimes tribunal was not intended. The examples mentioned in this article focus upon economic and political measures and do not in any way suggest judicial measures." [cite omitted]

It has also been argued that the measures contemplated under Article 41 are all measures to be undertaken by Member States, which is not the case with the establishment of the International Tribunal.

35.   The first argument does not stand by its own language. Article 41 reads as follows:

"The Security Council may decide what measures not involving the use of armed force are to be employed to give effect to its decisions, and it may call upon the Members of the United Nations to apply such measures. These may include complete or partial interruption of economic relations and of rail, sea, air, postal, telegraphic, radio, and other means of communication, and the severance of diplomatic relations." (United Nations Charter, art. 41.)

It is evident that the measures set out in Article 41 are merely illustrative **examples** which obviously do not exclude other measures. All the Article requires is that they do not involve "the use of force." It is a negative definition.

That the examples do not suggest judicial measures goes some way towards the other argument that the Article does not contemplate institutional measures implemented directly by the United Nations through one of its organs but, as the given examples suggest, only action by Member States, such as economic sanctions (though possibly coordinated through an organ of the Organization). However, as mentioned above, nothing in the Article suggests the limitation of the measures to those implemented by States. The Article only prescribes what these measures cannot be. Beyond that it does not say or suggest what they have to be. * * *

40. For the aforementioned reasons, the Appeals Chamber considers that the International Tribunal has been lawfully established as a measure under Chapter VII of the Charter.

* * *

41. Appellant challenges the establishment of the International Tribunal by contending that it has not been established by law. The entitlement of an individual to have a criminal charge against him determined by a tribunal which has been established by law is provided in Article 14, paragraph 1, of the International Covenant on Civil and Political Rights. It provides:

> "In the determination of any criminal charge against him, or of his rights and obligations in a suit at law, everyone shall be entitled to a fair and public hearing by a competent, independent and impartial tribunal established by law." (ICCPR, art. 14, para. 1.)

* * *

42. For the reasons outlined below, Appellant has not satisfied this Chamber that the requirements laid down in these three [n.b. human rights] conventions must apply not only in the context of national legal systems but also with respect to proceedings conducted before an international court. This Chamber is, however, satisfied that the principle that a tribunal must be established by law, as explained below, is a general principle of law imposing an international obligation which only applies to the administration of criminal justice in a municipal setting. * * *

46. An examination of the Statute of the International Tribunal, and of the Rules of Procedure and Evidence adopted pursuant to that Statute leads to the conclusion that it has been established in accordance with the rule of law. The fair trial guarantees in Article 14 of the International Covenant on Civil and Political Rights have been adopted almost verbatim in Article 21 of the Statute. Other fair trial guarantees appear in the Statute and the Rules of Procedure and Evidence * * *.

47. In conclusion, the Appeals Chamber finds that the International Tribunal has been established in accordance with the appropriate procedures under the United Nations Charter and provides all the necessary safeguards of a fair trial. It is thus "established by law." * * *

NOTES AND QUESTIONS

1. Why would the U.N. Security Council have chosen to use a Security Council resolution to create a Tribunal? What were the alternative methods for creating a court? Why weren't those chosen?

2.   Why is it permissible for the Security Council to create a court, even though admittedly the drafters of the U.N. Charter did not contemplate such a thing in Article 41? Do the SC origins of the two *ad hoc* criminal tribunals give them greater legitimacy, or less?

3.   What advantages come with SC creation of a court? Are all UN member states bound to follow the Security Council's directives? See Chapter 3. What happens if states choose not to cooperate with the Tribunals? In *Prosecutor v. Blaskic,* Case No. IT–95–14–T (Oct. 29, 1997) the Republic of Croatia challenged the ICTY's authority to issue a subpoena and refused to comply. The Appeals Chamber found that all member states had a duty to comply with Tribunal orders and that the Security Council could enforce such orders. How effective is this as a means of compliance?

4.   What are the goals articulated by the Security Council in creating the ICTY? Are these realistic goals? Are they consistent with the usual justifications for the applicability of the criminal law, such as retribution, deterrence, incapacitation or rehabilitation? Do those goals apply in the case of international prosecutions of government and military leaders acting to carry out a policy? Were there other goals at play here? What about assuaging guilt over not intervening more actively to stop the fighting or rescue civilians? Creating a precedent for international justice mechanisms? Avoiding placing collective blame on a people or ethnicity? Forestalling vigilante justice? Any others? Are these goals complementary or contradictory?

5.   The Statute of the ICTY includes four crimes, all of them already part of customary international law according to the Secretary–General's Report. They are grave breaches of the Geneva Conventions, other violations of the laws and customs of war, crimes against humanity, and genocide. Why was it important that these crimes were considered clearly prohibited in customary international law? Is there a problem with setting up a tribunal to judge crimes that occurred before the tribunal came into existence, by an organ that previously found that grave violations of humanitarian law have occurred? Or can any due process problems be dealt with through protection of defendants rights in the Statute and Rules of Procedure and Evidence? Those Rules basically incorporate the due process protections of Article 14 of the International Covenant on Civil and Political Rights.

6.   The first few years of the ICTY were rocky. The tribunal spent much of its time developing Rules of Procedure and Evidence, setting up its operations, and looking for money and political support. States, including the NATO forces which patrolled the territory after the 1995 Dayton Agreement, starting in December 1995, were reluctant to put troops at risk by arresting suspects; many on the tribunal's wanted list were seen at cafés and living quietly at home. The tribunal's early cases, in part for this reason, were small-time perpetrators who were found living in Germany (Tadić) or turned themselves in (Erdomović*). Over time, the Tribunal

---

* Erdemović turned himself in to an ABC news reporter.

improved its ability to apprehend the leaders and organizers of the war, including, in 2001, Slobodan Milosević, the former President of Serbia. Milosević was near the end of his 3–year trial when he died in detention in 2006. In 2008, the tribunal gained custody over Radovan Karadzić, former head of the so-called Bosnian Serb Republic. This leaves only one high-level commander, Ratko Mladić, at large as the Tribunal winds up its work. Between 1993 and 2009, the tribunal indicted 161 suspects, and held 86 trials, leading to 60 convictions and 11 acquittals.

7. *The relationship to national courts*: the Statute of the ICTY (like the ICTR, discussed below) gives the court primacy over national courts; this means that the ICTY gets to choose its cases, and to take cases away from the national courts if it so chooses. Initially, the ICTY distrusted national courts in the former Yugoslavia, considering them biased against defendants from other ethnic groups. It used its primacy power to impose "rules of the road" whereby national prosecutors had to check with the tribunal and get approval before starting local war crimes cases. This created bottlenecks and resentment. More recently, as the tribunal has wound down, both Bosnia and Serbia have created their own war crimes chambers, and Croatia has also tried a number of war crimes cases.

As the ICTY was barely getting underway, Hutu extremists in the tiny African country of Rwanda embarked on a genocidal campaign against the Tutsi minority and Hutus who opposed the campaign. Tensions between the two groups had been high for years, leading to a 1993 U.N.-brokered power-sharing accord. However, extreme Hutu nationalists opposed the accord; they organized anti-Tutsi militias and hate radio. When the president's plane was shot down in April 1994, violence erupted, leaving some 800,000 people dead within a four-month period. Most of the dead had been killed using machetes, hoes or other "low-tech" means that implied widespread popular participation in the crimes. The killing ended when Tutsi forces returned and drove the Hutu leadership and military into neighboring Congo. Congo eventually brought cases in the ICJ against Rwanda and Uganda for continuing armed cross-border actions. See Chapter 10. The Security Council, sensitive to criticism that it cared more about European dead than about Africans, in response created the International Criminal Tribunal for Rwanda in 1994. Its jurisdiction covered the year 1994 only.

While Rwanda, at the time a member of the Security Council, pushed hard for a tribunal, it voted against the final shape of the ICTR because it was based outside Rwanda (in Arusha, Tanzania). Moreover, it did not permit the death penalty, a punishment allowed under Rwandan law. The result for many years was that the "big fish" caught and sent to the ICTR were subject, at worst, to imprisonment, while the "little fish" tried by Rwandan courts could be executed. In 2007, as part of the effort to transfer remaining cases to Rwandan courts as the *ad hoc* Tribunals completed their work, Rwanda finally abolished its death penalty. The relationship between the Rwandan government and the ICTR has been problematic, with the government complaining about slow and ineffective prosecutions and disrespect of victims, but also using the ability to deny access to witnesses and evidence to avoid any investigation into the crimes of the Rwandan Patriotic Front, the military arm of the current government, during 1994.

The crimes encompassed by the ICTR Statute are similar, but not identical, to those of the ICTY. The two Tribunals share an appeals chamber, and until 2003, shared a chief prosecutor. They each consist of an Office of the Prosecutor, a registry which deals with administration and protection of victims and witnesses, and chambers of judges who sit in panels. They also share a set of Rules of Procedure and Evidence. Like the Statutes of the Tribunals, the Rules are an amalgam of common law and civil law. This has been challenging for the mix of common and civil-law lawyers practicing before the Tribunals. Along with the Statutes and Rules of the other international courts discussed below, they constitute the beginnings of an international criminal procedure.

One of the chief contributions of the *ad hoc* Tribunals, as mentioned at the beginning, has been their development of the meaning of the international crimes listed in their statutes: war crimes, crimes against humanity and genocide. Several useful digests exist of the Tribunals' work, including Human Rights Watch, http://www.hrw.org/reports/2004/ij/icty/index.htm. Websites including the Asser Institute in the Netherlands, http://www. asser.nl, and the International Committee for the Red Cross, http://www. icrc.org, provide useful databases on international humanitarian and criminal law more generally. Books summarizing the Tribunals' jurisprudence include RICHARD GOLDSTONE, FOR HUMANITY: REFLECTIONS OF A WAR CRIMES INVESTIGATOR (2000); MICHAEL P. SCHARF & VIRGINIA MORRIS, THE INTERNATIONAL CRIMINAL TRIBUNAL FOR RWANDA (2 vols.) (1998); MICHAEL SCHARF, BALKAN JUSTICE: THE STORY BEHIND THE FIRST INTERNATIONAL WAR CRIMES TRIAL SINCE NUREMBURG (1997); MICHAEL P. SCHARF & VIRGINIA MORRIS, AN INSIDER'S GUIDE TO THE INTERNATIONAL CRIMINAL TRIBUNAL FOR THE FORMER YUGOSLAVIA: A DOCUMENTARY HISTORY AND ANALYSIS (1995). The Tribunals are scheduled to finish their work, including appeals, by 2013, according to a letter from the President of the Tribunal to the President of the Security Council, dated May 14, 2009, S/2002/252.

The ICTR considered the definitions of genocide, crimes against humanity and war crimes in its first case.

The Prosecutor v. Jean–Paul Akayesu

International Criminal Tribunal for Rwanda
Case No. ICTR–96–4–T Judgment (Sept. 2, 1998)

* * *

The Accused

3.   Jean Paul AKAYESU, born in 1953 in Murehe sector, Taba commune, served as bourgmestre of that commune from April 1993 until June

1994. Prior to his appointment as bourgmestre, he was a teacher and school inspector in Taba.

4. As bourgmestre, Jean Paul AKAYESU was charged with the performance of executive functions and the maintenance of public order within his commune, subject to the authority of the prefect. He had exclusive control over the communal police, as well as any gendarmes put at the disposition of the commune. He was responsible for the execution of laws and regulations and the administration of justice, also subject only to the prefect's authority. * * *

Charges

12. As bourgmestre, Jean Paul AKAYESU was responsible for maintaining law and public order in his commune. At least 2000 Tutsis were killed in Taba between April 7 and the end of June, 1994, while he was still in power. The killings in Taba were openly committed and so widespread that, as bourgmestre, Jean Paul AKAYESU must have known about them. Although he had the authority and responsibility to do so, Jean Paul AKAYESU never attempted to prevent the killing of Tutsis in the commune in any way or called for assistance from regional or national authorities to quell the violence.

12A. Between April 7 and the end of June, 1994, hundreds of civilians (hereinafter "displaced civilians") sought refuge at the bureau communal. The majority of these displaced civilians were Tutsi. While seeking refuge at the bureau communal, female displaced civilians were regularly taken by armed local militia and/or communal police and subjected to sexual violence, and/or beaten on or near the bureau communal premises. Displaced civilians were also murdered frequently on or near the bureau communal premises. Many women were forced to endure multiple acts of sexual violence which were at times committed by more than one assailant. These acts of sexual violence were generally accompanied by explicit threats of death or bodily harm. The female displaced civilians lived in constant fear and their physical and psychological health deteriorated as a result of the sexual violence and beatings and killings.

12B. Jean Paul AKAYESU knew that the acts of sexual violence, beatings and murders were being committed and was at times present during their commission. Jean Paul AKAYESU facilitated the commission of the sexual violence, beatings and murders by allowing the sexual violence and beatings and murders to occur on or near the bureau communal premises. By virtue of his presence during the commission of the sexual violence, beatings and murders and by failing to prevent the sexual violence, beatings and murders, Jean Paul AKAYESU encouraged these activities ... [n.b. specific instances of killings, beatings and rape follow]. * * *

[Akayesu was charged with genocide, complicity in genocide, incitement of genocide, crimes against humanity (extermination, murder, torture), and war crimes, specifically violations of Common Article 3 of the Geneva Conventions which concern non-international armed conflict.]

[The definition of the crimes in the ICTR Statute:]

Article 2: Genocide

1. The International Tribunal for Rwanda shall have the power to prosecute persons committing genocide as defined in paragraph 2 of this article or of committing any of the other acts enumerated in paragraph 3 of this article.

2. Genocide means any of the following acts committed with intent to destroy, in whole or in part, a national, ethnical, racial or religious group, as such:

a) Killing members of the group;

b) Causing serious bodily or mental harm to members of the group;

c) Deliberately inflicting on the group conditions of life calculated to bring about its physical destruction in whole or in part

d) Imposing measures intended to prevent births within the group;

e) Forcibly transferring children of the group to another group.

3. The following acts shall be punishable:

a) Genocide;

b) Conspiracy to commit genocide;

c) Direct and public incitement to commit genocide;

d) Attempt to commit genocide;

e) Complicity in genocide.

Article 3: Crimes Against Humanity

The International Tribunal for Rwanda shall have the power to prosecute persons responsible for the following crimes when committed as part of a widespread or systematic attack against any civilian population on national, political, ethnic, racial or religious grounds:

a) Murder;

b) Extermination;

c) Enslavement;

d) Deportation;

e) Imprisonment;

f) Torture;

g) Rape;

h) Persecutions on political, racial and religious grounds;

i) Other inhumane acts.

Article 4: Violations of Article 3 common to the Geneva Conventions and of Additional Protocol II

The International Tribunal for Rwanda shall have the power to prosecute persons committing or ordering to be committed serious violations of Article 3 common to the Geneva Conventions of 12 August 1949 for the Protection of War Victims, and of Additional Protocol II thereto of 8 June 1977. These violations shall include, but shall not be limited to:

a) Violence to life, health and physical or mental well-being of persons, in particular murder as well as cruel treatment such as torture, mutilation or any form of corporal punishment;

b) Collective punishments;

c) Taking of hostages;

d) Acts of terrorism;

e) Outrages upon personal dignity, in particular humiliating and degrading treatment, rape, enforced prostitution and any form of indecent assault;

f) Pillage;

g) The passing of sentences and the carrying out of executions without previous judgment pronounced by a regularly constituted court, affording all the judicial guarantees which are recognised as indispensable by civilised peoples;

h) Threats to commit any of the foregoing acts.

8. In addition, Article 6 states the principle of individual criminal responsibility:

Article 6: Individual Criminal Responsibility

1. A person who planned, instigated, ordered, committed or otherwise aided and abetted in the planning, preparation or execution of a crime referred to in articles 2 to 4 of the present Statute, shall be individually responsible for the crime.

2. The official position of any accused person, whether as Head of State or Government or as a responsible Government official, shall not relieve such person of criminal responsibility nor mitigate punishment.

3. The fact that any of the acts referred to in articles 2 to 4 of the present Statute was committed by a subordinate does not relieve his or her superior of criminal responsibility if he or she knew or had reason to know that the subordinate was about to commit such acts or had done so and the superior failed to take the necessary and reasonable measures to prevent such acts or to punish the perpetrators thereof.

4. The fact that an accused person acted pursuant to an order of a Government or of a superior shall not relieve him or her of criminal responsibility, but may be considered in mitigation of punishment if the International Tribunal for Rwanda determines that justice so requires.
* * *

2.   Historical Context of the Events in Rwanda in 1994

78.   It is the opinion of the Chamber that, in order to understand the events alleged in the Indictment, it is necessary to say, however briefly, something about the history of Rwanda, beginning from the pre-colonial period up to 1994.

79.   Rwanda is a small, very hilly country in the Great Lakes region of Central Africa. Before the events of 1994, it was the most densely populated country of the African continent (7.1 million inhabitants for 26,338 square kilometres). Ninety per cent of the population lives on agriculture. Its per capita income is among the lowest in the world, mainly because of a very high population pressure on land.

80.   Prior to and during colonial rule, first, under Germany, from about 1897, and then under Belgium which, after driving out Germany in 1917, was given a mandate by the League of Nations to administer it, Rwanda was a complex and an advanced monarchy. The monarch ruled the country through his official representatives drawn from the Tutsi nobility. Thus, there emerged a highly sophisticated political culture which enabled the king to communicate with the people.

81.   Rwanda then, admittedly, had some eighteen clans defined primarily along lines of kinship. The terms Hutu and Tutsi were already in use but referred to individuals rather than to groups. In those days, the distinction between the Hutu and Tutsi was based on lineage rather than ethnicity. Indeed, the demarcation line was blurred: one could move from one status to another, as one became rich or poor, or even through marriage.

82.   Both German and Belgian colonial authorities, if only at the outset as far as the latter are concerned, relied on an elite essentially composed of people who referred to themselves as Tutsi, a choice which, according to Dr. Alison Desforges, was born of racial or even racist considerations. In the minds of the colonizers, the Tutsi looked more like them, because of their height and colour, and were, therefore, more intelligent and better equipped to govern.

83.   In the early 1930s, Belgian authorities introduced a permanent distinction by dividing the population into three groups which they called ethnic groups, with the Hutu representing about 84% of the population, while the Tutsi (about 15%) and Twa (about 1%) accounted for the rest. In line with this division, it became mandatory for every Rwandan to carry an identity card mentioning his or her ethnicity. The Chamber notes that the reference to ethnic background on identity cards was maintained, even after Rwanda's independence and was, at last, abolished only after the tragic events the country experienced in 1994. * * *

3.   Genocide in Rwanda in 1994?

* * *

118.   In the opinion of the Chamber, there is no doubt that considering their undeniable scale, their systematic nature and their atrociousness, the massacres were aimed at exterminating the group that was targeted. Many facts show that the intention of the perpetrators of these killings was to cause the complete disappearance of the Tutsi. In this connection, Alison Desforges, an expert witness, in her testimony before this Chamber on 25 February 1997, stated as follows: "on the basis of the statements made by certain political leaders, on the basis of songs and slogans popular among the Interahamwe, I believe that these people had the intention of completely wiping out the Tutsi from Rwanda so that—as they said on certain occasions—their children, later on, would not know what a Tutsi looked like, unless they referred to history books". Moreover, this testimony given by Dr. Desforges was confirmed by two prosecution witnesses, witness KK and witness OO, who testified separately before the Tribunal that one Silas Kubwimana had said during a public meeting chaired by the accused himself that all the Tutsi had to be killed so that someday Hutu children would not know what a Tutsi looked like.

119.   Furthermore, as mentioned above, Dr. Zachariah also testified that the Achilles' tendons of many wounded persons were cut to prevent them from fleeing. In the opinion of the Chamber, this demonstrates the resolve of the perpetrators of these massacres not to spare any Tutsi. Their plan called for doing whatever was possible to prevent any Tutsi from escaping and, thus, to destroy the whole group. Witness OO further told the Chamber that during the same meeting, a certain Ruvugama, who was then a Member of Parliament, had stated that he would rest only when no single Tutsi is left in Rwanda.

120.   Dr. Alison Desforges testified that many Tutsi bodies were often systematically thrown into the Nyabarongo river, a tributary of the Nile. Indeed, this has been corroborated by several images shown to the Chamber throughout the trial. She explained that the underlying intention of this act was to "send the Tutsi back to their place of origin", to "make them return to Abyssinia", in keeping with the allegation that the Tutsi are foreigners in Rwanda, where they are supposed to have settled following their arrival from the Nilotic regions.

122.   In light of the foregoing, it is now appropriate for the Chamber to consider the issue of specific intent that is required for genocide (mens rea or dolus specialis). In other words, it should be established that the above-mentioned acts were targeted at a particular group as such. In this respect also, many consistent and reliable testimonies, especially those of Major–General Dallaire, Dr. Zachariah, victim V, prosecution witness PP, defence witness DAAX, and particularly that of the accused himself unanimously agree on the fact that it was the Tutsi as members of an ethnic group which they formed in the context of the period in question, who were targeted during the massacres.

123.   Two facts, in particular, which suggest that it was indeed the Tutsi who were targeted should be highlighted: Firstly, at the roadblocks which were erected in Kigali immediately after the crash of the President's

plane on 6 April 1994 and, later on, in most of the country's localities, members of the Tutsi population were sorted out. Indeed, at these road-blocks which were manned, depending on the situation, either by soldiers, troops of the Presidential Guard and/or militiamen, the systematic check-ing of identity cards indicating the ethnic group of their holders, allowed the separation of Hutu from Tutsi, with the latter being immediately apprehended and killed, sometimes on the spot. Secondly, the propaganda campaign conducted before and during the tragedy by the audiovisual media, for example, "Radio Television des Milles Collines" (RTLM), or the print media, like the Kangura newspaper. These various news media overtly called for the killing of Tutsi, who were considered as the accom-plices of the RPF and accused of plotting to take over the power lost during the revolution of 1959. . . .

124.   In the opinion of the Chamber, all this proves that it was indeed a particular group, the Tutsi ethnic group, which was targeted. Clearly, the victims were not chosen as individuals but, indeed, because they belonged to said group; and hence the victims were members of this group selected as such. According to Alison Desforges's testimony, the Tutsi were killed solely on account of having been born Tutsi.

125.   Clearly therefore, the massacres which occurred in Rwanda in 1994 had a specific objective, namely the extermination of the Tutsi, who were targeted especially because of their Tutsi origin and not because they were RPF fighters. In any case, the Tutsi children and pregnant women would, naturally, not have been among the fighters.

126.   Consequently, the Chamber concludes from all the foregoing that genocide was, indeed, committed in Rwanda in 1994 against the Tutsi as a group. * * *

498.   Genocide is distinct from other crimes inasmuch as it embodies a special intent or dolus specialis. Special intent of a crime is the specific intention, required as a constitutive element of the crime, which demands that the perpetrator clearly seeks to produce the act charged. Thus, the special intent in the crime of genocide lies in "the intent to destroy, in whole or in part, a national, ethnical, racial or religious group, as such".

499.   Thus, for a crime of genocide to have been committed, it is necessary that one of the acts listed under Article 2(2) of the Statute be committed, that the particular act be committed against a specifically targeted group, it being a national, ethnical, racial or religious group. Consequently, in order to clarify the constitutive elements of the crime of genocide, the Chamber will first state its findings on the acts provided for under Article 2(2)(a) through Article 2(2)(e) of the Statute, the groups protected by the Genocide Convention, and the special intent or dolus specialis necessary for genocide to take place.

Killing members of the group (paragraph (a)):

500.   With regard to Article 2(2)(a) of the Statute, like in the Genocide Convention, the Chamber notes that the said paragraph states "meurtre"

in the French version while the English version states "killing". The Trial Chamber is of the opinion that the term "killing" used in the English version is too general, since it could very well include both intentional and unintentional homicides, whereas the term "meurtre", used in the French version, is more precise. It is accepted that there is murder when death has been caused with the intention to do so, as provided for, incidentally, in the Penal Code of Rwanda which stipulates in its Article 311 that "Homicide committed with intent to cause death shall be treated as murder".

* * *

Causing serious bodily or mental harm to members of the group (paragraph b)

502.   Causing serious bodily or mental harm to members of the group does not necessarily mean that the harm is permanent and irremediable.

503.   In the Adolf Eichmann case, who was convicted of crimes against the Jewish people, genocide under another legal definition, the District Court of Jerusalem stated in its judgment of 12 December 1961, that serious bodily or mental harm of members of the group can be caused

"by the enslavement, starvation, deportation and persecution [. . .] and by their detention in ghettos, transit camps and concentration camps in conditions which were designed to cause their degradation, deprivation of their rights as human beings, and to suppress them and cause them inhumane suffering and torture".

504.   For purposes of interpreting Article 2(2)(b) of the Statute, the Chamber takes serious bodily or mental harm, without limiting itself thereto, to mean acts of torture, be they bodily or mental, inhumane or degrading treatment, persecution. Deliberately inflicting on the group conditions of life calculated to bring about its physical destruction in whole or in part (paragraph c):

505.   The Chamber holds that the expression deliberately inflicting on the group conditions of life calculated to bring about its physical destruction in whole or in part, should be construed as the methods of destruction by which the perpetrator does not immediately kill the members of the group, but which, ultimately, seek their physical destruction.

506.   For purposes of interpreting Article 2(2)(c) of the Statute, the Chamber is of the opinion that the means of deliberate inflicting on the group conditions of life calculated to bring about its physical destruction, in whole or part, include, inter alia, subjecting a group of people to a subsistence diet, systematic expulsion from homes and the reduction of essential medical services below minimum requirement.

Imposing measures intended to prevent births within the group (paragraph d):

507.   For purposes of interpreting Article 2(2)(d) of the Statute, the Chamber holds that the measures intended to prevent births within the group, should be construed as sexual mutilation, the practice of sterilization, forced birth control, separation of the sexes and prohibition of

marriages. In patriarchal societies, where membership of a group is determined by the identity of the father, an example of a measure intended to prevent births within a group is the case where, during rape, a woman of the said group is deliberately impregnated by a man of another group, with the intent to have her give birth to a child who will consequently not belong to its mother's group.

508.   Furthermore, the Chamber notes that measures intended to prevent births within the group may be physical, but can also be mental. For instance, rape can be a measure intended to prevent births when the person raped refuses subsequently to procreate, in the same way that members of a group can be led, through threats or trauma, not to procreate.

Forcibly transferring children of the group to another group (paragraph e)

509.   With respect to forcibly transferring children of the group to another group, the Chamber is of the opinion that, as in the case of measures intended to prevent births, the objective is not only to sanction a direct act of forcible physical transfer, but also to sanction acts of threats or trauma which would lead to the forcible transfer of children.

510.   Since the special intent to commit genocide lies in the intent to "destroy, in whole or in part, a national, ethnical, racial or religious group, as such", it is necessary to consider a definition of the group as such. Article 2 of the Statute, just like the Genocide Convention, stipulates four types of victim groups, namely national, ethnical, racial or religious groups.

511.   On reading through the travaux préparatoires of the Genocide Convention, it appears that the crime of genocide was allegedly perceived as targeting only "stable" groups, constituted in a permanent fashion and membership of which is determined by birth, with the exclusion of the more "mobile" groups which one joins through individual voluntary commitment, such as political and economic groups. Therefore, a common criterion in the four types of groups protected by the Genocide Convention is that membership in such groups would seem to be normally not challengeable by its members, who belong to it automatically, by birth, in a continuous and often irremediable manner.

512.   Based on the Nottebohm decision rendered by the International Court of Justice, the Chamber holds that a national group is defined as a collection of people who are perceived to share a legal bond based on common citizenship, coupled with reciprocity of rights and duties.

513.   An ethnic group is generally defined as a group whose members share a common language or culture.

514.   The conventional definition of racial group is based on the hereditary physical traits often identified with a geographical region, irrespective of linguistic, cultural, national or religious factors.

515.   The religious group is one whose members share the same religion, denomination or mode of worship.

516.   Moreover, the Chamber considered whether the groups protected by the Genocide Convention, echoed in Article 2 of the Statute, should be limited to only the four groups expressly mentioned and whether they should not also include any group which is stable and permanent like the said four groups. In other words, the question that arises is whether it would be impossible to punish the physical destruction of a group as such under the Genocide Convention, if the said group, although stable and membership is by birth, does not meet the definition of any one of the four groups expressly protected by the Genocide Convention. In the opinion of the Chamber, it is particularly important to respect the intention of the drafters of the Genocide Convention, which according to the travaux préparatoires, was patently to ensure the protection of any stable and permanent group. * * *

520.   With regard to the crime of genocide, the offender is culpable only when he has committed one of the offences charged under Article 2(2) of the Statute with the clear intent to destroy, in whole or in part, a particular group. The offender is culpable because he knew or should have known that the act committed would destroy, in whole or in part, a group.

521.   In concrete terms, for any of the acts charged under Article 2 (2) of the Statute to be a constitutive element of genocide, the act must have been committed against one or several individuals, because such individual or individuals were members of a specific group, and specifically because they belonged to this group. Thus, the victim is chosen not because of his individual identity, but rather on account of his membership of a national, ethnical, racial or religious group. The victim of the act is therefore a member of a group, chosen as such, which, hence, means that the victim of the crime of genocide is the group itself and not only the individual.

522.   The perpetration of the act charged therefore extends beyond its actual commission, for example, the murder of a particular individual, for the realisation of an ulterior motive, which is to destroy, in whole or part, the group of which the individual is just one element.

523.   On the issue of determining the offender's specific intent, the Chamber considers that intent is a mental factor which is difficult, even impossible, to determine. This is the reason why, in the absence of a confession from the accused, his intent can be inferred from a certain number of presumptions of fact. The Chamber considers that it is possible to deduce the genocidal intent inherent in a particular act charged from the general context of the perpetration of other culpable acts systematically directed against that same group, whether these acts were committed by the same offender or by others. Other factors, such as the scale of atrocities committed, their general nature, in a region or a country, or furthermore, the fact of deliberately and systematically targeting victims on account of their membership of a particular group, while excluding the members of other groups, can enable the Chamber to infer the genocidal intent of a particular act.

524. Trial Chamber I of the International Criminal Tribunal for the former Yugoslavia also stated that the specific intent of the crime of genocide

"may be inferred from a number of facts such as the general political doctrine which gave rise to the acts possibly covered by the definition in Article 4, or the repetition of destructive and discriminatory acts. The intent may also be inferred from the perpetration of acts which violate, or which the perpetrators themselves consider to violate the very foundation of the group—acts which are not in themselves covered by the list in Article 4(2) but which are committed as part of the same pattern of conduct".

Thus, in the matter brought before the International Criminal Tribunal for the former Yugoslavia, the Trial Chamber, in its findings, found that

"this intent derives from the combined effect of speeches or projects laying the groundwork for and justifying the acts, from the massive scale of their destructive effect and from their specific nature, which aims at undermining what is considered to be the foundation of the group". * * *

702. In the light of the facts brought to its attention during the trial, the Chamber is of the opinion that, in Rwanda in 1994, the Tutsi constituted a group referred to as "ethnic" in official classifications. Thus, the identity cards at the time included a reference to "ubwoko" in Kinyarwanda or "ethnie" (ethnic group) in French which, depending on the case, referred to the designation Hutu or Tutsi, for example. The Chamber further noted that all the Rwandan witnesses who appeared before it invariably answered spontaneously and without hesitation the questions of the Prosecutor regarding their ethnic identity. Accordingly, the Chamber finds that, in any case, at the time of the alleged events, the Tutsi did indeed constitute a stable and permanent group and were identified as such by all. * * *

Crimes against Humanity—Historical development

563. Crimes against humanity were recognized in the Charter and Judgment of the Nuremberg Tribunal, as well as in Law No. 10 of the Control Council for Germany. * * *

565. Crimes against humanity are aimed at any civilian population and are prohibited regardless of whether they are committed in an armed conflict, international or internal in character. In fact, the concept of crimes against humanity had been recognised long before Nuremberg. On 28 May 1915, the Governments of France, Great Britain and Russia made a declaration regarding the massacres of the Armenian population in Turkey, denouncing them as "crimes against humanity and civilisation for which all the members of the Turkish government will be held responsible together with its agents implicated in the massacres". The 1919 Report of the Commission on the Responsibility of the Authors of the War and on Enforcement of Penalties formulated by representatives from several States

and presented to the Paris Peace Conference also referred to "offences against ... the laws of humanity". * * *

566. These World War I notions derived, in part, from the Martens clause of the Hague Convention (IV) of 1907, which referred to "the usages established among civilised peoples, from the laws of humanity, and the dictates of the public conscience". In 1874, George Curtis called slavery a "crime against humanity". Other such phrases as "crimes against mankind" and "crimes against the human family" appear far earlier in human history (see 12 N.Y.L. Sch. J. Hum. Rts. 545 (1995)).

567. The Chamber notes that, following the Nuremberg and Tokyo trials, the concept of crimes against humanity underwent a gradual evolution in the *Eichmann, Barbie, Touvier and Papon* cases. * * *

577. Article 7 of the Statute of the International Criminal Court defines a crime against humanity as any of the enumerated acts committed as part of a widespread or systematic attack directed against any civilian population, with knowledge of the attack. These enumerated acts are murder; extermination; enslavement; deportation or forcible transfer of population; imprisonment or other severe deprivation of physical liberty in violation of fundamental rules of international law; torture; rape, sexual slavery, enforced prostitution, forced pregnancy, enforced sterilization, or any other form of sexual violence of comparable gravity; persecution against any identifiable group or collectively on political, racial, national, ethnic, cultural, religious, gender or other grounds that are universally recognised as impermissible under international law, in connection with any act referred to in this article or any other crime within the jurisdiction of the Court; enforced disappearance of persons; the crime of apartheid; other inhumane acts of a similar character intentionally causing great suffering, or serious injury to body or mental or physical health.

Crimes against Humanity in Article 3 of the Statute of the Tribunal

578. The Chamber considers that Article 3 of the Statute confers on the Chamber the jurisdiction to prosecute persons for various inhumane acts which constitute crimes against humanity. This category of crimes may be broadly broken down into four essential elements, namely:

> (i) the act must be inhumane in nature and character, causing great suffering, or serious injury to body or to mental or physical health;

> (ii) the act must be committed as part of a wide spread or systematic attack;

> (iii) the act must be committed against members of the civilian population;

> (iv) the act must be committed on one or more discriminatory grounds, namely, national, political, ethnic, racial or religious grounds.

The act must be committed as part of a wide spread or systematic attack.

579. The Chamber considers that it is a prerequisite that the act must be committed as part of a wide spread or systematic attack and not

just a random act of violence. The act can be part of a widespread or systematic attack and need not be a part of both.

580.   The concept of "widespread" may be defined as massive, frequent, large scale action, carried out collectively with considerable seriousness and directed against a multiplicity of victims. The concept of "systematic" may be defined as thoroughly organised and following a regular pattern on the basis of a common policy involving substantial public or private resources. There is no requirement that this policy must be adopted formally as the policy of a state. There must however be some kind of preconceived plan or policy.

581.   The concept of "attack" maybe defined as a unlawful act of the kind enumerated in Article 3(a) to (i) of the Statute, like murder, extermination, enslavement etc. An attack may also be non violent in nature, like imposing a system of apartheid, which is declared a crime against humanity in Article 1 of the Apartheid Convention of 1973, or exerting pressure on the population to act in a particular manner, may come under the purview of an attack, if orchestrated on a massive scale or in a systematic manner.

The act must be directed against the civilian population

582.   The Chamber considers that an act must be directed against the civilian population if it is to constitute a crime against humanity. Members of the civilian population are people who are not taking any active part in the hostilities, including members of the armed forces who laid down their arms and those persons placed *hors de combat* by sickness, wounds, detention or any other cause. Where there are certain individuals within the civilian population who do not come within the definition of civilians, this does not deprive the population of its civilian character.

* * *

Applicability of Common Article 3 and Additional Protocol II

601.   The four 1949 Geneva Conventions and the 1977 Additional Protocol I thereto generally apply to international armed conflicts only, whereas Article 3 common to the Geneva Conventions extends a minimum threshold of humanitarian protection as well to all persons affected by a non-international conflict, a protection which was further developed and enhanced in the 1977 Additional Protocol II. In the field of international humanitarian law, a clear distinction as to the thresholds of application has been made between situations of international armed conflicts, in which the law of armed conflicts is applicable as a whole, situations of non-international (internal) armed conflicts, where Common Article 3 and Additional Protocol II are applicable, and non-international armed conflicts where only Common Article 3 is applicable. Situations of internal disturbances are not covered by international humanitarian law.

602.   The distinction pertaining to situations of conflicts of a non-international character emanates from the differing intensity of the conflicts. Such distinction is inherent to the conditions of applicability specified for Common Article 3 or Additional Protocol II respectively. Common

Article 3 applies to "armed conflicts not of an international character", whereas for a conflict to fall within the ambit of Additional Protocol II, it must "take place in the territory of a High Contracting Party between its armed forces and dissident armed forces or other organized armed groups which, under responsible command, exercise such control over a part of its territory as to enable them to carry out sustained and concerted military operations and to implement this Protocol". Additional Protocol II does not in itself establish a criterion for a non-international conflict, rather it merely develops and supplements the rules contained in Common Article 3 without modifying its conditions of application.

603. It should be stressed that the ascertainment of the intensity of a non-international conflict does not depend on the subjective judgment of the parties to the conflict. It should be recalled that the four Geneva Conventions, as well as the two Protocols, were adopted primarily to protect the victims, as well as potential victims, of armed conflicts. If the application of international humanitarian law depended solely on the discretionary judgment of the parties to the conflict, in most cases there would be a tendency for the conflict to be minimized by the parties thereto. Thus, on the basis of objective criteria, both Common Article 3 and Additional Protocol II will apply once it has been established there exists an internal armed conflict which fulfills their respective pre-determined criteria. * * *

608. It is today clear that the norms of Common Article 3 have acquired the status of customary law in that most States, by their domestic penal codes, have criminalized acts which if committed during internal armed conflict, would constitute violations of Common Article 3. It was also held by the ICTY Trial Chamber in the Tadic judgment that Article 3 of the ICTY Statute (Customs of War), being the body of customary international humanitarian law not covered by Articles 2, 4, and 5 of the ICTY Statute, included the regime of protection established under Common Article 3 applicable to armed conflicts not of an international character. This was in line with the view of the ICTY Appeals Chamber stipulating that Common Article 3 beyond doubt formed part of customary international law, and further that there exists a corpus of general principles and norms on internal armed conflict embracing Common Article 3 but having a much greater scope. * * *

609. However, as aforesaid, Additional Protocol II as a whole was not deemed by the Secretary–General to have been universally recognized as part of customary international law. The Appeals Chamber concurred with this view inasmuch as "[m]any provisions of this Protocol [II] can now be regarded as declaratory of existing rules or as having crystallised in emerging rules of customary law[ ]", but not all.

610. Whilst the Chamber is very much of the same view as pertains to Additional Protocol II as a whole, it should be recalled that the relevant Article in the context of the ICTR is Article 4(2) (Fundamental Guarantees) of Additional Protocol II. All of the guarantees, as enumerated in Article 4 reaffirm and supplement Common Article 3 and, as discussed above,

Common Article 3 being customary in nature, the Chamber is of the opinion that these guarantees did also at the time of the events alleged in the Indictment form part of existing international customary law.

[The Chamber went on to apply these definitions to the acts described in the indictments, as proven, and found Akayesu guilty of genocide; direct and public inducement to commit genocide and the crimes against humanity of extermination, murder, torture, rape and other inhuman acts. He was found not guilty of complicity in genocide and violations of the Geneval Convention. He was sentenced to life in prison.

NOTES AND QUESTIONS

1.   What is it about the targeting of national, racial, ethnic or religious groups for physical destruction that makes genocide a particularly heinous crime, the "crime of crimes?"

2.   In *Prosecutor v. Kristic*, the ICTY Appeals Chamber added a gloss to the elements of the crime: "It is well established that where a conviction for genocide relies on the intent to destroy a protected group 'in part,' the part must be a substantial part of that group. The aim of the Genocide Convention is to prevent the intentional destruction of entire human groups, and the part targeted must be significant enough to have an impact on the group as a whole...." *Kristic*, paras. 8–13.

3.   Could you prosecute the following as genocide?:

   a.   The deliberate killing of women, especially educated women, in Afghanistan?

   b.   The killing (or forcing into isolated camps) of HIV-positive persons?

   c.   The massive enforced disappearance of between 10,000 and 30,000 persons in Argentina in the mid 1970s?

   d.   The killing of over a million Cambodians, especially the middle class, the educated, or those wearing eye-glasses? See Hurst Hannum, *International Law and Cambodian Genocide: the Sounds of Silence*, 11 HUM. R. Q. 82 (1989). The Statute of the Extraordinary Chambers in the Courts of Cambodia (discussed below) includes the crime of genocide.

Is it sensible to limit the protected groups to national, ethnic[al], racial and religious groups? To stable and permanent groups? Are nationality or religion clearly permanent groups, if it's possible to change both? Should the definition depend on what the victim, or the perpetrator, defines as the relevant group? The jurisprudence talks about both an objective and a subjective element.

   Is this a reasonable limitation or a reflection of the post-Holocaust drafting history of the Genocide Convention? Or worse, an attempt to garner Soviet support for the Convention by excluding political or class-based groups like the *kulacs* and to ensure U.S. support by excluding cultural genocide? The drafting history of the Genocide Convention shows that political groups were covered to almost the end of the drafting process. Does your answer depend on whether prosecution for crimes against humanity is an option? See WILLIAM A. SCHABAS, GENOCIDE IN INTERNATIONAL LAW: THE CRIMES OF CRIMES, (2000); Beth Van Schaack, *The Definition of Crimes Against Humanity: Resolving the Incoherence*, 787 J. OF TRANS. L. & POL. 37, 1999. Some national courts have expanded the definition of genocide, often based on their own form of incorporation of the Convention definition into national law. See the broad definition of a "national group" in the Spanish cases applying Spain's universal jurisdiction law, e.g. *Chile (Pinochet and others) Case*, Nov. 5, 1998, available in English in Brody and Ratner, eds., THE PINOCHET PAPERS: THE CASE OF AUGUSTO PINOCHET IN SPAIN AND BRITAIN, (the Hague: Kluwer Law International, 2000) The drafting history of the Convention also makes clear that cultural destruction of groups, through assimilation or through destruction of their homeland, is not encompassed in the Convention definition. Should it be? What about protection of indigenous groups? See the U.N. Declaration on the Rights of Indigenous Peoples, G.A. Res. 61/295, U.N. Doc. A/RES/61/295, 13 Sept. 2007.

4. *Crimes Against Humanity*. Unlike war crimes and genocide, the London Charter creating the IMT was not followed by a specific convention defining crimes against humanity and their punishment in greater detail until 1998. Article 6(c) of the IMT, and its analogue in Control Council Law No. 10, formed the basis for modern definitions. Through interpretation in U.N. Resolutions and Principles, in national law and, eventually, in the Statutes of the ICTY and ICTR, the modern core of crimes against humanity emerged. The definition of crimes against humanity differs in the ICTY and ICTR based on differences in the contexts. The ICTY definition requires a nexus to armed conflict, although the jurisprudence of the Tribunal clarifies that this is a jurisdictional limitation, not part of the substantive definition of the offense. The ICTR definition requires no link to armed conflict, but does limit prosecution to offenses committed on national, political, ethnic, racial or religious grounds. Except in the context of the ICTR, there is no specific intent that the offenses be committed on persecutory grounds of any kind. One of the predicate crimes, however, is "persecution", and that crime does have such an intent.

5. Traditionally rape could be prosecuted as the war crime of unlawful violence against civilians. The *ad hoc* tribunals separated it out, defined it in international law, and made clear that rape and other forms of sexual violence can under the appropriate circumstances constitute a crime against humanity or even genocide as well as a war crime. See Kelly D. Askin, *Prosecuting Wartime Rape and Other Gender–Related Crimes Under International Law: Extraordinary Advances, Enduring Obstacles*, 21 Berkeley Journal of International Law 288 (2003); Patricia Viseur Sellers, *Sexual Violence and Peremptory Norms: The Legal Value of Rape*, 34 Case Western Reserve Journal of International Law 287 (2002).

2. BEYOND THE AD HOC TRIBUNALS: MIXED TRIBUNALS AND THE INTERNATIONAL CRIMINAL COURT

As mentioned at the beginning of this chapter, the ICTY and ICTR, despite their many achievements, also had some significant limitations.

They were set up during or after the conflicts, giving rise to due process challenges. Worse, they were set up by a political body, the Security Council, which has ignored equally (or more) heinous crimes elsewhere. They were expensive, slow, and remote. They did little or nothing to improve national legal systems or to train those from the territorial state who would have to do justice once the Tribunals dissolved. And they were often opaque and inaccessible to victims.

A number of responses emerged from these critiques. In an effort to reduce costs, leave a more permanent national legacy and reduce remoteness, the U.N. worked with governments or interim U.N. administrations in Sierra Leone, East Timor and Cambodia to create mixed (or hybrid) courts that sit mostly in-country and are composed of both national and international judges and staff. At the same time, countries stepped up work on a permanent International Criminal Court that would be available for any new situations of mass atrocity. And a number of states began using their authority under domestic and international law to bring prosecutions in their national courts, some of them based on universal jurisdiction. For example, the Spanish courts opened new investigations into crimes committed in Guatemala, El Salvador, Tibet, Gaza, Rwanda and elsewhere. Other national courts, especially in Peru, Chile and Argentina, overcame early domestic amnesty laws to hold high-ranking government officials (like Peruvian ex-President Fujimori, convicted in 2009) responsible for widespread or systematic crimes.

a.   MIXED OR HYBRID TRIBUNALS

Courts combining domestic and international personnel, law and location have been established to deal with international crimes committed in Sierra Leone, Kosovo, East Timor, and Cambodia. The Special Court for Sierra Leone (SCSL) was established in 2002 as the result of an agreement between the government and the U.N. to prosecute "persons who bear the greatest responsibility" for violations of international humanitarian law and Sierra Leonean law stemming from an armed conflict that lasted from 1991 to 2002. It held three major trials against groups of defendants from various factions (including both the rebels and government-aligned forces); a fourth trial, against former Liberian President Charles Taylor, who is accused of intervening in the conflict, is now underway.

The U.N. administration that ran Kosovo after the 1999 NATO intervention created mixed judicial panels due to the lack of trained local jurists and the ICTY's inability to handle all but a few cases. The Panels applied a mix of international and local law, and consisted of a majority of international judges sitting with Kosovar counterparts in war crimes trials. In East Timor as well, the U.N. administered the territory after a referendum on independence from Indonesia in 1999 led to an Indonesian campaign of destruction and terror. The U.N. administration set up three-judge panels composed of a majority of foreign judges, who heard cases of violations of international humanitarian law investigated by a Special Crimes unit. The Panels operated from 2000 until 2005, handing down sentences for crimes against humanity in 84 cases. Unfortunately, the success of the Panels was limited because most of those "most responsible" for the violations had fled to Indonesia, and the Indonesian government refused to extradite them or to conduct more than a handful of not-very-credible trials of its own.

After many years of negotiation, in 2003 the UN and the government of Cambodia forged agreement on a mixed tribunal to prosecute the remaining leadership of the Khmer Rouge, accused of creating a regime that murdered up to two million Cambodians between 1975 and 1979. The Extraordinary Chambers in the Courts of Cambodia have one national and one international co-prosecutor and a mixture of local and foreign judges; unlike the East Timor and Kosovo panels, the Cambodian version features a majority of Cambodian judges and staff. The ECCC's first trial got underway in 2009, although it is unclear how many defendants it will be able to try. The ECCC has also been particularly plagued by allegations of corruption and political interference from the government.

Finally, in 2007 the Security Council and the government of Lebanon agreed to set up a Special Tribunal for Lebanon is to prosecute persons responsible for the attack of 14 February 2005 resulting in the death of former Prime Minister Rafiq Hariri and in the death or injury of other persons. The Tribunal's jurisdiction could be extended beyond the bombing if the Tribunal finds that other attacks that occurred in Lebanon between 1 October 2004 and 12 December 2005 are connected to the bombing, and beyond 2005 if the government so requests. The Special Tribunal will apply national law but be an international entity, with a mix of Lebanese and foreign judges, an international Prosecutor and Registrar, and half the budget paid by the Lebanese government. It is, as of this writing, in pre-trial proceedings. Also notable, as a quasi mixed-tribunal effort is the Commission Against Impunity in Guatemala (CICIG), which combines international and local investigators and prosecutors preparing cases for the Guatemalan Attorney General's office to prosecute in the national courts. The CICIG acts as a supplementary prosecutor and can also recommend changes in practice and procedure to fight continued impunity.

Laura Dickinson, The Promise of Hybrid Courts
97 Am.J. Int'l L. 295 (2003)

In Kosovo and East Timor, the addition of international judges and prosecutors to cases involving serious human rights abuses may have enhanced the perceived legitimacy of the process, at least to some degree. In both contexts, the initial failure of UN authorities to consult with the local population in making governance decisions generally, and decisions about the judiciary specifically, sparked public outcry. Without normal political processes in place, of course, such consultation is inherently difficult. When no elected officials exist to give advice, and civil society is badly damaged by years of oppression and conflict, it is not at all clear precisely which people should be consulted without creating impressions of bias. Thus, in both Kosovo and East Timor the appointment of foreign judges to domestic courts to sit alongside local judges and the appointment of foreign prosecutors to team up with local prosecutors helped to create a framework for consultation that may have enhanced the general perception of the institution's legitimacy. . . .

The appointment of international judges to the local courts in these highly sensitive cases may also have helped to enhance the perception of the independence of the judiciary and therefore its legitimacy within a broad cross-section of the local population. . . .

The sharing of responsibilities among local and international officials is not a complete cure for legitimacy problems, of course. Indeed, such hybrid relationships can raise new questions about who is really controlling the process. . . .

The hybrid process offers advantages in the arena of capacity-building as well. The side-by-side working arrangements allow for on-the-job training that is likely to be more effective than abstract classroom discussions of formal legal rules and principles. And the teamwork can allow for sharing of experiences and knowledge in both directions. International actors have the opportunity to gain greater sensitivity to local issues, local culture, and local approaches to justice at the same time that local actors can learn from international actors. In addition, hybrid courts can serve as a locus for international funding efforts, thereby pumping needed funds into the rebuilding of local infrastructure.

To be sure, hybrid courts also face difficulties in capacity-building. A lack of resources has proven to be the most serious problem so far. . . .

With respect to the penetration and development of the norms of international humanitarian law, hybrid courts potentially offer still further benefits. Because the personnel of such institutions include both international and domestic judges, the opportunities are much greater for the cross-fertilization of international and domestic norms regarding accountability for mass atrocity. In a sense, the hybrid courts themselves create a network of international and domestic legal professionals, providing a setting in which they can interact, share experiences, and discuss the relevant norms, both in and out of the courtroom. * * *

NOTES AND QUESTIONS

1.   Dickinson postulates that these tribunals may increase legitimacy, capacity-building and uptake of international law norms, but that they suffer from resource problems. The resource challenges have been severe, since unlike the ICTY and ICTR the mixed tribunals have relied on voluntary funds. Compare the budget of the ICTR, $267 million for 2008, with the $36 million budget of the SCSL for the same year, and yet the Special Court has had a hard time recruiting personnel and carrying out investigations for lack of funds. Funding for the other mixed tribunals has been even more precarious.

2.   The Special Court has been successful on a number of fronts: it was the first court to indict a sitting African head of state, the first to rule on the

use and recruitment of child soldiers as a war crime, and the first to rule that forced marriage is a distinct crime against humanity separate from sexual slavery or rape. It has had an extensive outreach program, and for a number of years worked simultaneously with a Truth and Reconciliation Commission. On the other hand, the Court limited its purview to cases against less than a dozen accused, and its efforts to hold proceedings at the scene of the crime were undermined when the Sierra Leonean government decided it could not risk a trial of Charles Taylor in the area and the Court transferred the proceedings to The Hague.

3. One of the Court's most important decisions came on the question of whether a domestic amnesty law, granted as part of a peace agreement, could preclude international prosecution:

Prosecutor v. Kallon and Kamara, Decision on Challenge to Jurisdiction: Lomé Amnesty Law (Lomé Amnesty Decision)

Special Court for Sierra Leone
SCSL–2004–15–PT and SCSL–2004–16–PT (13 March 2004)

* * *

[The rebel defendants argued that the Special Court could not try them because they had been granted a full amnesty in Article IX of the Lomé Peace Accord between the government and the rebels. The Court held that the peace accord did not constitute a treaty. The Statute of the Special Court required prosecution for crimes including those that under domestic law were the subject of the Lomé amnesty.]

65. What rightly falls for consideration is not whether the undertaking in the Lomé Agreement made by the Government of Sierra Leone to grant an amnesty is binding on the Government of Sierra Leone, but whether such an undertaking could be effective in depriving this Court of the jurisdiction conferred on it by the treaty establishing it, and, if it could not be so effective, whether its existence is a ground for staying the proceedings by reason of the doctrine of abuse of process. * * *

67. The grant of amnesty or pardon is undoubtedly an exercise of sovereign power which, essentially, is closely linked, as far as crime is concerned, to the criminal jurisdiction of the State exercising such sovereign power. Where jurisdiction is universal, a State cannot deprive another State of its jurisdiction to prosecute the offender by the grant of amnesty. It is for this reason unrealistic to regard as universally effective the grant of amnesty by a State in regard to grave international crimes in which there exists universal jurisdiction. A State cannot bring into oblivion and forgetfulness a crime, such as a crime against international law, which other States are entitled to keep alive and remember. * * *

71. After reviewing international practice in regard to effectiveness or otherwise of amnesty granted by a State and the inconsistencies in state

practice as regards the prohibition of amnesty for crimes against humanity, Cassese conceptualised the status of international practice thus:

> There is not yet any general obligation for States to refrain from amnesty laws on these crimes. Consequently, if a State passes any such law, it does not breach a customary rule. Nonetheless if another State having in custody persons accused of international crimes decides to prosecute them although in their national State they would benefit from an amnesty law, such court would not thereby act contrary to general international law, in particular to the principle of respect for the sovereignty of other States.[50]

The opinion stated above is gratefully adopted. It is, therefore, not difficult to agree with the submission made on behalf of Redress that the amnesty granted by Sierra Leone cannot cover crimes under international law that are the subject of universal jurisdiction. In the first place, it stands to reason that a state cannot sweep such crimes into oblivion and forgetfulness which other states have jurisdiction to prosecute by reason of the fact that the obligation to protect human dignity is a peremptory norm and has assumed the nature of obligation *erga omnes*.[60]

72.   In view of the conclusions that have been arrived at in paragraph 69, it is clear that the question whether amnesty is unlawful under international law becomes relevant only in considering the question whether Article IX of the Lomé Agreement can constitute a legal bar to prosecution of the defendants by another State or by an international tribunal. There being no such bar, the remaining question is whether the undertaking contained in Article IX is good ground for holding that the prosecution of the defendants is an abuse of process of the Court.

82.   The submission by the Prosecution that there is a "crystallising international norm that a government cannot grant amnesty for serious violations of crimes under international law" is amply supported by materials placed before this Court. The opinion of both *amici curiae* that it has crystallised may not be entirely correct, but that is no reason why this court in forming its own opinion should ignore the strength of their argument and the weight of materials they place before the Court. It is accepted that such a norm is developing under international law. Counsel for Kallon [one of the defendants] submitted that there is, as yet, no universal acceptance that amnesties are unlawful under international law, but, as amply pointed out by Professor Orentlicher, there are several treaties requiring prosecution for such crimes. These include the 1948 Convention on the Prevention and Punishment of the Crime of Genocide,

---

50.   A. Cassese, *International Criminal Law* (Oxford, 2003), 315.

60.   See *Barcelona Traction, Light and Power Co. Case (Belgium v. Spain)* [1970] ICJ Reports 3; See also Mior, *The Law of Internal Armed Conflict*, 57. It has been suggested that three groups of [peremptory] norms exist: those protecting the foundations of law, peace and humanity; those rules of co-operation protecting fundamental common interests; and those protecting humanity to the extent of human dignity, personal and racial equality, life and personal freedom. See also I. Brownlie, *Principles of International Law* (6th Ed., 2003) where prohibition of crimes against humanity is incuded as an example of a *ius cogens* norm, p. 489.

the Convention Against Torture and Other Cruel, Inhuman or Degrading Treatment or Punishment, and the four Geneva conventions. There are also quite a number of resolutions of the UN General Assembly and the Security Council reaffirming a state obligation to prosecute or bring to justice. Redress has appended to its written submissions materials which include relevant conclusions of the Committee against Torture, findings of the Human Rights Commission, and relevant judgments of the Inter–American Court.

85.   Upon its establishment the Special Court assumed an independent existence and is not an agency of either the parties which executed the Agreement establishing the Court. It is described as "hybrid" or of "mixed jurisdiction" because of the nature of the laws it is empowered to apply. Its description as hybrid should not be understood as denoting that it is part of two or more legal systems. Prosecutions are not made in the name of Sierra Leone which plays no part in initiating or terminating prosecution and has no control whatsoever over the Prosecutor who exercises an independent judgment in his prosecutorial decision. The understanding of the United Nations in signing the Lomé Agreement is that the amnesty granted therein will not extend to such crimes covered by Articles 2 to 4 of the Statute of the Court. The understanding of Sierra Leone from the statement made on the inauguration of the Truth Commission was that the amnesty affected only prosecutions before national courts. All these are consistent with the provisions of Article 10 of the Statute and the universal jurisdiction of other states by virtue of the nature of the crime to prosecute the offenders. All these are factors which make the prayer that the proceedings be stayed by reason of abuse of process untenable. * * *

b. THE INTERNATIONAL CRIMINAL COURT

The 1948 Genocide Convention provided that the crime could be tried in the state where the acts took place, or in an international criminal court, which many thought would soon be created. The Cold War intervened, and the court was put on the back burner. Initially, the idea was to create a worldwide code of substantive crimes, to be followed by a Court. The International Law Commission created a Draft Code of Offenses Against the Peace and Security of Mankind in 1954, but then the project stalled. It was only in 1994, with the impetus of the ICTY and ICTR, that Trinidad and Tobago proposed a new international treaty to create a court that would try individuals for crimes including those discussed above as well as large-scale drug trafficking and organized crime. After several years of negotiations and drafts prepared by the International Law Commission, in the summer of 1998, delegates from 160 countries along with hundreds of non-governmental organizations gathered in Rome for a final, marathon negotiating session. The result was the Rome Statute establishing the International Criminal Court.

The Rome Statute includes four crimes: genocide, crimes against humanity, war crimes and the crime of aggression. However, delegates could not agree on language defining aggression (the successor to the crimes against peace charged at Nuremberg), and so the Statute indicates that the Court may not exercise jurisdiction over that crime until a provision is adopted defining the crime and setting out the conditions under which the Court can consider it. Are there specific issues that you can foresee with a Court deciding that aggression (or waging an aggressive war) has been committed, given what you know about the structure of the United Nations? A new attempt to define the crime will take place at the 2010 Review Conference.

The Court is an independent institution governed by an Assembly of State Parties that meets periodically. Its governing Statute, supplemented by Rules of Procedure and Evidence and by a document setting out the Elements of Crimes, reflects a mix of civil and common-law systems. Like the ICTY and ICTR, it has an Office of the Prosecutor, Trial and Appeal Chambers, and a Registry. It can only investigate crimes committed after July 1, 2002, the date the Statute entered into force.

The most contentious issues at the Rome Conference revolved around the triggers and preconditions to the Court's jurisdiction. The trigger question involves who—a state, the Security Council, other U.N. organs, and/or the prosecutor him-or herself—should be able to initiate an investigation, and to bring charges. What are the arguments in favor of allowing the Prosecutor to investigate without receiving authorization from states or the Security Council? Are there any concerns, especially from the perspective of a country like the U.S. that engages in extensive worldwide military operations? Take into account that in 1998 the Clinton administration in the U.S. was in the midst of the Monica Lewinsky investigation by Independent Prosecutor Ken Starr. Might this have colored the U.S.'s view of independent prosecutors?

Eventually, a compromise was reached between those concerned about the prosecutor's independence and those worried about possible over-reaching. Article 13 of the Rome Statute allows States Parties, the Security Council, and the Prosecutor to initiate an investigation. However, Article 15 provides in part:

> If the Prosecutor concludes that there is a reasonable basis to proceed with an investigation, he or she shall submit to the Pre–Trial Chamber a request for authorization of an investigation, together with any supporting material collected. Victims may make representations to the Pre–Trial Chamber, in accordance with the Rules of Procedure and Evidence.

> If the Pre–Trial Chamber, upon examination of the request and the supporting material, considers that there is a reasonable basis to proceed with an investigation, and that the case appears to fall within the jurisdiction of the Court, it shall authorize the commencement of the investigation, without prejudice to subsequent determinations by the Court with regard to the jurisdiction and admissibility of a case.

Does this adequately resolve the tension between independence and control of the Prosecutor?

With respect to the Security Council's role, the states at Rome agreed that it could refer cases, and that SC referrals would not require any other preconditions. But could the Council intervene to stop an ongoing investigation if it believed the Court's work would interfere with ongoing SC efforts at peacemaking? Article 16 reads:

No investigation or prosecution may be commenced or proceeded with under this Statute for a period of 12 months after the Security Council, in a resolution adopted under Chapter VII of the Charter of the United Nations, has requested the Court to that effect; that request may be renewed by the Council under the same conditions.

How does this Article deal with the veto power of the five permanent members? Is the onus on those seeking action or inaction?

The other extremely contentious issue in establishing the Court's jurisdiction was whether, in addition to becoming a party to the Statute, states would have to specially agree to an investigation that concerned their territory or their nationals. The U.S. and other countries expressed concern that without some limit, non-party states could nonetheless be subject to Court action, even without Security Council authorization. Until almost the last moment, the draft treaty allowed for jurisdiction if states possessing any of the jurisdictional ties we have studied—territory (where the crimes took place), nationality (of the offender), passive personality (nationality of the victim) or universality (custody of the defendant, even if no nationality or territorial ties) were parties to the Rome Treaty or accepted the Court's jurisdiction on a one-time basis. However, during the last couple of days, in an effort to convince wavering states to agree to the text, the following text, Article 12, was agreed upon:

1. A State which becomes a Party to this Statute thereby accepts the jurisdiction of the Court with respect to the crimes referred to in article 5.

2. In the case of article 13, paragraph (a) or (c), the Court may exercise its jurisdiction if one or more of the following States are Parties to this Statute or have accepted the jurisdiction of the Court in accordance with paragraph 3:

(a) The State on the territory of which the conduct in question occurred or, if the crime was committed on board a vessel or aircraft, the State of registration of that vessel or aircraft;

(b) The State of which the person accused of the crime is a national.

3. If the acceptance of a State which is not a Party to this Statute is required under paragraph 2, that State may, by declaration lodged with the Registrar, accept the exercise of jurisdiction by the Court with respect to the crime in question.

Does this precondition significantly limit the Court's potential reach, at least absent Security Council action? Under what conditions would the

Court have been able to prosecute Saddam Hussein or Augusto Pinochet, assuming their crimes happened after 2002?

Unlike the ICTY and ICTR which have primacy over national prosecutions, the ICC is a backstop to national courts, able to intervene only when national systems are "unwilling or unable" to do so. In other words, the ICC is based on the idea of "complementarity."

Article 17 of the Rome Statute reads:

1.   Having regard to paragraph 10 of the Preamble and article 1, the Court shall determine that a case is inadmissible where:

(a) The case is being investigated or prosecuted by a State which has jurisdiction over it, unless the State is unwilling or unable genuinely to carry out the investigation or prosecution;

(b) The case has been investigated by a State which has jurisdiction over it and the State has decided not to prosecute the person concerned, unless the decision resulted from the unwillingness or inability of the State genuinely to prosecute;

(c) The person concerned has already been tried for conduct which is the subject of the complaint, and a trial by the Court is not permitted under article 20, paragraph 3;

(d) The case is not of sufficient gravity to justify further action by the Court.

2.   In order to determine unwillingness in a particular case, the Court shall consider, having regard to the principles of due process recognized by international law, whether one or more of the following exist, as applicable:

(a) The proceedings were or are being undertaken or the national decision was made for the purpose of shielding the person concerned from criminal responsibility for crimes within the jurisdiction of the Court referred to in article 5;

(b) There has been an unjustified delay in the proceedings which in the circumstances is inconsistent with an intent to bring the person concerned to justice;

(d) The proceedings were not or are not being conducted independently or impartially, and they were or are being conducted in a manner which, in the circumstances, is inconsistent with an intent to bring the person concerned to justice.

3.   In order to determine inability in a particular case, the Court shall consider whether, due to a total or substantial collapse or unavailability of its national judicial system, the State is unable to obtain the accused or the necessary evidence and testimony or otherwise unable to carry out its proceedings.

Early on, the Office of the Prosecutor issued a policy document describing its views on the meaning of complementarity and how it would decide which cases to pursue.

Office of the Prosecutor, Paper on Some Policy Issues Before the Office of the Prosecutor

6 September 2003
Doc. ICC–OTP 2003

There is no impediment to the admissibility of a case before the Court where no State has initiated any investigation. There may be cases where inaction by States is the appropriate course of action. For example, the Court and a territorial State incapacitated by mass crimes may agree that a consensual division of labour is the most logical and effective approach. Groups bitterly divided by conflict may oppose prosecutions at each others' hands and yet agree to a prosecution by a Court perceived as neutral and impartial. There may also be cases where a third State has extra-territorial jurisdiction, but all interested parties agree that the Court has developed superior evidence and expertise relating to that situation, making the Court the more effective forum. In such cases there will be no question of "unwillingness" or "inability" under article 17.

It should however be recalled that the system of complementarity is principally based on the recognition that the exercise of national criminal jurisdiction is not only a right but also a duty of States. Indeed, the principle underlying the concept of complementarity is that States remain responsible and accountable for investigating and prosecuting crimes committed under their jurisdiction and that national systems are expected to maintain and enforce adherence to international standards.

Because of the nature of the crimes within the jurisdiction of the Court, the Prosecutor may be called upon to act in an environment very different from those experienced by national prosecutors. He may for example have to act in a situation of violence over which the State authorities have no control. The Prosecutor may also be asked to act in a situation where those who have the legitimate monopoly of force in a State are themselves the ones to commit the crimes, and the enforcement authorities in that State will consequently not be available to the Prosecutor. In circumstances such as these the Prosecutor will not be able to exercise his powers without the intervention of the international community, whether through the use of peacekeeping forces or otherwise; the Prosecutor will not be able to establish an office in the country concerned without being assured of its safety. He will also have to be assured that there will be the means available for investigation, protection of witnesses and arrest of suspects.

* * *

2.1. Who should be prosecuted?

Should the Office seek to bring charges against all alleged perpetrators? The Statute gives some guidance to answer this question. The Preamble affirms that "the most serious crimes of concern to the international community as a whole must not go unpunished". It continues that States Parties to the Statute are determined to establish a "permanent International Criminal Court in relationship with the United Nations system, with jurisdiction over the most serious crimes of concern to the international community as a whole". Accordingly, the Statute provides in article 5 that, "[t]he jurisdiction of the Court shall be limited to the most serious crimes of concern to the international criminal community as a whole". Article 17, dealing with admissibility, adds to the complementarity grounds one related to the gravity of a case. It states that the Court (which includes the Office of the Prosecutor) shall determine that a case is inadmissible where "the case is not of sufficient gravity to justify further action by the Court". The concept of gravity should not be exclusively attached to the act that constituted the crime but also to the degree of participation in its commission.

Furthermore, the Statute gives to the Prosecutor the power not to investigate or not to prosecute when such an investigation or prosecution would not serve the interests of justice.

The global character of the ICC, its statutory provisions and logistical constraints support a preliminary recommendation that, as a general rule, the Office of the Prosecutor should focus its investigative and prosecutorial efforts and resources on those who bear the greatest responsibility, such as the leaders of the State or organisation allegedly responsible for those crimes.

2.2.   Dealing with the "impunity gap"

The strategy of focussing on those who bear the greatest responsibility for crimes within the jurisdiction of the Court will leave an impunity gap unless national authorities, the international community and the Court work together to ensure that all appropriate means for bringing other perpetrators to justice are used. In some cases the focus of an investigation by the Office of the Prosecutor may go wider than high-ranking officers, if investigation of certain type of crimes or those officers lower down the chain of command is necessary for the whole case. For other offenders, alternative means for resolving the situation may be necessary, whether by encouraging and facilitating national prosecutions by strengthening or rebuilding national justice systems, by providing international assistance to those systems or by some other means.

* * *

NOTES AND QUESTIONS

1.   Are these the right criteria for deciding whether to take on a case? How do they compare to the proof of exhaustion of domestic remedies required

in human rights cases? Should they be different when discussing individual rather than state responsibility?

2. How exactly is the Court to weigh whether a state is "unable or unwilling"? What if the state has initiated investigations, but they have bogged down for months (or years)? What if a domestic amnesty law, statute of limitations or immunity rule precludes domestic prosecution? What if the state is prosecuting some but not all of the perpetrators? How many does it need to prosecute? These are some of the complications raised by Article 17. Note that interested states as well as the accused may challenge findings of admissibility.

c. THE COURT'S WORK TO DATE

As of 2009, the ICC has opened four investigations. Three of these, in northern Uganda, the Democratic Republic of the Congo, and the Central African Republic, have been state referrals. They have led to the issuance of 10 arrest warrants. Thomas Lubanga Dyilo, Germain Katanga and Mathieu Ngudjolo Chui are currently in the custody of the ICC. The suspect Bosco Ntaganda remains at large. Jean–Pierre Bemba Gombo was arrested in Belgium and transferred to the Court. One trial is now underway: Thomas Lubanga, head of a militia in the DRC, is accused of recruiting child soldiers, a war crime. Two other trials are set to start later this year.

The Lubanga trial has raised interesting questions about victim participation in the proceedings.

Fiona McKay, Victim Participation in Proceedings before the International Criminal Court

15 No. 3 HUMAN RIGHTS BRIEF 1 (2008)

One of the unique aspects of the International Criminal Court (ICC) compared to other international criminal tribunals is the element of victim participation. Victims may present their views and concerns to the ICC, where their interests are affected, potentially at any stage of the proceedings, from investigations to appeal. If an accused is convicted, the ICC may award reparations.

Such a role for victims in criminal proceedings is normal in some legal systems of the world, where victims can join criminal proceedings as civil parties. It is largely unfamiliar, however, to common law countries, like the United States, where victims may be called to testify as witnesses but play no further role in the proceedings and must bring a separate civil action if they wish to claim damages or another remedy for harm related to the crime. The closest process in the United States may be the notion of victim impact statements, whereby victims may address a court regarding the impact a crime had on them while the court considers sentencing. Before the ICC, victims may present their views to the ICC from a much earlier stage.

This innovation was introduced in order to give victims a voice in the proceedings and to address one of the deficiencies for which the *ad hoc* international criminal tribunals, such as those in the Former Yugoslavia and Rwanda, were criticized, namely the sense of alienation that many victims felt as a result of being left out of the proceedings, It was also intended to reflect developments in international standards that recognize greater rights for victims of crimes, including the right to reparation.

Many of the details of how this participation will work are currently being shaped. The participation of victims has been the subject of a considerable amount of the ICC's early jurisprudence, and a number of appeals are currently pending on key elements that will have a significant impact in determining what the role of victims before the ICC will be.

Aside from the legal issues, there are also very real, practical challenges involved in making the ICC's scheme for victims participation work. The Victims Participation and Reparations Section (VPRS) is one of several units in the ICC concerned with victims. The VPRS was established within the Registry of the ICC to assist victims and facilitate their access to the ICC, as well as to serve as the entry point for applications to participate in proceedings and to process such applications. Another unit of the ICC is responsible for protection and support (the Victims and Witnesses Unit), and two independent bodies have been established—an Office of Public Counsel for Victims to provide legal assistance and representation, and a Trust Fund for Victims of crimes within the ICC's jurisdiction and their families.

What Does "Participation" Mean?

According to Article 68(3) of the Rome Statute of the ICC (the Rome Statute):

> Where the personal interests of the victims are affected, the Court shall permit their views and concerns to be presented, and considered, at stages of the proceedings determined to be appropriate by the Court, and in a manner which is not prejudicial to or inconsistent with the rights of the accused and a fair and impartial trial.

Participating in proceedings should be distinguished from being called to testify as a witness. Some victims may be called as witnesses by one of the parties to give evidence that goes to the culpability or innocence of the accused, whereas appearing as a victim participant is entirely voluntary. Further, in participating, victims are pursuing their own interests, independent from the parties. Indeed, in the first major decision on victims' participation, dating from January 2006, the Pre–Trial Chamber dealing with the situation in the Democratic Republic of the Congo (DRC) noted that the Rome Statute grants victims an independent voice and role in the proceedings and that it should not be assumed that victims would be an ally of the Prosecutor.

On the other hand, victims' participation before the ICC does not go as far as the role of victims in legal systems based on the civil law tradition, where their role can be likened to that of a third party in the proceedings. Before the ICC they are not treated as full parties: for instance, to date their lawyers have not been permitted full access to the documents in the record of the proceedings.

Further, the judges sitting in relation to any particular phase of proceedings have a duty to manage the participation of victims during that phase and to ensure that it does not prejudice the rights of the accused or impede the efficiency of the proceedings.

The ICC's Rules envisage that a legal representative of a victim might question a witness, or even the accused, but only after seeking specific authorization from the Chamber. The Rules also provide that where there are a number of victims, a Chamber may order them to join together and choose a common legal representative, in the interests of ensuring the efficiency of the proceedings.

While the parties sought leave to appeal some of the early decisions on victims, the pre-trial chambers rejected such applications. More recently, several issues have come before the Appeals Chamber in the run up to the ICC's first trial, in the case of the *Prosecutor v. Thomas Lubanga Dyilo* (the *Lubanga* case). Following the transmission of the *Lubanga* case to the Trial Chamber for preparation for trial, a landmark decision on victims' participation of January 2008 gave rise to several appeals from both the defence and the prosecution, which are currently pending before the Appeals Chamber. The principal main issues at stake are noted below.

At Which Stages May Victims Participate?

The question of what should be the role of victims during the preliminary stages of proceedings has been a contentious one. The ICC's Statute and Rules provide some guidance on the matter, specifying, for instance, that victims may present their views and concerns in relation to decisions whether to proceed with an investigation or prosecution, in the context of challenges to jurisdiction or admissibility, and during a hearing to consider whether to confirm the charges against a person.

In an early decision from January 2006, the Pre–Trial Chamber dealing with the situation in the DRC decided that victims may participate even as early as the investigations phase, when the Prosecutor is still conducting investigations into which crimes might have been committed and who might be responsible, and before a case has been opened against any individual. According to Pre–Trial Chamber I, the personal interests of the victims are affected at this stage in a general manner, in that participation enables them to clarify facts, punish those responsible for crimes and seek reparation for harm suffered. The Chamber went on to distinguish between victims of a *situation* and of a specific *case*, an approach subsequently adopted by Pre–Trial Chamber II in relation to the Uganda situation. The Prosecutor challenged this approach, arguing that victim participation during an investigation could jeopardize the integrity and objectivity of the investigation as well as impact its efficiency and security. It was not until early 2008, however, that the issue came before the

Appeals Chamber, which is currently considering whether Article 68(3) of the Statute can be interpreted as providing for a procedural status of victim at the investigation stage of a situation and the pre-trial stage of a case.
* * *

The Trial Chamber also noted that victims may have very general and wide-ranging interests, such as in being allowed to express their views and concerns, verifying particular facts, protecting their dignity and ensuring their safety, and being recognized as victims, and that their interests were not limited to receiving reparations. As a result of applications from both the prosecution and the defence, the Appeals Chamber is currently considering the question of whether the harm alleged and the concept of "personal interests" must be linked with the charges against the accused.

What Will Victims Participating in Proceedings be Permitted to Do?

The ICC's rules relating to victim participation envisage that victims may give opening and closing statements at trial, and may request authorization to make interventions, including questioning witnesses. During the confirmation of charges hearing in the *Lubanga* case, a legal representative of a victim was permitted to put a question to a witness.

Another issue currently on appeal is whether victims participating in proceedings will be able to introduce evidence during trial. The Trial Chamber, in its decision on victims' participation of January 2008, held that victims participating in proceedings may be allowed to introduce and examine evidence if the Chamber finds it will assist in the determination of the truth.

* * *

NOTES AND QUESTIONS

1. In July 2008 the Appeals Chamber decided that (1) while victims do not have to be "direct" victims of the charges against the accused, they do have to have suffered personal harm; (2) that only victims of the crimes charged (once charges have been confirmed) will have the necessary personal interests to participate; and (3) confirmed the Trial Chambers decision that victims can introduce and examine evidence, including on issues touching on the guilt or innocence of the accused. *Prosecutor v. Lubanga,* Judgment on the Appeals of the Prosecutor and the Defence Against Trial Chamber I's Decision on Victim Participation of 18 January 2008, No. 01–04–01/06, 11 July 2008.

What are the competing interests at stake here? Why might the Prosecution and Defense have both challenged a Trial Chamber ruling granting broad participation rights to victims? Did the Appeals Chamber get the balance right?

If there are many victims, how are they all to be represented while respecting a defendant's right to a speedy trial? Is there a real concern that allowing victims an independent role can undermine the Prosecutor's trial strategy choices? How? What if the prosecutor wants to frame a narrow case to increase the possibility of conviction? Is that risk justified to allow victims to tell a more complete story of the crimes at issue? Does the answer depend on how you see the main purposes of the Court?

Many of the issues regarding participation of victims are considered in the Rules of Procedure and Evidence.

2.   Article 75 of the Rome Statute allows the Court to make provisions for reparation of victims. Reparations are to come from the confiscated assets of an accused or, where these are insufficient, from the Trust Fund for Victims. The Fund has its own governing Board, and can also provide funds not related to confiscated assets for the benefit of victims and affected communities. As of 2008, the TFV had assets of some €3,050,000 (over $4,000,000) although none of it had yet been awarded after a conviction.

3.   The Extraordinary Chambers in the Courts of Cambodia has even more vigorous provisions for victim participation. Victims are civil parties to the proceedings (in the French legal tradition) and participate fully.

4.   The arrest warrants in northern Uganda and in Sudan have been particularly controversial. In northern Uganda, there were complaints that the indictments and arrest warrants interfered with long-standing efforts at peace negotiations. The Court's supporters, in response, pointed to the fact that the LRA only came to the negotiating table after the arrest warrants were issued. In addition, critics complained that the arrest warrants were one-sided since the Ugandan army had also committed war crimes, and that Western-style trials did not resonate with the area's population, who would prefer reintegration mechanisms for fighters (especially former child soldiers) based on customary practice. In the case of Sudan (Darfur) there were similar concerns about interference with ongoing peace processes. Moreover, if the Security Council did not act to enforce the warrants, nor sanction states that refused to hand suspects over to the Court, the Court's effectiveness and credibility could be severely compromised. What do you think of these objections and criticisms? Is there really a conflict between peace and justice here, or is peace dependent on some measure of justice? Are there ways within the confines of the Rome Statute to deal with potential interference with peace talks? What about the issue of local customary practices? Is it possible to combine local reintegration practices with formal criminal prosecution? Is it desirable? What about the fact that these are called *international* crimes, that is, the repercussions extend beyond the local area and even beyond Uganda?

5.   *The United States and the ICC.* The U.S. has been a major backer of the ICTY and ICTR and of the mixed tribunals. At Rome, the U.S. had a large delegation, and many aspects of the Statute were heavily influenced by the U.S. In the end, largely due to Defense Department concerns about prosecutions of U.S. nationals, the U.S. joined six other countries (including Iraq, Libya and China) in voting against the treaty. Then–President Clinton signed the treaty just before leaving office, but expressed reservations about submitting it to the Senate for ratification. President George W. Bush's administration was at first implacably hostile to the ICC. The administration argued that the treaty, by allowing jurisdiction over nation-

als of non-party states when either the territorial or nationality state agreed, in effect bound non-party states without their consent. It also argued that the U.S., as the world's sole superpower, had special vulnerabilities and special responsibilities. He soon "unsigned" the Rome Statute (to understand the legal reason, see Article 18(a) of the Vienna Convention on the Law of Treaties), and Congress passed the American Servicemembers Protection Act, which forbid certain aid to non-NATO states that ratified the treaty and authorized the rescue of U.S. citizens arrested for transfer to the Court (hence it was known as the "Hague Invasion Act"). The U.S. also signed separate agreements with over 100 countries (known as "Article 98" agreements) pledging not to turn U.S. nationals in to the Court. However, by Bush's second term the U.S. stance had eased somewhat. The U.S. abstained when the Security Council voted to refer the situation in Darfur to the ICC, and since then has quietly provided some assistance to the Court on Darfur. What should the U.S. attitude toward the Court be now? Are there real risks to U.S. soldiers acting abroad, or do the complementarity provisions and other safeguards in the treaty sufficiently protect Americans from unwarranted investigations and prosecutions?

6. The ICC does not have its own police force or marshal's service to execute arrest warrants. It depends on national governments, especially members of the Assembly of States Parties of the ICC, to find and arrest suspects. So far, this mechanism has not proven particularly effective. What, if any, are the alternatives? Note this issue dovetails with episodic calls for the United Nations to have its own peacekeeping or peace enforcement capabilities.

7. In general, the Achilles heel of all efforts at international justice—national or transnational prosecutions, international criminal courts, mixed tribunals—has been the difficulties with finding and surrendering suspects. Even in the case of national prosecutions, extradition and judicial cooperation treaties are not well-suited to dealing with these types of crimes. Extradition is generally based on a network of bilateral and regional extradition treaties. The Conventions on Torture and Enforced Disappearance, as well as a number of anti-terrorism treaties, allow the treaty to serve as the basis for extradition if no other exists. Extradition will only be granted when the acts at issue constitute crimes in both countries (the "double criminality" rule), and when the crimes do not come within the political offense exception. Many countries also limit the extradition of nationals, and others will not extradite when the suspect might be sentenced to death. Judicial cooperation treaties generally try to streamline a cumbersome process of sharing documents, allowing investigation, or transferring documents or witness testimony from one country to another.

For more information on extradition and judicial cooperation, see BETH VAN SCHAACK AND RONALD SLYE, INTERNATIONAL CRIMINAL LAW AND ITS ENFORCEMENT, CASES AND MATERIALS (2007); M. CHERIF BASSIOUNI AND EDWARD WISE, AUT DEDERE AUT JUDICARE: THE DUTY TO EXTRADITE OR PROSECUTE IN INTERNATIONAL LAW (1995).

CHAPTER 6

EARTH LAW: COMMON SPACES AND THE PROTECTION OF THE ENVIRONMENT

In the middle of the 20th century, we saw our planet from space for the first time. Historians may eventually find that this vision had a greater impact on thought than did the Copernican revolution of the 16th century, which upset humans' self-image by revealing that the Earth is not the centre of the universe. From space, we see a small and fragile ball dominated not by human activity and edifice but by a pattern of clouds, oceans, greenery, and soils. Humanity's inability to fit its activities into that pattern is changing planetary systems fundamentally. Many such changes are accompanied by life-threatening hazards, from environmental degradation to nuclear destruction. These new realities, from which there is no escape, must be recognized and managed.

Towards Common Action: Proposals for Institutional and Legal Change, in Our Common Future, World Commission on Environment and Development, UN Doc. A/42/427 (1987).

As a physical matter, the earth is one. As an economic matter, as the size of our economy has grown, we have used an increasing amount of the world's resources and environmental services. The impacts of activities in one state increasingly spill over to others: toxic contaminants from industries in the U.S. and China ride the ocean currents to lodge in the bodies of Arctic seals, deforestation in one country affects rain patterns in its neighbors, and rising temperatures from increased carbon emissions will change life around the globe. As a legal matter, then, one would think that international law would be strongest and most developed in dealing with the regulation and protection of our common home. After all, all states have an interest in how other states behave with respect to the earth. For the most part, however, this has not been the case. Customary law concerning the use of the high seas does go back centuries, but many of the modern issues surrounding the oceans are of recent vintage. Laws regarding use of space and of common areas like Antarctica are also recent, as are the vast majority of environmental treaties. Even now, there is no overarching regime of environmental protection for Earth; there are more or less widely accepted principles, and an expanding welter of specialized treaties, guidelines, and programs. The looming threat of climate change, a major focus of this chapter, may begin to pull together aspects of our still piecemeal and scattered efforts to protect our home and its inhabitants through international law.

The Chapter starts by setting out the state of our world, including the major problems confronting it: climate change, loss of biodiversity, dangerous chemicals, growing population and consumption, and the environmental consequences of poverty. We introduce some of the basic ideas applicable to our efforts to deal with these problems through law. We will then consider some general principles of international environmental law and a brief history of their evolution.

We then consider specific environmental regimes, starting with what will no doubt evolve into the most complex set of rules and policies to date:

the climate change regime. We then turn to the law of common or shared spaces, those beyond national jurisdiction. While we will focus on the oceans, we will also glance briefly at river courses and fresh water, outer space and the poles. Then we will turn to the environmental protection regimes regarding the earth's living creatures, including animals, forests and biodiversity. Finally, we will briefly consider the regulation of the production and disposal of dangerous or toxic pollutants and chemicals.

Much of the current international activity on environment and sustainable development is carried out through existing and future treaty regimes. A common feature of many of these regimes is that the state parties meet regularly, in Conferences of the Parties (COPs) to evaluate, modify or create protocols to existing treaties. Almost all these treaty regimes have a Secretariat to keep track of and organize the multiple meetings of COPs and their subsidiary bodies. One way, therefore, to find current information on an area covered by a treaty regime is to look at the Secretariat's website. For ongoing (or past) treaty negotiations, a good resource is the Earth Negotiations Bulletin published by the International Institute for Sustainable Development, http://www.iisd.ca/. IISD also maintains listserves on specific environmental issues.

A.   THE STATE OF THE WORLD

Environmental Governance, in UN Environment Programme, Year Book 2009: New Science and Developments in Our Changing Environment*

available at http://www.unep.org/geo/yearbook/yb2009/

Introduction

Earth's ecosystems are under threat. Twenty per cent of the earth's land has been significantly degraded by human activity and 60 per cent of the planet's assessed ecosystems are now damaged or threatened. The irrefutable pattern is one of natural resource overexploitation while creating more waste than ecosystems can process.

The chemicals we use to produce energy, to control pests, to enhance productivity, to catalyze industrial processes, and to meet human health needs—as well as the chemicals we just discard—continue to weaken ecosystems and to imperil human health.

The changing climate is pushing many Earth systems towards critical thresholds that will alter regional and global environmental balances and already threaten stability at multiple scales. Alarmingly, we may have already passed tipping points that are irreversible within the time span of our current civilization.

In recent decades, the growing threat of climate change is demonstrated by a significant increase in the number and severity of storms, floods,

---

* Internal references omitted.

and droughts while the average number of seismic disasters, as devastating as they are, remained steady. New and ongoing conflicts can be both the result and cause of environmental degradation.

Industrial and environmental mismanagement is not a necessary component of development. Tools to minimize overexploitation and pollution are available. Using principles of industrial ecology, such as life cycle analysis and industrial symbiosis, can serve the public good and cultivate healthy communities.

Human beings, human societies, and the human economy are entirely integrated into the Earth system and into the Earth systems' economy— the geosphere, the biosphere, the atmosphere, and the ecosystems that knit it all together. Governance of that integration is one of the most important challenges of the 21st century.

Environmental degradation and industrial development were coupled during the industrial revolution and into modern times, but that relationship is not necessary and it cannot continue. Firm, informed, and enlightened environmental governance is necessary. The economic system that encouraged overexploitation of natural resources and production of waste is undergoing a complete redesign. This is the moment to ensure the next economic system does not repeat the mistakes of over exploitation and pollution.

ACHIEVING THE MILLENNIUM DEVELOPMENT GOALS

The Global Monitoring Report 2008 on progress towards achieving the United Nations Millennium Development Goals 2008 marks the midpoint toward the 2015 deadline for achieving the Millennium Development Goals (MDGs). The report finds that urgent action is needed to combat climate change that threatens the well-being of all countries, but particularly of poor countries and poor people. It also emphasizes that the goals of development and environmental sustainability are closely related and the paths to those goals have important synergies (World Bank 2008).

In the current global economic downturn, questions have arisen about priorities: Will environment and development objectives be lost in the new economic paradigm?

Pressures expected to increase

With business-as-usual policies, the proportion of people who suffer from hunger or whose income is less than US$1 a day will not be halved between 1990 and 2015 as expected in the targets set of the MDGs. The rate at which biodiversity is globally being lost will not be reduced by 2010. The impacts of climate change will not remain within agreed limits. The targets for water supply and especially sanitation will be nearly impossible to reach (UNDP 2008, UNFCCC 1992, World Bank 2008).

The environmental limitations ahead are exacerbated by additional pressures: The continuing growth of the world's population, their increasing material aspirations, and the natural resources that are being and will be exploited to satisfy those aspirations have major implications for ecosystem health, land use, and energy consumption.

The challenge is to meet these growing aspirations while ensuring environmental sustainablity (UN 2004, UN 2006a). Projecting population trends and devising methods to minimize the effects of rising population on resources cannot proceed outside of the environmental constraints or remain oblivious to the approaching thresholds that human activities have already provoked.

These aspirations could be met with less material input. The transition towards dematerialization of consumption could help decouple development from resource exploitation and associated environmental degradation * * *.

* * *

NOTES AND QUESTIONS

1. Recitations of the scope and scale of environmental problems tend to be overwhelming and depressing, and can lead to a reaction of paralysis or apathy in the face of huge, seemingly intractable problems. But although the problems are dire, and increasingly recognized as such, there are also hundreds of thousands of initiatives aimed at solving them. At a local, national and even occasionally global level people are working on alternative energy, green building, sustainable food supply, minimizing dangerous chemicals and wastes, rethinking transport and production of goods, and creating greater resilience in the face of potential disaster. These initiatives arise from the public sector, from academia, from private business, from thousands of non-governmental groups, and from innovative partnerships involving combinations of these actors. See, e.g. some of the public-private partnerships stimulated by the 2002 Johannesburg World Summit on Sustainable Development. These initiatives give cause for hope and are a call to action. As you learn more about efforts to use international law to address some of the challenges ahead, keep in mind both the urgency and the wide range of potential actors and actions involved. To what extent will solving these problems be a question of improved technology, or greater resources, and to what extent will it require fundamental changes in how we produce, consume, and interact?

2. What are the major environmental problems identified above, and how are they related to each other? How does climate change, for example, affect biodiversity? We shall take up some of the implications of climate change for other international environmental regimes below.

3. UNEP, created after the 1972 Stockholm Conference on the Environment, is the lead United Nations agency concerned with the environment. Other important international agencies concerned with the environment include the International Maritime Organization (IMO), the World Meteorological Organization, and the Intergovernmental Panel on Climate Change (IPCC). In addition, many of the major environmental treaties create their own structure, usually a Secretariat that services a Conference

of the Parties (COP). The COP meets regularly to consider implementation of the treaty and decide on further refinements or additional commitments.

4. Why does UNEP talk about poverty and the Millennium Development Goals as environmental issues? One of the fundamental changes in international environmental law has been an understanding that poverty both causes and is a consequence of environmental degradation, and that environmental problems must be solved hand in hand with economic ones. This idea, as we will see, underlies in part the concept of "sustainable development."

B. BASIC CONCEPTS OF INTERNATIONAL ENVIRONMENTAL LAW

Before turning to specific regimes or resources, it is useful to outline some of the basic ideas and principles that international environmental lawyers work with. Some of these ideas come from environmental economics and environmental law and policy more generally, and are applicable to both domestic and global environmental problems. Others involve widely-accepted commitments by states to principles guiding action across environmental problems. Often these principles emerge from a combination of repetition in numerous treaties and "soft law" instruments.

Until 1972 there was little in the way of general international environmental law. A few well-known arbitrations set basic rules regarding state responsibility for transboundary harm, but said little about state's responsibilities beyond the cross-border context. There were early conventions on whaling, fisheries, migratory animals and hazardous substances such as oil, but these were aimed primarily at rationalizing use of the resource, not at conservation. In many ways, global environmental concern arose from parallel concerns in many states at a national level: in the U.S., for example, the Clean Air Act's emission controls date to 1970. The rise of global concern over rivers that caught fire and forests dying from acid rain led to the first international conference on the environment, in Stockholm in 1972. The Declarations resulting from the Stockholm conference, and a second conference known as the U.N. Conference on Environment and Development (UNCED), in Rio de Janeiro in 1992, have proven influential in crystallizing state practice until then and outlining general principles, which have then been incorporated into numerous global and regional treaty instruments. While parts of these declarations are undoubtedly reflective of customary international law, others are more controversial.

1. THE POLLUTER–PAYS PRINCIPLE AND ENVIRONMENTAL ECONOMICS

The collective action problems that make international cooperation both necessary and difficult more generally are particularly acute in the environmental protection field. The following classic article explains one reason why:

Garrett Hardin, The Tragedy of the Commons

162 Science 1243–44 (1968)

* * * The tragedy of the commons develops in this way. Picture a pasture open to all. It is to be expected that each herdsman will try to keep as many cattle as possible on the commons. Such an arrangement may work reasonably satisfactorily for centuries because tribal wars, poaching, and disease keep the numbers of both man and beast well below the carrying capacity of the land. Finally, however, comes the day of reckoning, that is, the day when the long-desired goal of social stability becomes a reality. At this point, the inherent logic of the commons remorselessly generates tragedy.

As a rational being, each herdsman seeks to maximize his gain. Explicitly or implicitly, more or less consciously, he asks, "What is the utility *to me* of adding one more animal to my herd?" This utility has one negative and one positive component.

1.   The positive component is a function of the increment of one animal. Since the herdsman receives all the proceeds from the sale of the additional animal, the positive utility is nearly + 1.

2.   The negative component is a function of the additional overgrazing created by one more animal. Since, however, the effects of overgrazing are shared by all the herdsmen, the negative utility for any particular decision-making herdsman is only a fraction of – 1.

Adding together the component partial utilities, the rational herdsman concludes that the only sensible course for him to pursue is to add another animal to his herd. And another. . . . But this is the conclusion reached by each and every rational herdsman sharing a commons. Therein is the tragedy. Each man is locked into a system that compels him to increase his herd without limit—in a world that is limited. Ruin is the destination toward which all men rush, each pursuing his own best interest in a society that believes in the freedom of the commons. Freedom in a commons brings ruin to all. * * *

—————

Can you think of international environmental concerns that exemplify the problem? Note Hardin has been criticized because the commons he describes is really an open access regime, not one of common property, where rules do apply. See Ostrom, E. (1990) *Governing the Commons: The Evolution of Institutions for Collective Action* (Cambridge: Cambridge University Press). What about the high seas? The atmosphere? Do these have the kind of open access characteristics that will create a "tragedy" in fisheries, pollution or poaching of endangered species? Do states face the same kinds of incentives as our herder, in that if they limit their own use of common resources, other states will just take advantage, or will "free-ride" on their efforts to solve the problem? Is this an argument for strong international agreements?

Another concept often used in thinking about environmental problems is that of *externalities*. Why doesn't the herder in Hardin's example think about the cost of overgrazing? Because he only sees the cost to himself, not the cost to all—those costs are *external*. Similarly, a steel plant doesn't have to budget for the costs of the pollution coming out of its stack. As far as it's concerned, the air is free for the taking. Thus, the goal of much environmental policy is to internalize externalities. A related concept is that of market failure. Markets don't work well to price environmental amenities like clean air and water, or aesthetic value, and so prices don't send adequate signals to producers and consumers regarding the need to protect and conserve those resources.

What tools are available to deal with tragedies of the commons, externalities and market failures? Some major options include property rights, government regulation, financial incentives (taxes, penalties, subsidies) and information-based strategies. Property rights theoretically solve the problem because if the resources are yours and you can make money from them, you'll take care of them. Thus, states could allocate individual fishing quotas, or tradeable permits to emit a pollutant. Government regulation can take many forms: in the international environmental law context, so-called "command and control" regulation generally prohibits or limits the production, emission or disposal of certain toxic substances. Financial incentives aim to internalize externalities by raising the price to the polluter so that it aligns with the "true" social cost. They may include taxes, fines or the removal of subsidies for unsustainable practices. Liability regimes may also act to create price incentives for changed behavior, at least over time; with the exception of a few maritime treaties, liability has not been a favored strategy in international environmental law. Finally, information-based strategies seek to empower consumers and to mobilize shame through publicity. An ongoing debate in international environmental law, as in domestic environmental law, pits those who favor market-based or incentive-based solutions against those who prefer a regime of technology-or-health based limits set by governments.

One corollary to the idea of internalizing externalities can be expressed as the "polluter pays" principle, as expressed in the 1992 Rio Declaration on Environment and Development, UN Doc. A/CONF.151/26 (Vol. I) Chapter I, Annex I, 14 June, 1992:

Principle 16

National authorities should endeavour to promote the internalization of environmental costs and the use of economic instruments, taking into account the approach that the polluter should, in principle, bear the cost of pollution, with due regard to the public interest and without distorting international trade and investment.

2.   Equity Issues: Inter-generational Equity, Common but Differentiated Responsibilities, and Sustainable Development

Some of the principles of international environmental law involve fairness in sharing both environmental resources and the burdens of environmental protection and restoration. This includes fairness between current and future generations, between rich and poor countries and between the development needs of the poor and the need for environmental sustainability of economic growth.

a.   INTER-GENERATIONAL EQUITY

E. Brown Weiss, In Fairness to Future Generations, Conference on Human Rights, Public Finance, and the Development Process

8 Am. U. J. of Int'l L. and Pol'y 19–22 (1992)

Sustainable development is inherently an in*ter* generational question as well as an in*tra* generational question. Sustainable development relies on a commitment to equity with future generations. I suggest that this ethical and philosophical commitment acts as a constraint on a natural inclination to take advantage of our temporary control over the earth's resources, and to use them only for our own benefit without careful regard for what we leave to our children and their descendants. This may seem a self-centered philosophy, but it is actually embodied in the logic that controls economic decisions over the use of our resources in day-to-day life.

The recent and valid concern over environmental externalities focuses mainly on the costs that we and our contemporaries must bear when we pollute the air, water and soil by industrial expansion, deforestation and other aspects of economic development. Concern over these externalities is intended to ensure that the benefits from a contemplated action exceed its costs and that those who bear its costs are adequately compensated. But in practice the costs and benefits are assessed from the perspective of the present generation.

The discount rate, or in some ways the tyranny of the discount rate, ensures that short-term benefits nearly always outweigh long-term costs. For this reason it is useful to address the issue of sustainability philosophically and legally, as well as from an economic perspective. Sustainability requires that we look at the earth and its resources not only as an investment opportunity, but as a trust passed to us by our ancestors for our benefit, but also to be passed on to our descendants for their use.

This notion conveys both rights and responsibilities. Most importantly, it implies that future generations have rights too. These rights have meaning only if we, the living, respect them, and in this regard, transcend the differences among countries, religions, and cultures.

It is also important, as we discuss the appropriate economic instruments for sustainable economic development, to ensure the effective transfer of rights and responsibilities from one generation to the next. If we safeguard this transfer, then we can develop the economic instruments to ensure the most efficient use of resources to protect these rights and responsibilities. But we may continue to have difficulties until we firmly establish the transfer of rights and responsibilities as an entitlement.

Fortunately, the notion that each generation holds the earth as a trustee or steward for its descendants strikes a deep chord with all cultures, religions and nationalities. Nearly all human traditions recognize that we, the living, are sojourners on earth and temporary stewards of our resources. The theory of intergenerational equity states that we, the human species, hold the natural environment of our planet in common with other species, other people, and with past, present and future generations. As members of the present generation, we are both trustees, in a sense responsible for ensuring its integrity, and beneficiaries, with the right, the entitlement, to use and benefit from it for ourselves.

* * *

Declaration of the United Nations Conference on the Human Environment

Stockholm, June 5–16, 1972
1 I.L.M. 1416

Principle 1

Man has the fundamental right to freedom, equality and adequate conditions of life, in an environment of a quality that permits a life of dignity and well-being, and he bears a solemn responsibility to protect and improve the environment for present and future generations. * * *

Principle 2

The natural resources of the earth, including the air, water, land, flora and fauna and especially representative samples of natural ecosystems, must be safeguarded for the benefit of present and future generations through careful planning or management, as appropriate.

United Nations Conference on Environment and Development, Rio Declaration on Environment and Development

UN Doc. A/CONF.151/26 (Aug. 12, 1992)

Principle 3

The right to development must be fulfilled so as to equitably meet developmental and environmental needs of present and future generations.

b.   COMMON BUT DIFFERENTIATED RESPONSIBILITIES

Centre for International Sustainable Development Law, The Principle of Common but Differentiated Responsibilities

(2002) available at http://www.cisdl.org/pdf/brief_common.pdf

I.   Definition of the Principle of Common but Differentiated Responsibilities

The principle of "common but differentiated responsibility" evolved from the notion of the "common heritage of mankind" and is a manifestation of general principles of equity in international law. The principle recognises historical differences in the contributions of developed and developing States to global environmental problems, and differences in their respective economic and technical capacity to tackle these problems. Despite their common responsibilities, important differences exist between the stated responsibilities of developed and developing countries. The Rio Declaration states: "In view of the different contributions to global environmental degradation, States have common but differentiated responsibilities. The developed countries acknowledge the responsibility that they bear in the international pursuit of sustainable development in view of the pressures their societies place on the global environment and of the technologies and financial resources they command."

Similar language exists in the Framework Convention on Climate Change; parties should act to protect the climate system "on the basis of equality and in accordance with their common but differentiated responsibilities and respective capabilities."

The principle of common but differentiated responsibility includes two fundamental elements. The first concerns the common responsibility of States for the protection of the environment, or parts of it, at the national, regional and global levels. The second concerns the need to take into account the different circumstances, particularly each State's contribution to the evolution of a particular problem and its ability to prevent, reduce and control the threat. * * *

In practical terms, the principle has at least two consequences. First, it entitles, or may require, all concerned States to participate in international response measures aimed at addressing environmental problems. Second, it leads to environmental standards that impose differing obligations on States. The principle finds its roots prior to UNCED and is supported by state practice at the regional and global levels. * * *

Instances of common responsibility appear as early as 1949, where tuna and other fish were described as being "of common concern" to the parties by reason of their continued use by those parties. Other examples include outer space and the moon, on the other hand, are described as the "province of all mankind," waterfowl as "an international resource," natural and cultural heritage as "part of the world heritage of mankind as a whole," the conservation of wild animals as being "for the good of mankind" and resources of the seabed and ocean floor and subsoil as "the common heritage of mankind." Recent state practice supports the emergence of the concept of "common concern" as reflected in the Climate Change Convention, which acknowledges that "change in the Earth's climate and its adverse effects are a common concern of humankind," and the Biodiversity Convention which affirms that "biological diversity is a common concern of humankind." While each of these formulations differ, and must be understood and applied in the context of the circumstances in which they were adopted, the attributions of "commonality" share common consequences. Although state practice is inconclusive as to the precise legal nature of each formulation, certain legal responsibilities are attributable to all States with respect to these environmental media and natural resources under treaty or customary law. While the extent and legal nature of that responsibility will differ for each resource and instrument, the responsibility of each state to prevent harm, in particular through the adoption of environmental standards and international environmental obligations, can also differ.

Differentiated responsibility appears in a number of treaties. The 1972 London Convention requires measures to be adopted by parties "according to their scientific, technical and economic capabilities." The special needs of developing countries are expressly recognised at article 11(3) of the 1976 Barcelona Convention and in the preamble to the UN Convention on the Law of the Sea, where account is to be taken of their "circumstances and particular requirements," of their "specific needs and special circumstances," or of their "special conditions" and "the fact that economic and social development and eradication of poverty are the first and overriding priorities of the developing country parties." Other treaties identify the need to take account of States' "capabilities," "economic capacity," the "need for economic development," or the "means at their disposal and their capabilities."

The principle of differentiated responsibility has also been applied to treaties and other legal instruments for developed countries. Examples include the 1988 EC Large Combustion Directive, which sets different levels of emission reductions for each member state, the 1991 VOC Protocol, which allows parties to specify one of three different ways to achieve reduction, and the 1992 Maastricht Treaty which provides that: "Without prejudice to the principle that the polluter should pay, if a measure [. . .] involves costs deemed disproportionate for the public authorities of a member state, the Council shall, in the act adopting that measure, lay down appropriate provisions in the form of temporary derogations and/or financial support from the Cohesion Fund." Differentiation within developing countries is specified, for example, in the Climate Change Convention which recognises the "special needs and special circumstances of developing country parties, especially those that are particularly vulnerable to the adverse effects of climate change." Similarly, the Desertification Convention requires that "Parties [. . .] give priority to affected African country parties, in the light of the particular situation prevailing in that region, while not neglecting affected developing country parties in other regions."

Under the 1987 Montreal Protocol the special situation of developing countries entitles them, provided they meet certain conditions, to delay their compliance with control measures. Under the Climate Change Convention, the principle of common but differentiated responsibilities requires specific commitments only for developed country parties at this time, and allows for differentiation in reporting requirements. * * *

See also Ashfaq Khalfan and Marie–Claire Segger Cordonnier, Sustainable Development Law (Oxford: Oxford University Press, 2005).

Why are responsibilities differentiated between developed and developing countries in many environmental treaties? Is it because the developed countries created the problem and so should fix it, or because the developed countries have more resources, or both? As you look through the international environmental regimes we will study, see if you can find instances of application of the principle of common but differentiated responsibilities. We consider the law of common spaces and the common heritage in Section D below.

Note that other international regimes, notably the trade regime, also provide for different obligations for developed and developing countries. See, e.g. Part IV of the General Agreement on Tariffs and Trade, discussed in Chapter 7, or the Doha Ministerial *Declaration* of 14 November 2001 on the TRIPS Agreement and Public Health, Declaration on Compulsory Licensing of Pharmaceuticals (granting least developed countries ten extra years to implement patent obligations).

c. SUSTAINABLE DEVELOPMENT (INTRA-GENERATIONAL EQUITY)

Principle 4, Rio Declaration on Environment and Development

In order to achieve sustainable development, environmental protection shall constitute an integral part of the development process and cannot be considered in isolation from it.

Report of the World Commission on Environment and Development,* Our Common Future

pp. 54–76 (1987)

Sustainable development is development that meets the needs of the present without compromising the ability of future generations to meet their own needs. It contains within it two key concepts:

● the concept of "needs", in particular the essential needs of the world's poor, to which overriding priority should be given; and

_____

* Bruntland Commission.

- the idea of limitations imposed by the state of technology and social organization on the environment's ability to meet present and future needs. . . .

The satisfaction of human needs and aspirations is the major objective of development. The essential needs of vast numbers of people in developing countries for food, clothing, shelter, jobs—are not being met, and beyond their basic needs these people have legitimate aspirations for an improved quality of life. A world in which poverty and inequity are endemic will always be prone to ecological and other crises. Sustainable development requires meeting the basic needs of all and extending to all the opportunity to satisfy their aspirations for a better life.

Living standards that go beyond the basic minimum are sustainable only if consumption standards everywhere have regard for long-term sustainability. Yet many of us live beyond the world's ecological means, for instance in our patterns of energy use. Perceived needs are socially and culturally determined, and sustainable development requires the promotion of values that encourage consumption standards that are within the bounds of the ecological possible and to which all can reasonably aspire.

Meeting essential needs depends in part on achieving full growth potential, and sustainable development clearly requires economic growth in places where such needs are not being met. Elsewhere, it can be consistent with economic growth, provided the content of growth reflects the broad principles of sustainability and non-exploitation of others. But growth by itself is not enough. High levels of productive activity and widespread poverty can coexist, and can endanger the environment. Hence sustainable development requires that societies meet human needs both by increasing productive potential and by ensuring equitable opportunities for all.

The Gabcíkovo–Nagymaros Project

Hungary v. Slovakia
International Court of Justice
1997 I.C.J. Rep. 7 (Judgment of Sept. 25)

[This case was first taken up in Chapter 2 in the discussion of treaty performance. Here is a brief restatement of the facts and some of the main rulings in the case: On September 16, 1977 Hungary and Czechoslovakia entered into a Treaty concerning the construction and operation of a series of locks as a joint investment for the development of water resources, energy, transport, agriculture and other sectors of the national economies of both states. It was aimed at producing hydroelectricity, improving navigation on relevant sections of the River Danube and protection of the areas along the banks against flooding. Both states also undertook to ensure that water quality of the River Danube was not impaired as a result of the Project. Work began in 1978. The Danube is the second longest river in Europe and for 142 kilometers it forms the border between the two states. Due to intense criticism of the Project in Hungary in 1989, Hungary suspended and later on abandoned the Project. The Hungarian concerns and uncertainties stemmed from apprehension of environmental damage and the effect on Budapest's water supply. Hungary justified its conduct on a "state of ecological necessity" that constituted a circumstance that relieved it from incurring international responsibility. During that period Czechoslovakia started to investigate other solutions and decided on an alternative project, known as "Variant C," that entailed a unilateral diversion of the River Danube on its territory. Work on this began in 1991. Discussions broke down between the two states and in 1992 Hungary terminated the 1977 Treaty. In 1993 Slovakia became an independent state. As the successor state to Czechoslovakia, Slovakia's position was that Hungary was bound to carry out its Treaty obligations. Hungary presented five arguments in support of its unilateral termination of the joint Project. These were the existence of a state of necessity, the impossibility of performance of the Treaty, the occurrence of a fundamental change of circumstances, a material breach of the Treaty by Czechoslovakia and lastly the development of new norms of international law pertaining to the environment.]

140. * * * In order to evaluate the environmental risks, current standards must be taken into consideration. This is not only allowed by the wording of [the Treaty] * * *, but even prescribed, to the extent that these articles impose a continuing—and thus necessarily evolving—obligation on the parties to maintain the quality of the water and to protect nature.

The Court is mindful that, in the field of environmental protection, vigilance and prevention are required on account of the often irreversible character of damage to the environment and of the limitations inherent in the very mechanism of reparation of this type of damage.

Through the ages, mankind has, for economic and other reasons, constantly interfered with nature. In the past, this was often done without consideration of the effects upon the environment. Owing to new scientific insights and to a growing awareness of the risks for mankind—for present and future generations—of pursuit of such interventions at an unconsidered and unabated pace, new norms and standards have been developed, set forth in a number of instruments during the last two decades. Such new norms have to be taken into consideration, and such new standards given proper weight, not only when States contemplate new activities but also when continuing with activities begun in the past. This need to reconcile economic development with protection of the environment is aptly expressed in the concept of sustainable development. * * *

SEPARATE OPINION OF VICE–PRESIDENT WEERAMANTRY

This case raises a rich array of environmentally related legal issues. A discussion of some of them is essential to explain my reasons for voting as I have in this very difficult decision. * * *

The problem of steering a course between the needs of development and the necessity to protect the environment is a problem alike of the law of development and of the law of the environment. Both these vital and developing areas of law require, and indeed assume, the existence of a principle which harmonizes both needs.

To hold that no such principle exists in the law is to hold that current law recognizes the juxtaposition of two principles which could operate in collision with each other, without providing the necessary basis of principle for their reconciliation. The untenability of the supposition that the law sanctions such a state of normative anarchy suffices to condemn a hypothesis that leads to so unsatisfactory a result.

Each principle cannot be given free rein, regardless of the other. The law necessarily contains within itself the principle of reconciliation. That principle is the principle of sustainable development.

This case offers a unique opportunity for the application of that principle, for it arises from a Treaty which had development as its objective, and has been brought to a standstill over arguments concerning environmental considerations. * * *

(c) Sustainable Development as a Principle of International Law

After the early formulations of the concept of development, it has been recognized that development cannot be pursued to such a point as to result in substantial damage to the environment within which it is to occur. Therefore development can only be prosecuted in harmony with the reasonable demands of environmental protection. Whether development is sustainable by reason of its impact on the environment will, of course, be a question to be answered in the context of the particular situation involved.

It is thus the correct formulation of the right to development that that right does not exist in the absolute sense, but is relative always to its tolerance by the environment. The right to development as thus refined is clearly part of modern international law. It is compendiously referred to as sustainable development.

The concept of sustainable development can be traced back, beyond the Stockholm Conference of 1972, to such events as the Founex meeting of experts in Switzerland in June 1971; the conference on environment and development in Canberra in 1971; and United Nations General Assembly resolution 2849 (XXVI). It received a powerful impetus from the Stockholm Declaration which, by Principle 11, stressed the essentiality of development as well as the essentiality of bearing environmental considerations in mind in the developmental process. Moreover, many other Principles of that Declaration provided a setting for the development of the concept of sustainable development and more than one third of the Stockholm Declaration related to the harmonization of environment and development. The Stockholm Conference also produced an Action Plan for the Human Environment.

The international community had thus been sensitized to this issue even as early as the early 1970s, and it is therefore no cause for surprise that the 1977 Treaty [between Hungary and Czechoslovakia, ed.], in Articles 15 and 19, made special reference to environmental considerations.

Both Parties to the Treaty recognized the need for the developmental process to be in harmony with the environment and introduced a dynamic element into the Treaty which enabled the Joint Project to be kept in harmony with developing principles of international law.

Since then, it has received considerable endorsement from all sections of the international community, and at all levels.

Whether in the field of multilateral treaties, international declarations; the foundation documents of international organizations; the practices of international financial institutions; regional declarations and planning documents; or State practice, there is a wide and general recognition of the concept. [citing examples in each category]. * * *

The concept of sustainable development is thus a principle accepted not merely by the developing countries, but one which rests on a basis of worldwide acceptance.

In 1987, the Brundtland Report brought the concept of sustainable development to the forefront of international attention. In 1992, the Rio Conference made it a central feature of its Declaration, and it has been a focus of attention in all questions relating to development in the developing countries.

The principle of sustainable development is thus a part of modern international law by reason not only of its inescapable logical necessity, but also by reason of its wide and general acceptance by the global community.

The concept has a significant role to play in the resolution of environmentally related disputes. The components of the principle come from well-established areas of international law—human rights, State responsibility, environmental law, economic and industrial law, equity, territorial sovereignty, abuse of rights, good neighbourliness—to mention a few. It has also been expressly incorporated into a number of binding and far-reaching international agreements, thus giving it binding force in the context of those agreements. It offers an important principle for the resolution of tensions between two established rights. It reaffirms in the arena of international law that there must be both development and environmental protection, and that neither of these rights can be neglected.

The general support of the international community does not of course mean that each and every member of the community of nations has given its express and specific support to the principle—nor is this a requirement for the establishment of a principle of customary international law. * * *

(d) The Need for International Law to Draw upon the World's Diversity of Cultures in Harmonizing Development and Environmental Protection

This case, which deals with a major hydraulic project, is an opportunity to tap the wisdom of the past and draw from it some principles which can strengthen the concept of sustainable development, for every development project clearly produces an effect upon the environment, and humanity has lived with this problem for generations.

This is a legitimate source for the enrichment of international law, which source is perhaps not used to the extent which its importance warrants.

In drawing into international law the benefits of the insights available from other cultures, and in looking to the past for inspiration, international environmental law would not be departing from the traditional methods of international law, but would, in fact, be following in the path charted out by Grotius. Rather than laying down a set of principles a priori for the new discipline of international law, he sought them also a posteriori from the experience of the past, searching through the whole range of cultures available to him for this purpose. From them, he drew the durable principles which had weathered the ages, on which to build the new international order of the future. Environmental law is now in a formative stage, not unlike international law in its early stages. A wealth of past experience from a variety of cultures is available to it. It would be pity indeed if it were left untapped merely because of attitudes of formalism which see such approaches as not being entirely de rigueur.

I cite in this connection an observation of Sir Robert Jennings that, in taking note of different legal traditions and cultures, the International Court (as it did in the Western Sahara case):

> "was asserting, not negating, the Grotian subjection of the totality of international relations to international law. It seems to the writer, indeed, that at the present juncture in the development of the international legal system it may be more important to stress the imperative need to develop international law to comprehend within itself the rich diversity of cultures, civilizations and legal traditions ... "

Moreover, especially at the frontiers of the discipline of international law, it needs to be multi-disciplinary, drawing from other disciplines such as history, sociology, anthropology, and psychology such wisdom as may be relevant for its purpose. * * *

(e) Some Wisdom from the Past Relating to Sustainable Development

There are some principles of traditional legal systems that can be woven into the fabric of modern environmental law. They are specially pertinent to the concept of sustainable development which was well recognized in those systems. Moreover, several of these systems have particular relevance to this case, in that they relate to the harnessing of streams and rivers and show a concern that these acts of human interference with the course of nature should always be conducted with due regard to the protection of the environment. In the context of environmental wisdom generally, there is much to be derived from ancient civilizations and traditional legal systems in Asia, the Middle East, Africa, Europe, the Americas, the Pacific, and Australia—in fact, the whole world. This is a rich source which modern environmental law has left largely untapped. [Judge Weeramantry goes on to describe a number of ancient systems and precepts, including the concept of inter-generational equity] * * *

Observing that various societies have practised sustainable irrigation agriculture over thousands of years, and that modern irrigation systems rarely last more than a few decades, the authors pose the question whether it was due to the achievement of a "congruence of fit" between their methods and "the nature of land, water and climate". Modern environmental law needs to take note of the experience of the past in pursuing this "congruence of fit" between development and environmental imperatives.

By virtue of its representation of the main forms of civilization, this Court constitutes a unique forum for the reflection and the revitalization of those global legal traditions. There were principles ingrained in these civilizations as well as embodied in their legal systems, for legal systems include not merely written legal systems but traditional legal systems as well, which modern researchers have shown to be no less legal systems than their written cousins, and in some respects even more sophisticated and finely tuned than the latter.

Living law which is daily observed by members of the community, and compliance with which is so axiomatic that it is taken for granted, is not deprived of the character of law by the extraneous test and standard of reduction to writing. Writing is of course useful for establishing certainty, but when a duty such as the duty to protect the environment is so well accepted that all citizens act upon it, that duty is part of the legal system in question.

Moreover, when the Statute of the Court described the sources of international law as including the "general principles of law recognized by civilized nations", it expressly opened a door to the entry of such principles into modern international law.

(f) Traditional Principles That Can Assist in the Development of Modern Environmental Law

As modern environmental law develops, it can, with profit to itself, take account of the perspectives and principles of traditional systems, not merely in a general way, but with reference to specific principles, concepts, and aspirational standards.

Among those which may be extracted from the systems already referred to are such far-reaching principles as the principle of trusteeship of earth resources, the principle of intergenerational rights, and the principle that development and environmental conservation must go hand in hand. Land is to be respected as having a vitality of its own and being integrally linked to the welfare of the community. When it is used by humans, every opportunity should be afforded to it to replenish itself. Since flora and fauna have a niche in the ecological system, they must be expressly protected. There is a duty lying upon all members of the community to preserve the integrity and purity of the environment.

Natural resources are not individually, but collectively, owned, and a principle of their use is that they should be used for the maximum service of people. There should be no waste, and there should be a maximization of the use of plant and animal species, while preserving their regenerative powers. The purpose of development is the betterment of the condition of the people.

Most of them have relevance to the present case, and all of them can greatly enhance the ability of international environmental law to cope with problems such as these if and when they arise in the future. There are many routes of entry by which they can be assimilated into the international legal system, and modern international law would only diminish itself were it to lose sight of them—embodying as they do the wisdom which enabled the works of man to function for centuries and millennia in a stable relationship with the principles of the environment. This approach assumes increasing importance at a time when such a harmony between humanity and its planetary inheritance is a prerequisite for human survival.

Sustainable development is thus not merely a principle of modern international law. It is one of the most ancient of ideas in the human heritage. Fortified by the rich insights that can be gained from millennia of human experience, it has an important part to play in the service of international law.

NOTES AND QUESTIONS

1. How does Judge Weeramantry define sustainable development? How does his elaboration on the concept compare to the formulation in the Rio Declaration?

2. Is sustainable development a principle of customary international law? Why? What evidence would you point to? Is it a general principle of law? What evidence would you point to? Can it be both?

3. Traditional knowledge plays an important role as a concept in a number of areas of international law, including biodiversity (see Article 8(j) of the Convention on Biodiversity; Working Group on Article 8(j) http://www.cbd.int/convention/wg8j.shtml) and the rights of indigenous peoples, including the right to "maintain, control, protect and develop their cultural heritage, traditional knowledge and traditional cultural expressions" (see U.N. Declaration on the Rights of Indigenous Peoples, art. 31, G.A. Resolution 61/295, Adopted Sept. 13, 2007); International Labor Organization Convention No. 169, Indigenous and Tribal People's Convention, 1989. The World Intellectual Property Organization (WIPO) and UNESCO also have programs on traditional knowledge. Why are traditional knowledge and traditional (generally unwritten) legal systems important to environmental protection and restoration?

3.   SOVEREIGNTY OVER RESOURCES AND THE OBLIGATION TO AVOID TRANSBOUNDARY HARM

One of the oldest principles of international law is the responsibility of states to avoid harm to the territory of other states. In Roman law, this was known as *sic utere tuo, ut non alienum laedas,* meaning "use your property so as not to injure that of another". This principle was reaffirmed, *inter* alia, by the ICJ in the Corfu Channel case, where the Court held that Albania had violated "every State's obligation not to allow knowingly its territory to be used for acts contrary to the rights of other States." Corfu Channel (U.K. v. Albania), Merits, 1949 I.C.J. Rep. 4, 22 (Judgment of April 9). In the Trail Smelter Arbitration, United Nations, *Reports of International Arbitral Awards, Vol. III,* 1905–81 (1941), fumes from a Canadian smelter were damaging property and health in the State of Washington. After the two countries agreed to arbitration, the arbitral commission held that:

> "... under the principles of international law, as well as of the law of the United States, no State has the right to use or permit the use of its territory in such a manner as to cause injury by fumes in or to the territory of another or the properties or persons therein, when the case is of serious consequence and the injury is established by clear and convincing evidence."

How do these obligations square with the sovereign right of states to use and control over their territory, and in particular over their natural resources? The 1972 Stockholm Conference, in probably its most oft-repeated provision, stated in Principle 21 that:

States have, in accordance with the Charter of the United Nations and the principles of international law, the sovereign right to exploit their own resources pursuant to their own environmental policies, and the responsibility to ensure that activities within their jurisdiction or control do not cause damage to the environment of other States or of areas beyond the limits of national jurisdiction.

The Rio Declaration, ten years later, confirmed that

Principle 2

States have, in accordance with the Charter of the United Nations and the principles of international law, the sovereign right to exploit their own resources pursuant to their own environmental and developmental policies, and the responsibility to ensure that activities within their jurisdiction or control do not cause damage to the environment of other States or of areas beyond the limits of national jurisdiction.

Is the difference between the two formulations significant? Is Rio a step back from the point of view of privileging environmental protection? How exactly is a State supposed to manage the tension between the two parts of the Principle? Is this an absolute obligation, or one of due diligence (see Chapter 5). How much damage is enough to give rise to state responsibility? What about harm within the territory of a State that doesn't have immediately visible transboundary effects? Is there a duty to all states to avoid serious environmental harm? Is this an *erga omnes* obligation like those discussed in the ICJ's *Barcelona Traction Case,* discussed in Chapter 2?

The ICJ reaffirmed the customary nature of the prohibition on causing transboundary harm in a 1996 Advisory Opinion. The General Assembly asked the International Court of Justice in December 1994 for an Advisory

Opinion on the question of the legality of the threat or use of nuclear weapons. The Court advised that the threat or use of nuclear weapons was neither authorized nor prohibited by conventional or customary international law. However, states must comply with the U.N. Charter obligations contained in Articles 2(4) and 51. The extract below addresses the position of international environmental law in this debate.

Legality of the Threat or Use of Nuclear Weapons

International Court of Justice
1996 I.C.J. Rep. 226 (Advisory Opinion of July 8)

THE COURT:

* * *

29.   * * * [T]he environment is under daily threat and * * * the use of nuclear weapons could constitute a catastrophe for the environment. * * * The existence of the general obligation of States to ensure that activities within their jurisdiction and control respect the environment of other States or of other areas beyond national jurisdiction is now part of the corpus of international law relating to the environment.

30.   * * * [T]he issue is not whether the treaties relating to the protection of the environment are or are not applicable during an armed conflict, but rather whether the obligations stemming from these treaties were intended to be obligations of total restraint during military conflict.

The Court does not consider that the treaties in question could have intended to deprive a State of the exercise of its right to self-defence under international law because of its obligations to protect the environment. Nonetheless, States must take environmental considerations into account when assessing what is necessary and proportionate in the pursuit of legitimate military objectives. Respect for the environment is one of the elements that go to assessing whether an action is in conformity with the principles of necessity and proportionality.

[The Court then considered in support of this view, Principle 24 of the Rio Declaration, Articles 35(3) and 55 of Additional Protocol I to the Geneva Conventions and United Nations General Assembly Resolution 47/37 of November 25, 1992 on the Protection of the Environment in Times of Armed Conflict.]

33.   * * * The Court thus finds that while the existing international law relating to the protection of the environment does not specifically prohibit the use of nuclear weapons, it indicates important environmental factors that are properly to be taken into account in the context of the implementation of the principles and rules of the law applicable in armed conflict.

NOTES AND QUESTIONS

1.   Does the Court give any guidance as to exactly how military or civilian commanders should weigh the importance of environmental harm in decid-

ing on whether to threaten or use nuclear weapons? The principles of necessity and proportionality, discussed in Chapter 10 are the heart of international humanitarian law, but they operate, of themselves, at a high level of generality.

2.   Article 8(2)(b)(iv) of the Rome Statute creating the International Criminal Court deals with the war crime of intentionally causing "widespread, long-term and severe damage to the natural environment".

3.   What about the peaceful use of nuclear energy? Several Conventions provide for prompt notification and for mutual assistance in the case of a nuclear accident. See Convention on Early Notification of a Nuclear Accident and Convention on Assistance in the Case of a Nuclear Accident or Radiological Emergency, 25 I.L.M. 1370 and 1377 (1986).

4.   Uncertainty and the Precautionary Principle

The previous rule deals with state responsibility to avoid actual harm. What about risk of harm that has not yet materialized? Much of law and regulation is about planning for and dealing with contingencies and uncertainties. In international environmental law, these uncertainties are compounded by the underlying scientific uncertainty. We know little about how much carbon dioxide, for example, in the atmosphere will set off unstoppable melting of the polar ice sheets, or how the chemicals that surround us react synergistically with others in our bodies to disrupt our hormones. How do we regulate in the face of such uncertainty? Moreover, some of the uncertainties deal with irreversible harm, so that if we decide (or guess) wrong we cannot discover our error and return to the earlier state of affairs. Thus, if the atmosphere or a fishery is degraded past a point of no return, no amount of subsequent action will bring them back within a relevant timeframe. In addition, in the environmental area, even a very small risk, if it materializes, can prove catastrophic—should we regulate on the basis of such "worst case scenarios"?

The problem of acting in the face of incomplete and uncertain information gives rise, in the international environmental law context, to principles of prevention and precaution. First, the principle of prevention holds that it is better to prevent environmental harm in the first place than to remedy it afterwards. This rather common-sense proposition recognizes that after-the-fact remedies tend to be more expensive and complex than prevention, if indeed the damage can be remedied at all. As the Stockholm Declaration puts it:

Principle 6

The discharge of toxic substances or of other substances and the release of heat, in such quantities or concentrations as to exceed the capacity of the environment to render them harmless, must be halted in order to ensure that serious or irreversible damage is not inflicted upon ecosystems. . . .

Principle 7

States shall take all possible steps to prevent pollution of the seas by substances that are liable to create hazards to human health, to harm living resources and marine life, to damage amenities or to interfere with other legitimate uses of the sea.

Pollution prevention and waste minimization efforts, among others, follow from this principle. The more controversial response to uncertainty is the precautionary principle. The most well-known formulation is that in the Rio Declaration:

Principle 15

In order to protect the environment, the precautionary approach shall be widely applied by States according to their capabilities. Where there are threats of serious or irreversible damage, lack of full scientific certainty shall not be used as a reason for postponing cost-effective measures to prevent environmental degradation.

Consider also the Climate Change Framework Convention, Art. 3(3):

The Parties should take precautionary measures to anticipate, prevent or minimize the causes of climate change and mitigate its adverse effects. Where there are threats of serious or irreversible damage, lack of full scientific certainty should not be used as a reason for postponing such measures, taking into account that policies and measures to deal with climate change should be cost-effective so as to ensure global benefits at the lowest possible cost.

As an "approach" that simply means uncertainty can't be used to justify regulatory inaction, this is fairly uncontroversial. The dispute comes over a number of more ambitious formulations: first, that uncertainty justifies, and even compels, action to avoid potential harm. Second, that the precautionary principle shifts the burden of proof on regulation from the government to the proponent of the activity, even absent a conclusive showing of harm. Thus, a 1998 statement by a prominent group of environmental scientists concluded:

"We believe existing environmental regulations and other decisions, particularly those based on risk assessment, have failed to adequately protect human health and the environment, as well as the larger system of which humans are but a part.

We believe there is compelling evidence that damage to humans and the worldwide environment, is of such magnitude and seriousness that new principles for conducting human activities are necessary.

While we realize that human activities may involve hazards, people must proceed more carefully than has been the case in recent history. Corporations, government entities, organizations, communities, scientists and other individuals must adopt a precautionary approach to all human endeavors.

Therefore it is necessary to implement the Precautionary Principle: Where an activity raises threats of harm to the environment or human health, precautionary measures should be taken even if some cause and effect relationships are not fully established scientifically.

In this context the proponent of an activity, rather than the public bears the burden of proof."

Wingspread Statement on the Precautionary Principle, 25 January 1998, available at http://www.gdrc.org/u-gov/precaution–3.htm. See generally Jonathan B. Wiener, "Precaution," in The *Oxford Handbook of International Environmental Law*, D. Bodansky, E. Hey, J. Brunee, eds. (Oxford: Oxford University Press, 2007).

What are the implications of this statement? Does it mean, for example, that Hungary was allowed to abandon its treaty obligations in the *Gabcikovo Dam* case, above, based on a risk of harm to its shared rivercourse? The ICJ rejected this contention, holding that an argument based on necessity flowing from the risk of environmental damage would have to be imminent and "sufficiently certain." (para. 56) What about regulation based on risk assessment? Risk assessments try to determine how much exposure to a substance is tolerable to avoid certain negative health or environmental consequences (say, one cancer case per million people) and risk management then allows the activity up until that level. Would this procedure be prohibited in cases where there is some risk of harm at any level of the activity, as is the case with, for example, the majority of U.S. pollution and chemical-related regulatory programs? Compare to the interpretation of the WTO's SPS Agreement, discussed in Chapter 7. See David Wirth, "The Transatlantic GMO Dispute Against the European Communities: Some Preliminary Thoughts," in EU AND WTO LAW: HOW TIGHT IS THE LEGAL STRAITJACET FOR ENVIRONMENTAL PRODUCT REGULATION? (M. Pallemaerts, ed., VUB University Press, 2006; Boston College Law School Research Paper No. 100. Available at SSRN: http://ssrn.com/abstract=920474.) Would it mean that the makers of new chemicals would have to prove that they were conclusively safe before putting them on the market? How could they do that? See discussion of the EU's REACH program, below in Section C(4). Is there a risk that such a policy would stifle innovation, or leave older, riskier products on the market because newer ones could not pass the test required under this view of the precautionary principle? Could avoiding some risks increase others?

Scholars—and states—differ as to whether the precautionary principle has ripened into a norm of customary international law. It is cited in over 50 treaties or other instruments, including those involving ozone depletion, climate change, biosafety, biodiversity, and persistent organic pollutants as well as many regional instruments. However, the specific formulations differ, and little guidance on application is provided. Nonetheless, the trend is towards greater application and specificity, at both a global and national level. See cites in Wiener, notes 16–18.

5.   PROCEDURAL PRINCIPLES: NOTIFICATION, ASSESSMENT, AND PARTICIPATION

A final set of widely-accepted principles concern methods of ensuring optimal decisionmaking and implementation of environmental protection at both a global and national level. These include a general duty on states to cooperate, see Stockholm Declaration Principle 24, and several more specific manifestations:

a. NOTIFICATION

Rio Declaration Principle 19

States shall provide prior and timely notification and relevant information to potentially affected States on activities that may have a significant adverse transboundary environmental effect and shall consult with those States at an early stage and in good faith.

Note that the notifying state does not have to do anything in particular as a result of consultation, except presumably take their views into account "in good faith." What difficulties can you foresee with the application of this principle?

b. ENVIRONMENTAL ASSESSMENT (EIA)

In 1991 the U.N. Convention on Environmental Impact Assessment in a Transboundary Context was signed, 30 Int'l Leg.Mat. 809 (1991). This Convention provides, *inter alia,* for an assessment procedure that must be undertaken for any activity that is proposed that falls within Appendix I that is likely to cause significant adverse transboundary impact. There are provisions for notification and consultation of affected states parties and the public in those states.

The following year, UNCED affirmed the need for assessment:

Rio Declaration Principle 17

Environmental impact assessment, as a national instrument, shall be undertaken for proposed activities that are likely to have a significant adverse impact on the environment and are subject to a decision of a competent national authority.

Biodiversity Convention Article 14

1. Each Contracting Party, as far as possible and as appropriate, shall:

(a) Introduce appropriate procedures requiring environmental impact assessment of its proposed projects that are likely to have significant adverse effects on biological diversity with a view to avoiding or minimizing such effects and, where appropriate, allow for public participation in such procedures;

(b) Introduce appropriate arrangements to ensure that the environmental consequences of its programmes and policies that are likely to have significant adverse impacts on biological diversity are duly taken into account . . .

See also Climate Change Framework Convention Art. 4(1)(f); Law of the Sea Convention Art. 206, and many regional conventions. Note that the adverse impacts are not necessarily transboundary impacts; a number of treaties specifically provide that transboundary impacts are subject to environmental assessment. Most countries now have their own laws requiring EIAs in cases of potentially significant harm: in the U.S., the National Environmental Policy Act and its state analogs serve that purpose. Many commentators now consider environmental assessment a principle of customary law.

c. PARTICIPATION

Rio Declaration Principle 10

Environmental issues are best handled with participation of all concerned citizens, at the relevant level. At the national level, each individual shall have appropriate access to information concerning the environment that is held by public authorities, including information on hazardous materials and activities in their communities, and the opportunity to participate in decision-making processes. States shall facilitate and encourage public awareness and participation by making information widely available. Effective access to judicial and administrative proceedings, including redress and remedy, shall be provided.

The right to public participation, therefore, encompasses rights to information, to participation in decision-making, and to redress. Why are each of these rights important to effective environmental protection and restoration?

The most important elaboration of this right comes in the UN Economic Commission for Europe's Convention on Access to Information, Public Participation in Decisionmaking and Access to Justice in Environmental Matters, Doc. ECE–CEP–43 (25 June 1998), known as the Aarhus Convention for the Danish city where it was signed. The Convention covers some forty countries, most from Central and Eastern Europe, and includes provisions for national governments to provide all three rights.

Note also the overlap between these procedural rights and the rights to information, redress and political participation in the human rights regimes we have studied. See, e.g. Articles 19, 25 of the ICCPR.

We have considered some of the basic concepts and principles of international environmental law. We now turn to the specifics. We look first at the overarching environmental issue of this century: the accumulation of gases in the atmosphere that is changing the climate of our planet. We look at the problem, the emerging legal regime, and some of its ramifications for other areas of international law. We then consider the law of common spaces, common areas or, in other formulations, the common heritage of humankind. In this category we will study the Law of the Sea, of shared rivers, of Antarctica and of space. We then turn to two other categories of environmental treaties: those that protect the earth's living species, and those that concern the management of hazardous substances, especially chemicals and wastes. In each of these areas, we will draw out the connections and implications of climate change.

A caveat: as is true with many other subjects in this book, this chapter is a radically abbreviated version of an expanding and complex subject. For more information, consult the following reference books, among others: DANIEL BODANSKY, JUTTA BRUNNÉE AND ELLEN HEY, OXFORD HANDBOOK ON INTERNATIONAL ENVIRONMENTAL LAW (2007); ALEXANDRE KISS AND DINAH SHELTON, GUIDE TO INTERNATIONAL ENVIRONMENTAL LAW (2007), PHILIPPE SANDS, PRINCIPLES OF INTERNATIONAL ENVIRONMENTAL LAW, 2d ed. (2003).

C.   INCONVENIENT TRUTHS: OZONE DEPLETION AND CLIMATE CHANGE

1.   OZONE DEPLETION

The most successful international environmental treaty regime to date deals with the problem of ozone depletion. While ground-level ozone is an air pollutant, in the stratosphere the ozone layer is a protective screen that absorbs ultraviolet radiation and thus protects the earth from over-exposure. It is estimated that approximately ninety per cent of all the atmospheric ozone is to be found in the stratosphere. Chemicals, especially chlorofluorocarbons (CFCs), but also hydroflourocarbons (HFCs), carbon tetrachloride and methyl chloroform (solvents), methyl bromide (a soil fumigant) and halons (fire retardants), are known collectively as Ozone Depleting Chemicals (ODCs). When ODCs are released into the atmosphere they break down ozone molecules, causing a chain reaction that destroys stratospheric ozone. CFCs were used starting in the 1920s as less-flammable substitutes for existing gases in many consumer goods such as refrigerators, air conditioners, aerosol cans, solvents and styrofoam. As a result, more harmful UV rays reach the earth, causing increased skin cancers and immune system and eye problems, loss of agricultural productivity, changes in the oceans and other deleterious effects. CFCs, as well as many of their potential substitutes, are also potent greenhouse gases.

In 1985 the Vienna Convention for the Protection of the Ozone Layer, 1513 U.N.T.S. 293, 26 ILM 1516 (1987), became the first multilateral framework convention to deal with this dangerous problem. It came into force on September 22, 1988. Many of the ideas subsequently incorporated into modern international environmental law were first designed to deal with the problem of ozone depletion. The Vienna Convention is designed as a framework within which Protocols on specific substances or timetables can be later negotiated. The Convention recognizes the limits of then-existing scientific knowledge about ozone-depleting chemicals:

Article 2: General obligations

1.   The Parties shall take appropriate measures in accordance with the provisions of this Convention and of those protocols in force to which they are party to protect human health and the environment against adverse effects resulting or likely to result from human activities which modify or are likely to modify the ozone layer.

The Framework Convention does not contain a list of regulated substances, or a target for phasing them out. Instead, reflecting the uncertain science of the time, it is largely procedural, creating a permanent mechanism for considering and acting on the evolving science. It contemplates the creation of additional Protocols and of Annexes containing technical information, including lists of substances and control commitments. A complicated set of voting procedures balances the need for state consent with the need for expeditious action and the desire to avoid "free riders" who take advantage of other states' commitments to end or reduce their production and use.

Article 9: Amendments of the Convention or protocols

1.   Any Party may propose amendments to this Convention or to any protocol. Such amendments shall take due account, inter alia, of relevant scientific and technical considerations.

2.   Amendments to this Convention shall be adopted at a meeting of the Conference of the Parties. Amendments to any protocol shall be adopted at a meeting of the Parties to the protocol in question. ...

3.   The Parties shall make every effort to reach agreement on any proposed amendment to this Convention by consensus. If all efforts at consensus have been exhausted, and no agreement reached, the amendment shall as a last resort be adopted by a three-fourths majority vote of the Parties present and voting at the meeting, and shall be submitted by the Depositary to all Parties for ratification, approval or acceptance.

4.   The procedure mentioned in paragraph 3 above shall apply to amendments to any protocol, except that a two-thirds majority of the parties to that protocol present and voting at the meeting shall suffice for their adoption.

5.   Ratification, approval or acceptance of amendments shall be notified to the Depositary in writing. Amendments adopted in accordance with paragraphs 3 or 4 above shall enter into force between parties having accepted them on the ninetieth day after the receipt by the Depositary of notification of their ratification, approval or acceptance by at least three-fourths of the Parties to this Convention or by at least two-thirds of the parties to the protocol concerned, except as may otherwise be provided in such protocol. Thereafter the amendments shall enter into force for any other Party on the ninetieth day after that Party deposits its instrument of ratification, approval or acceptance of the amendments.

Article 10: Adoption and amendment of annexes

1.   The annexes to this Convention or to any protocol shall form an integral part of this Convention or of such protocol, as the case may be, and, unless expressly provided otherwise, a reference to this Convention or its protocols constitutes at the same time a reference to any annexes thereto. Such annexes shall be restricted to scientific, technical and administrative matters.

2.   Except as may be otherwise provided in any protocol with respect to its annexes, the following procedure shall apply to the proposal, adoption and entry into force of additional annexes to this Convention or of annexes to protocol:

(a) Annexes to this Convention shall be proposed and adopted according to the procedure laid down in article 9, paragraphs 2 and 3, while annexes to any protocol shall be proposed and adopted according to the procedure laid down in article 9, paragraphs 2 and 4;

(b) Any party that is unable to approve an additional annex to this Convention or annex to any protocol to which it is party shall so notify the Depositary, in writing, within six months from the date of the communication of the adoption by the Depositary. The Depositary shall without delay notify all Parties of any such notification received. A Party may at any time substitute an acceptance for a previous declaration of objection and the annexes shall thereupon enter into force for that Party;

(c) On the expiry of six months from the date of the circulation of the communication by the Depositary, the annex shall become effective for all Parties to this Convention or to any protocol concerned which have not submitted a notification in accordance with the provision of subparagraph (b) above. . . .

How does this procedure avoid the problems of consensus voting, which holds progress hostage to the last hold-out? Is it an "opt-in" or an "opt-out" procedure? How does it differ for the Convention itself, any Protocols thereto, and the Annexes to the Protocols? How is less than consensus-based voting consistent with the consent-based nature of international law?

The 1987 Montreal Protocol, which entered into force on January 1, 1989, 26 ILM 1541 (1987) provided the meat on the bones of the framework convention. It also pioneered several innovations that made it effective, and that have been used in various other treaties since then. The Protocol froze consumption levels of CFCs and halons, and required a phased reduction of CFC consumption over a number of years. Rather than set reductions chemical by chemical, the Protocol created a "basket" approach based on each chemical's ozone depleting potential; states could choose to reduce whichever ones they wanted so long as the required overall reductions in ODSs were achieved. These provisions gave greater flexibility, reduced costs, and signaled producers that there would be a market for substitutes if they were developed. The Protocol also required review of the control measures at least every four years. This allowed the legal regime to keep up with the evolving science.

The Protocol created several incentives for states, especially developing states, to join. Article 4 established trade measures aimed at avoiding free rider behavior. States commit to banning the import or export of controlled substances to or from non-parties. The Protocol also, and unusually, bans the import of products containing such substances from non-parties. Article 5 allows a developing country with less than .3 kilograms per capital consumption of controlled ODSs to delay its compliance with the phased reductions by ten years. The parties also agreed to facilitate access to environmentally safe alternatives, and the aid, subsidies, credits or other mechanisms to make them affordable, to developing states, but at that time made no concrete commitments. The Protocol also required eleven ratifications representing two-thirds of global consumption of the controlled substances. Ratification of both the Vienna Convention and the Montreal Protocol is practically universal (195 parties).

By 1990, it was clear that more stringent reductions were required. The 1990 London Adjustments and Amendments thereto, which entered into force on August 10, 1992, 30 ILM 537 (1991), created stepped-up phaseouts for CFCs and halons, and added phaseout schedules for a number of other substances. Developing countries, especially large countries like India and China with huge domestic markets for refrigerators and other CFC-using appliances, demanded a more concrete financial mechanism. They argued (as they would later in the climate negotiations) that their further development should not be constrained because developed countries had created a problem, or that at least they should be reimbursed for the incremental costs of changing over to substitutes. The result was the Multilateral Fund, which is tasked with providing technical and financial assistance to facilitate developing country compliance with the ozone regime. Pledges to the Fund amounted to US$2.2 billion from 1991 to 2007. Since London, periodic meetings of the parties have accelerated complete phaseouts of most ODSs. However, a new problem was created with the early CFC substitutes: some of them are potent greenhouse gases. Recent COPs of the Protocol have focused on phasing out some of these substitutes.

NOTES AND QUESTIONS

1. How does the Vienna Convention/Montreal Protocol regime express the general principles discussed in part A, especially those of common but differentiated responsibilities and precaution? How do the voting and entry into force provisions solve common problems in international lawmaking, including the disincentives for being an early ratifier of a treaty, and problems of free riding?

2. To what extent is the ozone regime a model for international lawmaking on climate change? How is the climate change problem different from that of ozone depletion? Take into account that a handful of large manufacturers, led by Dupont and the British company ICI, produced almost all ODS. Why might the manufacturers have eventually agreed to support the phasing out of CFCs? Richard Benedick, the chief U.S. negotiator of the Montreal Protocol, reflected years later on its success:

Richard Benedick, Avoiding Gridlock on Climate Change

Issues in Science and Technology 37–40 (Winter 2007)

We might draw some useful lessons from the ozone history. In the late 1970s, the ozone science was actually much more disputed than the climate science of today, and the major countries that produced and consumed chlorofluorocarbons (CFCs) were hopelessly deadlocked over the necessity for any controls at all. In this situation, the first international action on protecting the ozone layer was neither global, nor even a treaty. Rather, it was an informal accord among a loose coalition of like-minded nations, including Australia, Canada, Norway, Sweden, and the United States, to individually and separately ban the use of CFCs in aerosol spray cans.

This measure alone resulted in a temporary 30% drop in global CFC consumption (temporary because these "wonder chemicals" were continuing to find new uses in numerous industries.) But the action was nevertheless significant for the future. The resultant technological innovations demonstrated to the skeptics (in this case the European Community, Japan, and the Soviet Union) that controls were feasible, at least for this class of products. It also gave the United States and other proponents of a strong treaty the moral and practical high ground in later negotiations to restrict all uses of CFCs. Yet, if anyone had actually proposed a 30% reduction target, it would surely have been rejected as impossible.

An important lesson here is that a specific policy measure, not an abstract target, could stimulate unanticipated technological innovation. The policy measure drove the agreement on targets in the later ozone protocol, not vice versa. In contrast, the half-hearted performance of most governments with respect to climate policy measures has not matched their political rhetoric about the urgency of targets.

Another important lesson from the Montreal history was that not all countries need to agree in order to take a substantial step forward. It is also relevant to note that, in contrast to Kyoto, developing nations did accept limitations on their CFC consumption, but only when they were assured of equitable access to new technologies.

See also Richard Benedick, *Ozone Diplomacy* 5–7, 204–208 (Cambridge: Harvard University Press, 1991).

With these lessons in mind, we turn to the question of climate change, perhaps the most important and far-reaching environmental issue of this century.

2. CLIMATE CHANGE

a. THE SCIENCE

Climate change is a product of the "greenhouse effect." The gases created by burning of fossil fuels and other processes act like a greenhouse: sunlight passes through, but infra-red radiation is trapped close to the earth's surface, leading to overall warming. While carbon dioxide is the major culprit quantitatively, a number of other gases including methane, nitrous oxide, and hydroflourocarbons, perflourocarbons and sulfur hexafluoride are also powerful greenhouse gases (GHGs), as are the chloroflourocarbons (CFCs) regulated by the Montreal Protocol discussed above. Forests and plants store carbon dioxide (in the climate change regime they are discussed as "sinks"), and when they are cut down or burned that CO_2 escapes. Thus, almost every modern human activity, from burning fossil fuels for energy and transportation, to industrialized agriculture or accumulating wastes (which create methane), to clearing forests is implicated in the current and expected climactic changes. While climate change is sometimes called "global warming" this is actually something of a misnomer: although the overall effect is a warming of the earth's atmosphere, the effect in any particular place may be more severe weather, including more cold spells or precipitation as well as heat or drought.

b. THE IMPACTS OF CLIMATE CHANGE

Report, American Clean Energy and Security Act of 2009 [H.R. 2454]

Committee on Energy and Commerce, U.S. House of Representatives, 111TH Cong. Rept. #111–137, 277–320 (June 5, 2009)

THE IMPACTS OF CLIMATE CHANGE

The current and anticipated impacts of climate change have been increasingly well documented in the scientific literature. These impacts include effects on water scarcity and quality, the Arctic and Antarctic, warming and acidification of the world's oceans, sea level rise and coastal impacts, extreme weather events, public health, forests and wildfires, wildlife and endangered species, and national security.

INCREASING WATER SCARCITY AND DECLINING WATER QUALITY

One of the most dramatic impacts of global warming in the 21st century will be the exacerbation of already severe water scarcity—both in the United States and abroad. Freshwater scarcity and threats to water quality are increasing dramatically both in the United States and across the world. More than a billion people currently lack access to safe drinking water. By 2025, 1.8 billion people are expected to be living in regions experiencing water scarcity and "two-thirds of the world's population could be living under water stressed conditions." Climate change will greatly exacerbate current and future water stress. For example, the IPCC projects that by 2020, between 75 and 250 million people in Africa alone will experience an increase of water stress due to climate change. For Asia, the number is between 120 million and 1.2 billion people, and for Latin America it is 12 to 81 million.

Global warming is leading to rapid melting of land ice, glaciers, ice caps, and snow fields which over time will exacerbate water scarcity in many regions of the globe. One-sixth of the world population currently relies on meltwater from glaciers and snow cover for drinking water and irrigation for agriculture. . . .

Increased water stress due to climate change will disproportionately affect the dry tropics and dry regions at lower mid-latitudes—notably

Southeast Asia, southern Africa, Brazil, and the American Southwest. The United States is already experiencing water stress, which will worsen severely in the coming decades due to climate change. . . .

IMPACTS ON THE ARCTIC AND ANTARCTIC

The Arctic is one of the hotspots of global warming. Over the past 50 years average temperatures in the Arctic have increased as much as 7°F, five times the global average. In the next 100 years, some areas in the Arctic may see an increase in average temperatures as high as 13°F.

As temperatures rise in the Arctic, sea ice and glaciers are melting at an unprecedented and alarming rate. In 2007, a record 386,000 square miles of Arctic sea ice melted away, an area larger than Texas and Arizona combined and as big a decline in one year as has occurred over the last decade. In 2008, the sea ice extent was only slightly greater than in 2007, but the sea ice volume is likely the lowest on record due to the decline in multiyear old ice and the thinness of the remaining ice. Recent observations suggest that Arctic sea ice could completely disappear during the summer as early as 2020.

The Greenland ice sheet is melting at an alarming rate. Between 1979 and 2002, the extent of melting in Greenland has increased on average by 16 percent—an area roughly the size of Sweden. In the record-breaking year of 2005, parts of Greenland melted that have never melted during the 27–year–long satellite record.

A complete melting of Greenland would result in a rise in global sea level of more than 20 feet, with catastrophic consequences for coastal regions around the world. Furthermore, melting Arctic glaciers would contribute large amounts of fresh water into the ocean, potentially changing oceanic currents, damaging eco-systems and altering current weather conditions.

At the opposite end of world, massive amounts of water are stored in the two ice sheets of Antarctica. The larger East Antarctic ice sheet covers the majority of the continent, while the West Antarctic ice sheet has significant ice shelves partially floating in the ocean. In the spring of 2002, scientists were shocked to discover that an ice shelf the size of Rhode Island had disintegrated from the West Antarctica ice sheet in just over a month, rather than the millennium previously assumed. Until recently, it was believed that only coastal areas of the West Antarctic were vulnerable to melting. Satellite analysis has now revealed that large inland regions are also showing signs of the impacts of warming. NASA and university researchers have found clear evidence that an area the size of California melted in January 2005 in response to warm temperatures.

WARMING AND ACIDIFICATION OF THE WORLD'S OCEANS

The world's oceans will suffer devastating impacts as a result of global climate change. The oceans are already warming due to climate change. The oceans cover 70 percent of the Earth's surface and are critical components of the climate system for redistributing heat around the world and absorbing CO_2 from the atmosphere. According to the IPCC, global ocean temperature has risen by 0.18° F from 1961 to 2003. Since the ocean has a heat capacity 1,000 times greater than that of the atmosphere, it has taken up 20 times more heat than the atmosphere during this same period. As a result of the ocean's relatively large heat capacity, it has a great effect on the Earth's heat balance and how energy from solar radiation is distributed throughout the global environment.

Increasing atmospheric CO_2 concentrations are causing acidification of the oceans. * * *

Warming and acidification of ocean waters due to climate change are contributing to the collapse of coral reefs around the globe. Coral reefs are habitat for about a quarter of marine species, are the most diverse among marine ecosystems, and are already in a state of decline. * * *

Climate change threatens global fisheries. Warmer water and acidification not only harm coral reefs that function as fish hatcheries, but could also change the circulation of the world's ocean currents. Most fish species have a fairly narrow range of optimum temperatures due to temperature effects on their basic metabolism and the availability of food sources that have their own optimum temperature ranges. * * *

SEA LEVEL RISE AND COASTAL IMPACTS

Sea levels are already rising, and are predicted to rise by at least 1–2 feet by 2100—with the potential for a nearly 40–foot rise in sea level if the Greenland and West Antarctica ice sheets were to melt completely. The IPCC predicts that sea levels will rise by 8 to 24 inches above current levels by 2100, primarily due to thermal expansion from rising ocean temperatures with current emissions trends more consistent with the higher end of this range. However, how much and how quickly the polar ice sheets will melt in response to global warming is a critical question. Many scientists are increasingly concerned that the Greenland and West Antarctic ice sheets are melting at a greater rate than previously predicted. Because scientists do not fully understand the dynamics of ice sheet melting, the IPCC found that larger values of sea level rise could not be excluded. A complete melting of the Greenland ice sheet alone would cause a 20–foot rise in sea level, and complete melting of the West Antarctic ice sheet would cause a 16–foot sea level rise.

Sea level rise will have severe impacts on the world's coastal populations, including in the United States. Rising sea levels are already causing inundation of low-lying lands, erosion of wetlands and beaches, exacerbation of storm surges and flooding, and increases in the salinity of coastal estuaries and aquifers. The most dramatic near-term effects of sea level rise are being felt by inhabitants of small island states, the very existence of which is now endangered. Further, about one billion people live in areas within feet elevation of today's sea level, including many U.S. cities on the East Coast and Gulf of Mexico, almost all of Bangladesh, and areas occupied by more than 250 million people in China. In total, more than 70 percent of the world's population lives on coastal plains, and 11 of the world's 15 largest cities are on the coast.

In addition, rising sea level due to climate change will threaten drinking water supplies in coastal areas—causing intrusion of saltwater into both surface water and ground water. * * *

EXTREME WEATHER EVENTS

Global warming has already changed the intensity, duration, frequency, and geographic range of a variety of weather patterns and will continue to do so—with potentially severe impacts on the United States and the world. There is a broad scientific consensus that the United States is vulnerable to weather hazards that will be exacerbated by climate change. The cost of damages from weather disasters has increased markedly from the 1980s, rising to more than 100 billion dollars in 2007. In addition to a rise in total cost, the frequency of weather disasters costing more than one billion dollars has increased.

Global warming will lead to more extreme precipitation events and flooding. The IPCC has found that "[t]he frequency of heavy precipitation events has increased over most land areas, consistent with warming and observed increases of atmospheric water vapor." The U.S. Climate Change Science Program has concluded that heavy precipitation events averaged over North America have increased over the past 50 years.

Flooding and extreme precipitation events cost lives and can cause massive damages to infrastructure, property, and agricultural lands, as was highlighted by the flooding in the Midwestern United States in the summer of 2008. * * *

Increased sea surface temperatures are a critical determining factor in the strength of hurricanes, and some scientists predict that global warming will result in an increase in hurricane and tropical cyclone frequency and intensity. The IPCC has found observational evidence for the increase in intense hurricanes in the North Atlantic since the 1970s, correlated with increasing sea surface temperatures. Severe thunderstorms, hail, tornados, and winter storms may also increase. * * *

PUBLIC HEALTH

There is a broad consensus among experts within the worldwide public health community that climate change poses a serious risk to public health. The IPCC's Fourth Assessment report concluded that climate change's likely impacts on public health include:

● More frequent and more intense heat waves, leading to marked short-term increases in mortality.

● Increased numbers of people suffering from death, disease, and injury from floods, storms, fires and droughts.

● Increased cardio-respiratory morbidity and mortality associated with ground-level ozone pollution.

● Changes in the range of some infectious disease vectors.

● Increased malnutrition and consequent disorders, including those relating to child growth and development.

* * *

FORESTS AND WILDFIRES

The clearing and degradation of tropical forests is a major driver of global climate change. Forests cover about 30 percent of the Earth's land surface and hold almost half of the world's terrestrial carbon. They can act both as a source of carbon emissions to the atmosphere when cut, burned, or otherwise degraded and as a sink when they grow, removing carbon dioxide from the air through photosynthesis.

Since the 1950s, greenhouse gas emissions from land use change, including deforestation and degradation, have been significant, on the order of 20 to 50 percent of fossil fuel emissions. Deforestation and degradation currently account for 20 to 25 percent of global anthropogenic greenhouse gas emissions, roughly equivalent to the total fossil fuel emissions from the United States. These emissions come predominantly from deforestation of tropical rainforests.

Tropical forests play an especially crucial role. When forests are destroyed by fire, much of the carbon they store returns to the atmosphere, enhancing global warming. When a forest is cleared for crop or grazing land, the soils can become a large source of global warming emissions, depending on how farmers and ranchers manage the land. In places such as Indonesia, the soils of swampy lowland forests are rich in partially decayed organic matter, known as peat. During extended droughts, such as during El Niño events, the forests and the peat become flammable, especially if they have been degraded by logging or accidental fire. When they burn, they release huge volumes of CO_2 and other greenhouse gases.

There is growing scientific consensus that climate change is already increasing the frequency and intensity of wildfires in the United States, and this trend is likely to worsen in the coming decades. * * *

Global warming is also exacerbating insect infestations (most notably bark beetles), which in turn make forests more susceptible to wildfire. * * *

WILDLIFE AND ENDANGERED SPECIES

If climate change goes unchecked, it could lead to the extinction of up to 40 percent of the world's species by the latter half of this century. The International Union for the Conservation of Nature's [IUCN] 2008 annual report lists 38 percent of catalogued species as already threatened with extinction—including nearly 25 percent of all mammals. According to the IPCC's Fourth Assessment Report, "the resilience of many ecosystems is likely to be exceeded this century by an unprecedented combination of climate change, associated disturbances, (e.g. flooding, drought, wildfire, insects, ocean acidification), and other global change drivers.''

* * *

NATIONAL SECURITY IMPACTS

The current and projected impacts of global warming have serious national security consequences for the United States and our allies, in many cases acting as "threat multipliers." The security issues raised by global warming have received increasing scrutiny in the last few years both in Congress and in international venues, including a debate at the UN Security Council in April 2007. The first-ever U.S. government analysis of the security threats posed by global climate change was issued in June 2008 as the National Intelligence Assessment (NIA), *National Security Implications of Global Climate Change to 2030.* * * * In addition, U.S. and European military and security policy analysts have issued a number of public reports exploring the security consequences of global warming and potential responses. All of these reports emphasize concerns over a few key security impacts, including migration, water scarcity, infrastructure at risk from extreme weather, and new economic routes and access to new energy resources. In most cases, global warming is not creating "new" security threats, but rather is acting as a "threat multiplier."

Numerous impacts of global warming could ultimately increase both the temporary and permanent migration of people inside and across existing national borders—increasing risks of geopolitical instability. Nations dealing with an influx may have neither the resources nor the desire to support climate migrants. As in the past, movement of people into new territory can increase the likelihood of conflict and the potential need for intervention from U.S. and allied military forces.

Rising sea levels threaten low-lying island nations and populous coastal areas. Even if not totally inundated, rising sea levels can render these areas uninhabitable due to sea water incursion into fresh water resources and increased exposure to storms. For example, the risk of coastal flooding in Bangladesh is growing and could force 30 million people to search for higher ground in a country already known for political violence. India is already building a wall along its border with Bangladesh. The densely-populated and oil-rich Niger Delta is already the scene of conflict over the sharing of oil revenues. Land loss and increased risk of storms will exacerbate these tensions as well as the challenge of maintaining the existing oil infrastructure. Other important economic and agricultural coastal areas, like Egypt's Nile Delta and China's southeast coast, are also threatened from rising sea-levels and severe storms. Similar impacts in Central America and the Caribbean could add pressure to pre-existing migration patterns from those areas to the United States.

Increased water scarcity due to climate change exacerbates the risk of conflict over water resources. * * *

Finally, accelerating melting of Arctic sea ice is impacting the United States' strategic interests in the region. Russia has moved to stake claim to more than 460,000 square miles of territory, including areas with potential oil and natural gas resources. With the opening of the Northwest Passage for the first time in recorded history, the Prime Minister of Canada announced his intention to increase his country's military presence in the Arctic. Other circumpolar nations, including the United States, have begun to examine their potential claims on Arctic territory and identify necessary preparations for increased maritime traffic in the area.

THE ECONOMIC COSTS OF CLIMATE CHANGE

Climate change impacts of the types described above will have staggering economic impacts in the United States and the rest of the world in the coming decades * * *

Factoring in a wider range of harms such as health impacts and wildlife damages, these costs could reach 3.6 percent of GDP annually in the United States by 2100.

IMPACTS ON VULNERABLE COMMUNITIES

Climate change is predicted to have devastating impacts on the developing world, reversing gains in poverty reduction, food security and nutrition, health, and basic services and putting millions of lives at risk. Poor communities are especially vulnerable because they have less capacity to adapt to changes in climate and are more dependent on climate-sensitive resources such as local water and food supplies. Increased exposure to drought and water scarcity, more intense storms, floods, and other environmental pressures are projected to reverse many of the recent gains in poverty alleviation around the world, adding to the total of 2.6 billion people now living on $2 a day or less. By the end of the century, an additional 145–220 million people in South Asia and Sub Saharan Africa could fall below the $2 per day poverty level as a result of climate change impacts.

Poor communities and communities of color within the United States are vulnerable to climate change impacts as well, and suffer disproportionately from illnesses due to the social determinants of health. * * *

c.   THE EVOLVING LEGAL REGIME

1.) *The UN Framework Convention*

In 1988 UNEP and the World Meteorological Organization (WMO) established the Intergovernmental Panel on Climate Change to provide scientific and technical research on climate change. The United Nations General Assembly endorsed this in its Resolution on protection of Global Climate for Present and Future Generations of Mankind. See U.N.G.A. Res. 43/53, of December 6, 1988, reprinted in 28 ILM 1326 (1988). In its second Resolution on this topic the General Assembly supported UNEP and the WMO's initiative to initiate negotiations for a framework convention on climate change. See U.N.G.A. Res. 44/207, of December 22, 1989. On June 5, 1992, the United Nations Framework Convention on Climate Change was opened for signature, at UNCED. No reservations to this Convention are allowed. It entered into force on March 21, 1994. As of August, 2009 there were 192 states parties, including the United States.

The Framework Convention recognizes that climate change is a serious global problem and that emissions of carbon dioxide and other greenhouse gases must be reduced. It commits states parties to inventory greenhouse gases emitted from their territory, and to take climate change into account in formulating national policies. It provides for special consideration for countries that will be particularly affected by climate change, including island and desert states. It also contains the basic division of the world into developed (Annex I) and other countries. Each Annex I country is to:

> adopt national policies and take corresponding measures on the mitigation of climate change, by limiting its anthropogenic emissions of greenhouse gases and protecting and enhancing its greenhouse gas sinks and reservoirs. These policies and measures will demonstrate that developed countries are taking the lead in modifying longer-term trends in anthropogenic emissions consistent with the objective of the Convention, recognizing that the return by the end of the present decade to earlier levels of anthropogenic emissions of carbon dioxide and other greenhouse gases not controlled by the Montreal Protocol would contribute to such modification, and taking into account the differences in these Parties' starting points and approaches, economic structures and resource bases, the need to maintain strong and sustainable economic growth, available technologies and other individual circumstances, as well as the need for equitable and appropriate contributions by each of these Parties to the global effort regarding that objective. Art. 4(2)(a).

As you can see, the underlying political issue at Rio, as well as later in Kyoto (and also at Copenhagen in December 2009) was (and is) one of equity. The developing countries, citing the principle of common but differentiated responsibilities (see above) argued that because industrialized states had reaped the benefits of a non carbon-constrained world and had caused the problem, they should go first in making binding commitments to solve it. The developing states further argued that their continued development, and therefore the welfare of their peoples, required a cushion of further allowable carbon emissions. The developed countries, in turn, pointed out that an increasing proportion of carbon emissions come from developing countries, so that without their participation no real progress could be made. Furthermore, if only some country's emissions were limited, those not so limited would gain unfair trade advantages. In addition, there was no reason why these countries had to follow the same carbon-dependent trajectory rather than "leap-frogging" to new, clean energy as a basis for sustainable development.

The climate change regime is the attempt to square this circle. The Framework Convention also set in motion a process for further talks, including periodic conferences of the parties. It set up subsidiary bodies on science and on implementation. Like other framework conventions, it allows for the possibility of subsequent Protocols that may be adopted by some or all of the parties to the Convention.

The first Conference of the state parties to the Climate Convention was held in Berlin in 1995. The result was the "Berlin Mandate" which provided that the stated objectives of the developed states parties to reduce emissions of greenhouse gases to 1990 levels by 2000 were not adequate; it also aimed at producing a protocol or other agreement which would contain new emission reductions. The parties also decided to locate the Secretariat in Berlin. In 1996 the second meeting was held in Geneva and the third in 1997 in Kyoto, Japan. The big issue in Kyoto was whether or not developed states would agree to binding targets and timetables for emissions reductions. The Kyoto meeting was a cliff-hanger, not least because the U.S., which had raised objections to binding targets, at the last minute changed its position when then Vice–President Al Gore addressed the assembled delegates.

d. THE KYOTO PROTOCOL

The Kyoto Protocol was adopted on December 11, 1997. To enter into force, Kyoto had to be ratified by at least 55 countries, making up at least 55 percent of the emissions of the industrialized countries. Although the United States signed it, it was never submitted to the Senate for ratification (probably because the Senate, by a vote of 96–0, rejected it even before submission). European states were early supporters, Japan eventually came on board, and the Protocol entered into force on February 15, 2007 after Russia received special concessions and agreed to ratify. As of 2009 there are 184 parties.

The Protocol contains greenhouse gas emission reduction commitments (listed in Annex B of the Protocol) that are aimed at reducing the overall emissions of Annex I (developed) countries by at least 5% below 1990 levels in a period of initial commitments of 2008–2012. Annex I states are bound to reduce their emissions by a specified percentage from their baseline (generally 1990, with a few negotiated exceptions), while Annex II and III states (developing and "transitional" i.e. ex-Soviet) must reduce emissions but are not subject to specified targets. Targeted emissions reductions are calculated for a "basket" of gases, based on a formula reflecting their relative climate changing potency. The Protocol includes limited provisions for including "sinks" like forests in Annex I countries' net emissions calculations. We discuss the role of forests in climate change below, at Section C(4).

To reduce the costs of emissions reductions, the Protocol contains a number of market-based mechanisms. Please read articles 4(1), 6(1) and 12 in conjunction with the following analysis:

Harro van Asselt and Joyeeta Gupta, Stretching Too Far? Developing Countries and the Role of Flexibility Mechanisms Beyond Kyoto

28 Stan. Envtl. L.J. 311, 331 (2009)*

* * *

IIA. Flexibility Mechanisms in the Climate Regime: Background and History

[T]he Kyoto Protocol introduced three new market-based flexibility instruments: International emissions trading, [Joint Implementation] JI, and the [Clean Development Mechanism] CDM. The main rationale behind these flexibility mechanisms is cost effectiveness—ensuring that greenhouse gas emission reductions take place where they are cheapest.

International emissions trading can be classified as a "cap-and-trade" system, where a certain emission cap is set, and a fixed number of emission allowances are distributed. Article 17 of the Kyoto Protocol, in conjunction with Annex B—indicating the list of countries with binding targets—provides developed countries with an opportunity to realize the necessary emission reductions under the cap through emissions trading. If a country has low marginal abatement costs, it can sell its surplus allowances on the international market. Likewise, those countries with high marginal abatement costs can buy allowances at the market price. By putting a price on emissions, emissions trading can provide economic incentives for technological innovation, since new technologies can lead to greater reductions.

In implementing emissions trading, two broad methods for the initial allocation of allowances are commonly distinguished: allowances can be sold to the highest bidder ("auctioning"), or they can be allocated for free on the basis of historical or current emissions ("grandfathering"). * * *

In contrast with international emissions trading, both the CDM and JI can be classified as "baseline-and-credit" systems, through which credits can be earned by reducing greenhouse gas emissions against a constructed baseline. It is important to note that the mechanisms do not reduce greenhouse gas emissions; instead, they allow developed country investors to increase their emissions when they purchase credits.

Under the CDM, developed (Annex B) countries may form voluntary partnerships with non-Annex B countries to undertake greenhouse gas emission reduction projects. The dual purpose of the CDM as outlined in the Kyoto Protocol is to assist non-Annex B countries in achieving sustainable development through new technologies and efficiency techniques, while allowing Annex B countries to achieve their Kyoto targets at lower cost through certified emissions reductions (CERs), which may be counted against their national emission reduction targets. Whereas the CDM establishes the possibility for developed countries to cooperate with developing countries on greenhouse gas emission reduction projects, JI enables cooper-

---

* Footnotes omitted.

ation between two Parties to the Kyoto Protocol that both have binding quantitative commitments.

* * *

B.   Flexibility Mechanisms and Developing Countries: Structural Concerns

* * *

1.   Diffusing Western structures and values.

The first general objection to flexibility mechanisms is an ideological one that opposes imposition of one policy instrument on all countries. Through international emissions trading, Richman argues, Western structures and values are being diffused to developing countries. Some have deemed this to be a form of "carbon colonialism." * * * This commodification of the atmosphere could contribute to the diffusion of Western notions of cost effectiveness, free markets, law and economics, and property rights, even when it is unclear whether such notions favor, and are favored by, developing countries, or are compatible with environmental protection.

* * *

2.   Historical responsibility and shunning leadership.

For the second concern, the basic contention is that because developed countries have emitted greenhouse gases without regulatory constraints since preindustrial times, they are responsible for the observed and projected climate change impacts. Through emissions trading, however, developed countries can, to some extent, buy themselves out of their commitment to reduce emissions domestically, and receive credit for carbon reductions that result from their assistance to other countries. Even though the Kyoto Protocol demands that the use of flexibility mechanisms should be supplemental to domestic emission reductions, this "supplementarity" is not defined. Thus, it is possible for developed countries to evade their responsibility and leadership obligation, as there would be " 'virtual' compliance without physical compliance." By permitting credits from emissions trading, the incentives for domestic action are reduced, which could result in less—rather than more—technological innovation in the countries buying the credits.

Moreover, acceptance of the idea of grandfathering brings with it a rejection of the idea of allocations based on other rights. Under grandfathering, the polluter gets paid as countries are allocated emission rights more or less in accordance with their current emission levels, and the largest polluters can get compensated for reducing their emissions beyond their commitment levels. If this principle is accepted as legitimate, then allocating on the basis of other principles, such as the per capita principle, inevitably gets labeled as "hot air." "Hot air" in this context refers to providing allocations to countries in excess of their current pollution levels. The issue of hot air has also provoked other responses, not only in developing countries. It has been defined as the "degree to which a country's assigned amount exceeds what its emissions would be in the absence of any abatement measures." Effectively, it allows developed countries to increase their emissions by purchasing emission allowances from countries with economies in transition—mainly the countries that were part of the Former Soviet Union and its satellite states. Many of these latter countries are emitting far below their allocated levels as their economies have undergone extensive restructuring in the transition phase, and it will take some time before their economies recover. These countries could thus benefit from selling their surplus emissions. Buying emission allowances from these countries through international emissions trading would endanger the environmental integrity of the Kyoto Protocol, as the countries with economies in transition do not have to take any particular steps, at least in the short term, to reduce emissions. Although hot air would not technically lead Annex I countries to exceed their emission targets, the practical and ethical argument against it is that it can lead to higher emissions than would occur without emissions trading.

* * *

3. Differences in negotiating power.

After the adoption of the Kyoto Protocol, an extensive rulebook has developed on international emissions trading and the CDM. It is a daunting task for anyone to understand the detailed, and often complicated, rules and procedures. ... As a result, it is likely that the details of emissions trading at the global level will be based on experiences and proposals stemming from developed countries. * * *

4. High administrative burdens.

The design and implementation of emissions trading schemes pose new challenges to developed nations, as is illustrated by the European Union's struggle with the European emissions trading scheme. For developing countries, where institutional structures take different forms, this undertaking would be even more challenging. For any emissions trading scheme to function properly, countries need to fulfill certain basic conditions, which could imply high administrative costs. This includes establishing a reliable emissions monitoring, reporting and verification system, as well as putting in place a national registry for emission allowances. * * * Although the Kyoto Protocol does not yet extend international emissions trading to developing countries, it is important to keep this concern in mind in the light of calls to create a global carbon market.

C. The Clean Development Mechanism and Developing Countries

* * *

Increasingly, observers note that there is an inherent tension between the mechanism's objectives, and that tradeoffs are inevitable. The main criticism can be summarized as follows: the CDM focuses too much on ensuring that Annex B countries achieve their targets in a cost-effective fashion, and too little on ensuring sustainable development in non-Annex B countries. More specific concerns regarding the design of the mechanism are discussed below.

1.   Additionality and perverse incentives.

One of the key issues in the debate over the CDM involves the concept of additionality, the idea that a specific project activity would not have occurred without the CDM. The term "additionality" has various dimensions. A project could imply a trend break from current technological practice resulting in the transfer of best available technologies to the host country, which would make it technologically additional. A project could also be a more costly, but lower-emitting, alternative to common (baseline) practice, through which the project would satisfy the requirement of investment additionality. The additionality requirement aims to ensure that Annex B countries do not comply with their obligations under the Kyoto Protocol through the purchase of credits from projects that would have also been realized if this purchase had not taken place.

* * *

The concept of additionality also leads to consideration of another drawback of the CDM. Existing policies in CDM host countries naturally count as business-as-usual developments, and therefore emission reductions under these policies do not count. This creates a perverse incentive for host country governments to abstain from formulating greenhouse-gas-reducing policies and measures. The perversity lies in the fact that if countries adopt new and stricter environmental policies, their prospects of getting emission reductions funded under the CDM are reduced.

* * *

2.   Concentration of project types and sustainable development.

The Kyoto Protocol's Article 12 can be interpreted in such a way that it does not allow projects that do not contribute to sustainable development to be funded through the CDM. Determining which projects contribute to sustainable development and which ones do not, however, is highly context-specific and subjective. This difficulty is part of the reason why the definition of sustainable development is left up to the non-Annex B host countries. However, it is perhaps possible to indicate which projects have more benefits than others in terms of their contribution to sustainable development. At the very least, we would argue that contributing to sustainable development means something more than just reducing greenhouse gas emissions. Otherwise, every project that reduces emissions against a baseline would qualify as a CDM project that contributes to sustainable development. Yet, the reality is that most CDM funding flows to projects with high greenhouse gas emission reduction potential, but no or questionable non-climate sustainable development benefits.

* * *

3. Regional concentration of projects.

The CDM ideally provides an incentive for climate change mitigation projects throughout the developing world. However, soon after the start of the mechanism, it became clear that not everyone would benefit in the same way from the resources flowing from Annex B countries. The division of projects is very skewed, and in particular sub-Saharan African countries seem to have missed the boat when it comes to the CDM. * * * It can be argued that the distributional concerns regarding the CDM should be moderated to some extent if other variables—such as population, gross domestic product, and energy use—are taken into account.

* * *

NOTES AND QUESTIONS

1. How are the considerations involved in crafting a climate change regime different from those that confronted negotiators of the ozone depleting substances treaty? How do they compare on such parameters as number of producers, number of substances, number of sources, availability of substitutes (recall that at the time the ozone negotiations began there were no substitutes already on line), and uncertainty of the science? How should those differences affect the final shape of a post–2012 accord?

2. Look at the Kyoto Protocol. How are emissions reductions allocated (see Annex B)? Why do some Annex I countries have increased allocations? Note the special problems created by the 1990 baseline, which would reflect extremely low emissions from former Soviet states given the deep decrease in overall economic activity. How does the Protocol deal with this?

3. How effective do you think the market mechanisms used in the Kyoto Protocol to reduce carbon dioxide and other emissions can be? What are the advantages of using a cap and trade system, rather than a tax or a prohibition of certain technologies? What are the dangers? Note that emissions allowances traded are supposed to be "real, surplus, verifiable, permanent and enforceable". Is it possible to guarantee this? Under the emissions trading system set up under joint implementation by the European Union to meet its commitments, seven nations—Spain, Austria, Greece, Ireland, Portugal, Finland and Italy—actually increased their carbon dioxide emissions since 1990, although overall the EU insists it will meet its Kyoto targets by 2012.

4. An entire bureaucracy has grown up around the CDM, including project planners and certifiers. Many law firms are now developing specialties in emissions trading under Kyoto, especially given the existence of a European carbon market. In addition to the formal trading mechanisms of the treaty, "voluntary" carbon markets are emerging in anticipation of further development of the market mechanisms, especially U.S. entry into a cap-and-trade scheme. In 2007, the World Bank calculated the global carbon market at $64 billion, with the EU emissions trading scheme worth $50 billion of that trade. Climate exchanges have sprung up in London, Chicago and New York to trade carbon-related futures, and law firms as

well as consultants by the thousands are advising companies on how to operate in the new carbon markets. Is this a good sign for lowering greenhouse gas emissions to the extent that will be necessary, or not?

5.   During the decade of the 2000s, the U.S. was unable to pass federal legislation on climate change; states filled the vacuum. California, for example, passed AB 32, which required the state to make emissions reductions in line with Kyoto. In 2009, the House of Representatives finally passed the American Clean Energy and Security Act, H.R. 2454; the Senate has climate bills under consideration. The Obama administration, as this book goes to press, is playing an active role in the negotiations for a post-Kyoto regime.

It soon became clear that the Kyoto Protocol approach would be insufficient to stop climate change. Between 1997 and 2009, scientists increasingly raised the alarm that climate change was not some vague future problem, but a process that was happening now, at an accelerated pace. The popular media and public opinion began paying attention. Moreover, scientists agreed that even with the most ambitious plans for reducing carbon dioxide and other greenhouse emissions, enough emissions were already in the atmosphere that some degree of climate change is inevitable. The goal became to hold the degree of change to within 2 degrees Celsius, an amount at which the effects of a changing climate were thought manageable. "Business as usual" scenarios, in contrast, forecast a 4–5 degree minimum rise in temperature, with potentially catastrophic consequences. As countries prepared to meet at Copenhagen in December 2009, as this book goes to press, the outlines of a successor to the Kyoto Protocol began to take shape.

e.   THE FUTURE SHAPE OF THE CLIMATE REGIME: BALI TO COPENHAGEN AND BEYOND

Harro van Asselt and Joyeeta Gupta, Stretching Too Far? Developing Countries and the Role of Flexibility Mechanisms Beyond Kyoto*

28 STAN. ENVTL. L.J. 311, 329 (2009)

D.   Beyond Kyoto: Quo Vadis?

With the Protocol's rulebook largely in place, and implementation having begun in most of the ratifying countries, the question of how to proceed beyond Kyoto's commitment period became a key issue in international discussions. At COP–11 and COP/MOP–1, held in Montreal in December 2005, a first set of small steps was made to discuss and negotiate the future of international climate change governance. * * * In Montreal,

---

* Footnotes omitted.

it became apparent that developing countries still vigorously opposed even discussing the remote possibility of commitments.

The issue of future commitments was once again on the agenda at COP–12 and COP/MOP–2, held in Nairobi in November 2006. A decision was made there to hold a second review at the fourth COP/MOP in 2008, but that this review "shall not lead to new commitments for any Party." The Nairobi talks can be seen as merely a prelude to the discussions at the following COP and COP/MOP in Bali, Indonesia in December 2007. The Bali meeting was a crucial moment in the UNFCCC process to set in motion negotiations on a follow-up agreement to be concluded before the current Kyoto targets expire.

After intense negotiations that extended one day beyond schedule, Parties to the UNFCCC finally adopted a series of decisions referred to collectively as the "Bali Road Map." The key decision of COP–13 is known as the "Bali Action Plan." It launches "a comprehensive process to enable the full, effective and sustained implementation of the Convention through long-term cooperative action, now, up to, and beyond 2012, in order to reach an agreed outcome and adopt a decision at its fifteenth session." * * * The decision leaves open a number of key issues: it avoids any explicit, quantitative reference to a long-term objective, calling only for "deep cuts." It also does not specify any desirable short-to medium-term targets. Furthermore, the decision leaves open a wide range of possibilities for how a post–2012 agreement might look, and it does not explicitly preclude the option that negotiations under Article 3.9 of the Kyoto Protocol—on new commitments for Annex I countries—are linked to the negotiations under the UNFCCC. The decision also addresses the way in which developing countries could participate in a future agreement through "nationally appropriate mitigation commitments or actions." Although there was considerable pressure on developing countries to adopt "measurable, reportable and verifiable nationally appropriate mitigation actions," they were able to renegotiate the text to link the phrase "measurable, reportable and verifiable" to support by developed countries in the form of "technology, financing and capacity building," rather than to mitigation actions in developing countries.

The Bali action plan sets out four pillars—mitigation, adaptation, finance and technology—for future action. Negotiations moving forward are taking place in two separate working groups, one on further commitments under Kyoto and one on long-range action. It is unclear whether the next step, then, is one or two outcomes, and whether they are to take place under legal umbrella of the Kyoto Protocol, the UNFCCC, neither, or both. There are also debates as to what weight to give, and how to combine, different elements and constellations of commitments, including national programs (including voluntary ones), sector-by-sector commitments, ad-hoc groups of major emitters, and the like. And finally, all these decisions need to be made in such a way that large emitters like the U.S. and China can be brought on board.

The following excerpt suggests a more radical approach.

Paul Baer, et al., The Greenhouse Development Rights Framework: The Right to Development in a Climate Constrained World

pp. 85–92 (Berlin: Heinrich Boll Foundation, Christian Aid, EcoEquity and Stockholm Institute, rev'd 2d 2008) available at http://www.ecoequity.org.

The climate negotiations are adrift. They are, to be sure, entering a frenetic and unpredictable phase, but they are still, fundamentally, adrift. The breakthrough we require does not seem to be on the horizon, and with the level of North / South distrust high and the economic crisis casting everything into doubt, the dangers are clear. Chief among these, we fear, is a victory so incremental that it amounts to failure—one that appears to take us forward, but ultimately fails to engender the vastly increased resolve that will be required if we are to rapidly alter today's terrifying emissions trajectories.

* * * To avoid that fate, we require a simple, transparent, and compelling effort sharing framework, one that is robust enough to be universally applicable, and to make sense even when comparing wealthy, middle-income, and poor countries, each with skewed—and often highly skewed—income distributions. Such a framework must be built upon the principles of "common but differentiated responsibilities and respective capabilities," and, crucially, it will have to explicitly preserve a coherently defined right to sustainable development. These are the qualities that a differentiation scheme must have if it is to be more than a mere policy abstraction, if it is to serve as the backbone of a viable climate protection architecture.

The destination is, we believe, clearly captured by the GDRs framework. [The full report proposes Global Development Rights based on establishing a poverty threshold of about $7,500/per capita yearly income, and requiring countries to contribute to mitigation and adaptation efforts according to a formula based on the percentage of their population with incomes above that level, along with a responsibility formula based on their contributions to the problem by the population above the poverty threshold. This formula takes into account income inequality within states as well as among states.]

But a sense of the destination is not enough. We also need a way forward. For while ad hoc, tactical incrementalism would be a losing strategy, incrementalism of some sort is unavoidable. The divide between today's temporizing and tomorrow's mobilization will not be bridged in a single step. But since we must nonetheless take a next step, the question is: What is it going to be? Which is to say that the Copenhagen problem is, essentially, a sequencing problem.

At least we know that it cannot be another step like the one taken in Kyoto, way back in 1997. It is too late, and another step like that—arduous and protracted and small—would leave us in deep trouble. * * *

We can afford no further delay in launching a full-on global emergency climate mobilization. But neither can we yet rally the resolve and cooperation needed to put such a mobilization into place. In this fraught state, there is little choice but to allow ourselves an interim period of what we will call "trust building," though the term—which can be easily though incorrectly taken to imply further delay—is not ideal. Indeed, action and preparation for further action are the only really viable foundations for trust-building, and in any case this transition period should be as short as we can possibly manage, with only the stipulation that it be long enough to build the political foundations of a subsequent era of much more unified and ambitious action.

* * *

NOTES AND QUESTIONS

1.   For more on the challenges leading up to and beyond Copenhagen, see Joanna Depledge, *Crafting the Copenhagen Consensus: Some Reflections*, 17 Rev. EC & Int'l Envt'l L. 154 (2008). The Earth Negotiations Bulletin provides extensive documentation on the course of climate talks.

2.   Should a future climate regime build on the Kyoto Protocol as well as the UNFCCC, or should it abandon part of the Kyoto architecture, as suggested above? What else could be done that would move us faster towards bending emissions curves sharply downward? Would it make more sense to create a forum for a few high-emissions countries to negotiate among themselves? Some analysts have suggested a "multi-track approach" that combines global rules with "bottom-up" national and regional initiatives.

3.   Until recently, most focus in the climate debate was on mitigation. The latest science confirms that even with the most stringent mitigation measures conceivable there will still be some degree of warming, which will have serious effects on small island states, low-lying coastal regions, drylands and other particularly vulnerable areas. More attention has thus turned to the need to plan for, and finance, adaptation to climate change. The Bali meeting in 2007 finally made operational a 2% levy on CDM projects, payable into an Adaptation Fund. It is clear that much more will be required. Moreover, we can expect large movements of people within and across borders as their homes become unlivable. Current international law makes no provision for such "environmental refugees." Should the post-Kyoto negotiations tackle this issue? Or should it be left to other international organizations? Which?

4.   As we consider other international law regimes, consider how each of them will be impacted by climate change.

D.   THE LAW OF COMMON SPACES

As noted, certain areas of the planet are located beyond national jurisdictions. These include the high seas, outer space (including the moon) and, at least to some extent, Antarctica. These areas are subject to a common access regime of the kind that potentially gives rise to the "tragedy of the commons" discussed in Section B, above. As we will see, one response to the problems of a common access regime has been to "enclose" the commons, through the creation of legal regimes granting greater national control over resources that were previously common access. This is one way to understand the Law of the Sea regime, for example.

In addition to the idea of common areas, two related concepts bear mentioning. The "common heritage of humankind" emerged from the struggle, during the 1970s, of countries in Africa, Asia and Latin America to ensure a more equitable distribution of the world's resources through, for example, a New International Economic Order (see Chapter 7). The idea was that certain resources by definition belonged to the whole world, and therefore could not be appropriated and disposed of by any single country or group of countries. The most famous example is the seabed and its minerals, which, as we shall see, were the subject of Part XI of the Law of the Sea treaty, subsequently modified. However, as Jutta Brunnée points out, "the common management and fair allocation it [the common heritage concept] envisages could help address both the potential for over-exploitation and the inequities inherent in the general common area regime. And yet, it seems unlikely that the common heritage concept will deliver on that promise. Its focus on access to resources and benefits gets the concept entangled in and, it appears, sidelined by the competition that these preoccupations entail." Brunnée, "Common Areas, Common Heritage and Common Concern," in Bodansky, Brunnée and Hey, Oxford Handbook of International Environmental Law 550 (2007). The concept of "common concern" is far looser, and deals more with problems (like climate change or conservation of biodiversity) rather than geographically-bounded resources or areas. See Brunnée at 564–67.

1.   SEAS

As we have seen, most of the planet's land mass is divided into states, which exercise territorial jurisdiction over their land mass. But what about the water that surrounds us? Fully enclosed lakes and rivers, of course, are considered the state's internal waters and are within the control of the state in the same way land is. But what about the high seas, the coasts, or rivers that run through more than one state? Those are the subject of multiple, complex international regimes, consisting of a combination of treaties, customary law and general principles, on both a global and regional level. While we cannot hope to fully explore these regimes here, we present a sampling of some of the more salient aspects.

We start by considering the law applying to the oceans and coasts. For centuries, there has been a tension between the idea of the seas as a common area owned by, and accessible to, all, and the desire of states to control the area near their territory for purposes of resource use, security, and (more recently) environmental protection. In part, this was a tension between the big maritime trading powers (which favored freedom of the seas) and coastal states jealous of their ability to control, and profit from, the marine resources adjacent to their territory. This tension resulted over time in a complex set of rules regarding different levels of national control over seas at different distances from adjacent coasts.

a.   CODIFICATION OF THE LAW OF THE SEA

Navigation, fishing and extraction of minerals take place on or under the sea. For centuries, there has been an ongoing struggle over whether these activities can be engaged in freely by all states and their nationals almost anywhere in the sea or whether states can carve out maritime areas for their exclusive use and control. The law of the sea is one of the most dramatic examples of the dynamic evolution of international law. Even though codification has taken place as will be detailed in this Chapter, customary international law has and will continue to be a focal point in its future development.

Codification of the law of the sea began as early as 1930, at a conference of some 40 states held at The Hague under the auspices of the League of Nations, but it was not successful. Following work undertaken by the International Law Commission, more than 80 states participated in the 1958 Geneva conference on the law of the sea (UNCLOS I) and produced four conventions, which have all entered into force, codifying portions of the customary law and creating new law in some cases. They are:

1.   Convention on the Territorial Sea and the Contiguous Zone, which entered into force on September 10, 1964;

2.   Convention on the High Seas, which entered into force on September 30, 1962;

3.   Convention on the Continental Shelf, which entered into force on June 10, 1964;

4.   Convention on Fishing and Conservation of the Living Resources of the High Seas, in force on June 10, 1963.

Only the Convention on the High Seas states in the preamble that it is "generally declaratory of established principles of international law". In practice the Conventions on the Territorial Sea and the Contiguous Zone and the Continental Shelf were viewed as codifying certain aspects of customary international law as well. Reference should be made to the decision of the International Court of Justice in the *North Sea Continental Shelf* Cases, [1969] I.C.J. Rep. 3, in Chapter 2, concerning whether certain of the norms contained in the Convention on the Continental Shelf were paralleled in or had crystallized into customary international law.

After the second conference on the law of the sea (UNCLOS II) failed in 1960 to agree on the fundamental question of the breadth of the territorial sea, the General Assembly of the United Nations convened a third conference in 1973. Apart from the territorial sea and consequential questions concerning international straits and archipelagic states, other issues had also appeared outdating the 1958 Conventions, notably fishing rights beyond the territorial sea, pollution control and exploration and exploitation of oil, gas and minerals beyond national jurisdiction. After eleven sessions, from 1973 to 1982, UNCLOS III adopted the United Nations Convention on the Law of the Sea of December 10, 1982. The text contains 320 Articles and 9 Annexes.

The major sections of the LOS Convention both codify existing law and expand to new areas. The treaty sets out rules now accepted as customary regarding freedom of the high seas, and delimiting internal waters, territorial seas, and exclusive economic zones, each with their corresponding rights and responsibilities. The treaty contains the principles by which the zones are geographically determined. The zones are measured in nautical miles from "baselines" as provided by UNCLOS Articles 5–16. Waters on the landward side of the baselines form part of the state's "internal waters with exclusive jurisdiction" parallel to the rules for the state's adjacent land mass, including jurisdiction over foreign merchant vessels in ports and internal waters (unless otherwise provided by agreement between the coastal state and the flag state of the vessel). In addition, States are legally entitled to adopt a belt of "territorial seas" extending up to 12 miles seaward from the baseline (Part II) and many, including the U.S., have done so. In the territorial seas, states retain jurisdiction, but subject to foreign ships right of "innocent passage" and other rules. A "contiguous zone" may also be adopted for an additional 12 miles beyond the baseline for certain regulatory purposes. Farther out to sea to a maximum of 200 miles from the baseline, states may legally establish "exclusive economic zones", thereby obtaining sovereign rights to natural resources such as fish and minerals, and other rights specified in the convention. (Part V). Certain rights in the continental shelf are also provided (Part VI).

All parts of the seas not included in the zones referred to above are regulated as the "high seas" where the "freedom of the seas" principle reigns (Part VII). The Convention also contains detailed rules regarding the nationality of ships ("flag states") and limits to jurisdiction over ships under various circumstances. Responding to the concerns of a number of far-flung states, it contains special rules on archipelagic and island states. It contains a section, new at the time, on environmental protection of the seas from pollution and other harms (Part XII). (The International Maritime Organization also has extensive treaty rules re pollution from ships). It also contains novel dispute resolution procedures, including a new Tribunal on the Law of the Sea.

The most controversial part of the treaty is Part XI on seabed mining. It defines the "Area", defined in Article 1.1.(1) as the "sea-bed and ocean floor and subsoil thereof beyond the limits of national jurisdiction" (i.e., beyond the limits as outlined above). The treaty drafters, acting at a time when deep sea mining, especially of manganese modules, seemed both likely and lucrative, wanted to make sure that developing states shared in the coming mining bounty, and worried about the commercial enclosure of a global commons. Thus, they declared that "The Area and its resources are the 'common heritage of mankind'" (Article 136). "All rights in the resources of the Area are vested in mankind as a whole, on whose behalf" the International Sea-bed Authority established by the Convention acts, and no claim of sovereignty or appropriation is to be recognized (Article 137).

The aim was to arrive at a package-deal basically acceptable to all states and to adopt it by consensus. However, at the end of the Conference the then-new Reagan administration in the United States requested a vote after it failed to win changes in the deep seabed mining Articles. The 1982 Convention was then adopted in Montego Bay, Jamaica, by 130 states in favor to 4 against (Israel, Turkey, United States and Venezuela) with 17 abstentions. The Convention came into force on November 16, 1994, and as of January 2009, 157 states were parties. However, no member of the Group of Seven (the major developed countries) became a party in the 1980s due to dissatisfaction with some of the terms of Part XI.

In July 1990 informal consultations culminated in the adoption on July 28, 1994 by U.N. General Assembly Resolution 48/263 of the Agreement Relating to the Implementation of Part XI of the United Nations Convention on the Law of the Sea of 10 December, 1982. The Agreement was prompted by the desire to achieve universal participation in the 1982 Convention on the Law of the Sea and recognized that political and economic changes had necessitated the re-evaluation of some parts of Part XI (the deep-sea mining provisions). The Agreement entered into force July 28, 1996 and as of November 30, 2000 there were 100 states parties. The United States signed on November 16, 1994 but has not ratified. In his report to the President of the United States (upon which the President based a Message to the Senate, proposing Senate approval of the entire Convention) the Secretary of State wrote:

"... The legally binding changes set forth in the Agreement meet the objections of the United States to Part XI of the Convention. The United States and all other major industrialized states have signed the Agreement."

Would its provisions prevail over corresponding and inconsistent provisions of the Geneva Conventions of 1958, to which the United States is a party?

The Agreement and Part XI of the Convention are to be applied as a single instrument. In the event of inconsistency the provisions of the Agreement will apply. Of extreme importance is the fact that ratifications or accessions to the Convention following the adoption by the General

Assembly of the Agreement represent consent to be bound by the Agreement and consent to be bound by the Agreement is not permitted unless consent to be bound by the Convention is established. See B.H. Oxman, The 1994 Agreement and the Convention, 88 AJIL 687 (1994); L.B. Sohn, International Law Implications of the 1994 Agreement, *id.*, at 696; J. Charney, U.S. Provisional Application of the 1994 Deep Seabed Agreement, *id.*

1987 Restatement, Introductory Note to Part V, The Law of the Sea

American Law Institute, 1987

* * * [M]any * * * provisions of the Convention follow closely provisions in the 1958 conventions * * * which largely restated customary law as of that time. Other provisions in the LOS Convention set forth rules that, if not law in 1958, became customary law since that time, as they were accepted at the Conference by consensus and have influenced, and came to reflect, the practice of states. * * * In particular, in March 1983 President Reagan proclaimed a 200–nautical-mile exclusive economic zone for the United States and issued a policy statement in which the United States in effect agreed to accept the substantive provisions of the Convention, other than those dealing with deep sea-bed mining, in relation to all states that do so with respect to the United States. Thus, by express or tacit agreement accompanied by consistent practice, the United States, and states generally, have accepted the substantive provisions of the Convention, other than those addressing deep sea-bed mining, as statements of customary law binding upon them apart from the Convention. * * * In a few instances, however, there is disagreement whether a provision of the Convention reflects customary law. * * * Some provisions of the Convention, notably those accepting particular arrangements for settling disputes, clearly are not customary law and have not been accepted by express or tacit agreement.

b.   DRAWING THE LINES BETWEEN ZONES

Harry Schreiber, Ocean Governance and the Marine Fisheries Crisis: Two Decades of Innovation—and Frustration

20 Va. Envtl. L.J. 119 (2001) (Internal citations omitted)

When the UNCLOS agreement was signed in 1982, it was done amidst hopes that a new era of effective ocean governance would be inaugurated by the Convention, involving the universal acceptance of innovative principles in a comprehensive legal regime. When the final draft of UNCLOS was approved by formal vote in the March–April 1982 meeting of the Third United Nations Conference on the Law of the Sea, it represented the culmination of a treaty process that had its origins in technical and legal studies by the U.N. in the mid–1950s and descended directly from the Geneva conventions on oceans law signed in 1958. Unlike those earlier agreements, UNCLOS was an attempt at providing a broad-based, comprehensive approach to protecting the world's oceans, rather than an effort at codifying rules for particular problems or sectors of ocean use. UNCLOS was to be a framework document, treating nearly the entire range of outstanding oceans-law issues, from marine navigation, fisheries, and marine environment to the difficult question of maritime jurisdictional boundaries.

The 1982 UNCLOS agreement was necessarily a compromise package—a melange of bargains and trade-offs. One of the central themes in the long period of its negotiation had been the idea of the oceans as "the Common Heritage of Mankind," an idea proclaimed famously by Ambassador Arvid Pardo in U.N. General Assembly debates fifteen years earlier. This idea expressed the aspiration that UNCLOS would provide a firm foundation for a system of just and equitable allocation of ocean resources for the current generation's use. Equally, however, it was meant as a statement of legal norms indicating the moral imperative of protecting the marine environment and its resources—including fisheries, although it had been introduced at the time with reference specifically to seabed mineral resources—as a legacy for future generations. As a corollary to that central idea, the agreement specified duties and obligations of signatory states with regard to the sustainable use of ocean resources.

UNCLOS only incompletely realized these objectives. An abiding difficulty has been political in nature—the failure of the United States to ratify the Convention. . . . Nonetheless, the UNCLOS document did stand as a powerful expression of community-oriented altruistic principles, beyond questions relating to the seabed minerals issue. Of particular weight in the shaping of subsequent world discussion, as the fisheries crisis became evident, were the broad statements of principle in UNCLOS regarding general prescribed norms of ocean use, together with the requirements (such as duties to cooperate) that were placed upon signatory states in regard to sustainability in resource exploitation and protection of the marine environment from degradation. The new norms and obligations were broadly phrased, and were often vague; compliance was to be achieved largely by the consent of individual governments. Being largely rhetorical and aspirational, the obligations were seen by many critics as having little real use in controlling the practices of signatory states. Although such provisions of the agreement were in that sense only "soft law," UNCLOS provided a juridical foundation upon which more detailed and specific agreements could be built at a future time. . . .

The 1982 Convention also contained a provision requiring signatory states to submit disputes for adjudication and settlement, specifying choices as to mechanism and forum. This institutional and juridical thrust of UNCLOS culminated in the establishment of the U.N. Tribunal on the Law of the Sea. This body has handed down its first decisions and has already had an impact on the jurisprudence of international law. To many observers, compulsory submission of disputes for adjudication or settlement was perhaps the most important single substantive contribution to conflict reduction, institutional development, and long-term fostering of cooperation and community interests.

The foregoing features of UNCLOS were supportive of community interests and expressed altruistic and conservationist principles, usually in "soft law" terms. They were counter-balanced, however, by a strong reaffirmation and expansion of the prerogatives of traditional sovereignty, by which states could act legitimately in their own interests, with broad discretion, within the terms of the new rules of law. This obverse side of the Convention was embodied in the provisions authorizing the extension of coastal states' territorial seas out to a distance offshore of twelve miles, and also the authorization of Exclusive Economic Zones ("EEZs") out to the 200–mile line or the extent of the continental shelf. UNCLOS applied certain general constraints to coastal states' management policies regarding their EEZs, such as duties to cooperate. It also specified other types of obligations to protect fish stocks and the marine environment, applying them to flag state operations on the high seas as well as to management programs in the national EEZs.

As a practical matter, however, UNCLOS gave the coastal states nearly complete authority to determine unilaterally how to interpret and apply these provisions. As a result, the effectiveness of these new statements of law as constraints on fisheries policy and operations was doubtful from the outset. Because the inclusion of the 200–mile EEZ provision was so clearly contrary to the altruism required by the common heritage idea, this feature of UNCLOS evoked bitter criticism from many critics and participants in the negotiations—including Ambassador Pardo himself, who charged that the EEZ provision was a cynical betrayal of the convention's fundamental original purpose.

The decision to validate the ocean-enclosure movement through inclusion of the EEZ provision had an enormous impact upon the division of authority over marine fisheries, for an estimated 85% or more of commercially exploitable fish stocks and all then-known exploitable seabed mineral resources were located in the EEZ ocean areas. It was a virtual certainty, moreover, that UNCLOS and its high-sounding statements of principle could not prevent the EEZs from serving mainly as a form of protection against foreign competition in coastal fisheries. . . .

In fact, in the nearly two decades since UNCLOS validated the 200–mile EEZs, every coastal state with major fishing interests has failed to sustain the level of stocks in its fisheries. The picture today is one of almost universally negative results from unilateral management. Understandably, public attention has focused heavily upon issues on the blue-water high seas, such as the dramatic whaling situation and Canada's use of force in the "Turbot War" to stop Spanish fishing of straddling stocks in the Northwest Atlantic outside the Canadian EEZ outer boundary line. But the more mundane and long-term developments in the EEZ regimes (constituting 40% of the world's ocean waters) have played an even more significant role in producing the disaster that we now face in the marine fisheries globally.

* * *

NOTES AND QUESTIONS

1. What techniques described in Part B(1) of this chapter did the LOS Convention use to try to encourage fisheries conservation? Why, do you think, didn't the "enclosure of the seas" work? Fisheries treaties are considered below, with conservation of other living species.

2. Most of the controversies surrounding application of both the 1958 Conventions and the subsequent provisions of the LOS have involved drawing the right lines to demarcate the boundaries between various states territorial waters, EEZ and continental shelf, and those of other states. Some of the most intractable boundary-drawing problems arise from the difficulties in agreeing on a proper baseline, since the baseline determines the shape and size of the territorial and EEZ demarcations.

These controversies have taken up a considerable part of the docket of the International Court of Justice over the years, and have also been a significant part of the docket of the new International Tribunal for the Law of the Sea created by the UNCLOS.

c. ENVIRONMENTAL PROTECTION PROVISIONS IN THE UNCLOS

F. Orrego Vicuna, State Responsibility, Liability, and Remedial Measures Under International Law: New Criteria for Environmental Protection

pp. 124, 144–147, ENVIRONMENTAL CHANGE AND INTERNATIONAL LAW (E. Brown Weiss ed., 1992)

The 1982 Convention on the Law of the Sea and related treaties have significantly developed the rules of international law applicable to the preservation of the marine environment and illustrate the evolution of state responsibility. In point of fact, states are under the obligation to ensure that activities under their jurisdiction or control "are so conducted as not to cause damage by pollution to other States and their environment" and that any pollution arising from such activities "does not spread beyond the areas where they exercise sovereign rights." The activities included in this obligation are those undertaken both by the state and by entities of a private nature under state jurisdiction and control. It is also quite apparent that this provision covers not only transboundary effects of pollution but also harm to areas beyond national jurisdiction. In other words, the global scale of environmental effects is incorporated into this particular regime.

This regime encompasses all sources of pollution, a further indication of the broadening concern and scope of international law. In addition, a broad definition of pollution of the marine environment is included in this and other treaty regimes as an expression of the very same concern. Important IMO and related conventions have developed a well-structured normative regime dealing with specific questions of marine pollution particularly in terms of oil pollution, discharge and dumping of waste, and safety at sea.

In light of this more advanced regime, it follows quite naturally that international law has accepted holding a state responsible for pollution injuries resulting from a violation of its obligations in this field. Although the primary obligation to enforce the law is bestowed upon the flag state of the ships concerned, other states are not prevented from taking the necessary preventive or remedial actions. In addition to the powers allocated to the coastal state and the port state in given instances, there is the most important right of intervention on the high seas, which is ultimately related to a measure of self-help under international law. The obligation to notify is also prominent in this field. These developments of course do not prejudice the rules dealing specifically with issues such as the environmental consequences of seabed-mining operations, cooperation in emergencies, or the protection of fragile ecosystems.

Remedial measures have also evolved significantly in the area of the law of the sea. In addition to recourse to the general remedies provided for under international law, coastal and port states can participate actively by detaining and investigating ships and by instituting proceedings.

* * *

NOTES AND QUESTIONS

1.   Look at Part XII of the UNCLOS, especially the provisions related to enforcement. How do these provisions allocate responsibility for protection of the marine environment? Which state or states is responsible for preventing or cleaning up an oil spill that occurs transferring a hazardous chemical from a British oil platform in the North Sea (in the U.K.'s EEZ) to a Liberian-flagged ship carrying oil for a U.S. company to the U.S.? Are these provisions helpful in deciding this question? States commit to assessment of future activities, cooperation, consultation, and domestic legislation to implement these provisions. What else must states do?

As we have seen with other environmental regimes, the UNCLOS is intended to be a framework convention, to be developed and supplemented by future specific treaties on different forms and sources of pollution. Indeed, a detailed set of rules, including some of the few liability- and insurance-based regimes in international environmental law, governs pollution from ships. Conventions have been adopted dealing with, *inter alia,* design and construction of ships, oil pollution damage, a compensation fund and the dumping of wastes at sea.

2.   *Regional Seas.* The U.N. Environment Program (UNEP) has sponsored an extensive network of regional seas treaties to foster joint protection by coastal states. These continue to develop, but have been hampered by lack of domestic legislation in many states to implement the (sometimes extensive) treaty obligations involved. They focus on pollution from land-based sources, with differing degrees of specificity regarding how much, and what, can be dumped into waterways leading to a shared regional sea. There are

over 15 regional agreements dealing with the maritime environment, including those dealing with the Baltic Sea (1974); the Mediterranean Sea (1976 and 1980); the Kuwait area (1978), the West and Central African region (1981); the Wider Caribbean region (1983), the South Pacific region (1987), the Black Sea (1992), the Red Sea (1982) the South–East Pacific (1981) and the North–East Atlantic (1992). Most of these have subsequent Protocols detailing aspects of protection.

3. *Baselines and Climate Change.* As we have seen, the Law of the Sea Convention is predicated on being able to measure a baseline—generally the low-water line of the coast—from which the territorial sea, and from there the EEZ, can be calculated. But what happens if the sea level rises over time? How often must a state readjust its 12–mile and 200–mile zones based on changing baselines? As the Arctic seas melt at an accelerated pace, shipping lanes and resources previously frozen year round are now accessible. What potential problems do rising seas pose for the LOS regime?

Can you find provisions in UNCLOS for this circumstance? How should any conflicts be resolved? Should the expectations of the parties at the time they agreed to the current delimitation be given any weight? Are there other international law regimes, in addition to the LOS, that might be applicable? In 1991 an Arctic Environmental Protection Strategy was developed. The Arctic states are committed to international cooperation to ensure environmental protection in the region and its sustainable and equitable development, while protecting the cultures of indigenous peoples. *See* 30 ILM 1624 (1991). An Arctic Council is to coordinate such efforts. See 35 ILM 1386 (1996). Are there any doctrines of international law, including changed circumstances, that might apply? What about the ICJ's "evolutionary interpretation" concept, discussed in Chapter 2?

2.   ANTARCTICA

Antarctica is the only continent without significant human settlements. It contains 70% of the world's fresh water, and is home to a number of specially-adapted birds and marine mammals. Its huge ice fields play an important role in reflecting the sun's rays and in maintaining ocean currents. The continent today is threatened by climate change as well as by increasing scientific settlements and tourism, both of which create garbage and pollution.

As the ability to explore the poles increased at the beginning of the twentieth century, countries began staking claims to Antarctic territory, some of which overlapped. In 1959, the Antarctic Treaty, 19 ILM 860, provided an interim solution that persists until today. The treaty parties were Argentina, Australia, Belgium, Chile, France, Japan, New Zealand, Norway, South Africa, the USSR, the United Kingdom and the United States; most (but not all) of these states had staked territorial claims.

Article I

[Antarctica for peaceful purposes only]

1.   Antarctica shall be used for peaceful purposes only. There shall be prohibited, inter alia, any measures of a military nature, such as the

establishment of military bases and fortifications, the carrying out of military maneuvers, as well as the testing of any type of weapons.

2.   The present Treaty shall not prevent the use of military personnel or equipment for scientific research or for any other peaceful purposes.

Article II
[freedom of scientific investigation to continue]

Freedom of scientific investigation in Antarctica and cooperation toward that end, as applied during the International Geophysical Year, shall continue, subject to the provisions of the present Treaty.

Article IV
[territorial claims]

1.   Nothing contained in the present Treaty shall be interpreted as:

(a) a renunciation by any Contracting Party of previously asserted rights of or claims to territorial sovereignty in Antarctica;

(b) a renunciation or diminution by any Contracting Party of any basis of claim to territorial sovereignty in Antarctica which it may have whether as a result of its activities or those of its nationals in Antarctica, or otherwise;

(c) prejudicing the position of any Contracting Party as regards its recognition or nonrecognition of any other State's right of or claim or basis of claim to territorial sovereignty in Antarctica.

2.   No acts or activities taking place while the present Treaty is in force shall constitute a basis for asserting, supporting or denying a claim to territorial sovereignty in Antarctica. No new claim, or enlargement of an existing claim, to territorial sovereignty shall be asserted while the present Treaty is in force.

Article IX
[Treaty states to meet periodically]

1.   Representatives of the Contracting Parties named in the preamble to the present Treaty shall meet at the City of Canberra within two months after date of entry into force of the Treaty, and thereafter at suitable intervals and places, for the purpose of exchanging information, consulting together on matters of common interest pertaining to Antarctica, and formulating and considering, and recommending to their Governments, measures in furtherance of the principles and objectives of the Treaty including measures regarding:

(a) use of Antarctica for peaceful purposes only;

(b) facilitation of scientific research in Antarctica;

(c) facilitation of international scientific cooperation in Antarctica;

(d) facilitation of the exercise of the rights of inspection provided for in Article VII of the Treaty;

(e) questions relating to the exercise of jurisdiction in Antarctica;

(f) preservation and conservation of living resources in Antarctica.

2.   Each Contracting Party which has become a party to the present Treaty . . . shall be entitled to appoint representatives to participate in the meetings referred to in paragraph 1 of the present Article, during such time as the Contracting Party demonstrates its interest in Antarctica by conducting substantial scientific research activity there, such as the establishment of a scientific station or the dispatch of a scientific expedition.

Those signatories who conduct "substantial scientific research activity" in the Antarctic are known as Antarctic Treaty Consultative Parties (ATCPs) and meet regularly; in 2004 a Secretariat of the Treaty was established in Argentina. The Consultative Parties are to "exert appropriate efforts" to make sure that "no one engages in any activity in Antarctica contrary to the principles or purposes of the present Treaty." How are they to do that? What if non-parties to the Treaty want to conduct activities there?

Efforts to designate Antarctica a "common heritage of mankind" like the moon or the deep seabed have to date been unsuccessful. However, 15 additional nations (Brazil, Bulgaria, China, Ecuador, Finland, Germany, India, Italy, Netherlands, Poland, Peru, Republic of Korea, Sweden, Spain, and Uruguay) have achieved consultative status by acceding to the Treaty and by conducting substantial scientific research in Antarctica. Another 17 nations have acceded to the Antarctic Treaty: Austria, Canada, Colombia, Cuba, Czech Republic, Democratic Peoples Republic of Korea, Denmark, Greece, Guatemala, Hungary, Papua New Guinea, Romania, Slovak Republic, Switzerland, Turkey, Ukraine, and Venezuela. These nations agree to abide by the treaty and may attend consultative meetings as observers.

The Convention on the Conservation of Antarctic Marine Living Resources, 19 ILM 837, was adopted in 1980. It attempts to set limits on fishing of southern ocean species like the Patagonian toothfish (euphemistically sold as Chilean sea bass, and an over-exploited species) as well as on harvesting of krill. In 1991, the ATCPs signed a Protocol to the Antarctic Treaty on Environmental Protection, 30 ILM 1461. The protocol designates Antarctica "as a natural reserve, devoted to peace and science," prohibits all mining activity except for scientific research (this determination may be modified after 50 years), requires planning of all activities to minimize environmental impacts, and creates stringent EIA requirements. A 2005 Protocol on Liability establishes a strict liability regime for "environmental emergencies."

3.   OUTER SPACE AND THE MOON

The twentieth century saw the rise of the technologies of both air and space flight, and a concomitant evolution and creation of legal principles. Space law is in a holding pattern after a flurry of development incident to the orbital flight of Sputnik 1 in 1957, which produced a few, generalized international agreements, along with the creation of proto-law by the U.N. General Assembly and considerable additions to the scholarly legal literature. Flight operations of powered, steerable aircraft, both lighter-than-air and heavier-than-air, developed in World War I for military purposes. Between the two world wars, commercial aviation began, grew, and came under a number of legal controls, national and international. Virtually all of this law, unlike the law of the sea, is positive, rather than customary, in its origins. For instance, a freedom for aerial transit, like freedom on the "high seas," though advanced by early scholars, did not survive the Zeppelin bombing raids on London. The only free airspace today is that above the high seas.

In the course of its relatively brief and partial development, space law has had to deal with many problems, like where space begins. Is there a specific altitude? Or does the definition of space depend on the purpose to which it was put? How if at all, will advantages, such as orbits and substances from celestial bodies be shared? How will space debris or liability for it be handled? What should be the proper use of space for military operations? Space law as a specialty is still mainly in the hands of scholars and national and international officials. However, communications law has developed a practitioner specialty related to satellite ownership, financing, control, launching, and utilization.

Definition and Delimitation of Outer Space: Summary Report of a Discussion in the Legal Sub–Committee of the United Nations Committee on the Peaceful Uses of Outer Space, March–April 1984

21 UN Chronicle No. 4, p. 32 (1984)

Where does outer space begin? Does it have a physical boundary by which States could stake claim to areas above them? What problems would ensue from establishing legal definitions and boundaries?

The Legal Sub–Committee established a working group to deal with the problems of definition and delimitation of outer space and the character and use of the geostationary orbit. The working group, on a proposal of its Chairman, agreed on separate consideration of the two subjects. However, it felt time should also be allotted to consider the item as a whole.

Some countries maintained that a definition and delimitation of outer space was necessary and wanted a multilateral agreement, open to all States, to establish a specific altitude as the upper limit of air space. Related questions are whether outer space should be considered as beginning where air space ends; and at what altitude air space should be regarded as ending.

A number of nations favouring a "spatial definition" supported the Soviet proposal that the boundary between outer space and air space be at an altitude not exceeding 110 kms above sea level. Provision could be made for that to be changed in the future, by international agreement, should circumstances make it necessary, according to the proposal.

In the debate, the Soviet Union said delimitation and definition of outer space was needed to guarantee effectively a reliable legal basis for new spheres of space activity and to guarantee that the study and use of space would be carried out in the interests of all States. The problem of defining the boundary between the two types of space was important. That boundary was the limit of the height of the application of State sovereignty. Definition of the boundary was a means of establishing the area for applying international air and space law.

Bulgaria said the absence of a boundary between air and outer space opened the door to countless violations of State sovereignty. The absence of a clearly defined limit would compel States whose security would be threatened to enact measures to prevent such violation.

India said outer space should be defined and delimited because of the existence of different legal régimes for air and outer space. There was a need to provide a clear area for applying existing outer space law and facilitating the further development of that law to determine the upper limit of State sovereignty, to safeguard the security of national air space and prevent disputes between States.

Hungary said as there were two law régimes, of outer space and of air space, there could well be situations in the future which would raise the question as to which applied. Explicit definitions of outer space and air space were technically possible.

Nigeria said a definition was needed as a requirement for the full exercise of State sovereignty. Czechoslovakia said delimitation of space was important to preserve it for activities of a peaceful nature only.

Some States, while favouring the ''spatial definition'' approach, did not agree with the proposed altitude for the demarcation between air space and outer space. Kenya, for example, had some reservations regarding setting a specific distance in terms of delimiting outer space, as it seemed arbitrary. A definition of air space would be possible only after outer space had been defined.

Other delegations stated that: there was no present scientific basis for defining and delimiting outer space or for placing the boundary at any particular altitude; the development and application of the law of outer space had proceeded satisfactorily without such a definition or delimitation; and it would be unreasonable to adopt an arbitrary definition or delimitation which could give rise to difficulties and impede the development of space technology.

The United States said the establishment of a demarcation between outer space and air space in advance of a genuine and practical need for doing so would be an inherently arbitrary exercise having unforeseeable and almost certainly detrimental consequences for future outer space activities.

The United Kingdom said it was premature to define outer space, and was not convinced of the need for such a definition. The Netherlands said to draw a boundary between outer space and air space at a certain altitude was not only unnecessary but undesirable, as it could create problems that did not now exist.

Italy said a rigid and general delimitation of outer space did not meet the scientific criteria or respond to practical and functional criteria. A number of space agreements had been formulated without such a definition. A rigid definition would create major problems for certain smaller States in contradiction of the principle of free access to space activity.

Brazil said any definition could not be separated from the scientific knowledge available. The drawing of an arbitrary line to divide outer space and air space was always a possibility, but other approaches, such as spatial or functional, could be taken.

Some delegations considered that as the positions of delegations had not moved closer over many years, the Sub–Committee should, without prejudice to its future work on the question of the definition and delimitation of outer space, concern itself with such matters as the definition of "space objects" and "space activities". Others felt a consensus on the definition of a "space object" would be more difficult to achieve than on a definition and delimitation of outer space. . . .

NOTES AND QUESTIONS

1.   Why does it matter where outer space begins? In practice, states have not objected to the operation of satellites and other space objects above their territory, although as the skies become more and more saturated with communications satellites that may change. See Jason Krause, *Making Space Matter*, ABA JOURNAL, Mar. 2008.

Several international conventions address the legal problems of space. *The Outer Space Treaty* (Treaty on Principles Governing the Activities of States in the Exploration and Use of Outer Space, Including the Moon and Other Celestial Bodies), 18 U.S.T. 2410, 610 U.N.T.S. 205, entered into force for the United States on October 10, 1967. As of 2009, 100 States were parties. The following article indicates the generality of its provisions:

Article I

The exploration and use of outer space, including the moon and other celestial bodies, shall be carried out for the benefit and in the interests of all countries, irrespective of their degree of economic or scientific development, and shall be the province of all mankind.

Outer space, including the moon and other celestial bodies, shall be free for exploration and use by all States without discrimination of any kind, on a basis of equality and in accordance with international law, and there shall be free access to all areas of celestial bodies.

There shall be freedom of scientific investigation in outer space, including the moon and other celestial bodies, and States shall facilitate and encourage international co-operation in such investigation.

Article II

Outer space, including the moon and other celestial bodies, is not subject to national appropriation by claim of sovereignty, by means of use or occupation, or by any other means.

Article XII

All stations, installations, equipment and space vehicles on the Moon and other celestial bodies shall be open to representatives of other States Parties to the Treaty on a basis of reciprocity. . . .

Suppose that a state discovers a particularly rare and valuable mineral on the moon, which it is able to mine cheaply with manned or unmanned equipment. Does the treaty prohibit that state from exploiting the moon's resources for its own exclusive benefit? Can the state set up a base over which it has exclusive control so as to prevent another state from exploiting resources within that base? See Article XII. What law governs the state, not a party to the treaty, that wishes to claim a portion of the moon as its territory? Do the principles relating to the acquisition of territory on the surface of the earth apply? If so, what facts would support a claim that a state has lawfully acquired a portion of the moon as its territory?

In Dec. 1979, the General Assembly adopted an Agreement Governing the Activities of States on the Moon and other Celestial Bodies. Although the treaty came into force on July 11, 1984, it has very few adherents. Only 13 states were parties to the treaty in 2009. In addition to provisions dealing with notice of activities undertaken on the moon (and other celestial bodies), freedom of scientific investigation, and protection of the moon's environmental balance, the agreement looks ahead to an eventual partial internationalization of the moon. Article 11 provides:

States Parties to this Agreement hereby undertake to establish an international regime, including appropriate procedures, to govern the exploitation of the natural resources of the moon as such exploitation is about to become feasible. * * *

One of the main purposes of such an international regime is:

An equitable sharing by all States Parties in the benefits derived from those resources, whereby the interests and needs of the developing countries, as well as the efforts of those countries which have contributed either directly or indirectly to the exploration of the moon, shall be given special consideration.

To what extent do the treaties inhibit commercial exploitation of the moon's resources by a state party? Activity on the Moon does not seem to be contemplated by any "space power"; but, suppose, there should be a flurry of interest in the extraction of very valuable or security-important substances from the Moon, would we see a replay of Part XI of the Law of the Sea Convention?

The Convention on International Liability for Damage Caused by Space Objects, Mar. 29, 1972, 24 U.S.T. 2389, 961 U.N.T.S. 187, entered into force for the United States on October 9, 1973. 86 states were parties as of January 2008. The convention provides that the launching state shall be liable for damage caused by its space object absolutely in some cases, or for its fault in others. Claims procedure involves a Claims Commission, whose decision shall be binding if the parties have so agreed or whose award is recommendatory, "which the parties shall consider in good faith." (Article XIX). The Liability Convention defines "space object" as including the "component parts of a space object as well as its launch vehicle and parts thereof." How helpful is this definition? Can an astronaut be a "space object"? How about space debris?

4.   RIVERS AND WATERCOURSES

About 40% of the world's population lives near, and depends on, one of the 263 international river basins that covers 45.3% of the Earth's surface. Water is essential for life, both for drinking and for food production: 87% of water consumed is used in agriculture. Water scarcity is increasing. According to a 1997 assessment, by the year 2025, as much as two-thirds of the world's population will experience water "stress" due to increasing population and consumption, high withdrawals of water by upstream states, and heavy pollution loads. Commission on Sustainable Development, Comprehensive Assessment of the Freshwater Resources of the World, E/CN.17/1997/9. By 2009, those concerns had been augmented by concerns over melting glaciers and other effects of accelerating climate change on freshwater resources. While river basins are not, and were never considered, "common heritage," they are often the "shared heritage" of more than one state. The traditional law regarding watercourses now also has to be considered in light of climate change and of the movement towards articulating a human right to water.

Environmental protection of international rivers, lakes and drainage basins, including groundwater as well as surface water raises issues of shared utilization among states, including the quantity as well as quality of water. How should states share the resources of a single water basin when each has different needs and development plans, which might include agricultural irrigation, electricity-producing dams, flood control, drinking water for cities, recreation and tourism, or large-scale industrial uses as well as ecosystem protection and ecosystem services?

The basic rule is of equitable utilization or participation, as described below:

Sharon A. Williams, Public International Law and Water Quantity Management in a Common Drainage Basin: The Great Lakes

18 CASE W. R. J. OF INT'L L. 155, 165–168 (1986)

This theory of equitable utilization, currently described as equitable participation is clearly accepted by States and can be designated today as a rule of customary international law.

This theory was the basis for "equitable apportionment" in the case of Kansas v. Colorado [206 U.S. 46 (1907)] and was adopted as "equitable utilization" by the Helsinki Rules on the Uses of the Waters of International Rivers adopted by the International Law Association in 1966. The phrase "equitable participation" can be found in the [draft] articles on the Law of the Non–Navigational Uses of International Watercourses adopted by the International Law Commission. [Adopted by the General Assembly in 1997].

* * * Under these rules, basin states include all states whose territories contribute to the international drainage basin, whether or not they are "riparian" states. Thus, it is recognized in the Helsinki Rules (which although not a binding agreement between states, but rather a document produced by a non-governmental organization seeks to state the rules of customary international law) that underground waters may contribute to an international drainage basin. Article IV is illustrative of the key principle of the Rules, which is that every basin state in an international drainage basin has the right to reasonable use and an equitable share of the waters of the basin. The Rules reject outright the "Harmon Doctrine" of unlimited sovereignty. This rejection is based on state practice. A basin state is obligated to look to the rights and needs of other states and each is entitled to an equitable share. This latter concept is to provide the maximum benefit to each basin state from the waters in question, along with a minimum of detriment. . . .

Lake Lanoux Arbitration (France v. Spain)

12 U.N. REP. INT'L ARB. AWARDS 281 (1957)

[Spain objected to a French proposal to use Lake Lanoux for hydroelectric purposes, in that it would interfere with the flow of boundary waters contrary to an 1866 bilateral treaty. The arbitral tribunal first found for France, that its development scheme would not breach the bilateral treaty. In doing so it made an important finding concerning liability for environmental harm. The Tribunal then considered what conduct was expected of France in its relations with Spain over the project and Spain's contention that prior agreement of both States was needed.]

* * * States are today perfectly conscious of the importance of the conflicting interests brought into play by the industrial use of international rivers, and of the necessity to reconcile them by mutual concessions. The only way to arrive at such compromises of interests is to conclude agreements on an increasingly comprehensive basis. International practice reflects the conviction that States ought to strive to conclude such agreements: there would thus appear to be an obligation to accept in good faith all communications and contracts which could, by a broad comparison of interests and by reciprocal good will, provide States with the best conditions for concluding agreements. This point will be referred to again later on, when enquiring what obligations rest on France and Spain in connection with the contracts and the communications preceding the putting in hand of a scheme such as that relating to Lake Lanoux.

But international practice does not so far permit more than the following conclusion: the rule that States may utilize the hydraulic power of international watercourses only on condition of a *prior* agreement between the interested States cannot be established as a custom, even less as a general principle of law. * * *

The * * * question is to determine the method by which these interests can be safeguarded. If that method necessarily involves communications, it cannot be confined to purely formal requirements, such as taking note of complaints, protests or representations made by the downstream State. The Tribunal is of the opinion that, according to the rules of good faith, the upstream State is under the obligation to take into consideration the various interests involved, to seek to give them every satisfaction compatible with the pursuit of its own interests, and to show that in this regard it is genuinely concerned to reconcile the interests of the other riparian State with its own. * * *

As a matter of form, the upstream State has, procedurally, a right of initiative; it is not obliged to associate the downstream State in the elaboration of its schemes. If, in the course of discussions, the downstream State submits schemes to it, the upstream State must examine them, but it has the right to give preference to the solution contained in its own scheme provided that it takes into consideration in a reasonable manner the interests of the downstream State.

* * * In the case of Lake Lanoux, France has maintained to the end the solution which consists in diverting the waters of the Carol to the Ariege with full restitution. By making this choice France is only making use of a right; the development works of Lake Lanoux are on French territory, the financing of and the responsibility for the enterprise fall upon France, and France alone is the judge of works of public utility which are to be executed on her own territory, save for the provisions of Articles 9 and 10 of the Additional Act, which, however, the French scheme does not infringe.

On her side, Spain cannot invoke a right to insist on a development of Lake Lanoux based on the needs of Spanish agriculture. In effect, if France were to renounce all of the works envisaged on her territory, Spain could not demand that other works in conformity with her wishes should be carried out. Therefore, she can only urge her interests in order to obtain, within the framework of the scheme decided upon by France, terms which reasonably safeguard them.

It remains to be established whether this requirement has been fulfilled * * *.

When one examines the question of whether France, either in the course of the dealings or in her proposals, has taken Spanish interests into sufficient consideration, it must be stressed how closely linked together are the obligation to take into consideration, in the course of negotiations, adverse interests and the obligation to give a reasonable place to these interests in the solution finally adopted. A State which has conducted negotiations with understanding and good faith * * * is not relieved from giving a reasonable place to adverse interests in the solution it adopts simply because the conversations have been interrupted, even though owing to the intransigence of its partner. Conversely, in determining the manner in which a scheme has taken into consideration the interests involved, the way in which negotiations have developed, the total number of the interests which have been presented, the price which each Party was ready to pay to have those interests safeguarded, are all essential factors in establishing * * * the merits of that scheme.

[In conclusion, the Tribunal was of the view that France had sufficiently involved Spain in the preparations of the project.]

NOTES AND QUESTIONS

1. What exactly does the upstream state have to do to safeguard the interests of the downstream state? What does the downstream state have to do to safeguard its rights to the water? Can the downstream state "veto" the upstream state's use? If not, are its rights sufficiently protected? What problems could a downstream state's veto power cause? Do you think the tribunal was influenced by the fact that according to the facts of the case, France had completely replaced the diverted waters, and thus Spain did not allege any actual injury to water quantity or quality? What about the potential ecological harm to the river basin? Would increased attention to riparian ecology change the outcome if the case were decided today?

2. The Gabčikovo–Nagymaros (Hungary v. Slovakia) Dam case, introduced above, concerned the shared use of the Danube River. As noted, the countries entered into a treaty to construct a series of dams and barrages on the river, but Hungary later backed out, citing environmental concerns. Slovakia proceeded to dam part of the river entirely within its territory, diverting the river into a bypass canal (this is referred to in the opinion as "Variant C.") It justified the construction of Variant C as a countermeasure given Hungary's non-compliance with its treaty obligations. The International Court of Justice had this to say about the subject:

> 78. . . . [I]n practice, the operation of Variant C led Czechoslovakia to appropriate, essentially for its use and benefit, between 80 and 90 per cent of the waters of Danube before returning them to the main bed of the river, despite the fact that the Danube is not only a shared international watercourse but also an international boundary river. . . .

> 85. In the view of the Court, an important consideration is that the effects of a countermeasure must be commensurate with the injury suffered, taking account of the rights in question.

> In 1929, the Permanent Court of International Justice, with regard to navigation on the River Oder, stated as follows:

> "[the] community of interest in a navigable river becomes the basis of a common legal right, the essential features of which are the perfect

equality of all riparian States in the user of the whole course of the river and the exclusion of any preferential privilege of any one riparian State in relation to the others" (Territorial Jurisdiction of the International Commission of the River Oder, Judgment No. 16, 1929, P.C.I.J., Series A, No. 23, p. 27).

Modern development of international law has strengthened this principle for non-navigational uses of international watercourses as well, as evidenced by the adoption of the Convention of 21 May 1997 on the Law of the Non–Navigational Uses of International Watercourses by the United Nations General Assembly.

The Court considers that Czechoslovakia, by unilaterally assuming control of a shared resource, and thereby depriving Hungary of its right to an equitable and reasonable share of the natural resources of the Danube—with the continuing effects of the diversion of these waters on the ecology of the riparian area of the Szigetköz—failed to respect the proportionality which is required by international law.

86.   Moreover, as the Court has already pointed out (see paragraph 78), the fact that Hungary had agreed in the context of the original Project to the diversion of the Danube (and, in the Joint Contractual Plan, to a provisional measure of withdrawal of water from the Danube) cannot be understood as having authorized Czechoslovakia to proceed with a unilateral diversion of this magnitude without Hungary's consent.

What does this tell us about the nature of the obligations of states sharing a river basin?

3.   The 1997 Convention establishes the principle of equitable and reasonable utilization. Article 6 sets out the factors to be used in determining equitable utilization:

Factors relevant to equitable and reasonable utilization

1.   Utilization of an international watercourse in an equitable and reasonable manner within the meaning of article 5 requires taking into account all relevant factors and circumstances, including:

(a) Geographic, hydrographic, hydrological, climatic, ecological and other factors of a natural character;

(b) The social and economic needs of the watercourse States concerned;

(c) The population dependent on the watercourse in each watercourse State;

(d) The effects of the use or uses of the watercourses in one watercourse State on other watercourse States;

(e) Existing and potential uses of the watercourse;

(f) Conservation, protection, development and economy of use of the water resources of the watercourse and the costs of measures taken to that effect;

(g) The availability of alternatives, of comparable value, to a particular planned or existing use.

2.   In the application of article 5 or paragraph 1 of this article, watercourse States concerned shall, when the need arises, enter into consultations in a spirit of cooperation.

3.   The weight to be given to each factor is to be determined by its importance in comparison with that of other relevant factors. In determining what is a reasonable and equitable use, all relevant factors are to be considered together and a conclusion reached on the basis of the whole.

Are these the right factors? What if they point in different directions? Article 7 qualifies the "equitable utilization" principle thus:

"1. Watercourse States shall, in utilizing an international watercourse in their territories, take all appropriate measures to prevent the causing of significant harm to other watercourse States.

2.   Where significant harm nevertheless is caused to another watercourse State, the States whose use causes such harm shall, in the absence of agreement to such use, take all appropriate measures, having due regard for the provisions of articles 5 and 6, in consultation with the affected State, to eliminate or mitigate such harm and, where appropriate, to discuss the question of compensation."

How are the principles of equitable utilization and no significant harm reconcilable? What if equitable utilization would require significant harm to the downstream state? For some uses? Who decides what is significant in the absence of agreement? Which principle will upstream states champion? Downstream states? Developing countries, that might want to start new uses in the future? Which principle does the Convention seem to privilege? The Convention has not yet entered into force. Although it took over 20 years to negotiate, it does not have strong support from states. Why might that be? Could the difficulties of satisfying both upstream and downstream states in the same instrument be to blame? Like the Law of the Sea Convention, many of the provisions of the 1997 Convention are considered declaratory of customary international law. In addition, the "soft law" 1966 Helsinki Rules on the Uses of the Waters of International Rivers, *reprinted in* 52 ILM 484 (1967) and the subsequent 2004 Berlin Rules on Water Resources, both crafted by the (non-governmental) International Law Association, continue to be widely referenced. There are also specific regional or river basin agreements in Europe and Southern Africa that have influenced the development of customary international law in the area, especially the UNECE Convention on the Protection and Use of Transboundary Water Courses and Lakes, 31 ILM 1312 (1992), which entered into force on October 6, 1996 and which covers primarily European states. The Convention goes further in protecting water resources than the UN Watercourses Convention, incorporating principles of precaution, polluter pays and intergenerational equity as well as a broad definition of transboundary impact and specific obligations to control pollution in water-

courses. For more on the law of rivers and freshwater, see Steven McCaf-
frey, The Law of International Watercourses–Non-Navigational Uses
(2001); L. Boisson de Chaznournes and S.M.A. Salman, Water Resources and
International Law (2005).

4. *Canada–United States Great Lakes Cooperation.* The Great Lakes system had become extremely polluted by 1970 from many sources including
industrial and urban uses and maritime vessel wastes. A study and report
that revealed this convincingly was produced by the International Joint
Commission (IJC), a body set up in 1909 by the Boundary Waters Treaty,
U.S.T.S. 548, between the United States and Great Britain, on behalf of
Canada, to help settle and prevent disputes over the use of boundary
waters. Article IV of the 1909 Treaty declares that the boundary waters
"shall not be polluted on either side to the injury of health or property on
the other". The IJC's report led to the 1978 Canada–United States Great
Lakes Water Quality Agreement, 30 U.S.T.S., TIAS 9257, which supplements Article IV of the 1909 Treaty. The Agreement commits both states to
adopt common objectives and implement cooperative programs and measures to eliminate or reduce the discharge of pollutants into the basin
ecosystem. In discharging its responsibilities the IJC may conduct public
hearings and compel the testimony of witnesses and the production of
documents. A non-binding 2005 Great Lakes–St. Lawrence River Basin
Sustainable Water Resources Agreement among eight U.S. states and two
Canadian Provinces limits water withdrawals from the basin, applies
adaptive management and the precautionary principle, and provides for
extensive and detailed cooperation of the relevant states and provinces. It
complements a binding compact among the U.S. states on basin cooperation
that was signed into law in 2008.

E. Protection of Living Beings and Habitats

International environmental law uses a number of regimes and measures to protect the planet's biological resources, including species-specific,
ecosystem-wide and trade-based approaches. Despite a welter of multilateral and bilateral treaties and programs, we are facing a threat of massive
extinctions unseen since the time of the dinosaurs. According to the
International Union for the Conservation of Nature, at least 12% of birds,
30% of amphibians, 31% of reptiles, 21% of mammals and 57% of fish were
threatened or endangered as of 2008. Causes range from hunting and
overfishing to loss of habitat and pollution-induced die-offs. See http://www.
iucnredlist.org. Fisheries around the world are collapsing, and forests were
lost at an annual net rate of 7.3 million hectares a year from 2000–2005.
FAO 2005 Global Forest Resources Assessment. As you can probably guess
by now, climate change will exacerbate this problem, changing the habitat
of species faster than they can adapt and introducing new pathogens and
alien species.

We will proceed in much the same way international law has done: we
will start with the use, management and conservation of specific species,

including fish, whales, and "wildlife." We will look at the move from management to limits or prohibitions on taking, and at the use of trade restrictions in the Convention on International Trade in Endangered Species (CITES). We will then trace the broadening of concern to ecosystems as a whole, and to biological diversity as a value in itself, as reflected in the 1992 Biodiversity Convention. Several treaties or other instruments deal with specific habitats, including wetlands, forests and advancing deserts, or specific problems of genetic resources. We consider those next.

1. SPECIES CONSERVATION

The earliest attempts to conserve species were largely instrumental, aimed at maximizing sustainable yields in fish or conserving birds "useful to agriculture," as a 1902 treaty put it. Such treaties go back to the 1800s, and are usually species-specific. Examples include the Polar Bear Treaty (1974), the Migratory Bird Treaty (1916) or the North Pacific Fur Seal Treaty (1911).

a. FISHERIES

Recall Garrett Hardin's "Tragedy of the Commons." Global fisheries may be thought of as a classic example of the tragedy at work. Because no one owns the oceans or their contents, all states seek to maximize their fisheries yields. As a result, according to a 2008 FAO study, a bit more than half of all monitored fish stocks are now fully exploited, producing catches close to their maximum sustainable limits with no room for further expansion. Over a quarter are overexploited, depleted, or slowly recovering. Spectacular fisheries collapses have occurred, including the U.S. West Coast salmon fisheries and the rich banks off the coast of New England. In 2006 the global production from fishing and aquaculture combined reached approximately 144 million tons, of which 110 million were for human consumption. *FAO, The State of World Fisheries and Aquaculture 2008, available at* http://www.fao.org/docrep/011/i0250e/i0250e/htm.

Recall also the UNCLOS, which extended States' EEZs to 200 miles, thus in effect privatizing over 90% of fishing grounds. One might think that such privatization would lead states to take better care of their own resources, but in fact this has not occurred. States began subsidizing their fishing fleets, building up capacity and adding new technologies that made it easier to find, catch and freeze large amounts of fish on board ship. When close-in fishing predictably declined, they sent these long-distance fleets abroad, sometimes under different flags; illegal fishing fleets also blossomed. Fishing became especially intense in "donut holes" created where coastal nations EEZs left a small amount of space between them.

The UNCLOS contains a number of provisions concerning fisheries. See Articles 61–64 and 116–119 in the Documentary Supplement or online. Look at those provisions now.

NOTES AND QUESTIONS

1. Article 61 gives the coastal state the right to determine the allowable catch in its EEZ, subject to an obligation to take proper conservation and

management measures and to keep harvested species at levels that can produce "the maximum sustainable yield, as qualified by relevant environmental and economic factors"? What does this mean? Setting sustainable yields has proven to be highly problematic, as the science of predicting fish populations is quite difficult and uncertain; predictions of sustainable yield have often overshot the actual results. Are the goals of maximum yield and long-term species conservation compatible? Which does UNCLOS seem to privilege? How does the UNCLOS goal of maximum sustainable yield take into account bycatch (unwanted species caught in the course of fishing), or issues such as methods of fishing (driftnets, trawler factory ships) that have been thought to contribute to fisheries decline? Should the treaty treat small artisanal fisherfolk differently from large factory trawlers?

2.   The regional and subregional species specific organizations referred to in Article 118 are called regional fisheries management organizations (RFMOs). Examples include the Commission for the Conservation of Southern Bluefin Tuna (CCSBT), the International Commission for the Conservation of Atlantic Tunas (ICCAT), the Indian Ocean Tuna Commission (IOTC) and equivalent organizations for other species. According to the FAO, "the effectiveness of RFMOs is impaired by: the use of consensus decision-making; placing national interests ahead of good fisheries governance; an unwillingness of members to fund research in support of management; time-lagged implementation of management decisions; a focus on crisis management rather than everyday fisheries management; and the lack of a real connection between day-to-day fisheries management requirements and an annual meeting based on diplomatic practice. However, there is a growing consensus that these fundamental issues require resolution if RFMOs are to be reinvigorated and become truly effective vehicles for sustainable fisheries management." *FAO, supra.*

3.   Fish, unsurprisingly, do not recognize EEZs. How does UNCLOS deal with the problems of migratory fish and "straddling stocks?" In 1995, the 1995 Agreement for the Implementation of the Provisions of the 1982 UNCLOS Relating to the Conservation and Management of Straddling Fish Stocks and Highly Migratory Fish Stocks, U.N. Doc. A/CONF.164/37, 4 Aug. 1995 was negotiated.

David Freestone, A Decade of the Law of the Sea Convention: Is it a Success?*

39 GEO. WASH. INT'L L. REV. 499, 516 (2007)

The effective regulation of high seas fishing has been a perennial problem for international law. The 1982 UNCLOS effects a transfer of control to the coastal state over stocks within 200 nautical miles from the coastal baselines. The main exception to this coastal state control, covered by Article 63, is the regime of so-called "straddling stocks," fish species

* Footnotes omitted.

which move from EEZ to EEZ or from EEZ to high seas areas. The provisions of that article, however, like analogous articles in UNCLOS Part V, offer only what has been described by the International Law Association's EEZ Committee as "a minimum solution."

A review of the relevant provisions of the 1982 Convention indicates that the UNCLOS III sessions failed to solve this problem. For example, the provisions use phrases such as: States "shall seek to agree," "shall cooperate with a view to," "shall enter into negotiations with a view to. . . ." Although these are legal obligations, such provisions do not impose an obligation to agree, but simply to negotiate in good faith. Despite the fact that the Convention laid down basic principles, the articles are phrased in hortatory language which appears to be primarily concerned with accommodation of conflicting interests. Furthermore, none of the relevant provisions provide a remedy if agreement is not forthcoming; indeed, the Convention expressly excludes these issues from the general compulsory settlement techniques. This fact, as much as any, highlights that the defects in the UNCLOS high seas fishing regime were not inadvertent, but rather a failure to agree on these issues during the negotiation of the 1958 Geneva Convention on Fishing and Conservation of the Living Resources of the High Seas and at UNCLOS III.

A number of coastal states, frustrated by the inability of international bodies to remedy the defects of the UNCLOS, began pressing at the international level for action and threatened unilateral action to extend their jurisdiction beyond 200 nm in order to manage fish stocks in the high seas. In this sense, the UNCLOS is an unfinished agenda. The UN Fish Stocks Conference and ultimately the 1995 Agreement tried to address these issues, although up until the last minute, states differed considerably in opinion as to how best to approach them and, indeed, whether a binding agreement was the best approach. Some states, notably those with distant water fishing interests, such as Japan, preferred that the Conference produce a set of non-binding guidelines.

How did the 1995 Agreement change the 1982 Convention?

The final text of the 1995 Agreement contains fifty articles and two annexes. The Agreement is relevant to the interpretation and application of a number of key provisions of the UNCLOS, notably Articles 63, 64, and 116–120. Nevertheless, as Judge David Anderson has pointed out, the Agreement is a stand alone agreement in the sense that a state may become a party to the Agreement without becoming a party to UNCLOS and vice versa. However, the Agreement and the UNCLOS are fundamentally inter-related in the sense that one can be used to inform the interpretation of the other. The following section looks at the way the 1995 Agreement has changed or developed the 1982 Convention before making an assessment as to whether it is purely interpretative or has de facto modified the Convention.

The General Approach

The new approaches of the 1995 Agreement are apparent from the Preamble as well as the initial provisions of the Agreement relating to

conservation and management (Parts I and II). * * * Recital number seven
... declares an aspiration to improve upon previous fisheries management
treaties by recognizing the independent need to protect the marine environment through the protection of its biodiversity, maintenance of the integrity of marine ecosystems and the minimization of the risk of long term or
irreversible effects of fishing operations. This, albeit preambular statement,
means that the 1995 Agreement is the first global fisheries agreement to
recognize on a primary level the environmental significance of fishing
activities—not just for purposes of calculating the Total Allowable Catch
(TAC), but as an independent issue in its own right. The Agreement itself
recognizes this key concept, for example, in the precautionary approach.
* * *

In pursuance of an holistic, ecosystem approach, Article 3 indicates not
only that the Agreement applies to the conservation and management of
straddling and highly migratory stocks on the high seas, but also that
Articles 6 and 7 are to be applied to conservation and management
measures related to such stocks while in waters under national jurisdiction.
Coastal states are also obliged to utilize the principles of this agreement
(set out in Article 5) when managing such stocks within such waters.
Article 5 contains the general principles of stock management, Article 6 the
precautionary principle and Article 7 the requirements for coastal state and
distant water fishing state cooperation procedures vis-à-vis the implementation of conservation and management methodologies both within and
beyond the areas of national jurisdiction in all regional fisheries. Article 7
requires that "measures established for the high seas and those adopted
under national jurisdiction shall be compatible." This requirement does not
appear in the 1982 Convention and can be argued to be "progressive
development" of this regime, i.e., a change.

Article 5 identifies the framework of general principles to which coastal
states and "distant water fishing nations" (DWFNs) fishing on the high
seas must give effect, acting on a cooperative basis. Here, the emphasis is
on a proper balance between sustainability and utilization. What is significant about this key provision of the Agreement is that seven of the twelve
paragraphs relate to environmental sustainability and an ecosystem protection based on precaution and best scientific evidence, while one paragraph
deals with subsistence and artisanal fishers, two with data collection and
one with enforcement. Gone is the dominance of human consumption so
vividly expressed in the 1958 Convention.

Part III provides the framework for the most significant organizational
aspect of the Agreement in that it throws its weight behind international
cooperation through the development of new, and the enhancement of
existing, regional and subregional fishery management bodies....

What is significant about this new obligation is that failure to observe
this specific duty, (i.e. failure to become a member or participant in the
organization or arrangement) bars access to the fishery resources to which
the measures established by members or participants of the organization or
arrangement apply. For the first time, however, in international fisheries

law, "States which have a real (emphasis added) interest in the [straddling stock] fisheries concerned may become members of such organisations or participants in such arrangement" and the terms of participation of such organizations or arrangements shall not preclude such states from membership or participation, nor shall they be applied "in a manner which discriminates" against states with a "real" interest. There is a balance, however, in these provisions—the right of access to the resources requires membership of the regulatory organization; existing members may not, however, de facto deny access to the resources by denying participation to those with a legitimate (or in the wording of Article 8, "real") interest.

Given that the whole thrust of the Agreement is to focus the conservation and management of these stocks through regional organizations, the articles in Part III give some substance to what can legitimately be expected of such an agreement if it already exists, or of the minimum provisions which must be included in the constitutive instrument of a new body. Articles 9 to 12 provide a description of the jurisdiction, functions, membership, and character of sub-regional and regional fisheries management organizations. . . .

* * * In sum, Part III substantially develops the regime of the 1982 Law of the Sea Convention. Although Part III gives lip service to the concept of access to high seas resources, the regime clearly does not recognize unlimited access to these resources; rather, it recognizes a right for those states with a preexisting real interest to participate in existing Regional Fisheries Management Organizations, but does not give them a right to access the resources. This is a significant amendment to the traditional understanding of the language of the 1982 Convention. Similarly, the Agreement introduces a whole raft of additional mandatory requirements.

Do you agree that the 1995 Straddling Stock Convention modifies the understanding of the provisions of the UNCLOS? Does the underlying scientific change in how we understand the need for an ecosystem, rather than species-specific, approach explain this modification? How do you explain the fact that states can become parties to the 1995 Convention without being parties to the UNCLOS?

b. WHALES

One of the earliest species-specific conservation regimes deals with the various species of whales. Whales have long been hunted for food, oil, building materials and even clothing (think whalebone corsets), but by the turn of the twentieth century many whale species had been pursued to the brink of extinction. Several failed early efforts to manage the whale fishery led in 1946 to the International Convention on the Regulation of Whaling (ICRW), 161 U.N.T.S. 72. The Convention aims to "provide for the proper conservation of whale stocks and thus make possible the orderly development of the whaling industry." It is based on a Schedule of whale species and associated regulations, including limits on maximum catch, whaling areas and seasons, and types of gear. The Schedule may be amended based on scientific evidence by an International Whaling Commission (IWC) composed of member states. Contracting states agree to punish violations of the regulations by persons or vessels under their jurisdiction. However, the chief weakness of the Convention lies in the procedure for enforcing amendments: any state may object to a given amendment, and the amendment will then enter into force for all states that have not objected, but not for the objecting state. Article V.

In 1982, the IWC approved a "moratorium" on commercial whaling, pending a review of the scientific evidence on the viability and health of whale stocks. Although its Scientific Committee in 1994 presented a Revised Management Procedure that would regulate allowable catches, the IWC decided to continue the moratorium. It has been highly controversial. On the one hand, whaling nations like Iceland, Norway and Japan have protested that the moratorium ignores scientific findings that some minke whales can be caught without affecting the species' viability; and thus if sustainable yield is the goal the moratorium does not make sense. Thus, they argue that the regime has lost its original purpose and become a vehicle for animal rights activists. On the other, moratorium advocates argue that more work is needed on data gathering, understanding whale reproductive patterns, monitoring and enforcement, and that, in any case, whaling should now be outlawed since substitute products are now available and whales are sentient, intelligent beings that should not be hunted. As a result of these debates, Iceland pulled out of the IWC in 1992, (it rejoined in 2002) and Norway resumed commercial whaling in 1993. Japan continues to take significant numbers of minke whales, ostensibly for "scientific research" purposes.

Is the opt-out provision in the ICRW a fatal flaw? How could Norway resume commercial whaling while continuing to assert that it is part of the Convention? On the other hand, how is a permanent ban consistent with the ICRW's purpose? Why have most countries not exercised their right to reject amendments under Article V? U.S. domestic legislation allows the executive branch to impose sanctions on states acting contrary to the policies of the ICRW. The Pelly Amendment to the Fisherman's Protective Act of 1967, which is supplemented by the Packwood–Magnuson Amendments, allows sanctions to be imposed when foreign fisheries diminish the effectiveness of U.S. environmental laws. The Marine Mammal Protection Act prohibits U.S. nationals from taking whales. Is this an appropriate use of domestic legislation to provide teeth to an international conservation regime?

Is the IWC still a viable institution? In 1992, Norway, Iceland, Greenland (Denmark) and the Faeroe Islands created the North Atlantic Marine Mammal Commission to separately regulate their whaling activities. Why would Iceland then want to rejoin the IWC?

2.   CITES

For some animals and plants, the biggest threat to their survival comes from the demand for them in international trade. Elephant ivory, tiger bones, rhinoceros horns, tropical birds and rare orchids are all highly prized commodities that threaten the survival of the associated species. The 1973 Convention on International Trade in Endangered Species (CITES), 993 U.N.T.S. 243, 27 U.S.T.S. 1087; T.I.A.S. 8249 covers some 30,000 animals and plants. According to the CITES secretariat, "international wildlife trade is estimated to be worth billions of dollars and to include hundreds of millions of plant and animal specimens. The trade is diverse, ranging from live animals and plants to a vast array of wildlife products derived from them, including food products, exotic leather goods, wooden musical instruments, timber, tourist curios and medicines." *What is CITES?*, at http://www.cites.org/eng/disc/what.shtml. Most states (175 as of 2009) are parties to CITES.

CITES does not deal with habitat destruction, pollution or other non-trade related threats to species. Instead, CITES creates several levels of trade restrictions, depending on the level of threat to the species. It requires states to designate Management and Scientific authorities to issue permits and advise on technical issues; in the U.S., the Fish and Wildlife Service fulfils both functions. The levels of restriction, in decreasing order of severity, are as follows: Appendix I lists species threatened with extinction, and prohibits trade in them for "primarily commercial purposes." Any trade requires export as well as import permits, and a certification from the Management Authority of both exporting and importing states that the export will not be detrimental to the survival of the species and was legally obtained. This in effect bans most trade in Appendix I species and specimens derived from them. Appendix II includes species which, although not now threatened, may become so unless trade is regulated, while Appendix III includes all species which any Party regulates within its jurisdiction to prevent or restrict exploitation. Appendix II and III species only require export permits, but for Appendix II the exporting state's scientific authority must certify that the export will not be detrimental to the survival of the species. States are to take domestic measures to enforce the Convention and to punish violators.

Periodic meetings of the parties can modify the species listed in Appendix I and II by a two-thirds vote, depending on assessments of the health of the species. As is the case under the Whaling Convention, states can reserve to any amendments they disagree with while remaining part of CITES. Although most CITES listings are animals like apes, pandas, whales, tigers and elephants, in 2002 Central and South American big-leaf mahogany trees were listed under Appendix II.

The listing of the African elephant on Appendix I has been particularly controversial. Elephants range throughout central and eastern Africa, and their numbers fell dramatically through the 1980s due to habitat loss and poaching. After a quota system failed, the trade in elephant parts was banned in 1989, but Japan reserved the right to import raw ivory from some African states. The following article describes the next stages in the controversy.

African Elephant Ivory Sales Allowed Before Renewed Ban

ENV'T NEWS SERV., June 14, 2007, http://www.ens-newswire.com/ens/jun2007/2007-06-14-02.asp

THE HAGUE, The Netherlands, June 14, 2007 (ENS)—Ministers from the African elephant range states have for the first time achieved a consensus on how to address the controversial issue of international trade in elephant ivory. Some trade will be allowed before a nine year ban is imposed under the agreement reached today at the conference of Parties to the Convention on International Trade in Endangered Species, CITES.

CITES banned the international commercial ivory trade worldwide in 1989. But some southern African elephant range states have sought to sell ivory from healthy and well managed herds, saying they need the proceeds for conservation. Other African range states and most environmentalists say that even legal trade in ivory will increase the poaching of elephants.

Under the compromise forged in the pre-dawn hours this morning, each of four southern African countries will be permitted to make a single sale of ivory in addition to the one-off sale totaling 60 metric tons that was agreed in principle in 2002 and given the go-ahead by the CITES Standing Committee on June 2. The ivory for these new sales will consist of all government-owned stocks that have been registered and verified as of January 31, 2007. Each sale is to consist of a single shipment per destination and may only go to countries whose internal controls on ivory sales have been verified as being sufficient by the CITES Secretariat.

After these shipments have been completed no new proposals for further sales from these four countries are to be considered by CITES during a "resting period" of nine years that will begin as soon as the new sales have been completed. The four countries that will be permitted to market their ivory are Botswana, Namibia, South Africa and Zimbabwe.

NOTES AND QUESTIONS

1. Do you agree with Botswana and the other three countries that they should be allowed to sell ivory to raise money for conservation, or, as Kenya and others have argued, will a legal market in ivory simply serve as a cover for an illegal market, thus stimulating poaching? Does it depend in part on how well we can identify the source of ivory? If you were in charge of an alligator preserve in south Florida, would you allow people to shoot a certain (low) number of large male alligators in exchange for large amounts of money to support the local economy and pay for habitat improvements? Why or why not? Some people argue that the best way to preserve at least some wildlife is to make it more valuable alive than dead, providing incentives to local populations to protect "their" wildlife. Do you agree?

Are whale watching or eco-tourism adequate substitutes for whaling or the ivory trade?

2.   What other policies could protect endangered wildlife populations? What if the wildlife consists of a small, rather nondescript amphibian rather than charismatic megafauna like elephants? What if it has no known value to humans?

3.   THE BIODIVERSITY CONVENTION

By the 1980s it was clear that efforts to focus on single species or on the trade in wildlife were not enough to stop the steep decline in many wild animal and plant populations. Environmentalists began advocating an ecosystem approach that moved away from ad-hoc species-by-species considerations. At the same time, concern arose that the variability of life itself was being eroded, as agricultural breeding programs reduced the number of commercially viable variants of useful plants and animals, thereby increasing the vulnerability of the food supply to new diseases and pests, and as habitat loss, poaching and pollution took a toll. The role of wild species in providing the raw material for new medicines also prompted concern: over three quarters of all top prescription drugs used in the U.S. were derived from natural sources, many of them found in the ecosystems most under threat. For all these reasons, attention turned to conserving biodiversity more generally.

The 1992 UNCED conference produced two major framework conventions: the climate change convention we have already seen, and the Convention on Biological Diversity, 31 ILM 818 (1992) (CBD or Biodiversity Convention). The CBD covers "the conservation of biological diversity, the sustainable use of its components and the fair and equitable sharing of the benefits arising out of the utilization of genetic resources ..." Art. 1. Most countries (191 as of 2009), not including the United States, are parties. As was the case with the Climate Change Convention, serious rifts between northern (rich) countries and southern (poor) countries drove the negotiations. In this case, the South wanted to retain, and benefit from, control over most of the world's biological diversity, especially as those resources became relevant to the then-emerging biotechnology industry. They were especially concerned that biological resources—whether in the form of plants, fungi or genetic material—obtained in developing countries not then be subject to patent regimes that made them inaccessible to the very countries that had provided the raw material and that provided no benefit to the source countries. The North, for its part, wanted to ensure open access to such resources and protection of intellectual property rights. In this case, unlike in the cases of the deep seabed or space, it was the Northern countries that wanted the resource conceptualized as "common heritage" while the Southern countries wanted sovereign control over their own biological resources.

In the end, states agreed, for the first time, that conservation of biological resources, even those resources entirely contained within national borders, constitutes an issue of common concern properly the subject of international rulemaking. At the same time, they rejected the idea that biodiversity, especially genetic resources, was a "common heritage" of humanity to be freely available to all, and affirmed states' sovereignty over the biological and genetic resources within their borders. The idea, parallel to the discussion earlier regarding CITES, was that states would better protect the biological resources within their borders if these resources were potentially lucrative.

The relatively non-controversial parts of the CBD deal with *in-situ* conservation of biodiversity. The parties agreed to create national strategies, plans or programs to preserve biodiversity, and to integrate biodiversity protection into national planning more generally. They also committed themselves to establish a system of protected areas, control alien species, and regulate risks arising from biotechnology. They agreed to also adopt measures for *ex-situ* preservation of biodiversity, for example through seed banks, to promote the sustainable use of biological resources, and carry out impact assessments of projects that could impact biodiversity. Unfortunately, all these further obligations are qualified by language that states will act "as far as possible and as appropriate." What is left of these obligations given the qualifiers? Can they still have an impact?

The CBD's more controversial, and innovative, provisions concern access and benefit-sharing around the use of biological and genetic resources. One provision explicitly recognizes indigenous peoples and communities: article 8(j) commits states, subject to their national legislation, to "respect, preserve and maintain knowledge, innovations and practices of indigenous and local communities embodying traditional lifestyles relevant for the conservation and sustainable use of biological diversity and promote their wide application with the approval and involvement of the holders of such knowledge, innovations and practices and encourage the equitable sharing of the benefits arising from the utilization of such knowledge, innovations and practices." This represents a breakthrough in international law, combining human rights-type obligations of states to their own citizens with environmental protection provisions.

One of the CBD's stated aims is "the fair and equitable sharing of the benefits arising out of the utilization of genetic resources, including by appropriate access to genetic resources and by appropriate transfer of relevant technologies, taking into account all rights over those resources and to technologies, and by appropriate funding." The access and benefit-sharing provisions of the Convention are found in Articles 15 through 19, in the Documentary Supplement and online.

NOTES AND QUESTIONS

1. What is the bargain set out in these Articles? What do countries where biological and genetic resources are found commit to? What do countries with biotechnology industries commit to? How is the current patent regime, which allows for private patents on material synthesized from natural products, compatible with either Article 8(j) or with articles 15–19?

2. The United States has declined to join the CBD on grounds that the benefit-sharing articles do not sufficiently protect intellectual property rights. See SHARON L. SPRAY & KAREN LEAH MCGLOTHLIN, LOSS OF BIODIVERSITY 159–160 (2003).

3. Local peoples in India for thousands of years have known of the anti-insecticidal properties of the leaves of the neem tree. In 1971, U.S. timber importer Robert Larson began importing neem seed to the U.S. He eventually sold the patent for a pesticidal neem extract to the multinational chemical corporation, W. R. Grace and Co. See Emily Marden, *The Neem Tree Patent: International Conflict over the Commodification of Life*, 22 B.C. INT'L & COMP. L. REV. 279 (1999). What issues does this raise under the CBD? In response to the perceived appropriation of their genetic resources and local knowledge, a number of developing countries have passed national legislation allowing communities to register their existing knowledge or taken other steps to protect against "biopiracy." Is this a good solution? What else could be done? The trade-related aspects of intellectual property protection are contained in the World Trade Organization's Trade–Related Intellectual Property rights provisions (TRIPs). TRIPs allows states to deny patent protection to plants and animals so long as they provide alternative, *sui generis* protection. Article 27.3. For more on the complex relationships among the CBD, TRIPs, and other plant protection regimes, see Naomi Roht–Arriaza, *Of Seeds and Shamans: The Appropriation of the Scientific and Technical Knowledge of Indigenous and Local Communities*, 17 MICH. J. INT'L L. 919, 938 (1996).

4. The CBD Conference of the Parties has set up a number of working groups to implement its provisions. A Working Group on Access and Benefit Sharing has been tasked with drafting a further agreement implementing the convention articles on the subject. The Working Group on Article 8(j) has worked to increase indigenous and local community participation in the Convention process, developed guidelines for the conduct of cultural, environmental and social impact assessments (the Akwé:Kon Voluntary Guidelines), prepared a report on the status and trends of traditional knowledge and the identification of threats to the maintenance, preservation and application of traditional knowledge, and is working on elements of sui generis systems for the protection of traditional knowledge as well as elements of an ethical code of conduct. The Working Group on Protected Areas designs "tool kits" for the designation and management of protected areas, ecological corridors, marine sanctuaries and the like, while the Working Group on Review of Implementation tries to improve evaluation and monitoring.

5. Article 19(3) invites a Protocol on the safety of genetically modified organisms (GMOs). In 2000, states agreed to the Cartagena Protocol on Biosafety to the CBD, 31 ILM 1257 (2000). The Protocol sets out procedures, including notification and prior informed consent (considered below in section F), safe handling methods, and risk assessment and risk management obligations for living modified organisms. A less stringent procedure applies when such organisms are intended for direct use as food or feed, or for processing, for example soy or corn grown from genetically-modified seeds.

4.   PROTECTION OF SPECIFIC HABITATS

In addition to the Biodiversity Convention, a number of treaties focus on additional protection of spaces considered of particular importance. The World Heritage Convention and the Ramsar Convention on Wetlands start from the premises that certain defined areas need special protection. The Desertification Convention is mainly aimed at obtaining international support for African efforts to preserve arable land and at ensuring that local populations have a say in land-use policies. There is to date no specific treaty on forests, but the issue of forest preservation touches on a number of treaty regimes, finance and market-based efforts, and we consider them as a case study here.

a.   WORLD HERITAGE SITES

The 1972 UNESCO Convention for the Protection of the World Cultural and Natural Heritage, 1037 UNTS 151, 11 INT'L LEG.MAT. 1358 (1972), entered into force on December 17, 1975, protects those "parts of the cultural or natural heritage [that] are of outstanding interest and therefore need to be preserved as part of the world heritage of mankind as a whole." (Preamble). These world heritage sites, which may include monuments, cave dwellings, buildings, archeological sites, natural features, habitats for endangered species, or other natural sites, are threatened by decay as well as human activity. The Convention balances recognition of state sovereignty over these sites and the state's obligation to preserve such sites with the need for international help to do so, especially for poorer countries.

Under the Convention, each state is to designate its World Heritage sites and commits to protect and preserve them. The United States has listed, for example, the Grand Canyon. Other sites include Egypt's pyramids, famous cathedrals, and unique natural habitats. The Convention establishes a World Heritage Committee, elected from the states parties, to compile a World Heritage List from these designations. Article 11(4) tasks the Committee to also establish and keep up to date a List of World Heritage in Danger. This list may only contain property forming the part of the cultural and natural heritage that is threatened by serious and specific dangers. The Committee decides on international assistance, financial, technical or of another kind, to help states preserve their World Heritage sites. For this purpose, states parties pay into a voluntary fund administered by the Committee. For a list of World Heritage sites and information on the World Heritage system, see http://whc.unesco.org/en/about/.

b.   PROTECTION OF WETLANDS

A. Kiss and D. Shelton, International Environmental Law

p. 249 (1991)

* * * *The Convention on Wetlands of International Importance* was the first treaty based on the idea that the habitat of endangered species should

be the focus of protection. One of the first major conservation treaties, it is relatively simple in its structure. It is based on recognition that wetlands are among the most productive sources of ecological support on earth, acting as habitat for myriad species and as flood control regions.

The preamble affirms that wetlands constitute a resource of great economic, cultural, scientific and recreational value, the loss of which would be irreparable. Wetlands are defined in Article 1 as being areas of marsh, fen, peatland or water, whether natural or artificial, permanent or temporary, with water that is static or flowing, fresh, brackish or salt, including areas of marine water whose depth does not exceed six meters at low tide. Waterfowl, whose protection was the purpose of this convention, are defined as birds ecologically dependent on wetlands.

The original objective of the Convention was to protect the habitat of waterfowl. However, its importance has outstripped that objective as the ecological importance of wetlands has become recognized, particularly their role in supporting marine life. Unfortunately, during recent decades drainage operations and drought, as well as landfill, have considerably reduced the extent of wetlands.

The Convention on Wetlands of International Importance (RAMSAR Convention) entered into force on December 21, 1975. A Protocol to the Convention was adopted in 1982. See Protocol to Amend the Convention on Wetlands of International Importance especially as Waterfowl Habitat (Paris Protocol). See Simon Lyster, International Wildlife Law (1985), Navid, *The International Law of Migratory Species: The RAMSAR Convention*, 29 Nat. Res. J. 1001 (1989) and Bowman, *The RAMSAR Convention Comes of Age*, 42 Neth. Int'l L. Rev. (1995).

c. DESERTIFICATION

The 1994 United Nations Convention to Combat Desertification in Those Countries Experiencing Serious Drought and/or Deforestation, Particularly in Africa, 33 ILM 1328 (1994) is not aimed at protecting deserts *per se*; rather, the idea is that countries, especially in Africa, facing encroaching desertification, loss of arable soils, drought and related problems, need international support to confront the phenomenon. As Articles 2(2) and 4(1) and (2) indicate, the Convention foresees long term strategies that focus at the same time on improvements in the productivity of land and the rehabilitation, conservation and sustainable management of resources leading to improved living conditions.

Article 5 lays out the obligations of affected country parties. These include giving due priority to combating the problem of desertification and mitigating the effects of drought, allocating adequate resources in accordance with their circumstances and capabilities, addressing the underlying causes of desertification, paying special attention to the socio-economic factors that contribute to the desertification processes and promoting awareness and facilitating the participation of local populations, particularly women and youth with the support of NGOs. The extensive provisions on a "bottom up" approach stressing affected community participation in decision making are particularly innovative. As part of each COP, states organize a dialog with local NGOs to discuss the on-the-ground effectiveness of state plans and programs and to seek opportunities for collaboration.

In addition to a Secretariat and a Conference of the Parties, there is a committee on monitoring and implementation to consider state's reports on the progress of their national plans, a scientific committee, and a mechanism to coordinate funding efforts. The Convention has 193 states parties, including the United States.

d. FORESTS

The 1992 United Nations Conference on Environment and Development at Rio was unable to agree on a treaty on forests, and instead adopted a non-binding statement of principles on the protection of forests. Statement of Principles for a Global Consensus on the Management, Conservation and Sustainable Development of All Types of Forests, UN Doc. A/CONF. 151/6/Rev. 1; 31 ILM 818 (1992). At the time, a U.N. publication set out the importance of forest resources:

Earth Summit in Focus
No. 5, U.N. Department of Public Information, UN Doc. DPI/1198–92173 (Feb. 8, 1992)

Saving the Forests:

Forging a Global Compact

* * * The value of forests [is often] described in narrow economic terms, as an exploitable resource. However, in recent years a wider view has emerged of the varied functions forests serve, many of which have far-reaching economic and social implications. Increasingly, forests are seen:

- as homes for indigenous peoples.
- as "sinks" for converting carbon dioxide through photosynthesis into the oxygen needed to keep us alive.
- as protection for watersheds. Forests help prevent avalanches, floods, landslides and mud-flows, and protect hydroelectric power plants, irrigation and municipal water supplies.
- as wildlife habitats for a rich diversity of species of plant, animal and insect life. Tropical forests are believed to be home to more than half the species on earth, including medicinal plants and food crops. Fallen leaves are a primary source of humus, the topsoil which sustains plant life.
- as key players in maintaining crucial ecological balances, such as the annual cycle of sediments and flood water needed for the production of rice to feed hundreds of millions of people.

- as recreation areas.

- as fuel used daily by some two billion people in developing countries. Half the annual forest harvest is for fuel. Where forests are degraded, women must walk farther to find cooking fuel; but in some areas, there is no wood at all. By 2000, the fuel-wood deficit could reach 960 million cubic metres a year, the energy equivalent of $30 billion worth of oil annually.

* * *

Since 1992, the problem of deforestation has continued. At the same time, some efforts at implementing sustainable forestry, setting aside ecologically important forest resources, and including local populations in forest protection have been successful. At least, many governments have recognized that laws encouraging agricultural settlement of the forest frontier are counterproductive, and some have granted rights over forest lands to the peoples, especially indigenous peoples, who live there. Nonetheless, figuring out the right combination of legal regimes and economic incentives to reverse deforestation and forest degradation, much of it now based on illegal logging, to limit the replacement of natural forests with tree plantations (with their much impoverished biodiversity) and to protect the ecological services provided by forests, constitutes a major challenge. Consider the following options. Which ones seem promising? How can the different legal regimes—national and international—involved be harmonized?

(i) Post UNCED, efforts to draft a binding forestry agreement continued, to date without success. An Inter–Governmental Panel on Forests (1995–1997) was followed by an Inter–Governmental Forum on Forests (1997–2000), which was followed in turn by a permanent U.N. Forum on Forests starting in 2000. The Forest Principles set out the basic issue underlying the lack of progress towards a treaty:

> 1.(b) The agreed full incremental cost of achieving benefits associated with forest conservation and sustainable development requires increased international cooperation and should be equitably shared by the international community.

In other words, developing countries wanted control over the use and exploitation of forest resources, and were willing to conserve forests, but only if the developed countries chip in part of the cost of conservation. This continues to be the crux of the matter. Meanwhile, the UNFF has convened nine meetings which have produced a number of resolutions and even a draft treaty, but no progress towards a final text. As you read through the following materials, consider: would a treaty on forests be helpful? How? Are the existing treaty regimes on biodiversity, tropical timber, and climate change enough? What happens if their provisions are inconsistent?

(ii) The International Tropical Timber Agreement regulates the sale of tropical timber and provides a framework for cooperation between producing and consumer states. The ITTA was originally negotiated in 1983, but has been updated in 1994 and again in 2006. The International Tropical Timber Organization set up under the Agreement is primarily concerned with expanding trade in tropical wood, which is dominated by Asian countries as both producers and consumers; votes are allocated equally between producers and consumers. The 2006 version of the agreement asserts that its objective is to "promote the expansion and diversification of international trade in tropical timber from sustainably managed and legally harvested forests and to promote the sustainable management of tropical timber producing forests." Nonetheless, a nonbinding effort in 1990 to have all tropical timber be sustainably managed by 2000 failed, and it is not clear to what extent the sustainable forestry commitment translates into changed practices on the ground.

(iii) The 2007 U.N. Declaration on the Rights of Indigenous Peoples, which states that indigenous peoples have the rights to own, use, develop and control the lands, territories and resources that they possess by reason of traditional ownership or other traditional occupation or use, as well as those which they have otherwise acquired (Art. 26); to the conservation and protection of the environment and the productive capacity of their lands or territories and resources (Art. 29); and to determine and develop priorities and strategies for the development or use of their lands or territories and other resources (Art. 32). How does the Declaration impact forest policy in areas with indigenous forest dwellers?

(iv) The CBD protects forests as habitat for biodiversity, as we saw above. Efforts to protect forests as protected areas under the Biodiversity Convention have often come into conflict with the protection of indigenous and other local peoples' rights. As explained by the V IUCN World Parks Congress Durban Action Plan (2004):

"[T]he roles, knowledge and customary laws of indigenous peoples and local communities have frequently been disregarded or undervalued by the conservation community. For example, many protected areas have been established without adequate attention to, and respect for the rights of indigenous peoples, including mobile indigenous peoples, and local communities, especially their rights to lands, territories and resources, and their right freely to consent to activities that affect them. Furthermore, many indigenous peoples have been expelled from protected areas created in their territories, thereby severing their relationship with the land involved and undermining their cultural integrity. Indeed, indigenous peoples and local communities have often borne the costs of protected areas but received few benefits; this is particularly true of women."

One response has been a new emphasis on community-based forest management. Management of forest resources is devolved to the community level, in the understanding that local communities have the greatest interest in, and ability to, preserve the forests and derive benefit from them. Almost a quarter of the world's forests are now under community management. Local people may incorporate traditional techniques and practices into forest use and stewardship. Successful community forestry depends on adequate security of tenure and recognition of community rights to forest resources. A large number of community forestry projects, many of them funded by the World Bank, are underway.

(v) market-based methods I: Certification

The Forest Stewardship Council is a private organization that certifies that timber has been harvested in a sustainable manner. According to the organization's website, www.fsc.org, "The FSC label provides a credible link between responsible production and consumption of forest products, enabling consumers and businesses to make purchasing decisions that benefit people and the environment as well as providing ongoing business value." Certification of lumber is based on demonstrated compliance with a set of Principles, each with detailed guidelines:

Overview of the FSC Principles and Criteria

Principle 1.

Compliance with all applicable laws and international treaties

Principle 2.

Demonstrated and uncontested, clearly defined, long–term land tenure and use rights

Principle 3.

Recognition and respect of indigenous peoples' rights

Principle 4.

Maintenance or enhancement of long-term social and economic well-being of forest workers and local communities and respect of worker's rights in compliance with International Labour Organisation (ILO) conventions

Principle 5.

Equitable use and sharing of benefits derived from the forest

Principle 6.

Reduction of environmental impact of logging activities and maintenance of the ecological functions and integrity of the forest

Principle 7.

Appropriate and continuously updated management plan

Principle 8.

Appropriate monitoring and assessment activities to assess the condition of the forest, management activities and their social and environmental impacts

Principle 9.

Maintenance of High Conservation Value Forests (HCVFs) defined as environmental and social values that are considered to be of outstanding significance or critical importance

Principle 10.

In addition to compliance with all of the above, plantations must contribute to reduce the pressures on and promote the restoration and conservation of natural forests.

FSC-certified lumber commands a premium price. Can consumer preferences be harnessed to provide adequate protection for forests through efforts like the FSC? A similar organization exists for sustainably harvested seafood. See www.msc.org.

(vi) Market-based mechanisms II: Climate change flexible mechanisms and REDD

The Kyoto Protocol discusses forests as "sinks" and "reservoirs" of carbon. As you read through the following excerpts, recall the discussion of flexible market mechanisms in the Kyoto Protocol, including the Clean Development Mechanism, above.

David Takacs, Carbon Into Gold: Forest Carbon Offsets, Climate Change Adaptation, and International Law*

15 HASTINGS W.-N.W. J. ENV. L. & POL'Y 39, 56 (2009)

* * *

Forest Carbon Offsets (FCOs)

Half of the global terrestrial carbon pool is stored in forests. Tropical deforestation accounts for 11 percent to 28 percent of GHG emissions. Africa alone is losing nearly 10 million acres of forest each year. The UNDP reports that continued deforestation from Indonesia and Brazil alone equals 80 percent of the GHG emissions savings achieved if all Annex 1 nations were to meet their Kyoto Protocol goals in the 2008–2012 commitment period.

Northern investment in Southern forest preservation and reforestation is rapidly gaining currency both as one scheme to mitigate GHG buildup, and to help some communities and nations adapt to the ravages of global climate change. In an FCO, a project developer plants trees to reforest a degraded ecosystem, or ensures that a forest that would have otherwise been degraded or felled is, instead, preserved. The developer can then sell the carbon, in the form of CERs now sequestered in the trees and soil, for a contracted period of time. Proponents of FCOs argue that these projects will mitigate GHG accumulation globally, preserve vital ecosystems that help buffer the effects of global climate change and help sustain ecosystem services communities require locally, and also preserve biodiversity and generate ecologically sustainable new forms of wealth to community members living near forested lands. Preserving forests helps to stabilize local climate fluctuations, prevent drought, protect aquifers, maintain pollinator populations, stabilize soil, buffer communities from natural disasters, allow

---

* Footnotes omitted.

a source of sustainable forest products, and preserve forest-related options for the future.

* * *

Many Kyoto Protocol signatories were skeptical about these projects, and therefore circumscribed their inclusion as CDM-eligible. Skeptics claim that FCOs have problems with leakage (communities that formerly relied upon a forest are likely to cut trees elsewhere; a government may preserve one forest from planned logging and instead offer timber concessions elsewhere; logging companies denied concession rights in one country may instead cut timber in a neighboring country); permanence (forests burn or get chopped down); quantifiability (FCOs pose technical challenges of calculating present and future carbon stored in forests, particularly under different climate change scenarios); and additionality (project developers must show the project would not have been undertaken but for the FCO).

* * *

While the CDM has circumscribed their eligibility, FCOs are thriving as part of the broader voluntary carbon offset market. * * * Outside the bounds of formal regulation, a host of [multinational enterprises and international financial institutions] * * * are investing in these FCOs, with potential to wield powerful influence on how human and ecological communities are configured in distant lands. They are deriving their own codes of conduct for how they will proceed. . . .

* * * Traditional investment firms are getting into the carbon commodity business. For example, Merrill Lynch, in association with Australian business Carbon Conservation, has just announced that it is financing a high-profile, $US9–million deal to prevent deforestation on nearly 2 million acres in Aceh, Sumatra. Merrill Lynch hopes to sell the carbon credits (for which they're paying $US4 each) at a profit, and Carbon Conservation hopes to "become the amazon.com of the Amazon."

The UN recently created a Program to coordinate forest and climate policy. It is a subject for discussion in the post-2012 climate regime.

UN–REDD, About REDD

available at http://www.un-redd.org

Deforestation and forest degradation, through agricultural expansion, conversion to pastureland, infrastructure development, destructive logging, fires etc., account for nearly 20% of global greenhouse gas emissions, more than the entire global transportation sector and second only to the energy sector. It is now clear that in order to constrain the impacts of climate change within limits that society will reasonably be able to tolerate, the global average temperatures must be stabilized within two degrees Celsius. This will be practically impossible to achieve without reducing emissions from the forest sector, in addition to other mitigation actions.

REDD—Reducing Emissions from Deforestation and Forest Degradation in Developing Countries—is an effort to create a financial value for the carbon stored in forests, offering incentives for developing countries to reduce emissions from forested lands and invest in low-carbon paths to sustainable development.

It is predicted that financial flows for greenhouse gas emission reductions from REDD could reach up to US$30 billion a year. This significant North–South flow of funds could reward a meaningful reduction of carbon emissions and could also support new, pro-poor development, help conserve biodiversity and secure vital ecosystem services.

Further, maintaining forest ecosystems can contribute to increased resilience to climate change. To achieve these multiple benefits, REDD will require the full engagement and respect for the rights of Indigenous Peoples and other forest-dependent communities.

To "seal the deal" on climate change, REDD activities in developing countries must complement, not be a substitute for, deep cuts in developed countries' emissions. The decision to include REDD in a post-Kyoto regime must not jeopardize the commitment of Annex I countries to reduce their own emissions. Both will be critical to successfully address climate change.

NOTES AND QUESTIONS

1.   Which of these strategies seems promising for preserving forests? Are the multiple benefits of forest lands potentially in tension with each other? For example, reforesting with same-species, quick-growing eucalyptus or pine may improve carbon sequestration, but it has a negative effect on biodiversity, water resources and the ability of forest peoples to survive. How should these benefits be traded off against each other?

2.   If you represented a forest conservation NGO, would you put effort into negotiating a binding treaty on forests? Or would you argue that existing treaty and soft law is enough, and that the focus should be on local implementation? If you decided that a treaty was needed, what issues would you imagine most difficult? What would your positions be if you represented Ecuador or Brazil? Malaysia or Indonesia? A timber-importing state like Sweden? Would it matter if your forests were tropical or boreal? What other interest coalitions would be likely to form in such a negotiation?

3.   Does REDD seem like a promising strategy? What difficulties can you foresee given the experience with CDM and other market mechanisms?

F.   CHEMICALS AND HAZARDOUS WASTES

Industrial society produces a vast array of chemical substances, which are incorporated into products or used and thrown away. Some 75,000 chemicals are on the market, and another 1,500 appear each year. Some of these substances cause health and environmental problems for people, wildlife or ecosystems. They may cause acute poisoning, or long-term problems like cancer, birth defects, immune system suppression, or endocrine disruption. Of the millions of chemicals in circulation, very few have been tested for toxic or dangerous effects, and even fewer have been tested for their cumulative or synergistic effects with other chemicals. Chemicals are an international problem because they migrate: high levels of PCBs, DDT and other persistent organic chemicals, for example, have been found in the breast milk of the Inuit, even though no PCBs or DDT is used in their communities. Many chemicals, moreover, are important in international trade. States' regulatory regimes may differ so that chemicals banned or restricted in one country due to health or environmental effects are nonetheless sold in other countries where the risks are less well known. For example, many pesticides banned in the U.S. were exported for use in Mexico, and the produce was then imported into the U.S., creating a "circle of poison."

International law deals with chemicals and other hazardous substances in a number of ways. First, after the fact spills or transboundary accidents involving hazardous chemicals are dealt with under the rules regarding state responsibility (see Chapter 8) or under the small number of liability-based treaties that specify who is responsible for damages. Second, a number of agreements ban (or phase out) particularly harmful substances. The Montreal Protocol on the Protection of the Ozone Layer, considered in Part B, above, is one such agreement. The Protocol and its successive Amendments create tighter and tighter timetables for the phase out of ozone depleting chemicals, as well as add prohibited chemicals to the phase-out list. The 1972 London Dumping Convention deals with deliberate dumping of wastes into the sea. Its heart is a black list of substances that cannot be dumped, and a grey list of substances that require "special care." Several regional dumping agreements take a similar approach.

Starting in the 1990s, there has been a movement towards applying a more precautionary approach to chemicals and waste management. Thus, a 1996 Protocol to the London Dumping Convention (which entered into force in 2006) invokes the precautionary and polluter-pays principles, and changes from a listing approach to a "reverse list" in which the presumption is that if a substance does not appear on an annexed list, it cannot be dumped. The Stockholm Convention on Persistent Organic Chemicals (POPs treaty), considered below, also adopts this approach.

In addition to prohibition, a number of treaties deal with the implications of trade in hazardous substances or wastes. These include the Convention for the Application of Prior Informed Consent Procedure for Certain Hazardous Chemicals and Pesticides in International Trade (Rotterdam PIC Convention) and the Basel Convention on the Transboundary Movement of Hazardous Wastes and its regional analogs dealing with waste minimization and disposal. A final category of strategies involve the management of chemicals, including increased efforts to improve knowledge about their potential for harm. In this section we consider the EU's REACH regulation as well as global efforts.

1.   PROHIBITIONS ON CHEMICALS: FROM MONTREAL TO POPS

Peter L. Lallas, Current Development: The Stockholm Convention on Persistent Organic Pollutants

95 AM. J. INT'L L. 692 (2001)

The Stockholm Convention is designed to protect human health and the environment from persistent organic pollutants (POPs)—chemical substances that are persistent and toxic, that bioaccumulate in fatty tissue (achieving higher concentrations as they move up a particular food chain), and that are prone to long-range environmental transport. Among other things, the convention contains obligations to eliminate or severely restrict the production and use of a number of POP pesticides and industrial chemicals, to take strong measures to prevent or control the release of certain POPs that are formed as by-products of various combustion activities, and to ensure the safe and proper disposal or destruction of such substances when they become wastes. The convention initially applies to twelve POPs of particular concern—sometimes referred to as the "dirty dozen"—and includes a process and a set of criteria for adding new substances to the regime at a later date.

Several years of dialogue and negotiation preceded the conclusion of the Stockholm Convention at the fifth session of the POPs Intergovernmental Negotiating Committee (INC) in Johannesburg, South Africa, in December 2000. The convention may be viewed as a leading initiative in an increasingly prominent aspect of the global environmental agenda: action to address harm to human health and the environment from toxic substances.

The convention is also noteworthy for the manner in which it resolves certain recurring issues that have confronted the international community in other treaty negotiations. These issues include, for example: how to address differences among countries relating to capacity to comply and other factors (for example, whether and how to differentiate obligations); how to address scientific uncertainty; how to design a dynamic regime that can respond to both present and future needs; and, more generally, what combination of policy tools needs to be used in order to meet environmental policy goals and to avoid slipping to a "lowest common denominator" in protecting health and the environment.

In particular, the convention uses a variety of innovative approaches and "tools" to achieve its objectives and respond to the negotiating needs of the parties; it builds upon experiences and lessons from other treaties, and in some cases breaks new ground. Examples include: the use of what became known as country-specific exemptions that allow obligations to be "differentiated" among parties according to their *individual* circumstances;

the use of a relatively new legal tool, a register, to facilitate this process; the use of trade measures in a manner that is linked to the status of a particular substance under the convention; the special approach adopted to link efforts to reduce use of DDT with efforts to combat disease and death from malaria; the highly nuanced relationship between the Conference of the Parties (COP) and the expert group created under the convention to make recommendations regarding the addition of new substances; and the combination of approaches taken with respect both to the control of by-product contaminants and to the adoption of amendments to the convention.

A number of "prenegotiation" decisions regarding the scope and nature of the convention also played a major role in the ultimate outcome and, in the view of many, success of the negotiations. For example, rather than attempting to develop a broader "framework" convention that would cover all chemicals, a conscious decision was made to focus the treaty on POPs, to begin by including only the widely recognized list of twelve, and to set in place a process to add other POPs in the future. Interestingly, in the case of this particular treaty—unlike some others—the decision *not* to use a framework-convention approach (at least at the level of all chemicals) seemed to help maintain momentum for action.

* * *

The above process [regarding the procedure in Article 8 for adding new chemicals] represents a new approach for addressing a recurrent issue in treaty regimes: how to balance responsibilities between different parts of the institutional structure. This approach attempts to maintain the primary role of the POPs Review Committee in reviewing the science, while providing parties with the opportunity to appeal committee decisions to the COP.

Another important element in the Article 8 process for adding new substances is its approach to scientific uncertainty (the precaution issue). The screening criteria on persistence and bioaccumulation build in an element of expert judgment—and are not exclusively numerical or quantitative. Article 8(7)(a) also states, in particular, that the "lack of full scientific certainty shall not prevent the proposal from proceeding." Moreover, Article 9—which concerns the final decision by the COP whether or not to list a new substance—specifically directs that the COP, "taking due account of the recommendations of the Committee, including any scientific uncertainty, shall decide, in a precautionary manner, whether to list the chemical, and specify its related control measures."

* * *

Once the Article 8 process is completed, a decision by the COP to add a new substance is governed by the convention's amendment provisions, which also govern any revision to the screening criteria. In the negotiations concerning the addition of new substances, a key issue was whether to follow an "opt-in" approach, under which a country would not be bound until it formally submitted an instrument indicating its acceptance of an amendment, or an "opt-out" approach, under which a country would be bound by an amendment unless it explicitly opted out through notification under the convention. This issue was resolved by using a process previously used in only one other treaty, the UN Convention on Desertification, which sets forth an opt-out process but allows any individual country, at the time it becomes a party, to indicate that it will use, instead, an opt-in approach with respect to amendments. This still-rare mechanism had the value in the POPs negotiation of maintaining opt-out as a general approach but of also allowing those countries with a specific need (for example, relating to domestic procedures for ratification) to satisfy their own particular interests.

* * *

In negotiating the Stockholm Convention—as in many other situations—perhaps the most significant issue was whether to establish a separate, binding fund that would be administered by the convention, or to use an approach that relied on contributions into existing funding mechanisms (for example, the Global Environment Facility (GEF)). The dividing lines in the negotiation were clear: developing countries, in general, advocated the former (in particular, the approach taken in the Montreal Protocol), and developed countries, the latter.... In sum, instead of creating a separate, legally binding fund under the convention, this approach uses existing entities as the basic source of funding. At the same time, this approach provides a significant role to the parties in the construction and operation of the funding mechanism, is designed to ensure that new resources are brought to bear on the problems of implementation, and provides an apparently novel approach (the CAN—in effect, a clearinghouse for funding) to facilitate operations and fill gaps in matching needs and funding resources. The interim designation of GEF enables the funding mechanism to function pending final arrangements.

NOTES AND QUESTIONS

1. Look at the text of the POPs Convention. How does the POPs Convention compare with the Montreal Protocol on Ozone and the Kyoto Protocol on Climate Change with respect to flexibility, ability to respond to new scientific information, common but differentiated responsibilities, and funding for developing countries?

2. One reason the POPs Convention was relatively easy to negotiate is that most developed countries have already phased out most of the substances originally covered. This may explain why Article 8, regarding new listings, was such a source of tension.

3. The POPs Convention entered into force in 2004. It has 165 parties, not including the U.S. or Russia.

2.   CHEMICALS AND HAZARDOUS WASTES IN INTERNATIONAL TRADE

Countries differ greatly in the complexity and strength of their domestic regulatory regimes regarding chemicals, especially pesticides, and regarding the treatment of hazardous wastes. As these substances cross borders, therefore, there is a risk that countries with less developed or more lax regulations will not adequately protect against the health and safety risks, causing serious human health and environmental damage. A number of international regimes use similar techniques, including prior informed consent and technical assistance, to try to avoid these risks.

a.   THE ROTTERDAM CONVENTION AND PRIOR INFORMED CONSENT

In response to numerous instances of pesticide poisonings and other harmful effects of pesticides in developing countries where needed safeguards were unavailable or unused, in 1985 the UN Food and Agriculture Organization adopted a voluntary International Code of Conduct on the Distribution and Use of Pesticides. The United Nations Environment Program (UNEP) set up the London Guidelines for the Exchange of Information on Chemicals in International Trade in 1987. In 1989, both instruments were amended to include a voluntary prior informed consent (PIC) procedure. Notorious incidents of pesticide or chemical poisonings in states without the regulatory capacity to adequately control and monitor use of dangerous pesticides, and incidents of "dumping" of pesticides banned in developed countries in the developing world, created the impetus for a binding treaty on PIC. The result was the Rotterdam Convention, which was adopted in 1988 and entered into force, after the 50th ratification, in 2004. The PIC procedure as of 2009 applies to 24 banned or severely restricted pesticides, 6 severely hazardous pesticide formulations and 11 industrial chemicals.

Under the Convention, national authorities notify the Convention Secretariat whenever they take final regulatory action to severely restrict or ban a substance (or when the manufacturer voluntarily removes it from the market). The Secretariat notifies the Parties. If two or more regions ban or restrict the pesticide, it is, after review, listed on an Annex (Annex III) to be subject to the Prior Informed Consent procedure. Under this procedure, countries must decide whether they will allow imports of the chemical (and if so, under what conditions). If countries prohibit imports, they must do so for imports from every country and also prohibit domestic production of the chemical. Exporting countries must make sure that exporters do not send chemicals to any state that has not specifically agreed to import it. If an importing state does not respond to a query as to whether it will allow imports of the chemical, the exporting state is to assume that the importing state does not consent, except if the chemical is registered or has been previously used in the importing state. If an exporting country has banned or severely restricted a chemical but it is not yet listed on Annex III, it can only export it after sending safety data to the importing country and ensuring proper labeling.

The objective of all of this procedure is to ensure that importing states, especially developing states that may not have the infrastructure to properly evaluate and regulate chemical risks, make informed choices based on what other states have learned about the risks of particular chemicals. Does the procedure strike you as an effective one? What are its weaknesses? If you were a farmer in Gabon being sold a potent pesticide banned in the U.S. and Europe, how would the PIC procedure affect you, if at all? What if you were a Chinese exporter? What if the pesticide was only severely restricted in Denmark?

b. TRANSBOUNDARY MOVEMENT OF HAZARDOUS WASTES

The Prior Informed Consent procedure is at the heart of the current international regime for the management of hazardous wastes.

Such wastes are often shipped from developed countries with limited disposal space and high disposal costs to developing countries where disposal costs can be a fraction of the price. The practice can cause severe health and environmental problems in the receiving state, especially if the risks of the waste are unknown or inadequate disposal facilities exist. The spectacle of barges loaded with hazardous waste being turned away at port after port regularly reminds us of the need for international regulation of the transboundary trade in wastes.

The Basel Convention on the Transboundary Movement of Hazardous Wastes, entered into force May 5, 1992, 28 ILM 657 (1989) allows hazardous wastes to be exported only under certain circumstances and with the prior informed consent of the importing state. Hazardous wastes are defined as those that come from specified industrial processes or contain specific compounds, unless they do not possess hazardous characteristics like flammability, toxicity or corrosiveness. Those wastes considered hazardous in the domestic law of the export, import or transit country are also covered. The Convention is structured much like the Vienna Convention on Ozone Depleting Substances, with the ability to modify Annexes with less than unanimous approval of the parties. As of mid–2009 the Convention has 172 parties (the U.S. signed but has not ratified).

Parties may not export hazardous wastes to any state that has prohibited the import of such wastes, or, even if the state has not done so, without the written consent of the state. The exporting state, or the waste generator or exporter, must provide specified information to all concerned states on any transboundary movement of wastes. Even with consent, wastes cannot be exported or imported if the exporting or importing state "has reason to believe that the wastes in question will not be managed in an environmentally sound manner." The transboundary movement of hazardous wastes and other wastes is only allowed if:

"(a) The State of export does not have the technical capacity and the necessary facilities, capacity or suitable disposal sites in order to dispose of the wastes in question in an environmentally sound and efficient manner; or

(b) The wastes in question are required as a raw material for recycling or recovery industries in the State of import * * *."

The Convention bans waste shipments from a Party to or from a non-Party. However, a Party may enter into bilateral or regional arrangements with non-parties (as well as Parties) "provided that such agreements or arrangements do not derogate from the environmentally sound management of hazardous wastes and other wastes as required by this Convention. These agreements or arrangements shall stipulate provisions which are not less environmentally sound than those provided for by this Convention in particular taking into account the interests of developing countries." (Art. 11) The OECD countries have one such arrangement; the U.S. has bilateral agreements with Mexico and Canada.

Parties also take on domestic legislative requirements: to ensure that the generation of hazardous wastes and other wastes within it is reduced to a minimum, taking into account social, technological and economic aspects; ensure that persons involved in the management of hazardous wastes or other wastes within it take such steps as are necessary to prevent pollution ... and, if such pollution occurs, to minimize the consequences thereof for human health and the environment; take measures to prevent and punish conduct in contravention of the Convention, including combating illegal shipments of hazardous waste.

NOTES AND QUESTIONS

1. Look at the provisions of the Convention. How are they similar to those of the Montreal Protocol, discussed above? How are they similar to the Rotterdam PIC Convention? How different?

2. The Basel Convention does not actually ban any transboundary movement of hazardous waste. Why do you think that is so? Is there an argument for allowing such movements to countries where (a) recycling industries are a significant economic sector (b) there are economies of scale involved in specialized processing of certain waste materials, or (c) there is extensive sparsely settled dryland, so that costs of disposal are much cheaper than in more urbanized settings? Why or why not? Shouldn't states be encouraging recycling rather than requiring extensive consent procedures? How can they, under the convention, tell the difference between material shipped for disposal and material shipped for recycling?

3. What is an "environmentally sound manner"? The Convention leaves a definition up to the parties, and the COP has tended to define it on the basis of specific technical guidelines. Should it be defined differently for different states? What if states have different definitions in their national law?

4.   Many states, especially developing states, preferred a complete ban on shipments from developed to developing countries. The Bamako Convention on the Ban of Import into Africa and the Control of Transboundary Movement and Management of Hazardous Wastes Within Africa, 30 ILM 775 (1991), which came into force in 1998 and has been ratified by all 51 African states, requires parties to prohibit any imports of hazardous waste from outside Africa. By 1995, after several years of negotiation, the COP of the Basel Convention adopted an amendment banning waste exports from OECD or EU countries (or Lichtenstein) to other countries. How will this affect, say, exports of old computers from Germany to China for dismantling and recycling? Is that a good thing? What about exports from India to China? Why should those be treated differently? The Basel Ban as of 2009 has 65 parties, and is not yet in force.

3.   CHEMICALS MANAGEMENT

In addition to phaseouts, bans, and restrictions on trade, chemicals management also seeks ways to identify existing and emerging health and environmental risks and to encourage a shift to safer substitutes. The farthest-reaching application of the precautionary approach in chemicals management has been the European regulation called REACH (Registration, Evaluation and Assessment of Chemicals), Regulation 1907/2006 of 18 December 2006, Official Journal of the European Union L136/3 (2007).

The following article describes the importance of REACH:

John S. Applegate, Synthesizing TSCA and REACH: Practical Principles for Chemical Regulation Reform

35 ECOLOGY L.Q. 721 (2008)

* * *

The EU spent nearly a decade developing REACH....

* * *

While it simplified the existing regulatory structure for chemicals, REACH is by no means a simple piece of legislation. For present purposes, the basic regulatory process breaks down into four constituent parts, reflected in the elements of the REACH acronym: registration, evaluation, authorization, and restrictions. The first phase, registration, is primarily a data-gathering procedure. It covers all chemicals produced or imported in quantities above one metric ton per year, both new and existing (or "phase-in"), as well as certain substances found in other products. There are various exemptions for low-risk chemicals and polymers, but the European Chemical Authority expects to need to register thirty thousand chemicals and review eighty thousand dossiers by 2011.

Applications for the registration of any chemical must include a technical dossier, which is comprehensive information on the chemical's inherent properties, including a base set of toxicological information, graduated by production volume. For chemicals produced in quantities above ten metric tons, a much more extensive Chemical Safety Report is required, which includes toxicology and exposure data, as well as measures to reduce risks from the chemical. Chemical data, including those obtained in registration, is shared up and down the supply chain to avoid unnecessary testing.

The second phase, evaluation, involves three basic steps: an automatic "completeness check" for technical compliance with the REACH requirements; a dossier evaluation, which is essentially a quality control effort to assure that objectives like avoidance of animal testing and data sharing have occurred; and substance evaluation, which examines the risks posed by a substance and the measures taken to control the risks. Evaluation leads to the two final phases.

Authorization applies to substances "of very high concern" (VHC). VHC substances include carcinogens, mutagens, and reproductively toxic (CMR) substances; persistent, bioaccumulative, or toxic (PBT) substances; very persistent or very bioaccumulative (vPvB) substances; persistent organic pollutants (POPs); and other chronic hazards. Authorization is not limited to chemicals that meet the registration threshold amount of one metric ton. The primary objective of authorization is to ensure the progressive replacement of VHCs with safer alternatives; therefore, the centerpiece of the process is analysis of substitute substances. Each proponent of a VHC chemical must present a replacement chemical or at least a research plan for alternatives; if no alternatives are in prospect, then the chemical's use must be justified under a cost-benefit test. In addition, authorization requires that the substance be "adequately controlled," and if it cannot be adequately controlled (CMR substances, by definition, cannot be), then, again, its benefits must outweigh its risks. ECHA expects that about 1,500 substances will require authorization. It is expected that VHC substances will be banned entirely, authorized for a limited period, or authorized for very specific uses and conditions.

The final phase is restriction. While the objective of authorization is replacement, substances that are not subject to authorization but nevertheless pose hazards in their manufacture or use may have European Community-wide restrictions imposed on them to assure that health and environmental risks remain at acceptable levels. Such restrictions may be imposed centrally if the Commission, in cooperation with the member states, determines that the risk is not adequately controlled and that it needs to be addressed at the Community-wide level. The legal standard for acceptability is not stated other than a general commitment to a "high level of protection." Restrictions represent REACH's "safety net," or last resort, for ensuring chemical safety.

* * *

REACH explicitly seeks to eliminate the distinction between existing and new chemicals (and uses). Its purpose is to remedy the data gap for existing chemicals—what the White Paper calls "the burden of the past"—which will permit the application of a single, high level of safety to all chemicals, new and old. The general principle that chemicals must be shown to be safe before use also means that existing chemicals are subject to the same rigorous standards that a new chemical would be. * * *

Since REACH seeks to take a fundamentally precautionary approach to protecting the environment and human health when data are uncertain, REACH demands that better information be generated and that, in the absence of such information, chemicals be highly restricted or prohibited outright. As a consequence, the responsibility for generating new information is allocated to the proponent of the use of the chemical.

REACH makes the generation of information a priority. "The lack of data on the hazardous properties of chemicals was the driving force behind the development of a new chemicals policy in the EU," and so REACH moves the status quo from "no data, no problem" to "no data, no market" (the title of article 5 of REACH).

* * *

NOTES AND QUESTIONS

1. How does the REACH regulation shift the burden of proof? Is this useful? What incentives does it create for more robust data collection and evaluation? What checks are there on a company's submission of its own findings as a basis for regulation? Is it feasible to think that a regulatory authority can actually evaluate 30,000 chemicals in the next few years? In the U.S., the burden is on the regulatory agency to show that a chemical poses a risk; this has led to long delays and regulations regarding very few chemicals under the federal law, the Toxic Substances Control Act (TSCA), that deals with chemical testing and registration.

2. What are the implications of REACH for non-European chemical manufacturers? If they want to access the EU market, will they also have to conform to REACH? Does this create potential problems with the *de facto* imposition of European law on other states? If you represented a U.S. chemical producer, would you advise them to step up testing of their chemicals?

3. On a global level, UNEP has been orchestrating a "Strategic Approach to International Chemicals Management" (SAICM) aimed at ensuring, by 2020, "that chemicals or chemical uses that pose an unreasonable and otherwise unmanageable risk to human health and the environment based on a science-based risk assessment and taking into account the costs and benefits as well as the availability of safer substitutes and their efficacy, are no longer produced or used for such uses" and that "risks from unintended releases of chemicals that pose an unreasonable and otherwise unmanageable risk to human health and the environment based on a science-based risk assessment and taking into account the costs and benefits, are minimized." Global Plan of Action, Executive Summary, at 7(d)(i) and (ii) (2006). The SAICM, which is not a treaty but a voluntary "soft law" mechanism, also includes a periodic international conference on chemicals management.

G.   FINAL THOUGHTS

Frank Biermann, Reforming Global Environmental Governance: From UNEP towards a World Environment Organization

pp. 103, 104, Global Environmental Governance: Perspectives on the Current Debate
(Lydia Swart and Estelle Perry, eds. 2007)

In February 2007, 46 countries came together in Paris for a joint proposal to upgrade the United Nations Environment Programme to a Specialized Agency within the United Nations system. This proposal is not new. In fact, the debate on a special UN agency for the protection of the environment dates back more than thirty years to George Kennan's (1970) proposal for an international environmental agency. Now, with the recent support of one fourth of the community of nations, including many powerful countries from the North and South, the debate has reached a new stage.

In a nutshell, I propose to maintain the current system of issue specific international environmental regimes while strengthening environmental protection by upgrading UNEP from a mere UN program to a full fledged international organization with increased financial and staff resources and enhanced competencies and legal mandate. In this model, a WEO would function and have powers similar to other international organizations. Member States might then be inclined to shift some competencies related to the environment from those other bodies to the new WEO. In particular, the new organization would provide a venue for the co-location and eventually joint administration of the myriad convention secretariats. The organization would also have its own budget, based on assessed contributions by Member States, and it could make use of future innovative financial mechanisms, such as revenues from emissions trading regimes. Additional financial and staff resources could be devoted to the fields of awareness raising, technology transfer and the provision of environmental expertise to international, national and subnational levels. The elevation of UNEP to a world environment organization of this type could be modeled on the WHO or the International Labor Organization (ILO), that is, independent international organizations with their own membership, structure, and budget.

If UN Member States would agree on establishing a WEO as a UN Specialized Agency, this body would be based on a constitutive legal instrument that would require ratification of a certain number of states to become effective. The creation of such an organization would not require the legal acquiescence of all nations, and it would have autonomy over its own organizational design. A separate decision by the UN General Assembly would be needed to formally abolish UNEP and to transfer its staff and assets to the new agency.

Daniel C. Esty and Maria H. Ivanova, Making International Environmental Efforts Work: The Case for a Global Environmental Organization*

YALE CENTER FOR ENVIRONMENTAL LAW AND POLICY (2001)

1. Introduction

Poor performance in response to mounting global scale pollution and natural resource management challenges has spurred interest in rethinking global environmental governance and perhaps restructuring the current institutional architecture. Both former Soviet Union President Mikhail Gorbachev and French President Jacques Chirac have urged the establishment of a Global Environmental Organization. While more modest reform agendas, building on the status quo, might also be considered, the nature of the environmental problems at the global level and the inherent shortcomings of the existing structure argue strongly for a broader reconfiguration of the international environmental regime. Significant natural resources, from the ocean bed to the atmosphere, are shared regionally or globally. Yet, despite the multitude of treaties, conventions, and agencies, the current global environmental management system has failed to address and solve problems related to transboundary pollution spillovers and shared resources. A revitalized and strengthened policy mechanism and structure is needed to respond to the scale and complexity of the problems and to the changing context within which they have to be tackled. To this end, options for a new, flexible, and innovative approach to addressing global environmental problems needs to be developed. The world community would benefit from the presence of an authoritative environmental voice in the international arena and a recognized forum for national officials and other stakeholders to work cooperatively to address global issues.

In this paper, we advance the case for a Global Environmental Organization (GEO). Our proposal for a GEO builds on a careful analysis of the problems that must be addressed internationally and the key capacities that an international environmental body should possess. We outline a possible organizational structure, sketch out an implementation strategy, and address some of the arguments likely to be raised against creating a GEO.

* * *

The Global Environmental Governance System

It is now widely acknowledged that the current international environmental regime is performing poorly. From halting efforts to understand and confront the prospect of climate change to pressing issues of food safety, dissatisfaction among politicians, business people, environmental-

---

* Footnotes omitted.

ists, and the general public abounds. Some of the failings can be attributed to a history of management shortcomings and bureaucratic entanglements, but other aspects of the problem are deeper and more structural. Four major issues deserve particular focus:

2.1. Failed Collective Action

Environmental regulation at the global level requires an extraordinary degree of cooperation among nations. In academic lingo, it presents a difficult "collective action" problem. Because international environmental problems are diffuse—spread across space and time—incentives arise to ignore transboundary emissions and neglect the management of shared resources. Likewise, the concentration of abatement costs (borne fully within the country undertaking pollution control programs) and the diffusion of the benefits (spread across the world) makes free-riding on the efforts of others attractive. Quite simply, the spatial scale and temporal diffusion of international environmental issues makes the impacts of externalized harms hard to see—and thus the benefits of cooperation less than obvious. As a fundamental matter, unless countries perceive problems as real and thus recognize the advantages of collaboration, the transaction costs of organizing and sustaining international cooperation become overwhelming.

The fragmentation, gaps in issue coverage, and even contradictions among different treaties, organizations, and agencies with environmental responsibilities make international environmental policy coherence hard to achieve. A pervasive lack of data, information, and very limited policy transparency adds to the challenge, making even agreement on the scope of problems hard to get. This obscurity and confusion heightens the allure of letting others carry the environmental burden. But, of course, when everyone chooses to stand on the sidelines, no action is taken.

With limited exceptions (e.g., ozone layer protection), the global environmental scene in the last decade has involved too much watching and talking and too little effective action. On most issues, the results from the international environmental regime have fallen short of both expectations and needs. International coordination, issue identification, policy analysis, problem solving, and capacity building have been inadequate in many areas, including climate change, fisheries management, trade and environment, biodiversity, and desertification.

The pattern of sub-optimal policy outcomes can be traced to many sources: limited human and financial resources, bureaucratic inefficiencies, inadequate scientific underpinnings, and a lack of commitment to analytic rigor in a number of international bodies. But the core problem is, at least in part, structural. Other global challenges—international economic management, population control, and various world health problems (e.g., eradication of polio and small pox) have been addressed more successfully. In the international environmental domain, success has been achieved in a small number of cases where case specific institutional mechanisms sufficient to a particular problem emerged, the costs of the status quo and the benefits of action were realized, and political entrepreneurship was harnessed to develop effective, efficient, and innovative policy solutions. But the list of successes is short.

In brief, institutions matter. The international environmental architecture has proven itself incapable of living up to the challenges it faces. Change is required to better facilitate cooperation in response to global issues.

2.2. Fragmentation

International environmental responsibilities are spread across too many institutions with diffuse, overlapping, and even conflicting mandates. Thus, the United Nations Environment Programme (UNEP) competes for time, attention, and resources with more than a dozen other UN bodies (such as the Commission for Sustainable Development (CSD), the World Meteorological Organization (WMO), the International Oceanographic Commission (IOC), the UN Educational, Scientific and Cultural Organization (UNESCO) and others) with environmental responsibilities and interests. UNEP, UNDP, WMO, as well as the Organization for Economic Cooperation and Development (OECD) and the World Bank, for example, all have climate change programs underway with little coordination and no sense of strategic division of labor. In a similar vein, the World Humanity Action Trust Commission on Water has identified more than twenty bodies and specialized agencies within the UN system with water programs.

Adding to this fragmentation are the independent secretariats to numerous treaties including the Montreal Protocol (ozone layer protection), the Basel Convention (hazardous waste trade), the Convention on International Trade in Endangered Species (CITES), the Climate Change Convention, and many others. In fact, there are now over 500 multilateral environmental treaties, and 60 per cent of them have come into existence since the Stockholm Conference in 1972. Many of these agreements are limited in scope along issue and geographic areas. As pointed out in the report of UNEP's Executive Director on Multilateral Environmental Agreements, "[f]rom a combined global and regional perspective, the resultant proliferation of MEAs has placed an increasing burden on Parties and member states to meet their collective obligations and responsibilities to implement environmental conventions and related international agreements." When similar "treaty congestion" threatened to break down international efforts to regulate intellectual property, a single body, the World Intellectual Property Organization, was launched to consolidate global scale efforts and achieve scale economies in management. The environmental regime faces a similar pressing need for streamlining and coherence.

2.3. Deficient Authority

The existing international environmental institutions, especially UNEP, are hampered by narrow or vague mandates, small budgets, and limited political support. No one organization has the political authority, vitality, expertise, and profile to serve as the center of gravity for the international environmental regime and to exert sustained political influence in other global fora.

The contrast with other international regimes is striking. UNEP, set up as a program rather than as an autonomous agency, lacks the necessary legal authority, budget, and staff to manage (or even coordinate) global environmental policymaking. More critically, it has failed to attract and retain a first-rate staff. These weaknesses translate into poor performance and mean that the UNEP analyses and recommendations often do not carry much clout. A reputation for authoritativeness might alternatively have been established if UNEP had positioned itself as a "global public policy network," pulling in expertise from around the world. But this model was not developed either.

With an annual budget of $60 million, UNEP limps from one fiscal crisis to the next. The funding mechanism of "voluntary contributions" as opposed to "assessed contributions" leaves the organization vulnerable to the demands donors attach to financing. And the limited resources available have often been spread too thin. While set up as a mechanism for tackling global environmental issues, UNEP has been pushed to take on project responsibilities that it has neither the budget nor the structure to manage. Furthermore, political instability, serious personal safety issues, and a lack of a modern communications infrastructure in Nairobi have hampered progress.

The international environmental regime has thus become mired in a cycle of decline. UNEP's structural handicaps have led to its output being judged as modest and not very useful. This weak performance results in reduced political support, greater difficulty in attracting highly competent staff, and continuous budget problems as donors look elsewhere for ways to deploy their limited environmental resources. Results further deteriorate, and the downward spiral accelerates.

2.4. Insufficient Legitimacy

The existing international environmental regime has failed to adequately deal with the priorities of both developed and developing countries. As a result, there is little commitment across the world community to the success of the global environmental regime—and little sense of the importance or legitimacy lodged in the institutions that make up this regime. The Commission on Sustainable Development, set up to address economic, social, and environmental objectives in an integrated manner, has failed to galvanize the world community in support of sustainable development. It has not even succeeded in clarifying what the term means much less how it should be translated into a concrete action agenda.

Inattention on the part of industrialized countries to the need for a concerted worldwide effort to alleviate poverty has had significant spillovers into other issue areas. In many countries, there is a sense that the Rio Earth Summit compact—a simultaneous focus on the development needs of poorer countries and the environmental goals of wealthier nations—has not been kept. The North's limited initiatives to help to build environmental capacities in developing countries through financial and technological transfers has added to the sense of disillusionment with the current global environmental regime and its structures. While the United States, the EU, and Japan reject the charge that they failed to follow through on commitments made at Rio, the lack of progress on the international environmental policy front is palpable.

The inadequacy and dispersion of the existing financial mechanisms— scattered across the Global Environmental Facility, UN Development Programme, World Bank, and separate funds such as the Montreal Protocol Finance Mechanism—reinforces the perception of a lack of seriousness in the North about the plight of the South. Furthermore, fundamental principles of good governance such as representativeness, transparency, and accountability are still at issue in many of the institutions with environmental responsibilities. These procedural shortcomings undermine the legitimacy of the system as a whole.

Concerns arise not just from governments. The ongoing street protests by a range of environmental non-governmental organizations, from Washington to Prague, about the role of the World Bank and the IMF are emblematic of broader public dissatisfaction with how environmental issues are being managed at the global scale. These protests can also be seen as a signal of distress about the way globalization is unfolding and a sense that important values are being lost in the headlong rush for liberalized trade and economic growth.

2.5. Fiddling or fixing

A multi-prong agenda of refinements and reform could be developed to address these many issues. But the list of problems is so long and the baggage associated with the current regime is so heavy that, at some point, a fundamental restructuring rather than incremental tinkering becomes a better path forward. In the face of so many difficulties and the existing regime's poor track record, any presumption in favor of working with the status quo cannot be sustained. Moreover, as the analysis above suggests, the nub of the issue is structural, making a different starting point and a new institutional design advisable.

3.   Functions and Features of a GEO

The core function of a new Global Environmental Organization should be to fashion a coherent and effective international response to global-scale pollution control and natural resource management issues. At the national level, systems exist to regulate business, harness market forces, and ensure collective action in response to a range of environmental problems. With regard to the atmosphere, oceans, seabed, and other elements of the global (and regional) commons, such structures do not exist or are not functioning. Conceptually, a GEO fills an undeniable need for a mechanism to promote collective action at the international scale. Practically, a new body offers the chance to build a coherent and integrated environmental policymaking and management framework that addresses the challenges of a shared global ecosystem.

A GEO must, of course, accommodate the diverse needs of countries across the Earth and be responsive to the concerns of the increasing number of actors or stakeholders (business entities, environmental groups, and the broader set of non-governmental organizations that make up civil society) beyond national governments. And movement forward on the environmental front must be paired with a real commitment to poverty alleviation and economic growth across the world so that the vision of sustainable development can be achieved.

With these needs in mind, we see four core capacities as essential in a revitalized international environmental regime: (1) decision-making, (2) implementation, (3) monitoring, and (4) dispute resolution. A GEO should also be organized around good governance principles such as subsidiarity, integration, participation, transparency, and accountability.

3.1   Decision–Making

Sound environmental decision-making hinges on the availability of data, information, and analysis. To ensure sensitivity to the diversity of circumstances and values that exists across countries, any new body must be committed to open process and vigorous debate. A GEO should thus be capable of executing the following functions:

• Scientific assessment, including environmental data collection and analysis. Reliable data of high quality and comparability would support an integrated, ecosystem-based approach to problem definition and assessment. A strong data foundation would also permit much more vigorous initiatives to identify and disseminate information on best practices in the policy and technology realms. Long-term forecasting of environmental trends, early warnings of environmental risks, and intergenerational impact assessments could be devised on the basis of such data.

• Knowledge networking, drawing on a wide range of sources for information and data, problem identification, impact analysis, policy option development, and program evaluations. Given the inherent complexity and uncertainty of environmental policymaking, it is especially important that problems be approached from multiple perspectives so as to facilitate broad-based agreement on the best route forward.

• Rule-making, starting with the establishment of policy guidelines and international norms, which might, over time, develop into more formal rules. Broader access to data, information, and knowledge promotes consensus building on the scope of problems and ultimately movement toward broadly accepted norms. Laying the analytic groundwork for guidelines, identifying ways to address problems that require a "common but differentiated" response, and conducting international negotiations, especially with regard to transboundary externalities and the management of shared resources, would be critical functions.

3.2 Implementation

Ultimately, the implementation of global environmental agreements and compliance with international commitments becomes a matter of execution at the national and local levels. Building environmental capacity within nation-states is thus of critical importance. Comparative data and public disclosure of results represent critical tools in the push for international environmental progress. Shared information allows best practices, technologies, and policies to be identified, highlighting the opportunities for laggards to learn from those at the leading edge. Structured programs of financial, scientific, management, and technical assistance will also be needed, mobilizing both public and private resources and expertise.

3.3 Monitoring

The monitoring capacity of a GEO should include the continuous and systematic collection and evaluation of data on environmental performance and trends. Data and information lies at the heart of good decisionmaking. And while compliance monitoring should primarily be the function of regional or national organizations, a GEO could provide a central repository for such information and a mechanism for making the information available to concerned parties.

Development and systematic review of a core set of environmental indicators is central to good environmental decisionmaking. A common set of cross-country pollution control and natural resource metrics, data on trendlines, and a commitment to benchmarking at the national, regional, local, and corporate scales would enhance opportunities for policy progress. In addition, careful tracking of trends could provide the foundation for an early warning mechanism that would facilitate the timely forecasting and identification of environmental disasters and areas at risk.

3.4 Conflict Resolution

A GEO needs procedures to promote conflict resolution, including convening authority and agreed mechanisms for dispute settlement that draw on appropriate scientific and technical expertise. The structures developed need to take account of differences in levels of development as well as cultural and values diversity to promote ongoing cooperation and reconciliation.

3.5 Features of a GEO

The key attributes of a GEO should reflect the principles of good governance, including subsidiarity, an integrated approach to policymaking, broad-based participation, transparency and accountability. It is now widely recognized that under the "environmental" rubric fall a broad-based set of issues which require a multi-layered structure to address them. The principle of subsidiarity (and federalism), urging that decisions be taken at the most decentralized level that can competently address the issue at hand, is a core element of sound environmental policy. This principle suggests the need for division of labor among the various levels of governance and a carefully delineated and limited agenda for the global-scale environmental body. Focus will be a key to success for any revitalized international environmental body.

To be effective, a Global Environmental Organization should also be flexible and responsive to change. It should possess credibility among environmental groups and other NGOs, within the business community, and more broadly within the UN system. Analytic rigor, a commitment to sound science, a first-rate staff capable of convening experts from around the world, modern management, and an oversight mechanism are other essential features. Notably, the availability of adequate and predictable resources will be critical to the capabilities of a GEO.

A commitment to drawing into the international policymaking process the best data, thinking, analysis, and policy experience from the multinational economic institutions (WTO, World Bank, IMF), all the UN entities with environmental responsibilities (CSD, UNDP, UNCTAD, etc.), the private sector, non-governmental organizations, the academic community, and civil society at large would dramatically transform the global environmental decision-making. A GEO could provide the forum where such knowledge and expertise come together.

* * *

NOTES AND QUESTIONS

1. Is a GEO/WEO a good idea? Why or why not? Should it merely coordinate existing treaty secretariats, or should it attempt to integrate the multiple existing regimes? Is it an upgrade or a bottom-up revamping that is needed?

2. What else will it take to create the sense of purpose and urgency demanded by the scope and urgency of today's global environmental problems? How can lawyers be part of the solution?

CHAPTER 7

INTERNATIONAL ECONOMIC AND DEVELOPMENT LAW

We believe every person who is interested in or concerned about legal order in the world community needs to understand the basics covered in this chapter, e.g. the rapidly expanding, shifting and changing economic law sector of the international legal system. The materials chosen are broadly representative but are only a minimal introduction to specializations that are covered in advanced or graduate courses such as International Economic Law, International Business Transactions, the World Trade Organization, Foreign Trade Law, International Investment Law, and the like. Economic law seems to engage more private practitioners and big law firms than any other sector of international law. The monied levels of legal activity are so vast because the steadily increasing globalization of economic activity and the dramatic increases in world trade and direct foreign investment occurred in recent years while the legal regimes were being liberalized. Changes in trade and investment levels and possibly extensive changes in international and domestic regulation resulting from the world economic crisis beginning in 2008, might well change the above assessment dramatically in the long run.

Economic equality does not prevail in our world of both "legally equal states" and various types of other international entities linked to legally equal states. There are rich states, modestly endowed states, poor states, and the very poor. The economic condition of a state is a tremendous factor with respect to many aspects of international relations and international law. Very poor states may suffer from instability and difficulty extending human rights. Very wealthy states may expect exceptional treatment in international institutions and more readily resort to military force. While an equilibrium of assured economic equality cannot be fashioned, economists have long held out the promise that free trade and investment can result in global maximization of asset-uses and a more balanced share in wealth. Some of the legal situations as to each of these topics will be taken up in this chapter. But, first, consider illustrative problems sketched below as an introduction to the subject matter of this chapter.

Problem 1. **Denial of entry of foreign goods.** State A enjoys a large surplus of beef production, a surplus expected to continue and grow. Standards of health are quite high in State A, which fears imports from State B of meat and meat products derived from cattle produced with growth hormones. Following a "no risk" policy, State A forbids imports of such meat and products, despite the absence of convincing scientific evidence showing health related problems with the hormones. State A refuses to carry out an assessment of the possible risks.

Problem 2. **Denial of entry of foreign business capital.** A high technology computer hardware manufacturer in State X decides to set up production in State Y for State Y and nearby markets, using Y labor and materials. In order to encourage and protect State Y's internal industry in this and related fields, State Y refuses to permit the State X manufacturer to invest the requisite business capital in State Y and to commence operations there.

Problem 3. **Deprivation of rights flowing from ownership.** A corporation organized in State Z owns 100% of two corporations chartered in State Y, one for the manufacture of industrial machinery (Sub–A) and the other for the manufacture of heavy farm equipment (Sub–B). After a long period of economic downturn, State Y expropriates both subsidiaries, without affecting other foreign manufacturers operating on its territory. No compensation is offered or paid. State Y then transfers Sub–A's assets without cost to the brother of the Finance Minister and offers for sale in international markets the assets of Sub–B.

Notwithstanding the major activities and needs reflected in the above Problems, customary international law imposes no duties and creates no correlative rights governing them, except as in Problem 3, where the major capital-exporting states (or most of them) would argue that there is a rule of customary law requiring full compensation, while some capital-receiving (often also poor and developing) nations might disagree. Otherwise, the rules of the economic activity of international legal systems are almost entirely found in international agreements. Many of these rules are in constant evolution toward improvement but remain ambiguous, incomplete and manipulated in their application and in need of reform.

John H. Jackson, Global Economics and International Economic Law

1 J. INT'L ECON L. 1, 8 (1998)

3.   Understanding International Economic Law

It is appropriate to ask what we mean by "international economic law". This phrase can cover a very broad inventory of subjects: embracing the law of economic transactions; government regulation of economic matters; and related legal relations including litigation and international institutions for economic relations. Indeed, it is plausible to suggest that 90 per cent of international law work is in reality international economic law in some form or another. Much of this, of course, does not have the glamour or visibility of nation-state relations (use of force, human rights, intervention etc.), but does indeed involve many questions of international law and particularly treaty law. Increasingly, today's international economic law (IEL) issues are found on the front pages of the daily newspapers.

* * * Yet arguably in today's world the real challenges for understanding IEL and its impact on governments and private citizens' lives, suggest a focus on IEL as "regulatory law", similar to domestic subjects such as tax, labour, anti-trust, and other regulatory topics.

But apart from its breadth, what are some of the characteristics of IEL which, for example, might affect the approach to it of scholars or policy makers? The following are some tentative ventures to explore these characteristics, but they are obviously by no means complete.

* * * International economic law can not be separated or compartmentalized from general or "public" international law. The activities and cases relating to IEL contain much practice which is relevant to general principles of international law, especially concerning treaty law and practice. Conversely, general international law has considerable relevance to economic relations and transactions. * * *

––––––––––––

While international economic law has traditionally focused mainly on the regulation of international trade and investment, monetary cooperation and economic development, the global economic crisis beginning in 2008–2009 has stimulated interest in fostering additional international organization and legislative work to strengthen supervision and regulation of the world economy and finance. The G–20* London Summit Leader's State-

––––––––––––

* "The Group of Twenty (G–20) Finance ministers and Central bank governors was established in 1989 to bring together systemically important industrialized and developing economies to discuss issues in the global economy." (http://www.g20.org/about_what_is_g20.

ment of 2 April 2009, reproduced in part in the Documentary Supplement, contains a Declaration on *Strengthening the Financial System* in which they agreed

- to establish a new Financial Stability Board (FSB) with a strengthened mandate, as a successor to the Financial Stability Forum (FSF), including all G20 countries, FSF members, Spain, and the European Commission;

- that the FSB should collaborate with the IMF to provide early warning of macroeconomic and financial risks and the actions needed to address them;

- to reshape our regulatory systems so that our authorities are able to identify and take account of macro-prudential risks;

- to extend regulation and oversight to all systemically important financial institutions, instruments and markets. This will include, for the first time, systemically important hedge funds;

Moreover, at the G–20 Summit in Pittsburg on September 15, 2009, the G–20 carried on this work with additional policy and developments. See selections from leader statements in the Document Supplement.

This new financial work could lead to international legal measures as an important additional element of international economic law if it receives sufficient and sustained political support.

The Debate over Trade and Investment Liberalization

Open Markets Matter: The Benefits of Trade and Investment Liberalisation

OECD Policy Briefs, No. 6, p. 1 (1998)*

Never before have so many countries at such different levels of development been involved in so much activity aimed at progressively rolling back obstacles to freer trade and investment. Yet, paradoxically, at no time during the post-war period has the prospect of further liberalisation generated so much public anxiety, not least within those countries that built much of their prosperity on a liberal trade and investment order.

* * *

The debate over open markets has changed markedly in tone and substance. Support for liberalisation has eroded in some segments of civil society in recent years because of concerns about jobs, wages, the environment and national sovereignty. Waning support points to a deficit in

---

aspx). The G–20 is composed of representatives of 19 governments and the EU Council and Central Bank. The 2 April 2009 meeting was held at head of state level.

* For background on the OECD see Chapter 3, *supra*.

communications and in policy. The communications deficit can be remedied if the proponents of open markets explain clearly what trade and investment can and cannot do and what liberalisation is and is not responsible for. But it is not sufficient to point to incontrovertible evidence that liberalisation creates wealth or to the social and economic costs of failure to adjust to changing conditions. It is also necessary to confront the worries of citizens who are adversely affected by change. The challenge for policymakers is thus to design policies to help citizens and communities take advantage of the on-going, unprecedented, technology-driven structural transformation of national economies, a transformation in which trade and investment play a part, but only a part. * * *

What are the benefits of open markets?

* * *

The case for open markets rests on solid foundations. One of these is the fact that when individuals and companies engage in specialisation and exchange, a country will exploit its comparative advantage. It will devote its natural, human, industrial and financial resources to their highest and best uses. This will provide gains to firms and consumers alike. Another is the strong preference of people the world over for more, rather than less, freedom of choice.

A more open domestic market is not a handicap; it is a source of competitive strength. Exposure to international trade is a powerful stimulus to efficiency. Efficiency, in turn, contributes to economic growth and rising incomes.

Results speak for themselves. In the last decade, countries that have been more open have achieved double the annual average growth of others. Liberalisation from the Uruguay Round alone has delivered a global tax cut estimated to be worth more than $200 billion per annum: the equivalent of adding a new Korea or Switzerland to the world economy over the next ten years. Liberalisation benefits citizens in tangible ways: in the case of Australia, for example, its recent unilateral trade liberalisation has, in effect, put A$1,000 in the hands of the average Australian family.

* * *

What is the cost of protection?

One approach has been—and remains—to protect industry and workers against imports by raising trade barriers. Societies typically pay a high price when they resort to protection. Protection raises the price of both imports and domestic products, and restricts consumer choice. It defers change and raises its cost, inflicts damage on exporting firms by making them less competitive and almost invariably translates into greater long-term hardship.

The cost to consumers of protection in OECD countries has been estimated to be as much as US$300 billion. In the United States it has been estimated that if liberalisation were stopped right now, the wages of skilled workers would decline 2–5 per cent and unskilled wages would remain flat. Imposing a 30 per cent tariff on developing country exports would inflict even greater damage; it would cut the wages of unskilled workers by 1 per cent and those of skilled workers by 5 per cent.

Protection does not deliver what it promises. The average cost to consumers of a job protected exceeds the wages of employees whose jobs are saved. In one extreme case the consumer cost of saving a single job in one OECD country was estimated to be US$600,000 per annum. Even when the cost is lower, the fact remains that protection consumes resources that could more fruitfully be used to retrain or provide transitional income support to displaced workers, or to help firms develop new products or new businesses.

How should adjustment be approached?

The fact that resort to protection is not the answer is a vital message in its own right. But it is not the whole story. Policies are still needed to ease the plight of those in the front line of adjustment. It is just as important to stress, therefore, that there is, in fact, a better way.

Properly designed labour market and social policies that provide adequate income security while facilitating the redeployment of displaced workers into expanding firms and sectors, produce important equity and efficiency gains. The effectiveness of these policies will, of course, depend on the degree of flexibility in product and labour markets, and they cannot play this role in isolation from a range of other policies. In fact, a much broader strategy is called for, one capable of increasing the flexibility of markets, upgrading the skills of workers and raising workforce mobility. Areas such as regulatory reform, education, training, taxation, pension reform and the portability of health benefits (where that is an issue) need to be dealt with in a comprehensive way. This will ensure that citizens and communities are able to take advantage of and adjust to the foremost challenge they face, technology-driven structural change.

In sum, a balanced mix of policies is needed to reinforce adaptive capacity in the face of all structural changes, including those stemming from trade and investment liberalisation. Social protection policies also need to be reoriented to ensure that those who lose their jobs—including as a result of trade or investment liberalisation—are insured against excessive income loss during the period of search for a new job. There is no inevitable connection between increased openness and less social protection. In fact, increased international trade and investment is an additional reason to improve the efficiency of public systems of social protection, rather than a rationale for reducing them.

* * *

How does market openness affect national sovereignty?

There are concerns about the way in which market openness many affect national sovereignty. More particularly, there are concerns that increasing trade and investment flows, and multilateral rules for trade and investment, may erode the capacity of governments to exercise national "regulatory" sovereignty. That is, to decide the appropriate policies and regulatory approaches for their own country or region, on issues such as environmental protection or consumer health and safety, as well as on trade and investment matters. There is also a perception that multilateral agreements encourage or even require such regulatory standards to be reduced, eliminated or harmonised.

Trade and investment liberalisation in fact forms part of a country's overall strategy to maintain and even strengthen its capacity to determine its own future (and thus its sovereignty), by improving its competitiveness and raising incomes, and making it less vulnerable to external shocks. Thus liberalisation and regulatory reform are undertaken by national governments (whether unilaterally or in the context of international negotiations between sovereign governments) to enhance national interests. Such decisions are made precisely in order to gain the added security, stability and enhanced prospects for national welfare, that internationally agreed rules provide. An agreement such as the WTO is essentially an exercise of national sovereignty rather than a surrender of it.

Multilateral trade and investment agreements do not regard all national regulatory measures simply as unnecessary. Nor do they require the removal of all barriers to foreign trade and investment or that all of these be lowered. Indeed, governments retain the sovereign right to set their own objectives on such matters. The rules do require countries to prepare, implement and administer national regulations that affect foreign goods, services and investment in a transparent, non-arbitrary and non-discriminatory way. But that is because governments have taken a sovereign decision to abide by such rules. And they have done so because they recognise that such principles help to promote fairness and stability in an international economy in which all countries have a stake and from which they benefit themselves. Such agreements explicitly provide that high-quality effective national regulation be permitted to work properly in a number of areas. Where the rules place limits on recourse to certain trade or investment restrictions, for environmental or other purposes, this arises from the agreement of sovereign member countries that it is in their mutual interest to have each other do so. Moreover, the WTO rules and dispute settlement processes recognise that there can be legitimate grounds for exceptions from these rules in certain circumstances, or to achieve other policy objectives.

* * *

Joel R. Paul, Do International Trade Institutions Contribute to Economic Growth and Development?

44 Va. J. Int'l L. 285 (2003)

Proponents of trade liberalization routinely defend international trade institutions as engines of economic growth that benefit everyone. The justificatory rhetoric of trade institutions is so familiar that it operates as a background assumption of most informed persons. The purposes of the WTO, stated in the opening paragraph of its charter, include raising standards of living, ensuring full employment and a large and steadily growing volume of real income and effective demand, and expanding the production of and trade in goods and services, while allowing for the optimal use of the world's resources. Defenders of the WTO and NAFTA explicitly argue that trade leads to economic growth according to the theory of comparative advantage.

* * *

WTO proponents generally argue that according to the theory of comparative advantage, the WTO maximizes world welfare by lowering trade barriers. First, . . . these assumptions rarely conform to the realities of the contemporary international market. In the absence of these conditions, comparative advantage cannot show that trade leads to a more efficient allocation of resources. Second, empirical studies of the gains from trade cast doubt on the assumption that trade liberalization necessarily leads to worldwide economic growth. Indeed the gains from trade are often less than the sunk costs from lost resources that result from import competition. Third, even if trade liberalization creates economic growth in some circumstances, there is reason to doubt it improves social welfare. Fourth, the argument for trade liberalization ignores the important role that government plays in determining comparative advantage. In particular, government interference in the market often constructs comparative advantage.

. . . The proponents of the WTO and the FTAA claim that the benefits of trade are shared equally by the poorest countries and households. . . . [T]he weight of the evidence suggests that globalization has increased income inequality both among countries and within countries.

Neo-liberal economists acknowledge that international markets are distorted, and according to the theory of the second best, they prescribe government intervention in the market to correct some of these distortions. Under some circumstances, neo-liberal economists would favor trade regulation in response to external market failures. . . . [T]he legal obligations of the GATT are both inconsistent with its economic justification and a constraint on governments from taking the measures necessary to correct market failures and distortions. As a consequence, the rule structure of the GATT itself distorts the market or perpetuates market failures and may retard economic growth.

[I] offer a strong defense for international trade institutions as organs of conflict resolution and policy reconciliation. The WTO, in particular, has demonstrated remarkable effectiveness in resolving conflict, avoiding trade wars, and stabilizing regimes. I conclude that institutions like the WTO can have greater utility as political institutions than as engines of economic growth. Accordingly, international trade institutions are well suited to undertake policy measures for the protection of labor, human rights, and the environment.

———————

Hunter, Salzman and Zaelke, International Environmental Law and Policy

pp. 1239–1243 (2d ed. 2007)

ARGUMENTS AGAINST LIBERALIZED TRADE

To some, free trade is a paramount value in international relations. To others it is a threat against competing and equally important values. Despite the wealth maximizing effect of free trade and comparative advantage, there are a number of arguments that suggest unconstrained trade liberalization without appropriate safeguards will not maximize human welfare or approach sustainable development.

A major criticism of traditional trade theory is that it defines what is desirable in purely economic terms ... human wellbeing is dependent on more than monetary wealth. After basic physical needs have been met, our well-being is affected by relations of kinship, citizenship and our concrete experiences as a "person in community." These "intangibles" are an integral part of our humanity and cannot easily be valued in the marketplace of economic exchange—sometimes we may wish to opt for local solidarity over the opportunity to purchase cheaper imported products....

1.   ENVIRONMENTALLY DESTRUCTIVE GROWTH

The simplest criticism against increased trade is from an anti-growth or anti-globalization perspective. Current models of development have proven environmentally destructive, the argument goes, and because free trade will by definition increase commerce and development, increased trade will lead to further environmental degradation. Until we shift from a model of growth to one of development, trade liberalization should be opposed. This argument can take much more sophisticated forms but it is, at its core, a position against current forms of economic development and the institutions that promote such development.

2.   THREATS TO DOMESTIC SOCIAL PREFERENCES

Trade is often seen as a threat to a country's ability to choose worthwhile domestic goals—be they high levels of environmental protection, food security or an agrarian lifestyle, or support to certain domestic industries. Attaining these non-economic goals may require a willingness to forgo some of the economic benefits of free trade. A country may choose to levy tariffs on certain agricultural products to promote self-sufficiency in food or to prevent more efficient foreign producers from underselling domestic small family farmers. Alternatively, a society may want to establish a certain industry, but feel that tariff protections are required to ensure that the fledgling industry becomes sufficiently established to compete internationally.

Trade liberalization may affect social, environment and development priorities in a number of ways. It may change the pattern or nature of economic activity. It may increase trade in dangerous products such as hazardous waste or toxic chemicals that may threaten the environment in an importing country. Trade liberalization will also cause structural shifts between sectors as resources flow to the production of those products for which there is a comparative advantage. Naturally, within a given domestic economy, there will be some winners and some losers, but the lesson of comparative advantage is that in the aggregate, the domestic economy will be better off. Nevertheless, a society may be hesitant to allow certain sectors of the domestic economy to suffer severe setbacks even though on balance the economy might gain; the nature, as well as the scale and pace of economic change is important. Protecting the small family farmers, for example, may be a central social goal of the government. This phenomenon has been called the "conservative social welfare function," and it underlies many countries' tendency toward protectionist measures. A related critique of free trade is that the model of comparative advantage assumes limited international capital mobility, and that capital readjusts domestically to the most profitable activity, rather than flowing abroad. Yet this assumption is no longer valid in the modern international economy as capital is highly mobile. . . .

3. PRESSURE TO LOWER EXISTING ENVIRONMENTAL STANDARDS AND CHILL NEW STANDARDS

Similarly, the citizens of a country may want high levels of environmental protection, and fear that liberalized trade will cause a "race to the bottom" as countries relax or fail to enforce environmental standards in an attempt to gain market share. In response to foreign competition, it is feared, domestic producers will lobby for lower standards to maintain competitiveness in the global market and may even threaten to relocate to countries with lower environmental standards. . . . There has been a vigorous debate over the extent to which a race-to-the-bottom actually occurs. . . . But even if the race-to-the-bottom does not directly drive down standards, it can still result in "chilling" the development of new environmental [and social] law. . . .

4. PROTECTING NATIONAL DEFENSE AND SOVEREIGNTY

National defense is often advanced as a justification for opposing free trade policies. For example, a country may want to preserve its capacity to build airplanes or ships or to develop certain kinds of domestic infrastructure. A variation on this objection is that unfettered free trade increases reliance on external producers and leads to a loss of sovereignty by placing external powers in a position to influence domestic policy. . . .

5. INEQUITABLE DISTRIBUTION OF WEALTH AND UNSUSTAINABLE ECOLOGICAL SCALE

[C]ontinued economic growth is widening the gap between the rich and poor, and the resulting throughput of material resources is unsustainable at the present scale. . . .

NOTES AND QUESTIONS

1. As Hunter, Salzman and Zaelke go on to point out, the debate over the virtues and vices of trade and investment liberalization is not as simple as being for it or against it. Often, trade and investment can have simultaneous benefits and drawbacks. They may improve the wellbeing of people in, say, China, but also increase the scale and patterns of consumption in such a way as to increase inequalities and, by increasing the scope of human activity relative to the biosphere, increase pressure on the environment. With respect to labor, trade and investment may create new jobs but also exert downward pressure on wages. Foreign investment may decrease environmental damage by introducing new, less polluting technologies, but also increase environmental damage through "pollution havens" or increased long-distance transport of goods. How are we to pull apart the advantages and disadvantages? Is it a question of balancing trade objectives against other objectives? Who should do that balancing? These are some of the issues raised at the intersection of trade and investment law with environmental, human rights, national security and other areas of international law.

2. For more on the arguments in favor of increased liberalized trade, see JAGDISH BHAGWATI, FREE TRADE TODAY (2003); DOUGLAS IRWIN, FREE TRADE UNDER FIRE (2d ed. 2005); on the arguments against, see THE CASE AGAINST FREE TRADE: GATT, NAFTA, AND THE GLOBALIZATION OF CORPORATE POWER (Ralph Nader, ed., 1993).

A. INTERNATIONAL TRADE LAW

The shipment arrives at the frontier, usually pre-cleared, or delivered directly to a customs broker. The bill of lading describes the contents, using, if possible, the customs nomenclature of the receiving state. The goods are inspected for the accuracy and the veracity of the importer's classification. The customs inspector may change the classification and hence also the rate of duty, classifications being numerous, narrow, and sometimes surprisingly (or shockingly) variant as between items that seem not to be very different. (These differences may reflect hidden protectionism, sometimes ancient, with reasons forgotten.) If the importer does not accept a re-classification, a lawyer specializing in trade law has to be engaged to take the dispute through administrative review, and eventually, if necessary, judicial review. There is a whole body of specialist law about customs classification (and levy) issues. Note that the foregoing refers to trade in goods and things, not services. Services do not ordinarily receive customs classification for the levy of duties. Entry or denial is a matter of host state control not unlike those on foreign direct investments, treated in Section B.

There are import controls other than custom duties: quotas, sanitary and safety regulations, and importing state sanctions or other inducements to the exporting state to conform to some value or standard of interest to the import state. Quotas as to quantity or value have been often of more concern to foreign suppliers than customs duties, particularly when rates of duty have been reduced to low percentages of value, as they are now. You will see later that trade liberalization arrangements, such as the WTO, approach the rate of duty and quota problems along somewhat different lines. As to health, sanitary and safety regulations, contemporary news reports of American exporters' complaints about import country "assessment" delays and alleged overreaching standards have probably come to your attention. As you will see, some of most forthcoming rule systems in world trade, like health, safety and environment, can be used as subtle or not so subtle non-tariff barriers to otherwise desirable trade.

Prohibition of imports from a particular source for foreign policy reasons or national moral values (such as human rights) involves the legal pros and cons of "economic sanctions," at times in the form of boycotts. So do controls (including absolute prohibitions) on the export of materials and devices deemed of national security concern. Exports of most goods from the U.S. require notification to the government but no longer an export license. For security or foreign policy reasons, there are numerous restrictions appearing in an elaborate administrative regime that restricts such sensitive exports by product and destination country. Lawyers play important roles in this sector in advising clients in the face of heavy penalties for violation (including a possible ban on all exporting), and in the administrative and judicial review process governing U.S. exports.

Finally, as to the customs process: beyond what happens at the customs frontier, there are in the United States and elsewhere, rather vast and complicated administrative law procedures, and in the United States, federal judicial review. To these must now be added the growing international dimension, seen dramatically in the regulatory and dispute settlement systems of the World Trade Organization.

1. THE WORLD TRADE ORGANIZATION: THE MULTILATERAL TRADING SYSTEM

What is the World Trade Organization?
www.wto.org/wto 1999

The World Trade Organization (WTO) is the only international body dealing with the rules of trade between nations. At its heart are the WTO agreements, negotiated and signed by the bulk of the world's trading nations. These documents provide the legal ground-rules for international commerce.* They are essentially contracts, binding governments to keep

---

* The importance of this commerce may be seen in the trade statistics appearing on the WTO web site.

their trade policies within agreed limits. Although negotiated and signed by governments, the goal is to help producers of goods and services, exporters, and importers conduct their business.

Three main purposes

The system's overriding purpose is to help trade flow as freely as possible—so long as there are no undesirable side-effects. That partly means removing obstacles. It also means ensuring that individuals, companies and governments know what the trade rules are around the world, and giving them the confidence that there will be no sudden changes of policy. In other words, the rules have to be "transparent" and predictable.

Because the agreements are drafted and signed by the community of trading nations, often after considerable debate and controversy, one of the WTO's most important functions is to serve as a forum for trade negotiations.

A third important side to the WTO's work is dispute settlement. Trade relations often involve conflicting interests. Contracts and agreements, including those painstakingly negotiated in the WTO system, often need interpreting. The most harmonious way to settle these differences is through some neutral procedure based on an agreed legal foundation. That is the purpose behind the dispute settlement process written into the WTO agreements.

* * * The WTO began life on 1 January 1995, but its trading system is half a century older. Since 1948, the General Agreement on Tariffs and Trade (GATT) had provided the rules for the system. Before long it gave birth to an unofficial, *de facto* international organization, also known informally as GATT, and over the years GATT evolved through several rounds of negotiations.

The latest and largest round, was the Uruguay Round which lasted from 1986 to 1994 and led to the WTO's creation. Whereas GATT had mainly dealt with trade in goods, the WTO and its agreements now cover trade in services and in traded inventions, creations and designs (intellectual property).

* * *

Principles of the Trading System

The WTO agreements are lengthy and complex because they are legal texts covering a wide range of activities. They deal with: agriculture, textiles and clothing, banking, telecommunications, government purchases, industrial standards, food sanitation regulations, intellectual property, and much more. But a number of simple, fundamental principles run throughout all of these documents. These principles are the foundation of the multilateral trading system.

The principles

The trading system should be

—without discrimination—a country should not discriminate between its trading partners (they are all, equally, granted "most-favoured-nation" or MFN status); and it should not discriminate between its own and foreign products, services or nationals (they are given "national treatment").

—freer—with barriers coming down through negotiation.

—predictable—foreign companies, investors and governments should be confident that trade barriers (including tariffs, non-tariff barriers and other measures) should not be raised arbitrarily; more and more tariff rates and market-opening commitments are "bound" in the WTO.

—more competitive—by discouraging "unfair" practices such as export subsidies and dumping products at below cost to gain market share.

—more beneficial for less developed countries—by giving them more time to adjust, greater flexibility, and special privileges.

A closer look at these principles:

Trade without discrimination

1. Most-favoured-nation (MFN): treating other people equally

Under the WTO Agreements, countries cannot normally discriminate between their trading partners. Grant someone a special favour (such as a lower customs duty rate for one of their products) and you have to do the same for all other WTO members. This principle is known as most-favoured-nation (MFN) treatment. * * *

It is so important that it is the first article of the General Agreement on Tariffs and Trade (GATT), which governs trade in goods. MFN is also a priority in the General Agreement on Trade in Services (GATS) (Article 2) and the Agreement on Trade–Related Aspects of Intellectual Property Rights (TRIPS) (Article 4), although in each agreement the principle is handled slightly differently. Together, those three agreements cover all three main areas of trade handled by the WTO.

Why is it called "most-favoured"?

The name sounds like a contradiction. It suggests some kind of special treatment for one particular country, but in the WTO it actually means non-discrimination—treating virtually everyone equally.

What happens under the WTO is this. Each member treats all the other members equally as "most-favoured" trading partners. If a country improves the benefits that it gives to one trading partner, it has to give the same "best" treatment to all the other WTO members so that they all remain "most-favoured".

Most-favoured nation (MFN) status did not always mean equal treatment. In the 19th Century, when a number of early bilateral MFN treaties were signed, being included among a country's "most-favoured" trading partners was like being in an exclusive club because only a few countries enjoyed the privilege. Now, when most countries are in the WTO, the MFN club is no longer exclusive. The MFN principle ensures that each country treats its over-100 fellow-members equally. * * *

Some exceptions are allowed. For example, countries within a region can set up a free trade agreement that does not apply to goods from outside the group. Or a country can raise barriers against products from specific countries that are considered to be traded unfairly. And in services, countries are allowed, in limited circumstances, to discriminate. But the agreements only permit these exceptions under strict conditions. In general, MFN means that every time a country lowers a trade barrier or opens up a market, it has to do so for the same goods or services from all its trading partners—whether rich or poor, weak or strong.

2.   National treatment: treating foreigners and locals equally

Imported and locally-produced goods should be treated equally—at least after the foreign goods have entered the market. The same should apply to foreign and domestic services, and to foreign and local trademarks, copyrights and patents. This principle of "national treatment" (giving others the same treatment as one's own nationals) is also found in all the three main WTO agreements (Article 3 of GATT, Article 17 of GATS and Article 3 of TRIPS), although once again the principle is handled slightly differently in each of these.

National treatment only applies once a product, service or item of intellectual property has entered the market. Therefore, charging customs duty on an import is not a violation of national treatment even if locally-produced products are not charged an equivalent tax.

Freer trade: gradually, through negotiation

Lowering trade barriers is one of the most obvious means of encouraging trade. The barriers concerned include customs duties (or tariffs) and measures such as import bans or quotas that restrict quantities selectively. From time to time other issues such as red tape and exchange rate policies have also been discussed.

Since GATT's creation in 1947–48 there have been eight rounds of trade negotiations. At first these focused on lowering tariffs (customs duties) on imported goods. As a result of the negotiations, by the late 1980s industrial countries' tariff rates on industrial goods had fallen steadily to about 6.3% [by 2001 closer to 4%]. But by the 1980s, the negotiations had expanded to cover non-tariff barriers on goods, and to the new areas such as services and intellectual property. Opening markets can be beneficial, but it also requires adjustment. The WTO agreements allow countries to introduce changes gradually, through "progressive liberalization". Developing countries are usually given longer to fulfil their obligations.

* * *

Agreement Establishing the World Trade Organization*
www.wto.org, 33 ILM 1125 (1994)

Article II
Scope of the WTO

1. The WTO shall provide the common institutional framework for the conduct of trade relations among its Members in matters related to the agreements and associated legal instruments included in the Annexes to this Agreement.

2. The agreements and associated legal instruments included in Annexes 1, 2 and 3 (hereinafter referred to as "Multilateral Trade Agreements") are integral parts of this Agreement, binding on all Members.[1]

3. The agreements and associated legal instruments included in Annex 4 (hereinafter referred to as "Plurilateral Trade Agreements") are also part of this Agreement for those Members that have accepted them, and are binding on those Members. The Plurilateral Trade Agreements do not create either obligations or rights for Members that have not accepted them.

4. The General Agreement on Tariffs and Trade 1994 as specified in Annex 1A (hereinafter referred to as "GATT 1994") is legally distinct from the General Agreement on Tariffs and Trade, dated 30 October 1947, annexed to the Final Act Adopted at the Conclusion of the Second Session of the Preparatory Committee of the United Nations Conference on Trade and Employment, as subsequently rectified, amended or modified (hereinafter referred to as "GATT 1947").

Article III
Functions of the WTO

1. The WTO shall facilitate the implementation, administration and operation, and further the objectives, of this Agreement and of the Multilateral Trade Agreements, and shall also provide the framework for the implementation, administration and operation of the Plurilateral Trade Agreements.

2. The WTO shall provide the forum for negotiations among its Members concerning their multilateral trade relations in matters dealt with under the agreements in the Annexes to this Agreement. The WTO may also provide a forum for further negotiations among its Members concerning their multilateral trade relations, and a framework for the implementation of the results of such negotiations, as may be decided by the Ministerial Conference.

3. The WTO shall administer the Understanding on Rules and Procedures Governing the Settlement of Disputes (hereinafter referred to as the

---

* In 2009 the membership of the WTO consisted of 153 states and the European Communities.

1. The texts of Annexes 1–4 are found at 33 ILM 1125 (1994).

"Dispute Settlement Understanding" or "DSU") in Annex 2 to this Agreement.

4. The WTO shall administer the Trade Policy Review Mechanism (hereinafter referred to as the "TPRM") provided for in Annex 3 to this Agreement.

5. With a view to achieving greater coherence in global economic policy-making, the WTO shall cooperate, as appropriate, with the International Monetary Fund and with the International Bank for Reconstruction and Development and its affiliated agencies.

The WTO incorporates the provisions of the 1947 General Agreement on Tariffs and Trade (GATT), which deals primarily with goods. In addition, as noted above, since the 1980s the WTO has established rules on a wide variety of other issues. These include trade in services (GATS), trade-related aspects of intellectual property (TRIPs), trade-related investment measures (TRIMs), agriculture, and government procurement. The most recent Doha round of WTO negotiations at one point added competition (anti-trust) policy to this list, but as the current negotiations, as of 2009, are stalled, adding new issues seems to be off the table for now.

2.   THE WTO'S MANAGEMENT OF TRADE DISPUTES

Mitsuo Matsushita, et al., The World Trade Organization, Law, Practice and Policy
pp. 104–112 (2d ed. 2006)

* * *

One of the strengths of the WTO is the dispute settlement system, which came into operation on 1 January 1995. This system has rapidly become arguably the most important international tribunal. The WTO dispute settlement institutions function very much like a court of international trade: there is compulsory jurisdiction, disputes are settled largely by applying rules of law, decisions are binding on the parties and sanctions may be imposed if decisions are not observed.

* * *

Three institutions administer the WTO dispute settlement system. The first institution is the Dispute Settlement Body (DSB), which establishes panels, adopts panel and Appellate Body Reports, supervises the implementation of recommendations and rulings, and authorizes sanctions for failure to comply with dispute settlement decisions. The General Council of the WTO serves as the DSB, but the DSB has its own chairman and follows separate procedures from those of the General Council.

* * *

[I]n its interpretation of the covered agreements, panels and the Appellate Body are guided by "customary rules of interpretation of public international law", a reference to the Vienna Convention on the Law of Treaties. Interpretations of the WTO agreements by panels and the Appellate Body are not, however, definitive. Only the Ministerial Conference and the General Council have the authority to adopt definitive interpretations.

* * *

WTO panel and Appellate Body reports are binding on the parties to the dispute once the Dispute Settlement Body adopts them.

EC Measures Concerning Meat and Meat Products (Hormones)

WTO Appellate Body Report, European Communities, Approved 16 January, 1998
WT/DS26/AB/R. WT/DS48/AB/R

[These are appeals by the European Communities (EC), the U.S. and Canada from Panel Reports on complaints of the U.S. and Canada against the EC. The appeals relate to an EC ban on imports into the EC of meat and meat products of farm animals treated with certain growth hormones. A 1997 EC Directive prohibited the use of the hormones, and the sale and importation into the EC of the affected meat and products. A U.S. effort to counter an earlier, parallel EC Directive was successfully blocked by the EC in 1987 under the then applicable GATT 1947 Standards Code procedures requiring consensus to move forward. This early history is recounted in Dick, Note, 10 Mich. J. Int. L. 872 (1989).

Under the new WTO rules, the U.S. and Canada commenced the present proceeding challenging the 1997 Directive. They charged the EC with failing to comply with the WTO's Agreement on the Application of Sanitary and Phytosanitary Measures (SPS) which confirms the right of Members to take trade measures necessary to protect "human, animal or plant life or health" but only when the measures are consistent with this Agreement (Article 2.1). Reflecting concerns about Members using such measures as non-tariff trade barriers, ¶ 3 of Article 2 provides that:

3. Members shall ensure that their sanitary or phytosanitary measures do not arbitrarily or unjustifiably discriminate between Members where identical or similar conditions prevail, including between their own territory and that of other Members. Sanitary and phytosanitary measures shall not be applied in a manner which would constitute a disguised restriction on international trade.

Provisions governing the assessment of risk include the following article 5:

1. Members shall ensure that their sanitary and phytosanitary measures are based on an assessment, as appropriate to the circumstances, of the risks to human, animal or plant life, taking into account risk assessment techniques developed by the relevant international organizations.

2. In the assessment of risks, members shall take into account avail-able scientific evidence; relevant processes and production methods; relevant inspection, sampling and testing methods; prevalence of spe-cific diseases or pests; existence of pest-or disease-free areas; relevant ecological and environmental conditions; quarantine or other treat-ment.

A portion of the Appellate Body's Report follows.]

VI. The Relevance of the Precautionary Principle in the Interpretation of the *SPS Agreement*

120. We are asked by the European Communities to reverse the finding of the Panel relating to the precautionary principle. The Panel's finding and its supporting statements are set out in the Panel Reports in the following terms:

The European Communities also invokes the precautionary principle in support of its claim that its measures in dispute are based on a risk assessment. To the extent that this principle could be considered as part of customary international law *and* be used to interpret Articles 5.1 and 5.2 on the assessment of risks as a customary rule of interpretation of public international law (as that phrase is used in Article 3.2 of the DSU), we consider that *this principle would not override the explicit wording of Articles 5.1 and 5.2 outlined above*, in particular since the precautionary principle has been incorporated and given a specific meaning in Article 5.7 of the SPS Agreement. We note, however, that the European Communities has explicitly stated in this case that it is not invoking Article 5.7.

We thus find that *the precautionary principle cannot override our findings made above*, namely that the EC import ban of meat and meat products from animals treated with any of the five hormones at issue for growth promotion purposes, in so far as it also applies to meat and meat products from animals treated with any of these hormones *in accordance with good practice*, is, from a substantive point of view, not *based on a risk assessment*. (emphasis added by the Appellate Body).

121. The basic submission of the European Communities is that the precautionary principle is, or has become, "a general customary rule of international law" or at least "a general principle of law". Referring more specifically to Articles 5.1 and 5.2 of the *SPS Agreement*, applying the precautionary principle means, in the view of the European Communities, that it is not necessary for *all* scientists around the world to agree on the "possibility and magnitude" of the risk, nor for *all* or most of the WTO Members to perceive and evaluate the risk in the same way. It is also stressed that Articles 5.1 and 5.2 do not prescribe a particular type of risk assessment and do not prevent Members from being cautious in their risk assessment exercise. The European Communities goes on to state that its measures here at stake were precautionary in nature and satisfied the requirements of Articles 2.2 and 2.3, as well as of Articles 5.1, 5.2, 5.4, 5.5 and 5.6 of the *SPS Agreement*.

122.   The United States does not consider that the "precautionary principle" represents customary international law and suggests it is more an "approach" than a "principle". Canada, too, takes the view that the precautionary principle has not yet been incorporated into the corpus of public international law; however, it concedes that the "precautionary approach" or "concept" is "an *emerging* principle of law" which may in the future crystallize into one of the "general principles of law recognized by civilized nations" within the meaning of Article 38(1)(c) of the *Statute of the International Court of Justice*.

123.   The status of the precautionary principle in international law continues to be the subject of debate among academics, law practitioners, regulators and judges. The precautionary principle is regarded by some as having crystallized into a general principle of customary international *environmental* law. Whether it has been widely accepted by Members as a principle of *general* or *customary international law* appears less than clear. We consider, however, that it is unnecessary, and probably imprudent, for the Appellate Body in this appeal to take a position on this important, but abstract, question. We note that the Panel itself did not make any definitive finding with regard to the status of the precautionary principle in international law and that the precautionary principle, at least outside the field of international environmental law, still awaits authoritative formulation.

124.   It appears to us important, nevertheless, to note some aspects of the relationship of the precautionary principle to the *SPS Agreement*. First, the principle has not been written into the *SPS Agreement* as a ground for justifying SPS measures that are otherwise inconsistent with the obligations of Members set out in particular provisions of that Agreement. Secondly, the precautionary principle indeed finds reflection in Article 5.7 of the *SPS Agreement*. * * * Lastly, however, the precautionary principle does not, by itself, and without a clear textual directive to that effect, relieve a panel from the duty of applying the normal (i.e. customary international law) principles of treaty interpretation in reading the provisions of the *SPS Agreement*.

125.   We accordingly agree with the finding of the Panel that the precautionary principle does not override the provisions of Articles 5.1 and 5.2 of the *SPS Agreement*.

XIV.   Findings and Conclusions

* * *

255.   The Appellate Body recommends that the Dispute Settlement Body request the European Communities to bring the SPS measures found in this Report and in the Panel Reports, as modified by this Report, to be inconsistent with the SPS Agreement into conformity with the obligations of the European Communities under that Agreement.

NOTES AND QUESTIONS

1. How would you compare the WTO to other IOs, for example the U.N. or the EU?

2. How do you distinguish between "most favored nation" and "national" treatment in trade relations under the GATT 1994 Articles I and III.2 and .4? What elements must be present in order to establish a claim based on these concepts? In U.S. practice the "most favored nation" MFN formulation is giving way to "normal trade relations (NTR)". What do you suppose this new formulation means? Why is it gaining currency?

3. *An Earlier Hormones Case.* At the time the United States brought an earlier hormones case against the EC in the late 1980s under the then prevailing GATT rules, the disputes procedure required consensus to move forward. Progress in this case was stalled when the EC blocked a procedural decision. Had this case reached the enforcement stage, consensus would again have been required and doubtless again would not have been forthcoming. The 1994 WTO DSU is said to "reverse the consensus rule", requiring a consensus in order to prevent a specified action being taken rather to authorize an action to be taken. How would you expect the reversed consensus rule now in effect to bear on the outcome of the 1998 EC Hormones case reported above?

4. In the 1998 *EC Hormones* case, do you agree with the Appellate Body's view that a "risk assessment" is indeed required under Article 5.1 and 5.2 of the Sanitary and Phytosanitary Agreement (SPS), even though the importing authorities seek a "no risk" position for important reasons of public health? What is the potential non-tariff barrier problem in such cases?

5. After the Dispute Settlement Body acted favorably (by reverse consensus) on the above Appellate Body Report, the EC announced that it intended to fulfill its obligations and that it was examining the options for compliance. However, when the parties were unable to agree on the required "reasonable time for implementation", the EC requested that it be determined by binding arbitration under DSB rules. Unable to agree on an arbitrator, the parties requested the WTO Director–General to make the appointment in accord with the applicable rules. The EC requested 4 years (later reduced to 39 months), and the U.S. and Canada requested 10 months. The arbitrator adopted 15 months, expiring on 13 May 1999. The EC not having taken measures of compliance with the decision of the Dispute Settlement body, the United States and Canada faced the questions of (1) what additional procedures might be useful or required within the WTO, and (2) whether enforcement sanctions should be sought. These questions brought into play the WTO, the European Union and United States trade sanction rules addressed in Section 5 below.

6. An important reason why the EU prohibited beef hormones had to do with public fear and rejection of beef treated with these substances. How should the WTO deal with situations where even though a risk assessment might not indicate a serious risk to health, consumer preferences argue in

favor of a ban? How much leeway should states have in deciding how to assess and manage health and safety risks? Might states legitimately have varying preferences about these matters? The Appellate Body held that states do have to carry out risk assessments, but they do not have to present evidence that they relied on such an assessment in imposing an SPS measure, nor do they have to use a particular protocol or quantitative measure.

7.   How does the WTO Appellate Body's treatment of the precautionary principle compare to the materials in Chapter 6, on the principle? Is the use of the principle legitimate in this case? Or is it a cover for protectionist efforts?

3.   TRADE AND THE ENVIRONMENT: CONFLICT, COHERENCE OR BOTH

A recurring problem in the trade area is the intersection of trade law with domestic regulations that on their face seem aimed at legitimate regulatory protections: health, safety, the environment, labor rights, or the like. In practice, such rules may have disproportionately adverse effects on foreign producers or importers. Does that mean they are protectionist, or legitimate exercises of state sovereignty, or both? A famous dispute involving tuna and dolphins exemplifies the problem. Dolphins in the eastern tropical Pacific tend to swim above schools of yellowfin tuna. Tuna fishing fleets often set purse seine nets over the dolphins and associated tuna, maiming or killing many dolphins in the process. A U.S. law, the Marine Mammal Protection Act, prohibits U.S. fishing fleets from setting nets on dolphins, some of which are threatened or endangered. In order to pass the law, legislators agreed that it would be unfair to force the U.S. fleets to take expensive measures to protect dolphins while not requiring their foreign competitors to do the same. Thus, the Act required foreign fishing fleets serving the U.S. market to meet equivalent requirements. If they did not, they could not import tuna into the U.S. It turns out to be easier for the U.S. fleets to comply with the dolphin protection measures than it is for, say, the Mexican or Costa Rican fleets. Is the law protectionist, or a valid exercise of U.S. regulatory power vis-à-vis its own markets? Could different legislators have had one or the other rationale upmost in their minds when voting for the Act? In these "mixed motives" cases, how should the trade regime respond?

United States—Import of Certain Shrimp and Shrimp Products

AB–1998–4, Report of the Appellate Body, WT/DS58/AB/R
12 October 1998

[This case was introduced in Chapter 2 as an example of treaty interpretion. This excerpt considers the trade law aspects of the decision. Sea turtles are endangered species, listed on Appendix I of CITES and the

U.S. Endangered Species Act. Shrimp trawlers inadvertently catch sea turtles up, resulting in turtle death or injury. In 1987, the U.S. required all shrimpers to install turtle extruder devices (TEDs), an inexpensive technology that allows turtles to escape shrimping nets. The legislation, known as Section 609, also banned shrimp imports from countries that did not have in place a regulatory program and incidental sea turtle "take" rate comparable to that of the U.S. (except if the fishing environment posed no threat to turtles). Subsequent regulations embargoed all shrimp imports from countries that were not certified as using TEDs. India, Malaysia, Pakistan and Thailand brought a claim against the U.S. in 1997, claiming that Section 609 and its regulations constituted a quantitative restriction that violates Article XI of GATT. The U.S. responded that the measure was justified under Article XX of GATT, which allows otherwise prohibited trade restrictions in cases involving human, plant or animal life or health, morals, national security, use of prison labor, national treasures, or certain conservation-related measures. The initial panel found against the United States, and the U.S. appealed.]

* * *

125.   In claiming justification for its measure, the United States primarily invokes Article XX(g). Justification under Article XX(b) is claimed only in the alternative; that is, the United States suggests that we should look at Article XX(b)* only if we find that Section 609 does not fall within the ambit of Article XX(g). We proceed, therefore, to the first tier of the analysis of Section 609 and to our consideration of whether it may be characterized as provisionally justified under the terms of Article XX(g).

126.   Paragraph (g) of Article XX covers measures:

relating to the conservation of exhaustible natural resources if such measures are made effective in conjunction with restrictions on domestic production or consumption;

"Exhaustible Natural Resources"

127.   We begin with the threshold question of whether Section 609 is a measure concerned with the conservation of "exhaustible natural resources" within the meaning of Article XX(g). The Panel, of course, with its "chapeau-down" approach, did not make a finding on whether the sea turtles that Section 609 is designed to conserve constitute "exhaustible natural resources" for purposes of Article XX(g). In the proceedings before the Panel, however, the parties to the dispute argued this issue vigorously and extensively. India, Pakistan and Thailand contended that a "reasonable interpretation" of the term "exhaustible" is that the term refers to "finite resources such as minerals, rather than biological or renewable resources." . . .

---

* The text of Article XX(b) reads: "necessary to protect human, animal or plant life or health".

128.   We are not convinced by these arguments. Textually, Article XX(g) is not limited to the conservation of "mineral" or "non-living" natural resources. The complainants' principal argument is rooted in the notion that "living" natural resources are "renewable" and therefore cannot be "exhaustible" natural resources. We do not believe that "exhaustible" natural resources and "renewable" natural resources are mutually exclusive. One lesson that modern biological sciences teach us is that living species, though in principle, capable of reproduction and, in that sense, "renewable", are in certain circumstances indeed susceptible of depletion, exhaustion and extinction, frequently because of human activities. Living resources are just as "finite" as petroleum, iron ore and other non-living resources.

* * *

132.   We turn next to the issue of whether the living natural resources sought to be conserved by the measure are "exhaustible" under Article XX(g). That this element is present in respect of the five species of sea turtles here involved appears to be conceded by all the participants and third participants in this case. The exhaustibility of sea turtles would in fact have been very difficult to controvert since all of the seven recognized species of sea turtles are today listed in Appendix 1 of the Convention on International Trade in Endangered Species of Wild Fauna and Flora ("CITES"). The list in Appendix 1 includes "all species threatened with extinction which are or may be affected by trade." (emphasis added)

133.   Finally, we observe that sea turtles are highly migratory animals, passing in and out of waters subject to the rights of jurisdiction of various coastal states and the high seas. In the Panel Report, the Panel said:

> ... Information brought to the attention of the Panel, including documented statements from the experts, tends to confirm the fact that sea turtles, in certain circumstances of their lives, migrate through the waters of several countries and the high sea. ... (emphasis added)

The sea turtle species here at stake, i.e., covered by Section 609, are all known to occur in waters over which the United States exercises jurisdiction. Of course, it is not claimed that all populations of these species migrate to, or traverse, at one time or another, waters subject to United States jurisdiction. Neither the appellant nor any of the appellees claims any rights of exclusive ownership over the sea turtles, at least not while they are swimming freely in their natural habitat—the oceans. We do not pass upon the question of whether there is an implied jurisdictional limitation in Article XX(g), and if so, the nature or extent of that limitation. We note only that in the specific circumstances of the case before us, there is a sufficient nexus between the migratory and endangered marine populations involved and the United States for purposes of Article XX(g). ...

141. In its general design and structure, therefore, Section 609 is not a simple, blanket prohibition of the importation of shrimp imposed without regard to the consequences (or lack thereof) of the mode of harvesting employed upon the incidental capture and mortality of sea turtles. Focusing on the design of the measure here at stake, it appears to us that Section 609, cum implementing guidelines, is not disproportionately wide in its scope and reach in relation to the policy objective of protection and conservation of sea turtle species. The means are, in principle, reasonably related to the ends. The means and ends relationship between Section 609 and the legitimate policy of conserving an exhaustible, and, in fact, endangered species, is observably a close and real one. . . .

147. Although provisionally justified under Article XX(g), Section 609, if it is ultimately to be justified as an exception under Article XX, must also satisfy the requirements of the introductory clauses—the "chapeau"—of Article XX, that is,

Article XX

General Exceptions

Subject to the requirement that such measures are not applied in a manner which would constitute a means of arbitrary or unjustifiable discrimination between countries where the same conditions prevail, or a disguised restriction on international trade, nothing in this Agreement shall be construed to prevent the adoption or enforcement by any Member of measures: (emphasis added)

148. We begin by noting one of the principal arguments made by the United States in its appellant's submission. The United States argues: In context, an alleged "discrimination between countries where the same conditions prevail" is not "unjustifiable" where the policy goal of the Article XX exception being applied provides a rationale for the justification. If, for example, a measure is adopted for the purpose of conserving an exhaustible natural resource under Article XX(g), it is relevant whether the conservation goal justifies the discrimination. In this way, the Article XX chapeau guards against the misuse of the Article XX exceptions for the purpose of achieving indirect protection. . . . [A]n evaluation of whether a measure constitutes "unjustifiable discrimination [between countries] where the same conditions prevail" should take account of whether differing treatment between countries relates to the policy goal of the applicable Article XX exception. If a measure differentiates between countries based on a rationale legitimately connected with the policy of an Article XX exception, rather than for protectionist reasons, the measure does not amount to an abuse of the applicable Article XX exception. (emphasis added)

149. We believe this argument must be rejected. The policy goal of a measure at issue cannot provide its rationale or justification under the standards of the chapeau of Article XX. The legitimacy of the declared policy objective of the measure, and the relationship of that objective with the measure itself and its general design and structure, are examined under

Article XX(g), and the treaty interpreter may then and there declare the measure inconsistent with Article XX(g). If the measure is not held provisionally justified under Article XX(g), it cannot be ultimately justified under the chapeau of Article XX. On the other hand, it does not follow from the fact that a measure falls within the terms of Article XX(g) that that measure also will necessarily comply with the requirements of the chapeau. To accept the argument of the United States would be to disregard the standards established by the chapeau.

150.   We commence the second tier of our analysis with an examination of the ordinary meaning of the words of the chapeau. The precise language of the chapeau requires that a measure not be applied in a manner which would constitute a means of "arbitrary or unjustifiable discrimination between countries where the same conditions prevail" or a "disguised restriction on international trade." There are three standards contained in the chapeau: first, arbitrary discrimination between countries where the same conditions prevail; second, unjustifiable discrimination between countries where the same conditions prevail; and third, a disguised restriction on international trade. . . .

159.   The task of interpreting and applying the chapeau is, hence, essentially the delicate one of locating and marking out a line of equilibrium between the right of a Member to invoke an exception under Article XX and the rights of the other Members under varying substantive provisions (e.g., Article XI) of the GATT 1994, so that neither of the competing rights will cancel out the other and thereby distort and nullify or impair the balance of rights and obligations constructed by the Members themselves in that Agreement. The location of the line of equilibrium, as expressed in the chapeau, is not fixed and unchanging; the line moves as the kind and the shape of the measures at stake vary and as the facts making up specific cases differ.

160.   With these general considerations in mind, we address now the issue of whether the application of the United States measure, although the measure itself falls within the terms of Article XX(g), nevertheless constitutes "a means of arbitrary or unjustifiable discrimination between countries where the same conditions prevail" or "a disguised restriction on international trade". We address, in other words, whether the application of this measure constitutes an abuse or misuse of the provisional justification made available by Article XX(g). We note, preliminarily, that the application of a measure may be characterized as amounting to an abuse or misuse of an exception of Article XX not only when the detailed operating provisions of the measure prescribe the arbitrary or unjustifiable activity, but also where a measure, otherwise fair and just on its face, is actually applied in an arbitrary or unjustifiable manner. The standards of the chapeau, in our view, project both substantive and procedural requirements.

2.   "Unjustifiable Discrimination"

161.   We scrutinize first whether Section 609 has been applied in a manner constituting "unjustifiable discrimination between countries where

the same conditions prevail". Perhaps the most conspicuous flaw in this measure's application relates to its intended and actual coercive effect on the specific policy decisions made by foreign governments, Members of the WTO. Section 609, in its application, is, in effect, an economic embargo which requires all other exporting Members, if they wish to exercise their GATT rights, to adopt essentially the same policy (together with an approved enforcement program) as that applied to, and enforced on, United States domestic shrimp trawlers. As enacted by the Congress of the United States, the statutory provisions of Section 609(b)(2)(A) and (B) do not, in themselves, require that other WTO Members adopt essentially the same policies and enforcement practices as the United States. Viewed alone, the statute appears to permit a degree of discretion or flexibility in how the standards for determining comparability might be applied, in practice, to other countries. However, any flexibility that may have been intended by Congress when it enacted the statutory provision has been effectively eliminated in the implementation of that policy through the 1996 Guidelines promulgated by the Department of State and through the practice of the administrators in making certification determinations.

* * *

165.   Furthermore, when this dispute was before the Panel and before us, the United States did not permit imports of shrimp harvested by commercial shrimp trawl vessels using TEDs comparable in effectiveness to those required in the United States if those shrimp originated in waters of countries not certified under Section 609. In other words, shrimp caught using methods identical to those employed in the United States have been excluded from the United States market solely because they have been caught in waters of countries that have not been certified by the United States. The resulting situation is difficult to reconcile with the declared policy objective of protecting and conserving sea turtles. This suggests to us that this measure, in its application, is more concerned with effectively influencing WTO Members to adopt essentially the same comprehensive regulatory regime as that applied by the United States to its domestic shrimp trawlers, even though many of those Members may be differently situated. We believe that discrimination results not only when countries in which the same conditions prevail are differently treated, but also when the application of the measure at issue does not allow for any inquiry into the appropriateness of the regulatory program for the conditions prevailing in those exporting countries.

166.   Another aspect of the application of Section 609 that bears heavily in any appraisal of justifiable or unjustifiable discrimination is the failure of the United States to engage the appellees, as well as other Members exporting shrimp to the United States, in serious, across-the-board negotiations with the objective of concluding bilateral or multilateral agreements for the protection and conservation of sea turtles, before enforcing the import prohibition against the shrimp exports of those other Members. . . .

* * *

3. "Arbitrary Discrimination"

* * *

181. The certification processes followed by the United States thus appear to be singularly informal and casual, and to be conducted in a manner such that these processes could result in the negation of rights of Members. There appears to be no way that exporting Members can be certain whether the terms of Section 609, in particular, the 1996 Guidelines, are being applied in a fair and just manner by the appropriate governmental agencies of the United States. It appears to us that, effectively, exporting Members applying for certification whose applications are rejected are denied basic fairness and due process, and are discriminated against, vis-à-vis those Members which are granted certification. . . .

184. We find, accordingly, that the United States measure is applied in a manner which amounts to a means not just of "unjustifiable discrimination", but also of "arbitrary discrimination" between countries where the same conditions prevail, contrary to the requirements of the chapeau of Article XX. The measure, therefore, is not entitled to the justifying protection of Article XX of the GATT 1994. Having made this finding, it is not necessary for us to examine also whether the United States measure is applied in a manner that constitutes a "disguised restriction on international trade" under the chapeau of Article XX.

185. In reaching these conclusions, we wish to underscore what we have not decided in this appeal. We have not decided that the protection and preservation of the environment is of no significance to the Members of the WTO. Clearly, it is. We have not decided that the sovereign nations that are Members of the WTO cannot adopt effective measures to protect endangered species, such as sea turtles. Clearly, they can and should. And we have not decided that sovereign states should not act together bilaterally, plurilaterally or multilaterally, either within the WTO or in other international fora, to protect endangered species or to otherwise protect the environment. Clearly, they should and do.

186. What we have decided in this appeal is simply this: although the measure of the United States in dispute in this appeal serves an environmental objective that is recognized as legitimate under paragraph (g) of Article XX of the GATT 1994, this measure has been applied by the United States in a manner which constitutes arbitrary and unjustifiable discrimination between Members of the WTO, contrary to the requirements of the chapeau of Article XX. For all of the specific reasons outlined in this Report, this measure does not qualify for the exemption that Article XX of the GATT 1994 affords to measures which serve certain recognized, legitimate environmental purposes but which, at the same time, are not applied in a manner that constitutes a means of arbitrary or unjustifiable discrimination between countries where the same conditions prevail or a disguised restriction on international trade. As we emphasized in United States–Gasoline, WTO Members are free to adopt their own policies aimed at protecting the environment as long as, in so doing, they fulfill their

obligations and respect the rights of other Members under the WTO Agreement.

Findings and Conclusions

187.   For the reasons set out in this Report, the Appellate Body:

* * *

(b) reverses the Panel's finding that the United States measure at issue is not within the scope of measures permitted under the chapeau of Article XX of the GATT 1994, and

(c) concludes that the United States measure, while qualifying for provisional justification under Article XX(g), fails to meet the requirements of the chapeau of Article XX, and, therefore, is not justified under Article XX of the GATT 1994.

NOTES AND QUESTIONS

1.   Why did the Appellate Body find that the U.S. turtle protection law was not within the scope of Article XX? What else could the U.S. have done to protect turtles under these circumstances? According to the Appellate Body's reasoning, what *should* the U.S. have done? Why do you think the legislation was crafted in this way in the first place? Is it likely that the US shrimp industry wanted such a provision? Why?

2.   The Appellate Body takes the U.S. to task for not engaging in serious multilateral talks to create an international solution to the turtle/shrimp problem. In fact, the U.S. negotiated an Inter–American Convention on the Protection and Conservation of Sea Turtles, but did not achieve a similar convention outside the Americas. How much should a state be required to do multilaterally before it is permitted to use unilateral measures to save an endangered species? What if the U.S. had helped conclude a global agreement, but a rogue state refused to sign on and continued catching shrimp without TEDs?

3.   PPMs: a recurring source of disputes is the extent to which trade restrictions may be based on how a product is made rather than its intrinsic uses or characteristics. GATT requires that "like products" be treated alike no matter where they are from. But what is a "like product"? In the Tuna–Dolphin case described above, the Panel found that "[r]egulations governing the taking of tuna could not possibly affect tuna as a product." United States–Restrictions on Imports of Tuna, Report of the Panel, Sept. 3, 1991, para. 5.15. Should products be considered "unlike" if they are caught while protecting, rather than harming, dolphins or turtles? What about products made with child, or slave labor? Note Article XX permits the exclusion of the products of prison labor. Why do you think that is? Does the same rationale apply to other kinds of PPMs?

4.   The panel also faults the U.S. for imposing trade sanctions on all producers from certain countries, rather than just those producers who do not use TEDs (at paragraph 165). How could the U.S. distinguish between "compliant" and "non-compliant" shrimpers without reference to the

waters the shrimp were caught in? The WTO's Committee on Trade and Environment has spent many hours debating the GATT-legality of various eco-labeling, certification and other (mandatory or voluntary) information-based schemes to identify environmentally-preferable producers. Would a voluntary scheme like the Forest Stewardship Council certification discussed in Chapter 6 violate the provisions of GATT?

4. BILATERAL AND REGIONAL FREE TRADE AGREEMENTS AND CUSTOMS UNIONS

Robert McMahon, The Rise in Bilateral Free Trade Agreements

Council on Foreign on Relations (CFR), June 13, 2006
http://www.cfr.org/publication/10890/

Free trade agreements, many of which are bilateral, are arrangements in which countries give each other preferential treatment in trade, such as eliminating tariffs and other barriers on goods. Each country continues its trade policies, such as tariffs with countries outside the FTA. For example, in the U.S.-Australian FTA, which took effect in 2005, Australia lowered tariffs on most U.S. agricultural and manufactured goods, and the United States lowered tariffs on Australian beef, dairy and other items. Some U.S. regional free trade agreements, such as the Central America Free Trade Agreement, are essentially a series of bilateral deals between the United States and member countries.

* * *

On the domestic front, an increasing number of free trade agreements lower the price for consumer goods in the United States as well as the costs U.S. businesses pay for imported materials. Experts say more competition in local markets, while unsettling to some businesses, also spurs innovation and increases labor productivity. Bilateral deals also open up foreign markets to U.S. goods, increasing employment in those export sectors. Such deals usually provide a better climate for U.S. investors.

* * *

Are there negative repercussions to such deals?

Critics like Jagdish Bhagwati, [] CFR's senior fellow in international economics, say the United States is using such deals to bully smaller states, which want access to the large American market. They say Washington is able to insist on tough labor standards and intellectual property rules far in excess of requirements of the World Trade Organization. * * *

In recent years, provisions on labor and the environment have been included in some bilateral trade agreements entered into by the United States. The texts of these agreements can be found at www.ustr.gov. Selections from those provisions in the United States Trade Promotion

Agreement with Peru, which entered into force on February 1, 2009, are set forth in the Documentary Supplement.

Pascal Lamy, Proliferation of Regional Trade Agreements "Breeding Concern"

WTO Director General's Speech Opening the Conference on "Multilateralizing Regionalism", September 10, 2007 www.wto.org/english/news_e/sppl_e/sppl67_e.htm

We hear so much about regionalism these days, which is hardly surprising, considering that well over 200 of these agreements are operating and dozens more are in the making. There has been a veritable flurry of negotiating activity around regional trade deals in the last several years. And there has also been a vast quantity of recent writing on the subject, including last week's UNCTAD annual report.

* * *

I do not wish to be misunderstood. I am certainly not saying that regionalism is all bad. On the contrary, I believe many regional initiatives have made important contributions to economic welfare and doubtless to political stability as well. What I am talking about is the downside of an exponential expansion in RTAs. Where is the proliferation leading us in terms of trade and international economic relations more generally? Do we need to rethink our approach a bit to trade cooperation?

* * *

We often think and talk about how regionalism might be hurting multilateralism, either by bolstering discriminatory interests, or perhaps by fostering an anti-trade-openness posture, if regionalism is seen as a way of building protectionist structures behind enlarged closed markets. We also might worry about how focusing on building up the stock of RTAs might distract attention from multilateral processes.

But in ending what I would like to do is turn the question around. I would like to ask what the WTO might do to help avoid a situation in which these negative aspects of regional agreements prevail, and ultimately to promote multilateralization.

* * *

Thirdly, we should not forget that we have a negotiating mandate under Doha to look at the WTO rules governing regionalism. Now I know we have been doing this for a long time in different contexts and to very little effect, so my argument here would be that if we are concerned about the impact of burgeoning regionalism we should redouble our efforts here as well.

My final point is a derivative of the last one. I think it would be useful to look systematically at the characteristics and design of RTAs not only in terms of legal compliance questions, but also in terms of whether their architecture is more or less likely to foster multilateralization in the future. Perhaps we could think in terms of best practices in this regard.

GATT 1947, Article XXIV para. 4 Customs Unions and Free-trade Areas

www.wto.org

4.   The contracting parties recognize the desirability of increasing freedom of trade by the development, through voluntary agreements, of closer integration between the economies of the countries parties to such agreements. They also recognize that the purpose of a customs union or of a free-trade area should be to facilitate trade between the constituent territories and not to raise barriers to the trade of other contracting parties with such territories.

5.   Accordingly, the provisions of this Agreement shall not prevent, as between the territories of contracting parties, the formation of a customs union or of a free-trade area or the adoption of an interim agreement necessary for the formation of a customs union or of a free-trade area; *Provided* that:

(*b*) with respect to a free-trade area, or an interim agreement leading to the formation of a free-trade area, the duties and other regulations of commerce maintained in each of the constituent territories and applicable at the formation of such free-trade area or the adoption of such interim agreement to the trade of contracting parties not included in such area or not parties to such agreement shall not be higher or more restrictive than the corresponding duties and other regulations of commerce existing in the same constituent territories prior to the formation of the free-trade area, or interim agreement as the case may be; and

(*c*) any interim agreement referred to in subparagraphs (*a*) and (*b*) shall include a plan and schedule for the formation of such a customs union or of such a free-trade area within a reasonable length of time.

7.   (*a*) Any contracting party deciding to enter into a customs union or free-trade area, or an interim agreement leading to the formation of such a union or area, shall promptly notify the CONTRACTING PARTIES and shall make available to them such information regarding the proposed union or area as will enable them to make such reports and recommendations to contracting parties as they may deem appropriate.

(*b*) If, after having studied the plan and schedule included in an interim agreement referred to in paragraph 5 in consultation with the parties to that agreement and taking due account of the information made available in accordance with the provisions of subparagraph (*a*), the CONTRACTING PARTIES find that such agreement is not likely to result in the formation of a customs union or of a free-trade area within the period contemplated by the parties to the agreement or that such period is not a reasonable one, the CONTRACTING PARTIES shall make recommendations to the parties to the agreement. The parties shall not maintain or put into force, as the case may be, such agreement if they are not prepared to modify it in accordance with these recommendations.

The European Economic Community, discussed in Chapters 3 and 11, is a customs union, with a common external tariff, while the North American Free Trade Agreement (NAFTA) between Mexico, Canada and the U.S., is a free trade area. FTAs do away with tariffs and other barriers among the members but allow each member to set its own tariffs vis-à-vis non-members. The following article discusses some other differences between them:

Stephen Zamora, A Proposed North American Regional Development Fund: The Next Phase of North American Integration Under NAFTA*

40 LOY. U. CHI. L.J. 93, 94–115 (2008)

* * *

In adopting NAFTA as an ambitious blueprint for economic integration, the NAFTA governments carefully avoided any reference to the model of economic integration that has been pursued for half a century in Europe. More precisely, the governments of Canada, Mexico, and the United States chose to reject two important pillars of European unification: (1) free movement of workers, one of the fundamental freedoms of European unification; and (2) the harmonization of social welfare and environmental protections, which was deemed necessary to prevent "social dumping" in Europe—i.e., the migration of industries to regions of poorly paid workers and environmental degradation. The European Union (EU) is the most ambitious and successful economic, social, and political unification of separate nations ever achieved.

* * *

On January 1, 2009, NAFTA will celebrate its fifteenth birthday. After a decade and a half of existence, the agreement continues to stir controversy in all three member countries, with proponents citing the clear growth of intraregional trade and investment that has taken place since NAFTA's adoption, and opponents questioning the displacement of workers and uneven distribution of benefits.

The distribution of economic benefits and the effects of increased competition on workers were not considered during NAFTA negotiations. NAFTA's creators also minimized the importance of different levels of economic development between the United States and Canada on the one hand and Mexico on the other. They did so despite the fact that the per capita income of Mexico is approximately one-sixth that of the United States, and one-fifth that of Canada.

While recognizing that Mexico's economic strength and levels of employment lagged behind those of its NAFTA partners, NAFTA's proponents theorized that the agreement would spur economic growth in Mexico, reduce unemployment, and remove the impulse of Mexican workers to

---

* Footnotes omitted.

migrate to the United States for jobs. In the exchange of letters calling for the beginning of negotiations, the NAFTA parties made clear that immigration would be excluded from NAFTA, and the agreement includes only limited guarantees of freedom of movement for business persons. Yet while Mexico's economy did grow at a healthy rate for most of the decade following NAFTA's entry into force, the growth was "insufficient to address its long-run development challenges"—high levels of poverty, discussed below, and chronic unemployment and under-employment.

One side effect of endemic poverty in Mexico, coupled with a relatively healthy economy in the United States, has been a constant and increasing rate of "exportation" of unauthorized workers from Mexico to the United States. NAFTA has not changed this. . . . NAFTA has not rectified the lack of jobs and productivity of Mexican workers or stemmed the tide of migration to the United States. Mexico's opening to foreign competition, crowned with its entry into NAFTA, has caused economic dislocations in numerous sectors of the Mexican economy, including small-to medium-scale manufacturing and agricultural production. Whether the adoption of NAFTA, overall, has worsened the condition of Mexican workers is open to debate, but there is little question that NAFTA has not improved Mexican wages overall.

* * *

The North American Agreement on Labor Cooperation (NAALC) is the closest thing to a social charter in NAFTA, but its existence does not alter my previous conclusion that NAFTA's negotiators had no interest in trilateral cooperation on employment and social welfare issues. Added at the behest of U.S. negotiators to offset opposition to NAFTA by U.S. labor leaders, the NAALC was not designed to press for harmonization of legal protections in the NAFTA countries. Instead, the NAALC, like its sister agreement, the North American Agreement on Environmental Cooperation (NACEC), only committed the NAFTA Parties to enforcing whatever national laws were in existence—an obvious reference to U.S. and Canadian concerns over the lack of enforcement of Mexican environmental laws.

Administered by a Commission on Labor Cooperation (CLC) that consists of the labor ministers of the NAFTA Parties, the NAALC is charged with investigating citizens' complaints concerning the failure to enforce certain labor rights under the domestic law of the NAFTA Party. Certain key labor principles, such as right to strike and freedom of association, are not subject to the full range of CLC oversight of enforcement. The CLC administers a small trinational Secretariat to oversee the work of the Commission, but the Agreement depends on National Administrative Offices (NAOs) that are housed in the labor ministry of each NAFTA Party for enforcement.

The experience under the environmental side agreement has been modest to date, but with hopeful signs. By contrast, the experience of the NAALC has been an exercise in mismanagement and lack of governmental support.

5. THE OFFSHORING PROBLEM

Alan Blinder, Offshoring: The Next Industrial Revolution?

85 FOREIGN AFFAIRS 113 (2006)

* * * Once upon a time, the United Kingdom had a comparative advantage in textile manufacturing. Then that advantage shifted to New England, and so jobs were moved from the United Kingdom to the United States. Then the comparative advantage shifted once again—this time to the Carolinas—and jobs migrated south within the United States. Now the comparative advantage in textile manufacturing resides in China and other low-wage countries * * *

WHAT SORTS of jobs are at risk of being offshored? In the old days, when tradable goods were things that could be put in a box, the key distinction was between manufacturing and non-manufacturing jobs * * * But as the domain of tradable services expands, many service workers will also have to accept the new, and not very pleasant, reality * * *

WHAT is to be done about all of this? * * * In the first place, rich countries such as the United States will have to reorganize the nature of work to exploit their big advantage in non-tradable services * * * In the second place, the United States and other rich nations will have to transform their educational systems so as to prepare workers for the jobs that will actually exist in their societies. * * * One other important step for rich countries is to rethink the currently inadequate programs for trade adjustment assistance. * * * Thinking about adjustment assistance more broadly, the United States may have to repair and thicken the tattered safety net that supports workers who fall off the labor-market trapeze * * *

NOTES AND QUESTIONS

1. Trade adjustment assistance is available in the United States and in Europe, where existing programs are currently under review for purposes of improving coverage. Financial assistance is at times provided by companies, labor unions, states and local authorities. The United States and European Union programs are described in the materials cited below. See also, Lorand Bartels, *Social Issues: Labour, Environment and Human Rights, in* BILATERAL AND REGIONAL TRADE AGREEMENTS, ch. 13 (Lester and Mercurio eds. Forthcoming).

2. Do the provisions described below seem adequate to compensate the "losers" in free trade agreements? Is it even feasible to define who those people are given that job losses also arise from technological change and wage differentials not tied to free trade agreements? Isn't this just the operation of the free market, so that compensation schemes are akin to giving consolation prizes to buggy whip or VCR makers?

Trade Adjustment Assistance (TAA) and Alternative Trade Adjustment Assistance (ATAA) Services and Benefits

U.S. Dept. of Labor, April 27, 2007, www.doleta.gov/tradeact/benefits. cfm

Trade Adjustment Assistance (TAA) and Alternative Trade Adjustment Assistance (ATAA) help trade-affected workers who have lost their jobs as a result of increased imports or shifts in production out of the United States. Certified individuals may be eligible to receive one or more program benefits and services depending on what is needed to return them to employment.

The European Globalization Adjustment Fund

European Union, Commission Memo 06/486, Brussels, December 13, 2006 http://europa.eu/rapid/

1) Background

What is the new European Globalisation adjustment Fund (EGF)?

The opening of economies to international competition brings new opportunities in terms of competitiveness and the creation of high-quality jobs. However, trade openness can also have negative consequences for the most vulnerable and least qualified workers in some sectors and areas of the European Union.

The European Globalisation adjustment Fund (EGF) is a new instrument which will provide personalised support to workers who have been made redundant as a result of trade liberalisation, so that they can either remain in employment or find quickly a new job.

The EGF will thus express the Union's solidarity in complement to the support provided by the Member States at national, regional and local levels.

3. In addition to the EGF, the European Union provided extensive funds for "social cohesion," aimed at ameliorating the differences in levels of investment between the central, most developed Western European states and those, like Spain, Ireland and Greece, that came into the then-European Community at lower rates of per-capita income. These funds, described in Zamora, above, will come to over US$500 billion in the 2007–2013 period, fully a third of the EUs budget.

6. MULTILATERAL VERSUS UNILATERAL ENFORCEMENT SANCTIONS

a. WTO RULES

WTO Agreement, Annex 2: Understanding on Rules and Procedures Governing the Settlement of Disputes

Members hereby agree as follows:

Article 1: Coverage and Application

1. The rules and procedures of this Understanding shall apply to disputes brought pursuant to the consultation and dispute settlement

provisions of the agreements listed in Appendix 1 to this Understanding (referred to in this Understanding as the "covered agreements"). The rules and procedures of this Understanding shall also apply to consultations and the settlement of disputes between Members concerning their rights and obligations under the provisions of the Agreement Establishing the World Trade Organization (referred to in this Understanding as the "WTO Agreement") and of this Understanding taken in isolation or in combination with any other covered agreement.

Article 22: Compensation and the Suspension of Concessions

1.   Compensation and the suspension of concessions or other obligations are temporary measures available in the event that the recommendations and rulings are not implemented within a reasonable period of time. However, neither compensation nor the suspension of concessions or other obligations is preferred to full implementation of a recommendation to bring a measure into conformity with the covered agreements. Compensation is voluntary and, if granted, shall be consistent with the covered agreements.

2.   * * * If no satisfactory compensation has been agreed within 20 days after the date of expiry of the reasonable period of time, any party having invoked the dispute settlement procedures may request authorization from the DSB to suspend the application to the Member concerned of concessions or other obligations under the covered agreements.

4.   The level of the suspension of concessions or other obligations authorized by the DSB shall be equivalent to the level of the nullification or impairment.

6.   When the situation described in ¶ 2 occurs, the DSB, upon request, shall grant authorization to suspend concessions or other obligations * * * However, if the Member concerned objects to the level of suspension proposed, or claims that the principles and procedures set forth in ¶ 3 have not been followed * * * the matter shall be referred to arbitration. Such arbitration shall be carried out by the original panel, if members are available, or by an arbitrator appointed by the Director–General and shall be completed within 60 days after the date of expiry of the reasonable period of time. Concessions or other obligations shall not be suspended during the course of the arbitration.

b.   U.S. RULES

Enforcement of United States Rights Under Trade Agreements

19 USCA Sec. 2411 (Sec. 301 of U.S. Trade Act of 1974)

Sec. 2411. Actions by United States Trade Representative (Sec. 301)

(a) Mandatory action

(1) If the United States Trade Representative determines under section 2414(a)(1) of this title that—

(A) the rights of the United States under any trade agreement are being denied; or

(B) an act, policy, or practice of a foreign country—

(i) violates, or is inconsistent with, the provisions of, or otherwise denies benefits to the United States under, any trade agreement, or

(ii) is unjustifiable and burdens or restricts United States commerce; the Trade Representative shall take action authorized in subsection (c) of this section subject to the specific direction, if any, of the President regarding any such action, and shall take all other appropriate and feasible action within the power of the President that the President may direct the Trade Representative to take under this subsection, to enforce such rights or to obtain the elimination of such act, policy, or practice. Actions may be taken that are within the power of the President with respect to trade in any goods or services, or with respect to any other area of pertinent relations with the foreign country.

(2) The Trade Representative is not required to take action under paragraph (1) in any case in which—

(A) The Dispute Settlement Body (as defined in section 3531(5) of this title) has adopted a report, or a ruling issued under the formal dispute settlement proceeding provided under any other trade agreement finds, that—

(i) the rights of the United States under a trade agreement are not being denied, or

(ii) the act, policy, or practice—

(I) is not a violation of, or inconsistent with, the rights of the United States * * *

(c) Scope of authority

(1) For purposes of carrying out the provisions of subsection (a) or (b) of this section, the Trade Representative is authorized to—

(A) suspend, withdraw, or prevent the application of, benefits of trade agreement concessions to carry out a trade agreement with the foreign country referred to in such subsection;

(B) impose duties or other import restrictions on the goods of, and, notwithstanding any other provision of law, fees or restrictions on the services of, such foreign country for such time as the Trade Representative determines appropriate. * * *

c. EU RULES

The EU has also established procedures for protection against injurious illicit practices committed in the trade field by third countries. Current

EU law on this subject is contained in the Council's 1994 Regulation 3286/94 on trade barriers which establishes "Community procedures in the field of common commercial policy in order to ensure the exercise of the Communities' rights under international trade rules, in particular, those established under the auspices of the World Trade Organization". This Regulation broadens and strengthens the EUs procedures and potential for action in appropriate cases, while specifically conforming to the WTO associated rules.

Article 1 of Regulation 3286 provides that the procedures adopted in the Regulation are to ensure protection of the Community's rights aimed at:

(a) responding to obstacles to trade that have an effect on the market of the Community, with a view to removing the injury resulting therefrom;

(b) responding to obstacles to trade that have an effect on the market of a third country, with a view to removing the adverse trade effects resulting therefrom.

Pursuant to Article 12.2 where the Community's international obligations require the prior discharge of an international procedure for consultation or for the settlement of disputes, the measures referred to in paragraph 3 shall only be decided on after that procedure has been terminated * * *. Paragraph 3 of Article 12 states that:

3. Any commercial policy measures may be taken which are compatible with existing international obligations and procedures, notably:

(a) suspension or withdrawal of any concession resulting from commercial policy negotiations;

(b) the raising of existing customs duties or the introduction of any other charge on imports;

(c) the introduction of quantitative restrictions or any other measures modifying import or export conditions or otherwise affecting trade with the third country concerned.

d. AUTHORIZATION OF RETALIATION

WTO Authorizes Trade Retaliation Against EU in Beef Case

USIS Wahington File. Wendy Lubetkin, USIA European Correspondent
www.usia.gov

Geneva—The World Trade Organization (WTO) has formally authorized the United States and Canada to impose punitive duties on a selection of European Union (EU) imports in reaction to the EU's failure to comply with WTO rules in the transatlantic trade dispute over growth hormone-treated beef.

A July 26 meeting of the WTO Dispute Settlement Body authorized the United States to suspend tariff concessions on a range of imports from the EU worth $116.8 million a year, an amount previously determined by a group of WTO arbitrators.

Canada, also a party to the dispute, was authorized to impose sanctions in the amount of $Canadian 11.3 million.

"The requests by the U.S. and Canada were authorized today in accordance with the DSU [Dispute Settlement Understanding]," Ambassador Rita D. Hayes, deputy U.S. trade representative and U.S. permanent representative to the WTO, told a press briefing following the meeting.

"The United States intends to implement the suspension of tariff concessions and related obligations with respect to goods entered or withdrawn from the warehouse on or after July 29," she said.

Hayes emphasized, however, that the US, would prefer not to have to impose sanctions because "it does nothing to help our exports and is not to the benefit of our importers."

"The United States would prefer to settle this dispute," she said, "and we will continue to try to work with the EC [European Community] to find an acceptable solution."

The list of products subject to 100-percent ad valorem duties was made public by the Office of the U.S. Trade Representative (USTR) July 19. It includes a wide range of pork products, Roquefort cheese, foie gras, prepared mustard and truffles.

Asked whether the United States would take a "carousel" approach and change the products targeted for retaliation, Hayes said the USTR has the legal authority to change the list, but has no plans to do so at the current time.

Hayes said the United States was willing to consider compensation from the EU if the EU also offered some assurances that it would lift its barriers to U.S. beef.

"But, quite frankly, the EC's offer involving increased U.S. beef access was not adequate," she said. "The EC could not even provide assurances that this offer would in fact allow any U.S beef into the EC".

"We were also concerned that the EC would view compensation as a resolution of the dispute and the U.S. beef producers would never gain access," Hayes said. Under the WTO agreement, compensation is considered only a temporary measure for dealing with a situation like this.

Big Mac Targeted by French Farmers

3 BRIDGES WEEKLY TRADE NEWS DIGEST No. 34, 30 August 1999

French farmers have taken up arms (and apples) against U.S. agricultural trade policy in a series of demonstrations underway since early August. Protesting punitive tariffs imposed on EU products by the U.S. in the context of the dispute over EU banning imports of U.S. hormone-treated beef, farmers in southwest France dumped 10 tonnes of nectarines in front of a McDonalds on 20 August, followed the next day by farmers in Arles and Martigues dumping tonnes of fruit, vegetables and manure in front of a McDonald's there. These protests follow similar incidents by French farmers throughout the month.

* * *

McDonalds has become the target of choice for French farmers angered by the trade situation. The French Farmers' union Confédération Paysanne said in a statement that "Globalization is creating absurd economic conflicts," and that the protests aim to "allow farmers and others to feed themselves as they think best." French farmers have also called for a boycott of U.S. imports. Observers say these incidents show the unfairness of the Dispute Settlement System set up by the WTO: the authorized trade retaliation measures can hit small producers who had nothing to do with the initial conflict—rather than the Government—introducing a variation on the beggar-my-neighbor policies that the GATT was set up to prevent.

As tensions mounted last week, the U.S. Embassy in Paris said it would like to hold negotiations with EU officials to find a quick solution to the trade matter. The U.S. embassy said that the retaliatory tariffs were imposed "only as a last resort." The U.S. has so far argued that it would settle for nothing less than a lifting of the EU ban on hormone treated beef, while the EU has continually said it would not lift the ban until scientific risk assessments are completed.

———————

WTO proceedings in the *EC—Beef Hormone* Case continued. On 8 November 2004, the European Communities initiated proceedings asserting that the retaliatory measures should have been removed since the EC had already removed the measures found to be WTO-inconsistent in the *EC—Hormones* case. The specific issues raised by the EC included the following:

—the failure to remove the retaliatory measures despite the EC's removal of the WTO-inconsistent measures:

—the unilateral determinations that the new EC legislation is a continued WTO violation; and

—the failure to follow DSU Article 21.5 dispute settlement procedures to adjudicate the matter.

On 16 October 2008 the WTO Dispute Settlement Body, in a mixed decision, found that, while all parties had failed to follow certain procedures, the EU's new measures were not in compliance with the risk assessment requirement and that the US and Canada were not in violation of WTO rules by maintaining their sanctions against imports from the EU. Later the parties entered into consultations under WTO rules. The U.S. maintained the existing sanctions but announced that it would rotate the sanctions among other products and EU Member States in order to increase their impact, giving rise to further controversy. Under a determination announced on January 15, 2009, additional duties were to go into effect on April 23, 2009. Consultations among the parties continue at the time of writing.

Further developments in this dispute (No. DS321) may be found on the WTO web site at http://www.wto.org/english/tratop_e/dispu_e/cases_e/ds 320_e.htm.

On the broader issues of trade problems of the U.S. with the EC, consult the annual U.S. National Trade Estimate of Foreign Trade Barriers at www.ustr.gov/. For parallel reports of the EC on U.S. trade barriers, see http://europa.eu.int/comm/trade/ or Google: "European Union Report on United States Barriers to Trade and Investment".

NOTES AND QUESTIONS

1. How would you describe the differences between the U.S. Trade representative's retaliation power under § 301 and the EU powers under its protective Regulation 3286/94? Do you find the U.S. law to be compatible with the WTO's DSU rules? Why? Does the EU Regulation better conform to the DSU? Does § 301 authorize unilateral action by the U.S. without reference to the WTO? See the WTO case: *Panel on United States §§ 301–310 of the Trade Act of 1974*, WT/DS152/R, December 22, 1999, at http:// www.wto.org/english/tratop_e/dispu_e/cases_e/ds152_e.htm.

2. If the trade dispute is about beef, why punish European producers of pork products, Roquefort cheese, foie gras, prepared mustard and truffles? What do they have to do with it? How should the U.S.T.R. decide which products should be subject to sanctions?

3. In late 2009, after many years of controversy, the *EC Hormone* dispute had still not been resolved. Does this influence your views on trade sanctions?

B. FOREIGN DIRECT INVESTMENT

Successful trade operations frequently lead manufacturers to engage directly in more extended foreign operations, to license their key intellectual property rights to a foreign manufacturer to produce the traded goods, or more significantly for our purposes, to establish their own manufacturing facilities in foreign countries,* in the form of foreign direct investment (FDI).

---

* This Section deals with *direct* foreign investment, although portfolio investment is always another possible means of access to foreign business. Portfolio investment abroad can give the investor a stake in a manufacturing enterprise by purchase of shares of a foreign company, without control or operating responsibility and without a legal or physical presence in the country of operations. The risks of such investments normally fall on the investor who cannot expect significant assistance of its government if the investment goes wrong. For the portfolio investor there are normally fewer operational or foreign presence risks associated

The manufacturer with international trade experience is often well placed to seize upon opportunities of increasing its overall economic rewards through direct investment abroad, notwithstanding new and perhaps larger risks which may be encountered. Foreign direct investment (FDI) benefits may take many attractive forms. They may include capture of manufacturing profits which would not return to it in licensing of intellectual property. If the investment is made in a free trade-zone country, the new goods would have duty free access to other countries in the zone, as an investment in England provides duty-free access to the other 26 Member States of the European Union. There might well be reduced transport costs, advantageous wage rates and access to resources, lower social costs in local employment markets, less-costly environmental requirements, and so forth. Foreign direct investment carries the investor and its assets directly into the foreign country, with a number of far-reaching consequences. A manufacturer-investor typically transfers into the foreign country its production machinery, operating tools, and other tangible assets, as well as such intangible property as technology, operating procedures and trade secrets, in short all that is useful, available and economic for the new operations.

The investor also establishes a legal presence in the foreign country, usually a wholly owned subsidiary corporation formed under the law of that country. Direction and support are provided on-site by management and staff, some or all of whom may be employees of the investor, and with the investor they would be regarded as "aliens" by the host state, perhaps a new and uncertain status.

The new subsidiary soon finds itself under new legal controls, not only those of the investors home state, but also those of the host state. Both of these legal regimes function under the umbrella of a third regime, the rules of international law reflected in customary rules, Friendship, Commerce and Navigation type treaties, bilateral investment treaties (BITS) and other agreements, and in North America under NAFTA and globally under the WTO Agreements. This international legal dimension adds the potential of another unfamiliar element for the investor to contend with.

The foreign direct investor soon confronts the fact that the economic advantages it seeks abroad come with significant attachments in the form of fresh legal risks arising in unfamiliar locations. The new legal questions include:

The right of entry and terms of entry of the investor into the host country

The management and integrity of the investment once established

The terms of departure when this time comes

The settlement of disputes.

---

with direct investment abroad, except for the risk of loss or reduction in value of capital or income in cases of expropriation or other disruptive actions of the host government.

Hence it is no surprise that foreign investment lawyers in both the investor's home state and in the FDI host state have their tasks set out for themselves at all stages of the investment process.

For the successful resolution of the questions of right of entry, management and departure noted above, investors must look to their governments, which have established under international law an elaborate system of facilitative and protective rules. As in the trade field, there is little customary international law of investment, except probably for such basic rules as "fair and equitable treatment", "full protection and security" and the "minimum international standard" including "denial of justice". Rules governing the host country's expropriation of foreign property, the ultimate disaster for the investor, which is taken up extensively below, are more clearly a part of customary international law. However, the bulk of the law in this sector is found in the treaties mentioned above, and in their potential contribution to customary international law (see Tarcisio Gazzini, *The Role of Customary International Law in the Field of Foreign Investment, 8 J. of World Investment and Trade* 691 (2007)). The treaties govern much of the detail of investment rights, and more broadly reflect the national policies of the Contracting Parties. The major policy objective in this sector in recent years has been the movement to fuller freedom of investment.

Open Markets Matter: The Benefits of Trade and Investment

OECD POLICY BRIEFS, No. 6, p. 4, 1998

Why Is Foreign Investment Beneficial?

The case for opening markets to foreign direct investment is as compelling as it is for trade. More open economies enjoy higher rates of private investment, which is a major determinant of economic growth and job creation. FDI is actively courted by countries, not least because it generates spillovers such as improved management and better technology.* The benefits are tangible. As is true with firms that trade, firms and sectors where FDI is intense have higher average labour productivity and pay higher wages. Outward investment enables firms to remain competitive and thus supports employment at home. Investment abroad stimulates exports of machinery and other capital goods, and increases demand for intermediary products, know-how and specialised services. A study of OECD countries found that each $1.00 of outward foreign direct investment was associated with $2.00 of additional exports, and a trade surplus of $1.70. Without FDI those exports would be smaller, sustaining fewer of the more productive, better paying jobs that go with them.

Liberalisation can benefit developed and developing countries alike. As is the case for OECD countries, foreign investment brings higher wages,

---

* FDI trends and statistics are carried in the *UNCTAD: World Investment Report 2008* and successive annual Reports (http://www.unctad.org).

and is a major source of technology transfer and managerial skills in host developing countries. This contributes to rising prosperity in the developing countries concerned, as well as enhancing demand for higher value-added exports from OECD economies. In this way, developing countries are becoming major stake-holders in the trading system today, as is evidenced by estimates that close to one half of Uruguay Round welfare gains may accrue to them. * * *

OECD, Private Direct Investment for Development: Maximizing Benefits, Minimizing Costs

pp. 7, 22 (2002)

Potential drawbacks [of FDI] include a deterioration of the balance of payments as profits are repatriated (albeit often offset by incoming FDI), a lack of positive linkages with local communities, the potentially harmful environmental impact of FDI, especially in the extractive and heavy industries, social disruptions of accelerated commercialisation in less developed countries, and the effects on competition in national markets. Moreover, some host country authorities perceive an increasing dependence on internationally operating enterprises as representing a loss of political sovereignty. Even some expected benefits may prove elusive if, for example, the host economy, in its current state of economic development, is not able to take advantage of the technologies or know-how transferred through FDI.

* * *

The net benefits from FDI do not accrue automatically, and their magnitude differs according to host country and context. The factors that hold back the full benefits of FDI in some developing countries include the level of general education and health, the technological level of host-country enterprises, insufficient openness to trade, weak competition and inadequate regulatory frameworks. Conversely, a level of technological, educational and infrastructure achievement in a developing country does, other things being equal, equip it better to benefit from a foreign presence in its markets.

1.   INTERNATIONAL INVESTMENT AGREEMENTS

José Alvarez, The Emerging Foreign Direct Investment Regime

99 ASIL PROC. 94 (2005)

The emerging regime for foreign direct investment (FDI) consists of obligations imposed under some two thousand bilateral investment treaties (BITs), regional free trade agreements (FTAs), specialized multilateral treaties (such as the World Trade Organization [WTO]'s trade-related investment measures [TRIMs] and services agreements, the Organization for Economic Cooperation and Development's Code of Capital Movements, and Europe's Energy Charter), and soft law instruments (such as the World Bank's FDI Guidelines). The regime's impact is also suggested by the substantial recent rise in the number of investment disputes submitted to the International Centre for Settlement of Investment Disputes (ICSID) or under UN Commission on International Trade Law rules and by extensive FDI-friendly changes to national laws. These developments solidify the demise of the socialist alternative to capitalism and bury old demands for a "new international economic order" in a deluge of state practice; such developments provide tangible evidence that even (formally) Communist holdovers like China and Cuba have donned, albeit to different degrees, Thomas Friedman's "golden straightjacket."

The regime is based on the principle of comparative advantage. Its rules include absolute and relative rights for the foreign investor as well as the right to enforce these against the host state through international investor-dispute resolution. The regime puts foreign investors and international dispute settlers in the driver's seat. It undermines or renders unnecessary capital-exporting states' resort to either gunboat diplomacy or diplomatic espousal. Except for the WTO's TRIMs and services agreements, the regime relies on private attorneys general to enforce its norms. It is self-enforcing, since direct investor-state dispute settlement can displace national law and national venues for settling disputes. Even in the home of Carlos Calvo himself, Argentina now faces over thirty BIT claims whose face value is said to exceed nine times the Argentine national budget.

There are differing views about why lesser-developed countries (LDCs) have so willingly reversed course on FDI. Some say it's because these countries have finally learned that import substitution does not work and that they need to be "open for business." Others, like Andrew Guzman, argue that the "golden straightjacket" is an apt description of decisions forced upon *individual* LDCs by their competitive needs for capital, by the International Monetary Fund, and by their inability to act collectively. There are also differing assessments about whether the FDI regime has worked. If the aim of some of these treaties is to advance political-strategic alliances, there is little doubt investment treaties have achieved that. Furthermore, if the goal is to improve the lot of the foreign investor, the FDI regime has been successful in that realm. But if the goal of investment treaties is to increase the actual flow of FDI to LDCs, UN Conference on Trade and Development and World Bank studies to date have failed to establish any clear cause-and-effect relationship between concluding a BIT and an increase in FDI flows. While investment treaties may indeed fulfill a valuable signaling function, it is both difficult to quantify their effects on foreign investors' decisions and to measure the effects of investment treaties, given the sheer density of the regime. If the goal of the emerging regime was more ambitious and was to promote sustainable economic development in a way that would reduce the disparity between rich and poor, encourage less corrupt or more efficient governance, or promote liberal democracy and respect for human rights within the LDCs that have borne the brunt of making FDI-friendly reforms, the jury is still very much out on such assessments since it would require eliminating a lot of empirical "noise."

The FDI regime tries to produce converging expectations for host states, capital exporters, and investors without reliance on any single multilateral instrument or intergovernmental organization. Like the WTO, the FDI regime relies considerably on delegated power to adjudicators to fill in gaps in the law (as with respect to the meaning and content of ambiguous relative rights like "national treatment"). But unlike the WTO regime, adjudicative gap-filling occurs not through an orderly process with predictable timetables and procedures but through ad hoc arbitrations using different procedural rules and appointing authorities. "Appellate review" in the FDI regime is also haphazard. Forms of review may occur at the international level—as through ICSID annulment actions—or through revise, review, or annulment actions at the situs of the arbitration, but not through scrutiny by any single appellate body (as in the WTO).

The political, judicial, or other checks on investment arbitrators are of an entirely different kind from those in the WTO. Only some investment treaties, like the North American Free Trade Agreement (NAFTA), anticipate that the state parties can issue interpretations that can trump (or at least react to) arbitral rulings. Governments cannot screen the types of disputes that private parties are permitted to bring under investor-state arbitration, and arbitrators can provide direct relief to private parties. Unlike the WTO, national courts are more involved in the FDI regime since they can engage in limited review of arbitral decisions. In addition, some investment treaties permit direct actions in local court to enforce investor rights. The FDI regime's reliance on dispute settlement approximates the transnational forms of dispute settlement found in the Inter–American or European courts of human rights and differs from both classic state-to-state interstate dispute settlement (as in the International Court of Justice) and the intermediate form of dispute settlement that characterizes the WTO. The combination of private attorney-generals choosing which disputes to bring and which contentious legal arguments to push, the involvement of national courts, and the prospect of directly enforceable monetary awards greatly enhances the potential for adjudicative law making.

Mitsuo Matsushita, et al., The World Trade Organization, Law, Practice and Policy

p. 832 (2d ed. 2006)

Whereas there is a multilateral agreement on the liberalization of trade, there is no comprehensive multilateral agreement on investment. Investment liberalization has been carried out primarily through bilateral agreements, regional economic organizations, and in certain economic sectors. Bilaterally, trading partners commonly enter into so-called *bilateral investment treaties* (BITs), whereby agreement is reached on the conditions of foreign investment, the standards of compensation in case of expropriation, and investor remedies, which are often sought through investment-state arbitration. At the regional level, the *European Union* (EU) integration process aims, eventually, for a complete liberalization of investment (free movement of capital); in fact, free movement of capital is one of the four *fundamental freedoms* agreed by the EU Member States in the context of the *Treaty establishing the European Community* (ECT). The *North American Free Trade Agreement (NAFTA)* liberalizes investment between Mexico, the United States and Canada. At the multilateral level, a *sector-specific* attempt is reflected in the negotiations that led to the *Energy Charter Treaty*, which liberalizes investment in the energy sector among the parties to the treaty.

In the 1990s, a serious effort was made to negotiate a treaty on investment, known as the *Multilateral Agreement on Investment (MAI)*. Negotiated by the OECD, the *MAI* was intended to be incorporated as one of the covered agreements by the WTO (where it would have completed the triumvirate of global liberalization agreements covering goods, services, and investment). [But the *MAI* ultimately failed for a number of reasons, including problems of developing countries, problems of anti-globalization in public opinion as well as problems of environmental and labor protection.]

For many developing country governments as well as NGOs, the provisions of the proposed global investment agreement were "imbalanced." A representative NGO publication from the negotiations period summarized the concerns.

Third World Network, Earth Summit Plus 5 Briefing No. 6, The Multilateral Agreement on Investment (MAI): Impact on Sustainable Development

1997

Part 1: The MAI

The recent worldwide interest and controversy on foreign investment policy has been sparked by the proposal of some developed countries to introduce a legally-binding regime on foreign investment. This is taking place at two places: the WTO and OECD.

* * * The MAI is aimed at protecting and advancing the rights of international investors vis-à-vis host countries. The main elements are:

● The right of entry and establishment of foreign companies in almost all sectors, except security. This means the government will lose its authority to determine which foreign investor it would allow or disallow from entering the country, in all sectors.

● The right to full equity ownership. This means the government would not be allowed to impose a condition that foreign companies should allow a portion of their equity to be locally owned, or that they form joint ventures with local firms or with the state.

- National treatment. This means that the foreign company must be treated on equal or better terms than a local company. Governments will be prevented from granting better or more favourable treatment to local firms, for example in granting contracts or in allowing local banks to set up more branches etc.

- Removal of many regulations and conditions now imposed on foreign companies by the host government (e.g. movement of personnel; performance requirements; allowing foreign firms to take part in privatisation projects).

- Protection of the rights of foreign investors (including regarding non-discrimination, intellectual property, expropriation, compensation, transfer of funds, taxation) such as against closure or expropriation, or full compensation in the event of being asked to close or be taken over;

- Establish a dispute settlement system which makes the agreement legally-binding and enforceable.

The MAI is aimed at setting up an international regime for protection and advancement of international investors' rights. But correspondingly the rights and authority of the host country's government will be either removed or severely restricted.

Moreover, the MAI would impose no obligations on the foreign investor to respect the sovereignty or social and development objectives of the host country. But the host country's government would have many new and heavy obligations towards the foreign investor.

The MAI is therefore very imbalanced, in favour of the foreign investor's rights, and against the rights of the host country, the host government and the local firms (which would lose their present rights to receive more favourable treatment from their government and to be protected from bigger foreign firms so that they can survive and develop).

After the failure of the MAI and the lack of progress in WTO negotiations on investment, attention has turned to bilateral investment treaties. How many of the concerns raised about the MAI also apply to the standard BIT? Given the proliferation of BITs, would a multilateral process, however flawed, have been better?

Early on, the U.S. made provision for investment protection in a number of treaties of friendship, commerce and navigation (FCN Agreements). In *Asakura v. City of Seattle*, set forth in part below, the Supreme Court in 1924 applied the U.S. FCN with Japan in a case which demonstrates some of the basic elements of investment agreements and the relation of the FCN agreements to United States domestic law.

Asakura v. City of Seattle

United States Supreme Court
265 U.S. 332, 44 S.Ct. 515, 68 L.Ed. 1041 (1924)

■ Mr. Justice Butler delivered the opinion of the Court.

Plaintiff in error is a subject of the Emperor of Japan, and, since 1904, has resided in Seattle, Washington. Since July, 1915, he has been engaged in business there as a pawnbroker. The city passed an ordinance, which took effect July 2, 1921, regulating the business of pawnbroker and repealing former ordinances on the same subject. It makes it unlawful for any person to engage in the business unless he shall have a license, and the ordinance provides "that no such license shall be granted unless the applicant be a citizen of the United States." Violations of the ordinance are punishable by fine or imprisonment or both. Plaintiff in error brought this suit in the Superior Court of King County, Washington, against the city, its Comptroller and its Chief of Police to restrain them from enforcing the ordinance against him. He attacked the ordinance on the ground that it violates the treaty between the United States and the Empire of Japan, proclaimed April 5, 1911 * * *. He had about $5,000 invested in his business, which would be broken up and destroyed by the enforcement of the ordinance. The Superior Court granted the relief. On appeal, the [State] Supreme Court held the ordinance valid and reversed the decree. * * *

Does the ordinance violate the treaty? Plaintiff in error invokes and relies upon the following provisions: "The citizens or subjects of each of the High Contracting Parties shall have liberty to enter, travel and reside in the territories of the other to carry on trade, wholesale and retail, to own or lease and occupy houses, manufactories, warehouses and shops, to employ agents of their choice, to lease land for residential and commercial purposes, and generally to do anything incident to or necessary for trade upon the same terms as native citizens or subjects, submitting themselves to the laws and regulations there established. * * * The citizens or subjects of each * * * shall receive, in the territories of the other, the most constant protection, and security for their persons and property * * *."

A treaty made under the authority of the United States "shall be the supreme law of the land; and the judges in every State shall be bound thereby, any thing in the constitution or laws of any State to the contrary notwithstanding." Constitution, Art. VI, § 2.

* * * The treaty was made to strengthen friendly relations between the two nations. The provision quoted establishes the rule of equality between Japanese subjects while in this country and native citizens. Treaties for the protection of citizens of one country residing in the territory of another are numerous, and make for good understanding between nations. The treaty is binding within the State of Washington. * * * The rule of equality established by it cannot be rendered nugatory in any part of the United States by municipal ordinances or state laws. It stands on the same footing of supremacy as do the provisions of the Constitution and laws of

the United States. It operates of itself without the aid of any legislation, state or national; and it will be applied and given authoritative effect by the courts. * * *

The purpose of the ordinance complained of is to regulate, not to prohibit, the business of pawnbroker. But it makes it impossible for aliens to carry on the business. It need not be considered whether the State, if it sees fit, may forbid and destroy the business generally. Such a law would apply equally to aliens and citizens, and no question of conflict with the treaty would arise. The grievance here alleged is that plaintiff in error, in violation of the treaty, is denied equal opportunity.

* * * Decree reversed.

UNCTAD: Investment Instruments Online

http://www.unctadxi.org/templates/ (2008)

What are BITs?

Bilateral investment treaties (BITs) are agreements between two countries for the reciprocal encouragement, promotion and protection of investments in each other's territories by companies based in either country. Treaties typically cover the following areas: scope and definition of investment, admission and establishment, national treatment, most-favoured-nation treatment, fair and equitable treatment, compensation in the event of expropriation or damage to the investment, guarantees of free transfers of funds, and dispute settlement mechanisms, both state-state and investor-state.

For the past decade, UNCTAD has been actively monitoring and analysing the increase in the number of bilateral treaties (BITs) for the promotion and protection of foreign investments. A Compilation of about 1,800 available BITs is now accessible via a double-entry search engine.

UNCTAD Analysis of BITS

* * * The number of BITs increased dramatically during the 1990s. Their number rose from 385 in 1989 to a total of 2,265 in 2003. They now involve 176 countries.

UNCTAD has conducted a number of analytical studies on BITs: "Bilateral Investment Treaties 1959–1999" and "Bilateral Investment Treaties in the Mid–1990s". Analytical information on BITs has also been provided over the years in the World Investment Report Series.

BITs form only part of the international network of investment rules, which also include other bilateral, regional and multilateral trade agreements with investment provisions.

The Compendium on International Investment Instruments is now searchable on-line by keywords, country/region, categories (multilateral, regional, bilateral, non-governmental and prototype instruments) and dates. It seeks to provide a faithful record of the evolution of instruments relating to investment.

Kenneth J. Vandevelde, U.S. International Investment Agreements

p. 1 (2009)

1.1   THE BILATERAL INVESTMENT TREATY

Thirty years ago, the United States inaugurated a bilateral investment treaty (BIT) program. Since the beginning of the program, the principal purpose of the BITs has been to protect U.S. investment in foreign countries. The BITs are successors to the Friendship, Commerce, and Navigation (FCN) treaties that the United States had been negotiating since its War of Independence.

In the first 30 years of the program, the United States concluded 46 BITs with countries in every region of the world. During that same period the United States also concluded 11 free-trade agreements (FTAs) that included investment chapters modeled after the BITs.

The BIT program began in 1977 as a reaction to a large number of expropriations of foreign investment that had occurred in the postwar world and to the growing number of states that questioned whether customary international law required payment of full compensation for expropriated foreign investment. Several European states already had extensive BIT programs dating back to 1959, when Germany concluded the first BIT. The United States hoped to provide treaty protection beyond that accorded by customary international law, to develop a body of state practice in support of protection for foreign investment, and to establish a mechanism whereby its investors could obtain compensation from host states for unlawfully injured investments, without the involvement of the U.S. government.

Summary of U.S. Bilateral Investment Treaty (BIT) Program

Office of the U.S. Trade Representative
http://www.ustr.gov/Trade_Agreements/BIT/Section_Index.html
February 24, 2006

The U.S. bilateral investment treaty (BIT) program helps protect private investment, develop market-oriented policies in partner countries, and promote U.S. exports.

The BIT program's basic aims are to:

• Protect investment abroad in countries where investor rights are not already protected through existing agreements (such as modern treaties of friendship, commerce, and navigation, or free trade agreements);

• Encourage the adoption of market-oriented domestic policies that treat private investment in an open, transparent, and non-discriminatory way; and

• Support the development of international law standards consistent with these objectives.

U.S. BITs provide investments with six core benefits:

• First, U.S. BITs require that investors and their "covered investments" (that is, investments of a national or company of one BIT party in the territory of the other party) be treated as favorably as the host party treats its own investors and their investments or investors and investments from any third country. The BIT generally affords the better of national treatment or most-favored-nation treatment for the full life-cycle of investment—from establishment or acquisition, through management, operation, and expansion, to disposition.

• Second, BITs establish clear limits on the expropriation of investments and provide for payment of prompt, adequate, and effective compensation when expropriation takes place.

• Third, BITs provide for the transferability of investment-related funds into and out of a host country without delay and using a market rate of exchange.

• Fourth, BITs restrict the imposition of performance requirements, such as local content targets or export quotas, as a condition for the establishment, acquisition, expansion, management, conduct, or operation of an investment.

• Fifth, BITs give covered investments the right to engage the top managerial personnel of their choice, regardless of nationality.

• Sixth, BITs give investors from each party the right to submit an investment dispute with the government of the other party to international arbitration. There is no requirement to use that country's domestic courts.

The United States negotiates BITs on the basis of a model text. For further information on the BIT program, contact the bilateral investment treaty coordinators at 202–736–4906 (Department of State) or 202–395–9679 (Office of the U.S. Trade Representative).

NOTE

The United States has negotiated a variety of investment agreements, including the North American Free Trade Agreement (NAFTA) of 1994 (see Chapter 11 of that Agreement), the Central American–Dominican Republic Free Trade Agreement (2004) and some 40 BITS, mostly with developing countries. Selections from the 2004 U.S. Model Bilateral Investment Treaty (BIT) are set forth in the Documentary Supplement. In addition, the U.S. has negotiated a number of relatively soft Trade and Investment Framework Agreements (TIFAs) to serve as consultation mechanisms mostly with countries which have progressed to an early stage of opening their economies to international trade and investment. An example of a TIFA is the Agreement between the U.S. and Algeria of July 13, 2000, and selections from that Agreement are also included in the Documentary Supplement.

These agreements normally employ the expression "investment agreements" in the key operative provisions without elaboration or definition, so it is not surprising to find the issue of definition appearing in litigation, recently in the ICSID *Malaysian Historical Salvors Case* taken up below, following a word about ICSID.

About ICSID

http://icsid.worldbank.org/ICSID/ICSID/AboutICSID_Home.jsp

ICSID is an autonomous international institution established under the Convention on the Settlement of Investment Disputes between States and Nationals of Other States (the ICSID or the Washington Convention) with over one hundred and forty member States. The Convention sets forth ICSID's mandate, organization and core functions. The primary purpose of ICSID is to provide facilities for conciliation and arbitration of international investment disputes.

The ICSID Convention is a multilateral treaty formulated by the Executive Directors of the International Bank for Reconstruction and Development (the World Bank). It was opened for signature on March 18, 1965 and entered into force on October 14, 1966.

The Convention sought to remove major impediments to the free international flows of private investment posed by non-commercial risks and the absence of specialized international methods for investment dispute settlement. ICSID was created by the Convention as an impartial international forum providing facilities for the resolution of legal disputes between eligible parties, through conciliation or arbitration procedures. Recourse to the ICSID facilities is always subject to the parties' consent.

As evidenced by its large membership, considerable caseload, and by the numerous references to its arbitration facilities in investment treaties and laws, ICSID plays an important role in the field of international investment and economic development.

Today, ICSID is considered to be the leading international arbitration institution devoted to investor-State dispute settlement.

In the Matter of Malaysian Historical Salvors SDN BRD and the Government of Malasia

Ad Hoc Committee (ICSID Case No. ARB/05/10 (2009)), http://arbitration.fr/resources/ICSID–ARB–05–10–annulment.pdf

[This case arose initially under a marine salvage contract between the applicant Malaysian Historical Salvors (MHS), a British corporation, and the respondent Government of Malaysia, in a dispute over the sharing of the proceeds of the sale of the finds produced by the successful salvage operations.

In 1817 a British vessel, the *Diana,* sank in waters now part of the Malaysian territorial sea. Under the salvage contract MHS was to find the wreck and salvage the cargo for the Malaysian Government. After research and salvage operations over almost 4 years, MHS found the wreck and recovered almost 24,000 pieces of Chinese porcelain. Part of the porcelain was auctioned by Christie's for about $2.98 million, and a number of pieces were placed in the Malaysian National Museum.

In the initial ICSID arbitration, MHS alleged that it was not fully compensated under the contract, but the Sole Arbitrator dismissed the case for lack of jurisdiction, on the ground that the MHS resources applied to the work did not constitute an "investment" under Article 25(1) of the ICSID Convention (sometimes called the Washington Convention).

In the current proceedings before the ICSID ad Hoc Committee, MHS applied for the annulment of the initial ICSID award. In the current proceedings the Committee considered Article 25(1) which provides that:

> [t]he jurisdiction of the Centre shall extend to a legal dispute arising directly out of an investment, between a Contracting State (or any constituent subdivision or agency of a Contracting State) and a national of another Contracting State, which the parties to the dispute consent in writing to submit to the Centre.

The Committee also considered Article 1 of the bilateral investment agreement (BIT) between the United Kingdom and the Government of Malaysia. Article 1 of the BIT provides in part:

> [f]or the purposes of the Agreement, (1)(a) "investment" means every kind of asset and in particular, though not exclusively, includes: (iii) claims to money or to any performance under contract having a financial value (v) business transactions conferred by law or under contract, including concessions to search for, cultivate, extract or exploit natural resources.

In a 2–3 decision with the majority opinion written by former ICJ President Judge Stephen M. Schwebel, the Ad Hoc Committee annulled the initial award. Portions of that opinion and the dissent follow.]

DECISION ON THE APPLICATION FOR ANNULMENT

* * *

E.   ANALYSIS OF THE *AD HOC* COMMITTEE

56.   This case concerns the interpretation of treaties. The Vienna Convention on the Law of Treaties, a product of the extended codification processes of the International Law Commission of the United Nations led by a succession of exceptionally distinguished Special Rapporteurs, has been widely accepted, 108 States being party. Among the States that have ratified it are Malaysia and the United Kingdom. The Committee notes that the Vienna Convention as such is not applicable to the 1965 Washington Convention nor to the 1981 United Kingdom-Malaysia BIT. The Vienna Convention applies only to treaties which are concluded by States after its

entry into force with regard to such States. Malaysia became party to the Vienna Convention only in 1994. The non-retroactivity of the Vienna Convention is, however, "[w]ithout prejudice to the application of any rules set [in it] to which treaties would be subject under international law independently of the Convention." The Convention's provisions on the interpretation of treaties, embodied in Articles 31 and 32, while contested when adopted, have been accepted by the International Court of Justice and the international community as expressive not only of treaty commitment but of customary international law. The Committee thus considers itself on firm ground in resorting to the customary rules on interpretation of treaties as codified in the Vienna Convention.

57. The "ordinary meaning" [Vienna, Article 31] of the term "investment" is the commitment of money or other assets for the purpose of providing a return. In its context and in accordance with the object and purpose of the treaty—[Vienna Article 31]—which is to promote the flow of private investment to contracting countries by provision of a mechanism which, by enabling international settlement of disputes, conduces to the security of such investment—the term "investment" is unqualified. The purpose of the ICSID Convention was described in a draft of the Convention conveyed by the Bank's General Counsel to the Executive Directors of the Bank in these terms: " '[t]he purpose of' this Convention is to promote the resolution of disputes arising between the contracting States and nationals of other Contracting States by encouraging and facilitating recourse to international conciliation and arbitration." The meaning of the term "investment" may however be regarded as "ambiguous or obscure" under Article 32 of the Vienna Convention and hence justifying resort to the preparatory work of the Convention "to determine the meaning." As the pleadings in the instant case illustrate, there certainly have been marked differences among ICSID tribunals and among commentators on the meaning of "investment" as that term appears in Article 25(1) of the Convention. Thus the provision may be regarded as ambiguous. In any event, courts and tribunals interpreting treaties regularly review the *travaux preparatoires* whenever they are brought to their attention; it is mythological to pretend that they do so only when they first conclude that the term requiring interpretation is ambiguous or obscure.

63. What of the intentions of the Parties in concluding the Washington Convention? The term "investment" was deliberately left undefined. But light is shed on the intentions of the Parties in respect of that term by the Convention's *travaux preparatoires* as well as the Convention's interpretation, by the Executive Directors of the International Bank for Reconstruction and Development in adopting and opening it for signature.

64. The World Bank staff's initial proposal on "The Jurisdiction of the Center" provided, in Section 1(1): "The jurisdiction of the Center shall be limited to disputes between Contracting States and nationals of other Contracting States and shall be based on consent." Section 1(3) provided: "Except as otherwise agreed between the parties, the Center shall not exercise jurisdiction in respect of disputes involving claims of less than the

equivalent of one hundred thousand United States dollars determined as of 'the time of submission of the dispute," The comment on this proviso reads:

> Paragraph (3) places a monetary limit on claims to be submitted to the Center. Arbitration is a not inexpensive procedure and parties should not be forced to have resort to it if the amount claimed remains below a certain limit which, for purposes of illustration, has been put at the equivalent of U.S. $100,000.

66. The reaction of States and their representatives to these proposals was mixed. In the event, their specifications were rejected. While they elicited some support, the prevailing view was that there should be no monetary limit on claims submitted and that the contribution of money or other asset of economic value need not be for an indefinite period or for not less than five years. More than this, a British proposal that omitted any definition of the term "investment," on the ground that a definition would only create jurisdictional difficulties, "was adopted by a large majority in the Legal Committee."

67. That result was consistent with the position of the General Counsel of the Bank, Mr. Broches, who served as chairman of the regional meetings of legal experts of governments and of the Legal Committee. Thus,

> Mr. Broches called attention to the fact that the document did not limit or define the types of disputes which might be submitted to conciliation or arbitration under the auspices of the Center. It was difficult to find a satisfactory definition. There was the danger that recourse to the services of the Center might in a given situation be precluded because the dispute in question did not precisely qualify under the definition of the convention. There was the further danger that a definition might provide a reluctant party with an opportunity to frustrate or delay the proceedings by questioning whether the dispute was encompassed by the definition These possibilities suggested that it was inadvisable to define narrowly the kinds of disputes that could be submitted. Moreover, Mr. Broches added, a contracting state would be free to announce that it did not intend to use the facilities of the Center for particular kinds of disputes.

71. The preparatory work of the Convention as well as the Report of the Executive Directors thus shows that: (a) deliberately no definition of "investment" as that term is found in Article 25(1) was adopted; (b) a floor limit to the value of an investment was rejected; (c) a requirement of indefinite duration of an investment or of a duration of no less than five years was rejected; (d) the critical criterion adopted was the consent of the parties. By the terms of their consent, they could define jurisdiction under the Convention. Paragraph 23 of the Report provides that: "[c]onsent of the parties is the cornerstone of the jurisdiction of the Centre...." Paragraph 27 imports that the term "investment" was left undefined "given the essential requirement of consent by the parties." It continues that "States can make known in advance ... the classes of disputes which

they would or would not submit to the Centre," i.e., they could specify particularities of their consent.

73.   While it may not have been foreseen at the time of the adoption of the ICSID Convention when the number of bilateral investment treaties in force were few, since that date some 2800 bilateral, and three important multilateral, treaties have been concluded, which characteristically define investment in broad, inclusive terms such as those illustrated by the above-quoted Article 1 of the Agreement between Malaysia and the United Kingdom. Some 1700 of those treaties are in force, and the multilateral treaties, particularly the Energy Charter Treaty, which are in force, of themselves endow ICSID with an important jurisdictional reach. It is those bilateral and multilateral treaties which today are the engine of ICSID's effective jurisdiction. To ignore or depreciate the importance of the jurisdiction they bestow upon ICSID, and rather to embroider upon questionable interpretations of the term "investment" as found in Article 25(1) of the Convention, risks crippling the institution.

74.   In the light of this history of the preparation of the ICSID Convention and of the foregoing analysis of the Report of the Executive Directors in adopting it, the Committee finds that the failure of the Sole Arbitrator even to consider, let alone apply, the definition of investment as it is contained in the Agreement to be a gross error that gave rise to a manifest failure to exercise jurisdiction.

Dissenting Opinion of Judge Mohamed Shahabuddeen

2.   Regretfully, I have to forego the company of my distinguished colleagues. The question which separates me from them is whether a contribution to the economic development of the host State is a condition of an ICSID "investment." The Committee recalls the argument of the Applicant that it is not. The Committee's decision agrees with the Applicant's argument; I am of the opposite view.

4.   My main reasons for holding that economic development of the host State is a condition of an ICSID investment are these: *(a)*. However wide is the competence of parties to determine the terms of an investment, that competence is subject to some outer limits outside of their will, if only to measure the width of their competence within those limits. *(b)*. The outer limits in this case included a requirement that an investment must contribute to the economic development of the host State. *(c)*. The Tribunal was correct in finding that the contribution to the economic development of the host State had to be substantial or significant. *(d)*. The Tribunal was also correct in finding that the Applicant's outlay did not promote the economic development of Malaysia in a substantial or significant manner. *(e)*. It is a reversal of the logical process to begin the inquiry with a consideration of what is an investment under the 1981 * * * BIT. And, *(f)*, if the Tribunal erred in holding to these effects, it nevertheless did not manifestly exceed its powers.

34.   As recalled above, Article 31(1) of the Vienna Convention enjoins a search for the "ordinary meaning to be given to the terms of the treaty in

their context and in the light of its object and purpose." Whatever the strict sequence of the statutory steps, the search for the ordinary meaning of investment, sooner or later throws the searcher back on the understanding of the international legal community. The international community would have rejected out of hand the idea that any contribution to the economic development of the host State, however miniscule that contribution is, is sufficient to qualify the whole outlay as an "investment", within the meaning of Article 25(1) of the ICSID Convention. I am confident that the common understanding would have preferred the notion of a "substantial" or "significant" contribution as the Tribunal did.

35.   There is no basis for contending that the general understanding supports the opposite principle that effect has to be given even to minor but negligible matters—unless such a reading is required by the text. There is nothing to that effect in the governing text; Article 25(1) of the ICSID convention does not indicate the improbability of a very tiny contribution to economic development being sufficient to qualify the whole outlay as an ICSID investment. In my opinion, the concept of *de minimis* is a familiar and universal principle; it applies generally—barring a provision to the contrary.

2.   THE FOREIGN INVESTOR'S "RIGHT OF ESTABLISHMENT"

While many countries pursue liberal policies in welcoming FDI, there is apparently no customary international law that embodies the right of establishment. However, many international investment agreements typically provide for "national" and most favored nation (MFN) treatment on establishment issues. There is such protection in the Articles 3 and 4 of the 2004 Model BIT mentioned above, together with reference in Article 1 (definitions) to "investment authorization". Some countries have restrictions such as burdensome reviews regimes and permission requirements which can make entry quite difficult from a practical standpoint, as with the case of the Energy Charter Treaty (ECT) negotiations. The most that ECT negotiators have been able to obtain is a soft "best endeavors" type commitment (see the ECT references and discussion above in Chapter 3.)

Yet the United States has operated a relatively open system with the Committee on Foreign Investment in the United States (CFIUS), established under Section 721 of the Defense Production Act of 1950, known as the Exon–Florio amendments. U.S. law recently became potentially more restrictive under the Foreign Investment and National Security Act of 2007 (FINSA). Further information on the U.S legislation and administration can be found at www.treas.gov/. See also Robert Kimmitt, *Public Footprints in Private Markets*, 87 Foreign Affaires 119 (2008), particularly on the growing problem of sovereign wealth funds, and more generally in Ralph H. Folsom et al., *Principles of International Business Transactions*, Trade and Economic Relations 563, 652 (2005).

The U.S. Government Accounting Office (GAO) has also studied the foreign investment problems as seen in the following excerpts from its 2008 Report.

U.S. GAO Report: Foreign Investment Laws and Policies Regulating Foreign Investment in 10 Countries

http://www.gao.gov/highlights/d08320high.pdf, February 2008

Foreign acquisitions of U.S. companies can pose a significant challenge for the U.S. government because of the need to balance the benefits of foreign investment with national security concerns. The Exon–Florio amendment to the Defense Production Act authorizes the President to suspend or prohibit foreign acquisitions of U.S. companies that may harm national security.

To better understand how other countries deal with similar challenges, GAO [U.S. Government Accounting Office] was asked to identify how other countries address the issues that Exon–Florio is intended to address. Specifically, this report describes selected countries' (1) laws and policies enacted to regulate foreign investment to protect their national security interests and (2) implementation of those laws and policies.

This report updates a 1996 GAO report that describes how four major foreign investors in the United States—France, Germany, Japan, and the United Kingdom—monitored foreign investment in their own countries to protect national security interests. It also examines foreign investment in six additional countries: Canada, China, India, the Netherlands, Russia, and the United Arab Emirates (UAE). GAO reviewed selected laws and regulations and interviewed foreign government officials and others concerning their implementation and any planned changes to their foreign investment laws, regulations, and policies.

As is the case in the United States, the countries we reviewed have enacted laws and instituted policies regulating foreign investment, often to address national security concerns. However, each of the 10 countries has its own concept of national security that influences which particular investments may be restricted. As a result of the differing concepts, restrictions range from requiring approval of investments in a narrowly defined defense sector to broad restrictions on the basis of economic security and cultural policy. In addition, some countries have recently made changes to their laws and policies to more explicitly identify national security as an area of concern, in some cases as the result of controversial investments. Several countries have also introduced lists of strategic sectors in which foreign investment requires government review and approval.

While there are many unique characteristics of the systems employed by the 10 countries to regulate foreign investment, in many ways the systems are similar to each other, and to the U.S. process under Exon–Florio. Eight countries use a formal review process—usually conducted by a government economic body with input from government security bodies—

to review a transaction. Generally, national security is a primary factor or one of several factors considered in evaluating transactions. While the concepts of national security vary from country to country, all countries share concerns about a core set of issues. These include, for example, the defense industrial base, and more recently, investment in the energy sector and investment by state-owned enterprises and sovereign wealth funds. Most countries have established time frames for the review and can place conditions on transactions prior to approval. For example, a country may place national citizenship requirements on company board members.

However, unlike the voluntary notification under Exon–Florio, most countries' reviews are mandatory if the investment reaches certain dollar thresholds or if the buyer will obtain a controlling or blocking share in the acquired company. Further, unlike the United States, five countries allow decisions to be appealed through administrative means or in court.

Two countries do not have a formal review process. The Netherlands restricts entry into certain sectors such as public utilities, and the UAE restricts the extent of ownership allowed in all sectors without a review. In addition to the formal mechanisms, there are unofficial factors that may influence investment in each of the 10 countries. For example, in some countries an informal government preapproval for sensitive transactions may be needed.

NOTE

The Organization for Economic Cooperation and Development (OECD) and the International Monetary Fund (IMF) have been engaged in the task of developing guidelines on "best practices" on foreign sovereign wealth funds (SWFs) to ensure that their foreign investments are based upon economic rather than political or foreign policy objectives. At their June 4–5, 2008 meeting, OECD Ministers adopted unanimously with the adherence of Chile, Estonia and Slovenia, the following Declaration (CMIN(2008)8/FINAL):

> * * * Ministers endorsed the following policy principles for countries receiving SWF investments. These principles reflect long-standing OECD commitments that promote an open global investment environment. They are consistent with OECD countries' rights and obligations under the OECD investment instruments.
>
> Recipient countries should not erect protectionist barriers to foreign investment.
>
> Recipient countries should not discriminate among investors in like circumstances. Any additional investment restrictions in recipient countries should only be considered when policies of general application to both foreign and domestic investors are inadequate to address legitimate national security concerns.
>
> Where such national security concerns do arise, investment safeguards by recipient countries should be:
>
> transparent and predictable,

proportional to clearly-identified national security risks, and subject to accountability in their application.

_____

What are sovereign wealth funds (SWFs)? Simon Johnson, a writer for the IMF's Finance and Development magazine Vol. 44 No. 3, September 2007, www.imf.org, explained as follows:

The Rise of Sovereign Wealth Funds

Sovereign wealth funds are a fairly new name for something that's been around for quite a while: assets held by governments in another country's currency. All countries have foreign exchange reserves (these days, they're typically in dollars, euros, or yen). When a country, by running a current account surplus, accumulates more reserves than it feels it needs for immediate purposes, it can create a sovereign fund to manage those "extra" resources.

Sovereign funds have existed at least since the 1950s, but their total size worldwide has increased dramatically over the past 10–15 years. In 1990, sovereign funds probably held, at most, $500 billion; the current total is an estimated $2–3 trillion and, based on the likely trajectory of current accounts, could reach $10 trillion by 2012.

Currently, more than 20 countries have these funds, and half a dozen more have expressed an interest in establishing one. Still, the holdings remain quite concentrated, with the top five funds accounting for about 70 percent of total assets. Over half of these assets are in the hands of countries that export significant amounts of oil and gas. Norway has a large sovereign fund, as do places as disparate as Alaska, Canada, Russia, and Trinidad and Tobago. About one-third of total assets are held by Asian and Pacific countries, including Australia, China, and Singapore.

_____

The emergence of SWFs as important international investors has given rise to concerns in many counties, usually developed countries, where the SWF investments are made. The concerns stem from the possibility that these investments would be made for political as well as economic reasons and that they might destabilize financial markets.

3.   DIRECT AND INDIRECT EXPROPRIATION OF FOREIGN PROPERTY

3 Hackworth, Digest of International Law 661
U.S. Dept. of State, 1942

On March 18, 1938 the Mexican Government by decree undertook to expropriate the properties in Mexico of certain foreign-owned oil companies operating there, including a number of American-owned companies. In a statement to the press on March 30, 1938 the Secretary of State (Hull) said that this expropriation was "but one incident in a long series of incidents of this character" and accordingly raised "no new question". He said that the subject under consideration between the two Governments was "the matter of compensation for various properties of American citizens expropriated in the past few years" and that it was his earnest hope that a fair and equitable solution of the problem might soon be found. In a note of March 31 addressed to the American Ambassador in Mexico, the President of Mexico declared that his Government would "know how to honor its obligations of today and its obligations of yesterday".

On April 2, 1938 the Department of State instructed the Embassy in Mexico City to inquire when payment might be expected and what specific guaranty would be given that payment would be made.

In a statement released to the press on August 14, 1939 the Acting Secretary of State (Welles) said with reference to the position of the Government of the United States:

> In the decree of expropriation itself, and on numerous occasions subsequently, the Mexican Government recognized its liability to make compensation and stated its willingness to discuss terms with the petroleum companies concerned. Since that time there have been discussions between representatives of the Mexican Government and of the petroleum companies in an endeavor to come to some fair and equitable agreement. This Government has continuously and consistently sought to facilitate and to further these negotiations by conferring with both sides, first with one and then with the other.

* * *

It is of course evident that a solution of this controversy must be found in accordance with the basic principles of international law.

The position taken by the Government of the United States was further set forth in a note of April 3, 1940 from Secretary Hull to the Mexican Ambassador in Washington:

> The Government of the United States readily recognizes the right of a sovereign state to expropriate property for public purposes. This view has been stated in a number of communications addressed to your Government during the past two years and in conversations had with you during that same period regarding the expropriation by your Government of property belonging to American nationals. On each occasion, however, it has been stated with equal emphasis that the right to expropriate property is coupled with and conditioned on the obligation to make adequate, effective and prompt compensation. The legality of an expropriation is in fact dependent upon the observance of this requirement.

* * *

On March 16, 1940 you were good enough to hand to me an informal memorandum pursuant to our earlier discussions of the difficulties arising out of the expropriation by your Government of the oil properties belonging to American nationals. Without undertaking to pass in any way upon the memorandum as a whole, it is important to have a clarification of two or three of the points raised therein.

It is stated (a) that "the Mexican Government judges that the right of expropriation is beyond discussion", and (b) that "there exists no divergence of opinion between the Government of the United States and that of Mexico regarding the right of the Mexican State to expropriate any private property by payment of a just compensation, as Mexico is agreeable to paying such indemnity to the expropriated companies."

I am compelled to take exception to the statements that the "right of expropriation is beyond discussion" and that "there exists no divergence of opinion between the Government of the United States and that of Mexico" in this respect.

As above stated, in the opinion of the Government of the United States the legality of an expropriation is contingent upon adequate, effective and prompt compensation.

Expropriation provisions are common to BITs and recent free trade agreements. For example, Chapter 11 requires the NAFTA parties to:

1. afford U.S., Canadian, and Mexican investors "national treatment" (§ 1102);

2. comply with international law (including "fair and equitable treatment") in dealing with investments (§ 1105); and

3. refrain from acting in a way that either directly expropriates investors' property or, indirectly, is "tantamount to an expropriation" without compensation (§ 1110).

OECD, Resolution of the Council on the Draft Convention on the Protection of Foreign Property

pp. 3, 23 (12 October, 1967)

The Council

* * *

HAVING REGARD to the text of the Draft Convention on the Protection of Foreign Property and to the Notes and Comments constituting its interpretation (hereinafter called the "Draft Convention");

OBSERVING that the Draft Convention embodies recognised principles relating to the protection of foreign property, combined with rules to render more effective the application of these principles;

* * *

NOTING the conclusion of a Convention on the Settlement of Investment Disputes between States and Nationals of Other States;

I. REAFFIRMS the adherence of member States to the principles of international law embodied in the Draft Convention;

II. COMMENDS the Draft Convention as a basis for further extending and rendering more effective the application of these principles;

* * *

DRAFT CONVENTION ON THE PROTECTION OF FOREIGN PROPERTY

Article I
TREATMENT OF FOREIGN PROPERTY

(a) Each Party shall at all times ensure fair and equitable treatment to the property of the nationals of the other Parties. It shall accord within its territory the most constant protection and security to such property and shall not in any way impair the management, maintenance, use, enjoyment or disposal thereof by unreasonable or discriminatory measures. The fact that certain nationals of any State are accorded treatment more favourable than that provided for in this Convention shall not be regarded as discriminatory against nationals of a Party by reason only of the fact that such treatment is not accorded to the latter.

(b) The provisions of this Convention shall not affect the right of any Party to allow or prohibit the acquisition of property or the investment of capital within its territory by nationals of another Party.

Article 3
TAKING OF PROPERTY

No Party shall take any measures depriving, directly or indirectly, of his property a national of another Party unless the following conditions are complied with:

(i) The measures are taken in the public interest and under due process of law;

(ii) The measures are not discriminatory; and

(iii)The measures are accompanied by provision for the payment of just compensation. Such compensation shall represent the genuine value of the property affected, shall be paid without undue delay, and shall be transferable to the extent necessary to make it effective for the national entitled thereto.

NOTE

The U.N. General Assembly has adopted two principal resolutions on the subject of compensation in accordance with international law, but there exists an apparent conflict between the U.N General Assembly resolution of 1962 which follows and the next following U.N. Charter of Economic Rights and Duties of States of 1974. The former provides for international standards and the latter for national standards of compensation. In the *Texaco case,* below, the arbitrator had to make a determination as to which of the two instruments makes the proper statement of the customary international law on this subject.

Permanent Sovereignty Over Natural Resources

General Assembly Resolution 1803 (XVII), December 14, 1962
U.N. G.A.O.R. 17th Sess., Supp. No. 17 (A/5217), p. 15

The General Assembly,

Recalling its resolutions 523(VI) of 12 January 1952 and 626(VII) of 21 December 1952,

* * *

Declares that:

1.   The right of peoples and nations to permanent sovereignty over their natural wealth and resources must be exercised in the interest of their national development and of the well-being of the people of the State concerned.

4.   Nationalization, expropriation or requisitioning shall be based on grounds or reasons of public utility, security or the national interest which are recognized as overriding purely individual or private interests, both domestic and foreign. In such cases the owner shall be paid appropriate compensation, in accordance with the rules in force in the State taking such measures in the exercise of its sovereignty and in accordance with international law. In any case where the question of compensation gives rise to a controversy, the national jurisdiction of the State taking such measures shall be exhausted. However, upon agreement by sovereign States and other parties concerned, settlement of the dispute should be made through arbitration or international adjudication.

Charter of Economic Rights and Duties of States

General Assembly Resolution 3281 (XXIX)
UNGAOR 29th Sess. Supp. No. 31 (1974) 50, 14 I.L.M. 251 (1975), 12 December 1974

Article 2

1.   Every State has and shall freely exercise full Permanent sovereignty, including possession, use and disposal, over all its wealth, natural resources and economic activities.

2.   Each State has the right:

(a) To regulate and exercise authority over foreign investment within its national jurisdiction in accordance with its laws and regulations and in conformity with its national objectives and priorities. No State shall be compelled to grant preferential treatment to foreign investment;

(b) To regulate and supervise the activities of transnational corporations within its national jurisdiction and take measures to ensure that such activities comply with its laws, rules and regulations and conform with its economic and social policies. Transnational corporations shall not intervene in the internal affairs of a host State. Every State should, with full regard for its sovereign rights, co-operate with other States in the exercise of the right set forth in this subparagraph;

(c) To nationalize, expropriate or transfer ownership of foreign property, in which case appropriate compensation should be paid by the State adopting such measures, taking into account its relevant laws and regulations and all circumstances that the State considers pertinent. In any case where the question of compensation gives rise to a controversy, it shall be settled under the domestic law of the nationalizing State and by its tribunals, unless it is freely and mutually agreed by all States concerned that other peaceful means be sought on the basis of the sovereign equality of States and in accordance with the principle of free choice of means.

Texaco Overseas Petroleum Co. and California Asiatic Oil Co. v. The Government of the Libyan Arab Republic*

Dupuy, Sole Arbitrator, Award on the Merits, 1977
63 INTL L.REP. 389, 486 (1979)

[In this arbitration the plaintiffs sought relief from the Libyan government's nationalization of the plaintiffs' property. The Sole Arbitrator's award examines the effect of the U.N. General Assembly resolutions set forth immediately above. The arbitrator decided that the arbitration clause in the concession agreements referred to "international law" as the rule of decision, rather than the national law of the host state. Then the Sole Arbitrator directed himself to the content of the international law that was to govern. One aspect of that problem is dealt with here.]

83.   The general question of the legal validity of the Resolutions of the United Nations has been widely discussed by the writers. [citations omitted]

85.   * * *

The conditions under which Resolution 3281 (XXIX) proclaiming the Charter of Economic Rights and Duties of States, was adopted also show unambiguously that there was no general consensus of the States with respect to the most important provisions and in particular those concerning nationalization. Having been the subject matter of a roll-call vote, the Charter was adopted by 118 votes to 6, with 10 abstentions. The analysis of votes on specific sections of the Charter is most significant insofar as the present case is concerned. From this point of view, paragraph 2(c) of Article 2 of the Charter, which limits consideration of the characteristics of

---

* Text supplied by counsel for the plaintiffs. The text is available at 53 I.L.M. 389 (1979).

compensation to the State and does not refer to international law, was voted by 104 to 16, with 6 abstentions, all of the industrialized countries with market economies having abstained or having voted against it.

86. * * *

As this Tribunal has already indicated, the legal value of the resolutions which are relevant to the present case can be determined on the basis of circumstances under which they were adopted and by analysis of the principles which they state: With respect to the first point, the absence of any binding force of the resolutions of the General Assembly of the United Nations implies that such resolutions must be accepted by the members of the United Nations in order to be legally binding. In this respect, the Tribunal notes that only Resolution 1803 (XVII) of 14 December 1962 was supported by a majority of Member States representing all of the various groups. By contrast, the other Resolutions mentioned above, and in particular those referred to in the Libyan Memorandum, were supported by a majority of States but not by any of the developed countries with market economies which carry on the largest part of international trade.

87. With respect to * * * the appraisal of the legal value on the basis of the principles stated, it appears essential to this Tribunal to distinguish between those provisions stating the existence of a right on which the generality of the States has expressed agreement and those provisions introducing new principles which were rejected by certain representative groups of States and having nothing more than a de lege ferenda value only in the eyes of the States which have adopted them; as far as the others are concerned, the rejection of these same principles implies that they consider them as being contra lege. With respect to the former, which proclaim rules recognized by the community of nations, they do not create a custom but confirm one by formulating it and specifying its scope, thereby making it possible to determine whether or not one is confronted with a legal rule. As has been noted by Ambassador Castaneda, "[such resolutions] do not create the law; they have a declaratory nature of noting what does exist" (129 R.C.A.D.I. 204 (1970), at 315).

On the basis of the circumstances of adoption mentioned above and by expressing an opinio juris communes, Resolution 1803 (XVII) seems to this Tribunal to reflect the state of customary law existing in this field. Indeed, on the occasion of the vote on a resolution finding the existence of a customary rule, the States concerned clearly express their views. The consensus by a majority of States belonging to the various representative groups indicates without the slightest doubt universal recognition of the rules therein incorporated, i.e., with respect to nationalization and compensation the use of the rules in force in the nationalizing State, but all this in conformity with international law.

89. Such an attitude is further reinforced by an examination of the general practice of relations between States with respect to investments. This practice is in conformity, not with the provisions of Article 2(c) of the above-mentioned Charter conferring exclusive jurisdiction on domestic legislation and courts, but with the exception stated at the end of this

paragraph. Thus a great many investment agreements entered into between industrial States or their nationals, on the one hand, and developing countries, on the other, state, in an objective way, the standards of compensation and further provide, in case of dispute regarding the level of such compensation, the possibility of resorting to an international tribunal. In this respect, it is particularly significant in the eyes of this Tribunal that no fewer than 65 States, as of 31 October 1974, had ratified the Convention on the Settlement of Investment Disputes between States and Nationals of other States, dated March 18, 1965.

* * *

NOTES AND QUESTIONS

1. Thus the Tribunal declined to accept the majority vote in the General Assembly for texts stating international legal principles on expropriation of resources in the absence of a general consensus reflecting the views not only of the majority but also of the minority on that issue. The International Court of Justice employed similar reasoning in its opinion on the *Legality of the Threat or Use of Nuclear Weapons* (35 I.L.M. 809, paras. 68–71 (1996)).

2. What would be the risks to be foreseen in having a precise definition of "investments" in the ICSID Convention or in the BITS?

3. What possible problems might a host state foresee in granting uncontrolled or unrestricted rights of entry for investments originating from a BIT partner country? How would the home state and the investor view the same question? Should there be an overall international policy view of this question in terms of the generally accepted investment liberalization policy?

4. In *Asakura v. City of Seattle* what was the treaty basis of Mr. Asakura's claim? What if there had been a MFN type clause? What if there had been no treaty?

5. Do you see significant differences in the Hull Rule formulation as reported in Hackworth and the OECD formulation some 30 years later? How would you analyze the legal effect of the OECD Council Resolution on the draft convention on protection of foreign property?

6. Do you agree with the process by which Arbitrator Dupuy in the Texaco case resolved the apparent conflict between GA RES 1803 (XVII) on Permanent Sovereignty and GA RES 3281 (XXI) on the Economic Rights and Duties of States? Why?

7. Would you consider that the Hull Rule of "adequate, effective, and prompt" compensation is now established as a rule of customary international law applicable in cases in the absence of a treaty rule?

The Convention on the Settlement of Investment Disputes (ICSID), relied upon above by the sole arbitrator, results from a World Bank initiative directed toward pragmatic, development-related, ad hoc, settlements and arbitration. ICSID provides arbitration and conciliation facilities for disputes between states and investors, who might not be comfortable bringing disputes to the national courts of either the home or host state. Generally, in an ICSID arbitration the parties decide on the composition of the arbitral tribunal as well as the substantive rules to be applied. You will find an example of an important ICSID arbitration award below in the *LG&E Energy Corporation* case. ICSID does not formulate or require acceptance of legal rules as international law. Had it done so a considerable portion of the Bank's membership would not have accepted it. (See also the Banks Guidelines on the Treatment of Foreign Direct Investment (1992) 31 I.L.M. 1363 (1992)).

The Energy Charter Treaty

Done at Lisbon, December 17, 1995
ECT Secretariat, The Energy Charter Treaty and Related Documents, 2004,
34 I.L.M. 360 (1995)*

ARTICLE 13

EXPROPRIATION

(1) Investments of Investors of a Contracting Party in the Area of any other Contracting Party shall not be nationalized, expropriated or subjected to a measure or measures having effect equivalent to nationalization or expropriation (hereinafter referred to as "Expropriation") except where such Expropriation is:

   (a) for a purpose which is in the public interest

   (b) not discriminatory;

   (c) carried out under due process of law, and

   (d) accompanied by the payment of prompt, adequate and effective compensation.

Such compensation shall amount to the fair market value of the Investment expropriated at the time immediately before the Expropriation, or impending Expropriation became known in such a way as to affect the value of the Investment (hereinafter referred to as the "Valuation Date"). Such fair market value shall at the request of the Investor be expressed in a Freely Convertible Currency on the basis of the market rate of exchange existing for that currency on the Valuation Date. Compensation shall also include interest at a commercial rate established on a market basis from the date of Expropriation until the date of payment.

(2) The Investor shall have the right to prompt review under the law of the Contracting Party making the Expropriation by a judicial or other competent and independent authority of that Contracting Party, of its case,

---

* Entered into force on January 16, 1998. For current status see www.encharter.org. This Treaty represents one of the most recent and significant formulations of international law on expropriation. Signatories include the Russian Federation (since reported to be withdrawing) and many former members of the USSR, Eastern European and Asian countries as well as the EU and its Member States. The U.S. has not yet signed the treaty.

of the valuation of its Investment, and of the payment of compensation, in accordance with the principles set out in paragraph (1). * * *

LG&E Energy Corp. and Argentine Republic

ICSID Case No. ARB/02/1 (October 3, 2006)
46 I.L.M. 40 (2007)

[LG&E is a U.S. corporation investor in the Argentine gas industry which suffered serious losses in the Argentine economic crisis of the 1990s. In 1991 Argentina had enacted a Convertibility Law fixing the exchange rate for its currency against the dollar and also adopted a gas distribution licensing system providing for operators transportation and distribution tariffs to be calculated in dollars, tariffs which the Government could not change without the consent of the licensees. Thereafter LG&E was induced to purchase interests in 3 newly privatized gas companies which were operated under the licensing system. A later period of serious economic crisis of "catastrophic proportions", included severe devaluation of the national currency, strikes of millions of workers, a 25% unemployment rate, dramatically increased poverty and failures of national health services, widespread hunger and in one month the resignations of five successive presidential administrations, threatening the total collapse of the Government and the State. The Argentine Congressional responses included the adoption of a Public Emergency and Foreign Exchange System Reform Law that eliminated the above dollar tariffs protections and allegedly made it impossible for LG&E to continue its Argentine business as expected with the 3 gas companies.

Relying on the Bilateral Investment Agreement of 1994 between Argentina and the United States, LG&E initiated this ICSID arbitration, stating claims for breach of the standard of "fair equitable treatment", the rules against arbitrary measures and indirect expropriation of the LG&E investment without compensation, all in breach of the BIT and the rules of customary international law. The damages sought fell into the range of $248 to $268 million. Argentina denied the foregoing claims and interposed the defense of necessity under the circumstances of national economic crisis. The Arbitration Tribunal accepted the fair and equitable treatment as the basis for liability, rejected the arbitrary measures claim, and took up the expropriation and necessity issues in the portions of its unanimous opinion that follow.]

D. Considerations on Indirect Expropriation

1. Parties' Positions

176. LG&E seeks a declaration from this Tribunal that Argentina expropriated LG&E's investment in the Argentine gas-distribution sector without compensation in violation of Article IV of the Treaty, which provides, in part:

"1. Investments shall not be expropriated or nationalized either directly or indirectly through measures tantamount to expropriation or nationalization ('expropriation') except for a public purpose; in a non-discriminatory manner; upon payment of prompt, adequate and effective compensation; and in accordance with due process of law and the general principles of treatment provided for in Article II(2)."

177. LG&E articulates its expropriation claim as one of indirect expropriation. In other words, LG&E argues that the Argentine Government's treatment of Claimants' investment in the Licensees [the 3 corporations] constitutes an indirect expropriation of the investments because the value of LG&E's holdings in the Licenses has been reduced by more than 90% as a result of Respondent's abrogation of the principal guarantees of the tariff system * * *.

178. LG&E contends that, pursuant to Article IV of the Bilateral Treaty, it is entitled to compensation equivalent to the fair market value of the expropriated investment immediately before the expropriation was committed. Claimants pinpoint the date of expropriation in this case as the date on which Respondent's course of conduct finally resulted in the virtual destruction of the value of the investment—not later than August 2000, when the Argentine court enjoined implementation of the 17 July 2000 agreement * * *.

2. Tribunal's Analysis

185. In order to establish the sustainability of an indirect expropriation, the Tribunal must define the concept. Generally, bilateral treaties do not define what constitutes an expropriation—they just make an express reference to "expropriation" and add the language "any other action that has equivalent effects." Likewise, Article IV of the Bilateral Treaty does not define the term "expropriation" and does not establish which measures, actions or conduct would constitute acts tantamount to expropriation. Therefore, the Tribunal shall look to international law in determining the relevant criteria for evaluating this claim.

186. A State may, at its discretion, under Article IV of the Bilateral Treaty and in accordance with general principles of international law, make use of its sovereign power to expropriate private property with the purpose of satisfying a public interest. However, expropriation in any of its modalities requires due process and compensation under international law.

187. Although in scholarly authority two kinds of expropriation are known, we will obviously skip the direct one, understood as the forcible appropriation by the State of the tangible or intangible property of individuals by means of administrative or legislative action. The parties admit that the claim at issue does not involve a direct expropriation. In the case of the Argentine Republic, one could not say that it appropriated Claimants' investment, which is the indispensable requirement if one is to talk of direct expropriation. Instead, we shall limit ourselves to the assumption of the indirect expropriation, one qualified by the Bilateral Treaty itself as "measures tantamount to expropriation."

188.   Generally, the expression "equivalent to expropriation" or "tantamount to expropriation" found in most bilateral treaties, may refer both, to the so-called "creeping expropriation" and to the *de facto* expropriation. Their common point rests in the fact that the host State's actions or conduct do not involve "overt taking" but the taking occurs when governmental measures have "effectively neutralize[d] the benefit of property of the foreign owner." Ownership or enjoyment can be said to be "neutralized" where a party no longer is in control of the investment, or where it cannot direct the day-to-day operations of the investment. As to the differences, it is usual to say that indirect expropriation may show itself in a gradual or growing form—creeping expropriation—or through a sole and unique action, or through actions being quite close in time or simultaneous—*de facto* expropriation.

3.   Tribunal's Conclusion

198.   In the circumstances of this case, although the State adopted severe measures that had a certain impact on Claimants' investment, especially regarding the earnings that the Claimants expected, such measures did not deprive the investors of the right to enjoy their investment. * * * [T]he true interests at stake here are the investment's asset base, the value of which has rebounded since the economic crisis of December 2001 and 2002.

199.   Further, it cannot be said that Claimants lost control over their shares in the licensees, even though the value of the shares may have fluctuated during the economic crisis, or that they were unable to direct the day-to-day operations of the licensees in a manner different than before the measures were implemented.

200.   Thus, the effect of the Argentine State's actions has not been permanent on the value of the Claimants' shares', and Claimants' investment has not ceased to exist. Without a permanent, severe deprivation of LG&E's rights with regard to its investment, or almost complete deprivation of the value of LG&E's investment, the Tribunal concludes that these circumstances do not constitute expropriation.

E.   State of Necessity

1.   Parties' Positions

202.   Respondent pleads its defense as a "state of necessity" defense, available under Argentine law, Treaty in Articles XI and IV(3), as well as customary international law.

203.   Claimants reject Respondent's contentions regarding the alleged state of necessity defense. Claimants contend that Article XI is not applicable in the case of an economic crisis because the public order and essential security interests elements are intentionally narrow in scope, limited to security threats of a physical nature.

204.   Article XI of the Bilateral Treaty provides:

"This Treaty shall not preclude the application by either Party of measures necessary for the maintenance of public order, the fulfillment of its obligations with respect to the maintenance or restoration of international peace or security, or the protection of its own essential security interests."

205.   The Tribunal's analysis to determine the applicability of Article XI of the Bilateral Treaty is twofold. First, the Tribunal must decide whether the conditions that existed in Argentina during the relevant period were such that the State was entitled to invoke the protections included in Article XI of the Treaty. Second, the Tribunal must determine whether the measures implemented by Argentina were necessary to maintain public order or to protect its essential security interests, albeit in violation of the Treaty.

226.   In the judgment of the Tribunal, from 1 December 2001 until 26 April 2003, Argentina was in a period of crisis during which it was necessary to enact measures to maintain public order and protect its essential security interests.

229.   Thus, Argentina is excused under Article XI from liability for any breaches of the Treaty between 1 December 2001 and 26 April 2003. The reasons are the following:

230.   These dates coincide, on the one hand, with the Government's announcement of the measure freezing funds, which prohibited bank account owners from withdrawing more than one thousand pesos monthly and, on the other hand, with the election of President Kirchner. The Tribunal marks these dates as the beginning and end of the period of extreme crisis in view of the notorious events that occurred during this period.

231.   Evidence has been put before the Tribunal that the conditions as of December 2001 constituted the highest degree of public disorder and threatened Argentina's essential security interests. This was not merely a period of "economic problems" or "business cycle fluctuation" as Claimants described. * * * Extremely severe crises in the economic, political and social sectors reached their apex and converged in December 2001, threatening total collapse of the Government and the Argentine State.

232.   All of the major economic indicators reached catastrophic proportions in December 2001. An accelerated deterioration of Argentina's Gross Domestic Product (GDP) began in December 2001, falling 10 to 15 percent faster than the previous year. Private consumption dramatically dropped in the fourth quarter of 2001, accompanied by a severe drop in domestic prices.

237.   All of these devastating conditions—economic, political, social— in the aggregate triggered the protections afforded under Article XI of the Treaty to maintain order and control the civil unrest.

238.   The Tribunal rejects the notion that Article XI is only applicable in circumstances amounting to military action and war. Certainly, the conditions in Argentina in December 2001 called for immediate, decisive

action to restore civil order and stop the economic decline. To conclude that such a severe economic crisis could not constitute an essential security interest is to diminish the havoc that the economy can wreak on the lives of an entire population and the ability of the Government to lead. When a State's economic foundation is under siege, the severity of the problem can equal that of any military invasion.

240.   The Tribunal has determined that Argentina's enactment of the Emergency Law was a necessary and legitimate measure on the part of the Argentine Government. Under the conditions the Government faced in December 2001, time was of the essence in crafting a response. Drafted in just six days, the Emergency Law took the swift, unilateral action against the economic crisis that was necessary at the time. * * *

242.   * * * The severe devaluation of the peso against the dollar renders the Government's decision to abandon the calculation of tariffs in dollars reasonable. Similarly, the Government deemed that freezing gas tariffs altogether during the crisis period was necessary, and Claimants have not provided any reason as to why such measure would not provide immediate relief from the crisis.

243.   The Tribunal will now turn to Article IV(3) of the Treaty, which provides:

> "Nationals or companies of either Party whose investments suffer losses in the territory of the other Party owing to war or other armed conflict, revolution, *state of national emergency*, insurrection, civil disturbance or other similar events shall be accorded treatment by such other Party no less favorable than that accorded to its own nationals or companies or to nationals or companies of any third country, whichever is the more favorable treatment, as regards any measures it adopts in relation to such losses." (Emphasis added)

244.   Article IV(3) of the Treaty confirms that the States Party to the Bilateral Treaty contemplated the state of national emergency as a separate category of exceptional circumstances. That is in line with the Tribunal's interpretation of Article XI of the Treaty. Furthermore, the Tribunal has determined, as a factual matter that the grave crisis in Argentina lasted from 1 December 2001 until 26 April 2003. It has not been shown convincingly to the Tribunal that during that period the provisions of Article IV(3) of the Treaty have been violated by Argentina. On the contrary, during that period, the measures taken by Argentina were "across the board."

245.   In the previous analysis, the Tribunal has determined that the conditions in Argentina from 1 December 2001 until 26 April 2003 were such that Argentina is excused from liability for the alleged violation of its Treaty obligations due to the responsive measures it enacted. The concept of excusing a State for the responsibility for violation of its international obligations during what is called a "state of necessity" or "state of emergency" also exists in international law. While the Tribunal considers that the protections afforded by Article XI have been triggered in this case,

and are sufficient to excuse Argentina's liability, the Tribunal recognizes that satisfaction of the state of necessity standard as it exists in international law (reflected in Article 25 of the ILC's Draft Articles on State Responsibility) supports the Tribunal's conclusion.

246.   In international law, a state of necessity is marked by certain characteristics that must be present in order for a State to invoke this defense. As articulated by Roberto Ago, one of the mentors of the Draft Articles on State Responsibility, a state of necessity is identified by those conditions in which a State is threatened by a serious danger to its existence, to its political or economic survival, to the possibility of maintaining its essential services in operation, to the preservation of its internal peace, or to the survival of part of its territory. In other words, the State must be dealing with interests that are essential or particularly important.

247.   The United Nations Organization has understood that the invocation of a state of necessity depends on the concurrent existence of three circumstances, namely: a danger to the survival of the State, and not for its interests, is necessary; that danger must not have been created by the acting State; finally, the danger should be serious and imminent, so that there are no other means of avoiding it.

248.   The concept of state of necessity and the requirements for its admissibility lead to the idea of prevention: the State covers itself against the risk of suffering certain damages. Hence, the possibility of alleging the state of necessity is closely bound by the requirement that there should be a serious and imminent threat and no means to avoid it. Such circumstances, in principle, have been left to the State's subjective appreciation, a conclusion accepted by the International Law Commission. Nevertheless, the Commission was well aware of the fact that this exception, requiring admissibility, has been frequently abused by States, thus opening up a very easy opportunity to violate the international law with impunity. The Commission has set in its Draft Articles on State Responsibility very restrictive conditions to account for its admissibility, reducing such subjectivity.

(v) Conclusions of the Tribunal

266.   Based on the analysis of the state of necessity, the Tribunal concludes that, first, said state started on 1 December 2001 and ended on 26 April 2003; second, during that period Argentina is exempt of responsibility, and accordingly, the Claimants should bear the consequences of the measures taken by the host State; and finally, the Respondent should have restored the tariff regime on 27 April 2003, or should have compensated the Claimants, which did not occur. As a result, Argentina is liable as from that date to Claimants for damages.

NOTES AND QUESTIONS

1.   *LG&E* is not the only ICSID arbitration authority on the key issues of that case. In three parallel cases, ICSID arbitrators adopted contrary views on such issues as the measure of deference to paid the host state in crafting

emergency response measures, on the application of the BIT and the customary international law of necessity, on conflation of the two, and on the compliance of Argentina with the strict requirements of the I.L.C's statement of the rules on necessity. Overall the three other panels found Argentina to be fully responsible and liable to the investors for the harms suffered. Argentina's application for annulment of one of the other cases was rejected, largely on the ground that the technically limited scope of the Appellate Committee's jurisdiction. Background on the four cases and argument favoring the reasoning and outcome of *LG&E* are found in William Burke–White, "The Argentine Financial Crisis: State Liability Under BIT and the Legitimacy of the ICSID System", U. of Penn. Inst. for Law and Econ Research, Paper No. 08–01 (2008) http://ssrn.com/abstract= 1088837.

Disputes under investor-state arbitration clauses in BITs, as well as the parallel provisions of Chapter 11 of NAFTA, have raised difficult questions of social or environmental policy. Should engineering company Bechtel be able to claim compensation from Bolivia when the Bolivian government cancelled a contract for provision of water services after a company affiliate raised water rates, causing widespread protests that resulted in several deaths? Should a Canadian producer of gasoline additive MTBE be able to sue the U.S. because the State of California decides, on environmental grounds, to ban the additive? Consider the following description:

Sanford E. Gaines, International Decision: Methanex Corp. v. United States, Partial Award on Jurisdiction and Admissibility*

100 AM. J. INT'L L. 683 (2006)

During the 1990s, methyl tertiary butyl ether (MTBE) was the preferred oxygenate additive for California gasoline refiners striving to meet U.S. and California fuel standards intended to reduce air pollution. Beginning in 1996, however, MTBE contamination from leaking gasoline tanks forced dozens of cities in California to close wells that supplied municipal drinking water. In 1999, the governor of California directed state agencies to phase out the use of MTBE in California by the end of 2002. Methanol, an alcohol derived from natural gas, is a key ingredient in the manufacture of MTBE. On December 3, 1999, Methanex Corporation, a Canadian corporation that was the dominant supplier of methanol to California producers of MTBE, filed a claim for compensation of $970 million against the United States contesting the governor's action under the investor-state arbitration provisions of Chapter 11 ("Investment") of the North American Free Trade Agreement (NAFTA). In dismissing all elements of Methanex's claim, the arbitral tribunal found in both its partial (Partial) and final (Final) awards that it lacked jurisdiction under Chapter 11 because the

---

* Footnotes omitted.

California measures regulating MTBE were not ones "relating to" Methanex or its investments in methanol as required by NAFTA Article 1101. The tribunal also made decisions to enhance public participation in its proceedings. [Methanex challenged California's decision as violating NAFTA's Article 1105 minimum standard of fair and equitable treatment. Methanex also claimed the California measure was "both directly and indirectly tantamount to an expropriation" under Article 1110.]

Relevant to Methanex's claim, MTBE competes in the gasoline market against another oxygenate, ethanol, which is an alcohol fermented from corn or sugar. Archer Daniels Midland Company (ADM), a U.S. company, is the major producer of ethanol for the U.S. market.

* * *

The *Methanex* arbitration unfolded during a period when claims and awards in other NAFTA Chapter 11 arbitrations had persuaded many in the North American environmental community that NAFTA's investment provisions posed a serious, unexpected threat to local environmental protection measures. The Methanex filing and its high-value compensation claim created particular alarm in the North American environmental community. In the six-year history of NAFTA to that point, it was the fourth substantial investor claim under Chapter 11 seeking compensation because of local or national environmental measures. Canada had already settled one case and paid compensation.

The two other claims then pending against environmental measures resulted in partial or final awards of compensation that reinforced the anxiety in civil society. Substantively, environmentalists and others were especially critical of the awards' broad interpretations of Article 1105's "fair and equitable treatment" requirements and Article 1110's "tantamount to expropriation" language. Further fueling criticism of the NAFTA Chapter 11 arbitration process were the privacy of tribunal hearings, which were held behind closed doors, and the official inaccessibility of the pleadings and briefs during the early stages of the arbitration proceedings.

The *Methanex* awards should go some way to ease those concerns and thus to reshape the debate on investor-protection agreements.

* * *

The partial award is the first Chapter 11 ruling to confront the fundamental question whether an investor whose activities are not being directly regulated, but whose market is being substantially affected by government regulation of some other activity or product, can maintain a claim under Chapter 11. The *Methanex* tribunal correctly judged this to be a bridge too far, one that would open investor-state arbitration to virtually any investor financially affected by government action. For the reasons given by the United States and reiterated by the tribunal itself, a narrow reading of "legally significant connection" between investor and measure is especially comforting to governments that are considering environmental regulation, which almost invariably imposes economic costs, and sometimes even direct business losses, on a variety of private parties.

Even so, the tribunal and the United States recognized that in the context of NAFTA's national treatment obligation, a showing of specific intent in adopting a measure to discriminate against a foreign investor and in favor of a competing domestic investor would establish a connection that is "legally significant." That was precisely the thrust of Methanex's unsuccessful effort in the second round to show that Governor Davis intended not just to regulate MTBE, but, in particular, to disadvantage Methanex in favor of ADM. Similarly, failure to accord a foreign investor the minimum standard of treatment under international law (as required by Article 1105) would connect a measure and an investor in a "legally significant" way even when the underlying laws or regulations, if fairly applied, were beyond challenge.

* * *

Article 1105. The tribunal found no unfair treatment of Methanex that was violative of international law norms under Article 1105. Earlier Chapter 11 tribunals had read Article 1105 broadly. In reaction to these awards, the NAFTA Free Trade Commission (FTC), during the long course of the *Methanex* arbitration, issued an interpretation of Article 1105, which the tribunal properly treated as binding on it under NAFTA Article 1131(2). That interpretation expressly confines Article 1105 to the "customary international law minimum standard of treatment of aliens"; the terms " 'fair and equitable treatment' and 'full protection and security' do not require treatment in addition to or beyond" such customary international law. This narrow interpretation of the minimum standard of treatment to be accorded to foreign investors is favorable to environmental protection interests; it affords governments substantial latitude in their regulatory treatment of foreign investors and helps maintain a degree of parity between foreign investors and domestic investors with respect to the grounds on which they can successfully argue for compensation because of disparate or abusive treatment by the governing authorities.

Article 1110. The vexing interpretive question in Article 1110 is whether the phrase "tantamount to expropriation" merely clarifies the right to compensation for indirect expropriations, or whether it creates a broader right for compensation for measures with lesser effect on the investment. Distancing itself from some earlier tribunal awards that appeared to give "tantamount to expropriation" an unduly broad reading, the *Methanex* tribunal enunciated a restrictive approach in denying Methanex's claim of Article 1110 expropriation due to regulatory measures:

But as a matter of general international law, a non-discriminatory regulation for a public purpose, which is enacted in accordance with due process and which affects, inter alios, a foreign investor or investment is not deemed expropriatory and compensable unless specific commitments had been given by the regulating government to the then putative foreign investor contemplating investment that the government would refrain from such regulation. (Final, pt. IV.D, para. 7)

In conclusion, the *Methanex* awards gave readings to each of the critical articles of NAFTA Chapter 11 that set a high bar for investor claimants to vault over to gain compensation from host states. They reduce the chance for a successful claim, and thus the incentive for investors to mount challenges to national regulatory actions. This outcome is beneficial from the environmental and civil society perspectives; the substantial threat to national autonomy for bona fide regulation of business activities that many saw in early Chapter 11 awards appears to have receded, without depriving investors of the opportunity to challenge clearly discriminatory or abusive government behavior. Moreover, with the endorsement of the NAFTA Free Trade Commission, the *Methanex* tribunal also established important rights of civil society participation and observation in investor-state arbitrations. These outcomes give the *Methanex* Chapter 11 arbitration special significance for the continuing international dialogue about international protection of investor rights and the procedures for resolving foreign-investor claims against host country governments.

4.   THE GENERAL PROBLEM OF ENFORCEMENT

With the law of expropriation favorably developed to protect the investor, the way is now clearer for the investor to consider the choice of procedures for pursuing its claims. The investor may look with renewed confidence at procedures for direct action as a private party (negotiation, mediation, litigation in the host state); and if the views of its home government provide encouragement, the possibility of enlisting its supports its government at the international level might also be considered. The international system envisages both lines of action in appropriate cases.

However, investors might not find those procedures sufficient, either to ensure a reasonable possibility of relief, or to promise a sound basis for incurring the risks of new or increased foreign direct investment. For future FDI, the investor might examine other measures of protection which could be taken *before* the investment is made, namely insurance against expropriation risks. The World Bank's Multilateral Investment Guarantee Agency (MIGA) was created in 1988 to cover a number of non-commercial risks, including currency transfer, expropriation and similar measures, breach of contract by the host state, and war and civil disturbances. This Agency insures against partial or total loss from acts that reduce ownership or control but not against non-discriminatory acts of hosts in exercising regulatory authority. The World Banks insurance offers some multilateral advantages and the high standing of the Bank, without being closely identified directly with the U.S., unlike another investment insurance issuer, the American OPIC. OPIC is the U.S. government's Overseas Private Investment Corporation. OPIC's program of investment insurance can cover inconvertibility of currency, expropriation or confiscation of property, and property loss caused by war, revolution, insurrection or civil strife, plus business interruption due to any of the foregoing.

Another approach would be (or might not be) for governments to establish new procedures and remedies for the investor. One of these might be a proceeding by the investor in courts of the home state or other states against transferees or holders (traffickers) of the expropriated property, as provided for the Cuban nationalizations in the Helms–Burton Act to which we now turn.

Cuban Liberty and Democratic Solidarity (Libertad) Act of 1996 (Helms–Burton Act)

35 I.L.M. 357 (1996)

[Selected provisions of the Act governing a judicial remedy, liability, non-application of the act of state doctrine, waiver by the President, and exclusion of certain aliens may be found at the I.L.M. citation above. The essential elements for discussion are summarized in the text that follows.]

Brice Clagget, Title III of the Helms–Burton Act is Consistent With International Law

90 AM. J. INT'L LAW 434 (1996)

The Cuban Liberty and Democratic Solidarity (LIBERTAD) Act of 1996, otherwise known as the Helms–Burton Act, became law on March 12, 1996. Title III of the legislation creates a federal cause of action, on behalf of U.S. citizens whose property was confiscated without compensation by Cuba, against those who "traffic" in that property.[2] Several governments—notably Canada, Mexico and those of the European Union, whose corporate citizens are the principal "traffickers"—have denounced the legislation as an exercise of extraterritorial jurisdiction that violates customary international law. These governments apparently, see nothing wrong with permitting—even encouraging—their nationals to use and profit from property that rightfully belongs to others. The United States not only commands the moral high ground on this issue; it also has the better of the legal argument.

The genesis of Title III is found in two episodes separated by a generation: the massive confiscations of property by the Castro regime in the early 1960s, for which no reparation has been made; and, more recently, the collapse of the Soviet Union and the resulting termination of Soviet aid to Cuba, which has created severe economic and financial problems for the regime. One of its principal responses has become the solicitation of foreign investment in commercial enterprises. Such investment frequently involves property that was confiscated from U.S. or third-country nationals or from Cubans, many of whom have since become U.S. citizens.

A post-Castro government will have to deal with claims by both categories of U.S. nationals, as well as claims by confiscation victims who

---

2. "Traffics" is broadly defined in 4(13), 110 Stat. at 790–91, and includes any dealing in, use of or benefitting from confiscated property or causing, directing or profiting from trafficking by others. One purpose of the definition was to reach direct traffickers' affiliates that may be subject to U.S. jurisdiction. To be actionable, trafficking must be knowing and intentional, and it must begin or continue three months after August 1, 1996. * * *

remain in Cuba or have become naturalized in other countries. The principal techniques available for making reparation will be restitution in kind and monetary compensation, which have been adopted in varying degrees and combinations in countries emerging from totalitarian rule. Another possible method is what might be called substitution—conveyance to the claimant of property similar in nature and value to the confiscated property, or the issuance of "vouchers" that he can use to acquire property of his choice.

A post-Castro government will face staggering problems in attempting to do justice to the regimes victims while reviving the economy from the wreckage in which Castro will have left it. (The claims of preconfiscation U.S. nationals alone as certified by the Foreign Claims Settlement Commission, including interest, now total more than $6 billion.) Any just solution will necessarily involve a large measure of restitution or substitution, since the payment of full monetary compensation to claimants will be far beyond Cuba's resources.

* * *

Enactment of title III does no injustice to the "traffickers" who may become defendants. That Castro's confiscations were made without compensation, and also typically involved discrimination against U.S. nationals or political persecution of Cubans, is not one of the worlds best-kept secrets. Traffickers are fully aware that they are dealing in tainted property. It can be presumed that the culpability of dealing in stolen goods is a familiar concept to them from their own legal systems. Traffickers are knowingly taking the risk that the dispossessed owners or aggrieved states might take action against them.

A wealth of authority supports the view that confiscations that violate international law are not effective in passing title to property, and a state is under no obligation to recognize a title acquired by such a confiscation. Indeed, "[i]n respect to Cuban sugar and other United States assets seized in Cuba, a good case can certainly be made for an international legal *duty* of non-recognition of Castro's titles." British, French, Swiss, Austrian, Dutch and German courts are among those that have denied effect to foreign confiscations. Certainly, at a minimum, no consensus exists that an internationally unlawful confiscation *does* pass good title that a "purchaser" can rely on and that the United States is required to recognize or respect.

Thus, it seems difficult to make a serious argument that title III infringes international law to the extent that it permits suits by confiscation victims who were U.S. nationals at the time. To the contrary, title III applies and vindicates international law. As to these lawsuits, except for some of the details of the legislation, the United States is not even exercising its jurisdiction to prescribe, but only its jurisdiction to adjudicate. It is applying international law, not just its own law.

* * *

European Union: Demarches Protesting the Cuban Liberty and Democratic Solidarity (Libertad) Act

March 5, 1995
35 I.L.M. 397 (1996)

EUROPEAN UNION
DELEGATION OF THE EUROPEAN COMMISSION

The Presidency of the Council of the European Union and the European Commission present their compliments to the Department of State and wish to refer to the Cuban Liberty and Democratic Solidarity (LIBERTAD) Act of 1996.

The European Union (EU) has consistently expressed its opposition, as a matter of law and policy, to extraterritorial applications of U.S. jurisdiction which would also restrict EU trade in goods and services with Cuba, as already stated in various diplomatic demarches made in Washington last year, including a letter from Sir Leon Brittan to Secretary of State Warren Christopher. Although the EU is fully supportive of a peaceful transition in Cuba, it cannot accept that the U.S. unilaterally determine and restrict EU economic and commercial relations with third countries.

* * *

The EU cannot accept the prohibition for US-owned or controlled firms from financing other firms that might be involved in certain economic transactions with Cuba. The EU has stated on many occasions that such an extraterritorial extension of U.S. jurisdiction is unacceptable as a matter of law and policy. Therefore, the EU takes the position that the United States has no basis in international law to claim the right to regulate in any way transactions taking place outside the United States with Cuba undertaken by subsidiaries of US companies incorporated outside the U.S.

Nor can the EU accept the immediate impact of the legislation on the trade interests of the EU by prohibiting the entry of its sugars, syrups and molasses into the US, unless the former certifies that it will not import such products from Cuba. The EU considers such requests, designed to enforce a U.S. policy which is not applied by the EU, as illegitimate. Such measures would appear unjustifiable under GATT 1994 and would appear to violate the general principles of international law and sovereignty of independent states.

In these circumstances, the EU would appreciate it if you would inform Congress that the EU is currently examining the compatibility of this legislation with WTO rules and that the EU will react to protect all its legitimate rights.

* * *

Finally the EU objects, as a matter of principle, to those provisions that seek to assert extraterritorial jurisdiction of U.S. Federal courts over disputes between the U.S. and foreign companies regarding expropriated property located overseas. This measure would risk complicating not only third country economic relations with Cuba, but also any transitional process in Cuba itself. Furthermore, these provisions offer the possibility to U.S. firms for legal harassment against foreign competitors that choose to do business in Cuba. The threat of denial of a U.S. visa for corporate officers and shareholders accentuates this concern.

The EU considers that the collective effects of these provisions have the potential to cause grave damage to bilateral EU–US relations. For these reasons, the EU urges the U.S. Administration to use its influence to seek appropriate modifications to the proposed legislation, or if this should not be feasible, to prevent it from being enacted.

Should the legislation be adopted, the European Union intends to defend its legitimate interests in the appropriate international fora.

The Presidency of the Council of the European Union and the European Commission avail themselves of this opportunity to renew to the Department of State the assurances of their highest consideration.

European Union: Council Regulation (EC) No. 2271/96, Protecting Against the Effects of the Extra–Territorial Application of Legislation Adopted by a Third Country

November 22, 1996
O.J.E.C. 1996 (L. 309) 19, 36 I.L.M. 125 (1996)

THE COUNCIL OF THE EUROPEAN UNION,

* * *

HAS ADOPTED THIS REGULATION:

Article 1

This Regulation provides protection against and counteracts the effects of the extra-territorial application of the laws specified in the Annex* of this Regulation, including regulations and other legislative instruments, and of actions based thereon or resulting therefrom, where such application affects the interests of persons, referred to in Article 11, engaging in international trade and/or the movement of capital and related commercial activities between the Community and third countries. * * *

Article 2

Where the economic and/or financial interests of any person referred to in Article 11 are affected, directly or indirectly, by the laws specified in the Annex or by actions based thereon or resulting therefrom, that person shall inform the Commission accordingly * * *

Article 4

No judgment of a court or tribunal and no decision of an administrative authority located outside the Community giving effect, directly or

---

* The Annex refers to the Cuban Liberty and Democratic Solidarity (Libertad) Act of 1996 and specifically to Titles I, III and IV as well as to other U.S. laws and regulations.

indirectly, to the laws specified in the Annex or to actions based thereon or resulting therefrom, shall be recognized or be enforceable in any manner.

Article 5

No person referred to in Article 11 shall comply, whether directly or through a subsidiary or other intermediary person, actively or by deliberate omission, with any requirement or prohibition, including requests of foreign courts, based on or resulting, directly or indirectly, from the laws specified in the Annex or from actions based thereon or resulting therefrom.

Persons may be authorized, in accordance with the procedures provided in Articles 7 and 8, to comply fully or partially to the extent that noncompliance would seriously damage their interests or those of the Community. * * *

Article 6

Any person referred to in Article 11, who is engaging in an activity referred to in Article 1 shall be entitled to recover any damages, including legal costs, caused to that person by the application of the laws specified in the Annex or by actions based thereon or resulting therefrom. * * *

Without prejudice to other means available and in accordance with applicable law, the recovery could take the form of seizure and sale of assets held by those persons, entities, persons acting on their behalf or intermediaries within the Community, including shares held in a legal person incorporated within the Community.

Article 9

Each Member State shall determine the sanctions to be imposed in the event of breach of any relevant provisions of this Regulation. Such sanctions must be effective, proportional and dissuasive.

Article 11

This Regulation shall apply to:

1. any natural person being a resident in the Community and a national of a Member State,
2. any legal person incorporated within the Community,
4. any other natural person being a resident in the Community, unless that person is in the country of which he is a national,
5. any other natural person within the Community, including its territorial waters and air space and in any aircraft or on any vessel under the jurisdiction or control of a Member State, acting in a professional capacity.

Article 12

This Regulation shall enter into force on the day of its publication in the *Official Journal of the European Communities.*

This Regulation shall be binding in its entirety and directly applicable in all Member States. Done at Brussels, 22 November 1996.

European Union–United States: Memorandum of Understanding Concerning the U.S. Helms–Burton Act and the U.S. Iran and Libya Sanctions Act

April 11, 1997
36 I.L.M. 529 (1997)

Libertad Act

Both sides confirm their commitment to continue their efforts to promote democracy in Cuba. On the EU side, these efforts are set out in the Common Position adopted by the Council on 2 December 1996.

The U.S. reiterates its presumption of continued suspension of Title III during the remainder of the Presidents term so long as the EU and other allies continue their stepped up efforts to promote democracy in Cuba. Each side will encourage other countries to promote democracy and human rights in Cuba.

The EU and the U.S. agree to step up their efforts to develop agreed disciplines and principles for the strengthening of investment protection, bilaterally and in the context of the multilateral Agreement on Investment (MAI) or other appropriate international fora. Recognizing that the standard of protection governing expropriation and nationalization embodied in international law and envisioned in the MAI should be respected by all States, these disciplines should inhibit and deter the future acquisition of investments from any State which has expropriated or nationalized such investments in contravention of international law, and subsequent dealings in covered investments. Similarly, and in parallel, the EU and U.S. will work together to address and resolve through agreed principles the issue of conflicting jurisdictions, including issues affecting investors of another party because of their investments in third countries.

WTO Case

In the light of all of the above, the EU agrees to the suspension of the proceedings of the WTO panel. * * * This understanding reflects the fact that the U.S. Administration is obligated to implement the Libertad Act and ILSA. * * *

Jane A. Morse, A Breather on Title III, but no Changes for Helms–Burton

USIA Release 96071612, 16 July 1996
www.usinfo.state/gov/products/washfile/htm

WASHINGTON—President Bill Clinton's decision July 16 to wait another six months before allowing lawsuits to be filed under Title III of the Helms–Burton law against foreign companies invested in confiscated

U.S. properties in Cuba gives these companies a "breather." But it doesn't necessarily mean there will be changes in the law, according to an administrative official.

During a background briefing at the State Department, the official predicted that U.S. allies will not execute their threats of retaliation. "My presumption would be that the allies would not rush to judgment, because there is a six-month suspension in effect. There will be no lawsuits for six months against foreign companies...."

* * *

Title III of the law allows lawsuits to be filed in U.S. courts against foreign firms that own or operate the properties of U.S. citizens seized by the Cuban government after the 1959 Communist revolution. But U.S. allies around the world—most especially Europe, Canada, Mexico—have complained that the provision could deluge their companies in lawsuits. Some have threatened to retaliate.

U.S. administration officials have maintained that the United States will faithfully carry out the law, but in a way to minimize the effect on U.S. allies while maximizing the effect on the repressive Castro regime.

Clinton announced on July 16 that he would allow Title III to go into effect August 1 as provided for under the law, but he also said he would suspend the right to file lawsuits under Title III for six months. According to the administrative official, any claims are valid, "and the claims have legal standing; it's just that you cannot pursue them in the courts for six months." After that time, Clinton may once again consider his option for another waiver. [Note that this period of suspension was followed by successive suspensions.]

Organization of American States: Inter–American Juridical Committee Opinion Examining the U.S. Helms–Burton Act

August 27, 1996
35 I.L.M. 1322 (1996)

INTRODUCTION

1. This Opinion is adopted pursuant to the provisions of Resolution AG/doc.3375/96 approved by the General Assembly on 4 June 1996 during its XXVI regular period of sessions and entitled "Freedom of Trade and Investment in the Hemisphere" (Annex A), by which it instructed the Inter–American Juridical Committee, during this period of sessions, "to examine and decide upon the validity under international law of the Helms–Burton Act [known as the *"Cuban Liberty and Democratic Solidarity Act—Libertad Act"*] ... as a matter of priority, and to present its findings to the Permanent Council."

* * *

A. PROTECTION OF THE PROPERTY RIGHTS OF NATIONALS

* * *

6. In the light of the principles and norms set out in paragraph 5 above the Committee considers that the legislation under analysis does not conform to international law in each of the following respects:

a) The domestic courts of a claimant State are not the appropriate forum for the resolution of State-to-State claims.

b) The claimant State does not have the right to espouse claims by persons who were not its nationals at the time of injury.

c) The claimant State does not have the right to attribute liability to nationals of third States for a claim against a foreign State.

d) The claimant State does not have the right to attribute liability to nationals of third States for the use of expropriated property located in the territory of the expropriating State where such use conforms to the laws of this latter State, nor for the use in the territory of third States of intangible property or products that do not constitute the actual asset expropriated.

e) The claimant State does not have the right to impose liability on third parties not involved in a nationalization through the creation of liability not linked to the nationalization or unrecognized by the international law on this subject, thus modifying the juridical bases for liability.

f) The claimant State does not have the right to impose compensation in any amount greater than the effective damage, including interest, that results from the alleged wrongful act of the expropriating State.

g) The claimant State may not deprive a foreign national of the right in accordance with due process of law to effectively contest the bases and the quantum of claims that may affect his property.

h) Successful enforcement of such a claim against the property of nationals of a third State in a manner contrary to the norms of international law could itself constitute a measure tantamount to expropriation and result in responsibility of the claimant State.

B. EXTRATERRITORIALITY AND THE LIMITS IMPOSED BY INTERNATIONAL LAW ON THE EXERCISE OF JURISDICTION

7. The Committee understands that the legislation would result in the exercise of legislative or judicial jurisdiction over acts performed abroad by aliens on the basis of a concept termed "trafficking in confiscated properties."

8. The Committee has also examined the applicable norms of international law in respect of the exercise of jurisdiction by States and its limits on such exercise. In the opinion of the Committee, these norms include the following:

a) All States are subject to international law in their relations. No State may take measures that are not in conformity with international law without incurring responsibility.

b) All States have the freedom to exercise jurisdiction but such exercise must respect the limits imposed by international law. To the extent that such exercise does not comply with these limits, the exercising State will incur responsibility.

c) Except where a norm of international law permits, the State may not exercise its power in any form in the territory of another State. The basic premise under international law for establishing legislative and judicial jurisdiction is rooted in the principle of territoriality.

d) In the exercise of its territorial jurisdiction a State may regulate an act whose constituent elements may have occurred only in part in its territory: for example an act initiated abroad but consummated within its territory ("objective territoriality") or conversely an act initiated within its territory and consummated abroad ("subjective territoriality").

e) A State may justify the application of the laws of its territory only insofar as an act occurring outside its territory has a direct, substantial and foreseeable effect within its territory and the exercise of such jurisdiction is reasonable.

f) A State may exceptionally exercise jurisdiction on a basis other than territoriality only where there exists a substantial or otherwise significant connection between the matter in question and the State's sovereign authority, such as in the case of the exercise of jurisdiction over acts performed abroad by its nationals and in certain specific cases of the protection objectively necessary to safeguard its essential sovereign interests.

9. The Committee examined the provisions of the legislation that establish the exercise of jurisdiction on bases other than those of territoriality, and concluded that the exercise of such jurisdiction over acts of "trafficking in confiscated property" does not conform with the norms established by international law for the exercise of jurisdiction in each of the following respects:

a) A prescribing State does not have the right to exercise jurisdiction over acts of "trafficking" abroad by aliens unless specific conditions are fulfilled which do not appear to be satisfied in this situation.

b) A prescribing State does not have the right to exercise jurisdiction over acts of "trafficking" abroad by aliens under circumstances where neither the alien nor the conduct in question has any connection with its territory and where no apparent connection exists between such acts and the protection of its essential sovereign interests.

Therefore, the exercise of jurisdiction by a State over acts of "trafficking" by aliens abroad, under circumstances whereby neither the alien nor the conduct in question has any connection with its territory and there is no apparent connection between such acts and the protection of its essential sovereign interests, does not conform with international law.

CONCLUSION

10. For the above reasons the Committee concludes that in the significant areas described above the bases and potential application of the legislation which is the subject of this Opinion are not in conformity with international law * * * [and] this Resolution was approved unanimously.

Canada: Foreign Extraterritorial Measures Act

October 9, 1996
36 I.L.M. 111 (1996)

RECOGNITION AND ENFORCEMENT OF FOREIGN JUDGMENTS

7.1 Any judgment given under the law of the United States entitled Cuban Liberty and Democratic Solidarity (LIBERTAD) Act of 1996 shall not be recognized or enforceable in any manner in Canada.

8.1 Where an order may not be made under section 8 in respect of a judgment because the judgment has been satisfied outside Canada, or where a judgment has been given under the law of the United States entitled Cuban Liberty and Democratic Solidarity (LIBERTAD) Act of 1996, the Attorney General of Canada may, on application by a party against whom the judgment was given who is a Canadian citizen, a resident of Canada, a corporation incorporated by or under a law of Canada or a province or a person carrying on business in Canada, by order, declare that party may recover, under the provisions of section 9 that the Attorney General identifies, any or all amounts obtained from that party under the judgment, expenses incurred by that party, or loss or damage suffered by that party.

Mexico: Act to Protect Trade and Investment From Foreign Norms That Contravene International Law

October 23, 1996
36 I.L.M. 133 (1996)

Article 1

It is prohibited to any [Mexican and foreign] persons, whether natural and moral, public or private, who are located in [Mexico's] national territory; those [Mexican and foreign persons] whose acts take place or produce effects in said territory, totally or partially; as well as those [Mexican and foreign persons] who are subject to Mexican laws, to engage in acts that affect trade or investment when said acts are the consequence of the extraterritorial effects of foreign statutes.

A foreign statute is understood to have extraterritorial effects affecting Mexico's trade or investment when [said statute] has or may have any of the following objectives:

I.   To attempt to impose an economic blockade or restrict the flow of investment directed to a [given] country to provoke a change in its form of government;

II.   To allow claiming payments from individuals (particulares) derived from expropriations made in the country to which the blockade is applied; [or]

III.   To restrict the entry into the country which enacted the statute [to Mexican persons] as a means to accomplish the above-mentioned objectives.

Article 2

It is prohibited to [Mexican and foreign] persons mentioned in Article 1 of this Act to provide any [kind of] information, through any means, when requested by foreign courts or authorities, pursuant to the foreign statutes referred to in Article 1.

Article 3

Those affected [Mexican and foreign] persons must notify [both] the Secretariat of Foreign Affairs (Secretaria de Relaciones Exteriores or SRE) and the Secretariat of Commerce and Industrial Development (Secretaria de Comercio y Fomento Industrial or SECOFI) of the cases in which:

I.   Their activities or investment may be injured by the effects of the foreign statutes referred to in Article 1; and

II.   They receive requests or summons (requerimientos o notificaciones) issued pursuant to the foreign statutes referred to in Article 1.

Article 4

[Mexico's] National tribunals shall deny recognition to, and enforcement of any judgments, judicial resolutions (requerimientos judiciales) or arbitral awards rendered pursuant to the foreign statutes referred to in Article 1.

Article 5

Those [Mexican and foreign persons] who have been sentenced to pay an indemnification based upon a judgment or award rendered pursuant to the foreign statutes to which Article 1 refers, shall have the right to sue, before a federal court, the Plaintiff who filed the suit in a foreign country, for the payment of:

I.   Damages (en concepto de dano), and as the principal claim, the [monetary] amount established by the foreign judgment or award (suerte principal); and

II.   Injuries caused (perjuicios ocasionados), as well as the respective expenses and judicial costs (gastos y costas judiciales).

United Nations General Assembly, Necessity of Ending the Economic, Commercial and Financial Embargo Imposed by the United States of America Against Cuba

UN Doc. A/RES/63/7, 11 December 2008

The General Assembly,

* * *

Concerned at the continued promulgation and application by Member States of laws and regulations, such as that promulgated on 12 March 1996 known as the "Helms–Burton Act", the extraterritorial effects of which affect the sovereignty of other States, the legitimate interests of entities or persons under their jurisdiction and the freedom of trade and navigation,

* * *

2.   *Reiterates its call upon* all States to refrain from promulgating and applying laws and measures of the kind referred to in the preamble to the present resolution in conformity with their obligations under the Charter of the United Nations and international law, which, inter alia, reaffirm the freedom of trade and navigation;

3.   *Once again urges* States that have and continue to apply such laws and measures to take the necessary steps to repeal or invalidate them as soon as possible in accordance with their legal regime;

* * *

NOTES AND QUESTIONS

1.   In view of the disagreements between the *LG&E* award and the three other awards in parallel cases and in view of the finality of the four awards in those cases, what measures of institutional or other change would you consider to be appropriate for resolving this type of situation?

2.   After studying the OAS Juridical Committee Opinion above on Helms–Burton type situations, what conclusion would you draw on the issue of extraterritoriality as applied to Helms–Burton?

3.   Do the blocking measures of the EU, Canada and Mexico help resolve the legal issue in Helms–Burton type situations? Or do they represent defensive measures which may simply lead to a stalemate? Under these circumstances, what procedures are open to the U.S and the others to resolve this kind of impasse? Note that one possibility suggested in the readings was to negotiate a multilateral agreement authorizing and regulating a solution. This was attempted in the OECD MAI negotiations, but secondary economic boycotts and illegal expropriations figured among the issues that brought about the failure of these negotiations.

4.   Further Reading: Rudolf Dolzer and Christoph Schreuer, Principles of International Investment Law (2008); Andreas E. Lowenfeld, International Economic Law (2d ed., 2007); OECD, International Investment Law (2008); Kenneth J. Vandevelde, U.S. International Investment Agreements (2009).

C.   Development—A Brief Survey

This Section takes up briefly some of the chief centers of legal interest in the world of international development. Of course much of the earlier Sections on trade and investment contain important elements that apply to developing countries. This is true for the basic trade rules, the WTO and dispute settlement, bilateral and regional trade agreements in Section B and for the bilateral investment agreements (BITS), the rules about the international standards for treatment of aliens, and the nationalization of foreign property in Section C, all features where the governing rules are relatively well developed as hard law. In addition, special provisions of trade agreements apply to developing countries. For example, Part IV of the GATT, TRIPs and other trade provisions have special rules for developing countries, U.S. trade law contains special preferences for goods from developing countries, and the latest trade round was supposed to be the "development round." As you will see below, much of the remainder of development "law" is quite broadly supported but is relatively uncertain. It tends to be softer law, framed more as institutional, policy or aspirational statements than legally binding formulations, however important its content may be to the developed as well as developing countries.

What are developing countries? The reference to developed and developing countries invites questions about the meaning of those and related terms. In the decades following World War II, the new states moving out from under the colonial system and others with relatively low levels of development were identified as the "less developed countries" (LDCs), but that eventually gave way to the more progressive "developing countries", with the later appearing as a sub-category of "least developed countries", now also called LDCs. It was at this time that an articulated policy of helping poor countries develop came into being at the international level. Policy makers at times employ the distinction between "rich countries" "poor countries" and "poorest" countries, or between "northern" and "southern" countries (or the global south). More recently some of the most successful developing countries have become known as "emerging countries" (e.g. the BRIC countries: Brazil, Russia, India and China), and there are "countries in transition" (formerly under communist regimes). What difference do these descriptors make? What assumptions underlie each of them? Various organizations, including the UN, WTO, OECD, maintain useful official lists of developing countries.

What is development? The UN Declaration on the Right to Development recognizes in para. 2 of the Preamble that

* * * development is a comprehensive economic, social, cultural and political process, which aims at the constant improvement of the well-being of the entire population and of all individuals on the basis of their active, free and meaningful participation in development and in the fair distribution of benefits resulting therefrom (A/RES/41/128, 1986).

And in Article 1.1

1. The right to development is an inalienable human right by virtue of which every human person and all peoples are entitled to participate in, contribute to, and enjoy economic, social, cultural and political development, in which all human rights and fundamental freedoms can be fully realized.

In more concrete terms, development objectives can be seen as including enhanced levels of production of goods and services (growth), access to world trade on WTO or more favorable terms, balanced trade, sufficient levels of investment to meet economic needs, sound government financing, sound currency exchange rates, democratic governance, elimination of bribery and other forms of corruption, poverty reduction, crisis reduction, sufficient health, education and social services, environment protection, and recognition, and all as not falling far below world averages of performance in those fields.

More recently, theorists have questioned the de facto emphasis on growth and open markets as the principal indicator of development. The UN Development Programme (UNDP) has developed a broad set of indicators that go far beyond GDP. The following explains the Human Development Index:

National wealth has the potential to expand people's choices. However, it may not. The manner in which countries spend their wealth, not the wealth itself, is decisive. Moreover, an excessive obsession with the creation of material wealth can obscure the ultimate objective of enriching human lives . . .

In many instances, countries with higher average incomes have higher average life expectancies, lower rates of infant and child mortality and higher literacy rates, and consequently a higher human development index (HDI). But these associations are far from perfect. In inter-country comparisons, income variations tend to explain not much more than half the variation in life expectancy, or in infant and child mortality. And they explain an even smaller part of the differences in adult literacy rates.

Although there is a definite correlation between material wealth and human well-being, it breaks down in far too many societies. Many countries have high GNP per capita, but low human development indicators and vice versa.

UNDP Human Development Index, available at http://hdr.undp.org/en/media/HDR_20072008_EN_Indicator_tables.pdf.

Consider the latest version of the HDI. Are the country rankings surprising? To what extent are the HDI indicators correlated with GNP? How could one use these indicators to drive policy? Recent editions of the HDI index also compare countries on gender inequality and on income inequality within countries as measures of development.

UNDP and other international development agencies have been strongly influenced by the work of economist Amartya Sen. Sen posits that the aim of development is to enlarge the sphere of human capabilities to do things that the person has reason to value, "expanding the real freedoms that people enjoy." Amartya Sen, Development as Freedom (New York: Knopf, 1999), p. 3. He further argues that, in order to stimulate development, we must remove "major sources of unfreedom" like poverty, tyranny, social deprivation and the like, and that by doing so, "free and sustainable agency emerges as a major engine of development." Id. Sen's work, and extensions of it by Martha Nussbaum and others, has led to increasing attention to distributional factors, human rights observance, the central role of women in development, and the rule of law as important determinants of development.

The acceptance of the principle of sustainable development, discussed in Chapter 6, has also influenced development thinking more generally. Environmental economists point out that traditional markers of growth like per capita GDP include services, for example, waste disposal or disaster clean up, that actually involve negative contributors to well being, and such markers do not take into account environmental services provided by natural resources. They propose a "green accounting" that would change the way GDP is measured, and therefore also the measures of which countries are "developing" which are not. They also propose that, given current environmental conditions, a steady-state economy, rather than perpetual growth, should be the goal. See, e.g. HERMAN DALY AND JOHN E. COBB, FOR THE COMMON GOOD (1994).

Is there a "right" of countries to development? That would certainly correspond to the ordinary meaning of the language from the 1986 General Assembly Resolution quoted above. And that was reconfirmed by the 1993 World Conference on Human Rights Vienna Declaration (Article 10, UNGA A/Conf.157/23, 12 July 1993). Both of these actions are entitled to great weight, even though they are not legislative acts in the normal sense, for they both suffer two infirmities, (1) that they are framed in such a high degree of abstraction that lawyers would encounter serious difficulty in reducing them to workable legal concepts, and (2) they do not seem to have become rules of international law under the familiar concepts of Article 38 of the ICJ Statute: legally binding treaties, customary practice accepted as law and general principles of law recognized by nations as law. (and see the opinion of arbitrator Dupuy in the *Texaco Overseas Petroleum* case above in Section C).

However, there is the possibility of evolution of the UN Declaration, as with the 1948 Human Rights Declaration, where "the consensus of the international community on the meaning of that right * * * may eventually generate legally binding obligations related to that right." Arjun Sengupta, *The Human Right of Development, in* Development As a Human Right: Legal, Political, and Economic Dimensions, Bård A. Andreassen and Stephen P. Marks, eds. (2006). Thus for the time being one might characterize the Declaration as expressing a political and perhaps a moral obligation but not yet a legal one in international law. The emergence of a legal rule could come later by evolution after elaboration, refinement and fuller expression of detail in the undertakings. Meanwhile, there are interesting legal expressions of competence of international organizations in the development field which throw additional light on the law of development and governments' reasonable expectations.

What are the relevant competences and roles of international organizations in the field of development? The principal international organization active in development is of course the United Nations which is empowered in Article 55 of the Charter to promote "higher standards of living, full employment and conditions of economic progress and development" and "solutions of international economic, social, health and related problems". Development work in the UN and the Specialized Agencies is coordinated by the Economic and Social Committee (ECOSOC) with the assistance of the UN Development Program (UNDP) which is the operational network advocating change and connecting countries to knowledge, experience and resources of others. UNDP is funded by voluntary contributions of UN members, sets goals for their levels of Official Development Assistance (ODA) to developing countries, and directly administers a number of development funds. For some time, the goal has been for rich countries to provide 0.7% of their gross national income as foreign assistance, but only four OECD states met that goal in 2008. (The U.S. foreign assistance budget came to less than 0.2%, the worst percentage of any OECD country).

UN Members have pledged to achieve the Millennium Development Goals (MDGs), including the overarching goal of cutting poverty in half by 2015. UNDP's network links and coordinates global and national efforts to reach these Goals, focusing on the challenges of democratic governance, poverty reduction, provision of clean water and sanitation, education, maternal and child health, crisis prevention and recovery, environment and energy, and HIV/AIDS. More information on the MDGs is at http://www.undp.org/mdg and at www.un.org/millenniumgoals/

UNDP's work is enhanced by its representation directly in 166 countries (see http://www.undp.org/about). In addition, UNCTAD (United Nations Conference on Trade and Development) "promotes the development-friendly integration of developing countries into the world economy" largely concerning trade and commodities, investment technology and enterprise development, macroeconomic policies, debt and development financing (see http://www.unctad.org/). Within the UN membership there is the "Group of 77" in which the developing countries can "articulate their collective interests and enhance their collective negotiating capacity". The Group of 77 has now grown to some 130 states, a clear majority in the General

Assembly while the original name is retained for historical reasons. See http://www.g77.org.

What are international financial institutions and how do they work? In addition to direct development assistance under the UN system, low cost or grant financing and technical assistance are provided by two other international organizations closely related to the UN, the International Bank for Reconstruction and Development (World Bank) (formed at the Bretton Woods Conference during World War II) and the Bank's International Development Association (IDA). These lending institutions are not operated for profit. The Bank is market based, using its high credit rating to pass low loan interest rates on to "middle income and credit worthy" developing countries. The IDA provides interest-free credit and grants to "the poorest countries in the world." Together they aim at financing "for education, health, infrastructure, communication and many other purposes." This Bank work is financed primarily by selling AAA bonds on world markets; IDA financing is largely by contributions of 40 donor countries (see http://www.worldbank.org/). A World Bank affiliate, the International Finance Corporation, finances private sector investment, mobilizing capital in the international financial markets, and providing advisory services to businesses and governments. In addition, the Multilateral Investment Guarantee Agency (MIGA) provides political risk insurance and technical support for foreign direct investment in developing countries. The World Bank is also known for having established the International Centre for the Settlement of Investment Disputes (ICSID), discussed above in Section B. While the Bank and the IDA have worldwide membership comparable to the United Nations, there are in addition regional development banks, the Asian, African, and Inter–American Development Banks and the European Bank for Reconstruction and Development, also formed by governments to provide financing for developing countries, each in its own region. Unlike the UN, however, the Banks' voting structure is weighted by each country's capital contributions.

The other principal financial organization created with the World Bank at the Bretton Woods conference is the International Monetary Fund (IMF), designed to "ensure the stability of the international monetary system". Composed of some 185 states, the IMF provides advice, serves as a forum for member states, makes financing temporarily available to aid in overcoming balance of payments problems, and provides technical assistance and training. After the post-war recovery of Europe and Japan, the IMF directed its lending and assistance functions largely to the developing countries and later to the transition countries of Central and Eastern Europe. (See http://www.imf.org). The IMF has helped many developing countries with balance of payments issues, such as shortages of foreign exchange necessary to finance imports, and in advising on the remedies necessary to prevent future imbalances. At times the IMF has required commitments of recipient countries to applying difficult IMF remedies before agreeing to advance the necessary funds. These structural adjustment programs (SAPs), which often require cuts in government spending and opening of markets, have been criticized for exacerbating problems (for example during the Asian crisis of the mid–1990s) and for being incompatible with the emphasis on increased government spending on health, education and other services proposed in the MDGs.

As a result of increasingly strident critiques of the World Bank's operations, including both project finance and macroeconomic SAP requirements, in 1993 the Bank's leadership agreed to create a novel dispute resolution mechanism. The mechanism, the Inspection Panel, allows "affected parties" to bring to the attention of the Bank's management violations of the Bank's own policies on environmental and social issues.

Enrique R. Carrasco and Alison K. Guernsey, The World Bank's Inspection Panel: Promoting True Accountability Through Arbitration*

41 CORNELL INT'L L.J. 577 (2008)

In September 1993, the World Bank (the Bank) created the Inspection Panel (the Panel). The creation of the Panel was, at the time, an unprecedented effort to increase the Bank's accountability. Prior to the establishment of the Panel, the Bank had engaged in a number of projects that devastated local populations and caused significant environmental damage. One highly visible project involved the Sardar Sarovar Dam on the Narmada River in India. In the late 1980s, the Bank advanced India a loan to build a dam that would supply water to 30 million people and irrigate crops to feed another 20 million. The project was deeply flawed, however, requiring the unanticipated relocation of thousands of people and threatening to cause widespread soil erosion.

Lewis Preston, then President of the World Bank, commissioned an independent review of the project, known as the Morse Commission (the Commission). The Commission's report revealed that the Bank had pervasively failed to follow its own social and environmental policies in project lending. Another internal review of the Bank, known as the Wapenhans Report, described a "culture of approval" at the Bank—an attitude that emphasized increasing the Bank's loan portfolio without adequately taking into account the social and environmental consequences of the project lending. After unrelenting pressure from environmental and human rights non-governmental organizations (NGOs), the World Bank established the Inspection Panel with the hope of bringing transparency to the Bank's project lending.

The Inspection Panel is comprised of three members who are appointed by the World Bank, but the Panel is ostensibly independent from the larger institution. Generally, the Panel is charged with investigating complaints filed by parties in borrower countries who believe that the Bank is violating its policies or procedures in the design, preparation, or implementation of a Bank-funded project. The Panel deals exclusively with claims

---

* Footnotes omitted.

relating to the International Bank of Reconstruction and Development (IBRD), which focuses on providing loans to "middle income and creditworthy poor countries" and the International Development Association (IDA), which "focuses on the poorest countries in the world." The Panel's jurisdiction does not extend to the risk-mitigation or private-sector investment arms of the World Bank.

To bring a claim to the Panel, the party requesting investigation (Requester) must believe that actual or likely harm will result from the Bank's failure to adhere to its policies and procedures. Requesters must also bring their concerns to the Bank's attention before filing a claim. The Panel's functions and procedures are outlined in its Operating Procedures and its founding Resolution. As of May 2008, there have been fifty-two requests for inspections.

Despite its novelty when it was established in 1993, there are many critiques of the Panel. Generally, critics question whether the Panel truly increases the accountability of the World Bank on the whole. Critics often point out that the Panel has a limited substantive mandate and no ability to grant relief. Furthermore, the Panel fails to give affected people a true voice in the outcome of an investigation. After the Panel receives the claim, the Bank rarely considers the affected communities' desires for resolution. In essence, the Panel is compliance-oriented and problem-solving is not a principal focus.

NOTES AND QUESTIONS

1. The Inspection Panel is an innovation in international law, allowing access (albeit limited) to the decisions of international financial institutions. More or less parallel complaint or ombudsman functions now exist at the IMF and the regional development banks as well. All of these mechanisms are advisory, leaving decisions on whether to continue to the bank's governing board. How effective does the Inspection Panel structure seem? At the time it was created, U.S. government representatives tried to create a body independent of the World Bank to consider complaints, but failed. Should the panel have to take international legal obligations of the borrowing state, not just its own regulations, into account? Can the Bank simply weaken its internal regulations and avoid scrutiny of its actions?

2. How could the "right to development" become operationalized? Is it a useful concept? Who is the rights-holder? Who is the right effective against? How would one know if the right has been violated?

3. Human rights bodies have become more active in recent years on development issues, especially under the rubric of economic, social and cultural rights. For example, they have issued general comments on the right to water, or appointed special rapporteurs on poverty or the role of international financial institutions. At the same time, development agencies have taken up the language of "rights-based development." Is this convergence useful, or does it blur the relevant issues?

4. Further Reading: RUMA SARKAR, INTERNATIONAL DEVELOPMENT LAW (2009); Mac Darrow and Louis Arbour, *The Pillar of Glass: Human Rights in the Development Operations of the United Nations*, 103 AM. J. INT'L L. 446 (2009); G. SAMPSON, THE WTO AND GLOBAL GOVERNANCE (eds., 2008); United Nations Development Program, *Making the Law Work for Every One*, JOSE ANTONIO OCAMPO AND ROB VOS, UNEVEN ECONOMIC DEVELOPMENT (2008); United Nations, *The Millennium Development Goals Report* (2008); Arjun Sengupta, *The Human Right of Development, in* DEVELOPMENT AS A HUMAN RIGHT: IN LEGAL, POLITICAL, AND ECONOMIC DIMENSIONS 9 (Bård A. Andreassen and Stephen P. Marks eds., 2006).

CHAPTER 8

STATE RESPONSIBILITY

When an international obligation is breached international responsibility is incurred. International law contains rules and principles to determine when a state is responsible for an act or omission in breach of an international obligation. These rules and principles are known as the law of state responsibility. We look to the law of state responsibility (state responsibility for short) to determine if the breach in question may be attributed to the state, whether the state has an excuse or justification for its action, and, if not, what the consequences of the breach may be for the state. This is a fundamental area of international law, and, yet, there is no treaty on the subject. The League of Nations attempted to codify the law of state responsibility at a conference in 1930 but failed. The United Nations International Law Commission (ILC) identified state responsibility in 1949 as an important subject for codification. It began work toward a treaty in 1956. In 2001, the ILC finally presented its completed work to the UN General Assembly, but not in the form of a treaty. Instead, it presented a set of "articles." The General Assembly acknowledged the Articles in Resolution 56/83 (Dec. 12, 2001). The ILC has not foreclosed eventually including the Articles in a treaty, but, in 2009, the international community appears content to refer to the Articles on State Responsibility when questions arise respecting state responsibility. *See also* the ILC's Draft Articles on the Responsibility of International Organizations, http://untreaty.un.org/ilc/reports/2005/2005report.htm (referred to in Chapter 3 above.)

763

A.   GENERAL PRINCIPLES OF RESPONSIBILITY

Responsibility of States for Internationally Wrongful Acts

http://untreaty.unorg/ilc/texts/instruments/english/draft ̈articles/9_6_2001.pdf

CHAPTER I   GENERAL PRINCIPLES

Article 1
Responsibility of a State for its internationally wrongful acts

Every internationally wrongful act of a State entails the international responsibility of that State.

Article 2
Elements of an internationally wrongful act of a State

There is an internationally wrongful act of a State when conduct consisting of an action or omission:

(*a*) Is attributable to the State under international law; and

(*b*) Constitutes a breach of an international obligation of the State.

Article 3
Characterization of an act of a State as internationally wrongful

The characterization of an act of a State as internationally wrongful is governed by international law. Such characterization is not affected by the characterization of the same act as lawful by internal law.

The Factory at Chorzów

Permanent Court of International Justice
Ser. A, no. 9 at 21 (Judgment of July 26, 1927)

[As mentioned in Chapter 3, after the First World War, the representatives to the Paris Peace Conference made a number of territorial settlements attempting to create the conditions for peace following the conflict. One of the most important led to the establishment of the Second Polish Republic in 1918. In 1922, a region that had been under German sovereignty since 1742, Upper Silesia, was incorporated into Poland. Germany and Poland concluded a treaty, the Geneva Convention, to provide for an orderly process to pay compensation for certain kinds of financial losses suffered by Germany as a result of the transfer. Disputes under the convention were to be resolved by the Permanent Court of International Justice. In one case, *Certain German Interests in Polish Upper Silesia*, 1926 P.C.I.J. (Ser. A, No. 7), the court found that Poland had breached its obligation to Germany in failing to pay for a nitrate factory that had been built by a joint venture of the German government and a private German company. When Germany tried to collect the compensation following the judgment, Poland resisted. Finally, Germany returned to the court for a ruling as to Poland's obligation to pay. Poland argued that the court did not have jurisdiction because in Poland's view the Geneva Convention only gave the PCIJ jurisdiction to determine the breach of a substantive obligation, not the consequences of the breach. The PCIJ disagreed and in one of the most important statements about state responsibility said:]

It is a principle of international law that the breach of an engagement involves an obligation to make reparation in an adequate form. Reparation therefore is the indispensable complement of a failure to apply a convention and there is no necessity for this to be stated in the convention itself. Differences relating to reparations, which may be due by reason of failure to apply a convention, are consequently differences relating to its application.

NOTES AND QUESTIONS

1. Do you think the UN should request that the ILC draft a treaty on state responsibility? What is the source of this law in the absence of a treaty? As you read the materials in this chapter consider why it took the ILC 46 years to produce a non-treaty on state responsibility.

2. The prominent British legal philosopher of the last century, H.L.A. Hart, famously said that international law did indeed qualify as law but that it was a primitive legal system owing to the fact that it is made up only of primary rules and lacks secondary rules. Is not the law of state responsibility a set of secondary rules? What other secondary rules have you seen so far in this book? See H.L.A. HART, THE CONCEPT OF LAW (1961).

3. Consider the implications of "state" responsibility. You have already seen the developments in the area of individual accountability. Since governments are run by individuals, should not the officials involved in a breach of international law be the ones held responsible? If the state is held responsible, is that not implicating an entire population in wrongdoing? Does this make more sense in cases of states with democratic forms of government because the leaders are chosen by the population and, therefore, arguably have some responsibility for the decisions of government officials to violate international law? Consider the move to "smart sanctions" by the UN that target state leaders rather than the entire population. See SMART SANCTIONS: TARGETING ECONOMIC STATECRAFT (David Cortright & George Lopez eds., 2002).

Are there types of wrongs that may only be committed by the state as a whole? Greenhouse gas emissions? Unfair trade practices?

Article 19
International crimes and international delicts

* * *

2. An internationally wrongful act which results from the breach by a State of an international obligation so essential for the protection

of fundamental interests of the international community that its breach is recognized as a crime by the community as a whole constitutes an international crime.

3.   Subject to paragraph 2, and on the basis of the rules of international law in force, an international crime may result, inter alia, from:

(a) a serious breach of an international obligation of essential importance for the maintenance of international peace and security, such as that prohibiting aggression;

(b) a serious breach of an international obligation of essential importance for safeguarding the right of self-determination of peoples, such as that prohibiting the establishment or maintenance by force of colonial domination;

(c) a serious breach on a widespread scale of an international obligation of essential importance for safeguarding the human being, such as those prohibiting slavery, genocide and apartheid;

(d) a serious breach of an international obligation of essential importance for the safeguarding and preservation of the human environment, such as those prohibiting massive pollution of the atmosphere or of the seas.

4.   Any internationally wrongful act which is not an international crime in accordance with paragraph 2 constitutes an international delict.

4.   For many years, the ILC rapporteurs on state responsibility included an article on crimes of states.

James Crawford, the last rapporteur on state responsibility, explains why Article 19 was finally deleted:

The existence of obligations towards the international community as a whole was affirmed by the International Court in the Barcelona Traction case * * *. [Previous rapporteurs] sought to translate that idea into the Draft Articles by reference to the notion of international crimes of states * * *:

* * *

There is nothing inherent in the State as such which excludes it from being the subject of penal sanctions. * * * But a crucial difficulty with taking the idea of "international crimes" further was that even its supporters were extremely reluctant to accept a full-scale penal regime or indeed any punitive elements at all.

JAMES CRAWFORD, THE INTERNATIONAL LAW COMMISSION'S ARTICLES ON STATE RESPONSIBILITY 16–19 (2002). What remains of the distinction between ordinary wrongs and more serious ones is the following:

Article 48
Invocation of responsibility by a State other than an injured State

1.   Any State other than an injured State is entitled to invoke the responsibility of another State in accordance with paragraph 2 if:

(*a*) The obligation breached is owed to a group of States including that State, and is established for the protection of a collective interest of the group; or

(*b*) The obligation breached is owed to the international community as a whole.

2. Any State entitled to invoke responsibility under paragraph 1 may claim from the responsible State:

(*a*) Cessation of the internationally wrongful act, and assurances and guarantees of non-repetition in accordance with article 30; and

(*b*) Performance of the obligation of reparation in accordance with the preceding articles, in the interest of the injured State or of the beneficiaries of the obligation breached. * * *

Does the move from state crimes to Article 48 indicate a move toward or away from an international community?

5. For further reading on state responsibility in general, see INTERNATIONAL RESPONSIBILITY TODAY, ESSAYS IN MEMORY OF OSCAR SCHACHTER (Maurizio Ragazzi ed., 2005); JAMES CRAWFORD, THE INTERNATIONAL LAW COMMISSION'S ARTICLES ON STATE RESPONSIBILITY, INTRODUCTION, TEXT AND COMMENTARIES (2001).

B. ATTRIBUTION

Perhaps the most important international issue addressed in all of the law of state responsibility today is that of attribution. States act through individuals: government officials, military officers, police, contractors, and others. It is clear that the state will be held responsible if these individuals breach international law in the course of their duties. It is also clear that the state will not be held responsible for violations of international law by private parties with no ties to the government—except to the extent the state should have exercised greater due diligence. (See Chapter 5.) The law of state responsibility sets out the principles of attribution—when the acts of individuals may be attributed to the state. When, exactly, acts by individuals may be attributed to the state is an important question of international law. This question has arisen, in particular, with respect to the law violations committed by organized armed groups. When reading the cases below, note the important implications of attributing the acts of such groups to a state.

Responsibility of States for Internationally Wrongful Acts

http://untreaty.unorg/ilc/texts/instruments/english/draft articles/9_6_2001.pdf

Article 4
Conduct of organs of a State

1. The conduct of any State organ shall be considered an act of that State under international law, whether the organ exercises legislative,

executive, judicial or any other functions, whatever position it holds in the organization of the State, and whatever its character as an organ of the central Government or of a territorial unit of the State.

2.   An organ includes any person or entity which has that status in accordance with the internal law of the State.

Article 5
Conduct of persons or entities exercising elements of governmental authority

The conduct of a person or entity which is not an organ of the State under article 4 but which is empowered by the law of that State to exercise elements of the governmental authority shall be considered an act of the State under international law, provided the person or entity is acting in that capacity in the particular instance.

Article 6
Conduct of organs placed at the disposal of a State by another State

The conduct of an organ placed at the disposal of a State by another State shall be considered an act of the former State under international law if the organ is acting in the exercise of elements of the governmental authority of the State at whose disposal it is placed.

Article 7
Excess of authority or contravention of instructions

The conduct of an organ of a State or of a person or entity empowered to exercise elements of the governmental authority shall be considered an act of the State under international law if the organ, person or entity acts in that capacity, even if it exceeds its authority or contravenes instructions.

Article 8
Conduct directed or controlled by a State

The conduct of a person or group of persons shall be considered an act of a State under international law if the person or group of persons is in fact acting on the instructions of, or under the direction or control of, that State in carrying out the conduct.

Article 9
Conduct carried out in the absence or default of the official authorities

The conduct of a person or group of persons shall be considered an act of a State under international law if the person or group of persons is in fact exercising elements of the governmental authority in the absence or default of the official authorities and in circumstances such as to call for the exercise of those elements of authority.

Article 10
Conduct of an insurrectional or other movement

1.   The conduct of an insurrectional movement which becomes the new Government of a State shall be considered an act of that State under international law.

2.   The conduct of a movement, insurrectional or other, which succeeds in establishing a new State in part of the territory of a pre-existing State or in a territory under its administration shall be considered an act of the new State under international law.

3.   This article is without prejudice to the attribution to a State of any conduct, however related to that of the movement concerned, which is to be considered an act of that State by virtue of articles 4 to 9.

Article 11
Conduct acknowledged and adopted by a State as its own

Conduct which is not attributable to a State under the preceding articles shall nevertheless be considered an act of that State under international law if and to the extent that the State acknowledges and adopts the conduct in question as its own.

1.   CONTROL

Military and Paramilitary Activities In and Against Nicaragua

Nicaragua v. U.S.
International Court of Justice
1986 I.C.J. Rep. 14 (Judgment of June 27)

[This case was introduced in Chapter 2. Recall that it concerned charges brought by Nicaragua against the United States for mining the harbors of Nicaragua's capital, Managua, for overflight of Nicaraguan territory, and for supporting forces seeking to overthrow the Sandinista government of Nicaragua. These forces were collectively known as the "*contras*." One faction was the FDN. The *contras* committed numerous violations of international human rights and humanitarian law. Nicaragua argued that owing to U.S. support, the *contras'* violations of international law were attributable to the U.S. Here is the ICJ's key finding on that charge.]

107.   To sum up, despite the secrecy which surrounded it, at least initially, the financial support given by the Government of the United States to the military and paramilitary activities of the *contras* in Nicaragua is a fully established fact. The legislative and executive bodies of the respondent State have moreover, subsequent to the controversy which has been sparked off in the United States, openly admitted the nature, volume and frequency of this support. Indeed, they clearly take responsibility for it, this government aid having now become the major element of United States foreign policy in the region. As to the ways in which such financial support has been translated into practical assistance, the Court has been able to reach a general finding.

108.   Despite the large quantity of documentary evidence and testimony which it has examined, the Court has not been able to satisfy itself that the respondent State "created" the *contra* force in Nicaragua. It seems certain that members of the former Somoza National Guard, together with

civilian opponents to the Sandinista régime, withdrew from Nicaragua soon after that régime was installed in Managua, and sought to continue their struggle against it, even if in a disorganized way and with limited and ineffectual resources, before the Respondent took advantage of the existence of these opponents and incorporated this fact into its policies vis-à-vis the régime of the Applicant. Nor does the evidence warrant a finding that the United States gave "direct and critical combat support", at least if that form of words is taken to mean that this support was tantamount to direct intervention by the United States combat forces, or that all *contra* operations reflected strategy and tactics wholly devised by the United States. On the other hand, the Court holds it established that the United States authorities largely financed, trained, equipped, armed and organized the FDN.

109.   What the Court has to determine at this point is whether or not the relationship of the *contras* to the United States Government was so much one of dependence on the one side and control on the other that it would be right to equate the *contras,* for legal purposes, with an organ of the United States Government, or as acting on behalf of that Government. Here it is relevant to note that in May 1983 the assessment of the Intelligence Committee, in the Report referred to in paragraph 95 above, was that the *contras* "constitute[d] an independent force" and that the "only element of control that could be exercised by the United States" was "cessation of aid". Paradoxically this assessment serves to underline, *a contrario,* the potential for control inherent in the degree of the contras' dependence on aid. Yet despite the heavy subsidies and other support provided to them by the United States, there is no clear evidence of the United States having actually exercised such a degree of control in all fields as to justify treating the *contras* as acting on its behalf.

110.   So far as the potential control constituted by the possibility of cessation of United States military aid is concerned, it may be noted that after 1 October 1984 such aid was no longer authorized, though the sharing of intelligence, and the provision of "humanitarian assistance" * * * may continue. Yet, according to Nicaragua's own case, and according to press reports, *contra* activity has continued. In sum, the evidence available to the Court indicates that the various forms of assistance provided to the *contras* by the United States have been crucial to the pursuit of their activities, but is insufficient to demonstrate their complete dependence on United States aid. On the other hand, it indicates that in the initial years of United States assistance the *contra* force was so dependent. However, whether the United States Government at any stage devised the strategy and directed the tactics of the *contras* depends on the extent to which the United States made use of the potential for control inherent in that dependence. The Court already indicated that it has insufficient evidence to reach a finding on this point. It is *a fortiori* unable to determine that the *contra* force may be equated for legal purposes with the forces of the United States. This conclusion, however, does not of course suffice to resolve the entire question of the responsibility incurred by the United States through its assistance to the *contras.*

111.   In the view of the Court it is established that the *contra* force
has, at least at one period, been so dependent on the United States that it
could not conduct its crucial or most significant military and paramilitary
activities without the multi-faceted support of the United States. This
finding is fundamental in the present case. Nevertheless, adequate direct
proof that all or the great majority of *contra* activities during that period
received this support has not been, and indeed probably could not be,
advanced in every respect. It will suffice [for] the Court to stress that a
degree of control by the United States Government, as described above, is
inherent in the position in which the *contra* force finds itself in relation to
that Government.

112.   To show the existence of this control, the Applicant argued
before the Court that the political leaders of the *contra* force had been
selected, installed and paid by the United States; it also argued that the
purpose herein was both to guarantee United States control over this force,
and to excite sympathy for the Government's policy within Congress and
among the public in the United States. According to the affidavit of Mr.
Chamorro, who was directly concerned, when the FDN was formed the
name of the organization, the members of the political junta, and "the
members of the general staff were all chosen or approved by the CIA"; later
the CIA asked that a particular person be made head of the political
directorate of the FDN, and this was done. However, the question of the
selection, installation and payment of the leaders of the *contra* force is
merely one aspect among others of the degree of dependency of that force.
This partial dependency on the United States authorities, the exact extent
of which the Court cannot establish, may certainly be inferred *inter alia*
from the fact that the leaders were selected by the United States. But it
may also be inferred from other factors, some of which have been examined
by the Court, such as the organization, training and equipping of the force,
the planning of operations, the choosing of targets and the operational
support provided.

113.   The question of the degree of control of the *contras* by the
United States Government is relevant to the claim of Nicaragua attributing
responsibility to the United States for activities of the *contras* whereby the
United States has, it is alleged, violated an obligation of international law
not to kill, wound or kidnap citizens of Nicaragua. The activities in
question are said to represent a tactic which includes "the spreading of
terror and danger to non-combatants as an end in itself with no attempt to
observe humanitarian standards and no reference to the concept of military
necessity". In support of this, Nicaragua has catalogued numerous incidents, attributed to "CIA-trained mercenaries" or "mercenary forces", of
kidnapping, assassination, torture, rape, killing of prisoners, and killing of
civilians not dictated by military necessity. The declaration of Commander
Carrion annexed to the Memorial lists the first such incident in December
1981, and continues up to the end of 1984. Two of the witnesses called by
Nicaragua (Father Loison and Mr. Glennon) gave oral evidence as to events
of this kind. By way of examples of evidence to provide "direct proof of the
tactics adopted by the *contras* under United States guidance and control",

the Memorial of Nicaragua offers a statement, reported in the press, by the ex-FDN leader Mr. Edgar Chamorro, repeated in the latter's affidavit, of assassinations in Nicaraguan villages; the alleged existence of a classified Defence Intelligence Agency report of July 1982, reported in the *New York Times* on 21 October 1984, disclosing that the *contras* were carrying out assassinations; and the preparation by the CIA in 1983 of a manual of psychological warfare. At the hearings, reliance was also placed on the affidavit of Mr. Chamorro.

114.   In this respect, the Court notes that according to Nicaragua, the *contras* are no more than bands of mercenaries which have been recruited, organized, paid and commanded by the Government of the United States. This would mean that they have no real autonomy in relation to that Government. Consequently, any offences which they have committed would be imputable to the Government of the United States, like those of any other forces placed under the latter's command. In the view of Nicaragua, "*stricto sensu,* the military and paramilitary attacks launched by the United States against Nicaragua do not constitute a case of civil strife. They are essentially the acts of the United States." If such a finding of the imputability of the acts of *the contras* to the United States were to be made, no question would arise of mere complicity in those acts, or of incitement of the *contras* to commit them.

115.   The Court has taken the view (paragraph 110 above) that United States participation, even if preponderant or decisive, in the financing, organizing, training, supplying and equipping of the *contras,* the selection of its military or paramilitary targets, and the planning of the whole of its operation, is still insufficient in itself, on the basis of the evidence in the possession of the Court, for the purpose of attributing to the United States the acts committed by the *contras* in the course of their military or paramilitary operations in Nicaragua. All the forms of United States participation mentioned above, and even the general control by the respondent State over a force with a high degree of dependency on it, would not in themselves mean, without further evidence, that the United States directed or enforced the perpetration of the acts contrary to human rights and humanitarian law alleged by the applicant State. Such acts could well be committed by members of the *contras* without the control of the United States. For this conduct to give rise to legal responsibility of the United States, it would in principle have to be proved that that State had effective control of the military or paramilitary operations in the course of which the alleged violations were committed.

116.   The Court does not consider that the assistance given by the United States to the *contras* warrants the conclusion that these forces are subject to the United States to such an extent that any acts they have committed are imputable to that State. It takes the view that the *contras* remain responsible for their acts, and that the United States is not responsible for the acts of the *contras,* but for its own conduct vis-à-vis Nicaragua, including conduct related to the acts of the *contras*. What the Court has to investigate is not the complaints relating to alleged violations

of humanitarian law by the *contras,* regarded by Nicaragua as imputable to the United States, but rather unlawful acts for which the United States may be responsible directly in connection with the activities of the *contras.* The lawfulness or otherwise of such acts of the United States is a question different from the violations of humanitarian law of which the *contras* may or may not have been guilty. It is for this reason that the Court does not have to determine whether the violations of humanitarian law attributed to the *contras* were in fact committed by them. * * *

* * *

Prosecutor v. Tadić

International Criminal Tribunal for Yugoslavia, Appeals Chamber
IT–94–1–A (July 15, 1999)

99.   In dealing with the question of the legal conditions required for individuals to be considered as acting on behalf of a State, i.e., as *de facto* State officials, a high degree of control has been authoritatively suggested by the International Court of Justice in *Nicaragua*.

100.   The issue brought before the International Court of Justice was whether a foreign State, the United States, because of its financing, organising, training, equipping and planning of the operations of organised military and paramilitary groups of Nicaraguan rebels (the so-called *contras*) in Nicaragua, was responsible for violations of international humanitarian law committed by those rebels. The Court held that a high degree of control was necessary for this to be the case. It required that (i) a Party not only be in effective control of a military or paramilitary group, but that (ii) the control be exercised with respect to the specific operation in the course of which breaches may have been committed. The Court went so far as to state that in order to establish that the United States was responsible for "acts contrary to human rights and humanitarian law" allegedly perpetrated by the Nicaraguan *contras,* it was necessary to prove that the United States had specifically "directed or enforced" the perpetration of those acts.

* * *

[The Appeals Chamber went on to discuss why it found the effective control test unpersuasive before setting out the test that it found in customary international law.]

130.   Precisely what measure of State control does international law require for organized military groups? Judging from international case law and State practice, it would seem that for such control to come about, it is not sufficient for the group to be financially or even militarily assisted by a State. This proposition is confirmed by the international practice concerning national liberation movements. Although some States provided movements such as the PLO, SWAPO or the ANC with a territorial base or with economic and military assistance (short of sending their own troops to aid them), other States, including those against which these movements were fighting, did not attribute international responsibility for the acts of the

movements to the assisting States. *Nicaragua* also supports this proposition, since the United States, although it aided the *contras* financially, and otherwise, was not held responsible for their acts (whereas on account of this financial and other assistance to the *contras,* the United States was held by the Court to be responsible for breaching the principle of non-intervention as well as "its obligation . . . not to use force against another State." This was clearly a case of responsibility for the acts of its own organs).

131.   In order to attribute the acts of a military or paramilitary group to a State, it must be proved that the State wields overall control over the group, not only by equipping and financing the group, but also by coordinating or helping in the general planning of its military activity. Only then can the State be held internationally accountable for any misconduct of the group. However, it is not necessary that, in addition, the State should also issue, either to the head or to members of the group, instructions for the commission of specific acts contrary to international law.

Application of the Convention on the Prevention and Punishment of the Crime of Genocide

Bosnia v. Serbia
International Court of Justice
2007 I.C.J. Rep. (Judgment of Feb. 26)

* * *

VI.   The facts invoked by the Applicant, in relation to Article II

(1) The background

231.   In this case the Court is seised of a dispute between two sovereign States, each of which is established in part of the territory of the former State known as the Socialist Federal Republic of Yugoslavia, concerning the application and fulfilment of an international convention to which they are parties, the Convention on the Prevention and Punishment of the Crime of Genocide. The task of the Court is to deal with the legal claims and factual allegations advanced by Bosnia and Herzegovina against Serbia and Montenegro * * *.

* * *

(2) The entities involved in the events complained of

235.   It will be convenient next to define the institutions, organizations or groups that were the actors in the tragic events that were to unfold in Bosnia and Herzegovina. Of the independent sovereign States that had emerged from the break-up of the SFRY, two are concerned in the present proceedings: on the one side, the FRY (later to be called Serbia and Montenegro), which was composed of the two constituent republics of Serbia and Montenegro; on the other, the Republic of Bosnia and Herzegovina. At the time when the latter State declared its independence (15 October 1991), the independence of two other entities had already been

declared: in Croatia, the Republika Srpska Krajina, on 26 April 1991, and the Republic of the Serb People of Bosnia and Herzegovina, later to be called the Republika Srpska, on 9 January 1992 (paragraph 233 above). The Republika Srpska never attained international recognition as a sovereign State, but it had de facto control of substantial territory, and the loyalty of large numbers of Bosnian Serbs. [The army of the Republika Srpska was also known by its Serb initials "VRS".]

236.   The Parties both recognize that there were a number of entities at a lower level the activities of which have formed part of the factual issues in the case, though they disagree as to the significance of those activities. Of the military and paramilitary units active in the hostilities, there were in April 1992 five types of armed formations involved in Bosnia: first, the Yugoslav People's Army (JNA), subsequently the Yugoslav Army (VJ); second, volunteer units supported by the JNA and later by the VJ, and the Ministry of the Interior (MUP) of the FRY; third, municipal Bosnian Serb Territorial Defence (TO) detachments; and, fourth, police forces of the Bosnian Serb Ministry of the Interior. The MUP of the Republika Srpska controlled the police and the security services, and operated, according to the Applicant, in close co-operation and co-ordination with the MUP of the FRY. On 15 April 1992, the Bosnian Government established a military force, based on the former Territorial Defence of the Republic, the Army of the Republic of Bosnia and Herzegovina (ARBiH), merging several non-official forces, including a number of paramilitary defence groups, such as the Green Berets, and the Patriotic League, being the military wing of the Muslim Party of Democratic Action. The Court does not overlook the evidence suggesting the existence of Muslim organizations involved in the conflict, such as foreign Mujahideen, although as a result of the withdrawal of the Respondent's counter-claims, the activities of these bodies are not the subject of specific claims before the Court.

* * *

[The court reviews facts related to fighting and detention camps. The worst single incident concerned Srebrenica:]

278.   The atrocities committed in and around Srebrenica are nowhere better summarized than in the first paragraph of the Judgment of the Trial Chamber in the Krstić case:

> "The events surrounding the Bosnian Serb take-over of the United Nations ('UN') 'safe area' of Srebrenica in Bosnia and Herzegovina, in July 1995, have become well known to the world. Despite a UN Security Council resolution declaring that the enclave was to be 'free from armed attack or any other hostile act', units of the Bosnian Serb Army ('VRS') launched an attack and captured the town. Within a few days, approximately 25,000 Bosnian Muslims, most of them women, children and elderly people who were living in the area, were uprooted and, in an atmosphere of terror, loaded onto overcrowded buses by the Bosnian Serb forces and transported across the confrontation lines into Bosnian Muslim-held territory. The military-aged Bosnian Muslim men of Srebrenica, however, were consigned to a separate fate. As thou-

sands of them attempted to flee the area, they were taken prisoner, detained in brutal conditions and then executed. More than 7,000 people were never seen again." (IT–98–33–T, Judgment, 2 August 2001, para. 1; footnotes omitted.)

* * *

297. The Court concludes that the acts committed at Srebrenica falling within Article II*(a)* and *(b)* of the [Genocide] Convention were committed with the specific intent to destroy in part the group of the Muslims of Bosnia and Herzegovina as such; and accordingly that these were acts of genocide, committed by members of the VRS in and around Srebrenica from about 13 July 1995. * * *

* * *

376. * * * Having * * * concluded * * * in the specific case of the massacres at Srebrenica in July 1995, that acts of genocide were committed in operations led by members of the VRS, the Court now turns to the question whether those acts are attributable to the Respondent.

* * *

VII. The question of responsibility for events at Srebrenica under Article III, paragraph *(a)*, of the Genocide Convention

* * *

389. The issue also arises as to whether the Respondent might bear responsibility for the acts of the "Scorpions" in the Srebrenica area. In this connection, the Court will consider whether it has been proved that the Scorpions were a de jure organ of the Respondent. It is in dispute between the Parties as to when the "Scorpions" became incorporated into the forces of the Respondent. The Applicant has claimed that incorporation occurred by a decree of 1991 (which has not been produced as an Annex). The Respondent states that "these regulations [were] relevant exclusively for the war in Croatia in 1991" and that there is no evidence that they remained in force in 1992 in Bosnia and Herzegovina. The Court observes that, while the single State of Yugoslavia was disintegrating at that time, it is the status of the "Scorpions" in mid–1995 that is of relevance to the present case. In two of the intercepted documents presented by the Applicant * * *, there is reference to the "Scorpions" as "MUP of Serbia" and a unit of Ministry of Interiors of Serbia. The Respondent identified the senders of these communications, Ljubiša Borovčanin and Savo Cvjetinović, as being "officials of the police forces of Republika Srpska". The Court observes that neither of these communications was addressed to Belgrade. Judging on the basis of these materials, the Court is unable to find that the "Scorpions" were, in mid–1995, *de jure* organs of the Respondent. Furthermore, the Court notes that in any event the act of an organ placed by a State at the disposal of another public authority shall not be considered an act of that State if the organ was acting on behalf of the public authority at whose disposal it had been placed.

390. The argument of the Applicant however goes beyond mere contemplation of the status, under the Respondent's internal law, of the persons who committed the acts of genocide; it argues that Republika Srpska and the VRS, as well as the paramilitary militias known as the "Scorpions", the "Red Berets", the "Tigers" and the "White Eagles" must be deemed, notwithstanding their apparent status, to have been *"de facto organs"* of the FRY, in particular at the time in question, so that all of their acts, and specifically the massacres at Srebrenica, must be considered attributable to the FRY, just as if they had been organs of that State under its internal law; reality must prevail over appearances. The Respondent rejects this contention, and maintains that these were not de facto organs of the FRY.

391. The first issue raised by this argument is whether it is possible in principle to attribute to a State conduct of persons—or groups of persons—who, while they do not have the legal status of State organs, in fact act under such strict control by the State that they must be treated as its organs for purposes of the necessary attribution leading to the State's responsibility for an internationally wrongful act. The Court has in fact already addressed this question, and given an answer to it in principle, in its Judgment of 27 June 1986 in the case concerning *Military and Paramilitary Activities in and against Nicaragua* (Nicaragua v. United States of America) (Merits, Judgment, I.C.J. Reports 1986, pp. 62–64). In paragraph 109 of that Judgment the Court stated that it had to

> "determine ... whether or not the relationship of the contras to the United States Government was so much one of dependence on the one side and control on the other that it would be right to equate the contras, for legal purposes, with an organ of the United States Government, or as acting on behalf of that Government" (p. 62).

Then, examining the facts in the light of the information in its possession, the Court observed that

> "there is no clear evidence of the United States having actually exercised such a degree of control in all fields as to justify treating the contras as acting on its behalf" (para. 109), and went on to conclude that "the evidence available to the Court ... is insufficient to demonstrate [the contras'] complete dependence on United States aid", so that the Court was "unable to determine that the contra force may be equated for legal purposes with the forces of the United States" (pp. 62–63, para. 110).

392. The passages quoted show that, according to the Court's jurisprudence, persons, groups of persons or entities may, for purposes of international responsibility, be equated with State organs even if that status does not follow from internal law, provided that in fact the persons, groups or entities act in "complete dependence" on the State, of which they are ultimately merely the instrument. In such a case, it is appropriate to look beyond legal status alone, in order to grasp the reality of the relationship between the person taking action, and the State to which he is so

closely attached as to appear to be nothing more than its agent: any other solution would allow States to escape their international responsibility by choosing to act through persons or entities whose supposed independence would be purely fictitious.

393.   However, so to equate persons or entities with State organs when they do not have that status under internal law must be exceptional, for it requires proof of a particularly great degree of State control over them, a relationship which the Court's Judgment quoted above expressly described as "complete dependence". It remains to be determined in the present case whether, at the time in question, the persons or entities that committed the acts of genocide at Srebrenica had such ties with the FRY that they can be deemed to have been completely dependent on it; it is only if this condition is met that they can be equated with organs of the Respondent for the purposes of its international responsibility.

394.   The Court can only answer this question in the negative. At the relevant time, July 1995, neither the Republika Srpska nor the VRS could be regarded as mere instruments through which the FRY was acting, and as lacking any real autonomy. While the political, military and logistical relations between the federal authorities in Belgrade and the authorities in Pale, between the Yugoslav army and the VRS, had been strong and close in previous years (see paragraph 238 above), and these ties undoubtedly remained powerful, they were, at least at the relevant time, not such that the Bosnian Serbs' political and military organizations should be equated with organs of the FRY. It is even true that differences over strategic options emerged at the time between Yugoslav authorities and Bosnian Serb leaders; at the very least, these are evidence that the latter had some qualified, but real, margin of independence. Nor, notwithstanding the very important support given by the Respondent to the Republika Srpska, without which it could not have "conduct[ed] its crucial or most significant military and paramilitary activities" (I.C.J. Reports 1986, p. 63, para. 111), did this signify a total dependence of the Republika Srpska upon the Respondent.

395.   The Court now turns to the question whether the "Scorpions" were in fact acting in complete dependence on the Respondent. The Court has not been presented with materials to indicate this. The Court also notes that, in giving his evidence, General Dannatt, when asked under whose control or whose authority the paramilitary groups coming from Serbia were operating, replied, "they would have been under the command of Mladić and part of the chain of the command of the VRS". The Parties referred the Court to the *Stanišić and Simatović* case (IT–03–69, pending); notwithstanding that the defendants are not charged with genocide in that case, it could have its relevance for illuminating the status of the "Scorpions" as Serbian MUP or otherwise. However, the Court cannot draw further conclusions as this case remains at the indictment stage. In this respect, the Court recalls that it can only form its opinion on the basis of the information which has been brought to its notice at the time when it gives its decision, and which emerges from the pleadings and documents in

the case file, and the arguments of the Parties made during the oral exchanges.

The Court therefore finds that the acts of genocide at Srebrenica cannot be attributed to the Respondent as having been committed by its organs or by persons or entities wholly dependent upon it, and thus do not on this basis entail the Respondent's international responsibility.

* * *

(4) The question of attribution of the Srebrenica genocide to the Respondent on the basis of direction or control

396. As noted above * * *, the Court must now determine whether the massacres at Srebrenica were committed by persons who, though not having the status of organs of the Respondent, nevertheless acted on its instructions or under its direction or control, as the Applicant argues in the alternative; the Respondent denies that such was the case.

397. The Court must emphasize, at this stage in its reasoning, that the question just stated is not the same as those dealt with thus far. It is obvious that it is different from the question whether the persons who committed the acts of genocide had the status of organs of the Respondent under its internal law; nor however, and despite some appearance to the contrary, is it the same as the question whether those persons should be equated with State organs *de facto*, even though not enjoying that status under internal law. The answer to the latter question depends, as previously explained, on whether those persons were in a relationship of such complete dependence on the State that they cannot be considered otherwise than as organs of the State, so that all their actions performed in such capacity would be attributable to the State for purposes of international responsibility. Having answered that question in the negative, the Court now addresses a completely separate issue: whether, in the specific circumstances surrounding the events at Srebrenica the perpetrators of genocide were acting on the Respondent's instructions, or under its direction or control. An affirmative answer to this question would in no way imply that the perpetrators should be characterized as organs of the FRY, or equated with such organs. It would merely mean that the FRY's international responsibility would be incurred owing to the conduct of those of its own organs which gave the instructions or exercised the control resulting in the commission of acts in breach of its international obligations. In other words, it is no longer a question of ascertaining whether the persons who directly committed the genocide were acting as organs of the FRY, or could be equated with those organs—this question having already been answered in the negative. What must be determined is whether FRY organs— incontestably having that status under the FRY's internal law—originated the genocide by issuing instructions to the perpetrators or exercising direction or control, and whether, as a result, the conduct of organs of the Respondent, having been the cause of the commission of acts in breach of its international obligations, constituted a violation of those obligations.

398. On this subject the applicable rule, which is one of customary law of international responsibility, is laid down in Article 8 of the ILC Articles on State Responsibility as follows:

"Article 8

Conduct directed or controlled by a State

The conduct of a person or group of persons shall be considered an act of a State under international law if the person or group of persons is in fact acting on the instructions of, or under the direction or control of, that State in carrying out the conduct."

399. This provision must be understood in the light of the Court's jurisprudence on the subject, particularly that of the 1986 Judgment in the case concerning *Military and Paramilitary Activities in and against Nicaragua* (Nicaragua v. United States of America) referred to above (paragraph 391). In that Judgment the Court, as noted above, after having rejected the argument that the *contras* were to be equated with organs of the United States because they were "completely dependent" on it, added that the responsibility of the Respondent could still arise if it were proved that it had itself "directed or enforced the perpetration of the acts contrary to human rights and humanitarian law alleged by the applicant State" (I.C.J. Reports 1986, p. 64, para. 115); this led to the following significant conclusion:

"For this conduct to give rise to legal responsibility of the United States, it would in principle have to be proved that that State had effective control of the military or paramilitary operations in the course of which the alleged violations were committed." (Ibid., p. 65.)

400. The test thus formulated differs in two respects from the test—described above—to determine whether a person or entity may be equated with a State organ even if not having that status under internal law. First, in this context it is not necessary to show that the persons who performed the acts alleged to have violated international law were in general in a relationship of "complete dependence" on the respondent State; it has to be proved that they acted in accordance with that State's instructions or under its "effective control". It must however be shown that this "effective control" was exercised, or that the State's instructions were given, in respect of each operation in which the alleged violations occurred, not generally in respect of the overall actions taken by the persons or groups of persons having committed the violations.

401. The Applicant has, it is true, contended that the crime of genocide has a particular nature, in that it may be composed of a considerable number of specific acts separate, to a greater or lesser extent, in time and space. According to the Applicant, this particular nature would justify, among other consequences, assessing the "effective control" of the State allegedly responsible, not in relation to each of these specific acts, but in relation to the whole body of operations carried out by the direct perpetrators of the genocide. The Court is however of the view that the particular characteristics of genocide do not justify the Court in departing from the

criterion elaborated in the Judgment in the case concerning *Military and Paramilitary Activities in and against Nicaragua* (Nicaragua v. United States of America) (see paragraph 399 above). The rules for attributing alleged internationally wrongful conduct to a State do not vary with the nature of the wrongful act in question in the absence of a clearly expressed *lex specialis*. Genocide will be considered as attributable to a State if and to the extent that the physical acts constitutive of genocide that have been committed by organs or persons other than the State's own agents were carried out, wholly or in part, on the instructions or directions of the State, or under its effective control. This is the state of customary international law, as reflected in the ILC Articles on State Responsibility.

402.   The Court notes however that the Applicant has further questioned the validity of applying, in the present case, the criterion adopted in the *Military and Paramilitary Activities* Judgment. It has drawn attention to the Judgment of the ICTY Appeals Chamber in the *Tadić* case (IT–94–1–A, Judgment, 15 July 1999). In that case the Chamber did not follow the jurisprudence of the Court in the Military and Paramilitary Activities case: it held that the appropriate criterion, applicable in its view both to the characterization of the armed conflict in Bosnia and Herzegovina as international, and to imputing the acts committed by Bosnian Serbs to the FRY under the law of State responsibility, was that of the "overall control" exercised over the Bosnian Serbs by the FRY; and further that that criterion was satisfied in the case * * *. In other words, the Appeals Chamber took the view that acts committed by Bosnian Serbs could give rise to international responsibility of the FRY on the basis of the overall control exercised by the FRY over the Republika Srpska and the VRS, without there being any need to prove that each operation during which acts were committed in breach of international law was carried out on the FRY's instructions, or under its effective control.

403.   The Court has given careful consideration to the Appeals Chamber's reasoning in support of the foregoing conclusion, but finds itself unable to subscribe to the Chamber's view. First, the Court observes that the ICTY was not called upon in the *Tadić* case, nor is it in general called upon, to rule on questions of State responsibility, since its jurisdiction is criminal and extends over persons only. Thus, in that Judgment the Tribunal addressed an issue which was not indispensable for the exercise of its jurisdiction. As stated above, the Court attaches the utmost importance to the factual and legal findings made by the ICTY in ruling on the criminal liability of the accused before it and, in the present case, the Court takes fullest account of the ICTY's trial and appellate judgments dealing with the events underlying the dispute. The situation is not the same for positions adopted by the ICTY on issues of general international law which do not lie within the specific purview of its jurisdiction and, moreover, the resolution of which is not always necessary for deciding the criminal cases before it.

404.   This is the case of the doctrine laid down in the *Tadić* Judgment. Insofar as the "overall control" test is employed to determine whether or

not an armed conflict is international, which was the sole question which the Appeals Chamber was called upon to decide, it may well be that the test is applicable and suitable; the Court does not however think it appropriate to take a position on the point in the present case, as there is no need to resolve it for purposes of the present Judgment. On the other hand, the ICTY presented the "overall control" test as equally applicable under the law of State responsibility for the purpose of determining—as the Court is required to do in the present case—when a State is responsible for acts committed by paramilitary units, armed forces which are not among its official organs. In this context, the argument in favour of that test is unpersuasive.

405. It should first be observed that logic does not require the same test to be adopted in resolving the two issues, which are very different in nature: the degree and nature of a State's involvement in an armed conflict on another State's territory which is required for the conflict to be characterized as international, can very well, and without logical inconsistency, differ from the degree and nature of involvement required to give rise to that State's responsibility for a specific act committed in the course of the conflict.

406. It must next be noted that the "overall control" test has the major drawback of broadening the scope of State responsibility well beyond the fundamental principle governing the law of international responsibility: a State is responsible only for its own conduct, that is to say the conduct of persons acting, on whatever basis, on its behalf. That is true of acts carried out by its official organs, and also by persons or entities which are not formally recognized as official organs under internal law but which must nevertheless be equated with State organs because they are in a relationship of complete dependence on the State. Apart from these cases, a State's responsibility can be incurred for acts committed by persons or groups of persons—neither State organs nor to be equated with such organs—only if, assuming those acts to be internationally wrongful, they are attributable to it under the rule of customary international law reflected in Article 8 * * *. This is so where an organ of the State gave the instructions or provided the direction pursuant to which the perpetrators of the wrongful act acted or where it exercised effective control over the action during which the wrong was committed. In this regard the "overall control" test is unsuitable, for it stretches too far, almost to breaking point, the connection which must exist between the conduct of a State's organs and its international responsibility.

* * *

413. In the light of the information available to it, the Court finds, as indicated above, that it has not been established that the massacres at Srebrenica were committed by persons or entities ranking as organs of the Respondent * * *. It finds also that it has not been established that those massacres were committed on the instructions, or under the direction of organs of the Respondent State, nor that the Respondent exercised effective

control over the operations in the course of which those massacres, which
* * * constituted the crime of genocide, were perpetrated.

* * *

414.   Finally, the Court observes that none of the situations, other
than those referred to in Articles 4 and 8 of the ILC's Articles on State
Responsibility, in which specific conduct may be attributed to a State,
matches the circumstances of the present case in regard to the possibility of
attributing the genocide at Srebrenica to the Respondent. The Court does
not see itself required to decide at this stage whether the ILC's Articles
dealing with attribution, apart from Articles 4 and 8, express present
customary international law, it being clear that none of them apply in this
case. The acts constituting genocide were not committed by persons or
entities which, while not being organs of the FRY, were empowered by it to
exercise elements of the governmental authority (Art. 5), nor by organs
placed at the Respondent's disposal by another State (Art. 6), nor by
persons in fact exercising elements of the governmental authority in the
absence or default of the official authorities of the Respondent (Art. 9);
finally, the Respondent has not acknowledged and adopted the conduct of
the perpetrators of the acts of genocide as its own (Art. 11).

[The court did find that Serbia had breached its obligations under the
Genocide Convention to prevent and punish the crime of genocide. The
court imposed certain remedies for these breaches discussed in the last
section of this chapter: Consequences of Wrongfulness.]

2.   ADOPTION

Case Concerning United States Diplomatic and Consular Staff in Tehran

United States v. Iran
1980 I.C.J. Rep. 3 (Judgment of May 24)

* * *

17.   At approximately 10:30 a.m. on 4 November 1979, during the
course of a demonstration of approximately 3,000 persons, the United
States Embassy compound in Tehran was overrun by a strong armed group
of several hundred people. The Iranian security personnel are reported to
have simply disappeared from the scene; at all events it is established that
they made no apparent effort to deter or prevent the demonstrators from
seizing the Embassy's premises. The invading group (who subsequently
described themselves as "Muslim Student Followers of the Imam's Policy",
and who will hereafter be referred to as "the militants") gained access by
force to the compound and to the ground floor of the Chancery building.
Over two hours after the beginning of the attack, and after the militants
had attempted to set fire to the Chancery building and to cut through the
upstairs steel doors with a torch, they gained entry to the upper floor; one
hour later they gained control of the main vault. The militants also seized

the other buildings, including the various residences, on the Embassy compound. In the course of the attack, all the diplomatic and consular personnel and other persons present in the premises were seized as hostages, and detained in the Embassy compound; subsequently other United States personnel and one United States private citizen seized elsewhere in Tehran were brought to the compound and added to the number of hostages.

18.   During the three hours or more of the assault, repeated calls for help were made from the Embassy to the Iranian Foreign Ministry, and repeated efforts to secure help from the Iranian authorities were also made through direct discussions by the United States Charge d'affaires, who was at the Foreign Ministry at the time, together with two other members of the mission. From there he made contact with the Prime Minister's Office and with Foreign Ministry officials. A request was also made to the Iranian Charge d'affaires in Washington for assistance in putting an end to the seizure of the Embassy. Despite these repeated requests, no Iranian security forces were sent in time to provide relief and protection to the Embassy. In fact when Revolutionary Guards ultimately arrived on the scene, despatched by the Government "to prevent clashes", they considered that their task was merely to "protect the safety of both the hostages and the students", according to statements subsequently made by the Iranian Government's spokesman, and by the operations commander of the Guards. No attempt was made by the Iranian Government to clear the Embassy premises, to rescue the persons held hostage, or to persuade the militants to terminate their action against the Embassy.

* * *

21.   The premises of the United States Embassy in Tehran have remained in the hands of militants; and the same appears to be the case with the Consulates at Tabriz and Shiraz. Of the total number of United States citizens seized and held as hostages, 13 were released on 18–20 November 1979, but the remainder have continued to be held up to the present time. The release of the 13 hostages was effected pursuant to a decree by the Ayatollah Khomeini addressed to the militants, dated 17 November 1979, in which he called upon the militants to "hand over the blacks and the women, if it is proven they did not spy, to the Ministry of Foreign Affairs so that they may be immediately expelled from Iran".

22.   The persons still held hostage in Iran include, according to the information furnished to the Court by the United States, at least 28 persons having the status, duly recognized by the Government of Iran, of "member of the diplomatic staff" within the meaning of the Vienna Convention on Diplomatic Relations of 1961; at least 20 persons having the status, similarly recognized, of "member of the administrative and technical staff" within the meaning of that Convention; and two other persons of United States nationality not possessing either diplomatic or consular status. Of the persons with the status of member of the diplomatic staff, four are members of the Consular Section of the Mission.

23.   Allegations have been made by the Government of the United States of inhumane treatment of hostages; the militants and Iranian authorities have asserted that the hostages have been well treated, and have allowed special visits to the hostages by religious personalities and by representatives of the International Committee of the Red Cross. The specific allegations of ill-treatment have not however been refuted. Examples of such allegations, which are mentioned in some of the sworn declarations of hostages released in November 1979, are as follows: at the outset of the occupation of the Embassy some were paraded bound and blindfolded before hostile and chanting crowds; at least during the initial period of their captivity, hostages were kept bound, and frequently blindfolded, denied mail or any communication with their government or with each other, subjected to interrogation, threatened with weapons.

24.   Those archives and documents of the United States Embassy which were not destroyed by the staff during the attack on 4 November have been ransacked by the militants. Documents purporting to come from this source have been disseminated by the militants and by the Government-controlled media.

* * *

56.   The principal facts material for the Court's decision on the merits of the present case have been set out earlier in this Judgment. Those facts have to be looked at by the Court from two points of view. First, it must determine how far, legally, the acts in question may be regarded as imputable to the Iranian State. Secondly, it must consider their compatibility or incompatibility with the obligations of Iran under treaties in force or under any other rules of international law that may be applicable. The events which are the subject of the United States' claims fall into two phases which it will be convenient to examine separately.

* * *

58.   No suggestion has been made that the militants, when they executed their attack on the Embassy, had any form of official status as recognized "agents" or organs of the Iranian State. Their conduct in mounting the attack, overrunning the Embassy and seizing its inmates as hostages cannot, therefore, be regarded as imputable to that State on that basis. Their conduct might be considered as itself directly imputable to the Iranian State only if it were established that, in fact, on the occasion in question the militants acted on behalf of the State, having been charged by some competent organ of the Iranian State to carry out a specific operation. The information before the Court does not, however, suffice to establish with the requisite certainty the existence at that time of such a link between the militants and any competent organ of the State.

59.   Previously, it is true, the religious leader of the country, the Ayatollah Khomeini, had made several public declarations inveighing against the United States as responsible for all his country's problems. In so doing, it would appear, the Ayatollah Khomeini was giving utterance to the general resentment felt by supporters of the revolution at the admis-

sion of the former Shah to the United States. The information before the Court also indicates that a spokesman for the militants, in explaining their action afterwards, did expressly refer to a message issued by the Ayatollah Khomeini, on 1 November 1979. In that message the Ayatollah Khomeini had declared that it was "up to the dear pupils, students and theological students to expand with all their might their attacks against the United States and Israel, so they may force the United States to return the deposed and criminal shah, and to condemn this great plot" (that is, a plot to stir up dissension between the main streams of Islamic thought). In the view of the Court, however, it would be going too far to interpret such general declarations of the Ayatollah Khomeini to the people or students of Iran as amounting to an authorization from the State to undertake the specific operation of invading and seizing the United States Embassy. To do so would, indeed, conflict with the assertions of the militants themselves who are reported to have claimed credit for having devised and carried out the plan to occupy the Embassy. Again, congratulations after the event, such as those reportedly telephoned to the militants by the Ayatollah Khomeini on the actual evening of the attack, and other subsequent statements of official approval, though highly significant in another context shortly to be considered, do not alter the initially independent and unofficial character of the militants' attack on the Embassy. * * *

61.   * * * By a number of provisions of the Vienna Conventions of 1961 and 1963, Iran was placed under the most categorical obligations, as a receiving State, to take appropriate steps to ensure the protection of the United States Embassy and Consulates, their staffs, their archives, their means of communication and the freedom of movement of the members of their staffs.

62.   Thus, after solemnly proclaiming the inviolability of the premises of a diplomatic mission, Article 22 of the 1961 Convention continues in paragraph 2:

> *"The receiving State is under a special duty to take all appropriate steps to protect the premises of the mission against any* intrusion or damage and to prevent any disturbance of the peace of the mission or impairment of its dignity." (Emphasis added.)

So, too, after proclaiming that the person of a diplomatic agent shall be inviolable, and that he shall not be liable to any form of arrest or detention, Article 29 provides:

> "The receiving State shall treat him with due respect and *shall take all appropriate steps to prevent any attack on his person, freedom or dignity*." (Emphasis added.)

The obligation of a receiving State to protect the inviolability of the archives and documents of a diplomatic mission is laid down in Article 24, which specifically provides that they are to be "inviolable at any time and wherever they may be". Under Article 25 it is required to "accord full facilities for the performance of the functions of the mission", under Article

26 to "ensure to all members of the mission freedom of movement and travel in its territory", and under Article 27 to "permit and protect free communication on the part of the mission for all official purposes".

Analogous provisions are to be found in the 1963 Convention regarding the privileges and immunities of consular missions and their staffs (Art. 31, para. 3, Arts. 40, 33, 28, 34 and 35). In the view of the Court, the obligations of the Iranian Government here in question are not merely contractual obligations established by the Vienna Conventions of 1961 and 1963, but also obligations under general international law.

63. The facts set out in paragraphs 14 to 27 above establish to the satisfaction of the Court that on 4 November 1979 the Iranian Government failed altogether to take any "appropriate steps" to protect the premises, staff and archives of the United States' mission against attack by the militants, and to take any steps either to prevent this attack or to stop it before it reached its completion. They also show that on 5 November 1979 the Iranian Government similarly failed to take appropriate steps for the protection of the United States Consulates at Tabriz and Shiraz. In addition they show, in the opinion of the Court, that the failure of the Iranian Government to take such steps was due to more than mere negligence or lack of appropriate means.

64. The total inaction of the Iranian authorities on that date in face of urgent and repeated requests for help contrasts very sharply with its conduct on several other occasions of a similar kind. Some eight months earlier, on 14 February 1979, the United States Embassy in Tehran had itself been subjected to the armed attack mentioned above * * * in the course of which the attackers had taken the Ambassador and his staff prisoner. On that occasion, however, a detachment of Revolutionary Guards, sent by the Government, had arrived promptly, together with a Deputy Prime Minister, and had quickly succeeded in freeing the Ambassador and his staff and restoring the Embassy to him. On 1 March 1979, moreover, the Prime Minister of Iran had sent a letter expressing deep regret at the incident, giving an assurance that appropriate arrangements had been made to prevent any repetition of such incidents, and indicating the willingness of his Government to indemnify the United States for the damage. On 1 November 1979, only three days before the events which gave rise to the present case, the Iranian police intervened quickly and effectively to protect the United States Embassy when a large crowd of demonstrators spent several hours marching up and down outside it. Furthermore, on other occasions in November 1979 and January 1980, invasions or attempted invasions of other foreign embassies in Tehran were frustrated or speedily terminated.

65. A similar pattern of facts appears in relation to consulates. In February 1979, at about the same time as the first attack on the United States Embassy, attacks were made by demonstrators on its Consulates in Tabriz and Shiraz; but the Iranian authorities then took the necessary steps to clear them of the demonstrators. On the other hand, the Iranian authorities took no action to prevent the attack of 5 November 1979, or to

restore the Consulates to the possession of the United States. In contrast, when on the next day militants invaded the Iraqi Consulate in Kermanshah, prompt steps were taken by the Iranian authorities to secure their withdrawal from the Consulate. Thus in this case, the Iranian authorities and police took the necessary steps to prevent and check the attempted invasion or return the premises to their rightful owners.

66.   As to the actual conduct of the Iranian authorities when faced with the events of 4 November 1979, the information before the Court establishes that, despite assurances previously given by them to the United States Government and despite repeated and urgent calls for help, they took no apparent steps either to prevent the militants from invading the Embassy or to persuade or to compel them to withdraw. Furthermore, after the militants had forced an entry into the premises of the Embassy, the Iranian authorities made no effort to compel or even to persuade them to withdraw from the Embassy and to free the diplomatic and consular staff whom they had made prisoner.

67.   This inaction of the Iranian Government by itself constituted clear and serious violation of Iran's obligations to the United States under the provisions of Article 22, paragraph 2, and Articles 24, 25, 26, 27 and 29 of the 1961 Vienna Convention on Diplomatic Relations, and Articles 5 and 36 of the 1963 Vienna Convention on Consular Relations. Similarly, with respect to the attacks on the Consulates at Tabriz and Shiraz, the inaction of the Iranian authorities entailed clear and serious breaches of its obligations under the provisions of several further articles of the 1963 Convention on Consular Relations. So far as concerns the two private United States nationals seized as hostages by the invading militants, that inaction entailed, albeit incidentally, a breach of its obligations under Article II, paragraph 4, of the 1955 Treaty of Amity, Economic Relations, and Consular Rights which, in addition to the obligations of Iran existing under general international law, requires the parties to ensure the most constant protection and security to each other's nationals in their respective territories.

* * *

69.   The second phase of the events which are the subject of the United States' claims comprises the whole series of facts which occurred following the completion of the occupation of the United States Embassy by the militants, and the seizure of the Consulates at Tabriz and Shiraz. The occupation having taken place and the diplomatic and consular personnel of the United States' mission having been taken hostage, the action required of the Iranian Government by the Vienna Conventions and by general international law was manifest. Its plain duty was at once to make every effort, and to take every appropriate step, to bring these flagrant infringements of the inviolability of the premises, archives and diplomatic and consular staff of the United States Embassy to a speedy end, to restore the Consulates at Tabriz and Shiraz to United States control, and in general to re-establish the status quo and to offer reparation for the damage.

70.   No such step was, however, taken by the Iranian authorities. At a press conference on 5 November the Foreign Minister, Mr. Yazdi, conceded that "according to international regulations the Iranian Government is dutybound to safeguard the life and property of foreign nationals". But he made no mention of Iran's obligation to safeguard the inviolability of foreign embassies and diplomats; and he ended by announcing that the action of the students "enjoys the endorsement and support of the government, because America herself is responsible for this incident". As to the Prime Minister, Mr. Bazargan, he does not appear to have made any statement on the matter before resigning his office on 5 November.

71.   In any event expressions of approval of the take-over of the Embassy, and indeed also of the Consulates at Tabriz and Shiraz, by militants came immediately from numerous Iranian authorities, including religious, judicial, executive, police and broadcasting authorities. Above all, the Ayatollah Khomeini himself made crystal clear the endorsement by the State both of the take-over of the Embassy and Consulates and of the detention of the Embassy staff as hostages. At a reception in Qom on 5 November, the Ayatollah Khomeini left his audience in no doubt as to his approval of the action of the militants in occupying the Embassy, to which he said they had resorted "because they saw that the shah was allowed in America". Saying that he had been informed that the "centre occupied by our young men ... has been a lair of espionage and plotting", he asked how the young people could be expected "simply to remain idle and witness all these things". Furthermore he expressly stigmatized as "rotten roots" those in Iran who were "hoping we would mediate and tell 'the young people' to leave this place". The Ayatollah's refusal to order the young people to put an end to their occupation of the Embassy, or the militants in Tabriz and Shiraz to evacuate the United States Consulates there, must have appeared the more significant when, on 6 November, he instructed 'the young people' who had occupied the Iraqi Consulate in Kermanshah that they should leave it as soon as possible. The true significance of this was only reinforced when, next day, he expressly forbade members of the Revolutionary Council and all responsible officials to meet the special representatives sent by President Carter to try and obtain the release of the hostages and evacuation of the Embassy."

72.   At any rate, thus fortified in their action, the militants at the Embassy at once went one step farther. On 6 November they proclaimed that the Embassy, which they too referred to as "the U.S. centre of plots and espionage", would remain under their occupation, and that they were watching "most closely" the members of the diplomatic staff taken hostage whom they called "U.S. mercenaries and spies".

73.   The seal of official government approval was finally set on this situation by a decree issued on 17 November 1979 by the Ayatollah Khomeini. His decree began with the assertion that the American Embassy was "a centre of espionage and conspiracy" and that "those people who hatched plots against our Islamic movement in that place do not enjoy international diplomatic respect". He went on expressly to declare that the

premises of the Embassy and the hostages would remain as they were until the United States had handed over the former Shah for trial and returned his property to Iran. This statement of policy the Ayatollah qualified only to the extent of requesting the militants holding the hostages to "hand over the blacks and the women, if it is proven that they did not spy, to the Ministry of Foreign Affairs so that they may be immediately expelled from Iran". As to the rest of the hostages, he made the Iranian Government's intentions all too clear:

> "The noble Iranian nation will not give permission for the release of the rest of them. Therefore, the rest of them will be under arrest until the American Government acts according to the wish of the nation."

74.   The policy thus announced by the Ayatollah Khomeini, of maintaining the occupation of the Embassy and the detention of its inmates as hostages for the purpose of exerting pressure on the United States Government was complied with by other Iranian authorities and endorsed by them repeatedly in statements made in various contexts. The result of that policy was fundamentally to transform the legal nature of the situation created by the occupation of the Embassy and the detention of its diplomatic and consular staff as hostages. The approval given to these facts by the Ayatollah Khomeini and other organs of the Iranian State, and the decision to perpetuate them, translated continuing occupation of the Embassy and detention of the hostages into acts of that State. The militants, authors of the invasion and jailers of the hostages, had now become agents of the Iranian State for whose acts the State itself was internationally responsible. On 6 May 1980, the Minister for Foreign Affairs, Mr. Ghotbzadeh, is reported to have said in a television interview that the occupation of the United States Embassy had been "done by our nation". Moreover, in the prevailing circumstances the situation of the hostages was aggravated by the fact that their detention by the militants did not even offer the normal guarantees which might have been afforded by police and security forces subject to the discipline and the control of official superiors.

75.   During the six months which have elapsed since the situation just described was created by the decree of the Ayatollah Khomeini, it has undergone no material change. * * *

* * *

90.   On the basis of the foregoing detailed examination of the merits of the case, the Court finds that Iran, by committing successive and continuing breaches of the obligations laid upon it by the Vienna Conventions of 1961 and 1963 on Diplomatic and Consular Relations, the Treaty of Amity, Economic Relations, and Consular Rights of 1955, and the applicable rules of general international law, has incurred responsibility towards the United States. As to the consequences of this finding, it clearly entails an obligation on the part of the Iranian State to make reparation for the injury thereby caused to the United States. Since however Iran's breaches of its obligations are still continuing, the form and amount of such reparation cannot be determined at the present date.

3. DUE DILIGENCE

James Gathii, Irregular Forces and Self-Defense Under the UN Charter*

in THE MEANING OF ARMED CONFLICT IN INTERNATIONAL LAW (Mary Ellen O'Connell ed., forthcoming)

* * *

[Professor Yoram Dinstein, argues that irrespective of attribution to a state of an armed attack by a non-state actor, the defending state may counter-attack on the territory from where the attack originated. Professor Gathii explains that international law does not permit omitting assessment of attribution:]

In the Global Counter–Terrorism Strategy, the General Assembly required States to "refrain from organizing, instigating, facilitating, participating in, financing, encouraging or tolerating terrorist activities and to take appropriate practical measures to ensure that our respective territories are not used for terrorist installations or training camps, or for the preparation or organization of terrorist acts intended to be committed against other States or their citizens." This statement, while encompassing the obligations stated by the resolutions of the Security Council, also adds the additional prohibition against tolerating terrorist activities. In *Congo v. Uganda*, the ICJ linked the toleration of rebels within a State's territory to a State's duty of vigilance. It noted this was a separate issue from active support of such rebels. Thus, the increased responsibilities in these Security Council resolutions impose affirmative international obligations on States irrespective of whether the conduct of irregular forces may be attributed to the State itself. Such duties add an additional form of accountability and further emphasize the point made in the seminal article: "State Responsibility For Injuries to Aliens Occasioned by Terrorist Activities," where Professors Lillich and Paxman concluded that "[a] state is responsible for the acts of individuals only when it has failed to fulfill its international obligations to prevent such acts. [Thus], for a State to incur responsibility it must be shown that, under the circumstances of the particular case, the State failed to maintain the required level of vigilance or 'due diligence' to prevent the injury." Thus, rules of state responsibility determine when a state is responsible for the conduct of non-state actors. Attribution of the conduct of non-state actors to a State for purposes of the right to use force in self-defense still requires the much higher threshold of whether there was so much or complete dependence on one side, and control on the other such that the non-State actor would be regarded as acting on behalf of the State. This test for establishing when a non-State actor can be regarded as an organ of a State was affirmed in the ICJ's judgment in the *Case Concerning the Application of the Convention on the Prevention and Punishment of the Crime of Genocide (Bosnia and Herzego-*

---

* Footnotes omitted.

vina v. Serbia and Montenegro). The views of individual judges of the ICJ who would eliminate the requirements of direction and control as prerequisites to attributing non-State actor conduct to a State cannot be a substitute for consent based norms of international law.

NOTES AND QUESTIONS

1. Compare what you have read about attribution in this section with the definition of "torture" found in the UN Convention Against Torture (CAT). Although the ILC's Articles on State Responsibility and the CAT were both developed by the UN, they were developed by different UN bodies and serve different purposes. Do you think these two documents reflect similar or different attitudes toward attribution? Where do these two documents fit in your understanding of the growing area of individual accountability? (See Chapter 5) Indeed, the Articles were completed after the Rome Statute of the International Criminal Court. Should they not have provided more guidance on when the state as a whole is held responsible and when individuals?

2. Gathii writes in another publication that

> [State] responsibility for war destruction in *AAPL v. Sri Lanka* [has] evolved in an ever-tightening obligation on States to take preventive measures to avoid loss or damage to the property of alien investors in the context of war and domestic unrest. Therefore, although ICSID Tribunals cite *AAPL v. Sri Lanka* for the proposition that full security and protection do not embody absolute obligations, the effect of these decisions has been to effectively heighten the obligations of States for war destruction toward such absoluteness and strictness.

> This heightened standard of State responsibility for war destruction is clearly demonstrated when one compares the standard of vigilance States have in the investor context, with that in the context of ensuring their territory is not used for purposes inimical to other States. In *Democratic Republic of Congo v. Uganda,* the International Court of Justice (ICJ) strongly suggested that the duty of due diligence or vigilance expected of a government with respect to rebel activity that may result in violating the rights of a neighboring State may be lower if the geographical terrain was remote and difficult. In fact, this is the customary international legal standard of due diligence that imposes a reasonable, rather than an absolute, standard of conduct. Under such a standard, a State is assumed to have the means to provide protection. As such if its ability to provide protection was remote, liability would not automatically attach. In addition, this standard is based on the assumption that a State had the opportunity to "prevent the act but failed to do so." Taken together, these tests require before imposition of liability that the conduct of the State be "judged by [its] reasonableness under the circumstances." This, in my view, is the approach taken by the ICJ in *Congo v. Uganda.*

James Thuo Gathii, War, Commerce and International Law (forthcoming) (footnotes omitted.)

Should there be differing standards for due diligence for different categories of international law rules? Gathii is citing various arbitral awards. Should arbitral tribunals decide these questions?

3. Why is there still support for the test of attribution found in the Tadić case? What are the advantages of the Tadić test over the ICJ's control test? International law scholars have a tendency to overloook due diligence. Could that explain the resistance to the ICJ test? See Chapter 5 above and the discussion of due diligence in the human rights context. See also Chapter 12 and the discussion of "fragmentation." How serious a problem is it for international law if different international courts rule differently on issues such as the test of attribution?

4. *See* Mary Ellen O'Connell, *Enhancing The Status of Non–State Actors Through A Global War on Terror*, 43 COLUM. J. TRANSNAT'L L. 435, 448–49 (2005); Richard B. Lillich & John M. Paxman, *State Responsibility For Injuries to Aliens Occasioned by Terrorist Activities*, 26 AM. U. L. REV. 217, 230–31 (1977).

C. CIRCUMSTANCES PRECLUDING WRONGFULNESS

Responsibility of States for Internationally Wrongful Acts

http://untreaty.unorg/ilc/texts/instruments/english/draft ̈articles/9_6_2001.pdf

Article 20
Consent

Valid consent by a State to the commission of a given act by another State precludes the wrongfulness of that act in relation to the former State to the extent that the act remains within the limits of that consent.

Article 21
Self-defence

The wrongfulness of an act of a State is precluded if the act constitutes a lawful measure of self-defence taken in conformity with the Charter of the United Nations.

Article 22
Countermeasures in respect of an internationally wrongful act

The wrongfulness of an act of a State not in conformity with an international obligation towards another State is precluded if and to the extent that the act constitutes a countermeasure taken against the latter State in accordance with chapter II of part three.

Article 23
Force majeure

1. The wrongfulness of an act of a State not in conformity with an international obligation of that State is precluded if the act is due to force

majeure, that is the occurrence of an irresistible force or of an unforeseen event, beyond the control of the State, making it materially impossible in the circumstances to perform the obligation.

2.   Paragraph 1 does not apply if:

(*a*) The situation of force majeure is due, either alone or in combination with other factors, to the conduct of the State invoking it; or

(*b*) The State has assumed the risk of that situation occurring.

Article 24
Distress

1.   The wrongfulness of an act of a State not in conformity with an international obligation of that State is precluded if the author of the act in question has no other reasonable way, in a situation of distress, of saving the author's life or the lives of other persons entrusted to the author's care.

2.   Paragraph 1 does not apply if:

(*a*) The situation of distress is due, either alone or in combination with other factors, to the conduct of the State invoking it; or

(*b*) The act in question is likely to create a comparable or greater peril.

Article 25
Necessity

1.   Necessity may not be invoked by a State as a ground for precluding the wrongfulness of an act not in conformity with an international obligation of that State unless the act:

(*a*) Is the only way for the State to safeguard an essential interest against a grave and imminent peril; and

(*b*) Does not seriously impair an essential interest of the State or States towards which the obligation exists, or of the international community as a whole.

2.   In any case, necessity may not be invoked by a State as a ground for precluding wrongfulness if:

(*a*) The international obligation in question excludes the possibility of invoking necessity; or

(*b*) The State has contributed to the situation of necessity.

Article 26
Compliance with peremptory norms

Nothing in this chapter precludes the wrongfulness of any act of a State which is not in conformity with an obligation arising under a peremptory norm of general international law.

1.   General Defenses

Rainbow Warrior

New Zealand v. France
France–New Zealand Arbitration Tribunal, April 30, 1990

Jimenez de Arechaga, *Chairman;* Sir Kenneth Keith and Professor Bredin, *Members*

SUMMARY: The facts:—In July 1985 a team of French agents sabotaged and sank the *Rainbow Warrior,* a vessel belonging to Greenpeace International, while it lay in harbor in New Zealand. One member of the crew was killed. Two of the agents, Major Mafart and Captain Prieur, were subsequently arrested in New Zealand and, having pleaded guilty to charges of manslaughter and criminal damage, were sentenced by a New Zealand court to ten years imprisonment. A dispute arose between France, which demanded the release of the two agents, and New Zealand, which claimed compensation for the incident. New Zealand also complained that France was threatening to disrupt New Zealand trade with the European Communities unless the two agents were released.

The two countries requested the Secretary–General of the United Nations to mediate and to propose a solution in the form of a ruling, which both Parties agreed in advance to accept. The Secretary–General's ruling, which was given in 1986, required France to pay U.S. $7 million to New Zealand and to undertake not to take certain defined measures injurious to New Zealand trade with the European Communities. The ruling also provided that Major Mafart and Captain Prieur were to be released into French custody but were to spend the next three years on an isolated French military base in the Pacific. The two States concluded an agreement in the form of an exchange of letters on 9 July 1986 ("the First Agreement"), which provided for the implementation of the ruling. Under the terms of the First Agreement, Major Mafart and Captain Prieur were to be

> ... transferred to a French military facility on the island of Hao for a period of not less than three years. They will be prohibited from leaving the island for any reason, except with the mutual consent of the two governments.

The actual transfer took place on 23 July 1986.

Following concern about Major Mafart's health, a French medical team advised that he be evacuated to France for treatment on 10 December 1987. On 11 December France sought New Zealand's consent to this "urgent, health-related transfer" but New Zealand's request that its own medical team should also examine Mafart before he was repatriated was denied when France refused to allow a New Zealand military aircraft carrying a doctor to land at Hao. On 14 December 1987 Mafart left Hao without the consent of New Zealand. Following medical treatment in Paris, Mafart was permitted to remain in France. New Zealand doctors who examined Mafart after his return to Paris agreed that he could not have been satisfactorily examined in Hao but denied that the evacuation was an emergency measure and concluded that Mafart's health was not such as to preclude his being returned to Hao after the treatment had been concluded.

Captain Prieur was repatriated in May 1988. On 3 May 1988 the French authorities notified New Zealand that she was expecting her first child and asked consent to her repatriation. New Zealand again requested that an independent medical examination be made. France acceded to this request and a New Zealand doctor was due to arrive in Hao on 6 May. On 5 May, however, the French authorities notified New Zealand that Captain Prieur's father was dying of cancer and that her immediate evacuation had thus become necessary. She was repatriated on 5 May 1988 without the consent of New Zealand and never returned to Hao.

The 1986 Agreement contained provision for arbitration of any dispute arising out of the agreement. After New Zealand invoked this provision, France and New Zealand concluded a further agreement on 14 February 1989 ("the Supplementary Agreement"), designating the three arbitrators and dealing with the procedure for the arbitration.

* * *

The Applicable Law

* * *

75. * * * [B]oth the customary Law of Treaties and the customary Law of State Responsibility are relevant and applicable. The customary Law of Treaties, as codified in the Vienna Convention, proclaimed in Article 26, under the title "*Pacta sunt servanda*" that

"Every treaty in force is binding upon the parties to it and must be performed by them in good faith."

This fundamental provision is applicable to the determination whether there have been violations of that principle, and in particular, whether material breaches of treaty obligations have been committed.

Moreover, certain specific provisions of customary law in the Vienna Convention are relevant in this case, such as Article 60, which gives a precise definition of the concept of a material breach of a treaty, and Article 70, which deals with the legal consequences of the expiry of a treaty.

One the other hand, the legal consequences of a breach of a treaty, including the determination of the circumstances that may exclude wrongfulness (and render the breach only apparent) and the appropriate remedies for breach are subjects that belong to the customary Law of State Responsibility.

The reason is that the general principles of International Law concerning State responsibility are equally applicable in the case of breach of treaty obligation, since in the international law field there is no distinction between contractual and tortuous responsibility, so that any violation by a State of any obligation, of whatever origin, gives rise to State responsibility and consequently, to the duty of reparation. The particular treaty itself might of course limit or extend the general Law of State Responsibility, for instance by establishing a system of remedies for it.

The Permanent Court proclaimed this fundamental principle in the Chorzow Factory (Jurisdiction) case, stating:

> "It is a principle of international law that the breach of an engagement involves an obligation to make reparation in an adequate form. Reparation, therefore, is the indispensable complement of a failure to apply a convention." (P.C.I.J., Series A, Nos. 9, 21 (1927).)

And the present Court has said:

> "It is clear that refusal to fulfill a treaty obligation involves international responsibility." (Peace Treaties (second phase) 1950, ICJ Reports 221, 228) * * *

The conclusion to be reached on this issue is that, without prejudice to the terms of the agreement which the Parties signed and the applicability of certain important provisions of the Vienna Convention on the Law of Treaties, the existence in this case of circumstances excluding wrongfulness as well as the questions of appropriate remedies, should be answered in the context and in the light of the customary Law of State Responsibility.

Circumstances Precluding Wrongfulness

76.   Under the title "Circumstances Precluding Wrongfulness" the International Law Commission proposed in Articles 29 to 35 a set of rules which include three provisions, on *force majeure* and fortuitous event (Article 31), distress (Article 32), and state of necessity (Article 33), which may be relevant to the decision on this case.

* * * [T]here are several reasons for excluding the applicability of the excuse of *force majeure* in this case. As pointed out in the report of the International Law Commission, Article 31 refers to "a situation facing the subject taking the action, which leads it, as it were, *despite itself,* to act in a manner not in conformity with the requirements of an international obligation incumbent on it" * * *. *Force majeure* is "generally invoked to justify *involuntary,* or at least unintentional conduct" it refers "to an irresistible force or an unforeseen external event against which it has no remedy and which makes it 'materially impossible' for it to act in conformity with the obligation," since "no person is required to do the impossible" * * *.

In conclusion, New Zealand is right in asserting that the excuse of *force majeure* is not of relevance in this case because the test of its applicability is of absolute and material impossibility, and because a circumstance rendering performance more difficult or burdensome does not constitute a case of *force majeure*. Consequently, this excuse is of no relevance in the present case.

78.   * * * The commentary of the International Law Commission explains that "distress" means a situation of extreme peril in which the

organ of the State which adopts that conduct has, at that particular moment, no means of saving himself or persons entrusted to his care other than to act in a manner not in conformity with the requirements of the obligation in question (Ybk. cit. 1979, p. 133, para. 1).

The Report adds that in international practice distress, as a circumstance capable of precluding the wrongfulness of an otherwise wrongful act of the State, "has been invoked and recognized primarily in cases involving the violation of a frontier of another State, particularly its airspace and its sea—for example, when the captain of a State vessel in distress seeks refuge from storm in a foreign port without authorization, or when the pilot of a State aircraft lands without authorization on foreign soil to avoid an otherwise inevitable disaster" * * *.

Both parties recognized that the return of Major Mafart to Hao depended mainly on his state of health. Thus, the French Ministry of Foreign Affairs in its note of 30 December 1987 to the New Zealand Embassy referring to France's respect for the 1986 Agreement had said that Major Mafart will return to Hao when his state of health allowed.

Consequently, there was no valid ground for Major Mafart continuing to remain in metropolitan France and the conclusion is unavoidable that this omission constitutes a material breach by the French Government of the First Agreement.

For the foregoing reasons the Tribunal:

> by a majority declares that the French Republic did not breach its obligations to New Zealand by removing Major Mafart from the island of Hao on 13 December 1987;

> declares that the French Republic committed a material and continuing breach of its obligations to New Zealand by failing to order the return of Major Mafart to the island of Hao as from 12 February 1988.

94.   * * * [I]t appears that during the day of 5 May the French Government suddenly decided to present the New Zealand Government with the *fait accompli* of Captain Prieur's hasty return for a new reason, the health of Mrs. Prieur's father, who was seriously ill, hospitalized for cancer. Indisputably the health of Mrs. Prieur's father, who unfortunately would die on 16 May, and the concern for allowing Mrs. Prieur to visit her dying father constitute humanitarian reasons worthy of consideration by both Governments under the 1986 Agreement. But the events of 5 May (French date) prove that the French Republic did not make efforts in good faith to obtain New Zealand's consent. First of all, it must be remembered that France and New Zealand agreed that Captain Prieur would be examined in Hao on 6 May, which would allow her to return to France immediately. For France, in this case, it was only a question of gaining 24 or 36 hours. Of course, the health of Mrs. Prieur's father, who had been hospitalized for several months, could serve as grounds for such acute and sudden urgency; but, in this case, New Zealand would have had to be

informed very precisely and completely, and not be presented with a decision that had already been made.

However, when the French Republic notified the Ambassador of New Zealand on 5 May at 11:00 a.m. (French time), the latter was merely told that Mrs. Dominique Prieur's father, hospitalized for cancer treatment, was dying. Of course, it was explained that the New Zealand Government could verify "the validity of this information" using a physician of its choice, but the telegram the French Minister of Foreign Affairs sent to the Embassy of France in Wellington on 5 May 1988 clearly stated that the decision to repatriate was final. And this singular announcement was addressed to New Zealand: "After all, New Zealand should understand that it would be incomprehensible for both French and New Zealand opinion for the New Zealand Government to stand in the way of allowing Mrs. Prieur to see her father on his death bed ..." Thus, New Zealand was really not asked for its approval, as compliance with France's obligations required, even under extremely urgent circumstances; it was indeed demanded so firmly that it was bound to provoke a strong reaction from New Zealand.

95.   The events that follow confirm that the French Government's decision had already been made and that it produced a foreseeable reaction. Indeed, at 9:30 p.m. (French time) on 5 May, the Ambassador of New Zealand in Paris announced that the New Zealand Government was not prepared to approve Mrs. Prieur's departure from Hao, for the reason given that very morning by the French Government. But the New Zealand Government explained that the "response and New Zealand's offer concerning the consequences of Mrs. Prieur's pregnancy were still valid." France, therefore, could have expected the procedure agreed upon by reason of Mrs. Prieur's pregnancy to be respected. Quite on the contrary, the French Government informed the New Zealand Ambassador at 10:30 p.m. that "the French officer is thus leaving immediately for Paris;" and Mrs. Prieur actually left Hao on board a special flight at 11:30 p.m. (Paris time). It would be very unlikely that the special flight leaving Hao at 11:30 p.m. had not been planned and organized before 10:30 p.m., when the French decision was intimated, and even before 9:30 p.m., the time of New Zealand's response. Indeed the totality of facts prove that, as of the morning of Thursday, 5 May, France had decided that Captain Prieur would leave Hao during the day, with or without New Zealand's approval.

96.   Pondering the reasons for the haste of France, New Zealand contended that Captain Prieur's "removal took place against the backdrop of French presidential elections in which the Prime Minister was a candidate" and New Zealand pointed out that Captain Prieur's departure and arrival in Paris had been widely publicized in France. During the oral proceedings, New Zealand produced the text of an interview given on 27 September 1989 by the Prime Minister at the relevant time, explaining the following on the subject of the "Turenge couple": "I take responsibility for the decision that was made, and could not imagine how these two officers could be abandoned after having obeyed the highest authorities of the State. Because it was the last days of my Government, I decided to bring

Mrs. Prieur, who was pregnant, back from the Pacific atoll where she was stationed. Had I failed to do so, she would surely still be there today." New Zealand alleges that the French Government acted in this way for reasons quite different from the motive or pretext invoked. The Tribunal need not search for the French Government's motives, nor examine the hypotheses alleged by New Zealand. It only observes that, during the day of 5 May 1988, France did not seek New Zealand's approval in good faith for Captain Prieur's sudden departure; and accordingly, that the return of Captain Prieur, who left Hao on Thursday, 5 May at 11:30 p.m. (French time) and arrived in Paris on Friday, 6 May, thus constituted a violation of the obligations under the 1986 Agreement.

This violation seems even more regrettable because, as of 12 February 1988, France had been in a state of continuing violation of its obligations concerning Major Mafart, as stated above, which normally should have resulted in special care concerning compliance with the Agreement in Captain Prieur's case.

97. Moreover, France continued to fall short of its obligations by keeping Captain Prieur in Paris after the unfortunate death of her father on 16 May 1988. No medical report supports or demonstrates the original claim by French authorities to the effect that Captain Prieur's pregnancy required "particular care" and demonstrating that "the medical facilities on Hao are not equipped to carry out the necessary medical examinations and to give Mrs. Prieur the care required by her condition." There is no evidence either which demonstrates that the facilities in Papeete, originally suggested by the New Zealand Ambassador in Paris, were also inadequate; on the contrary, positive evidence has been presented by New Zealand as to their adequacy and sophistication.

The Only medical report in the files concerning Captain Prieur's health is one from Dr. Croxson, dated 21 July 1988, which appears to discard the necessity of particular care for a pregnancy which is "proceeding uneventfully." This medical report adds that "no special arrangements for later pregnancy or delivery are planned, and I formed the opinion that management would be conducted on usual clinical criteria for a 39–year–old, fit, healthy woman in her first pregnancy."

So, the record provides no justification for the failure to return Captain Prieur to Hao some time after the death of her father.

98. The fact that "pregnancy in itself normally constitutes a contra-indication for overseas appointment" is not a valid explanation, because the return to Hao was not "an assignment" to service, or an assignment or military posting, for the reasons already indicated in the case of Major Mafart.

Likewise, the fact that Captain Prieur benefited, under French regulations, from "military leave which she had not taken previously:" as well as "the maternity and nursing leaves established by French law:" may be measures provided by French military laws or regulations.

But in this case, as in that of Major Mafart, French military laws or regulations do not constitute the limit of the obligations of France or of the consequential rights deriving for New Zealand from those obligations. The French rules "governing military discipline" are referred to in the fourth paragraph of the First Agreement not as the limit of New Zealand rights, but as the means of enforcing the stipulated conditions and ensuring that they "will be strictly complied with." Moreover, French military laws or regulations can never be invoked to justify the breach of a treaty. As the French Counter–Memorial properly stated: "the principle according to which the existence of a domestic regulation can never be an excuse for not complying with an international obligation is well established, and France subscribes to it completely."

99.   In summary, the circumstances of distress, of extreme urgency and the humanitarian considerations invoked by France may have been circumstances excluding responsibility for the unilateral removal of Major Mafart without obtaining New Zealand's consent, but clearly these circumstances entirely fail to justify France's responsibility for the removal of Captain Prieur and from the breach of its obligations resulting from the failure to return the two officers to Hao (in the case of Major Mafart once the reasons for their removal had disappeared). There was here a clear breach of its obligations and a breach of a material character.

100.   * * * The facts show that the essential object or purpose of the First Agreement was not fulfilled, since the two agents left the island before the expiry of the three-year period.

This leads the Tribunal to conclude that there have been material breaches by France of its international obligations.

* * *

Duration of the Obligations

102.   The Parties in this case are in complete disagreement with respect to the duration of the obligations assumed by France * * *.

New Zealand contends that the obligation in the Exchange of Letters envisaged that in the normal course of events both agents would remain on Hao for a continuous period of three years. It point out that the First Agreement does not set an expiry date for the three year term but rather describes the term as being for "a period of not less than three years." According to the New Zealand Government, this is clearly not a fixed period ending on a predetermined date. "The three-year period, in its context, clearly means the period of time to be spent by Major Mafart and Captain Prieur on Hao rather than a continuous or fixed time span. In the event of an interruption to the three year period, the obligation assumed by France to ensure that either or both agents serve the balance of the three years would remain." Consequently, concludes the Government of New Zealand, "France is under an ongoing obligation to return Major Mafart and Captain Prieur to Hao to serve out the balance of their three-year confinement."

103.   For its part, the French Government answers: "it is true that the 1986 Agreement does not fix the exact date of expiry of the specific regime that it sets up for the two agents. But neither does it fix the exact date that this regime will take effect." The reason, adds the French Government, is that in paragraph 7 of the First Agreement, it is provided that the undertakings relating to "the transfer of Major Mafart and Captain Prieur will be implemented not later than 25 July 1986." * * *

105.   The characterization of the breach as one extending or continuing in time, in accordance with Article 25 of the draft on State Responsibility (see para. 101), confirms the previous conclusion concerning the duration of the relevant obligations by France under the First Agreement.

According to Article 25, "the time of commission of the breach" extends over the entire period during which the unlawful act continues to take place. France committed a continuous breach of its obligations, without any interruption or suspension, during the whole period when the two agents remained in Paris in breach of the Agreement.

If the breach was a continuous one, as established in paragraph 101 above, that means that the violated obligation also had to be running continuously and without interruption. The "time of commission of the breach" constituted an uninterrupted period, which was not and could not be intermittent, divided into fractions or subject to intervals. Since it had begun on 22 July 1986, it had to end on 22 July 1989, at the expiry of the three years stipulated.

Thus, while France continues to be liable for the breaches which occurred before 22 July 1989, it cannot be said today that France is *now* in breach of its international obligations.

106.   This does not mean that the French Government is exempt from responsibility on account of the previous breaches of its obligations, committed while these obligations were in force.

Article 70(1) of the Vienna Convention on the Law of Treaties provides that:

"the termination of a treaty under its provisions . . .

b) does not affect any right, obligation or legal situation of the parties created through the execution of the treaty prior to its termination."

Referring to claims based on the previous infringement of a treaty which had since expired, Lord McNair stated:

"such claims acquire an existence independent of the treaty whose breach gave rise to them" (ICJ Reports, 1952, p. 63).

In this case it is undisputed that the breaches of obligation incurred by the French Government discussed in paragraphs 88 and 101 of the award—the failure to return Major Mafart and the removal of and failure to return Captain Prieur—were committed at a time when the obligations assumed in the First Agreement were still in force.

Consequently, the claims advanced by New Zealand have an existence independent of the expiration of the First Agreement and entitle New Zealand to obtain adequate relief for these breaches.

For the foregoing reason the Tribunal:

by a majority declares that the obligations of the French Republic requiring the stay of Major Mafart and Captain Prieur on the island of Hao ended on 22 July 1989.

* * *

For the foregoing reasons the Tribunal:

declares that the condemnation of the French Republic for its breaches of its treaty obligations to New Zealand, made public by the decision of the Tribunal, constitutes in the circumstances appropriate satisfaction for the legal and moral damage caused to New Zealand.

For the foregoing reasons the Tribunal:

in light of the above decisions, recommends that the Governments of the French Republic and of New Zealand set up a fund to promote close and friendly relations between the citizens of the two countries, and that the Government of the French Republic make an initial contribution equivalent to U.S. Dollars 2 million to that fund.

Subsequent to the *Rainbow Warrior* arbitration, Major Mafart was promoted to the rank of Colonel and decorated for distinguished service before leaving the French Army. In 1995, Captain Prieur published her memoires of the affair under the title AGENTE SECRETE. See LE MONDE, May 12, 1995, p. 14, Col. 1. Ultimately France and New Zealand reconciled.

For another case discussing the interrelationship of treaty rules on breach and the rules of state responsibility see the *Gabčíkovo–Nagymaros* case, included in Chapter 2 above.

Case Concerning United States Diplomatic and Consular Staff in Tehran

United States v. Iran
1980 I.C.J. Rep. 3 (Judgment of May 24)

80.   The facts of the present case, viewed in the light of the applicable rules of law, thus speak loudly and clearly of successive and still continuing breaches by Iran of its obligations to the United States under the Vienna Conventions of 1961 and 1963, as well as under the Treaty of 1955. Before drawing from this finding the conclusions which flow from it, in terms of the international responsibility of the Iranian State vis-à-vis the United States of America, the Court considers that it should examine one further point. The Court cannot overlook the fact that on the Iranian side, in often

imprecise terms, the idea has been put forward that the conduct of the Iranian Government, at the time of the events of 4 November 1979 and subsequently, might be justified by the existence of special circumstances.

81.   In his letters of 9 December 1979 and 16 March 1980, as previously recalled, Iran's Minister for Foreign Affairs referred to the present case as only "a marginal and secondary aspect of an overall problem". This problem, he maintained, "involves, *inter alia,* more than 25 years of continual interference by the United States in the internal affairs of Iran, the shameless exploitation of our country, and numerous crimes perpetrated against the Iranian people, contrary to and in conflict with all international and humanitarian norms". In the first of the two letters he indeed singled out amongst the "crimes" which he attributed to the United States an alleged complicity on the part of the Central Intelligence Agency in the coup d'etat of 1953 and in the restoration of the Shah to the throne of Iran. Invoking these alleged crimes of the United States, the Iranian Foreign Minister took the position that the United States' Application could not be examined by the Court divorced from its proper context, which he insisted was "the whole political dossier of the relations between Iran and the United States over the last 25 years".

82.   The Court must however observe, first of all, that the matters alleged in the Iranian Foreign Minister's letters of 9 December 1979 and 16 March 1980 are of a kind which, if invoked in legal proceedings, must clearly be established to the satisfaction of the tribunal with all the requisite proof. The Court, in its Order of 15 December 1979, pointed out that if the Iranian Government considered the alleged activities of the United States in Iran legally to have a close connection with the subject-matter of the Application it was open to Iran to present its own case regarding those activities to the Court by way of defence to the United States' claims. The Iranian Government, however, did not appear before the Court. Moreover, even in his letter of 16 March 1980, transmitted to the Court some three months after the issue of that Order, the Iranian Foreign Minister did not furnish the Court with any further information regarding the alleged criminal activities of the United States in Iran, or explain on what legal basis he considered these allegations to constitute a relevant answer to the United States' claims. The large body of information submitted by the United States itself to the Court includes, it is true, some statements emanating from Iranian authorities or from the militants in which reference is made to alleged espionage and interference in Iran by the United States centered upon its Embassy in Tehran. These statements are, however, of the same general character as the assertions of alleged criminal activities of the United States contained in the Foreign Minister's letters, and are unsupported by evidence furnished by Iran before the Court. Hence they do not provide a basis on which the Court could form a judicial opinion on the truth or otherwise of the matters there alleged.

83.   In any case, even if the alleged criminal activities of the United States in Iran could be considered as having been established, the question would remain whether they could be regarded by the Court as constituting

a justification of Iran's conduct and thus a defence to the United States' claims in the present case. The Court, however, is unable to accept that they can be so regarded. This is because diplomatic law itself provides the necessary means of defence against, and sanction for, illicit activities by members of diplomatic or consular missions.

84.   The Vienna Conventions of 1961 and 1963 contain express provisions to meet the case when members of an embassy staff, under the cover of diplomatic privileges and immunities, engage in such abuses of their functions as espionage or interference in the internal affairs of the receiving State. It is precisely with the possibility of such abuses in contemplation that Article 41, paragraph 1, of the Vienna Convention on Diplomatic Relations, and Article 55, paragraph 1, of the Vienna Convention on Consular Relations, provide

> "Without prejudice to their privileges and immunities, it is the duty of all persons enjoying such privileges and immunities to respect the laws and regulations of the receiving State. They also have a duty not to interfere in the internal affairs of that State."

Paragraph 3 of Article 41 of the 1961 Convention further states: "The premises of the mission must not be used in any manner incompatible with the functions of the missions . . .": an analogous provision, with respect to consular premises is to be found in Article 55, paragraph 2, of the 1963 Convention.

85.   Thus, it is for the very purpose of providing a remedy for such possible abuses of diplomatic functions that Article 9 of the 1961 Convention on Diplomatic Relations stipulates:

> "1.   The receiving State may at any time and without having to explain its decision, notify the sending State that the head of the mission or any member of the diplomatic staff of the mission is *persona non grata* or that any other member of the staff of the mission is not acceptable. In any such case, the sending State shall, as appropriate, either recall the person concerned or terminate his functions with the mission. A person may be declared *non grata* or not acceptable before arriving in the territory of the receiving State.
>
> 2.   If the sending State refuses or fails within a reasonable period to carry out its obligations under paragraph I of this Article, the receiving State may refuse to recognize the person concerned as a member of the mission."

The 1963 Convention contains, in Article 23, paragraphs I and 4, analogous provisions in respect of consular officers and consular staff. Paragraph I of Article 9 of the 1961 Convention, and paragraph 4 of Article 23 of the 1963 Convention, take account of the difficulty that may be experienced in practice of proving such abuses in every case or, indeed, of determining exactly when exercise of the diplomatic function, expressly recognized in Article 3(1)(*d*) of the 1961 Convention, of "ascertaining by all lawful means conditions and developments in the receiving State" may be considered as involving such acts as "espionage" or "interference in internal affairs". The way in which Article 9, paragraph I, takes account of any such difficulty is by providing expressly in its opening sentence that the receiving State may "at any time and without having to explain its decision" notify the sending State that any particular member of its diplomatic mission is "*persona non grata*" or "not acceptable" (and similarly Article 23, paragraph 4, of the 1963 Convention provides that "the receiving State is not obliged to give to the sending State reasons for its decision"). Beyond that remedy for dealing with abuses of the diplomatic function by individual members of a mission, a receiving State has in its hands a more radical remedy if abuses of their functions by members of a mission reach serious proportions. This is the power which every receiving State has, at its own discretion, to break off diplomatic relations with a sending State and to call for the immediate closure of the offending mission.

86. The rules of diplomatic law, in short, constitute a self-contained regime which, on the one hand, lays down the receiving State's obligations regarding the facilities, privileges and immunities to be accorded to diplomatic missions and, on the other, foresees their possible abuse by members of the mission and specifies the means at the disposal of the receiving State to counter any such abuse. These means are, by their nature, entirely efficacious, for unless the sending State recalls the member of the mission objected to forthwith, the prospect of the almost immediate loss of his privileges and immunities, because of the withdrawal by the receiving State of his recognition as a member of the mission, will in practice compel that person, in his own interest, to depart at once. But the principle of the inviolability of the persons of diplomatic agents and the premises of diplomatic missions is one of the very foundations of this long-established regime, to the evolution of which the traditions of Islam made a substantial contribution. The fundamental character of the principle of inviolability is, moreover, strongly underlined by the provisions of Articles 44 and 45 of the Convention of 1961 (cf. also Articles 26 and 27 of the Convention of 1963). Even in the case of armed conflict or in the case of a breach in diplomatic relations those provisions require that both the inviolability of the members of a diplomatic mission and of the premises, property and archives of the mission must be respected by the receiving State. Naturally, the observance of this principle does not mean—and this the Applicant Government expressly acknowledges—that a diplomatic agent caught in the act of committing an assault or other offence may not, on occasion, be briefly arrested by the police of the receiving State in order to prevent the commission of the particular crime. But such eventualities bear no relation at all to what occurred in the present case.

87. In the present case, the Iranian Government did not break off diplomatic relations with the United States; and in response to a question put to him by a Member of the Court, the United States Agent informed the Court that at no time before the events of 4 November 1979 had the Iranian Government declared, or indicated any intention to declare, any member of the United States diplomatic or consular staff in Tehran *persona non grata*. The Iranian Government did not, therefore, employ the remedies placed at its disposal by diplomatic law specifically for dealing with activities of the kind of which it now complains. Instead, it allowed a group of militants to attack and occupy the United States Embassy by force, and to seize the diplomatic and consular staff as hostages; instead, it

has endorsed that action of those militants and has deliberately maintained their occupation of the Embassy and detention of its staff as a means of coercing the sending State. It has, at the same time, refused altogether to discuss this situation with representatives of the United States. The Court, therefore, can only conclude that Iran did not have recourse to the normal and efficacious means at its disposal, but resorted to coercive action against the United States Embassy and its staff.

88.   In an address given on 5 November 1979, the Ayatollah Khomeini traced the origin of the operation carried out by the Islamic militants on the previous day to the news of the arrival of the former Shah of Iran in the United States. That fact may no doubt have been the ultimate catalyst of the resentment felt in certain circles in Iran and among the Iranian population against the former Shah for his alleged misdeeds, and also against the United States Government which was being publicly accused of having restored him to the throne, of having supported him for many years and of planning to go on doing so. But whatever be the truth in regard to those matters, they could hardly be considered as having provided a justification for the attack on the United States Embassy and its diplomatic mission. Whatever extenuation of the responsibility to be attached to the conduct of the Iranian authorities may be found in the offence felt by them because of the admission of the Shah to the United States, that feeling of offence could not affect the imperative character of the legal obligations incumbent upon the Iranian Government which is not altered by a state of diplomatic tension between the two countries. Still less could a mere refusal or failure on the part of the United States to extradite the Shah to Iran be considered to modify the obligations of the Iranian authorities, quite apart from any legal difficulties, in internal or international law, there might be in acceding to such a request for extradition.

89.   Accordingly, the Court finds that no circumstances exist in the present case which are capable of negativing the fundamentally unlawful character of the conduct pursued by the Iranian State on 4 November 1979 and thereafter. This finding does not however exclude the possibility that some of the circumstances alleged, if duly established, may later be found to have some relevance in determining the consequences of the responsibility incurred by the Iranian State with respect to that conduct, although they could not be considered to alter its unlawful character.

2.   COUNTERMEASURES

Case Concerning the Air Services Agreement of 27 March 1946*

United States v. France
Arbitral Tribunal established by the *Compromis* of 11 July 1978
9 December 1978

Riphagen, President; Ehrlich and Reuter, Arbitrators

II.   THE FACTS

1.   An Exchange of Notes of 5 April 1960 relating to the Air Services Agreement concluded between the United States of America and France on

---

* Footnotes omitted.

27 March 1946 authorises air carriers designated by the United States to operate to Paris via London (without traffic rights between London and Paris) services to and from United States West Coast points. A carrier so designated, Pan American World Airways (hereinafter referred to as Pan Am) intermittently operated services over this route until 2 March 1975.

2.   On 20 February 1978, pursuant to French legislation requiring flight schedules to be filed thirty days in advance, Pan Am informed the competent French authority, the *Direction generale de l'Aviation civile* (hereinafter referred to as *D.G.A.C.*), of its plan to resume its West Coast—London–Paris service (without traffic rights between London and Paris) on 1 May 1978 with six weekly flights in each direction. The operation of this service was to involve a change of gauge, in London; from a Boeing 747 aircraft to a smaller Boeing 727 on the outward journey and from a Boeing 727 to a larger Boeing 747 on the return journey.

3.   On 14 March 1978, the *D.G.A.G.* refused to approve Pan Am's plan on the ground that it called for a change of gauge in the territory of a third State and thus was contrary to Section VI of the Annex to the 1946 Air Services Agreement, which deals with changes of gauge in the territory of the Contracting Parties only. The United States Embassy in Paris having, on 22 March 1978, requested the French Foreign Ministry to re-consider the decision of the *D.G.A.G.*, the matter then became the subject of discussions and of diplomatic exchanges between the two Parties, the United States arguing that Pan Am's proposed change of gauge in London was consistent with the 1946 Air Services Agreement and France contending that it was not and reserving its right to take appropriate measures.

4.   On 1 and 2 May 1978, when Pan Am operated for the first time its renewed West Coast–London–Paris service with a change of gauge in London, the French police confined themselves to drawing up reports of what they considered to be unlawful flights. Another flight having taken place on 3 May, Pan Am's Boeing 727 aircraft was surrounded by French police upon arrival at Paris Orly Airport, and its captain was instructed to return to London without having disembarked the passengers or freight. Thereupon Pan Am's flights were suspended.

5.   On 4 May, the United States proposed that the issue be submitted to binding arbitration, on the understanding that Pan Am would be permitted to continue its flights pending the arbitral award. On 9 May, the United States Civil Aeronautics Board (hereinafter referred to as CA.B.) issued a first Order putting into operation phase 1 of Part 213 of its Economic Regulations by requiring the French companies Air France and Union de transports aeriens (U.T.A.) to file, within prescribed time-limits, all their existing flight schedules to and from the United States as well as any new schedules. After having unsuccessfully attempted to have this

Order stayed and revised by the CA.B. or the United States courts, the two companies complied with it on 30 May 1978 by filing their schedules.

6.   In a Note dated 13 May 1978, the French Embassy in Washington had in the meantime acknowledged Pan Am's Suspension of its flights to Paris and had informed the United States Department of State of France's agreement "to the principle of recourse to arbitration." At the same time, the Embassy had objected to the unilateral measure decreed by the Order of the CA.B. prior to the exhaustion of the means of direct negotiations; it had proposed that such negotiations be held and had noted that French local remedies had not been exhausted; finally, it had warned the Department of State that the pursuit of a course of unilateral measures "would have damaging consequences for the French airline companies and create an additional dispute regarding legality and compensation."

7.   On 18 May 1978, Pan Am requested the Administrative Tribunal of Paris to annul as being *ultra vires* the decision taken by the *D.G.A.C.* on 14 March 1978 to disapprove Pan Am's flight schedule. This request is still pending. In a motion filed on 31 May, Pan Am asked that the decision of 14 March 1978 be stayed. This motion was denied on 11 July on the ground that implementation of that decision would not cause irreparable harm.

8.   In the meantime, on 31 May 1978, the C.A.B. issued a second Order under Part 213 of its Economic Regulations. This Order, which was subject to stay or disapproval by the President of the United States within ten days and which was to be implemented on 12 July, was to prevent Air France from operating its thrice-weekly flights to and from Los Angeles and Paris via Montreal for the period during which Pan Am would be barred from operating its West Coast–London–Paris service with change of gauge in London.

9.   The second Part 213 Order was not implemented, however. Legal experts of both Parties having met on 1 and 2 June in Washington, on 28 and 29 June in Paris, and on 10 and 11 July in Washington, a *Compromis* of Arbitration was signed between the United States and France on 11 July 1978. This *Compromis* reads as follows:

* * *

V.   QUESTION (A)

43.   The first question to be decided by the Tribunal is as follows:

Does a United States-designated carrier have the right to operate West Coast–Paris service under the Air Services Agreement between the United States and France with a change of gauge in London (transshipment to a smaller aircraft on the outward journey and to a larger aircraft on the return journey)?

[After a thorough review of the text and evidence per the Vienna Convention on the Law of Treaties, the Tribunal found that a change of gauge on continuous flights was permitted by the treaty.]

VI. QUESTION (B)

* * *

[T]he Tribunal will consider, in turn, the principle of the legitimacy of "counter-measures" and the limits on these measures in the light either of the existence of a machinery of negotiations or of a mechanism of arbitration or judicial settlement.

81.   Under the rules of present-day international law, and unless the contrary results from special obligations arising under particular treaties, notably from mechanisms created within the framework of international organisations, each State establishes for itself its legal situation vis-à-vis other States. If a situation arises which, in one State's view, results in the violation of an international obligation by another State, the first State is entitled, within the limits set by the general rules of international law pertaining to the use of armed force, to affirm its rights through "counter-measures."

82.   At this point, one could introduce various doctrinal distinctions and adopt a diversified terminology dependent on various criteria, in particular whether it is the obligation allegedly breached which is the subject of the counter-measures or whether the latter involve another obligation, and whether or not all the obligations under consideration pertain to the same convention. The Tribunal, however, does not think it necessary to go into these distinctions for the purposes of the present case. Indeed, in the present case, both the alleged violation and the counter-measure directly affect the operation of air services provided for in the Agreement and the Exchange of Notes of 5 April 1960.

83.   It is generally agreed that all counter-measures must, in the first instance, have some degree of equivalence with the alleged breach; this is a well-known rule. In the course of the present proceedings; both Parties have recognised that the rule applies to this case, and they both have invoked it. It has been observed, generally, that judging the "proportionality" of counter-measures is not an easy task and can at best be accomplished by approximation. In the Tribunal's view, it is essential, in a dispute between States, to take into account not only the injuries suffered by the companies concerned but also the importance of the questions of principle arising from the alleged breach. The Tribunal thinks that it will not suffice, in the present case, to compare the losses suffered by Pan Am on account of the suspension of the projected services with the losses which the French companies would have suffered as a result of the counter-measures; it will also be necessary to take into account the importance of the positions of principle which were taken when the French authorities prohibited changes of gauge in third countries. If the importance of the issue is viewed within the framework of the general air transport policy adopted by the United States Government and implemented by the conclusion of a large number of international agreements with countries other than France, the measures taken by the United States do not appear to be clearly disproportionate when compared to those taken by France. Neither

Party has provided the Tribunal with evidence that would be sufficient to affirm or reject the existence of proportionality in these terms, and the Tribunal must be satisfied with a very approximative appreciation.

84.   Can it be said that the resort to such counter-measures which are contrary to international law but justified by a violation of international law allegedly committed by the State against which they are directed, is restricted if it is found that the Parties previously accepted a duty to negotiate or an obligation to have their dispute settled through a procedure of arbitration or of judicial settlement?

85.   It is tempting to assert that when Parties enter into negotiations, they are under a general duty not to aggravate the dispute, this general duty being a kind of emanation of the principle of good faith.

86.   Though it is far from rejecting such an assertion, the Tribunal is of the view that, when attempting to define more precisely such a principle, several essential considerations must be examined.

87.   First, the duty to negotiate may, in present times, take several forms and thus have a greater or lesser significance. There is the very general obligation to negotiate which is set forth by Article 33 of the Charter of the United Nations and the content of which can be stated in some quite basic terms. But there are other, more precise obligations.

88.   The Tribunal recalls the terms of Article VIII of the 1946 Agreement, which reads as follows:

> In a spirit of close collaboration, the aeronautical authorities of the two Contracting Parties will consult regularly with a view to assuring the observance of the principles and the implementation of the provisions outlined in the present Agreement and its Annex.

> This Article provides for an obligation of continuing consultation between the Parties. In the context of this general duty, the Agreement establishes a clear mandate to the Parties to make good faith efforts to negotiate on issues of potential controversy. Several other provisions of the Agreement and the Annex state requirements to consult in specific circumstances, when the possibility of a dispute might be particularly acute. Finally, Article X imposes on the Parties a special consultation requirement when, in spite of previous efforts, a dispute has arisen.

89.   But the present problem is whether, on the basis of the above-mentioned texts, counter-measures are prohibited. The Tribunal does not consider that either general international law or the provisions of the Agreement allow it to go that far.

90.   Indeed, it is necessary carefully to assess the meaning of counter-measures in the framework of proportionality. Their aim is to restore equality between the Parties and to encourage them to continue negotiations with mutual desire to reach an acceptable solution. In the present case, the United States of America holds that a change of gauge is permissible in third countries; that conviction defined its position before

the French refusal came into play; the United States counter-measures restore in a negative way the symmetry of the initial positions.

91.   It goes without saying that recourse to counter-measures involves the great risk of giving rise, in turn, to a further reaction, thereby causing an escalation which will lead to a worsening of the conflict. Counter-measures therefore should be a wager on the wisdom, not on the weakness of the other Party. They should be used with a spirit of great moderation and be accompanied by a genuine effort at resolving the dispute. But the Arbitral Tribunal does not believe that it is possible, in the present state of international relations, to lay down a rule prohibiting the use of counter-measures during negotiations, especially where such counter-measures are accompanied by an offer for a procedure affording the possibility of accelerating the solution of the dispute.

92.   That last consideration is particularly relevant in disputes concerning air service operations: the network of air services is in fact an extremely sensitive system, disturbances of which can have wide and unforeseeable consequences.

93.   With regard to the machinery of negotiations, the actions by the United States Government do not appear, therefore, to run counter to the international obligations of that Government.

94.   However, the lawfulness of such counter-measures has to be considered still from another viewpoint. It may indeed be asked whether they are valid in general, in the case of a dispute concerning a point of law, where there is arbitral or judicial machinery which can settle the dispute. Many jurists have felt that while arbitral or judicial proceedings were in progress, recourse to counter-measures, even if limited by the proportionality rule, was prohibited. Such an assertion deserves sympathy but requires further elaboration. If the proceedings form part of an institutional framework ensuring some degree of enforcement of obligations, the justification of countermeasures will undoubtedly disappear, but owing to the existence of that framework rather than solely on account of the existence of arbitral or judicial proceedings as such.

95.   Besides, the situation during the period in which a case is not yet before a tribunal is not the same as the situation during the period in which that case is *sub judice*. So long as a dispute has not been brought before the tribunal, in particular because an agreement between the Parties is needed to set the procedure in motion, the period of negotiation is not over and the rules mentioned above remain applicable. This may be a regrettable solution, as the Parties in principle did agree to resort to arbitration or judicial settlement, but it must be conceded that under present-day international law States have not renounced their right to take counter-measures in such situations. In fact, however, this solution may be preferable as it facilitates States' acceptance of arbitration or judicial settlement procedures.

96.   The situation changes once the tribunal is in a position to act. To the extent that the tribunal has the necessary means to achieve the

objectives justifying the countermeasures, it must be admitted that the right of the Parties to initiate such measures disappears. In other words, the power of a tribunal to decide on interim measures of protection, regardless of whether this power is expressly mentioned or implied in its statute (at least as the power to formulate recommendations to this effect), leads to the disappearance of the power to initiate counter-measures and may lead to an elimination of existing counter-measures to the extent that the tribunal so provides as an interim measure of protection. As the object and scope of the power of the tribunal to decide on interim measures of protection may be defined quite narrowly, however, the power of the Parties to initiate or maintain counter-measures, too, may not disappear completely.

97.   In a case under the terms of a provision like Article X of the Air Services Agreement of 1946, as amended by the Exchange of Notes of 19 March 1951, the arbitration may be set in motion unilaterally. Although the arbitration need not be binding, the Parties are obliged to "use their best efforts under the powers available to them to put into effect the opinion expressed" by the Tribunal. In the present case, the Parties concluded a *Compromis* that provides for a binding decision on Question (A) and expressly authorises the Tribunal to decide on interim measures.

98.   As far as the action undertaken by the United States Government in the present case is concerned, the situation is quite simple. Even if arbitration under Article X of the Agreement is set in motion unilaterally, implementation may take time, and during this period counter-measures are not excluded; a State resorting to such measures, however, must do everything in its power to expedite the arbitration. This is exactly what the Government of the United States has done.

99.   The Tribunal's Reply to Question (B) consists of the above observations as a whole. These observations lead to the conclusion that, under the circumstances in question, the Government of the United States had the right to undertake the action that it undertook under Part 213 of the Economic Regulations of the C.A.B.

* * *

Thomas Franck, Proportionality*

102 AM. J. INT'L L. 742–752 (2008)

IV.   The Principle of Proportionality and
Disproportionality in Trade Disputes

The concept of "proportionality" is a prominent feature of the dispute settlement system of the World Trade Organization. The term appears explicitly in two footnotes to the WTO Agreement on Subsidies and Countervailing Measures (SCM Agreement). More broadly, the set of rules governing trade disputes (regarding a violation of WTO law) requires that

---

* Footnotes omitted.

any countermeasure authorized by the WTO Dispute Settlement Body (DSB) be "equivalent" to the "nullification or impairment" resulting from the trade law violation. Due attention to the concepts of equivalence and proportionality has permeated the process adopted by arbitral panels in implementing the WTO agreements.

The WTO Dispute Settlement Understanding (DSU) sets out detailed procedures for resolving trade disputes. If a WTO member is found to be violating WTO law and the member does not correct the violation, the DSB may authorize the suspension of concessions or other obligations. This remedy, which is referred to as "retaliation" or "SCOO," is available only to the aggrieved party, who is then free to impose it. Since such lawful retaliation is the principal means for enforcing the trade regime's rules in the event of their violation, the system permits an aggrieved party considerable leeway in fashioning the appropriate countermeasure while also subordinating its discretion to a second opinion on its proportionality. To put the matter succinctly: The violation of a reciprocal obligation creates an opportunity for the injured party to seek relief by the imposition of a countermeasure. That the countermeasure does not exceed limits imposed by proportionality is superintended by the dispute settlement procedure.

For certain disputes regarding subsidies, the regular DSU procedures are supplemented by more specific procedures in the SCM Agreement. Under those procedures, the aggrieved party may seek authorization to take what are termed "countermeasures." When the WTO law violation being complained of is a prohibited subsidy, the SCM rules provide for the remedy of "appropriate countermeasures." To clarify the meaning of the term "appropriate," the SCM Agreement contains two footnotes stating that "[t]his expression is not meant to allow countermeasures that are disproportionate in light of the fact that the subsidies dealt with under these provisions are prohibited."

For a case involving a prohibited subsidy, the procedural rules are straightforward. The SCM, in its Article 4 on remedies, allows a state to challenge measures that allegedly constitute export subsidies made unlawful by Article 3. If not resolved by negotiations, such a challenge may be referred to a panel by the DSB. If the panel finds that the disputed measure is a prohibited subsidy, it must be withdrawn. And if, within a stipulated time, the unlawful measure is not rescinded, the DSB may authorize the complainant state (under Article 4.10) to take "appropriate countermeasures," a term that, as noted above, a footnote explains "is not meant to allow countermeasures that are disproportionate." Several arbitration panels have given substance to the double-negative term "not ... disproportionate," thereby casting light on its logical concomitant, the principle of proportionality.

The "not ... disproportionate" qualifier is not used in the WTO Agreement beyond prohibited subsidies because, for any other violation of WTO law, the permissible extent of countermeasures is specified in a positive way. For example, for violations involving actionable subsidies, Article 7.9 of part III of the SCM provides that the countermeasures must be "commensurate" with the degree and nature of the adverse effects caused by the subsidy. This standard is similar to the more general remedy for other infractions of the trade regime found in Article 22.4 of the DSU. It provides that the level of retaliation (or SCOO) authorized after a finding of violations "shall be equivalent to the level of the nullification or impairment" of its treaty obligations found to have been incurred by the actions of the offending party. The latter, however, may object that the countermeasure sought is not "equivalent" to the level of "nullification or impairment" (Article 22.6), and demand arbitration to determine whether the impact exceeds the level of trade nullification or impairment found to have been caused by the unlawful measure.

It will be readily apparent that these texts incorporate somewhat different notions of what constitutes a permissible countermeasure. Under the part of the SCM Agreement that pertains to prohibited subsidies, the complaining state is authorized to take "appropriate countermeasures" which are "not disproportionate." Under DSU Articles 22.4 and 22.7, which set a standard applicable to any dispute, the retaliation must be "equivalent" to the trade "nullification and impairment" produced by an offending state's unlawful actions affecting trade. It thus appears that, depending on the applicable provision under which retaliatory measures have been taken, arbitrators are meant to conduct either an *instrumental* inquiry as to whether the retaliatory means were appropriate to the purpose of having the violations stopped, or a *comparative* inquiry as to the equivalence between damage inflicted by the wrongful act and that inflicted by the countermeasures taken. Both streams of WTO arbitration suggest proportionality, although they do so in different ways.

Several arbitral panels have applied these provisions and examined the differences between them. In the 1999 *Banana* dispute between the United States and the European Union, the main issue was a discriminatory tariff disadvantaging U.S. exports. Since the cause of action concerned tariffs, not subsidies, the DSU's "equivalence" standard was applied. Comparing the SCM standard of "appropriateness" with the DSU standard of "equivalence," the arbitral panel concluded that "the ordinary meaning of '*equivalent*' implies a higher degree of correspondence, identity or stricter balance between the level of the proposed suspension and the level of nullification or impairment" caused by the unlawful measure. Implicitly, the proportionality required by the SCM standard was seen as not requiring so strict an equivalence between an unlawful measure and the corresponding "appropriate" countermeasure. The panel also applied the stricter "equivalence" standard when it compared "the value of relevant EC imports from the United States under the present banana import regime (the actual situation) with [what] their value [would have been] under a WTO-consistent regime." The effect of the decision was to narrow significantly the band of indeterminacy surrounding the terms "equivalent" and "appropriate." The arbitration further made a jurisprudentially significant distinction between permissibly equivalent countermeasures and those that were impermissible because they were punitive.

Equivalence was again the preferred standard for determining allowable levels of retaliation by Canada against the European Community in response to the latter's failure to rescind a scientifically unsupported ban on Canadian hormone-treated beef exports. Applying the stricter standard, the arbitration compared Canada's actual exports with those that probably would have been achieved but for the distortion brought about by the unlawful constraint. In this way, by a process of public reasoning that applies interpretative rulings made in one case to subsequent cases, the jurisprudence of proportionality gradually progresses toward a degree of determinacy that the treaty text does not provide, reinforcing the text's legitimacy. * * *

Although the standard of equivalence is generally applied in WTO disputes, the matter remains less clear with regard to retaliation in response to prohibited subsidies, where the SCM sets the standard at "appropriateness." In a dispute between Canada and Brazil, the arbitrators allowed the former to impose countermeasures on the latter to the full value of the latter's subsidies for global sales of Brazilian airplanes, rather than limiting the countermeasures to an amount strictly equivalent to the actual loss sustained by Canada. The arbitrator noted that the object of the "appropriateness" standard was not merely to compensate the complaining state for actual losses, but also to induce withdrawal of the offending subsidies themselves. Thus, while a "countermeasure remains 'appropriate' as long as it is not *disproportionate*," that proportionality is not to be calculated simply by estimating the effect of the unlawful measure on the complaining state because "a countermeasure based on the actual level of nullification or impairment will have less or no inducement effect and the subsidizing country may not withdraw the measure at issue."

The finding of the arbitrators points to the conclusion in law that a coercive measure is proportionate as long as it does not exceed the amount necessary to bring about a reversal of the state's noncompliance with a legal obligation. Rejecting Brazil's claim that the Canadian countermeasures were punitive, the arbitrators distinguished between measures "intended to ensure that the State in breach of its obligations bring its conduct into conformity with its international obligations" and those that contain "an additional dimension meant to sanction the action of that State." The decision appears to have accepted that a proportionate countermeasure cannot always have precisely the same weight as the measure provoking it. It also accepted that retaliation, to be effective, cannot always be configured as a mirror image of the offending measure. For example, Canada could not simply grant a countervailing subsidy like Brazil's to its own aircraft export industry "because other Members than the parties compete with the products of the parties" and thus would be adversely affected.

The arbitration concluded that "a countermeasure is 'appropriate' *inter alia* if it *effectively* induces compliance." As a result, Canada's countermeasures could be exerted at whatever level is appropriate to "inducing the withdrawal of the prohibited subsidy." In effect, an "appropriate" countermeasure may be more onerous than one calculated to be merely "equivalent" to the wrong inflicted, as long as it is not "disproportionate" to the objective of ending illegal conduct. Thus, when determining the proportionality of SCOO countermeasures, the test is calculated somewhat differently for prohibited subsidies than for other types of WTO violations. This distinction, however, is justified both by the applicable text and purpose of the SCM and DSU, and by the consistent arbitral jurisprudence emerging case by case.

* * *

The DSU, as we have seen, provides for arbitration to determine whether restrictive policies of one state party violate the rules of the regime and thereby cause quantifiable harm to another party. Yet not all restraints are illegal. Article XX of the GATT provides a list of "general exceptions" to the prohibitions on quantitative and discriminatory restraints on trade. It states:

[N]othing in this Agreement shall be construed to prevent the adoption or enforcement by any contracting party of measures:

(*a*) necessary to protect public morals;

(*b*) necessary to protect human, animal or plant life or health;

. . .

(*d*) necessary to secure compliance with laws or regulations which are not inconsistent with the provisions of this Agreement. . . . The key term "necessary" has been interpreted by several GATT dispute panels. Assessing whether a restrictive provision of the United States Tariff Act of 1930 was commensurate with clause (d) of Article XX, a 1990 decision stipulated that "a contracting party cannot justify a measure inconsistent with [a] GATT provision as 'necessary . . .' if an alternative measure which it could reasonably be expected to employ and which is not inconsistent with other GATT provisions is available to it." The party claiming, by reference to one of the provisos of Article XX, the exceptional right not to implement a GATT obligation "is bound to use, among the measures reasonably available to it, that which entails the least degree of inconsistency with other GATT provisions." The same principle was applied in construing the legality of a Thai restriction on the importation of cigarettes, a violation of GATT that was claimed to be a health measure permitted under Article XX(b). The arbitration concluded that the restraint on cigarette imports was allowable "only if there were no alternative measure consistent with the [GATT], or less inconsistent with it." More adjudications have helped make Article XX's initially elastic principle more concrete.

* * *

In another dispute, one between Canada and the European Union, the Appellate Body held that Canada had failed to establish that measures excluding its asbestos exports from the European market were "inconsistent with the obligations of the European Communities under the covered agreements," concluding, rather, that they were within the permissible exception ("necessary to protect human ... health") of Article XX(b). Specifically, the appellate tribunal found the exclusion "necessary" to France's objective of eliminating all asbestos, and refused to heed Canada's call to consider whether comparable levels of health protection could not have been achieved by a more selective form of prohibition. It concluded that the government's chosen health policy—zero asbestos—could not be challenged as unreasonable on the ground that a different strategy would have been almost as efficacious in protecting the public health. France's recourse to the exception permitted by Article XX(b) could not be reviewed by examining whether a slightly more relaxed policy might yield comparable levels of health protection with a lesser impact on trade. The tribunal could merely inquire whether the trade restriction was necessary to achieve the government's chosen policy, not whether another policy might achieve a comparable level of health protection. That is, it is up to the state to determine whether it seeks to eliminate, or merely to mitigate, the consequences of another state's action that affects its people's health. If the state decides to eliminate the threat entirely, any means necessary to achieve that objective falls within the ambit of a discretionary countermeasure available to achieve that end. Lesser means, capable of effecting mitigation but not eradication, are not "reasonably available alternatives" to which it must have recourse. This reading makes predictable the finding by the Appellate Body of the proposition that the "necessity" of U.S. laws imposing restraints with a significant restrictive trade impact on Antiguan gambling services is not negated by the U.S. refusal of an invitation to engage in bilateral or multilateral consultations and/or negotiations with the complainant. The mere fact that "the United States did not enter into consultations with Antigua" to find other means to protect its "public morals or to maintain public order" did not demonstrate that less restrictive means were available and that the means actually deployed were therefore unnecessary. It has been deduced from the cases that the jurisprudence recognizes a form of presumption:

[I]f the regulatory objective relates to some highly valued interest such as the protection of human life, then the challenged regulation will be upheld if there is any doubt as to the ability of the proposed alternative to achieve the same level of efficacy. This practice may be understood as a recognition of the fact that the costs of an erroneous decision—loss of life—would be extremely high, and that even a small probability of an erroneous decision counsels against condemning the measure under scrutiny.

Where, however, the regulatory objective is to protect some lesser interest than life or health, the standard chosen to review a restraint on trade will tend to be more rigorous.

Similar "least restrictive means requirements" are attached to exceptions set out in several other trade agreements that postdate the GATT. As with exceptions to treaty-based social rights protecting individual rights and freedoms (see below), so in the area of trade "the proportionality principle refers to the obligation to choose the *means least restrictive* of a certain societal interest" defined by a widely ratified international legal instrument. Thus, the proportionality of measures taken under the Sanitary and Phytosanitary Agreement has been reviewed by arbitration panels and in appeals to the Appellate Body. In the *Salmon* case, for example, Canada alleged that Australia's ban on fresh, frozen, or chilled salmon violated the SPS Agreement's requirement that health-protective constraints on imports not be "more trade-restrictive than required to achieve their appropriate level of sanitary or phytosanitary protection, taking into account technical and economic feasibility." The test, confirmed by the Appellate Body, stipulates that a measure will be found to be more restrictive than necessary (i.e., disproportionate) when (1) another measure is reasonably available to provide SPS protection, and (2) this alternative measure would achieve the appropriate level of protection, and (3) the alternative would be significantly less restrictive of trade. According to the tribunal, it is the complaining party that bears the burden of proving these three elements. This test incorporates in the context of international trade law a specialized aspect of the proportionality principle. The ubiquitous reference to the requirement that least restrictive measures be taken when the violation of a free trade norm is claimed to be necessary to protect a party's lawful interest is also echoed in such diverse fields as the law of warfare and the law of human rights, where similar principles have been formulated to limit recourse to exceptions. Whenever a code of law makes provision for a state of exception or necessity, there is likely also to be found, in treaty text and in judicial interpretations, some version of the "least restrictive means" principle. The application of that rule, which we will examine more closely in the context of human rights law, involves the rendering of a disinterested second opinion as to the proportionality of the exceptional measure taken by a party asserting a legitimate interest but derogating from the requirements of a treaty regime.

Observers have duly noted that neither the treaty texts, nor the pre-GATT arbitral panels have offered "much guidance as to how the necessity and least restrictive means requirements are to be implemented in practice.... [B]ut the WTO decisions to date strongly suggest that cost-benefit logic lies at the center of analysis." Some version of cost-benefit analysis indeed lies at the heart of many applications of the principle of proportionality. In both the European Community's and the Council of Europe's law (see below), in matters ranging from the regulation of property to constraints on human rights, the proportionality principle has emerged as "one of the most important unwritten principles commonly invoked" before the European Court of Justice and the European Court of Human Rights to challenge the effect of regulations on the rights of persons.

* * *

NOTES AND QUESTIONS

1. *No Mistake.* The Articles on State Responsibility do not include an article on mistake. According to Mary Ellen O'Connell, there is evidence that states treat mistakes as precluding wrongfulness:

With respect to mistake, according to Oppenheim, no general principle exists in international law as to a fault standard in the commission of a wrong. Some international law rules indicate a fault standard; others do not. International law scholars who generally find that international law supports only an objective, not a subjective fault standard would reject mistake as an excuse. This seems to be the position of the Articles on State Responsibility, which do include mistake as a circumstance that precludes wrongfulness. Crawford takes the view, in his Third Report as Special Rapporteur, that no excuse of good-faith mistake is recognized in international law. The circumstances that do preclude wrongfulness include necessity, duress, *force majeure*, self defense, consent, and countermeasures. Arguably, these are better thought of as excuses rather than "circumstances precluding wrongfulness," but for our purposes the important point is that they do not apparently require an inquiry into subjective fault. If the objective fact of *force majeure* can be shown, for example, the state has committed no wrong or the wrong can be excused. Thus, we tend not to speak of whether officials "intended" a result or "knew" a result would occur.

Mistake, by contrast, will require a showing of what government officials knew. Did they act in a good-faith but mistaken belief that they were correct as to a question of law or an important fact? In the claims and counterclaims of states, the examples suggest that states will be excused for good-faith mistakes. The cases of passenger planes being shot down support this conclusion. If mistake is accepted as an excuse in those cases, the argument for mistake is even stronger for countermeasures cases. Countermeasures should be reversible, so any harm is only temporary. In the *Tuna–Dolphin* case under the 1947 General Agreement on Tariffs and Trade (GATT) between the U.S. and Mexico, the U.S. used countermeasures against Mexico to induce it to protect dolphins in the course of tuna harvesting. A GATT panel eventually found the United States had no right to take countermeasures and the U.S. ended them. The panel report gives no indication that the United States owed Mexico compensation for having instituted unlawful countermeasures. In a later case on similar facts, a WTO appellate body found in the *Shrimp–Turtle* case that the United States was again using countermeasures inconsistently with its GATT obligations. The measures had to be reformed, but no responsibility was found for the original inadequate measures.

MARY ELLEN O'CONNELL, THE POWER AND PURPOSE OF INTERNATIONAL LAW, INSIGHTS FROM THE THEORY AND PRACTICE OF ENFORCEMENT 248–49 (2008) (footnotes omitted.)

2. Are countermeasures properly grouped with the other "circumstances precluding wrongfulness"? Are they not much more than that? In addition to specific treaty-based limits on the use of countermeasures as well as the general principles of proportionality and necessity, what other limits exist in international law on resort to countermeasures by states and international organizations? What limits should exist?

3. We have seen that states have different kinds of obligations under international law. Does your perspective on the role of state responsibility change when a state breaches an obligation *erga omnes*, such as those under international human rights law? Should the same counter-measures be available for all breaches or should breaches of human rights trigger different counter-measures? For more on this topic, see Karl Zemanak, *Does the Prospect of Incurring Responsibility Improve the Observance of International Law?*, in INTERNATIONAL RESPONSIBILITY TODAY: ESSAYS IN MEMORY OF OSCAR SCHACTER 126–34 (Maurizio Ragazzi, ed. 2005).

4. For more on countermeasures, see MARY ELLEN O'CONNELL, THE POWER AND PURPOSE OF INTERNATIONAL LAW, chs. 6 & 7 (2008); OMER Y. ELAGAB, THE LEGALITY OF NON-FORCIBLE COUNTER-MEASURES IN INTERNATIONAL LAW (1988); AND ELISABETH ZOLLER, PEACETIME UNILATERAL COUNTERMEASURES (1984).

D. CONSEQUENCES OF WRONGFULNESS

Article 30
Cessation and non-repetition

The State responsible for the internationally wrongful act is under an obligation:

(*a*) To cease that act, if it is continuing;

(*b*) To offer appropriate assurances and guarantees of non-repetition, if circumstances so require.

Article 31
Reparation

1. The responsible State is under an obligation to make full reparation for the injury caused by the internationally wrongful act.

2. Injury includes any damage, whether material or moral, caused by the internationally wrongful act of a State.

Article 32
Irrelevance of internal law

The responsible State may not rely on the provisions of its internal law as justification for failure to comply with its obligations under this part.

* * *

Article 35
Restitution

A State responsible for an internationally wrongful act is under an obligation to make restitution, that is, to re-establish the situation which existed before the wrongful act was committed, provided and to the extent that restitution:

(*a*) Is not materially impossible;

(*b*) Does not involve a burden out of all proportion to the benefit deriving from restitution instead of compensation.

Article 36
Compensation

1.   The State responsible for an internationally wrongful act is under an obligation to compensate for the damage caused thereby, insofar as such damage is not made good by restitution.

2.   The compensation shall cover any financially assessable damage including loss of profits insofar as it is established.

Article 37
Satisfaction

1.   The State responsible for an internationally wrongful act is under an obligation to give satisfaction for the injury caused by that act insofar as it cannot be made good by restitution or compensation.

2.   Satisfaction may consist in an acknowledgement of the breach, an expression of regret, a formal apology or another appropriate modality.

3.   Satisfaction shall not be out of proportion to the injury and may not take a form humiliating to the responsible State.

Application of the Convention on the Prevention and Punishment of the Crime of Genocide

Bosnia v. Serbia
International Court of Justice
2007 I.C.J. Rep. (Judgment of Feb. 26)

XI.   The question of reparation

459.   Having thus found that the Respondent has failed to comply with its obligations under the Genocide Convention in respect of the prevention and punishment of genocide, the Court turns to the question of reparation. The Applicant, in its final submissions, has asked the Court to decide that the Respondent

> "must redress the consequences of its international wrongful acts and, as a result of the international responsibility incurred for ... violations of the Convention on the Prevention and Punishment of the Crime of Genocide, must pay, and Bosnia and Herzegovina is entitled to receive, in its own right and as *parens patriae* for its citizens, full compensation for the damages and losses caused" (submission 6(*b*)).

The Applicant also asks the Court to decide that the Respondent

> "shall immediately take effective steps to ensure full compliance with its obligation to punish acts of genocide under the Convention on the Prevention and Punishment of the Crime of Genocide or any other act prohibited by the Convention and to transfer individuals accused of genocide or any other act prohibited by the Convention to the Interna-

tional Criminal Tribunal for the former Yugoslavia and to fully co-operate with this Tribunal" (submission 6(a)),

and that the Respondent "shall provide specific guarantees and assurances that it will not repeat the wrongful acts complained of, the form of which guarantees and assurances is to be determined by the Court" (submission 6(d)). These submissions, and in particular that relating to compensation, were however predicated on the basis that the Court would have upheld, not merely that part of the Applicant's claim as relates to the obligation of prevention and punishment, but also the claim that the Respondent has violated its substantive obligation not to commit genocide, as well as the ancillary obligations under the Convention concerning complicity, conspiracy and incitement, and the claim that the Respondent has aided and abetted genocide. The Court has now to consider what is the appropriate form of reparation for the other forms of violation of the Convention which have been alleged against the Respondent and which the Court has found to have been established, that is to say breaches of the obligations to prevent and punish.

460. The principle governing the determination of reparation for an internationally wrongful act is as stated by the Permanent Court of International Justice in the *Factory at Chorzów* case: that "reparation must, so far as possible, wipe out all the consequences of the illegal act and reestablish the situation which would, in all probability, have existed if that act had not been committed" (*P.C.I.J. Series A, No. 17*, p. 47: see also Article 31 of the ILC's Articles on State Responsibility). In the circumstances of this case, as the Applicant recognizes, it is inappropriate to ask the Court to find that the Respondent is under an obligation of *restitutio in integrum*. Insofar as restitution is not possible, as the Court stated in the case of the *Gabčíkovo-Nagymaros Project (Hungary/Slovakia)*, "[i]t is a well-established rule of international law that an injured State is entitled to obtain compensation from the State which has committed an internationally wrongful act for the damage caused by it" (*I.C.J. Reports 1997*, p. 81, para. 152.; cf. *Legal Consequences of the Construction of a Wall in the Occupied Palestinian Territory, Advisory Opinion, I.C.J. Reports 2004*, p. 198, paras. 152–153; see also Article 36 of the ILC's Articles on State Responsibility). It is therefore appropriate to consider what were the consequences of the failure of the Respondent to comply with its obligations under the Genocide Convention to prevent and punish the crime of genocide, committed in Bosnia and Herzegovina, and what damage can be said to have been caused thereby.

461. The Court has found that the authorities of the Respondent could not have been unaware of the grave risk of genocide once the VRS forces had decided to take possession of the Srebrenica enclave, and that in view of its influence over the events, the Respondent must be held to have had the means of action by which it could seek to prevent genocide, and to have manifestly refrained from employing them * * *. To that extent therefore it failed to comply with its obligation of prevention under the Convention. The obligation to prevent the commission of the crime of

genocide is imposed by the Genocide Convention on any State party which, in a given situation, has it in its power to contribute to restraining in any degree the commission of genocide.

To make this finding, the Court did not have to decide whether the acts of genocide committed at Srebrenica would have occurred anyway even if the Respondent had done as it should have and employed the means available to it. This is because, as explained above, the obligation to prevent genocide places a State under a duty to act which is not dependent on the certainty that the action to be taken will succeed in preventing the commission of acts of genocide, or even on the likelihood of that outcome. It therefore does not follow from the Court's reasoning above in finding a violation by the Respondent of its obligation of prevention that the atrocious suffering caused by the genocide committed at Srebrenica would not have occurred had the violation not taken place.

462.   The Court cannot however leave it at that. Since it now has to rule on the claim for reparation, it must ascertain whether, and to what extent, the injury asserted by the Applicant is the consequence of wrongful conduct by the Respondent with the consequence that the Respondent should be required to make reparation for it, in accordance with the principle of customary international law stated above. In this context, the question just mentioned, whether the genocide at Srebrenica would have taken place even if the Respondent had attempted to prevent it by employing all means in its possession, becomes directly relevant, for the definition of the extent of the obligation of reparation borne by the Respondent as a result of its wrongful conduct. The question is whether there is a sufficiently direct and certain causal nexus between the wrongful act, the Respondent's breach of the obligation to prevent genocide, and the injury suffered by the Applicant, consisting of all damage of any type, material or moral, caused by the acts of genocide. Such a nexus could be considered established only if the Court were able to conclude from the case as a whole and with a sufficient degree of certainty that the genocide at Srebrenica would in fact have been averted if the Respondent had acted in compliance with its legal obligations. However, the Court clearly cannot do so. As noted above, the Respondent did have significant means of influencing the Bosnian Serb military and political authorities which it could, and therefore should, have employed in an attempt to prevent the atrocities, but it has not been shown that, in the specific context of these events, those means would have sufficed to achieve the result which the Respondent should have sought. Since the Court cannot therefore regard as proven a causal nexus between the Respondent's violation of its obligation of prevention and the damage resulting from the genocide at Srebrenica, financial compensation is not the appropriate form of reparation for the breach of the obligation to prevent genocide.

463.   It is however clear that the Applicant is entitled to reparation in the form of satisfaction, and this may take the most appropriate form, as the Applicant itself suggested, of a declaration in the present Judgment that the Respondent has failed to comply with the obligation imposed by

the Convention to prevent the crime of genocide. As in the *Corfu Channel (United Kingdom* v. *Albania)* case, the Court considers that a declaration of this kind is "in itself appropriate satisfaction" (*Merits, Judgment, I.C.J. Reports 1949*, pp. 35, 36), and it will, as in that case, include such a declaration in the operative clause of the present Judgment. The Applicant acknowledges that this failure is no longer continuing, and accordingly has withdrawn the request made in the Reply that the Court declare that the Respondent "has violated *and is violating* the Convention" (emphasis added).

464.   The Court now turns to the question of the appropriate reparation for the breach by the Respondent of its obligation under the Convention to punish acts of genocide; in this respect, the Applicant asserts the existence of a continuing breach, and therefore maintains *(inter alia)* its request for a declaration in that sense. As noted above * * * the Applicant includes under this heading the failure "to transfer individuals accused of genocide or any other act prohibited by the Convention to the International Criminal Tribunal for the former Yugoslavia and to fully co-operate with this Tribunal"; and the Court has found that in that respect the Respondent is indeed in breach of Article VI of the Convention (paragraph 449 above). A declaration to that effect is therefore one appropriate form of satisfaction, in the same way as in relation to the breach of the obligation to prevent genocide. However, the Applicant asks the Court in this respect to decide more specifically that "Serbia and Montenegro shall immediately take effective steps to ensure full compliance with its obligation to punish acts of genocide under the Convention on the Prevention and Punishment of the Crime of Genocide or any other act prohibited by the Convention and to transfer individuals accused of genocide or any other act prohibited by the Convention to the International Criminal Tribunal for the former Yugoslavia and to fully co-operate with this Tribunal."

465.   It will be clear from the Court's findings above on the question of the obligation to punish under the Convention that it is satisfied that the Respondent has outstanding obligations as regards the transfer to the ICTY of persons accused of genocide, in order to comply with its obligations under Articles I and VI of the Genocide Convention, in particular in respect of General Ratko Mladić * * *. The Court will therefore make a declaration in these terms in the operative clause of the present Judgment, which will in its view constitute appropriate satisfaction.

466.   In its final submissions, the Applicant also requests the Court to decide "that Serbia and Montenegro shall provide specific guarantees and assurances that it will not repeat the wrongful acts complained of, the form of which guarantees and assurances is to be determined by the Court". As presented, this submission relates to all the wrongful acts, i.e. breaches of the Genocide Convention, attributed by the Applicant to the Respondent, thus including alleged breaches of the Respondent's obligation not itself to commit genocide, as well as the ancillary obligations under the Convention concerning complicity, conspiracy and incitement. Insofar as the Court has not upheld these claims, the submission falls. There remains however the

question whether it is appropriate to direct that the Respondent provide guarantees and assurances of non-repetition in relation to the established breaches of the obligations to prevent and punish genocide. The Court notes the reasons advanced by counsel for the Applicant at the hearings in support of the submission, which relate for the most part to "recent events [which] cannot fail to cause concern as to whether movements in Serbia and Montenegro calling for genocide have disappeared". It considers that these indications do not constitute sufficient grounds for requiring guarantees of non-repetition. The Applicant also referred in this connection to the question of non-compliance with provisional measures, but this matter has already been examined above * * * and will be mentioned further below. In the circumstances, the Court considers that the declaration referred to in * * * above is sufficient as regards the Respondent's continuing duty of punishment, and therefore does not consider that this is a case in which a direction for guarantees of non-repetition would be appropriate.

467. Finally, the Applicant has presented the following submission:

"That in failing to comply with the Orders for indication of provisional measures rendered by the Court on 8 April 1993 and 13 September 1993 Serbia and Montenegro has been in breach of its international obligations and is under an obligation to Bosnia and Herzegovina to provide for the latter violation symbolic compensation, the amount of which is to be determined by the Court."

The provisional measures indicated by the Court's Order of 8 April 1993, and reiterated by the Order of 13 September 1993, were addressed specifically to the Respondent's obligation "to prevent commission of the crime of genocide" and to certain measures which should "in particular" be taken to that end (*I.C.J. Reports 1993*, p. 24, para. 52(A)(1) and (2)).

468. Provisional measures under Article 41 of the Statute are indicated "pending [the] final decision" in the case, and the measures indicated in 1993 will thus lapse on the delivery of the present Judgment (cf. *Anglo-Iranian Oil Co. (United Kingdom v. Iran), Preliminary Objections, Judgment, I.C.J. Reports 1952*, p. 114; *Military and Paramilitary Activities in and against Nicaragua (Nicaragua v. United States of America), Jurisdiction and Admissibility, Judgment, I.C.J. Reports 1984*, p. 442, para. 112). However, as already observed (paragraph 452 above), orders made by the Court indicating provisional measures under Article 41 of the Statute have binding effect, and their purpose is to protect the rights of either party, pending the final decision in the case.

469. The Court has found above (paragraph 456) that, in respect of the massacres at Srebrenica in July 1995, the Respondent failed to take measures which would have satisfied the requirements of paragraphs 52(A)(1) and (2) of the Court's Order of 8 April 1993 (reaffirmed in the Order of 13 September 1993). The Court however considers that, for purposes of reparation, the Respondent's non-compliance with the provisional measures ordered is an aspect of, or merges with, its breaches of the substantive obligations of prevention and punishment laid upon it by the

Convention. The Court does not therefore find it appropriate to give effect to the Applicant's request for an order for symbolic compensation in this respect. The Court will however include in the operative clause of the present Judgment, by way of satisfaction, a declaration that the Respondent has failed to comply with the Court's Orders indicating provisional measures.

470.   The Court further notes that one of the provisional measures indicated in the Order of 8 April and reaffirmed in that of 13 September 1993 was addressed to both Parties. The Court's findings in paragraphs 456 to 457 and 469 are without prejudice to the question whether the Applicant did not also fail to comply with the Orders indicating provisional measures.

In 2008, in the *Avena* case, Mexico asked the ICJ to rule on the consequences of a United States failure to comply with an ICJ order of preliminary measures and final judgment. That case is taken up in the next Chapter as part of the discussion of the ICJ and enforcement of its orders and judgments.

NOTES AND QUESTIONS

1.   In the *Gabčíkovo–Nagaymoros* case discussed in Chapter 2, the ICJ found the treaty agreed to by Hungary and Slovokia to create a barrage system in the Danube was still in effect. The court found the parties had an obligation to continue to work together until a satisfactory situation was reached. The court found that both parties owed damages to the other for failures to comply with the treaty to the point of the case. The court hints that the damages could be offset (paras. 148–150). The ICJ has found in a number of cases that parties have an obligation to negotiate. How reasonable is this as a remedy for states party to a dispute? Is it a more reasonable remedy among states and international organizations than perhaps among human beings and businesses?

2.   Note Franck's discussion of remedies in trade disputes mentions the WTO Dispute Settlement Body's concern about the potential negative impact of trade sanctions on third parties.

3.   For more on the subject of remedies, see CHRISTINE GRAY, JUDICIAL REMEDIES IN INTERNATIONAL LAW (1987).

CHAPTER 9

INTERNATIONAL DISPUTE RESOLUTION

Section A.   Non–Binding Methods.
            1. Negotiation and Consultation.
            2. Mediation and Good Offices.
            3. Fact-finding and Conciliation.
Section B.   Binding Methods.
            1. Arbitration.
            2. Adjudication.

For as long as groups have tried to settle disputes or to gain advantages with respect to other groups using violence, they have also sought to do so using peaceful means. Indeed, the history of international law could be told as a history of the attempt to replace resort to violence with the use of peaceful means for the settlement of disputes. With the adoption of the United Nations Charter in 1945, the use of force was finally outlawed and states took on the obligation to settle disputes peacefully:

United Nations Charter

CHAPTER I   PURPOSES AND PRINCIPLES

Article 2

3. All Members shall settle their international disputes by peaceful means in such a manner that international peace and security, and justice, are not endangered.

4. All Members shall refrain in their international relations from the threat or use of force against the territorial integrity or political independence of any state, or in any other manner inconsistent with the Purposes of the United Nations.

CHAPTER VI   PACIFIC SETTLEMENT OF DISPUTES

Article 33

1. The parties to any dispute, the continuance of which is likely to endanger the maintenance of international peace and security, shall, first of all, seek a solution by negotiation, enquiry, mediation, conciliation, arbitra-

tion, judicial settlement, resort to regional agencies or arrangements, or other peaceful means of their own choice.

The methods listed in Article 33(1) of the Charter are all methods accepted in international law as means of peaceful settlement. Having just read Chapter 8 on state responsibility, would you add anything to the list? What is the nature of the Charter obligation to use these methods? Must states resolve disputes?

Each of the methods found in Article 33 will be examined in this chapter according to the classic division between methods that produce binding outcomes and methods that produce non-binding outcomes. O'Connell writes of the importance of these methods, not only for the direct avoidance of violence, but also for the development of international law, which in general, if indirectly, also supports the avoidance of violence:

> A legal system cannot settle social issues by means of substantive rules alone. Procedures are necessary to interpret, apply and enforce the rules and to handle those questions for which the rules are inadequate. The role of legal procedures in the international legal system may be even more important than in national systems. As international law has no legislature for the development of substantive rules, gaps are more likely to exist and, with the accelerated pace of international life, are increasingly likely. The procedures of negotiation, good offices, mediation, inquiry, conciliation, arbitration and judicial settlement have grown up to meet the dispute settlement needs of international society. All these procedures are experiencing a renaissance since the end of the Cold War both in response to globalization and as a result of the end of Cold War obstacles to cooperation in solving international society's issues; each procedure is continually being put to new uses and being further developed to meet new needs.

> The open question remains, however, as to whether the traditional mechanisms will keep pace with international society's future needs. Will they prove adequate to deal with questions over boundaries, ensure free and fair trade, regulating use of the Internet, protecting the environment, promoting respect for human rights and so on? Or will we need thorough modification or complete revision to handle these issues and, most importantly, disputes that can threaten the peace? In an age of weapons of mass destruction, the work of international lawyers in the field of peaceful settlement of disputes is as compelling as in any previous era. It continues to be their challenge to design dispute settlement mechanisms of the future that will preserve the peace.

Mary Ellen O'Connell, *Introduction in* INTERNATIONAL DISPUTE RESOLUTION xxvi (Mary Ellen O'Connell ed., 2003)(Library of Essays in International Law). *See also*, J.G. MERRILLS, INTERNATIONAL DISPUTE SETTLEMENT (4th ed.

2005), INTERNATIONAL ORGANIZATIONS AND INTERNATIONAL DISPUTE SETTLEMENT: TRENDS AND PROSPECTS (Laurence Boisson de Chazournes et al. eds., 2003), and JOHN G. COLLIER & A. VAUGHAN LOWE, THE SETTLEMENT OF DISPUTES IN INTERNATIONAL LAW: INSTITUTIONS AND PROCEDURES (1999).

A. NON-BINDING METHODS

1. NEGOTIATION AND CONSULTATION

Charles Manga Fombad, Consultation and Negotiation in the Pacific Settlement of International Disputes*

1 AFRICAN J. INT'L & COMP. L. 707 (1989)

* * *

The Concepts of Consultation and Negotiation

The terms "negotiations" and "consultations" are often used interchangeably. This usage is correct in many instances where these two concepts constitute part of a unified process. There however exists a distinction between the two concepts which is of great practical importance, especially with regards to their role in the pacific settlement of international disputes.

"Negotiation" is a broad complex notion which at first sight appears easy to define and understand but on detail analysis will reveal its multiple dimensions. For our purposes and in the context of pacific settlement of international disputes, the most satisfactory definition is that stated in the dissenting opinion of Judge MOORE in the *Mavrommatis Palestine Concessions* case, where he said:

> "... in the international sphere and in the sense of International Law, negotiation is the legal and orderly administrative process by which Governments, in the exercise of their unquestionable powers, conduct their relations with another and discuss, adjust and settle, their differences."

This definition brings out three important features of negotiation:

(i) It makes it clear that negotiations are a legal process and as such must operate and function within the general framework of International Law.

(ii) From the broad formulation, it covers both "ad hoc" and permanent or institutional negotiations, as well as bilateral and multilateral negotiations, and

---

* Most footnotes omitted.

(iii) The fact that negotiations provide a medium both for general discussions and affecting adjustments which help towards both preventing, or avoiding potential disputes and resolving actual disputes that have arisen.

The effectiveness of negotiations in any particular dispute will therefore depend on the interaction of these three factors. But, negotiation, defined in these broad terms, also covers and incorporates the notion of "consultation".

"Consultation" per se is a rather complex legal notion that eludes a precise definition. It could however be described as consisting of the formal or informal, "ad hoc" or permanent, bilateral or multilateral discussions and conversations between states aimed at resolving their differences although it is more often to avoid or prevent potential rather than actual disputes. Consultation as such, unlike negotiation *stricto sensu,* relates more to situations and issues of potential controversy rather than actual disputes.

Mavrommatis Palestine Concessions

Greece v. United Kingdom
Permanent Court of International Justice
1924 P.C.I.J. Ser. A, No. 2 (Judgment of Aug. 30)

■ DISSENTING OPINION BY MR. MOORE.

I regret that I am obliged to dissent from the judgment of the Court in the present case.

By the present application *(Requête),* filed on May 13th, 1924, the Greek Government, appearing as a plaintiff, has asked the Court in the exercise of compulsory jurisdiction to require the British Government to appear and, as defendant, answer on the merits a claim for damages preferred on behalf of M. Mavrommatis, a Greek subject, in respect of certain concessions which he obtained and of others which he had wished to obtain from the Turkish authorities in Palestine. All these concessions, actual and proposed, relate to public works, services, or "utilities". Two of them, respectively relating to the construction and operation of electric tramways and the supply of electric light and power at Jerusalem, and to the supply of drinking water to the same city, were definitively concluded with the local Turkish authorities on January 27th, 1914. It is alleged that M. Mavrommatis had begun to carry out these concessions by depositing in bank a sum of money and by submitting detailed plans for the approval of the authorities, when, on the outbreak of war he availed himself, with the consent of the authorities, of a provision in the concessions for the postponement of construction in case of *force majeure.* A second group relates to the construction and operation of electric tramways and the supply of electric light and power and of drinking water in the city of Jaffa, and the irrigation of its gardens from the waters of El–Hodja. It is alleged that M. Mavrommatis, under agreements signed on January 27th, 1914, deposited a provisional security and made preliminary surveys; that on

January 28th, 1916, concessions were signed by the local authorities, but that, under a new Turkish law, such concessions had to be confirmed by Imperial *firman*; that the documents were sent to Constantinople, and were returned to Jerusalem with a request for the change of a single and immaterial descriptive word, and that the issue of the *firman* involved a mere formality, when, in consequence of the outbreak of war between Greece and Turkey, M. Mavrommatis was obliged to leave the Ottoman dominions and the Imperial *firman* was not promulgated. The third concessionary group related to the irrigation of the valley of the Jordan. Here, again, it is alleged that, under a verbal agreement in 1911 with the competent authorities, surveys and reports were made, that plans and the draft of a contract were submitted, and that a provisional security was deposited; but it is further stated that, by the Turkish law, the contract required the consent of the Imperial Government after approval by the Parliament, and that this approval was not obtained because the outbreak of the war prevented the Parliament from assembling. In conclusion, the application asks the Court to give judgment that the Government of Palestine and consequently also the British Government has since 1921 "wrongfully refused to recognise to their full extent the rights acquired by M. Mavrommatis under the contracts and agreements concluded by him with the Ottoman authorities in regard to the works specified above", and that the British Government should make reparation for the consequent loss, estimated at £234, 339, together with interest at six per cent from July 20th, 1923, the date on which the estimate was made.

In the Case *(Memoire)* subsequently filed on behalf of the Greek Government, the claim for damages in respect of the Jordan valley transactions is abandoned, as a proof, so the Case states, that where the claimant feels some doubt as to the international value of his rights, he is not disposed to press them. But the Court is then asked to give judgment against the British Government for the sum of £121,045 in respect of the Jerusalem concessions, and of £113,294 in respect of the Jaffa group, together with interest in each case at the rate of six per cent from July 20th, 1923, up to the date on which the judgment is given. The total of these two sums is the same as the total amount claimed before the Jordan group was withdrawn.

* * *

There are certain elementary conceptions common to all systems of jurisprudence, and one of these is the principle that a court of justice is never justified in hearing and adjudging the merits of a cause of which it has not jurisdiction. Nowhere is this more clearly laid down than in the great French repository of jurisprudence by Dalloz, where it is stated that, as jurisdiction is essentially a question of public order, it being a matter of general interest that no authority shall transgress the limits to which its action is confined, an exception to the competence of a tribunal may be taken at any stage of the proceedings, so that, even though the Parties be silent, the tribunal, if it finds that competence is lacking, is bound of its own motion to dismiss the case * * *.

* * *

This principle is peculiarly applicable to the Permanent Court of International Justice. By Article 36 of the Statute, the limited compulsory jurisdiction, which it was originally proposed to apply to all adhering States, now extends only to States which expressly declare that they accept it; and for this purpose there is attached to the Statute a special protocol, the nature of which is indicated by the title "optional clause" *(disposition facultative)*. This "optional clause" has not been signed either by Great Britain or by Greece, so that, for the exercise of compulsory jurisdiction in the present case, grounds must be found elsewhere.

The Greek Government having assigned as grounds for the present compulsory claim Articles 26 and II of the Palestine Mandate, I will now consider the terms and effect of these articles.

Article 26 reads as follows:

"The Mandatory agrees that, if any dispute whatever should arise between the Mandatory and another Member of the League of Nations relating to the interpretation or the application of the provisions of the Mandate, such dispute, if it cannot be settled by negotiation, shall be submitted to the Permanent Court of International Justice provided for by Article 14 of the Covenant of the League of Nations."

* * *

To the jurisdiction of the Court under Article 26 the concurrence of three conditions is indispensable. These conditions are: First, there must be a "dispute" between the Mandatory and another Member of the League of Nations; secondly, the dispute must relate to "the interpretation or the application of the provisions of the Mandate"; thirdly, it must appear that the dispute "cannot be settled by negotiation". Taking as a whole all that is set forth in the present application *(Requête)* and the supporting documents, I am of opinion that none of these conditions is fulfilled. I will discuss the first and third together.

The first condition—the existence of a dispute between the Mandatory and another Member of the League—is not met merely by the filing of a suit by the one government against the other in this Court. There must be a pre-existent difference, certainly in the sense and to the extent that the government which professes to have been aggrieved should have stated its claims and the grounds on which they rest, and that the other government should have had an opportunity to reply, and if it rejects the demands, to give its reasons for so doing. Moreover, if it rejects some of the demands, but admits others, it is entitled to know why the compromise thus offered is not acceptable. These propositions, tested by the ordinary conceptions of fair dealing as between man and man, should seem to be self-evident; nor would it be difficult to cite cases in which governments have abandoned their claims on considering the arguments adduced on the other side.

But it must also appear—and this is the third condition—that the dispute, if any is shown to exist, "cannot be settled by negotiation". This condition did not originate with the mandates. On the contrary, long before mandates were heard of, a similar clause was inserted in scores of general arbitration treaties, as a vital condition of their acceptance and operation. These treaties for the most part still exist. The condition in question does not mean that the difference must be of such a nature that it is not susceptible of settlement by negotiation; nor does it mean that resort to the Court is precluded so long as the alleged wrong-doer may profess a willingness to negotiate. The clause must receive a reasonable interpretation; but an interpretation cannot be reasonable which in effect nullifies the condition.

An international "dispute which cannot be settled by negotiation", cannot, upon the pending application *(requête)* and supporting proof, be said now to exist, either in law or in fact.

When Article 26 of the Mandate provides for the submission to the Permanent Court of International Justice of disputes which "cannot be settled by negotiation", it necessarily means disputes between governments. The article, by its very terms, includes only disputes which may arise "between the Mandatory and another Member of the League of Nations". This obviously does not include a dispute between the Mandatory and M. Mavrommatis. Had M. Mavrommatis been a Member of the League of Nations, it would have been unnecessary for his government to appear here; but, under Article 26, it is only of disputes between governments that the Court has jurisdiction, and, when the article speaks of the settlement of such disputes by negotiation, it also necessarily means negotiation between governments.

Moreover, in deciding whether such negotiation has taken place, the Court is not at liberty to interpret the word "negotiation" as a process by which governments are enabled to evade their obligations. Although this superficial view may to some extent popularly prevail, yet, in the international sphere and in the sense of international law, negotiation is the legal and orderly administrative process by which governments, in the exercise of their unquestionable powers, conduct their relations one with another and discuss, adjust and settle, their differences. Many celebrated judicial decisions might be cited to show the respect paid to this principle by national courts, and it is equally binding on international courts, which exercise their powers only with the consent of nations.

The theory that the Greek Government, at any moment when it might see fit to intervene, might be considered as having been a party to the discussions which M. Mavrommatis and his attorneys carried on directly with the British Colonial Office from 1921 to 1923, cannot be accepted. It is a common thing for aliens to negotiate with a government both concerning contracts or concessions which they desire to obtain and concerning contracts or concessions which the government is alleged to have failed to keep. Often the negotiations are thus directly carried on because it is perfectly understood that the subject matter is not a proper one for diplomatic intervention; and it can never be argued that the government, because it negotiated with the claimant, admitted the right of his government to espouse his cause. On the other hand, in the treatment of the points at issue, and in the making of proposals and counter-proposals, the alien claimant is not hampered by the international obligations which might limit or even preclude the interposition of his government, if he should ask it to make his claim the subject of an international demand.

It is an elementary principle that, when a government officially intervenes on behalf of its citizen, it makes his claim its own, and may settle the claim on such terms as it may conceive to be proper. From this it necessarily results that the government, in taking up the claim, is subject to all the limitations resulting from any obligations which it may have contracted towards the government against which the claim is made; and it cannot pretend to be freed from those limitations by reason of the fact that they were not observed in the negotiations which its citizen previously carried on with the other government. On the other hand, the private citizen, in placing his claim in his government's hands, must be held to have accepted the necessary legal consequences of his action.

* * *

Applicability of the Obligation to Arbitrate Under Section 21 of the United Nations Headquarters Agreement of 26 June 1947

International Court of Justice
1988 I.C.J. Rep.12 (Advisory Opinion of April 26)

7. The question upon which the opinion of the Court has been requested is whether the United States of America (hereafter referred to as "the United States"), as a party to the United Nations Headquarters Agreement, is under an obligation to enter into arbitration. The Headquarters Agreement of 26 June 1947 came into force in accordance with its terms on 21 November 1947 by exchange of letters between the Secretary–General and the United States Permanent Representative. The Agreement was registered the same day with the United Nations Secretariat, in accordance with Article 102 of the Charter. In section 21, paragraph (a), it provides as follows:

> "Any dispute between the United Nations and the United States concerning the interpretation or application of this agreement or of any supplemental agreement, which is not settled by negotiation or other agreed mode of settlement, shall be referred for final decision to a tribunal of three arbitrators, one to be named by the Secretary–General, one to be named by the Secretary of State of the United States, and the third to be chosen by the two, or, if they should fail to agree upon a third, then by the President of the International Court of Justice."

* * *

9. In May 1987 a Bill (S.1203) was introduced into the Senate of the United States, the purpose of which was stated in its title to be "to make unlawful the establishment or maintenance within the United States of an office of the Palestine Liberation Organization".

* * *

11. On 22 October 1987, the view of the Secretary–General was summed up in the following statement made by the Spokesman for the Secretary–General (subsequently endorsed by the General Assembly in resolution 42/210 B):

> "The members of the PLO Observer Mission are, by virtue of resolution 3237 (XXIX), invitees to the United Nations. As such, they are covered by sections 11, 12 and 13 of the Headquarters Agreement of 26 June 1947. There is therefore a treaty obligation on the host country to permit PLO personnel to enter and remain in the United States to carry out their official functions at United Nations Headquarters."

In this respect, it may be noted that section 11 of the Headquarters Agreement provides that

> "The federal, state or local authorities of the United States shall not impose any impediments to transit to or from the headquarters district of: (1) representatives of Members ... or the families of such representatives ...; ... (5) other persons invited to the headquarters district by the United Nations ... on official business ..."

Section 12 provides that "The provisions of Section 11 shall be applicable irrespective of the relations existing between the Governments of the persons referred to in that section and the Government of the United States." Section 13 provides, *inter alia*, that "Laws and regulations in force in the United States regarding the entry of aliens shall not be applied in such manner as to interfere with the privileges referred to in Section 11."

* * *

15. On 22 December 1987 the Foreign Relations Authorization Act, Fiscal Years 1988 and 1989, was signed into law by the President of the United States. Title X thereof, the Anti–Terrorism Act of 1987 was, according to its terms, to take effect 90 days after that date. On 5 January 1988 the Acting Permanent Representative of the United States to the United Nations, Ambassador Herbert Okun, in a reply to the Secretary–General's letters of 7 and 21 December 1987, informed the Secretary–General of this. The letter went on to say that

> "Because the provisions concerning the PLO Observer Mission may infringe on the President's constitutional authority and, if implemented, would be contrary to our international legal obligations under the United Nations Headquarters Agreement, the Administration intends, during the ninety-day period before this provision is to take effect, to engage in consultations with the Congress in an effort to resolve this matter."

16.   On 14 January 1988 the Secretary–General again wrote to Ambassador Walters. After welcoming the intention expressed in Ambassador Okun's letter to use the ninety-day period to engage in consultations with the Congress, the Secretary–General went on to say:

> "As you will recall, I had, by my letter of 7 December, informed you that, in the view of the United Nations, the United States is under a legal obligation under the Headquarters Agreement of 1947 to maintain the current arrangements for the PLO Observer Mission, which have been in effect for the past 13 years. I had therefore asked you to confirm that if this legislative proposal became law, the present arrangements for the PLO Observer Mission would not be curtailed or otherwise affected, for without such assurance, a dispute between the United Nations and the United States concerning the interpretation and application of the Headquarters Agreement would exist ..."

Then, referring to the letter of 5 January 1988 from the Permanent Representative and to declarations by the Legal Adviser to the State Department, he observed that neither that letter nor those declarations

> "constitute the assurance that I had sought in my letter of 7 December 1987 nor do they ensure that full respect for the Headquarters Agreement can be assumed. Under these circumstances, a dispute exists between the Organization and the United States concerning the interpretation and application of the Headquarters Agreement and I hereby invoke the dispute settlement procedure set out in Section 21 of the said Agreement.

> According to Section 21(a), an attempt has to be made at first to solve the dispute through negotiations, and I would like to propose that the first round of the negotiating phase be convened on Wednesday, 20 January 1988 ..."

17.   Beginning on 7 January 1988, a series of consultations were held; from the account of these consultations presented to the General Assembly by the Secretary–General in the Report referred to in the request for advisory opinion, it appears that the positions of the parties thereto were as follows:

> "the [United Nations] Legal Counsel was informed that the United States was not in a position and not willing to enter formally into the dispute settlement procedure under section 21 of the Headquarters Agreement; the United States was still evaluating the situation and had not yet concluded that a dispute existed between the United Nations and the United States at the present time because the legislation in question had not yet been implemented. The Executive Branch was still examining the possibility of interpreting the law in conformity with the United States obligations under the Headquarters Agreement regarding the PLO Observer Mission, as reflected in the arrangements currently made for the Mission, or alternatively of providing assurances that would set aside the ninety-day period for the coming into force of the legislation." (A/42/915, para. 6.)

18.   The United Nations Legal Counsel stated that for the Organization the question was one of compliance with international law. The Headquarters Agreement was a binding international instrument the obligations of the United States under which were, in the view of the Secretary–General and the General Assembly, being violated by the legislation in question. Section 21 of the Agreement set out the procedure to be followed in the event of a dispute as to the interpretation or application of the Agreement and the United Nations had every intention of defending its rights under that Agreement. He insisted, therefore, that if the PLO Observer Mission was not to be exempted from the application of the law, the procedure provided for in Section 21 be implemented and also that technical discussions regarding the establishment of an arbitral tribunal take place immediately. The United States agreed to such discussions but only on an informal basis. Technical discussions were commenced on 28 January 1988. Among the matters discussed were the costs of arbitration, its location, its secretariat, languages, rules of procedure and the form of the compromise between the two sides (*ibid.*, paras. 7–8).

* * *

24.   On 11 March 1988 the Acting Permanent Representative of the United States to the United Nations wrote to the Secretary–General, referring to General Assembly resolution 42/229 A and 42/229 B and stating as follows:

> "I wish to inform you that the Attorney General of the United States has determined that he is required by the Anti–Terrorism Act of 1987 to close the office of the Palestine Liberation Organization Observer Mission to the United Nations in New York, irrespective of any obligations the United States may have under the Agreement between the United Nations and the United States regarding the Headquarters of the United Nations. If the PLO does not comply with the Act, the Attorney General will initiate legal action to close the PLO Observer Mission on or about March 21, 1998, the effective date of the Act. This course of action will allow the orderly enforcement of the Act. The United States will not take other actions to close the Observer Mission pending a decision in such litigation. Under the circumstances, the United States believes that submission of this matter to arbitration would not serve a useful purpose."

This letter was delivered by hand to the Secretary–General by the Acting Permanent Representative of the United States on 11 March 1988. On receiving the letter, the Secretary–General protested to the Acting Permanent Representative and stated that the decision taken by the United States Government as outlined in the letter was a clear violation of the Headquarters Agreement between the United Nations and the United States.

25.   On the same day, the United States Attorney General wrote to the Permanent Observer of the PLO to the United Nations to the following effect:

"I am writing to notify you that on March 21, 1988, the provisions of the 'Anti–Terrorism Act of 1987' * * * will become effective. The Act prohibits, among other things, the Palestine Liberation Organization ('PLO') from establishing or maintaining an office within the jurisdiction of the United States. Accordingly, as of March 21, 1988, maintaining the PLO Observer Mission to the United Nations in the United States will be unlawful.

The legislation charges the Attorney General with the responsibility of enforcing the Act. To that end, please be advised that, should you fail to comply with the requirements of the Act, the Department of Justice will forthwith take action in United States federal court to ensure your compliance."

26.   Finally, on the same day, in the course of a press briefing held by the United States Department of Justice, the Assistant Attorney General in charge of the Office of Legal Counsel said as follows, in reply to a question:

"We have determined that we would not participate in any forum, either the arbitral tribunal that might be constituted under Article XXI, as I understand it, of the UN Headquarters Agreement, or the International Court of Justice. As I said earlier, the statute [i.e., the Anti–Terrorism Act of 1987] has superseded the requirements of the UN Headquarters Agreement to the extent that those requirements are inconsistent with the statute, and therefore, participation in any of these tribunals that you cite would be to no useful end. The statute's mandate governs, and we have no choice but to enforce it."

* * *

33.   In the present case, the Court is not called upon to decide whether the measures adopted by the United States in regard to the Observer Mission of the PLO to the United Nations do or do not run counter to the Headquarters Agreement. The question put to the Court is not about either the alleged violations of the provisions of the Headquarters Agreement applicable to that Mission or the interpretation of those provisions. The request for an opinion is here directed solely to the determination whether under section 21 of the Headquarters Agreement the United Nations was entitled to call for arbitration, and the United States was obliged to enter into this procedure. Hence the request for an opinion concerns solely the applicability to the alleged dispute of the arbitration procedure provided for by the Headquarters Agreement. It is a legal question within the meaning of Article 65, paragraph 1, of the Statute. There is in this case no reason why the Court should not answer that question.

34.   In order to answer the question put to it, the Court has to determine whether there exists a dispute between the United Nations and the United States, and if so whether or not that dispute is one "concerning the interpretation or application of" the Headquarters Agreement within the meaning of section 21 thereof. If it finds that there is such a dispute it

must also, pursuant to that section, satisfy itself that it is one "not settled by negotiation or other agreed mode of settlement".

35.   As the Court observed in the case concerning *Interpretation of Peace Treaties with Bulgaria, Hungary and Romania*, "whether there exists an international dispute is a matter for objective determination" (*I.C.J. Reports 1950*, p. 74). In this respect the Permanent Court of International Justice, in the case concerning *Mavrommatis Palestine Concessions* (*P.C.I.J., Series A, No. 2*, p.11), had defined a dispute as "a disagreement on a point of law or fact, a conflict of legal views or of interests between two persons". This definition has since been applied and clarified on a number of occasions. In the Advisory Opinion of 30 March 1950 the Court, after examining the diplomatic exchanges between the States concerned, noted that "the two sides hold clearly opposite views concerning the question of the performance or non-performance of certain treaty obligations" and concluded that "international disputes have arisen" (*Interpretation of Peace Treaties with Bulgaria, Hungary and Romania, First Phase, I.C.J. Reports 1950*, p. 74). Furthermore, in its Judgement of 21 December 1962 in the *South West Africa* case, the Court made it clear that in order to prove the existence of a dispute

> "it is not sufficient for one party to a contentious case to assert that a dispute exists with the other party. A mere assertion is not sufficient to prove the existence of a dispute any more than a mere denial of the existence of the dispute proves its non-existence. Nor is it adequate to show that the interests of the two parties to such a case are in conflict. It must be shown that the claim of one party is positively opposed by the other." (*South West Africa, I.C.J. Reports 1962*, p. 328).

* * *

38.   In the view of the Court, where one party to a treaty protests against the behaviour or a decision of another party, and claims that such behavior or decision constitutes a breach of the treaty, the mere fact that the party accused does not advance any argument to justify its conduct under international law does not prevent the opposing attitudes of the parties from giving rise to a dispute concerning the interpretation or application of the treaty.

* * *

41.   The Court must further point out that the alleged dispute relates solely to what the United Nations considers to be its rights under the Headquarters Agreement. The purpose of the arbitration procedure envisaged by that Agreement is precisely the settlement of such disputes as may arise between the Organization and the host country without any prior recourse to municipal courts, and it would be against both the letter and the spirit of the Agreement for the implementation of that procedure to be subjected to such prior recourse. It is evident that a provision of the nature of section 21 of the Headquarters Agreement cannot require the exhaustion of local remedies as a condition of its implementation.

* * *

55.   The Court considers that, taking into account the United States attitude, the Secretary–General has in the circumstances exhausted such possibilities of negotiation as were open to him. The Court would recall in this connection the dictum of the Permanent Court of International Justice in the *Mavrommatis Palestine Concessions* case that "the question of the importance and chances of success of diplomatic negotiations is essentially a relative one. Negotiations do not of necessity always presuppose a more or less lengthy series of notes and dispatches; it may suffice that a discussion should have been commenced, and this discussion may have been very short; this will be the case if a deadlock is reached, or if finally a point is reached at which one of the Parties definitely declares himself unable, or refuses, to give way, and there can therefore be no doubt that the dispute cannot be settled by diplomatic negotiation" (*P.C.I.J., Series A, No. 2*, p. 13).

When in the case concerning *United States Diplomatic and Consular Staff in Tehran* the attempts of the United States to negotiate with Iran "had reached a deadlock, owing to the refusal of the Iranian Government to enter into any discussion of the matter", the Court concluded that "In consequence, there existed at that date not only a dispute but, beyond any doubt, a 'dispute . . . not satisfactorily adjusted by diplomacy' within the meaning of" relevant jurisdictional text (*I.C.J. Reports* 1980, p. 27, para. 51). In the present case, the Court regards it as similarly beyond any doubt that the dispute between the United Nations and the United States is one "not settled by negotiation" within the meaning of section 21 *(a)* of the Headquarters Agreement.

* * *

58.   For these reasons,

THE COURT,

Unanimously,

Is of the opinion that the United States of America, as a party to the Agreement between the United Nations and the United States of America regarding the Headquarters of the United Nations of 26 June 1947, is under an obligation, in accordance with section 21 of that Agreement, to enter into arbitration for the settlement of the dispute between itself and the United Nations.

Interpretation of the Agreement of 25 March 1951 Between the WHO and Egypt

International Court of Justice
1980 I.C.J. Rep. 73 (Advisory Opinion of Dec. 20)

[Following Egypt's entering into a peace agreement with Israel at Camp David in 1978, some members of the World Health Organization (WHO) sought to have a regional office of the WHO removed from Egypt. Doing so required terminating the Host State Agreement. The ICJ said it also required more:]

48.   * * * [T]he Court takes as its starting point the mutual obligations incumbent upon Egypt and the Organization to co-operate in good faith with respect to the implications and effects of the transfer of the Regional Office from Egypt. The Court does so the more readily as it considers those obligations to be the very basis of the legal relations between the Organization and Egypt under general international law, under the Constitution of the Organization and under the agreements in force between Egypt and the Organization. The essential task of the Court in replying to the request is, therefore, to determine the specific legal implications of the mutual obligations incumbent upon Egypt and the Organization in the event of either of them wishing to have the Regional Office transferred from Egypt.

49.   The Court considers that in the context of the present case the mutual obligations of the Organization and the host State to co-operate under the applicable legal principles and rules are as follows:

—In the first place, those obligations place a duty both upon the Organization and upon Egypt to consult together in good faith as to the question under what conditions and in accordance with what modalities a transfer of the Regional Office may be effected.

—Secondly, in the event of its being finally decided that the Regional Office shall be transferred from Egypt, their mutual obligations of co-operation shall place a duty upon the Organization and Egypt to consult together and to negotiate regarding the various arrangements needed to effect the transfer from the existing to the new site in an orderly manner and with a minimum of prejudice to the work of the Organization and the interests of Egypt.

—Thirdly, those mutual obligations place a duty upon the party which wishes to effect the transfer to give a reasonable period of notice to the other party for the termination of the existing situation regarding the Regional Office at Alexandria, taking due account of all the practical arrangements needed to effect an orderly and equitable transfer of the Office to its new site.

Those, in the view of the Court, are the implications of the general legal principles and rules applicable in the event of the transfer of the seat of a Regional Office from the territory of a host State. Precisely what periods of time may be involved in the observance of the duties to consult and negotiate, and what period of notice of termination should be given, are matters which necessarily vary according to the requirements of the particular case. In principle, therefore, it is for the parties in each case to determine the length of those periods by consultation and negotiation in good faith. Some indications as to the possible periods involved, as the Court has said, can be seen in provisions of host agreements, including Section 37 of the Agreement of 25 March 1951, as well as in Article 56 of the Vienna Convention on the Law of Treaties and in the corresponding article of the International Law Commission's draft articles on treaties between States and international organizations or between international organizations. But what is reasonable and equitable in any given case must depend on its particular circumstances. Moreover, the paramount consideration both for the Organization and the host State in every case must be their clear obligation to co-operate in good faith to promote the objectives and purposes of the Organization as expressed in its Constitution; and this too means that they must in consultation determine a reasonable period of time to enable them to achieve an orderly transfer of the Office from the territory of the host State.

NOTES AND QUESTIONS

1. What makes negotiation a "legal process" deserving of inclusion with other legal processes such as arbitration and adjudication? Can you argue that negotiation is both the most and the least important dispute settlement procedure?

2. We have seen WTO Dispute Settlement Body decisions in prior chapters e.g. *Shrimp–Turtle* (Chapters 2 and 7). Before resort to the panel and appellate procedures of the Dispute Settlement Understanding (DSU), WTO members must first attempt "consultations," then:

Article 4(7)

If the consultations fail to settle a dispute within 60 days after the date of the receipt of the request for consultations, the complaining party may request the establishment of a panel. The complaining party may request a panel during the 60–day period if the consulting parties jointly consider that consultations have failed to settle the dispute.

The DSU does not define "consultations." Consider Fombad's definitions of consultations and negotiation. Might the DSU actually be referring to negotiation rather than consultation? How likely is it that a carefully negotiated legal text like the DSU has incorporated an inaccurate term? Recall the term used by the WTO for periodic discussions toward new agreements. How important is it to use precise and uniform terms in the area of dispute resolution?

3. In the *Fisheries* Case (U.K. v. Iceland), 1974 I.C.J. Rep. 3 (Judgment of 25 July) the ICJ told Iceland and the UK (and Germany in a companion case) to negotiate in good faith. Good faith is the general standard of conduct for parties to any dispute settlement process. Despite its importance, the ICJ and other courts seem not to have defined it. Here is a definition from a book on the subject. Good faith is

directly related to honesty, fairness and reasonableness * * * determined at any particular time by the compelling standards of honesty, fairness and reasonableness prevailing in the international community at that time.

J.F. O'CONNOR, GOOD FAITH IN INTERNATIONAL LAW 121 (1991). Does this definition help? Would you know how to advise a client about to enter into negotiations as to what is required?

Is bad faith an easier concept to apply than good faith? In the arbitration between Peru and Chile to settle a territorial dispute following the Pacific War, Peru alleged that Chile was acting in bad faith. The arbitrator found "the record fails to show that Chile has ever arbitrarily refused to negotiate with Peru * * *. Such causes of delay as a cabinet crisis, a revolution, the illness of a minister, the death of a president—political contingencies which did not lie beyond the contemplation of the Parties—cannot be charged to either side as constituting a willful refusal to proceed with negotiations." *Tacna–Arica Arbitration* (Peru v. Chile), 2 R.I.A.A. 921, 929–33 (1925). Can you think of other examples of bad faith that might arise in multilateral or bilateral negotiation? What remedies are appropriate?

4. Compare bilateral negotiations, like the negotiation of the Headquarters Agreement between the U.S. and the UN, and multilateral negotiations, like the negotiations that resulted in the World Trade Organization (WTO) and the DSU or the United Nations Convention on the Law of the Sea (UNCLOS). Multilateral negotiation aimed at drafting a treaty is commonly known as "conference negotiation." Can you argue that conference negotiation is not negotiation but rather a different procedure, perhaps even a new category of procedure? The UNCLOS negotiations lasted from 1973–1982 and involved almost all states in the international community. To reach a decision, new methods were employed like package deals and consensus decision-making.

Consensus decision-making, which is now standard in conference negotiations, means:

> General agreement or collective opinion by those most interested in the matter. In common use, the term can range in meaning from unanimity to a simple majority vote. In public policy facilitation and multilateral international negotiations, however, the term refers to a general agreement reached after discussions and consultations, usually without voting. Unanimity is required only to the extent that it means an absence of major objections.

DOUGLAS H. YARN, DICTIONARY OF CONFLICT RESOLUTION 122 (1999).

6. In *Mavrommatis*, the dispute was at first between a private person and a state—Mavrommatis and Britain. Subsequently, the Greek government took up the case. The dispute then entered upon a new phase and the domain of international law. Typically before a state can make a claim against another state on behalf of a national, the national must have exhausted whatever local remedies are available. The ICJ dismissed a case brought by Switzerland on behalf of its national against the U.S. because the national had not exhausted all the judicial remedies available in the U.S. It had not appealed to the Supreme Court. The ICJ said, "the State where the violation occurred should have an opportunity to redress it by its own means, within the framework of its own domestic legal system." *Interhandel* (Switz. v. U.S.), 1959 I.C.J. Rep. 6, 27 (Mar. 21). The practice of adopting a national's claim and the doctrine of exhaustion of local remedies are two important concepts in the international law on dispute

resolution. We have seen the adoption principle before, for example, in the *Nottebohm* case in Chapter 3.

7. For further reading on negotiation and consultation, see, FREDERIC L. KIRGIS, JR., PRIOR CONSULTATION IN INTERNATIONAL LAW, A STUDY OF STATE PRACTICE (1983).

2. MEDIATION AND GOOD OFFICES

The term "good offices" refers to a third party who simply brings disputing parties together, helping them to get negotiations underway. Mediation generally involves more, including helping parties develop proposals. If the mediator offers a solution of her own, the mediation begins to meld into conciliation, a procedure discussed in the next section. Good offices and mediation are often provided by international organizations or agencies (the term used in UN Charter Article 33), governments, and individuals.

Good offices and mediation are the least developed of all dispute settlement methods in terms of applicable law. While both appear in most lists of dispute resolution mechanisms, in treaties, and elsewhere, we apparently have no cases concerning either method from any international court. And, indeed, these methods have rarely been the subject of legal scholarship.

Both good offices and mediation differ in a significant respect from negotiation because both introduce a third party into the dispute. One rule clearly applies to their use—all parties must expressly consent to the third party's participation. Even when mediation is provided for in a treaty, see, e.g., WTO DSU Article 5, the parties need to participate in choosing the mediator; thus, mediation has never worked in an "automatic" way where the parties have simply had to accept the appointment of a mediator.

Undoubtedly the participants in mediation must act in good faith in a negotiation. We can deduce this rule from negotiation and the rules governing other dispute resolution mechanisms. It has not been pronounced, to date, by a court or tribunal.

The United Nations Secretary–General has developed lending good offices or acting as a mediator in disputes threatening to deteriorate into armed conflict as an integral part of his job. That was not always the case. In the centuries–old border conflict between Cambodia and Thailand, the Secretary–General in 1966 initiated a good-offices mission to the countries on his own authority. On August 16, 1966, the Secretary–General advised the Security Council that on the invitation of the parties he had appointed a representative to attempt to mediate the border dispute. The following letters were sent in response.

a. *Letter from N. Fedorenko, Permanent Representative [of the U.S.S.R.] to the President of the Security Council. 27 Aug. 1966:*

With reference to the Secretary–General's letter dated 26 August 1966 addressed to the President of the Security Council (S/7402), stating his intention to appoint a Special Representative to help to eliminate tension between Cambodia and Thailand, I consider it necessary to emphasize that under the United Nations Charter decisions on matters connected with action by the United Nations relating to the maintenance of international peace and security are taken by the Security Council. When the Security Council takes a decision on the particular candidate put forward for the post after consultation with the parties concerned, the Soviet Union will have no objection to make.

I should be grateful if you would arrange for this letter to be circulated as an official Security Council document. Accept, Sir, etc.

(Signed) N. FEDORENKO

Representative of the USSR

in the Security Council

b. *Letter from Raul Quijano, Deputy Permanent Representative of the Argentine Republic Addressed to the President of the Security Council. 30 Sept. 1966*

I have the honour to refer to the letter dated 27 August 1966 from the Permanent Representative of the Union of Soviet Socialist Republics to the United Nations addressed to the President of the Security Council (S/7478). The Argentine Government wishes to state that it cannot share the views expressed by the Permanent Representative of the USSR concerning the decision taken by the Secretary–General, in consultation with the Governments of Cambodia and Thailand, to appoint Ambassador Herbert de Ribbing as his Special Representative in these two countries. My Government considers that the action taken by the Secretary–General is fully justified and falls within the competence conferred upon him by the Charter of the United Nations.

In the light of the provisions of Article 99 of the Charter and the directives addressed by the General Assembly to the Secretary–General concerning his functions and responsibilities, my Government has no doubt whatever that the Secretary–General has the authority, and even the duty, to keep himself informed on all matters which may threaten the maintenance of international peace and security and to exert the utmost effort to relieve situations which may become threats to international peace and security. Most particularly, when a dispute arises between two or more countries, it lies within the authority of the Secretary–General to offer his good offices to the parties concerned, either directly or through a representative, to reduce tension and resolve the disagreement between them. The Secretary–General's appointment of a representative for this purpose is, in my Government's view, subject to only two requirements: that he should consult the parties concerned and obtain their consent to his appointment of a representative and that he should inform the Security Council of his decision.

(Signed) Raul QUIJANO
Deputy Permanent Representative
of the Argentine
Republic to the United Nations
Charge d'affaires a.1.

Review the relevant Charter provisions. Who do you think is correct?

NOTES AND QUESTIONS

1. Compare negotiation with mediation and good offices. What are the advantages and disadvantages of mediation and good offices as dispute settlement mechanisms compared with negotiation? Why do disputants turn to mediators? Why do third parties offer to act as mediators or offer good offices? In what circumstances would a third party offer good offices and when mediation?

2. The Secretary General did not succeed in the Thai–Cambodia dispute. His attempt followed a judgment by the ICJ, which had also failed to resolve matters. See *Temple of Preah Vihear* (Cambodia v. Thailand), 1962 I.C.J. Rep. 6 (Judgment of June 15). In April 2009, the Thai prime minister referred the dispute to the summit of South East Asian Nations (ASEAN):

> Thai Prime Minister Abhisit Vejjajiva said Sunday that clashes between Thai and Cambodian military units along the two countries['] disputed border will be raised at Asean Summit in Pattaya.
>
> Speaking in his weekly TV talk, Abhisit said tensions at the disputed border had existed for some years, but had become more worrisome since July last year, after Unesco granted world heritage status to the ancient Preah Vihear temple. The latest incident broke out last Friday when soldiers of the two countries clashed twice near the ancient temple. Two Thai soldiers and two Cambodian soldiers died in the fighting while nine Thai soldiers were wounded. Abhisit also expressed his condolences to families of Thai soldiers who were killed and wounded in the fighting.
>
> Abhisit said he had earlier discussed with his Cambodian counterpart Hun Sen that the border dispute should be settled by the Thai–Cambodian joint border committee (JBC). The border committee will meet in Phnom Penh on Monday and Tuesday. The meeting was planned before last week's clashes took place.
>
> The prime minister said both Deputy Prime Minister Suthep Thaugsuban and Defence Minister Gen. Prawit Wongsuwan have been in sustained contact with the concerned Cambodian authorities to settle the "misunderstanding" and he said he expects that the problem has now eased.

Thai PM to Refer Thai–Cambodian Border Dispute to ASEAN Summit, THE NATION (April 5, 2009) http://www.nationmultimedia.com/2009/04/05/ national/national_30099692.php (some paragraph breaks omitted.)

Why do you suspect that border disputes have a history of leading to armed conflict? Most boundary judgments by the ICJ have led to peaceful settlement—the Thailand and Cambodia case is an exception. The problem appears to be that while the ICJ determined on which side of the border an ancient and revered temple stood, it was not asked to make a full determination of the boundary. Should it have provided it anyway? See Section B.2 below.

3.   Recall the role of the EU as a mediator in the dispute between Hungary and Slovakia over the Gabčíkovo–Nagymoros project (see Chapter 2). The EU persuaded the states to take their dispute to the ICJ. This was an example of a regional agency assisting in peaceful dispute settlement. The EU was in a good position to influence the parties given that both Hungary and Slovakia were seeking membership in the EU. Why do you think the EU provided this assistance to non-member states?

4.   Do you accept the argument that mediation should at least be subject to the obligation of good faith? Why or why not? If mediation were subject to good faith, what would that mean? What specific obligations would be implied? A duty to keep confidences? A duty on the mediator to be neutral? What does neutrality in mediation mean? Can international law impose an obligation of neutrality on a mediator, for example Jimmy Carter or Nelson Mandela, acting in his personal capacity?

5.   While there are many books detailing particular attempts at mediation of international disputes and books on the art of mediation, we have found no book-length treatment of the international law aspects of mediation or good offices.

3.   FACT-FINDING AND CONCILIATION

In the late 19th and early 20th centuries, states began developing new formal procedures for dispute resolution—commissions of inquiry and conciliation. Inquiry, also called fact-finding, is a process that aims to resolve disputes by settling issues of fact. It is a process more typically found in international than national law. Conciliation is a process that

> . . . combines elements of both INQUIRY and MEDIATION. . . . Created in the twentieth century under various bilateral and multilateral treaties and approved in the UN charter (art. 33, para. 1), conciliation has two basic functions: to investigate and clarify the facts in dispute, and to attempt to bring the parties into agreement by suggesting mutually acceptable solutions to the problem.

DOUGLAS H. YARN, DICTIONARY OF CONFLICT RESOLUTION 106–07 (1999).

Both procedures typically employ a commission of persons, often subject-matter experts, to investigate and report. Inquiry and conciliation commissions typically hear witness testimony, review documents, and make site inspections. At the close of proceedings, a non-binding report is issued. It is this report that distinguishes inquiry and conciliation from mediation and arbitration. In mediation, no report is issued, and, in arbitration, the decision is typically binding.

Significant institutional development of international commissions of inquiry as a technique in the peaceful resolution of disputes began with the Hague Conventions of 1899 and 1907, although informal international commissions of inquiry had been employed before. Seven commissions of inquiry were established under the two Hague Conventions. The commissions all possessed the following characteristics: (1) resort to the commissions was voluntary; (2) only minor disputes were referred; (3) each was *ad hoc;* (4) each commission was constituted so as to insure neutral dominance; (5) the report was recommendatory only; (6) commissions could investigate only factual differences.

Between 1913 and 1915 the U.S. signed over 30 bilateral treaties, all entitled "Treaty for the Advancement of Peace," with other American states and with several European states. The force behind the negotiation of the treaties was William Jennings Bryan, who made his acceptance of the office of Secretary of State dependent upon President Wilson accepting promotion of commissions of inquiry as an aspect of U.S. foreign policy. While there are obvious similarities between the Hague and Bryan Commissions, the differences are more significant. Where the Hague Conventions provided for *ad hoc* commissions to be established by agreement between the parties, the Bryan treaties established permanent commissions within guidelines provided by the Conventions, under the Hague Conventions, the jurisdiction of the commissions was severely limited to disputes of an incidental nature, involving neither national honor "nor vital interests." In addition, the commissions' terms of reference under the Conventions were usually limited to findings of fact rather than conclusions of law.

Between 1920 and 1940, the League of Nations handled 30 disputes. Most of these were border and territorial disputes stemming from the disintegration of the Austro–Hungarian, Turkish, and Russian empires. Franco–British solidarity accounted for the League's success in resolving most of the disputes, which arose in the 1920s. This solidarity, however, proved insufficient to deal with the aggressive acts of other great powers in the 1930s.

The lessons learned from these efforts by the League, as well as those carried out under the 1899 and 1907 Hague Conventions, suggest that there are two essential elements of successful fact-finding efforts to aid in the peaceful settlement of international disputes: first, the parties must, to a certain degree, accept peaceful settlement as a customary means of dispute resolution; and second, the parties must believe that there is a credible threat of community sanction to enforce those means. There is a direct correlation between these two factors. As the first increases in the depth of its tradition, the necessity of the second decreases proportionally.

The United Nations took up where the League left off. The Greek crisis was the first dispute to confront the UN. Following World War II,

Greece suffered internal dissent and insurrection. The Acting Chair of the Greek delegation sent a letter to the Secretary–General, asking him to bring the problem to the attention of the UN pursuant to articles 34 and 35 of the Charter. The Greek Government claimed that a condition of insurgency existed only in its northern provinces and that the insurgents were being trained and supplied by its northern neighbors, Yugoslavia, Albania, and Bulgaria.

The Security Council invited the representatives of the states involved to present their cases before the Council on December 10, 1946. After hearing the arguments the Security Council voted unanimously to establish a Fact–Finding Commission to investigate the alleged border violations and to report its conclusions to the Council.

Despite being denied access to three of the four states for most of its tenure, the Commission's investigation was thorough and relatively successful. The Commission concluded that Yugoslavia and, to a lesser degree, Albania and Bulgaria, supported the guerrilla warfare in Greece. The Commission found that most of the violence had taken place in the three most northern Greek provinces, but that the level of violence did not constitute a civil war. The majority of the members of the Security Council approved the Commission's Report, but the former USSR and Poland did not. The USSR vetoed the execution of the measures called for in the Commission's Report, concluding that the evidence in the report demonstrated that a state of civil war did exist throughout Greece and was the result of internal causes. See, 1946–47 Y.B.U.N. 369.

Following the Security Council's refusal to execute the Report, the General Assembly created the United Nations Special Committee on the Balkans (UNSCOB). The Assembly ordered UNSCOB to observe compliance with its collateral call for the four involved states to "establish good neighborly relations, establish frontier agreements, settle the refugee problems and study the possibility of transferring minority groups along the border." UNSCOB had authority to investigate within each of the four states, although only Greece ultimately allowed the observer force into their country. Nevertheless, UNSCOB was successful in collecting information and ultimately provided unambiguous evidence that the three northern neighbor states were essential accomplices in the Greek insurgency. Armed with these reports, the General Assembly condemned the actions of Yugoslavia, Albania, and Bulgaria.

NOTES AND QUESTIONS

1. Compare mediation, inquiry and conciliation. What are the advantages and disadvantages of mediation compared with inquiry and conciliation? What are the advantages and disadvantages of inquiry compared with conciliation?

2. The famous 1949 Geneva Conventions provide for commissions of inquiry in the case of a dispute over the conduct of armed conflict. *See* 1949 Geneva Convention IV Relative to the Protection of Civilian Persons in Time of War, 75 UNTS 287, art. 149:

At the request of a Party to the conflict, an inquiry shall be instituted, in a manner to be decided between the interested Parties, concerning any alleged violation of the Convention.

If agreement has not been reached concerning the procedure for the inquiry, the Parties should agree on the choice of an umpire who will decide upon the procedure to be followed.

Once the violation has been established, the Parties to the conflict shall put an end to it and shall repress it with the least possible delay.

During 2000–2002, two commissions of inquiry were formed to investigate conflict in the Middle East. One was the Mitchell Commission, formed in November 2000 to investigate the origins of the violence that broke out in September 2000 between Palestinians and Israelis. Matthew Less, *U.S. Names Panel to Probe Mideast Violence Ahead of White House Talks,* AGENCE FRANCE-PRESSE, Nov. 7, 2000. The Commission issued its report in May 2001. *See* Sharm el Sheikh Fact–Finding Committee, *at* www.usinfo. state.gov/regional/nea.

A year later, UN Secretary General Kofi Annan formed a fact-finding commission to look into claims of a massacre by Israeli troops in the Jenin Palestinian Refugee Camp. John Lancaster, *Israel Sets Conditions for Jenin Camp Probe; UN Team to Investigate Circumstances of Assault,* WASH. POST, Apr. 21, 2002, at A16. Eventually, Israel blocked the Commission. John Lancaster and Craig Whitlock, *Israel Reverses Position on Probe of Jenin Assault; U.N. Inquiry Delayed Over U.S. Urging,* WASH. POST, Apr. 24, 2002, at A01.

3. In 1976, Chilean agents carried out one of their most brazen criminal acts pursuant to "Operation Condor." They used a car bomb in the heart of downtown Washington, D.C. to assassinate Chile's former ambassador to the U.S., Orlando Letelier, and his American assistant, Ronni Moffitt. Operation Condor is described in discussions of the *Pinochet* case in Chapters 1, 4 and 5. The United States had only a single agreement with Chile that required resort to a compulsory dispute settlement process—one of the old Bryan Treaties. The treaty mandated the establishment of a commission of inquiry. The U.S. asked the commission to inquire into what compensation is due for such a bombing. Chile never accepted liability in the case but did eventually pay the compensation. See *Re Letelier and Moffitt* (Chile–United States of America International Commission), 11 Jan. 1992, 88 I.L.R. 727.

Should this case have encouraged the United States to seek more and better agreements for settling disputes with other states? Or is this the very sort of case that involves individual criminal wrong-doing? Why should the state of Chile be required to pay damages for what was ordered by Pinochet and carried out by his agents?

4. See also, Declaration on Fact–Finding by the United Nations in the Field of the Maintenance of International Peace and Security, G. A. Res. 59, U.N. GAOR, 46th Sess., U.N. Doc. A/Res/46/59 (1992) and United

Nations Model Rules for the Conciliation of Disputes between States, U.N. Doc A/Res/50/50, Dec. 11, 1995.

B. BINDING METHODS

Arbitration is a method of binding dispute settlement that has been a feature of international life since antiquity. Permanent arbitral tribunals and courts are a newer feature of international dispute resolution. Peace movements in the United States and Britain had campaigned for alternatives to war throughout the 19th century. They turned to the establishment of permanent institutions for peaceful settlement after the U.S. triumph over Britain in 1872 in the *Alabama Claims* arbitration. The arbitrators had found that Great Britain was liable for the actions of the *Alabama* and Confederate ships that had wreaked serious damage to Northern shipping and the Union Navy. The Confederacy had contracted with a British shipbuilder in Liverpool to construct the ships. The U.S. had warned Britain that allowing the ships to sail would violate Britain's neutral duties. The British accepted this position but apparently failed to act diligently to prevent the ships from joining the Confederate Navy. After the War, the United States made demands on the UK for compensation, which were rejected. After some years of negotiation and even threats of military action, the two parties finally agreed to arbitrate the matter. The arbitrators found for the United States and awarded the U.S. $15.5 million in gold for the direct damage claims. Less than a year after the decision, on September 9, 1873, Great Britain paid the full amount to the U.S. Treasury. The case was a sensation and was held up as a triumph of peaceful settlement. It electrified the peace movements, which immediately began efforts toward the establishment of permanent machinery for the peaceful settlement of disputes. By 1899, the peace movements had succeeded in placing the issue of permanent institutions for peaceful settlement the agenda of the Hague Peace Conference. The delegates agreed to the establishment of the Permanent Court of Arbitration. See the Website of the PCA, http://www.pca-cpa.org. See also, CHARLES DEBENEDETTI, THE PEACE REFORM IN AMERICAN HISTORY (1980).

In the international legal system, parties must consent to participate in a binding method of dispute resolution. The system does not have true compulsory jurisdiction. Some advances have been made over the years, however, toward general, compulsory dispute resolution. In particular, parties may agree in advance of a dispute to use a particular mechanism. If at the time of the dispute one party no longer wishes to have resort to the mechanism, it is nevertheless bound. In this generally voluntarist system, the jurisdiction provisions in the treaties establishing courts and tribunals are closely scrutinized in cases where one party is resisting resort to the mechanism. Such scrutiny will be seen in many of the cases in this section. Other general principles governing adjudication are litigated in such cases, as well. Issues such as standing of the parties to bring a claim (seen for example in the *Nottebohm* case, *supra*) or whether the claim is ripe or moot may result in a court or tribunal declining to accept jurisdiction. We do not have space to go into detail respecting these issues, but we do observe that with the many obstacles it may seem extraordinary that cases ever proceed at the international level. In fact, more and more do all the time. Consider why this is so and the impact on the development of an international community of having disputes settled in courts and tribunals of law.

1.   Arbitration

United Nations Handbook on the Pacific Settlement of Disputes Between States

p. 55 (1992)

168.   The 1899 and 1907 Hague Conventions for the Pacific Settlement of International Disputes described the object of international arbitration as the settlement of disputes between States by judges chosen by the parties themselves and on the basis of respect for law. They further provided that recourse to the procedure implied submission in good faith to the award of the tribunal. Accordingly, one of the basic characteristics of arbitration is that it is a procedure which results in binding decisions upon the parties to the dispute.

169.   The power to render binding decisions is, therefore, a characteristic which arbitration shares with the method of judicial settlement by international courts whose judgements are not only binding but also, as in the case of the International Court of Justice, final and without appeal, as indicated in article 60 of the I.C.J. Statute. For this reason, arbitration and judicial settlement are both usually referred to as compulsory means of settlement of disputes.

170.   However, while both arbitration and judicial settlement are similar in that respect, the two methods of settlement are nevertheless structurally different from each other. Arbitration, in general, is constituted by mutual consent of the states parties to a specific dispute where such parties retain considerable control over the process through the power of appointing arbitrators of their own choice. By contrast, judicial settlement relies upon pre-constituted international courts or tribunals, the composition of which is not to the same extent subject to control by the parties to the dispute.

* * *

(a) *Types of arbitration agreements*

174.   Consent of the parties to arbitration may be expressed prior to or after the occurrence of a dispute. Parties may agree to submit all or special categories of future disputes to arbitration. Such commitment may be made in multilateral or bilateral treaties entirely devoted to the peaceful settlement of disputes.[116] A more common method is by inclusion of a

---

116.   One of the well-known multilateral general dispute settlement agreements is the Hague Convention for the Pacific Settlement of International Disputes of 18 October 1907. It

compromissory clause in a treaty, by which parties agree to submit all or part of their future disputes regarding that treaty to arbitration. Parties may also agree to go to arbitration by a special agreement or a *compromis* after the occurrence of a dispute.

* * *

David D. Caron, The Nature of the Iran–United States Claims Tribunal and the Evolving Structure of International Dispute Resolution*

84 Am. J. Int'l L. 104 (1990)

The Iran–United States Claims Tribunal[1] has been called "the most significant arbitral body in history"; its awards, "a gold mine of information for perceptive lawyers." In a recent international commercial arbitration, however, an arbitrator reportedly stated that decisions of the Tribunal, although on point, were not persuasive because the Tribunal, after all, involves a special type of arbitration. This arbitrator is not alone. A lecturer at the Hague Academy of International Law, speaking on international commercial arbitration, reportedly did not refer to the Tribunal's

---

was one of the more successful first attempts to design a multilateral convention aimed specifically at proposing a variety of means and procedures for the peaceful settlement of disputes. The Convention establishes a system of arbitration for which new agencies were created. The most important part of the Convention was devoted to the organization and the operation of the Permanent Court of Arbitration. The Permanent Court was created with the object of facilitating an immediate recourse to arbitration of international disputes which could not be settled by diplomacy.

The Revised General Act for the Pacific Settlement of International Disputes of 1949 is another important multilateral general dispute settlement agreement. Chapter III is devoted to arbitration. The chapter provides a system for the establishment of the tribunal, including the mode of appointment and number of arbitrators, the cases of vacancies and so forth. Under article 21 of the Revised General Act the parties may agree to a different mode of establishing the tribunal. See United Nations, *Treaty Series,* vol. 71, p. 101.

An example of a bilateral treaty wholly devoted to the peaceful settlement of disputes is the Treaty for Conciliation, Judicial Settlement and Arbitration (with annexes) between the United Kingdom of Great Britain and Northern Ireland and Switzerland, signed at London on 7 July 1965. Chapter IV of the Treaty is devoted to arbitration. It sets out the number of arbitrators, their nationality and their appointment. It also deals with the question of vacancy and the scope of the competence of the arbitration tribunal. The annex to this Treaty contains recommended rules of procedure for the arbitration tribunal that the parties may wish to choose. Under article 15 of the Treaty the parties may agree to a different mode of establishment of the arbitral tribunal. * * *

* Some footnotes omitted.

1. The Iran–United States Claims Tribunal was established in 1981 pursuant to the Declaration of the Government of the Democratic and Popular Republic of Algeria (hereinafter General Declaration) and the Declaration of the Government of the Democratic and Popular Republic of Algeria concerning the Settlement of Claims by the Government of the United States of America and the Government of the Islamic Republic of Iran (hereinafter Claims Settlement Declaration), collectively referred to as the Algiers Accords. For the text of the Accords, see 1 Iran–United States Claims Tribunal Reports [hereinafter Iran–U.S. C.T.R.1 3 (1981–2), 75 AJIL 418 (1981)].

jurisprudence because he did not find it relevant to his work for the same reason. Viewed as a gigantic experiment in international dispute resolution rather than merely a claims settlement device for this particular group of disputes, the Tribunal thus appears (at least to some) to yield decisions of unclear precedential value. Millions of dollars have been spent on its operation and hundreds of awards rendered, yet an apparently not uncommon perception is that the work of this, in some respects unique, institution is not applicable elsewhere.

In one sense, the doubt about the relevance of the Tribunal's work reflects a more fundamental uncertainty about the proper place of the Tribunal and its work within traditional categories of international dispute resolution. Like any truly nagging question, that fundamental uncertainty comes to be phrased in various ways. A phrasing frequently used by scholars inquires into the "nature" of the Tribunal. The assumption apparently underlying this question is that there are basically two distinct types of international arbitration: interstate arbitration such as the *Beagle Channel* arbitration between Chile and Argentina (sometimes referred to here as public international arbitration); and international commercial arbitration such as proceedings between private companies before the International Chamber of Commerce (ICC) (sometimes more broadly referred to here as private international arbitration). Practitioners often regard the inquiry into the nature of the process as irrelevant to lawyering until it is pointed out that many practical questions, such as the enforceability of an award and the ability to challenge an award, turn upon the answer.

* * *

Interstate Arbitration

The internal world of interstate arbitration typically is created and defined by treaty. The agreement to arbitrate and (where applicable) the treaty establishing the responsible institution are the most relevant treaties. The external world may be of little significance for two reasons. So far as the relationship of the customary international legal system to the arbitration is concerned, the international lawmaking capability of the parties may lead to a merging of the internal/external models. The models can collapse into one because states by their agreements both define the internal world of the arbitration *and* modify the applicable international law. In this sense, international law leaves the structuring and conduct of the arbitration entirely in the control of the parties. Consequently, the prime question is whether by their agreement to arbitrate the state parties intend to adopt, supplement or, instead, replace entirely the customary international law that governs such processes. Many agreements to ad hoc arbitration are quite brief and are intended to rest upon the pertinent customary international practice. Even a brief agreement, however, may raise the question whether aspects of customary practice have been displaced.

II. The Legal System Supervising the Iran–U.S. Claims Tribunal

One of the most innovative and intellectually satisfying aspects of the Algiers Accords is that they establish for the Iran–United States Claims Tribunal a rather complete internal world. There is little need for the parties to request assistance from powers external to the Tribunal. The UNCITRAL Arbitration Rules provide for an appointing authority to resolve disputes between the parties over the composition of the Tribunal. More importantly, the Algiers Accords established a fund, the Security Account, with a portion of the Iranian assets that the United States had frozen. With the Algerian Government acting as escrow agent for the Security Account pursuant to the Tribunal's instructions, the Security Account assures the availability of funds to satisfy most awards of the Tribunal.

* * *

Another factor in analyzing the Tribunal's relationship to the external legal world is the Tribunal's three primary jurisdictional grants. It must be asked whether the legal system supervising the arbitral process before the Tribunal is a function of the particular basis of jurisdiction. First, the Tribunal may hear "claims of nationals of the United States against Iran and claims of nationals of Iran against the United States" (claims of nationals). Second, the Tribunal has jurisdiction over "official claims of the United States and Iran against each other arising out of [certain] contractual arrangements between them" (official claims). Third, the Tribunal may hear disputes between Iran and the United States concerning the interpretation or performance of any provision of the General Declaration or the interpretation or application of the Claims Settlement Declaration (interpretive disputes). * * *

* * *

Treaty Between the United States and the Russian Federation Concerning the Encouragement and Reciprocal Protection of Investment, April 3, 1992

31 I.L.M. 794 (1992)

Article VII

1. Any dispute between the Parties concerning the interpretation or application of the Treaty which is not resolved through consultations or other diplomatic channels, shall be submitted, upon the request of either Party, to an arbitral tribunal for binding decision in accordance with the applicable rules of international law. In the absence of an agreement by the Parties to the contrary, the UNCITRAL Rules, except to the extent modified by the Parties, shall govern.

2. Within two months of receipt of a request, each Party shall appoint an arbitrator. The two arbitrators shall select a third arbitrator as Chairman, who is a national of a third State. The UNCITRAL Rules for

appointing members of three member panels shall apply to the appointment of the arbitral panel, except that the appointing authority referenced in those rules shall be the Secretary–General of the Permanent Court of Arbitration.

3.   Unless otherwise agreed, all submissions shall be made and all hearings shall be completed within six months of the date of selection of the third arbitrator, and the Tribunal shall render its decisions within two months of the date of the final submissions or the date of the closing of the hearings, whichever is later.

4.   Expenses of the Chairman, the other arbitrators, and other costs of the proceedings shall be paid for equally by the Parties. The Tribunal may, however, at its discretion, direct that a higher proportion of the costs be paid by one of the Parties.

Arbitration between a state party and a national or company of the other party is provided in Article VI. Arbitration of certain international law questions is provided in Article 5 of the Investment Incentive Agreement between the United States and the Russian Federation, April 3, 1992, 31 I.L.M. 777 (1992).

NOTES AND QUESTIONS

1.   What are the advantages for disputing parties of resort to binding arbitration versus non-binding methods? What are the disadvantages?

2.   The ICJ has been so busy in recent years that parties in some disputes have opted for arbitration to get a speedier decision. *See, e.g.*, the case of the Ethiopia–Eritrea Boundary Arbitration. *Ethiopia, Eritrea at Odds Over Border Ruling; Both Sides Claim International Commission's Support for Their Land Claims*, WASH. POST, Apr. 14, 2002, at A21.

3.   The basis of authority in arbitration is that parties have given their consent to engage in it. How stringent should arbitrators be in looking for consent? Should they seek to expand binding dispute resolution by a canon of construction that favors finding consent? Consider this question again after reading the ICJ's *Nicaragua* case in the next section.

4.   Recall that in the *Air Services* arbitration, discussed in Chapter 8, France believed the agreement to arbitrate was the remedy for any dispute arising under the air services agreement with the U.S. The Tribunal found that despite the arbitration provision, and pending the formation of the tribunal, countermeasures were lawful. Do you agree with this reasoning? Here are the Articles on State Responsibility respecting countermeasures and dispute settlement provisions:

Article 22
Countermeasures in respect of an internationally wrongful act

The wrongfulness of an act of a State not in conformity with an international obligation towards another State is precluded if and to the extent that the act constitutes a countermeasure taken against the latter State in accordance with chapter II of part three.

Article 50

Obligations not affected by countermeasures

2. A State taking countermeasures is not relieved from fulfilling its obligations:

(a) Under any dispute settlement procedure applicable between it and the responsible State * * *.

International Law Commission Document, Responsibility of States for Internationally Wrongful Acts, *see* G.A. Res. 56/83, UN. Doc. A/RES/56/83 (2002).

5. The United States has many agreements such as the one with Russia excerpted here—bilateral investment agreements or "BITs." These were discussed in Chapter 7, *supra*. Note that many investment treaties specify dispute resolution at the World Bank's International Center for the Settlement of Investment Disputes (ICSID). See the Website of ICSID for the treaty establishing it, its procedural rules, arbitral awards, and pending cases, http://www.worldbank.org/icsid.

6. For further reading on international arbitration, *see*, INTERNATIONAL MASS CLAIMS PROCESSES: LEGAL AND PRACTICAL PERSPECTIVES (Howard M. Holtzman & Edda Kristjánsdóttir eds., 2007); THE UNCITRAL ARBITRATION RULES: A COMMENTARY (David D. Caron et al. eds., 2006); WAYNE MAPP, THE IRAN-UNITED STATES CLAIMS TRIBUNAL. THE FIRST TEN YEARS 1981–1991 (1993); W. MICHAEL REISMAN, SYSTEMS OF CONTROL IN INTERNATIONAL ADJUDICATION AND INTERNATIONAL ARBITRATION: BREAK-DOWN AND REPAIR (1992); STEPHEN M. SCHWEBEL, INTERNATIONAL ARBITRATION: THREE SALIENT PROBLEMS (1987); J. GILLIS WETTER, THE INTERNATIONAL ARBITRATION PROCESS: PUBLIC AND PRIVATE (1979) and ALEXANDER M. STUYT, SURVEY OF INTERNATIONAL ARBITRATIONS, 1794– 1970 (1972).

2. ADJUDICATION

a. INTERNATIONAL COURTS

Up to this point in the book you have seen references to many international courts: the ICJ, the European Court of Justice, the Nuremberg Tribunal, human rights courts, the Law of the Sea Tribunal, the WTO Appellate body, the ICTY, ICTR, ICC, and others. Plainly the 19th century movement to establish courts succeeded in the 20th century. Some believe the efforts might have succeeded too well as the proliferation of courts has disadvantages for international law, along with definite advantages. After a discussion of the many new courts of the international community, we will proceed to look in detail at one of the oldest international courts, the ICJ, and one of the newest, the ICC.

Sir Robert Y. Jennings, The Proliferation of Adjudicatory Bodies: Dangers and Possible Answers

pp. 2–7, ASIL Bulletin, No. 9 (Nov. 1995)

* * *

The Quiet Revolution in International Law

* * *

Most governments make a lot of treaties every year, and an increasing number of them are not the old political kind of treaties one used to read about in history books; they are treaties that affect the life of every one of us daily in our ordinary occupations. These are interpreted and applied by municipal courts and there, I think, is a very big change, certainly in my time as an international lawyer. More and more, international law is a little doubtfully international law as it were; the boundary between municipal law and international law has been breaking down. To take an example, the great body of air law: one can still give a lecture on the international law of the air, but if you wanted to advise an air company, for example, on what is happening in the real world, just to be an international lawyer would not be very much use. You would have to know at least some municipal law and about its enforcement by municipal courts. You would have to be something of a comparativist. And you would certainly have to be something of a private international lawyer, as well as a public international lawyer.

So that is the first thing I wanted to do; to put the problem in the perspective of the very considerable change in the nature of international law and the breaking down of those old barriers. The idea I was taught as an undergraduate that public international law was something on a special plane of its own and quite different from municipal law and the work of municipal court, is no longer even approximately true. So it is not surprising perhaps that, in this crucial and new context, there has been a proliferation of adjudicating tribunals of various kinds.

Reasons Requiring the Establishment of New Tribunals

There are a number of reasons for having more tribunals. There is of course the regional idea; that is people sometimes prefer a local tribunal. One recently established tribunal of that kind is the Badinter Commission, established under the auspices of the Peace Conference on Yugoslavia, where there was the feeling that security within Europe was a European problem. It was perhaps unfortunate that the first big problem that occurred before it turned out not to be European at all, but universal. The efforts were about as successful as all the other efforts—whether on a regional or a universal scale—in dealing with the problem of the former Yugoslavia which is still with us.

But there is this idea, and I think it is reasonable, that local tribunals sometimes can understand the local requirements better than more general tribunals. One may think, for example, of the criticisms that used to be leveled against the ICJ about the *Asylum* case by South American states, which felt that the local tradition of asylum in an embassy was not really properly understood by what was then, a predominantly European court. On the other hand, it is also true that it is possible for a universal court to understand local variations. I think the chamber of the ICJ in the *Honduras/El Salvador* case coped pretty well with the problem of *uti possidetis juris*; indeed, it was difficult not to understand it after all the explanations we heard from counsel in the course of that case.

* * *

Then there are courts and tribunals established for special subjects, such as the courts of human rights. The European Court of Human Rights, for example, was established on a European basis because of the European Convention and because it was possible to provide machinery with teeth to enforce human rights in this regional group, which was not possible on a larger basis. That is obviously a very good reason for having a special, regional tribunal.

* * *

There are also the international criminal courts, the proposed general one [which is now in existence: the International Criminal Court], the one for former Yugoslavia and the one for Rwanda; the last two, peculiar tribunals because they were established by the Security Council under the machinery for the keeping of the peace. Thus, they are purely *ad hoc* and should come to an end when their purpose is accomplished. But how far the tribunals will assist in establishing peace in those regions remains to be seen.

* * *

The Dangers of Proliferation

There are thus various good reasons for producing more tribunals of different kinds, but the problem really is the possible dangers that could arise from this proliferation. I think the main point can be put this way: looking at it as a whole, you see that this proliferation has been flourishing, but without system. It is simply that tribunals have been thought of and produced from time to time for local and other reasons, but the result as a whole is a mess. And to put it in better words, there is a recent article written by my colleague Judge Shahabuddeen, whom I quote:

> The adjudicating machinery on the international plane consists of a number of tribunals, some instituted on a bilateral basis, others on a multilateral basis, but with nothing to hold them together in a coherent system. They all make decisions which can influence the development of international law. If that influence can amount to law-making in the case of all of them, the absence of hierarchical authority to impose order is a prescription for conflicting precepts.

Now, that is probably the main danger of proliferation, the fragmentation of international law; and by fragmentation I do not mean the very proper local variations for particular purposes. It so happens that the Strasbourg Court of Human Rights has produced for me the ideal case to illustrate this danger. In * * * the case of *Loizidou v. Turkey*, a complaint against Turkey was brought by Cyprus before the European Court about the alleged difficulty of a Cypriot national of the Greek community who wanted to visit the family property in the Turkish part of Cyprus. The question first before the Court was a question of competence or jurisdiction. The Convention has a clause providing for declaration by governments accepting the jurisdiction of the Strasbourg Court and that clause is, word for word, based on Article 36(2) of the Statute of the ICJ, the optional clause. So the same machinery was provided and governments that wish to accept the jurisdiction of the Court did so by making a declaration. Most of them, and apparently practically all of them, if they wished to accept the jurisdiction, did so unconditionally by simply filing a declaration. Turkey acted differently. It agreed to the application of the Convention and the competence of the Court in respect of "matters coming within Article 1 of the Convention and performed within the boundary of the national territory of the Republic of Turkey," a reservation obviously intended to exclude the northern part of Cyprus from the jurisdiction of the tribunal.

The decision of the Court on this matter—the merits have not yet come before the Court—was that it did have jurisdiction and the reasoning was as follows. First, other governments in accepting the Court's jurisdiction had accepted it without reservation. Therefore, in the light of this consistent practice, the making of reservations was not permissible. The Court went on to say that the decisions of the ICJ to this matter, which of course had been pleaded before them, were irrelevant because of the special character of the Strasbourg Court. The surprising thing to me is that it is not unlike the famous separate opinion of Judge Lauterpacht, where he felt that the "automatic" reservation of France to its optional declaration was invalid and void because contrary to the Statute. He agreed, however, with the majority of the Court that the reservation was unseverable and that therefore the French attempt to create jurisdiction was itself invalid. To the contrary, the Strasboug Court decided that the Turkish "invalid" reservation was severable and therefore Turkey must be taken to have accepted the competence of the Court without any reservation at all. The passage of the Court's decision that I want to mention is:

> The fundamental difference in the role and purpose of the respective tribunals [that is Strasbourg and the Hague], coupled with the existence of a practice of unconditional acceptance, provided a compelling basis for distinguishing Convention practice from that of the International Court.

Now, of course, one can say this is merely a question of jurisdiction, and not of substance, but there are red lights there. It indicates that tendency of particular tribunals to regard themselves as different, as separate little empires which must as far as possible be augmented. Of course, one can appreciate that the Strasbourg Court, applying and interpreting the European Convention, is in a different position from the ICJ applying a universal system of international law. It might be acceptable to rely on the regional differences for a question of jurisdiction; but obviously, there is a possibility that the technique might also be extended to matters of substance. This could lead to a law of human rights increasingly different from the universal system, which is part of general international law, and under the custody of the ICJ. I merely point out the danger. I have no solution, all I can say is that I am sure this tendency will increase rather than decrease. We ought to be thinking about it.

Possible Answers

Coming back to this question of the control raised by Judge Shahabuddeen, what can we do about this glut of tribunals with no hierarchical pattern? We do not even have a list of these different tribunals anywhere easily available, much less an analysis. Well, one thinks immediately of the ICJ, the principal judicial organ of the United Nations, as possibly providing the head of some sort of hierarchy, a court of last resort, of appeal, review or cassation. But there are difficulties about that and the principal one is Article 34(1) of the Statute of the Court, which says that only states may be parties before the Court. It means that for the contentious jurisdiction at any rate, it is not easy to think of any machinery for tribunals dealing with other entities than states having recourse to the Court. It may happen incidentally sometimes in a contentious case. It did happen in the Guinea–Bissau case. The Court did pass upon an arbitral award which was, according to the agreement establishing the arbitration, to have been final. The Court confirmed the validity of the award, but it did hear the case. So there is a sort of precedent there. The other difficulty with the International Court's attempt to control these other tribunals would be that, according to Article 34(1), it does not have contentious jurisdiction over any of the international organizations which exist in the international sphere. This is a most extraordinary position. It is extraordinary that you have this UN system of law, a universal system of international law, you have a principal judicial organ of the United Nations and no state or government can cite an international organization before the ICJ; for example, in regard of allegedly *ultra vires* activities. Maybe the International Court itself is not the proper instrument, but there ought to be some way of getting international organizations, a well as other entities, before the tribunals.

* * *

Article 34(1) of the Statute of the International Court is the embodiment of the Westphalian legal order. I suppose something can be done. Another colleague of the Court, Judge Guillaume has suggested that there might be a possibility of reference by other tribunals to the Court, corresponding to Article 177 of the Rome Treaty [renumbered EC Article 234]. They might be encouraged to ask the Court for advice on questions of international law. The advisory jurisdiction of the ICJ is much more flexible, and it could accommodate a procedure of reference. Whether tribunals would in fact refer is perhaps doubtful; but at any rate, even if there were the possibility, it might serve as a beginning for some sort of order and system.

* * *

NOTES AND QUESTIONS

1. Why did states make the leap from arbitral tribunals to permanent courts? In addition to the materials in this chapter, refer again to the historical introduction in Chapter 1.

2. Do you agree with Sir Robert that the proliferation of courts could be a challenge for the unity of international law? Recall the discussion of attribution to the state of the acts of militant groups. Recall the discussion in Chapter 8 of the ICJ, in effect, "overruling" the International Criminal Tribunal for the former Yugoslavia in finding in *Bosnia v. Serbia* that the proper test is control not cooperation as the ICTY has held in *Tadić*. This was a far more direct assertion of overall authority by the ICJ as the guardian of international law than was seen in the case cited by Sir Robert between Senegal and Guinea–Bissau. Should the ICJ take on this role? Sir Robert thought so, but, of course, he was a long-serving judge of the ICJ!

3. For further reading on international courts, see CHITTHARANJAN F. AMERASINGHE, JURISDICTION OF SPECIFIC INTERNATIONAL TRIBUNALS (2009); THE INTERNATIONAL JUDGE: AN INTRODUCTION TO THE MEN AND WOMEN WHO DECIDE THE WORLD'S CASES (Daniel Terris et al. eds., 2007).

1.) The International Court of Justice

Stephen Schwebel, Fifty Years of the World Court: A Critical Appraisal

90 ASIL PROC. 339 (1996)

Now what of the record of the Court the last fifty years? That record may indeed be said to stretch back to 1922, to the initiation of the Permanent Court of International Justice (PCIJ). That Court proved to be an outstandingly successful innovation in the affairs of mankind. Between 1922 and 1940, it dealt with sixty-six cases. Thirty-eight were contentious and twenty-eight advisory; twelve were settled out of court. The PCIJ demonstrated that an international court of justice could work. Its judgments were generally well received and virtually uniformly implemented; its advisory opinions were given great weight by the League Council and the states and organizations on whose behalf the Council flexibly transmitted questions. The only opinion that attracted widespread criticism was the *Customs Union* opinion, in which the Court narrowly held that the proposed customs union between Germany and Austria was incompatible with the Peace Treaties regime of 1919.

In the 1920s, in a period of international detente, the Court flourished. In the 1930s, with the rise of international tensions engendered by what came to be known as the Axis Powers, the Court declined. Significant an institution as the Court was, and concerned as it was with a number of cases arising out of the Peace Treaties, and with tensions between Germany and Poland, it could hardly prevent the Second World War. The history of the interwar period suggests that, rather than international adjudication producing peace, peace is conducive to international adjudication. It demonstrated as well that an international court could and did make great contributions to the development of international law.

Reconsideration in 1945

It is a striking fact that the founders of the United Nations from the outset agreed that the League of Nations would be dissolved and displaced by the United Nations but that the Permanent Court of International Justice would be maintained by the International Court of Justice. Statesmen and lawyers never for a moment doubted that the Court should be preserved.

They were not prepared to agree on much more. The International Court of Justice is the immediate offspring of the Permanent Court. The United Nations Charter provides that its Statute is based upon the Statute of the Permanent Court. The ICJ Statute is in large measure unchanged, down to the very numbering of its articles. Its jurisdiction is similarly consensual and hence sharply limited. The two great states that had never become parties to the Statute of the Permanent Court, the United States and the Soviet Union, were no more willing in 1945 to accept statutory provision for compulsory jurisdiction than had been the United Kingdom, Italy and Japan in 1920. Recalling the unsuccessful battles in the Senate over adherence to the Statute of the Permanent Court, the State Department was unwilling to risk ratification of the Charter of which the Statute was part. The USSR had an ideological antipathy toward submitting to international adjudication, which began to soften only with the advent of Gorbachev.

But in 1945 there were a few significant innovations. The International Court of Justice is an organ of the United Nations, whereas the Permanent Court was not an organ of the League; an important result is that all members of the United Nations ipso facto are parties to the Statute. Provision was introduced authorizing the Court to form a chamber for dealing with a particular case. And Article 94 of the Charter provides that each member of the United Nations must undertake to comply with the Court's decision in any case to which it is a party and that the Security Council may make recommendations or decide upon measures to give effect to the judgment.

The International Court of Justice has fifteen judges, as did the PCIJ. They too sit in the Peace Palace in The Hague. The International Court of Justice inherited not only the quarters, the archives, the registry, the rules, and the jurisdiction of the Permanent Court; it inherited its jurisprudence as well. Counsel in argument before the Court, judges in their deliberations, and the Court in its judgments and advisory opinions, invoke the jurisprudence of the Permanent Court as they invoke the jurisprudence of this Court.

An Appraisal of the International Court of Justice

Jurisdiction. The hope at San Francisco was that, by preserving adherences to the compulsory jurisdiction of the Permanent Court under the optional clause and treaties specifying recourse to the Court for settlement of disputes arising thereunder, and by fresh adherences by United Nations members under these titles, the jurisdiction of the Court would grow.

In fact, for some years jurisdiction under the optional clause contracted, in numbers and content. Not only did fewer states—relative to the large expansion in the number of independent states—adhere to the optional clause[, m]any of the states that did adhere, did so with far-reaching reservations unknown in the League era. Sir Humphrey Waldock was moved to write his well-known article on "The Decline of the Optional Clause," a decline whose angle widened when France and the United States withdrew their adherences altogether.

But more recently, that trend has turned upward. Currently fifty-nine states adhere to the Court's compulsory jurisdiction under the optional clause, out of 187 parties to the Statute. The geographical spread is wide, and it now includes states from Eastern Europe as well as Africa and Asia. Yet in percentage terms far fewer states adhere than in 1939, when thirty-six out of forty-eight parties to the Statute of the Permanent Court adhered to the optional clause. In all, then, the record on this count is mixed. While the number of adherences appears to be slowly increasing, the majority of states remains outside the system and that majority today includes four of the five permanent members of the Security Council.

All this said, it is clear that the optional clause as a meaningful source of the Court's jurisdiction has not disappeared. On the contrary, significant cases have been brought on the basis of it in recent years.

Some 264 treaties provide that disputes arising thereunder may at the instance of a party be submitted to the Court for determination. Some 106 of these treaties are multilateral. With the passing of the ideological opposition to the Court's jurisdiction of the former Soviet Union and its former allies, and with much greater recourse to the Court by states of the developing world, it is to be expected that more and more treaties, multilateral and bilateral, will invest the Court with jurisdiction. It is equally to be expected that there will continue to be special agreements between states to take disputes to the Court.

As it is, despite the limitations on its jurisdiction, the Court today is busy and as busy as it has been since 1922. The Court has evolved a jurisdictional jurisprudence which is unique in its complexity and subtlety. In the construction of its jurisdiction, it has been criticized at times for undue conservatism; at other times, for excessive liberalism. Having not infrequently dissented in matters of jurisdiction and admissibility, I cannot say that I think that such diverse criticism shows that the Court has achieved the golden mean. But in this sphere as in others, I believe that its record is, with relatively few exceptions, rather good.

Recourse to the Court. Recourse to the International Court of Justice has been uneven; it has had its ups and downs. There were a considerable number of contentious cases and advisory proceedings in the period 1946–1966. Then, for more than a dozen years, the Court experienced a sharp diminution in cases. With the bringing of the *Hostages* case, in 1979, pace in and publicity about the Court quickened. In the 1980s, recourse to the Court burgeoned. In recent years, the Court has had as many as thirteen cases on its docket.

Why this is so is not clear. Some speculate that increased recourse to the Court by developing states flows from an increase in confidence in the Court engendered by its judgments in *Military and Paramilitary Activities in and against Nicaragua*. If so, that would be paradoxical, since those judgments gave rise to unprecedented criticism of the Court, above all in the United States, but also in some other states and among many international legal scholars.

Whatever the cause, the fact is that the Court is no longer underemployed. Indeed, so busy is it that, if its workload continues to increase, it may have to enlarge significantly its Registry and the services it renders— as by the addition of clerks to judges—and reform the Court's ponderous procedures. Those procedures are designed to accord considerable latitude to sovereign litigants, while affording each of the fifteen judges the fullest opportunity for shaping the Court's judgments and opinions. But they evolved in times of less recourse to the Court. The Court is falling behind in its expeditious disposition of cases, and there are understandable proposals for accelerating the pace of its work. Yet the financial pressures on the Court of which I have spoken cut the other way.

* * *

The Prospects of the Court

If the Statute remains unchanged. The Statute of the Court cannot be easily amended, governed as it is in this respect by the amendment provisions of the United Nations Charter: that is, adoption and ratification by two-thirds of the membership of the United Nations, including all the permanent members of the Security Council.

Taking the Statute as it is, the Court today is accomplishing much. Tomorrow it may accomplish more still, if its flow of cases is maintained and expanded. That is true, whether the cases are large or small in import. For the Court to play a significant role in the settlement of international disputes and the development of international law, it is not necessary for international disputes of great moment to be submitted to it. What is important is that states increasingly acquire the habit of submitting legal disputes not otherwise settled—and most disputes are and should be otherwise settled—to the Court. It is likely that the more they do, the more they will do.

Not only are most international disputes rightly settled without judicial recourse[, n]umbers of disputes that have been submitted to the Court have been settled in the course of litigation, occasionally with the Court's encouragement. That may be no less desirable on an international plane than it is on national and local planes.

If the Statute were to be amended. If the Statute were to be amended, the scope for change—progressive, but also regressive—would be wide. Any amendments would require the most careful consideration, which these remarks do not purport to offer. A few tentative thoughts:

- The amendment that may at once be the most desirable and the most portentous and problematic is that of amending Article 34's provision that only states may be parties in contentious cases before the Court. But if the gates are to be opened, how wide? Presumably, to include intergovernmental international organizations. Even that relatively modest innovation would entail multiple difficulties. But nongovernmental international organizations? Corporations incorporated under national law? Private associations? Individuals? The prospects are daunting.

- Extending the capacity to request advisory opinions from UN organs and the UN specialized agencies so as to include other intergovernmental international organizations should be sympathetically canvassed. The UN Secretary–General should be authorized to request advisory opinions on legal questions arising within the scope of his responsibilities (the latter step requires no Charter amendment).

- Affording other international courts the facility of appeal to the International Court of Justice merits consideration. As specialized international courts multiply, the importance of preserving the position of the International Court of Justice grows, lest various international courts develop conflicting interpretations of international law.

- Enabling the highest national courts to refer questions of international law in cases arising before them to the International Court of Justice for its opinion on those questions, the case being remitted to the national court for disposition thereafter, is another proposed innovation that may deserve examination.

- Lengthening the current judicial term of office of nine years to fifteen years, but specifying that it shall not be subject to renewal, might enhance the independence of the members of the Court.

* * *

A.) Contentious Cases

United Nations, Handbook on the Pacific Settlement of Disputes Between States
p. 70 (1992)

* * *

(a) *Jurisdiction, competence and initiation of the process*

202.   Settlement of international disputes by international courts is subject to State acceptance of jurisdiction over such disputes. This recogni-

tion may be expressed by way of a special agreement between the States parties *(compromis)* conferring jurisdiction upon a court in a particular dispute, or by a compromissory clause providing for an agreed or unilateral reference of a dispute to a court, or by other means. In the event of a dispute as to whether a court has jurisdiction, the matter is settled by the decision of the court. For example, the court may rule on questions of competence or other substantive preliminary objections that can be raised by a respondent State. Issues relating to procedural preliminary objections under the rule of exhaustion of local remedies are also heard.

(i) *Special agreement*

203.   Article 36, paragraph 1, of the Statute of the International Court of Justice provides that the "jurisdiction of the Court comprises all cases which the parties refer to it", which is done normally by way of notification to the Registry of a special agreement *(compromis)* concluded by the parties for that purpose. The Special Agreement of 23 May 1976 concerning the Delimitation of the Continental Shelf (Libya/Malta), for example, provides:

"The Government of the Republic of Malta and the Government of the Libyan Arab Republic agree to recourse to the International Court of Justice as follows:

"*Article I,*

"The Court is requested to decide the following questions:

"What principles and rules of international law are applicable to the delimitation of the area of the continental shelf which appertains to the Republic of Malta and the area of continental shelf which appertains to the Libyan Arab Republic and how in practice such principles and rules can be applied by the two parties in this particular case in order that they may without difficulty delimit such areas by an agreement * * *."

205.   Article 36, paragraph 1, of the Statute * * * provides also that the jurisdiction * * * comprises "all matters specially provided for * * * in treaties and conventions in force". There are numerous treaties containing such a compromissory clause, some of which provide for unilateral reference of all or certain categories of disputes to the International Court of Justice. At the global level, for example, under the General Act for the Pacific Settlement of International Disputes of 26 September 1928 and 28 April 1949 all legal disputes are subject to compulsory adjudication by the Court, unless the parties agree to submit them to arbitration or conciliation. * * *

206.   At the regional level, * * * the European Convention for the Peaceful Settlement of Disputes of 29 April 1957, * * * provides for the submission of all international legal disputes to the International Court of Justice.

(iii) *Other means of conferring jurisdiction*

207. * * * States parties to the Statute of the [International Court of Justice] have the option of making a declaration under Article 36, paragraph 2, of the Statute by which they accept in advance the jurisdiction of the Court "in all legal disputes concerning *(a)* the interpretation of a treaty; *(b)* any question of international law; *(c)* the existence of any fact which, if established, would constitute a breach of an international obligation; *(d)* the nature or extent of the reparation to be made for the breach of an international obligation". States are bound by this declaration only with respect to States which have also made such a declaration. The declaration may be made unconditionally or on condition of reciprocity on the part of several or certain States, or for a certain time. Optional clauses of compulsory jurisdiction also exist with respect to the European Court of Human Rights and the Inter–American Court of Human Rights.

208. By contrast, other treaties establishing an international court automatically confer jurisdiction to that court with respect to its scope of activities. The States parties do not need and do not have the option to make a declaration of acceptance of the compulsory jurisdiction of that court. Thus, by becoming a party to the Treaties establishing the European Communities, member States automatically subject themselves to the jurisdiction of the Court of Justice of the European Communities for disputes connected with the application and interpretation of the Treaties. States parties to the 1982 United Nations Convention on the Law of the Sea *ipso facto* accept the compulsory jurisdiction of various forums for the settlement of law of the sea disputes. However, under the Convention, States parties have to make a declaration on the choice of the forum for judicial settlement established thereunder.

(iv) *Initiation of process*

209. Contentious proceedings before international courts are instituted either unilaterally by one of the parties to a dispute or jointly by the parties, depending upon the terms of the relevant agreement in force between them.[202] Thus, if under the agreement the parties have accepted the compulsory jurisdiction of the International Court of Justice in respect of the dispute, then proceedings may be instituted unilaterally by the applicant State. In the absence of such a prior acceptance, however, proceedings can only be brought before international courts on the basis of the mutual consent of the parties.

210. The procedure for instituting contentious proceedings is defined in the basic statute of the respective international courts. The Statute of the International Court of Justice provides under Article 40 as follows:

---

202. In some regional courts, cases may be brought to them by entities other than states (e.g., the European Commission of Human Rights with respect to the European Court of Human Rights; the Council or the Commission with respect to the Court of Justice of the European Communities; the Inter–American Commission on Human Rights with respect to the Inter–American Court of Human Rights) or even by individuals (e.g., the Court of Justice of the European Communities). * * *

"1. Cases are brought before the Court, as the case may be, either by the notification of the special agreement or by a written application addressed to the Registrar. In either case the subject of the dispute and the parties shall be indicated.

"2. The Registrar shall forthwith communicate the application to all concerned.

"3. He shall also notify the Members of the United Nations through the Secretary–General, and also any other States entitled to appear before the Court."

* * *

Examples of Declarations Under Article 36(2) of the Statute of the International Court of Justice

International Court of Justice, Yearbook 1990–1991 at 93 (1992) [Translation from French]

Nicaragua

On behalf of the Republic of Nicaragua I recognize as compulsory unconditionally the jurisdiction of the Permanent Court of International Justice. Geneva, 24 September 1929. (Signed) T.F. MEDINA.

International Court of Justice, Yearbook 1984–1985 at 99 (1985)

United States of America

I, Harry S. Truman, President of the United States of America, declare on behalf of the United States of America, under Article 36, paragraph 2, of the Statute of the International Court of Justice, and in accordance with the Resolution of 2 August 1946 of the Senate of the United States of America (two-thirds of the Senators present concurring therein), that the United States of America recognizes as compulsory *ipso facto* and without special agreement, in relation to any other State accepting the same obligation, the jurisdiction of the International Court of Justice in all legal disputes hereafter arising concerning

a.   the interpretation of a treaty;

b.   any question of international law;

c.   the existence of any fact which, if established, would constitute a breach of an international obligation;

d.   the nature or extent of the reparation to be made for the breach of an international obligation;

Provided, that this declaration shall not apply to

a.   disputes the solution of which the parties shall entrust to other tribunals by virtue of agreements already in existence or which may be concluded in the future; or

b. disputes with regard to matters which are essentially within the domestic jurisdiction of the United States of America as determined by the United States of America; or

c. disputes arising under a multilateral treaty, unless (1) all parties to the treaty affected by the decision are also parties to the case before the Court, or (2) the United States of America specially agrees to jurisdiction; and

Provided further, that this declaration shall remain in force for a period of five years and thereafter until the expiration of six months after notice may be given to terminate this declaration.

Done at Washington this fourteenth day of August 1946.

(*Signed*) Harry S. Truman.

————

The declaration was terminated on October 7, 1985.

Case Concerning Military and Paramilitary Activities In and Against Nicaragua

Nicaragua v. United States
International Court of Justice
1984 I.C.J.Rep. 392 (Judgment of Nov. 26)

[On April 9, 1984, the Government of Nicaragua filed an application instituting proceedings against the United States with respect to its military and paramilitary activities in Nicaragua.

On April 6, 1984, *i.e.* three days before the filing, the Secretary of State of the United States sent to the Secretary–General of the United Nations the letter which follows.]

* * *

I have the honor on behalf of the Government of the United States of America to refer to the Declaration of my Government of August 26, 1946, concerning the acceptance by the United States of America of the compulsory jurisdiction of the International Court of Justice, and to state that the aforesaid Declaration shall not apply to disputes with any Central American state or arising out of or related to events in Central America; any of which disputes shall be settled in such manner as the parties to them may agree.

Notwithstanding the terms of the aforesaid Declaration, this proviso shall take effect immediately and shall remain in force for two years, so as to foster the continuing regional dispute settlement process which seeks a negotiated solution to the interrelated political, economic and security problems of Central America.

* * * 23 International Legal Materials 670 (1984).

[The United States appeared and pleaded that the court lacked jurisdiction relying, *inter alia*, on its letter of April 6, 1984, and on proviso (c) of its reservations to its acceptance of the compulsory jurisdiction of the court.

By eleven votes to five, the court held that it had jurisdiction to entertain the application of Nicaragua on the basis of Article 36, paragraphs 2 and 5 of the ICJ Statute. It rejected the United States' arguments based on the letter of April 6, 1984, as will be seen in the discussion that follows:]

57. The terms of the 1984 notification, introducing substantial changes in the United States Declaration of Acceptance of 1946, have been quoted above; they constitute an important element for the development of the Court's reasoning. The 1984 notification has two salient aspects: on the one hand it states that the 1946 Declaration of acceptance shall not apply to disputes with any Central American State or arising out of or related to events in Central America; on the other hand it states that it is to take effect immediately, notwithstanding the terms of the 1946 Declaration, and is to remain in force for two years.

* * *

59. Declarations of acceptance of the compulsory jurisdiction of the Court are facultative, unilateral engagements, that States are absolutely free to make or not to make. In making the declaration a State is equally free either to do so unconditionally and without limit of time for its duration, or to qualify it with conditions or reservations. In particular, it may limit its effect to disputes arising after a certain date; or it may specify how long the declaration itself shall remain in force, or what notice (if any) will be required to terminate it. However, the unilateral nature of declarations does not signify that the State making the declaration is free to amend the scope and the contents of its solemn commitments as it pleases. * * *

60. In fact, the declarations, even though they are unilateral acts, establish a series of bilateral engagements with other States accepting the same obligation of compulsory jurisdiction, in which the conditions, reservations and time-limit clauses are taken into consideration. In the establishment of this network of engagements, which constitutes the Optional–Clause system, the principle of good faith plays an important role; the Court has emphasized the need in international relations for respect for good faith and confidence in particularly unambiguous terms. * * *

61. The most important question relating to the effect of the 1984 notification is whether the United States was free to disregard the clause of six months' notice which, freely and by its own choice, it had appended to its 1946 Declaration. In so doing the United States entered into an obligation which is binding upon it vis-à-vis other States parties to the Optional–Clause system. Although the United States retained the right to modify the contents of the 1946 Declaration or to terminate it, a power which is inherent in any unilateral act of a State, it has, nevertheless

assumed an inescapable obligation towards other States accepting the Optional Clause, by stating formally and solemnly that any such change should take effect only after six months have elapsed as from the date of notice.

62.   The United States has argued that the Nicaraguan 1929 Declaration, being of undefined duration, is liable to immediate termination, without previous notice, and that therefore Nicaragua has not accepted "the same obligation" as itself for the purposes of Article 36, paragraph 2, and consequently may not rely on the six months' notice proviso against the United States. The Court does not however consider that this argument entitles the United States validly to act in non-application of the time-limit proviso included in the 1946 Declaration. The notion of reciprocity is concerned with the scope and substance of the commitments entered into, including reservations, and not with the formal conditions of their creation, duration or extinction. It appears clearly that reciprocity cannot be invoked in order to excuse departure from the terms of a State's own declaration, whatever its scope, limitations or conditions. As the Court observed in the *Interhandel* case:

> "Reciprocity enables the State which has made the wider acceptance of the jurisdiction of the Court to rely upon the reservations to the acceptance laid down by the other party. There the effect of reciprocity ends. It cannot justify a State, in this instance, the United States, in relying upon a restriction which the other party, Switzerland, has not included in its own Declaration." * * *

The maintenance in force of the United States Declaration for six months after notice of termination is a positive undertaking, flowing from the time-limit clause, but the Nicaraguan Declaration contains no express restriction at all. It is therefore clear that the United States is not in a position to invoke reciprocity as a basis for its action in making the 1984 notification which purported to modify the content of the 1946 Declaration. On the contrary it is Nicaragua that can invoke the six months' notice against the United States—not of course on the basis of reciprocity, but because it is an undertaking which is an integral part of the instrument that contains it.

* * *

65.   In sum, the six months' notice clause forms an important integral part of the United States Declaration and it is a condition that must be complied with in case of either termination or modification. Consequently, the 1984 notification, in the present case, cannot override the obligation of the United States to submit to the compulsory jurisdiction * * * vis-à-vis Nicaragua, a State accepting the same obligation.

* * *

[The court then rejected the United States' arguments based on proviso (c) of its reservations, *i.e.* the so-called multilateral treaty (Vandenberg) reservation.]

* * *

72.   The multilateral treaty reservation in the United States Declaration has some obscure aspects, which have been the subject of comment since its making in 1946. There are two interpretations of the need for the presence of the parties to the multilateral treaties concerned in the proceedings before the Court as a condition for the validity of the acceptance of the compulsory jurisdiction by the United States. It is not clear whether what are "affected", according to the terms of the proviso, are the treaties themselves or the parties to them. Similar reservations to be found in certain other declarations of acceptance, such as those of India, El Salvador and the Philippines, refer clearly to "all parties" to the treaties. The phrase "all parties to the treaty affected by the decision" is at the centre of the present doubts. The United States interprets the reservation in the present case as referring to the States parties affected by the decision of the Court, merely mentioning the alternative interpretation, whereby it is the treaty which is "affected", so that all parties to the treaty would have to be before the Court, as "an *a fortiori* case". This latter interpretation need not therefore be considered. The argument of the United States relates specifically to El Salvador, Honduras and Costa Rica, the neighbour States of Nicaragua, which allegedly would be affected by the decision of the Court.

73.   It may * * * be noted that the multilateral treaty reservation could not bar adjudication by the Court of all Nicaragua's claims, because Nicaragua * * * does not confine those claims only to violations of the four multilateral conventions referred to above (paragraph 68). On the contrary, Nicaragua invokes a number of principles of customary and general international law that, according to the Application, have been violated by the United States. The Court cannot dismiss the claims of Nicaragua under principles of customary and general international law, simply because such principles have been enshrined in the texts of the conventions relied upon by Nicaragua. The fact that the above-mentioned principles, recognized as such, have been codified or embodied in multilateral conventions does not mean that they cease to exist and to apply as principles of customary law, even as regards countries that are parties to such conventions. Principles such as those of the non-use of force, non-intervention, respect for the independence and territorial integrity of States, and the freedom of navigation, continue to be binding as part of customary international law, despite the operation of provisions of conventional law in which they have been incorporated. Therefore, since the claim before the Court in this case is not confined to violation of the multilateral conventional provisions invoked, it would not in any event be barred by the multilateral treaty reservation in the United States 1946 Declaration.

* * *

75.   The United States Declaration uses the word "affected", without making it clear who is to determine whether the States referred to are, or are not, affected. The States themselves would have the choice of either instituting proceedings or intervening for the protection of their interests, in so far as these are not already protected by Article 59 of the Statute. As for the Court, it is only when the general lines of the judgment to be given

become clear that the States "affected" could be identified. By way of example we may take the hypothesis that if the Court were to decide to reject the Application of Nicaragua on the facts, there would be no third State's claim to be affected. Certainly the determination of the States "affected" could not be left to the parties but must be made by the Court.

76.   At any rate, this is a question concerning matters of substance relating to the merits of the case: obviously the question of what states may be "affected" by the decision on the merits is not in itself a jurisdictional problem. The present phase of examination of jurisdictional questions was opened by the Court itself by its Order of 10 May 1984, not by a formal preliminary objection submitted by the United States; but it is appropriate to consider the grounds put forward by the United States for alleged lack of jurisdiction in the light of the procedural provisions for such objections. That being so, and since the procedural technique formerly available of joinder of preliminary objections to the merits has been done away with since the 1972 revision of the Rules of Court, the Court has no choice but to avail itself of Article 79, paragraph 7, of the present Rules of Court, and declare that the objection based on the multilateral treaty reservation of the United States Declaration of Acceptance does not possess, in the circumstances of the case, an exclusively preliminary character, and that consequently it does not constitute an obstacle for the Court to entertain the proceedings instituted by Nicaragua under the Application of 9 April 1984.

* * *

U.S. Withdrawal From the Proceedings Initiated by Nicaragua in the ICJ

Statement, Jan. 18, 1985
United States Department of State Bulletin 64 (Mar. 1985)

The United States has consistently taken the position that the proceedings initiated by Nicaragua in the International Court of Justice (ICJ) are a misuse of the Court for political purposes and that the Court lacks jurisdiction and competence over such a case. The Court's decision of November 26, 1984, finding that it has jurisdiction, is contrary to law and fact. With great reluctance, the United States has decided not to participate in further proceedings in this case.

* * *

The conflict in Central America, * * * is an inherently political problem that is not appropriate for judicial resolution. The conflict will be solved only by political and diplomatic means—not through a judicial tribunal. The ICJ was never intended to resolve issues of collective security and self-defense and is patently unsuited for such a role. Unlike domestic courts, the World Court has jurisdiction only to the extent that nation-states have consented to it. When the United States accepted the Court's compulsory jurisdiction in 1946, it certainly never conceived of such a role for the Court in such controversies. Nicaragua's suit against the United States—which includes an absurd demand for hundreds of millions of dollars in reparations—is a blatant misuse of the Court for political and propaganda purposes.

* * *

This decision is erroneous as a matter of law and is based on a misreading and distortion of the evidence and precedent.

* * *

[After stating some reasons for this assertion, the Department continued]: For these reasons, we are forced to conclude that our continued participation in this case could not be justified.

* * *

U.S. Terminates Acceptance of ICJ Compulsory Jurisdiction

Secretary's Letter to UN
United States Department of State Bulletin 67 (Jan. 1986)

Secretary General, Oct. 7, 1985.

* * *

I have the honor on behalf of the Government of the United States of America to refer to the declaration of my Government of 26 August 1946, as modified by my note of 6 April 1984, concerning the acceptance by the United States of America of the compulsory jurisdiction of the International Court of Justice, and to state that the aforesaid declaration is hereby terminated, with effect six months from the date hereof.

* * *

Legal Advisor Soafer's statement defending this action also appears in the *State Department Bulletin*, January 1986. For a statement supporting compulsory jurisdiction, see U.S. Decision to Withdraw from the International Court of Justice, Hearing before the Subcommittee on Human Rights and International Organizations of the House Committee on Foreign Affairs, 99th Cong., 1st Sess. 92–109 (1986) (statement of Burns H. Weston and Bessie D. Murray for the Independent Commission on Respect for International Law).

The final action in the case was taken in 1991. In March 1988, the Sandinista government asked the ICJ to order the United States to pay $12 billion in damages. The Court made no ruling before February 25, 1990, however, when the Sandinistas were voted out of office. The new government, which had received generous financial support during the campaign from the United States, did not withdraw the country's request at the

Court, so, in late 1990, the United States informed Nicaragua's new leader, Mrs. Chamarro, that a $300 million aid package would be held until the case was withdrawn. Scott Wallace, *Evading Justice*, NATION, 476, Oct. 29, 1990, 1990 WLNR 3501240. In September 1991, Nicaragua formally requested that the Court remove the case from its list. In 1991 the Agent for Nicaragua informed the Court that Nicaragua did not wish to go on with these proceedings, and the Legal Advisor of the Department of State advised the Court that the United States welcomed the Nicaraguan request for discontinuance of the proceedings in this case. *See* 31 I.L.M. 103 (1992). The Order removing the case from the Court's list was made on 26 September, 1991. 1991 I.C.J. Rep. 47; 31 I.L.M. 103 (1992). *See also* Mary Ellen O'Connell, *The Nicaragua Case, Preserving World Peace and the World Court*, *in* INTERNATIONAL LAW STORIES 339 (John Noyes et al. eds. 2007).

Case Concerning East Timor

Portugal v. Australia
International Court of Justice
1995 I.C.J. Rep. 90 (Judgment of June 30)

11.   The Territory of East Timor corresponds to the eastern part of the island of Timor; it includes the island of Atauro, 25 kilometres to the north, the islet of Jaco to the east, and the enclave of Oe–Cusse in the western part of the island of Timor. Its capital is Dili, situated on its north coast. The south coast of East Timor lies opposite the north coast of Australia, the distance between them being approximately 430 kilometres.

In the sixteenth century, East Timor became a colony of Portugal; Portugal remained there until 1975. The western part of the island came under Dutch rule and later became part of independent Indonesia.

12.   In resolution 1542 (XV) of 15 December 1960 the United Nations General Assembly recalled "differences of views ... concerning the status of certain territories under the administrations of Portugal and Spain and described by these two States as 'overseas provinces' of the metropolitan State concerned"; and it also stated that it considered that the territories under the administration of Portugal, which were listed therein (including "Timor and dependencies") were non-self-governing territories within the meaning of Chapter XI of the Charter. Portugal, in the wake of its "Carnation Revolution", accepted this position in 1974.

13.   Following internal disturbances in East Timor, on 27 August 1975 the Portuguese civil and military authorities withdrew from the mainland of East Timor to the island of Atauro. On 7 December 1975 the armed forces of Indonesia intervened in East Timor. On 8 December 1975 the Portuguese authorities departed from the island of Atauro, and thus left East Timor altogether. Since their departure, Indonesia has occupied the Territory, and the Parties acknowledge that the Territory has remained under the effective control of that State. Asserting that on 31 May 1976 the people of East Timor had requested Indonesia "to accept East Timor as an

integral part of the Republic of Indonesia", on 17 July 1976 Indonesia enacted a law incorporating the Territory as part of its national territory.

18. * * * Australia and Indonesia then turned to the possibility of establishing a provisional arrangement for the joint exploration and exploitation of the resources of an area of the continental shelf. A Treaty to this effect was eventually concluded between them on 11 December 1989, whereby a "Zone of Cooperation" was created "in an area between the Indonesian Province of East Timor and Northern Australia". Australia enacted legislation in 1990 with a view to implementing the Treaty; this law came into force in 1991. * * *

* * *

19. In these proceedings Portugal maintains that Australia, in negotiating and concluding the 1989 Treaty, in initiating performance of the Treaty, in taking internal legislative measures for its application, and in continuing to negotiate with Indonesia, has acted unlawfully, in that it has infringed the rights of the people of East Timor to self-determination and to permanent sovereignty over its natural resources, infringed the rights of Portugal as the administering Power, and contravened Security Council resolutions 384 and 389. * * *

* * *

23. The Court will now consider Australia's principal objection, to the effect that Portugal's Application would require the Court to determine the rights and obligations of Indonesia. The declarations made by the Parties under Article 36, paragraph 2, of the Statute do not include any limitation which would exclude Portugal's claims from the jurisdiction thereby conferred upon the Court. Australia, however, contends that the jurisdiction so conferred would not enable the Court to act if, in order to do so, the Court were required to rule on the lawfulness of Indonesia's entry into and continuing presence in East Timor, on the validity of the 1989 Treaty between Australia and Indonesia, or on the rights and obligations of Indonesia under that Treaty, even if the Court did not have to determine its validity. Portugal agrees that if its Application required the Court to decide any of these questions, the Court could not entertain it. The Parties disagree, however, as to whether the Court is required to decide any of these questions in order to resolve the dispute referred to it.

24. Australia argues that the decision sought from the Court by Portugal would inevitably require the Court to rule on the lawfulness of the conduct of a third State, namely Indonesia, in the absence of that State's consent. In support of its argument, it cites the Judgment in the case concerning *Monetary Gold Removed from Rome in 1943*, in which the Court ruled that, in the absence of Albania's consent, it could not take any decision on the international responsibility of that State since "Albania's legal interests would not only be affected by a decision, but would form the very subject-matter of the decision" (I.C.J. Reports 1954, p. 32).

25. In reply, Portugal contends, first, that its Application is concerned exclusively with the objective conduct of Australia, which consists in having

negotiated, concluded and initiated performance of the 1989 Treaty with Indonesia, and that this question is perfectly separable from any question relating to the lawfulness of the conduct of Indonesia. According to Portugal, such conduct of Australia in itself constitutes a breach of its obligation to treat East Timor as a non-self-governing territory and Portugal as its administering Power; and that breach could be passed upon by the Court by itself and without passing upon the rights of Indonesia. The objective conduct of Australia, considered as such, constitutes the only violation of international law of which Portugal complains.

26.   The Court recalls in this respect that one of the fundamental principles of its Statute is that it cannot decide a dispute between States without the consent of those States to its jurisdiction. This principle was reaffirmed in the Judgment given by the Court in the case concerning *Monetary Gold Removed from Rome in 1943* and confirmed in several of its subsequent decisions * * *.

27.   The Court notes that Portugal's claim that, in entering into the 1989 Treaty with Indonesia, Australia violated the obligation to respect Portugal's status as administering Power and that of East Timor as a non-self-governing territory, is based on the assertion that Portugal alone, in its capacity as administering Power, had the power to enter into the Treaty on behalf of East Timor; that Australia disregarded this exclusive power, and, in so doing, violated its obligations to respect the status of Portugal and that of East Timor.

The Court also observes that Australia, for its part, rejects Portugal's claim to the exclusive power to conclude treaties on behalf of East Timor, and the very fact that it entered into the 1989 Treaty with Indonesia shows that it considered that Indonesia had that power. Australia in substance argues that even if Portugal had retained that power, on whatever basis, after withdrawing from East Timor, the possibility existed that the power could later pass to another State under general international law, and that it did so pass to Indonesia; Australia affirms moreover that, if the power in question did pass to Indonesia, it was acting in conformity with international law in entering into the 1989 Treaty with that State, and could not have violated any of the obligations Portugal attributes to it. Thus, for Australia, the fundamental question in the present case is ultimately whether, in 1989, the power to conclude a treaty on behalf of East Timor in relation to its continental shelf lay with Portugal or with Indonesia.

28.   The Court has carefully considered the argument advanced by Portugal which seeks to separate Australia's behaviour from that of Indonesia. However, in the view of the Court, Australia's behaviour cannot be assessed without first entering into the question why it is that Indonesia could not lawfully have concluded the 1989 Treaty, while Portugal allegedly could have done so; the very subject-matter of the Court's decision would necessarily be a determination whether, having regard to the circumstances in which Indonesia entered and remained in East Timor, it could or could not have acquired the power to enter into treaties on behalf of East Timor

relating to the resources of its continental shelf. The Court could not make such a determination in the absence of the consent of Indonesia.

* * *

In the Court's view, Portugal's assertion that the right of peoples to self-determination, as it evolved from the Charter and from United Nations practice, has an *erga omnes* character, is irreproachable. The principle of self-determination of peoples has been recognized by the United Nations Charter and in the jurisprudence of the Court *(see Legal Consequences for States of the Continued Presence of South Africa in Namibia (South West Africa) notwithstanding Security Council Resolution 276 (1970), Advisory Opinion, I.C.J. Reports 1971, pp. 31–32, paras. 52–53; Western Sahara, Advisory Opinion, I.C.J. Reports 1975, pp. 31–33, paras. 54–59)*; it is one of the essential principles of contemporary international law. However, the Court considers that the *erga omnes* character of a norm and the rule of consent to jurisdiction are two different things. Whatever the nature of the obligations invoked, the Court could not rule on the lawfulness of the conduct of a State when its judgment would imply an evaluation of the lawfulness of the conduct of another State which is not a party to the case. Where this is so, the Court cannot act, even if the right in question is a right *erga omnes*.

* * *

35. The Court concludes that it cannot, in this case, exercise the jurisdiction it has by virtue of the declarations made by the Parties under Article 36, paragraph 2, of its Statute because, in order to decide the claims of Portugal, it would have to rule, as a prerequisite, on the lawfulness of Indonesia's conduct in the absence of that State's consent. This conclusion applies to all the claims of Portugal, for all of them raise a common question: whether the power to make treaties concerning the continental shelf resources of East Timor belongs to Portugal or Indonesia, and, therefore, whether Indonesia's entry into and continued presence in the Territory are lawful. * * *

* * *

———

As the *Nicaragua* and *East Timor* cases indicate, the ICJ has generally taken a conservative view of its jurisdiction. The next set of cases involving the Vienna Convention on Consular Relations and issues of compliance and enforcement of ICJ judgments suggests that in some circumstances, the court might view its authority more broadly.

Statute of the International Court of Justice

Article 59

The decision of the Court has no binding force except between the parties and in respect of that particular case.

Article 60

The judgment is final and without appeal. In the event of dispute as to the meaning or scope of the judgment, the Court shall construe it upon the request of any party.

United Nations Charter

Article 94

1. Each Member of the United Nations undertakes to comply with the decision of the International Court of Justice in any case to which it is a party.

2. If any party to a case fails to perform the obligations incumbent upon it under a judgment rendered by the Court, the other party may have recourse to the Security Council, which may, if it deems necessary, make recommendations or decide upon measures to be taken to give effect to the judgment.

The Security Council has yet to act to enforce an ICJ judgment. During the *Nicaragua* case, Nicaragua made a request to the Security Council, but the request was vetoed by the United States. Should the permanent members of the Security Council be allowed to veto requests for assistance in enforcing judgments of the ICJ? See Richard B. Bilder, *The United States and the World Court in the Post-"Cold War" Era*, 40 Cath. U. L. Rev. 251, 255 (1991) (citing United Nations Security Council: Excerpts from Verbatim Records discussing I.C.J. Judgment in Nicaragua v. United States, 25 I.L.M. 1337, 1352, 1363 (1986)).

Avena and Other Mexican Nationals

Mexico v. United States
International Court of Justice
2004 I.C.J. Rep. (Judgment of Mar. 31)

49. In its final submissions Mexico asks the Court to adjudge and declare that, "the United States of America, in arresting, detaining, trying, convicting, and sentencing the 52 Mexican nationals on death row described in Mexico's Memorial, violated its international legal obligations to Mexico, in its own right and in the exercise of its right to diplomatic protection of its nationals, by failing to inform, without delay, the 52 Mexican nationals after their arrest of their right to consular notification and access under Article 36(1)(b) of the Vienna Convention on Consular Relations, and by depriving Mexico of its right to provide consular protection and the 52 nationals' right to receive such protection as Mexico would provide under Article 36(1)(a) and (c) of the Convention."

50. The Court has already in its Judgment in the *LaGrand* case described Article 36, paragraph 1, as "an interrelated régime designed to

facilitate the implementation of the system of consular protection" (I.C.J. Reports 2001, p. 492, para. 74).

* * *

61.   The Court thus now turns to the interpretation of Article 36, paragraph 1(b), having found * * * above that it is applicable to the 52 persons listed in paragraph 16. It begins by noting that Article 36, paragraph 1(b), contains three separate but interrelated elements: the right of the individual concerned to be informed without delay of his rights under Article 36, paragraph 1(b); the right of the consular post to be notified without delay of the individual's detention, if he so requests; and the obligation of the receiving State to forward without delay any communication addressed to the consular post by the detained person.

* * *

90.   The Court accordingly concludes that, with respect to each of the individuals listed in paragraph 16, * * * the United States has violated its obligation under Article 36, paragraph 1(b), of the Vienna Convention to provide information to the arrested person.

* * *

Article 36, paragraph 2

107.   In its third final submission Mexico asks the Court to adjudge and declare that "the United States violated its obligations under Article 36(2) of the Vienna Convention by failing to provide meaningful and effective review and reconsideration of convictions and sentences impaired by a violation of Article 36(1)."

108.   Article 36, paragraph 2, provides:

"The rights referred to in paragraph 1 of this article shall be exercised in conformity with the laws and regulations of the receiving State, subject to the proviso, however, that the said laws and regulations must enable full effect to be given to the purposes for which the rights accorded under this article are intended."

109.   In this connection, Mexico has argued that the United States

"By applying provisions of its municipal law to defeat or foreclose remedies for the violation of rights conferred by Article 36—thus failing to provide meaningful review and reconsideration of severe sentences imposed in proceedings that violated Article 36—... has violated, and continues to violate, the Vienna Convention."

* * *

Legal Consequences of the breach

* * *

119.   The general principle on the legal consequences of the commission of an internationally wrongful act was stated by the Permanent Court of International Justice in the *Factory at Chorzów* case as follows: "It is a principle of international law that the breach of an engagement involves an

obligation to make reparation in an adequate form." (*Factory at Chorzów, Jurisdiction*, 1927, P.C.I.J., Series A, No. 9, p. 21.) * * *

120. In the *LaGrand* case the Court made a general statement on the principle involved as follows:

"The Court considers in this respect that if the United States, notwithstanding its commitment [to ensure implementation of the specific measures adopted in performance of its obligations under Article 36, paragraph 1(b)], should fail in its obligation of consular notification to the detriment of German nationals, an apology would not suffice in cases where the individuals concerned have been subjected to prolonged detention or convicted and sentenced to severe penalties. In the case of such a conviction and sentence, it would be incumbent upon the United States to allow the review and reconsideration of the conviction and sentence by taking account of the violation of the rights set forth in the Convention. This obligation can be carried out in various ways. The choice of means must be left to the United States." (I.C.J. Reports 2001, pp. 513–514, para. 125.)

121. Similarly, in the present case the Court's task is to determine what would be adequate reparation for the violations of Article 36. It should be clear from what has been observed above that the internationally wrongful acts committed by the United States were the failure of its competent authorities to inform the Mexican nationals concerned, to notify Mexican consular posts and to enable Mexico to provide consular assistance. It follows that the remedy to make good these violations should consist in an obligation on the United States to permit review and reconsideration of these nationals' cases by the United States courts, as the Court will explain further in paragraphs 128 to 134 below, with a view to ascertaining whether in each case the violation of Article 36 committed by the competent authorities caused actual prejudice to the defendant in the process of administration of criminal justice.

* * *

123. It is not to be presumed, as Mexico asserts, that partial or total annulment of conviction or sentence provides the necessary and sole remedy. In this regard, Mexico cites the recent Judgment of this Court in the case concerning the *Arrest Warrant of 11 April 2000* (Democratic Republic of the Congo v. Belgium), in which the "Court ordered the cancellation of an arrest warrant issued by a Belgian judicial official in violation of the international immunity of the Congo Minister for Foreign Affairs." However, the present case has clearly to be distinguished from the *Arrest Warrant* case. In that case, the question of the legality under international law of the act of issuing the arrest warrant against the Congolese Minister for Foreign Affairs by the Belgian judicial authorities was itself the subject-matter of the dispute. Since the Court found that act to be in violation of international law relating to immunity, the proper legal consequence was for the Court to order the cancellation of the arrest warrant in question (I.C.J. Reports 2002, p. 33). By contrast, in the present case it is not the convictions and sentences of the Mexican nationals which

are to be regarded as a violation of international law, but solely certain breaches of treaty obligations which preceded them.

* * *

135.   Mexico, in the latter part of its seventh submission, has stated that "this obligation [of providing review and reconsideration] cannot be satisfied by means of clemency proceedings." Mexico elaborates this point by arguing first of all that "the United States's reliance on clemency proceedings is wholly inconsistent with its obligation to provide a remedy, as that obligation was found by this Court in *LaGrand*."

* * *

138.   The Court would emphasize that the "review and reconsideration" prescribed by it in the *LaGrand* case should be effective. Thus it should "tak [e] account of the violation of the rights set forth in [the] Convention" (I.C.J. Reports 2001, p. 516, para. 128(7)) and guarantee that the violation and the possible prejudice caused by that violation will be fully examined and taken into account in the review and reconsideration process. Lastly, review and reconsideration should be both of the sentence and of the conviction.

* * *

140.   As has been explained in paragraphs 128 to 134 above, the Court is of the view that, in cases where the breach of the individual rights of Mexican nationals under Article 36, paragraph 1(b), of the Convention has resulted, in the sequence of judicial proceedings that has followed, in the individuals concerned being subjected to prolonged detention or convicted and sentenced to severe penalties, the legal consequences of this breach have to be examined and taken into account in the course of review and reconsideration. The Court considers that it is the judicial process that is suited to this task.

Request for Interpretation of the Judgment of 31 March in the Case Concerning *Avena and Other Mexican Nationals*

Mexico v. United States
International Court of Justice
2009 I.C.J. Rep. (Judgment of Jan. 19)

11.   The Court recalls that in paragraph 153(9) of the *Avena* Judgment the Court had found that:

"the appropriate reparation in this case consists in the obligation of the United States of America to provide, by means of its own choosing, review and reconsideration of the convictions and sentences of the Mexican nationals referred to in subparagraphs (4), (5), (6) and (7) above, by taking account both of the violation of the rights set forth in Article 36 of the [Vienna] Convention [on Consular Relations] and of paragraphs 138 to 141 of this Judgment".

12. Mexico asked for an interpretation as to whether paragraph 153(9) expresses an obligation of result and requested that the Court should so state, as well as issue certain orders to the United States "pursuant to the foregoing obligation of result" (see paragraph 9 above).

13. Mexico's Request for interpretation of paragraph 153(9) of the Court's Judgment of 31 March 2004 was made by reference to Article 60 of the Statute. That Article provides that "[t]he judgment is final and without appeal. In the event of dispute ['contestation' in the French version] as to the meaning or scope of the judgment, the Court shall construe it upon the request of any party."

14. The United States informed the Court that it agreed that the obligation in paragraph 153(9) was an obligation of result and, there being no dispute between the Parties as to the meaning or scope of the words of which Mexico requested an interpretation, Article 60 of the Statute did not confer jurisdiction on the Court to make the interpretation (see para. 41 of the Order of 16 July 2008). In its written observations of 29 August 2008, the United States also contended that the absence of a dispute about the meaning or scope of paragraph 153(9) rendered Mexico's Application inadmissible.

15. The Court notes that its Order of 16 July 2008 on provisional measures was not made on the basis of prima facie jurisdiction. Rather, the Court stated that "the Court's jurisdiction on the basis of Article 60 of the Statute is not preconditioned by the existence of any other basis of jurisdiction as between the parties to the original case" (Order, para. 44).

The Court also affirmed that the withdrawal by the United States from the Optional Protocol to the Vienna Convention on Consular Relations Concerning the Compulsory Settlement of Disputes since the rendering of the *Avena* Judgment had no bearing on the Court's jurisdiction under Article 60 of the Statute (*ibid.*, para. 44).

16. In its Order of 16 July 2008, the Court had addressed whether the conditions laid down in Article 60 "for the Court to entertain a request for interpretation appeared to be satisfied" (*ibid.*, para. 45), observing that "the Court may entertain a request for interpretation of any judgment rendered by it provided that there is a 'dispute as to the meaning or scope of [the said] judgment'" (*ibid.*, para. 46).

17. In the same Order, the Court pointed out that "the French and English versions of Article 60 of the Statute are not in total harmony" and that the existence of a dispute/"contestation" under Article 60 was not subject to satisfaction of the same criteria as that of a dispute ("différend" in the French text) as referred to in Article 36, paragraph 2, of the Statute (Order, para. 53). The Court nonetheless observed that "it seems both Parties regard paragraph 153 (9) of the *Avena* Judgment as an international obligation of result" (*ibid.*, para. 55).

18. However, the Court also observed that

"the Parties nonetheless apparently hold different views as to the meaning and scope of that obligation of result, namely, whether that understanding is shared by all United States federal and state authorities and whether that obligation falls upon those authorities" (*ibid.*, para. 55).

19.   The Court stated that the decision rendered on the request for the indication of provisional measures "in no way prejudges any question that the Court may have to deal with relating to the Request for interpretation" (*ibid.*, para. 79).

20.   Accordingly, in the present procedure it is appropriate for the Court to review again whether there does exist a dispute over whether the obligation in paragraph 153(9) of the *Avena* Judgment is an obligation of result. The Court will also at this juncture need to consider whether there is indeed a difference of opinion between the Parties as to whether the obligation in paragraph 153(9) of the *Avena* Judgment falls upon all United States federal and state authorities.

21.   As is clear from the settled jurisprudence of the Court, a dispute must exist for a request for interpretation to be admissible (*Request for Interpretation of the Judgment of 20 November 1950 in the Asylum Case (Colombia* v. *Peru), Judgment, I.C.J. Reports 1950*, p. 402 *Application for Revision and Interpretation of the Judgment of 24 February 1982 in the Case concerning the* Continental Shelf (Tunisia/Libyan Arab Jamahiriya) *(Tunisia* v. *Libyan Arab Jamahiriya), Judgment, I.C.J. Reports 1985*, pp. 216–217, para. 44; see also *Request for Interpretation of the Judgment of 11 June 1998 in the Case concerning the* Land and Maritime Boundary between Cameroon and Nigeria (Cameroon *v.* Nigeria), Preliminary Objections *(Nigeria* v. *Cameroon), Judgment, I.C.J. Reports 1999 (I)*, p. 36, para. 12).

* * *

24.   Mexico referred in particular to the actions of the United States federal Executive, claiming that certain actions reflected the United States disagreement with Mexico over the meaning or scope of the *Avena* Judgment. According to Mexico, this difference of views manifested itself in the position taken by the United States Government in the Supreme Court: that the *Avena* Judgment was not directly enforceable under domestic law and was not binding on domestic courts without action by the President of the United States; and further that the obligation under Article 94 of the United Nations Charter to comply with judgments of the Court fell solely upon the political branches of the States parties to the Charter. In Mexico's view, "the operative language [of the *Avena* Judgment] establishes an obligation of result reaching all organs of the United States, including the federal and state judiciaries, that must be discharged irrespective of domestic law impediments". Mexico maintains that the United States Government's narrow reading of the means for implementing the Judgment led to its failure to take all the steps necessary to bring about compliance by all authorities concerned with the obligation borne by the United States. In particular, Mexico noted that the United States Government had not sought to intervene in support of Mr. Medellín's petition for a stay of execution before the United States Supreme Court. This course of conduct

is alleged to reflect a fundamental disagreement between the Parties concerning the obligation of the United States to bring about a specific result by any necessary means. Mexico further argues that the existence of a dispute is also shown by the fact that the competent executive, legislative and judicial organs at the federal and Texas state levels have taken positions in conflict with Mexico's as to the meaning or scope of paragraph 153 (9) of the *Avena* Judgment.

* * *

28.   The United States has insisted that it fully accepts that paragraph 153(9) of the *Avena* Judgment constitutes an obligation of result. It therefore continues to assert that there is no dispute over whether paragraph 153(9) expresses an obligation of result, and thus no dispute within the meaning of the condition in Article 60 of the Statute. Mexico contends, making reference to certain omissions of the federal government to act and of certain actions and statements of organs of government or other public authorities, that in reality the United States does not accept that it is under an obligation of result; and that therefore there is indeed a dispute under Article 60.

29.   It is for the Court itself to decide whether a dispute within the meaning of Article 60 of the Statute does indeed exist (see *Interpretation of Judgments Nos. 7 and 8 (Factory at Chorzów), Judgment No. 11, 1927, P.C.I.J., Series A, No. 13*, p. 12).

* * *

43.   * * * [E]ven if a dispute in the present case were ultimately found to exist within the meaning of Article 60 of the Statute. The Parties' different stated perspectives on the existence of a dispute reveal also different contentions as to whether paragraph 153(9) of the *Avena* Judgment envisages that a direct effect is to be given to the obligation contained therein.

44.   The *Avena* Judgment nowhere lays down or implies that the courts in the United States are required to give direct effect to paragraph 153(9). The obligation laid down in that paragraph is indeed an obligation of result which clearly must be performed unconditionally; non-performance of it constitutes internationally wrongful conduct. However, the Judgment leaves it to the United States to choose the means of implementation, not excluding the introduction within a reasonable time of appropriate legislation, if deemed necessary under domestic constitutional law. Nor moreover does the *Avena* Judgment prevent direct enforceability of the obligation in question, if such an effect is permitted by domestic law. In short, the question is not decided in the Court's original Judgment and thus cannot be submitted to it for interpretation under Article 60 of the Statute (*Request for Interpretation of the Judgment of 20 November 1950 in the Asylum Case (Colombia v. Peru), Judgment, I.C.J. Reports 1950*, p. 402).

45.   Mexico's argument * * * concerns the general question of the effects of a judgment of the Court in the domestic legal order of the States

parties to the case in which the judgment was delivered, not the "meaning or scope" of the *Avena* Judgment, as Article 60 of the Court's Statute requires. By virtue of its general nature, the question underlying Mexico's Request for interpretation is outside the jurisdiction specifically conferred upon the Court by Article 60. Whether or not there is a dispute, it does not bear on the interpretation of the *Avena* Judgment, in particular of paragraph 153(9).

46.   For these reasons, the Court cannot accede to Mexico's Request for interpretation.

* * *

47.   Before proceeding to the additional requests of Mexico, the Court observes that considerations of domestic law which have so far hindered the implementation of the obligation incumbent upon the United States, cannot relieve it of its obligation. A choice of means was allowed to the United States in the implementation of its obligation and, failing success within a reasonable period of time through the means chosen, it must rapidly turn to alternative and effective means of attaining that result.

* * *

48.   In the context of the proceedings instituted by the Application requesting interpretation, Mexico has presented three additional claims to the Court. First, Mexico asks the Court to adjudge and declare that the United States breached the Order indicating provisional measures of 16 July 2008 by executing Mr. Medellín on 5 August 2008 without having provided him with the review and reconsideration required under the *Avena* Judgment. Second, Mexico also regards that execution as having constituted a breach of the *Avena* Judgment itself. Third, Mexico requests the Court to order the United States to provide guarantees of non-repetition.

49.   The United States argues that the Court lacks jurisdiction to entertain the supplemental requests made by Mexico. As regards Mexico's claim concerning the alleged breach of the Order of 16 July 2008, the United States is of the opinion, first, that the lack of a basis of jurisdiction for the Court to adjudicate Mexico's Request for interpretation extends to this ancillary claim. Second, and in the alternative, the United States suggests that such a claim, in any event, goes beyond the jurisdiction of the Court under Article 60 of the Statute. Similarly, the United States submits that there is no basis of jurisdiction for the Court to entertain Mexico's claim relating to an alleged violation of the *Avena* Judgment. Finally, the United States disputes the Court's jurisdiction to order guarantees of non-repetition.

* * *

50.   Concerning Mexico's claim that the United States breached the Court's Order indicating provisional measures of 16 July 2008 by executing Mr. Medellín, the Court observes that in that Order it found that "it appears that the Court may, under Article 60 of the Statute, deal with the

Request for interpretation" (Order, para. 57). The Court then indicated in its Order that:

> "The United States of America shall take all measures necessary to ensure that Messrs. José Ernesto Medellín Rojas, César Roberto Fierro Reyna, Rubén Ramírez Cárdenas, Humberto Leal García, and Roberto Moreno Ramos are not executed pending judgment on the Request for interpretation submitted by the United Mexican States, unless and until these five Mexican nationals receive review and reconsideration consistent with paragraphs 138 to 141 of the Court's Judgment delivered on 31 March 2004 in the case concerning *Avena and Other Mexican Nationals (Mexico* v. *United States of America)." (Ibid.,* para. 80 (II)*(a)*.)

51.   There is no reason for the Court to seek any further basis of jurisdiction than Article 60 of the Statute to deal with this alleged breach of its Order indicating provisional measures issued in the same proceedings. The Court's competence under Article 60 necessarily entails its incidental jurisdiction to make findings about alleged breaches of the Order indicating provisional measures. That is still so even when the Court decides, upon examination of the Request for interpretation, as it has done in the present case, not to exercise its jurisdiction to proceed under Article 60.

52.   Mr. Medellín was executed in the State of Texas on 5 August 2008 after having unsuccessfully filed an application for a writ of *habeas corpus* and applications for stay of execution and after having been refused a stay of execution through the clemency process. Mr. Medellín was executed without being afforded the review and reconsideration provided for by * * * the *Avena* Judgment, contrary to what was directed by the Court in its Order indicating provisional measures of 16 July 2008.

53.   The Court thus finds that the United States did not discharge its obligation under the Court's Order of 16 July 2008, in the case of Mr. José Ernesto Medellín Rojas.

54.   The Court further notes that the Order of 16 July 2008 stipulated that five named persons were to be protected from execution until they received review and reconsideration or until the Court had rendered its Judgment upon Mexico's Request for interpretation. The Court recalls that the obligation upon the United States not to execute Messrs. César Roberto Fierro Reyna, Rubén Ramírez Cárdenas, Humberto Leal García, and Roberto Moreno Ramos pending review and reconsideration being afforded to them is fully intact by virtue of subparagraphs (4), (5), (6), (7) and (9) of paragraph 153 of the *Avena* Judgment itself. The Court further notes that the other persons named in the *Avena* Judgment are also to be afforded review and reconsideration in the terms there specified.

55.   The Court finally recalls that, as the United States has itself acknowledged, until all of the Mexican nationals referred to in subparagraphs (4), (5), (6) and (7) of paragraph 153 of the *Avena* Judgment have had their convictions and sentences reviewed and reconsidered, by taking account of Article 36 of the Vienna Convention on Consular Relations and

paragraphs 138 to 141 of the *Avena* Judgment, the United States has not complied with the obligation incumbent upon it.

* * *

56.   As regards the additional claim by Mexico asking the Court to declare that the United States breached the *Avena* Judgment by executing José Ernesto Medellín Rojas without having provided him review and reconsideration consistent with the terms of that Judgment, the Court notes that the only basis of jurisdiction relied upon for this claim in the present proceedings is Article 60 of the Statute, and that that Article does not allow it to consider possible violations of the Judgment which it is called upon to interpret.

57.   In view of the above, the Court finds that the additional claim by Mexico concerning alleged violations of the *Avena* Judgment must be dismissed.

* * *

58.   Lastly, Mexico requests the Court to order the United States to provide guarantees of non-repetition (point (2)*(c)* of Mexico's submissions) so that none of the Mexican nationals mentioned in the *Avena* Judgment is executed without having benefited from the review and reconsideration provided for by the operative part of that Judgment.

59.   The United States disputes the jurisdiction of the Court to order it to furnish guarantees of non-repetition, principally inasmuch as the Court lacks jurisdiction under Article 60 of the Statute to entertain Mexico's Request for interpretation or, in the alternative, since the Court cannot, in any event, order the provision of such guarantees within the context of interpretation proceedings.

60.   The Court finds it sufficient to reiterate that its *Avena* Judgment remains binding and that the United States continues to be under an obligation fully to implement it.

NOTES AND QUESTIONS

1.   Recall that the United States invoked the Vienna Convention on Consular Relations optional protocol in 1979 when Americans were seized in Iran and held hostage. *United States Diplomatic and Consular Staff in Tehran* (U.S. v. Iran), 1980 I.C.J. 3 (May 24) (discussed in Chapter 8 above.) The U.S. attempted to negotiate their release. When it failed, it went to the ICJ for provisional measures of protection. The ICJ ordered the immediate release of the hostages in a unanimous decision of the court at the height of the Cold War. The U.S. went on to win a highly favorable decision on the merits a few months later. Iran did not immediately release the hostages, but the ICJ's decisions played a key role in the eventual settlement of the crisis. The U.S., European states, and others froze Iranian assets upon the seizure of the hostages. States began to question whether they had a right to do so to enforce the rights of another state. The ICJ made clear the importance of compliance with the Vienna Convention and did not critique the sanctions imposed on Iran. Assets were held

until Iran agreed to release the hostages and join a claims process for paying damages to thousands of Americans injured in the course of the Iranian revolution. The Iran–U.S. Claims Tribunal continues to operate today.

The next three cases to be brought to the ICJ under the optional protocol were brought against the United States for failing to provide consular notice to the citizens of other countries in the U.S. The U.S.'s main argument in all three cases was that the U.S. federal government is limited in imposing obligations on U.S. States in these cases so that remedies imposed on the U.S. by the ICJ are pointless. The U.S. has not denied its failure to comply with its obligations. After losing the third case, Secretary of State Condoleeza Rice withdrew the U.S. from the optional protocol. She explained:

> So we will continue to live up to our obligations under the Vienna Convention. We will continue to believe in the importance of consular notification. But this particular optional protocol was in our federal system being interpreted in ways that we thought were inappropriate for a system in which there is a jurisdictional issue between the federal government and the states. And that's really what this is about.

Briefing En Route to Mexico, Secretary Condoleeza Rice, Mexico City, Mexico, Mar. 10, 2005.

2. For the U.S. Supreme Court case indicated in the *Request for Interpretation*, see *Medellín v. Texas*, 552 U.S. 491, 128 S.Ct. 1346, 170 L.Ed.2d 190 (2008), discussed in the final section of this chapter.

3. Note that the U.S. record respecting international courts and tribunals is mixed: The U.S. has been one of the ICJ's main champions as well as detractors. As discussed at the outset of this section, major popular movements in the U.S. and Britain supported courts and tribunals for the peaceful settlement of disputes. In the 20th century popular and official support in the U.S. appears to have declined from the high point when U.S. Secretary of State Elihu Root tried to persuade the other participants in the 1907 Hague Conference to found an international court. Nevertheless, the U.S. is still party to dozens of treaties that include commitments to settle any disputes before the ICJ. The United States has been a party to more cases before the ICJ than any other state. Russia and China, both with judges on the ICJ, have never been a party to a single case before the court. While U.S. antipathy for the International Criminal Court is well known, it is less well known that the U.S. was the prime mover behind compulsory dispute resolution at the WTO. The U.S. is also the most frequent party to dispute settlement at the WTO. What might explain this mixed record respecting adjudication? For some insights, see, THE SWORD AND THE SCALES, THE UNITED STATES AND INTERNATIONAL COURTS AND TRIBUNALS (Cesare P.R. Romano ed., 2009).

4. What might create greater enthusiasm for the ICJ not just in the U.S. but throughout the world? Currently only about one-third of the states in the world are party to the ICJ's optional compulsory jurisdiction. The United Kingdom is the only permanent member of the Security Council

that currently accepts the optional clause. Why not require all permanent members to commit to compulsory jurisdiction as a sign of true commitment to international law and as an indication that they are qualified to hold the privilege of exercising the veto?

5. Why do you think that Australia resisted the ICJ taking the *East Timor* case? Did Australia not want to know whether it was acting lawfully in entering into a treaty with Indonesia that implicated the rights of the Timorese people?

B.) ADVISORY OPINIONS

United Nations, Handbook on the Pacific Settlement of Disputes Between States

p. 70 (1992)

(v) *Advisory opinions*

212. International courts may be empowered to give an advisory opinion on a legal question relating to an existing international dispute between States referred to them by an international entity. The opinion does not bind the requesting entity, or any other body, or any State. Nevertheless, procedure in advisory cases, as in contentious cases, involves elaborate written and oral proceedings in accordance with the predetermined rules of the court in question, and as such advisory opinions could assume the character of judicial pronouncements which, while not binding, might entail practical consequences * * *.

We have already seen advisory opinions of the ICJ, recall the *Headquarters Agreement* (Chapters 1 and 9) *Reparations for Injury* case (Chapter 3), the *Reservations* case (Chapter 2), and the *WHO* case in this chapter. The next excerpt is one of the ICJ's most controversial advisory opinions to date. Consider why as you read it.

Legality of the Threat or Use of Nuclear Weapons

Advisory Opinion
International Court of Justice
1996 I.C.J. Rep. 226

10. The Court must first consider whether it has the jurisdiction to give a reply to the request of the General Assembly for an Advisory Opinion and whether, should the answer be in the affirmative, there is any reason it should decline to exercise any such jurisdiction.

The Court draws its competence in respect of advisory opinions from Article 65, paragraph 1, of its Statute. Under this Article, the Court "may give an advisory opinion on any legal question at the request of whatever body may be authorized by or in accordance with the Charter of the United Nations to make such a request".

11.   For the Court to be competent to give an advisory opinion, it is thus necessary at the outset for the body requesting the opinion to be "authorized by or in accordance with the Charter of the United Nations to make such a request". The Charter provides in Article 96, paragraph 1, that:

"The General Assembly or the Security Council may request the International Court of Justice to give an advisory opinion on any legal question."

Some States which oppose the giving of an opinion by the Court argued that the General Assembly and Security Council are not entitled to ask for opinions on matters totally unrelated to their work. They suggested that, as in the case of organs and agencies acting under Article 96, paragraph 2, of the Charter, and notwithstanding the difference in wording between that provision and paragraph 1 of the same Article, the General Assembly and Security Council may ask for an advisory opinion on a legal question only within the scope of their activities.

In the view of the Court, it matters little whether this interpretation of Article 96, paragraph 1, is or is not correct; in the present case, the General Assembly has competence in any event to seise the Court. Indeed, Article 10 of the Charter has conferred upon the General Assembly a competence relating to "any questions or any matters" within the scope of the Charter. Article 11 has specifically provided it with a competence to "consider the general principles ... in the maintenance of international peace and security, including the principles governing disarmament and the regulation of armaments". Lastly, according to Article 13, the General Assembly "shall initiate studies and make recommendations for the purpose of ... encouraging the progressive development of international law and its codification".

* * *

13.   The Court must furthermore satisfy itself that the advisory opinion requested does indeed relate to a "legal question" within the meaning of its Statute and the United Nations Charter.

The Court has already had occasion to indicate that questions

"framed in terms of law and rais[ing] problems of international law are by their very nature susceptible of a reply based on law ... [and] appear ... to be questions of a legal character" *(Western Sahara, Advisory Opinion, I.C.J. Reports* 1975, p. 18, para. 15).

The question put to the Court by the General Assembly is indeed a legal one, since the Court is asked to rule on the compatibility of the threat or use of nuclear weapons with the relevant principles and rules of international law. To do this, the Court must identify the existing principles and rules, interpret them and apply them to the threat or use of nuclear weapons, thus offering a reply to the question posed based on law.

The fact that this question also has political aspects, as, in the nature of things, is the case with so many questions which arise in international life, does not suffice to deprive it of its character as a "legal question" and to "deprive the Court of a competence expressly conferred on it by its Statute" *(Application for Review of Judgement No. 158 of the United Nations Administrative Tribunal, Advisory Opinion, I.C.J. Reports* 1973, p. 172, para. 14). Whatever its political aspects, the Court cannot refuse to admit the legal character of a question which invites it to discharge an essentially judicial task, namely, an assessment of the legality of the possible conduct of States with regard to the obligations imposed upon them by international law [Citations omitted].

Furthermore, as the Court said in the Opinion it gave in 1980 concerning the *Interpretation of the Agreement of 25 March 1951 between the WHO and Egypt:*

> "Indeed, in situations in which political considerations are prominent it may be particularly necessary for an international organization to obtain an advisory opinion from the Court as to the legal principles applicable with respect to the matter under debate ..." *(Interpretation of the Agreement of 25 March* 1951 *between the WHO and Egypt, Advisory Opinion, I.C.J. Reports 1980,* p. 87, para. 33.) The Court moreover considers that the political nature of the motives which may be said to have inspired the request and the political implications that the opinion given might have are of no relevance in the establishment of its jurisdiction to give such an opinion.

14. Article 65, paragraph 1, of the Statute provides: "The Court *may* give an advisory opinion ..." (Emphasis added.) This is more than an enabling provision. As the Court has repeatedly emphasized, the Statute leaves a discretion as to whether or not it will give an advisory opinion that has been requested of it, once it has established its competence to do so. In this context, the Court has previously noted as follows:

> "The Court's Opinion is given not to the States, but to the organ which is entitled to request it; the reply of the Court, itself an 'organ of the United Nations', represents its participation in the activities of the Organization, and, in principle, should not be refused." * * *

The Court has constantly been mindful of its responsibilities as "the principal judicial organ of the United Nations" (Charter, Art. 92). When considering each request, it is mindful that it should not, in principle, refuse to give an advisory opinion. In accordance with the consistent jurisprudence of the Court, only "compelling reasons" could lead it to such a refusal [Citations omitted]. There has been no refusal, based on the discretionary power of the Court, to act upon a request for advisory opinion in the history of the present Court; in the case concerning the *Legality of the Use by a State of Nuclear Weapons in Armed Conflict,* the refusal to give the World Health Organization the advisory opinion requested by it was justified by the Court's lack of jurisdiction in that case. The Permanent Court of International Justice took the view on only one occasion that it could not reply to a question put to it, having regard to the very particular circumstances of the case, among which were that the question directly concerned an already existing dispute, one of the States parties to which was neither a party to the Statute of the Permanent Court nor a Member of the League of Nations, objected to the proceedings, and refused to take part in any way *(Status of Eastern Carelia, P.C.I.J., Series B, No. 5)*.

15. Most of the reasons adduced in these proceedings in order to persuade the Court that in the exercise of its discretionary power it should decline to render the opinion requested by General Assembly resolution 49/75K were summarized in the following statement made by one State in the written proceedings:

> "The question presented is vague and abstract, addressing complex issues which are the subject of consideration among interested States and within other bodies of the United Nations which have an express mandate to address these matters. An opinion by the Court in regard to the question presented would provide no practical assistance to the General Assembly in carrying out its functions under the Charter. Such an opinion has the potential of undermining progress already made or being made on this sensitive subject and, therefore, is contrary to the interest of the United Nations Organization." (United States of America, Written Statement, pp. 1–2; * * *).

In contending that the question put to the Court is vague and abstract, some States appeared to mean by this that there exists no specific dispute on the subject-matter of the question. In order to respond to this argument, it is necessary to distinguish between requirements governing contentious procedure and those applicable to advisory opinions. The purpose of the advisory function is not to settle—at least directly—disputes between States, but to offer legal advice to the organs and institutions requesting the opinion (cf. *Interpretation of Peace Treaties I.C.J. Reports 1950*, p. 71). The fact that the question put to the Court does not relate to a specific dispute should consequently not lead the Court to decline to give the opinion requested.

Moreover, it is the clear position of the Court that to contend that it should not deal with a question couched in abstract terms is "a mere affirmation devoid of any justification", and that "the Court may give an advisory opinion on any legal question, abstract or otherwise" * * *

* * *

16. Certain States have observed that the General Assembly has not explained to the Court for what precise purposes it seeks the advisory opinion. Nevertheless, it is not for the Court itself to purport to decide whether or not an advisory opinion is needed by the Assembly for the performance of its functions. The General Assembly has the right to decide for itself on the usefulness of an opinion in the light of its own needs.

* * *

18.   Finally, it has been contended by some States that in answering the question posed, the Court would be going beyond its judicial role and would be taking upon itself a law-making capacity. It is clear that the Court cannot legislate, and, in the circumstances of the present case, it is not called upon to do so. Rather its task is to engage in its normal judicial function of ascertaining the existence or otherwise of legal principles and rules applicable to the threat or use of nuclear weapons. The contention that the giving of an answer to the question posed would require the Court to legislate is based on a supposition that the present corpus juris is devoid of relevant rules in this matter. The Court could not accede to this argument; it states the existing law and does not legislate. This is so even if, in stating and applying the law, the Court necessarily has to specify its scope and sometimes note its general trend.

19.   In view of what is stated above, the Court concludes that it has the authority to deliver an opinion on the question posed by the General Assembly, and that there exist no "compelling reasons" which would lead the Court to exercise its discretion not to do so.

An entirely different question is whether the Court, under the constraints placed upon it as a judicial organ, will be able to give a complete answer to the question asked of it. However, that is a different matter from a refusal to answer at all.

NOTES AND QUESTIONS

1.   How would you characterize the status of ICJ advisory opinions? Are these opinions obligatory, and, if so, in what sense and on whom? Or as advice to the requesting organ, are they merely hortatory but to be taken into account? Are they any more or less binding than other decisions of the ICJ? *See* UN Charter Article 96 and ICJ Statute Articles 65–68. Compare Charter Article 94, which provides for Security Council assistance in enforcing judgments binding on states.

2.   What procedures might be employed to make advisory opinions formally binding in the sense of Charter Article 94 as applied to contentious cases? What would be the effect of an agreement providing that "[t]he opinion of the Court shall be accepted as decisive by the parties?" *See* in the Documentary Supplement, Section 30 of the Convention on the Privileges and Immunities of the United Nations.

3.   Organs and agencies authorized to request advisory opinions under Charter Article 94 are limited to 5 UN organs (General Assembly, Security Council, Economic and Social Council, Trusteeship Council and the Interim Committee of the General Assembly) and UN Specialized Agencies (see listing in Chapter 3, Section C.1 below). Judge Sir Robert Jennings suggested (in the excerpt above) that access to the Court's advisory jurisdiction be expanded. He and others would include the Secretary–General and even other public international organizations not directly affiliated with the United Nations, such as the Council of Europe, OECD, NATO, the OAS. Why not expand to states? Or to non-state parties such as NGOs, companies and individuals? How might that be done in formal terms?

4. Recall the case of *Yassin Abdullah Kadi v. Council of the European Union and Commission of the European Communities*, E.C.J., Cases C–402/05 and C–415 P (Sept. 3, 2008) discussed in Chapter 3. In that case the European Court of Justice held that the UK approach to complying with a UN Security Council program for controlling the financing of terrorist organizations denied people due process. Should a regional court have the authority in international law to rule on the legality of Security Council action? Is that not the job of the ICJ? What if, as in this case, the Security Council fails to request an advisory opinion to clarify the matter? Even if it did, would the ECJ have to respect the decision? Is the ECJ ruling on the Security Council's action?

5. In some cases, states have viewed the request for an advisory opinion as a way to get around the need for states to give their consent to jurisdiction in contentious cases. Some have said this about, notably, *Legal Consequences of the Construction of a Wall in the Occupied Palestinian Territories*, 2004 I.C.J. Rep. 136; *Applicability of Article VI, Section 22 of the Convention on the Privileges and Immunities of the United Nations* 1989 I.C.J. Rep. 177, and *Western Sahara*, 1975 I.C.J. Rep. 12. If the the intention of the UN organ requesting the opinion is to do an end-round around Article 36 of the ICJ Statute, should the ICJ decline to take the case? Would that not pose a different sort of jurisprudential problem?

6. Should the decisions of the ICJ in contentious cases and advisory opinions have a *stare decisis* quality? Do they have precedential value in any case? Is there a distinction to be made on these issues between contentious cases and advisory opinions? Have you noticed how the ICJ actually treats its decisions and opinions on parallel issues presented in later cases? How would you compare the ICJ practice to the notion of *stare decisis* in the common law world? Can you distinguish its treatment of contentious cases versus advisory opinions? Is this relevant to the question, are advisory opinions binding?

7. For further reading on the ICJ, see, Fifty Years of the International Court of Justice: Essays in Honour of Sir Robert Jennings (Vaughan Lowe & Malgosia Fitzmaurice eds., 1996); Mohamed Shahabuddeen, Precedent in the World Court (1996); Arthur Eyffinger, The International Court of Justice, 1946–1996 (1996); Shabtai Rosenne, The World Court: what it is and how it works (1995).

2.) *The International Criminal Court*

In Chapter 5 you were introduced to international criminal courts, including the International Criminal Court (ICC). In this chapter we consider whether criminal courts are fora for peaceful settlement of disputes. In other words, does the ICC promote peace or justice or both? What does it say about the evolution of international law that before working out problems regarding enforcement of ICJ decisions, a court for individual accountability has been formed? In its short decade of existence and before any cases have been decided by the ICC, the court has already become the subject of a vast literature and activism. Indeed, it is now the subject of specialized courses. Why this enthusiasm among international law scholars and human rights advocates? By contrast, the United States has had a generally negative attitude at the official level. President Clinton's representative to the Rome conference to negotiate the ICC Statute voted against the final text. President Clinton did sign the treaty during his final days as president, apparently to allow the United States to continue to participate in discussions relevant to the court, but President Bush had Undersecretary of State John Bolton remove President Clinton's signature. Press Statement, International Criminal Court: Letter to UN Secretary General Kofi Annan (May 2, 2002).

Arguably, criminal courts are not a proper topic for this chapter which concerns peaceful settlement of disputes. Do criminal courts help maintain peace and security? Professors Luigi Condorelli and Santiago Villaplando argue that the Security Council began forming criminal tribunals to help maintain peace and security in the world:

> Through the establishment of the ICTY and the ICTR, the Security Council gave a new dimension to the exercise of its powers for the maintenance of international peace and security, by becoming active in the field of the prosecution of international crimes. In this perspective, the Rome Statute takes over from the Security Council's pioneering action and consolidates the progress accomplished in the field of international criminal law. But it also provides for a new instrument at the Security Council's disposal for the fulfillment of its primary responsibility under the UN Charter. By establishing a permanent international criminal court, providing for the basic rules that govern its functioning and defining its jurisdiction, and then by allowing the security Council to "trigger" the proceedings before the Court, the Rome Statute encourages and considerably simplifies this UN organ's action. In the future, the prosecution of international crimes could be initiated immediately, without the need to establish new tribunals and to define their constitutive elements. In other words, in 1998, the States participating in the Rome Conference seemed to make a "gift" to the Security Council for the accomplishment of its duties under the Charter.

Luigi Condorelli & Santiago Villalpando, *Can the Security Council Extend the ICC's Jurisdiction? in* I THE ROME STATUTE OF THE INTERNATIONAL CRIMINAL COURT: A COMMENTARY 571, 571–72 (Antonio Cassese et al. eds., 2002).

Christopher Blakesley, Report on the Obstacles to the Creation of a Permanent War Crimes Tribunal

18 FLETCHER FOR. WORLD AFF. 77, 78, 81–86, 97–98 (1994)*

The usual and most appropriate method for establishing an international criminal tribunal would be a convention. All member states, howev-

---

* Footnotes omitted.

er, are likely under a binding obligation to take whatever action is required to enforce the statute under U.N. Charter, Chapter VII. The Secretary–General suggested that the treaty approach would be too long and arduous; drafting an instrument and obtaining the required ratifications for entry into force would not be reconcilable with the urgency expressed by the Security Council in Resolution 808 (Secretary–General's Report, at ¶ ¶ 2021). Thus, it was recommended that the authority or legal basis for the tribunal be predicated on Chapter VII of the U.N. Charter, which covers Action with respect to Threats to the Peace, Breaches of the Peace, and Acts of Aggression. The creation of the tribunal would be a "measure to maintain or restore international peace and security, following the requisite determination of the existence of a threat to the peace, breach of the peace or act of aggression." Article 41 of the U.N. Charter provides: "The Security Council may decide what measures not involving the use of armed force are to be employed to give effect to its decisions, and it may call upon the members of the United Nations to apply such measures." Article 42 adds: "Should the Security Council consider that measures provided for in Article 41 would be inadequate or have proved to be inadequate, it may take such action by air, sea, or land forces as may be necessary to maintain or restore international peace and security. Such action may include demonstrations, blockade, and other operations by air, sea, or land forces of Members of the [U.N.]" The argument is that if the use of force is allowed as a "measure" under Article 42, a fortiori, the creation of an ad hoc international criminal court should also be allowed. In "the particular case of the former Yugoslavia, the Secretary–General believes that the establishment of the International Tribunal by means of a Chapter VII decision would be legally justified, both in terms of the object and purpose of the decision [as indicated in the purpose statement in his report] and of past Security Council practice." [Sec.Gen.Report §§ 24,27]. The Secretary–General's Report relating to the atrocities there noted that the creation of the Tribunal for the prosecution of the alleged breaches of international humanitarian law will apply existing law, including the Geneva Conventions of 1949, and that the Security Council would not be creating law or purporting to legislate.

* * *

About the Court

http://www.icc-cpi.int/Menus/ICC/About + the + Court/

The International Criminal Court (ICC), governed by the Rome Statute, is the first permanent, treaty based, international criminal court established to help end impunity for the perpetrators of the most serious crimes of concern to the international community.

The ICC is an independent international organisation, and is not part of the United Nations system. Its seat is at The Hague in the Netherlands. Although the Court's expenses are funded primarily by States Parties, it also receives voluntary contributions from governments, international organisations, individuals, corporations and other entities.

The international community has long aspired to the creation of a permanent international court, and, in the 20th century, it reached consensus on definitions of genocide, crimes against humanity and war crimes. The Nuremberg and Tokyo trials addressed war crimes, crimes against peace, and crimes against humanity committed during the Second World War.

In the 1990s after the end of the Cold War, tribunals like the International Criminal Tribunal for the former Yugoslavia and for Rwanda were the result of consensus that impunity is unacceptable. However, because they were established to try crimes committed only within a specific time-frame and during a specific conflict, there was general agreement that an independent, permanent criminal court was needed. On 17 July 1998, the international community reached an historic milestone when 120 States adopted the Rome Statute, the legal basis for establishing the permanent International Criminal Court.

The Rome Statute entered into force on 1 July 2002 after ratification by 60 countries.

Rome Statute on the Establishment of an International Criminal Court

July 17, 1998, U.N. Doc. *A/CONF.183/9.*

Article 5
Crimes within the jurisdiction of the Court

1.   The jurisdiction of the Court shall be limited to the most serious crimes of concern to the international community as a whole. The Court has jurisdiction in accordance with this Statute with respect to the following crimes:

(a) The crime of genocide;

(b) Crimes against humanity;

(c) War crimes;

(d) The crime of aggression.

2.   The Court shall exercise jurisdiction over the crime of aggression once a provision is adopted in accordance with articles 121 and 123 defining the crime and setting out the conditions under which the Court shall exercise jurisdiction with respect to this crime. Such a provision shall be consistent with the relevant provisions of the Charter of the United Nations.

International Criminal Court	ICC–ASP/7/SWGCA/INF.1
Assembly of States Parties	Distr.: General
	19 February 2009
	Original: English

Seventh session (second resumption)
New York
9–13 February 2009

Discussion paper on the crime of aggression proposed by the Chairman (revision January 2009)

Annex

Draft amendments to the Rome Statute of the International Criminal Court on the Crime of Aggression

1.   *Article 5, paragraph 2, of the Statute is deleted.*

2.   *The following text is inserted after article 8 of the Statute:*

Article 8 bis

Crime of aggression

1.   For the purpose of this Statute, "crime of aggression" means the planning, preparation, initiation or execution, by a person in a position effectively to exercise control over or to direct the political or military action of a State, of an act of aggression which, by its character, gravity and scale, constitutes a manifest violation of the Charter of the United Nations.

2.   For the purpose of paragraph 1, "act of aggression" means the use of armed force by a State against the sovereignty, territorial integrity or political independence of another State, or in any other manner inconsistent with the Charter of the United Nations.

Any of the following acts, regardless of a declaration of war, shall, in accordance with United Nations General Assembly resolution 3314 (**XXIX**) of 14 December 1974, qualify as an act of aggression:

(a) The invasion or attack by the armed forces of a State of the territory of another State, or any military occupation, however temporary, resulting from such invasion or attack, or any annexation by the use of force of the territory of another State or part thereof;

(b) Bombardment by the armed forces of a State against the territory of another State or the use of any weapons by a State against the territory of another State;

(c) The blockade of the ports or coasts of a State by the armed forces of another State;

(d) An attack by the armed forces of a State on the land, sea or air forces, or marine and air fleets of another State;

(e) The use of armed forces of one State which are within the territory of another State with the agreement of the receiving State, in contravention of the conditions provided for in the agreement or any extension of their presence in such territory beyond the termination of the agreement;

(f) The action of a State in allowing its territory, which it has placed at the disposal of another State, to be used by that other State for perpetrating an act of aggression against a third State;

(g) The sending by or on behalf of a State of armed bands, groups, irregulars or mercenaries, which carry out acts of armed force against another State of such gravity as to amount to the acts listed above, or its substantial involvement therein.

3. *The following text is inserted after article 15 of the Statute:*

Article 15 bis

Exercise of jurisdiction over the crime of aggression

1. The Court may exercise jurisdiction over the crime of aggression in accordance with article 13, subject to the provisions of this article.

2. Where the Prosecutor concludes that there is a reasonable basis to proceed with an investigation in respect of a crime of aggression, he or she shall first ascertain whether the Security Council has made a determination of an act of aggression committed by the State concerned. The Prosecutor shall notify the Secretary–General of the United Nations of the situation before the Court, including any relevant information and documents.

3. Where the Security Council has made such a determination, the Prosecutor may proceed with the investigation in respect of a crime of aggression.

4. (Alternative 1) In the absence of such a determination, the Prosecutor may not proceed with the investigation in respect of a crime of aggression,

Option 1—end the paragraph here.

Option 2—add: unless the Security Council has, in a resolution adopted under Chapter VII of the Charter of the United Nations, requested the Prosecutor to proceed with the investigation in respect of a crime of aggression.

4. (Alternative 2) Where no such determination is made within [6] months after the date of notification, the Prosecutor may proceed with the investigation in respect of a crime of aggression,

Option 1—end the paragraph here.

Option 2—add: provided that the Pre–Trial Chamber has authorized the commencement of the investigation in respect of a crime of aggression in accordance with the procedure contained in article 15;

Option 3—add: provided that the General Assembly has determined that an act of aggression has been committed by the State referred to in article 8 bis;

Option 4—add: provided that the International Court of Justice has determined that an act of aggression has been committed by the State referred to in article 8 bis.

5.   A determination of an act of aggression by an organ outside the Court shall be without prejudice to the Court's determination of an act of aggression under this Statute.

6.   This article is without prejudice to the provisions relating to the exercise of jurisdiction with respect to other crimes referred to in article 5.

4.   The following text is inserted after article 25, paragraph 3 of the Statute:

3 bis In respect of the crime of aggression, the provisions of this article shall apply only to persons in a position effectively to exercise control over or to direct the political or military action of a State.

NOTES AND QUESTIONS

1.   In July 2008, the ICC issued the following press release on its most dramatic action to that point:

ICC Prosecutor presents case against Sudanese President, Hassan Ahmad AL BASHIR, for genocide, crimes against humanity and war crimes in Darfur

ICC–OTP–20080714–PR341

Situation: Darfur, Sudan

ICC Prosecutor Luis Moreno–Ocampo has presented evidence today showing that Sudanese President, Omar Hassan Ahmad AL BASHIR committed the crimes of genocide, crimes against humanity and war crimes in Darfur.

Three years after the Security Council requested him to investigate in Darfur, and based on the evidence collected, the Prosecutor has concluded there are reasonable grounds to believe that Omar Hassan Ahmad AL BASHIR bears criminal responsibility in relation to 10 counts of genocide, crimes against humanity and war crimes. * * *

Sudan immediately broke off peace talks with some Darfuri militias taking place in Qatar. It also expelled a number of aid NGOs accusing them of assisting the ICC and, thereby, violating their duties of neutrality and impartiality. Do you think it was worth issuing the indictment in light of these repercussions? Could the prosecutor appropriately take such things into account in deciding whether or not to issue an indictment? Would this require an answer to the question of whether the ICC is an institution primarily for the promotion of peace or primarily for the promotion of justice? A year after the indictment there is no indication Bashir will be sent to the ICC. See the Website of the ICC for other pending cases, http://www.icc-cpi.net.

2.   Do you think prosecuting the crime of aggression may strengthen the prohibition on the use of force—the central topic of Chapter 10? If you were doubtful about the ICC as an institution to promote peace, will adding the crime of aggression allay your doubts? Should Ocampo bring charges of aggression against the Darfuri rebels for first resorting to force? If he did would that hurt or help his case against Bashir in the eyes of the world?

3.   In addition to removing President Clinton's signature from the Rome Statute, the Bush Administration took other unprecedented actions aimed at undermining the ICC. It requested, for example, that states party to the Rome Statute sign bilateral agreements with the U.S. promising not to send any U.S. national to the ICC. Such bilateral agreements put states into conflict with their Rome Statute obligations. The U.S. abandoned the effort by 2006. In 2005 the Bush Administration allowed the Security Council to refer the case of Sudan to the prosecutor. Why do you think President Bush and members of Congress felt such strong opposition to the ICC? Why did the opposition recede?

4.   For further reading on the ICC, its history and role in support of peace, *see*, BRUCE BROOMHALL, INTERNATIONAL JUSTICE AND THE INTERNATIONAL CRIMINAL COURT: BETWEEN SOVEREIGNTY AND THE RULE OF LAW (2003); LEILA NADYA SADAT, THE INTERNATIONAL CRIMINAL COURT AND THE TRANSFORMATION OF INTERNATIONAL LAW: JUSTICE FOR THE NEW MILLENNIUM (2002); THE INTERNATIONAL CRIMINAL COURT: THE MAKING OF THE ROME STATUTE–ISSUES, NEGOTIATIONS, RESULTS (Roy S. Lee ed., in cooperation with the Project on International Courts and Tribunals, 1999).

5.   For further reading on courts other than the ICJ and ICC, *see*, TRUDI HARTZENBERG, WTO DISPUTE SETTLEMENT: AN AFRICAN PERSPECTIVE (2008); INTERNATIONAL COURTS FOR THE TWENTY-FIRST CENTURY (MARK W. JANIS ED., 1992); COMPLIANCE WITH JUDGMENTS OF INTERNATIONAL COURTS (M.K. BULTERMAN & M. KUIJER eds., 1996); THE INTERNATIONAL TRIBUNAL FOR THE LAW OF THE SEA: LAW AND PRACTICE (P. CHANDRASEKHARA RAO & RAHMATULLAH KHAN eds., 2001).

b. NATIONAL COURTS

Despite the growth of international courts and tribunals, national courts very likely continue to decide more international law issues on an annual basis than all international forums combined. Recall the case discussed in Chapter 1, *U.S. v. PLO*, a dispute between the UN and the U.S. over the PLO Mission to the UN. The judgment led to the end of that dispute. Similar examples are found in every chapter. In this section, we look at three decisions concerning the enforcement or implementation of ICJ judgments by national courts.

Committee of U.S. Citizens Living in Nicaragua v. Reagan

District of Columbia Circuit Court of Appeals
859 F.2d 929 (1988)

■ MIKVA, CIRCUIT JUDGE:

Appellants, comprising organizations and individuals who oppose United States policy in Central America, claim to have suffered physical, economic and other injuries from the war in Nicaragua. These facts form the backdrop to this lawsuit.

The suit finds its genesis, however, in a 1986 decision by the International Court of Justice (ICJ), which held that America's support of military actions by the so-called "Contras" against the government of Nicaragua violated both customary international law and a treaty between the United States and Nicaragua. The ICJ concluded that the United States "is under a duty immediately to cease and to refrain from all such acts as may constitute breaches of the foregoing legal obligations." 1986 I.C.J. 14, 149. Included among those acts were the "training, arming, equipping, financing and supplying [of] the *contra* forces." *Id.* at 146.

Prior to the ICJ's decision, the United States withdrew from the merits phase of the court's proceedings, contending that the court lacked jurisdiction over Nicaragua's application. Since the decision, the President has requested and Congress has approved continued funding for the Contras of the sort that the ICJ found illegal. In addition, the U.S. used its veto power in the United Nations (U.N.) Security Council to block consideration of a resolution enforcing the ICJ decision.

Unhappy with their government's failure to abide by the ICJ decision and believing that continued funding of the Contras injures their own interests, appellants filed suit in the United States District Court for the District of Columbia. The suit sought injunctive and declaratory relief against the funding of the Contras on grounds that such funding violates the Administrative Procedure Act, the first and fifth amendments of the United States Constitution, Article 94 of the U.N. Charter, and customary international law.

* * *

B. Appellants Have No Basis in Domestic Law for Enforcing the ICJ Judgment

1. *The status of international law in the United States' domestic legal order*

Appellants argue that the United States' decision to disregard the ICJ judgment and to continue funding the Contras violates three types of international law. First, contravention of the ICJ judgment is said to violate part of a United States treaty, namely Article 94 of the U.N. Charter. That article provides that "[e]ach Member of the United Nations undertakes to comply with the decision of the International Court of Justice in any case to which it is a party." U.N. Charter art. 94. Second, disregard of the ICJ judgment allegedly violates principles of customary international law. One such principle holds that treaties in force shall be observed. Appellants contend that another such principle requires parties to ICJ decisions to adhere to those decisions. Third, the United States may have violated peremptory norms of international law. Such norms, often referred to as *jus cogens* (or "compelling law"), enjoy the highest status in international law and prevail over both customary international law and treaties. Appellants' contention that the United States has violated *jus cogens* forms their primary argument before this court. They contend that the obligation of parties to an ICJ judgment to obey that judgment is not merely a customary rule but actually a peremptory norm of international law.

For purposes of the present lawsuit, the key question is not simply whether the United States has violated any of these three legal norms but whether such violations can be remedied by an American court or whether they can only be redressed on an international level. In short, do violations of international law have domestic legal consequences? The answer largely depends on what form the "violation" takes. Here, the alleged violation is the law that Congress enacted and that the President signed, appropriating funds for the Contras. When our government's two political branches, acting together, contravene an international legal norm, does this court have any authority to remedy the violation? The answer is "no" if the type of international obligation that Congress and the President violate is either a treaty or a rule of customary international law. If, on the other hand, Congress and the President violate a peremptory norm (or *jus cogens*), the domestic legal consequences are unclear. We need not resolve this uncertainty, however, for we find that the principles appellants characterize as peremptory norms of international law are not recognized as such by the community of nations.

* * *

Our conclusion is strengthened when we consider those few norms that arguably do meet the stringent criteria for jus cogens. The recently revised Restatement acknowledges two categories of such norms: "the principles of the United Nations Charter prohibiting the use of force," Restatement § 102 comment k, and fundamental human rights law that prohibits genocide, slavery, murder, torture, prolonged arbitrary detention, and racial discrimination. Id. § 702 & comment n; see also Randall, *Universal Jurisdiction Under International Law*, 66 Tex.L.Rev. 785, 830 (1988); *Whiteman, Jus Cogens In International Law, With a Projected List*, 7 Ga.J.Int'l & Comp.L. 609, 625–26 (1977). But see Restatement § 331 comment e (doctrine of jus cogens is of such "uncertain scope" that a "domestic court should not on its own authority refuse to give effect to an agreement on the ground that it violates a peremptory norm").

Such basic norms of international law as the proscription against murder and slavery may well have the domestic legal effect that appellants suggest. That is, they may well restrain our government in the same way that the Constitution restrains it. If Congress adopted a foreign policy that resulted in the enslavement of our citizens or of other individuals, that policy might well be subject to challenge in domestic court under international law. Such a conclusion was indeed implicit in the landmark decision in Filartiga v. Pena–Irala, 630 F.2d 876 (2d Cir.1980), which upheld jurisdiction over a suit by a Paraguayan citizen against a Paraguayan police chief for the death by torture of the plaintiff's brother. The court concluded that "official torture is now prohibited by the law of nations." Id. at 884 (footnote omitted). The same point has been echoed in our own court. Judge Edwards observed in Tel–Oren v. Libyan Arab Republic, 726 F.2d 774 (D.C.Cir.1984), cert. denied, 470 U.S. 1003, 105 S.Ct. 1354, 84 L.Ed.2d 377 (1985), that "commentators have begun to identify a handful of heinous actions—each of which violates definable, universal and obligatory norms," id. at 781 (Edwards, J., concurring), and that these include, at a minimum, bans on governmental "torture, summary execution, genocide, and slavery." Id. at 791 n. 20; see also Letelier v. Republic of Chile, 488 F.Supp. 665 (D.D.C.1980) (upholding jurisdiction over claim that foreign government brought about assassination of its own citizen living in the United States, in violation of international law and the U.S. Constitution).

[12] We think it clear, however, that the harm that results when a government disregards or contravenes an ICJ judgment does not generate the level of universal disapprobation aroused by torture, slavery, summary execution, or genocide. Appellants try to bootstrap the ICJ's judgment against the United States into a form of jus cogens by pointing out that the judgment relies on a peremptory norm of international law—that is, that the ICJ invoked the norm proscribing aggressive use of force between nations when it rendered its decision in the Nicaragua case. This argument, however, confuses the judgment itself with the ICJ's rationale for that judgment. The gravamen of appellants' complaint is that compliance with an ICJ judgment is a nonderogable norm of international law, not that a particular judgment constitutes collateral estoppel against the United States as to its violation of a nonderogable norm. Were appellants to advance the latter contention, they would be applying nonmutual, offensive collateral estoppel against the federal government, which generally is not permitted even in domestic law cases, see United States v. Mendoza, 464 U.S. 154, 104 S.Ct. 568, 78 L.Ed.2d 379 (1984), much less in international law cases where our government disputes the prior court's jurisdiction. In sum, appellants' attempt to enjoin funding of the Contras on the ground that it violates a peremptory norm of international law by contravening an ICJ judgment is unavailing. The ICJ judgment does not represent such a peremptory norm.

* * *

III.   CONCLUSION

There is no question that, in the second half of the twentieth century, the protections afforded individuals under international law have greatly expanded. At one time, international law concerned itself chiefly with relations among states, occasionally with relations between a state and citizens of other states, and almost never with a nation's treatment of its own citizens. *See, e.g.,* Sohn, *The New International Law: Protection of the Rights of Individuals Rather than States,* 32 Am.U.L.Rev. 1, 9 (1982). That has now changed, *id.* at 9–11, and government officials can be held responsible for certain egregious violations of their own citizens' rights. *See, e.g., Filartiga v. Pena–Irala,* 630 F.2d 876 (2d Cir.1980) (international law proscribes "official torture"). Notwithstanding these changes, however, the expanded law of nations does not encompass the principles that appellants advance in this lawsuit. No principle of *jus cogens* protects citizens from harm that may result from their own government's contravention of an ICJ decision. Nor has the expansion of international law altered the principle of domestic law that congressional enactments cannot violate but can only supersede prior inconsistent treaties or customary norms of international law. For these reasons, we dismiss so much of appellants' cause of action as is based on international law.

We also find that appellants' fifth amendment cause of action fails to state a claim on which relief can be granted, though for somewhat different reasons. We do not conclude that Congress' pursuit of a foreign policy could never give rise to a deprivation of rights cognizable in domestic courts. We say only that what constitutes a deprivation of our citizens' liberty and property "without due process of law" must be gauged by the circumstances—in this case, Congress' pursuit of foreign policy objectives. The risk to Americans that Congress accepted in deciding to fund the Contras may or may not satisfy the standard for "reckless" conduct as a matter of domestic tort law. But appellants' factual averments concerning the Contras' injuries to Americans in Nicaragua cannot support a constitutional claim against the United States for its support of that foreign "resistance" movement. Accordingly, appellants' fifth amendment claims are also dismissed.

Bruno Simma & Carsten Hoppe, The *LaGrand* Case: A Story of Many Miscommunications*

pp. 402–03 *in* INTERNATIONAL LAW STORIES (John Noyes et al. eds., 2007)

On September 19, 2006, a Chamber of the Bundesverfassungsgerichthof (Federal Constitutional Court) in Karlsruhe decided unanimously that a violation of the individual right enshrined in Articles 36 [of the Vienna Convention on Consular Relations] in criminal proceedings amounted to a violation of the constitutional right to a fair trial, and remanded the underlying cases back to the competent criminal courts, obligating them to "take account of" the decisions of the ICJ in *LaGrand* and *Avena* in interpreting and applying Article 36. Article 36 was confirmed as being directly applicable in German domestic law. Further, decisions of the ICJ were said to be persuasive even in cases in which Germany was not a party; they have a "normative guiding function" and share the binding quality of international law in the German system.

---

* Footnotes omitted.

Medellín v. Texas*

United States Supreme Court
552 U.S. 491, 128 S.Ct. 1346, 170 L.Ed.2d 190 (2008)

■ Chief Justice Roberts delivered the opinion of the Court. . . .

I.

In 1969, the United States, upon the advice and consent of the Senate, ratified the Vienna Convention on Consular Relations (Vienna Convention or Convention), Apr. 24, 1963, [1970] 21 U.S.T. 77, T.I.A.S. No. 6820, and the Optional Protocol Concerning the Compulsory Settlement of Disputes to the Vienna Convention (Optional Protocol or Protocol), Apr. 24, 1963, [1970] 21 U.S.T. 325, T.I.A.S. No. 6820 * * *.

* * *

Article 36 of the Convention was drafted to "facilitat[e] the exercise of consular functions." Art. 36(1), 21 U.S.T., at 100. It provides that if a person detained by a foreign country "so requests, the competent authorities of the receiving State shall, without delay, inform the consular post of the sending State" of such detention, and "inform the [detainee] of his righ[t]" to request assistance from the consul of his own state. Art. 36(1)(b), *id.*, at 101.

The Optional Protocol provides a venue for the resolution of disputes arising out of the interpretation or application of the Vienna Convention. Art. 1, 21 U.S.T., at 326. Under the Protocol, such disputes "shall lie within the compulsory jurisdiction of the International Court of Justice" and "may accordingly be brought before the [ICJ] . . . by any party to the dispute being a Party to the present Protocol." *Ibid.*

The ICJ is "the principal judicial organ of the United Nations." United Nations Charter, Art. 92, 59 Stat. 1051, T. S. No. 993 (1945). It was established in 1945 pursuant to the United Nations Charter. The ICJ Statute—annexed to the U.N. Charter—provides the organizational framework and governing procedures for cases brought before the ICJ. Statute of the International Court of Justice (ICJ Statute), 59 Stat. 1055, T. S. No. 993 (1945).

Under Article 94(1) of the U.N. Charter, "[e]ach Member of the United Nations undertakes to comply with the decision of the [ICJ] in any case to which it is a party." 59 Stat. 1051 * * *

By ratifying the Optional Protocol to the Vienna Convention, the United States consented to the specific jurisdiction of the ICJ with respect to claims arising out of the Vienna Convention. On March 7, 2005, subsequent to the ICJ's judgment in *Avena*, the United States gave notice of withdrawal from the Optional Protocol to the Vienna Convention. Letter from Condoleezza Rice, Secretary of State, to Kofi A. Annan, Secretary–General of the United Nations * * *.

---

* Footnotes omitted.

Petitioner José Ernesto Medellín, a Mexican national, has lived in the United States since preschool. A member of the "Black and Whites" gang, Medellín was convicted of capital murder and sentenced to death in Texas for the gang rape and brutal murders of two Houston teenagers * * *.

Medellín first raised his Vienna Convention claim in his first application for state post conviction relief. The state trial court held that the claim was procedurally defaulted because Medellín had failed to raise it at trial or on direct review. The trial court also rejected the Vienna Convention claim on the merits, finding that Medellín had "fail[ed] to show that any nonnotification of the Mexican authorities impacted on the validity of his conviction or punishment." *Id.*, at 62. The Texas Court of Criminal Appeals affirmed. *Id.*, at 64–65.

Medellín then filed a habeas petition in Federal District Court. The District Court denied relief, holding that Medellín's Vienna Convention claim was procedurally defaulted and that Medellín had failed to show prejudice arising from the Vienna Convention violation. See *Medellín* v. *Cockrell*, Civ. Action No. H–01–4078 (SD Tex., June 26, 2003), App. to Brief for Respondent 86–92.

While Medellín's application for a certificate of appealability was pending in the Fifth Circuit, the ICJ issued its decision in *Avena*. The ICJ held that the United States had violated Article 36(1)(b) of the Vienna Convention by failing to inform the 51 named Mexican nationals, including Medellín, of their Vienna Convention rights. 2004 I.C.J., at 53–55. In the ICJ's determination, the United States was obligated "to provide, by means of its own choosing, review and reconsideration of the convictions and sentences of the [affected] Mexican nationals." *Id.*, at 72. The ICJ indicated that such review was required without regard to state procedural default rules. *Id.*, at 56–57.

The Fifth Circuit denied a certificate of appealability. *Medellín* v. *Dretke*, 371 F. 3d 270, 281 (2004). The court concluded that the Vienna Convention did not confer individually enforceable rights. *Id.*, at 280. The court further ruled that it was in any event bound by this Court's decision in *Breard* v. *Greene*, 523 U.S. 371, 375 (1998) (*per curiam*), which held that Vienna Convention claims are subject to procedural default rules, rather than by the ICJ's contrary decision in *Avena*. 371 F. 3d, at 280.

This Court granted certiorari. *Medellín* v. *Dretke*, 544 U.S. 660, 661 (2005) (*per curiam*) (*Medellín I*). Before we heard oral argument, however, President George W. Bush issued his Memorandum to the United States Attorney General, providing:

> I have determined, pursuant to the authority vested in me as President by the Constitution and the laws of the United States of America, that the United States will discharge its international obligations under the decision of the International Court of Justice in [*Avena*], by having State courts give effect to the decision in accordance with general principles of comity in cases filed by the 51 Mexican nationals addressed in that decision. App. to Pet. for Cert. 187a.

Medellín, relying on the President's Memorandum and the ICJ's decision in *Avena*, filed a second application for habeas relief in state court. *Ex parte Medellín*, 223 S. W. 3d 315, 322–323 (Tex. Crim. App. 2006). Because the state-court proceedings might have provided Medellín with the review and reconsideration he requested, and because his claim for federal relief might otherwise have been barred, we dismissed his petition for certiorari as improvidently granted. *Medellín I, supra*, at 664.

The Texas Court of Criminal Appeals subsequently dismissed Medellín's second state habeas application as an abuse of the writ. 223 S. W. 3d, at 352. In the court's view, neither the *Avena* decision nor the President's Memorandum was "binding federal law" that could displace the State's limitations on the filing of successive habeas applications. *Ibid.* We again granted certiorari. 550 U.S. ___ (2007).

II

Medellín first contends that the ICJ's judgment in *Avena* constitutes a "binding" obligation on the state and federal courts of the United States. He argues that "by virtue of the Supremacy Clause, the treaties requiring compliance with the *Avena* judgment are *already* the 'Law of the Land' by which all state and federal courts in this country are 'bound.' " Reply Brief for Petitioner 1. Accordingly, Medellín argues, *Avena* is a binding federal rule of decision that pre-empts contrary state limitations on successive habeas petitions.

No one disputes that the *Avena* decision—a decision that flows from the treaties through which the United States submitted to ICJ jurisdiction with respect to Vienna Convention disputes—constitutes an *international* law obligation on the part of the United States. But not all international law obligations automatically constitute binding federal law enforceable in United States courts. The question we confront here is whether the *Avena* judgment has automatic *domestic* legal effect such that the judgment of its own force applies in state and federal courts.

This Court has long recognized the distinction between treaties that automatically have effect as domestic law, and those that—while they constitute international law commitments—do not by themselves function as binding federal law. The distinction was well explained by Chief Justice Marshall's opinion in *Foster* v. *Neilson*, 2 Pet. 253, 315 (1829), overruled on other grounds, *United States* v. *Percheman*, 7 Pet. 51 (1833), which held that a treaty is "equivalent to an act of the legislature," and hence self-executing, when it "operates of itself without the aid of any legislative provision." *Foster, supra,* at 314. When, in contrast, "[treaty] stipulations are not self-executing they can only be enforced pursuant to legislation to carry them into effect." *Whitney* v. *Robertson*, 124 U.S. 190, 194 (1888). In sum, while treaties "may comprise international commitments . . . they are not domestic law unless Congress has either enacted implementing statutes or the treaty itself conveys an intention that it be 'self-executing' and is ratified on these terms." *Igartúa–De La Rosa* v. *United States*, 417 F. 3d 145, 150 (CA1 2005) (en banc) (Boudin, C. J.). * * *

A

The interpretation of a treaty, like the interpretation of a statute, begins with its text. *Air France* v. *Saks*, 470 U.S. 392, 396–397 (1985). Because a treaty ratified by the United States is "an agreement among sovereign powers," we have also considered as "aids to its interpretation" the negotiation and drafting history of the treaty as well as "the post ratification understanding" of signatory nations. *Zicherman* v. *Korean Air Lines Co.*, 516 U.S. 217, 226 (1996); see also *United States* v. *Stuart*, 489 U.S. 353, 365–366 (1989); *Choctaw Nation* v. *United States*, 318 U.S. 423, 431–432 (1943).

As a signatory to the Optional Protocol, the United States agreed to submit disputes arising out of the Vienna Convention to the ICJ. The Protocol provides: "Disputes arising out of the interpretation or application of the [Vienna] Convention shall lie within the compulsory jurisdiction of the International Court of Justice." Art. I, 21 U.S.T., at 326. Of course, submitting to jurisdiction and agreeing to be bound are two different things. A party could, for example, agree to compulsory nonbinding arbitration. Such an agreement would require the party to appear before the arbitral tribunal without obligating the party to treat the tribunal's decision as binding. See, *e.g.*, North American Free Trade Agreement, U.S.-Can.-Mex., Art. 2018(1), Dec. 17, 1992, 32 I. L. M. 605, 697 (1993) ("On receipt of the final report of [the arbitral panel requested by a Party to the agreement], the disputing Parties shall agree on the resolution of the dispute, which normally shall conform with the determinations and recommendations of the panel").

The most natural reading of the Optional Protocol is as a bare grant of jurisdiction. It provides only that "[d]isputes arising out of the interpretation or application of the [Vienna] Convention shall lie within the compulsory jurisdiction of the International Court of Justice" and "may accordingly be brought before the [ICJ] ... by any party to the dispute being a Party to the present Protocol." Art. I, 21 U.S.T., at 326. The Protocol says nothing about the effect of an ICJ decision and does not itself commit signatories to comply with an ICJ judgment. The Protocol is similarly silent as to any enforcement mechanism.

The obligation on the part of signatory nations to comply with ICJ judgments derives not from the Optional Protocol, but rather from Article 94 of the United Nations Charter—the provision that specifically addresses the effect of ICJ decisions. Article 94(1) provides that "[e]ach Member of the United Nations *undertakes to comply* with the decision of the [ICJ] in any case to which it is a party." 59 Stat. 1051 (emphasis added). The Executive Branch contends that the phrase "undertakes to comply" is not "an acknowledgement that an ICJ decision will have immediate legal effect in the courts of U.N. members," but rather "a *commitment* on the part of U.N. Members to take *future* action through their political branches to comply with an ICJ decision." Brief for United States as *Amicus Curiae* in *Medellín I*, O. T. 2004, No. 04–5928, p. 34.

We agree with this construction of Article 94. The Article is not a directive to domestic courts. It does not provide that the United States "shall" or "must" comply with an ICJ decision, nor indicate that the Senate that ratified the U.N. Charter intended to vest ICJ decisions with immediate legal effect in domestic courts. Instead, "[t]he words of Article 94 . . . call upon governments to take certain action." *Committee of United States Citizens Living in Nicaragua* v. *Reagan*, 859 F. 2d 929, 938 (CADC 1988) (quoting *Diggs* v. *Richardson*, 555 F. 2d 848, 851 (CADC 1976); internal quotation marks omitted) * * *.

The remainder of Article 94 confirms that the U.N. Charter does not contemplate the automatic enforceability of ICJ decisions in domestic courts. Article 94(2)—the enforcement provision—provides the sole remedy for noncompliance: referral to the United Nations Security Council by an aggrieved state. 59 Stat. 1051 * * *.

("[I]f a state fails to perform its obligations under a judgment of the [ICJ], the other party may have recourse to the Security Council"); *id.*, at 286 (statement of Leo Paslovsky, Special Assistant to the Secretary of State for International Organizations and Security Affairs) ("[W]hen the Court has rendered a judgment and one of the parties refuses to accept it, then the dispute becomes political rather than legal. It is as a political dispute that the matter is referred to the Security Council") * * *

If ICJ judgments were instead regarded as automatically enforceable domestic law, they would be immediately and directly binding on state and federal courts pursuant to the Supremacy Clause. Mexico or the ICJ would have no need to proceed to the Security Council to enforce the judgment in this case. Noncompliance with an ICJ judgment through exercise of the Security Council veto—always regarded as an option by the Executive and ratifying Senate during and after consideration of the U.N. Charter, Optional Protocol, and ICJ Statute—would no longer be a viable alternative. There would be nothing to veto. In light of the U.N. Charter's remedial scheme, there is no reason to believe that the President and Senate signed up for such a result.

In sum, Medellín's view that ICJ decisions are automatically enforceable as domestic law is fatally undermined by the enforcement structure established by Article 94. His construction would eliminate the option of noncompliance contemplated by Article 94(2), undermining the ability of the political branches to determine whether and how to comply with an ICJ judgment. . . .

C

Our conclusion that *Avena* does not by itself constitute binding federal law is confirmed by the "postratification understanding" of signatory nations. See *Zicherman,* 516 U.S., at 226. There are currently 47 nations that are parties to the Optional Protocol and 171 nations that are parties to the Vienna Convention. Yet neither Medellín nor his *amici* have identified a single nation that treats ICJ judgments as binding in domestic courts * * *.

Medellín and the dissent cite *Comegys v. Vasse,* 1 Pet. 193 (1828), for the proposition that the judgments of international tribunals are automatically binding on domestic courts. See *post,* at 9; Reply Brief for Petitioner 2; Brief for Petitioner 19–20. That case, of course, involved a different treaty than the ones at issue here; it stands only for the modest principle that the terms of a treaty control the outcome of a case. We do not suggest that treaties can never afford binding domestic effect to international tribunal judgments—only that the U.N. Charter, the Optional Protocol, and the ICJ Statute do not do so. And whether the treaties underlying a judgment are self-executing so that the judgment is directly enforceable as domestic law in our courts is, of course, a matter for this Court to decide. See *Sanchez–Llamas, supra,* at 353–354.

Our holding does not call into question the ordinary enforcement of foreign judgments or international arbitral agreements. Indeed, we agree with Medellín that, as a general matter, "an agreement to abide by the result" of an international adjudication—or what he really means, an agreement to give the result of such adjudication domestic legal effect—can be a treaty obligation like any other, so long as the agreement is consistent with the Constitution. See Brief for Petitioner 20. The point is that the particular treaty obligations on which Medellín relies do not of their own force create domestic law.

[Justice Stevens concurred in the result.]

■ JUSTICE BREYER, with whom JUSTICE SOUTER and JUSTICE GINSBURG join, dissenting.

The Constitution's Supremacy Clause provides that "all Treaties . . . which shall be made . . . under the Authority of the United States, shall be the supreme Law of the Land; and the Judges in every State shall be bound thereby." Art. VI, cl. 2. The Clause means that the "courts" must regard "a treaty . . . as equivalent to an act of the legislature, whenever it operates of itself without the aid of any legislative provision." *Foster* v. *Neilson*, 2 Pet. 253, 314 (1829) (majority opinion of Marshall, C.J.).

In the *Avena* case the International Court of Justice (ICJ) (interpreting and applying the Vienna Convention on Consular Relations) issued a judgment that requires the United States to reexamine certain criminal proceedings in the cases of 51 Mexican nationals. *Case Concerning Avena and Other Mexican Nationals (Mex. v. U.S.)*, 2004 I.C.J. 12 (Judgment of Mar. 31) *(Avena)*. The question here is whether the ICJ's *Avena* judgment is enforceable now as a matter of domestic law, *i.e.*, whether it "operates of itself without the aid" of any further legislation.

The United States has signed and ratified a series of treaties obliging it to comply with ICJ judgments in cases in which it has given its consent to the exercise of the ICJ's adjudicatory authority. Specifically, the United States has agreed to submit, in this kind of case, to the ICJ's "compulsory jurisdiction" for purposes of "compulsory settlement." Optional Protocol Concerning the Compulsory Settlement of Disputes (Optional Protocol or Protocol), Art. I, Apr. 24, 1963, [1970] 21 U.S.T. 325, 326 T.I.A.S. No. 6820 (capitalization altered). And it agreed that the ICJ's judgments would have "binding force ... between the parties and in respect of [a] particular case." United Nations Charter, Art. 59, 59 Stat. 1062, T.S. No. 993 (1945). President Bush has determined that domestic courts should enforce this particular ICJ judgment. Memorandum to the Attorney General (Feb. 28, 2005), App. to Pet. for Cert. 187a (hereinafter President's Memorandum). And Congress has done nothing to suggest the contrary. Under these circumstances, I believe the treaty obligations, and hence the judgment, resting as it does upon the consent of the United States to the ICJ's jurisdiction, bind the courts no less than would "an act of the [federal] legislature." *Foster*, *supra*, at 314. * * *

Mexico claimed that state authorities within the United States had failed to notify the arrested persons of their Vienna Convention rights and, by applying state procedural law in a manner which did not give full effect to the Vienna Convention rights, had deprived them of an appropriate remedy. *Ibid.* The ICJ judgment in *Avena* requires that the United States reexamine "by means of its own choosing" certain aspects of the relevant state criminal proceedings of 51 of these individual Mexican nationals. *Id.,* at 62 * * *.

[T]ext and history, along with subject matter and related characteristics will help our courts determine whether, as Chief Justice Marshall put it, the treaty provision "addresses itself to the political ... department[s]" for further action or to "the judicial department" for direct enforcement. *Foster*, 2 Pet., at 314; see also *Ware*, 3 Dall., at 244 (opinion of Chase, J.) ("No one can doubt that a treaty may stipulate, that certain acts shall be done by the Legislature; that other acts shall be done by the Executive; and others by the Judiciary") * * *.

[I]n accepting Article 94(1) of the Charter, "[e]ach Member ... undertakes to comply with the decision" of the ICJ "in any case to which it is a party." 59 Stat. 1051. And the ICJ Statute (part of the U.N. Charter) makes clear that, a decision of the ICJ between parties that have consented to the ICJ's compulsory jurisdiction has *"binding force ...* between the parties and in respect of that particular case." Art. 59, *id.,* at 1062 (emphasis added). Enforcement of a court's judgment that has "binding force" involves quintessential judicial activity....

And even if I agreed with JUSTICE STEVENS that the language is perfectly ambiguous (which I do not), I could not agree that "the best reading ... is ... one that contemplates future action by the political branches." *Ante*, at 3. The consequence of such a reading is to place the fate of an international promise made by the United States in the hands of a single State. See *ante*, at 4–6. And that is precisely the situation that the Framers sought to prevent by enacting the Supremacy Clause. See 3 Story 696 (purpose of Supremacy Clause "was probably to obviate" the "difficulty" of system where treaties were "dependent upon the good will of the states for their execution"); see also *Ware*, 3 Dall., at 277–278 (opinion of Iredell, J.) * * *

[I]nsofar as today's holdings make it more difficult to enforce the judgments of international tribunals, including technical non-politically-controversial judgments, those holdings weaken that rule of law for which our Constitution stands. Compare Hughes Defends Foreign Policies in Plea for Lodge, N.Y. Times, Oct. 31, 1922, p. 1, col. 1, p. 4, col. 1 (then-Secretary of State Charles Evans Hughes stating that "we favor, and always have favored, an international court of justice for the determination according to judicial standards of justiciable international disputes"); Mr. Root Discusses International Problems, N.Y. Times, July 9, 1916, section 6, book review p. 276 (former Secretary of State and U.S. Senator Elihu Root stating that " 'a court of international justice with a general obligation to submit all justiciable questions to its jurisdiction and to abide by its judgment is a primary requisite to any real restraint of law' "); Mills, The Obligation of the United States Toward the World Court, 114 Annals of the American Academy of Political and Social Science 128 (1924) (Congressman Ogden Mills describing the efforts of then-Secretary of State John Hay, and others, to establish a World Court, and the support therefor).

These institutional considerations make it difficult to reconcile the majority's holdings with the workable Constitution that the Founders envisaged. They reinforce the importance, in practice and in principle, of asking Chief Justice Marshall's question: Does a treaty provision address the "Judicial" Branch rather than the "Political Branches" of Government. See *Foster*, 2 Pet., at 314. And they show the wisdom of the well-established precedent that indicates that the answer to the question here is "yes." * * *

V

In sum, a strong line of precedent, likely reflecting the views of the Founders, indicates that the treaty provisions before us and the judgment of the International Court of Justice address themselves to the Judicial Branch and consequently are self-executing. In reaching a contrary conclusion, the Court has failed to take proper account of that precedent and, as a result, the Nation may well break its word even though the President seeks to live up to that word and Congress has done nothing to suggest the contrary. For the reasons set forth, I respectfully dissent.

[The case will be discussed further in Chapter 11 *International Law in National Courts.*]

NOTES AND QUESTIONS

1. Is *Medellín* fundamentally a judgment enforcement or treaty enforcement case? Why does this basic characterization make a decisive difference? United States courts enforce judgments of many foreign and international courts and tribunals as an exercise of their judicial function. Is there some reason why two cases from the ICJ (*Nicaragua* and *Avena*) met resistance in being treated as other judgment enforcement cases? *Medellín* and *Committee of U.S. Citizens* have similar outcomes for the plaintiffs in-

volved, but their treatment of international law and the ICJ seem quite distinct. Point to some differences.

2.   What do you think of the German Federal Constitutional court's treatment of *LaGrand*? Does it seem in keeping with Sir Robert Jenning's proposal for the ICJ to be considered the court of last resort for international law questions? If you think so and see this as a good thing, how might the German position be spread? Could you see American courts eventually adopting this view?

3.   The Reuters News Service carried the following story of the aftermath of *Medellín v. Texas* and *Request for Interpretation*:

Texas defies World Court with execution

Wed Aug 6, 2008 12:10 a.m. EDT

By Ed Stoddard

DALLAS, Aug. 5 (Reuters)—Texas defied the World Court and executed a Mexican national by lethal injection on Tuesday over the objections of the international judicial body and neighboring Mexico.

Jose Medellín, 33, was pronounced dead at 9:57 p.m. CDT (0257 GMT) in the state's death chamber in Huntsville, the Texas Department of Criminal Justice said. He had been condemned for the 1993 rape and murder of 16–year–old Elizabeth Pena in Houston and lost his bid late Tuesday for a last-minute stay from the U.S. Supreme Court.

The World Court last month ordered the U.S. government to "take all measures necessary" to halt the upcoming executions of five Mexicans including Medellín's on the grounds that they had been deprived of their right to consular services after their arrests.

Medellín's execution is sure to anger neighboring Mexico and analysts have said it could make life rough for Americans arrested abroad if other countries decide to evoke the U.S. example and deprive them of their right to consular services. This typically means diplomats will visit and provide legal advice to their nationals being held by authorities. * * *

(Some paragraph breaks omitted.)

4.   At time of writing, *Avena* is the only ICJ judgment where a party is awaiting compliance with the final judgment. Does this surprise you? The ICJ's record of compliance is, in fact, quite strong. Why do you think this is? Admittedly, its decisions number in the hundreds, not the thousands as with other courts. Still, would it be better if the jurisdiction requirements remained stringent and the court retained its high rate of compliance or should the world move to greater use of the ICJ, even if that means greater non-compliance?

5.   Now that you have had an overview of the complete system of international dispute settlement, what would you propose for improving it? What are the greatest weaknesses? What are the greatest strengths?

6. For further reading on national courts in the system of international dispute settlement, see, ENFORCING INTERNATIONAL HUMAN RIGHTS IN DOMESTIC COURTS (Benedetto Conforti & Francesco Francioni eds., 1999): INTERNATIONAL LAW DECISIONS IN NATIONAL COURTS (Thomas M. Franck & Gregory H. Fox eds., 1996); BENEDETTO CONFORTI, INTERNATIONAL LAW AND THE ROLE OF DOMESTIC LEGAL SYSTEM (1993); and CHRISTOPH SCHEUER, DECISIONS OF INTERNATIONAL INSTITUTIONS BEFORE DOMESTIC COURTS (1981).

CHAPTER 10

INTERNATIONAL LAW AND THE USE OF FORCE

International law on the use of force is one of the oldest parts of international law. Limits on inter-group conflict can be found in antiquity—whether restrictions on when a group may resort to armed conflict, restrictions on permissible targets of force, or on acceptable weapons. Indeed, a large part of the history of international law concerns the development of ever-greater restraints on the right to resort to force and the means and methods of warfare. The law on resort to force is often referred to by the Latin term, *jus ad bellum*. This law today is based on the United Nations Charter and is the first topic of this chapter. The law governing the conduct of force, also known as the *jus in bello*, is based on the 1949 Geneva Conventions, the Hague Conventions of 1899 and 1907, and numerous conventions restricting the use of weapons.

The Roman jurist Cicero is credited with saying that "in war law is silent" (*silent enim leges inter armes*). The very fact that so much law on war or armed conflict exists stands as evidence against this view. A primary purpose of all law is the peaceful settlement of disputes. In human communities, governing by force eventually evolved into governing by law. The right to use force within a community came to be restricted to law enforcement authorities; the right to use force between communities has also become evermore restricted. The Peace of Westphalia of 1648 laid down certain principles designed to prevent new conflicts among Europe's newly emerging states and instituted means to enforce them, including collective action against wrongdoers and a requirement to employ negotiation or arbitration before resort to force. Restricting force was a primary purpose and prerequisite of the new system of international law.

Despite its necessity, no one believes the law on the use of force works as well as it should. The world is constantly the scene of armed conflict, often characterized by the commission of war crimes. As you read this chapter consider what can be done to strengthen this venerable area of international law. For more on this subject, *see*, MARY ELLEN O'CONNELL, INTERNATIONAL LAW AND THE USE OF FORCE, CASES AND MATERIALS (2d ed. 2009), CHRISTINE GRAY, INTERNATIONAL LAW ON THE USE OF FORCE (2008), STEPHEN C. NEFF, WAR AND THE LAW OF NATIONS, A GENERAL HISTORY (2005), and YORAM DINSTEIN, WAR, AGGRESSION AND SELF-DEFENSE (4th ed. 2005).

A. RESORT TO ARMED FORCE

1. DEVELOPMENTS PRECEDING THE UN CHARTER

We can trace the origins of today's law on resort to war to Roman law and earlier. The 5th century bishop Augustine of Hippo, drew on Roman law, Greek philosophy, Christian scripture, and other ideas to form what would become the Just War Doctrine. Augustine wished to persuade pacifist Christians that using limited force in a just cause could be consistent with Christian values. International law still permits the use of coercion in a limited way to achieve certain permitted ends. Thus, Augustine's Just War Doctrine remains at the foundation of contemporary thinking about the justifications for resort to war.

The Just War Doctrine was and remains today an aspect of natural law. Augustine and his successors reasoned on the basis of the natural order and the common good when resort to armed force could justified. By the 19th century, positivism replaced natural law theory as the dominant explanation of the authority of international law. From this, some scholars concluded that, as no positive law restricted resort to war, states could resort to war at will. In fact, throughout the 19th century governments consistently justified resort to war in the old Just War terms. The concept had deep moral roots and was not so easily dismissed.

The famous exchange of correspondence between Britain's Lord Ashburton and the U.S. Secretary of State Webster over the *Caroline* incident is an example of 19th century attention to legal detail in resort to armed force. For a full account of the episode, *see*, John E. Noyes, The Caroline, *International Law Limits on Resort to Force, in* INTERNATIONAL LAW STORIES 263 (John E. Noyes et al. eds., 2008).

The Caroline

Charles Cheney Hyde, International Law 239 (1945)

[During an insurrection in Canada in 1837, the insurgents secured recruits and supplies from the American side of the border. There was an encampment of one thousand armed men organized at Buffalo, and located at Navy Island in Upper Canada; there was another encampment of insurgents at Black Rock, on the American side. The Caroline was a small steamer employed by these encampments. On December 29, 1837, while moored at Schlosser, on the American side of the Niagara River, and while occupied by some thirty-three American citizens, the steamer was boarded by an armed body of men from the Canadian side, who attacked the occupants. The latter merely endeavored to escape. Several were wounded; one was killed on the dock; only twenty-one were afterwards accounted for. The attacking party fired the steamer and set her adrift over Niagara Falls. In 1841, upon the arrest and detention of one Alexander McLeod, in New York, on account of his alleged participation in the destruction of the vessel, Lord Palmerston avowed responsibility for the destruction of the Caroline as a public act of force in self-defense, by persons in the British service. He therefore demanded McLeod's release. McLeod was, however, tried in New York, and acquitted. In 1842 the two Governments agreed on principle that the requirements of self-defense might necessitate the use of force. Mr. Webster, Secretary of State, denied, however, that the necessity existed in this particular case, while Lord Ashburton, the British Minister, apologized for the invasion of American territory. Said Mr. Webster in the course of a communication to the British Minister, August 6, 1842:]

The President sees with pleasure that your Lordship fully admits those great principles of public law, applicable to cases of this kind, which this government has expressed; and that on your part, as on ours, respect for the inviolable character of the territory of independent states is the most essential foundation of civilization. And while it is admitted on both sides that there are exceptions to this rule, he is gratified to find that your Lordship admits that such exceptions must come within the limitations stated and the terms used in a former communication from this department to the British plenipotentiary here. Undoubtedly it is just, that, while it is admitted that exceptions growing out of the great law of self-defense do exist, those exceptions should be confined to cases in which the "necessity of that self-defence is instant, overwhelming, and leaving no choice of means, and no moment for deliberation." In an earlier letter to the British authorities, Mr. Webster included a requirement of proportionality: "It will be for [Her Majesty's Government] to show, also, that the local authorities of Canada, even supposing the necessity of the moment authorized them to enter territories of the United States at all, did nothing unreasonable or excessive; since the act, justified by the necessity of self-defence, must be limited by that necessity, and kept clearly within it." Mr. Webster to Mr.

Fox (April 24, 1841), 29 British and Foreign State Papers 1129, 1138 (1857).

* * *

Despite the continuing viability of the Just War Doctrine and other rules on resort to force, legal scholars did push for treaties regulating resort to force in order to have positive law instruments that fit better within the prevailing positivist law theory of international law. These scholars had effective allies in the form of peace movements in many countries, popular movements working to outlaw war. These movements succeeded in getting the topic of alternatives to war onto the agenda of the First Hague Peace Conference of 1899. At the Second Hague Peace Conference of 1907, they managed to get one type of war outlawed (war to collect contract debts) and to get a firmer mandate for resort to peaceful settlement of dispute before resort to war:

The Hague Convention of 1907 for the Pacific Settlement of International Disputes

* * *

PART I.   THE MAINTENANCE OF GENERAL PEACE

Article 1. With a view to obviating as far as possible recourse to force in the relations between states, the *Contracting* Powers agree to use their best efforts to insure the pacific settlement of international differences.

PART II.   GOOD OFFICES AND MEDIATIONS

Article 2. In case of serious disagreement or dispute, before an appeal to arms, the *Contracting* Powers agree to have recourse, as far as circumstances allow, to the good offices or mediation of one or more friendly powers.

Article 3. Independently of this recourse, the *Contracting* Powers deem it expedient *and desirable* that one or more powers, strangers to the dispute, should, on their own initiative and as far as circumstances may allow, offer their good offices or mediation to the states at variance.

Powers strangers to the dispute have the right to offer good offices or mediation even during the course of hostilities. The exercise of this right can never be regarded by either of the parties in dispute as an unfriendly act.

* * *

Plainly, the Hague Convention did not prevent the outbreak of the First World War. After that devastating conflict, states tried again to limit resort to war through binding international instruments.

The Covenant of the League of Nations

THE HIGH CONTRACTING PARTIES, In order to promote international co-operation and to achieve international peace and security by the acceptance of obligations not to resort to war by the prescription of open, just and honourable relations between nations by the firm establishment of the understandings of international law as the actual rule of conduct among Governments, and by the maintenance of justice and a scrupulous respect for all treaty obligations in the dealings of organised peoples with one another Agree to this Covenant of the League of Nations.

* * *

ARTICLE 10.

The Members of the League undertake to respect and preserve as against external aggression the territorial integrity and existing political independence of all Members of the League. In case of any such aggression or in case of any threat or danger of such aggression the Council shall advise upon the means by which this obligation shall be fulfilled.

* * *

ARTICLE 12.

The Members of the League agree that if there should arise between them any dispute likely to lead to a rupture, they will submit the matter either to arbitration or to inquiry by the Council, and they agree in no case to resort to war until three months after the award by arbitrators or the report by the Council. In any case under this Article the award of the arbitrators shall be made within a reasonable time, and the report of the Council shall be made within six months after the submission of the dispute.

Treaty Providing for the Renunciation of War as an Instrument of National Policy

August 27, 1928, 46 Stat. 2343 T.S. No. 796, 2 Bevans 732*

ARTICLE I

The High Contracting Parties solemnly declare in the names of their respective peoples that they condemn recourse to war for the solution of international controversies, and renounce it, as an instrument of national policy in their relations with one another.

---

* Also known as the Kellogg–Briand Pact or Pact of Paris.

ARTICLE II

The High Contracting Parties agree that the settlement or solution of all disputes or conflicts of whatever nature or of whatever origin they may be, which may arise among them, shall never be sought except by pacific means.

The Hague Conventions, the League Covenant, and the Kellogg–Briand Pact all failed to prevent resort to war in 1939. These treaties did, however, form the basis of charges against German and Japanese leaders who had started the war. They were charged with crimes against the peace—waging war in violation of treaties.

The Nürnberg Charter, 1945

Charter of the International Military Tribunal
59 Stat. 1544, 1546*

Article 2. The Tribunal shall consist of four members, each with an alternate. One member and one alternate shall be appointed by each of the Signatories. * * *

Article 6. The Tribunal established by the Agreement referred to in Article 1 hereof for the trial and punishment of the major war criminals of the European Axis countries shall have the power to try and punish persons who, acting in the interests of the European Axis countries, whether as individuals or as members of organizations, committed any of the following crimes. The following acts, or any of them, are crimes coming within the jurisdiction of the Tribunal for which there shall be individual responsibility:

(a) CRIMES AGAINST PEACE: namely, planning, preparation, initiation or waging of a war of aggression, or a war in violation of international treaties, agreements or assurances, or participation in a common plan or conspiracy for the accomplishment of any of the foregoing;

(b) WAR CRIMES: namely, violations of the laws or customs of war. Such violations shall include, but not be limited to, murder, ill-treatment or deportation to slave labor or for any other purpose of civilian population of or in occupied territory, murder or ill-treatment of prisoners of war or persons on the seas, killing of hostages, plunder of public or private property, wanton destruction of cities, towns or villages, or devastation not justified by military necessity;

---

* The Charter was annexed to an Agreement for the Prosecution and Punishment of the Major War Criminals of the European Axis, which came into force on signature, August 8, 1945, by France, the U.S.S.R., the U.K., and the U.S. 11 WHITEMAN's DIGEST 881–82 (1968). In the U.S. it was treated as an executive agreement and was not submitted to the Senate as a treaty for the latter's advice and consent.

(c) CRIMES AGAINST HUMANITY: namely, murder, extermination, enslavement, deportation, and other inhumane acts committed against any civilian population, before or during the war;[1] or persecutions on political, racial or religious grounds in execution of or in connection with any crime within the jurisdiction of the Tribunal, whether or not in violation of the domestic law of the country where perpetrated.

Leaders, organizers, instigators and accomplices participating in the formulation or execution of a common plan or conspiracy to commit any of the foregoing crimes are responsible for all acts performed by any persons in execution of such plan.

Article 7. The official position of defendants, whether as Heads of State or responsible officials in Government Departments, shall not be considered as freeing them from responsibility or mitigating punishment.

Article 8. The fact that the Defendant acted pursuant to order of his Government or of a superior shall not free him from responsibility, but may be considered in mitigation of punishment if the Tribunal determines that justice so requires.

Article 9. At the trial of any individual member of any group or organization the Tribunal may declare (in connection with any act of which the individual may be convicted) that the group or organization of which the individual was a member was a criminal organization.

After receipt of the Indictment the Tribunal shall give such notice as it thinks fit that the prosecution intends to ask the Tribunal to make such declaration and any member of the organization will be entitled to apply to the Tribunal for leave to be heard by the Tribunal upon the question of the criminal character of the organization. The Tribunal shall have power to allow or reject the application. If the application is allowed, the Tribunal may direct in what manner the applicants shall be represented and heard.

Article 10. In cases where a group or organization is declared criminal by the Tribunal, the competent national authority of any Signatory shall have the right to bring individuals to trial for membership therein before national, military or occupation courts. In any such case the criminal nature of the group or organization is considered proved and shall not be questioned.

Article 11. Any person convicted by the Tribunal may be charged before a national, military or occupation court, referred to in Article 10 of this Charter, with a crime other than of membership in a criminal group or organization and such court may, after convicting him, impose upon him punishment independent of and additional to the punishment imposed by the Tribunal for participation in the criminal activities of such group or organization.

---

1. [The contracting governments signed a protocol at Berlin on Oct. 6, 1945 * * * which provides that this semi-colon in the English text should be changed to a comma.]

Article 12. The Tribunal shall have the right to take proceedings against a person charged with crimes set out in Article 6 of this Charter in his absence, if he has not been found or if the Tribunal, for any reason, finds it necessary, in the interests of justice, to conduct the hearing in his absence.

Article 26. The judgment of the Tribunal as to the guilt or the innocence of any Defendant shall give the reasons on which it is based, and shall be final and not subject to review.

Article 27. The Tribunal shall have the right to impose upon a Defendant, on conviction, death or such other punishment as shall be determined by it to be just. * * *

2. THE UNITED NATIONS CHARTER

Preamble

WE THE PEOPLES OF THE UNITED NATIONS DETERMINED

- to save succeeding generations from the scourge of war, which twice in our lifetime has brought untold sorrow to mankind, and

- to reaffirm faith in fundamental human rights, in the dignity and worth of the human person, in the equal rights of men and women and of nations large and small, and

- to establish conditions under which justice and respect for the obligations arising from treaties and other sources of international law can be maintained, and

- to promote social progress and better standards of life in larger freedom,

AND FOR THESE ENDS

- to practice tolerance and live together in peace with one another as good neighbors, and

- to unite our strength to maintain international peace and security, and

- to ensure, by the acceptance of principles and the institution of methods, that armed force shall not be used, save in the common interest, and

- to employ international machinery for the promotion of the economic and social advancement of all peoples,

HAVE RESOLVED TO COMBINE OUR EFFORTS TO ACCOMPLISH THESE AIMS

Accordingly, our respective Governments, through representatives assembled in the city of San Francisco, who have exhibited their full powers found to be in good and due form, have agreed to the present Charter of the

United Nations and do hereby establish an international organization to be known as the United Nations.

———————

As with the Preamble, the Charter's Chapter I on purposes and principles emphasizes the UN's purpose of preserving the peace as well the promotion of human rights and economic development. Article 2(4) is at the heart of the legal strategy to maintain peace.

UN Charter, Chapter I Purposes and Principles

Article 1

The Purposes of the United Nations are:

1. To maintain international peace and security, and to that end: to take effective collective measures for the prevention and removal of threats to the peace, and for the suppression of acts of aggression or other breaches of the peace, and to bring about by peaceful means, and in conformity with the principles of justice and international law, adjustment or settlement of international disputes or situations which might lead to a breach of the peace;

* * *

Article 2

The Organization and its Members, in pursuit of the Purposes stated in Article 1, shall act in accordance with the following Principles:

* * *

4. All Members shall refrain in their international relations from the threat or use of force against the territorial integrity or political independence of any state, or in any other manner inconsistent with the Purposes of the United Nations.

5. All Members shall give the United Nations every assistance in any action it takes in accordance with the present Charter, and shall refrain from giving assistance to any state against which the United Nations is taking preventive or enforcement action.

* * *

7. Nothing contained in the present Charter shall authorize the United Nations to intervene in matters which are essentially within the domestic jurisdiction of any state or shall require the Members to submit such matters to settlement under the present Charter; but this principle shall not prejudice the application of enforcement measures under Chapter VII.

* * *

UN Charter, Chapter VII

Article 39

The Security council shall determine the existence of any threat to the peace, breach of the peace, or act of aggression and shall make recommendations, or decide what measures shall be taken in accordance with Article 41 and 42, to maintain or restore international peace and security.

* * *

Article 41

The Security Council may decide what measures not involving the use of armed force are to be employed to give effect to its decisions, and it may call upon the Members of the United Nations to apply such measure. These may include complete or partial interruption of economic relations and of rail, sea, air, postal telegraphic, radio, and other means of communication, and the severance of diplomatic relations.

Article 42

Should the Security Council consider that measures provided for in Article 41 would be inadequate or have proved to be inadequate, it may take such action by air, sea, or land forces as may be necessary to maintain or resotre international peace and security. Such action may include demonstrations, blockade, and other operations by air, sea, or land forces of Members of the United Nations.

* * *

Article 51

Nothing in the present Charter shall impair the inherent right of individual or collective self-defense if an armed attack occurs against a Member of the United Nations, until the Security Council has taken measures necessary to maintain international peace and security. Measures taken by Members in the exercise of this right of self-defense shall be immediately reported to the Security Council and shall not in any way affect the authority and responsibility of the Security Council under the present Charter to take at any time such action as it deems necessary in order to maintain or restore international peace and security.

UN Charter, Chapter VIII

Article 52

1. Nothing in the present Charter precludes the existence of regional arrangements or agencies for dealing with such matters relating to the maintenance of international peace and security as are appropriate for regional action, provided that such arrangements or agencies and their

activities are consistent with the Purposes and Principles of the United Nations.

* * *

Article 53

1. The Security Council shall, where appropriate, utilize such regional arrangements or agencies for enforcement action under its authority. But no enforcement action shall be taken under regional arrangements or by regional agencies without the authorization of the Security Council * * *.

* * *

a. SELF DEFENSE

The aim of the Charter drafters was to generally prohibit force in Article 2(4), allowing only a narrow exception to states in Article 51. The exception in Article 51 is for self-defense. The force exercised must have the purpose of defense. In the *Corfu Channel* case, the ICJ's first case on the use of force decided in 1949, the court underscored the broad prohibition on force.

1.) The Purpose of Defense

The *Corfu Channel* case arose when, on May 15, 1946, Albanian shore batteries fired on British warships passing through the north end of the Corfu Channel, formed by the Greek island of Corfu and the Albanian mainland. The British sent four more warships through the Channel on October 22, 1946, prepared to return fire. Two of the British vessels struck mines, causing damage and loss of life. Three weeks later, in what they called, "Operation Retail," the British sent minesweepers, protected by war ships, back to the Channel where they collected 22 mines.

The Corfu Channel Case

United Kingdom v. Albania
International Court of Justice
1949 I.C.J. Rep. 4, 29–35 (Judgment of April 9)

* * *

Having regard to these various considerations, the Court has arrived at the conclusion that the North Corfu Channel should be considered as belonging to the class of international highways through which passage cannot be prohibited by a coastal State in time of peace.

On the other hand, it is a fact that the two coastal States did not maintain normal relations, that Greece had made territorial claims precisely with regard to a part of Albanian territory bordering on the Channel, that Greece had declared that she considered herself technically in a state of war with Albania, and that Albania, invoking the danger of Greek incursions, had considered it necessary to take certain measures of vigilance in this region. The Court is of opinion that Albania, in view of these exceptional circumstances, would have been justified in issuing regulations in respect of the passage of warships through the Strait, but not in prohibiting such passage or in subjecting it to the requirement of special authorization.

For these reasons the Court is unable to accept the Albanian contention that the Government of the United Kingdom has violated Albanian sovereignty by sending the warships through the Strait without having obtained the previous authorization of the Albanian Government.

In these circumstances, it is unnecessary to consider the more general question, much debated by the Parties, whether States under international law have a right to send warships in time of peace through territorial waters not included in a Strait.

The Albanian Government has further contended that the sovereignty of Albania was violated because the passage of the British warships on October 22nd, 1946, was not an *innocent passage*. The reasons advanced in support of this contention may be summed up as follows: The passage was not an ordinary passage, but a political mission; the ships were manoeuvring and sailing in diamond combat formation with soldiers on board; the position of the guns was not consistent with innocent passage; the vessels passed with crews at action stations; the number of the ships and their armament surpassed what was necessary in order to attain their object and showed an intention to intimidate and not merely pass; the ships had received orders to observe and report upon the coastal defences and this order was carried out.

It is shown by the Admiralty telegram of September 21st, cited above, and admitted by the United Kingdom Agent, that the object of sending the warships through the Strait was not only to carry out a passage for purposes of navigation, but also to test Albania's attitude. As mentioned above, the Albanian Government, on May 15th, 1946, tried to impose by means of gunfire its view with regard to the passage. As the exchange of diplomatic notes did not lead to any clarification, the Government of the United Kingdom wanted to ascertain by other means whether the Albanian Government would maintain its illegal attitude and again impose its view by firing at passing ships. The legality of this measure taken by the Government of the United Kingdom cannot be disputed, provided that it was carried out in a manner consistent with the requirements of international law. The "mission" was designed to affirm a right which had been unjustly denied. The Government of the United Kingdom was not bound to abstain from exercising its right of passage, which the Albanian Government had illegally denied.

It remains, therefore, to consider whether the *manner* in which the passage was carried out was consistent with the principle of innocent passage and to examine the various contentions of the Albanian Government in so far as they appear to be relevant. When the Albanian coastguards at St. George's Monastery reported that the British warships were sailing in combat formation and were manoeuvring, they must have been under a misapprehension.

It is shown by the evidence that the ships were not proceeding in combat formation, but in line, one after the other, and that they were not manoeuvring until after the first explosion. Their movements thereafter were due to the explosions and were made necessary in order to save human life and the mined ships. It is shown by evidence of witnesses that the contention that soldiers were on board must be due to a misunderstanding probably arising from the fact that the two cruisers carried their usual detachment of marines.

It is known from the above-mentioned order issued by the British Admiralty on August 10th, 1946, that ships, when using the North Corfu Strait, must pass with armament in fore and aft position. That this order was carried out during the passage on October 22nd is stated by the Commander-in-Chief, Mediterranean, in a telegram of October 26th to the Admiralty. The guns were, he reported, "trained fore and aft, which is their normal position at sea in peace time, and were not loaded".

* * *

Having thus examined the various contentions of the Albanian Government in so far as they appear to be relevant, the Court has arrived at the conclusion that the United Kingdom did not violate the sovereignty of Albania by reason of the acts of the British Navy in Albanian waters on October 22nd, 1946.

* * *

In addition to the passage of the United Kingdom warships on October 22nd, 1946, the second question in the Special Agreement relates to the acts of the Royal Navy in Albanian waters on November 12th and 13th, 1946. This is the minesweeping operation called "Operation Retail" by the Parties during the proceedings. This name will be used in the present Judgment.

* * *

The United Kingdom Government does not dispute that "Operation Retail" was carried out against the clearly expressed wish of the Albanian Government. It recognizes that the operation had not the consent of the international mine clearance organizations, that it could not be justified as the exercise of a right of innocent passage, and lastly that, in principle, international law does not allow a State to assemble a large number of warships in the territorial waters of another State and to carry out minesweeping in those waters. The United Kingdom Government states that the operation was one of extreme urgency, and that it considered itself entitled to carry it out without anybody's consent.

The United Kingdom Government put forward two reasons in justification. First, the Agreement of November 22nd, 1945, signed by the Governments of the United Kingdom, France, the Soviet Union and the United States of America, authorizing regional mine clearance organizations, such as the Mediterranean Zone Board, to divide the sectors in their respective zones amongst the States concerned for sweeping. Relying on the circumstance that the Corfu Channel was in the sector allotted to Greece by the Mediterranean Zone Board on November 5th, i.e., before the signing of the above-mentioned Agreement, the United Kingdom Government put forward a permission given by the Hellenic Government to resweep the navigable channel.

The Court does not consider this argument convincing. It must be noted that, as the United Kingdom Government admits, the need for resweeping the Channel was not under consideration in November 1945; for previous sweeps in 1944 and 1945 were considered as having effected complete safety. As a consequence, the allocation of the sector in question to Greece, and therefore, the permission of the Hellenic Government which is relied on, were both of them merely nominal. It is also to be remarked that Albania was not consulted regarding the allocation to Greece to the sector in question, despite the fact that the Channel passed through Albanian territorial waters.

But, in fact, the explosions of October 22, 1946, in a channel declared safe for navigation, and one which the United Kingdom Government, more than any other government, had reason to consider safe, raised quite a different problem from that of a routine sweep carried out under the orders of the mine clearance organizations. These explosions were suspicious; they raised a question of responsibility.

Accordingly, this was the ground on which the United Kingdom Government chose to establish its main line of defence. According to that Government, the *corpora delicti* must be secured as quickly as possible, for fear they should be taken away, without leaving traces, by the authors of the mine-laying or by the Albanian authorities. This justification took two distinct forms in the United Kingdom Government's arguments. It was presented first as a new and special application of the theory of intervention, by means of which the State intervening would secure possession of evidence in the territory of another State, in order to submit it to an international tribunal and thus facilitate its task.

The Court cannot accept such a line of defence. The Court can only regard the alleged right of intervention as the manifestation of a policy of force, such as has, in the past, given rise to most serious abuses and such as cannot, whatever be the present defects in international organization, find a place in international law. Intervention is perhaps still less admissible in the particular form it would take here; for, from the nature of things, it would be reserved for the most powerful States, and might easily lead to perverting the administration of international justice itself. The United Kingdom Agent, in his speech in reply, has further classified "Operation Retail" among methods of self-protection or self-help. The Court cannot accept this defence either. Between independent States, respect for territorial sovereignty is an essential foundation of international relations. The Court recognizes that the Albanian Government's complete failure to carry out its duties after the explosions, and the dilatory nature of its diplomatic notes, are extenuating circumstances for the action of the United Kingdom Government. But to ensure respect for international law, of which it is the organ, the Court must declare that the action of the British Navy co[n]stituted a violation of Albanian sovereignty.

This declaration is in accordance with the request made by Albania through her Counsel, and is in itself appropriate satisfaction. The method of carrying out "Operation Retail" has also been criticized by the Albanian Government, the main ground of complaint being that the United Kingdom, on that occasion, made use of an unnecessarily large display of force, out of proportion to the requirements of the sweep. The Court thinks that this criticism is not justified. It does not consider that the action of the British Navy was demonstration of force for the purpose of exercising political pressure on Albania. The responsible naval commander, who kept his ships at a distance from the coast, cannot be reproached for having employed an important covering force in a region where twice within a few months his ships had been the object of serious outrages.

2.) *Armed Attack*

Following the *Corfu Channel* case, the next significant debate on the right of states to use armed force broke out in connection with the Suez Canal Crisis of 1954–56. Professor Henkin relates that the argument that the pre-Charter rules on self-defense survived the adoption of the Charter surfaced during the Suez crisis. *See*, Louis Henkin, *Use of Force: Law and U.S. Policy*, *in* MIGHT V. RIGHT, INTERNATIONAL LAW AND THE USE OF FORCE 45 (Louis Henkin et al. eds., 1989). Britain argued during the crisis that Israel had the right to use force in lawful self-defense against Egypt even before Egypt attacked it. Egypt was in the midst of a massive military build-up and had already indicated its hostile intent toward Israel. Britain argued this was enough to justify an Israeli preemptive strike on Egypt before Egypt had the opportunity to develop a military force that could overwhelm Israel. States generally rejected this argument. The use of force by all parties in the Suez crisis was widely condemned, including by both the United States and the Soviet Union. Israel again attacked Egypt on June 5, 1967. The Six Day War is widely cited as an example to support the principle that a state may indeed use force in anticipation of an armed attack even where one has not yet occurred. In reporting on its initial use of force to the Security Council, however, Israel did not argue that it acted in anticipation of an attack, but rather that Egyptian forces had actually crossed into Israeli-held territory. By June 17, when the General Assembly began its debate on the conflict, Israel's foreign minister no longer spoke of actual Egyptian attacks, but only of Egyptian forces approaching Israel's borders. *See* 1967 U.N.Y.B 175–77, 196. Following the Six Day War, a number of scholars began to interpret Article 51 as allowing force in anticipatory self-defense, where an attack was imminent or occurring, even if it had not yet occurred. The 1981 Security Council debate on Israel's bombing of a nuclear reactor in Iraq, turned very much on the requirement of "imminence":

Security Council Consideration of a Complaint by Iraq, 8 June 1981

36 UN SCOR, 2280–2288 mtgs (1981)

Mr. Blum (Israel):

57. On Sunday, 7 June 1981, the Israeli Air Force carried out an operation against the Iraqi atomic reactor called "Osirak". That reactor

was in its final stages of construction near Baghdad. The pilots' mission was to destroy it. They executed their mission successfully.

58.   In destroying Osirak, Israel performed an elementary act of self-preservation, both morally and legally. In so doing, Israel was exercising its inherent right of self-defence as understood in general international law and as preserved in Article 51 of the Charter of the United Nations.

59.   A threat of nuclear obliteration was being developed against Israel by Iraq, one of Israel's most implacable enemies. Israel tried to have the threat halted by diplomatic means. Our efforts bore no fruit. Ultimately we were left with no choice. We were obliged to remove that mortal danger. We did it cleanly and effectively. The Middle East has become a safer place. We trust that the international community has also been given pause to make the world a safer place.

60.   Those facts and the potentials for a safer world are widely recognized. Several States in the Middle East and beyond are sleeping more easily today in the knowledge that Saddam Hussein's nuclear-arms potential has been smashed.

* * *

97.   The Government of Israel, like any other Government, has the elementary duty to protect the lives of its citizens. In destroying Osirak last Sunday, Israel was exercising its inherent and natural right to self-defence, as understood in general international law and well within the meaning of Article 51 of the Charter of the United Nations.

98.   Commenting on the meaning of Article 51 of the Charter, Sir Humphrey Waldock, now President of the International Court of Justice, stated in a lecture delivered at The Hague Academy of International Law in 1952 that

> "it would be a travesty of the purposes of the Charter to compel a defending State to allow its assailant to deliver the first and perhaps fatal blow. ... To read Article 51 otherwise is to protect the aggressor's right to the first strike."

99.   In a similar vein, Professor Morton Kaplan and Nicholas de B. Katzenbach wrote in their book, *The Political Foundations of International Law*:

> "Must a state wait until it is too late before it may defend itself? Must it permit another the advantages of military build-up, surprise attack, and total offense, against which there may be no defense? It would be unreasonable to expect any State to permit this—particularly when given the possibility that a surprise nuclear blow might bring about total destruction, or at least total subjugation, unless the attack were forestalled."

100.   Professor Derek Bowett of Cambridge University, in his authoritative work on *Self–Defense in International Law*, observed:

"No state can be expected to await an initial attack, which in the present state of armaments, may well destroy the state's capacity for further resistance and so jeopardize its very existence."

101.   So much for the legalities of the case. Still, we have been accused of acting unlawfully. Presumably it is lawful for a sovereign State to create an instrument capable of destroying several hundred thousand Israelis; it is unlawful to halt that fatal process before it reaches completion.

102.   The decision taken by my Government in the exercise of its right of self-defence, after the unusual international procedures and avenues had proven futile, was one of the most agonizing we have ever had to take. We sought to act in a manner which would minimize the danger to all concerned, including a large segment of Iraq's population. We waited until the eleventh hour after the diplomatic clock had run out hoping against hope that Iraq's nuclear arms project would be brought to a halt. Our Air Force was only called in when, as I have said, we learned on the basis of completely reliable information that there was less than a month to go before Osirak might have become critical. Our Air Force's operation was consciously launched on a Sunday, and timed for late in the day, the assumption that the workers on the site, including foreign experts employed at the reactor, would have left. That assumption proved correct, and the loss of human life, which we sincerely regret, was minimal.

103.   I should add that those same considerations worked in the opposite direction as regards Iraq's other nuclear facilities and constrained Israel from taking action against the smaller Western-supplied research reactor, as well as a small Soviet research reactor. Both of those facilities are operational and if attacked, could release substantial amounts of radiation.

104.   In this connection, I wish to deny in the most categorical terms the false allegation made here by the Minister for Foreign Affairs of Iraq—who had the courtesy to leave the Chamber when I started my statement—that Iraq's nuclear installations were attacked by Israel on a date prior to 7 June.

105.   With regard to the statement of the Foreign Minister of Baghdad as a whole, let me just observe that he added yet another tale to the *Tales of 1,001 Nights*, which, if I am not mistaken, were all written, like his statement, in Baghdad.

* * *

118.   MR. CAID ESSEBSI (Tunisia) (*interpretation from French*): Since the announcement of the atrocious act committed on Sunday, 7 June, against one of our Member States, Iraq, the eyes of the world have turned to the United Nations and to this supreme body entrusted with the task of maintaining international peace and security, as well as respect for the fundamental principles of the Charter. * * *

129.   I need hardly recall here that, according to the Definition of Aggression contained in the annex to resolution 3314 (XXIX) adopted by the General Assembly on 14 December 1974, bombardment by the armed

forces of a State against the territory of another State, regardless of a declaration of war, constitutes an act of aggression. I need hardly recall article 5 of the Definition of Aggression, which states:

> "1. No consideration of whatever nature, whether political, economic, military or otherwise, may serve as a justification for aggression.

> 2. A war of aggression is a crime against international peace. Aggression gives rise to international responsibility."

130.   In our view that is the only appropriate response to Israel's quibbling. We refuse to give undue weight to considerations not founded on generally accepted international rules that are based on principle and law.

* * *

MR. PARSONS (UNITED KINGDOM):

"The Government have already made plain their view that armed attack in such circumstances cannot be justified. It represents a grave breach of international law."

Mrs. Thatcher was asked about the fact that, whereas Iraq has signed the nuclear Non–Proliferation Treaty and accepted IAEA safeguards, Israel has not. She replied:

"The Government firmly support the Non–Proliferation Treaty and wish that more countries would become signatories."

She went on to say:

"A tragedy of this case was that Iraq was a signatory to the Agreement and had been inspected, but neither of these facts protected her. It was an unprovoked attack, which we must condemn. Just because a country is trying to manufacture energy from nuclear sources, it must not be believed that she is doing something totally wrong."

It has been argued that the Israeli attack was an act of self-defence. But it was not a response to an armed attack on Israel by Iraq. There was no instant or overwhelming necessity for self-defence. Nor can it be justified as a forcible measure of self-protection. The Israeli intervention amounted to a use of force which cannot find a place in international law or in the Charter and which violated the sovereignty of Iraq. It has also been argued that, whatever the legal rights and wrongs of the matter, the international community privately breathed a sigh of relief after the Israeli raid, the suggestion being that the Iraqi Government will not now have a nuclear-weapon potential for some further time to come. That is certainly not the case so far as my Government is concerned. We do not believe that Iraq had the capacity to manufacture fissile material for nuclear weapons.

Answering an assertion of this kind in the House of Commons, my Prime Minister replied:

"Had there been such an attack on Israel of the kind that there has just been on Iraq, I should totally and utterly have condemned it. I therefore totally and utterly condemn the attack on Iraq."

* * *

151.   The PRESIDENT (*interpretation from Spanish*): I shall now put to the vote the draft resolution in document S/14556.

A vote was taken by show of hands.

The draft resolution was adopted unanimously. *

152.   The PRESIDENT (*interpretation from Spanish*): I shall now call on those members of the Council who have asked to be allowed to speak following the vote.

* * *

156.   Mrs. KIRKPATRICK (United States of America): Like other members of the Council, the United States does not regard the resolution just adopted as a perfect one.

157.   With respect to the resolution, I must point out that my country voted against the resolution of IAEA which is referred to in the present resolution. We continue to oppose it. In addition, our judgement that Israeli actions violated the Charter of the United Nations is based solely on the conviction that Israel failed to exhaust peaceful means for the resolution of this dispute. Finally, we also believe that the question of appropriate redress must be understood in the full legal context of the relationships that exist in the region.

158.   Nothing in this resolution will affect my Government's commitment to Israel's security and nothing in these reservations affects my Government's determination to work with all Governments of the region willing to use appropriate means to enhance the peace and security of the area.

* * *

197.   Mr. AL–QAYSI (Iraq): I apologize to you, Mr. President, and the members of the Council for having asked to be allowed to speak for a few minutes in this late hour.

198.   My purpose in doing so is to recall that the representative of Israel at the end of his statement called this a moment of truth for all of us. Let us see how he has abided by that motto of his statement.

199.   The representative of Israel saw fit in his statement of 12 June [*2280th meeting*] before the Council and in his statement today to quote from an article by Sir Humphrey Waldock, the President of the International Court of Justice. He has also quoted from other sources in a vain attempt to substantiate his allegations. Let us see what the truth of that quotation was.

200.   Sir Humphrey Waldock said exactly the following:

"The Charter prohibits the use of force except in self-defence. The Charter obliges Members to submit to the Council or Assembly any dispute dangerous to peace which they cannot settle. Members have therefore an imperative duty to invoke the jurisdiction of the United

---

* Resolution 487 (1981), see p. 252, below.

Nations whenever a grave menace to their security develops carrying the probability of armed attack. But, if the action of the United Nations is obstructed, delayed or inadequate and the armed attack becomes manifestly imminent, then it would be a travesty of the purposes of the Charter to compel a defending State to allow its assailant to deliver the first and perhaps fatal blow. If an armed attack is imminent within the strict doctrine of the *Caroline*, then it would seem to bring the case within Article 51. To read Article 51 otherwise is to protect the aggressor's right to the first stroke.''

201.   That is what was said by Sir Humphrey Waldock in the article referred to by the representative of Israel. Yet, the representative of Israel on two occasions deemed it fit to quote Sir Humphrey Waldock as having said:

"It would be a travesty of the purposes of the Charter to compel a defending State to allow its assailant to deliver the first and perhaps fatal blow. ... To read Article 51 otherwise is to protect the aggressor's right to the first strike.'' [*Para.* 81 above.]

Military and Paramilitary Activities in and Against Nicaragua

Nicaragua v. United States
International Court of Justice
1986 I.C.J. 14 (Judgment of June 27)

193.   The general rule prohibiting force allows for certain exceptions. In view of the arguments advanced by the United States to justify the acts of which it is accused by Nicaragua, the Court must express a view on the content of the right of self-defence, and more particularly the right of collective self-defence. First, with regard to the existence of this right, it notes that in the language of Article 51 of the United Nations Charter, the inherent right (or "droit naturel") which any State possesses in the event of an armed attack, covers both collective and individual self-defence. Thus, the Charter itself testifies to the existence of the right of collective self-defence in customary international law. Moreover, just as the wording of certain General Assembly declarations adopted by States demonstrates their recognition of the principle of the prohibition of force as definitely a matter of customary international law, some of the wording in those declarations operates similarly in respect of the right of self-defence (both collective and individual). Thus, in the declaration quoted above on the Principles of International Law concerning Friendly Relations and Co-operation among States in accordance with the Charter of the United Nations, the reference to the prohibition of force is followed by a paragraph stating that:

"nothing in the foregoing paragraphs shall be construed as enlarging or diminishing in any way the scope of the provisions of the Charter concerning cases in which the use of force is lawful''.

This resolution demonstrates that the States represented in the General Assembly regard the exception to the prohibition of force constituted by the right of individual or collective self-defence as already a matter of customary international law.

194.   With regard to the characteristics governing the right of self-defence, since the Parties consider the existence of this right to be established as a matter of customary international law, they have concentrated on the conditions governing its use. In view of the circumstances in which the dispute has arisen, reliance is placed by the Parties only on the right of self-defence in the case of an armed attack which has already occurred, and the issue of the lawfulness of a response to the imminent threat of armed attack has not been raised. Accordingly the Court expresses no view on that issue. The Parties also agree in holding that whether the response to the attack is lawful depends on observance of the criteria of the necessity and the proportionality of the measures taken in self-defence. Since the existence of the right of collective self-defence is established in customary international law, the Court must define the specific conditions which may have to be met for its exercise, in addition to the conditions of necessity and proportionality to which the Parties have referred.

195.   In the case of individual self-defence, the exercise of this right is subject to the State concerned having been the victim of an armed attack. Reliance on collective self-defence of course does not remove the need for this. There appears now to be general agreement on the nature of the acts which can be treated as constituting armed attacks. In particular, it may be considered to be agreed that an armed attack must be understood as including not merely action by regular armed forces across an international border, but also "the sending by or on behalf of a State of armed bands, groups, irregulars or mercenaries, which carry out acts of armed force against another State of such gravity as to amount to" (*inter alia*) an actual armed attack conducted by regular forces, "or its substantial involvement therein". This description, contained in Article 3, paragraph (*g*), of the Definition of Aggression annexed to General Assembly resolution 3314 (XXIX), may be taken to reflect customary international law. The Court sees no reason to deny that, in customary law, the prohibition of armed attacks may apply to the sending by a State of armed bands to the territory of another State, if such an operation, because of its scale and effects, would have been classified as an armed attack rather than as a mere frontier incident had it been carried out by regular armed forces. But the Court does not believe that the concept of "armed attack" includes not only acts by armed bands where such acts occur on a significant scale but also assistance to rebels in the form of the provision of weapons or logistical or other support. Such assistance may be regarded as a threat or use of force, or amount to intervention in the internal or external affairs of other States. It is also clear that it is the State which is the victim of an armed attack which must form and declare the view that it has been so attacked. There is no rule in customary international law permitting another State to exercise the right of collective self-defence on the basis of its own assessment of the situation. Where collective self-defence is invoked, it is to be

expected that the State for whose benefit this right is used will have declared itself to be the victim of an armed attack.

* * *

227. The Court will first appraise the facts in the light of the principle of the non-use of force, examined in paragraphs 187 to 200 above. What is unlawful, in accordance with that principle, is recourse to either the threat or the use of force against the territorial integrity or political independence of any State. For the most part, the complaints by Nicaragua are of the actual use of force against it by the United States. Of the acts which the Court has found imputable to the Government of the United States, the following are relevant in this respect:

— the laying of mines in Nicaraguan internal or territorial waters in early 1984 * * *;

— certain attacks on Nicaraguan ports, oil installations and a naval base * * *.

These activities constitute infringements of the principle of the prohibition of the use of force, defined earlier, unless they are justified by circumstances which exclude their unlawfulness, a question now to be examined. The Court has also found (paragraph 92) the existence of military manoeuvres held by the United States near the Nicaraguan borders; and Nicaragua has made some suggestion that this constituted a "threat of force", which is equally forbidden by the principle of non-use of force. The Court is however not satisfied that the manoeuvres complained of, in the circumstances in which they were held, constituted on the part of the United States a breach, as against Nicaragua, of the principle forbidding recourse to the threat or use of force.

228. Nicaragua has also claimed that the United States has violated Article 2, paragraph 4, of the Charter, and has used force against Nicaragua in breach of its obligation under customary international law in as much as it has engaged in

"recruiting, training, arming, equipping, financing, supplying and otherwise encouraging, supporting, aiding, and directing military and paramilitary actions in and against Nicaragua" (Application, para. 26 (a) and (c)).

So far as the claim concerns breach of the Charter, it is excluded from the Court's jurisdiction by the multilateral treaty reservation. As to the claim that United States activities in relation to the *contras* constitute a breach of the customary international law principle of the non-use of force, the Court finds that, subject to the question whether the action of the United States might be justified as an exercise of the right of self-defence, the United States has committed a prima facie violation of that principle by its assistance to the *contras* in Nicaragua, by "organizing or encouraging the organization of irregular forces or armed bands for incursion into the territory of another State", and "participating in acts of civil strife in another State", in the terms of General Assembly resolution 2625 (XXV). According to that resolution, participation of this kind is contrary to the principle of the prohibition of the use of force when the acts of civil strife referred to "involve a threat or use of force". In the view of the Court, while the arming and training of the *contras* can certainly be said to involve the threat or use of force against Nicaragua, this is not necessarily so in respect of all the assistance given by the United States Government. In particular, the Court considers that the mere supply of funds to the *contras*, while undoubtedly an act of intervention in the internal affairs of Nicaragua, as will be explained below, does not in itself amount to a use of force.

229. The Court must thus consider whether, as the Respondent claims, the acts in question of the United States are justified by the exercise of its right of collective self-defence against an armed attack. The Court must therefore establish whether the circumstances required for the exercise of this right of self-defence are present and, if so, whether the steps taken by the United States actually correspond to the requirements of international law. For the Court to conclude that the United States was lawfully exercising its right of collective self-defence, it must first find that Nicaragua engaged in an armed attack against El Salvador, Honduras or Costa Rica.

230. As regards El Salvador, the Court has found * * * that it is satisfied that between July 1979 and the early months of 1981, an intermittent flow of arms was routed via the territory of Nicaragua to the armed opposition in that country. The Court was not however satisfied that assistance has reached the Salvadorian armed opposition, on a scale of any significance, since the early months of 1981, or that the Government of Nicaragua was responsible for any flow of arms at either period. Even assuming that the supply of arms to the opposition in El Salvador could be treated as imputable to the Government of Nicaragua, to justify invocation of the right of collective self-defence in customary international law, it would have to be equated with an armed attack by Nicaragua on El Salvador. As stated above, the Court is unable to consider that, in customary international law, the provision of arms to the opposition in another State constitutes an armed attack on that State. Even at a time when the arms flow was at its peak, and again assuming the participation of the Nicaraguan Government, that would not constitute such armed attack.

* * *

237. Since the Court has found that the condition *sine qua non* required for the exercise of the right of collective self-defence by the United States is not fulfilled in this case, the appraisal of the United States activities in relation to the criteria of necessity and proportionality takes on a different significance. As a result of this conclusion of the Court, even if the United States activities in question had been carried on in strict compliance with the canons of necessity and proportionality, they would not thereby become lawful. If however they were not, this may constitute an additional ground of wrongfulness. On the question of necessity, the Court observes that the United States measures taken in December 1981 (or, at the earliest, March of that year * * *) cannot be said to correspond

to a "necessity" justifying the United States action against Nicaragua on the basis of assistance given by Nicaragua to the armed opposition in El Salvador. First, these measures were only taken, and began to produce their effects, several months after the major offensive of the armed opposition against the Government of El Salvador had been completely repulsed (January 1981), and the actions of the opposition considerably reduced in consequence. Thus it was possible to eliminate the main danger to the Salvadorian Government without the United States embarking on activities in and against Nicaragua. Accordingly, it cannot be held that these activities were undertaken in the light of necessity. Whether or not the assistance to the *contras* might meet the criterion of proportionality, the Court cannot regard the United States activities summarized in paragraphs 80, 81 and 86, i.e., those relating to the mining of the Nicaraguan ports and the attacks on ports, oil installations, etc., as satisfying that criterion. Whatever uncertainty may exist as to the exact scale of the aid received by the Salvadorian armed opposition from Nicaragua, it is clear that these latter United States activities in question could not have been proportionate to that aid. Finally on this point, the Court must also observe that the reaction of the United States in the context of what it regarded as self-defence was continued long after the period in which any presumed armed attack by Nicaragua could reasonably be contemplated.

238.   Accordingly, the Court concludes that the plea of collective self-defence against an alleged armed attack on El Salvador, Honduras or Costa Rica, advanced by the United States to justify its conduct toward Nicaragua, cannot be upheld; and accordingly that the United States has violated the principle prohibiting recourse to the threat or use of force by the acts listed in paragraph 227 above, and by its assistance to the *contras* to the extent that this assistance "involve[s] a threat or use of force" * * *.

* * *

3.) The Responsible Party

Oil Platforms

Iran v. United States
International Court of Justice
2003 I.C.J. 161 (Judgment of Nov. 6)

23.   * * * The actions giving rise to both the claim and the counter-claim occurred in the context of the general events that took place in the Persian Gulf between 1980 and 1988, in particular the armed conflict that opposed Iran and Iraq. That conflict began on 22 September 1980, when Iraqi forces advanced into the western areas of Iranian territory, and continued until the belligerent parties accepted a ceasefire in the summer of 1988, pursuant to United Nations Security Council resolution 598 (1987) of 20 July 1987. During the war, combat occurred in the territories of both States, but the conflict also spread to the Persian Gulf * * *.

* * *

25.   Two specific attacks on shipping are of particular relevance in this case. On 16 October 1987, the Kuwaiti tanker *Sea Isle City*, reflagged to the United States, was hit by a missile near Kuwait harbor. The United States attributed this attack to Iran and three days later, on 19 October 1987, it attacked Iranian offshore oil production installations, claiming to be acting in self-defense. United State naval forces launched an attack against [Iranian oil platforms] * * * [The platforms] were destroyed in the attack.

* * *

61.   In short, the Court has examined with great care the evidence and arguments presented on each side, and finds that the evidence indicative of Iranian responsibility for the attack on the *Sea Isle City* is not sufficient to support the contentions of the United States. The conclusion to which the Court has come on this aspect of the case is thus that the burden of proof of the existence of an armed attack by Iran on the United States, in the form of the missile attack on the *Sea Isle City*, has not been discharged.

4.) *Necessity and Proportionality*

The ICJ refers to the need to respect the principles of necessity and proportionality in both the *Corfu Channel* and *Nicaragua* cases. It dealt with these principles in greater detail in its advisory opinion on *Nuclear Weapons* and in the *Oil Platforms* case, both excerpted here.

Legality of the Threat or Use of Nuclear Weapons

International Court of Justice
1996 I.C.J. Rep. 226 (Advisory Opinion of Jul. 8)

37.   The Court will now address the question of the legality or illegality of recourse to nuclear weapons in the light of the provisions of the Charter relating to the threat or use of force.

38.   The Charter contains several provisions relating to the threat and use of force. In Article 2, paragraph 4, the threat or use of force against the territorial integrity or political independence of another State or in any other manner inconsistent with the purposes of the United Nations is prohibited. That paragraph provides:

> "All Members shall refrain in their international relations from the threat or use of force against the territorial integrity or political independence of any State, or in any other manner inconsistent with the Purposes of the United Nations."

This prohibition of the use of force is to be considered in the light of other relevant provisions of the Charter. In Article 51, the Charter recognizes the inherent right of individual or collective self-defence if an armed attack occurs. A further lawful use of force is envisaged in Article 42, whereby the

Security Council may take military enforcement measures in conformity with Chapter VII of the Charter.

39.   These provisions do not refer to specific weapons. They apply to any use of force, regardless of the weapons employed. The Charter neither expressly prohibits, nor permits, the use of any specific weapon, including nuclear weapons. A weapon that is already unlawful *per se*, whether by treaty or custom, does not become lawful by reason of its being used for a legitimate purpose under the Charter.

40.   The entitlement to resort to self-defence under Article 51 is subject to certain constraints. Some of these constraints are inherent in the very concept of self-defence. Other requirements are specified in Article 51.

41.   The submission of the exercise of the right of self-defence to the conditions of necessity and proportionality is a rule of customary international law. As the Court stated in the case concerning *Military and Paramilitary Activities in and against Nicaragua (Nicaragua v. United States of America)*: there is a ''specific rule whereby self-defence would warrant only measures which are proportional to the armed attack and necessary to respond to it, a rule well established in customary international law'' (*I.C.J. Reports 1986*, p. 94, para. 176). This dual condition applies equally to Article 51 of the Charter, whatever the means of force employed.

42.   The proportionality principle may thus not in itself exclude the use of nuclear weapons in self-defence in all circumstances. But at the same time, a use of force that is proportionate under the law of self-defence, must, in order to be lawful, also meet the requirements of the law applicable in armed conflict which comprise in particular the principles and rules of humanitarian law.

43.   Certain States have in their written and oral pleadings suggested that in the case of nuclear weapons, the condition of proportionality must be evaluated in the light of still further factors. They contend that the very nature of nuclear weapons, and the high probability of an escalation of nuclear exchanges, mean that there is an extremely strong risk of devastation. The risk factor is said to negate the possibility of the condition of proportionality being complied with. The Court does not find it necessary to embark upon the quantification of such risks; nor does it need to enquire into the question whether tactical nuclear weapons exist which are sufficiently precise to limit those risks: it suffices for the Court to note that the very nature of all nuclear weapons and the profound risks associated therewith are further considerations to be borne in mind by States believing they can exercise a nuclear response in self-defence in accordance with the requirements of proportionality.

NOTES AND QUESTIONS

1.   *Cyberwar* Computers have come to dominate the battlefield. Troops and supplies are positioned with the aid of global positioning systems (''GPS''). ''Smart'' munitions allow for pin-point accuracy from great distances. Sensors, spy drones and satellites constantly gather information. Comput-

ers have been used to spread propaganda. Russian and Chechen forces used the Internet for this purpose as early as 1994. In these capacities computers are simply enhancing traditional warfare. GPS systems replace paper and ink maps; logistics officers use digital catalogues instead of reams of paper, and bombs strike within inches of a targets rather than kilometers. Internet propaganda represents the evolution of a classic technique. We do not need new international law to deal with these uses. We are, however, beginning to see new uses of computers that may need new regulation.

Other forms of cyber attack are unique to computers, however, such practices as denial of service (DoS) attacks, data modification, and the hacking of government infrastructure. In 2003, the Pentagon and various American intelligence agencies formulated a plan to use cyber attacks along with physical attacks in the invasion of Iraq. The plan centered on freezing billions of dollars in Saddam Hussein's government bank accounts in order to cripple the Iraqi financial system before coalition troops entered the country. The Bush administration dropped the plan citing concerns about the potential fallout of such an attack, including the possibility that financial destabilization of large areas of the Middle East could set off a worldwide financial crisis. John Markoff and Thom Shanker, *Halted '03 Iraq Plan Illustrates U.S. Fear of Cyberwar Risk*, N.Y. TIMES, Aug. 2, 2009. Destructive cyberattacks have also been carried out by lone hackers.

Do we need new international law for these new forms of attack using computers?

2. *Terrorism*. Terrorist attacks have generally been treated as criminal acts because they have all the hallmarks of crimes, not armed attacks that can give rise to the right of self-defense. *See* LOUISE RICHARDSON, WHAT TERRORISTS WANT: UNDERSTANDING THE ENEMY, CONTAINING THE THREAT (2006). Ingrid Detter DeLupis explains: "International terrorism implies the intermittent use or threat of force against person(s) to obtain certain political objectives of international relevance from a third party. But at the same time the intermittent factor, which is a hallmark of terrorism, excludes it from constituting war per se." LAW OF WAR 25 (2d ed. 2000). The United States, nevertheless, declared it was in a "global war on terrorism" following the 9/11 attacks. Is it relevant that other states suffering terrorist attacks after 9/11 (the UK, Spain, Indonesia, India) did not declare war? Does it matter or should it matter that the U.S. suffered more casualties on 9/11 than in the attacks in these other states? What are the advantages of declaring war? What are the disadvantages? Will states generally be able to respond to a terrorist attack meeting all of the elements of lawful use of force in self-defense: with the purpose of defense, following a significant armed attack, against the responsible state, and respecting necessity and proportionality? *See* Mary Ellen O'Connell, *Lawful Self–Defense to Terrorism*, 63 U. OF PITTSBURGH L.R. 889 (2002). See also, generally on the subject of terrorism and international law, CHRISTOPHER L. BLAKESLEY, TERRORISM AND ANTI-TERRORISM: A NORMATIVE AND PRACTICAL ASSESSMENT (2006).

3.   *Consent.* Should there be any limits on a government's right to request outside assistance in suppressing violence on its territory? Traditionally, once an opponent to a government gained enough strength to seriously challenge the government militarily, it reached a stage of belligerency. States wishing to maintain neutral rights had to withdraw from supporting either side. Does this rule still make sense today? What if the government requesting help was democratically elected and the opponents are seeking to seize power? What if the opponents promise to hold elections if they succeed in overthrowing an unelected government? On issues of consent and withdrawal of consent for military assistance, see, *Armed Activities on the Territory of the Congo* (D.R.C. v. Uganda), 2005 I.C.J. Rep. (Judgment of Dec. 19).

4.   For a discussion of the current law of occupation, see, *Legal Consequences of the Construction of a Wall in the Occupied Palestinian Territory*, 2004 I.C.J. Rep. 136 (Advisory Opinion of July 9) and *Armed Activities on the Territory of the Congo* (D.R.C. v. Uganda) 2005 I.C.J. Rep. (Judgment of Dec. 19).

5.   For further reading on self-defense, see, MARY ELLEN O'CONNELL, THE POWER AND PURPOSE OF INTERNATIONAL LAW, ch. 4 (2008); YORAM DINSTEIN, WAR, AGGRESSION, AND SELF-DEFENCE (4th ed. 2005), and STANIMIR A. ALEXANDROV, SELF-DEFENSE AGAINST THE USE OF FORCE IN INTERNATIONAL LAW (1996).

b.   COLLECTIVE USE OF FORCE

In discussing unilateral action, we also discussed related collective action, in particular, collective self-defense. In this section we turn to collective action by previously organized groups. We start with the form of collective action envisaged in the UN Charter—action mandated by the Security Council. We will see that the Charter's plan for Security Council responses to threats to the peace, breaches of the peace and acts of aggression has never been fully implemented. Rather, the Security Council has reacted to various crisis situations in ways either approximating the Charter provisions (the Korean and the Gulf Wars) or in innovative ways, extrapolating from the Charter (peacekeeping and peace enforcement).

In addition to collective action through the United Nations, we also look at security arrangements developed to respond to security threats and humanitarian crises. Review the provisions of Chapter VII of the Charter, reproduced above, before considering the case of the Cuban Missile Crisis and the Organization of American States (OAS) and the Kosovo Crisis and the North Atlantic Treaty Organization (NATO). *See generally* on this subject, COLLECTIVE SECURITY LAW (Nigel D. White ed., 2003).

1.) *UNITED NATIONS COLLECTIVE ACTION*

The Security Council was organized as a standing body with clear responsibility to act on behalf of all victims of unlawful force. It may mandate action by members when it adopts a resolution by nine affirmative votes, if no permanent member vetoes the resolution. Under Chapter VII Articles 43 and 45, the Council was to have troops available with which to act. It could also call on regional agencies to act on its behalf. Thus, the Council was to be a uniquely powerful organization in the area of peace and security. These articles call for member states to make agreements with the United Nations to provide troops for use by the Council when acting under Article 39 to respond to threats to or breaches of the peace. These agreements were never formed. Instead, when the UN has called on armed forces it has done so on an *ad hoc* basis. In 1948 and 1949 it sent truce observers to the Middle East and to the border area between India and Pakistan. Then in 1950 North Korea invaded South Korea with the aim of unifying the peninsula. The Security Council authorized a United Nations force under the command of the United States to intervene and push North Korea back. The authorization was only possible because the Soviet Union was boycotting the Council at the time in protest over the failure to seat a representative of the People's Republic of China in place of the Nationalist Chinese representative.

When the Soviet Union returned to the Council, the U.S. tried to devise an alternative to Security Council authorization for the use of force by going to the General Assembly, where, in those days, it could count on a majority of countries to support its position. In November 1950, the Assembly adopted the "Uniting for Peace" Resolution, setting out that the Assembly had the power to discuss and make recommendations on matters of peace and security if the Council found itself deadlocked. Members were also to hold armed forces ready in the event that the Council failed to act. The Uniting for Peace Resolution was first used in 1956 when Britain and France vetoed Security Council resolutions during the Suez crisis. The General Assembly demanded that the two countries withdraw their troops from Egypt, and they did. The Soviet Union, however, paid no attention at all to a similar demand when it invaded Hungary also in 1956. The Uniting for Peace Resolution has played only a limited role since its adoption, but it has reappeared in the Report of the Secretary General, Implementing the Responsibility to Protect, UN Doc. A/63/677, pp. 9, 22–27 (Jan. 12, 2009). (Responsibility to Protect or "R2P" is discussed at the end of this section.) After reading the *Certain Expenses* case below and considering the UN Charter principles respecting the powers of the General Assembly in Chapter IV. What is the role of the General Assembly in peace and security matters?

The closest the Security Council has come to functioning as foreseen by the Charter drafters was in the case of the 1990–1991 Iraqi invasion of Kuwait and successful liberation by a coalition of states led by the United States. *See* UN Security Council Resolutions 660 (1990), 667 (1990), 687 (1991) and 688 (1991) and Mary Ellen O'Connell, *Enforcing the Prohibition on the Use of Force: The U.N.'s Response to Iraq's Invasion of Kuwait*, 15 S. ILL. U. L.J. 453, 479–80 (1991).

A.) PEACEKEEPING

The term peacekeeping does not appear in the Charter. The Council has no express authority to send peacekeepers. But UN lawyers have always argued that under Chapter VI of the Charter the Security Council has authority to recommend to states a variety of measures for peaceful settlement of disputes and under Chapter VII it may send the troops of member states to conflict areas. Putting these provisions together, international lawyers believe the necessary Charter authority can be found. The authority is in Chapter VI ½. To remain within this paradigm, peacekeepers must have the consent of all parties, deploy only following a ceasefire, and use limited force. Thereby, the UN would be able to avoid interfering in the political struggle underlying such conflicts. These are the elements of classic peacekeeping doctrine.

Before the end of the Cold War, seventeen such peacekeeping missions were organized. These missions aided compliance with cease-fires by literally imposing blue-helmeted soldiers between warring factions or setting up observer posts to report breaches of the cease-fire. Peacekeepers were not, however, peace enforcers—they did not take coercive action to compel compliance with a cease-fire. This factor was key to a decision by the International Court of Justice that the General Assembly—and not just the Security Council—had the authority to organize peacekeeping missions. During the complicated Congo Crisis of 1960, the General Assembly, acting under the Uniting for Peace Resolution called for troops to go to support the newly-independent Congolese government. France and the Soviet Union opposed the intervention and refused to pay the expenses associated with it. GEORGES ABI-SAAB, INTERNATIONAL CRISES AND THE ROLE OF LAW: THE UNITED NATIONS OPERATION IN THE CONGO 1960–1964 (1978).

The General Assembly asked the International Court of Justice for an advisory opinion regarding the obligation of UN members to pay for peacekeeping expenses incurred by the General Assembly.

Certain Expenses of the United Nations

International Court of Justice
1962 I.C.J. Rep. 151–156, 162–170, 179 (Advisory Opinion of July 20)

* * *

The power of the Court to give an advisory opinion is derived from Article 65 of the Statute. The power granted is of a discretionary character. In exercising its discretion, the International Court of Justice, like the Permanent Court of International Justice, has always been guided by the principle which the Permanent Court stated in the case concerning the Status of Eastern Carelia on 23 July 1923: "The Court, being a Court of Justice, cannot, even in giving advisory opinions, depart from the essential rules guiding their activity as a Court" (P.C.I.J., Series B, No. 5, p. 29). Therefore, and in accordance with Article 65 of its Statute, the Court can give an advisory opinion only on a legal question. If a question is not a legal one, the Court has no discretion in the matter; it must decline to give the opinion requested. But even if the question is a legal one, which the Court is undoubtedly competent to answer, it may nonetheless decline to do so. As this Court said in its Opinion of 30 March 1950, the permissive character of Article 65 "gives the Court the power to examine whether the circumstances of the case are of such a character as should lead it to decline to answer the Request" (*Interpretation of Peace Treaties with Bulgaria, Hungary and Romania (First Phase), I.C.J. Reports 1950, p. 72*). But, as the Court also said in the same Opinion, "the reply of the Court, itself an 'organ of the United Nations', represents its participation in the activities of the Organization, and, in principle, should not be refused" (*ibid.*, p. 71). Still more emphatically, in its Opinion of 23 October 1956, the Court said that only "compelling reasons" should lead it to refuse to give a requested advisory opinion (*Judgments of the Administrative Tribunal of the I.L.O. upon complaints made against the Unesco, I.C.J. Reports 1956, p. 86*).

The Court finds no "compelling reason" why it should not give the advisory opinion which the General Assembly requested by its resolution 1731 (XVI). It has been argued that the question put to the Court is intertwined with political questions, and that for this reason the Court should refuse to give an opinion. It is true that most interpretations of the Charter of the United Nations will have political significance, great or small. In the nature of things it could not be otherwise. The Court, however, cannot attribute a political character to a request which invites it to undertake an essentially judicial task, namely, the interpretation of a treaty provision.

In the preamble to the resolution requesting this opinion, the General Assembly expressed its recognition of "its need for authoritative legal guidance". In its search for such guidance it has put to the Court a legal question—a question of the interpretation of Article 17, paragraph 2, of the Charter of the United Nations. In its Opinion of 28 May 1948, the Court made it clear that as "the principal judicial organ of the United Nations", it was entitled to exercise in regard to an article of the Charter, "a multilateral treaty, an interpretative function which falls within the normal exercise of its judicial powers" (*Conditions of Admission of a State to Membership in the United Nations (Article 4 of the Charter), I.C.J. Reports 1947–1948, p. 61*).

The Court, therefore, having been asked to give an advisory opinion upon a concrete legal question, will proceed to give its opinion.

The question on which the Court is asked to give its opinion is whether certain expenditures which were authorized by the General Assembly to cover the costs of the United Nations operations in the Congo (hereinafter referred to as ONUC) and of the operations of the United Nations Emergency Force in the Middle East (hereinafter referred to as UNEF), "constitute 'expenses of the Organization' within the meaning of Article 17, paragraph 2, of the Charter of the United Nations".

* * *

The general purposes of Article 17 are the vesting of control over the finances of the Organization, and the levying of apportioned amounts of the expenses of the Organization in order to enable it to carry out the functions of the Organization as a whole acting through its principal organs and such subsidiary organs as may be established under the authority of Article 22 or Article 29.

Article 17 is the only article in the Charter which refers to budgetary authority or to the power to apportion expenses, or otherwise to raise revenue, except for Articles 33 and 35, paragraph 3, of the Statute of the Court which have no bearing on the point here under discussion. Nevertheless, it has been argued before the Court that one type of expenses, namely those resulting from operations for the maintenance of international peace and security, are not "expenses of the Organization" within the meaning of Article 17, paragraph 2, of the Charter, inasmuch as they fall to be dealt with exclusively by the Security Council, and more especially through agreements negotiated in accordance with Article 43 of the Charter.

The argument rests in part upon the view that when the maintenance of international peace and security is involved, it is only the Security Council which is authorized to decide on any action relative thereto. It is argued further that since the General Assembly's power is limited to discussing, considering, studying and recommending, it cannot impose an obligation to pay the expenses which result from the implementation of its recommendations. This argument leads to an examination of the respective functions of the General Assembly and of the Security Council under the Charter, particularly with respect to the maintenance of international peace and security.

Article 24 of the Charter provides:

"In order to ensure prompt and effective action by the United Nations, its Members confer on the Security Council primary responsibility for the maintenance of international peace and security . . . ."

The responsibility conferred is "primary", not exclusive. This primary responsibility is conferred upon the Security Council, as stated in Article 24, "in order to ensure prompt and effective action". To this end, it is the Security Council which is given a power to impose an explicit obligation of compliance if for example it issues an order or command to an aggressor under Chapter VII. It is only the Security Council which can require enforcement by coercive action against an aggressor.

* * *

"The General Assembly may discuss any questions relating to the maintenance of international peace and security brought before it by any Member of the United Nations, or by the Security Council, or by a State which is not a Member of the United Nations in accordance with Article 35, paragraph 2, and, except as provided in Article 12, may make recommendations with regard to any such question to the State or States concerned or to the Security Council, or to both. Any such question on which action is necessary shall be referred to the Security Council by the General Assembly either before or after discussion."

The Court considers that the kind of action referred to in Article 11, paragraph 2, is coercive or enforcement action. This paragraph, which applies not merely to general questions relating to peace and security, but also to specific cases brought before the General Assembly by a State under Article 35, in its first sentence empowers the General Assembly, by means of recommendations to States or to the Security Council, or to both, to organize peacekeeping operations, at the request, or with the consent, of the States concerned. This power of the General Assembly is a special power which in no way derogates from its general powers under Article 10 or Article 14, except as limited by the last sentence of Article 11, paragraph 2. This last sentence says that when "action" is necessary the General Assembly shall refer the question to the Security Council. The word "action" must mean such action as is solely within the province of the Security Council. It cannot refer to recommendations which the Security Council might make, as for instance under Article 38, because the General Assembly under Article 11 has a comparable power. The "action" which is solely within the province of the Security Council is that which is indicated by the title of Chapter VII of the Charter, namely "Action with respect to threats to the peace, breaches of the peace, and acts of aggression". If the word "action" in Article 11, paragraph 2, were interpreted to mean that the General Assembly could make recommendations only of a general character affecting peace and security in the abstract, and not in relation to specific cases, the paragraph would not have provided that the General Assembly may make recommendations on questions brought before it by States or by the Security Council. Accordingly, the last sentence of Article 11, paragraph 2, has no application where the necessary action is not enforcement action.

The practice of the Organization throughout its history bears out the foregoing elucidation of the term "action" in the last sentence of Article 11, paragraph 2. Whether the General Assembly proceeds under Article 11 or under Article 14, the implementation of its recommendations for setting up commissions or other bodies involves organizational activity—action—in connection with the maintenance of international peace and security. Such implementation is a normal feature of the functioning of the United Nations. Such committees, commissions or other bodies or individuals, constitute, in some cases, subsidiary organs established under the authority of Article 22 of the Charter. The functions of the General Assembly for which it may establish such subsidiary organs include, for example, investigation, observation and supervision, but the way in which such subsidiary organs are utilized depends on the consent of the State or States concerned.

The Court accordingly finds that the argument which seeks, by reference to Article 11, paragraph 2, to limit the budgetary authority of the General Assembly in respect of the maintenance of international peace and security, is unfounded.

It has further been argued before the Court that Article 43 of the Charter constitutes a particular rule, a *lex specialis*, which derogates from the general rule in Article 17, whenever an expenditure for the maintenance of international peace and security is involved. Article 43 provides that Members shall negotiate agreements with the Security Council on its initiative, stipulating what "armed forces, assistance and facilities, including rights of passage, necessary for the purpose of maintaining international peace and security'', the Member state will make available to the Security Council on its call. According to paragraph 2 of the Article:

> "Such agreement or agreements shall govern the numbers and types of forces, their degree of readiness and general location, and the nature of the facilities and assistance to be provided."

The argument is that such agreements were intended to include specifications concerning the allocation of costs of such enforcement actions as might be taken by direction of the Security Council, and that it is only the Security Council which has the authority to arrange for meeting such costs.

With reference to this argument, the Court will state at the outset that, for reasons fully expounded later in this Opinion, the operations known as UNEF and ONUC were not *enforcement* actions within the compass of Chapter VII of the Charter and that therefore Article 43 could not have any applicability to the cases with which the Court is here concerned. However, even if Article 43 were applicable, the Court could not accept this interpretation of its text for the following reasons.

There is nothing in the text of Article 43 which would limit the discretion of the Security Council in negotiating such agreements. It cannot be assumed that in every such agreement the Security Council would insist, or that any Member State would be bound to agree, that such State would bear the entire cost of the "assistance" which it would make available including, for example, transport of forces to the point of operation, complete logistical maintenance in the field, supplies, arms and ammunition, etc. If, during negotiations under the terms of Article 43, a Member State would be entitled (as it would be) to insist, and the Security Council would be entitled (as it would be) to agree, that some part of the expense should be borne by the Organization, then such expense would form part of the expenses of the Organization and would fall to be apportioned by the General Assembly under Article 17. It is difficult to see how it could have been contemplated that all potential expenses could be envisaged in such agreements concluded perhaps long in advance. Indeed, the difficulty or impossibility of anticipating the entire financial impact of enforcement measures on Member States is brought out by the terms of Article 50 which provides that a State, whether a Member of the United Nations or not, "which finds itself confronted with special economic problems arising from the carrying out of those [preventive or enforcement] measures, shall have the right to consult the Security Council with regard to a solution of those problems". Presumably in such a case the Security Council might determine that the overburdened State was entitled to some financial assistance; such financial assistance, if afforded by the Organization, as it might be, would clearly constitute part of the "expenses of the Organization". The economic problems could not have been covered in advance by a negotiated agreement since they would be unknown until after the event and in the case of non-Member States, which are also included in Article 50, no agreement at all would have been negotiated under Article 43.

Moreover, an argument which insists that all measures taken for the maintenance of international peace and security must be financed through agreements concluded under Article 43, would seem to exclude the possibility that the Security Council might act under some other Article of the Charter. The Court cannot accept so limited a view of the powers of the Security Council under the Charter. It cannot be said that the Charter has left the Security Council impotent in the face of an emergency situation when agreements under Article 43 have not been concluded.

Articles of Chapter VII of the Charter speak of "situations" as well as disputes, and it must lie within the power of the Security Council to police a situation even though it does not resort to enforcement action against a State. The costs of actions which the Security Council is authorized to take constitute "expenses of the Organization within the meaning of Article 17, paragraph 2".

The Court has considered the general problem of the interpretation of Article 17, paragraph 2, in the light of the general structure of the Charter and of the respective functions assigned by the Charter to the General Assembly and to the Security Council, with a view to determining the meaning of the phrase "the expenses of the Organization". The Court does not find it necessary to go further in giving a more detailed definition of such expenses. The Court will, therefore, proceed to examine the expenditures enumerated in the request for the advisory opinion. In determining whether the actual expenditures authorized constitute "expenses of the Organization within the meaning of Article 17, paragraph 2, of the Charter", the Court agrees that such expenditures must be tested by their relationship to the purposes of the United Nations in the sense that if an expenditure were made for a purpose which is not one of the purposes of the United Nations, it could not be considered an "expense of the Organization".

The purposes of the United Nations are set forth in Article 1 of the Charter. The first two purposes as stated in paragraphs 1 and 2, may be summarily described as pointing to the goal of international peace and security and friendly relations. The third purpose is the achievement of economic, social, cultural and humanitarian goals and respect for human rights. The fourth and last purpose is: "To be a center for harmonizing the actions of nations in the attainment of these common ends."

The primary place ascribed to international peace and security is natural, since the fulfillment of the other purposes will be dependent upon the attainment of that basic condition. These purposes are broad indeed, but neither they nor the powers conferred to effectuate them are unlimited. Save as they have entrusted the Organization with the attainment of these common ends, the Member States retain their freedom of action. But when the Organization takes action which warrants the assertion that it was appropriate for the fulfillment of one of the stated purposes of the United Nations, the presumption is that such action is not *ultra vires* the Organization.

If it is agreed that the action in question is within the scope of the functions of the Organization but it is alleged that it has been initiated or carried out in a manner not in conformity with the division of functions among the several organs which the Charter prescribes, one moves to the internal plane, to the internal structure of the Organization. If the action was taken by the wrong organ, it was irregular as a matter of that internal structure, but this would not necessarily mean that the expense incurred was not an expense of the Organization. Both national and international law contemplate cases in which the body corporate or politic may be bound, as to third parties, by an *ultra vires* act of an agent.

In the legal systems of States, there is often some procedure for determining the validity of even a legislative or governmental act, but no analogous procedure is to be found in the structure of the United Nations. Proposals made during the drafting of the Charter to place the ultimate authority to interpret the Charter in the International Court of Justice were not accepted; the opinion which the Court is in course of rendering is an *advisory* opinion. As anticipated in 1945, therefore, each organ must, in the first place at least, determine its own jurisdiction. If the Security Council, for example, adopts a resolution purportedly for the maintenance of international peace and security and if, in accordance with a mandate or authorization in such resolution, the Secretary–General incurs financial obligations, these amounts must be presumed to constitute "expenses of the Organization".

* * *

The obligation is one thing: the way in which the obligation is met—that is from what source the funds are secured—is another. The General Assembly may follow any one of several alternatives: it may apportion the cost of the item according to the ordinary scale of assessment; it may apportion the cost according to some special scale of assessment; it may utilize funds which are voluntarily contributed to the Organization; or it may find some other method or combination of methods for providing the necessary funds. In this context, it is of no legal significance whether, as a matter of book-keeping or accounting, the General Assembly chooses to have the item in question included under one of the "standard" established sections of the "regular" budget or whether it is separately listed in some special account or fund. The significant fact is that the item is an expense of the Organization and under Article 17, paragraph 2, the General Assembly therefore has authority to apportion it.

At the outset of this opinion, the Court pointed out that the text of Article 17, paragraph 2, of the Charter could lead to the simple conclusion that "the expenses of the Organization" are the amounts paid out to defray the costs of carrying out the purposes of the Organization. It was further indicated that the Court would examine the resolutions authorizing the expenditures referred to in the request for the advisory opinion in order to ascertain whether they were incurred with that end in view. The Court has made such an examination and finds that they were so incurred. The Court has also analyzed the principal arguments which have been advanced against the conclusion that the expenditures in question should be considered as "expenses of the Organization within the meaning of Article 17, paragraph 2, of the Charter of the United Nations", and has found that these arguments are unfounded. Consequently, the Court arrives at the conclusion that the question submitted to it in General Assembly resolution 1731 (XVI) must be answered in the affirmative.

For a number of years following the *Certain Expense* case, UN members continued to negotiate how to pay for peacekeeping. There were years more of negotiation before a separate account for peacekeeping expenses was established, to be paid voluntary. The financing of the Congo operation was not the only contentious issue. The UN troops that went to the Congo were supposed to intervene to counter Belgian intervention on the eve Congolese independence. The UN, however, ended up fighting alongside the central government against the people of Katanga province who were attempting to secede. The UN strove to remain neutral but could not and, thus, tipped the political balance. Future peacekeeping missions for the remainder of the Cold War were established only where both the U.S. and the Soviet Union agreed.

B.) Peace Enforcement

With the end of the Cold War in the late 1980s, permanent members of the Security Council ceased blocking every move of an adversary with the veto. The Council voted unanimously to condemn Iraq's invasion of Kuwait. Following the successful liberation of Kuwait, Security Council members and the UN Secretary General began to think more expansively about the UN's role in world peace. *See* the Secretary General's Agenda for Peace, UN Doc. S/24111–A/47/277 (1992). The Council began to authorize missions to respond to humanitarian crises, crises that had not traditionally been interpreted as violations of "international peace." The missions themselves were given authority to use force to actually enforce the peace or end the crisis in contrast with traditional peacekeeping missions that could only use force in personal self-defense. The new missions have come to be called "peace enforcement." The Security Council has typically referred to "Chapter VII" of the Charter in authorizing them and it usually authorizes the missions to use "all necessary means" to carry out their actions. Despite these significant changes, the troops in the field carrying out the missions still wear the UN blue helmet and are usually still referred to as "peacekeepers."

The first departure from traditional peacekeeping toward peace enforcement can be traced to the establishment of the Iraqi Exclusion Zone in April 1991 just at the end of major fighting in the Gulf War. As the fighting to liberate Kuwait was ending, the Kurds of northern Iraq and the Shia in the south began rebellions against the Iraqi government, apparently either to secede from Iraq or at least to establish an autonomous region. This development seems to have caught the UN and the coalition off guard. Both resisted initial calls for intervention. The United States took the position that it could not intervene militarily to support the uprisings because intervention would be unlawful interference in Iraq's internal affairs. The French agreed with this legal assessment, yet argued that "[t]he law is one thing, but the safeguard of a population is another, quite as precious, to which humanity cannot be indifferent." FIN. TIMES, April 5, 1991, at 4 (Statement of French Foreign Minister Roland Dumas).

France could not, however, persuade the other permanent members of the Security Council to authorize force to liberate the Kurds or Shia. Instead, the Council ordered only humanitarian aid on the Kurds' behalf. In Resolution 688, the Council found that Iraqi attacks on the Kurds constituted a threat to peace in the region. In the subsequent operative paragraphs of the resolution, the Council called on Iraq to end its repression of the Kurds and to allow international humanitarian assistance to reach northern Iraq. This was as far as the Council could go without inviting a Chinese veto or failing to get the required two-thirds vote of the fifteen-member Council. As it was, China and India abstained from supporting the resolution, while Cuba, Yemen and Zimbabwe voted against it. All stated they believed the resolution interfered in Iraq's internal affairs.

Providing humanitarian aid was arguably not interference with internal affairs and therefore is not unlawful. Creating the protective zone, however, went well beyond distributing humanitarian aid. There is a question whether such a move was really authorized by the Security Council. The British have argued that Resolution 688, read together with Resolution 678 (which authorized all means to bring peace to the region), did provide authority to create the zone as part of the response to Iraq's violation of international peace. It appears that Iraq gave consent to the establishment of the zone in May 1991. It was then that Coalition forces left the area and United Nations "police" entered.

In mid-summer 1991, fighting broke out in Yugoslavia between the province of Croatia, which had declared its independence, and the Yugoslav federal government. This conflict also raised the question of UN intervention in civil war.

In the early months of the war, the UN played no role. The European Community (EC) wished to mediate the conflict, declaring it a European matter. But the EC had not succeeded in getting a cease-fire by mid-September. The Security Council then became involved, beginning with Resolution 713, which imposed an arms embargo on the entire territory of the former Yugoslavia. This embargo had the consent of Belgrade, and thus avoided a Chinese veto. In November 1991, Zagreb and Belgrade agreed to the formation of a peacekeeping force, the United Nations Protection Force (UNPROFOR), to act as a buffer under Resolution 743.

In July 1995, UNPROFOR was supposed to be policing a ceasefire in the town of Srebrenica between Bosnian Muslims and Bosnian Serbs. As the ceasefire broke down, UNPROFOR did not prevent it, but did continue to give Muslims the illusion they would be protected. The following is an excerpt from a Report by the UN Secretary General to the General Assembly.

Report of the Secretary–General Pursuant to General Assembly Resolution 53/35 The Fall of Srebrenica

UN Doc. A/54/549 (15 Nov. 1999)

* * *

2. On 16 November 1995, the International Tribunal for the Former Yugoslavia indicted Radovan Karadžić ("President of the Republika Srpska") and Ratko Mladić, (Commander of the Bosnian Serb Army) for their alleged, direct responsibility for the atrocities committed in July 1995 against the Bosnian Muslim population of the United Nations-designated safe area of Srebrenica. After a review of the evidence submitted by the Prosecutor, Judge Riad confirmed the indictment, stating that:

> "After Srebrenica fell to besieging Serbian forces in July 1995, a truly terrible massacre of the Muslim population appears to have taken place. The evidence tendered by the Prosecutor describes scenes of unimaginable savagery: thousands of men executed and buried in mass graves, hundreds of men buried alive, men and women mutilated and slaughtered, children killed before their mothers' eyes, a grandfather forced to eat the liver of his own grandson. These are truly scenes from hell, written on the darkest pages of human history."

3. The United Nations had a mandate to "deter attacks" on Srebrenica and five other "safe areas" in Bosnia and Herzegovina. Despite that mandate, up to 20,000 people, overwhelmingly from the Bosnian Muslim community, were killed in and around the safe areas. In addition, a majority of the 117 members of the United Nations Protection Force (UNPROFOR) who lost their lives in Bosnia and Herzegovina died in or around the safe areas.

* * *

11. Following the declaration of independence by Slovenia, fighting broke out between Slovenian forces and predominantly Serb forces of the Yugoslav People's Army (JNA). The fighting, however, lasted for only 10 days, with light casualties on both sides. The conflict ended with the Brioni agreement of 7 July 1991, and was followed, over the coming months, by the withdrawal of JNA forces and de facto independence for Slovenia. In Croatia, the fighting was much more serious. The declaration of independence led to an increase in the armed clashes which had been taking place for several months, pitting Croatian forces against both the JNA and Croatian Serb militias. These clashes descended into full-scale warfare in August 1991 and continued until 2 January 1992, when a ceasefire was signed in Sarajevo under the auspices of the United Nations. Shortly thereafter, the parties to the conflict in Croatia "fully and unconditionally" accepted the "concept for a United Nations peacekeeping operation in Yugoslavia" presented by the Personal Envoy of the Secretary–General,

Cyrus Vance ("the Vance Plan"). At the end of this phase of the fighting in Croatia, Serb forces remained in de facto control of approximately one third of the Republic of Croatia.

* * *

350.   By the end of the day on 13 July, there were virtually no Bosniac males left in the former "safe area" of Srebrenica. Almost all were in one of four categories:

(1) Those alive and making their way through the woods towards Government-held territory;

(2) Those who had been killed on that journey;

(3) Those who had surrendered themselves to the Serbs in Potocari or on the way to Government-held territory, and who had already been killed;

(4) Those who had surrendered themselves to the Serbs in Potocari or on the way to Government-held territory, and who were being moved to Bratunac, pending relocation to execution and burial sites.

351.   The United Nations military observers and Dutchbat were aware that Bosniac men were being detained in Bratunac, but did not know the precise numbers or locations. There is now strong evidence that between 4,000 and 5,000 Bosniac males were being held there in various locations around town: a warehouse; an old school; three lines of trucks and buses; and a football field. The Dutchbat* soldiers being detained in Bratunac, meanwhile, were in different locations (the Hotel Fontana and the Technical School, both of which are close to the football field).

352.   Although the precise details of what happened to the men of Srebrenica on 13 July have been reconstructed only after subsequent enquiry over the past four years, there was concern at the time, and at least five written messages were sent on that day, expressing alarm about potential human rights abuses having been committed or that potentially might be committed.

* * *

361.   It has since been learned that the Bosnian Serbs began the systematic extermination of the thousands of Bosniac males being held in Bratunac in the early morning hours of 14 July. At that time, they began loading the Bosniacs into vehicles and transporting them to different locations in the wider area. Those locations turned out to be extermination sites, where there is strong evidence to suggest that all of those men were executed over the next two to three days (with the exception of a handful of individuals who survived by hiding under or among the dead bodies). * * *

* * *

---

* "Dutchbat" refers to a battalion of peacekeeping troops from The Netherlands.

498.   The fall of Srebrenica is replete with lessons for this Organization and its Member States—lessons that must be learned if we are to expect the peoples of the world to place their faith in the United Nations. There are occasions when Member States cannot achieve consensus on a particular response to active military conflicts, or do not have the will to pursue what many might consider to be an appropriate course of action. The first of the general lessons is that when peacekeeping operations are used as a substitute for such political consensus they are likely to fail. There is a role for peacekeeping—a proud role in a world still riven by conflict—and there is even a role for protected zones and safe havens in certain situations; but peacekeeping and war fighting are distinct activities which should not be mixed. Peacekeepers must never again be deployed into an environment in which there is no ceasefire or peace agreement. Peacekeepers must never again be told that they must use their peacekeeping tools—lightly armed soldiers in scattered positions—to impose the ill-defined wishes of the international community on one or another of the belligerents by military means. If the necessary resources are not provided—and the necessary political, military and moral judgments are not made—the job simply cannot be done.

499.   Protected zones and safe areas can have a role in protecting civilians in armed conflict, but it is clear that either they must be demilitarized and established by the agreement of the belligerents, as in the case of the "protected zones" and "safe havens" recognized by international humanitarian law, or they must be truly safe areas, fully defended by a credible military deterrent. The two concepts are absolutely distinct and must not be confused. It is tempting for critics to blame the UNPROFOR units in Srebrenica for its fall, or to blame the United Nations hierarchy above those units. Certainly, errors of judgment were made—errors rooted in a philosophy of impartiality and non-violence wholly unsuited to the conflict in Bosnia—but this must not divert us from the more fundamental mistakes. The safe areas were established by the Security Council without the consent of the parties and without the provision of any credible military deterrent. They were neither protected areas nor safe havens in the sense of international humanitarian law, nor safe areas in any militarily meaningful sense. Several representatives on the Council, as well as the Secretariat, noted this problem at the time, warning that, in failing to provide a credible military deterrent, the safe area policy would be gravely damaging to the Council's reputation and, indeed, to the United Nations as a whole.

* * *

———————

Between 1991 and 2009, there have been almost 50 UN peacekeeping missions. In 2009, there were 16 active UN peacekeeping missions, many with peace enforcement mandates. Despite the tragedies of Rwanda and Srebrenica, the UN continues to send Blue Helmets to crisis areas of the world. Some improvements have been made especially within the UN's

Department of Peacekeeping Operations. Yet, many of the missions continue to be characterized by too few troops, troops that lack proper training and equipment, unclear mandates, and uncertain exit strategies. The Security Council wants to respond to crises like those in the Congo, Haiti, Liberia, Sudan, and other places, but it consistently has difficulty getting states to contribute troops and funds for these missions. It nevertheless sends missions and is also open to flexible arrangements, such as authorizing particular willing states to send troops into crisis situations not under the auspices of the UN. The US and France sent troops in this posture to Haiti under Security Council Resolution 1529 (2004). The most serious problem of sending Blue Helmets to more crises than the UN can actually manage professionally has been problems of indiscipline and even criminal behavior, including sexual violence, by peacekeepers. *See* Human Rights Watch, UN: Tackle Wrongdoing by Peacekeepers (May 1, 2008) http://www.hrw.org/en/news/2008/05/01/un-tackle-wrongdoing-peacekeepers?print.

2.) Non–UN Collective Uses of Force

In October 1962, the United States detected that the Soviet Union was installing missile launchers on the island of Cuba within easy striking distance of the U.S. The Kennedy Administration decided to establish a naval blockade to prevent Soviet ships from reaching Cuba with remaining material to complete the missile launchers. The US called the blockade a "quarantine" to deflect from the fact that a naval blockade is a use of force prohibited under Article 2(4) of the Charter, unless the blockading state has an exception for its use—self-defense or authorization. The U.S. understood changing the term was not enough and also sought a legal justification for the blockade. The U.S. did not want to claim self-defense because then it would have to characterize the missiles as the equivalent of an armed attack. The U.S. itself had missiles in Turkey that the Soviets could equally have characterized as an armed attack. So the U.S. turned to authorization, but with the Soviets possessing the veto, the State Department's lawyers devised an alternative to requesting authorization from the Security Council.

State Department Memorandum Legal Basis for the Quarantine of Cuba, October 23, 1962

The quarantine against shipments of offensive weapons to Cuba has been imposed by the United States in accordance with a recommendatory resolution of the Organ of Consultation established by the Inter–American Treaty of Reciprocal Assistance (Rio Treaty). The validity of the action in international law depends on affirmative answers to two questions:

(1) Was the action of the Organ of Consultation authorized by the Rio Treaty; and (2) Is the action consistent with the provisions of the UN Charter to which the Rio Treaty is by its own terms and by the terms of the Charter subordinate?

1. Authorization Under the Rio Treaty

The Rio Treaty, together with related agreements, constitute the Inter–American system. The paramount purpose of this system, as stated in the Treaty, is:

> "to assure peace, through adequate means, to provide for effective reciprocal assistance to meet armed attacks against any American State, and . . . to deal with threats of aggression against any of them."

The Treaty provides for collective action, not only in the case of armed attack, which is covered by Article 3, but also:

> "If the inviolability or the integrity of the territory or the sovereignty or political independence of any American State should be affected by an aggression which is not an armed attack . . . or by any other fact or situation that might endanger the peace of America. . . ." (Article 6.)

In such cases, the Organ of Consultation, comprised of the Foreign Ministers of the Member States or representatives specifically designated for the purpose, is to,

> "meet immediately in order to agree on the measures which must be taken in case of aggression to assist the victim of the aggression or, in any case, the measures which should be taken for the common defense and for the maintenance of the peace and security of the Continent." (Article 6.)

The Organ of Consultation acts "by a vote of two-thirds of the Signatory States which have ratified the Treaty." (Article 17.)

The Treaty is equally explicit as to the measures which may be taken by the Organ of Consultation in any case covered by Article 6. These measures are listed in Article 8 and specifically include "use of armed force". Article 20 further specifies that decisions to take any of the measures listed in Article 8 shall be binding except that "no State shall be required to use armed force without its consent."

The action of the OAS in the present case falls readily within the framework of the procedures established by the Treaty. The Inter–American system has long recognized that the adherence by the present Government of Cuba to Sino–Soviet Communism is inconsistent with the principles of the Inter–American system, and has created a situation endangering the peace of the hemisphere. As early as the Seventh Meeting of Foreign Ministers of the Organization of American States in 1960, the Organization "condemned the intervention or the threat of intervention of extra-continental communist powers in the hemisphere. . . ." The Eighth Meeting, at Punta del Este in 1962, went further. It declared that "the continental unity and democratic institutions of the hemisphere are now in danger." The source of that danger was the "subversive offensive of communist Governments." Among the "outstanding facts in this intensified offensive" was "the existence of a Marxist–Leninist government in Cuba which is publicly aligned with the doctrine and foreign policy of the communist powers." (Resolution I, Final Act, Eighth Meeting of Consultation of Ministers of Foreign Affairs Serving as Organ of Consultation in Application of the Inter–American Treaty of Reciprocal Assistance.) At that meeting, the Organization took the first collective measures designed to deal with the threat. It prohibited all trade in arms with Cuba, and excluded the present government of that country from participation in the organs of the Inter–American system.

"More recently, on October 2 and 3 of this year, the Foreign Ministers of the American States, meeting informally in Washington, reiterated that 'the Soviet Union's intervention in Cuba threatens the unity of the Americas and its democratic institutions'" and that this called for the adoption of special measures, both individual and collective.

Against this background the Council of the Organization of American States met on October 23 and constituted itself as Organ of Consultation in accordance with Article 12 of the Rio Treaty. The Organ considered the evidence before it of the secret introduction of Soviet strategic missiles into Cuba in the face of Soviet and Cuban assurances to the contrary. It concluded that it was confronted with a situation that might endanger the peace of America within the meaning of Article 6. This considered judgment brought into play the authority to take one or more of the measures listed in Article 8. The resolution adopted by the Organ exercises this authority. It recommends

> "that the member states, in accordance with Articles 6 and 8 of the Inter–American Treaty of Reciprocal Assistance, take all measures, individually and collectively including the use of armed force which they may deem necessary to ensure that the Government of Cuba cannot continue to receive from the Sino–Soviet powers military material and related supplies which may threaten the peace and security of the Continent and to prevent the missiles in Cuba with offensive capability from ever becoming an active threat to the peace and security of the Continent."

The recommendation contained in the Resolution for the use of armed force if necessary was thus fully authorized by the terms of the Rio Treaty and adopted in accordance with its procedure. The quarantine being imposed is specifically designed "to ensure that the Government of Cuba cannot continue to receive from the Sino–Soviet powers" the offensive weapons which threaten the peace and security of the Continent. It represents a minimal use of force to achieve the stated objectives. The United States action thus falls within the terms of the OAS Resolution.

2.   The UN Charter

(a) Regional Organizations

The Resolution of the Organ of Consultation and the quarantine imposed by the United States pursuant to that Resolution are entirely consistent with the Charter of the United Nations.

The Charter specifically recognizes regional organizations and assigns to them an important place in carrying out the purposes of the United Nations. Article 52(1) states that:

"Nothing in the present Charter precludes the existence of regional arrangements or agencies for dealing with such matters relating to the maintenance of international peace and security as are appropriate for regional action, provided that such arrangements or agencies and their activities are consistent with the Purposes and Principles of the United Nations."

Article 52(2) provides that United Nations National Members that have entered into "such arrangements" or who have constituted "such agencies" must "make every effort to achieve pacific settlement of local disputes through such regional arrangements or by such regional agencies before referring them to the Security Council." Paragraph 3 of the same Article requires the Security Council to "encourage the development of pacific settlement of local disputes through such regional arrangements or by such regional agencies...." Article 54 provides that, "The Security Council shall at all times be kept fully informed of activities undertaken or in contemplation under regional arrangements or by regional agencies for the maintenance of international peace and security." In accordance with this provision, the Organ of Consultation provided that the Security Council would be informed of the contents of the Resolution of October 23rd.

The Charter limits the activities of regional organizations only in the Article 52(1) proviso that such activities must be "consistent with the Purposes and Principles of the United Nations." The Rio Treaty plainly meets this requirement. It was enacted by the High Contracting Parties "to improve the procedure for the pacific settlement of their controversies," in full accord with Article 52(2). The High Contracting Parties expressly reiterated "their will to remain united in an Inter–American system consistent with the purposes and principles of the United Nations." The Resolution and its implementation by the quarantine are in complete accordance with those purposes and principles. These measures are designed, in the opening words of the Charter, "to maintain international peace". They represent "effective collective measures for the prevention and removal of threats to the peace." Article I(i).

The importance of regional agencies in the maintenance of peace and security was recognized in the earliest conceptions of the United Nations. The draft proposal which was prepared at the initial conference at Dumbarton Oaks is virtually the same as Chapter VIII of the Charter.

The framers of the Charter met in San Francisco in 1945 after the basic outlines of the most significant regional arrangement, the Organization of American States, were already established. The meeting was held subsequent to the Conference of the American Republics at which the Act of Chapultepec was approved. This Act recommended the execution of a treaty to establish a regional arrangement, and specifically provided that the "use of armed force to prevent or repel aggression" constituted "regional action which might appropriately be taken by the regional arrangements." The debates at the San Francisco Conference concerning regional organizations were held against this background, and the Organization of American States provided the principal context for the discussions.

When Article 52 was debated at the San Francisco Conference, the Chairman of the committee charged with considering regional arrangements, speaking as the delegate of Colombia, made the following statement concerning the relationship between the Inter–American system and Chapter VIII of the Charter:

> "The Act of Chapultepec provides for the collective defense of the hemisphere and establishes that if an American nation is attacked all the rest consider themselves attacked. Consequently, such action as they may take to repel aggression, authorized by the article which was discussed in the subcommittee yesterday, is legitimate for all of them. Such action would be in accord with the Charter, by the approval of the article, and a regional arrangement may take action, provided it does not have improper purposes as, for example, joint aggression against another state. From this, it may be deduced that the approval of this article implies that the Act of Chapultepec is not in contravention of the Charter."

No delegate disputed this statement and it must be viewed as generally accepted. The very language of the Act of Chapultepec as well as its purposes were adopted by the Rio Treaty. It is evident that the Treaty created the very type of arrangement contemplated by the Charter.

The records of the Conference reveal that a major role was envisaged for regional arrangements under the Charter. Mr. Perez, the Minister of Foreign Affairs of Venezuela, said, "It is in the interests of all that any conflicts which may arise should be solved as quickly as possible in a satisfactory manner, and no one doubts that regional systems are most appropriate to this effect." The delegate from Mexico, Ambassador Najera noted, "In the chapter to which I am referring, the first consideration of the delegations of the American nations was to safeguard their greatest achievement, the most precious flower of cooperation for security through peaceful means." * * *

The history of events since the San Francisco Conference demonstrates the wisdom of the Charter's framers in entrusting to regional organizations the responsibility for handling regional disputes. Such organizations have close contact with the problems within their regions and thus can exercise considered and informed judgment in dealing with these problems. The Organization of American States is the prime example of this. The political process by which it must operate ensures that action will only be taken after careful analysis. Measures to protect peace and security can only be directed or recommended by a vote of two-thirds of the High Contracting Parties. Article 20 of the Treaty expressly provides that no State may be directed to use armed force without its consent. The Organ of Consultation may only recommend but cannot compel the use of armed force. By the presence of such safeguards, this regional organization is able to take effective action with assurance that such action will be consistent with the limitations imposed by the United Nations Charter. It has taken such action in regard to Cuba by its October 23 Resolution, as implemented by the United States quarantine.

(b) Article 53

Article 53(1) of the UN Charter provides:

"The Security Council shall, where appropriate, utilize such regional arrangements or agencies for enforcement action under its authority. But no enforcement action shall be taken under regional arrangements or by regional agencies without the authorization of the Security Council...."

The quarantine measures here under consideration as approved by the Organ of Consultation do not constitute "enforcement action". Accordingly, these measures do not require Security Council authorization.

Twice before the Security Council has rejected the contention that the activities of a regional organization constituted "enforcement action" within the meaning of Article 53 of the Charter. In September, 1960, the Council met to consider an allegation by the Soviet Union that a decision of the Organ of Consultation to take certain diplomatic and embargo measures against the Government of the Dominican Republic constituted "enforcement action". The Security Council did not accept that allegation. Earlier this year, Cuba asked the Security Council to consider decisions taken by the American Republics at Punta del Este, claiming that they required Security Council authorization. Again the Council disagreed.

Thus, it appears from the practice of the Security Council, that measures taken by a regional organization to deal with a threat to the peace, are not necessarily "enforcement action" even though they are obligatory in character. When, as here, they are recommendatory in character, it is clear that they cannot involve "enforcement action".

The construction of the phrase "enforcement action" is supported by its use elsewhere in the Charter. The expression appears at several places in the Charter in addition to Article 53. For example, Article 2, paragraph 5 obligates the Members of the United Nations to "refrain from giving assistance to any state against which the United Nations is taking preventive or enforcement action". And Article 5 provides that

"A Member of the United Nations against which preventive or enforcement action has been taken by the Security Council may be suspended from the exercise of the rights and privileges of membership by the General Assembly upon the recommendation of the Security Council."

The "preventive" and "enforcement" action mentioned in these articles refers to action which the Council is authorized to take under Articles 40, 41, and 42. Article 40 provides for taking of "preventive action" in the form of provisional measures. Such measures are orders of the Council with which Member States are bound to comply. Articles 41 and 42 empower the Council to enforce its decisions by calling upon United Nations Members to apply certain measures or by taking action directly through air, sea, or land forces which are at the disposal of the Security Council. Again, in acting under Articles 41 and 42, the Security Council does more than recommend to Members steps which they might take to meet a threat to peace and security. Rather it decides upon measures and issues orders of enforcement which Member States are obligated under the Charter to carry out.

Council actions under Articles 40, 41, and 42 are to be distinguished from recommendations made by the Council under Article 39 or by the General Assembly in the discharge of its responsibilities as set forth in Chapter IV of the Charter. In the exercise of its powers under Article 10 and 11, the General Assembly has on a number of occasions in the past recommended the use of armed force. The actions of the UN to repel aggression in Korea and to maintain order in the Congo are two such occasions. These actions were taken despite the contention made long ago that such measures constituted "action" which could only be taken by the Security Council. Since the Assembly's powers are only recommendatory in the field of peace and security, the exercise of these powers by the Assembly could not be considered either "preventive" or "enforcement" action.

This distinction between a Security Council measure which is obligatory and constitutes "action," on the one hand, and a measure which is recommended either by the Council or by the General Assembly on the other, is supported by the Advisory Opinion of the International Court of Justice, "Certain Expenses of the United Nations" (July 20, 1962). The Court held that the measures taken by the GA and the Security Council in Suez and the Congo were not enforcement action, in part, because they were only recommendatory as to participating States. Specifically, the Court stated:

> "The word (action) must mean such action as is solely within the province of the Security Council. It cannot refer to recommendations which the Security Council might make, as for instance under Article 38, because the General Assembly under Article II has a comparable power. The (action) which is solely within the province of the Security Council is that which is indicated by the title of Chapter VII of the Charter, namely (Action with respect to threats to the peace, breaches of the peace, and acts of aggression). If the word (action) in Article II, paragraph 2, were interpreted to mean that the General Assembly could make recommendations only of a general character affecting peace and security in the abstract, and not in relation to specific cases, the paragraph would not have provided that the General Assembly may make recommendations on questions brought before it by States or by the Security Council. Accordingly, the last sentence of Article II, paragraph 2, has no application where the necessary action is not enforcement action."

Thus, in the context of United Nations bodies, "enforcement action" does not include action by a United Nations body which is not obligatory on all the Members. As used in Article 53(1), "enforcement action" refers to action by a regional organization rather than to action by an organ of the United Nations, but the words must be given the same meaning in this context. It follows that "enforcement action", as the phrase appears in Article 53(1), does not comprehend action taken by a regional organization which is only recommendatory to the Members of the Organization.

As was pointed out above, the Resolution authorizing the quarantine was agreed upon pursuant to Article 6 of the Rio Treaty. As a recommendation of the "use of armed force", it was specifically authorized by Article 8 of that Treaty. And it is, by the express terms of Article 20, the one measure which, when agreed upon by the Organ of Consultation, Member States are not obligated to carry out. Since States signatories of the Rio Treaty are not obligated to carry out the Resolution recommending quarantine, it does not constitute "enforcement action" under Article 53(1), and is therefore not subject to Security Council authorization.

———————

The Kosovo Crisis During the remainder of 1997 and into 1998, the Kosovo Liberation Army (KLA) claimed more than 50 attacks on Serbs in Kosovo and were labeled a terrorist organization by the United States. On February 27, 1998, the KLA ambushed and killed four Serb police. Over the weekend of 28 February to 1 March 1998, Serb police killed at least twenty ethnic Albanians, apparently in revenge for the killing of the Serb police by the KLA.

On 7 March 1998, U.S. Secretary of State Madeleine Albright announced in Rome that the U.S. would not stand idly by. Many blamed the United States for not intervening to stop the 1994 genocide in Rwanda and the 1995 massacre at Srebrenica, Bosnia. Comparisons were also being made to the U.S. failure in the 1930s to do more to stop the Holocaust of European Jews. So, on 9 March, Albright and Germany's Foreign Minister Klaus Kinkel announced in Bonn that they favored intervening in Kosovo— at least diplomatically. The U.S., however, was apparently also prepared to use force. Yet, the UN Charter restricts the right of states to use force except in self-defense to an armed attack or with Security Council authorization.

Nevertheless, human rights activists and journalists began calling Serbian treatment of Albanians in Kosovo ethnic cleansing and even genocide. They began demanding that the United States and the European Union act militarily. By 31 March the Security Council had adopted Resolution 1160 that imposed economic sanctions on Yugoslavia. Economic sanctions, however, did not persuade the parties to develop a peaceful solution. By the end of August about 300,000 people in the province were displaced. In September 1998, the Security Council passed another resolution. Resolution 1199 strengthened the sanctions, but did not authorize force. Despite this fact, on 13 October 1998, NATO members agreed to authorize the use of force in Yugoslavia even though they did not have an explicit United Nations Security Council mandate to do so. The U.S. was not worried about the legal situation in that Albright and Defense Secretary William Cohen had argued for months before that NATO could act without Security Council authorization.

NATO requires consensus to authorize such an operation. Germany had been arguing against a NATO use of force without Security Council authorization. By October 1998, however, Germany had just held national elections. The out-going government of Helmut Kohl took into account the views of the in-coming government regarding the action. The first official act of Foreign Minister-designate, Joschka Fischer, of the traditionally anti-NATO Green Party, was to agree to a decision for NATO to use armed force against Yugoslavia. In explaining the decision, Germany and most of the NATO members involved made arguments quite similar to those used by the U.S. in the Cuban Missile Crisis: Even if NATO had not exactly met the requirements of the UN Charter, it had come close to meeting the requirements, and the deviation from strict compliance would neither set a bad precedent nor likely harm the Charter regime. They pointed to the fact that Security Council Resolution 1199 referred to Chapter VII of the Charter. Chapter VII provides the authority for the Council to order military and other action in the face of a threat or breach of international peace. In addition to Resolution 1199, winter was coming and people would die in the mountains if they remained. Further, some NATO members might have approved the action not really believing that force would actually be used, thinking a threat would be enough. Finally, the Russians had indicated to the U.S. that if no explicit resolution was requested, they would not protest the ACTORD at the Security Council. None of this changes the fact, however, that in October 1998, NATO agreed to violate the UN Charter.

The actual violation did not occur that autumn. U.S. Ambassador Richard Holbrooke succeeded in brokering an agreement with Yugoslavia's president, Slobodan Milosevic. The agreement called for the positioning of 2000 unarmed human rights monitors and gave confidence to those who had fled their homes to return. In the end only 1400 monitors were deployed, but the vast majority of refugees did go home. Still it was an unstable situation. According to the *International Herald Tribune*: "U.S. intelligence reported almost immediately [following the Agreement] that the Kosovo rebels intended to draw NATO into its fight for independence by provoking Serbian forces into further atrocities." Barton Gellman, *The Path to Crisis: How the United States and Its Allies Went to War*, INT'L HERALD TRIB., 19 April 1999 at 2. More attacks did occur. One incident, in particular, apparently pushed America's leadership to decide for war.

On the morning of 16 January 1999, the bodies of 45 people were found shot to death, in the Kosovo village of Racak. Twenty-three people were found in a ravine and another 22 scattered throughout the village. Guy Dinmore, *Villagers Slaughtered in Kosovo Atrocity*, WASH. POST, 17 Jan.

1999. For a detailed account of the numbers killed in the conflict during 1998, *see* Human Rights Watch, World Report 1999 (visited 7 Aug. 1999) <http://www.hrw.org/hrw/worldreport99/europe/yugoslavia.html> (the report mentions several hundred fatalities). Originally it was reported that the 45 individuals were men, women and children in Racak. It was later clarified that it was in fact 43 men and 2 women. The men were between ages 16 and 60, though several men were classified as "elderly." All of the victims were found in civilian clothing and unarmed. Members of the Kosovo Liberation Army took journalists and human rights monitors to the ravine and then to where the other 22 bodies lay in the village. U.S. diplomat William Walker declared it a "massacre" of civilians "at close range in execution fashion."

Despite the ambiguous facts around the Racak incident, the monitors were withdrawn, and the Contact Group turned to discussions of a peace-keeping force for Kosovo. Talks continued intermittently near Paris during February and March between the Contact Group, Yugoslavia, and representatives of the Kosovo Albanians. The aim was to get both sides to agree to a plan drafted by the U.S., the "Rambouillet Accord." The Kosovo Albanians at first resisted the plan but were finally persuaded to agree. The Serbs were not persuaded, despite Albright's ultimatum that NATO would use force against them if they did not. Rather, the Serbs began massing 40,000 troops in Kosovo close to the international borders. On 24 March 1999, NATO began a bombing campaign over Yugoslavia. NATO had no legal right to do so since the Security Council provided no authorization. NATO issued no statement setting out a legal justification for the action, nor did the United States. The U.S. President and Secretary of State Albright made references to humanitarian disaster, though not to any right of humanitarian intervention.

The bombing continued for 78 days, triggering a mass exodus of refugees and widespread killing of civilians by Yugoslav regular forces, militias, and by NATO bombs. Human rights groups charge that NATO killed approximately 500 civilians in violation of the laws of war. The bombing only ended when the Russians intervened with Milosevic to persuade him to pull his forces from Kosovo. Milosevic himself was in office for another year because even his strongest opponents rallied around him when their country was attacked. When Serb forces left Kosovo, Serb residents fled as Kosovo Albanians began the systematic killing of Serbs and other minorities. In 2008, Kosovo Albanians declared the independence of Kosovo. The legality of this declaration is the subject of an advisory opinion request by the UN General Assembly. See Mary Ellen O'Connell, *Die Forderung nach humanitären Interventionen–eine kritische Betrachtung*, im DAS RECHT UND DIE MACHT. BEITRÖGE ZUM VÖLKERRECHT UND VLKERSTRAFRECHT AM BEGINN DES 21. Jahrhunderts (Gerd Hankel ed., 2008). (*The Claims for Humanitarian Intervention, A Critical Observation*, *in* LAW AND POWER, CONTRIBUTIONS TO INTERNATIONAL LAW AND INTERNATIONAL CRIMINAL LAW AT THE BEGINNING OF THE 21ST CENTURY).

It was the Kosovo Crisis that led the Canadian government to convene a commission, the International Commission on Intervention and State Sovereignty (ICISS), to look into future uses of force in humanitarian crises situations. The commission coined the phrase "responsibility to protect." INTERNATIONAL COMMISSION ON INTERVENTION AND STATE SOVEREIGNTY, THE RESPONSIBILITY TO PROTECT (2001). For the most part, the Report reinforces existing international law, especially human rights obligations of states. It does, however include a significant departure from the Charter in the following passage:

E. If the Security Council rejects a proposal or fails to deal with it in a reasonable time, alternative options are:

I. consideration of the matter by the General Assembly in Emergency Special Session under the "Uniting for Peace" procedure; and

II. action within area of jurisdiction by regional or sub-regional organizations under Chapter VIII of the Charter, subject to their seeking *subsequent* authorization from the Security Council.

There is a large literature explaining the R2P concept: *see, e.g.,* Gareth Evans, President, Int'l Crisis Group and Co–Chair, Int'l Comm'n on Intervention and State Sovereignty, Keynote Address to United Nations Univ./Int'l Crisis Group Conference: Prevention of Mass Atrocities: From Mandate to Realisation (Oct. 10, 2007), *available at* http://www.crisisgroup.org/home/index.cfm?id=5116&1=1, and SABINE VON SCHORLEMER, THE RESPONSIBILITY TO PROTECT AS AN ELEMENT OF PEACE, RECOMMENDATIONS FOR ITS OPERATIONALISATION, POLICY PAPER 28 (Development and Peace Foundation, Dec. 2007).

In 2005, at the World Summit in New York, representatives of all UN members adopted the following document:

United Nations   A/RES/60/1

General Assembly   Distr.: General
24 October 2005

Sixtieth session
Agenda items 46 and 120

Resolution adopted by the General Assembly

[*without reference to a Main Committee (A/60/L.1)*]

60/1. 2005 World Summit Outcome

The General Assembly

Adopts the following 2005 World Summit Outcome:

2005 World Summit Outcome

I. Values and principles

1. We, Heads of State and Government, have gathered at United Nations Headquarters in New York from 14 to 16 September 2005.

2. We reaffirm our faith in the United Nations and our commitment to the purposes and principles of the Charter of the United Nations and international law, which are indispensable foundations of a more peaceful, prosperous and just world, and reiterate our determination to foster strict respect for them.

* * *

78. We reiterate the importance of promoting and strengthening the multilateral process and of addressing international challenges and problems by strictly abiding by the Charter and the principles of international law, and further stress our commitment to multilateralism.

79. We reaffirm that the relevant provisions of the Charter are sufficient to address the full range of threats to international peace and security. We further reaffirm the authority of the Security Council to mandate coercive action to maintain and restore international peace and security. We stress the importance of acting in accordance with the purposes and principles of the Charter.

80. We also reaffirm that the Security Council has primary responsibility in the maintenance of international peace and security. We also note the role of the General Assembly relating to the maintenance of international peace and security in accordance with the relevant provisions of the Charter.

* * *

138. Each individual State has the responsibility to protect its populations from genocide, war crimes, ethnic cleansing and crimes against humanity. This responsibility entails the prevention of such crimes, including their incitement, through appropriate and necessary means. We accept that responsibility and will act in accordance with it. The international community should, as appropriate, encourage and help States to exercise this responsibility and support the United Nations in establishing an early warning capability.

139. The international community, through the United Nations, also has the responsibility to use appropriate diplomatic, humanitarian and other peaceful means, in accordance with Chapters VI and VIII of the Charter, to help to protect populations from genocide, war crimes, ethnic cleansing and crimes against humanity. In this context, we are prepared to take collective action, in a timely and decisive manner, through the Security Council, in accordance with the Charter, including Chapter VII, on a case-by-case basis and in cooperation with relevant regional organizations as appropriate, should peaceful means be inadequate and national authorities are manifestly failing to protect their populations from genocide, war crimes, ethnic cleansing and crimes against humanity. We stress the need for the General Assembly to continue consideration of the responsibility to protect populations from genocide, war crimes, ethnic cleansing and crimes against humanity and its implications, bearing in mind the principles of the

Charter and international law. We also intend to commit ourselves, as necessary and appropriate, to helping States build capacity to protect their populations from genocide, war crimes, ethnic cleansing and crimes against humanity and to assisting those which are under stress before crises and conflicts break out.

NOTES AND QUESTIONS

1.   The Charter has been subject to some creative interpretation: peace-keeping was invented out of Chapters VI and VII. The Security Council ignores provisions on creating troop agreements with states (Article 45) by simply authorizing willing volunteers to go to war in the name of the UN, as in the Korean and the Gulf Wars. Given that these interpretations have been tolerated, why not conclude that the General Assembly has the right to authorize force under the Uniting for Peace resolution or that NATO has the right to authorize force in Kosovo? What impact does the World Summit Outcome document have on any of these developments respecting the Charter?

2.   What can be done to improve UN peacekeeping? Perhaps the UN should get out of the peacekeeping business? Is there another organization that might do better? In addition to NATO, several other organizations have intervened in humanitarian crises: the African Union (Sudan), the Economic Community of West African States (ECOWAS) (Liberia and Sierre Leone) and the Organization of Eastern Caribbean States (Grenada). Check the record of these interventions. Does it support or detract from the UN taking the lead in peacekeeping and peace enforcement or does the record rather say something in general about military intervention in humanitarian crises regardless of who intervenes?

3.   For further reading on collective uses of force, see, ERIKA DE WET, THE CHAPTER VII POWERS OF THE UNITED NATIONS SECURITY COUNCIL (2004); TREVOR FINDLAY, THE USE OF FORCE IN UN PEACE OPERATIONS (2002) and N.D. WHITE, THE UNITED NATIONS AND THE MAINTENANCE OF INTERNATIONAL PEACE AND SECURITY (1990).

3.   THE CRIME OF AGGRESSION

Review the discussions in Chapters 5 and 9 of the International Criminal Court. Recall that as of 2009, work was moving ahead to include the crime of aggression in the ICC Statute. No person has been convicted by an international court for the crime of aggression since World War II.

Draft Amendments to the Rome Statute of the International Criminal Court on the Crime of Aggression

ICC–ASP/7/SWGCA/INF.1 (Feb. 19, 2009)

Article 8 bis

Crime of aggression

1.   For the purpose of this Statute, "crime of aggression" means the planning, preparation, initiation or execution, by a person in a position effectively to exercise control over or to direct the political or military

action of a State, of an act of aggression which, by its character, gravity and scale, constitutes a manifest violation of the Charter of the United Nations.

2.   For the purpose of paragraph 1, "act of aggression" means the use of armed force by a State against the sovereignty, territorial integrity or political independence of another State, or in any other manner inconsistent with the Charter of the United Nations.

Any of the following acts, regardless of a declaration of war, shall, in accordance with United Nations General Assembly resolution 3314 (XXIX) of 14 December 1974, qualify as an act of aggression:

(a) The invasion or attack by the armed forces of a State of the territory of another State, or any military occupation, however temporary, resulting from such invasion or attack, or any annexation by the use of force of the territory of another State or part thereof;

(b) Bombardment by the armed forces of a State against the territory of another State or the use of any weapons by a State against the territory of another State;

(c) The blockade of the ports or coasts of a State by the armed forces of another State;

(d) An attack by the armed forces of a State on the land, sea or air forces, or marine and air fleets of another State;

(e) The use of armed forces of one State which are within the territory of another State with the agreement of the receiving State, in contravention of the conditions provided for in the agreement or any extension of their presence in such territory beyond the termination of the agreement;

(f) The action of a State in allowing its territory, which it has placed at the disposal of another State, to be used by that other State for perpetrating an act of aggression against a third State;

(g) The sending by or on behalf of a State of armed bands, groups, irregulars or mercenaries, which carry out acts of armed force against another State of such gravity as to amount to the acts listed above, or its substantial involvement therein.

NOTES AND QUESTIONS

1.   Given the history of the law restricting resort to force, is it appropriate to prosecute for aggression? In the Kosovo Crisis, who might be prosecuted for aggression? Even if prosecuting for aggression creates challenges, can this serious international crime be ignored if the ICC plans to prosecute other serious international crimes?

2.   For further reading, see, OSCAR SOLERA, DEFINING THE CRIME OF AGGRESSION (2007) and THE INTERNATIONAL CRIMINAL COURT AND THE CRIME OF AGGRESSION (Mauro Politi and Giuseppe Nesi eds., 2004).

B.   CONDUCT OF ARMED CONFLICT

1.   DEVELOPMENTS PRECEDING THE 1949 GENEVA CONVENTIONS

Telford Taylor, Nuremberg and Vietnam
p. 20 (1970)

What, then, are the "laws of war"? They are of ancient origin, and followed two main streams of development. The first flowed from medieval notions of knightly chivalry. Over the course of the centuries the stream has thinned to a trickle; it had a brief spurt during the days of singlehanded aerial combat, and survives today in rules (often violated) prohibiting various deceptions such as the use of the enemy's uniforms or battle insignia, or the launching of a war without fair warning by formal declaration.

The second and far more important concept is that the ravages of war should be mitigated as far as possible by prohibiting needless cruelties, and other acts that spread death and destruction and are not reasonably related to the conduct of hostilities. The seeds of such a principle must be nearly as old as human society, and ancient literature abounds with condemnation of pillage and massacre. In more recent times, both religious humanitarianism and the opposition of merchants to unnecessary disruptions of commerce have furnished the motivation for restricting customs and understandings. In the 17th century these ideas began to find expression in learned writings, especially those of the Dutch jurist-philosopher Hugo Grotius.

The formalization of military organization in the 18th-century brought the establishment of military courts, empowered to try violations of the laws of war as well as other offenses by soldiers. During the American Revolution, both Captain Nathan Hale and the British Major John Andre were convicted as spies and ordered to be hanged, the former by a British military court and the latter by a "Board of General Officers" appointed by George Washington. During the Mexican War, General Winfield Scott created "military commissions," with jurisdiction over violations of the laws of war committed either by American troops against Mexican civilians, or vice versa.

Up to that time the laws of war had remained largely a matter of unwritten tradition, and it was the United States, during the Civil War, that took the lead in reducing them to systematic, written form. In 1863 President Lincoln approved the promulgation by the War Department of "Instructions for the Government of Armies of the United States in the Field," prepared by Francis Lieber, a German veteran of the Napoleonic wars, who emigrated to the United States and became professor of law and political science at Columbia University. These comprised 159 articles, covering such subjects as "military necessity," "punishment of crimes against the inhabitants of hostile countries," "prisoners of war," and "spies." It was by a military commission appointed in accordance with these instructions that Mary Surratt and the others accused of conspiring to assassinate Lincoln were tried.

In the wake of the Crimean War, the Civil War and the Franco–Prussian War of 1870 there arose, in Europe and America, a tide of sentiment for codification of the laws of war and their embodiment in international agreements. The principal fruits of that movement were the series of treaties known today as the Hague and Geneva Conventions. For present purposes, the most important of these are the Fourth Hague Convention of 1907, and the Geneva Prisoner of War, Red Cross, and Protection of Civilians Conventions of 1929 and 1949.

"The right of belligerents to adopt means of injuring the enemy is not unlimited," declared Article 22 of the Fourth Hague Convention, and ensuing articles specify a number of limitations: Enemy soldiers who surrender must not be killed, and are to be taken prisoner; captured cities and towns must not be pillaged, nor "undefended" places bombarded; poisoned weapons and other arms "calculated to cause unnecessary suffering" are forbidden. Other provisions make it clear that war is not a free-for-all between the populations of the countries at war; only members of the armed forces can claim protection of the laws of war, and if a noncombatant civilian takes hostile action against the enemy he is guilty of a war crime. When an army occupies enemy territory, it must endeavor to restore public order, and respect "family honor and rights, the lives of persons, and private property, as well as religious convictions and practices."

Rules requiring humane treatment of prisoners, and for protection of the sick and wounded, are prescribed in the Geneva Conventions. While there is no general treaty on naval warfare, the Ninth Hague Convention prohibited the bombardment of undefended "ports," and the London Naval Treaty of 1930 condemned submarine sinkings of merchant vessels, unless passengers and crews were first placed in "safety."

In all of these treaties, the laws of war are stated as general principles of conduct, and neither the means of enforcement nor the penalties for violations are specified. The substance of their provisions, however, has been taken into the military law of many countries, and is often set forth in general orders, manuals of instruction, or other official documents. In the United States, for example, the Lieber rules of 1863 were replaced in 1914 by an army field manual which, up-dated, is still in force under the title "The Law of Land Warfare." It is set forth therein that the laws of war are part of the law of the United States, and that they may be enforced against both soldiers and civilians, including enemy personnel, by general courts-martial, military commissions, or other military or international tribunals.

Comparable though not identical publications have been issued by the military authorities of Britain, France, Germany and many other countries. These documents, and the treaties on which they are largely based, are regarded as a comprehensive but not necessarily complete exposition of what is really a body of international common law—the laws of war.

Since the mid–19th century, with increasing frequency, the major powers have utilized military courts for the trial of persons accused of war crimes. An early and now famous trial, depicted in a successful Broadway play, was the post-Civil War proceeding against the Confederate Major Henry Wirz on charges of responsibility for the death of thousands of Union prisoners in the Andersonville prison camp, of which he had been commandant. War crimes tribunals were convened by the United States after the Spanish–American War, and by the British after the Boer War.

Following the defeat of Germany in the First World War, the Allies demanded that nearly 900 Germans accused of war crimes, including military and political leaders, be handed over for trial on war crimes charges. The Germans resisted the demand, and in the upshot they were allowed to try their own "war criminals." The trials in 1921 and 1922 were not conducted by military courts, but by the Supreme Court of Germany, sitting in Leipzig. From the Allied standpoint they were a fiasco, as only a handful of accused were tried, and of these nearly all were acquitted or allowed to escape their very short prison sentences. The German court did, however, affirm that violations of the laws of war are punishable offenses, and in the Llandovery Castle case sentenced two German U-boat officers to four-year prison terms (from which both soon escaped) for complicity in the torpedoing of a British hospital ship and the shelling and sinking of her lifeboats. * * *

Frits Kalshoven, Geneva

pp. 10–11 CONSTRAINTS ON THE WAGING OF WAR (1987)

* * *

The tragic events, successively, of the Spanish Civil War and the Second World War provided the incentive for yet another major revision and further development of the law of Geneva. To this end a diplomatic conference met in 1949 in Geneva, once again at the instigation of the ICRC and by invitation of the Swiss Government. The three Conventions in force (one of 1907 and two of 1929) were substituted by new Conventions, giving improved versions of many existing rules and filling lacunae that practice had brought to light. To give just one example, the armed resistance in several European countries under German occupation during the Second World War led to the express recognition that members of organized resistance movements which fulfil a number of (severe) conditions would qualify as prisoners of war.

Then the law of Geneva was enriched by an entirely novel Convention on the protection of civilian persons in time of war. This Convention serves to protect two categories of civilians in particular: enemy civilians in the territory of a belligerent party, and the inhabitants of occupied territory; categories of civilians, that is, who as a consequence of the armed conflict find themselves in the power of the enemy. With this latest addition the law of Geneva had come to comprise four Conventions, dealing with the wounded and sick on land; the wounded, sick and shipwrecked at sea; prisoners of war; and protected civilians.

The Diplomatic Conference of 1949 produced one further innovation of such major importance that it needs to be mentioned here. Thus far, the Conventions of Geneva had always been regarded as applicable primarily in wars between States. The Spanish Civil War had demonstrated the difficulty of making the parties to such an internal armed conflict respect even the most basic principles of the law of Geneva. In the light of this experience the Conference decided, on the one hand, that the Conventions would continue to apply in their entirety to international armed conflicts. On the other hand, it introduced into all four Conventions of 1949 a common Article 3, "applicable in the case of armed conflict not of an international character occurring in the territory of one of the High Contracting Parties", and providing for such an event a list of fundamental rules the parties are "bound to apply, as a minimum". The adoption of the Article signified a tremendous step forward in that it proved the possibility of laying down rules of international law expressly and exclusively addressing the situation of internal armed conflict.

2.   THE 1949 GENEVA CONVENTIONS AND OTHER AGREEMENTS

All states are today party to the 1949 Geneva Conventions. Indeed, the 1949 Conventions along with the UN Charter have more parties than most other treaties. According to Kalshoven, "The law of Geneva serves to provide protection for all those who, as a consequence of an armed conflict, have fallen into the hands of the adversary. The protection envisaged here is, hence, not protection against the violence of war itself, but against the arbitrary power which one belligerent party acquires in the course of the war over persons belonging to the other party." Thus, Geneva law focuses most essentially on combatants no longer fighting (*hors de combat*) and civilians. The excerpts below include some of the most important provisions in the Prisoners and the Civilians Conventions. All four conventions contain Common Article 3, also reproduced below. This article is a sort of restatement of the core principles for the treatment of persons in any armed conflict. The 1949 Geneva Conventions were intended to have broad application. The drafters designed them to apply in all armed conflicts, not just cases of traditional or declared war. Should there be any doubt about the conditions necessary for the application of the Conventions, it is to be resolved in favor of extending protections.

Geneva Convention Relative to the Treatment of Prisoners of War of August 12, 1949

75 U.N.T.S. 135 (1950)

* * *

PART I—GENERAL PROVISIONS

Article 1

The High Contracting Parties undertake to respect and to ensure respect for the present Convention in all circumstances.

Article 2

In addition to the provisions which shall be implemented in peace time, the present Convention shall apply to all cases of declared war or of any other armed conflict which may arise between two or more of the High Contracting Parties, even if the state of war is not recognized by one of them.

The Convention shall also apply to all cases of partial or total occupation of the territory of a High Contracting Party, even if the said occupation meets with no armed resistance.

Although one of the Powers in conflict may not be a party to the present Convention, the Powers who are parties thereto shall remain bound by it in their mutual relations. They shall furthermore be bound by the Convention in relation to the said Power, if the latter accepts and applies the provisions thereof.

Article 3

In the case of armed conflict not of an international character occurring in the territory of one of the High Contracting Parties, each Party to the conflict shall be bound to apply, as a minimum, the following provisions:

(1) Persons taking no active part in the hostilities, including members of armed forces who have laid down their arms and those placed *hors de combat* by sickness, wounds, detention, or any other cause, shall in all circumstances be treated humanely, without any adverse distinction founded on race, colour, religion or faith, sex, birth or wealth, or any other similar criteria.

To this end, the following acts are and shall remain prohibited at any time and in any place whatsoever with respect to the above-mentioned persons:

(a) violence to life and person, in particular murder of all kinds, mutilation, cruel treatment and torture;

(b) taking of hostages;

(c) outrages upon personal dignity, in particular humiliating and degrading treatment;

(d) the passing of sentences and the carrying out of executions without previous judgment pronounced by a regularly constituted court affording all the judicial guarantees, which are recognized as indispensable by civilized peoples.

(2) The wounded and sick shall be collected and cared for. An impartial humanitarian body, such as the International Committee of the Red Cross, may offer its services to the Parties to the conflict.

The Parties to the conflict should further endeavour to bring into force, by means of special agreements, all or part of the other provisions of the present Convention.

The application of the preceding provisions shall not affect the legal status of the Parties to the conflict.

Article 4

A.   Prisoners of war, in the sense of the present Convention, are persons belonging to one of the following categories, who have fallen into the power of the enemy:

(1) Members of the armed forces of a Party to the conflict as well as members of militias or volunteer corps forming part of such armed forces.

(2) Members of other militias and members of other volunteer corps, including those of organized resistance movements, belonging to a Party to the conflict and operating in or outside their own territory, even if this territory is occupied, provided that such militias or volunteer corps, including such organized resistance movements, fulfil the following condition:

(a) that of being commanded by a person responsible for his subordinates;

(b) that of having a fixed distinctive sign recognizable at a distance;

(c) that of carrying arms openly;

(d) that of conducting their operations in accordance with the laws and customs of war.

* * *

(6) Inhabitants of a non-occupied territory, who on the approach of the enemy spontaneously take up arms to resist the invading forces, without having had time to form themselves into regular armed units, provided they carry arms openly and respect the laws and customs of war.

* * *

Article 5

The present Convention shall apply to the persons referred to in Article 4 from the time they fall into the power of the enemy and until their final release and repatriation.

Should any doubt arise as to whether persons, having committed a belligerent act and having fallen into the hands of the enemy, belong to any of the categories enumerated in Article 4, such persons shall enjoy the protection of the present Convention until such time as their status has been determined by a competent tribunal.

* * *

PART II—GENERAL PROTECTION OF PRISONERS OF WAR

* * *

Article 13

Prisoners of war must at all times be humanely treated. Any unlawful act or omission by the Detaining Power causing death or seriously endangering the health of a prisoner of war in its custody is prohibited, and will be regarded as a serious breach of the present Convention. In particular, no prisoner of war may be subjected to physical mutilation or to medical or scientific experiments of any kind which are not justified by the medical, dental or hospital treatment of the prisoner concerned and carried out in his interest.

Likewise, prisoners of war must at all times be protected, particularly against acts of violence or intimidation and against insults and public curiosity.

PART IV—EXECUTION OF THE CONVENTION

SECTION I—GENERAL PROVISIONS

Article 127

The High Contracting Parties undertake, in time of peace as in time of war, to disseminate the text of the present Convention as widely as possible in their respective countries, and in particular, to include the study thereof in their programmes of military and, if possible, civil instruction, so that the principles thereof may become known to all their armed forces and to the entire populations.

Any military or other authorities, who in time of war assume responsibilities in respect of prisoners of war, must possess the text of the Convention and be specially instructed as to its provisions.

* * *

Article 129

The High Contracting Parties undertake to enact any legislation necessary to provide effective penal sanctions for person committing, or ordering to be committed, any of the grave breaches of the present Convention defined in the following Article.

Each High Contracting Party shall be under the obligation to search for persons alleged to have committed, or to have ordered to be committed, such grave breaches, and shall bring such persons, regardless of their nationality, before its own courts. It may also, if it prefers, and in accordance with the provisions of its own legislation, hand such persons over for trial to another High Contracting Party concerned, provided such High Contracting Party has made out a prima facie case.

Each High Contracting Party shall take measure necessary for the suppression of all acts contrary to the provisions of the present Convention other than grave breaches denied in the following Article.

* * *

Article 130

Grave breaches to which the preceding Article relates shall be those involving any of the following acts, if committed against person or property protected by the Convention: willful killing, torture or inhuman treatment, including biological experiments, willfully causing great suffering or serious injury to body or health compelling a prisoner of war to serve in the forces of the hostile Power, or willfully depriving a prisoner of the rights of fair and regular trial prescribed in this Convention.

Geneva Convention Relative to the Protection of Civilian Persons in Time of War of August 12, 1949

5 U.N.T.S. 287 (1950)

Articles 1–3 [See PW arts. 1–3, above]

Article 4

Persons protected by the Convention are those who, at a given moment, and in any manner whatsoever, find themselves, in case of a conflict or occupation, in the hands of a Party to the conflict or Occupying Power of which they are not nationals.

* * *

Article 27

Protected persons are entitled, in all circumstances, to respect for their persons, their honour, their family rights, their religious convictions and practices, and their manners and customs. They shall at all times be humanely treated, and shall be protected especially against all acts of violence or threats thereof and against insults and public curiosity.

Women shall be especially protected against any attack on their honour, in particular against rape, enforced prostitution, or any form of indecent assault.

Without prejudice to the provisions relating to their state of health, age and sex, all protected persons shall be treated with the same consideration by the Party to the conflict in whose power they are, without any adverse distinction based, in particular, on race, religion or political opinion.

However, the Parties to the conflict may take such measures of control and security in regard to protected persons as may be necessary as a result of the war.

Article 28

The presence of a protected person may not be used to render certain points or areas immune from military operations.

Article 29

The Party to the conflict in whose hands protected persons may be, is responsible for the treatment accorded to them by its agents, irrespective of any individual responsibility which may be incurred.

* * *

Article 31

No physical or moral coercion shall be exercised against protected persons, in particular to obtain information from them or from third parties.

Article 32

The High Contracting Parties specifically agree that each of them is prohibited from taking any measure of such character as to cause the physical suffering or extermination of protected persons in their hands. This prohibition applies not only to murder, torture, corporal punishment, mutilation and medical or scientific experiments not necessitated by the medical treatment of a protected person, but also to any other measures of brutality whether applied by civilian or military agents.

Article 33

No protected person may be punished for an offence he or she has not personally committed. Collective penalties and likewise all measures of intimidation or of terrorism are prohibited.

Pillage is prohibited.

* * *

SECTION III—OCCUPIED TERRITORIES

Article 49

Individual or mass forcible transfers, as well as deportations of protected persons from occupied territory to the territory of the Occupying Power or to that of any other country, occupied or not, are prohibited, regardless of their motive.

Nevertheless, the Occupying Power may undertake total or partial evacuation of a given area if the security of the population or imperative military reasons so demand. Such evacuations may not involve the displacement of protected persons outside the bounds of the occupied territory except when for material reasons it is impossible to avoid such displacement. Persons thus evacuated shall be transferred back to their homes as soon as hostilities in the area in question have ceased. * * *

The Occupying Power shall not detain protected persons in an area particularly exposed to the dangers of war unless the security of the population or imperative military reasons so demand.

The Occupying Power shall not deport or transfer parts of its own civilian population into the territory it occupies.

* * *

Article 53

Any destruction by the Occupying Power of real or personal property belonging individually or collectively to private persons, or to the State, or to other public authorities, or to social or cooperative organizations, is prohibited, except where such destruction is rendered absolutely necessary by military operations.

Article 54

The Occupying Power may not alter the status of public officials or judges in the occupied territories, or in any way apply sanctions to or take any measures of coercion or discrimination against them, should they abstain from fulfilling their functions for reasons of conscience.

This prohibition does not prejudice the application of the second paragraph of Article 51. It does not affect the right of the Occupying Power to remove public officials from their posts.

Article 55

To the fullest extent of the means available to it, the Occupying Power has the duty of ensuring the food and medical supplies of the population; it should, in particular, bring in the necessary foodstuffs, medical stores and other articles if the resources of the occupied territory are inadequate.

* * *

PART IV—EXECUTION OF THE CONVENTION

SECTION I—GENERAL PROVISIONS

* * *

Article 144
[See PW Art. 127 above.]

* * *

Article 146
[See PW Art. 129, above.]

Article 147

Grave breaches to which the preceding Article relates shall be those involving any of the following acts, if committed against persons or property protected by the present Convention: willful killing, torture or inhuman treatment, including biological experiments, willfully causing great suffering or serious injury to body or health, unlawful deportation or transfer or unlawful confinement of a protected person, compelling a protected person to serve in the forces of a hostile Power, or willfully depriving a protected person of the rights of fair and regular trial prescribed in the present Convention, taking of hostages and extensive destruction and appropriation of property, not justified by military necessity and carried out unlawfully and wantonly.

———————

The Biafran War in Nigeria (1967–70) and the Vietnam War (1958–1974), among others, motivated the ICRC to attempt to increase the protections of victims in armed conflict. Biafra cost between 2 and 3 million civilian lives, mostly from hunger and disease. Biafra demonstrated that parties needed to respect Common Article 3, but, also, that Common Article 3 plainly had gaps that needed filling. In Vietnam, the problem of guerilla fighters and the torture and abuse of American prisoners by the North Vietnamese were prominent issues. The ICRC wanted to signal to all warring parties that Common Article 3 was customary law and binding on them, whether or not they were parties to the Conventions. The ICRC began undertaking studies and engaging in consultations on supplementing the 1949 Conventions as early as the 1960s. By 1974 two draft protocols were ready for presentation to a diplomatic conference. What became Protocol I was designed to extend the protections of victims of international armed conflict. The other draft, eventually Protocol II, aimed at increasing the protections in noninternational armed conflicts. During the four years of negotiations, the delegates decided to include wars against colonial domination and alien occupation in Protocol I. This decision was criticized by a number of delegations, including the United States. And in the end, Protocol II emerged a simpler instrument than the ICRC originally planned—only 28 Articles. Nevertheless, those contained important additions as a supplement to Common Article 3.

Protocol II applies in only a narrower range of non-international armed conflict—arguably narrower than Article 3. According to Article 1(1), it applies when an armed conflict takes place

> [i]n the territory of a High Contracting Party between its armed forces and dissident armed forces or other organized armed groups which, under responsible command, exercise such control over a part of its territory as to enable them to carry out sustained and concerted military operations and to implement this Protocol.

Protocol II does not apply to "situations of international disturbances and tensions, such as riots, isolated and sporadic acts of violence and other acts of a similar nature." (AP II, Art. 1(2)) Despite Protocol II's narrow scope, states included Article 3(2) to provide further protection of domestic jurisdiction:

> Nothing in this Protocol shall be invoked as a justification for intervening, directly or indirectly, for any reason whatever, in the armed conflict or in the internal or external affairs of the High Contracting Party in the territory of which that conflict occurs.

Where Protocol II does apply, the provisions on humanitarian assistance enhance those of the Common Article 3. On December 12, 1977, the United States signed Additional Protocols I & II. During the Reagan Administration, the State Department did a thorough review of the Protocols and decided to submit APII to the Congress for advice and consent on the question of ratification. With respect to API, it decided that it would not submit it for advice and consent but rather declare certain provisions binding as customary international law. As of July 2004, the United States had not become party to either Protocol, but over 150 other states, including the United Kingdom, are parties.

1977 Geneva Protocol I Additional to the Geneva Conventions of 12 August 1949, and Relating to the Protection of Victims of International Armed Conflicts

1125 U.N.T.S. 3 (1979)

Article 75—Fundamental guarantees

1.   In so far as they are affected by a situation referred to in Article 1 of this Protocol, persons who are in the power of a Party to the conflict and who do not benefit from more favourable treatment under the Conventions or under this Protocol shall be treated humanely in all circumstances and shall enjoy, as a minimum, the protection provided by this Article without any adverse distinction based upon race, colour, sex, language, religion or belief, political or other opinion, national or social origin, wealth, birth or other status, or on any other similar criteria. Each Party shall respect the person, honour, convictions and religious practices of all such persons.

2.   The following acts are and shall remain prohibited at any time and in any place whatsoever, whether committed by civilian or by military agents:

(*a*) violence to the life, health, or physical or mental wellbeing of persons, in particular:

    (i) murder;

    (ii) torture of all kinds, whether physical or mental;

    (iii) corporal punishment; and

    (iv) mutilation;

(*b*) outrages upon personal dignity, in particular humiliating and degrading treatment, enforced prostitution and any form of indecent assault;

(*c*) the taking of hostages;

(*d*) collective punishments; and

(*e*) threats to commit any of the foregoing acts.

3.   Any person arrested, detained or interned for actions related to the armed conflict shall be informed promptly, in a language he understands, of

the reasons why these measures have been taken. Except in cases of arrest or detention for penal offences, such persons shall be released with the minimum delay possible and in any event as soon as the circumstances justifying the arrest, detention or internment have ceased to exist.

4. No sentence may be passed and no penalty may be executed on a person found guilty of a penal offence related to the armed conflict except pursuant to a conviction pronounced by an impartial and regularly constituted court respecting the generally recognized principles of regular judicial procedure * * *.

* * *

1998 Rome Statute of the International Court

UN Doc. A/CONF.183/9* (July 17, 1998)

Article 8—War crimes

1. The Court shall have jurisdiction in respect of war crimes in particular when committed as part of a plan or policy or as part of a large-scale commission of such crimes.

2. For the purpose of this Statute, "war crimes" means:

(*a*) Grave breaches of the Geneva Conventions of 12 August 1949, namely, any of the following acts against persons or property protected under the provisions of the relevant Geneva Convention:

(i) Wilful killing;

(ii) Torture or inhuman treatment, including biological experiments;

(iii) Wilfully causing great suffering, or serious injury to body or health;

(iv) Extensive destruction and appropriation of property, not justified by military necessity and carried out unlawfully and wantonly;

(v) Compelling a prisoner of war or other protected person to serve in the forces of a hostile Power;

(vi) Wilfully depriving a prisoner of war or other protected person of the rights of fair and regular trial;

(vii) Unlawful deportation or transfer or unlawful confinement;

(viii) Taking of hostages.

(*b*) Other serious violations of the laws and customs applicable in international armed conflict, within the established framework of international law, namely, any of the following acts:

(i) Intentionally directing attacks against the civilian population as such or against individual civilians not taking direct part in hostilities;

---

* Corrections issued Sept. 1998.

(ii) Intentionally directing attacks against civilian objects, that is, objects which are not military objectives;

(iii) Intentionally directing attacks against personnel, installations, material, units or vehicles involved in a humanitarian assistance or peacekeeping mission in accordance with the Charter of the United Nations, as long as they are entitled to the protection given to civilians or civilian objects under the international law of armed conflict;

(iv) Intentionally launching an attack in the knowledge that such attack will cause incidental loss of life or injury to civilians or damage to civilian objects or widespread, long-term and severe damage to the natural environment which would be clearly excessive in relation to the concrete and direct overall military advantage anticipated;

(v) Attacking or bombarding, by whatever means, towns, villages, dwellings or buildings which are undefended and which are not military objectives * * *.

3.   Enforcement of the *Jus in Bello*

Prisoners of War Ethiopia's Claim 4 (Part 3), (Partial Award)*

Eritrea Ethiopia Claims Commission (July 1, 2003)
www.pca-cpa.org

I.   INTRODUCTION

A.   Summary of the Positions of the Parties

1.   This Claim ("Ethiopia's Claim 4;" "ETO4") has been brought to the Commission by the Claimant, the Federal Democratic Republic of Ethiopia ("Ethiopia"), pursuant to Article 5 of the Agreement between the Government of the Federal Democratic Republic of Ethiopia and the Government of the State of Eritrea of December 12, 2000 ("the Agreement"). The Claim seeks a finding of the liability of the Respondent, the State of Eritrea ("Eritrea"), for loss, damage and injury suffered by the Claimant as a result of the Respondent's alleged unlawful treatment of its Prisoners of War ("POWs") who were nationals of the Claimant. In its Statement of Claim, the Claimant requested monetary compensation, and in its Memorial, it proposed that compensation be determined by a mass claims process based upon the five permanent camps in which those POWs were held.

2.   The Respondent asserts that it fully complied with international law in its treatment of POWs.

* * *

---

* Some footnotes omitted.

C. General Comment

12. As the findings in this Award and in the related Award in Eritrea's Claim 17 describe, there were significant difficulties in both Parties' performance of important legal obligations for the protection of prisoners of war. Nevertheless, the Commission must record an important preliminary point that provides essential context for what follows. Based on the extensive evidence adduced during these proceedings, the Commission believes that both Parties had a commitment to the most fundamental principles bearing on prisoners of war. Both parties conducted organized, official training programs to instruct their troops on procedures to be followed when POWs are taken. In contrast to many other contemporary armed conflicts, both Eritrea and Ethiopia regularly and consistently took POWs. Enemy personnel who were *hors de combat* were moved away from the battlefield to conditions of greater safety. Further, although these case involve two of the poorest countries in the world, both made significant efforts to provide for the sustenance and care of the POWs in their custody.

13. There were deficiencies of performance on both sides, sometimes significant, occasionally grave. Nevertheless, the evidence in these cases shows that both Eritrea and Ethiopia endeavored to observe their fundamental humanitarian obligations to collect and protect enemy soldiers unable to resist on the battlefield. The Awards in these cases, and the difficulties that they identify, must be read against this background.

* * *

2. Eritrea's Refusal to Permit the ICRC to Visit POWs

55. From the outset of the armed conflict in 1998, the ICRC was permitted by Ethiopia to visit the Eritrean POWs and the camps in which they were held. It was also permitted to provide relief to them and to assist them in corresponding with their families in Eritrea, although there is evidence that Eritrea refused to permit communications from those POWs to be passed on to their families. In Eritrea, the ICRC had a limited role in the 1998 repatriation of seventy sick or wounded POWs, but all efforts by the ICRC to visit the Ethiopian POWs held by Eritrea were refused by Eritrea until August 2000, just after Eritrea acceded to the 1949 Geneva Conventions. The Commission must decide whether, as alleged by Ethiopia, such refusal by Eritrea constituted a violation of its legal obligations under the applicable law.

56. Eritrea argues that the right of access by the ICRC to POWs is a treaty-based right and that the provisions of Geneva Convention III granting such access to the ICRC should not be considered provisions that express customary international law. While recognizing that most of the provisions of the Convention have become customary law, Eritrea asserts that the provisions dealing with the access of the ICRC are among the detailed or procedural provisions that have not attained such status.

57. That the ICRC did not agree with Eritrea is demonstrated by a press statement it issued on May 7, 1999, in which it recounted its visits to POWs and interned civilians held by Ethiopia and said: "In Eritrea,

meanwhile, the ICRC is pursuing its efforts to gain access, as required by the Third Geneva Convention, to Ethiopian POWs captured since the conflict erupted last year."

58.   The ICRC is assigned significant responsibilities in a number of articles of the Convention. These provisions make clear that the ICRC may function in at least two different capacities—as a humanitarian organization providing relief and as an organization providing necessary and vital external scrutiny of the treatment of POWs, either supplementary to a Protecting Power or as a substitute when there is no Protecting Power. There is no evidence before the Commission that Protecting Powers were proposed by either Ethiopia or Eritrea, and it seems evident that none was appointed. Nevertheless, the Convention clearly requires external scrutiny of the treatment of POWs and, in Article 10, where there is no Protecting Power or other functioning oversight body, it requires Detaining Powers to "accept . . . the offer of the services of a humanitarian organization, such as the International Committee of the Red Cross, to assume the humanitarian functions performed by Protecting Powers under the present Convention." In that event, Article 10 also provides that all mention of Protecting Powers in the Convention applies to such substitute organizations.

59.   The right of the ICRC to have access to POWs is not limited to a situation covered by Article 10 in which it serves as a substitute for a Protecting Power. Article 126 specifies clear and critical rights of Protecting Powers with respect to access to camps and to POWs, including the right to interview POWs without witnesses, and it states that the delegates of the ICRC "shall enjoy the same prerogatives." Ethiopia relies primarily on Article 126 in its allegation that Eritrea violated its legal obligations by refusing the ICRC access to its POWs.

60.   Professor Levie points out in his monumental study of the treatment of POWs in international armed conflicts that the ICRC "has played an indispensable humanitarian role in every armed conflict for more than a century."[28] He also notes that, in addition to the work by the many Protecting Powers, the ICRC played a vital role in protecting POWs during the Second World War, when it made a total of 11,175 visits to installations where POWs and civilian internees were confined. Levie also lists the places where the ICRC and protecting powers have been excluded in recent times—the Soviet Union (1940–45), North Korea and the Peoples Republic of China (1950–53), and North Vietnam (1965–73). It is common knowledge that the treatment of POWs by the named Parties in those four places where the ICRC was unlawfully excluded was far worse than that required by the standards of applicable law. The long term result of these exclusions has been a reinforcement of the general understanding of the crucial role played by outside observers in the effective functioning of the legal regime for the protection of POWs.

---

28.   Howard S. Levie, *Prisoners of War in International Armed Conflict, in* INTERNATIONAL LAW STUDIES, Volume 59, p. 312 (United States Naval War College Press 1978).

61. The Commission cannot agree with Eritrea's argument that provisions of the Convention requiring external scrutiny of the treatment of POWs and access to POWs by the ICRC are mere details or simply implementing procedural provisions that have not, in half a century, become part of customary international law. These provisions are an essential part of the regime for protecting POWs that has developed in international practice, as reflected in Geneva Convention III. These requirements are, indeed, "treaty-based" in the sense that they are articulated in the Convention; but, as such, they incorporate past practices that had standing of their own in customary law, and they are of such importance for the prospects of compliance with the law that it would be irresponsible for the Commission to consider them inapplicable as customary international law. As the International Court of Justice said in its Advisory Opinion on the Legality of the Threat or Use of Nuclear Weapons:

> 79. It is undoubtedly because a great many rules of humanitarian law applicable in armed conflict are so fundamental to the respect of the human person and "elementary considerations of humanity" as the Court put it in its Judgment of 9 April 1949 in the *Corfu Channel Case* (*I.C.J. Reports* 1949, p. 22), that the Hague and Geneva Conventions have enjoyed a broad accession. Further these fundamental rules are to be observed by all States whether or not they have ratified the conventions that contain them, because they constitute intransgressible principles of international customary law.

62. For the above reasons, the Commission holds that Eritrea violated customary international law from May 1998 until August 2000 by refusing to permit the ICRC to send its delegates to visit all places where Ethiopian POWs were detained, to register those POWs, to interview them without witnesses, and to provide them with the customary relief and services. Consequently, Eritrea is liable for the suffering caused by that refusal.

3. Mistreatment of POWs at Capture and its Immediate Aftermath

63. Of the thirty Ethiopian POW declarants, at least twenty were already wounded at capture and nearly all testified to treatment of the sick or wounded by Eritrean forces upon capture at the front and during evacuation. Consequently, in addition to the customary international law standards reflected in Geneva Convention III, the Commission also applies the standards reflected in the Geneva Convention for the Amelioration of the Condition of the Wounded and Sick in Armed Forces in the Field on August 12, 1949 ("Geneva Convention I"). For a wounded or sick POW, the provisions of Geneva Convention I apply along with Geneva Convention III. Among other provisions, Article 12 of Geneva Convention I demands respect and protection of wounded or sick members of the armed forces in "all circumstances."

64. A State's obligation to ensure humane treatment of enemy soldiers can be severely tested in the heated and confused moments immediately following capture or surrender and during evacuation from the battlefront to the rear. Nevertheless, customary international law as reflected in Geneva Conventions I and III absolutely prohibits the killing of

POWs, requires the wounded and sick to be collected and cared for, the dead to be collected, and demands prompt and humane evacuation of POWs.

a. Abusive Treatment

65. Ethiopia alleged that Eritrean troops regularly beat and frequently killed Ethiopians upon capture and its immediate aftermath. Ethiopia presented a *prima facie* case, through clear and convincing evidence, to support this allegation.

66. One-third of the Ethiopian POW declarations contain accounts of Eritrean soldiers deliberately killing Ethiopian POWs, most wounded, at capture or evacuation. Particularly troubling are accounts in three declarations of Eritrean officers ordering troops to kill Ethiopian POWs or beating them for not doing so. More than half of the Ethiopian POW declarants described repeated and brutal beatings, both at the front and during evacuation, including blows purposefully inflicted on wounds. Fortunately, these accounts were countered to a degree by several other accounts from Ethiopian declarants of Eritrean officers and soldiers intervening to curtail physical abuse and prevent killings.

67. In rebuttal, Eritrea offered detailed and persuasive evidence that Eritrean troops and officers had received extensive instruction during their basic training, both on the basic requirements of the Geneva Conventions on the taking of POWs and on the policies and practices of the Eritrean People's Liberation Front ("EPLF") in the war against the prior Ethiopian government, the Derg, for independence, which had emphasized the importance of humane treatment of prisoners. What is lacking in the record, however, is evidence of what steps Eritrea took, if any, to ensure that its forces actually put this extensive training to use in the field. There is no evidence that Eritrea conducted inquiries into incidents of physical abuse or pursued disciplinary measures under Article 121 of Geneva Convention III.

68. The Commission concludes that Eritrea has not rebutted the *prima facie* case presented by Ethiopia and, consequently, holds that Eritrea failed to comply with the fundamental obligation of customary international law that POWs, even when wounded, must be protected and may not, under any circumstances, be killed. Consequently, Eritrea is liable for failing to protect Ethiopian POWs from being killed at capture or its immediate aftermath, and for permitting beatings and other physical abuse of Ethiopian POWs at capture or its immediate aftermath.

b. Medical Care Immediately Following Capture

69. Ethiopia alleges that Eritrea failed to provide necessary medical attention to Ethiopian POWs after capture and during evacuation, as required under customary international law reflected in Geneva Conventions I (Article 12) and III (Articles 20 and 15). Many Ethiopian declarants testified that their wounds were not cleaned and bandaged at or shortly after capture, leading to infection and other complications. Eritrea present-

ed rebuttal evidence that its troops provided rudimentary first aid as soon as possible, including in transit camps.

70.   The Commission believes that the requirement to provide POWs with medical care during the initial period after capture must be assessed in light of the harsh conditions on the battlefield and the limited extent of medical training and equipment available to front line troops. On balance, and recognizing the logistical and resource limitations faced by both Parties to the conflict, the Commission finds that Eritrea is not liable for failing to provide medical care to Ethiopian POWs at the front and during evacuation.

c.   Evacuation Conditions

71.   Ethiopia also alleges that, in addition to poor medical care, Eritrea failed to ensure humane evacuation conditions. As reflected in Articles 19 and 20 of Geneva Convention III, the Detaining Power is obliged to evacuate prisoners humanely, safely and as soon as possible from combat zones; only if there is a greater risk in evacuation may the wounded or sick be temporarily kept in the combat zone, and they must not be unnecessarily exposed to danger. The measure of a humane evacuation is that, as set out in Article 20, POWs should be evacuated "in conditions similar to those for the forces of the Detaining Power."

72.   Turning first to the timing of evacuation, Eritrea submitted clear and convincing evidence that, given the reality of battle, the great majority of Ethiopians POWs were evacuated from the various fronts in a timely manner. Despite one disquieting incident in which a wounded Ethiopian POW allegedly was forced to spend a night on top of a trench while artillery exchanges occurred and his Eritrean captors took refuge in the trench, the Commission concludes that Eritrea generally took the necessary measures to evacuate its prisoners promptly.

73.   Timing aside, the Ethiopian POW declarants described extremely onerous conditions of evacuation. The POWs were forced to walk from the front for hours or days over rough terrain, often in pain from their own wounds, often carrying wounded comrades and Eritrean supplies, often in harsh weather, and often with little or no food and water. Eritrea offered rebuttal evidence that its soldiers faced nearly the same unavoidably difficult conditions, particularly given the lack of paved roads in Eritrea.

74.   Subject to the holding above concerning unlawful physical abuse during evacuation and with one exception, the Commission finds that Eritrean troops satisfied the legal requirements for evacuations from the battlefield under the harsh geographic, military and logistical circumstances. The exception is the Eritrean practice of seizing the footwear of all Ethiopian POWs, testified to by many declarants. Although the harshness of the terrain and weather on the marches to the camps may have been out of Eritrea's control, to force the POWs to walk barefoot in such conditions unnecessarily compounded their misery. The Commission finds Eritrea liable for inhumane treatment during evacuations from the battlefield as a

result of its forcing Ethiopian POWs to go without footwear during evacuation marches.

d. Coercive Interrogation

75. Ethiopia alleges frequent abuse in Eritrea's interrogation of POWs, commencing at capture and evacuation. International law does not prohibit the interrogation of POWs, but it does restrict the information they are obliged to reveal and prohibits torture or other measures of coercion, including threats and "unpleasant or disadvantageous treatment of any kind." [Article 17.]

76. Ethiopia presented clear and convincing evidence, unrebutted by Eritrea, that Eritrean interrogators frequently threatened or beat POWs during interrogation, particularly when they were dissatisfied with the prisoner's answers. The Commission must conclude that Eritrea either failed to train its interrogators in the relevant legal restraints or to make it clear that they are imperative. Consequently, Eritrea is liable for permitting such coercive interrogation.

* * *

4. Physical and Mental Abuse in POW Camps

81. Ethiopia's evidence of physical and mental abuse of Ethiopian POWs in Eritrean POW camps takes several forms. First, there was the testimony before the Commission of a former POW; second, Ethiopia filed with its Memorial forty signed declarations, including thirty by former POWs in which they described their treatment while captive; third, Ethiopia filed many unsigned statements and claims forms of former POWs; and fourth, Ethiopia filed data it had drawn from the claims forms of other former POWs. The Commission has relied heavily on the first two of these forms of evidence, as it considers the others of uncertain probative value for the proof of liability.

82. The testimony at the hearing of a former POW and the declarations of the other POWs are consistent and persuasive that the Eritrean guards at the various POW camps relied often upon brutal force for the enforcement of rules and as means of punishment. All thirty POW declarations described frequent beatings of POWs by camp guards. Several guards accused of regularly abusing POWs were identified by name in numerous declarations. The evidence indicates that many of the same guards remained in charge as the numbers of POWs increased and as they were moved from one camp to another, and the conclusion is unavoidable that guards who regularly beat POWs were not replaced as a result. Beatings with wooden sticks were common and, on occasion, resulted in broken bones and lack of consciousness. There were multiple, consistent accounts that, at Digdigta, several POWs who had attempted to escape were beaten senseless, with one losing an eye, prior to their disappearance. Being forced to hold heavy objects over one's head for long periods of time, being punched or kicked, being required to roll on stony or thorny ground, to look at the sun, and to undergo periods of confinement in hot metal containers were notable among the other abuses, all of which violated customary

international law, as exemplified by Articles 13, 42, 87 and 89 of Geneva Convention III. Regrettably, the evidence also indicates that the camp commanders did little to restrain these abuses and, in some cases, even threatened POWs by telling them that, as there was (prior to the first ICRC visits in August 2000) no list of prisoners, they could do anything they wanted to the POWs and could not be held accountable.

83.   In addition to the fear and mental anguish that accompanied these physical abuses, there is clear evidence that some POWs, particularly Tigrayans, were treated worse than others and that several POWs were treated as deserters and given favored treatment. (Those given favored treatment were not among those who signed the thirty declarations relied on by Ethiopia on this issue.) Such discrimination is, of course, prohibited by Article 16 of Geneva Convention III.

84.   The evidence is persuasive that beatings were common at all camps: Barentu, Embakala, Digdigta, Afabet and Nakfa. Solitary confinement of three months or more occurred at least at Digdigta and Afabet. At Nakfa, much of the evidence of beatings and other brutal punishments relates to POWs away from camp working on labor projects and occurred when fatigue slowed their work. After ICRC visits began, there is some evidence that POWs were threatened with physical punishment if they reported abuses to the ICRC.

85.   Eritrea introduced little, if any, evidence to counter Ethiopia's evidence of physical and mental abuse of POWs. Eritrea sought to undermine the credibility of Ethiopia's witnesses by pointing to some discrepancies in their declarations or testimony on medical and food issues. Eritrea also asserted that the allegations of physical abuse were not sufficiently specific to make it possible to investigate or rebut them. However, Eritrea chose not to introduce any witnesses from among its camp commanders, and it did not unequivocally deny that specific abuses, such as the beating of the attempted escapees at Digdigta, had occurred.

86.   In conclusion, the Commission holds that Eritrea violated international law from May 1998 until the last Ethiopian POWs were released and repatriated in August 2002 by permitting the pervasive and continuous physical and mental abuse of Ethiopian POWs in Eritrean POW camps. Consequently, Eritrea is liable for such abuse.

* * *

6.   Inadequate Medical Care in Camps

104.   A Detaining Power has the obligation to provide in its POW camps the medical assistance on which the POWs depend to heal their battle wounds and to prevent further damage to their health. This duty is particularly crucial in camps with a large population and a greater risk of transmission of contagious diseases. 105. The protections provided by Articles 15, 20, 29, 30, 31, 109 and 110 of Geneva Convention III are unconditional. These rules, which are based on similar rules in Articles 4, 13, 14, 15 and 68 of the Geneva Convention Relative to the Treatment of Prisoners of War of July 27, 1929, are part of customary international law.

106.   Many of these rules are broadly phrased and do not characterize precisely the quality or extent of medical care necessary for POWs. Article 15 speaks of the "medical attention *required* by their state of health;" Article 30 requires infirmaries to provide prisoners "the attention they *require*" (emphasis added). The lack of definition regarding the quality or extent of care "required" led to difficulties in assessing this claim. Indeed, standards of medical practice vary around the world, and there may be room for varying assessments of what is required in a specific situation. Moreover, the Commission is mindful that it is dealing here with two countries with very limited resources.

107.   Nevertheless, the Commission believes certain principles can be applied in assessing the medical care provided to POWs. The Commission began by considering Article 15's concept of the maintenance of POWs, which it understands to mean that a Detaining Power must do those things required to prevent significant deterioration of a prisoner's health. Next, the Commission paid particular attention to measures that are specifically required by Geneva Convention III, such as the requirements for segregation of prisoners with infectious diseases and for regular physical examinations.

* * *

c.   The Commission's Conclusions

116.   Overall, while the Commission is satisfied from the evidence that Eritrea made efforts to provide medical care and that some care was available at each permanent camp, Eritrea's evidence is inadequate to allow the Commission to form judgements regarding the extent or quality of health care sufficient to overcome Ethiopia's *prima facie* case.

117.   The camp clinic logs (where readable) do show that numerous POWs went to the clinics, but they cannot establish that care was appropriate or that all POWs in need of medical attention were treated in a timely manner over the full course of their captivity. For example, from the records it appears that the clinics did not register patients on a daily basis. Under international humanitarian law, a POW has the right to seek medical attention on his or her own initiative and to receive the continuous medical attention required by his or her state of health—which requires daily access to a clinic.

118.   International humanitarian law also requires that POWs be treated at a specialized hospital or facility when required medical care cannot be given in a camp clinic. The hospital records submitted by Eritrea, however, are not sufficient to establish that all POWs in need of specialized treatment were referred to hospitals. Moreover, a quantitative analysis of those records shows that, while a few relate to treatment in the first half of 1999 at Digdigta, nearly one half relate to the period from August to December 2000 and one quarter to 2001 and 2002, *i.e.*, the time period after Eritrea acceded to the Geneva Conventions and ICRC camp visits started. Only a few records relate to treatment between July 1999 and May

2000, when the POWs were detained at Afabet, and none relates to the time when Barentu and Embakala were open.

119. Likewise, the medicine supply reports submitted by Eritrea indicate that Eritrea distributed some drugs and vitamins to the POWs, but they do not prove that Eritrea provided adequate drugs to all POWs in the camps. It is striking that, according to the evidence submitted, Eritrea apparently distributed substantially more Vitamin A, B and C and multivitamins to POWs after August 2000 than before.

120. Preventive care is a matter of particular concern to the Commission. As evidenced by their prominence in Geneva Convention III, regular medical examinations of all POWs are vital to maintaining good health in a closed environment where diseases are easily spread. The Commission considers monthly examinations of the camp population to be a preventive measure forming part of the Detaining Power's obligations under international customary law.

121. The Commission must conclude that Eritrea failed to take several important preventative care measures specifically mandated by international law. In assessing this issue, the Commission looked not just to Ethiopia but also to Eritrea, which administered the camps and had the best knowledge of its own practices.

122. As noted, Ethiopia submitted several declarations indicating that no regular medical examinations took place. Eritrea failed to submit records in rebuttal demonstrating that personal POW medical data, including weight records, were maintained on a regular basis. It appears that health inspections were performed only in the last months of captivity.

123. The evidence also reflects that Eritrea failed to segregate certain infected prisoners. POWs are particularly susceptible to contagious diseases such as tuberculosis, and customary international law (reflecting proper basic health care) requires that infected POWs be isolated from the general POW population. Several Ethiopian POW declarants describe how tuberculosis patients were lodged with the other POWs, evidence which was not effectively rebutted by Eritrea. The camp authorities should have detected contagious diseases as early as possible and organized special wards.

124. Accordingly, the Commission holds that Eritrea violated international law from May 1998 until the last Ethiopian POWs were released and repatriated in August 2002, by failing to provide Ethiopian POWs with the required minimum standard of medical care. Consequently, Eritrea is liable for this violation of customary international law.

125. In closing, the Commission notes its recognition that Eritrea and Ethiopia cannot, at least at present, be required to have the same standards for medical treatment as developed countries. However, scarcity of finances and infrastructure cannot excuse a failure to grant the minimum standard of medical care required by international humanitarian law. The cost of such care is not, in any event, substantial in comparison with the other costs imposed by the armed conflict.

* * *

Prosecutor v. Stanislav Galić

International Criminal Tribunal for the former Yugoslavia
Case No. IT–98–29–T, Dec. 5, 2003

I. INTRODUCTION

1. Trial Chamber I of the International Tribunal (the "Trial Chamber") is seized of a case which concerns events surrounding the military encirclement of the city of Sarajevo in 1992 by Bosnian Serb forces.

2. The Prosecution alleges that "The siege of Sarajevo, as it came to be popularly known, was an episode of such notoriety in the conflict in the former Yugoslavia that one must go back to World War II to find a parallel in European history. Not since then had a professional army conducted a campaign of unrelenting violence against the inhabitants of a European city so as to reduce them to a state of medieval deprivation in which they were in constant fear of death. In the period covered in this Indictment, there was nowhere safe for a Sarajevan, not at home, at school, in a hospital, from deliberate attack".

3. In the course of the three and a half years of the armed conflict in and around Sarajevo, three officers commanded the unit of the Bosnian–Serb Army ("VRS") operating in the area of Sarajevo, the Sarajevo Romanija Corps ("SRK"). The second of those three officers, Major–General Stanislav Galić, is the accused in this case ("the Accused"). He was the commander for the longest period, almost two years, from around 10 September 1992 to 10 August 1994. The Prosecution alleges that over this period he conducted a protracted campaign of sniping and shelling against civilians in Sarajevo. Two schedules to the Indictment "set forth a small representative number of individual incidents for specificity of pleading". At the end of the Prosecution case and pursuant to Rule 98 *bis* of the Rules of Procedure and Evidence of the International Tribunal, the Trial Chamber decided upon the Defence Motion for Acquittal that the Prosecution had failed to prove some of these scheduled sniping incidents.

4. The Prosecution alleges that General Galić incurs individual criminal responsibility under Articles 7(1) and 7(3) of the Statute for his acts and omissions in relation to the crime of terror (count 1), attacks on civilians (counts 4 and 7), murder (counts 2 and 5) and inhumane acts (counts 3 and 6) committed against civilians in the city of Sarajevo.

* * *

(ii) Discussion

41. Although the Indictment refers in general terms to Article 51 of Additional Protocol I, the Trial Chamber understands the first sentence of the second paragraph of that article to be the legal basis of the charges of attack on civilians in Counts 4 and 7. This sentence will hereinafter be referred to as "the first part" of the second paragraph of Article 51 of Additional Protocol I, or simply as the "first part of Article 51(2)".

42. The constitutive elements of the offence of attack on civilians have not yet been the subject of a definitive statement by the Appeals

Chamber. In only two cases before the Tribunal have persons been charged and tried of attack on civilians under Article 3 of the Statute pursuant to Article 51(2) of Additional Protocol I. In each case a brief exposition was given of the offence, together with the offence of attacks on civilian property. In the *Blašić* case the Trial Chamber observed in relation to the *actus reus* that "the attack must have caused deaths and/or serious bodily injury within the civilian population or damage to civilian property. [. . .] Targeting civilians or civilian property is an offence when not justified by military necessity." On the *mens rea* it found that "such an attack must have been conducted intentionally in the knowledge, or when it was impossible not to know, that civilians or civilian property were being targeted not through military necessity". The Trial Chamber in the *Kordić* and *Cerkez* case held that "prohibited attacks are those launched deliberately against civilians or civilian objects in the course of an armed conflict and are not justified by military necessity. They must have caused deaths and/or serious bodily injuries within the civilian population or extensive damage to civilian objects".

43.   The Trial Chamber follows the above-mentioned jurisprudence to the extent that it states that an attack which causes death or serious bodily injury within the civilian population constitutes an offence. As noted above, such an attack when committed wilfully is punishable as a grave breach of Additional Protocol I. The question remains whether attacks resulting in non-serious civilian casualties, or in no casualties at all, may also entail the individual criminal responsibility of the perpetrator under the type of charge considered here, and thus fall within the jurisdiction of the Tribunal, even though they do not amount to grave breaches of Additional Protocol I. The present Indictment refers only to killing and wounding of civilians; therefore the Trial Chamber does not deem it necessary to express its opinion on that question.

44.   The Trial Chamber does not however subscribe to the view that the prohibited conduct set out in the first part of Article 51(2) of Additional Protocol I is adequately described as "targeting civilians when not justified by military necessity". This provision states in clear language that civilians and the civilian population as such should not be the object of attack. It does not mention any exceptions. In particular, it does not contemplate derogating from this rule by invoking military necessity.

45.   The Trial Chamber recalls that the provision in question explicitly confirms the customary rule that civilians must enjoy general protection against the danger arising from hostilities. The prohibition against attacking civilians stems from a fundamental principle of international humanitarian law, the principle of distinction, which obliges warring parties to distinguish *at all times* between the civilian population and combatants and between civilian objects and military objectives and accordingly to direct their operations only against military objectives. In its Advisory Opinion on the Legality of Nuclear Weapons, the International Court of Justice described the principle of distinction, along with the principle of protection of the civilian population, as "the cardinal principles contained in the texts

constituting the fabric of humanitarian law" and stated that "States must never make civilians the object of attack [. . .]."

46.   Part IV of Additional Protocol I, entitled "Civilian Population" (articles 48 to 58), develops and augments earlier legal protections afforded to civilians through specific rules aimed at guiding belligerents to respect and protect the civilian population and individual civilians during the conduct of hostilities. The general prohibition mentioned above forms [an] integral part of and is complemented and reinforced by this set of rules. In order to properly define the conduct outlawed in the first part of Article 51 (2) of Additional Protocol I, this rule must be interpreted in light of the ordinary meaning of the terms of Additional Protocol I, as well as of its spirit and purpose.

47.   As already stated, the first part of Article 51(2) of Additional Protocol I proscribes making the civilian population as such, or individual civilians, the object of attack. According to Article 50 of Additional Protocol I, "a civilian is any person who does not belong to one of the categories of persons referred to in Article 4(A)(1), (2), (3) and (6) of the Third Geneva Convention and in Article 43 of Additional Protocol I." For the purpose of the protection of victims of armed conflict, the term "civilian" is defined negatively as anyone who is not a member of the armed forces or of an organized military group belonging to a party to the conflict. It is a matter of evidence in each particular case to determine whether an individual has the status of civilian.

48.   The protection from attack afforded to individual civilians by Article 51 of Additional Protocol I is suspended when and for such time as they directly participate in hostilities. To take a "direct" part in the hostilities means acts of war which by their nature or purpose are likely to cause actual harm to the personnel or matériel of the enemy armed forces. As the *Kupreskić* Trial Chamber explained:

> the protection of civilian and civilian objects provided by modern international law may cease entirely or be reduced or suspended [. . .] if a group of civilians takes up arms [. . .] and engages in fighting against the enemy belligerent, they may be legitimately attacked by the enemy belligerent whether or not they meet the requirements laid down in Article 4(A)(2) of the Third Geneva Convention of 1949.

Combatants and other individuals directly engaged in hostilities are considered to be legitimate military targets.

49.   The civilian population comprises all persons who are civilians, as defined above. The use of the expression "civilian population *as such*" in Article 51(2) of Additional Protocol I indicates that "the population must never be used as a target or as a tactical objective".

50.   The presence of individual combatants within the population does not change its civilian character. In order to promote the protection of civilians, combatants are under the obligation to distinguish themselves at all times from the civilian population; the generally accepted practice is

that they do so by wearing uniforms, or at least a distinctive sign, and by carrying their weapons openly. In certain situations it may be difficult to ascertain the status of particular persons in the population. The clothing, activity, age, or sex of a person are among the factors which may be considered in deciding whether he or she is a civilian. A person shall be considered to be a civilian for as long as there is a doubt as to his or her real status. The Commentary to Additional Protocol I explains that the presumption of civilian status concerns "persons who have not committed hostile acts, but whose status seems doubtful because of the circumstances. They should be considered to be civilians until further information is available, and should therefore not be attacked". The Trial Chamber understands that a person shall not be made the object of attack when it is not reasonable to believe, in the circumstances of the person contemplating the attack, including the information available to the latter, that the potential target is a combatant.

51.   As mentioned above, in accordance with the principles of distinction and protection of the civilian population, only military objectives may be lawfully attacked. A widely accepted definition of military objectives is given by Article 52 of Additional Protocol I as "those objects which by their nature, location, purpose or use make an effective contribution to military action and whose total or partial destruction, capture or neutralization, in the circumstances ruling at the time, offers a definite military advantage". In case of doubt as to whether an object which is normally dedicated to civilian purposes is being used to make an effective contribution to military action, it shall be presumed not to be so used. The Trial Chamber understands that such an object shall not be attacked when it is not reasonable to believe, in the circumstances of the person contemplating the attack, including the information available to the latter, that the object is being used to make an effective contribution to military action.

52.   "Attack" is defined in Article 49 of Additional Protocol I as "acts of violence against the adversary, whether in offence or in defence." The Commentary makes the point that "attack" is a technical term relating to a specific military operation limited in time and place, and covers attacks carried out both in offence and in defence. The jurisprudence of the Tribunal has defined "attack" as a course of conduct involving the commission of acts of violence. In order to be punishable under Article 3 of the [ICTY] Statute, these acts have to be carried out during the course of an armed conflict.

53.   In light of the discussion above, the Trial Chamber holds that the prohibited conduct set out in the first part of Article 51(2) is to direct an attack (as defined in Article 49 of Additional Protocol I) against the civilian population and against individual civilians not taking part in hostilities.

54.   The Trial Chamber will now consider the mental element of the offence of attack on civilians, when it results in death or serious injury to body or health. Article 85 of Additional Protocol I explains the intent required for the application of the first part of Article 51(2). It expressly qualifies as a grave breach the act of *wilfully* "making the civilian popula-

tion or individual civilians the object of attack''. The Commentary to Article 85 of Additional Protocol I explains the term as follows:

> *wilfully*: the accused must have acted consciously and with intent, i.e., with his mind on the act and its consequences, and willing them (''criminal intent'' or ''malice aforethought''); this encompasses the concepts of ''wrongful intent'' or ''recklessness'', viz., the attitude of an agent who, without being certain of a particular result, accepts the possibility of it happening; on the other hand, ordinary negligence or lack of foresight is not covered, i.e., when a man acts without having his mind on the act or its consequences.

The Trial Chamber accepts this explanation, according to which the notion of ''wilfully'' incorporates the concept of recklessness, whilst excluding mere negligence. The perpetrator who recklessly attacks civilians acts ''wilfully''.

55. For the *mens rea* recognized by Additional Protocol I to be proven, the Prosecution must show that the perpetrator was aware or should have been aware of the civilian status of the persons attacked. In case of doubt as to the status of a person, that person shall be considered to be a civilian. However, in such cases, the Prosecution must show that in the given circumstances a reasonable person could not have believed that the individual he or she attacked was a combatant.

56. In sum, the Trial Chamber finds that the crime of attack on civilians is constituted of the elements common to offences falling under Article 3 of the Statute, as well as of the following specific elements:

> 1. Acts of violence directed against the civilian population or individual civilians not taking direct part in hostilities causing death or serious injury to body or health within the civilian population.

> 2. The offender wilfully made the civilian population or individual civilians not taking direct part in hostilities the object of those acts of violence.

57. As regards the first element, the Trial Chamber agrees with previous Trial Chambers that indiscriminate attacks, that is to say, attacks which strike civilians or civilian objects and military objectives without distinction, may qualify as direct attacks against civilians. It notes that indiscriminate attacks are expressly prohibited by Additional Protocol I. This prohibition reflects a well-established rule of customary law applicable in all armed conflicts.

58. One type of indiscriminate attack violated the principle of proportionality. The practical application of the principle of distinction requires that those who plan or launch an attack take all feasible precautions to verify that the objectives attacked are neither civilians nor civilian objects, so as to spare civilians as much as possible. Once the military character of a target has been ascertained, commanders must consider whether striking this target is ''expected to cause incidental loss of life, injury to civilians, damage to civilian objectives or a combination thereof, which would be

excessive in relation to the concrete and direct military advantage anticipated.'' If such casualties are expected to result, the attack should not be
pursued. The basic obligation to spare civilians and civilian objects as much
as possible must guide the attacking party when considering the proportionality of an attack. In determining whether an attack was proportionate
it is necessary to examine whether a reasonably well-informed person in
the circumstances of the actual perpetrator, making reasonable use of the
information available to him or her, could have expected excessive civilian
casualties to result from the attack.

59.   To establish the *mens rea* of a disproportionate attack the Prosecution must prove, instead of the above-mentioned *mens rea* requirement,
that the attack was launched wilfully and in knowledge of circumstances
giving rise to the expectation of excessive civilian casualties.

60.   The Trial Chamber considers that certain apparently disproportionate attacks may give rise to the inference that civilians were actually
the object of attack. This is to be determined on a case-by-case basis in light
of the available evidence.

61.   As suggested by the Defence, the parties to a conflict are under an
obligation to remove civilians, to the maximum extent feasible from the
vicinity of military objectives and to avoid locating military objectives
within or near densely populated areas. However, the failure of a party to
abide by this obligation does not relieve the attacking side of its duty to
abide by the principles of distinction and proportionality when launching
an attack.

(f) Conclusion

62.   The Trial Chamber finds that an attack on civilian[s] can be
brought under Article 3 by virtue of customary international law and, in
the instant case, also by virtue of conventional law and is constituted of
acts of violence willfully directed against the civilian population or individual civilians not taking direct part in hostilities causing death or serious
injury to body or health within the civilian population.

* * *

The next two excerpts concern the lawful conditions of detention. The
first focuses on consequences for the detaining power when conditions do
not meet the international legal standard. The second excerpt concerns
consequences for an individual found guilty of abusing combatant detainees. Between May 1998 and June 2000, Eritrea and Ethiopia fought a bitter
and costly war over their mutual boundary that left tens of thousands dead.
As part of the peace agreement, in addition to agreeing to settle the
boundary dispute, the two states agreed to establish a commission to settle
claims growing out of the conduct of the war.

Hamdan v. Rumsfeld*

Supreme Court of the United States
548 U.S. 557, 126 S.Ct. 2749, 165 L.Ed.2d 723 (2006)

■ JUSTICE STEVENS announced the judgment of the Court and delivered the opinion of the Court [and an opinion with respect to Parts V and VI–D–iv, in which JUSTICES SOUTER, GINSBURG, and BREYER joined.]

Petitioner Salim Ahmed Hamdan, a Yemeni national, is in custody at an American prison in Guantánamo Bay, Cuba. In November 2001, during hostilities between the United States and the Taliban (which then governed Afghanistan), Hamdan was captured by militia forces and turned over to the U.S. military. In June 2002, he was transported to Guantánamo Bay. Over a year later, the President deemed him eligible for trial by military commission for then-unspecified crimes. After another year had passed, Hamdan was charged with one count of conspiracy "to commit . . . offenses triable by military commission." Hamdan [petitioned] for [a] writ of habeas corpus. [We] conclude that the military commission convened to try Hamdan lacks power to proceed because its structure and procedures violate both the Uniform Code of Military Justice (UCMJ) and the Geneva Conventions.

* * *

IV.

The military commission, a tribunal neither mentioned in the Constitution nor created by statute, was born of military necessity, [foreshadowed] by earlier tribunals like the Board of General Officers that General Washington convened to try British Major John Andre for spying during the Revolutionary War. [Exigency] alone, of course, will not justify the establishment and use of penal tribunals not contemplated by Article I, § 8 and Article III, § 1 of the Constitution unless some other part of that document authorizes a response to the felt need. And that authority, if it exists, can derive only from the powers granted jointly to the President and Congress in time of war. The Constitution makes the President the "Commander in Chief" of the Armed Forces, Art. II, § 2, cl. 1, but vests in Congress the powers to "declare War . . . and make Rules concerning Captures on Land and Water," Art. I, § 8, cl. 11, to "raise and support Armies," cl. 12, to "define and punish . . . Offences against the Law of Nations," cl. 10, and "To make Rules for the Government and Regulation of the land and naval Forces," cl. 14. [Whether] the President may constitutionally convene military commissions "without the sanction of Congress" in cases of "controlling necessity" is a question this Court has not answered definitively, and need not answer today. For we held in Quirin that Congress had, through Article of War 15 [adopted in 1916], sanctioned the use of military commissions in such circumstances. Article 21 of the UCMJ, the language of which is substantially identical to the old

---

* Excerpted from KATHLEEN M. SULLIVAN and GERALD GUNTHER, CONSTITUTIONAL LAW 282–89 (16th ed. 2007).

Article 15, [was] preserved by Congress after World War II. [But] even Quirin did not view the authorization as a sweeping mandate for the President to "invoke military commissions when he deems them necessary." Rather, [Quirin] recognized that Congress had simply preserved what power, under the Constitution and the common law of war, the President had had before 1916 to convene military commissions—with the express condition that the President and those under his command comply with the law of war.

The Government would have us [find] in either the AUMF or the DTA specific, overriding authorization for the very commission that has been convened to try Hamdan. Neither of these congressional Acts, however, expands the President's authority to convene military commissions. First, while we assume that the AUMF activated the President's war powers, and that those powers include the authority to convene military commissions in appropriate circumstances, there is nothing in the text or legislative history of the AUMF even hinting that Congress intended to expand or alter the authorization set forth in Article 21 of the UCMJ. [Although] the DTA, unlike either Article 21 or the AUMF, was enacted after the President had convened Hamdan's commission, it contains no language authorizing that tribunal or any other at Guantánamo Bay. [Together,] the UCMJ, the AUMF, and the DTA at most acknowledge a general Presidential authority to convene military commissions in circumstances where justified under the "Constitution and laws," including the law of war.

V.

The common law governing military commissions may be gleaned from past practice and what sparse legal precedent exists. Commissions historically have been used in three situations. First, they have substituted for civilian courts at times and in places where martial law has been declared. [Second,] commissions have been established to try civilians "as part of a temporary military government over occupied enemy territory or territory regained from an enemy where civilian government cannot and does not function." The third type of commission, convened as an "incident to the conduct of war" when there is a need "to seize and subject to disciplinary measures those enemies who in their attempt to thwart or impede our military effort have violated the law of war," [serves to] determine, typically on the battlefield itself, whether the defendant has violated the law of war. The last time the U.S. Armed Forces used the law-of-war military commission was during World War II. In Quirin, this Court sanctioned President Roosevelt's use of such a tribunal to try Nazi saboteurs captured on American soil during the War. [Since] Guantánamo Bay is neither enemy-occupied territory nor under martial law, the law-of-war commission is the only model available. [The] charge against Hamdan [alleges] a conspiracy extending over a number of years, from 1996 to November 2001. [This offense] is not triable by law-of-war military commission. There is no suggestion that Congress has, in exercise of its constitutional authority to "define and punish ... Offences against the Law of Nations," U.S. Const., Art. I, § 8, cl. 10, positively identified "conspiracy" as a war crime. [While] Congress, through Article 21 of the UCMJ, has "incorporated by reference" the common law of war, which may render triable by military commission certain offenses not defined by statute, [the] precedent must be plain and unambiguous, [and that] burden is far from satisfied here. The crime of "conspiracy" has rarely if ever been tried as such in this country by any law-of-war military commission not exercising some other form of jurisdiction, and does not appear in either the Geneva Conventions or the Hague Conventions—the major treaties on the law of war. [Finally,] international sources confirm that the crime charged here is not a recognized violation of the law of war. [None] of the major treaties governing the law of war identifies conspiracy as a violation thereof. [The] International Military Tribunal at Nuremberg, over the prosecution's objections, pointedly refused to recognize as a violation of the law of war conspiracy to commit war crimes.

[Because] the charge does not support the commission's jurisdiction, the commission lacks authority to try Hamdan. [Hamdan] is charged not with an overt act for which he was caught redhanded in a theater of war and which military efficiency demands be tried expeditiously, but with an *agreement* the inception of which long predated the attacks of September 11, 2001 and the AUMF. That may well be a crime [prosecutable by court-martial or in federal court] but it is not an offense that "by the law of war may be tried by military commission."

* * *

VI.

Whether or not the Government has charged Hamdan with an offense against the law of war cognizable by military commission, the commission lacks power to proceed. The UCMJ conditions the President's use of military commissions on compliance not only with the American common law of war, but also with the rest of the UCMJ itself [and] with the "rules and precepts of the law of nations," including, inter alia, the four Geneva Conventions signed in 1949. The procedures that the Government has decreed will govern Hamdan's trial by commission violate these laws.

A.   [Every commission] must have a presiding officer and at least three other members, all of whom must be commissioned officers. [The] accused is entitled to appointed military counsel and may hire civilian counsel at his own expense. [The] accused also is entitled to a copy of the charge(s) against him, both in English and his own language (if different), to a presumption of innocence, and to certain other rights typically afforded criminal defendants in civilian courts and courts-martial. These rights are subject, however, to one glaring condition: The accused and his civilian counsel may be excluded from, and precluded from ever learning what evidence was presented during, any part of the proceeding that either the Appointing Authority or the presiding officer decides to "close." [The rules also] permit the admission of any evidence that, in the opinion of the presiding officer, "would have probative value to a reasonable person." Under this test, not only is testimonial hearsay and evidence obtained through coercion fully admissible, but neither live testimony nor witnesses' written statements need be sworn.

B.   [Hamdan objects] that the procedures' admitted deviation from those governing courts-martial itself renders the commission illegal, [that] he may [be] convicted based on evidence he has not seen or heard, and that any evidence admitted against him need not comply with the admissibility or relevance rules typically applicable in criminal trials and court-martial proceedings.

C.   [Article 36] of the UCMJ [provides that] the rules applied to military commissions must be the same as those applied to courts-martial unless such uniformity proves impracticable. [Nothing] in the record before us demonstrates that it would be impracticable to apply court-martial rules in this case. [The] only reason offered [is] the danger posed by international terrorism. Without for one moment underestimating that danger, it is not evident to us why it should require, in the case of Hamdan's trial, any variance from the rules that govern courts-martial. The absence of any showing of impracticability is particularly disturbing when considered in light of the clear and admitted failure to apply one of the most fundamental protections afforded not just by the Manual for Courts–Martial but also by the UCMJ itself: the right to be present. [Under] the circumstances, then, the rules applicable in courts-martial must apply.

* * *

D.   The procedures adopted to try Hamdan also violate the Geneva Conventions.

* * *

i.   The Court of Appeals [held] that "the 1949 Geneva Convention does not confer upon Hamdan a right to enforce its provisions in court." * * * For regardless of the nature of the rights conferred on Hamdan, they are * * * part of the law of war. And compliance with the law of war is the condition upon which the authority set forth in Article 21 is granted.

* * *

ii.   * * * The Court of Appeals [also] reasoned that the war with al Qaeda evades the reach of the Geneva Conventions. We [disagree.] [Although] al Qaeda, unlike Afghanistan, is not [a] signatory of the Conventions, there is at least one provision of the Geneva Conventions that applies here even if the relevant conflict is not one between signatories. Article 3 [provides] that in a "conflict not of an international character occurring in the territory of one of the [signatories], each Party to the conflict shall be bound to apply, as a minimum," certain provisions [including one that] prohibits "the passing of sentences and the carrying out of executions [upon detainees] without previous judgment pronounced by a regularly constituted court affording all the judicial guarantees which are recognized as indispensable by civilized peoples."

* * *

iii.   Common Article 3, then, is applicable here and [requires] that Hamdan be tried by a "regularly constituted court." ["The] regular military courts in our system are the courts-martial established by congressional statutes." At a minimum, a military commission "can be 'regularly constituted' by the standards of our military justice system only if some practical need explains deviations from court-martial practice." [No] such need has been demonstrated here.

* * *

iv.   * * * "The judicial guarantees which are recognized as indispensable by civilized peoples" [must] be understood to incorporate at least the barest of those trial protections that have been recognized by customary international law. Many of these are described in Article 75 of Protocol I to the Geneva Conventions of 1949, adopted in 1977. [Among] the rights set forth in Article 75 is the "right to be tried in [one's] presence." [The military commission procedures] dispense with the principles, articulated in Article 75 and indisputably part of the customary international law, that an accused must, absent disruptive conduct or consent, be present for his trial and must be privy to the evidence against him.

* * *

v.   [Common Article 3] obviously tolerates a great degree of flexibility in trying individuals captured during armed conflict; its requirements are general ones, crafted to accommodate a wide variety of legal systems. But requirements they are nonetheless. The commission that the President has convened to try Hamdan does not meet those requirements.

* * *

VII.

* * *

* * * It bears emphasizing that Hamdan does not challenge, and we do not today address, the Government's power to detain him for the duration of active hostilities in order to prevent such harm. But in undertaking to try Hamdan and subject him to criminal punishment, the Executive is bound to comply with the Rule of Law that prevails in this jurisdiction. * * *

* * *

Boumediene v. Bush

United States Supreme Court
553 U.S. ___, 128 S.Ct. 2229, 171 L.Ed.2d 41 (2008)

■ JUSTICE KENNEDY delivered the opinion of the Court.

Petitioners are aliens designated as enemy combatants and detained at the United States Naval Station at Guantánamo Bay, Cuba. There are others detained there, also aliens, who are not parties to this suit.

Petitioners present a question not resolved by our earlier cases relating to the detention of aliens at Guantánamo: whether they have the constitutional privilege of habeas corpus, a privilege not to be withdrawn except in conformance with the Suspension Clause, Art. I, 9, cl. 2. ["The Privilege of the Writ of Habeas Corpus shall not be suspended, unless when in Cases of Rebellion or Invasion the public safety may require it."] We hold these petitioners do have the habeas corpus privilege. Congress has enacted a statute, the Detainee Treatment Act of 2005 (DTA), 119 Stat. 2739, that provides certain procedures for review of the detainees' status. We hold that those procedures are not an adequate and effective substitute for habeas corpus. Therefore § 7 of the Military Commissions Act of 2006(MCA), 28 U.S.C.A. 2241(e) (Supp.2007), operates as an unconstitutional suspension of the writ. We do not address whether the President has authority to detain these petitioners nor do we hold that the writ must issue. These and other questions regarding the legality of the detention are to be resolved in the first instance by the District Court.

* * *

We hold that Art. I, 9, cl. 2, of the Constitution has full effect at Guantánamo Bay. If the privilege of habeas corpus is to be denied to the detainees now before us, Congress must act in accordance with the requirements of the Suspension Clause. Cf. Hamdi, (SCALIA, J., dissenting) ("[I]ndefinite imprisonment on reasonable suspicion is not an available option of treatment for those accused of aiding the enemy, absent a suspension of the writ"). This Court may not impose a *de facto* suspension by abstaining from these controversies. See Hamdan, ("[A]bstention is not appropriate in cases . . . in which the legal challenge 'turn[s] on the status of the persons as to whom the military asserted its power'") (quoting Schlesinger v. Councilman,). The MCA does not purport to be a formal suspension of the writ; and the Government, in its submissions to us, has not argued that it is. Petitioners, therefore, are entitled to the privilege of habeas corpus to challenge the legality of their detention.

[Concurring and dissenting opinions omitted]

NOTES AND QUESTIONS

1.   The International Committee of the Red Cross undertook an extensive study of the rules of customary international law that have emerged since the adoption of the 1949 Conventions. The results may be found in I & II JEAN-MARIE HENCKAERTS AND LOUISE DOSWALD-BECK, CUSTOMARY INTERNATIONAL HUMANITARIAN LAW (2005). The customary international law rules respecting weapons are included in the next section.

2.   Throughout the materials in this section you have seen reference to four fundamental rules governing the conduct of conflict: distinction, necessity, proportionality, and humanity. Can you argue for and against the proposition that they are *jus cogens* norms? Have you encountered other rules or principles in this chapter that are *jus cogens*?

3.   In the Ethiopia–Eritrea Prisoner of War claims, the Commission notes that Eritrea and Ethiopia cannot be held to the same standard as developed countries for medical treatment. They can be held to a minimum standard. What does this mean for IHL? Are the United States, Britain, and other developed states expected to provide a higher level of medical treatment of POWs or is it also only required to provide the same minimum as Ethiopia and Eritrea? What about other areas of the *jus in bello*? If a state can afford to use high-tech weapons that strike targets "surgically" causing fewer casualties to civilians, must the state purchase and use such a weapons? Is it held to a different proportionality standard than poorer states?

4.   *When does armed conflict end?* Upon the cessation of hostilities, prisoners-of-war must be released or charged with a crime and tried before a regular court. In the Ethiopia–Eritrea conflict, the hostilities presumably ended when there was an effective cease-fire in June 2002. A peace settlement system was only agreed to, however, in December 2002. When will the hostilities end for the detainees at Guantánamo Bay? In early 2009, President Obama announced the prison at Guantánamo Bay would be closed. Many detainees there would be released from U.S. custody, but the President foresees holding some indefinitely without trial. Does the U.S. have the right to do so? See *Executive Order–Review and Disposition of Individuals Detained at the Guantánamo Bay Naval Base and Closure of the Facility*, Jan. 25, 2009.

5.   For further reading on the law governing conduct of armed conflict, see, THE HANDBOOK OF HUMANITARIAN LAW IN ARMED CONFLICT (Dieter Fleck 2d ed., 2007); A.P.V. ROGERS, LAW ON THE BATTLEFIELD (2d ed. 2004); REFLECTIONS ON LAW AND ARMED CONFLICTS: THE SELECTED WORKS ON THE LAWS OF WAR BY THE LATE PROFESSOR COLONEL G.I.A. D. DRAPER, OBE (Michael A. Meyer & Hilaire McCoubrey eds., 1998).

C.   WEAPONS RESTRICTIONS

How weapons are used and against who was very much part of the discussion of the fundamental principles of the *jus in bello*—particularly the principles of humanity and distinction. We find the origins in today's international law on weapons in such agreements as the 1868 St. Petersburg Declaration banning explosive projectiles. The 1907 Hague Regulations, annexed to Hague Convention IV of 1907, contain certain provisions relevant to weapons, such as the ban on poison and weapons causing unnecessary suffering. (Article 23) The Regulations also caution that "the means of injuring the enemy is not unlimited." (Article 22) After the First World War, states declared the use of "asphyxiating and other gasses" prohibited. Attempts were also made to regulate weapons, notably at the 1922 Washington Naval Conference to limit arsenals of ships and submarines and in the 1923 Hague Rules of Air Warfare. The Air Rules were never adopted. After the Second World War, states and organizations renewed efforts toward the control of some weapons and the outright prohibition of others. These efforts took the form of a series of treaties devoted to specific types of weapons. This section introduces six important treaties containing outright bans on weapons in the two traditional categories: weapons of mass destruction (WMD) and conventional weapons. It also considers throughout important customary international law rules and general principles. For more on the law regulating the means and methods of war, *see*, Stefan Oeter, *Methods and Means of Combat, in* THE HANDBOOK OF INTERNATIONAL HUMANITARIAN LAW 119 (Dieter Fleck ed., 2008).

1.   WEAPONS OF MASS DESTRUCTION

The United States Department of Defense defines weapons of mass destruction (WMDs) as "weapons that are capable of a high order of destruction and/or of being used in such a manner as to destroy large numbers of people." Nuclear weapons are the ultimate WMD. The destructive power and lasting devastation has led to determined effort to prevent their ever being used again. The Nuclear Non–Proliferation Treaty (NPT) of 1968 seeks to prevent the spread of nuclear weapons and is discussed below.

While nuclear weapons are an invention of the 20th century, the other primary categories of WMD, chemical (CW) and biological weapons (BW) have existed in some form for thousands of years. They have progressed from poisoning arrows and water supplies in Ancient Greece and catapulting plague infected bodies during the Middle Ages to small pox blankets and the use of poison gases such as mustard gas during the World Wars. The world's most recent exposure to the use of chemical weapons on a large scale took place during the Iran–Iraq War when Saddam Hussein used chemical weapons including mustard, sarin, and VX gases against both Iranian forces as well as the Iraqi Kurdish village of Halabja, killing nearly 5000 of his own citizens. See Report of the Mission Dispatched by the Secretary–General to Investigate Allegations of the use of Chemical Weapons in the Conflict Between the Islamic Republic of Iran and Iraq. UN Doc. S/17922 (12 March 1986). The use of CW/BW on a smaller scale by terrorist organizations is also a matter of concern. Some of the better-known examples of such terrorism include the 1995 Aum Shinrikyo sarin gas attack on the Tokyo subway system and the 2001 anthrax attacks in the United States. More recently, terrorist bombers in Iraq have taken to adding chlorine gas to improvised explosive devices (IEDs) creating dirty bombs.

The 1993 Chemical Weapons Convention (CWC) and the 1972 Biological Weapons Convention (BWC) ban the possession and use of these weapons. They are discussed below. For more on this topic, *see*, FREDERICK N. MATTIS, BANNING WEAPONS OF MASS DESTRUCTION (2009).

a.   NUCLEAR WEAPONS

On July 1, 1968, the international community adopted the Treaty on the Non–Proliferation of Nuclear Weapons. This treaty did not ban nuclear weapons for all states—just most of them. Under the terms of the treaty, the five declared nuclear weapons states in 1968 were permitted to retain some of their weapons. They had to agree, however, to aid in the preventing all other states from acquiring them. As of 2009, only four other states had managed to acquire nuclear weapons: India, Israel, North Korea and Pakistan. North Korea, however, had already taken credible steps to dismantle its program. Considerable efforts were being made to prevent Iran from acquiring weapons.

Legality of the Threat or Use of Nuclear Weapons
International Court of Justice
1996 I.C.J. Rep. 226 (Advisory Opinion of July 8)

1. The question upon which the advisory opinion of the Court has been requested is set forth in resolution 49/75 K adopted by the General Assembly of the United Nations (hereinafter called the "General Assembly") on 15 December 1994. By a letter dated 19 December 1994, received in the Registry by facsimile on 20 December 1994 and filed in the original on 6 January 1995, the Secretary–General of the United Nations officially communicated to the Registrar the decision taken by the General Assembly to submit the question to the Court for an advisory opinion. Resolution 49/75 K, the English text of which was enclosed with the letter, reads as follows:

> *"The General Assembly,*
>
> *Conscious* that the continuing existence and development of nuclear weapons pose serious risks to humanity,
>
> *Mindful* that States have an obligation under the Charter of the United Nations to refrain from the threat or use of force against the territorial integrity or political independence of any State,

* * *

34. The Court concludes that the most directly relevant applicable law governing the question of which it was seised, is that relating to the use of force enshrined in the United Nations Charter and the law applicable in armed conflict which regulates the conduct of hostilities, together with any specific treaties on nuclear weapons that the Court might determine to be relevant.

* * *

35. In applying this law to the present case, the Court cannot however fail to take into account certain unique characteristics of nuclear weapons.

The Court has noted the definitions of nuclear weapons contained in various treaties and accords. It also notes that nuclear weapons are explosive devices whose energy results from the fusion or fission of the atom. By its very nature, that process, in nuclear weapons as they exist today, releases not only immense quantities of heat and energy, but also powerful and prolonged radiation. According to the material before the

Court, the first two causes of damage are vastly more powerful than the damage caused by other weapons, while the phenomenon of radiation is said to be peculiar to nuclear weapons. These characteristics render the nuclear weapon potentially catastrophic. The destructive power of nuclear weapons cannot be contained in either space or time. They have the potential to destroy all civilization and the entire ecosystem of the planet.

The radiation released by a nuclear explosion would affect health, agriculture, natural resources and demography over a very wide area. Further, the use of nuclear weapons would be a serious danger to future generations. Ionizing radiation has the potential to damage the future environment, food and marine ecosystem, and to cause genetic defects and illness in future generations.

36.   In consequence, in order correctly to apply to the present case the Charter law on the use of force and the law applicable in armed conflict, in particular humanitarian law, it is imperative for the Court to take account of the unique characteristics of nuclear weapons, and in particular their destructive capacity, their capacity to cause untold human suffering, and their ability to cause damage to generations to come.

* * *

37.   The Court will now address the question of the legality or illegality of recourse to nuclear weapons in the light of the provisions of the Charter relating to the threat or use of force.

38.   The Charter contains several provisions relating to the threat and use of force. In Article 2, paragraph 4, the threat or use of force against the territorial integrity or political independence of another State or in any other manner inconsistent with the purposes of the United Nations is prohibited. That paragraph provides: "All Members shall refrain in their international relations from the threat or use of force against the territorial integrity or political independence of any State, or in any other manner inconsistent with the Purposes of the United Nations."

This prohibition of the use of force is to be considered in the light of other relevant provisions of the Charter. In Article 51, the Charter recognizes the inherent right of individual or collective self-defence if an armed attack occurs. A further lawful use of force is envisaged in Article 42, whereby the Security Council may take military enforcement measures in conformity with Chapter VII of the Charter.

39.   These provisions do not refer to specific weapons. They apply to any use of force, regardless of the weapons employed. The Charter neither expressly prohibits, nor permits, the use of any specific weapon, including nuclear weapons. A weapon that is already unlawful per se, whether by treaty or custom, does not become lawful by reason of its being used for a legitimate purpose under the Charter.

40.   The entitlement to resort to self-defence under Article 51 is subject to certain constraints. Some of these constraints are inherent in the very concept of self defence. Other requirements are specified in Article 51.

41. The submission of the exercise of the right of self-defence to the conditions of necessity and proportionality is a rule of customary international law. As the Court stated in the case concerning Military and Paramilitary Activities in and against Nicaragua (Nicaragua v. United States of America) (I.C.J. Reports 1986, p. 94, para. 176): "there is a specific rule whereby self-defence would warrant only measures which are proportional to the armed attack and necessary to respond to it, a rule well established in customary international law". This dual condition applies equally to Article 51 of the Charter, whatever the means of force employed.

42. The proportionality principle may thus not in itself exclude the use of nuclear weapons in self-defence in all circumstances. But at the same time, a use of force that is proportionate under the law of self-defence, must, in order to be lawful, also meet the requirements of the law applicable in armed conflict which comprise in particular the principles and rules of humanitarian law.

43. Certain States have in their written and oral pleadings suggested that in the case of nuclear weapons, the condition of proportionality must be evaluated in the light of still further factors. They contend that the very nature of nuclear weapons, and the high probability of an escalation of nuclear exchanges, mean that there is an extremely strong risk of devastation. The risk factor is said to negate the possibility of the condition of proportionality being complied with. The Court does not find it necessary to embark upon the quantification of such risks; nor does it need to enquire into the question whether tactical nuclear weapons exist which are sufficiently precise to limit those risks: it suffices for the Court to note that the very nature of all nuclear weapons and the profound risks associated therewith are further considerations to be borne in mind by States believing they can exercise a nuclear response in self-defence in accordance with the requirements of proportionality.

44. Beyond the conditions of necessity and proportionality, Article 51 specifically requires that measures taken by States in the exercise of the right of self-defence shall be immediately reported to the Security Council; this article further provides that these measures shall not in any way affect the authority and responsibility of the Security Council under the Charter to take at any time such action as it deems necessary in order to maintain or restore international peace and security. These requirements of Article 51 apply whatever the means of force used in self-defence.

45. The Court notes that the Security Council adopted on 11 April 1995, in the context of the extension of the Treaty on the Non–Proliferation of Nuclear Weapons, resolution 984 (1995) by the terms of which, on the one hand, it "[t]akes note with appreciation of the statements made by each of the nuclear-weapon States (S/1995/261, S/1995/262, S/1995/263, S/1995/264, S/1995/265), in which they give security assurances against the use of nuclear weapons to non-nuclear-weapon States that are Parties to the Treaty on the Non–Proliferation of Nuclear Weapons," and, on the other hand, it

"[w]elcomes the intention expressed by certain States that they will provide or support immediate assistance, in accordance with the Charter, to any non-nuclear-weapon State Party to the Treaty on the Non–Proliferation of Nuclear Weapons that is a victim of an act of, or an object of a threat of, aggression in which nuclear weapons are used".

46.   Certain States asserted that the use of nuclear weapons in the conduct of reprisals would be lawful. The Court does not have to examine, in this context, the question of armed reprisals in time of peace, which are considered to be unlawful. Nor does it have to pronounce on the question of belligerent reprisals save to observe that in any case any right of recourse to such reprisals would, like self-defence, be governed inter alia by the principle of proportionality.

47.   In order to lessen or eliminate the risk of unlawful attack, States sometimes signal that they possess certain weapons to use in self-defence against any State violating their territorial integrity or political independence. Whether a signalled intention to use force if certain events occur is or is not a "threat" within Article 2, paragraph 4, of the Charter depends upon various factors. If the envisaged use of force is itself unlawful, the stated readiness to use it would be a threat prohibited under Article 2, paragraph 4. Thus it would be illegal for a State to threaten force to secure territory from another State, or to cause it to follow or not follow certain political or economic paths. The notions of "threat" and "use" of force under Article 2, paragraph 4, of the Charter stand together in the sense that if the use of force itself in a given case is illegal for whatever reason the threat to use such force will likewise be illegal. In short, if it is to be lawful, the declared readiness of a State to use force must be a use of force that is in conformity with the Charter. For the rest, no State whether or not it defended the policy of deterrence suggested to the Court that it would be lawful to threaten to use force if the use of force contemplated would be illegal.

48.   Some States put forward the argument that possession of nuclear weapons is itself an unlawful threat to use force. Possession of nuclear weapons may indeed justify an inference of preparedness to use them. In order to be effective, the policy of deterrence, by which those States possessing or under the umbrella of nuclear weapons seek to discourage military aggression by demonstrating that it will serve no purpose, necessitates that the intention to use nuclear weapons be credible. Whether this is a "threat" contrary to Article 2, paragraph 4, depends upon whether the particular use of force envisaged would be directed against the territorial integrity or political independence of a State, or against the Purposes of the United Nations or whether, in the event that it were intended as a means of defence, it would necessarily violate the principles of necessity and proportionality. In any of these circumstances the use of force, and the threat to use it, would be unlawful under the law of the Charter.

49.   Moreover, the Security Council may take enforcement measures under Chapter VII of the Charter. From the statements presented to it the

Court does not consider it necessary to address questions which might, in a given case, arise from the application of Chapter VII.

50. The terms of the question put to the Court by the General Assembly in resolution 49/75K could in principle also cover a threat or use of nuclear weapons by a State within its own boundaries. However, this particular aspect has not been dealt with by any of the States which addressed the Court orally or in writing in these proceedings. The Court finds that it is not called upon to deal with an internal use of nuclear weapons.

* * *

51. Having dealt with the Charter provisions relating to the threat or use of force, the Court will now turn to the law applicable in situations of armed conflict. It will first address the question whether there are specific rules in international law regulating the legality or illegality of recourse to nuclear weapons per se; it will then examine the question put to it in the light of the law applicable in armed conflict proper, i.e. the principles and rules of humanitarian law applicable in armed conflict, and the law of neutrality.

* * *

52. The Court notes by way of introduction that international customary and treaty law does not contain any specific prescription authorizing the threat or use of nuclear weapons or any other weapon in general or in certain circumstances, in particular those of the exercise of legitimate self-defence. Nor, however, is there any principle or rule of international law which would make the legality of the threat or use of nuclear weapons or of any other weapons dependent on a specific authorization. State practice shows that the illegality of the use of certain weapons as such does not result from an absence of authorization but, on the contrary, is formulated in terms of prohibition.

* * *

53. The Court must therefore now examine whether there is any prohibition of recourse to nuclear weapons as such; it will first ascertain whether there is a conventional prescription to this effect.

54. In this regard, the argument has been advanced that nuclear weapons should be treated in the same way as poisoned weapons. In that case, they would be prohibited under:

(a) the Second Hague Declaration of 29 July 1899, which prohibits "the use of projectiles the object of which is the diffusion of asphyxiating or deleterious gases";

(b) Article 23 (a) of the Regulations respecting the laws and customs of war on land annexed to the Hague Convention IV of 18 October 1907, whereby "it is especially forbidden: ... to employ poison or poisoned weapons"; and

(c) the Geneva Protocol of 17 June 1925 which prohibits "the use in war of asphyxiating, poisonous or other gases, and of all analogous liquids, materials or devices".

55. The Court will observe that the Regulations annexed to the Hague Convention IV do not define what is to be understood by "poison or poisoned weapons" and that different interpretations exist on the issue. Nor does the 1925 Protocol specify the meaning to be given to the term "analogous materials or devices". The terms have been understood, in the practice of States, in their ordinary sense as covering weapons whose prime, or even exclusive, effect is to poison or asphyxiate. This practice is clear, and the parties to those instruments have not treated them as referring to nuclear weapons.

56. In view of this, it does not seem to the Court that the use of nuclear weapons can be regarded as specifically prohibited on the basis of the above-mentioned provisions of the Second Hague Declaration of 1899, the Regulations annexed to the Hague Convention IV of 1907 or the 1925 Protocol (see paragraph 54 above).

57. The pattern until now has been for weapons of mass destruction to be declared illegal by specific instruments. The most recent such instruments are the Convention of 10 April 1972 on the Prohibition of the Development, Production and Stockpiling of Bacteriological (Biological) and Toxin Weapons and on their destruction which prohibits the possession of bacteriological and toxic weapons and reinforces the prohibition of their use and the Convention of 13 January 1993 on the Prohibition of the Development, Production, Stockpiling and Use of Chemical Weapons and on Their Destruction which prohibits all use of chemical weapons and requires the destruction of existing stocks. Each of these instruments has been negotiated and adopted in its own context and for its own reasons. The Court does not find any specific prohibition of recourse to nuclear weapons in treaties expressly prohibiting the use of certain weapons of mass destruction.

58. In the last two decades, a great many negotiations have been conducted regarding nuclear weapons; they have not resulted in a treaty of general prohibition of the same kind as for bacteriological and chemical weapons. However, a number of specific treaties have been concluded in order to limit [possession and use.]

* * *

(c) [A]s to the Treaty on the Non–Proliferation of Nuclear Weapons, at the time of its signing in 1968 the United States, the United Kingdom and the USSR gave various security assurances to the non-nuclear-weapon States that were parties to the Treaty. In resolution 255 (1968) the Security Council took note with satisfaction of the intention expressed by those three States to

"provide or support immediate assistance, in accordance with the Charter, to any non-nuclear-weapon State Party to the Treaty on the Non–Proliferation ... that is a victim of an act of, or an object of a threat of, aggression in which nuclear weapons are used".

On the occasion of the extension of the Treaty in 1995, the five nuclear-weapon States gave their non-nuclear-weapon partners, by means of separate unilateral statements on 5 and 6 April 1995, positive and negative security assurances against the use of such weapons. All the five nuclear-weapon States first undertook not to use nuclear weapons against non-nuclear-weapon States that were parties to the Treaty on the Non–Proliferation of Nuclear Weapons. However, these States, apart from China, made an exception in the case of an invasion or any other attack against them, their territories, armed forces or allies, or on a State towards which they had a security commitment, carried out or sustained by a non-nuclear-weapon State party to the Non–Proliferation Treaty in association or alliance with a nuclear-weapon State. Each of the nuclear-weapon States further undertook, as a permanent Member of the Security Council, in the event of an attack with the use of nuclear weapons, or threat of such attack, against a non-nuclear-weapon State, to refer the matter to the Security Council without delay and to act within it in order that it might take immediate measures with a view to supplying, pursuant to the Charter, the necessary assistance to the victim State (the commitments assumed comprising minor variations in wording). The Security Council, in unanimously adopting resolution 984 (1995) of 11 April 1995, cited above, took note of those statements with appreciation. It also recognized

> "that the nuclear-weapon State permanent members of the Security Council will bring the matter immediately to the attention of the Council and seek Council action to provide, in accordance with the Charter, the necessary assistance to the State victim";

and welcomed the fact that

> "the intention expressed by certain States that they will provide or support immediate assistance, in accordance with the Charter, to any non-nuclear-weapon State Party to the Treaty on the Non–Proliferation of Nuclear Weapons that is a victim of an act of, or an object of a threat of, aggression in which nuclear weapons are used."

60. Those States that believe that recourse to nuclear weapons is illegal stress that the conventions that include various rules providing for the limitation or elimination of nuclear weapons in certain areas (such as the Antarctic Treaty of 1959 which prohibits the deployment of nuclear weapons in the Antarctic, or the Treaty of Tlatelolco of 1967 which creates a nuclear-weapon-free zone in Latin America), or the conventions that apply certain measures of control and limitation to the existence of nuclear weapons (such as the 1963 Partial Test–Ban Treaty or the Treaty on the Non–Proliferation of Nuclear Weapons) all set limits to the use of nuclear weapons. In their view, these treaties bear witness, in their own way, to the emergence of a rule of complete legal prohibition of all uses of nuclear weapons.

61. Those States who defend the position that recourse to nuclear weapons is legal in certain circumstances see a logical contradiction in reaching such a conclusion. According to them, those Treaties, such as the

Treaty on the Non–Proliferation of Nuclear Weapons, as well as Security Council resolutions 255 (1968) and 984 (1995) which take note of the security assurances given by the nuclear-weapon States to the non-nuclear-weapon States in relation to any nuclear aggression against the latter, cannot be understood as prohibiting the use of nuclear weapons, and such a claim is contrary to the very text of those instruments. For those who support the legality in certain circumstances of recourse to nuclear weapons, there is no absolute prohibition against the use of such weapons. The very logic and construction of the Treaty on the Non–Proliferation of Nuclear Weapons, they assert, confirm this. This Treaty, whereby, they contend, the possession of nuclear weapons by the five nuclear-weapon States has been accepted, cannot be seen as a treaty banning their use by those States; to accept the fact that those States possess nuclear weapons is tantamount to recognizing that such weapons may be used in certain circumstances. Nor, they contend, could the security assurances given by the nuclear-weapon States in 1968, and more recently in connection with the Review and Extension Conference of the Parties to the Treaty on the Non–Proliferation of Nuclear Weapons in 1995, have been conceived without out its being supposed that there were circumstances in which nuclear weapons could be used in a lawful manner. For those who defend the legality of the use, in certain circumstances, of nuclear weapons, the acceptance of those instruments by the different non-nuclear-weapon States confirms and reinforces the evident logic upon which those instruments are based.

62.   The Court notes that the treaties dealing exclusively with acquisition, manufacture, possession, deployment and testing of nuclear weapons, without specifically addressing their threat or use, certainly point to an increasing concern in the international community with these weapons; the Court concludes from this that these treaties could therefore be seen as foreshadowing a future general prohibition of the use of such weapons, but they do not constitute such a prohibition by themselves. As to the treaties of Tlatelolco and Rarotonga and their Protocols, and also the declarations made in connection with the indefinite extension of the Treaty on the Non–Proliferation of Nuclear Weapons, it emerges from these instruments that:

(a) a number of States have undertaken not to use nuclear weapons in specific zones (Latin America; the South Pacific) or against certain other States (non-nuclear-weapon States which are parties to the Treaty on the Non–Proliferation of Nuclear Weapons);

(b) nevertheless, even within this framework, the nuclear-weapon States have reserved the right to use nuclear weapons in certain circumstances; and

(c) these reservations met with no objection from the parties to the Tlatelolco or Rarotonga Treaties or from the Security Council.

63.   These two treaties, the security assurances given in 1995 by the nuclear-weapon States and the fact that the Security Council took note of them with satisfaction, testify to a growing awareness of the need to liberate the community of States and the international public from the

dangers resulting from the existence of nuclear weapons. The Court more-over notes the signing, even more recently, on 15 December 1995, at Bangkok, of a Treaty on the Southeast Asia Nuclear–Weapon–Free Zone, and on 11 April 1996, at Cairo, of a treaty on the creation of a nuclear-weapons-free zone in Africa. It does not, however, view these elements as amounting to a comprehensive and universal conventional prohibition on the use, or the threat of use, of those weapons as such.

* * *

64.   The Court will now turn to an examination of customary interna-tional law to determine whether a prohibition of the threat or use of nuclear weapons as such flows from that source of law. As the Court has stated, the substance of that law must be "looked for primarily in the actual practice and opinio juris of States" (Continental Shelf (Libyan Arab Jamahiriya/Malta), Judgment, I.C.J. Reports 1985, p. 29, para. 27).

65.   States which hold the view that the use of nuclear weapons is illegal have endeavoured to demonstrate the existence of a customary rule prohibiting this use. They refer to a consistent practice of non-utilization of nuclear weapons by States since 1945 and they would see in that practice the expression of an opinio juris on the part of those who possess such weapons.

66.   Some other States, which assert the legality of the threat and use of nuclear weapons in certain circumstances, invoked the doctrine and practice of deterrence in support of their argument. They recall that they have always, in concert with certain other States, reserved the right to use those weapons in the exercise of the right to self-defence against an armed attack threatening their vital security interests. In their view, if nuclear weapons have not been used since 1945, it is not on account of an existing or nascent custom but merely because circumstances that might justify their use have fortunately not arisen.

67.   The Court does not intend to pronounce here upon the practice known as the "policy of deterrence". It notes that it is a fact that a number of States adhered to that practice during the greater part of the Cold War and continue to adhere to it. Furthermore, the Members of the internation-al community are profoundly divided on the matter of whether non-recourse to nuclear weapons over the past fifty years constitutes the expression of an opinio juris. Under these circumstances the Court does not consider itself able to find that there is such an opinio juris.

68.   According to certain States, the important series of General Assembly resolutions, beginning with resolution 1653 (XVI) of 24 Novem-ber 1961, that deal with nuclear weapons and that affirm, with consistent regularity, the illegality of nuclear weapons, signify the existence of a rule of international customary law which prohibits recourse to those weapons. According to other States, however, the resolutions in question have no binding character on their own account and are not declaratory of any customary rule of prohibition of nuclear weapons; some of these States have also pointed out that this series of resolutions not only did not meet

with the approval of all of the nuclear-weapon States but of many other States as well.

69.   States which consider that the use of nuclear weapons is illegal indicated that those resolutions did not claim to create any new rules, but were confined to a confirmation of customary law relating to the prohibition of means or methods of warfare which, by their use, overstepped the bounds of what is permissible in the conduct of hostilities. In their view, the resolutions in question did no more than apply to nuclear weapons the existing rules of international law applicable in armed conflict; they were no more than the "envelope" or instrumentum containing certain preexisting customary rules of international law. For those States it is accordingly of little importance that the instrumentum should have occasioned negative votes, which cannot have the effect of obliterating those customary rules which have been confirmed by treaty law.

70.   The Court notes that General Assembly resolutions, even if they are not binding, may sometimes have normative value. They can, in certain circumstances, provide evidence important for establishing the existence of a rule or the emergence of an opinio juris. To establish whether this is true of a given General Assembly resolution, it is necessary to look at its content and the conditions of its adoption; it is also necessary to see whether an opinio juris exists as to its normative character. Or a series of resolutions may show the gradual evolution of the opinio juris required for the establishment of a new rule.

71.   Examined in their totality, the General Assembly resolutions put before the Court declare that the use of nuclear weapons would be "a direct violation of the Charter of the United Nations"; and in certain formulations that such use "should be prohibited". The focus of these resolutions has sometimes shifted to diverse related matters however, several of the resolutions under consideration in the present case have been adopted with substantial numbers of negative votes and abstentions; thus, although those resolutions are a clear sign of deep concern regarding the problem of nuclear weapons, they still fall short of establishing the existence of an opinio juris on the illegality of the use of such weapons.

72.   The Court further notes that the first of the resolutions of the General Assembly expressly proclaiming the illegality of the use of nuclear weapons, resolution 1653 (XVI) of 24 November 1961 (mentioned in subsequent resolutions), after referring to certain international declarations and binding agreements, from the Declaration of St. Petersburg of 1868 to the Geneva Protocol of 1925, proceeded to qualify the legal nature of nuclear weapons, determine their effects, and apply general rules of customary international law to nuclear weapons in particular. That application by the General Assembly of general rules of customary law to the particular case of nuclear weapons indicates that, in its view, there was no specific rule of customary law which prohibited the use of nuclear weapons; if such a rule had existed, the General Assembly could simply have referred to it and would not have needed to undertake such an exercise of legal qualification.

73. Having said this, the Court points out that the adoption each year by the General Assembly, by a large majority, of resolutions recalling the content of resolution 1653 (XVI), and requesting the member States to conclude a convention prohibiting the use of nuclear weapons in any circumstance, reveals the desire of a very large section of the international community to take, by a specific and express prohibition of the use of nuclear weapons, a significant step forward along the road to complete nuclear disarmament. The emergence, as lex lata, of a customary rule specifically prohibiting the use of nuclear weapons as such is hampered by the continuing tensions between the nascent opinio juris on the one hand, and the still strong adherence to the practice of deterrence on the other.

* * *

74. The Court not having found a conventional rule of general scope, nor a customary rule specifically proscribing the threat or use of nuclear weapons per se, it will now deal with the question whether recourse to nuclear weapons must be considered as illegal in the light of the principles and rules of international humanitarian law applicable in armed conflict and of the law of neutrality.

75. A large number of customary rules have been developed by the practice of States and are an integral part of the international law relevant to the question posed. The "laws and customs of war" as they were traditionally called were the subject of efforts at codification undertaken in The Hague (including the Conventions of 1899 and 1907), and were based partly upon the St. Petersburg Declaration of 1868 as well as the results of the Brussels Conference of 1874. This "Hague Law" and, more particularly, the Regulations Respecting the Laws and Customs of War on Land, fixed the rights and duties of belligerents in their conduct of operations and limited the choice of methods and means of injuring the enemy in an international armed conflict. One should add to this the "Geneva Law" (the Conventions of 1864, 1906, 1929 and 1949), which protects the victims of war and aims to provide safeguards for disabled armed forces personnel and persons not taking part in the hostilities. These two branches of the law applicable in armed conflict have become so closely interrelated that they are considered to have gradually formed one single complex system, known today as international humanitarian law. The provisions of the Additional Protocols of 1977 give expression and attest to the unity and complexity of that law.

76. Since the turn of the century, the appearance of new means of combat has without calling into question the longstanding principles and rules of international law rendered necessary some specific prohibitions of the use of certain weapons, such as explosive projectiles under 400 grammes, dum-dum bullets and asphyxiating gases. Chemical and bacteriological weapons were then prohibited by the 1925 Geneva Protocol. More recently, the use of weapons producing "non-detectable fragments", of other types of "mines, booby traps and other devices", and of "incendiary weapons", was either prohibited or limited, depending on the case, by the Convention of 10 October 1980 on Prohibitions or Restrictions on the Use of Certain Conven-

tional Weapons Which May Be Deemed to Be Excessively Injurious or to Have Indiscriminate Effects. The provisions of the Convention on "mines, booby traps and other devices" have just been amended, on 3 May 1996, and now regulate in greater detail, for example, the use of antipersonnel land mines.

77.   All this shows that the conduct of military operations is governed by a body of legal prescriptions. This is so because "the right of belligerents to adopt means of injuring the enemy is not unlimited" as stated in Article 22 of the 1907 Hague Regulations relating to the laws and customs of war on land. The St. Petersburg Declaration had already condemned the use of weapons "which uselessly aggravate the suffering of disabled men or make their death inevitable". The aforementioned Regulations relating to the laws and customs of war on land, annexed to the Hague Convention IV of 1907, prohibit the use of "arms, projectiles, or material calculated to cause unnecessary suffering" (Art. 23).

78.   The cardinal principles contained in the texts constituting the fabric of humanitarian law are the following. The first is aimed at the protection of the civilian population and civilian objects and establishes the distinction between combatants and non-combatants; States must never make civilians the object of attack and must consequently never use weapons that are incapable of distinguishing between civilian and military targets. According to the second principle, it is prohibited to cause unnecessary suffering to combatants: it is accordingly prohibited to use weapons causing them such harm or uselessly aggravating their suffering. In application of that second principle, States do not have unlimited freedom of choice of means in the weapons they use.

The Court would likewise refer, in relation to these principles, to the Martens Clause, which was first included in the Hague Convention II with Respect to the Laws and Customs of War on Land of 1899 and which has proved to be an effective means of addressing the rapid evolution of military technology. A modern version of that clause is to be found in Article 1, paragraph 2, of Additional Protocol I of 1977, which reads as follows:

> "In cases not covered by this Protocol or by other international agreements, civilians and combatants remain under the protection and authority of the principles of international law derived from established custom, from the principles of humanity and from the dictates of public conscience."

In conformity with the aforementioned principles, humanitarian law, at a very early stage, prohibited certain types of weapons either because of their indiscriminate effect on combatants and civilians or because of the unnecessary suffering caused to combatants, that is to say, a harm greater than that unavoidable to achieve legitimate military objectives. If an envisaged use of weapons would not meet the requirements of humanitarian law, a threat to engage in such use would also be contrary to that law.

79.   It is undoubtedly because a great many rules of humanitarian law applicable in armed conflict are so fundamental to the respect of the human person and "elementary considerations of humanity" as the Court put it in its Judgment of 9 April 1949 in the Corfu Channel case (I.C.J. Reports 1949, p. 22), that the Hague and Geneva Conventions have enjoyed a broad accession. Further these fundamental rules are to be observed by all States whether or not they have ratified the conventions that contain them, because they constitute intransgressible principles of international customary law.

80.   The Nuremberg International Military Tribunal had already found in 1945 that the humanitarian rules included in the Regulations annexed to the Hague Convention IV of 1907 "were recognized by all civilized nations and were regarded as being declaratory of the laws and customs of war" *(International Military Tribunal, Trial of the Major War Criminals, 14 November 1945–1 October 1946, Nuremberg, 1947, Vol. 1, p. 254).*

81.   The Report of the Secretary–General pursuant to paragraph 2 of Security Council resolution 808 (1993), with which he introduced the Statute of the International Tribunal for the Prosecution of Persons Responsible for Serious Violations of International Humanitarian Law Committed in the Territory of the Former Yugoslavia since 1991, and which was unanimously approved by the Security Council (resolution 827 (1993)), stated:

"In the view of the Secretary–General, the application of the principle *nullum crimen sine lege* requires that the international tribunal should apply rules of international humanitarian law which are beyond any doubt part of customary law . . . The part of conventional international humanitarian law which has beyond doubt become part of international customary law is the law applicable in armed conflict as embodied in the Geneva Conventions of 12 August 1949 for the Protection of War Victims; the Hague Convention (IV) Respecting the Laws and Customs of War on Land and the Regulations annexed thereto of 18 October 1907; the Convention on the Prevention and Punishment of the Crime of Genocide of 9 December 1948; and the Charter of the International Military Tribunal of 8 August 1945."

82.   The extensive codification of humanitarian law and the extent of the accession to the resultant treaties, as well as the fact that the denunciation clauses that existed in the codification instruments have never been used, have provided the international community with a corpus of treaty rules the great majority of which had already become customary and which reflected the most universally recognized humanitarian principles. These rules indicate the normal conduct and behaviour expected of States.

83.   It has been maintained in these proceedings that these principles and rules of humanitarian law are part of *jus cogens* as defined in Article 53 of the Vienna Convention on the Law of Treaties of 23 May 1969. The question whether a norm is part of the *jus cogens* relates to the legal character of the norm. The request addressed to the Court by the General

Assembly raises the question of the applicability of the principles and rules of humanitarian law in cases of recourse to nuclear weapons and the consequences of that applicability for the legality of recourse to these weapons. But it does not raise the question of the character of the humanitarian law which would apply to the use of nuclear weapons. There is, therefore, no need for the Court to pronounce on this matter.

84.   Nor is there any need for the Court to elaborate on the question of the applicability of Additional Protocol I of 1977 to nuclear weapons. * * *

85.   Turning now to the applicability of the principles and rules of humanitarian law to a possible threat or use of nuclear weapons * * *.

* * *

94.   The Court would observe that none of the States advocating the legality of the use of nuclear weapons under certain circumstances, including the "clean" use of smaller, low yield, tactical nuclear weapons, has indicated what, supposing such limited use were feasible, would be the precise circumstances justifying such use; nor whether such limited use would not tend to escalate into the all-out use of high yield nuclear weapons. This being so, the Court does not consider that it has a sufficient basis for a determination on the validity of this view.

95.   Nor can the Court make a determination on the validity of the view that the recourse to nuclear weapons would be illegal in any circumstance owing to their inherent and total incompatibility with the law applicable in armed conflict. Certainly, as the Court has already indicated, the principles and rules of law applicable in armed conflict at the heart of which is the overriding consideration of humanity make the conduct of armed hostilities subject to a number of strict requirements. Thus, methods and means of warfare, which would preclude any distinction between civilian and military targets, or which would result in unnecessary suffering to combatants, are prohibited. In view of the unique characteristics of nuclear weapons, to which the Court has referred above, the use of such weapons in fact seems scarcely reconcilable with respect for such requirements. Nevertheless, the Court considers that it does not have sufficient elements to enable it to conclude with certainty that the use of nuclear weapons would necessarily be at variance with the principles and rules of law applicable in armed conflict in any circumstance.

96.   Furthermore, the Court cannot lose sight of the fundamental right of every State to survival, and thus its right to resort to self-defence, in accordance with Article 51 of the Charter, when its survival is at stake. Nor can it ignore the practice referred to as "policy of deterrence", to which an appreciable section of the international community adhered for many years. The Court also notes the reservations which certain nuclear-weapon States have appended to the undertakings they have given, notably under the Protocols to the Treaties of Tlatelolco and Rarotonga, and also under the declarations made by them in connection with the extension of the Treaty on the Non–Proliferation of Nuclear Weapons, not to resort to such weapons.

97.   Accordingly, in view of the present state of international law viewed as a whole, as examined above by the Court, and of the elements of fact at its disposal, the Court is led to observe that it cannot reach a definitive conclusion as to the legality or illegality of the use of nuclear weapons by a State in an extreme circumstance of self-defence, in which its very survival would be at stake.

* * *

E.   By seven votes to seven, by the President's casting vote,

It follows from the above-mentioned requirements that the threat or use of nuclear weapons would generally be contrary to the rules of international law applicable in armed conflict, and in particular the principles and rules of humanitarian law;

However, in view of the current state of international law, and of the elements of fact at its disposal, the Court cannot conclude definitively whether the threat or use of nuclear weapons would be lawful or unlawful in an extreme circumstance of self-defence, in which the very survival of a State would be at stake;

IN FAVOUR: *President* Bedjaoui; *Judges* Ranjeva, Herczegh, Shi, Fleischhauer, Vereschetin, Ferrari Bravo;

AGAINST: *Vice–President* Schwebel; *Judges* Oda, Guillaume, Shahabuddeen, Weeramantry, Koroma, Higgins.

F.   Unanimously,

There exists an obligation to pursue in good faith and bring to a conclusion negotiations leading to nuclear disarmament in all its aspects under strict and effective international control.

President Bedjaoui, Judges Herczegh, Shi, Vereshchetin and Ferrari Bravo append declarations to the Advisory Opinion of the Court. Judges Guillaume, Ranjeva and Fleischhauer append separate opinions to the Advisory Opinion of the Court. Vice–President Schwebel, Judges Oda, Shahabuddeen, Weeramantry, Koroma and Higgins append dissenting opinions to the Advisory Opinion of the Court.

b.   CHEMICAL AND BIOLOGICAL WEAPONS

Jack M. Beard, The Shortcomings of Indeterminacy in Arms Control Regimes: The Case of the Biological Weapons Convention

101 Am. J Int'l. L. 271 (2007)*

Although its use in warfare has been relatively rare, disease is said to have been employed as a weapon as early as the Middle Ages. Practical considerations, however, greatly limited the use of biological agents as weapons, particularly as they were difficult to produce, store, and deploy,

---

* Footnotes omitted.

and were as likely to harm friendly forces as the enemy. Nascent efforts by states to regulate the increasingly destructive new weapons near the end of the nineteenth century included agreements banning the use of certain poisons and asphyxiating gases but not biological weapons. In spite of early efforts to ban asphyxiating gases, chemical weapons (CW) were used extensively in World War I and caused hundreds of thousands of casualties. After the war, widely publicized accounts of the suffering and death associated with CW led to various attempts by states formally and effectively to outlaw the use of all chemical weapons.

At a multilateral arms control conference in 1925 addressing the nonuse of poisonous gases, a prohibition on "the use of bacteriological methods of warfare" was proposed for the first time. The work of this conference resulted in the conclusion of the Geneva Protocol for the Prohibition of Poisonous Gases and Bacteriological Methods of Warfare on June 17, 1925 (Geneva Protocol), which banned the use of both chemical and biological weapons. However, banning biological weapons, in contrast to chemical weapons, was a new legal concept in 1925. Since any practical threat presented by these weapons in 1925 was merely imagined, the authors of the Geneva Protocol in effect sought to ban a weapon of the future. In doing so, states demonstrated the power of biological weapons to cause considerable fear and insecurity on a largely abstract level.

As an international agreement, the Geneva Protocol was significantly limited in the scope of its application. The text banned the use, in war, of biological weapons only against other states parties (not states generally) and did not ban the possession or development of these weapons. Many states also made reservations declaring that the obligations under the Protocol would cease to be binding on them if enemy states failed to respect its prohibitions, effectively making it a prohibition on the "first use" of chemical and biological weapons. Thus, the Protocol's de facto recognition of a potential defensive or deterrent basis for these weapons—coupled with the absence of any prohibition on their development, acquisition, possession, manufacture, or transfer—resulted in a legal framework that allowed states to conduct BW research, develop new biological weapons, and ultimately engage in BW arms races.

The BW Arms Race

The fears generated by biological weapons and the security dilemmas that states have faced in arming against BW threats have historically been compounded by fundamental identification problems associated with the development of these weapons. Since disease occurs naturally, a troubling question of intention has often arisen when the scientific or military establishments in adversary states have been reported to be in possession of components or technology with BW applications. It was in fact the fear of nonexistent weapons, the potential impact of technological advances, and the misperception of threats that first inspired several states to begin to develop their own BW programs shortly after the legal ban on their use was formalized in 1925. In a remarkable testament to the power of these concerns, "misperceptions of enemy interest" appear to have compelled several states to begin building biological weapons soon after the Geneva Protocol was signed.

Events in World War II further demonstrated the power of BW misperceptions to magnify security dilemmas and motivate states to pursue BW programs. Although after the war the lack of any large-scale German BW program was established, both Britain and the United States had misperceived a serious German BW threat during the war and responded by developing their own BW programs. Both countries also concluded that the best defensive arsenal should include offensive biological weapons and in 1942 Britain conducted tests that for the first time proved the effectiveness of bombs with BW agents.

American efforts at the close of World War II to limit access to captured scientists responsible for Japan's infamous BW experiments on humans increased Soviet suspicions of U.S. intentions regarding new BW capabilities and set the stage for the Cold War BW arms race. While the United States had not shown great interest in BW research programs in the 1930s, efforts to build a BW program expanded rapidly at the end of World War II and funding was dramatically increased. After adopting a policy in 1956 to be "prepared to use chemical and bacteriological weapons in general war," the United States embarked on extensive programs to test the lethality, survivability, and dispersal characteristics of biological agents.

Choosing Indeterminacy and No Transparency: The Creation of the BWC

At the height of the massive BW arms race in the midst of the Cold War, President Richard M. Nixon took the dramatic and unexpected step on November 25, 1969, of unilaterally renouncing the possession and use by the United States of "lethal biological agents and weapons, and all other methods of biological warfare," and declaring that all biological research in the future would be confined to "defensive measures such as immunization and safety measures." Although the stated goal was to advance world peace, the questionable military utility of biological weapons significantly influenced the opinions of U.S. decision makers. In spite of newly developed practical applications, President Nixon and U.S. military leaders had serious reservations about the effectiveness of biological weapons and believed that nuclear forces provided both sufficient and superior strategic deterrence for the United States.

As the United States proceeded to destroy its BW arsenal, the United Kingdom continued its attempt to achieve a worldwide treaty banning biological weapons. In 1969 the British and Americans were able to agree on the final wording of such a treaty, but the Soviet Union adamantly opposed the effort even after the British removed language requiring enforceable verification measures. In August 1970, the Soviets suddenly dropped their objections to the proposal, and within a year the Americans, the British, and the Soviets were able to report the draft BWC to the United Nations for its approval. The BWC was opened for signature on April 10, 1972, and the United States became a party on January 22, 1975.

* * *

In negotiating the design of agreements, states may face a wide range of trade-offs in substance, structure, and obligation that include hard and soft levels of legalization, and thus yield different types of commitments and different degrees of difficulty in achieving these agreements. Various forms of soft law are touted by scholars as an easier way for states facing these choices to achieve desired objectives, to accommodate different interests through short-term compromises, and to provide the flexibility to address uncertainties and other issues. In the case of the final compromise BWC text, the design elements chosen by the drafting parties—hard legally binding obligations, soft structure (lacking any access to transparency measures), and soft indeterminate language—reflected a complex set of preferences. Both the United States and Britain, like the Soviet Union, were clearly not eager to accept the sovereignty costs and security limitations associated with either precise requirements or intrusive inspections.

Ambiguity in the BWC advanced important security objectives for the United States and Britain. The Western militaries in particular were unwilling to accept any clarifying distinctions between "peaceful" and prohibited BW activities, which resulted in the intentional placement by the Western powers of a fatal ambiguity at the heart of the BWC. While indeterminate provisions and a lack of transparency created a real possibility of future undetected defections, the ultimate national security interests of the Western powers were thought to be safeguarded in 1972 by powerful strategic nuclear deterrents. In the context of bipolar Cold War security and competition, the BWC drafting parties thus perceived a rational basis for eschewing both precision in their commitments and serious monitoring mechanisms, but this decision would have far-reaching consequences for the BWC regime when it was forced to confront BW proliferation challenges beyond the Cold War paradigm.

Overview of the Indeterminate Provisions in the BWC

The central obligation of the BWC is found in Article I, which requires each state party "never in any circumstances to develop, produce, stockpile or otherwise acquire or retain ... [m]icrobial or other biological agents, or toxins whatever their origin or method of production." This comprehensive ban, however, is limited in the same sentence to apply only to agents or toxins if they are "of types and in quantities that have no justification for prophylactic, protective or other peaceful purposes." The BWC offers no definitions of or clarifying rules on the types of biological agents that have "no justification for prophylactic, protective or other peaceful purposes." Similarly, both the obligation imposed upon states parties in Article II to destroy or convert to peaceful purposes all prohibited agents, toxins, weapons, or equipment in their possession and the prohibition in Article III preventing states parties from transferring prohibited agents, toxins, weapons, or equipment are explicitly made dependent on what might be included within the scope of the indeterminate phrase "peaceful purposes" found in Article I. To provide for domestic enforcement of its treaty obligations, each BWC state party is required to take the necessary measures within its territory to prohibit and prevent the development, production, stockpiling, acquisition, or retention of unlawful agents, toxins, weapons, and equipment. Once again, however, determining the extent of this prohibition depends on the vagaries of the term "peaceful purposes" as set forth in Article I. With respect to international enforcement, the BWC provides that a state party may submit a complaint of noncompliance to the UN Security Council, but the Convention does not specify any clear legal requirements or rules to invoke in lodging such a complaint, which must establish a "breach of obligations deriving from the provisions of the Convention."

The lack of any determinate rules or criteria in the BWC also raises troubling issues with respect to the obligation of states parties to facilitate "the fullest possible exchange of equipment, materials and scientific and technological information for the use of bacteriological (biological) agents and toxins for peaceful purposes." With no definition of what constitutes "peaceful purposes," how can any state determine precisely what should be exchanged to the fullest possible extent, on the one hand, and what should be restricted, on the other, to prevent the proliferation of biological weapons? The lack of such a definition similarly complicates the obligation to implement the BWC so as to avoid hampering international cooperation and exchanges in "peaceful" biological activities.

* * *

By 1994 it was generally acknowledged that voluntary CBMs [confidence building measures] were a failure, prompting a Special Conference of States Parties to establish the "Ad Hoc Group of States Parties" (Ad Hoc Group) to negotiate a more effective and legally binding verification regime for the BWC. The weakness of the existing BWC regime was made more apparent in the summer of 1995 when Iraq acknowledged that it had maintained an offensive BW program from 1975 until January 1991, even though it had previously claimed that it did not possess any biological weapons. Amid rising concerns about the BWC's ineffectiveness and Iraqi defiance of new UN inspections, the fourth review conference met in late 1996 and discussed the work of the Ad Hoc Group. After four and a half more years of negotiations, a "composite text" of a BWC draft protocol containing compromise language for outstanding bracketed issues was submitted by the chairman of the Ad Hoc Group and considered in April 2001.

On July 25, 2001, the U.S. ambassador to the twenty-fourth session of the Ad Hoc Group stunned delegates by unexpectedly rejecting the composite text of the draft protocol, arguing that it "would put national security and confidential business information at risk" and that it would "do little to deter those countries seeking to develop biological weapons." Other than noting general national security risks and the proprietary concerns of the U.S. pharmaceutical industry, the United States offered no specific reasons for its actions, leading domestic and international observers to complain that the decision had been heavily influenced by the drug companies.

The U.S. criticism of the draft protocol's ineffectiveness was all the more unexpected in view of the many changes that had previously been made in the text based on American objections. When the fifth review conference convened on November 19, 2001, the United States sought to terminate the Ad Hoc Group's discussion of legally binding multilateral measures altogether. Rejecting the draft protocol as a "flawed text" that would neither detect nor deter proliferators, the U.S. representative also named specific states that he said were not complying with the BWC obligations. With the draft protocol effectively dead, the fifth review conference was hastily adjourned and any further discussion of similar multilateral initiatives was suspended.

Unsuccessful BWC reform efforts thus have been accompanied by allegations of extensive noncompliance, underscoring the regime's failings while exacerbating perceived threats that can contribute to further defections. In the absence of both effective transparency measures and determinate rules to define illicit activity, governments and nonproliferation experts remain in substantial disagreement over which states to accuse of misconduct or to include on lists of states possessing or pursuing BW programs. Although the U.S. government has obviously not included itself on any list of states of BW concern, many nonproliferation experts disagree and contend that the United States is itself contributing to an insecure BW environment by conducting research in expansive "biodefense" programs that appears to violate the BWC.

* * *

While transnational actors will continue to contribute to BW nonproliferation efforts and are likely to benefit from determinate rules in the BWC, state actors with security-driven preferences hold the key to establishing an effective ban on biological weapons. In 1972, in an attempt to achieve various short-term security objectives in the context of bipolar Cold War strategies, the most powerful state actors chose the short-term benefits and expediency of soft indeterminate provisions and soft structural approaches in designing a "hard" legally binding BWC regime. In the context of modern BW proliferation problems, however, these states now have a self-interested security basis for eschewing this type of soft law approach. The United States in particular has reason to reevaluate, in light of its long-term national security interests, the rejection of BWC reform policies that it embraced prior to adopting a position based on myopic interests and unilateralist sentiments. Although a soft law approach based on indeterminacy may be beneficial in other contexts, the long-term impact of its psychological and rational mechanisms in modern arms control and multilateral security instruments presents fundamental problems that pose a different research agenda.

Convention on the Prohibition of the Development, Production and Stockpiling of Bacteriological (Biological) and Toxin Weapons and on Their Destruction of 1972

1015 U.N.T.S. 163

Article I

Each State Party to this Convention undertakes never in any circumstances to develop, produce, stockpile or otherwise acquire or retain:

(1) Microbial or other biological agents, or toxins whatever their origin or method of production, of types and in quantities that have no justification for prophylactic, protective or other peaceful purposes;

(2) Weapons, equipment or means of delivery designed to use such agents or toxins for hostile purposes or in armed conflict.

Article II

Each State Party to this Convention undertakes to destroy, or to divert to peaceful purposes, as soon as possible but not later than nine months after entry into force of the Convention, all agents, toxins, weapons, equipment and means of delivery specified in article I of the Convention, which are in its possession or under its jurisdiction or control. In implementing the provisions of this article all necessary safety precautions shall be observed to protect populations and the environment.

Article III

Each State Party to this Convention undertakes not to transfer to any recipient whatsoever, directly or indirectly, and not in any way to assist, encourage, or induce any State, group of States or international organizations to manufacture or otherwise acquire any of the agents, toxins, weapons, equipment or means of delivery specified in article I of this Convention.

Article IV

Each State Party to this Convention shall, in accordance with its constitutional processes, take any necessary measures to prohibit and prevent the development, production, stockpiling, acquisition, or retention of the agents, toxins, weapons, equipment and means of delivery specified in article I of the Convention, within the territory of such State, under its jurisdiction or under its control anywhere.

* * *

Article VI

(1) Any State Party to this convention which finds that any other State Party is acting in breach of obligations deriving from the provisions of the Convention may lodge a complaint with the Security Council of the United Nations. Such a complaint should include all possible evidence confirming its validity, as well as a request for its consideration by the Security Council.

* * *

Article VIII

Nothing in this Convention shall be interpreted as in any way limiting or detracting from the obligations assumed by any State under the Protocol for the Prohibition of the Use in War of Asphyxiating, Poisonous or Other

Gases, and of Bacteriological Methods of Warfare, signed at Geneva on June 17, 1925.

* * *

Convention on the Prohibition of the Development, Production, Stockpiling and Use of Chemical Weapons and on Their Destruction

32 I.L.M. 800 (1993)

ARTICLE I
GENERAL OBLIGATIONS

1. Each State Party to this Convention undertakes never under any circumstances:

(a) To develop, produce, otherwise acquire, stockpile or retain chemical weapons, or transfer, directly or indirectly, chemical weapons to anyone;

(b) To use chemical weapons;

(c) To engage in any military preparations to use chemical weapons;

(d) To assist, encourage or induce, in any way, anyone to engage in any activity prohibited to a State Party under this Convention.

2. Each State Party undertakes to destroy chemical weapons it owns or possesses, or that are located in any place under its jurisdiction or control, in accordance with the provisions of this Convention.

3. Each State Party undertakes to destroy all chemical weapons it abandoned on the territory of another State Party, in accordance with the provisions of this Convention.

4. Each State Party undertakes to destroy any chemical weapons production facilities it owns or possesses, or that are located in any place under its jurisdiction or control, in accordance with the provisions of this Convention.

5. Each State Party undertakes not to use riot control agents as a method of warfare.

ARTICLE II
DEFINITIONS AND CRITERIA

For the purposes of this Convention:

1. "Chemical Weapons" means the following, together or separately:

(a) Toxic chemicals and their precursors, except where intended for purposes not prohibited under this Convention, as long as the types and quantities are consistent with such purposes;

(b) Munitions and devices, specifically designed to cause death or other harm through the toxic properties of those toxic chemicals specified in subparagraph (a), which would be released as a result of the employment of such munitions and devices;

(c) Any equipment specifically designed for use directly in connection with the employment of munitions and devices specified in subparagraph (b).

2.   CONVENTIONAL WEAPONS

a.   LANDMINES

International Committee of the Red Cross, Banning Anti–Personnel Mines—The Ottawa Treaty Explained
www.icrc.org (1998)

Introduction

The Ottawa treaty is part of the international response to the humanitarian crisis caused by the global proliferation of anti-personnel mines. Millions of these deadly weapons are already contaminating more than 70 countries, creating one of the most serious man-made problems of our time. Their long-term impact upon individuals, communities, and entire societies is startling. Recognizing the seriousness of the problem, countries from all regions of the world voluntarily came together in 1997 and negotiated the Ottawa treaty, an international agreement comprehensively banning the development, production, stockpiling, transfer and use of antipersonnel mines, and requiring their destruction. This treaty is an outstanding achievement because it marks the first time that countries—through international humanitarian law—have agreed to ban completely a weapon already in widespread use. In setting a clear international standard against anti-personnel mines, the Ottawa treaty represents a decisive first step in the long-term goal of addressing the scourge of landmines and clearing the world of these horrific weapons.

1.1   The need for a ban treaty

Landmines are powerful and unforgiving devices. Unlike other weapons of war, most of which must be aimed and fired, anti-personnel landmines are "victim" actuated. That is, they are designed to be detonated by a person stepping on or handling the device, or by disturbing a tripwire attached to it.[2] Once emplaced, anti-personnel mines are indiscriminate in their effects and, unless removed or detonated, long lasting. Even today, landmines laid during the Second World War continue to be discovered and, on occasion, to kill or wound, more than 50 years after the end of the conflict. Landmines cannot "distinguish" between the soldier and the civilian. They kill or maim a child playing football just as readily as a

---

2. Anti-vehicle mines, on the other hand, are designed to be detonated by the weight of a vehicle. When left on roadways that are not used solely by military personnel, they also take their toll on civilian lives and injuries. Anti-vehicle mines are discussed further below.

soldier on patrol. Especially in post-conflict societies, it is most often the civilian going about his or her daily activities that is the unfortunate victim.

While all war wounds are horrific, the injuries inflicted by anti-personnel mines are particularly severe. These weapons are designed to kill, or, more often, to disable permanently their victims. They are specifically constructed to shatter limbs and lives beyond repair. The detonation of a buried anti-personnel "blast" mine rips off one or both legs of the victim and drives soil, grass, gravel, metal, the plastic fragments of the mine casing, pieces of the shoe, and shattered bone up into the muscles and lower parts of the body. Thus, in addition to the traumatic amputation of the limb, there is a serious threat of secondary infection. As wounds such as these are not often seen by civilian doctors, treating a mine injured patient can be a challenge to the most competent surgeon. If they survive a landmine blast, the victims typically require multiple operations and prolonged rehabilitative treatment. Unfortunately, most mine accidents occur in countries with limited medical and rehabilitative resources. Access to proper treatment and care is thus difficult or impossible. Moreover, transportation to a medical facility immediately following an accident is often arduous. In some countries it may take victims between six and 24 hours to get to a hospital capable of treating them. Many die before reaching any medical facility. Following the provision of medical care, most mine victims will require extensive rehabilitative treatment. Not only must amputees be fitted with artificial limbs to ensure mobility, but their loss of dignity and their psychological distress must also be addressed. Few survivors have access to such long-term care and assistance programmes. Even if rehabilitated, many victims are disabled, cannot work or provide for their families, and are likely to suffer intense anxiety, with little hope of improving their situation. In addition to the devastating impact on individual lives, mines also have severe social and economic consequences, particularly for a country attempting to rebuild after the end of an armed conflict. The presence of mines can leave large portions of the national territory unusable. Farmland, grazing pastures and other food-producing areas may be rendered inaccessible and, as a result, the ability of a community to feed itself is impaired. Mined roads and railways make the movement of persons and goods, including the delivery of humanitarian aid, extremely difficult. Mine clearance, although essential, is a slow, dangerous and expensive process.

Although international humanitarian law and traditional military doctrine have set clear requirements for the "responsible" use of anti-personnel mines, too often these rules have not been implemented. Research conducted on behalf of the International Committee of the Red Cross (ICRC) by military experts has shown that in 26 conflicts since the beginning of the Second World War, anti-personnel mines have only rarely been deployed in accordance with the existing legal and military requirements. Even well-trained professional armies have found it extremely difficult to use mines correctly in combat situations.

Furthermore, mines have increasingly been used as part of a brutal and systematic war against civilians, especially in the bitter internal conflicts that have come to characterize warfare in the late twentieth century. It is these tragic realities which make the anti-personnel mine a particularly abhorrent weapon and which have led the ICRC and many other organizations and individuals to call for its prohibition and stigmatization. The use of poison gas and exploding bullets has already been stigmatized and condemned by the international community. Both are weapons of war that are considered as violating the most basic principles of humanity however and whenever they are used. Now, with the adoption of the Ottawa treaty, anti-personnel mines will also be considered as a weapon which carries a level of humanitarian costs that far outweighs their limited military value.

1.2   The existing law

In 1990, the ICRC and other humanitarian organizations began to document a dramatically high number of civilian mine casualties. Many of the victims were wounded during periods when no fighting was taking place or after the end of hostilities. Subsequently, the ICRC, National Red Cross and Red Crescent Societies and the International Campaign to Ban Landmines (ICBL)—an international coalition of non-governmental organizations—began efforts to raise awareness about the devastating effects of these weapons and press for an end to their use. During the years leading up to the conclusion of the Ottawa treaty in 1997, these efforts were the dominant force in mobilizing public opinion, stimulating military and political debate, and ensuring that the plight of the victims and communities living under the threat of landmines was not forgotten.

The use of anti-personnel landmines is restricted by international law, specifically international humanitarian law, which contains several general rules applicable to these weapons. Two of the most important provisions are derived from the customary rules of warfare and are consequently binding on all sides in every situation of armed conflict:

a) Parties to a conflict must always distinguish between civilians and combatants, and civilians must not be attacked. In accordance with this principle, any weapon that is inherently indiscriminate must never be used.

b) It is prohibited to use weapons which are "of a nature to cause superfluous injury or unnecessary suffering". This means that any weapon designed to cause more injury than required to take a soldier "out of action" (i.e. one intended to inflict gratuitous suffering), even when directed solely against combatants, is unlawful and must not be used.

In addition to these general customary rules, more detailed provisions specific to anti-personnel mines are contained in various international agreements. Prior to the conclusion of the Ottawa treaty, the principal agreement governing the use of landmines was the 1980 UN Convention on

Certain Conventional Weapons (CCW).[3] Protocol II of this treaty specifically regulates mines, booby-traps and other devices. Since this is an international legal agreement, as opposed to international customary law, it applies only to those countries which agree to be bound by its terms.

As the civilian impact of landmines grew more apparent, it became evident that existing provisions of the CCW were too weak and were not being adequately followed in many of the recent conflicts where mines were being used. Following a formal request by France in 1993, governments agreed to meet and review the treaty and, in particular, to strengthen the provisions of Protocol II dealing with anti-personnel mines. Following two years of meetings of government experts in Geneva, the Review Conference of the CCW opened in Vienna in September 1995. Hopes were high that substantial and meaningful prohibitions and restrictions on landmines would be agreed by the governments taking part in the negotiations. However, although the Conference successfully adopted a new protocol banning the use and transfer of blinding laser weapons, talks to prohibit or strictly limit the production, transfer and use of anti-personnel mines became deadlocked and the conference was adjourned without any new limitations being placed on these weapons.

The Review Conference was reconvened in Geneva for two sessions in 1996. Although this time changes to the mines protocol were agreed upon, the ICRC, the ICBL and many governments considered the results disappointing and inadequate. The provisions drafted were extremely complex and many doubted whether they would or even could be effectively implemented in most situations of armed conflict. Few believed that the amended protocol would be sufficient to stem the proliferation of the weapon and consequently to reduce the number of civilian landmine casualties. At the closing session of the Review Conference, the Canadian government announced its intention to invite pro-ban countries and interested organizations and agencies to attend a conference later in the year convened to develop strategies aimed at effectively ending the affliction caused by landmines. The scene was set for the beginning of what would be termed the "Ottawa process".

1.3   The Ottawa process

The Canadian-sponsored strategy conference, Towards a Global Ban on Anti–Personnel Mines, took place in Ottawa in October 1996 with the active support of 50 governments, the JCRC, the ICBL and the United Nations. On 5 October 1996, the conference adopted the Ottawa Declaration, which committed the participants to carrying out a plan of action intended to increase resources for mine clearance and victim assistance and to working to ensure that a ban treaty was concluded at the earliest possible date. At the closing of this Conference, the Canadian government once again seized the initiative by inviting all governments to come to

---

3.   The full title is the United Nations Convention on Prohibitions or Restrictions on the Use of Certain Conventional Weapons Which May Be Deemed to Be Excessively Injurious or to Have Indiscriminate Effects.

Ottawa in December 1997 to sign a treaty prohibiting the production, stockpiling, transfer and use of anti-personnel mines. The "Ottawa process" had been officially launched.

International support for a ban on landmines continued to build. In December 1996, the UN General Assembly passed Resolution 51/45S, which called upon all countries to conclude a new international agreement totally prohibiting anti-personnel mines "as soon as possible". A total of 157 countries voted in favour of this resolution, none opposed it, and only 10 abstained from the voting. To support the Ottawa process, the Austrian government prepared a draft text of the ban treaty and circulated it to interested governments and organizations. This draft, which was subsequently revised a number of times, was the basis of the ban treaty concluded in Oslo in September 1997.

International discussion on the draft text began in Vienna in February 1997 at a meeting hosted by the Austrian government. In its address to the meeting, the ICRC called for a comprehensive ban treaty based on an unambiguous definition of an anti-personnel mine. In April 1997, the German government hosted a special meeting to discuss possible verification measures to be included in a total ban treaty. Views were divided between those who stressed the central importance of establishing a humanitarian norm against anti-personnel mines and others who considered effective verification mechanisms to be essential to the success of the treaty.

The formal follow-up to the 1996 Ottawa conference took place in Brussels from 24–27 June 1997. The Brussels International Conference for a Global Ban on Anti–Personnel Mines was attended by representatives of 154 countries. It was the largest gathering of governments to date for a conference devoted specifically to the issue of landmines. On the closing day, 97 governments signed the Brussels Declaration, launching formal negotiations on a comprehensive landmine ban treaty, greater international cooperation and assistance for mine clearance and the destruction of all stockpiled and cleared anti-personnel mines. The Declaration called for the convening of a diplomatic conference in Oslo to negotiate such a treaty on the basis of the draft prepared by the Austrian government.

In accordance with the Brussels Declaration, which by now had been signed by 107 countries, formal treaty negotiations took place from 1 to 18 September 1997 at the Oslo Diplomatic Conference on an International Total Ban on Anti–Personnel Land Mines, hosted by the Norwegian government. Ninety-one countries took part in the negotiations as full participants and 38 countries were present as observers, as were the ICRC, the ICBL and the UN.

The Oslo Diplomatic Conference proved to be a tremendous success. Propelled by its South African Chairman, Ambassador Jakob Selebi, on 18 September the Conference solemnly adopted the Convention on the Prohibition of the Use, Stockpiling, Production and Transfer of Anti–Personnel Mines and on their Destruction—the "Ottawa treaty". The treaty was opened for signature at a ceremony on 3 and 4 December 1997, when representatives from a total of 121 countries signed it on behalf of their governments. It came into force on 1 March 1999, the fastest entry into force ever for a multilateral arms related treaty. An overview of the content of the treaty is set out in the pages that follow.

Convention on the Prohibition of the Use, Stockpiling, Production and Transfer of Anti-personnel Mines and on Their Destruction

18 September 1997

Preamble

The States Parties,

Determined to put an end to the suffering and casualties caused by anti-personnel mines, that kill or maim hundreds of people every week, mostly innocent and defenceless civilians and especially children, obstruct economic development and reconstruction, inhibit the repatriation of refugees and internally displaced persons, and have other severe consequences for years after emplacement,

Believing it necessary to do their utmost to contribute in an efficient and coordinated manner to face the challenge of removing anti-personnel mines placed throughout the world, and to assure their destruction,

Wishing to do their utmost in providing assistance for the care and rehabilitation, including the social and economic reintegration of mine victims,

Recognizing that a total ban of anti-personnel mines would also be an important confidence-building measure,

Welcoming the adoption of the Protocol on Prohibitions or Restrictions on the Use of Mines, Booby–Traps and Other Devices, as amended on 3 May 1996, annexed to the Convention on Prohibitions or Restrictions on the Use of Certain Conventional Weapons Which May Be Deemed to Be Excessively Injurious or to Have Indiscriminate Effects, and calling for the early ratification of this Protocol by all States which have not yet done so,

* * *

Emphasizing the desirability of attracting the adherence of all States to this Convention, and determined to work strenuously towards the promotion of its universalization in all relevant for a including, inter alia, the United Nations, the Conference on Disarmament, regional organizations, and groupings, and review conferences of the Convention on Prohibitions or Restrictions on the Use of Certain Conventional Weapons Which May Be Deemed to Be Excessively Injurious or to Have Indiscriminate Effects,

Basing themselves on the principle of international humanitarian law that the right of the parties to an armed conflict to choose methods or means of warfare is not unlimited, on the principle that prohibits the employment in armed conflicts of weapons, projectiles and materials and methods of warfare of a nature to cause superfluous injury or unnecessary suffering and on the principle that a distinction must be made between civilians and combatants,

Have agreed as follows:

Article 1
General obligations

1. Each State party undertakes never under any circumstances:

(a) To use anti-personnel mines;

(b) To develop, produce, otherwise acquire, stockpile, retain or transfer to anyone, directly or indirectly, anti-personnel mines;

(c) To assist, encourage or induce, in any way, anyone to engage in any activity prohibited to a State Party under this Convention.

2. Each State Party undertakes to destroy or ensure the destruction of all anti-personnel mines in accordance with the provisions of this Convention.

Article 2
Definitions

1. "Anti-personnel mine" means a mine designed to be exploded by the presence, proximity or contact of a person and that will incapacitate, injure or kill one or more persons. Mines designed to be detonated by the presence, proximity or contact of a vehicle as opposed to a person, that are equipped with anti-handling devices, are not considered anti-personnel mines as a result of being so equipped.

2. "Mine" means a munition designed to be placed under, on or near the ground or other surface area and to be exploded by the presence, proximity or contact of a person or a vehicle.

* * *

b. CLUSTER MUNITIONS

Nout van Woudenberg, The Long and Winding Road Towards an Instrument on Cluster Munitions

12 J. CONFLICT & SECURITY L. 447 (2007)*

1. The Cluster Munition Problem in a Nutshell

Cluster munitions have been used for many years and were first employed during the Second World War. The first country to do so was Germany, which dropped a bomb commonly known as the "butterfly bomb" during air raids on the United Kingdom. Since then, cluster munitions have been repeatedly used in armed conflicts. Examples are

---

* Footnotes omitted.

Indochina (1950s to the early 1970s), the Gulf War (1991), Russia/Chechnya (1994–1996), Kosovo (1999), Afghanistan 2001–2002, Iraq 2003 and Lebanon (2006).

At least 75 countries worldwide have stockpiled cluster munitions, and 34 of them are known to produce in total over 210 types of cluster munitions. Cluster munitions have actually been used in at least 25 countries. The use of cluster munitions almost inevitably results in [explosive remnants of war] ERW, since it must be assumed that some of the submunitions do not explode and are therefore left behind at the end of a conflict. This may occur, for example, because of a defective detonation mechanism, production errors or lengthy storage or if submunitions land on a soft rather than a hard surface. The problem of cluster munitions has been well summarised by Eric Myjer:

> After every conflict in which explosives have been used—but also during one—there remains a category of unexploded ordnance [UXO] which might later lead to explosions causing great physical harm or even death to civilians of all ages when they come into contact with the UXO.
>
> However, they do not only cause much human suffering but also impede the development of the countries affected, particularly in the economic field. It is estimated that there have been some 100,000 victims of cluster munitions worldwide. Moreover, the area affected by a cluster bomb in practice seems to be larger than assumed by producers and users of such munitions.

The debate centres on two issues. First, there is the question of whether efforts should be focused on improving compliance, on the assumption that current international humanitarian law is adequate or whether, if the current law is not considered adequate or precise enough, a legal instrument specifically designed for cluster weapons should be introduced. And, second, if it is assumed that an instrument must be introduced to deal with cluster weapons; there is the question of whether there should be a ban on all cluster weapons or only on certain types, for example, cluster weapons that cause unacceptable humanitarian harm.

Those who oppose the use of cluster munitions cite the technical unreliability of the weapon and the fact that unexploded munitions sometimes still claim victims many years after the end of a conflict. They argue that the weapon has insufficient capacity to distinguish and discriminate, particularly when used against military targets in the vicinity of civilian areas. Advocates of the use of cluster munitions generally concede that the chance that the submunitions will not hit the target is inherently greater than in the case of a possible alternative weapon, but point out that on the other hand, the explosive charge of a submunition is considerably more limited. Given the smaller explosive charge of the submunition and the released air pressure, and in view of the category of targets for which cluster weapons are needed, they argue that the chance of collateral damage is smaller than in the case of other weapons whose explosive charge is much greater. Moreover, where use is made of an alternative to cluster weapons, more missions are needed in order to cover the same area. As more aircraft therefore have to be deployed over enemy territory, the risks to one's own forces increase. There is also the element of surprise: cluster munitions enable a military airfield, for example, to be hit in one go, whereas unitary munitions allow more time to move combat aircraft on the ground to safety.

As regards the discussion on a new instrument, the rules of treaty law still play a role. According to the rules of international law, a more recent treaty takes precedence over an earlier treaty if they address the same subject matter and are concluded between the same states. In addition, a more specific treaty takes precedence over a more general one. This could therefore mean that, if not properly coordinated, a new treaty on cluster munitions might take precedence over, and therefore detract from the existing instruments of international law (such as the Red Cross Conventions and Protocols and Protocol V to the Conventional Weapons Convention—as regards these instruments, see also Sections 3.A and 4.C). This would be undesirable in view of the importance of these instruments in international law. Various states and the ICRC therefore argue that a new convention should explicitly provide that it is complementary to the existing instruments of international law.

2.   What Are Cluster Munitions?

Cluster munitions exist in various forms. The most common are artillery projectiles and aircraft bombs. Unlike ordinary munitions, cluster munitions do not explode all at once but break up into smaller units—submunitions—which come down across a wide area and then explode. As various enemy units or targets (such as armoured vehicle columns and groups of aircraft at airfields) can thus be attacked simultaneously in a particular area, cluster munitions are more effective than standard munitions in operations of this kind. The number of submunitions in a cluster weapon can vary greatly.

This showed that the UN has defined cluster munitions as "[c]ontainers designed to disperse or release multiple submunitions". This definition is therefore restricted to the container. Submunitions are defined by the UN as "any munition that, to perform its task, separates from a parent munition". There is no standard definition of a cluster weapon or cluster munitions. In June 2007, the Geneva International Centre for Humanitarian Demining (GICHD) analysed existing and proposed definitions. The Cluster Munition Coalition uses the following definition: A cluster munition is a weapon comprising multiple explosive submunitions which are dispensed from a container. An explosive submunition is a munition designed to be dispensed in multiple quantities from a container and to detonate prior to, on, or after impact.

During the Third Review Conference of the Conventional Weapons Convention (CCW, see also Section 4.A) in November 2007, a group of 25 countries led by Norway called for the introduction of an instrument on cluster munitions. Cluster munitions were described in the declaration as "air-carried or ground-launched dispensers that contain submunitions, and where each such dispenser is designed to eject submunitions containing explosives designed to detonate on, prior to, or immediately after impact on the identified target."

In June 2007, Germany submitted a proposal to a CCW meeting for a CCW Protocol on Cluster Munitions. The proposed definition of cluster munitions is as follows:

Cluster munitions means an air-carried or ground-launched dispenser that contains submunitions with explosives. Each cluster munition is designed to eject submunitions over a pre-defined area target. Cluster munitions does not mean a dispenser that contains:

(a) direct-fire submunitions,

(b) flare and smoke ammunitions,

(c) landmines,

(d) submunitions that are inert post impact, or

(e) less than ten submunitions with explosives.

The German view is that this definition is consistent with the result of the common understanding of cluster munitions within the meetings of military and technical experts held in the context of the CCW.

The German proposal also contains a separate definition of submunition: "Submunition of cluster munitions means a munition which contains explosives and separates from a parent munition. Submunitions are designed to detonate on, prior to, or immediately after impact on the identified target."

The United Kingdom also produced a paper containing a definition of cluster munitions and submunitions in June 2007. Cluster munition is defined as "[a] dispenser or container, other than direct fire munitions, that releases more than [x] submunitions. Each duster munition is designed to eject submunitions over a pre-defined area target. A dispenser or container that contains pyrotechnic, flare, smoke or non explosive submunitions is not a cluster munition." Submunition is defined as "[a] munition that to perform its task separates from a dispenser or container. A submunition is designed to detonate on, prior to, or immediately after impact." Submunitions are categorised according to their design purpose, function, warhead and guidance system; accordingly:

A basic submunition means a munition that contains explosives but no guidance system or fail-safe mechanism.

For the discussion in Lima * * * the co-chairs of the conference presented a discussion paper on "a legally binding international instrument that will prohibit the use, production, transfer and stockpiling of cluster munitions that cause unacceptable harm to civilians". This paper used the following definition of cluster munition: "Air carried dispersal systems or air delivered, surface or sub-surface launched containers, that are designed to disperse explosive submunitions intended to detonate following separation from the container or dispenser, unless they are designed to, manually or automatically, aim, detect and engage point targets, or are meant for smoke or flaring, or unless their use is regulated or prohibited under other treaties."

The definition used in the subsequent discussion paper for the meeting in Vienna from 5 to 7 December 2007 (see below, Section G.C) is more akin to the definition used by the UN. It proposes that for the purposes of the Convention, "cluster munition" means a munition that is designed to disperse or release explosive submunitions, and includes those explosive submunitions. It does not mean the following:

> "Explosive submunitions" means munitions that, in order to perform their task, separate from a parent munition and are designed to function by detonating an explosive charge prior to, on or immediately after impact.

Dublin Convention on Cluster Munitions
May 2008

The States Parties to this Convention,

Deeply concerned that civilian populations and individual civilians continue to bear the brunt of armed conflict,

Determined to put an end for all time to the suffering and casualties caused by cluster munitions at the time of their use, when they fail to function as intended or when they are abandoned,

Concerned that cluster munition remnants kill or maim civilians, including women and children, obstruct economic and social development, including through the loss of livelihood, impede post-conflict rehabilitation and reconstruction, delay or prevent the return of refugees and internally displaced persons, can negatively impact on national and international peace-building and humanitarian assistance efforts, and have other severe consequences that can persist for many years after use,

Deeply concerned also at the dangers presented by the large national stockpiles of cluster munitions retained for operational use and *determined* to ensure their rapid destruction,

Basing themselves on the principles and rules of international humanitarian law, in particular the principle that the right of parties to an armed conflict to choose methods or means of warfare is not unlimited, and the rules that the parties to a conflict shall at all times distinguish between the civilian population and combatants and between civilian objects and military objectives and accordingly direct their operations against military objectives only, that in the conduct of military operations constant care shall be taken to spare the civilian population, civilians and civilian objects and that the civilian population and individual civilians enjoy general protection against dangers arising from military operations,

HAVE AGREED as follows:

Article 1
General obligations and scope of application

1.   Each State Party undertakes never under any circumstances to:

(a) Use cluster munitions;

(b) Develop, produce, otherwise acquire, stockpile, retain or transfer to anyone, directly or indirectly, cluster munitions;

(c) Assist, encourage or induce anyone to engage in any activity prohibited to a State Party under this Convention.

2.   Paragraph 1 of this Article applies, *mutatis mutandis,* to explosive bomblets that are specifically designed to be dispersed or released from dispensers affixed to aircraft.

3.   This Convention does not apply to mines.

* * *

NOTES AND QUESTIONS

1.   The 2005 Customary International Humanitarian Law Study identifies two general principles respecting the use of weapons in general and twelve prohibited weapons. The Study includes a note respecting nuclear weapons that refers to the ICJ's *Nuclear Weapons* advisory opinion discussed above but no rule with respect to nuclear weapons. The rules relevant to weapons included in the Study are the following:

> Rule 70. The use of means and methods of warfare which are of a nature to cause superfluous injury or unnecessary suffering is prohibited.

> Rule 71. The use of weapons which are by nature indiscriminate is prohibited.

> Rule 72. The use of poison or poisoned weapons is prohibited.

> Rule 73. The use of biological weapons is prohibited.

> Rule 74. The use of chemical weapons is prohibited.

> Rule 75. The use of riot-control agents as a method of warfare is prohibited.

> Rule 76. The use of herbicides as a method of warfare is prohibited [in certain cases]. . . .

> Rules 77. The use of bullets which expand or flatten easily in the human body is prohibited.

> Rule 78. The anti-personnel use of bullets which explode within the human body is prohibited.

> Rule 79. The use of weapons the primary effect of which is to injure by fragments which are not detectable by X-rays in the human body is prohibited.

> Rule 80. The use of booby-traps which are in any way attached to or associated with objects or persons entitled to special protection under

international humanitarian law or with objects that are likely to attract civilians is prohibited.

Rule 81. When landmines are used, particular care must be taken to minimize their indiscriminate effects. . . .

Rule 84. If incendiary weapons are used, particular care must be taken to avoid, and in any event to minimize, incidental loss of civilian life, injury to civilians and damage to civilian objects. . . .

Rule 86. The use of laser weapons that are specifically designed, [as a combat function] . . ., to cause permanent blindness to unenhanced vision is prohibited.

See I JEAN-MARIE HENCKAERTS AND LOUISE DOSWALD-BECK, CUSTOMARY INTERNATIONAL HUMANITARIAN LAW (RULES) Part IV (2005).

2. The ICRC Study finds that the use of landmines is not prohibited in all circumstances under international law. It does find the use of landmines is restricted. The United States Department of State issued the following statement with respect to U.S. policy on landmines:

U.S. Dep't of State Fact Sheet No. 2007/999, United States Leadership in Clearing Landmines and Saving Lives (Nov. 13, 2007):

[December 2007] marks the 9th anniversary of the entry into force of Amended Protocol II to the Convention on Certain Conventional Weapons (CCW), the world's first landmine treaty, and to which the United States is a party. We take this opportunity to reiterate United States landmine policy and actions.

POLICY: The military capabilities provided by landmines remain necessary for the United States to protect its armed forces and ensure the success of their mission. The United States is also committed to eliminating the humanitarian risks posed by all landmines—both anti-personnel and anti-vehicle. It stands with those who seek to protect innocent civilians from these weapons. However, the United States has not signed the Ottawa Convention because it fails to balance legitimate military requirements with humanitarian concerns.

ACTIONS: In 1992 the United States banned the export of its anti-Personnel mines. In 1999 it removed its last minefield, which protected its base in Guantánamo Bay, Cuba, and ratified Amended Protocol II. In 2004 the United States committed to never employ a "persistent" (long-lived) landmine after 2010, relying instead only on short-duration, self-destructing/self-deactivating mines that cease to be a threat within hours or days after combat. In 2005, the United States banned the use of non-detectable mines, both anti-personnel and anti-vehicle, surpassing the requirements of both landmine treaties. In 2006, the United States, joined by 24 other states, issued a declaration at the Third Review Conference of the CCW, committing each government to make anti-vehicle mines used outside of perimeter-marked areas detectable, not to use such mines outside a perimeter-marked area if they are not self-destructing or self-neutralizing, to prevent the transfer of such mines that do not meet these criteria, and then only to transfer such mines to states accepting this policy.

Since 1993, the United States has spent over $1.2 billion dollars in nearly 50 mine-affected countries and regions for: clearance of mines and explosive remnants of war (most of which are of foreign origin); mine risk education; survivors assistance; landmine surveys; research and development on better ways to detect and clear mines; training foreign deminers and mine action managers; and destroying at-risk stocks of arms and munitions. Thanks in part to United States' help, the annual landmine casualty rate has dropped from over 26,000 four years ago to around 5,000 today, and Costa Rica, Djibouti, EI Salvador, Guatemala, Honduras, Kosovo, Macedonia, Namibia, and Suriname have achieved mine "impact-free" status. Nicaragua should follow suit in 2008....

Is this statement an example of an objection by the United States to maintain persistent objector status in the face of a developing rule of customary international law? Does it accomplish any other purpose?

3.   There are few if any cases in which individuals have been held to account for the use of prohibited weapons. Saddam Hussein was tried and executed in 2007 for the murder of scores of persons suspected of being involved in a plot to assassinate him in the village of Dujail, Iraq. He was not tried for ordering the use of chemical weapons against Iranians in the Iran–Iraq War as confirmed by the UN in reports such as the ones excerpted above. See Nehal Bhuta, *Fatal Errors, The Trial and Appeal Judgments in the Dujail Case,* 6 J. INT'L CRIM. JUST. 39 (2008).

Vietnamese citizens have tried to bring civil law suits against Dow Chemical for the manufacture of Agent Orange and other herbicides used by the United States during the Vietnam War. The plaintiffs argued that the use of Agent Orange violated the customary prohibition on the use of poison and the infliction of unnecessary suffering and, therefore, was the type of violation for which they could sue under the 1789 Alien Tort Claims Act, 28 U.S.C. § 1350 (ATCA). Under the U.S. Supreme Court's decision in *Sosa v. Alvarez–Machain,* 542 U.S. 692, 124 S.Ct. 2739, 159 L.Ed.2d 718 (2004), the violations encompassed under ATCA must be specific and universally recognized as an obligation under international law. The use of poison might meet such a test, but the plaintiffs did not present evidence that the United States had intended to use Agent Orange to poison people. *Vietnam Association for Victims of Agent Orange v. Dow Chemical Co.,* 517 F.3d 104 (2d Cir. 2008).

4.   Is there any possibility of prohibiting suicide bombing or improvised explosive devices on the ground that such methods or weapons are too indiscriminate to be lawful? How could it be done effectively within the means available in international law? Note that these low-tech methods have killed many times more persons in the recent decades than WMDs.

5.   Of the three areas surveyed in this chapter, law on resort to armed conflict, law on the conduct of armed conflict, and arms control, in which is it most urgent that the international community make progress? In which area is progress most likely?

CHAPTER 11

INTERNATIONAL LAW IN NATIONAL AND REGIONAL SYSTEMS

Section A. The United Kingdom.
Section B. The United States.
Section C. Argentina.
Section D. European Union.
Section E. France.
Section F. South Africa.

Throughout this book you have seen the interconnections among various legal systems. In this chapter we focus on that subject directly. We have chosen six diverse national and regional jurisdictions that the authors have studied in depth. We present them in chronological order of the date of the adoption of the constitution or constituent instrument. For each we will look at constitutional principles touching on the reception of international law in the national systems, as well as specific principles governing the reception of treaties and customary international law. This chapter is limited to the reception of international law in other systems and does not concern national or regional legal controls over foreign policy-making or security policy. That subject is left for specialized courses, which in the United States are often designated "foreign affairs and the constitution" or "national security law." Nor is the chapter concerned with the reach of national or regional law abroad; that topic was taken up in Chapter 4 above. This chapter concerns the various ways legal systems are organized for applying and enforcing international law.

Recall that this subject was briefly introduced in Chapter 1. D.P. O'Connell set out four theories for how national systems (or "municipal" systems as he refers to them) tend to be oriented vis-à-vis international law:

> Almost every case in a municipal court in which a rule of international law is asserted to govern the decision raises the problem of the relationship of international law and municipal law; * * * There are four possible attitudes towards the question:
>
> (a) That international law has primacy over municipal law in both international and municipal decisions. This is the *monist* theory.
>
> (b) That international law has primacy over municipal law in international decisions, and municipal law has primacy over international law in municipal decisions. This is the *dualist* theory.

(c) That municipal law has primacy over international law in both international and municipal decisions. This is a species of monism in reverse.

(d) That there should be no supposition of conflict between international law and municipal law.

1 D.P. O'CONNELL, INTERNATIONAL LAW 38 (1970). As you read about the various approaches described in this chapter, consider whether a system is a monist, dualist, reverse monist, or no conflict system. We think you will find that the systems have tendencies toward one or the other of these theories but no system is purely monist, dualist, or anything else. *See also*, Eileen Denza, *The Relationship between Municipal and International Law*, *in* INTERNATIONAL LAW, ch. 14 (Malcolm Evans ed., 2003).

A. UNITED KINGDOM

In the United Kingdom, international law is traditionally described as playing only a minor role in judicial decisions. Consistent with a monist approach, customary international law is usually considered automatically incorporated into domestic law, while the dualist theory explains treaties: they must be transformed through domestic legislation in order to be enforceable by English courts. These principles remain true as a general matter, but exceptions and variations abound.

1. CONSTITUTIONAL CONSIDERATIONS

In accordance with its unwritten constitution, Parliament has the power to establish and to change the law of the UK. The conduct of foreign affairs, including the making of treaties, remains under the royal prerogative (i.e., carried out by the executive of the government in power). Nevertheless, the government remains broadly accountable to Parliament in the area of foreign policymaking. The UK does not require the supremacy of international legal obligations over the national constitution.

With the passage of the European Communities Act of 1972, however, the UK now accepts into UK law features of the Community legal order—in particular direct applicability of Council and Commission regulations.

2. TREATIES

British law views treaties as purely executive, rather than legislative, acts. In order to become part of domestic law, the treaty must be "transformed" into domestic law by being "incorporated" through the adoption of relevant legislation. Except to the extent that a treaty becomes incorporated into the laws of the UK by statute, the courts of the UK are generally considered to have no power to enforce treaty rights and obligations at the request of either a sovereign government or of a private individual. This maintains the supremacy of Parliament by ensuring that the executive alone cannot alter national law by means of a treaty rather than through the legislative process.

The European Convention on Human Rights and the various treaties establishing the European Economic Community and the European Union have been incorporated into British law by the Human Rights Act 1998 and the European Communities Act 1972. The UK rarely assumes international commitments without giving internal effect to them and subjects all treaties to rigorous scrutiny of national implementation before ratification. On the other hand, there is evidence that even respecting treaties, the UK is not a strict dualist system. For example, the United Kingdom Human Rights Act of 1998, provides: "So far as it is possible to do so, primary legislation and subordinate legislation must be read and given effect in a way which is compatible with the [European] Convention rights." This legislation resulted from a perception that a better system of incorporating the European Convention on Human Rights into United Kingdom law would result in more effective enforcement of its provisions.

UK courts had already developed a pattern of seeking to avoid conflict where divergence from international law arises at the national level. The approach was set out by Lord Denning in *Salomon v. Commissioners of Customs and Excise*, 2 QB 116 (1967), where he said of a treaty which could not directly be relied on but which formed part of the background of the statutory provision in issue:

> I think we are entitled to look at it because it is an instrument which is binding in international law and we ought always to interpret our statutes as to be in conformity with international law.

J.H. Rayner v. Department of Trade and Industry
Maclaine Watson v. Department of Trade and Industry

Court of Appeals (England)
[1988] 3 All ER 257 (Tin Council)

■ (KERR, NOURSE and RALPH GIBSON L.JJ.)

SUMMARY: *The facts* :—The International Tin Council ("ITC") was an international organization constituted, at the relevant time, under the Sixth International Tin Agreement ("ITA6"). The members of the ITC were 23 States, including the United Kingdom, and the European Economic Community. The headquarters of the ITC were in London. The object of the ITC was to promote an orderly market in tin, preventing excessive fluctuations in the price. To this end the ITC operated a buffer stock, buying tin when the market price fell below a certain level and selling tin from the buffer stock when the price rose too high. Article 16 of ITA provided that the ITC should have legal personality and, in particular, the capacity to contract, to acquire and dispose of movable and immovable property and to institute legal proceedings. The provisions of Article 16 were repeated in Article 3 of the ITC–United Kingdom Headquarters

Agreement, 1972. Article 8 of the Headquarters Agreement provided that the ITC was to enjoy immunity from jurisdiction and execution subject to certain exceptions. The Headquarters Agreement was given effect in English law by the International Tin Council (Immunities and Privileges) Order 1972 ("the 1972 Order"), an Order in Council made under the provisions of the International Organizations Act 1968. Article 5 of the 1972 Order provided that the ITC was to have the legal capacities of a body corporate, while Article 6 stipulated that the ITC should be immune from suit and legal process except in certain cases. Neither ITA6 nor the Headquarters Agreement was incorporated into English law.

In October 1985 the ITC announced that it was unable to meet its commitments and ceased trading, owing debts of several hundred million pounds to its creditors. Several of these creditors instituted proceedings against the members of the ITC.

* * *

[In three separate cases] plaintiffs sued the Department of Trade and Industry ("DTI"), representing the United Kingdom and the other 22 Member States of the ITC. In the *Rayner* and *Six Banks* actions the plaintiffs also sued the Commission of the European Communities. In the *Multi–Brokers* action the plaintiffs sued the European Economic Community (rather than the Commission) and the ITC itself, as well as the DTI and the other Member States. The plaintiffs in all the actions contended that the members of the ITC were liable for debts incurred by, or in the name of, the ITC. In the High Court, Staughton J. held that the statement of claim disclosed no cause of action. The plaintiffs appealed against that judgment. In *Maclaine Watson and Co Ltd v. Department of Trade and Industry*, another tin trading company brought proceedings against the DTI to enforce a judgment for over £6 million which had been entered against the ITC. The plaintiffs contended that the members of the ITC were jointly and severally liable for the debt. In the High Court, Millett J. held that the statement of claim disclosed no reasonable cause of action and ordered that it be struck out. The plaintiffs appealed against the judgment.

Before the Court of Appeal the plaintiffs in the various actions advanced three alternative submissions:

(a) that the ITC was not a legal entity distinct from its members, so that contracts concluded in the name of the ITC were in fact concluded by all the members of the ITC;

(b) that if the ITC did possess legal personality, that personality did not absolve the members from liability, so that the members were liable concurrently with the ITC for debts incurred by the ITC or had secondary liability if the ITC failed to honour those debts;

(c) that the constitution of the ITC was such that it had contracted as agent for its members.

The defendants disputed all three submissions, maintaining that in both English and international law the ITC was an entity distinct from its members and able to contract without engaging their liability and that nothing in ITA6 could give rise to any relationship of principal and agent. They also argued that the interpretation of ITA6 was non-justiciable in the English courts since the treaty had not been incorporated into English law, with the result that the plaintiffs could not rely upon ITA6 to sustain their submissions that the ITC's legal personality did not absolve its members from liability or that the ITC had acted as agent for its members. In addition, the defendants, other than the DTI, maintained that, in relation to submissions (b) and (c) advanced by the plaintiff they were entitled to sovereign immunity, the Member States relying upon the State Immunity Act 1978, while the EEC maintained that it was entitled to sovereign immunity at common law.

Held *(Nourse L.J. dissenting in part):—The appeals were dismissed.*

(1) (unanimously) The ITC had legal personality separate and distinct from its members. Although Article 5 of the 1972 Order did not make the ITC a body corporate in English law, the ITC was undoubtedly a legal entity distinct from its members on the plane of international law and the 1972 Order recognized that fact. Moreover, the provisions of the Order conferring immunities upon the ITC and creating certain exceptions to those immunities so that the ITC might be held liable in particular cases would be meaningless unless the ITC had a separate legal existence * * *.

* * *

The issues in outline

The legal problems involved in these proceedings are unprecedented, not only in our courts but evidently anywhere. It would be inappropriate to consider them solely by reference to English law in isolation. They concern all international organisations operating in similar circumstances and require analysis on the plane of public international law and of the relationship between international law and the domestic law of this country.

Turning to the latter, in pursuance of the I.T.A. treaties and a "Headquarters Agreement" between the I.T.C. and the United Kingdom concluded in 1972, the I.T.C. was granted "the legal capacities of a body corporate" in this country by an Order in Council made in 1972 which continued in force in relation to I.T.A.6. But the I.T.C. was not incorporated. Its status remained formally unchanged, and it was common ground that in international law it had "legal personality." The conferment of "the legal capacities of a body corporate" is a time honoured phrase which has been in use for more than 30 years in our domestic legislation in relation to the facilities granted in this country to international organisations created by treaty. But its meaning and effect have never been considered. In the present situation it raises acute problems about the status of the I.T.C. and the claims made directly against its members. Are they under any liability, either concurrently with the I.T.C. or secondarily in the event that the I.T.C. defaults on its obligations? Or can they claim to be in the same position as the shareholders of a limited liability company because the

I.T.C. has been given the capacity to contract in its own name and did so? Alternatively, can the members be held liable as undisclosed principals on whose behalf the I.T.C. contracted as agent?

Then there are other problems. The I.T.C. was granted immunities from suit and legal process except (so far as relevant) in respect of the enforcement of arbitration awards. The London Metal Exchange contracts contained arbitration clauses and resulted in large awards in favour of the broker plaintiffs against the I.T.C. But only one of the bank loans was made subject to a provision for arbitration, so that the failure to repay the others can only result in judgments against the I.T.C. It now claims immunity in respect of them, and it resists the application for a winding up order on the ground that this would be inappropriate in relation to an international organisation and that such an order would in any event not fall within the exception of enforcement of an arbitration award.

Next, there is the doctrine of the "non-justiciability" in our courts of rights and obligations arising under treaties—such as I.T.A. 1 to 6—which have not been incorporated into our domestic law. The scope and effect of this doctrine is uncertain and poses many problems in the present context. In particular, it is invoked as a defence to the receivership application on the ground that a receiver, standing in the shoes of the I.T.C would be unable to enforce in our courts whatever claims (if any) the I.T.C. might have against its members, since these would require the interpretation and application of I.T.A.6.

* * *

Justiciability

Various aspects of the limits of justiciability fall to be considered in different contexts in these appeals. The topic is usually referred to as "the doctrine of non-justiciability." It is convenient to discuss this doctrine in general terms at this stage in the context of unincorporated treaties, i.e. treaties which have not been incorporated into our law. bearing in mind that in our law—unlike in the case of many other systems—treaties are not self-executing.

Many of the leading cases and dicta on the non-justiciability of unincorporated treaties are referred to in the judgment of Staughton J. [1987] B.C.L.C. 667, 687 et seq. and 701 et seq. I do not think that it is necessary to review these again here. But some general considerations should be borne in mind.

The main one is that any question whether or not a matter connected with an unincorporated treaty is justiciable must depend on the nature of the issue which is under consideration and not on whether the arguments or evidence placed before the court require reference to the contents of an unincorporated treaty. Thus, with all respect to the passage in the judgment of Staughton J., at p. 703B–F, as well as to many of the submissions addressed to us on these appeals, reliance on the doctrine of non-justiciability may all too easily involve an approach which tends to preclude all reference to the terms of a treaty and to inhibit the duty of the court to decide justiciable issues. This carries non-justiciability much too far. In considering the limits of the doctrine one must remember that it only rests on two general principles, leaving aside any overlap with non-justiciability in relation to acts of state, etc. of the kind discussed in *Buttes Gas and Oil Co. v. Hammer (No. 3)* [1982] A.C. 888. The first is that since unincorporated treaties have no legislative effect, they do not form part of the law of this country: see e.g. *Attorney–General for Canada v. Attorney–General for Ontario* [1937] A.C. 326, 347, *per* Lord Atkin. No private rights or obligations can therefore be derived from the provisions of such treaties. Secondly, although treaties are agreements intended to be binding upon the parties to them, they are not contracts which our courts can enforce: see e.g. *Cook v. Sprigg* [1899] A.C. 572, 578, and *British Airways Board v. Laker Airways Ltd.* [1984] Q.B. 142, 192D, C.A. and [1985] A.C. 58, 85H and 86A, H.L.(E.). Any issue between the parties to an unincorporated treaty is a non-justiciable issue in our courts. But that is as far as the doctrine goes. It does not preclude the decision of justiciable issues which arise against the background of an unincorporated treaty in a way which renders it necessary or convenient to refer to, and consider, the contents of the treaty. Indeed, any contest as to whether or not an issue connected with an unincorporated treaty is justiciable will usually require some reference to the treaty. Apart from this, a court must be free to inform itself fully of the contents of a treaty whenever these are relevant to the decision of any issue which is not in itself a non-justiciable issue. There are many precedents of high authority which demonstrate this * * *. To keep in mind the proper bounds of non-justiciability in relation to unincorporated treaties is in my view of importance for the consideration of all three of the plaintiffs' submissions A, B and C.

First, submissions A and B necessarily involve consideration of the legal nature of the I.T.C., using this expression in the widest sense and for the present without distinguishing between its nature in international law and municipal law. However, the court has no means of informing itself about the nature of the I.T.C. otherwise than by looking at its constitution, which is only to be found in I.T.A.6. The only instrument having direct effect in our municipal law is the Order of Council of 1972. But article 4 tells us no more than that the I.T.C. is "an organisation" in international law, and article 5 does no more than to confer "capacities" upon this organisation without purporting to define, or to alter, its legal nature in any way, whatever this might be. So the court must consider I.T.A.6 against the background of international law in order to inform itself about the nature of the I.T.C. And for that purpose one must also reject any suggestion that when a court looks at an unincorporated treaty, it is then precluded from applying any process of interpretation to its provisions. This was submitted on all sides from time to time in different contexts. However, reading a treaty involves seeking to understand it, and this may necessarily involve some interpretation of its terms.

The second reason why the principles of non-justiciability do not preclude resort to I.T.A.6 or to the Headquarters Agreement is that both are of assistance in the interpretation of the Order in Council of 1972. In relation to articles 4 and 5 of the Order this may only be a restatement of what I have said above. But article 6.1(c) refers expressly to articles of the Headquarters Agreement which have not been incorporated in the Order and which cannot therefore be applied without reference to that treaty. And articles 8 and 10 to 13 inclusive, read together with article 2, necessarily require consideration of I.T.A.6.

I have not found it necessary to cite from any of the numerous authorities to which we were referred in order to support these conclusions. They are in line with the dicta of Diplock L.J. in *Salomon v. Commissioners of Customs and Excise* [1967] 2 Q.B. 116, 132, and of Lord Diplock in *Garland v. British Railway Engineering Ltd.* [1983] 2 A.C. 751, 771. But in the present peculiarly international context one should in any event not shrink from adopting a liberal approach to the right to consider unincorporated treaties in order to interpret our consequential domestic legislation. Thus, given the problems and uncertainties of interpreting the Order in Council of 1972 passed in consequence of I.T.A.4 and the Headquarters Agreement, in the same way mutatis mutandis as numerous other similar Orders in consequence of numerous other similar treaties, it appears excessively insular, and perhaps in these times almost absurd, to prohibit reference to the underlying international instruments as an aid to the intended effect of the Orders. But in case this might be thought to be going too far I should refer to two statements of high authority which are of particular assistance in the present context, and I take them chronologically. In *Pan–American World Airways Inc. v. Department of Trade* [1976] 1 Lloyd's Rep. 257, 261, Scarman L.J. said:

> "There is one other situation in which, in my opinion, it is proper for our courts to take note of an international convention. It arises when two courses are reasonably open to the court: but one would lead to a decision inconsistent with Her Majesty's international obligations under the convention while the other would lead to a result consistent with those obligations. If statutory words have to be construed or a legal principle formulated in an area of the law where Her Majesty has accepted international obligations, our courts—who of course, take notice of the acts of Her Majesty done in the exercise of her sovereign power—will have regard to the convention as part of the full content or background of the law. Such a convention, especially a multilateral one, should then be considered by courts even though no statute expressly or impliedly incorporates it into our law."

Secondly, there is a passage in the speech of Lord Bridge of Harwich in Shearson Lehman Brothers Inc. v. Maclaine Watson & Co. Ltd. [17] (No. 2) [1988] 1 W.L.R. 16, 24D, which is of direct assistance. It was concerned with article 7 of the Order in Council of 1972 but is of general application for present purposes. Apart from appearing to indicate that in his view reference to the Headquarters Agreement was not precluded, Lord Bridge (in whose speech all their Lordships concurred) said that he derived assistance from "a consistent practice in domestic legislation, enacted to give effect to treaties concluded by the United Kingdom with international organisations . . .''

The importance of these passages is that they call for the rejection of a major argument on behalf of the plaintiffs made at the outset of these appeals in support of submission A. This was founded on the fact that the words in articles 4 and 5 of the Order of 1972 were the same as those which had originally been used in the Diplomatic Privileges (Extension) Act 1944 and that they must therefore have the same meaning in 1972 as they had in 1944. In consequence, to quote from the ''skeleton argument'' of Maclaine Watson: ''the instruments . . . relating to other international organisations and which are all subsequent to the Act of 1944 are not admissible to construe [the Order of 1972].'' Furthermore, it was said that the legislation beginning in 1944 which culminated in the International Organisations Act 1968 effectively prescribed the wording of articles 4 and 5 for the purposes of the Order of 1972 relating to the I.T.C., and therefore precluded any consideration of the nature of the I.T.C. under I.T.A.6, the Headquarters Agreement and international law generally.

I had difficulty in following these submissions and hope that I do not do them any injustice. But their purpose was to seek to compel the court to ignore entirely that I.T.A.6 and the Headquarters Agreement provided expressly that the I.T.C. ''shall have legal personality,'' in articles 3 and 16.1 respectively. Equally, their purpose was to render it impermissible for the court to know and take into account that the great majority of treaties setting up international organisations has expressly provided, by the use of the same or similar words, that the organisation was to be a legal entity on the plane of international law. It was said that the English courts are allowed to know no more about the I.T.C. than that it was an ''organisation'' as mentioned in article 4 of the Order of 1972 and that the courts therefore had to remain wholly uninformed about the nature of this organisation on the plane of international law.

I have already said enough to make it clear that in my view all these submissions are untenable. The court is under a duty to inform itself as best it can about the juridical nature of the I.T.C. in order to consider upon what legal entity, body, organisation or concept the capacities of a body corporate have been conferred by article 5 of the Order, and for the purpose of deciding the justiciable issues raised by the contention that the members of the I.T.C. are liable to the plaintiffs for the contractual debts of the I.T.C.

This not only permits, but requires, the court to consider I.T.A.6 and the Headquarters Agreement so far as necessary. It also requires the court to determine what are the relevant principles of international law in so far as their ascertainment may be necessary for the determination of the issues between the parties. While these must of course ultimately be decided by English law, it does not by any means follow that international law is irrelevant in deciding upon the position of the parties under English law.

I have spent some time on these initial submissions of the plaintiffs because in my view they involve an erroneous application of the doctrine of non-justiciability in relation to unincorporated treaties, and because the proper scope of this doctrine bears upon so many aspects of these appeals. But in fairness to the plaintiffs it should be noted that these extreme submissions were only advanced for the purposes of submission A, and that submissions A, B and C are wholly alternative and therefore permissibly inconsistent with each other. Thus, as will be seen later, the plaintiffs' approach to non-justiciability in relation to submission B—particularly as advanced by Mr. Burnton on behalf of the banks—was wholly in line with the views expressed above and not seriously contested by the defendants. On the other hand, in relation to submission C the roles were reversed, since it was the concern of the defendants to seek to exclude recourse to I.T.A.6 when the plaintiffs were claiming that this was permissible.

* * *

English law and international law

For up to two and a half centuries it has been generally accepted amongst English judges and jurists that international law forms part of the law of this country, at all events if it can be shown that there is an established rule which, first, is derived from one or more of the recognised sources of international law and, secondly, has already been carried into English law by statute, judicial decision or ancient custom. It would seem that the second of these requirements, which is based on what is known as the doctrine of transformation, could not be satisfied without the prior satisfaction of the first, but the circumstances of the present case require that they be separately identified. Beyond this common ground there was formerly a significant difference of opinion. The doctrine of transformation had a rival in the doctrine of incorporation, which holds that the rules of international law from time to time in force are automatically incorporated into the common law and, subject always to statute, are supreme. That rivalry was resolved in favour of incorporation by the decision of this court * * *.

The effect of the doctrine of incorporation on the present case is that an English court, in pursuance of the direction given to it by article 4 of the Order of 1972, must attribute to the I.T.C.'s contracts such effect as is currently assigned to them by international law, notwithstanding that there is no statute, judicial decision nor ancient custom to hand. But there remains the difficulty, already acknowledged, that there is no established rule of international law which bears on the matter. Does this mean that an English court has no alternative but to apply its own established rule?

The proposition that international law can only form part of English law if there is an established rule in point is supported by the views of several respected judges, their authority being by no means diminished by the fact that some of them were expressed in support of the doctrine of transformation: see *Reg. v. Keyn* (1876) 2 Ex.D. 63, 202–203, Cockburn C.J. and *West Rand Central Gold Mining Co. Ltd. v. The King* [1905] 2 K.B. 391, 406–408, Lord Alverstone C.J., Wills and Kennedy JJ. Perhaps the clearest statement was made by Lord Macmillan in *Compania Naviera Vascongado v. S.S. Cristina* [1938] A.C. 485, 497:

> "Now, it is a recognised prerequisite of the adoption in our municipal law of a doctrine of public international law that it shall have attained the position of general acceptance by civilised nations as a rule of international conduct, evidenced by international treaties and conventions, authoritative text-books, practice and judicial decisions. It is manifestly of the highest importance that the courts of this country before they give the force of law within this realm to any doctrine of international law should be satisfied that it has the hallmarks of general assent and reciprocity."

In none of those cases was the English court, as it is here, directed by an Order in Council to form a view of the nature of an international organisation and the effect of its contracts in international law. In such a case and in the absence of an established rule, it is argued that the court must do its best, on the material available to it, to arrive at the view of the matter which international law would be most likely to take. * * * [In support of this position][t]he next judgment relied on by Mr. Burnton was that of the Privy Council in *In re Piracy Jure Gentium* [1934] A.C. 586, where an order in council directed the judicial committee to hear and consider the question whether actual robbery was an essential element of the crime of piracy jure gentium or whether a frustrated attempt to commit a piratical robbery was enough to constitute the offence. Viscount Sankey L.C., in delivering the report of the Board, said, at pp. 588–589:

> "In considering such a question, the Board is permitted to consult and act upon a wider range of authority than that which it examines when the question for determination is one of municipal law only. The sources from which international law is derived include treaties between various states, state papers, municipal Acts of Parliament and the decisions of municipal courts and last, but not least, opinions of jurisconsults or text-book writers. It is a process of inductive reasoning. It must be remembered that in the strict sense international law still has no legislature, no executive and no judiciary, though in a certain sense there is now an international judiciary in The Hague Tribunal and attempts are being made by the League of Nations to draw up codes of international law. Speaking generally, in embarking upon international law, their Lordships are to a great extent in the realm of opinion, and in estimating the value of opinion it is permissible not only to seek a consensus of views, but to select what appear to be the better views upon the question."

Finally, Mr. Burnton referred us to a passage from the judgment of the Privy Council delivered by Lord Atkin in *Chung Chi Cheung v. The King* [1939] A.C. 160, 167–168, but I do not find that that adds anything of significance to the present inquiry. To these citations may be added the following from the judgment of Lord Denning M.R. in *Trendtex Trading Corporation v. Central Bank of Nigeria* [1977] Q.B. 529, 552–553:

"It is, I think, for the courts of this country to define the rule as best they can, seeking guidance from the decisions of the courts of other countries, from the jurists who have studied the problem, from treaties and conventions and, above all, defining the rule in terms which are consonant with justice rather than adverse to it. An uncertain question of international law is one which cannot be settled by reference either to an opinion of the International Court of Justice or to some usage, custom or general principle of law recognised by all civilised nations. The authorities show that where it is necessary for an English court to decide such a question, and whatever the doubts and difficulties, it can and must do so; being guided by municipal legislation and judicial decisions, treaties and conventions and the opinions of international jurists; and, where no consensus is there found, by those opinions which are the most nearly consistent with reason and justice. Broadly stated, the uncertain question which confronts us in the present case is whether the members of the I.T.C. are liable for its debts. It is a question which must be answered either in the affirmative or in the negative. It is a question to which international law can no more refuse an answer than municipal law."

* * *

Lastly, I would refer to the work of Professor Ignaz Seidl–Hohenveldern of the University of Vienna, *Corporations in and under International Law* (1987). A brief citation is sufficient for this purpose, from p. 73:

"International organisations and common inter-state enterprises, however, have two features in common: they are formed by several states for the pursuit of a common purpose and these states have endowed them with a separate personality, applying a general principle of civil law to relations established under international law."

It would, as I think, be astonishing if international law were found to be to any different effect. The repeated use of the phrase "legal personality," or variants of it, in the multi-lateral treaties listed in the schedule could not have been intended by the states, who were parties to the treaties, to have no effect in international law so that the organisation, upon which they expressed the intention of conferring legal personality, continued as an association of, and not an entity separate from, the members. In *In re Reparation for Injuries Suffered in Service of United Nations* [1949] I.C.J.R. 174, the International Court of Justice had to consider whether the United Nations, under its charter, had international personality so as to be able to bring an international claim. As already mentioned above, the charter did not express an intention by the founding states that the United Nations should have international legal personality. The court concluded, at pp. 179–180:

"the organisation was intended to exercise and enjoy ... functions and rights which can only be explained on the basis of the possession of a large measure of international personality and the capacity to operate upon an international plane. ... It must be acknowledged that its members, by entrusting certain functions to it, with the attendant duties and responsibilities, have clothed it with the competence required to enable those functions to be effectively discharged. Accordingly the court has come to the conclusion that the organisation is an international person. That is not the same thing as saying that it is a state, which it certainly is not, or that its legal personality and rights and duties are the same as those of a state. ... Whereas a state possesses the totality of international rights and duties recognised by international law, the rights and duties of an entity such as the organisation must depend upon its purposes and functions as specified or implied in its constituent documents and developed in practice.''

It appears to me to be clear that international law would regard the possession of legal personality under international law by an international organisation, expressly conferred by its constituent documents, as causing the organisation to have existence separate from the members who formed it and capable of acting in law independently of its members. The rights and duties of the organisation, and the consequences in international law of its actions for the liability of its members by reason of their membership would have to be determined by consideration to the constituent documents of the organisation in the light of any relevant rule of international law.

The international obligation assumed by the United Kingdom to the I.T.C. in the Headquarters Agreement, that the I.T.C. should have legal personality under our law, was therefore, in my judgment, an obligation to afford such legal personality as would cause the I.T.C. to be an entity distinct from its members and capable of acting and contracting on its own behalf and without, at the same time and automatically, engaging the primary liability of the members under its contracts. In short, the organisation would not be a form of partnership as known to English law. Further the obligation assumed by the United Kingdom under the United Nations Convention of February 1946, to the effect that the United Nations should have ''juridical personality,'' was to the same effect. That obligation was assumed before the date of any of the authorities cited to us, but I would hold that the effect of legal personality in international law must be taken to have been the same in 1946, and when the Act of 1944 was passed, as it is shown to have been before and after 1972.

I would add that the international obligation assumed by the United Kingdom was, in my judgment, limited to the provision for the I.T.C. of separate legal personality and did not extend to the securing in English law of the enforceability of any other attributes of the international legal personality of the I.T.C. which under international law might be derived from the terms of its then constituent document, I.T.A.4. That limit upon the obligation assumed by the United Kingdom under I.T.A.4 and the Headquarters Agreement is apparent from the terms of the Headquarters Agreement of which article 3 says only that the council shall have legal personality. There cannot be derived from that provision any obligation to enact in this country any particular attributes of that personality whether concerned with liability or non-liability of the members.

In the result, the first and main submission for the plaintiffs must, in my judgment, fail. The I.T.C. has at all times had legal personality separate from its members and of such a nature that, when it contracts in its own name, it contracts for itself and it does not thereby engage its members by reason only of their membership in any direct and primary liability upon its contracts.

3.   CUSTOMARY INTERNATIONAL LAW

As previously discussed, customary international law is automatically incorporated into English law and need not be transformed by a parliamentary act. Indeed, the occasions on which rules of customary international law fail to be applied by English courts are relatively few. Those cases that have dealt with the role of customary international law in English domestic law have concerned limited situations of jurisdiction and dealing with immunities of foreign States and governments and of diplomatic agents or with territorial waters.

The seminal case establishing the status and process of incorporation of customary international law in the English system was *Trendtex Trading Corporation v. Central Bank of Nigeria.*

Trendtex Trading Corporation v. Central Bank of Nigeria

England, Queen's Bench, 1977
[1977] Q.B. 529, 553–554

[The issue was whether the bank was entitled to sovereign immunity i.e., whether it was immune from suit in the courts of England.

At the time the suit was brought, the applicable rule of customary international law did not require the court to grant the immunity. Lord Denning discussed the manner in which this rule of international law became part of the law of England. A portion of his opinion follows.]

* * *

A fundamental question arises. * * * What is the place of international law in our English law? One school of thought holds to the doctrine of *incorporation*. It says that the rules of international law are incorporated into English law automatically and considered to be part of English law unless they are in conflict with an Act of Parliament. The other school of thought holds to the doctrine of *transformation*. It says that the rules of international law are not to be considered as part of English law except in so far as they have been already adopted and made part of our law by the decisions of the judges, or by Act of Parliament, or long established custom. The difference is vital when you are faced with a change in the rules of international law. Under the doctrine of incorporation, when the rules of international law change, our English law changes with them. But, under the doctrine of transformation, the English law does not change. It is bound by precedent. It is bound down to those rules of international law which have been accepted and adopted in the past. It cannot develop as international law develops.

(i) *The doctrine of incorporation.* The doctrine of incorporation goes back to 1737 in *Buvot v. Barbut* [sic] (1736) 3 Burr. 1481 * * * in which Lord Talbot L.C. (who was highly esteemed) made a declaration which was taken down by young William Murray (who was of counsel in the case) and adopted by him in 1764 when he was Lord Mansfield C.J. in *Triquet v. Bath* (1764) 3 Burr. 1478:

> Lord Talbot declared a clear opinion—"That the law of nations in its full extent was part of the law of England." * * *

> That doctrine was accepted, not only by Lord Mansfield himself, but also by Sir William Blackstone, and [numerous] other great names.

* * *

(iii) *Which is correct?* * * * I now believe that the doctrine of incorporation is correct. Otherwise I do not see that our courts could ever recognise a change in the rules of international law. It is certain that international law does change. I would use of international law the words which Galileo used of the earth: "But it does move." International law does change: and the courts have applied the changes without the aid of any Act of Parliament. * * *

(iv) *Conclusion on this point.* Seeing that the rules of international law have changed—and do change—and that the courts have given effect to the changes without any Act of Parliament, it follows to my mind inexorably that the rules of international law, as existing from time to time, do form part of our English law. It follows, too, that a decision of this court—as to what was the ruling of international law 50 or 60 years ago—is not binding on this court today. International law knows no rule of stare decisis. * * *

* * *

———

This old rule of absolute State immunity had become embedded, or "transformed" into English common law by a series of judicial decisions such as *Thai–Europe Tapioca Service Ltd. v. Government of Pakistan*[a] and *The Phillipine Admiral.*[b] Under the English rules on precedent, these customary rules on state immunity, now incorporated into English common law, could be reversed only by the House of Lords as the supreme appellate body. The Court of Appeal in *Trendex* held that the Central Bank was not

---

a. 1 W.L.R. 1485 (1975) (holding that a foreign State or its government enjoys sovereign immunity in respect to proceedings against itself or its property, whether the action arose out of a government or a commercial activity or transaction).

b. A.C. 373 (1977) (holding that no immunity existed in respect of commercial activities if the action was *in rem*, but that the Court was bound by its own previous decisions to hold immunity did exist in respect to such activities if the action was *in personam* (like that in *Trendtex*)).

an organ of the Nigerian State and so did not share Nigeria's sovereign immunity. Most significant was that Lord Denning, presiding over the Court in the case, went on to expressly hold that even had the action been against the Nigerian government itself, the government would not have been able to rely on the plea of immunity, since the transaction out of which the action arose was commercial, not governmental in nature, and which was no longer protected under customary international law. He explained that the English rules on precedent did not apply. Rather, customary international law as incorporated into English law meant that when the rules of customary international law changed, so too did the English law. Lord Denning stated:

> International law does change, and courts have applied the changes without the aid of any Act of Parliament. Thus, when the rules of international law were changed (by the force of public opinion) so as to condemn slavery, the English courts were justified in applying the modern rules of international law . . .

The view laid forth by Lord Denning in *Trendex* was later confirmed by *Maclaine Watson v. DTI supra.*

Another issue of application of international law in domestic courts is whether a rule of customary international law is directly effective such that an individual may rely on it as a source of rights at the national level. The English case of *Bennett v. Horseferry Magistrates Court*[c] involved an individual who was abducted by the South African police. Such a forcible abduction arguably constituted outrageous conduct in violation of customary international law. The House of Lords by majority held that the courts should decline as a matter of discretion to exercise criminal jurisdiction. Lord Bridge stated:

> When it is shown that the law enforcement agency responsible for bringing a prosecution has only been enabled to do so by participating in violations of international law and of the laws of another state in order to secure the presence of the accused within the territorial jurisdiction of the court, I think that respect for the rule of law demand that the court take cognisance of that circumstance.[d]

In the context of customary international law, the case of *Alcom v. Republic of Columbia and others*[e] raised the question whether attachment or execution of a judgment could take place against the ordinary bank account of a diplomatic mission. The question had not been expressly regulated by the UK State Immunity Act 1978. The House of Lords accepted that international law required such immunity from legal process to be granted. Lord Diplock observed that the position in international law at the date of passing of the State Immunity Act was not sufficient to conclude the question of construction, and said:

---

c. 3 All ER 138 (1993).

d. *Id.* at 155.

e. 2 All ER 6 (1984).

It makes it highly unlikely that Parliament intended to require the United Kingdom Courts to act contrary to International Law unless the clear language of the Statute compels such a conclusion; but it does not do more than this.

NOTES AND QUESTIONS

1. "Neither the dualists nor the monists have given a satisfactory answer to the problem of the relationship between international law and municipal law." What is the evidence of the truth of this statement in British law?

2. *Non–Justiciable Norms v. Peremptory Norms.* Where questions of international law are central to a claim, English courts have often held that they are not competent to address the issue. Lord Wilberforce articulated a general principle of judicial restraint in the House of Lords in the case of *Buttes Gas and Oil Co v. Hammer*, [1982] A.C. 888, 1981 WL 187889. While the claim on its face was one of defamation and the defence one of jurisdiction, the underlying issue concerned a dispute over the extent of the territorial waters of Sharjah in the Persian Gulf and the right to exploit natural resources below these waters. The case required investigating the conduct of Umm al Qaiwain, Iran, the UK, and Sharjah. Lord Wilberforce for the majority found that there were no judicial standards for an English court to judge the issues of international law. He explained:

> . . . the court would be in a judicial non-man's land; the court would be asked to review transactions in which four sovereign states were involved, which they had brought to a precarious settlement, after diplomacy and the use of force, and to say that at least part of these were "unlawful" under international law.

In *Kuwait Airways Corporation v. Iraqi Airways*, 2 A.C. 883 (2002), the House of Lords determined that the act of state doctrine set forth in the *Buttes* case was limited by public policy and did not apply to acts of foreign states within their own territory where the act flagrantly violated fundamental rules of public international law. The case resulted from the taking by Iraqi forces during their invasion of ten commercial aircraft belonging to Kuwait Airways Corporation (KAC) and their transfer, by decree of the Revolutionary Command Council, to the state-owned Iraqi Airways Company. Some of the aircraft were later destroyed by coalition bombing during the conflict to liberate Kuwait and others were flown to and sheltered by Iran. KAC claimed the return of the aircraft or payment of their value and damages. The House of Lords found for KAC and determined that this case fell within an exception to the act of state doctrine; namely that a foreign act of state in its own territory would not be recognized if such recognition was against English public policy. The majority decided that, as Iraq's invasion of Kuwait violated international law (invoking unincorporated Security Council resolutions, *jus cogens* norms, and customary international law), English public policy would not give effect to transfers of title resulting therefrom.

This was the first time the public policy exception was applied to a commercial claim. In *Oppenheimer v. Cattermole*, [1976] A.C. 249 (1975), the court refused to recognize a racially discriminatory and confiscatory law of the National Socialist Government of Germany because it breached fundamental principles of human rights law. In *Occidental Petroleum v. Ecuador*, the Court of Appeals followed *Kuwait Airways* and determined that there were no unmanageable standards in this case dealing with the construction of an investment agreement between a state and private party rather than a dispute between states involving a treaty. The Court concluded:

> The case is not concerned with an attempt to invoke at the national legal level a Treaty which operates only at the international level. It concerns a Treaty intended by its signatories to give rise to rights in favour of private investors capable of enforcement, to an extent specified by the Treaty wording, in consensual arbitration against one or other of its signatory States. For the English Court to treat the extent of such rights as non-justiciable would appear to us to involve an extension, rather than an application, of existing doctrine developed in different contexts.

In *R. (on the application of Abbasi and another) v. Secretary of State for Foreign and Commonwealth Affairs and another* (above), Lord Phillips carved out a special area of justiciability where human rights are involved in concluding "this court does not need the statutory context in order to be free to express a view in relation to what it conceives to be a clear breach of international law, particularly in the context of human rights." Abbasi, Al ER 70 at para. 57.

Recall that the principle of judicial restraint in regards to state immunity was considered in the *Pinochet* case, *Al Adsani v. Kuwait,* and *Jones v. Saudi Arabia* discussed in Chapter 4 above.

3. For additional reading, see, Katherine Reece *The Changing Status of International Law in English Domestic Law*, NETHERLANDS INT'L L. REV. 371 (2006); J.G. Collier, *Is International Law Really Part of the Laws of England?*, 38 INT'L & COMP. L. Q. 924 (1989).

B. THE UNITED STATES

1. CONSTITUTIONAL CONSIDERATIONS

Constitution of the United States

Article I, Section 10

No State shall enter into any Treaty, Alliance, or Confederation; grant Letters of Marque and Reprisal; coin Money; emit Bills of Credit; make any Thing but gold and silver Coin a Tender in Payment of Debts; pass any Bill of Attainder, ex post facto Law, or Law impairing the Obligation of Contracts, or grant any Title of Nobility.

No State shall, without the Consent of the Congress, lay any Imposts or Duties on Imports or Exports, except what may be absolutely necessary for executing its inspection Laws: and the net Produce of all Duties and Imposts, laid by any State on Imports or Exports, shall be for the Use of the Treasury of the United States; and all such Laws shall be subject to the Revision and Control of the Congress.

No State shall, without the Consent of Congress, lay any Duty of Tonnage, keep Troops, or Ships of War in time of Peace, enter into any Agreement or Compact with another State, or with a foreign Power, or engage in War, unless actually invaded, or in such imminent Danger as will not admit of delay.

Article II, Section 2

The President shall be Commander in Chief of the Army and Navy of the United States, and of the Militia of the several States, when called into the actual Service of the United States; * * *.

He shall have Power, by and with the Advice and Consent of the Senate, to make Treaties, provided two thirds of the Senators present concur; and he shall nominate, and by and with the Advice and Consent of the Senate, shall appoint Ambassadors, * * *.

Article II, Section 3

He shall from time to time give to the Congress Information of the State of the Union, and recommend to their Consideration such Measures as he shall judge necessary and expedient; he may, on extraordinary Occasions, convene both Houses, or either of them, and in Case of Disagreement between them, with Respect to the Time of Adjournment, he may adjourn them to such Time as he shall think proper; he shall receive Ambassadors and other public Ministers; he shall take Care that the Laws be faithfully executed, and shall Commission all the Officers of the United States.

Article VI

All Debts contracted and Engagements entered into, before the Adoption of this Constitution, shall be as valid against the United States under this Constitution, as under the Confederation.

This Constitution, and the Laws of the United States which shall be made in Pursuance thereof; and all Treaties made, or which shall be made, under the Authority of the United States, shall be the supreme Law of the Land; and the Judges in every State shall be bound thereby, any Thing in the Constitution or Laws of any State to the Contrary notwithstanding.

* * *

Amendment X

The powers not delegated to the United States by the Constitution, nor prohibited by it to the States, are reserved to the States respectively, or to the people.

2.   TREATIES

Ware v. Hylton

Supreme Court of the United States, 1796
3 U.S. (3 Dall.) 199, 1 L.Ed. 568

■ CHASE, JUSTICE.—The Defendants in error, on the 7th day of July, 1774, passed their penal bond to Farrell and Jones, for the payment of £.2,976 11 [shillings] 6 [pence], of good British money; but the condition of the bond, or the time of payment, does not appear on the record.

On the 20th of October, 1777, the legislature of the commonwealth of Virginia, passed a law to sequester British property. In the 3d section of the law, it was enacted, "that it should be lawful for any citizen of Virginia, owing money to a subject of Great Britain, to pay the same, or any part thereof, from time to time, as he should think fit, into the loan office, taking thereout a certificate for the same, in the name of the creditor, with an indorsement, under the hand of the commissioner of the said office, expressing the name of the payer; and shall deliver such certificate to the governor and the council, whose receipt shall discharge him from so much of the debt. And the governor and the council shall, in like manner, lay before the General Assembly, once in every year, an account of these certificates, specifying the names of the persons by, and for whom they were paid; and shall see to the safe keeping of the same; subject to the future directions of the legislature: provided, that the governor and the council may make such allowance, as they shall think reasonable, out of the interest of the money so paid into the loan office, to the wives and children, residing in the state, of such creditor."

On the 26th of April, 1780, the Defendants in error, paid into the loan office of Virginia, part of their debt, to wit, 3,111 1–9 dollars, equal to £.933 14 0 Virginia currency; and obtained a certificate from the commissioners of the loan office, and a receipt from the governor and the council of Virginia, agreeably to the above, in part recited law.

The Defendants in error being sued, on the above bond, in the Circuit Court of Virginia, pleaded the above law, and the payment above stated, in bar of so much of the Plaintiff's debt. The plaintiff, to avoid this bar, replied the fourth article of the Definitive Treaty of Peace, between Great Britain and the United States, of the 3d of September, 1783. To this replication there was a general demurrer and joinder. The Circuit Court allowed the demurrer, and the plaintiff brought the present writ of error. The case is of great importance, not only from the property that depends on the decision, but because the effect and operation of the treaty are necessarily involved. * * *

The first point raised by the council for the Plaintiff in error was, that the legislature of Virginia had no right to make the law, of the 20th October, 1777 * * *. If this objection is established, the judgment of the

Circuit Court must be reversed; because it destroys the Defendant's plea in bar, and leaves him without defence to the Plaintiff's action.

This objection was maintained on different grounds by the Plaintiff's council. One of them contended, that the legislature of Virginia had no right to confiscate any British property, because Virginia was part of the dismembered empire of Great Britain, and the Plaintiff and Defendants were, all of them, members of the British nation, when the debt was contracted, and therefore, that the laws of independent nations do not apply to the case; and, if applicable, that the legislature of Virginia was not justified by the modern law and practice of European nations, in confiscating private debts. In support of this opinion, he cited Vattel who expresses himself thus: "The sovereign has naturally the same right over what his subjects may be indebted to enemies. Therefore, he may confiscate debts of this nature, if the term of payment happen in the time of war. But at present, in regard to the advantage and safety of Commerce, all the sovereigns of Europe have departed from this rigour * * * "

* * *

I am of opinion that the exclusive right of confiscating, during the war, all and every species of British property, within the territorial limits of Virginia, resided only in the Legislature of that commonwealth. * * *

* * *

The 4th article of the treaty is in these words: "It is agreed that creditor, on either side, shall meet with no lawful impediment to the recovery of the full value, in sterling money, of all bona fide debts, heretofore contracted."

* * * I will adopt the following remarks, which I think applicable, and which may be found in Dr. Rutherforth and Vattel. * * * The intention of the framers of the treaty, must be collected from a view of the whole instrument, and from the words made use of by them to express their intention, or from probable or rational conjectures. If the words express the meaning of the parties plainly, distinctly, and perfectly, there ought to be no other means of interpretation; but if the words are obscure, or ambiguous, or imperfect, recourse must be had to other means of interpretation, and in these three cases, we must collect the meaning from the words, or from probable or rational conjectures, or from both. When we collect the intention from the words only, as they lie in the writing before us, it is a literal interpretation; and indeed if the words, and, the construction of a writing, are clear and precise, we can scarce call it interpretation to collect the intention of the writer from thence. The principal rule to be observed in literal interpretation, is to follow that sense, in respect both of the words, and the construction, which is agreeable to common use.

* * *

■ WILSON, JUSTICE,

* * *

* * * Even if Virginia had the power to confiscate, the treaty annuls the confiscation. The fourth article is well expressed to meet the very case: it is not confined to debts existing at the time of making the treaty; but is extended to debts heretofore contracted. It is impossible by any glossary, or argument, to make the words more perspicuous, more conclusive, than by a bare recital. Independent, therefore, of the Constitution of the United States, (which authoritatively inculcates the obligation of contracts) the treaty is sufficient to remove every impediment founded on the law of Virginia. The State made the law; the State was a party to the making of the treaty: a law does nothing more than express the will of a nation; and a treaty does the same. Under this general view of the subject, I think the judgment of the Circuit Court ought to be reversed.

[The court agreed, although some justices found the plight of the debtor who had paid his debt under the law of Virginia, very troublesome. The opinion of Justice Tredell is particularly anguished.]

Missouri v. Holland*

United States Supreme Court, 1920
252 U.S. 416, 40 S.Ct. 382, 64 L.Ed. 641

■ MR. JUSTICE HOLMES delivered the opinion of the court.

This is a bill in equity brought by the State of Missouri to prevent a game warden of the United States from attempting to enforce the Migratory Bird Treaty Act of July 3, 1918, and the regulations made by the Secretary of Agriculture in pursuance of the same. The ground of the bill is that the statute is an unconstitutional interference with the rights reserved to the States by the Tenth Amendment, and that the acts of the defendant done and threatened under that authority invade the sovereign right of the State and contravene its will manifested in statutes. The State also alleges a pecuniary interest, as owner of the wild birds within its borders and otherwise, admitted by the Government to be sufficient, but it is enough that the bill is a reasonable and proper means to assert the alleged quasi sovereign rights of a State. A motion to dismiss was sustained by the District Court on the ground that the act of Congress is constitutional. The State appeals.

On December 8, 1916, a treaty between the United States and Great Britain was proclaimed by the President. It recited that many species of birds in their annual migrations traversed certain parts of the United States and of Canada, that they were of great value as a source of food and in destroying insects injurious to vegetation, but were in danger of extermination through lack of adequate protection. It therefore provided for specified close[d] seasons and protection in other forms, and agreed that the two powers would take or propose to their law-making bodies the necessary measures for carrying the treaty out. The above mentioned Act of July 3, 1918, entitled an act to give effect to the convention, prohibited the

---

* Some citations omitted.

killing, capturing or selling any of the migratory birds included in the terms of the treaty except as permitted by regulations compatible with those terms, to be made by the Secretary of Agriculture. Regulations were proclaimed [in] 1918. It is unnecessary to go into any details, because, the question raised is the general one whether the treaty and statute are void as an interference with the rights reserved to the States.

To answer this question it is not enough to refer to the Tenth Amendment, reserving the powers not delegated to the United States, because by Article II, § 2, the power to make treaties is delegated expressly, and by Article VI treaties made under the authority of the United States, along with the Constitution and laws of the United States made in pursuance thereof, are declared the supreme law of the land. If the treaty is valid there can be no dispute about the validity of the statute under Article I, § 8, as a necessary and proper means to execute the powers of the Government. The language of the Constitution as to the supremacy of treaties being general, the question before us is narrowed to an inquiry into the ground upon which the present supposed exception is placed.

It is said that a treaty cannot be valid if it infringes the Constitution, that there are limits, therefore, to the treatymaking power, and that one such limit is that what an act of Congress could not do unaided, in derogation of the powers reserved to the States, a treaty cannot do. An earlier act of Congress that attempted by itself and not in pursuance of a treaty to regulate the killing of migratory birds within the States had been held bad in the District Court. Those decisions were supported by arguments that migratory birds were owned by the States in their sovereign capacity for the benefit of their people, and that under cases like Geer v. Connecticut, this control was one that Congress had no power to displace. The same argument is supposed to apply now with equal force.

Whether the two cases cited were decided rightly or not they cannot be accepted as a test of the treaty power. Acts of Congress are the supreme law of the land only when made in pursuance of the Constitution, while treaties are declared to be so when made under the authority of the United States. It is open to question whether the authority of the United States means more than the formal acts prescribed to make the convention. We do not mean to imply that there are no qualifications to the treaty-making power; but they must be ascertained in a different way. It is obvious that there may be matters of the sharpest exigency for the national well being that an act of Congress could not deal with but that a treaty followed by such an act could, and it is not lightly to be assumed that, in matters requiring national action, "a power which must belong to and somewhere reside in every civilized government" is not to be found. What was said in that case with regard to the powers of the States applies with equal force to the powers of the nation in cases where the States individually are incompetent to act. We are not yet discussing the particular case before us but only are considering the validity of the test proposed. With regard to that we may add that when we are dealing with words that also are a constituent act, like the Constitution of the United States, we must realize that they have called into life a being the development of which could not have been foreseen completely by the most gifted of its begetters. It was enough for them to realize or to hope that they had created an organism; it has taken a century and has cost their successors much sweat and blood to prove that they created a nation. The case before us must be considered in the light of our whole experience and not merely in that of what was said a hundred years ago. The treaty in question does not contravene any prohibitory words to be found in the Constitution. The only question is whether it is forbidden by some invisible radiation from the general terms of the Tenth Amendment. We must consider what this country has become in deciding what that Amendment has reserved.

The State as we have intimated founds its claim of exclusive authority upon an assertion of title to migratory birds, an assertion that is embodied in statute. No doubt it is true that as between a State and its inhabitants the State may regulate the killing and sale of such birds, but it does not follow that its authority is exclusive of paramount powers. To put the claim of the State upon title is to lean upon a slender reed. Wild birds are not in the possession of anyone; and possession is the beginning of ownership. The whole foundation of the State's rights is the presence within their jurisdiction of birds that yesterday had not arrived, tomorrow may be in another State and in a week a thousand miles away. If we are to be accurate we cannot put the case of the State upon higher ground than that the treaty deals with creatures that for the moment are within the state borders, that it must be carried out by officers of the United States within the same territory, and that but for the treaty the State would be free to regulate this subject itself.

As most of the laws of the United States are carried out within the States and as many of them deal with matters which in the silence of such laws the State might regulate, such general grounds are not enough to support Missouri's claim. Valid treaties of course "are as binding within the territorial limits of the States as they are elsewhere throughout the dominion of the United States." No doubt the great body of private relations usually fall within the control of the State, but a treaty may override its power. We do not have to invoke the later developments of constitutional law for this proposition; it was recognized early with regard to statutes of limitation, and even earlier, as to confiscation, in *Ware v. Hylton*. It was assumed by Chief Justice Marshall with regard to the escheat of land to the State in *Chirac v. Chirac*. So as to a limited jurisdiction of foreign consuls within a State. *Wildenhus's* Case. It only remains to consider the application of established rules to the present case.

Here a national interest of very nearly the first magnitude is involved. It can be protected only by national action in concert with that of another power. The subject-matter is only transitorily within the State and has no permanent habitat therein. But for the treaty and the statute there soon might be no birds for any powers to deal with. We see nothing in the Constitution that compels the Government to sit by while a food supply is cut off and the protectors of our forests and our crops are destroyed. It is not sufficient to rely upon the States. The reliance is vain, and were it otherwise, the question is whether the United States is forbidden to act. We are of opinion that the treaty and statute must be upheld.

[A]ffirmed. MR. JUSTICE VAN DEVANTER and MR. JUSTICE PITNEY dissent.

Asakura v. City of Seattle*

United States Supreme Court, 1924
265 U.S. 332, 44 S.Ct. 515, 68 L.Ed. 1041

■ Mr. Justice Butler DELIVERED THE OPINION OF THE COURT.

Plaintiff in error is a subject of the Emperor of Japan, and, since 1904, has resided in Seattle, Washington. Since July, 1915, he has been engaged in business there as a pawnbroker. The city passed an ordinance, which took effect July 2, 1921, regulating the business of pawnbroker and repealing former ordinances on the same subject. It makes it unlawful for any person to engage in the business unless he shall have a license, and the ordinance provides "that no such license shall be granted unless the applicant be a citizen of the United States." Violations of the ordinance are punishable by fine or imprisonment or both. Plaintiff in error brought this suit in the Superior Court of King County, Washington, against the city, its Comptroller and its Chief of Police to restrain them from enforcing the ordinance against him. He attacked the ordinance on the ground that it violates the treaty between the United States and the Empire of Japan, proclaimed April 5, 1911 * * *. He had about $5,000 invested in his business, which would be broken up and destroyed by the enforcement of the ordinance. The Superior Court granted the relief. On appeal, the [State] Supreme Court held the ordinance valid and reversed the decree.

* * *

Does the ordinance violate the treaty? Plaintiff in error invokes and relies upon the following provisions: "The citizens or subjects of each of the High Contracting Parties shall have liberty to enter, travel and reside in the territories of the other to carry on trade, wholesale and retail, to own or lease and occupy houses, manufactories, warehouses and shops, to employ agents of their choice, to lease land for residential and commercial purposes, and generally to do anything incident to or necessary for trade upon the same terms as native citizens or subjects, submitting themselves to the laws and regulations there established. * * * The citizens or subjects of each * * * shall receive, in the territories of the other, the most constant protection, and security for their persons and property * * *."

A treaty made under the authority of the United States "shall be the supreme law of the land; and the judges in every State shall be bound thereby, any thing in the constitution or laws of any State to the contrary notwithstanding." Constitution, Art. VI, § 2.

---

* Citations omitted.

* * * The treaty was made to strengthen friendly relations between the two nations. The provision quoted establishes the rule of equality between Japanese subjects while in this country and native citizens. Treaties for the protection of citizens of one country residing in the territory of another are numerous, and make for good understanding between nations. The treaty is binding within the State of Washington. * * * The rule of equality established by it cannot be rendered nugatory in any part of the United States by municipal ordinances or state laws. It stands on the same footing of supremacy as do the provisions of the Constitution and laws of the United States. It operates of itself without the aid of any legislation, state or national; and it will be applied and given authoritative effect by the courts. * * *

The purpose of the ordinance complained of is to regulate, not to prohibit, the business of pawnbroker. But it makes it impossible for aliens to carry on the business. It need not be considered whether the State, if it sees fit, may forbid and destroy the business generally. Such a law would apply equally to aliens and citizens, and no question of conflict with the treaty would arise. The grievance here alleged is that plaintiff in error, in violation of the treaty, is denied equal opportunity.

* * * Decree reversed.

————

The following case was included in Chapter 4 in the discussion of jurisdiction and extradition treaties. We return to it again as an indication of the attitude of the U.S. government toward treaties.

United States v. Alvarez–Machain*

United States Supreme Court
504 U.S. 655, 112 S.Ct. 2188, 119 L.Ed.2d 441 (1992)

■ REHNQUIST, C.J. The issue in this case is whether a criminal defendant, abducted to the United States from a nation with which it has an extradition treaty, thereby acquires a defense to the jurisdiction of this country's courts. We hold that he does not, and that he may be tried in federal district court for violations of the criminal law of the United States.

Respondent, Alvarez–Machain, is a citizen and resident of Mexico. He was indicted for participating in the kidnap and murder of United States Drug Enforcement Administration (DEA) special agent Enrique Camarena–Salazar and a Mexican pilot working with Camarena, Alfredo Zavala–Avelar.

The DEA believes that respondent, a medical doctor, participated in the murder by prolonging agent Camarena's life so that others could further torture and interrogate him. On April 2, 1990, respondent was

—————————
* Some citations are omitted.

forcibly kidnaped from his medical office in Guadalajara, Mexico, to be flown by private plane to EI Paso, Texas, where he was arrested by DEA officials. The District Court concluded that DEA agents were responsible for respondent's abduction, although they were not personally involved in it.*

Respondent moved to dismiss the indictment, claiming that his abduction constituted outrageous governmental conduct, and that the District Court lacked jurisdiction to try him because he was abducted in violation of the *[U.S.–Mexico] Extradition Treaty*. The District Court rejected the outrageous governmental conduct claim, but held that it lacked jurisdiction to try respondent because his abduction violated the Extradition Treaty. The district court discharged respondent and ordered that he be repatriated to Mexico . . .

The Court of Appeals affirmed the dismissal of the indictment and the repatriation of respondent, relying on its decision in *[U.S. v. VerdugoUrquidez]*. . . . Although the Treaty does not expressly prohibit such abductions, the Court of Appeals held that the "purpose" of the Treaty was violated by a forcible abduction, * * * which, along with a formal protest by the offended nation, would give a defendant the right to invoke the Treaty violation to defeat jurisdiction of the district court to try him. The Court of Appeals further held that the proper remedy for such a violation would be dismissal of the indictment and repatriation of the defendant to Mexico.

In the instant case, the Court of Appeals affirmed the district court's finding that the United States had authorized the abduction of respondent, and that letters from the Mexican government to the United States government served as an official protest of the Treaty violation. Therefore, the Court of Appeals ordered that the indictment against respondent be dismissed and that respondent be repatriated to Mexico * * *. We granted certiorari * * * and now reverse.

* * *

In construing a treaty, as in construing a statute, we first look to its terms to determine its meaning. * * * The Treaty says nothing about the obligations of the United States and Mexico to refrain from forcible abductions of people from the territory of the other nation, or the consequences under the Treaty if such an abduction occurs. * * *

More critical to respondent's argument is Article 9 of the Treaty:

1.   Neither Contracting Party shall be bound to deliver up its own nationals, but the executive authority of the requested Party shall, if not prevented by the laws of that Party, have the power to deliver them up if, in its discretion, it be deemed proper to do so.

---

* Apparently, DEA officials had attempted to gain respondent's presence in the United States through informal negotiations with Mexican officials, but were unsuccessful. DEA officials then, through a contact in Mexico, offered to pay a reward and expenses in return for the delivery of respondent to the United States. *U.S. v. Caro–Quintero*, 745 F.Supp. at 602–04.

2. If extradition is not granted pursuant to paragraph 1 of this Article, the requested Party shall submit the case to its competent authorities for the purpose of prosecution, proved that Party has jurisdiction over the offense.

According to respondent, Article 9 embodies the terms of the bargain which the United States struck: if the United States wishes to prosecute a Mexican national, it may request that individual's extradition. Upon a request from the United States, Mexico may either extradite the individual, or submit the case to the proper authorities for prosecution in Mexico. In this way, respondent reasons, each nation preserved its right to choose whether its nationals would be tried in its own courts or by the courts of the other nation. This preservation of rights would be frustrated if either nation were free to abduct nationals of the other nation for the purposes of prosecution. More broadly, respondent reasons, as did the Court of Appeals, that all the processes and restrictions on the obligation to extradite established by the Treaty would make no sense if either nation were free to resort to forcible kidnaping to gain the presence of an individual for prosecution in a manner not contemplated by the Treaty. * * *

We do not read the Treaty in such a fashion. Article 9 does not purport to specify the only way in which one country may gain custody of a national of the other country for the purposes of prosecution. In the absence of an extradition treaty, nations are under no obligation to surrender those in their country to foreign authorities for prosecution. * * * Extradition treaties exist so as to impose mutual obligations to surrender individuals in certain defined sets of circumstances, following established procedures * * *. The Treaty provides a mechanism which would not otherwise exist, requiring, under certain circumstances, the United States and Mexico to extradite individuals to the other country, and establishing the procedures to be followed when the Treaty is invoked.

The history of negotiation and practice under the Treaty also fails to show that abductions outside of the Treaty constitute a violation of the Treaty. As the Solicitor General notes, the Mexican government was made aware, as early as 1906, of the *Ker* doctrine, and the United States' position that it applied to forcible abductions made outside of the terms of the U.S.– Mexico Extradition Treaty.* Nonetheless, the current version of the Treaty,

---

* In correspondence between the United States and Mexico growing out of the 1905 Martinez incident, in which a Mexican national was abducted from Mexico and brought to the United States for trial, the Mexican charge wrote to the Secretary of State protesting that as Martinez' arrest was made outside of the procedures established in the extradition treaty, "the action pending against the man can not rest [on] any legal foundation." * * * The Secretary of State responded that the exact issue raised by the Martinez incident had been decided by Ker, and that the remedy open to the Mexican government, namely a request to the United States for extradition of Martinez' abductor had been granted by the United States * * *. Respondent and the Court of Appeals stress a statement made in 1881 by Secretary of State James Blaine to the governor of Texas to the effect that the extradition treaty in its form at that time did not authorize unconsented abductions from Mexico. * * * This misses the mark, however, for the Government's argument is not that the Treaty authorizes the abduction of respondent; but that the Treaty does not prohibit the abduction.

signed in 1978, does not attempt to establish a rule that would in any way curtail the effect of *Ker*. Moreover, although language which would grant individuals exactly the right sought by respondent had been considered and drafted as early as 1935 by a prominent group of legal scholars sponsored by the faculty of Harvard Law School, no such clause appears in the current treaty.**

Thus, the language of the Treaty, in the context of its history, does not support the proposition that the Treaty prohibits abductions outside of its terms. The remaining question, therefore, is whether the Treaty should be interpreted so as to include an implied term prohibiting prosecution where the defendant's presence is obtained by means other than those established by the Treaty. . . .

Respondent contends that the Treaty must be interpreted against the backdrop of customary international law, and that international abductions are "so clearly prohibited in international law" that there was no reason to include such a clause in the Treaty itself * * *. The international censure of international abductions is further evinced, according to respondent, by the [U.N. and O.A.S. Charters]. * * * Respondent does not argue that these sources of international law prove an independent basis for the right respondent asserts not to be tried in the United States, but rather that they should inform the interpretation of the Treaty terms.

The Court of Appeals deemed it essential, * * * for the individual defendant to assert a right under the Treaty, that the affected foreign government had registered a protest * * *. Respondent agrees that the right exercised by the individual is derivative of the nation's right under the Treaty, since nations are authorized, notwithstanding the terms of an extradition treaty, to voluntarily render an individual to the other country on terms completely outside of those proved in the Treaty. The formal protest * * * ensures that the "offended" nation actually objects to the abduction and has not in some way voluntarily rendered the individual for prosecution. Thus the Extradition Treaty only prohibits gaining the defendant's presence by means other than those set forth in the Treaty when the nation from which the defendant was abducted objects.

This argument seems to us inconsistent with the remainder of respondent's argument. The Extradition Treaty has the force of law, and if, as respondent asserts, it is self-executing, it would appear that a court must enforce it on behalf of an individual regardless of the offensiveness of the * * * practice of one nation to the other nation * * *

More fundamentally, the difficulty with the support respondent garners from international law is that none of it relates to the practice of nations in relation to extradition treaties. In *Rauscher*, we implied a term in the Webster–Ashburton Treaty because of the practice of nations with regard to extradition treaties. In the instant case, respondent would imply terms in the Extradition Treaty from the practice of nations with regards

---

** The U.S. and Mexico signed, in spring 1994, a treaty supplement, which now explicitly prohibits such abductions.

to international law more generally. Respondent would have us find that the Treaty acts as a prohibition against a violation of the general principle of international law that one government may not "exercise its police power in the territory of another state." * * * There are many actions which could be taken by a nation that would violate this principle, including waging war, but it cannot seriously be contended an invasion of the United States by Mexico would violate the terms of the Extradition Treaty. . . . In sum, to infer from this Treaty and its terms that it prohibits all means of gaining the presence of an individual outside of its terms goes beyond established precedent and practice * * *. The general principles cited by respondent simply fail to persuade us that we should imply in the U.S.–Mexico Extradition Treaty a term prohibiting international abductions.

Respondent and his *amici* may be correct that respondent's abduction was "shocking," * * *, and that it may be in violation of general international law principles. Mexico has protested the abduction of respondent through diplomatic notes * * *, and the decision of whether respondent should be returned to Mexico, as a matter outside of the Treaty, is a matter for the Executive Branch. *[The Mexican Government has requested the extradition of two individuals who allegedly participated in the abduction from Mexico].* We conclude, however, that respondent's abduction was not in violation of the [U.S.–Mexico Extradition Treaty], * * *.

■ JUSTICE STEVENS, with whom JUSTICE BLACKMUN and JUSTICE O'CONNOR join, dissenting.

* * * The case is unique for several reasons. It does not involve an ordinary abduction by a private kidnaper, or bounty hunter, as in *Ker* * * *; nor does it involve the apprehension of an American fugitive who committed a crime in one State and sought asylum in another, as in *Frisbie* * * * Rather, it involves this country's abduction of another country's citizen; it also involves a violation of the territorial integrity of that other country, with which this country has signed an extradition treaty.

A Mexican citizen was kidnaped in Mexico and charged with a crime committed in Mexico; his offense allegedly violated both Mexican and American law. Mexico has formally demanded on at least two separate occasions that he be returned to Mexico and has represented that he will be prosecuted and punished for his alleged offense. It is clear that Mexico's demand must be honored if this official abduction violated the 1978 [U.S.–Mexico] Extradition Treaty * * * In my opinion, a fair reading of the treaty in light of our decision in *[U.S. v. Rauscher]* * * *, and applicable principles of international law, leads inexorably to the conclusion that the District Court, and the Court of Appeals for the Ninth Circuit * * * correctly construed that instrument.

* * *

I

The Extradition Treaty with Mexico is a comprehensive document * * *. The parties announced their purpose in the preamble: The two

Governments desire "to cooperate more closely in the fight against crime and, to this end, to mutually render better assistance in matters of extradition." From the preamble, through the description of the parties' obligations with respect to offenses committed within as well as beyond the territory of a requesting party, the delineation of the procedures and evidentiary requirements for extradition, the special provisions for political offenses and capital punishment, and other details, the Treaty appears to have been designed to cover the entire subject of extradition.

* * *

* * * Thus, the Extradition Treaty, as understood in the context of cases that have addressed similar issues, suffices to protect the defendant from prosecution despite the absence of any express language in the Treaty itself purporting to limit this Nation's power to prosecute a defendant over whom it had lawfully acquired jurisdiction.

Although the Court's conclusion in *Rauscher* was supported by a number of judicial precedents, the holdings in these cases were not nearly as uniform as the consensus of international opinion that condemns one Nation's violation of the territorial integrity of a friendly neighbor.[21] It is shocking that a party to an extradition treaty might believe that it has secretly reserved the right to make seizures of citizens in the other party's territory. Justice Story found it shocking enough that the United States would attempt to justify an American seizure of a foreign vessel in a Spanish port: "But, even supposing, for a moment, that our laws had required an entry of the Apollon, in her transit, does it follow, that the power to arrest her was meant to be given, after she had passed into the exclusive territory of a foreign nation? We think not. *It would be monstrous to suppose that our revenue officers were authorized to enter into foreign ports and territories, for the purpose of seizing vessels which had offended against our laws. It cannot be presumed that Congress would voluntarily justify such a clear violation of the laws of nations.*" The *Apollon,* 9 Wheat. 362, 370–371 (1824) *(emphasis added).*[22]

---

21. When Abraham Sofaer, Legal Adviser of the State Department, was questioned at a congressional hearing, he resisted the notion that such seizures were acceptable: " 'Can you imagine us going into Paris and seizing some person we regard as a terrorist * * *? [H]ow would we feel if some foreign nation—let us take the United Kingdom—came over here and seized some terrorist suspect in New York City, or Boston, or Philadelphia, * * * because we refused through the normal channels of international, legal communications, to extradite that individual?' " Bill To Authorize Prosecution of Terrorists and Others Who Attack U.S. Government Employees and Citizens Abroad: Hearing before the Subcommittee on Security and Terrorism of the Senate Committee on the Judiciary, 99th Cong., 1st Sess., 63 (1985).

22. Justice Story's opinion continued: "The arrest of the offending vessel must, therefore, be restrained to places where our jurisdiction is complete, to our own waters, or to the ocean, the common highway of all nations. It is said, that there is a revenue jurisdiction, which is distinct from the ordinary maritime jurisdiction over waters within the range of a common shot from our shores. And the provisions in the Collection Act of 1799, which authorize a visitation of vessels within four leagues of our coasts, are referred to in proof of the assertion. But where is that right of visitation to be exercised? In a foreign territory, in the exclusive jurisdiction of another sovereign? Certainly not; for the very terms of the act confine it to the ocean, where all nations have a common right, and exercise a common sovereignty. And over

The law of Nations, as understood by Justice Story in 1824, has not changed. Thus, a leading treatise explains: "A State must not perform acts of sovereignty in the territory of another State." * * *

"It is * * * a breach of International Law for a State to send its agents to the territory of another State to apprehend persons accused of having committed a crime. Apart from other satisfaction, the first duty of the offending State is to hand over the person in question to the State in whose territory he was apprehended." * * * Commenting on the precise issue raised by this case, the chief reporter for the American Law Institute's Restatement of Foreign Relations used language reminiscent of Justice Story's characterization of an official seizure in a foreign jurisdiction as "monstrous:"

> When done without consent of the foreign government, abducting a person from a foreign country is a gross violation of international law and gross disrespect for a norm high in the opinion of mankind. It is a blatant violation of the territorial integrity of another state; it eviscerates the extradition system (established by a comprehensive network of treaties involving virtually all states).

III

A critical flaw pervades the Court's entire opinion. It fails to differentiate between the conduct of private citizens, which does not violate any treaty obligation, and conduct expressly authorized by the Executive Branch * * *, which unquestionably constitutes a flagrant violation of international law, and in my opinion, also constitutes a breach of our treaty obligations. Thus, at the outset, the Court states the issue as "whether a criminal defendant, abducted to the United States from a nation with which it has an extradition treaty, thereby acquires a defense to the jurisdiction of this country's courts." * * * That, of course, is the question decided in *Ker v. Illinois;* it is not, however, the question presented for decision today.

The importance of the distinction between a court's exercise of jurisdiction over either a person or property that has been wrongfully seized by a private citizen, or even by a state-law enforcement agent, on the one hand, and the attempted exercise of jurisdiction predicated on a seizure by federal officers acting beyond their authority conferred by treaty, on the other, [was recognized in 1933, in *Cook v. U.S.* 288 U.S. 102] * * *.

[*Discussing common law rules of seizure*] [T]he objection to the seizure is not that it was wrongful merely because made by one upon whom the government had not conferred authority to seize at the place where the seizure was made. The objection is that the Government itself lacked power

---

what vessels is this right of visitation to be exercised? By the very words of the act, over our own vessels, and over foreign vessels bound to our ports, and over no others. To have gone beyond this, would have been an usurpation of exclusive sovereignty on the ocean, and an exercise of an universal right of search, a right which has never yet been acknowledged by other nations, and would be resisted by none with more pertinacity than by the American." The Apollon, 9 Wheat., at 371–373.

to seize, since by the Treaty it had imposed a territorial limitation upon its own authority. The Treaty fixes the conditions under which a "vessel may be seized and taken into a [U.S. port], * * * for adjudication in accordance with applicable laws. Thereby, Great Britain agreed that adjudication may follow a rightful seizure. Our Government, lacking power to seize, lacked power, because of the Treaty, to subject the vessel to our laws. To hold that adjudication may follow a wrongful seizure would go far to nullify the purpose and effect of the Treaty * * *.''

The Court's failure to differentiate between private abductions and official invasions of another sovereign's territory also accounts for its misplaced reliance on the 1935 proposal made by the Advisory Committee on Research in International Law * * *. [Where] the text * * * plainly states, it would have rejected the rule of [*Ker*]. The failure to adopt that recommendation does not speak to the issue the Court decides today. The Court's admittedly "shocking" disdain for customary and conventional international law principles, * * * is thus entirely unsupported by case law and commentary.

IV

As the Court observes at the outset of its opinion, there is reason to believe that respondent participated in an especially brutal murder of an American law enforcement agent. That fact, if true, may explain the Executive's intense interest in punishing respondent in our courts. Such an explanation, however, proves no justification for disregarding the Rule of Law that this Court has a duty to uphold. That the Executive may wish to reinterpret the Treaty to allow for an action that the Treaty in no way authorizes should not influence this Court's interpretation. Indeed, the desire for revenge exerts "a kind of hydraulic pressure * * * before which even well settled principles of law will bend," *Northern Securities Co. v. U.S.* * * * (1904) (Holmes, J., dissenting), but it is precisely at such moments that we should remember and be guided by our duty "to render judgment evenly and dispassionately according to law, as each is given understanding to ascertain and apply it." The way that we perform that duty in a case of this kind sets an example that other tribunals in other countries are sure to emulate.

The significance of this Court's precedents is illustrated by a recent decision of the Court of Appeal of the Republic of South Africa. Based largely on its understanding of the import of this Court's cases—including our decision in *Ker* * * *—that court held that the prosecution of a defendant kidnapped by agents of South Africa in another country must be dismissed. *S v. Ebrahim,* S. Afr. L. Rep. (Apr.–June 1991). The Court of Appeal of South Africa—indeed, I suspect most courts throughout the civilized world will be deeply disturbed by the "monstrous" decision the Court announces today. For every Nation that has an interest in preserving the Rule of Law is affected, directly or indirectly, by a decision of this character. As Thomas Paine warned, an "avidity to punish is always dangerous to liberty" because it leads a Nation "to stretch, to misinterpret, and to misapply even the best of laws." To counter that tendency, he reminds us: "He that would make his own liberty secure must guard even his enemy from oppression; for if he violates this duty he establishes a precedent that will reach to himself."

MCC–Marble Ceramic Center, Inc. v. Ceramic Nuova d'Agostino, S.p.A.

Eleventh Circuit Court of Appeals
144 F.3d 1384 (1998)

BACKGROUND

The plaintiff-appellant, MCC–Marble Ceramic, Inc. ("MCC"), is a Florida corporation engaged in the retail sale of tiles, and the defendant-appellee, Ceramica Nuova d'Agostino S.p.A. ("D'Agostino") is an Italian corporation engaged in the manufacture of ceramic tiles. In October 1990, MCC's president, Juan Carlos Mozon, met representatives of D'Agostino at a trade fair in Bologna, Italy and negotiated an agreement to purchase ceramic tiles from D'Agostino based on samples he examined at the trade fair. Monzon, who spoke no Italian, communicated with Gianni Silingardi, then D'Agostino's commercial director, through a translator, Gianfranco Copelli, who was himself an agent of D'Agostino. The parties apparently arrived at an oral agreement on the crucial terms of price, quality, quantity, delivery and payment. The parties then recorded these terms on one of D'Agostino's standard, pre-printed order forms and Monzon signed the contract on MCC's behalf. According to MCC, the parties also entered into a requirements contract in February 1991, subject to which D'Agostino agreed to supply MCC with high grade ceramic tile at specific discounts as long as MCC purchased sufficient quantities of tile. MCC completed a number of additional order forms requesting tile deliveries pursuant to that agreement.

MCC brought suit against D'Agostino claiming a breach of the February 1991 requirements contract when D'Agostino failed to satisfy orders in April, May, and August of 1991. In addition to other defenses, D'Agostino responded that it was under no obligation to fill MCC's orders because MCC had defaulted on payment for previous shipments. In support of its position, D'Agostino relied on the pre-printed terms of the contracts that MCC had executed. The executed forms were printed in Italian and contained terms and conditions on both the front and reverse. According to an English translation of the October 1990 contract, the front of the order form contained the following language directly beneath Monzon's signature:

> [T]he buyer hereby states that he is aware of the sales conditions stated on the reverse and that he expressly approves of them with special reference to those numbered 1–2–3–4–5–6–7–8.

R2–126, Exh. 3 ¶ 5 ("Maselli Aff."). Clause 6(b), printed on the back of the form states:

[D]efault or delay in payment within the time agreed upon gives D'Agostino the right to . . . suspend or cancel the contract itself and to cancel possible other pending contracts and the buyer does not have the right to indemnification or damages.

Id. ¶ 6.

D'Agostino also brought a number of counterclaims against MCC, seeking damages for MCC's alleged nonpayment for deliveries of tile that D'Agostino had made between February 28, 1991 and July 4, 1991. MCC responded that the tile it had received was of a lower quality than contracted for, and that, pursuant to the CISG, MCC was entitled to reduce payment in proportion to the defects. D'Agostino, however, noted that clause 4 on the reverse of the contract states, in pertinent part:

> Possible complaints for defects of the merchandise must be made in writing by means of a certified letter within and not later than 10 days after receipt of the merchandise. . . .

Maselli Aff. ¶ 6. Although there is evidence to support MCC's claims that it complained about the quality of the deliveries it received, MCC never submitted any written complaints.

MCC did not dispute these underlying facts before the district court, but argued that the parties never intended the terms and conditions printed on the reverse of the order form to apply to their agreements. As evidence for this assertion, MCC submitted Monzon's affidavit, which claims that MCC had no subjective intent to be bound by those terms and that D'Agostino was aware of this intent. MCC also filed affidavits from Silingardi and Copelli, D'Agostino's representatives at the trade fair, which support Monzon's claim that the parties subjectively intended not to be bound by the terms on the reverse of the order form. The magistrate judge held that the affidavits, even if true, did not raise an issue of material fact regarding the interpretation or applicability of the terms of the written contracts and the district court accepted his recommendation to award summary judgment in D'Agostino's favor. MCC then filed this timely appeal.

DISCUSSION

* * *

The parties to this case agree that the CISG governs their dispute because the United States, where MCC has its place of business, and Italy, where D'Agostino has its place of business, are both States Party to the Convention.[5] *See* CISG, art. 1.[6] Article 8 of the CISG governs the interpre-

---

5. The United States Senate ratified the CISG in 1986, and the United States deposited its instrument of ratification at the United Nations Headquarters in New York on December 11, 1986. *See Preface to Convention, reprinted at* 15 U.S.C. app. 52 (1997). The Convention entered into force between the United States and the other States Parties, including Italy, on January 1, 1988. *See id.; Filanto S.p.A. v. Chilewich Int'l Corp.,* 789 F.Supp. 1229, 1237 (S.D.N.Y.1992).

tation of international contracts for the sale of goods and forms the basis of MCC's appeal from the district court's grant of summary judgment in D'Agostino's favor.[7] MCC argues that the magistrate judge and the district court improperly ignored evidence that MCC submitted regarding the parties' subjective intent when they memorialized the terms of their agreement on D'Agostino's preprinted form contract, and that the magistrate judge erred by applying the parol evidence rule in derogation of the CISG.

I. Subjective Intent Under the CISG

Contrary to what is familiar practice in United States courts, the CISG appears to permit a substantial inquiry into the parties' subjective intent, even if the parties did not engage in any objectively ascertainable means of registering this intent.[8] Article 8(1) of the CISG instructs courts to interpret the "statements . . . and other conduct of a party . . . according to his intent" as long as the other party "knew or could not have been unaware" of that intent. The plain language of the Convention, therefore, requires an inquiry into a party's subjective intent as long as the other party to the contract was aware of that intent.

---

6. Article 1 of the CISG states in relevant part:

(1) This Convention applies to contracts of sale of goods between parties whose places of business are in different States:

(a) When the States are Contracting States. . . .

CISG, art. 1.

7. Article 8 provides:

(1) For the purposes of this Convention statements made by and other conduct of a party are to be interpreted according to his intent where the other party knew or could not have been unaware what that intent was.

(2) If the preceding paragraph is not applicable, statements made by and conduct of a party are to be interpreted according to the understanding a reasonable person of the same kind as the other party would have had in the same circumstances.

(3) In determining the intent of a party or the understanding a reasonable person would have had, due consideration is to be given to all relevant circumstances of the case including the negotiations, any practices which the parties have established between themselves, usages and any subsequent conduct of the parties.

CISG, art. 8.

8. In the United States, the legislatures, courts, and the legal academy have voiced a preference for relying on objective manifestations of the parties' intentions. For example, Article Two of the Uniform Commercial Code, which most states have enacted in some form or another to govern contracts for the sale of goods, is replete with references to standards of commercial reasonableness. *See e.g.,* U.C.C. § 2–206 (referring to reasonable means of accepting an offer); *see also Lucy v. Zehmer,* 196 Va. 493, 503, 84 S.E.2d 516, 522 (1954) ("Whether the writing signed . . . was the result of a serious offer . . . and a serious acceptance . . ., or was a serious offer . . . and an acceptance in secret jest . . ., in either event it constituted a binding contract of sale between the parties."). Justice Holmes expressed the philosophy behind this focus on the objective in forceful terms: "The law has nothing to do with the actual state of the parties' minds. In contract, as elsewhere, it must go by externals, and judge parties by their conduct." Oliver W. Holmes, *The Common Law* 242 (Howe ed.1963) *quoted in* John O. Honnold, *Uniform Law for International Sales under the 1980 United Nations Convention* § 107 at 164 (2d ed.1991) (hereinafter Honnold, *Uniform Law*).

In this case, MCC has submitted three affidavits that discuss the purported subjective intent of the parties to the initial agreement concluded between MCC and D'Agostino in October 1990. All three affidavits discuss the preliminary negotiations and report that the parties arrived at an oral agreement for D'Agostino to supply quantities of a specific grade of ceramic tile to MCC at an agreed upon price. The affidavits state that the "oral agreement established the essential terms of quality, quantity, description of goods, delivery, price and payment." See R3–133 ¶ 9 ("Silingardi Aff."); R1–51 ¶ 7 ("Copelli Aff."); R1–47 ¶ 7 ("Monzon Aff."). The affidavits also note that the parties memorialized the terms of their oral agreement on a standard D'Agostino order form, but all three affiants contend that the parties *subjectively* intended not to be bound by the terms on the reverse of that form despite a provision directly below the signature line that expressly and specifically incorporated those terms.

The terms on the reverse of the contract give D'Agostino the right to suspend or cancel all contracts in the event of a buyer's non-payment and require a buyer to make a written report of all defects within ten days. As the magistrate judge's report and recommendation makes clear, if these terms applied to the agreements between MCC and D'Agostino, summary judgment would be appropriate because MCC failed to make any written complaints about the quality of tile it received and D'Agostino has established MCC's non-payment of a number of invoices amounting to $108,389.40 and 102,053,846.00 Italian lira.

Article 8(1) of the CISG requires a court to consider this evidence of the parties' subjective intent. Contrary to the magistrate judge's report, which the district court endorsed and adopted, article 8(1) does not focus on interpreting the parties' statements alone. Although we agree with the magistrate judge's conclusion that no "interpretation" of the contract's *terms* could support MCC's position, article 8(1) also requires a court to consider subjective intent while interpreting the *conduct* of the parties. The CISG's language, therefore, requires courts to consider evidence of a party's subjective intent when signing a contract if the other party to the contract was aware of that intent at the time. This is precisely the type of evidence that MCC has provided through the Silingardi, Copelli, and Monzon affidavits, which discuss not only Monzon's intent as MCC's representative but also discuss the intent of D'Agostino's representatives and their knowledge that Monzon did not intend to agree to the terms on the reverse of the form contract. This acknowledgment that D'Agostino's representatives were aware of Monzon's subjective intent puts this case squarely within article 8(1) of the CISG, and therefore requires the court to consider MCC's evidence as it interprets the parties' conduct.

II.   Parol Evidence and the CISG

Given our determination that the magistrate judge and the district court should have considered MCC's affidavits regarding the parties' subjective intentions, we must address a question of first impression in this circuit: whether the parol evidence rule, which bars evidence of an earlier oral contract that contradicts or varies the terms of a subsequent or contemporaneous written plays any role in cases involving the CISG. We begin by observing that the parol evidence rule, contrary to its title, is a substantive rule of law, not a rule of evidence. *See* II E. Allen Farnsworth, *Farnsworth on Contracts,* § 7.2 at 194 (1990). The rule does not purport to exclude a particular type of evidence as an "untrustworthy or undesirable" way of proving a fact, but prevents a litigant from attempting to show "the fact itself—the fact that the terms of the agreement are other than those in the writing." *Id.* As such, a federal district court cannot simply apply the parol evidence rule as a procedural matter—as it might if excluding a particular type of evidence under the Federal Rules of Evidence, which apply in federal court regardless of the source of the substantive rule of decision. *Cf. id.* § 7.2 at 196.

The CISG itself contains no express statement on the role of parol evidence. *See* Honnold, Uniform Law § 110 at 170. It is clear, however, that the drafters of the CISG were comfortable with the concept of permitting parties to rely on oral contracts because they eschewed any statutes of fraud provision and expressly provided for the enforcement of oral contracts. *Compare* CISG, art. 11 (a contract of sale need not be concluded or evidenced in writing) *with* U.C.C. § 2–201 (precluding the enforcement of oral contracts for the sale of goods involving more than $500). Moreover, article 8(3) of the CISG expressly directs courts to give "due consideration . . . to all relevant circumstances of the case including the negotiations . . ." to determine the intent of the parties. Given article 8(1)'s directive to use the intent of the parties to interpret their statements and conduct, article 8(3) is a clear instruction to admit and consider parol evidence regarding the negotiations to the extent they reveal the parties' subjective intent.

* * *

Our reading of article 8(3) as a rejection of the parol evidence rule, * * * is in accordance with the great weight of academic commentary on the issue. As one scholar has explained:

> The language of Article 8(3) that "due consideration is to be given to *all relevant* circumstances of the case" seems adequate to override any domestic rule that would bar a tribunal from considering the relevance of other agreements. . . . Article 8(3) relieves tribunals from domestic rules that might bar them from "considering" any evidence between the parties that is relevant. This added flexibility for interpretation is consistent with a growing body of opinion that the "parol evidence rule" has been an embarrassment for the administration of modern transactions.

Honnold, Uniform Law § 110 at 170–71. * * * [A]lthough jurisdictions in the United States have found the parol evidence rule helpful to promote good faith and uniformity in contract, as well as an appropriate answer to the question of how much consideration to give parol evidence, a wide number of other States Party to the CISG have rejected the rule in their

domestic jurisdictions. One of the primary factors motivating the negotiation and adoption of the CISG was to provide parties to international
contracts for the sale of goods with some degree of certainty as to the
principles of law that would govern potential disputes and remove the
previous doubt regarding which party's legal system might otherwise apply.
See Letter of Transmittal from Ronald Reagan, President of the United
States, to the United States Senate, reprinted at 15 U.S.C. app. 70, 71
(1997). Courts applying the CISG cannot, therefore, upset the parties'
reliance on the Convention by substituting familiar principles of domestic
law when the Convention requires a different result. We may only achieve
the directives of good faith and uniformity in contracts under the CISG by
interpreting and applying the plain language of article 8(3) as written and
obeying its directive to consider this type of parol evidence.

This is not to say that parties to an international contract for the sale
of goods cannot depend on written contracts or that parol evidence regarding subjective contractual intent need always prevent a party relying on a
written agreement from securing summary judgment. To the contrary,
most cases will not present a situation (as exists in this case) in which both
parties to the contract acknowledge a subjective intent not to be bound by
the terms of a pre-printed writing. In most cases, therefore, article 8(2) of
the CISG will apply, and objective evidence will provide the basis for the
court's decision. See Honnold, *Uniform Law* § 107 at 164–65. Consequently, a party to a contract governed by the CISG will not be able to avoid the
terms of a contract and force a jury trial simply by submitting an affidavit
which states that he or she did not have the subjective intent to be bound
by the contract's terms. *Cf. Klopfenstein v. Pargeter,* 597 F.2d 150, 152 (9th
Cir.1979) (affirming summary judgment despite the appellant's submission
of his own affidavit regarding his subjective intent: "Undisclosed, subjective intentions are immaterial in [a] commercial transaction, especially
when contradicted by objective conduct. Thus, the affidavit has no legal
effect even if its averments are accepted as wholly truthful."). Moreover, to
the extent parties wish to avoid parol evidence problems they can do so by
including a merger clause in their agreement that extinguishes any and all
prior agreements and understandings not expressed in the writing.

Considering MCC's affidavits in this case, however, we conclude that
the magistrate judge and the district court improperly granted summary
judgment in favor of D'Agostino. * * *

* * * Accordingly, we REVERSE the district court's grant of summary
judgment and REMAND this case for further proceedings consistent with
this opinion.

———

The next case was first included in Chapter 9. Review the facts and
opening sections there. Here we focus on the Supreme Court's discussion of
"self-executing" versus "non-self executing treaties" in the U.S. legal

system and the U.S. president's respect to authority with implementing international law.

Medellín v. Texas*

Supreme Court of the United States
552 U.S. 491, 128 S.Ct. 1346, 170 L.Ed.2d 190 (2008)

■ CHIEF JUSTICE ROBERTS delivered the opinion of the Court. . . .

III

Medellín next argues that the ICJ's judgment in *Avena* is binding on state courts by virtue of the President's February 28, 2005 Memorandum. The United States contends that while the *Avena* judgment does not of its own force require domestic courts to set aside ordinary rules of procedural default, that judgment became the law of the land with precisely that effect pursuant to the President's Memorandum and his power to establish binding rules of decision that preempt contrary state law. Accordingly, we must decide whether the President's declaration alters our conclusion that the *Avena* judgment is not a rule of domestic law binding in state and federal courts.

A

The United States maintains that the President's constitutional role uniquely qualifies him to resolve the sensitive foreign policy decisions that bear on compliance with an ICJ decision and to do so expeditiously. Brief for United States as *Amicus Curiae* 11, 12. We do not question these propositions. In this case, the President seeks to vindicate United States interests in ensuring the reciprocal observance of the Vienna Convention, protecting relations with foreign governments, and demonstrating commitment to the role of international law. These interests are plainly compelling.

Such considerations, however, do not allow us to set aside first principles. The President's authority to act, as with the exercise of any governmental power, must stem either from an act of Congress or from the Constitution itself. *Youngstown Sheet & Tube v. Sawyer*, 343 U.S. 579, 585 (1952); *Dames & Moore v. Regan*, 453 U.S. 654, 668 (1981).

Justice Jackson's familiar tripartite scheme provides the accepted framework for evaluating executive action in this area. First, "[w]hen the President acts pursuant to an express or implied authorization of Congress, his authority is at its maximum, for it includes all that he possesses in his own right plus all that Congress can delegate." *Youngstown*, 343 U.S., at 635 (Jackson, J., concurring). Second, "[w]hen the President acts in absence of either a congressional grant or denial of authority, he can only rely upon his own independent powers, but there is a zone of twilight in which he and Congress may have concurrent authority, or in which its distribu-

---

* Footnotes omitted.

tion is uncertain." *Id.*, at 637. In this circumstance, Presidential authority can derive support from congressional inertia, indifference or quiescence. *Ibid.* Finally, "[w]hen the President takes measures incompatible with the expressed or implied will of Congress, his power is at its lowest ebb, and the Court can sustain his actions only by disabling the Congress from acting upon the subject." *Id.*, at 637–638.

B

The United States marshals two principal arguments in favor of the President's authority to establish binding rules of decision that preempt contrary state law. The Solicitor General first argues that the relevant treaties give the President the authority to implement the *Avena* judgment and that Congress has acquiesced in the exercise of such authority. The United States also relies upon an independent international dispute-resolution power wholly apart from the asserted authority based on the pertinent treaties. * * *

1

The United States maintains that the President's Memorandum is authorized by the Optional Protocol and the U.N. Charter. Brief for United States as *Amicus Curiae* 9. That is, because the relevant treaties "create an obligation to comply with *Avena*," they "*implicitly* give the President authority to implement that treaty-based obligation." *Id.*, at 11 (emphasis added). As a result, the President's Memorandum is well grounded in the first category of the *Youngstown* framework.

We disagree. The President has an array of political and diplomatic means available to enforce international obligations, but unilaterally converting a non-self-executing treaty into a self-executing one is not among them. The responsibility for transforming an international obligation arising from a non-self-executing treaty into domestic law falls to Congress. As this Court has explained, when treaty stipulations are "not self-executing they can only be enforced pursuant to legislation to carry them into effect." *Whitney*, 124 U.S., at 194. * * *

The requirement that Congress, rather than the President, implement a non-self-executing treaty derives from the text of the Constitution, which divides the treaty-making power between the President and the Senate. The Constitution vests the President with the authority to "make" a treaty. Art. II, § 2. If the Executive determines that a treaty should have domestic effect of its own force, that determination may be implemented "in mak[ing]" the treaty, by ensuring that it contains language plainly providing for domestic enforceability. If the treaty is to be self-executing in this respect, the Senate must consent to the treaty by the requisite two-thirds vote, *ibid.*, consistent with all other constitutional restraints.

Once a treaty is ratified without provisions clearly according it domestic effect, however, whether the treaty will ever have such effect is governed by the fundamental constitutional principle that "[t]he power to make the necessary laws is in Congress; the power to execute in the

President." *Hamdan v. Rumsfeld*, 548 U.S. 557 (2006) (quoting *Ex parte Milligan*, 4 Wall. 2, 139 (1866) (opinion of Chase, C. J.)); see U.S. Const., Art. I, § 1 ("All legislative Powers herein granted shall be vested in a Congress of the United States"). As already noted, the terms of a non-self-executing treaty can become domestic law only in the same way as any other law—through passage of legislation by both Houses of Congress, combined with either the President's signature or a congressional override of a Presidential veto. See Art. I, § 7. Indeed, "the President's power to see that the laws are faithfully executed refutes the idea that he is to be a lawmaker." *Youngstown*, 343 U.S., at 587.

A non-self-executing treaty, by definition, is one that was ratified with the understanding that it is not to have domestic effect of its own force. That understanding precludes the assertion that Congress has implicitly authorized the President—acting on his own—to achieve precisely the same result. We therefore conclude, given the absence of congressional legislation, that the non-self-executing treaties at issue here did not "express[ly] or implied[ly]" vest the President with the unilateral authority to make them self-executing. *See id.*, at 635 (Jackson, J., concurring). Accordingly, the President's Memorandum does not fall within the first category of the Youngstown framework.

Indeed, the preceding discussion should make clear that the non-self-executing character of the relevant treaties not only refutes the notion that the ratifying parties vested the President with the authority to unilaterally make treaty obligations binding on domestic courts, but also implicitly prohibits him from doing so. When the President asserts the power to enforce a non-self-executing treaty by unilaterally creating domestic law, he acts in conflict with the implicit understanding of the ratifying Senate. His assertion of authority, insofar as it is based on the pertinent non-self-executing treaties, is therefore within Justice Jackson's third category, not the first or even the second. See *id.*, at 637–638 * * *

The United States nonetheless maintains that the President's Memorandum should be given effect as domestic law because "this case involves a valid Presidential action in the context of Congressional 'acquiescence'." Brief for United States as *Amicus Curiae* 11, n. 2. Under the *Youngstown* tripartite framework, congressional acquiescence is pertinent when the President's action falls within the second category—that is, when he "acts in absence of either a congressional grant or denial of authority." 343 U.S., at 637 (Jackson, J., concurring). Here, however, as we have explained, the President's effort to accord domestic effect to the *Avena* judgment does not meet that prerequisite.

In any event, even if we were persuaded that congressional acquiescence could support the President's asserted authority to create domestic law pursuant to a non-self executing treaty, such acquiescence does not exist here. The United States first locates congressional acquiescence in Congress's failure to act following the President's resolution of prior ICJ controversies. A review of the Executive's actions in those prior cases, however, cannot support the claim that Congress acquiesced in this particular exercise of Presidential authority, for none of them remotely involved transforming an international obligation into domestic law and thereby displacing state law.[14]

2

We thus turn to the United States' claim that—independent of the United States' treaty obligations—the Memorandum is a valid exercise of the President's foreign affairs authority to resolve claims disputes with foreign nations. *Id.*, at 12–16. The United States relies on a series of cases in which this Court has upheld the authority of the President to settle foreign claims pursuant to an executive agreement. See *Garamendi*, 539 U.S., at 415; *Dames & Moore*, 453 U.S., at 679–680; *United States* v. *Pink*, 315 U.S. 203, 229 (1942); *United States* v. *Belmont*, 301 U.S. 324, 330 (1937). In these cases this Court has explained that, if pervasive enough, a history of congressional acquiescence can be treated as a "gloss on 'Executive Power' vested in the President by § 1 of Art. II." *Dames & Moore, supra,* at 686 (some internal quotation marks omitted). This argument is of a different nature than the one rejected above. Rather than relying on the United States' treaty obligations, the President relies on an independent source of authority in ordering Texas to put aside its procedural bar to successive habeas petitions. Nevertheless, we find that our claims-settlement cases do not support the authority that the President asserts in this case. The claims-settlement cases involve a narrow set of circumstances: the making of executive agreements to settle civil claims between American

---

14. Rather, in the *Case Concerning Military and Paramilitary Activities in and Against Nicaragua (Nicar* v. *U.S.),* 1986 I. C. J. 14 (Judgment of June 27), the President determined that the United States would *not* comply with the ICJ's conclusion that the United States owed reparations to Nicaragua. In the *Case Concerning Delimitation of the Maritime Boundary in the Gulf of Maine Area (Can.* v. *U.S.),* 1984 I. C. J. 246 (Judgment of Oct. 12), a federal agency—the National Oceanic and Atmospheric Administration—issued a final rule which complied with the ICJ's boundary determination. The *Case Concerning Rights of Nationals of the United States of America in Morocco (Fr.* v. *U.S.),* 1952 I.C.J. 176 (Judgment of Aug. 27), concerned the legal status of United States citizens living in Morocco; it was not enforced in United States courts. The final two cases arose under the Vienna Convention. In the *La grand Case (F.R.G.* v. *U.S.),* 2001 I.C.J. 466 (Judgment of June 27), the ICJ ordered the review and reconsideration of convictions and sentences of German nationals denied consular notification. In response, the State Department sent letters to the States "encouraging" them to consider the Vienna Convention in the clemency process. Brief for United States as *Amicus Curiae* 20–21. Such encouragement did not give the ICJ judgment direct effect as domestic law; thus, it cannot serve as precedent for doing so in which Congress might be said to have acquiesced. In the *Case Concerning the Vienna Convention on Consular Relations (Para.* v. *U.S.),* 1998 I. C. J. 248 (Judgment of Apr. 9), the ICJ issued a provisional order, directing the United States to "take all measures at its disposal to ensure that [Breard] is not executed pending the final decision in [the ICJ's] proceedings." *Breard*, 523 U.S., at 374 (internal quotation marks omitted). In response, the Secretary of State sent a letter to the Governor of Virginia requesting that he stay Breard's execution. *Id.*, at 378. When Paraguay sought a stay of execution from this Court, the United States argued that it had taken every measure at its disposal: because "our federal system imposes limits on the federal government's ability to interfere with the criminal justice systems of the States," those measures included "only persuasion," not "legal compulsion." Brief for United States as *Amicus Curiae*, O.T. 1997, No. 97–8214, p. 51. This of course is precedent contrary tithe proposition asserted by the Solicitor General in this case.

citizens and foreign governments or foreign nationals. See, *e.g.*, *Belmont, supra*, at 327. They are based on the view that "a systematic, unbroken, executive practice, long pursued to the knowledge of the Congress and never before questioned," can "raise a presumption that the [action] had been[taken] in pursuance of its consent." *Dames & Moore, supra*, at 686 (some internal quotation marks omitted). As this Court explained in *Garamendi*,

> Making executive agreements to settle claims of American nationals against foreign governments is a particularly longstanding practice.... Given the fact that the practice goes back over 200 years, and has received congressional acquiescence throughout its history, the conclusion that the President's control of foreign relations includes the settlement of claims is indisputable. 539 U.S., at 415 (internal quotation marks and brackets omitted).

Even still, the limitations on this source of executive power are clearly set forth and the Court has been careful to note that "[p]ast practice does not, by itself, create power." *Dames & Moore, supra*, at 686.

The President's Memorandum is not supported by a "particularly longstanding practice" of congressional acquiescence, see *Garamendi, supra*, at 415, but rather is what the United States itself has described as "unprecedented action," Brief for United States as *Amicus Curiae* in *Sanchez–Llamas*, O.T. 2005, Nos. 05–51 and 04–10566, pp. 29–30. Indeed, the Government has not identified a single instance in which the President has attempted (or Congress has acquiesced in) a Presidential directive issued to state courts, much less one that reaches deep into the heart of the State's police powers and compels state courts to reopen final criminal judgments and set aside neutrally applicable state laws. Cf. *Brecht* v. *Abrahamson*, 507 U.S. 619, 635 (1993) ("States possess primary authority for defining and enforcing the criminal law") (quoting *Engle* v. *Isaac*, 456 U.S. 107, 128 (1982); internal quotation marks omitted). The Executive's narrow and strictly limited authority to settle international claims disputes pursuant to an executive agreement cannot stretch so far as to support the current Presidential Memorandum * * *.

It is so ordered.

■ JUSTICE STEVENS, concurring in the judgment.

There is a great deal of wisdom in JUSTICE BREYER's dissent. I agree that the text and history of the Supremacy Clause, as well as this Court's treaty-related cases, do not support a presumption against self-execution. See *post*, at 5–10. I also endorse the proposition that the Vienna Convention on Consular Relations, Apr. 24, 1963, [1970] 21 U.S.T. 77, T.I.A.S. No. 6820, "is itself self-executing and judicially enforceable." *Post*, at 19. Moreover, I think this case presents a closer question than the Court's opinion allows. In the end, however, I am persuaded that the relevant treaties do not authorize this Court to enforce the judgment of the International Court of Justice (ICJ) in *Case Concerning Avena and Other*

Mexican Nationals (Mex. v. *U.S.)*, 2004 I.C.J. 12 (Judgment of Mar. 31) (*Avena*) * * *.

Under the express terms of the Supremacy Clause, the United States' obligation to "undertak[e] to comply" with the ICJ's decision falls on each of the States as well as the Federal Government. One consequence of our form of government is that sometimes States must shoulder the primary responsibility for protecting the honor and integrity of the Nation. Texas' duty in this respect is all the greater since it was Texas that—by failing to provide consular notice in accordance with the Vienna Convention—ensnared the United States in the current controversy. Having already put the Nation in breach of one treaty, it is now up to Texas to prevent the breach of another * * *.

■ JUSTICE BREYER, with whom JUSTICE SOUTER and JUSTICE GINSBURG join, dissenting.

The Constitution's Supremacy Clause provides that "all Treaties . . . which shall be made . . . under the Authority of the United States, shall be the supreme Law of the Land; and the Judges in every State shall be bound thereby." Art. VI, cl. 2. The Clause means that the "courts" must regard "a treaty . . . as equivalent to an act of the legislature, whenever it operates of itself without the aid of any legislative provision." *Foster* v. *Neilson*, 2 Pet. 253, 314 (1829) (majority opinion of Marshall, C. J.). * * *

NOTES AND QUESTIONS

1. *Treaty Making in the United States.* The U.S. Constitution says in Article II, section 2 that the president has the power to make treaties with the advice and consent of two-thirds of the Senators present. So in the case of many treaties, the president submits the treaty to the Senate and it is voted on before the president may ratify the treaty. The United States, however, is party to thousands of treaties. Many of these are in need of amendment and modification. The process of getting advice and consent is too cumbersome to cope with the needs of contemporary international relations, resulting in the practice by which the president makes agreements under his sole authority as so-called "executive agreements." In some cases, the Congress gives the president authority to make commitments in advance of negotiations. This is often the case in trade negotiations, where the president is given "fast-track" authority. Regardless of the progress internal to the U.S., if an official with evident authority enters into a treaty, the U.S. will generally be bound on the international plane. The Vienna Convention on the Law of Treaties does contain the following provision in Article 46:

Provisions of internal law regarding competence
to conclude treaties

1.   A State may not invoke the fact that its consent to be bound by a treaty has been expressed in violation of a provision of its internal law regarding competence to conclude treaties as invalidating its consent

unless that violation was manifest and concerned a rule of its internal law of fundamental importance.

2.   A violation is manifest if it would be objectively evident to any State conducting itself in the matter in accordance with normal practice and in good faith.

While this provision might have been included particularily with the U.S. in mind, query whether states can today be held to know when it is required to get the Senate's advice and consent and when not.

2.   The majority in *Alvarez–Machain* states that the parties to the extradition treaty silently reserved the right to resort to self-help, if deemed expedient. Do nations have the right or legal authority to resort to such self-help? The extradition treaty did not explicitly prohibit abduction. Is the defendant's argument that the treaty implicitly does this a strong one? Is this at odds with the whole rationale behind having extradition treaties that protect state sovereignty and the human rights of the person sought? The U.S. and Mexico have negotiated and entered into a new extradition treaty, which specifies explicitly that extradition is the sole means of obtaining custody of a fugitive for prosecution. See, Cruz, Villereal & Velasco, *Oued listo el tratado de extradition y sera signado a mas tardar en abril: Tello*, EL UNIVERSAL (Mexico City) Feb. 20, 1994, at p. 31, col. 1.

3.   *Dismissal of the charges against Alvarez–Machain* On remand, the district court judge dismissed the case against Alvarez for want of evidence, noting that it was nothing more than the "wildest speculation." He was allowed to return home. *See*, Mydans, *Judge Clears Mexican in Agent's Killing*, N.Y. Times, A12, Dec. 15, 1992.

4.   Alvarez–Machain sued the U.S. Government and the individuals involved in his abduction and alleged torture. Abduction by U.S. authorities is obviously illegal under international law. Is it illegal under U.S. law? Could or should this lead to civil penalties or criminal prosecution in the offended nation; in the offending nation? Would some form of immunity be a defense? See *Sosa v. Alvarez–Machain* below.

5.   *Reflection on U.S. Treaty Commitments*. Detlev Vagts has written:

> The mood in the United States about treaty commitments has turned distinctly negative. This has gone so far as to dismay both actual and potential treaty partners of the United States and, in general, all who are concerned about the performance of the country in the realm of international law * * *. The American reaction is most striking with respect to a willingness to disregard existing treaty obligations * * *. A series of opinions by the Supreme Court have struck observers abroad and in the United States as extremely restrictive in that sense. Clearly, no international tribunal would be likely to have construed the Extradition Treaty with Mexico as did the Court in *United States v. Alvarez–Machain*. Such a tribunal would have found, by interpreting the treaty in "good faith," that the United States had an obligation not to bypass the treaty by kidnaping the defendant from Mexican soil, an acknowledged violation of customary international law. The following year, in

Sale v. Haitian Centers Council, Inc., [509 U.S. 155 (1993)] the Supreme Court's reading of the United Nations Protocol on the Status of Refugees and the associated portions of our immigration legislation strained the text to free the United States to intercept Haitian refugees on the high seas. The Court found support for that conclusion very largely in negotiating history consisting of statements by the Swiss delegation that, one infers, were trying both to justify Switzerland's exclusion of Jews fleeing the Holocaust in 1942 and to allow future exclusions of "mass migrations." The earlier *Aerospatiale* case [482 U.S. 522 (1987)] freed U.S. courts to continue to require foreign litigants in U.S. courts to provide discovery under the Federal Rules of Civil Procedure rather than make parties seeking that information resort to international cooperative measures set forth in the Hague Convention. The result in all three cases was to prevent treaty commitments from altering the way we are used to doing things.

Detlev Vagts, *Taking Treaties Less Seriously,* 92 AM. J. INT'L L. 458 (1998). Michael Van Alstine continues the thought:

[U.S.] jurisprudence remains rooted in the * * * premise that treaties solely reflect a "contract" between sovereign nations. The consequence has been an inflated view of both the subjective intent of "the parties" and the degree of appropriate deference to the views of the Executive Branch in interpretive inquiries. * * * [T]he common practical outcome of treaty interpretation by the Court has been of a distinctly conservative nature. * * * [T]he Court has consistently refused to view a treaty as a body of integrated norms that is capable of generating internal solutions for gaps in its provisions. Instead, when faced with an unsettled question under a treaty, the common approach has been to retreat to otherwise applicable domestic law, "whatever may be the imperfections or difficulties' this may leave in the fulfillment of the international law project."

Michael Van Alstine, *Dynamic Treaty Interpretation,* 146 U. PA. L. REV. 687 (1998).

6.   Note Justice Stevens emphasis on the point that the courts should not assume treaties are non-self-executing. What is a non-self-executing treaty? Why is the CISG a self-executing treaty but the Vienna Convention on Consular Relations, the Statute of the International Court of Justice and UN Charter Article 94 are not? Is this perhaps a case of comparing apples and oranges? Was President Bush seeking to enforce an ICJ judgment, or the ICJ Statute and the other treaties mentioned by the majority?

7.   Chief Justice Roberts states that there is a clear distinction between the president creating claims process procedures that involve removing claims of American nationals from the courts and sending them to international courts (e.g. The Iran–U.S. Claims Tribunal) and enforcing an International Court of Justice judgment. Are you persuaded? Compare what is involved in the two presidential actions. Claims cases generally involve money damages, the *Medellin* case involves the rights of a person facing a

capital sentence. Should the nature of the underlying rights play a role in how the Supreme Court views presidential power?

3.   CUSTOMARY INTERNATIONAL LAW

We have already seen a number of important cases discussing the place of customary international law in U.S. law. The most important of these was *Paquette Habana*, discussed in Chapter 2. Justice Souter relies on that case and others in reaching the Supreme Court's decision in *Sosa*.

Sosa v. Alvarez–Machain

United States Supreme Court
542 U.S. 692, 124 S.Ct. 2739, 159 L.Ed.2d 718 (2004)

■ JUSTICE SOUTER delivered the opinion of the Court.

The two issues are whether respondent Alvarez–Machain's allegation that the Drug Enforcement Administration instigated his abduction from Mexico for criminal trial in the United States supports a claim against the Government under the Federal Tort Claims Act (FTCA or Act), 28 U.S.C. §§ 1346(b)(1), 2671–2680, and whether he may recover under the Alien Tort Statute (ATS), 28 U.S.C. § 1350. We hold that he is not entitled to a remedy under either statute.

I

We have considered the underlying facts before, *United States v. Alvarez–Machain,* 504 U.S. 655, 112 S.Ct. 2188, 119 L.Ed.2d 441 (1992). In 1985, an agent of the Drug Enforcement Administration (DEA), Enrique Camarena–Salazar, was captured on assignment in Mexico and taken to a house in Guadalajara, where he was tortured over the course of a 2–day interrogation, then murdered. Based in part on eyewitness testimony, DEA officials in the United States came to believe that respondent Humberto Alvarez–Machain (Alvarez), a Mexican physician, was present at the house and acted to prolong the agent's life in order to extend the interrogation and torture. *Id.,* at 657, 112 S.Ct. 2188.

In 1990, a federal grand jury indicted Alvarez for the torture and murder of Camarena–Salazar, and the United States District Court for the Central District of California issued a warrant for his arrest. 331 F.3d 604, 609 (C.A.9 2003) (en banc). The DEA asked the Mexican Government for help in getting Alvarez into the United States, but when the requests and negotiations proved fruitless, the DEA approved a plan to hire Mexican nationals to seize Alvarez and bring him to the United States for trial. As so planned, a group of Mexicans, including petitioner Jose Francisco Sosa, abducted Alvarez from his house, held him overnight in a motel, and brought him by private plane to El Paso, Texas, where he was arrested by federal officers. *Ibid.*

Once in American custody, Alvarez moved to dismiss the indictment on the ground that his seizure was "outrageous governmental conduct,"

Alvarez–Machain, 504 U.S., at 658, 112 S.Ct. 2188, and violated the extradition treaty between the United States and Mexico. The District Court agreed, the Ninth Circuit affirmed, and we reversed, *id.,* at 670, 112 S.Ct. 2188, holding that the fact of Alvarez's forcible seizure did not affect the jurisdiction of a federal court. The case was tried in 1992, and ended at the close of the Government's case, when the District Court granted Alvarez's motion for a judgment of acquittal.

In 1993, after returning to Mexico, Alvarez began the civil action before us here. He sued Sosa, Mexican citizen and DEA operative Antonio Garate–Bustamante, five unnamed Mexican civilians, the United States, and four DEA agents. 331 F.3d, at 610. So far as it matters here, Alvarez sought damages from the United States under the FTCA, alleging false arrest, and from Sosa under the ATS, for a violation of the law of nations. The former statute authorizes suit "for ... personal injury ... caused by the negligent or wrongful act or omission of any employee of the Government while acting within the scope of his office or employment." 28 U.S.C. § 1346(b)(1). The latter provides in its entirety that "[t]he district courts shall have original jurisdiction of any civil action by an alien for a tort only, committed in violation of the law of nations or a treaty of the United States." § 1350.

The District Court granted the Government's motion to dismiss the FTCA claim, but awarded summary judgment and $25,000 in damages to Alvarez on the ATS claim. A three-judge panel of the Ninth Circuit then affirmed the ATS judgment, but reversed the dismissal of the FTCA claim. 266 F.3d 1045 (2001).

A divided en banc court came to the same conclusion. 331 F.3d, at 641. As for the ATS claim, the court called on its own precedent, "that [the ATS] not only provides federal courts with subject matter jurisdiction, but also creates a cause of action for an alleged violation of the law of nations." *Id.,* at 612.

The Circuit then relied upon what it called the "clear and universally recognized norm prohibiting arbitrary arrest and detention," *id.,* at 620, to support the conclusion that Alvarez's arrest amounted to a tort in violation of international law. On the FTCA claim, the Ninth Circuit held that, because "the DEA had no authority to effect Alvarez's arrest and detention in Mexico," *id.,* at 608, the United States was liable to him under California law for the tort of false arrest, *id.,* at 640–641.

We granted certiorari in these companion cases to clarify the scope of both the FTCA and the ATS. 540 U.S. 1045, 124 S.Ct. 807, 157 L.Ed.2d 692 (2003). We now reverse in each.

* * *

III

Alvarez has also brought an action under the ATS against petitioner Sosa, who argues (as does the United States supporting him) that there is no relief under the ATS because the statute does no more than vest federal courts with jurisdiction, neither creating nor authorizing the courts to recognize any particular right of action without further congressional action. Although we agree the statute is in terms only jurisdictional, we think that at the time of enactment the jurisdiction enabled federal courts to hear claims in a very limited category defined by the law of nations and recognized at common law. We do not believe, however, that the limited, implicit sanction to entertain the handful of international law *cum* common law claims understood in 1789 should be taken as authority to recognize the right of action asserted by Alvarez here.

A

Judge Friendly called the ATS a "legal Lohengrin," *IIT v. Vencap, Ltd.,* 519 F.2d 1001, 1015 (C.A.2 1975); "no one seems to know whence it came," *ibid.,* and for over 170 years after its enactment it provided jurisdiction in only one case. The first Congress passed it as part of the Judiciary Act of 1789, in providing that the new federal district courts "shall also have cognizance, concurrent with the courts of the several States, or the circuit courts, as the case may be, of all causes where an alien sues for a tort only in violation of the law of nations or a treaty of the United States." Act of Sept. 24, 1789, ch. 20, § 9, 1 Stat. 77.

The parties and *amici* here advance radically different historical interpretations of this terse provision. Alvarez says that the ATS was intended not simply as a jurisdictional grant, but as authority for the creation of a new cause of action for torts in violation of international law. We think that reading is implausible. As enacted in 1789, the ATS gave the district courts "cognizance" of certain causes of action, and the term bespoke a grant of jurisdiction, not power to mold substantive law. See, *e.g.,* The Federalist No. 81, pp. 447, 451 (J. Cooke ed. 1961) (A.Hamilton) (using "jurisdiction" interchangeably with "cognizance"). The fact that the ATS was placed in § 9 of the Judiciary Act, a statute otherwise exclusively concerned with federal-court jurisdiction, is itself support for its strictly jurisdictional nature. Nor would the distinction between jurisdiction and cause of action have been elided by the drafters of the Act or those who voted on it. As Fisher Ames put it, "there is a substantial difference between the jurisdiction of the courts and the rules of decision." 1 Annals of Cong. 807 (Gales ed. 1834). It is unsurprising, then, that an authority on the historical origins of the ATS has written that "section 1350 clearly does not create a statutory cause of action," and that the contrary suggestion is "simply frivolous." Casto, The Federal Courts' Protective Jurisdiction over Torts Committed in Violation of the Law of Nations, 18 Conn. L.Rev. 467, 479, 480 (1986) (hereinafter Casto, Law of Nations); cf. Dodge, The Constitutionality of the Alien Tort Statute: Some Observations on Text and Context, 42 Va. J. Int'l L. 687, 689 (2002). In sum, we think the statute was intended as jurisdictional in the sense of addressing the power of the courts to entertain cases concerned with a certain subject.

But holding the ATS jurisdictional raises a new question, this one about the interaction between the ATS at the time of its enactment and the ambient law of the era. Sosa would have it that the ATS was stillborn because there could be no claim for relief without a further statute expressly authorizing adoption of causes of action. *Amici* professors of federal jurisdiction and legal history take a different tack, that federal courts could entertain claims once the jurisdictional grant was on the books, because torts in violation of the law of nations would have been recognized within the common law of the time. Brief for Vikram Amar et al. as *Amici Curiae*. We think history and practice give the edge to this latter position.

1

"When the *United States* declared their independence, they were bound to receive the law of nations, in its modern state of purity and refinement." *Ware v. Hylton,* 3 Dall. 199, 281, 1 L.Ed. 568 (1796) (Wilson, J.). In the years of the early Republic, this law of nations comprised two principal elements, the first covering the general norms governing the behavior of national states with each other: *"the science which teaches the rights subsisting between nations or states, and the obligations correspondent to those rights,"* E. de Vattel, Law of Nations, Preliminaries § 3 (J. Chitty et al. transl. and ed. 1883) (hereinafter Vattel) (footnote omitted), or "that code of public instruction which defines the rights and prescribes the duties of nations, in their intercourse with each other," 1 J. Kent, Commentaries on American Law *1. This aspect of the law of nations thus occupied the executive and legislative domains, not the judicial. See 4 W. Blackstone, Commentaries on the Laws of England 68 (1769) (hereinafter Commentaries) ("[O]ffences against" the law of nations are "principally incident to whole states or nations").

The law of nations included a second, more pedestrian element, however, that did fall within the judicial sphere, as a body of judge-made law regulating the conduct of individuals situated outside domestic boundaries and consequently carrying an international savor. To Blackstone, the law of nations in this sense was implicated "in mercantile questions, such as bills of exchange and the like; in all marine causes, relating to freight, average, demurrage, insurances, bottomry ...; [and] in all disputes relating to prizes, to shipwrecks, to hostages, and ransom bills." *Id.,* at 67. The law merchant emerged from the customary practices of international traders and admiralty required its own transnational regulation. And it was the law of nations in this sense that our precursors spoke about when the Court explained the status of coast fishing vessels in wartime grew from "ancient usage among civilized nations, beginning centuries ago, and gradually ripening into a rule of international law...." *The Paquete Habana,* 175 U.S. 677, 686, 20 S.Ct. 290, 44 L.Ed. 320 (1900).

There was, finally, a sphere in which these rules binding individuals for the benefit of other individuals overlapped with the norms of state relationships. Blackstone referred to it when he mentioned three specific offenses against the law of nations addressed by the criminal law of England: violation of safe conducts, infringement of the rights of ambassadors, and piracy. 4 Commentaries 68. An assault against an ambassador, for example, impinged upon the sovereignty of the foreign nation and if not adequately redressed could rise to an issue of war. See Vattel 463–464. It was this narrow set of violations of the law of nations, admitting of a judicial remedy and at the same time threatening serious consequences in international affairs, that was probably on minds of the men who drafted the ATS with its reference to tort.

2

Before there was any ATS, a distinctly American preoccupation with these hybrid international norms had taken shape owing to the distribution of political power from independence through the period of confederation. The Continental Congress was hamstrung by its inability to "cause infractions of treaties, or of the law of nations to be punished," J. Madison, Journal of the Constitutional Convention 60 (E. Scott ed. 1893), and in 1781 the Congress implored the States to vindicate rights under the law of nations. In words that echo Blackstone, the congressional resolution called upon state legislatures to "provide expeditious, exemplary and adequate punishment" for "the violation of safe conducts or passports, . . . of hostility against such as are in amity . . . with the United States, . . . infractions of the immunities of ambassadors and other public ministers . . . [and] infractions of treaties and conventions to which the United States are a party." 21 Journals of the Continental Congress 1136–1137 (G. Hunt ed.1912) (hereinafter Journals of the Continental Congress). The resolution recommended that the States "authorise suits . . . for damages by the party injured, and for compensation to the United States for damage sustained by them from an injury done to a foreign power by a citizen." *Id.,* at 1137; cf. Vattel 463–464 ("Whoever offends . . . a public minister . . . should be punished . . . , and . . . the state should, at the expense of the delinquent, give full satisfaction to the sovereign who has been offended in the person of his minister"). Apparently only one State acted upon the recommendation, see Public Records of the State of Connecticut, 1782, pp. 82, 83 (L. Larabee ed.1982) (1942 compilation, exact date of Act unknown), but Congress had done what it could to signal a commitment to enforce the law of nations.

Appreciation of the Continental Congress's incapacity to deal with this class of cases was intensified by the so-called Marbois incident of May 1784, in which a French adventurer, De Longchamps, verbally and physically assaulted the Secretary of the French Legion in Philadelphia. See *Republica v. De Longchamps,* 1 Dall. 111, 1 L.Ed. 59 (O.T. Phila.1784). Congress called again for state legislation addressing such matters, and concern over the inadequate vindication of the law of nations persisted through the time of the Constitutional Convention. See 1 Records of the Federal Convention of 1787, p. 25 (M. Farrand ed.1911) (speech of J. Randolph). During the Convention itself, in fact, a New York City constable produced a reprise of the Marbois affair and Secretary Jay reported to Congress on the Dutch Ambassador's protest, with the explanation that " 'the federal government does not appear . . . to be vested with any judicial Powers competent to the

Cognizance and Judgment of such Cases.' " Casto, Law of Nations 494, and n. 152.

The Framers responded by vesting the Supreme Court with original jurisdiction over "all Cases affecting Ambassadors, other public ministers and Consuls." U.S. Const., Art. III, § 2, and the First Congress followed through. The Judiciary Act reinforced this Court's original jurisdiction over suits brought by diplomats, see 1 Stat. 80, ch. 20, § 13, created alienage jurisdiction, § 11, and, of course, included the ATS, § 9. See generally Randall, Federal Jurisdiction over International Law Claims: Inquiries into the Alien Tort Statute, 18 N.Y.U.J. Int'l L. & Pol. 1, 15–21 (1985) (hereinafter Randall) (discussing foreign affairs implications of the Judiciary Act); W. Casto, The Supreme Court in the Early Republic 27–53 (1995).

3

Although Congress modified the draft of what became the Judiciary Act, see generally Warren, New Light on the History of the Federal Judiciary Act of 1789, 37 Harv. L.Rev. 49 (1923), it made hardly any changes to the provisions on aliens, including what became the ATS, see Casto, Law of Nations 498. There is no record of congressional discussion about private actions that might be subject to the jurisdictional provision, or about any need for further legislation to create private remedies; there is no record even of debate on the section. Given the poverty of drafting history, modern commentators have necessarily concentrated on the text, remarking on the innovative use of the word "tort," see, *e.g.,* Sweeney, A Tort only in Violation of the Law of Nations, 18 Hastings Int'l & Comp. L. Rev. 445 (1995) (arguing that "tort" refers to the law of prize), and the statute's mixture of terms expansive ("all suits"), see, *e.g.,* Casto, Law of Nations 500, and restrictive ("for a tort only"), see, *e.g.,* Randall at 28–31 (limiting suits to torts, as opposed to commercial actions, especially by British plaintiffs). The historical scholarship has also placed the ATS within the competition between federalist and antifederalist forces over the national role in foreign relations. *Id.,* at 22–23 (nonexclusiveness of federal jurisdiction under the ATS may reflect compromise). But despite considerable scholarly attention, it is fair to say that a consensus understanding of what Congress intended has proven elusive.

Still, the history does tend to support two propositions. First, there is every reason to suppose that the First Congress did not pass the ATS as a jurisdictional convenience to be placed on the shelf for use by a future Congress or state legislature that might, someday, authorize the creation of causes of action or itself decide to make some element of the law of nations actionable for the benefit of foreigners. The anxieties of the preconstitutional period cannot be ignored easily enough to think that the statute was not meant to have a practical effect. Consider that the principal draftsman of the ATS was apparently Oliver Ellsworth, previously a member of the Continental Congress that had passed the 1781 resolution and a member of the Connecticut Legislature that made good on that congressional request. See generally W. Brown, The Life of Oliver Ellsworth (1905). Consider, too, that the First Congress was attentive enough to the law of nations to recognize certain offenses expressly as criminal, including the three mentioned by Blackstone. See An Act for the Punishment of Certain Crimes Against the United States, § 8, 1 Stat. 113–114 (murder or robbery, or other capital crimes, punishable as piracy if committed on the high seas), and § 28, *id.,* at 118 (violation of safe conducts and assaults against ambassadors punished by imprisonment and fines described as "infract[ions of] the law of nations"). It would have been passing strange for Ellsworth and this very Congress to vest federal courts expressly with jurisdiction to entertain civil causes brought by aliens alleging violations of the law of nations, but to no effect whatever until the Congress should take further action. There is too much in the historical record to believe that Congress would have enacted the ATS only to leave it lying fallow indefinitely.

The second inference to be drawn from the history is that Congress intended the ATS to furnish jurisdiction for a relatively modest set of actions alleging violations of the law of nations. Uppermost in the legislative mind appears to have been offenses against ambassadors, see *id.,* at 118; violations of safe conduct were probably understood to be actionable, *ibid.,* and individual actions arising out of prize captures and piracy may well have also been contemplated, *id.,* at 113–114. But the common law appears to have understood only those three of the hybrid variety as definite and actionable, or at any rate, to have assumed only a very limited set of claims. As Blackstone had put it, "offences against this law [of nations] are principally incident to whole states or nations," and not individuals seeking relief in court. 4 Commentaries 68.

4

The sparse contemporaneous cases and legal materials referring to the ATS tend to confirm both inferences, that some, but few, torts in violation of the law of nations were understood to be within the common law. In *Bolchos v. Darrel,* 3 F. Cas. 810 (No. 1,607) (S.C. 1795), the District Court's doubt about admiralty jurisdiction over a suit for damages brought by a French privateer against the mortgagee of a British slave ship was assuaged by assuming that the ATS was a jurisdictional basis for the court's action. Nor is *Moxon v. The Fanny,* 17 F. Cas. 942 (No. 9,895) (D.Pa.1793), to the contrary, a case in which the owners of a British ship sought damages for its seizure in United States waters by a French privateer. The District Court said in dictum that the ATS was not the proper vehicle for suit because "[i]t cannot be called a suit for a tort only, when the property, as well as damages for the supposed trespass, are sought for." *Id.,* at 948. But the judge gave no intimation that further legislation would have been needed to give the District Court jurisdiction over a suit limited to damages.

Then there was the 1795 opinion of Attorney General William Bradford, who was asked whether criminal prosecution was available against Americans who had taken part in the French plunder of a British slave colony in Sierra Leone. 1 Op. Atty. Gen. 57. Bradford was uncertain, but he made it clear that a federal court was open for the prosecution of a tort action growing out of the episode:

> "But there can be no doubt that the company or individuals who have been injured by these acts of hostility have a remedy by a *civil* suit in the courts of the United States; jurisdiction being expressly given to these courts in all cases where an alien sues for a tort only, in violation of the laws of nations, or a treaty of the United States. . . ." *Id.,* at 59.

Although it is conceivable that Bradford (who had prosecuted in the Marbois incident, see Casto, Law of Nations 503, n. 201) assumed that there had been a violation of a treaty, 1 Op. Atty. Gen., at 58, that is certainly not obvious, and it appears likely that Bradford understood the ATS to provide jurisdiction over what must have amounted to common law causes of action.

B

Against these indications that the ATS was meant to underwrite litigation of a narrow set of common law actions derived from the law of nations, Sosa raises two main objections. First, he claims that this conclusion makes no sense in view of the Continental Congress's 1781 recommendation to state legislatures to pass laws authorizing such suits. Sosa thinks state legislation would have been "absurd," Reply Brief for Petitioner Sosa 5, if common law remedies had been available. Second, Sosa juxtaposes Blackstone's treatise mentioning violations of the law of nations as occasions for criminal remedies, against the statute's innovative reference to "tort," as evidence that there was no familiar set of legal actions for exercise of jurisdiction under the ATS. Neither argument is convincing.

The notion that it would have been absurd for the Continental Congress to recommend that States pass positive law to duplicate remedies already available at common law rests on a misunderstanding of the relationship between common law and positive law in the late 18th century, when positive law was frequently relied upon to reinforce and give standard expression to the "brooding omnipresence" of the common law then thought discoverable by reason. As Blackstone clarified the relation between positive law and the law of nations, "those acts of parliament, which have from time to time been made to enforce this universal law, or to facilitate the execution of [its] decisions, are not to be considered as introductive of any new rule, but merely as declaratory of the old fundamental constitutions of the kingdom; without which it must cease to be a part of the civilized world." 4 Commentaries 67. Indeed, Sosa's argument is undermined by the 1781 resolution on which he principally relies. Notwithstanding the undisputed fact (per Blackstone) that the common law afforded criminal law remedies for violations of the law of nations, the Continental Congress encouraged state legislatures to pass criminal statutes to the same effect, and the first Congress did the same, *supra,* at 2758.

Nor are we convinced by Sosa's argument that legislation conferring a right of action is needed because Blackstone treated international law offenses under the rubric of "public wrongs," whereas the ATS uses a word, "tort," that was relatively uncommon in the legal vernacular of the day. It is true that Blackstone did refer to what he deemed the three principal offenses against the law of nations in the course of discussing criminal sanctions, observing that it was in the interest of sovereigns "to animadvert upon them with a becoming severity, that the peace of the world may be maintained," 4 Commentaries 68. But Vattel explicitly linked the criminal sanction for offenses against ambassadors with the requirement that the state, "at the expense of the delinquent, give full satisfaction to the sovereign who has been offended in the person of his minister." Vattel 463–464. Cf. Stephens, Individuals Enforcing International Law: The Comparative and Historical Context, 52 DePaul L.Rev. 433, 444 (2002) (observing that a "mixed approach to international law violations, encompassing both criminal prosecution . . . and compensation to those injured through a civil suit, would have been familiar to the founding generation"). The 1781 resolution goes a step further in showing that a private remedy was thought necessary for diplomatic offenses under the law of nations. And the Attorney General's Letter of 1795, as well as the two early federal precedents discussing the ATS, point to a prevalent assumption that Congress did not intend the ATS to sit on the shelf until some future time when it might enact further legislation.

In sum, although the ATS is a jurisdictional statute creating no new causes of action, the reasonable inference from the historical materials is that the statute was intended to have practical effect the moment it became law. The jurisdictional grant is best read as having been enacted on the understanding that the common law would provide a cause of action for the modest number of international law violations with a potential for personal liability at the time.

IV

We think it is correct, then, to assume that the First Congress understood that the district courts would recognize private causes of action for certain torts in violation of the law of nations, though we have found no basis to suspect Congress had any examples in mind beyond those torts corresponding to Blackstone's three primary offenses: violation of safe conducts, infringement of the rights of ambassadors, and piracy. We assume, too, that no development in the two centuries from the enactment of § 1350 to the birth of the modern line of cases beginning with *Filartiga v. Pena–Irala,* 630 F.2d 876 (C.A.2 1980), has categorically precluded federal courts from recognizing a claim under the law of nations as an element of common law; Congress has not in any relevant way amended § 1350 or limited civil common law power by another statute. Still, there are good reasons for a restrained conception of the discretion a federal court should exercise in considering a new cause of action of this kind. Accordingly, we think courts should require any claim based on the present-day law of nations to rest on a norm of international character accepted by the civilized world and defined with a specificity comparable to the features of the 18th-century paradigms we have recognized. This requirement is fatal to Alvarez's claim.

A

A series of reasons argue for judicial caution when considering the kinds of individual claims that might implement the jurisdiction conferred by the early statute. First, the prevailing conception of the common law has changed since 1789 in a way that counsels restraint in judicially applying internationally generated norms. When § 1350 was enacted, the accepted conception was of the common law as "a transcendental body of law outside of any particular State but obligatory within it unless and until changed by statute." *Black and White Taxicab & Transfer Co. v. Brown and Yellow Taxicab & Transfer Co.,* 276 U.S. 518, 533, 48 S.Ct. 404, 72 L.Ed. 681 (1928) (Holmes, J., dissenting). Now, however, in most cases where a court is asked to state or formulate a common law principle in a new context, there is a general understanding that the law is not so much found or discovered as it is either made or created. Holmes explained famously in 1881 that

> "in substance the growth of the law is legislative . . . [because t]he very considerations which judges most rarely mention, and always with an apology, are the secret root from which the law draws all the juices of life. I mean, of course, considerations of what is expedient for the community concerned." The Common Law 31–32 (Howe ed.1963).

One need not accept the Holmesian view as far as its ultimate implications to acknowledge that a judge deciding in reliance on an international norm will find a substantial element of discretionary judgment in the decision.

Second, along with, and in part driven by, that conceptual development in understanding common law has come an equally significant rethinking of the role of the federal courts in making it. *Erie R. Co. v. Tompkins,* 304 U.S. 64, 58 S.Ct. 817, 82 L.Ed. 1188 (1938), was the watershed in which we denied the existence of any federal "general" common law, *id.,* at 78, 58 S.Ct. 817, which largely withdrew to havens of specialty, some of them defined by express congressional authorization to devise a body of law directly, *e.g., Textile Workers v. Lincoln Mills of Ala.,* 353 U.S. 448, 77 S.Ct. 912, 1 L.Ed.2d 972 (1957) (interpretation of collective-bargaining agreements); Fed. Rule Evid. 501 (evidentiary privileges in federal-question cases). Elsewhere, this Court has thought it was in order to create federal common law rules in interstitial areas of particular federal interest. *E.g., United States v. Kimbell Foods, Inc.,* 440 U.S. 715, 726–727, 99 S.Ct. 1448, 59 L.Ed.2d 711 (1979). And although we have even assumed competence to make judicial rules of decision of particular importance to foreign relations, such as the act of state doctrine, see *Banco Nacional de Cuba v. Sabbatino,* 376 U.S. 398, 427, 84 S.Ct. 923, 11 L.Ed.2d 804 (1964), the general practice has been to look for legislative guidance before exercising innovative authority over substantive law. It would be remarkable to take a more aggressive role in exercising a jurisdiction that remained largely in shadow for much of the prior two centuries.

Third, this Court has recently and repeatedly said that a decision to create a private right of action is one better left to legislative judgment in the great majority of cases. *Correctional Services Corp. v. Malesko,* 534 U.S. 61, 68, 122 S.Ct. 515, 151 L.Ed.2d 456 (2001); *Alexander v. Sandoval,* 532 U.S. 275, 286–287, 121 S.Ct. 1511, 149 L.Ed.2d 517 (2001). The creation of a private right of action raises issues beyond the mere consideration whether underlying primary conduct should be allowed or not, entailing, for example, a decision to permit enforcement without the check imposed by prosecutorial discretion. Accordingly, even when Congress has made it clear by statute that a rule applies to purely domestic conduct, we are reluctant to infer intent to provide a private cause of action where the statute does not supply one expressly. While the absence of congressional action addressing private rights of action under an international norm is more equivocal than its failure to provide such a right when it creates a statute, the possible collateral consequences of making international rules privately actionable argue for judicial caution.

Fourth, the subject of those collateral consequences is itself a reason for a high bar to new private causes of action for violating international law, for the potential implications for the foreign relations of the United States of recognizing such causes should make courts particularly wary of impinging on the discretion of the Legislative and Executive Branches in managing foreign affairs. It is one thing for American courts to enforce constitutional limits on our own State and Federal Governments' power, but quite another to consider suits under rules that would go so far as to claim a limit on the power of foreign governments over their own citizens, and to hold that a foreign government or its agent has transgressed those limits. Cf. *Sabbatino, supra,* at 431–432, 84 S.Ct. 923. Yet modern international law is very much concerned with just such questions, and apt to stimulate calls for vindicating private interests in § 1350 cases. Since many attempts by federal courts to craft remedies for the violation of new norms of international law would raise risks of adverse foreign policy consequences, they should be undertaken, if at all, with great caution. Cf. *Tel–Oren v. Libyan Arab Republic,* 726 F.2d 774, 813 (C.A.D.C.1984) (Bork, J., concurring) (expressing doubt that § 1350 should be read to require "our courts [to] sit in judgment of the conduct of foreign officials in their own countries with respect to their own citizens").

The fifth reason is particularly important in light of the first four. We have no congressional mandate to seek out and define new and debatable violations of the law of nations, and modern indications of congressional understanding of the judicial role in the field have not affirmatively encouraged greater judicial creativity. It is true that a clear mandate appears in the Torture Victim Protection Act of 1991, 106 Stat. 73, providing authority that "establish[es] an unambiguous and modern basis for" federal claims of torture and extrajudicial killing, H.R.Rep. No. 102–367, pt. 1, p. 3 (1991). But that affirmative authority is confined to specific subject matter, and although the legislative history includes the remark that § 1350 should "remain intact to permit suits based on other norms that already exist or may ripen in the future into rules of customary international law," *id.,* at 4, Congress as a body has done nothing to promote such suits. Several times, indeed, the Senate has expressly declined to give the federal courts the task of interpreting and applying international human rights law, as when its ratification of the International Covenant on Civil and Political Rights declared that the substantive provisions of the document were not self-executing. 138 Cong. Rec. 8071 (1992).

B

These reasons argue for great caution in adapting the law of nations to private rights. Justice Scalia, *post,* p. 2769 (opinion concurring in part and concurring in judgment), concludes that caution is too hospitable, and a word is in order to summarize where we have come so far and to focus our difference with him on whether some norms of today's law of nations may ever be recognized legitimately by federal courts in the absence of congressional action beyond § 1350. All Members of the Court agree that § 1350 is only jurisdictional. We also agree, or at least Justice SCALIA does not dispute, *post,* at 2770, 2772–2773, that the jurisdiction was originally understood to be available to enforce a small number of international norms that a federal court could properly recognize as within the common law enforceable without further statutory authority. Justice Scalia concludes, however, that two subsequent developments should be understood to preclude federal courts from recognizing any further international norms as judicially enforceable today, absent further congressional action. As described before, we now tend to understand common law not as a discoverable reflection of universal reason but, in a positivistic way, as a product of human choice. And we now adhere to a conception of limited judicial power first expressed in reorienting federal diversity jurisdiction, see *Erie R. Co. v. Tompkins,* 304 U.S. 64, 58 S.Ct. 817, 82 L.Ed. 1188 (1938), that federal courts have no authority to derive "general" common law.

Whereas Justice Scalia sees these developments as sufficient to close the door to further independent judicial recognition of actionable international norms, other considerations persuade us that the judicial power should be exercised on the understanding that the door is still ajar subject to vigilant doorkeeping, and thus open to a narrow class of international norms today. *Erie* did not in terms bar any judicial recognition of new substantive rules, no matter what the circumstances, and post-*Erie* understanding has identified limited enclaves in which federal courts may derive some substantive law in a common law way. For two centuries we have affirmed that the domestic law of the United States recognizes the law of nations. See, *e.g., Sabbatino,* 376 U.S., at 423, 84 S.Ct. 923 ("[I]t is, of course, true that United States courts apply international law as a part of our own in appropriate circumstances"); [18] *The Paquete Habana,* 175 U.S., at 700, 20 S.Ct. 290 ("International law is part of our law, and must be ascertained and administered by the courts of justice of appropriate jurisdiction, as often as questions of right depending upon it are duly presented for their determination"); *The Nereide,* 9 Cranch 388, 423, 3 L.Ed. 769 (1815) (Marshall, C.J.) ("[T]he Court is bound by the law of nations which is a part of the law of the land"); see also *Texas Industries, Inc. v. Radcliff Materials, Inc.,* 451 U.S. 630, 641, 101 S.Ct. 2061, 68 L.Ed.2d 500 (1981) (recognizing that "international disputes implicating . . . our relations with foreign nations" are one of the "narrow areas" in which "federal common law" continues to exist). It would take some explaining to say now that federal courts must avert their gaze entirely from any international norm intended to protect individuals. We think an attempt to justify such a position would be particularly unconvincing in light of what we know about congressional understanding bearing on this issue lying at the intersection of the judicial and legislative powers. The First Congress, which reflected the understanding of the framing generation and included some of the Framers, assumed that federal courts could properly identify some international norms as enforceable in the exercise of § 1350 jurisdiction. We think it would be unreasonable to assume that the First Congress would have expected federal courts to lose all capacity to recognize enforceable international norms simply because the common law might lose some metaphysical cachet on the road to modern realism. Later Congresses seem to have shared our view. The position we take today has been assumed by some federal courts for 24 years, ever since the Second Circuit decided *Filartiga v. Pena–Irala,* 630 F.2d 876 (C.A.2 1980), and for practical purposes the point of today's disagreement has been focused since the exchange between Judge Edwards and Judge Bork in *Tel–Oren v. Libyan Arab Republic,* 726 F.2d 774 (C.A.D.C.1984). Congress, however, has not only expressed no disagreement with our view of the proper exercise of the judicial power, but has responded to its most notable instance by enacting legislation supplementing the judicial determination in some detail. See *supra,* at 2763 (discussing the Torture Victim Protection Act).

While we agree with Justice Scalia to the point that we would welcome any congressional guidance in exercising jurisdiction with such obvious potential to affect foreign relations, nothing Congress has done is a reason for us to shut the door to the law of nations entirely. It is enough to say that Congress may do that at any time (explicitly, or implicitly by treaties or statutes that occupy the field), just as it may modify or cancel any judicial decision so far as it rests on recognizing an international norm as such.

---

18. *Sabbatino* itself did not directly apply international law, see 376 U.S., at 421–423, 84 S.Ct. 923, but neither did it question the application of that law in appropriate cases, and it further endorsed the reasoning of a noted commentator who had argued that *Erie* should not preclude the continued application of international law in federal courts, 376 U.S., at 425, 84 S.Ct. 923 (citing Jessup, The Doctrine of Erie Railroad v. Tompkins Applied to International Law, 33 Am. J. Int'l L. 740 (1939)).

C

We must still, however, derive a standard or set of standards for assessing the particular claim Alvarez raises, and for this action it suffices to look to the historical antecedents. Whatever the ultimate criteria for accepting a cause of action subject to jurisdiction under § 1350, we are persuaded that federal courts should not recognize private claims under federal common law for violations of any international law norm with less definite content and acceptance among civilized nations than the historical paradigms familiar when § 1350 was enacted. See, *e.g., United States v. Smith,* 5 Wheat. 153, 163–180, 5 L.Ed. 57 (1820) (illustrating the specificity with which the law of nations defined piracy). This limit upon judicial recognition is generally consistent with the reasoning of many of the courts and judges who faced the issue before it reached this Court. See *Filartiga, supra,* at 890 ("'[F]or purposes of civil liability, the torturer has become— like the pirate and slave trader before him—*hostis humani generis,* an enemy of all mankind'"); *Tel–Oren, supra,* at 781 (Edwards, J., concurring) (suggesting that the "limits of section 1350's reach" be defined by "a handful of heinous actions—each of which violates definable, universal and obligatory norms"); see also *In re Estate of Marcos Human Rights Litigation,* 25 F.3d 1467, 1475 (C.A.9 1994) ("Actionable violations of international law must be of a norm that is specific, universal, and obligatory"). And the determination whether a norm is sufficiently definite to support a cause of action should (and, indeed, inevitably must) involve an element of judgment about the practical consequences of making that cause available to litigants in the federal courts.

Thus, Alvarez's detention claim must be gauged against the current state of international law, looking to those sources we have long, albeit cautiously, recognized.

"[W]here there is no treaty, and no controlling executive or legislative act or judicial decision, resort must be had to the customs and usages of civilized nations; and, as evidence of these, to the works of jurists and commentators, who by years of labor, research and experience, have made themselves peculiarly well acquainted with the subjects of which they treat. Such works are resorted to by judicial tribunals, not for the speculations of their authors concerning what the law ought to be, but for trustworthy evidence of what the law really is." *The Paquete Habana,* 175 U.S., at 700, 20 S.Ct. 290.

To begin with, Alvarez cites two well-known international agreements that, despite their moral authority, have little utility under the standard set out in this opinion. He says that his abduction by Sosa was an "arbitrary arrest" within the meaning of the Universal Declaration of Human Rights (Declaration), G.A. Res. 217A (III), U.N. Doc. A/810 (1948). And he traces the rule against arbitrary arrest not only to the Declaration, but also to article nine of the International Covenant on Civil and Political Rights (Covenant), Dec. 16, 1966, 999 U.N.T.S. 171, to which the United States is a party, and to various other conventions to which it is not. But the Declaration does not of its own force impose obligations as a matter of international law. See Humphrey, The UN Charter and the Universal Declaration of Human Rights, in The International Protection of Human Rights 39, 50 (E. Luard ed.1967) (quoting Eleanor Roosevelt calling the Declaration " 'a statement of principles . . . setting up a common standard of achievement for all peoples and all nations' " and " 'not a treaty or international agreement . . . impos[ing] legal obligations' "). And, although the Covenant does bind the United States as a matter of international law, the United States ratified the Covenant on the express understanding that it was not self-executing and so did not itself create obligations enforceable in the federal courts. See *supra,* at 2763. Accordingly, Alvarez cannot say that the Declaration and Covenant themselves establish the relevant and applicable rule of international law. He instead attempts to show that prohibition of arbitrary arrest has attained the status of binding customary international law.

Here, it is useful to examine Alvarez's complaint in greater detail. As he presently argues it, the claim does not rest on the cross-border feature of his abduction. Although the District Court granted relief in part on finding a violation of international law in taking Alvarez across the border from Mexico to the United States, the Court of Appeals rejected that ground of liability for failure to identify a norm of requisite force prohibiting a forcible abduction across a border. Instead, it relied on the conclusion that the law of the United States did not authorize Alvarez's arrest, because the DEA lacked extraterritorial authority under 21 U.S.C. § 878, and because Federal Rule of Criminal Procedure 4(d)(2) limited the warrant for Alvarez's arrest to "the jurisdiction of the United States." It is this position that Alvarez takes now: that his arrest was arbitrary and as such forbidden by international law not because it infringed the prerogatives of Mexico, but because no applicable law authorized it.

Alvarez thus invokes a general prohibition of "arbitrary" detention defined as officially sanctioned action exceeding positive authorization to detain under the domestic law of some government, regardless of the circumstances. Whether or not this is an accurate reading of the Covenant, Alvarez cites little authority that a rule so broad has the status of a binding customary norm today. He certainly cites nothing to justify the federal courts in taking his broad rule as the predicate for a federal lawsuit, for its implications would be breathtaking. His rule would support a cause of action in federal court for any arrest, anywhere in the world, unauthorized by the law of the jurisdiction in which it took place, and would create a cause of action for any seizure of an alien in violation of the Fourth Amendment, supplanting the actions under Rev. Stat. § 1979, 42 U.S.C. § 1983, and *Bivens v. Six Unknown Fed. Narcotics Agents,* 403 U.S. 388, 91 S.Ct. 1999, 29 L.Ed.2d 619 (1971), that now provide damages remedies for such violations. It would create an action in federal court for arrests by state officers who simply exceed their authority; and for the violation of any limit that the law of any country might place on the authority of its own officers to arrest. And all of this assumes that Alvarez could establish that Sosa was acting on behalf of a government when he made the arrest, for otherwise he would need a rule broader still.

Alvarez's failure to marshal support for his proposed rule is underscored by the Restatement (Third) of Foreign Relations Law of the United States (1986), which says in its discussion of customary international human rights law that a "state violates international law if, as a matter of state policy, it practices, encourages, or condones . . . prolonged arbitrary detention." 2 *Id.*, § 702. Although the Restatement does not explain its requirements of a "state policy" and of "prolonged" detention, the implication is clear. Any credible invocation of a principle against arbitrary detention that the civilized world accepts as binding customary international law requires a factual basis beyond relatively brief detention in excess of positive authority. Even the Restatement's limits are only the beginning of the enquiry, because although it is easy to say that some policies of prolonged arbitrary detentions are so bad that those who enforce them become enemies of the human race, it may be harder to say which policies cross that line with the certainty afforded by Blackstone's three common law offenses. In any event, the label would never fit the reckless policeman who botches his warrant, even though that same officer might pay damages under municipal law. *E.g., Groh v. Ramirez*, 540 U.S. 551, 124 S.Ct. 1284, 157 L.Ed.2d 1068 (2004).

Whatever may be said for the broad principle Alvarez advances, in the present, imperfect world, it expresses an aspiration that exceeds any binding customary rule having the specificity we require. Creating a private cause of action to further that aspiration would go beyond any residual common law discretion we think it appropriate to exercise. It is enough to hold that a single illegal detention of less than a day, followed by the transfer of custody to lawful authorities and a prompt arraignment, violates no norm of customary international law so well defined as to support the creation of a federal remedy.

* * *

The judgment of the Court of Appeals is

Reversed.

NOTES AND QUESTIONS

1.   Are *jus cogens* norms also part of federal common law? See *Siderman, Committee of U.S. Citizens Living in Nicaragua*, and *Filartiga*, discussed in earlier chapters.

2.   What is the test the Court sets out for when the law of nations can be applied as federal common law, at least within the context of section 1350? What is the relevance of Justice Souter's list of reasons for caution by lower court judges applying *Sosa*?

3.   *Treaties & Customary International Law. Alvarez–Machain's* essential argument was that customary international law prohibits official abduction and requires repatriation. Did the Court gratuitously disparage customary international law as a source of law for decision in the case? Or, can the case be read as one that actually provides subtle support for the customary rule, but not the remedy sought? Extradition is the agreed-upon legal

method for rendering fugitives to another's justice. Could Justice Rehnquist's opinion in *Alvarez–Machain* actually be read as holding only that releasing the fugitive would not be the proper remedy? Does *Sosa* repair any damage done to customary international law in *Alvarez-Machain*?

4.   For more on international law in the United States, see, DAVID BEDERMAN, THE CLASSICAL FOUNDATIONS OF THE AMERICAN CONSTITUTION: PREVAILING WISDOM (2008); JOHN F. MURPHY, THE UNITED STATES AND THE RULE OF LAW IN INTERNATIONAL AFFAIRS (2004); LOUIS HENKIN, FOREIGN AFFAIRS AND THE CONSTITUTION (2d ed. 1996).

C.   ARGENTINA

1.   CONSTITUTIONAL PROVISIONS

Section 31.—This Constitution, the laws of the Nation enacted by Congress in pursuance thereof, and treaties with foreign powers, are the supreme law of the Nation; and the authorities of each province are bound thereby, notwithstanding any provision to the contrary included in the provincial laws or constitutions, except for the province of Buenos Aires, the treaties ratified after the Pact of November 11, 1859.

Section 75.—Congress is empowered: . . .

22.—To approve or reject treaties concluded with other nations and international organizations, and concordats with the Holy See. Treaties and concordats have a higher constitutional status than laws.

The American Declaration of the Rights and Duties of Man; the Universal Declaration of Human Rights; the American Convention on Human Rights; the International Covenant on Economic, Social and Cultural Rights; the International Covenant on Civil and Political Rights and its Optional Protocol; the Convention on the Prevention and Punishment of Genocide; the International Convention on the Elimination of all Forms of Racial Discrimination; the Convention on the Elimination of all Forms of Discrimination against Women; the Convention against Torture and other Cruel, Inhuman or Degrading Treatment or Punishment; the Convention on the Rights of the Child; in the full force of their provisions, they have constitutional hierarchy, do not repeal any section of the First Part of this Constitution and are to be understood as complementing the rights and guarantees recognized herein. They shall only be denounced, in such event, by the National Executive Power after the approval of two-thirds of all the members of each House.

In order to attain constitutional hierarchy, other treaties and conventions on human rights shall require the vote of two-thirds of all the members of each House, after their approval by Congress.

24.—To approve treaties of integration which delegate powers and jurisdiction to supranational organizations under reciprocal and equal conditions, and which respect the democratic order and human rights. The rules derived therefrom have a higher hierarchy than laws.

The approval of these treaties with Latin American States shall require the absolute majority of all the members of each House. In the case of treaties with other States, the National Congress, with the absolute majority of the members present of each House, shall declare the advisability of the approval of the treaty which shall only be approved with the vote of the absolute majority of all the members of each House, one hundred and twenty days after said declaration of advisability.

The denunciation of the treaties referred to in this subsection shall require the prior approval of the absolute majority of all the members of each House.

Section 116.—The Supreme Court and the lower courts of the Nation are empowered to hear and decide all cases arising under the Constitution and the laws of the Nation * * * and under the treaties made with foreign nations; * * *

Section 118.—The trial of all ordinary criminal cases not arising from the right to impeach granted to the House of Deputies, shall be decided by jury once this institution is established in the Nation. The trial shall be held in the province where the crime has been committed; but when committed outside the territory of the Nation against customary international law, the trial shall be held at such place as Congress may determine by a special law.

Janet Koven Levit, The Constitutionalization of Human Rights in Argentina: Problem or Promise?*

37 COLUM. J. TRANSNAT'L L. 281 (1999)

* * *

Unlike many Latin American constitutions, Argentina's Constitution was a portrait of longevity, dating from 1853. Argentina's Constitution largely echoed the U.S. Constitution, especially regarding separation of powers and federalism. The 1853 Constitution did not explicitly address human rights treaties, or even international law in general. Like the U.S. Constitution, the 1853 Constitution divided power over international treaties among the three independent branches: "The Congress shall approve or disapprove of treaties concluded with other nations"; the Executive shall conclude and sign treaties with foreign powers and receive their ministers; and the federal courts shall have jurisdiction over matters pertaining to international treaties.

From 1976 through 1983, Argentina suffered a brutal military dictatorship, during which thousands "disappeared." These severe human rights

---

* Footnotes omitted.

abuses were the backdrop to subsequent democratization efforts and, ultimately, the 1994 constitutional reform.

* * *

Substantively, while international human rights norms infiltrate national constitutions to greater or lesser degrees, Argentina's Constitution is a unique, verbatim replica of these treaties. In terms of status, Argentina is the only country that grants human rights treaties constitutional standing. * * * South American constitutions fall into one of two broad groups. The first group includes constitutions that incorporate the "spirit" of human rights treaties. In general, these constitutions are skeletal reflections of international human rights treaties, incorporating many core rights—core ideas—but lacking the flesh to make these rights as robust as their treaty-based counterparts. The second group, on the other hand, incorporates the texture and nuances of international treaty-based rights.

The constitutions which place international law on a par with domestic law expose international norms to subsequent statutory invalidation. International treaty norms thus become vulnerable and manipulable, depending on the sentiments and mood of transient legislatures. The Peruvian Constitution clearly states that treaties are a part of "national law." The Venezuelan Constitution requires the legislature to pass laws validating all international treaties or conventions, relegating these international norms to the status of a domestic law. Other constitutions do not explicitly address the status of international law, but divide power over international treaties among the executive, who concludes treaties, and the legislative branch, which ratifies treaties. Domestic constitutional law interpreting these provisions frequently relegates international treaties to the status of a domestic statute.

On the other hand, some constitutions explicitly elevate international norms, or a specific group of international norms. Paraguay's Constitution ranks sources of law, with international treaties and conventions falling below its Constitution but above "laws dictated by Congress." Colombia's Constitution elevates international treaties that "recognize human rights and that prohibit their limitation in states of emergency." Ecuador's Constitution is not explicit in its treatment of international human rights norms; it sanctifies "fundamental human rights" and guarantees "free and effective exercise and enjoyment of the civil, political, economic, social and cultural rights enunciated in declarations, pacts, agreements and other international instruments in force," while it relegates international treaties or agreements to the status of a "secondary" or non-constitutional norm. Juxtaposing these constitutional provisions, one can logically conclude that international treaty norms float somewhere between the Constitution and domestic law in Ecuador's domestic legal hierarchy.

Other constitutions leave the status of international norms ambiguous. Chile's Constitution, for example, mimics the constitutional division of power among the executive and the legislative branches found in the Uruguayan and Bolivian Constitutions, suggesting that international norms would be on a par with domestic norms. Yet, a relatively recent amendment to Chile's Constitution charges state agencies with the duty "to respect and promote the rights guaranteed" in international treaties, suggesting that such norms are cloaked with special domestic standing.

* * *

Argentina's 1994 constitutional reform altered the Constitution's standing in terms of status and substance. Article 75(22) endowed nine international human rights treaties with constitutional standing, and otherwise reaffirmed the Supreme Court's decisions by providing all other international treaties with supra-statutory standing. Thus, domestic law cannot trump an international norm, and certain international human rights norms, to be interpreted in harmony with the rest of the 1994 Constitution, stand on par with the Constitution itself.

In terms of substance, it is important first to examine Argentina's new Constitution independent of Article 75(22) * * *. Without Article 75(22), Argentina's Constitution remains highly reminiscent of its predecessor and similar to those constitutions that reflect the spirit, rather than the scope, of human rights treaties. * * *

Now consider the effect of Article 75(22). The Argentine Constitution is no longer a succinct document containing 110 constitutional provisions but rather a compendium of the constitutional text and the nine human rights treaties which, by virtue of their constitutional status, are effectively incorporated into the constitutional text. Therefore, every right, every privilege, every guarantee, that the anointed human rights treaties grant are part of Argentina's Constitution. Whereas some constitutions merely incorporate the spirit of human rights treaties and others more accurately reflect their scope and breadth, Argentina's Constitution takes a further step: wholesale incorporation of the treaties themselves. The Constitution now mirrors these select human rights treaties, identical in scope, form, and substance. In this sense, Argentina's actions are unique in South America and, arguably, the world.

The effect of Argentina's constitutionalization of human rights treaties can be seen in the Argentine courts' jurisprudence on prosecuting military officers responsible for bombings, forced disappearances and other international (and national) crimes in the context of the 1970s "dirty war" period. When a civilian government returned to power in 1983, it prosecuted the highest military commanders for human rights violations, leading to the "trial of the Juntas" and prison sentences for several junta leaders. However, under military pressure, the government eventually passed a "due obedience law" that acted as a *de facto* amnesty, shielding almost all the remaining military and police from prosecutions for criminal acts committed during the period of military rule. Over the subsequent years, family members of those killed and human rights lawyers brought cases seeking to expand loopholes in the law and eventually to overturn it on grounds of incompatibility with international law.

The case that led to judicial nullification of the amnesty law began with the kidnapping of Claudia Victoria Poblete, who was eight months old when she was abducted together with her parents and held in a clandestine detention center. Her father, José Liborio Poblete, was a Chilean disability rights activist who used a wheelchair. Her mother, Gertrudis Marta Hlaczik, was a psychology student. The couple was killed and the baby was turned over to a police lieutenant colonel and his wife. After years of investigation, the lieutenant colonel was accused and convicted of kidnapping a minor—a crime specifically excluded from the amnesty law. The court also issued arrest warrants for two notorious torturers, Juan Antonio del Cerro and Julio Héctor Simón and seven other military officers for the kidnapping of Claudia Poblete and the disappearance of her parents. On November 1, 2000, del Cerro and Simón were arrested for the crime. The court noted that it was absurd to investigate what happened to the child, who after all was still alive, but not look into the deaths of the child's parents arising under the same set of facts. For that, the amnesty laws had to be brushed aside. In March 2001, Judge Gabriel Cavallo declared the due obedience law null and void. The case was upheld by the Appellate Court. In 2005, the Supreme Court affirmed:

Simón, Julio Héctor and Others re Illegitimate Deprivation of Freedom

Supreme Court of Justice of the Nation
Cause No. 17.768c, 14 June 2005

15) That, in effect, beginning with the Constitutional modification of 1994, the Argentine state has assumed with respect to international law and, especially, with regard to the Inter–American human rights system, a series of constitutionally-mandated obligations, which have been increasingly consolidated and specified in their reach and content, and have moved in the direction of limiting the power of local law to pardon or avoid the prosecution of acts like those under consideration here.

16) That while it is true that art. 75, inc. 20 of the Constitution maintains the legislature's power to issue general amnesties, that power has been limited in its reach. In principle, amnesty laws have historically been used as instruments of social pacification.... However, to the extent they allow the "forgetting" of grave human rights violations, they contradict the provisions of the American Convention on Human Rights and the International Covenant on Civil and Political Rights and, therefore, are constitutionally prohibited.

17) That, as this court has recognized, the jurisprudence of the Inter–American Court of Human Rights, along with the directives of the Inter–American Commission, are a required source of interpretation of the duties and obligations derived from the American Convention on Human Rights. [The Court goes on to apply the Inter–American Court's ruling invalidating amnesty laws in Peru to the Argentine context, finding that the Inter–American Court would similarly invalidate the Argentine amnesty.]

* * *

Therefore, the Court

3.   Declares, in any case, without any effect Laws 23.492 and 23.521 and any act based on them that could impede the advance of the criminal prosecutions underway, or the trial and possible conviction of the accused, or that could hinder in any way the investigations being carried out by the appropriate authorities, into crimes against humanity committed within Argentine territory.

2.   TREATIES

Even before the 1994 Constitutional reform, the Argentine courts had declared that treaties were federal law and were superior to "ordinary" legislation. The landmark *Ekmekdijan* case involved freedom of expression and the "right of reply."

Ekmekdjian, Miguel A. c/ Sofovich, Gerardo and others

Supreme Court of Justice
July 7, 1992; Fallos 315:1492

[Petitioner was deeply upset that he had been denied a "right of reply" to insulting statements about Jesus and the Virgin Mary that were made on television. He sued the TV host when the host refused to read a response to the insults on his television program, "Saturday Night." He alleged that this violated his constitutional rights as well as the provisions of the American Convention on Human Rights. The Court first established that this was a conflict between two rights: freedom of expression and the right of reply. It went on to consider whether contrary national law was superior to the rights found in the American Convention, a duly ratified treaty.]

15) In our legal system, the right of reply has been established in Article 14 of the American Convention, which, having been approved by Law 23,054 and ratified on September 5, 1984, is the supreme law of the land according to art. 31 of the Constitution. We consider whether—as petitioner affirms—this article is directly applicable in our internal law or if, on the contrary, it requires legislative implementation.

16) In that sense, violation of an International treaty may occur either because internal laws require action contrary to the treaty, or because of a lack of internal laws to make its implementation possible. Both sets of circumstances would be contrary to the prior treaty ratification and would mean the lack of compliance with or repudiation of the treaty, with the harmful consequences that could follow.

17) A ratified treaty is organically federal, since the Executive concludes and signs treaties, the Congress rejects or approves them by federal law, and the Executive confirms the approved treaties through a federal act. The derogation of an international treaty by a Congressional statute violates the distribution of powers imposed by the Constitution, because it could overturn this complex federal act of completing a treaty. It would be

an unconstitutional incursion of the legislature into the province of the executive branch, which is solely responsible for the conduct of foreign policy.

18) The Vienna Convention on the Law of Treaties, approved by law 19,865, ratified by the Executive on December 5, 1972 and in force since January 27, 1980, confers primacy to International law over domestic law. This hierarchy is now part of Argentine law. The Convention is a constitutionally valid treaty that assigns priority to International treaties over domestic law in the domestic law, that is, it recognizes the primacy of International over domestic law. This has changed the [prior precedents].

19) The necessary application of Article 27 of the Vienna Convention means that the Argentine state must give priority to the treaty in case of a conflict with a contrary domestic statute or with the omission of passing laws that, in effect, would imply non-compliance with the International treaty.

20) Along the same lines, when the nation ratifies a treaty, it takes on an International obligation for its judicial and administrative organs to apply the treaty, so long as its provisions are sufficiently concrete to allow their immediate application. A norm is self-executing when it refers to a concrete situation where it can operate immediately without the need for Congressionally-created institutions. In the case of article 14.1 its language is clear and unequivocal and creates, in the situations it describes, a right to reply or clarification, although it leaves to further legislation the details of its reglementation * * *. The textual interpretation according to which "all persons have the right to * * *" removes any doubt about the self-executing nature of the provision. The same is not true of other articles which establish that "the law should recognize" (art. 17) or "it shall be prohibited by law" (art. 13.5).

21) Interpretation of the American Convention should, moreover, be guided by the jurisprudence of the Inter-american Court of Human Rights, which has as one of its objectives the interpretation of the Convention. * * *

3. CUSTOMARY INTERNATIONAL LAW

The defendants in the *Simón* case argued, among other things, that the crimes at issue had long been subject to the statute of limitations, so that even if the amnesty laws were annulled, prosecution was now barred. To the extent the revival of criminal investigations was based on the Convention on the Non–Applicability of Statutes of Limitation and on the Inter–American Convention on Enforced Disappearances, those treaties were ratified subsequent to the charged events and, therefore, and that reviving prosecutions was a breach of the principle of legality. The Supreme Court in an earlier case had addressed that issue, as well as the role of customary international law in Argentine courts.

Arancibia Clavel, Enrique Lautaro, and others, re Aggravated Homicide and Illicit Association and Others

Supreme Court of Justice
Cause No. 15/6/93–B, August 24, 2004

[Arancibia Clavel was accused of being a member of the Chilean secret police. He was sent to Argentina to murder Chilean general Carlos Prats and his wife, who had sought refuge after the 1973 Chilean coup in Argentina. Prats and his wife were killed in 1974 when a bomb exploded at their Buenos Aires home. Arancibia argued that the statute of limitations forbid prosecution.]

16) Offenses like genocide, torture, forced disappearance, homicide and any other type of acts aimed at persecuting and exterminating political opponents—including being part of a group dedicated to carrying out these crimes—may be considered crimes against humanity, because they violate customary international law as prescribed in article 118 of the Constitution. * * *

19) The statute of limitations in criminal cases is closely connected to the principle of legality, therefore an *ex post facto* law that is detrimental to the accused could not be applied * * *.

21) The exception to this rule involves those acts that constitute crimes against humanity, which continue to affect the whole of society given their magnitude and significance. This means that they are still of concern not only to national society but also to the international community.

28) That this [Convention on the Non–Applicability of Statutory Limitation for War Crimes and Crimes Against Humanity, ratified by Argentina after the passage of the amnesty law] merely affirms the existing imprescriptibility of these crimes, which means it is simply recognizing an already existent norm (of *jus cogens*) as part of customary international law.

33) That therefore the acts for which Arancibia Clavel was convicted were already not subject to a statute of limitations under international law at the moment they were committed. Thus, there is no retrospective application of the Convention, but rather application of a rule of customary international law in place since the 1960s, and to which the Argentine state adhered.

34) That, understanding that at the time they were committed, the facts under investigation were considered crimes against humanity under international human rights law legally binding for the Argentine state, the logical consequence is the inevitability of their prosecution and their imprescriptibility.

The Federal Court of Appeals for Buenos Aires, in a similar case, had earlier elaborated on the role of customary international law in the Argentine legal system:

Massera re Appeals

Federal Appeals Court of Buenos Aires
No. 30514 September 15, 1999

The evolution of law, especially international law—which is not fixed but rather in permanent and dynamic development, has implied a noticeable change in the juridical panorama.

In accordance with public international law, the alleged acts [of forced disappearance] in addition to being continuing crimes until the fate and whereabouts of the disappeared person are established, are not subject to a statute of limitations because they are crimes against humanity, no matter when committed.

[The Court then takes notice, as evidence of the existence of a customary international law norm, of ratified and unratified treaties, the Nuremberg Charter, cases from the U.S. and the U.K., proposed codes of conduct, the opinions of judges of the Inter–American Court of Human Rights, and the Rome Statute.]

Notwithstanding the inapplicability of many of these treaties, it is clear that the notion of crimes against humanity is inextricable from the need for its prosecution without time limits, and that what we can call an "international custom" has developed in that regard around which these multiple manifestations of international law have converged. * * *

The application of customary international law has been obligatory since 1853, thanks to the specific reference in [constitutional] article 118–ex 102—which was aimed at making sure national courts would be able to prosecute international crimes.

Similarly, in accordance with articles 116 and 117 of the Constitution, the Supreme Court has made clear that customary International law and general principles of law—sources of International law according to Article 38 of the ICJ Statute—are directly applicable in our legal system. Thus, in numerous cases the high court has referred to "customary law" and the "general principles of international law" in diverse contexts. * * * The importance and applicability of that referred to in article 118 has been the subject of case law * * * as well as doctrine, which holds that article 118 should be broadly interpreted so that through that article International Criminal Law and International Human Rights law become part of our constitutional order. * * *

NOTES AND QUESTIONS

1.   Would it be a good idea for other countries to copy Argentina's 1994 constitution in its treatment of human rights treaties? Why or why not? Would you include other sorts of treaties? International humanitarian law? Environmental law? Is it a good idea to further import the jurisprudence of the Inter–American Court of Human Rights? What if the bodies interpreting the various human rights instruments come to different conclusions about what certain language means? Would you also include similar provisions on regional (but not global) trade agreements?

2.   The amnesty laws were also annulled by Legislative Decree 25.779 of September 2, 2003. The retrospective effect of the annulment was confirmed in the Supreme Court decision excerpted. Does the concurrence of the legislature increase the legitimacy of the Court's decision? Then–President Kirchner also supported annulment of the laws.

3.   Is it a violation of the principle of legality—also known as *nullum poena sine lege*—to allow renewed prosecutions long after the statute of limitations would have barred them for "ordinary" crimes like murder and kidnapping? Why or why not? Critics of the decision pointed to the lack of extensive state practice behind the Court's determinations on the existence of customary international law. Is it licit to allow extensive references to treaties (and jurisprudence of human rights courts) that came into being after the crimes had been committed? Why or why not?

4.   For further reading, see Naomi Roht-Arriaza, The Pinochet Effect, ch. 4 (2006); Christine A.E. Bakker, *A Full Stop to Amnesty in Argentina: The* Simón *Case*, 3 J. of Int'l Crim. J. 1106 (2005).

D.   European Union

1.   Constitutional Considerations

The EU described above in Chapter 3 is a product of international law by virtue of its having been established by international treaties, in the same way that the United Nations and other international organizations have been created by their respective treaties. Moreover, the EU depends upon international law for its status, fundamental powers and rights in the international system.

Article 5 of the Vienna Convention on the Law of Treaties provides that:

> The present Convention applies to any treaty which is the constituent instrument of an international organization and to any treaty adopted within an international organization without prejudice to any relevant rules of the organization.

The EU is thus governed by the texts of its constituent treaties, by the Vienna Convention, by treaties to which the EU is a contracting party, and by the applicable rules of customary international law. The constituent treaties and secondary legislation of the EU are binding on the EU and its institutions as well as its Member States, individuals, firms and other entities operating in the European Union, as developed in EU legislation and the decisions of the European Court of Justice.

These principles have also been envisaged in the Treaty of Lisbon, (O.J.E.U. C 115.1, 9 May 2008.) which is entered into force in 2009. Note that in Article 3(5) of the Lisbon Treaty on the European Union (TEU) the Union is required to contribute to the "strict observance and development of international law, including respect for the principles of the United

Nations Charter", and the reformed TEU Articles 10(2)(b) and 21(1) mention "respect for the principles of international law", and Article 21.2(b) refers to consolidation and support for the principles of international law. In the new Lisbon Treaty on the Functioning of the European Union, Article 77(4) refers to international law in applying policy on border questions and in Article 214 provides for humanitarian aid operations to be "conducted in accordance with international law". In these respects Lisbon seems to track prior understanding and practice. The EU is fully bound by the principles and rules of international law, participates in its development generally, and creates international law by entering into international treaties, by judgments of the European Court of Justice and by other actions.

While there is no formal "Constitution" for the EU, the constituent treaties mentioned above serve a like function in setting out the status, scope, powers, functions and limitations of the EU in terms of basic law.

2.   Application of Treaties and Customary International Law

In the European Court of Justice, direct application of treaties and customary international law to the EU and within the EU is demonstrated in the *Van Gend en Loos* and *Racke* cases. In the *Kadi* case the Court quashed an EU (EC) Regulation giving effect to a decision of the UN Security Council where that Regulation was found to have infringed certain fundamental rights under EU law. These cases represent some of the principle building blocks of the EU. Excerpts from the judgments in these cases follow.

van Gend en Loos v. Nederlandse Administratie der Belastingen

European Court of Justice
Case 26/62, [1963] ECR 1

[In 1960 the plaintiff Van Gend & Loos company imported a chemical known as ureaformaldehyde from Germany into the Netherlands. At the time of the import, the Dutch authorities had classified the product in a certain customs category and imposed a duty of 8%. When the Rome Treaties came into force in 1958, however, the Community had imposed a duty of only 3% on that product. The plaintiff argues that the higher duty of 8% was imposed in violation of Article 12 (since renumbered Article 25) of the EC Treaty which prohibits Member States from increasing the customs and duties on imports or exports once the Treaty had taken effect, one of the keystones of the common market.]

Grounds of judgment

B—*On the substance of the Case*

The first question * * * is whether Article 12 [since renumbered Article 25] of the Treaty has direct application in national law in the sense that nationals of Member States may on the basis of this Article lay claim to rights which the national court must protect.

To ascertain whether the provisions of an international treaty extend so far in their effects it is necessary to consider the spirit, the general scheme and the wording of those provisions * * *.

With regard to the general scheme of the Treaty as it relates to customs duties and charges having equivalent effect it must be emphasized that Article 9 [since renumbered Article 23], which bases the Community upon a customs union, includes as an essential provision the prohibition of these customs duties and charges. This provision is found at the beginning of the part of the Treaty which defines the 'Foundations of the Community'. It is applied and explained by Article 12.

The wording of Article 12 contains a clear and unconditional prohibition which is not a positive but a negative obligation. This obligation, moreover, is not qualified by any reservation on the part of states which would make its implementation conditional upon a positive legislative measure enacted under national law. The very nature of this prohibition makes it ideally adapted to produce direct effects in the legal relationship between Member States and their subjects.

The implementation of Article 12 does not require any legislative intervention on the part of the states. The fact that under this Article it is the Member States who are made the subject of the negative obligation does not imply that their nationals cannot benefit from this obligation.

In addition the argument based on Articles 169 and 170 [since renumbered Articles 226 and 227] of the Treaty put forward by the three Governments which have submitted observations to the Court in their statements of case is misconceived. The fact that these Articles of the Treaty enable the Commission and the Member States to bring before the Court a State which has not fulfilled its obligations does not mean that individuals cannot plead these obligations, should the occasion arise, before a national court, any more than the fact that the Treaty places at the disposal of the Commission ways of ensuring that obligations imposed upon those subject to the Treaty are observed, precludes the possibility, in actions between individuals before a national court, of pleading infringements of these obligations.

A restriction of the guarantees against an infringement of Article 12 by Member States to the procedures under Article 169 and 170 would remove all direct legal protection of the individual rights of their nationals. There is the risk that recourse to the procedure under these Articles would be ineffective if it were to occur after the implementation of a national decision taken contrary to the provisions of the Treaty.

The vigilance of individuals concerned to protect their rights amounts to an effective supervision in addition to the supervision entrusted by

Articles 169 and 170 to the diligence of the Commission and of the Member States.

It follows from the foregoing considerations that, according to the spirit, the general scheme and the wording of the Treaty, Article 12 must be interpreted as producing direct effects and creating individual rights which national courts must protect.

Firma A. Racke GmbH & Co. v. Hauptzollamt Mainz

European Court of Justice
Case C–162/96, [1998] ECR I–3655

[An importer of wine from Serbia to Gernany, Racke benefitted from tariff preferences on imports of wine from Yugoslavia under a Cooperation Agreement between the EC and the former Yugoslavia. Because of the war in the former Yugoslavia, the EC Council adopted Regulation No. 3300/91 which suspended trade concessions provided in that Agreement. In these proceedings in the German Bundesfinanzhof, Racke challenged the suspension regulation on the ground that it was adopted in violation of customary international law and was thus invalid. He argued that the wine tariff provisions for Yugoslavia fell under the customary rule of *pacta sunt servanda*, that treaties are binding and must be observed, against the contention that the suspension was proper under circumstances of a "fundamental change in the parties' situations", or *rebus sic stantibus*. The Bundesfinanzhof made this preliminary reference to the European Court of Justice of Justice under an EC Treaty procedure ("preliminary ruling", which will be taken up in subsection 4 below) to consider whether under EU law a private claimant in a national court may invoke rules of general international law against a decision to suspend the operation of an international agreement. In other words, are relevant provisions of customary international law superior to the law between the Community and Yugoslavia found in the language of the Cooperation Agreement?]

Judgment

[11]   In accordance with Article 60 of the Cooperation Agreement, the Council adopted Decision 91/602/EEC of 25 November 1991 denouncing the Cooperation Agreement between the European Economic Community and the Socialist Federal Republic of Yugoslavia (OJ 1991 L 325, p. 23). * * *

[18]   Racke has appealed on a point of law against that decision to the Bundesfinanzhof, which first considers the question whether unilateral suspension of the Cooperation Agreement complies with the conditions laid down in Article 62(1) of the Vienna Convention on the Law of Treaties of 23 May 1969 (the "Vienna Convention").

[19]   Article 62 of the Vienna Convention provides:

"1. A fundamental change of circumstances which has occurred with regard to those existing at the time of the conclusion of a treaty, and which was not foreseen by the parties, may not be invoked as a ground for terminating or withdrawing from the treaty unless:

(a) the existence of those circumstances constituted an essential basis of the consent of the parties to be bound by the treaty; and

(b) the effect of the change is radically to transform the extent of obligations still to be performed under the treaty.

* * * 3. If, under the foregoing paragraphs, a party may invoke a fundamental change of circumstances as a ground for terminating or withdrawing from a treaty it may also invoke the change as a ground for suspending the operation of the treaty."

[20] In the view of the national court, the break-up of Yugoslavia into several new States and the hostilities within Yugoslavia, which were factors to be regarded as a political change, involved a fundamental change in the material circumstances underlying the consent of the contracting parties bound by the Cooperation Agreement. On the other hand, the change did not appear radically to have altered the extent of the obligations under the Cooperation Agreement, which was essentially an economic agreement * * *

Question 1

[24] By way of a preliminary observation, it should be noted that even though the Vienna Convention does not bind either the Community or all its Member States, a series of its provisions, including Article 62, reflect the rules of international law which lay down, subject to certain conditions, the principle that a change of circumstances may entail the lapse or suspension of a treaty. Thus the International Court of Justice held that "[t]his principle, and the conditions and exceptions to which it is subject, have been embodied in Article 62 of the Vienna Convention on the Law of Treaties, which may in many respects be considered as a codification of existing customary law on the subject of the termination of a treaty relationship on account of change of circumstances" (judgment of 2 February 1973, Fisheries Jurisdiction (United Kingdom v. Iceland), ICJ Reports 1973, p. 3, paragraph 36).

The jurisdiction of the Court

[25] The Commission has expressed doubts as to the jurisdiction of the Court to rule on the first question because it relates to the validity of the disputed regulation under rules of customary international law. Even though the regulation constitutes an act of the Community within the meaning of subparagraph (b) of the first paragraph of Article 177 [since renumbered Article 234] of the Treaty, the preliminary rulings procedure does not permit the development of an argument based on international law alone, and in particular on the principles governing the termination of treaties and the suspension of their operation.

[26] As the Court has already held in Joined Cases 21/72 to 24/72 *International Fruit Company v. Produktschap voor Groenten en Fruit* [1972] ECR 1219, paragraph 5, the jurisdiction of the Court to give preliminary rulings under Article 177 of the Treaty concerning the validity of acts of the Community institutions cannot be limited by the grounds on which the validity of those measures may be contested.

[27]   Since such jurisdiction extends to all grounds capable of invalidating those measures, the Court is obliged to examine whether their validity may be affected by reason of the fact that they are contrary to a rule of international law (International Fruit Company, paragraph 6).

[28]   The Court therefore has jurisdiction to rule on the first question.

The validity of the disputed regulation

* * *

[31]   The Court has consistently held that a provision of an agreement concluded by the Community with non-member countries must be regarded as being directly applicable when, regard being had to its wording and the purpose and nature of the agreement itself, the provision contains a clear and precise obligation which is not subject, in its implementation or effects, to the adoption of any subsequent measure (see, in particular, Case 12/86 *Demirel v. Stadt Schwabisch Gmund* [1987] ECR 3719, paragraph 14).

[33]   By its very wording, that provision requires Community measures to implement it in order to enable the annual Community tariff quota to be opened in accordance with the detailed rules laid down by Article 2(1) and (2) of the Additional Protocol, the Community having no discretion as to the adoption of those measures. The Community is obliged to carry out, within a certain period, an exact calculation of customs duties in accordance with those provisions.

[34]   It follows that, as regards the preferential customs treatment for which it makes provision, Article 22(4) of the Cooperation Agreement is capable of conferring rights upon which individuals may rely before national courts.

[37]   It next needs to be examined whether, when invoking in legal proceedings the preferential customs treatment granted to him by Article 22(4) of the Cooperation Agreement, an individual may challenge the validity under customary international law rules of the disputed regulation, suspending the trade concessions granted under that Agreement as from 15 November 1991 * * *

[40]   It is important to note at the outset that the question referred by the national court concerns only the validity of the disputed regulation under rules of customary international law.

[41]   As far as the Community is concerned, an agreement concluded by the Council with a non-member country in accordance with the provisions of the EC Treaty is an act of a Community institution, and the provisions of such an agreement form an integral part of Community law (see Demirel, cited above, paragraph 7).

[45]   It should be noted in that respect that, as is demonstrated by the Courts judgment in Case C–286/90 *Poulsen and Diva Navigation* [1992] ECR I–6019, paragraph 9, the European Community must respect international law in the exercise of its powers. It is therefore required to comply with the rules of customary international law when adopting a regulation

suspending the trade concessions granted by, or by virtue of, an agreement which it has concluded with a non-member country.

[46]   It follows that the rules of customary international law concerning the termination and the suspension of treaty relations by reason of a fundamental change of circumstances are binding upon the Community institutions and form part of the Community legal order * * *.

[51]   In those circumstances, an individual relying in legal proceedings on rights which he derives directly from an agreement with a non-member country may not be denied the possibility of challenging the validity of a regulation which, by suspending the trade concessions granted by that agreement, prevents him from relying on it, and of invoking, in order to challenge the validity of the suspending regulation, obligations deriving from rules of customary international law which govern the termination and suspension of treaty relations * * *.

[57]   Whilst it is true, as Racke argues, that a certain volume of trade had to continue with Yugoslavia and that the Community could have continued to grant tariff concessions, the fact remains, as the Advocate General has pointed out in paragraph 93 of his Opinion, that application of the customary international law rules in question does not require an impossibility to perform obligations, and that there was no point in continuing to grant preferences, with a view to stimulating trade, in circumstances where Yugoslavia was breaking up * * *.

Yassin Abdullah Kadi et al. v. Council of the European Union and the Commission of the European Communities

European Court of the Justice, Grand Chamber
Joined Cases C–402/5 P and C–415/05 P, [2008] ECR I–0000

[These proceedings arose out of the efforts of the European Union to implement a number of U.N. Security Council resolutions directed against terrorist activities associated with Usama bin Laden, the Al–Qaeda network and the Taliban in Afganistan. The Security Council had found under Charter VII of the U.N. Charter that the suppression of international terrorism was essential to the maintenance of international peace and security. In Resolution 1267 (1999) the Security Council decided that all States must freeze funds and other financial assets of the Talaban, and established a Sanctions Committee to implement that decision and to designate the particular persons and entities to whom it would apply. The Sanctions Committee designated Mr. Kadi among others whose funds and financial assets were to be frozen.

The EU Council in turn adopted Regulation (EC) 881/2002 which applied the U.N freeze regime to the EU, and led to further actions which applied the freeze to particular individuals and entities, including Mr. Kadi. Mr. Kadi then brought an action in the EU Court of First Instance (CFI) seeking annulment of that Regulation on grounds of breaches of fundamental rights, including the right to be heard and right of respect for property. Following the CFI's judgment denying relief, Mr. Kadi appealed to the ECJ. In a landmark judgment, the ECJ annulled the EC Regulation and thus recognized the higher authority of the EU fundamental rights within the EU.]

281   In this connection it is to be borne in mind that the Community is based on the rule of law, inasmuch as neither its Member States nor its institutions can avoid review of the conformity of their acts with the basic constitutional charter, the EC Treaty, which established a complete system of legal remedies and procedures designed to enable the Court of Justice to review the legality of acts of the institutions (Case 294/83 *Les Verts* v. *Parliament* [1986] ECR 1339, paragraph 23).

282   It is also to be recalled that an international agreement cannot affect the allocation of powers fixed by the Treaties or, consequently, the autonomy of the Community legal system, observance of which is ensured by the Court by virtue of the exclusive jurisdiction conferred on it by Article 220 EC, jurisdiction that the Court has, moreover, already held to form part of the very foundations of the Community (see, to that effect, Opinion 1/91 [1991] ECR I–6079, paragraphs 35 and 71, and Case C–459/03 *Commission* v. *Ireland* [2006] ECR I–4635, paragraph 123 and case-law cited).

283   In addition, according to settled case-law, fundamental rights form an integral part of the general principles of law whose observance the Court ensures. For that purpose, the Court draws inspiration from the constitutional traditions common to the Member States and from the guidelines supplied by international instruments for the protection of human rights on which the Member States have collaborated or to which they are signatories. In that regard, the ECHR [European Court of human Rights] has special significance (see, inter alia, Case C–305/05 *Ordre des barreaux francophones et germanophone and Others* [2007] ECRI–5305, paragraph 29 and case-law cited).

284   It is also clear from the case-law that respect for human rights is a condition of the lawfulness of Community acts (Opinion 2/94, paragraph 34) and that measures incompatible with respect for human rights are not acceptable in the Community (Case C–112/00 *Schmidberger* [2003] ECR I–5659, paragraph 73 and case-law cited).

285   It follows from all those considerations that the obligations imposed by an international agreement cannot have the effect of prejudic-ing the constitutional principles of the EC Treaty, which include the principle that all Community acts must respect fundamental rights, that respect constituting a condition of their lawfulness which it is for the Court to review in the framework of the complete system of legal remedies established by the Treaty.

286   In this regard it must be emphasised that, in circumstances such as those of these cases, the review of lawfulness thus to be ensured by the

Community judicature applies to the Community act intended to give effect to the international agreement at issue, and not to the latter as such.

287   With more particular regard to a Community act which, like the contested regulation, is intended to give effect to a resolution adopted by the Security Council under Chapter VII of the Charter of the United Nations, it is not, therefore, for the Community judicature, under the exclusive jurisdiction provided for by Article 220 EC, to review the lawfulness of such a resolution adopted by an international body, even if that review were to be limited to examination of the compatibility of that resolution with jus cogens.

288   However, any judgment given by the Community judicature deciding that a Community measure intended to give effect to such a resolution is contrary to a higher rule of law in the Community legal order would not entail any challenge to the primacy of that resolution in international law.

291   In this respect it is first to be borne in mind that the European Community must respect international law in the exercise of its powers (*Poulsen and Diva Navigation*, paragraph 9, and *Racke*, paragraph 45), the Court having in addition stated, in the same paragraph of the first of those judgments, that a measure adopted by virtue of those powers must be interpreted, and its scope limited, in the light of the relevant rules of international law.

292   Moreover, the Court has held that the powers of the Community provided for by Articles 177 EC to 181 EC in the sphere of cooperation and development must be exercised in observance of the undertakings given in the context of the United Nations and other international organisations (Case C–91/05 *Commission* v. *Council* [2008] ECR I–0000, paragraph 65 and case-law cited).

293   Observance of the undertakings given in the context of the United Nations is required just as much in the sphere of the maintenance of international peace and security when the Community gives effect, by means of the adoption of Community measures taken on the basis of Articles 60 EC and 301 EC, to resolutions adopted by the Security Council under Chapter VII of the Charter of the United Nations.

294   In the exercise of that latter power it is necessary for the Community to attach special importance to the fact that, in accordance with Article 24 of the Charter of the United Nations, the adoption by the Security Council of resolutions under Chapter VII of the Charter constitutes the exercise of the primary responsibility with which that international body is invested for the maintenance of peace and security at the global level, a responsibility which, under Chapter VII, includes the power to determine what and who poses a threat to international peace and security and to take the measures necessary to maintain or restore them.

296   Although, because of the adoption of such an act, the Community is bound to take, under the EC Treaty, the measures necessitated by that act, that obligation means, when the object is to implement a resolution of the Security Council adopted under Chapter VII of the Charter of the United Nations, that in drawing up those measures the Community is to

take due account of the terms and objectives of the resolution concerned and of the relevant obligations under the Charter of the United Nations relating to such implementation.

298   It must however be noted that the Charter of the United Nations does not impose the choice of a particular model for the implementation of resolutions adopted by the Security Council under Chapter VII of the Charter, since they are to be given effect in accordance with the procedure applicable in that respect in the domestic legal order of each Member of the United Nations. The Charter of the United Nations leaves the Members of the United Nations a free choice among the various possible models for transposition of those resolutions into their domestic legal order.

299   It follows from all those considerations that it is not a consequence of the principles governing the international legal order under the United Nations that any judicial review of the internal lawfulness of the contested regulation in the light of fundamental freedoms is excluded by virtue of the fact that that measure is intended to give effect to a resolution of the Security Council adopted under Chapter VII of the Charter of the United Nations.

300   What is more, such immunity from jurisdiction for a Community measure like the contested regulation, as a corollary of the principle of the primacy at the level of international law of obligations under the Charter of the United Nations, especially those relating to the implementation of resolutions of the Security Council adopted under Chapter VII of the Charter, cannot find a basis in the EC Treaty.

302   It is true also that Article 297 EC implicitly permits obstacles to the operation of the common market when they are caused by measures taken by a Member State to carry out the international obligations it has accepted for the purpose of maintaining international peace and security.

303   Those provisions cannot, however, be understood to authorise any derogation from the principles of liberty, democracy and respect for human rights and fundamental freedoms enshrined in Article 6(1) EU as a foundation of the Union.

304   Article 307 EC may in no circumstances permit any challenge to the principles that form part of the very foundations of the Community legal order, one of which is the protection of fundamental rights, including the review by the Community judicature of the lawfulness of Community measures as regards their consistency with those fundamental rights.

305   Nor can an immunity from jurisdiction for the contested regulation with regard to the review of its compatibility with fundamental rights, arising from the alleged absolute primacy of the resolutions of the Security Council to which that measure is designed to give effect, find any basis in the place that obligations under the Charter of the United Nations would occupy in the hierarchy of norms within the Community legal order if those obligations were to be classified in that hierarchy.

306   Article 300(7) EC provides that agreements concluded under the conditions set out in that article are to be binding on the institutions of the Community and on Member States.

307   Thus, by virtue of that provision, supposing it to be applicable to the Charter of the United Nations, the latter would have primacy over acts of secondary Community law (see, to that effect, Case C–308/06 *Intertanko and Others* [2008] ECR I–0000, paragraph 42 and case-law cited).

308   That primacy at the level of Community law would not, however, extend to primary law, in particular to the general principles of which fundamental rights form part.

314   In the instant case it must be declared that the contested regulation cannot be considered to be an act directly attributable to the United Nations as an action of one of its subsidiary organs created under Chapter VII of the Charter of the United Nations or an action falling within the exercise of powers lawfully delegated by the Security Council pursuant to that chapter.

323   * * * [A]lthough it is now open to any person or entity to approach the Sanctions Committee directly, submitting a request to be removed from the summary list at what is called the "focal" point, the fact remains that the procedure before that Committee is still in essence diplomatic and intergovernmental, the persons or entities concerned having no real opportunity of asserting their rights and that committee taking its decisions by consensus, each of its members having a right of veto.

324   The Guidelines of the Sanctions Committee, as last amended on 12 February 2007, make it plain that an applicant submitting a request for removal from the list may in no way assert his rights himself during the procedure before the Sanctions Committee or be represented for that purpose, the Government of his State of residence or of citizenship alone having the right to submit observations on that request.

325   Moreover, those Guidelines do not require the Sanctions Committee to communicate to the applicant the reasons and evidence justifying his appearance in the summary list or to give him access, even restricted, to that information. Last, if that Committee rejects the request for removal from the list, it is under no obligation to give reasons.

326   It follows from the foregoing that the Community judicature must, in accordance with the powers conferred on it by the EC Treaty, ensure the review, in principle the full review, of the lawfulness of all Community acts in the light of the fundamental rights forming an integral part of the general principles of Community law, including review of Community measures which, like the contested regulation, are designed to give effect to the resolutions adopted by the Security Council under Chapter VII of the Charter of the United Nations.

327   The Court of First Instance erred in law, therefore, when it held, in paragraphs 212 to 231 of *Kadi* and 263 to 282 of *Yusuf and Al Barakaat*, that it followed from the principles governing the relationship between the international legal order under the United Nations and the Community legal order that the contested regulation, since it is designed to give effect to a resolution adopted by the Security Council under Chapter VII of the Charter of the United Nations affording no latitude in that respect, must

enjoy immunity from jurisdiction so far as concerns its internal lawfulness save with regard to its compatibility with the norms of jus cogens.

328   The appellants' grounds of appeal are therefore well founded on that point, with the result that the judgments under appeal must be set aside

* * *

On those grounds, the Court (Grand Chamber) hereby:

2.   Annuls Council Regulation (EC) No 881/2002 of 27 May 2002 imposing certain specific restrictive measures directed against certain persons and entities associated with Usama bin Laden, the Al–Qaeda network and the Taliban * * *.

3.   EU TREATY–MAKING POWERS

Legal power to enter into international agreements is specifically provided for the EU in Article 24 of the TEU and for the EC in Article 300 of the TEC, both of which are set forth in the Documentary Supplement. The procedures in the TEU and the TEC have some similarities in the pattern of the procedure for entering into agreements, although the TEU authorization applies to agreements made in implementation of the Common Foreign and Security Policy Title of the TEU and the TEC refers broadly to the agreements pursuant to provisions of the TEC. In both cases, the agreements are made by the Council. When the prescribed procedures are followed, the agreements become binding on the institutions of the EU and in the case of the EC the agreements are binding on Member States as well.

For the EC, Article 300 provides that the initial step in treaty making is a recommendation of a new agreement by the Commission to the Council which, normally acting by majority may then authorize the Commission to open the necessary negotiations. The Commission conducts the negotiations in consultation with Council committees and pursuant to its directives. The Council concludes agreements after following the procedures for consultation with the European Parliament (EP), and in specified situations (agreements creating institutional cooperation or important budgetary implications, for example), the consent of the EP must be obtained.

New rules for the EU to conclude agreements are featured in Article 37 of the proposed Lisbon Treaty on the EU and in Articles 216–218 of the proposed Treaty on the Functioning of the EU. These Articles are also found in the Documentary Supplement.

Commission of the European Communities v. Council of the European Communities [The ERTA or AETR Case]

European Court of Justice
Case 22/70, [1971] ECR 263

Grounds of Judgment

[1]   By an application lodged on 19 May 1970 the Commission of the European Communities has requested the annulment of the Council's

proceedings of 20 March 1970 regarding the negotiation and conclusion by the Member States of the Community, under the auspices of the United Nations Economic Commission for Europe, of the European Agreement Concerning the Work of Crews of Vehicles Engaged in International Road Transport (AETR).

* * *

[6]   The Commission takes the view that Article 75 [since renumbered Article 71] of the Treaty, which conferred on the Community powers defined in wide terms with a view to implementing the common transport policy, must apply to external relations just as much as to domestic measures in the sphere envisaged.

[7]   It believes that the full effect of this provision would be jeopardized if the powers which it confers, particularly that of laying down "any appropriate provisions", within the meaning of subparagraph (1)(c) of the article cited, did not extend to the conclusion of agreements with third countries.

[8]   Even if, it is argued, this power did not originally embrace the whole sphere of transport, it would tend to become general and exclusive as and where the common policy in this field came to be implemented.

[9]   The Council, on the other hand, contends that since the Community only has such powers as have been conferred on it, authority to enter into agreements with third countries cannot be assumed in the absence of an express provision in the Treaty.

[13]   Article 210 [since renumbered Article 281] provides that "The Community shall have legal personality".

[14]   This provision, placed at the head of Part Six of the Treaty, devoted to 'General and Final Provisions', means that in its external relations the Community enjoys the capacity to establish contractual links with third countries over the whole field of objectives defined in Part One of the Treaty, which Part Six supplements.

[15]   To determine in a particular case the Community's authority to enter into international agreements, regard must be had to the whole scheme of the Treaty no less than to its substantive provisions.

[16]   Such authority arises not only from an express conferment by the Treaty—as is the case with Articles 113 [since renumbered Article 131] and 114 [since repealed] for tariff and trade agreements and with Article 238 [since renumbered Article 310] for association agreements—but may equally flow from other provisions of the Treaty and from measures adopted, within the framework of those provisions, by the Community institutions.

[17]   In particular, each time the Community, with a view to implementing a common policy envisaged by the Treaty, adopts provisions laying down common rules, whatever form these may take, the Member States no longer have the right, acting individually or even collectively, to undertake obligations with third countries which affect those rules.

[18]   As and when such common rules come into being, the Community alone is in a position to assume and carry out contractual obligations towards third countries affecting the whole sphere of application of the Community legal system.

[19]   With regard to the implementation of the provisions of the Treaty the system of internal Community measures may not therefore be separated from that of external relations.

[20]   Under Article 3(e), the adoption of a common policy in the sphere of transport is specially mentioned amongst the objectives of the Community.

[21]   Under Article 5, [since renumbered Article 10] the Member States are required on the one hand to take all appropriate measures to ensure fulfilment of the obligations arising out of the Treaty or resulting from action taken by the institutions and, on the other, hand, to obtain from any measure which might jeopardize the attainment of the objectives of the Treaty.

[22]   If these two provisions are read in conjunction, it follows that to the extent to which Community rules are promulgated for the attainment of the objectives of the Treaty, the Member States cannot, outside the framework of the Community institutions, assume obligations which might affect those rules or alter their scope.

[23]   According to Article 74, [since renumbered Article 70] the objectives of the Treaty in matters of transport are to be pursued within the framework of a common policy.

[24]   With this in view, Article 75(1) [since renumbered Article 71.1] directs the Council to lay down common rules and, in addition, "any other appropriate provisions".

[25]   By the terms of subparagraph (a) of the same provision, those common rules are applicable "to international transport to or from the territory of a Member State or passing across the territory of one or more Member States".

[26]   This provision is equally concerned with transport from or to third countries, as regards that part of the journey which takes place on Community territory.

[27]   It thus assumes that the powers of the Community extend to relationships arising from international law, and hence involve the need in the sphere in question for agreements with the third countries concerned.

[28]   Although it is true that Articles 74 and 75 do not expressly confer on the Community authority to enter into international agreements, nevertheless the bringing into force, on 25 March 1969, of Regulation No 543/69 of the Council on the harmonization of certain social legislation relating to road transport (OJ L 77, p. 49) necessarily vested in the Community power to enter into any agreements with third countries relating to the subject-matter governed by that regulation.

[29]   This grant of power is moreover expressly recognized by Article 3 of the said regulation which prescribes that: "The Community shall enter

into any negotiations with third countries which may prove necessary for the purpose of implementing this regulation''.

[30] Since the subject-matter of the AETR falls within the scope of Regulation no 543/69, the Community has been empowered to negotiate and conclude the agreement in question since the entry into force of the said regulation.

[31] These Community powers exclude the possibility of concurrent powers on the part of Member States, since any steps taken outside the framework of the Community institutions would be incompatible with the unity of the Common Market and the uniform application of Community law....

4. Direct Applicability of EU Legislation in the Member States

The discussion above focused on the application of the EU constituent treaties and international law to the EU(EC) as a legal entity, as well as to the Member States, individuals and entities in the EU, much in the same way as international law generally might (or might not) apply to the U.S. as a federal state. In this sub-section, the focus is upon the situation of the EU itself as a legislator in the international legal system, with the issue shifting to EU law (regulations, directives and decisions identified in TEC Article 249 set forth below) and their direct application to Member States, individuals and entities, presenting the question of the relation of EU law to the Member State's national legal orders. This issue may be compared to the direct application of U.S. federal law to the states under the Supremacy clause (Article VI of the U.S. Constitution).

The cases that follow deal with direct application (*Costa*), the superiority of EU law to national law (*Factortame*), and the unusual and successful procedure, called ''preliminary rulings'' established in EC Article 234 to ensure that these results will be achieved in practice.

Consolidated Version of the Treaty Establishing the European Community

J.O. E.U., C 325 24 2002

Article 249 (ex Article 189).

In order to carry out their task and in accordance with the provisions of this Treaty, the European Parliament acting jointly with the Council, the Council and the Commission shall make regulations and issue directives, take decisions, make recommendations or deliver opinions.

A regulation shall have general application. It shall be binding in its entirety and directly applicable in all Member States.

A directive shall be binding, as to the result to be achieved, upon each Member State to which it is addressed, but shall leave to the national authorities the choice of form and methods.

A decision shall be binding in its entirety upon those to whom it is addressed.

Recommendations and opinions shall have no binding force.

Costa v. ENEL

European Court of Justice
Case [1964] ECR 585

[Facts: omitted]

Grounds of Judgment

By contrast with ordinary international treaties, the EEC Treaty has created its own legal system which, on the entry into force of the Treaty, became an integral part of the legal systems of the Member States and which their courts are bound to apply.

By creating a Community of unlimited duration, having its own institutions, its own personality, its own legal capacity and capacity of representation on the international plane and, more particularly, real powers stemming from a limitation of sovereignty or a transfer of powers from the States to the Community, the Member States have limited their sovereign rights, albeit within limited fields, and have thus created a body of law which binds both their nationals and themselves.

The integration into the laws of each Member State of provisions which derive from the Community, and more generally the terms and the spirit of the Treaty, make it impossible for the States, as a corollary, to accord precedence to a unilateral and subsequent measure over a legal system accepted by them on a basis of reciprocity. Such a measure cannot therefore be inconsistent with that legal system. The executive force of Community law cannot vary from one State to another in deference to subsequent domestic laws, without jeopardizing the attainment of the objectives of the Treaty set out in Article 5(2) [since renumbered Article 10] and giving rise to the discrimination prohibited by Article 7 [since repealed].

The obligations undertaken under the Treaty establishing the Community would not be unconditional, but merely contingent, if they could be called in question by subsequent legislative acts of the signatories * * *.

The precedence of Community law is confirmed by Article 189 [since renumbered Article 249], whereby a regulation "shall be binding" and "directly applicable in all Member States". This provision, which is subject to no reservation, would be quite meaningless if a State could unilaterally nullify its effects by means of a legislative measure which could prevail over Community law.

It follows from all these observations that the law stemming from the Treaty, an independent source of law, could not, because of its special and original nature, be overridden by domestic legal provisions, however framed, without being deprived of its character as Community law and without the legal basis of the Community itself being called into question.

The transfer by the States from their domestic legal system to the Community legal system of the rights and obligations arising under the Treaty carries with it a permanent limitation of their sovereign rights, against which a subsequent unilateral act incompatible with the concept of the Community cannot prevail. Consequently Article 177 [renumbered Article 234, set forth below] is to be applied regardless of any domestic law, whenever questions relating to the interpretation of the Treaty arise * * *.

The Queen v. Secretary of State for Transport, ex parte: Factortame Ltd. and Others

European Court of Justice
Case C–213/89, [1990] ECR I–2433

[Facts: Several companies incorporated under the laws of the United Kingdom were operating in the fisheries sector. They contested the validity under Community law of a U.K. statute of 1988 which modified the requirements for registration of fishing vessels. Factortame Limited and others instituted proceedings for judicial review and sought a declaration that the Act did not apply to them on the ground that such application would be contrary to Community law. The companies also sought an order prohibiting the authorities from treating the registration of vessels under an older Act (prior to the 1988 statute) as having ceased, and interim relief pending final outcome of the case. The Queen's Bench Court granted interim relief and ordered the Secretary of State for Transport not to apply the Act to the applicants pending final judgment (upon receipt of a preliminary ruling of the Court of Justice) or further order of the court. The Secretary of State for Transport successfully appealed to the Court of Appeal which held that courts of the United Kingdom did not have the power to suspend, by means of interim relief, the application of statutes or to grant an injunction against the Crown. The House of Lords ultimately confirmed the position of the Court of Appeal but referred to the Court of Justice the issue of the extent of power of national courts to grant interim relief where rights claimed under Community law were involved.]

Judgment

[17]   * * * [T]he preliminary question raised by the House of Lords seeks essentially to ascertain whether a national court which, in a case before it concerning Community law, considers that the sole obstacle which precludes it from granting interim relief is a rule of national law, must disapply that rule.

[18]   For the purpose of replying to that question, it is necessary to point out that in its judgment of 9 March 1978 in Case 106/77 *Amministrazione delle finanze dello Stato v. Simmenthal SpA* [1978] ECR 629 the Court held that directly applicable rules of Community law "must be fully and uniformly applied in all the Member States from the date of their entry into force and for so long as they continue in force" (paragraph 14) and

that "in accordance with the principle of the precedence of Community law, the relationship between provisions of the Treaty and directly applicable measures of the institutions on the one hand and the national law of the Member States on the other is such that those provisions and measures * * * by their entry into force render automatically inapplicable any conflicting provision of * * * national law" (paragraph 17).

[19]   In accordance with the case-law of the Court, it is for the national courts, in application of the principle of cooperation laid down in Article 5 [renumbered Article 10] of the EEC Treaty, to ensure the legal protection which persons derive from the direct effect of provisions of Community law * * *.

[20]   The Court has also held that any provision of a national legal system and any legislative, administrative or judicial practice which might impair the effectiveness of Community law by withholding from the national court having jurisdiction to apply such law the power to do everything necessary at the moment of its application to set aside national legislative provisions which might prevent, even temporarily, Community rules from having full force and effect are incompatible with those requirements, which are the very essence of Community law (judgment of 9 March 1978 in *Simmenthal*, cited above, paragraphs 22 and 23).

[21]   It must be added that the full effectiveness of Community law would be just as much impaired if a rule of national law could prevent a court seised of a dispute governed by Community law from granting interim relief in order to ensure the full effectiveness of the judgment to be given on the existence of the rights claimed under Community law. It follows that a court which in those circumstances would grant interim relief, if it were not for a rule of national law, is obliged to set aside that rule.

[22]   That interpretation is reinforced by the system established by Article 177 [renumbered Article 234] of the EEC Treaty whose effectiveness would be impaired if a national court, having stayed proceedings pending the reply by the Court of Justice to the question referred to it for a preliminary ruling, were not able to grant interim relief until it delivered its judgment following the reply given by the Court of Justice.

[23]   Consequently, the reply to the question raised should be that Community law must be interpreted as meaning that a national court which, in a case before it concerning Community law, considers that the sole obstacle which precludes it from granting interim relief is a rule of national law must set aside that rule * * *.

Consolidated Version of the Treaty Establishing the European Community

J.O. E.U., C 325 24 2002

Article 234 (ex Article 177)

The Court of Justice shall have jurisdiction to give preliminary rulings concerning:

(a) the interpretation of this Treaty;

(b) the validity and interpretation of acts of the institutions of the Community and of the ECB;

(c) the interpretation of the statutes of bodies established by an act of the Council, where those statutes so provide.

Where such a question is raised before any court or tribunal of a Member State, that court or tribunal may, if it considers that a decision on the question is necessary to enable it to give judgment, request the Court of Justice to give a ruling thereon.

Where any such question is raised in a case pending before a court or tribunal of a Member State against whose decisions there is no judicial remedy under national law, that court or tribunal shall bring the matter before the Court of Justice.

It should be noted that provisions essentially parallel to the above Article 234 are contained in the proposed Lisbon Treaty on the Functioning of the European Union, Article 267, set forth in the Documentary Supplement.

Criminal Proceedings against Jean–Claude Levy

European Court of Justice
Case C–158/91, [1993] ECR I–4287

Judgment

[1] By judgment of 22 May 1991, received at the Court on 18 June 1991, the Tribunal de Police (local criminal court), Metz (France), referred for a preliminary ruling under Article 177 [renumbered Article 234] of the EEC Treaty a question on the interpretation of Articles 1 to 5 of Council Directive 76/207/EEC of 9 February 1976 on the implementation of the principle of equal treatment for men and women as regards access to employment, vocational training and promotion, and working conditions (OJ 1976 L 39, p. 40, hereinafter "the directive").

[2] That question arose in criminal proceedings brought by the Ministère Public (Public Prosecuor) and the Direction du Travail et de lEmploi (Department of Labour and Employment) against Jean–Claude Levy, Director of Nouvelle Falor SA, who is accused of having employed, on 22 March 1990, 23 women on night work, contrary to Article L 213–1 of the French Code du Travail (hereinafter "the French Code"), an infringement which is punishable by a fine pursuant in particular to Article R 261–7 of that code.

[3] Those provisions were adopted in order to implement Convention No 89 of 9 July 1948 of the International Labour Organization on night work for women in industry (hereinafter "the ILO Convention"), whose

ratification was authorized in France by Law No 53–603 of 7 July 1953. The instrument of ratification was registered by the Director General of the International Labour Office on 21 September 1953.

[4]   The wording of Article 3 of the ILO Convention, which is essentially set out in the French Code, provides that:

> "Women without distinction of age shall not be employed during the night in any public or private industrial undertaking, or in any branch thereof, other than an undertaking in which only members of the same family are employed."

[5]   In the proceedings before the Tribunal de Police, Metz, Mr. Levy, the defendant, claimed that the French Code was incompatible with Article 5 of the directive, which provides that:

> "Member States shall take the measures necessary to ensure that any laws, regulations and administrative provisions contrary to the principle of equal treatment shall be abolished."

[6]   The Tribunal de Police thereupon decided to stay the proceedings and to * * * refer the following question to the Court of Justice for a preliminary ruling:

> "Are Articles 1 to 5 of Directive 76/207/EEC of 9 February 1976 to be interpreted as meaning that national legislation prohibiting night work solely for women amounts to discrimination, having regard inter alia to Article 3 of Convention No 89 of the International Labour Organisation prohibiting night work for women, to which France is a signatory?" * * *

[9]   In Case C–345/89 *Stoeckel* [1991] ECR I–4047, the Court held that Article 5 of the directive is sufficiently precise to impose on the Member States the obligation not to lay down by legislation the principle that night work by women is prohibited, even if that is subject to exceptions, where night work by men is not prohibited. It follows that, in principle, a national court is under a duty to give full effect to that rule, refusing to apply any conflicting provision of national legislation (see the judgment in Case 106/77 *Amministrazione delle Finanze dello Stato v. Simmenthal* [1978] ECR 629).

[10]   In this case, the question referred for a preliminary ruling seeks essentially to ascertain whether a national court is under the same obligation where the national provision which is alleged to be incompatible with Community law is intended to implement an agreement, such as the ILO Convention, which was concluded by the Member State concerned with other Member States and non-member countries prior to the entry into force of the EEC Treaty (hereinafter "earlier international agreement").

[11]   The first paragraph of Article 234 [since renumbered Article 307] of the Treaty provides that the rights and obligations arising from agreements concluded before the entry into force of the Treaty between one or more Member States on the one hand, and one or more non-member countries on the other, are not affected by the provisions of the Treaty.

Nonetheless, the second paragraph obliges the Member States to take all appropriate steps to eliminate any incompatibilities between such an agreement and the Treaty. Article 234 is of general scope and applies to any international agreement, irrespective of subject-matter, which is capable of affecting the application of the Treaty (see Case 812/79 *Attorney General v. Burgoa* [1980] ECR 2787, paragraph 6).

[12] According to the judgment in Case 10/61 *Commission v. Italy* [1962] ECR 1, the purpose of the first paragraph of Article 234 of the Treaty is to make clear, in accordance with the principles of international law, that application of the Treaty does not affect the commitment of the Member State concerned to respect the rights of non-member countries under an earlier agreement and to comply with its corresponding obligations. It follows that, in that provision, the terms "rights and obligations" refer, as regards "rights", to the rights of non-member countries and, as regards "obligations", to the obligations of Member States.

[13] Consequently, in order to determine whether a Community rule may be deprived of effect by an earlier international agreement, it is necessary to examine whether that agreement imposes on the Member State concerned obligations whose performance may still be required by non-member countries which are parties to it.

[14] In that respect, the Commission maintains that, since the Court ruled in Stoeckel, cited above, that the concern for protection which originally inspired the principle of the prohibition on night work for women is no longer well founded, the Member States are required, by virtue of Article 5(2)(c) of the directive, to take the measures necessary to revise those laws, regulations and administrative provisions which are contrary to the principle of equal treatment. Where the laws which are to be revised result from the conclusion of earlier international agreements, such as the ILO Convention, the measures to be taken by the Member States are the same as the "appropriate steps" to which they must resort, pursuant to the second paragraph of Article 234 of the Treaty, in order to eliminate the incompatibilities established between those international agreements and Community law, namely the extension of the prohibition on night work to workers of the opposite sex or the abrogation of the earlier international agreement.

[15] The Commission adds that, in any event, the obligation arising from the ILO Convention not to have women working at night cannot allow a Member State not to observe the principle of equal treatment of men and women, a fundamental human right respect for which forms an integral part of the general principles of law protected by the Court of Justice (see the judgment in Case 11/70 *Internationale Handelsgesellschaft v. Einfuhr- und Vorratsstelle Getreide* [1970] ECR 1125). It argues that, according to the case-law of the European Court of Human Rights (see, in particular, the judgment of 28 May 1985 Abdulaziz, Cabales and Balkandali Series A, No 94), a difference of treatment between men and women must be justified on objective and reasonable grounds and there must be a reasonable relationship of proportionality between the means employed and the

aim sought to be realised. In view of the similarity of the risks to which both men and women who work at night are exposed, a difference of treatment between men and women may only be justified by the need to protect the biological condition of women.

[18]   The Commission also bases its argument on the development of international law in that field and, in particular, on the Convention for the Elimination of all Forms of Discrimination against Women, concluded in New York on 18 December 1979 (hereinafter "the New York Convention"), ratified by France on 14 December 1983, and on developments within the International Labour Organization itself. * * *

[19]   It is true that the provisions of an international agreement may be deprived of their binding force if it appears that all the parties to the agreement have concluded a subsequent agreement whose provisions are so far incompatible with those of the earlier one that the two agreements are not capable of being applied at the same time (see Article 59(1)(b) of the Vienna Convention on the Law of Treaties of 21 March 1986).

[20]   In the present case, if it were apparent from the development of international law, as recalled by the Commission, that the prohibition on night work for women, provided for in the ILO Convention, had been annulled by virtue of subsequent agreements binding on the same parties, the first paragraph of Article 234 of the Treaty would not be applicable. There would then be nothing to prevent the national court from applying Article 5 of the directive as interpreted by the Court in Stoeckel, cited above, and disapplying any national provisions conflicting therewith.

[21]   However, in proceedings for a preliminary ruling, it is not for this Court but for the national court to determine which obligations are imposed by an earlier international agreement on the Member State concerned and to ascertain their ambit so as to be able to determine the extent to which they constitute an obstacle to the application of Article 5 of the directive.

[22]   In view of the foregoing considerations, the answer to the question submitted for a preliminary ruling must be that the national court is under an obligation to ensure that Article 5 of Directive 76/207 is fully complied with by refraining from applying any conflicting provision of national legislation, unless the application of such a provision is necessary in order to ensure the performance by the Member State concerned of obligations arising under an agreement concluded with non-member countries prior to the entry into force of the EEC Treaty * * *.

NOTES AND QUESTIONS

1.   Are you satisfied with the justification above for the proposition that the EU is fully bound by the principles and rules of customary international law as well as treaty law? What international law authorities would you select to support your views on this question?

2.   Speaking of the *Kadi* opinion in the ECJ, an editorial writer stated:

"Whereas *Medellín* [See Section B on the U.S. above] was generally excoriated as the low water mark of American constitutional and judicial insularity, gruesomely resulting in the actual execution of the principals, *Kadi* was mostly hailed as an example of the more progressive and open attitude of the ECJ, with the proof of the pudding in the eating—overturning the Council Regulations which gave effect to the measures adopted against the defendants pursuant to the Security Council Resolutions, and doing so on the grounds that they violate fundamental rights and protections applicable within the legal order of the EU. There the gallows; —*chez nous* liberty. Happy ending.

It is so, however, only to those for whom outcomes are more important than process and reasoning. For, at a deeper level, *Kadi* looks very much like the European cousin of *Medellín*.

Joseph Weiler, *Kadi–Europe's Medellín*, 19 EUR. J. INT'L L. 895 (2008). How would *you* compare these two important cases? Would the implementation of *Kadi* result in an EU infringement of international law? Would the process and reasoning have been different in the 2008 *Kadi case* above if the provisions offending human rights had been clearly and fully stated in the Security Council's Resolutions? Would U.N. Charter Articles 25 and 103 tend to force a different outcome?

3.   How would you summarize the implied powers of the European communities in the light of the ERTA Judgment?

4.   Another problem of competence to enter into treaties has arisen within the EU: the competence of the Commission to enter into treaties on its own without following the procedure in ECT Article 300 (ex Article 228) requiring actions by the Council. In 1991 the Commission, acting alone without Council approval, entered into an agreement with the United States regarding cooperation on the application of EU competition and U.S. antitrust laws. This Agreement was declared void by the ECJ in *French Republic v. Commission of the European Communities*, Case C–327/91 [1991] ECR I–3641, in which the Court states that:

> [41]   ... Even though the Commission has the power, internally, to take individual decisions applying the rules of competition, a field covered by the agreement, that internal power is not such as to alter the allocation of powers between the Community institutions with regard to the conclusion of international agreements, which is determined by Article 228 of the treaty....

Similar problems have arisen in the United States in assessing the treaty power and the President's "executive agreement" power under the Constitution. Executive agreements as well as Article II. 2 Treaties (requiring advice and consent of the Senate) are binding upon the United States under international law. For consideration of the scope of the executive agreement power in the United States, see Section B above.

5.   What are the distinctions between the various EU actions described in TEC Article 249: regulations, directives, decisions, recommendations and opinions?

6.   Does it surprise you to see the U.K. House of Lords in *Factortame* and a French Criminal Court in the *Levy* referring the EU law issues to the

ECJ under Article 234 of the TEC, where the ECJ's judgment is final and binding on the national courts on such issues?

On the broader international level, there is no such jurisdiction of the ICJ where requests for advisory opinions, for example, may be filed with the Court only by qualified organs of certain international organizations, and contentious case jurisdiction is limited to disputes between states, as seen in U.N Charter Chapter XIV and Article 36 of the Statute of the ICJ.

Considering this Article 234 EU process for unifying judicial decisions on international legal issues in Member State courts, what would you propose for a parallel or similar procedure for international law generally? Would you favor some such procedure? Do you think the U.S. could accept it? Do you think this could be envisaged as a possible broadening of the ICJ's jurisdiction sometime in the future?

7. The ECJ judgment in *Levy* above was not the end of the problem of that case. France later terminated its participation in the ILO Convention but declined to rescind the offending provision of the Code du Travail (Labor Code). The Commission then commenced a proceeding against France for a declaration that, in failing to rescind the Code provision, France remained in violation of the anti-discrimination Directive. France defended on the ground that there was no longer any discrimination because the Code could not be enforced following termination of the Convention. However, the ECJ held for the Commission, finding that "individuals are in a position of uncertainty as to their legal situation and exposed to unwarranted criminal proceedings" (para. 16). [*Commission of the European Communities v. French Republic*, Case C–197/96, [1997] ECR I–1489.]

In the circumstances of the Levy case, would you favor the policy supporting the ILO Convention or the EU Directive approach to night labor by women? What do you think might have changed between French ratification of the ILO Convention in 1953 and the adoption of the EC Directive of 1976?

8. Further reading: Daniel Bethlehem, *International Law, European Community Law, National Law: Three Systems in Search of a Framework, in* INTERNATIONAL LAW ASPECTS OF THE EUROPEAN UNION 169 (Martii Kostenniemi ed., 1998); Grainne De Burca, *The EU, The European Court of Justice and the International Legal Order after Kadi.* 1 HARV. INT'L L. J. (2009) (Fordham Law Legal Studies Research Paper No. 1321313. Available at SSRN: http://ssrn.com/abstract=1321313); THE EUROPEANISATION OF INTERNATIONAL LAW: THE STATUS OF INTERNATIONAL LAW IN THE EU AND ITS MEMBER STATES (Jan Wouters, et al. eds., 2008).

E. FRANCE

1. CONSTITUTIONAL CONSIDERATIONS

The 1958 Constitution of the French Fifth Republic contains a number of provisions of varying specificity defining the relationship of the French state and international law. The most general provision is perhaps the vaguest, the Preamble which adopts by reference a fragment of the 1946 Constitution Preamble, paragraph 14, stating:

> The French Republic, faithful to its traditions, complies with the rules of public international law. It undertakes no war for conquest and never employs its forces against the liberty of any people.*

Despite its uncertain status and ambiguity, this text may be taken as a statement of general application of customary international law as well as treaty obligations of France. The Constitution of 1958 also makes provision for negotiation, adoption, ratification and application of treaties seen in Subsection 3 below, including the rule of Article 55 that treaties "have an authority superior to that of laws".

The French Constitution was amended in 1992 to accommodate the European Community by the addition of Article 88–1 which provides:

> The Republic shall participate in the European Communities and in the European Union constituted by States that have freely chosen, by virtue of the Treaties that established them, to exercise some of their powers in common.

The effect of this provision on EU secondary legislation as part of international law in the French national system is taken up in Subsection 3 below with the discussion of treaties in the French system.

2.   CUSTOMARY INTERNATIONAL LAW

Customary international law enjoys an uncertain status in France, in part because of the status of the paragraph 14 problem of ambiguity noted above. Does the paragraph 14 presence in the Preamble rather than in the operational Articles weaken its effect? Does its presence only by reference back to the 1946 Preamble rather than in the 1958 Preamble weaken it further? Does paragraph 14 impose a legal obligation corresponding to its terms or is it merely a non-binding political statement of fact—which could be accurate or not?

This textual problem accompanies other doubts about customary law which suffers from uncertainty in a legal culture more accustomed to relying upon written law (loi écrite) in codes and other legislation on the national level and written treaties on the international level. Custom is seen as difficult to prove, as requiring research on a broad international scale, and as ambiguous and subjective in its applications, all of which are compounded when an attempt is made to impose international customary law on French nationals. (See S. Sur, *Progrès et Limites de la Rèception du Droit International en Droit Francais*, in Droit International et Droits Internes, Dévelopements Récents, 227, Paris, 1998).

So how can judges be expected to approach the problems in paragraph 14? The answer to that question depends on whether the issue comes before the Conseil Constitutionel (Constitutional Council) which is compe-

---

* Translation by the authors.

tent to rule on the constitutionality of French legislation, the Cour de Cassation (Supreme Court for Review of Ordinary (Civil and Criminal) Cases) or the Conseil d'Etat (Supreme Court for the Administrative System). In this division of judicial functions in France, judges in the three judicial systems have different approaches, yet for practical purposes they are equal in rank. In short, the Constitutional Council (Conseil Constitutional) has been known, when examining the constitutionality of French legislation, to consider whether the legislation violates any provision of customary international law ("loi non-écrite") in the rare cases where that issue is presented. The Cour de Cassation has squarely faced the question and decided to apply customary international law in appropriate cases, as will be seen below in the *Khadhafi* and *Saudi* cases. However, the Conseil d'Etat for its part is not known to apply customary rules at all, although this may be changing, as will also be seen below in *Aquarone*. (See Dominique Carreau, *Droit International*, p. 475, 477 Paris 2007). So there can be no simple answer to the question.

You will notice that in cases arising in the three French Court systems, decision texts are most often quite sparse, giving little more than the barest but necessary statement of the judgment, authorities and reasoning, which common law lawyers may find surprising.

Gaddafi [Khadafi]

France, Cour de Cassation, March 13, 2001
125 INT. L. REP. 490, 508 (2004)

The Court has considered the general principles of international law.

International custom precludes Heads of State in office from being the subject of proceedings before the criminal courts of a foreign State, in the absence of specific provisions to the contrary binding on the parties concerned.

* * * [Civil parties allege complicity in the destruction of property by an explosive substance causing death and involving a terrorist undertaking, against Muammar Gaddafi, Head of State in office of the Libyan Arab Republic. They allege that Gaddafi was implicated in the attack committed on 19 September 1985 against a DC 10 aircraft of the company UTA which, by exploding above Niger, caused the death of 170 persons, several of whom were of French nationality.

In upholding the order of the examining magistrate that it was appropriate to initiate proceedings, notwithstanding the contrary arguments of the *Ministère public*, the judges in the Court of Appeal considered that, whilst the immunity of foreign Heads of State was still recognized by the international community, including France, no immunity could cover complicity in the destruction of property as a result of an explosion causing death and involving a terrorist undertaking.

[This Court considers] however, that in giving this ruling, when in the current state of international law the alleged crime, however serious, did not constitute one of the exceptions to the principle of the jurisdictional immunity of foreign Heads of State in office, the Chambre d'accusation of the Court of Appeal misconstrued the above-mentioned principle.

The judgment under appeal is therefore subject to cassation. * * *

In this case the Cour de Cassation applied directly the rule of international law on the immunity of heads of state:

> The Court has considered the general principles of international law. International custom precludes Heads of State in office from being the subject of proceedings before the criminal courts of a foreign State, in the absence of specific provisions to the contrary binding on the parties concerned.

X v. Saudi School in Paris and Saudi Arabia

France, Cour de Cassation
No. 220, ILDC 777 (June 20, 2003)

Ms Naira X was hired in 1993 by the government of Saudi Arabia as an Arabic teacher in the Saudi School in Paris, an institution created and owned by Saudi Arabia. The school refused to register her for French national social insurance. She sued the school in order to obtain her registration for such insurance, as well as damages for the loss that resulting from the refusal of registration. Saudi Arabia intervened in the proceedings claiming that the complaint was inadmissible on the grounds of its jurisdictional sovereign immunity, which the labour tribunal and Court of Appeal of Paris accepted. In a decision dated 7 September 2000, the Court of Appeal of Paris held that the school was protected by Saudi Arabia's jurisdictional immunity. It had decided earlier that the Saudi school formed part of Saudi Arabia and thus constituted the same legal person as that state. Naira X appealed to the Court of Cassation, arguing that in the circumstances of the case neither the Saudi state, nor the school, could enjoy immunity.

Quashing the decision of 7 September 2000, the Cour de Cassation held that considering the principles of international law governing sovereign immunities, foreign states enjoy jurisdictional immunity only in so far as the act giving rise to the dispute, by its nature or purpose, is an exercise of the sovereignty and is not an act *gestionis*.* A state decision not requiring the registration of an employee was merely an ordinary act of state administration. Neither the fact that Naira X had taken part in the Saudi

---

* See Chapter 4, Section B above for discussion of the distinction between governmental sovereign or "public" acts, which are entitled to immunity, and governmental "private", *gestionis* or administrative acts, which are not. This is the now widely accepted restrictive view of sovereign immunity.

public service of education, nor the character of some clauses of her employment contract, were decisive factors for immunity to be relied upon.

In contrast, however, the Conseil d'Etat has not so explicitly faced the question of incorporation of customary international law into internal French administrative law, yet in *In Re Aquarone* left the clear impression that customary international law is included in the overall body of law that the Conseil d'Etat is charged to respect, although not to the point of prevailing over domestic law.

In Re: Aquarone

101 Rev. Gen. Dr. Int Pub. 838 (1997), Report by Stefan A. Riesenfeld, in *International Decisions*, 92 AJIL 764 (1998)

In this case, the French Council of State, * * * in a carefully crafted opinion, the highest administrative court of France rejected the petition and the claim of immunity from taxation of his retirement pay by Aquarone, a former Registrar of the International Court of Justice * * * In reaching its conclusion, the [Court] held "... that neither Article [55 of the Constitution] nor any other provision of constitutional value prescribes or implies that the administrative judge shall give priority to customary international law over a statute in the case of a conflict between these two types of norms." The [Court] concluded that, "therefore, in rejecting the contention of Mr. Aquarone, on the ground that the inconsistency between French tax law and rules of customary law of that character was immaterial, the administrative court of appeal, which also found that the custom invoked did not exist, did not commit a legal error."

In ruling as it did, the [Court] followed the conclusions of the government Commissioner, G. Bachelier, who had argued, inter alia, that this pay was exempted * * * under rules of customary international law, which prevailed over inconsistent statutes by virtue of paragraph 14 of the Preamble to the Constitution of 1946 * * *.

Bachelier agreed with the administrative court of appeal of Lyon that this provision is not necessarily devoid of any effect in internal law but, conversely, does not have the effect of conferring upon the rules of customary international law or even upon the principles of international law an authority superior to that of a statute, which Article 55 of the Constitution attributes only to treaties or agreements, regularly ratified or approved, from the date of publication.

a.   PIRACY IN THE INDIAN OCEAN AND GULF OF ADEN

France and other countries regularly apply customary international law without making specific reference to it, as in many recent cases of piracy and the rule of universal jurisdiction (for more on piracy, see

Chapter 1 above; and for more on universal jurisdiction, see Chapter 4, Section A.4).

Reuters reported on April 16, 2009 that the French navy had detained 11 Somali pirates who had tried to seize a Liberian merchant ship, noting that the French navy was operating under the EU's anti-piracy mission that also involves German, Spanish and Italian forces (Irish Times.com). The New York Times posted a story on April 24 stating that the French navy had delivered the 11 Somalis to Kenya for trial under Section 60(1) of the Kenyan penal code: "Any person who, in territorial waters or the high seas, commits any act of piracy jure gentium is guilty of the offence of piracy." Today more than three dozen Somali pirates are being held in prison at Mombasa, Kenya. The French navy was, of course, exercising international legal rights under universal jurisdiction in turning over the 11 Somali pirates to Kenyan authorities, and that rule would also provide the legal basis for other countries taking parallel actions.

3.   TREATIES

Starting with the procedure for ratifying a treaty for France, the Courts play an important role in managing the internal application of treaties. Under Article 52 of the Constitution of 1958, the President of the Republic is authorized to negotiate and to ratify treaties. Article 54 provides for issues of the constitutionality of a treaty to be brought before the Conseil Constitutionel by the President, the Prime Minister, the President of the Assembly or of the Senate, or by 60 members of the Assembly or of the Senate. If the Conseil finds that a proposed treaty obligation contains a clause contrary to the Constitution, the authorization to ratify or approve the international engagement in question may take place only after the revision of the Constitution. This far-reaching power of the Conseil has been invoked successfully in a number of cases, including successive amendments of the EU treaties, most recently the Treaty of Rome on the Statute of the International Criminal Court in 1999 and the Treaty of Lisbon in 2007.

As seen below in a sparse decision, the *International Criminal Court* case shows how the Article 54 process results in a constitutional change, in that case on the issue of the ICC's jurisdiction, in order to permit the President to ratify the new treaty. Later the Constitution was modified and the Treaty was duly ratified.

Re Establishment of the International Criminal Court

France, Constitutional Council, January 22, 1999
Decision No. 98–408, 125 ILR 475

The Constitutional Council decides:

Article I—The authorization to ratify the Convention establishing the International Criminal Court requires a revision of the Constitution.

NOTE

[By the publisher, ILR] Following the decision of the Constitutional Council, a Draft Law was presented to the French Parliament amending the Constitution so as to enable the Convention containing the Statute of the International Criminal Court to be ratified by France. The Law, promulgated by the French President on 8 July 1999, following its adoption by the Parliament, inserted into the Constitution Article 53(2) which provides: "The Republic may recognize the jurisdiction of the International Criminal Court under the conditions laid down in the Convention signed on 18 July 1998."

Issues of the compatibility of two other treaties with the Constitution came before the Constitutional Council in *International treaties relating to the abolition of capital punishment, Constitutional complaint procedure*, ILDC 761(FR 2005). Both treaties contained provisions on the abolition of capital punishment. Both were signed for France and awaited ratification. The issue was whether either or both required amendment of the Constitution. Under Article 54 of the Constitution, the test is whether an international agreement would affect constitutionally protected rights or freedoms or would undermine the essential conditions of national sovereignty, in which cases the agreement could not be ratified without prior Constitutional amendment. The Council concluded that one of these agreements, a Protocol to the Convention on Protection of Human Rights, did not offend the sovereignty provision because the agreement could be denounced, leaving France free from the Protocol's death penalty restraint if necessary. However, the other agreement, a protocol to the Covenant on Civil and Political Rights, contained no provision on denunciation, and thus would bind France irrevocably even if exceptional dangers would threaten the existence of the state. Under these circumstances, the Council found that the exercise of national sovereignty would be affected, and the Constitution would have to be amended before ratification of the protocol to the Covenant. In 2007 the French Parliament meeting in Congress with both houses acting together, amended the Constitution to provide that "no one can be sentenced to the death penalty".

Procedure of ratification. Depending on the circumstances, treaties may be ratified or approved in France under one of three different procedures. The first is found in Article 53 of the Constitution which adopts a list of treaties that may be ratified only by virtue of a law; i.e., treaties of peace, trade treaties, treaties and agreements relative to international organization, those which engage the finances of the state, those which modify provisions of a legislative nature, those relating to the status of persons, and those which include cession, exchange or addition of territory, and in the latter case the action is valid only with the consent of the affected populations. From this enumeration, there is an inference from Article 25 that the President of the Republic is empowered by a second procedure to act on his own to ratify treaties and agreements which do not fall within the enumeration. A third procedure enables the President to submit to a referendum in accordance with Article 11 of the Constitution any draft law tending to authorize ratification of a treaty which (without being contrary to the Constitution) would have effects on the functioning of French institutions. A recent example is the 2005 Treaty Establishing a Constitution for Europe, which was submitted by referendum in France, The Netherlands and others, but was rejected by the French and Netherlands' populations. Although called a "Constitution" it was not a free-standing instrument like the U.S. Constitution but was submitted as a treaty to replace the prior EU treaties. Despite ratification by some two-thirds of EU Member States, the actions of France and the Netherlands populations effectively shelved the "Constitution" as such and led to the preparation of the Treaty of Lisbon containing much of the contents of the defeated Constitution.

Once a treaty has been ratified, questions of conflict with later internal French law may arise. The hierarchy of treaties and laws in cases of conflict is treated specifically in Article 55 of the 1958 Constitution as follows:

> Treaties or agreements have, once they are published, a superior authority than laws, provided, for each agreement or treaty, that it is applied by the other party.

In the case of later enactment of conflicting laws, Article 55 thus presents a Constitutional denial of the familiar "last in time" doctrine seen in the United States and elsewhere. Even where the treaty is "first in time", Article 55 recognizes the superior status of the treaty as against later laws, so long as the other party is itself applying the treaty. This was challenged in the Cour de Cassation's *Jacques Vabre* case below.

Administration des Douanes v. Société Cafés Jacques Vabre

France, Cour de Cassation (Chambres Reunies), 1975
2 Common Market Law Reports 336 (1975)

[See more of this opinion in Chapter 1, Section A.3 above.

French Customs applied a discriminatory tax law to plaintiff Jacques Vabre's imports of certain coffee products at a rate higher than that applied to those products manufactured and sold in France itself. Plaintiff argued that the discriminatory tax on its imports violated Article 95 of the Rome Treaty of 1957 on the establishment of the EEC. Article 95 provided that:

> No Member State shall impose, directly or indirectly, on the products of other Member States any internal taxation of any kind in excess of that imposed directly or indirectly on similar domestic products.

Plaintiff also argued that the Treaty should trump the later legislation under Article 55 of the Constitution which provided that treaties "have an authority superior to that of laws". The French Customs argued, on the other hand, that the law in question was "later in time" and should prevail in such cases.]

In his submissions, the Procureur Général (M. Adolphe Touffait), argued the Article 55 point, stating:

* * *

The idea emerges irresistibly that there can be no international relations if the diplomatic agreements can be put in balk by unilateral decisions of the contracting powers, and the duty of the State to respect its international obligations becomes a fundamental principle * * *.

An analysis of the texts, in accord with the international ethic intended by the makers of the Constitutions of 1946 and 1958, thus ineluctably leads to the consideration that the concept of superiority of treaties over statutes only has sense with regard to statutes subsequent to the treaty, as it is clear that the international legal order can only be realised and developed if the States loyally apply the treaties they have signed, ratified and published.

In its Judgment the Cour de Cassation then concluded:

* * * [T]he treaty of 25 March 1957 [Treaty of Rome], which by virtue of the above mentioned Article of the Constitution has an authority greater than that of statutes, institutes a separate legal order integrated with that of the Member States. Because of that separateness, the legal order which it has created is directly applicable to the nationals of those States and is binding on their courts. Therefore, the Cour d'Appel was correct and did not exceed its powers in deciding that Article 95 of the Treaty was to be applied in the instant case, and not section 265 of the Customs Code, even though the latter was later in date.

NOTE

Having seen the historic divergence of views between the Cour de Cassation and the Conseil d'Etat on the treatment of customary international law, one would probably expect to find echoes of that divergence in the Article 55 problem as seen in *Jacques Vabre*, and that would be correct. For years the Conseil d'Etat considered that it was without jurisdiction to apply Article 55 and thus turned away administrative cases that would have called for application of the treaty in the face of an inconsistent later law. But in the *affaire Nicolo* in 1989, the Conseil d'Etat apparently found that indeed it had jurisdiction to decide the Article 55 issue, but without saying so explicitly. In the end the Conseil found in *Nicolo* that there was no incompatibility between the earlier treaty and later law, and thus did not reach the main question, yet the jurisdiction question was necessarily involved in the finding of no incompatibility (the brief Opinion of the Conseil and conclusions of the government's commissioner are found in French in *Documents d'études*, No. 6.02 p. 57, Paris, 1990), and see D. Carreau, *Droit International* Ch. 11, Paris, 2007 and P–M Dupuy *Droit International Public* § 435, Paris, 2002 on these and related questions.

Self–Executing Treaties (direct application) in France

X v. Y and anor
France, Cour de Cassation, June 14, 2005
No. 1810, ILDC 770

In 2000, Sophie X, a French citizen, and David Washington Y, an American citizen, were married in the United States. They lived together in the United States with their daughter Charlotte until March 2003 when the wife came to France with her daughter on holiday. On 31 March 2003, she notified her husband that she had decided to stay indefinitely in France with Charlotte. Mr. Washington sought, in application of the Hague Convention on the Civil Aspects of International Child Abduction, (the "Hague Convention"), the immediate return of his child to the United States. Before the Aix-en-Provence Court of Appeal in France, Mrs. Washington invoked Article 13(b) of the Hague Convention which prevented a child from being returned when "there is a grave risk that his or her return would expose the child to physical or psychological harm or otherwise place the child in an intolerable situation". The court dismissed the argument and ordered Charlotte immediate return to her father. Mrs. Washington lodged an appeal before the Court of Cassation, claiming, among other things, that the decision of the Court of Appeal violated Article 3(1) of Convention on the Rights of the Child (CRC), which provided that "[i]n all actions concerning children ... the best interests of the child shall be a primary consideration". But the Court of Cassation noted that the Court of Appeal had not found that there was evidence of a risk to the child in being returned to her father, that child's best interests had been taken into account by the Court and that Article 3(1) of the CRC which was *directly applicable (self-executing)* and could be invoked before French courts, had been satisfied. Under these circumstances the child should be ordered to be returned to her father. Mrs. Washington's appeal was rejected.

Iraq State v. Corporation Dumez GTM SA

France, Cour de Cassation, April 25, 2006
No. 679, ILDC 771

Following contractual relations between the Commission of Military Works of the Iraqi State and the French corporation Dumez, Iraq refused to pay the company for its services. According to Iraqi legislation adopted on 16 September 1990, the referral of a case to Iraqi courts and arbitrators was forbidden to foreign corporations. Consequently, the corporation's request for the seizure of certain funds detained in France by the Iraqi

State before a French judge was granted, The Court of Appeals considered that UN Security Council Resolution 687 April 3, 1991 on the cease-fire following the successful liberation of Kuwait demanding "that Iraq adhere scrupulously to all of its obligations concerning servicing and repayment of its foreign debt", was directly applicable before the national judges of State Parties to the Charter. However, the Cour de Cassation held that binding resolutions of the UN Security Council have no direct effect in France as long as their provisions have not been incorporated in the national legal order. In such cases, they can be taken into account as a "legal fact". The Appeal Court's judgment was quashed, as Resolution 687 had not been incorporated into the national legal order, and the Court had not respected the principle of state immunity from suit. The acceptance by the Iraqi State of Resolution 687 did not amount to a waiver of its immunity.

Gardedieu v. France

France, Council of State, February 8, 2007
IDC 738 (FR 2007)

Working as a dentist, Mr Gardedieu had contributed to a national French Pension system for many years. In response to a decree raising contributions to the system, Mr Gardedieu refused to pay the required sums, and his challenge was successful in a French court. While these proceedings were continuing, a 1994 Act sought to validate the increase of contributions in "all *ongoing* proceedings". Ruling on Mr. Gardedieu's against this Act, the Council of State held that

> State responsibility for legislative acts could be engaged by reason of the state's obligation to guarantee respect for international conventions by public authorities. The state was liable to compensate for damage resulting from the operation of a law adopted in violation of international commitments.

The 1994 Act was contrary to Article 6(1) of the Convention for the Protection of Human Rights and Fundamental Freedoms (4 November 1950) 213 UNTS 222; 312 ETS 5, entered into force 3 September 1953 ("ECHR") since the intervention of Parliament into ongoing proceedings had violated the right to a fair trial. The legislator had validated an increase in contributions whose legality was under judicial review. This was not justified by any imperatives relating to the national interest, regardless of the financial interests put forward by the legislator.

State liability was engaged and Mr. Gardedieu was entitled to compensation for the damage he had sustained.

a. WAR CRIMES, CRIMES AGAINST HUMANITY AND TORTURE

As would be expected in the aftermath of the multitude of grievous violations of the law of war and the suffering the French experienced in World War II, France has been especially active in this area of international law, in its internal law, prosecutions and support for the International criminal Court. As France became liberated and immediately after the war, many judicial and informal responsive measures were taken. In 1964 France adopted legislation to remove the rule of prescription (that is rules similar to statutes of limitation) in cases of crimes against humanity as defined by the U.N. General Assembly. This brought those crimes into French law, making possible the highly publicized prosecutions of Klaus Barbie, (German), Paul Touvier (French), and Maurice Papon (French). They were each convicted of complicity to commit crimes against humanity in judgments that were affirmed by the Cour de Cassation (see Leila Nadya Sadat, *The Nuremberg Paradox*, 61 HASTINGS L.J. __ (2009)).

French courts like others have encountered difficulties in finding universal jurisdiction authority in the internal law of their respective countries. See Brigitte Stern, *Universal jurisdiction over crimes against humanity under French law—grave breaches of the Geneva Convention—genocide—torture—human rights violations in Bosnia and Rwanda*, 93 AM. J. INT'L L. 525, 528 (1999). Professor Stern states that there are:

> two different general articles on universal jurisdiction in the Code de procédure pénale: Articles 689 and 689–1.

> The first article, Article 689, provides that "[t]he authors or accomplices of offenses committed outside the territory of the Republic can be sued in the French courts and judged by them ... whenever an international convention grants jurisdiction to the French courts." This article contemplates self-executing conventions. It makes no reference to the presence of the suspect in France.

> The second article, Article 689–1, provides that, according to international conventions cited in the following articles (689 to 689), universal jurisdiction exists for the offenses enumerated in these conventions, if the suspect is found in France. This article applies to conventions that, according to its terms, are not self-executing. An example is Article 5 of the Torture Convention.

The establishment of the International Criminal Court might well make these problems more manageable.

b. TORTURE BY THE FRENCH ARMY DURING THE ALGERIAN WAR

In 2001, an 83 year old retired French general, Paul Aussaresses, confessed publicaly that he had routinely tortured and murdered numbers of victims in the course of the civil war in Algeria which eventually led to independence of that country. He served as the head of the French secret service in Algeria and as deputy to the commander General Massu. The shocking details of his actions appeared in his autobiography entitled: *"Pour la France: Services Spéciaux"* 1942–1954 (2001) and in *"The Battle of the Casbah: Terrorism and Counterterrorism in Algeria"* 1955–1957 (2004). Following a public outcry in France, he showed no remorse, claiming that his actions were necessary in the circumstances. The General could not be prosecuted in France because he was covered by a 1968 general amnesty relating to the Algerian war. However, various French administrative actions could be taken. He was stripped of his military rank, his right to wear any military uniforms, and lost other military honors. In addition a civil action was brought against him by the Ligue des droits de l'homme (League of the Rights of Man) on a charge of "apology for war crimes" resulting in a money judgment that survived appeal to the Cour de Cassastion. See The New York Times, May 5, 2001 (nyt.com) and BBC News, November 26, 2001 (news.bbc.co.uk).

Ould Dah v. France

European Court of Human Rights
Register Press Release No. 13113/03, March 30, 2009

[This torture case shows the French application of universal jurisdiction in the trial and conviction of Ould Dah in a French court for acts of torture committed in another country, in this case Mauritania. In *Ould Dah* the ECHR recognizes the French exercise of jurisdiction under the Convention against Torture and Other Cruel, Inhuman or Degrading Treatment or Punishment. See Chapter 4 above on universal jurisdiction and Chapter 5 above on the subject of torture. The summary of the opinion of the ECHR below is taken from the ASIL's International Law in Brief, 3 April 2009 available at, asil.org. See also the ECHR's Press Release on this case and the decision on the ECHR web site, www.echr.coe.int.]

In its recent decision to dismiss the case of Ould Dah on the basis that it was manifestly ill-founded, the European Court of Human Rights "reiterated that the prohibition of torture occupied a prominent place in international law and that the prohibition was binding."

The case centers on the conviction of Ould Dah, a Mauritanian army officer, for acts of torture committed between 1990 and 1991 against prisoners held in Mauritania. Mr. Dah argued that by imposing the sentence amounting to 10 years of imprisonment for alleged acts of torture, France had violated Article 7 of the European Convention on Human Rights (no penalty without law) because he benefited from an amnesty law passed in Mauritania in 1993. The plaintiff also claimed that he could not foresee being prosecuted in France for acts that had taken place in Mauritania. Finally, according to the plaintiff, "torture had not been classified under French law as an autonomous offence at the relevant time and that the provisions of the new Criminal Code had been applied to him retrospectively."

The Court dismissed the plaintiff's arguments, "observ[ing] that at the material time the United Nations Convention against Torture of 1984 had already come into force and had been incorporated into French law." Furthermore, " 'absolute necessity' of prohibiting and penalising torture thus justified, in the exercise of universal jurisdiction (i.e. the right of States to prosecute the perpetrators of acts of torture committed outside their own jurisdiction), not only that the French courts declared that they had jurisdiction to try the case, but also that they would apply French law.

Otherwise, application of the Mauritanian amnesty law, which served merely to grant impunity to the perpetrators of torture, would deprive the universal jurisdiction provided for by the United Nations Convention of 1984 of its substance."

4.   SECONDARY EU LAW

Review the material on the European Union in Chapter 3, and in Section D above.

Chloé Charpie, The Status of (Secondary) Community Law in the French Internal Order: The Recent Case–Law of the *Conseil Constitutional and the Conseil d'Etat*

3 EUROPEAN CONSTITUTIONAL LAW REVIEW 436, 462 (2007)

Recently, the *Conseil constitutionnel* and the *Conseil d'Etat* have clarified the relationship between French constitutional law and Community law. The courts will refrain from testing the constitutionality of acts implementing unconditionally and precisely phrased provisions of a [Community] directive, except when France's constitutional identity is questioned (*Conseil constitutionnel*) or when no equivalent protection is offered at the Community level (*Conseil d'Etat*). Thereby, both French courts ensure respect for Community duties, inter alia, by also testing Acts of Parliament against unconditionally and precisely phrased provisions of the directive they purport to implement (*Conseil constitutionnel*), while at the same time reinforcing the supremacy of the Constitution in the French legal order. Nevertheless, not all has been settled. For instance, there remains opposition between the position of these French courts on the one hand, which reiterate the idea of the supremacy of the Constitution, and the principle of the Community law's primacy asserted by the [Community's] Court of Justice on the other hand. Moreover, the contents and scope of the French courts' case-law remain unclear at points. This is the case for France's constitutional identity, for instance, the new concept used by the Conseil constitutionnel. The question also remains of what the Conseil d'Etat will do when it is faced with an Act of Parliament contrary to constitutional provisions that are also encountered in Union law. * * *

Société Arcelor Atlantique et Lorraine and Ors v. France

France, Council of State February 8, 2007
No. 287110, ILDC 739

A 2003 EC Directive established a scheme for greenhouse gas emission allowance trading within the European Community ("EC"), and by decree in 2004 France incorporated the Directive into the Code of Environment, making the scheme applicable to the steel companies. Upon failing to have the Decree repealed, the steel companies requested the Council of State to overturn the Decree. In particular, they put forward the principle of equality, arguing that the Decree made the scheme applicable to steel without including the aluminium and plastic industries, their competitors.

The Council of State rejected the application so far as it contested the French authorities' decision to transpose the 2003 Directive into French law, including its applicability to the steel sector industries, required by the Directive. It was within the jurisdiction of the Council of State to search for the existence of a general principle of Community law that guaranteed these principles' effectiveness. The judge merely had to examine whether the 2003 Directive did respect the Constitution, and to dismiss the application if it did so. If there was any doubt, he or she could use the preliminary ruling reference to the European Court of Justice ("ECJ").* If faced with a lack of any relevant European principle, the judge could directly ascertain the conformity of the decree with French constitutional principles. European principles did guarantee the right to property and free enterprise, and were fully respected. The judgment was suspended in respect of the principle of equality. It seemed necessary to request the ECJ about the consistency of the Directive with the European principle of equal treatment, as this text made the scheme applicable to the steel sector without including in its scope the aluminium and plastic industries.

NOTES AND QUESTIONS

1. Study in Chapter 1 above the Submissions of the Procureur General in the *Jacques Vabre* case on the relations between international law and internal law. Note that in the end the judgment in that case relied solely on Article 55 of the French Constitution set forth above. What then became of the Procureur's suggestion? Usually it would be followed. Would you classify France as dualist, monist or a mix of the two?

2. How would you summarize the relation of international law and domestic law in France compared to the United States?

3. In this book other cases concerning the direct application of international law include the following: *Barrandon v. United States of America* (Chapter 4, Section B *Republic of Zaire v. Duclaux,* Chapter 4, Section C).

4. Further Reading: Ronny Abraham, *L'Articulation du Droit Interne at du Droit International*, in La France et le Droit International Paris, (G. CAHIN, F. POIRAT, S. SZUREK, eds., 2007); Thomas M. Franck and Arun K. Thiruvengadam, *International Law and Constitution*–Making, 2 Chinese J. of Int'l L. 467 (2002); JEAN COMBACU AND SERGE SUR, DROIT INTERNATIONAL PUBLIC (8th ed., 2008).

F. SOUTH AFRICA

The South African Constitution of 1996, passed after the end of the apartheid regime, is one of the most modern in the world. It contains an

---

* On the preliminary reference by EU Member States of EU legal issues to the ECJ, see discussion below in Subsection D.4, Article 234.

extensive Bill of Rights largely modeled on the international human rights treaties discussed in Chapter 5. It creates a Constitutional Court; that Court has developed an extensive jurisprudence interpreting the Bill of Rights provisions. Among the most well-known decisions of that Court are those involving the right to housing (Grootboom), the right of access to antiretroviral drugs to contain the IIIV virus (Treatment Action Center), the prohibition on corporal punishment in schools (Christian Education case), the rights of minorities to be educated in their own language (Gauteng education bill) and others. See Erika de Wet, *The "Friendly but Cautious" Reception of International Law in the Jurisprudence of the South African Court: Some Critical Remarks*, 28 FORDHAM INT'L L.J. 1529 (2005).

An early Constitutional law case abolished the death penalty, relying in part on a survey of international and comparative law. The relevant constitutional provisions, and then an excerpt from that decision, follow.

1.   CONSTITUTIONAL CONSIDERATIONS

South African Constitution

11.   Life

Everyone has the right to life.

39.   Interpretation of Bill of Rights

 1.   When interpreting the Bill of Rights, a court, tribunal or forum

  a.   must promote the values that underlie an open and democratic society based on human dignity, equality and freedom;

  b.   must consider international law; and

  c.   may consider foreign law.

 2.   When interpreting any legislation, and when developing the common law or customary law, every court, tribunal or forum must promote the spirit, purport and objects of the Bill of Rights.

 3.   The Bill of Rights does not deny the existence of any other rights or freedoms that are recognised or conferred by common law, customary law or legislation, to the extent that they are consistent with the Bill.

232.   Customary international law

Customary international law is law in the Republic unless it is inconsistent with the Constitution or an Act of Parliament.

233.   Application of international law

When interpreting any legislation, every court must prefer any reasonable interpretation of the legislation that is consistent with international law over any alternative interpretation that is inconsistent with international law.

The State v. T. Makwanyane and M. Mchunu*

Constitutional Court of the Republic of South Africa, Case No. CCT/3/94 (1995)

JUDGMENT

[1]   CHASKALSON P: The two accused in this matter were convicted in the Witwatersrand Local Division of the Supreme Court on four counts of murder, one count of attempted murder and one count of robbery with aggravating circumstances. They were sentenced to death on each of the counts of murder and to long terms of imprisonment on the other counts. They appealed to the Appellate Division of the Supreme Court against the convictions and sentences. The Appellate Division dismissed the appeals against the convictions and came to the conclusion that the circumstances of the murders were such that the accused should receive the heaviest sentence permissible according to law. Section 277(1)(a) of the Criminal Procedure Act No. 51 of 1977 prescribes that the death penalty is a competent sentence for murder.

* * *

International and Foreign Comparative Law

[33]   The death sentence is a form of punishment which has been used throughout history by different societies. It has long been the subject of controversy. As societies became more enlightened, they restricted the offences for which this penalty could be imposed. The movement away from the death penalty gained momentum during the second half of the present century with the growth of the abolitionist movement. In some countries it is now prohibited in all circumstances, in some it is prohibited save in times of war, and in most countries that have retained it as a penalty for crime, its use has been restricted to extreme cases. According to Amnesty International, 1,831 executions were carried out throughout the world in 1993 as a result of sentences of death, of which 1,419 were in China, which means that only 412 executions were carried out in the rest of the world in that year. Today, capital punishment has been abolished as a penalty for murder either specifically or in practice by almost half the countries of the world including the democracies of Europe and our neighbouring countries, Namibia, Mozambique and Angola. In most of those countries where it is retained, as the Amnesty International statistics show, it is seldom used.

[34]   In the course of the arguments addressed to us, we were referred to books and articles on the death sentence, and to judgments dealing with challenges made to capital punishment in the courts of other countries and in international tribunals. The international and foreign authorities are of value because they analyse arguments for and against the death sentence and show how courts of other jurisdictions have dealt with this vexed issue. For that reason alone they require our attention. They may also have to be considered because of their relevance to section 35(1) of the Constitution [above]

---

* Footnotes omitted.

[35]   Customary international law and the ratification and accession to international agreements is dealt with in *section* 231 of the Constitution which sets the requirements for such law to be binding within South Africa. In the context of *section* 35(1), public international law would include non-binding as well as binding law. They may both be used under the section as tools of interpretation. International agreements and customary international law accordingly provide a framework within which Chapter Three can be evaluated and understood, and for that purpose, decisions of tribunals dealing with comparable instruments, such as the United Nations Committee on Human Rights, the Inter–American Commission on Human Rights, the Inter–American Court of Human Rights, the European Commission on Human Rights, and the European Court of Human Rights, and in appropriate cases, reports of specialised agencies such as the International Labour Organisation may provide guidance as to the correct interpretation of particular provisions of Chapter Three.

[36]   Capital punishment is not prohibited by public international law, and this is a factor that has to be taken into account in deciding whether it is cruel, inhuman or degrading punishment within the meaning of section 11(2). International human rights agreements differ, however, from our Constitution in that where the right to life is expressed in unqualified terms they either deal specifically with the death sentence, or authorise exceptions to be made to the right to life by law. This has influenced the way international tribunals have dealt with issues relating to capital punishment, and is relevant to a proper understanding of such decisions.

[37]   Comparative "bill of rights" jurisprudence will no doubt be of importance, particularly in the early stages of the transition when there is no developed indigenous jurisprudence in this branch of the law on which to draw. Although we are told by section 35(1) that we "may" have regard to foreign case law, it is important to appreciate that this will not necessarily offer a safe guide to the interpretation of Chapter Three of our Constitution. This has already been pointed out in a number of decisions of the Provincial and Local Divisions of the Supreme Court, and is implicit in the injunction given to the Courts in section 35(1), which in permissive terms allows the Courts to "have regard to" such law. There is no injunction to do more than this.

[38]   When challenges to the death sentence in international or foreign courts and tribunals have failed, the constitution or the international instrument concerned has either directly sanctioned capital punishment or has specifically provided that the right to life is subject to exceptions sanctioned by law. The only case to which we were referred in which there were not such express provisions in the Constitution, was the decision of the Hungarian Constitutional Court. There the challenge succeeded and the death penalty was declared to be unconstitutional.

[39]   Our Constitution expresses the right to life in an unqualified form, and prescribes the criteria that have to be met for the limitation of entrenched rights, including the prohibition of legislation that negates the essential content of an entrenched right. In dealing with comparative law,

we must bear in mind that we are required to construe the South African Constitution, and not an international instrument or the constitution of some foreign country, and that this has to be done with due regard to our legal system, our history and circumstances, and the structure and language of our own Constitution.

[56] We can derive assistance from public international law and foreign case law, but we are in no way bound to follow it.

[The Court then surveys the treatment of the death penalty in the United States, Canada, Germany, India, Tanzania, and Hungary and by the U.N. Human Rights Committee and by the European Court of Human Rights, and, after extensive discussion of the legal and policy arguments on both sides, decides that the death penalty is unconstitutional.]

2.   TREATIES

The 1996 Constitution provides:

231.   International agreements

1.   The negotiating and signing of all international agreements is the responsibility of the national executive.

2.   An international agreement binds the Republic only after it has been approved by resolution in both the National Assembly and the National Council of Provinces, unless it is an agreement referred to in subsection (3).

3.   An international agreement of a technical, administrative or executive nature, or an agreement which does not require either ratification or accession, entered into by the national executive, binds the Republic without approval by the National Assembly and the National Council of Provinces, but must be tabled in the Assembly and the Council within a reasonable time.

4.   Any international agreement becomes law in the Republic when it is enacted into law by national legislation; but a self-executing provision of an agreement that has been approved by Parliament is law in the Republic unless it is inconsistent with the Constitution or an Act of Parliament.

5.   The Republic is bound by international agreements which were binding on the Republic when this Constitution took effect.

John Dugard, South Africa*

in The Role of Domestic Courts in Treaty Enforcement (David Sloss, ed., 2009)

While a court must consider treaties to which South Africa is not a party in interpreting the Bill of Rights, no such rule exists in respect of treaties to which South Africa is not a party where the Bill of Rights is not an issue. A treaty to which South Africa is not a party is *res inter alios acta*

---

* Footnotes omitted.

and may not be considered *qua* treaty, although it may be considered as evidence of a customary rule.

Different considerations apply in respect of a treaty to which South Africa is a party but that has not been incorporated into municipal law. In the first instance, a municipal court may have recourse to an unincorporated treaty in order to interpret an ambiguous statute. Secondly, an unincorporated treaty may be taken into account in a challenge to the validity of delegated legislation on the grounds of unreasonableness....

An increasing number of statutes refer expressly to international law and some make it clear that the statute is to be interpreted to accord with international law. For instance, the Promotion of Equality and Prevention of Unfair Discrimination Act provides that any person interpreting the Act may be "mindful" of international law; the Implementation of the Rome Statute of the International Criminal Court Act provides that a court applying the Act must consider both conventional and customary international law; the Labour Relations Act of 1995 proclaims as one of the primary objects of the Act "to give effect to the obligations incurred by the Republic as a member state of the International Labour Organization" and requires the Act to be interpreted in compliance with the public international law obligations of the Republic; the Refugees Act provides that the Act "must be interpreted and applied with due regard" to the principal refugee conventions, other relevant conventions and the Universal Declaration of Human Rights. Such statutes confirm the principle expounded in sec. 233 of the Constitution that legislation is to be interpreted in accordance with international law.

* * * The Constitution is the supreme law of South Africa. A treaty enacted into law by national legislation in accordance with sec. 231(4) of the Constitution will enjoy the status accorded to it by the act of incorporation: a treaty enacted into law by Act of Parliament will be treated as an Act of Parliament, whereas a treaty enacted into law by subordinate legislation will be treated as subordinate legislation. A non-self-executing treaty binding on South Africa internationally, but not incorporated into municipal law, will have no direct force of law, but may be used to interpret an ambiguous statute or to challenge subordinate, delegated legislation. A self-executing treaty will obviously, in terms of sec. 231(4), give way to both the Constitution and an Act of Parliament. Probably such a self-executing treaty will take priority over delegated legislation, in the event of a conflict. Whereas apartheid South Africa accepted, and indeed approved, a contradiction between international law and domestic law, the new South African legal order seeks to ensure that there will be no conflict between the two. Section 233 and 39 of the Constitution and several statutes are designed to achieve such harmony.

NOTES AND QUESTIONS

1. What difference does it make that reference to international and comparative law is built into the South African constitution? Into statutes?

2.   One criticism of the South African Constitutional Court's jurisprudence is that it seems to give equal weight to treaties, and decisions of treaty bodies, that are ratified and those that are unratified. Thus, the European Court of Human Rights jurisprudence receives much more extensive treatment than that of the African Commission on Human Rights. *See* de Wet, cited above. Why might this be? Is it a mistake on the part of the Court, or is ratification irrelevant if the only use of international and comparative law is interpretative of the South African Bill of Rights?

CHAPTER 12

INTERNATIONAL LAW FOR THE FUTURE

Section A.   **Law in a Divided World.**
          1. Diversity and Law.
          2. Regionalism.
          3. Exceptionalism.
Section B.   **Law of Community.**
          1. Universal Law–Making.
          2. Universal Rules, Norms, and Principles.
          3. Community Building.

In this final chapter of the book, we present two contrasting visions of what international law is today. The purpose is to invite you to think about the international law of the future. Try to detect future trends from these perspectives on the present. How do you foresee the future of international law? International law is a human construct. We can have some impact on how it develops. Do you see future scenarios we should work to avoid? Despite the fact we are responsible for international law, there are constraints on building the sort of international law we may want. What are those constraints? Consider as you read the material in this chapter how free we are to shape international law as we want. Consider also the view of some (from both left and right political persuasions) that the only international law we can get is so fraught with negative consequences that the whole "project" should be abandoned. What do these critics propose in place of international law? Anything?

The first vision is of international law as the law of a divided world, a world divided by state boundaries, privileges, cultures, and gender. Aspects of international life have pull away from the universal toward particular international law, including law for various groupings of states, whether Christian, liberal-democratic, socialist or others. The concept of cultural relativity and the rise of regional or hegemonic powers have also undercut the claims of universality for international law, leaving us with an international law that is little more than a set of weak principles loosely linking a divided world.

The second vision is of international law as the law of a community. This vision holds that international law's most important characteristic, now and in the future, is its universality. In Chapter 1 we said that "[e]arly international law scholars conceived of law as having universal application and importance to people everywhere. As the state system developed, international law developed along with it to serve the needs of states." (p. 1) International law was to be a law binding on all equally. It was to be a universal law for all subjects. In the words of Addis Adeno, it is a community of diversity. (*See* Chapter 1 *supra.*)

A.   LAW IN A DIVIDED WORLD

The perspective just discussed supports the claim that international law can be described as universal law. Another perspective raises doubts as to whether international law is or can be universal. This section explores claims that international law is better described as "particular" than universal.

1.   CULTURAL DIVERSITY

Some scholars emphasize that international law originated in a European, Christian culture certainly not shared by all states today. They doubt the possibility of successful universal international law, theorizing that it requires a close-knit group sharing cultural, religious, or political commitments—true communities. The first to hold such views were European international law scholars of the 19th century. Their views happened also to support European imperialism.

Alexander Orakhelashvili, The Idea of European International Law*

17 EUR. J. INT'L L. 315, 318–319 (2006)

To illustrate the essence of the idea of European international law it is necessary to examine how this idea was developed by its proponents. Among English-speaking jurists, Wheaton contended that international law had always been limited to civilized and Christian people of Europe or to those of European origin. Wheaton denied the existence of the universal law of nations which all mankind, savage and civilized, Christian and Pagan, recognized, professed to obey, or in fact, did obey. He admitted that the law of nations could apply outside Europe, but that it was necessarily inferior to European international law. This attitude implies a perception of inequality and exclusion of those who find themselves at lower stages of civilization.

---

* Footnotes omitted.

The relevance of civilization in terms of the ambit of the law of nations and its limitation to nations of European origin was most vigorously developed by Lorimer, whose approach to international law was based on natural law conceptions which teach that all rights and duties have their origin in, and are limited by, the facts of natural life. Consequently, "Law of nations is the law of nature, realised in the relations of separate political communities." Lorimer denied that international law could exist at earlier stages of history and argued that "[e]ven now the same rights and duties do not belong to savages and civilised man". To contradict the idea of universality of international law, Lorimer developed his idea of recognition and pointed out how nations with different levels of civilization can participate in the international legal system:

> The sphere of plenary political recognition extends to all the existing States of Europe, with their colonial dependencies, in so far as these are peopled by persons of European birth or descent; and to the States or North and South America which have vindicated their independence of the European States of which they were colonies.
>
> The sphere of partial political recognition extends to Turkey in Europe and Asia, and to the old historical States of Asia which have not become European dependencies—viz., to Persia and the other separate States of Central Asia, to China, Siam, and Japan.
>
> The sphere of natural, or mere human recognition, extends to the residue of mankind, though here we ought, perhaps, to distinguish between the progressive and non-progressive races.
>
> It is with the first of these spheres alone that the international jurist has directly to deal.
>
> [However, he] must take cognisance of the relations in which civilised communities are placed to the partially civilised communities which surround them. He is not bound to apply the positive law of nations to savages, or even to barbarians, as such; but he is bound to ascertain the points at which, and the directions in which, barbarians or savages come within the scope of partial recognition. In the case of the Turks we have had a bitter experience of extending the rights of civilisation to barbarians who have proved to be incapable of performing its duties, and who possibly do not even belong to the progressive races of mankind.

These criteria are not based on empirical evidence of the norms and principles of international law, but on certain assumed perceptions, or even prejudices, as to how differentiated the application of international law should be with regard to different nations. Genetic and racial characteristics of nations are among Lorimer's principal considerations.

Lorimer further argued that even when diplomatic relations have been established between a semi-barbarous state and a civilized state, recognition of the former does not extend to its municipal law, either public or private, except as regards its own citizens within its own frontiers. The recognizing states consequently maintain separate courts, exercising within the borders of the partially recognized state what is known as consular jurisdiction, to adjudicate on "all questions between the citizens of the recognising States, *inter se*, and, in many cases, between them and the citizens of the partially recognised State".

Barbary states could never be recognized by European nations because, so Lorimer attributed to them, they are burdened by their criminal intention and the consequent absence of rational will. Therefore, the conquest of Algeria by France was not a violation of international law; it was "an act of discipline which the bystander was entitled to exercise in the absence of police". Had Algeria come to respect the rights of life and property, its history would not have permanently deprived it of the right to recognition.

In addition, if a European state annexes a non-European state, then "Law follows fact very closely, and a very short prescription will give an international title." At the same time, Lorimer advocated the forcible domination over what he called semibarbarous states:

> Colonisation, and the reclamation of barbarians and savages, if possible in point of fact, are duties morally and jurally inevitable; and where circumstances demand the application of physical force, they fall within necessary objects of war. On this ground, the wars against China and Japan, to compel these countries to open their ports, may be defended.

Lorimer had to confront the realities of international life, including the fact that European nations had legal relations with non-Europeans and would even, as was the case with Turkey, admit them into the European family of nations. On this Lorimer observed that Turkey's position was "anomalous" and complained that the 1856 Treaty of Paris, which admitted Turkey to the advantages of the public law of Europe, placed British and Turkish representatives on an equal footing: "It is scarcely possible to imagine a more absurd or even ludicrous result of the failure of positive international law to recognise the relative side of the doctrine of recognition." Lorimer went on to argue that "[s]emi-barbarous States like China, Turkey and Japan, whose municipal law and the judgments of whose courts are not recognised by civilized nations" were excluded from full participation in international law.

The works of Westlake do not reveal any direct influence by Lorimer, but certainly express an identical social sentiment, which in all probability shaped the attitude of both authors. According to Westlake, international society, which develops international law by means of its controlling opinion, "is composed of all the States of European blood, that is of all the European and American States except Turkey, and of Japan". At the same time, some Christian countries, such as "Abyssinia, backward in civilisation" and "the little republic of Liberia", cannot contribute to the development and enforcement of international law. Westlake referred to international society as being identical to European society, and considered that the norms of international law could emerge if the "general consensus of opinion within the limits of European civilisation is in favour of the rule". International society, thus composed, "exercises the right of admitting States to parts of its law without admitting them to the whole of it".

Westlake acknowledged that non-European countries were treated on the level of ordinary international law in their relations with European states; they maintained treaty and diplomatic relations with European states, could acquire territorial title and could benefit from the laws of war in the same way as European states. Nevertheless, "Turkey and Persia, China, Japan, Siam and some other countries have civilizations differing from the European" and this required that Europeans and Americans in such countries be protected by separate legal systems under their consuls. European habits and traditions are based on monogamous marriage and respect for women, Westlake argued, and such habits cannot be protected by judiciaries in non-European civilization. To allow such consular jurisdiction to function, the territorial states should maintain regular law and order; if not, then "the position of foreigners would be so untenable that either their conquest of the country in question or the termination of their residence in it would soon follow."

Westlake understood international law as a tool for ensuring the supremacy of the interests of "peoples of European blood" over those of the inhabitants of the territories they colonized. "The white man's needs" was of paramount concern and required the establishment in the native areas of a government that suited those needs, a government which the natives were not intelligent enough to understand. What they could understand though was the concept of property and they were able to transfer the property title to the whites "with full knowledge of what they were doing". Agreements with native chiefs, Westlake declared, "ought to be strictly limited to the things which the natives can understand, among which property and its transfer are commonly to be found". Westlake did not specify whether there was anything else, apart from property transfer, that natives were capable of understanding.

In treating the problem of international legal personality, Oppenheim spoke of the category of "full-Sovereign States", each one of equal standing, although Turkey's position was anomalous due to the regime of capitulations that operated there. But "doubtful was the position of all non-Christian States such as China, Korea, Siam, Persia, and further Abyssinia", even if Christian.

Their civilisation is essentially so different from that of the Christian States that international intercourse with them of the same kind has been hitherto impossible. And neither their Governments nor their population are at present able to understand the Law of Nations and to take up an attitude which is in conformity with all the rules of this law.

Such states could not, according to Oppenheim, be full international persons: their personality covered only those areas in which they were accepted by the "Family of Nations". In other fields, especially with regard to war, they were treated by Christian powers according to discretion. Therefore, the key to Oppenheim's approach was the cultural and religious difference of non-European nations, which ultimately rendered them so intellectually inferior as to be unable to understand international law. Hall likewise excluded uncivilized and semi-civilized nations from the ambit of international law, arguing that such barbarous communities were not mature enough for the administration of European law as between themselves.

Despite its firm foundation in universalist thinking, international law as universal law in fact conflicted with certain interests of European states in the 18th and 19th centuries. Their ambition to build empires by conquering non-Western peoples clashed with the ideas of universal rights, equality of political communities, non-intervention, and the like. Some European legal scholars interested in promoting the subjugation of non-European peoples developed concepts explaining away the universality of international law in the name of promoting *eventual* universal law. Conquest was excused as a path that would one day lead to statehood and inclusion in the family of nations. The imperial state would support the development of the colony so that it could eventually enter into international law as a fully sovereign state.

As Antony Anghie and others explain, this justification required a concomitant theory of international law that could exclude non-Western political communities. The theory asserted that international law could only encompass "civilized" states. Thus, colonies could be excluded and could be dominated by imperial powers, which were the "mature", and, therefore, the "authentic" subjects of international law. Positivism, which was replacing natural law as the dominant theory of international law in the 19th century, turned out to be a useful legal theory for imperial states as it more readily accommodated exclusion than classical natural law, which embraced all. These theories and views of European writers such as Lorimer and Wheaton have resulted in a critical movement that also doubts the possibility and even the desirability of international law for all.

Makau Mutua, What Is TWAIL?*
94 ASIL Proc. 35 2000

The regime of international law is illegitimate. It is a predatory system that legitimizes, reproduces and sustains the plunder and subordination of the Third World by the West. Neither universality nor its promise of global order and stability make international law a just, equitable, and legitimate code of global governance for the Third World. The construction and universalization of international law were essential to the imperial expan-

----

* Footnotes omitted.

sion that subordinated non-European peoples and societies to European conquest and domination. Historically, the Third World has generally viewed international law as a regime and discourse of domination and subordination, not resistance and liberation. This broad dialectic of opposition to international law is defined and referred to here as Third World Approaches to International Law (TWAIL).

TWAIL is not a recent phenomenon. It stretches back to the decolonization movement that swept the globe after World War II. Bandung was the symbolic birthplace of TWAIL, although the North–South confrontation draws heavily from Latin American opposition to the domination of the Third World by the industrialized West. This confrontation has its roots in the anti-colonial movement. TWAIL is a response to decolonization and the end of direct European colonial rule over non-Europeans. It basically describes a response to a condition, and is both reactive and proactive. It is reactive in the sense that it responds to international law as an Imperial project. But it is proactive because it seeks the internal transformation of conditions in the Third World.

TWAIL is driven by three basic, interrelated and purposeful objectives. The first is to understand, deconstruct, and unpack the uses of international law as a medium for the creation and perpetuation of a racialized hierarchy of international norms and institutions that subordinate non-Europeans to Europeans. Second, it seeks to construct and present an alternative normative legal edifice for international governance. Finally, TWAIL seeks through scholarship, policy, and politics to eradicate the conditions of underdevelopment in the Third World.

The present inquiry into the meaning and purposes of TWAIL rejects attempts by some scholars, particularly those of postmodern and postcolonial persuasions, to diminish the importance of scholarship and political movements and strategies deployed by earlier Third World voices and political leaders as tools against the imperial projects of the West. There is no doubt that much of the scholarship in this genre has made enormous contributions to the struggle to unravel the cruelties that have and are being inflicted on the Third World by the West. More important, these new scholars have shown how Third World scholars and states have at times been complicit, albeit unwittingly, in their own oppression. They have pointed to gaps and mistakes in conception and analysis.

Certainly, antiessentialist critiques of earlier Third World scholarship are welcome, necessary, and pivotal in the development of an alternative project of international law. But the Third World is real. It not only exists in what some in the West regard as the vacuous minds of Third World scholars and political leaders, but in the lives of those who live its daily cruelties. It is therefore important to realize that today's Third World scholars and political actors stand on the shoulders of Bandung and the Group of 77, among other important milestones of the Third World challenge to European hegemony. The challenge of TWAIL today is to carry that struggle forward, and to realize that the script of resistance and liberation is a historical continuum, taken sometimes in small, localized, and painful steps.

One can identify two broad thematic trends in Third World scholarship and politics over the last half century. On the one hand, some Third World states and intellectuals have struggled in hostile environments to change the subordinate status of the Third World in relation to the West. I call these thinkers and political actors *affirmative reconstructionists*. Some have been radical actors, seeking a total transformation of international law and the Third World. But many have been moderate reformers, lacking the vision or will to demand a radical overhaul.

But I contend that both the *radical* and *reformist* trends form a *progressive* whole that accounts for the complexity and diversity of TWAIL. In any case, both trends are united in their opposition to official international law. It is their legacy that must be carried forward. On the other hand, the full complexity of the nature of domination would be incomplete without the fact of collaboration. The Third World has also been littered with collaborationist intellectuals and political leaders. I call the members of this betrayer class the *minimalist assimilationists*. It is their legacy that must be rejected.

In this lecture I seek to define and systematize the emergent discipline of TWAIL. I identify the historical bases for the TWAIL movement and discuss the basic philosophical and political interests of the movement. The lecture examines the fundamental assumptions and purposes of traditional international law, and how they make TWAIL a necessary project. Also, it explores the vexed interplay between international law and Third World statehood and conditions, and the continued dependence of the Third World on the West. Finally, it articulates a signpost, an agenda for the reconstruction of international law through the TWAIL prism.

International law claims to be universal, although its creators have unambiguously asserted its European and Christian origins. In fact, Hugo Grotius, widely regarded as the "father" of international law, traced the discipline to Francisco de Vitoria, a sixteenth-century Spanish Christian theologian and legal scholar. In a celebrated passage, a prominent Third World Jurist has observed that international law is premised on Europe as the center, Christianity as the basis for civilization, capitalism as innate in humans, and imperialism as a necessity. As demonstrated by early European scholarship, international law developed in—and was instrumental in—the encounter between Europe and the rest of the world. The notion of sovereignty itself was the key to justifying, managing, and legitimizing colonialism, wherein a small number of European states fanned across the globe and took over more than three quarters of it for their own aggrandizement. As well put by Anghie:

> The colonial confrontation was not a confrontation between two sovereign states, but between a sovereign European state and a non-European state that, according to the positivist jurisprudence of the time, was lacking in sovereignty. Such a confrontation poses no conceptual difficulties for the positivist jurist who basically resolves the issue by arguing that the sovereign state can do as it wishes with regard to the non-sovereign entity, which lacks the legal personality to assert any legal opposition.

Since the state is the central and most important actor in international law, sovereign statehood, as defined by European imperial powers, was the difference between freedom and the conquest and occupation of a people or society. The colonization of independent, non-European lands by Europeans was therefore justified, whether it was through military conquest, fraud, or intimidation. Since colonization was part of the manifest destiny of Europeans, and "good" for non-Europeans in any case, any method deployed in its pursuit was morally and legally just. Brutal force, including the most barbaric actions imaginable, was applied by Europeans in the furtherance of colonialism. Anghie writes that

> The violence of positivist language in relation to non-European peoples is hard to overlook. Positivists developed an elaborate vocabulary for denigrating these peoples, presenting them as suitable objects for conquest, and legitimizing the most extreme violence against them, all in the furtherance of the civilizing mission—the discharge of the white man's burden.

Reporting on the colonial conquest, an African newspaper noted in 1885 that "[t]he world has, perhaps, never witnessed a robbery on so large a scale." Lamenting Africa's helplessness to prevent these gross violations, the newspaper observed that "this 'Christian' business can only end, at no distant date, in the annihilation of the natives." By the end of the nineteenth century, international law had been universalized through the imperial conquests and the subjection of Africa, Asia, and the Pacific to European powers. North, Central and South America had been claimed by various European powers in the preceding four centuries. The "Age of Empire" thus witnessed the forced assimilation of non-European peoples into international law, a regime of global governance that issued from European thought, history, culture, and experience. * * * Immediately after World War II, many colonies overthrew the yoke of direct colonial rule. But they quickly realized that political independence was largely illusory. Although now formally free, Third World states were still bonded—politically, legally, and economically—to the West. The United Nations, formed after World War II by the dominant Western powers, aimed to create and maintain *global order* through peace, security, and cooperation among states. The new global order had two important legitimating features. Non–European powers were now recognized as having the right to self-determination, which was a repudiation of direct colonialism. Second, states were to be governed by human rights. Ostensibly, the United Nations was the neutral, universal and fair guardian of the new order. But in reality, European hegemony over global affairs was simply transferred to the big powers—the United States, Britain, France, the Soviet Union, and China—which allotted themselves permanent seats at the Security Council, the most powerful UN organ. The primacy of the Security Council over the UN General Assembly, which would be dominated by Third World states, made a mockery of the notion of sovereign equality among states. Third World states now became fodder in the new bipolar Cold War vise, whose center was still the West. As noted by others, the use of the United Nations as a front by the big powers "simply changed the form of European hegemony, not its substance."

In the economic arena, Third World states found themselves vised by the Bretton Woods institutions—the World Bank, International Monetary Fund (IMP), and General Agreement on Tariffs and Trade (GATT)—multinational corporations and the Western states. In the eyes of all of these institutions, the newly emergent states remained marginal, and at the mercy of Western capital. Mwalimu Julius Nyerere, the late President of Tanzania and an original TWAIL statesman, defined "the meaning and practice of neo-colonialism" as the inability of Third World states to change their dependency upon and exploitation by the former imperial powers. Crushing debt, which the West advanced to corrupt, undemocratic regimes, now ensures that many countries in Africa, Asia, and Latin America cannot create meaningful development programs. Yet the international financial institutions refuse to do the right thing and either write off or forgive the debt.

It was these realities that gave rise to the *twailian* Group of 77 and its proposals for, among others, the ill-fated New International Economic Order (NIEO). Today, globalization and the ubiquity of free markets, and the push for a single global market, simply underscore these evil imbalances which characterize the international order. The World Trade Organisation (WTO), which has an opaque undemocratic bureaucracy, is the latest in a series of international institutions perpetuating Western hegemony over the rest of the world.

––––––––––

In addition to the North–South division and the European-non-European division, states in the world are divided between states with liberal-democratic forms of government and those without. David Fidler argues this division is as significant for the possibility of universal law as the others.

David P. Fidler, The Return of the Standard of Civilization*

2 CHI. J. INT'L L. 137 (2001)

III. THE NEW STANDARD OF CIVILIZATION: FROM WESTPHALIAN CIVILIZATION TO LIBERAL, GLOBALIZED CIVILIZATION

The international legal profession's preference to forget the embarrassing [concept of "standard of civilization" (SOC)] * * * runs counter to current discourse that raises the importance of civilizations and their role in world affairs. The international lawyer's reluctance to approach the SOC is understandable; but, when we analyze what is happening today in international law, it is hard not to see a process that echoes what took place under the old SOC: the values and principles of Western civilization

––––––––––

* Footnotes omitted.

are (1) being held up as the rallying point for global action; and (2) being used as criteria to judge the performance and legitimacy of "backward" countries. As in the past, international law today carries the values of Western civilization forward and provides means for their imposition on other countries and cultures. In the post-Cold War world, the triumph of liberalism within Western civilization has spawned a new SOC. This new standard dominates thinking about the role and substance of international law in Westphalian civilization. The resulting convergence of the new standard of civilization and international law creates the vision of a liberal, globalized civilization, which is a more radical and far-reaching concept than Westphalian civilization.

Although the old standard of civilization helped build Westphalian civilization, this civilization was mechanical. It did not deeply harmonize government, economics, and law. Much of the 20th century witnessed hot and cold wars fought to determine what philosophy would control Westphalian civilization. Western civilization suffered two World Wars and the Cold War in a struggle of ideologies. Because the West had historically been the hegemon, its prevailing ideology would determine the destiny of the Westphalian civilization. With the end of the Cold War, liberalism emerged victorious.

The liberal victory has been discernable in international law and international relations theory. In international law, liberal dominance appears in the prominence given to free trade, democratic governance, human rights, the rule of law, and good governance. In international relations theory, liberalism has attracted attention. Scholars working with liberalism have divided the world into liberal and nonliberal zones. The liberal zone, according to Benedict Kingsbury, is "constituted by liberal states practising a higher degree of legal civilization, to which other states will be admitted only when they met the requisite standards." Kingsbury further argues that dividing the planet into zones of liberal and nonliberal States with "the liberal West as the vanguard of a transformed global legal order" contains a "new standard of civilization" promulgated "to promote the advancement of the backward." As Kingsbury suggests, the new SOC arises in the wake of liberalism's victory, the collapse of alternative ideologies, and the decline in the geopolitical importance of the non-Western developing world. In addition, no non-Western culture is universalizable like liberalism. No other civilization appears to have the potential to be the ghost in the Westphalian machine.

As argued in Part II, the old SOC, doctrinally speaking, was limited. The new standard is more ambitious and intrusive. If the old standard connects with pluralistic rationalism, then the new standard aims for solidaristic rationalism. Under the new SOC, international law is a tool of political, economic, and legal harmonization and homogenization on a scale that dwarfs what was seen in the 19th and early 20th centuries. The civilizational conquest started under the old SOC is now being carried deeper into the hearts of non-Western cultures through international law.

For those who espouse liberalism as the new standard of civilization, the world is divided between liberal and "nonliberal" states, with international law incorporating the values of liberal states only. The mission of international law is to move all states to liberalism. Until that is accomplished, international law will not be characterized by universally-held values but only by the values of one group of states. A variation of this view would give a privileged place to liberalism and/or liberal states. If a state wished to make a reservation to a human rights treaty, for example, one that clashed with liberal values, liberal states should reject it. It is better, from this perspective, to have fewer members of a treaty regime than to have a treaty regime not fully compatible with liberalism.

Related to the view that international law works only among "civilized states" is the view that the world is too culturally diverse to support one body of international law. The belief in the need for a close association between culture and successful law that is embedded in the concept of civilization is also reflected in the thinking around the concept of cultural relativity.

Much has been written by critical theorists, Third World scholars, feminist scholars and others associated with the post-modern movement on how international law, and particularly human rights law, reflects materialist, European, Christian, imperialist, racist, militarist, and/or male perspectives. The Universal Declaration of Human Rights and the International Covenant on Civil and Political Rights, for example, ostensibly reflect the West's privileging of liberalism and individualism. Other cultures and perspectives, by contrast, stress community, duties as well as rights, the natural environment, economic rights, the role of women and spirituality. To accept international law is to risk weakening these alternative values and priorities. For people to commit to one version of international law or one version of human rights would seem to require sacrificing our diverse cultures and their unique way of viewing the world. Not only could commitment to international law risk the loss of culture, from some perspectives it means commitment to a universal law that has supported imperialism, militarism, male supremacy, racism, and other pathologies of human history. International law has allowed—even required—the subjugation of peoples and the suppression of distinct cultures. Therefore, it cannot arguably be viewed today as legitimate, as worthy to be law for all people.

Dianne Otto, Rethinking the "Universality" of Human Rights Law

29 COLUM. HUM. RTS. L. REV. 1 (1997–1998)

A. Cultural Relativism and Universality: The Bangkok Declaration and its Aftermath

That a universal law of human rights has the potential to erase cultural diversity is hardly disputable. In 1947, the American Anthropological Society cautioned the U.N. Commission on Human Rights about this danger during the drafting of the UDHR. The Society pointed to the West's history of "ascribing cultural inferiority" to non-European peoples, which has led to the "demoralization of human personality and the disintegration of human rights."[25] They outlined the challenge confronting the drafters as follows:

> The problem is thus to formulate a statement of human rights that will do more than just phrase respect for the individual as an individual. It must also take into full account the individual as a member of the social group of which he [or she] is a part.... It must embrace and recognize the validity of many different ways of life.[26]

Despite the best intentions of the drafters to produce an "innocent"[27] UDHR that was without political and cultural allegiances, poststructural critiques of modern knowledges indicate why this was impossible. The achievement of universality in a transcendent sense relies on the modern assumption that objective, True knowledge is possible, and that the historical, situated contingencies of the production and interpretation of knowledge can be transcended by modern scientific or dialectical methods. In contrast, a poststructural perspective understands all knowledge/Truth as the contingent product of particular, situated ways of comprehending the world and the outcome of a complex of power relations.

In contemporary debates, the "universalists," who are primarily Northern states, predict that even the slightest "dilution" of universalism will give the green light to tyrannical governments, torturers, and mutilators of women. The universalist position completely denies that the existing universal standards may themselves be culturally specific and allied to dominant regimes of power. As political philosopher Daniel Bell observes, "[e]ven some of the most thoughtful proponents of human rights in the West do not admit the possibility that every society need not settle on exactly the same conception of vital human interests."[31] At the same time, "cultural relativist" counterarguments from Southern states entrench an intense polarization of views. The relativist position advances alternative claims to universal Truth that have their foundations in non-European cultural traditions and rejects the current human rights paradigm as oppressive for developing states with different cultures.

---

25. American Anthropological Association, *Statement on Human Rights,* 49 Am. Anthropologist 539 (1947), *reprinted in* Henry J. Steiner & Philip Alston, International Human Rights in Context: Law, Politics, Morals 198 (1996).

26. *Id.* at 198, 200.

27. *See* Jane Flax, *The End of Innocence, in* Feminists Theorize the Political 445, 447 (Judith Butler & Joan W. Scott eds., 1992). The author describes the knowledge of Western philosophy as "innocent" in its assumption that it is possible to discover "some sort of truth which can tell us how to act in the world in ways that benefit or are for the (at least ultimate) good of all." *Id.*

31. Daniel A. Bell, *The East Asian Challenge to Human Rights: Reflections on an East West Dialogue,* 18 Hum. Rts. Q. 641, 667 (1996).

A useful starting point for a critical analysis of the contemporary debate is the 1993 Bangkok Declaration, which was devised by proponents of the cultural relativist position at the Regional Meeting for Asian–Pacific states in preparation for the WCHR.[32] Surprisingly, given the polarized rhetoric of the debate, the Bangkok Declaration welcomes the "increased attention" to human rights,[33] reaffirms commitment to the UDHR,[34] encourages the ratification of the International Covenant on Civil and Political Rights (ICCPR) and the International Covenant on Economic, Social and Cultural Rights (ICESCR),[35] and stresses the "universality, objectivity and non-selectivity of all human rights."[36] Even accounting for the geopolitical posturing that inspired the Bangkok Declaration, this language does not in fact depart from the underlying normative framework and principles of the U.N. Charter and the UDHR, although the strongly-critical reactions to it from Northern states and many nongovernmental organizations (NGOs)[37] suggest otherwise. The Bangkok Declaration does not take issue with the foundational philosophical assumptions of human rights orthodoxy about human "dignity" or "reason." Nor does it question the generational categorizations or the overarching commitment to equality in human rights law.

However, the Bangkok Declaration does endorse various positions and priorities that are consistent with those which the NAM has been espousing for many years.[38] In confirming the interdependence and indivisibility of human rights, it stresses the "inherent interrelationship between development, democracy, universal enjoyment of all human rights, and social justice"[39] and urges giving "equal emphasis to all categories of human rights."[40] In listing types of human rights violations, the Bangkok Declaration includes "foreign aggression and occupation, and the establishment of illegal settlements in occupied territories."[41] Such inclusions reflect the ongoing concern about imperialism and neocolonialism in the South. The Bangkok Declaration also emphasizes that adherence to human rights

---

32. The Bangkok Declaration, Mar. 29–Apr. 3, 1993, *reprinted in* Human Rights and Chinese Values 205–09 (Michael C. Davis ed., 1995).

33. *Id.* at pmbl., ¶ 4.

34. *Id.* at pmbl., ¶ 3, art. 1. It should be noted that this position may be changing. Dr. Mahathir, the Prime Minister of Malaysia, has recently suggested that a review of the UDHR is necessary because it was "formulated by the super-powers which did not understand the needs of poor countries." Mark Baker, *Row as Malaysia Seeks to Rewrite the Book on Human Rights*, The Age (Melbourne), July 30, 1997, at 1.

35. The Bangkok Declaration, * * * at pmbl., ¶ 7.

36. *Id.* at pmbl., ¶ 9, art. 7.

37. Asian Cultural Forum on Development, *Our Voice: Bangkok NGO Declaration on Human Rights,* Reports of the Asia Pacific NGO Conference on Human Rights and NGOs' Statements to the Asia Regional Meeting 106 (1993).

38. Virginia A. Leary, *The Asian Region and the International Human Rights Movement, in* Asian Persp. on Hum. Rts. 13, 16–18 (Claude E. Welch & Virginia A Leary eds., 1990).

39. The Bangkok Declaration, *supra* note 32, at pmbl., ¶ 11.

40. *Id.* at art. 10.

41. *Id.* at art. 14.

standards ought to be encouraged by consensus and "not through confrontation and the imposition of incompatible values."[42] All of these positions are cogently supported by reference to U.N. Charter principles of self-determination, sovereignty, territorial integrity, and international cooperation.

It is the Bangkok Declaration's emphasis on state sovereignty and nonintervention that reads as rejecting or qualifying the universality of human rights standards, particularly in its statement about the significance of cultural difference:

> [W]hile human rights are universal in nature, they must be considered in the context of a dynamic and evolving process of international norm-setting, bearing in mind the significance of national and regional particularities and various historical, cultural and religious backgrounds.[43]

Yet, as Bilahari Kausikan from Singapore's Ministry of Foreign Affairs argues in his unofficial capacity, surely this statement only describes what is obvious—that all human rights are in a constant process of evolution which relies on debate and contending claims.[44] Speaking at the American Society of International Law Annual Meeting two years after the WCHR, he stated that the "Western overreaction to this simple description of reality—that moreover explicitly recognized the ideal of universality . . . still poisons the atmosphere and fuels misunderstanding."[45]

The "poisonous" atmosphere reached its zenith at the WCHR. The United States and others accused the Southern states, who argued for some consideration of cultural specificities,[46] of promoting a "screen behind which authoritarian governments could perpetrate human rights abuses."[47] The defensive response from Indonesia's Foreign Minister Ali Alatas, as spokesperson for the NAM at the WCHR, was that Asian states "have not come to Vienna to engage in confrontation, nor to advocate an alternative conception of human rights, based on some nebulous notion of 'cultural relativism' as spuriously adopted by some quarters."[48]

The official outcome of this confrontation, adopted by consensus by the 172 states in attendance, was the reaffirmation of the universality of

---

42. *Id.* at pmbl., ¶ 10, arts. 4, 5. Article 4 expressly rejects making development assistance conditional on human rights and Article 5 abhors any use of human rights as an instrument of political pressure.

43. *Id.* at art. 8.

44. Bilahari Kausikan, *An Asian Approach to Human Rights,* 89 Am. Soc'y Int'l L. Proc. 146, 148 (1995).

45. *Id.*

46. These states included China, Columbia, Cuba, Indonesia, Iran, Iraq, Libya, Malaysia, Mexico, Myanmar, Pakistan, Singapore, Syria, Vietnam, and Yemen.

47. Christina M. Cerna, *Universality of Human Rights and Cultural Diversity: Implementation of Human Rights in Different Socio–Cultural Contexts,* 16 Hum. Rts. Q. 740,741 (1994) [hereinafter Cerna, *Universality*].

48. Christina M. Cerna, *East Asian Approaches to Human Rights,* 89 Am. Soc'y Int'l L. Proc. 152, 155 (1995) [hereinafter Cerna, *East Asian*].

human rights, repeated throughout the Vienna Declaration and Programme of Action[49] almost to the point of redundancy, as human rights theorist Christina Cerna notes.[50] However, the commitment to universality was also qualified in paragraph 5 in language reminiscent of the Bangkok Declaration:

All human rights are universal, indivisible and interdependent and interrelated. The international community must treat human rights globally in a fair and equal manner, on the same footing, and with the same emphasis. While the significance of national and regional particularities and various historical, cultural and religious backgrounds must be borne in mind, it is the duty of States, regardless of their political, economic and cultural systems, to promote and protect all human rights and fundamental freedoms.[51]

That the overall outcome can be read as supporting either the universalist or relativist position reflects the paralysis of the debate and leaves the issue firmly on the international human rights agenda for another day.

An opportunity to reopen the debate came two years later, in the shape of the FWCW. The preparatory processes saw a solid confirmation of the polarized positions that had been marked out in Vienna between the universalists and relativists. The antipathy between the two sides was compounded by the capriciousness of some states from the cultural relativity camp who inserted "universality" into the draft conference documents in such a way that it operated as a modifier and thereby served the relativist rather than the universalist agenda. For example, phrases like "universally recognized" and "universally accepted" human rights limited the scope of human rights to those that had been formally accepted by *all* states—arguably very few. This action undermined the credibility of the positions taken by more conciliatory Southern spokespeople like Alatas and also strengthened the hand of Northern conservatives who were eager to vilify the non-Western cultural relativists.

The result was the bracketing of universality every time it appeared in the draft conference documents, indicating that the use of the word was contentious.[52] Also, a footnote in the section on women's health which addressed the important issues of sexuality and reproduction sought to ensure that all the health actions outlined were not universally applicable but subject to domestic regulation consistent with "the various religious and ethical values and cultural backgrounds of [a state's] people."[53] The

---

49. *Report of the World Conference on Human Rights, Vienna Declaration and Programme of Action,* Vienna, June 1993, at ¶¶ 1, 5, 18, 32, 37, U.N. Doc. A/CONF.157/24 (1993) [hereinafter WCHR Report].

50. Cerna, *Universality, supra* note 47, 742.

51. *WCHR Report, supra* note 49, at ¶ 5.

52. The use of square brackets indicates that states have not agreed on the wording in the brackets.

53. *Draft Platform for Action,* Fourth World Conference on Women, at 43, U.N. Doc. NCONF.177/L.1 (1995).

debate seethed for the entire FWCW and the participants did not finish negotiations until its closing hours.[54] In the end, the footnote was deleted, the egregious use of "universality" was expunged, and the Vienna language that affirmed universality while repeating that "cultural and religious backgrounds must be borne in mind"[55] was retained. Deepening the ambiguity of this clause, the same paragraph goes on to say that "full respect for various religious and ethical values ... should contribute to the full enjoyment by women of their human rights...."[56]

The debate about universality highlights the centrality of concepts of gender, particularly the control of women's reproductive and sexual identities, to the universal knowledges of global regimes of power. It also raises many important questions about the modern egalitarian ideals reflected in human rights discourse and their potential to promote a world without domination. However, it is not these issues that are at the "real" center of the debate, as I will argue in the following Part.

This critical perspective focuses mostly on human rights and the cultural divergences seen in that subfield of international law. The critique rarely extends to the whole of international law. Even with respect to human rights, some cultural relativists do accept that a core of significant human rights are binding universally regardless of culture. Norms against aggression, slavery, torture, apartheid, and genocide—the *jus cogens* norms—are accepted as universal. It is other human rights, such as freedom of expression or women's rights that need to respect cultural context. Interestingly, some universal instruments have been shaped to reflect this perspective. The Cairo Declaration on Human Rights and the Bangkok Declaration on Human Rights, in 1990 and 1993, respectively, reflect the objection to primarily Western values in international human rights law. These regional instruments proclaim that while the recognition of human rights is, indeed, universal, any definition of such rights must reflect one particular cultural context.

2. REGIONALISM

Implicit in the Cairo and Bangkok declarations is the view that while international law may not work well in all subject areas at the international level, it may at the regional level. The cultural relativity debate has also led some to argue for regionalism to replace universalism as the structural basis of international law. This argument is not recent. During the negotiation of the United Nations Charter (1938–1945), the debate over the advantages of a universal organization versus one focused on regionalism

---

54. Dianne Otto, *Holding Up Half the Sky, but for Whose Benefit? A Critical Analysis of the Fourth World Conference on Women,* 6 Austl. Feminist L.J. 7, 19 (1996).

55. *Report of the Fourth World Conference on Women,* Fourth World Conference on Women, ¶ 9, U.N. Doc. NCONF.177/20 (1995).

56. *Id.*

played a prominent role. Britain's Prime Minister Churchill proposed a federation of regions, but this was rejected in favor of a universal organization. Indeed, only Chapter VIII of the UN Charter discusses regions in any detail and then only to make clear that while regional security organizations may exist, they are subordinate to the Security Council. Still, the arguments for regionalism persist, especially among those who perceive that the United Nations has not fulfilled its potential. Regional groups of states arguably share more culturally, politically, and economically, and, may, therefore, have a stronger basis for cooperation. They may share the common culture believed to make law possible, especially law on culturally-specific topics such as human rights. The success of the European Union (EU) and the European human rights system are prime examples invoked by advocates of regional international law.

The argument about regions appears to be one about how international law might work better and not an argument about what international law is today. In particular, it does not speak to whether international law is universal law or can be. Occasionally references are made to "European international law", which would suggest international law is not universal but has unique features for different regions. Yet within the European Union, a distinction is made between EU law and the broader international law in which the EU is situated. The same can be said about the regional human rights regimes of Africa, the Americas and Europe. While distinctive treaties are being interpreted and applied, this work is done in the context of general international law. Colombia invoked "American international law" as supporting a regional custom permitting free passage in the *Asylum Case.*

The Asylum Case

Colombia v. Peru
International Court of Justice
1950 I.C.J. Rep. 266 (Judgment of Nov. 20)

The Colombian Government has finally invoked "American international law in general". In addition to the rules arising from agreements which have already been considered, it has relied on an alleged regional or local custom peculiar to Latin–American States.

The Party which relies on a custom of this kind must prove that this custom is established in such a manner that it has become binding on the other Party. The Colombian Government must prove that the rule invoked by it is in accordance with a constant and uniform usage practised by the States in question, and that this usage is the expression of a right appertaining to the State granting asylum and a duty incumbent on the territorial State. This follows from Article 38 of the Statute of the Court, which refers to international custom "as evidence of a general practice accepted as law".

In support of its contention concerning the existence of such a custom, the Colombian Government has referred to a large number of extradition treaties which, as already explained, can have no bearing on the question now under consideration. It has cited conventions and agreements which do not contain any provision concerning the alleged rule of unilateral and definitive qualification such as the Montevideo Convention of 1889 on international penal law, the Bolivarian Agreement of 1911 and the Havana Convention of 1928. It has invoked conventions which have not been ratified by Peru, such as the Montevideo Conventions of 1933 and 1939. The Convention of 1933 has, in fact, been ratified by not more than eleven States and the Convention of 1939 by two States only.

It is particularly the Montevideo Convention of 1933 which Counsel for the Colombian Government has also relied on in this connexion. It is contended that this Convention has merely codified principles which were already recognized by Latin–American custom, and that it is valid against Peru as a proof of customary law. The limited number of States which have ratified this Convention reveals the weakness of this argument, and furthermore, it is invalidated by the preamble which states that this Convention modifies the Havana Convention.

Finally, the Colombian Government has referred to a large number of particular cases in which diplomatic asylum was in fact granted and respected. But it has not shown that the alleged rule of unilateral and definitive qualification was invoked or—if in some cases it was in fact invoked—that it was, apart from conventional stipulations, exercised by the States granting asylum as a right appertaining to them and respected by the territorial States as a duty incumbent on them and not merely for reasons of political expediency. The facts brought to the knowledge of the Court disclose so much uncertainty and contradiction, so much fluctuation and discrepancy in the exercise of diplomatic asylum and in the official views expressed on various occasions, there has been so much inconsistency in the rapid succession of conventions on asylum, ratified by some States and rejected by others, and the practice has been so much influenced by considerations of political expediency in the various cases, that it is not possible to discern in all this any constant and uniform usage, accepted as law, with regard to the alleged rule of unilateral and definitive qualification of the offence.

The Court cannot therefore find that the Colombian Government has proved the existence of such a custom. But even if it could be supposed that such a custom existed between certain Latin–American States only, it could not be invoked against Peru which, far from having by its attitude adhered to it, has, on the contrary, repudiated it by refraining from ratifying the Montevideo Conventions of 1933 and 1939, which were the first to include a rule concerning the qualification of the offence in matters of diplomatic asylum.

In the written Pleadings and during the oral proceedings, the Government of Colombia relied upon official communiqués published by the Peruvian Ministry of Foreign Affairs on October 13th and 26th, 1948, and the Government of Peru relied upon a Report of the Advisory Committee of the Ministry of Foreign Affairs of Colombia dated September 2nd, 1937; on the question of qualification, these documents state views which are contrary to those now maintained by these Governments. The Court, whose duty it is to apply international law in deciding the present case, cannot attach decisive importance to any of these documents.

For these reasons, the Court has arrived at the conclusion that Colombia, as the State granting asylum, is not competent to qualify the offence by a unilateral and definitive decision, binding on Peru.

* * *

In its second submission, the Colombian Government asks the Court to adjudge and declare:

> "That the Republic of Peru, as the territorial State, is bound in the case now before the Court, to give the guarantees necessary for the departure of M. Victor Raul Raya de la Torre from the country, with due regard to the inviolability of his person."

This alleged obligation of the Peruvian Government does not entirely depend on the answer given to the first Colombian submission relating to the unilateral and definitive qualification of the offence. It follows from the first two articles of the Havana Convention that, even if such a right of qualification is not admitted, the Colombian Government is entitled to request a safe-conduct under certain conditions.

The first condition is that asylum has been regularly granted and maintained. It can be granted only to political offenders who are not accused or condemned for common crimes and only in urgent cases and for the time strictly indispensable for the safety of the refugee. These points relate to the Peruvian counterclaim and will be considered later to the extent necessary for the decision of the present case.

The second condition is laid down in Article 2 of the Havana Convention:

> "Third: The Government of the State may require that the refugee be sent out of the national territory within the shortest time possible; and the diplomatic agent of the country who has granted asylum may in turn require the guarantees necessary for the departure of the refugee from the country with due regard to the inviolability of his person."

Do you see international law becoming, "international law of the Americas," "European international law," "African international law," "Asian international law," etc. ?

3.   EXCEPTIONALISM

By the start of the 21st century, the unique power of the United States led some scholars to renew the concept of "hegemonic international law," where a hegemonic power has a privileged place in the international legal system.

Detlev F. Vagts, Hegemonic International Law*

95 Am. J. Int'l L. 843 (2001)

One increasingly sees the United States designated as the hegemonic (or indispensable, dominant, or preeminent) power. Those employing this terminology include former officials of high rank as well as widely read publicists. The French, for their part, use the term "hyper-power." A passage by Charles Krauthammer in *Time* best captures the spirit: "America is no mere international citizen. It is the dominant power in the world, more dominant than any since Rome. Accordingly, America is in a position to reshape norms, alter expectations and create new realities. How? By unapologetic and implacable demonstrations of will."

The idea of hegemony has begun to work its way into the world of international law to the point where a session of the annual meeting of the American Society of International Law in 2000 was dedicated to "the single superpower." A new undersecretary of state, John Bolton, while still at the American Enterprise Institute, wrote in an article entitled *Is There Really "Law" in International Affairs?* that we "should be unashamed, unapologetic, uncompromising American constitutional hegemonists."

* * *

II.   HIL AS NORMATIVE

The received body of international law is based on the idea of the equality of states. The United Nations Charter in Article 2(1) proclaims that it is "based on the principle of the sovereign equality of all its Members." In 1979 the General Assembly reinforced that idea by passing a resolution entitled "Inadmissibility of the Policy of Hegemonism in International Relations" (which the United States and three other members opposed). To get to HIL, one must discard or seriously modify this principle. Note that equality is questioned by another influential body of international law thinking, the one that asserts that a different law prevails among liberal democracies than in the rest of the world. HIL advocates would also say that norms cannot stray too far from reality and must therefore recognize inequalities of power. Schmitt spoke in terms of concrete order thinking and sought to move thinking on both German constitutional law and international law to focus on where power was located and what followed from that, including inequality between states. Even classical publicists of international law acknowledged the role that power, and disparities in power, played in their subject. In the scholarship of international relations, power has been a central object of study ever since the work of Hans Morgenthau.

One might thus conclude that no law graces the hegemon's universe and this is what Bolton seems to say. But the historical record shows that it can be convenient for the hegemon to have a body of law to work with, provided that it is suitably adapted. Moreover, those subject to its domina-

---

* Footnotes omitted.

tion may need clear indications of what is expected of them. The hegemon is also a trading party and the world of trade needs rules. While Bolton's national security world may be rather free of rules, his colleague, Special Trade Representative Robert Zoellick, has to operate in the highly legalized universe of the World Trade Organization.

III. HIL AND INTERVENTION

A shift to HIL most specially requires setting aside the norm of nonintervention into the internal affairs of states. Indeed, Bolton's objection to international law centers particularly on its attempted use to hamper unilateral intervention by the United States. German thinking about hegemony centered on defending the legitimacy of German intervention within Europe for such purposes as protecting persons of German origin and attacking the appropriateness of intervention by nations outside the continent. The United States, as all students of history know, openly asserted through the Monroe Doctrine the right to exclude other powers from the Western Hemisphere. It is less generally remembered that the United States also assumed for itself the right to intervene militarily within that territory. In earlier years that assumption was quite overt and legalized. Schmitt hailed Article III of the 1903 Treaty on Relations with Cuba as a piece of hegemonic drafting. It stated:

> The Government of Cuba consents that the United States may exercise the right to intervene for the preservation of Cuban independence, the maintenance of a government adequate for the protection of life, property, and individual liberty, and for discharging the obligations with respect to Cuba imposed by the Treaty of Paris on the United States, now to be assumed and undertaken by the Government of Cuba.

An early fan of indeterminacy, Schmitt noted that indeterminacy in this agreement gave the key to the hegemonic power, which had the right to interpret the law, a doctrine he labeled "decisionism." Since President Franklin D. Roosevelt withdrew the marines from Haiti and Nicaragua, we have been more circumspect about intervention but have not ceased the practice. Indeed, even without United Nations blessings we have projected military force into areas outside Latin America such as Sudan, Afghanistan, Libya, and the former Yugoslavia. A true hegemon would have reverted to the practice of overt intervention and would have demonstrated its unapologetic and implacable will by not canceling air cover for the Bay of Pigs invasion. Whatever changes that would require in international law would have been made.

IV. HIL AND TREATIES

Treaties, since they represent constraints at some level on unilateral action by the parties, irritate hegemonists. In particular, they would avoid agreements creating international regimes or organizations that might enable lesser powers to form coalitions that might frustrate the hegemon. Of course, a hegemon can use an international organization to magnify its authority by a judicious combination of voting power and leadership, as the United States has often done. A dominant power can minimize the problem by refusing to enter into treaties it finds inconvenient; one need not call the roll of these agreements, starting with the Law of the Sea Convention and the Vienna Convention on the Law of Treaties and running to the convention on land mines. The hegemon can pronounce as customary law those portions of such a convention that suit its interests while ignoring the rest. Bent on ridding itself of an existing obligation, a power can resort to the *clausula rebus sic stantibus,* even if others have difficulty finding those circumstances. German international lawyers paid special attention to this doctrine. Of course, a hegemon must set aside the rule enshrined in the Vienna Convention that treaties obtained through coercion are invalid. The Reich's prevailing on Czechoslovakia to agree to the protectorate in 1939 exemplifies what the drafters of that rule had in mind.

United States thinkers have increasingly chosen the route of declaring that treaties do not have legally binding effect. The American hegemonist school of thought specializes in resorting to the later-in-time rule, which puts internal laws above international law as a matter of American constitutional doctrine. According to Bolton, treaties are thus left with only political and moral standing. Illustrative of the point is his showcasing of *Chae Chang Ping* as decisive. But this decision can boast no more than a dubious relation to politics and morality. The misleading quality of Bolton's treatment starts by skipping the name of the case at the top of the page in the *United States Reports*—"The Chinese Exclusion Case." The *Chinese Exclusion Case,* as it is generally known, is a monument to the shameful heritage of American racism—"an abiding embarrassment" as Professor Henkin says. Even though China was then a militarily feeble state, the political ramifications of the statute involved in the case were so mortifying that it was quietly undermined by another agreement. Memories are longer in Beijing than in Washington and these aspects of the case have not been forgotten there. To entrust a man who has written this straightforward celebration of America's power to break treaties with the task of negotiating new agreements is ironic. It stands in contrast to the more efficient double-facedness of Frederick the Great, who prefaced his ruthless pursuit of dominance in Europe by publishing *Anti–Machiavel* in which he denounced the Florentine international relations expert for counseling the Prince not to feel bound by his agreements.

V.   HIL AND CUSTOMARY INTERNATIONAL LAW

A hegemon confronts customary international law differently from other countries. In terms of the formation of customary law, such a power can by its abstention prevent the emerging rule from becoming part of custom. It is disputed how nearly unanimous the acceptance of a rule must be for it to meet the requirement of Article of the Statute of the International Court of Justice that it be "general practice." Abstention by a hegemonic power does seem to be enough to keep it from being general. For example, the dissenters from the ruling in *The Paquete Habana* that fishing boats were exempt from capture said that "[i]t is difficult to conceive of a law of the sea of universal obligation to which Great Britain has not acceded." By the same token, a customary rule against executing those who commit crimes while under eighteen cannot be confirmed if it is not joined in by the United States—not to mention its sympathizers, such as Iran and Iraq. This implies that, whereas a lesser state might find itself bound by custom even if it failed to sign a treaty that had gained overwhelming assent, a hegemon could safely abstain. If a custom has crystallized, the hegemon can disregard it more safely than a treaty rule and have its action hailed as creative. Bolton finds it even easier to dispose of customary international law than treaties:

> Customary international law changes under this definition when state practice changes, which led former Attorney General Bill Barr to opine: "Well, as I understand it, what you're saying is the only way to change international law is to break it." This telling remark shows the incoherence of treating "customary international law" as law.

Attorney General Barr will be remembered as the author of the policy of extraterritorial abductions in lieu of extradition, which led to the kidnapping involved in *United States v. Alvarez–Machain*.

In a hegemonic system, the hegemon may pick and choose the rules it cares to observe. Law is no longer universal in application, but follows a two-level approach. Hegemony is more or less the opposite of the world of many regions, as just discussed. Under hegemony the world has one dominant state, surrounded by many lesser states. The Westphalian principles at the foundation of international law are negated, especially the principle of equality. Some proponents of U.S. power characterize the international system in the early 21st century as just such a two-tiered legal system and have argued for U.S. rights and duties different from other states and commensurate with its power.

Related to this position is the view that national systems, perhaps especially the U.S. system, or religious systems, such as Sharia, are superior to the international one. For some this may be true of only some areas of the law, such as criminal law and procedure or human rights. Others have a view that international is generally inferior, lacking a written constitution, elected law-makers, and regular courts.

B. LAW OF COMMUNITY

Those who see international law as the law of a community do not deny that the world is characterized by division. They hold the view, however, that we can shape international law to transcend what divides us, whether power, culture or ideology. The need for law that provides common regulation of global issues and that allows for common commitment to important moral norms is wanted and supported. Powerful phenomena have for centuries moved international law ever closer toward true universality. New means of law-making, old imperialism, and dynamic globalization have all influenced the trend toward universality. Universality is perhaps the most important gift international law offers the world.

1.   Universal Law-Making

Law-making through methods that are widely inclusive, involving participants from all corners of the globe is now a standard feature of international relations. With the end of the Cold War and the revolution in international communications, international law-making truly opened up to world-wide participation. Today, not only states, but inter-governmental organizations, non-governmental organizations, corporations, and individuals everywhere can and do participate in the development of international law, helping ensure that the law will reflect wide consensus and be applied and respected universally. The drafting of the Rome Statute for the International Criminal Court in 1998, the Landmines Convention in 1997, and the negotiation of a protocol on climate change to replace the Kyoto Protocol are examples where large numbers of diverse voices were heard in the creation of new law. The wide participation in these law-making efforts was facilitated by the new developments in communications. Information about the issues was widely disseminated by the media. Coalitions were formed of like-minded groups around the world over the Internet. Travel became faster and cheaper, allowing individuals to attend preparatory meetings and negotiating conferences. Widespread knowledge of English allowed interaction far beyond the circle of classically-trained official diplomats.

Participation in international law making today might be cited as more universal than ever before, but universalists can point to the wide participation in law-making that is part of the history of international law. In the classical account modern international law emerged with the state system at the end of Europe's Thirty Year's War in 1648 and the signing of treaties known collectively as the Peace of Westphalia. The method used to create the Peace of Westphalia, multi-party negotiation, included as many as 176 representatives negotiating on behalf of 194 European rulers. Geoffrey Parker, The Thirty Years' War 178 (1987).

This basic approach to creating agreements has been replicated ever since on an ever wider and more sophisticated basis. Throughout the 19th century, European states continued to act through multi-party negotiations, known as "congresses" or "conferences". The Hague Peace Conferences of 1899 and 1907 created obligations of peaceful settlement, the Permanent Court of Arbitration and improvements in the law of war; the Paris Peace Conference of 1918 created the League of Nations, and the San Francisco Conference of 1945 created the United Nations. All of these events have been important milestones in a trend toward ever-greater participation in law-making.

After the creation of the United Nations, the UN became an important forum for initiating new international law, both treaty and customary rules. The United Nations General Assembly has included the vast majority of the world's states since the UN's founding. Entities with observer status have been allowed to participate in the work of the United Nations along with specially-invited participants. Informal participation has also been a consistent feature of United Nations-sponsored law-making. The UN Security Council, International Law Commission, UN specialized agencies, and ad hoc diplomatic conferences have all served since 1945, but especially from the 1960s forward, as forums for starting new initiatives in international law.

Important examples of multilateral conferences resulting in important new international law before the end of the Cold War include the 1972 Stockholm Conference on the Human Environment and the Third United Nations Conference on the Law of the Sea ending in 1982. By 1993, Jonathan Charney noted that these developments marked an evolution in international law-making that was not only resulting in the more rapid development of international law but also law more widely accepted as legitimate because of the wider participation in the law-making process.

In addition to wider, more universal participation in law-making international law, advances in communication have resulted in greater interaction and the related need for more international law. Globalization, a phenomenon associated with expanded communication and participation of people from all over the planet in the same activities, is a powerful development that brings with it the need for common, worldwide rules for regulating issues that reach around the globe, such as trade, environmental protection, intellectual property protection, disease prevention, and crime suppression. International law is the natural source of such common rules. The need for law in a world community experiencing globalization is likely to foster the trend toward more rapid creation of new international law through ever-wider participation, and, thus toward universality.

W. Michael Reisman, The Democratization of Contemporary International Law–Making Processes and the Differentiation of Their Application

pp. 21–24, DEVELOPMENTS OF INTERNATIONAL LAW IN TREATY MAKING (Wolfrum and Röben, eds., 2005)

I do not believe that there is a crisis in international law-making, but rather a crisis in the *perception* of the law-making process in international law. Given the characteristics of the international system, I submit that international law-making is working about as well as can be expected. Its "problems" arise from the nature of the contemporary international social and political systems within which the law-making process operates. Those problems are an ineluctable part of the practice of modern international law and constitute one of the reasons why the study and practice of international law are so much more intellectually, challenging and operationally difficult than their counterparts in domestic law.

* * *

There are many factors that have facilitated the democratization of international law-making and, in particular, the expansion of private sector international law-making. One has been the end of the Cold War, which has removed many constraints that had confined the activities of smaller actors. Another factor has been the technological revolution, providing the communications infrastructure available to non-state actors. Indeed, the international activities of modern non-governmental actors are inseparable from and probably inconceivable without the Internet. Coincident with the new communications opportunities has been the phenomenon of "privatization," involving the voluntary withdrawal in some states of the state apparatus from activities that were previously deemed to be inherently "public," as well as the disintegration and collapse of public services in others. These revolutions have coincided with the opening of national markets to international investors who undertake to perform the now privatized activities along with the entry of NGO service providers to fill governmental vacuums. Along with these radical transformations, one cannot ignore the rapidity of change in a science-based and technological civilization which has required state law-making institutions to resign a substantial amount of competence to the informal law-making of the economic sectors concerned, because national legislatures have simply been unable to keep up.

Thus the modalities through which international law is being prescribed now range over a wide spectrum. At one end, we find treaties and other international agreements, the classical form of international lawmaking. Close to it we find delegated law-making, the preeminent example of which is the Security Council when it operates under Chapter VII of the Charter; incipient developments may also be detected in some environmental treaties. Beyond that, there is a vast area in which expectations of authority on particular courses of right behavior are established and supported by diverse sanctions applied through a wide range of modalities. This dynamic and open process of communication involves a wide-range of non-state actors who play critical roles in the shaping and sustaining of expectations of right behavior. In contrast to classical international law-making, much of which is *lex scripta,* the open process of law-making is more dynamic and fluid, often responding to perceptions of crisis. Nonetheless, it is marked by a number of constant and unprecedented features, foremost among them the general demand for human rights and the general intolerance of cruel and violent behavior by state elites.

Legal purists may dismiss the dynamic form of international lawmaking as "political" or "moral." The purists are correct that this is a process of norm generation that does not conform to many of the policies we demand of conventional law-making. But they err in dismissing it. The political decision maker, whether operating in a democratic system which requires responsiveness to constituencies, or in an authoritarian system which reduces but does not eliminate the need for such responsiveness, can no longer ignore this dynamic form of law-making. This is the imperative version of what is presented as right that appears in editorials of the leading newspapers, is repeated relentlessly in the visual and audial media and that comes to be reflected in popular expectations. Those expectations, in turn, are recorded in incessant opinion polls which are then checked regularly by nervous decision-makers and their "spin-meisters." Since I view the lawyer's task as seeking to understand in order to influence decision, I cannot exclude this corollary process from a meaningful conception of international law.

In sum, in contemporary international law, we encounter two broad forms of international law-making, one essentially oligarchical, restricted to the representatives of states, the other more democratic, but not necessarily egalitarian. While there is a certain inter-play between the two forms of international law-making, they are often distinct in their outcomes. At the land-mines conference or the Rome conference, the influence of non-governmental organizations on the formal law-making process was manifest and, sometimes, even dominant. But the outcome of that process was still a familiar instrument of formal international law. In the more dynamic process, some of the law production is more evanescent, even capricious, though none the less influential on decision-makers.

Not surprisingly, the two systems often produce quite different results. In the past, the discrepancy between classic international law-making by treaty and by custom was attributable to the relative durability of *lex scripta,* whose decay rate is quite slow, and the comparatively more rapid transformation of expectations by *consuetudo.* But both of these streams were the result of state activity. In the modern system, the discrepancy is due to the different policy objectives pursued by states in treaty-making and non-state actors in their prescriptive endeavors.

Thomas Franck, Legitimacy In the International System

82 AM. J. INT'L L. 705 (1988)

The surprising thing about international law is that nations ever obey its strictures or carry out its mandates. This observation is made not to register optimism that the half-empty glass is also half full, but to draw attention to a pregnant phenomenon: that most states observe systemic rules much of the time in their relations with other states. That they should do so is much more interesting than, say, the fact that most citizens usually obey their nation's laws, because the international system is organized in a voluntarist fashion, supported by so little coercive authority. This unenforced rule system can obligate states to profess, if not always to manifest, a significant level of day-to-day compliance even, at times, when that is not in their short-term self-interest. The element or paradox attracts our attention and challenges us to investigate it, perhaps in the hope of discovering a theory that can illuminate more generally the occurrence of voluntary normative compliance and even yield a prescription for enhancing aspects of world order. * * *

Legitimacy is used here to mean that quality of a rule *which derives from* a *perception on the part of those to whom it is addressed that it has come into being in accordance with right process.* Right process includes the notion of valid sources but also encompasses literary, socio-anthropological and philosophical insights. The elements of right process that will be discussed below are identified as affecting decisively the degree to which any rule is perceived as legitimate. * * *

A series of events connected with the role of the U.S. Navy in protecting U.S.-flagged vessels in the Persian Gulf serves to illustrate the paradoxical phenomenon of uncoerced compliance in a situation where the rule conflicts with perceived self-interest. Early in 1988, the Department of Defense became aware of a ship approaching the gulf with a load of Chinese-made Silkworm missiles en route to Iran. The Department believed the successful delivery of these potent weapons would increase materially the danger to both protected and protecting U.S. ships in the region. It therefore argued for permission to intercept the delivery. The Department of State countered that such a search and seizure on the high seas, under the universally recognized rules of war and neutrality, would constitute aggressive blockade, an act tantamount to a declaration of war against Iran. In the event, the delivery ship and its cargo of missiles were allowed to pass. Deference to systemic rules had won out over tactical advantage in the internal struggle for control of U.S. policy.

Why should this have been so? In the absence of a world government and a global coercive power to enforce its laws, why did the U.S. Government, with its evident power to do as it wished, choose to "play by the rules" despite the considerable short-term strategic advantage to be gained by seizing the Silkworms before they could be delivered? Why did preeminent American power defer to the rules of the sanctionless system? At least part of the answer to this question, quietly given by the State Department to the Department of Defense, is that the international rules of neutrality have attained a high degree of recognized legitimacy and must not be violated lightly. Specifically, they are well understood, enjoy a long pedigree and are part of a consistent framework of rules—the *jus in bello* governing and restraining the use of force in conflicts. To violate a set of rules of such widely recognized legitimacy, the State Department argued, would transform the U.S. posture in the gulf from that of a neutral to one of belligerency. That could end Washington's role as an honest broker seeking to promote peace negotiations. It would also undermine the carefully crafted historic "rules of the game" applicable to wars, rules that are widely perceived to be in the interest of all states. * * *

Four elements—the indicators of rule legitimacy in the community of states—are identified and studied in this essay. They are *determinacy, symbolic validation, coherence* and *adherence* (to a normative hierarchy). To the extent rules exhibit these properties, they appear to exert a strong pull on states to comply with their commands. To the extent these elements are not present, rules seem to be easier to avoid by a state tempted to pursue its short-term self-interest. This is not to say that the legitimacy of a rule can be deduced solely by counting how often it is obeyed or disobeyed. While its legitimacy may exert a powerful pull on state conduct, yet other pulls may be stronger in a particular circumstance. The chance to take a quick, decisive advantage may overcome the counterpull of even a highly legitimate rule. In such circumstances, legitimacy is indicated not by obedience, but by the discomfort disobedience induces in the violator. (Student demonstrations sometimes are a sensitive indicator of such discomfort.) The variable to watch is not compliance but the strength of the compliance pull, whether or not the rule achieves actual compliance in any one case.

Each rule has an inherent pull power that is independent of the circumstances in which it is exerted, and that varies from rule to rule. This pull power is its index of legitimacy. For example, the rule that makes it improper for one state to infiltrate spies into another state in the guise of diplomats is formally acknowledged by almost every state, yet it enjoys so low a degree of legitimacy as to exert virtually no pull towards compliance. As Schachter observes, "some 'laws,' though enacted properly, have so low a degree of probable compliance that they are treated as 'dead letters' and * * * some treaties, while properly concluded, are considered 'scraps of paper.'" By way of contrast, we have noted, the rules pertaining to belligerency and neutrality actually exerted a very high level of pull on Washington in connection with the Silkworm missile shipment in the Persian Gulf.

Perhaps the most self-evident of all characteristics making for legitimacy is textual *determinacy*. What is meant by this is the ability of the text to convey a clear message, to appear transparent in the sense that one can see through the language to the meaning. Obviously, rules with a readily ascertainable meaning have a better chance than those that do not regulate the conduct of those to whom the rule is addressed or exert a compliance pull on their policymaking process. Those addressed will know precisely what is expected of them, which is a necessary first step towards compliance.

To illustrate the point, compare two textual formulations defining the boundary of the underwater continental shelf. The 1958 Convention places the shelf at "a depth of 200 meters or, beyond that limit, to where the depth of the superjacent waters admits of the exploitation of the natural resources of the said areas." The 1982 Convention on the Law of the Sea, on the other hand, is far more detailed and specific. It defines the shelf as "the natural prolongation of * * * land territory to the outer edge of the continental margin, or to a distance of 200 nautical miles from the baselines from which the breadth of the territorial sea is measured," but takes into account such specific factors as "the thickness of sedimentary rocks" and imposes an outermost limit that "shall not exceed 100 nautical miles from the 2,500 meter isobath," which, in turn, is a line connecting the points where the waters are 2,500 meters deep. The 1982 standard, despite its complexity, is far more determinate than the elastic standard in the 1958 Convention, which, in a sense, established no rule at all. Back in

1958, the parties simply covered their differences and uncertainties with a formula, whose content was left in abeyance pending further work by negotiators, courts, and administrators and by the evolution of customary state practice. The vagueness of the rule did permit a flexible response to further advances in technology, a benefit inherent in indeterminacy.

Indeterminacy, however, has costs. Indeterminate normative standards not only make it harder to know what conformity is expected, but also make it easier to justify noncompliance. Put conversely, the more determinate the standard, the more difficult it is to resist the pull of the rule to compliance and to justify noncompliance. Since few persons or states wish to be perceived as acting in obvious violation of a generally recognized rule of conduct, they may try to resolve the conflicts between the demands of a rule and their desire not to be fettered, by "interpreting" the rule permissively. A determinate rule is less elastic and thus less amenable to such evasive strategy than an indeterminate one. * * *

To summarize: the legitimacy of a rule is affected by its degree of determinacy. Its determinacy depends upon the clarity with which it is able to communicate its intent and to shape that intent into a specific situational command. This, in turn, can depend upon the literary structure of the rule, its ability to avoid *reductio ad absurdum* and the availability of a process for resolving ambiguities in its application. * * *

As determinacy is the linguistic or literary-structural component of legitimacy, so *symbolic validation, ritual* and *pedigree* provide its cultural and anthropological dimension. As with determinacy, so here, the legitimacy of the rule—its ability to exert pull to compliance and to command voluntary obedience—is to be examined in the light of its ability to communicate. In this instance, however, what is to be communicated is not so much content as *authority:* the authority of a rule, the authority of the originator of a validating communication and, at times, the authority bestowed on the recipient of the communication. The communication of authority, moreover, is symbolic rather than literal. We shall refer to these symbolically validating communications as cues.

All ritual is a form of symbolic validation, but the converse is not necessarily true. *Pedigree* is a different subset of cues that seek to enhance the compliance pull of rules or rule-making institutions by emphasizing their historical origins, their cultural or anthropological deep-rootedness. * * * Professor Schachter has observed that a body of rules produced by the UN legislative drafting body, the International Law Commission, will be more readily accepted by the nations "after [the Commission] has devoted a long period in careful study and consideration of precedent and practice." Moreover, the authority will be greater if the product is labeled *codification—that* is, the interpolation of rules from deep-rooted evidence of state practice—"than if it were presented as a 'development" (that is, as new law)," even though the Commission (as a subsidiary of the General Assembly) is equally empowered by the UN Charter to promote "the progressive development of international law and its codification." The compliance pull of a rule is enhanced by a demonstrable lineage. A new rule will have greater difficulty finding compliance, and even evidence of its good sense may not fully compensate for its lack of breeding. Nevertheless, a new rule may be taken more seriously if it arrives on the scene under the aegis of a particularly venerable sponsor such as a widely ratified multilateral convention, or a virtually unanimous decision of the International Court of Justice. * * *

* * * Symbols of pedigree and rituals are firmly imbedded in state diplomatic practice. The titles ("ambassador extraordinary and plenipotentiary"), prerogatives and immunities of ambassadors, consuls and others functioning in a representative capacity are among the oldest of symbols and rites associated with the conduct of international relations. The sending state, by the rituals of accreditation, endows its diplomats with pedigree. They become, in time-honored tradition, a symbolic reification of the nation ("full powers" or *plenipotentiary),* a role that is ritually endorsed by the receiving state's ceremony accepting the envoy's credentials. These ceremonies, incidentally, are as old as they are elaborate and are performed with as remarkably faithful uniformity in Communist citadels as in royal palaces. Once accredited and received, an ambassador *is* the embodiment of the nation. The status of ambassador, once conferred, carries with it inherent rights and duties that do not depend on the qualities of the person, or on the condition of relations between the sending and receiving states, or on the relative might of the sending state. To insult or harm this envoy, no matter how grievous the provocation, is to attack the sending state. Moreover, when an envoy, acting officially, agrees to something, the envoy's state is bound, usually even if the envoy acted without proper authorization. The host state normally is entitled to rely on the word of an ambassador as if his or her state were speaking.

The venerable ritual practices of diplomacy are almost universally observed, and the rules that govern diplomacy are widely recognized as imbued with a high degree of legitimacy, being both descriptive and predictive of nearly invariable state conduct and reflecting a strong sense of historically endowed obligation. When the rules are violated—as they have been by Iran and Libya in recent years—the international community tends to respond by rallying around the rule, as the Security Council and the International Court of Justice demonstrated when the Iranian regime encouraged the occupation of the U.S. Embassy in Tehran. Violations of the elaborate rules pertaining to embassies and immunities usually lead the victim state to terminate its diplomatic relations with the offender. The offended state—as Britain demonstrated after the St. James Square shooting—usually takes care not to retaliate by means that the rules do not permit.

Both determinacy and symbolic validation are connected to a further variable: coherence. The effect of incoherence on symbolic validation can be illustrated by reference to diplomatic practices pertaining to the ritual validation of governments and states. The most important act of pedigreeing in the international system is the deep-rooted, traditional act that endows a new government, or a new state, with symbolic status. When the endowing is done by individual governments, it is known as *recognition*. The symbolic conferral of status is also performed collectively through a global organization like the United Nations when the members vote to admit a new nation to membership, or when the General Assembly votes to accept the credentials of the delegates representing a new government.

These two forms of validation are important because they enhance the status of the validated entity; that is, the new state or government acquires legitimacy, which, in turn, carries entitlements and obligations equal to those of other such entities. Such symbolic validation cannot alter the empirically observable reality of power disparity among states and governments, nor, properly understood, does it give off that cue. It does, however, purport to restrict what powerful states legitimately may do with their advantage over the weak. It is a cue that prompts the Soviets, however reluctantly, to do a lot of explaining when they invade Afghanistan. The pedigreed statehood of Afghanistan, together with the determinacy of the rules against intervention by one state in the internal affairs of another, then combine to render those Soviet explanations essentially unacceptable, global scorn evidencing the inelastic determinacy of the applicable rules. * * *

To summarize: coherence, and thus legitimacy, must be understood in part as defined by factors derived from a notion of community. Rules become coherent when they are applied so as to preclude capricious checkerboarding. They preclude caprice when they are applied consistently or, if inconsistently applied, when they make distinctions based on underlying general principles that connect with an ascertainable purpose of the rules and with similar distinctions made throughout the rule system. The resultant skein of underlying principles is an aspect of community, which, in turn, confirms the status of the states that constitute the community. Validated membership in the community accords equal capacity for rights and obligations derived from its legitimate rule system.

By focusing on the connections between specific rules and general underlying principles, we have emphasized the horizontal aspect of our central notion of a community of legitimate rules. However, there are vertical aspects of this community that have even more significant impact on the legitimacy of rules. * * *

* * * A rule * * * is more likely to obligate if it is made within the procedural and institutional framework of an organized community than if it is strictly an ad hoc agreement between parties in the state of nature. The same rule is still more likely to obligate if it is made within the hierarchically structured procedural and constitutional framework of a sophisticated community rather than in a primitive community lacking such secondary rules about rules. * * * Of course, there *are* lawmaking institutions in the system. One has but to visit a highly structured multinational negotiation such as the decade-long Law of the Sea Conference of the 1970s to see a kind of incipient legislature at work. The Security Council, the decision-making bodies of the World Bank and, perhaps, the UN General Assembly also somewhat resemble the cabinets and legislatures of national governments, even if they are not so highly

disciplined and empowered as the British Parliament, the French National Assembly or even the U.S. Congress. Moreover, there *are* courts in the international system: not only the International Court of Justice, the European Community Court and the regional human rights tribunals, but also a very active network of quasi-judicial committees and commissions, as well as arbitral tribunals established under such auspices as the Algiers agreement ending the Iran hostage crisis. Arbitrators regularly settle investment disputes under the auspices and procedures of the World Bank and the International Chamber of Commerce. Treaties and contracts create jurisdiction for these tribunals and establish rules of evidence and procedure.

The international system thus appears on close examination to be a more developed community than critics sometimes allege. It has an extensive network of horizontally coherent rules, rule-making institutions, and judicial and quasi-judicial bodies to apply the rules impartially. Many of the rules are sufficiently determinate for states to know what is required for compliance and most states obey them most of the time. Those that do not, tend to feel guilty and to lie about their conduct rather than defy the rules openly. The system also has means for changing, adapting and repealing rules.

Most nations, most of the time, are both rule conscious and rule abiding. Why this is so, rather than that it is so, is also relevant to an understanding of the degree to which an international community has developed in practice. This silent majority's sense of obligation derives primarily not from explicit consent to specific treaties or custom, but from *status*. Obligation is perceived to be owed *to a community of states as a necessary reciprocal incident of membership in the community*. Moreover, that community is defined by secondary rules of process as well as by primary rules of obligation: states perceive themselves to be participants in a structured process of continual interaction that is governed by secondary rules of process (sometimes called rules of recognition), of which the UN Charter is but the most obvious example. The Charter is a set of rules, but it is also about how rules are to be made by the various institutions established by the Charter and by the subsidiaries those institutions have created, such as the International Law and Human Rights Commissions. * * * In the world of nations, each of these described conditions of a sophisticated community is observable today, even though imperfectly. This does not mean that its rules will never be disobeyed. It does mean, however, that it is usually possible to distinguish rule compliance from rule violation, and a valid rule or ruling from an invalid one. It also means that it is not necessary to await the millennium of Austinian-type world government to proceed with constructing—perfecting—a system of rules and institutions that will exhibit a powerful pull to compliance and a self-enforcing degree of legitimacy.

2.   UNIVERSAL RULES, NORMS, AND PRINCIPLES

Many, if not the vast majority of international law rules and principles emerging from universal law-making techniques are intended for universal application. Fundamental principles found in the law of the sea or international environmental law, for example, apply universally. International law has had such fundamental principles since the emergence of the system in the 17th century and these are featured as examples of why international law is universal law. In addition, basic structural rules—rules on how international law is made, applied and enforced—apply to all subjects of the law. Additionally, international law's higher principles are argued to apply to all.

Among the principles that were agreed implicitly or explicitly in the Peace of Westphalia were the principles of sovereign equality and the related principles of non-intervention and territorial integrity. The principle that the law applied equally to all states was a universal principle that, in turn, supported the universality of international law in general was at the heart of international law, assuring the equality application of the law or its universality. Equality was an understandable principle to feature in a system heavily influenced by natural law thinkers such as Hugo Grotius. Equality supported universalism and universalism "was an inescapable consequence of natural law."

Grotius understood all law to apply universally. He accepted the possibility of treaties among Europeans and non-Europeans, as well as Catholics and Protestants. He stressed the need for tolerance for some difference throughout his great treatise, *The Law of War and Peace* (1625). Tolerance makes the possibility of agreement to universal law possible. Grotius drew on Greek, Roman, Indian, Hebrew, and other cultures in addition to his own to explain law. His theory of law was universalist, as was his methodology. The international law he explained was consequently universalist as well.

Grotian ideas about international law were developed on the basis of earlier work done by, in particular, the 16th century Spanish Scholastics. The Scholastics also worked from the perspective of universal natural law. Vitoria and Las Casas, for example, advocated the view that native peoples in the Americas had rights. Universal natural law embraced them as well as Europeans, meaning Europeans could not simply slaughter or enslave them as if they had no rights. The Scholastics were, in turn, influenced by earlier jurists. The Roman jurist Gaius who lived in the 2nd century saw in the Roman *jus gentium* a universal law. Gaius contrasted the *jus civile*, which governed the internal affairs of a community, with the *jus gentium* governing relations among peoples on the basis of natural reason. The *jus gentium* was subsequently looked to by medieval and post-medieval scholars as a body of universal law, binding on all nations. By the time of Westphalia and until the decline of natural law theory, international law had a firm foundation in universalist theory and principles. As positivism steadily replaced natural law as the dominant theory in international law by the early 20th century, natural law's universalism nevertheless persisted.

Alexander Orakhelashvili, The Idea of European International Law

17 EUR. J. INT'L. L. 315, 347 (2006)

The idea of European international law as developed by its proponents has from the outset been a racist idea that misrepresented the real character of international law.

As is clear, universal international law is possible both from naturalist and positivist perspectives. International law has always been universal both because its natural law element inherently implies universality as upheld by classical writers, and also because state practice as an aspect of positive law has consistently supported its universality.

Consequently, European international law is an ideology based not on evidence, but on prejudice and chauvinism generated from a sense of racial, cultural and religious superiority over those who are different. It thus translated into the concept of legal exclusivity, which was never realized in practice. Indeed, the concept never became reality because of the conceptual and practical impossibility of legal exclusivity in the international legal system.

There is thus no need to revive the idea of exclusivity reflected in "European international law" within the framework of modern European projects. There appears to be an increasing awareness today that regional projects like these are derived from, and operate in accordance with, general international law. Accumulated experience proves that international legal reasoning should be rid of the clichés of European international law and the related implications of the continuous tradition of Eurokitsch based on the misinterpretation of legal institutions right up to the end of the 20th century. This will help us to properly confront and better understand the legal principles and institutions in our already complex world of international law.

Yet, positivism and imperialism gave some support to the universality of law. As mentioned, a justification for colonialism was that it would serve to bring all peoples eventually into international law. In addition, European states did not conquer every non-European place. They needed international law to regulate trade with non-colonial, non-European countries that were not bound by European laws and customs. European imperialists and the United States demanded concessions and other rights which could only be made binding by international law. Imposing these obligations on non-Western communities gave those communities duties under international law. Rights could only follow. Thus, imperialism, despite its deep immorality, gave some support to universal international law. Consent to treaties had to have meaning if colonial powers were to hold treaty parties to their agreements.

Another aspect of international law that supports the universality argument is that the sources of international law are the same for all rules. The three primary sources of international law are treaties, custom, and general principles. International law perhaps more than national law relies on consent to bind, and this aspect of the law may seem to undermine its universality. It is true that states may withhold consent to a treaty or may make reservations to some treaties and avoid being bound by treaties in whole or in part. The international community is developing ways to obligate states under treaties without strict consent. Tomuschat has pointed out that the need for new regulation has resulted in obligations even absent express consent. Christian Tomuschat, *Obligations Arising for States Without or Against Their Will*, 241 Recueil des Cours 241 (1993). For the most part, however, it remains the case that not all states are bound by all treaties or all treaty provisions. Still, the rules governing the formation, interpretation, and termination of treaties are the same for all treaties and to this extent the law of treaties in general, if not particular treaties, is universal law.

The other primary sources of international law, custom and general principles, are less dependent on consent and will tend to apply to all with only rare exceptions. Some states may avoid the application of a particular rule of customary international law through persistent objection from the start of the formation of the rule. This is such a rare occurrence, however, that customary international law may be thought of as generating universally applicable rules. The general principles of international law is also a source of universal rules. In fact, general principles are more universally applicable than treaties or customary rules because subjects of international law have no apparent means to opt-out of them. Courts have tended to identify two ways of finding general principles: They are either principles found commonly in legal systems, such as the nationality of corporations, or principles inherent in law or society, such as good faith and proportionality. Like inherent general principles, *jus cogens* norms are also conceived as universal. The norms are understood expressly to apply universally. (See Chapter 2 above.) Recall that the International Court of Justice (ICJ) recognized a right of all states to participate in the enforcement of such norms in the *Barcelona Traction Case*:

> In view of the importance of the rights involved, all States can be held to have an interest of a legal nature in their protection; they are obligations *erga omnes* ... Such obligations derive, for example, in contemporary international law, from the outlawing of acts of aggression, and of genocide, as also from the principles and rules concerning the basic rights of the human person, including protection from slavery and racial discrimination. Some of the corresponding rights of protection have entered into the body of general international law; others are conferred by international instruments of a universal or quasi-universal character.

Barcelona Traction, Light and Power Company Ltd. (Canada v. Belgium) 1972 I.C.J. Rep., paras. 33–34.

Fragmentation of International Law: Difficulties Arising from the Diversification and Expansion of International Law (Chair of the Study Group, Martti Koskenniemmi)*

Report of the International Law Commission, 58th Session, A/61/10 (1 May–9 June and 3 July–11 August 2006)

I. Background

* * *

247. The rationale for the Commission's treatment of fragmentation is that the emergence of new and special types of law, so-called "self-contained regimes" and geographically or functionally limited treaty-systems, creates problems of coherence in international law. New types of specialized law do not emerge accidentally but seek to respond to new technical and functional requirements. The emergence of "environmental law", for example, is a response to growing concern over the state of the international environment. "Trade law" develops as an instrument to respond to opportunities created by comparative advantage in international economic relations. "Human rights law" aims to protect the interests of individuals and "international criminal law" gives legal expression to the "fight against impunity". Each rule-complex or "regime" comes with its own principles, its own form of expertise and its own "ethos", not necessarily identical to the ethos of neighbouring specializations. "Trade law" and "environmental law", for example, have highly specific objectives and rely on principles that may often point in different directions. In order for the new law to be efficient, it often includes new types of treaty clauses or practices that may not be compatible with old general law or the law of some other specialized branch. Very often new rules or regimes develop precisely in order to deviate from what was earlier provided by the general law. When such deviations become general and frequent, the unity of the law suffers.

* * *

II. Conclusions of the work of the Study Group

251. The conclusions reached in the work of the Study Group are as follows:

1. General

(1) *International law as a legal system*. International law is a legal system. Its rules and principles (i.e. its norms) act in relation to and should be interpreted against the background of other rules and principles. As a legal system, international law is not a random collection of such norms. There are meaningful relationships between them. Norms may thus exist at higher and lower hierarchical levels, their formulation may involve

---

* Some footnotes omitted.

greater or lesser generality and specificity and their validity may date back to earlier or later moments in time.

(2) In applying international law, it is often necessary to determine the precise relationship between two or more rules and principles that are both valid and applicable in respect of a situation. For that purpose the relevant relationships fall into two general types:

- *Relationships of interpretation*. This is the case where one norm assists in the interpretation of another. A norm may assist in the interpretation of another norm for example as an application, clarification, updating, or modification of the latter. In such situation, both norms are applied in conjunction.

- *Relationships of conflict*. This is the case where two norms that are both valid and applicable point to incompatible decisions so that a choice must be made between them. The basic rules concerning the resolution of normative conflicts are to be found in the VCLT.

(3) *The VCLT*. When seeking to determine the relationship of two or more norms to each other, the norms should be interpreted in accordance with or analogously to the VCLT and especially the provisions in its articles 31–33 having to do with the interpretation of treaties.

(4) *The principle of harmonization*. It is a generally accepted principle that when several norms bear on a single issue they should, to the extent possible, be interpreted so as to give rise to a single set of compatible obligations.

2.   The maxim *lex specialis derogat legi generali*

(5) *General principle*. The maxim *lex specialis derogat legi generali* is a generally accepted technique of interpretation and conflict resolution in international law. It suggests that whenever two or more norms deal with the same subject matter, priority should be given to the norm that is more specific.

* * *

3.   Special (self-contained) regimes

(11) *Special ("self-contained") regimes as lex specialis*. A group of rules and principles concerned with a particular subject matter may form a special regime ("Self-contained regime") and be applicable as *lex specialis*. Such special regimes often have their own institutions to administer the relevant rules.

* * *

(14) *The relationship between special regimes and general international law*. A special regime may prevail over general law under the same conditions as *lex specialis* generally (see conclusions (8) and (10) above).

(15) *The role of general law in special regimes: Gap-filling*. The scope of special laws is by definition narrower than that of general laws. It will thus frequently be the case that a matter not regulated by special law will

arise in the institutions charged to administer it. In such cases, the relevant general law will apply.

(16) *The role of general law in special regimes: Failure of special regimes.* Special regimes or the institutions set up by them may fail. Failure might be inferred when the special laws have no reasonable prospect of appropriately addressing the objectives for which they were enacted. It could be manifested, for example, by the failure of the regime's institutions to fulfil the purposes allotted to them, persistent non-compliance by one or several of the parties, desuetude, withdrawal by parties instrumental for the regime, among other causes. Whether a regime has "failed" in this sense, however, would have to be assessed above all by an interpretation of its constitutional instruments. In the event of failure, the relevant general law becomes applicable.

4.   Article 31(3)(c) VCLT

(17) *Systemic integration.* Article 31(3)(c) VCLT provides one means within the framework of the VCLT, through which relationships of interpretation (referred to in conclusion (2) above) may be applied. It requires the interpreter of a treaty to take into account "any relevant rules of international law applicable in relations between the parties". The article gives expression to the objective of "systemic integration" according to which, whatever their subject matter, treaties are a creation of the international legal system and their operation is predicated upon that fact.

(18) *Interpretation as integration in the system.* Systemic integration governs all treaty interpretation, the other relevant aspects of which are set out in the other paragraphs of articles 31–32 VCLT. These paragraphs describe a process of legal reasoning, in which particular elements will have greater or less relevance depending upon the nature of the treaty provisions in the context of interpretation. In many cases, the issue of interpretation will be capable of resolution with the framework of the treaty itself. Article 31 (3) (c) deals with the case where material sources external to the treaty are relevant in its interpretation. These may include other treaties, customary rules or general principles of law.[1022]

* * *

5.   Conflicts between successive norms

(24) *Lex posterior derogat legi priori.* According to article 30 VCLT, when all the parties to a treaty are also parties to an earlier treaty on the

---

1022.   In the *Oil Platforms* case *(Iran v. United States of America) (Merits) I.C.J. Reports 2003*, at para. 41, the Court spoke of the relations between a bilateral treaty and general international law by reference to article 31(3)(c) as follows: "Moreover, under the general rules of treaty interpretation, as reflected in the 1969 Vienna Convention on the Law of Treaties, interpretation must take into account 'any relevant rules of international law applicable in the relations between the parties' (Article 31, paragraph 3(c)). The Court cannot accept that Article XX, paragraph 1(d), of the 1955 Treaty was intended to operate wholly independently of the relevant rules of international law ... The application of the relevant rules of international law relating to this question thus forms an integral part of the task of interpretation entrusted to the Court by ... the 1955 Treaty."

same subject, and the earlier treaty is not suspended or terminated, then it applies only to the extent its provisions are compatible with those of the later treaty. This is an expression of the principle according to which "later law supersedes earlier law".

(25) *Limits of the "lex posterior" principle.* The applicability of the *lex posterior* principle is, however, limited. It cannot, for example, be automatically extended to the case where the parties to the subsequent treaty are not identical to the parties of the earlier treaty.

* * *

6. Hierarchy in international law: *Jus cogens*, Obligations *erga omnes*, Article 103 of the Charter of the United Nations

(31) *Hierarchical relations between norms of international law.* The main sources of international law (treaties, custom, general principles of law as laid out in Article 38 of the Statute of the International Court of Justice) are not in a hierarchical relationship *inter se.*[1029] Drawing analogies from the hierarchical nature of domestic legal system is not generally appropriate owing to the differences between the two systems. Nevertheless, some rules of international law are more important than other rules and for this reason enjoy a superior position or special status in the international legal system. This is sometimes expressed by the designation of some norms as "fundamental" or as expressive of "elementary considerations of humanity"[1030] or "intransgressible principles of international law".[1031] What effect such designations may have is usually determined by the relevant context or instrument in which that designation appears.

(32) *Recognized hierarchical relations by the substance of the rules: Jus cogens.* A rule of international law may be superior to other rules on account of the importance of its content as well as the universal acceptance of its superiority. This is the case of peremptory norms of international law (*jus cogens*, Article 53 VCLT), that is, norms "accepted and recognized by the international community of States as a whole from which no derogation is permitted".[1032]

(33) *The content of jus cogens.* The most frequently cited examples of *jus cogens* norms are the prohibition of aggression, slavery and the slave trade, genocide, racial discrimination, apartheid and torture, as well as

---

1029.   In addition, Article 38(d) mentions "judicial decisions and the teachings of the most highly qualified publicists of the various nations, as subsidiary means for the determination of rules of law".

1030.   *Corfu Channel case (United Kingdom v. Albania) I.C.J. Reports 1949,* p. 22.

1031.   *Legality of the Threat or Use of Nuclear Weapons case,* Advisory Opinion, *I.C.J. Reports 1996,* para. 79.

1032.   Article 53 VCLT: A treaty is void if, at the time of its conclusion, it conflicts with a peremptory norm of general international law. For the purposes of the present Convention, a peremptory norm of general international law is a norm accepted and recognized by the international community of States as a whole as a norm from which no derogation is permitted and which can be modified only by a subsequent norm of general international law having the same character.

basic rules of international humanitarian law applicable in armed conflict, and the right to self-determination.[1033] Also other rules may have a *jus cogens* character inasmuch as they are accepted and recognized by the international community of States as a whole as norms from which no derogation is permitted.

(34) *Recognized hierarchical relations by virtue of a treaty provision: Article 103 of the Charter of the United Nations.* A rule of international law may also be superior to other rules by virtue of a treaty provision. This is the case of Article 103 of the United Nations Charter by virtue of which "In the event of a conflict between the obligations of the Members of the United Nations under the . . . Charter and their obligations under any other international agreement, their obligations under the . . . Charter shall prevail."

(35) *The scope of Article 103 of the Charter.* The scope of Article 103 extends not only to the Articles of the Charter but also to binding decisions made by United Nations organs such as the Security Council.[1034] Given the character of some Charter provisions, the constitutional character of the Charter and the established practice of States and United Nations organs, Charter obligations may also prevail over inconsistent customary international law.

(36) *The status of the United Nations Charter.* It is also recognized that the United Nations Charter itself enjoys special character owing to the fundamental nature of some of its norms, particularly its principles and purposes and its universal acceptance.[1035]

(37) *Rules specifying obligations owed to the international community as a whole: Obligations erga omnes.* Some obligations enjoy a special status owing to the universal scope of their applicability. This is the case of obligations *erga omnes*, that is obligations of a State towards the international community as a whole. These rules concern all States and all States can be held to have a legal interest in the protection of the rights involved. Every State may invoke the responsibility of the State violating such obligations.

(38) *The relationship between jus cogens norms and obligations erga omnes.* It is recognized that while all obligations established by *jus cogens* norms, as referred to in conclusion (33) above, also have the character of

---

1033. *Official Records of the General Assembly, Fifty-sixth Session, Supplement 10* (A/56/10), commentary to article 40 of the draft articles on State Responsibility, paras. (4)–(6). See also commentary to article 26, para. (5).

See also *Case concerning armed activities on the territory of the Congo* (Democratic Republic of the Congo v. Rwanda) I.C.J. Reports 2006, para. 64.

1034. *Questions of Interpretation and Application of the 1971 Montreal Convention arising from the Aerial Incident at Lockerbie (Libyan Arab Jamahiriya v. United States of America) (Provisional Measures)* I.C.J. Reports 1998, para. 42 and *Case concerning Questions of Interpretation and Application of the 1971 Montreal Convention arising from the Aerial Incident at Lockerbie (Libyan Arab Jamahiriya v. the United Kingdom) (Provisional Measures)* I.C.J. Reports 1992, paras. 39–40.

1035. See Article 2(6) of the Charter of the United Nations.

erga omnes obligations, the reverse is not necessarily true. Not all *erga omnes* obligations are established by peremptory norms of general international law. This is the case, for example, of certain obligations under "the principles and rules concerning the basic rights of the human person",[1039] as well as of some obligations relating to the global commons.[1040]

* * *

(40) *The relationship between jus cogens and the obligations under the United Nations Charter.* The United Nations Charter has been universally accepted by States and thus a conflict between *jus cogens* norms and Charter obligations is difficult to contemplate. In any case, according to Article 24(2) of the Charter, the Security Council shall act in accordance with the Purposes and Principles of the United Nations which include norms that have been subsequently treated as *jus cogens*.

* * *

The growing body of courts and tribunals can help ensure universality by employing certain approaches to decision-making. Formalism, for example, is a legal method that strives for objective analysis of law, minimizing reliance on personal opinion, personal moral views, or the personal policy of the one analyzing the law. Formal analysis of a treaty is based on strict adherence to the treaty text as opposed to the reader interpreting words to reach personal objectives. Formal analysis of customary law is based on careful assessment of practice and *opinio juris*.

3.   COMMUNITY BUILDING

The excerpts in this section discuss on-going practices within the international system that promote the continuing development of international community. The final excerpt indicates what more should be done to create truly universal law for the world community.

Dianne Otto, Rethinking the "Universality" of Human Rights Law*

29 COLUM. HUM. RTS. L. REV. 1 (1997–1998)

Universality still has a role in a transformative paradigm, but it is universality understood as dialogue, in the sense of struggle against domination, rather than as a disciplinary civilizing mission of Europe.

1039.   *Barcelona Traction case* * * *.

1040.   The obligations are illustrated by article 1 of the Treaty on Principles Governing the Activities of States in the Exploration and Use of Outer Space, including the Moon and Other Celestial Bodies, United Nations, *Treaty Series*, vol. 610, p. 205 and article 136 of the United Nations Convention on the Law of the Sea, United Nations, *Treaty Series*, vol. 1834, p. 396.

* Some footnotes omitted.

Many human rights theorists and activists advocate the importance of dialogue.[126] Postcolonial theorist Raimundo Pannikar, for example, suggests that while human value exists only in a particular cultural context, "there may be cross-cultural values and a cross-cultural critique is indeed possible."[127] He advocates a "healthy pluralism" whereby people are made aware that human rights is only one of a plurality of windows through which different cultures imagine human dignity.[128] However, this kind of approach, while consistent with the CRT idea of multiple consciousness, can easily slip into the rainbow coalition classification wherein anything becomes acceptable, without some "methodological precautions," to borrow a Foucauldian idea.[129] I prefer to use the term "ethics."

The articulation of ethical struggle is, in my view, at the center of the transformative project of universality. Smart is correct when she says:

> [I]f we abandon the idea of an ultimate Truth or correctness, then we have to allow ethics back into the discussion. Ethics should not be the subtext on which we rely to negate oppositional stances, they should be openly addressed.

Also, Harris, arguing for *disenchantment* with the presumed cohesion of modern identity categories, stresses that solidarity is produced by struggle that includes moral and ethical struggle, not solely political struggle. I suggest three ethical struggles, not an exhaustive list, that are critical to the idea of transformative universality in human rights law. These struggles might perhaps be likened to the principles that have guided, though admittedly not necessarily progressively, the development of the law of equity in the common law.[132]

First, transformative dialogue can take place only in a context where participants acknowledge and address disparities in power.[133] Human rights lawyer Abdullahi An–Na'im highlights this issue when he says that "ideally participants [in dialogue] should feel on an equal footing but, given existing power relations, those in a position to do so might seek ways of redressing the imbalance."[134] I would go much farther and insist that transparency of the operations of global networks of power, of exploitation and domination,

---

126.   * * * Abdullahi An–Na'im, *Islam, Islamic Law and the Dilemma of Cultural Legitimacy for Universal Human Rights, in* Human Rights in Cross–Cultural Perspective: A Quest For Consensus 31 (Abdullahi An–Na'im ed., 1992).

127.   Raimundo Pannikar, *Is The Notion of Human Rights a Western Concept?, 120* Diogenes 76, 87–88 (1982).

128.   *Id.* at 79.

129.   Foucault, *Two Lectures, * * * at 96.*

132.   Michael Chesterman, *Equity in the Law, in* A Just Society? Essays in Equity in Australia 51, 63 (P.N. Troyed., 1981); *see also* Sir Anthony Mason, *Themes and Prospects, in* Essays in Equity 242 (Paul Finn ed., 1985).

133.   Anne Orford, *Citizenship, Sovereignty and Globalization: Teaching International Law in the Post–Soviet Era,* 6 Legal Educ. Rev. 251, 251–52 (1995).

134.   Abdullahi An–Na'im, *What Do We Mean By Universal?,* 5 Index on Censorship 120, 122 (1994).

is a vitally important component of transformative dialogue. Human rights tribunals and monitoring mechanisms must be redesigned to take account of inequalities in power, in order to find ways to admit the voices of modernity's Others and incommensurables. This reshaping goes well beyond the modern project of expanding the pluralist democratic polity by including the views of Others. It involves acting ethically by interrogating any privileges we might enjoy as a result of Europe's masculinist hegemony, and taking responsibility for the associated relations of dominating power. In other words, transformative strategies involve transformation of the self[135] as concomitant to rethinking the systems of which we are all a part.

Second, transformative dialogue involves the *unlearning* of privileged epistemologies by those who benefit from them. We have an ethical responsibility to recognize and positively assert the diversity of the world. Spivak raises this issue in the context of the possibility of dialogue between European feminists and subaltern women:

> In seeking to learn to speak to (rather than listen to or speak for) the historically muted subject of the subaltern woman, the postcolonial intellectual *systematically* "unlearns" female privilege. This systematic unlearning involves learning to critique postcolonial discourse with the best tools it can provide and not simply substituting the lost figure of the colonized.

This unlearning means making a radical break from "the ferocious standardizing benevolence" of European knowledges that force the translation of difference into the terms of the dominant discourse. Speaking *to* and *among* Europe's Others and incommensurables requires acknowledging one's own positionality, resisting the hierarchization and erasure of difference, and opening oneself to uncertainty—attributes that are unfamiliar to modernity. It requires too that international lawyers and human rights activists confront, in our work, Chakrabarty's ethical question of whether "genuinely 'nonviolative' relations between the Self (the 'West') and its Other" are possible.

Third, transformative dialogue must also be based on an ethical commitment to address the *material* aspects of human dignity, and thus to promote global economic justice and substantive equality. As the Soviet Union pointed out in 1948, gross disparities in social, economic, and political power contradict the idea of universal principles. As these inequalities are deepened by post-Cold War economic restructuring,[139] transformative dialogue between the various interests of the people of the world, without a redistribution of wealth, becomes ever more inconceivable.[140] The

---

135. *See* Tracey E. Higgins, *Anti–Essentialism, Relativism and Human Rights,* 19 Harv. Women's L.J. 89, at 115 (1996).

139. *See* Julie Stephens, *Running Interface: An Interview with Gayatri Chakravorty Spivak,* 7 Austl. Women's Book Rev. 19, 20 (1995); *see also* J. Brecher & T. Costello, Global Village or Global Pillage: Economic Restructuring From the Bottom Up (1994).

140. *See* Martti Koskenniemi, *The Future of Statehood,* 32 Harv. Int'l L.J. 397, 403–04 (1991).

dialogue of transformative universality must make the ethical move of embracing, in its practice, the indivisibility of the pursuit of individual and collective liberty, and the achievement of global material justice. At the very least, this move means ensuring that the concept of human rights includes social rights and economic justice.

Thus, universality, in the transformative sense, involves continuous political and ethical struggle between differences and across incommensurabilities. These struggles, as I have argued, are usefully informed by aspects of both modern and poststructural ideals and practices. Following Harris, universality rethought in this way might be understood as lying in the tensions or intersections between modernism and poststructuralism. There are many other intersections which might inform transformative universality, two of which are particularly relevant to human rights discourse: one, the tension between local and global knowledges; two, the tension between the interests of the individual and the collective interests of their community.

Turning to the first issue, the problem of the relationship between the local and the global has always been present in human rights law. However, to assert the local in a transformative paradigm is not to claim greater authenticity or validity for certain knowledges over others. Nor is the meaning of *local* equivalent to the nation-state as it is often understood in international law. Instead, local knowledges can be found in many locations that are not necessarily territorially defined. For example, the *locality* of women's or sexuality movements or of subaltern peoples may traverse many territorially local constituencies, and may even be transnational in certain instances.

In this way, transformative universality opens spaces for dialogue within and beyond the nation-state, in transnational as well as intranational solidarities. It also readmits the embodied and situated subject to human rights discourse; displacing the preconstituted, universal Subject (Man) of modernity. A transformative notion of local might be likened to international legal theorist James Boyle's image of the unreified expression of politics that would accompany a rejection of the Enlightenment search for essences in international law.[141] Rather than addressing the imponderables of the relationship between local and global knowledges by searching for an absolute statement, the relationship should be recognized as one of the productive intersections which are integral to transformative dialogue. As postcolonial feminist Chantal Mouffe explains this process, "[u]niversalism is not rejected but particularized."[142]

---

141. James Boyle, *Ideals and Things: International Legal Scholarship and the Prison-House of Language*, 26 Harv. Int'l L.J. 327, 330–32 (1985).

142. *See* Chantal Mouffe, *Radical Democracy: Modern or Postmodern?, in* Universal Abandon? The Politics of Postmodernism 31, 36 (Andrew Ross ed., 1988).

Jean Porter, Ministers of Law: Authority, Reason, and the Natural Law*

(forthcoming)

A. The claims of humanity and the authority of international law

The authority of the nation-state is properly bounded by the authoritative rights claims of individuals—if we are persuaded by this, then we will more readily accept the claim that the authoritative claims of nation-states are also bounded by international law. Yet international law, like customary law, has long been regarded as problematic, especially for those who hold that legal force depends on the formal enactment on the part of a legitimate, authoritative lawmaker. The difficulty from this perspective is of course simply that there is no agency that can credibly claim comprehensive law-making authority over all the peoples of the world. In many instances, international law seems to emerge from what are, in effect, the customary practices of nations and peoples. Even those norms which look most like formal enactments—treaties, trade agreements, the decrees and conventions of international bodies, and the like—are grounded in the free agreements of formally equal political authorities, rather than the enactments of some formally acknowledged legal authority. For the early legal positivists, who claimed that the lawgiver must rely on some authority above that of the community, these were insurmountable obstacles.

This particular construal of legal authority was decisively undermined by Hart, who as we have seen argues that the authority of the lawgiver is on the contrary dependent on the community, operating through a contingent rule of recognition. Seen from a natural law perspective, these rules of recognition are expressions of the political authority of the community itself, which has a reasonable claim to regulate its own affairs in such a way as to sustain a common way of life. Thus, there is nothing necessarily problematic about the claim that international law can be genuinely law, even though it is not formally enacted. As we have seen, the same may be said, in an extended but legitimate sense, of customary law.

However, international law is problematic in another way, seen from a natural law perspective—and not only from that perspective. On a natural law account, political and legal authority stem from the authority of the community, insofar as the institutions of governance and the legal system serve the purposes of safeguarding and expressing the values and commitments that sustain the common life of the polity. International law does not, and by its intrinsic character cannot represent the authority of a cohesive community in this way. Whatever else it may be, international law is first and foremost a set of norms or practices pertaining to the activities of collective entities, and secondarily, to individuals as they move across and outside the boundaries of organized political communities. And cosmopolitan fantasies to the contrary notwithstanding, the peoples and individuals of the world cannot form a polity in the relevant sense. The sheer fact of

---

* Footnotes omitted.

human diversity, and the irreducible plurality of cultures and ways of life stemming from that diversity, rule out the possibility of developing a deep, substantive conception of human happiness and the common good in which all the peoples of the world can share.

And yet, it is manifestly the case that the nations of the world do acknowledge and comply with the norms of international law, at least in most instances, even when compliance works against a nation's immediate interests. Nor should this state of affairs surprise us. Even though the peoples of the world do not form a polity, unified by shared ideals and commitments, nonetheless we do share enough to engage in processes of rhetorical deliberation and persuasion. We share a common humanity, and while this does not by itself yield a comprehensive, concrete moral system, or much less sufficient basis for a comprehensive formal law, it does provide a basis for shared agreement on at least the outer limits of tolerable behavior, and the scope and force of the most exigent demands for mutual aid. What is more, ongoing processes of rhetorical persuasion have given rise to a considerable body of shared agreements with respect to a very wide range of matters, including everything from mundane agreements on the proper use of shared resources to the intricacies of shared economic structures. These are themselves conventional and contingent— they may well have been decided differently—but to a considerable extent they are so deeply entrenched as to seem natural, and to provide an uncontroversial framework within which more specific rules and agreements can be worked out as needed. As contingent expressions of judgement, which nonetheless stem from natural considerations, they reflect genuine expressions of authority, the authority of humanity itself arranging its own affairs in those contexts in which shared activity calls for some such arrangements. Thus, even though the peoples of the world do not constitute a polity, they do nonetheless constitute a kind of extended community by virtue of their ongoing mutual interactions and the limited yet vitally important shared interests that can only be pursued in common. We can therefore speak, in an extended but legitimate way, of a world community bearing its own proper self-governing authority.

This authority is in turn expressed (*inter alia*) by norms of international law, which are constituted as such through common consent. To a very considerable extent, the specific norms in question emerge through the customary practices of the nations. As Theodor Meron points out, "General practice of states which is accepted and observed as law, i.e. from a sense of legal obligation builds norms of customary international law." Acknowledged customary law, in turn, is typically codified through treaties and other instruments of international law, but as Meron goes on to observe, "It is, of course, not the treaty norm, but the customary norm with identical content, that binds such states." This, as he goes on to say, helps to explain why the norms of customary international law can be regarded as binding on nation-states generally, even those who do not accept the treaty or instrument in question. Thus understood, treaties and other instruments are thus not enactments that create new laws, but attempts to formulate what is regarded as already existing law—identified, debated, and eventually given formal expression through the familiar processes of rhetorical persuasion, carried out in the court of world opinion. What is more, actual courts once again serve as the gatekeepers for the law, adjudicating the claims of collective entities and individuals on the basis of their best sense of what, substantively, the practices comprising international law are, and what they imply. To a very considerable extent, even more perhaps than with judges operating within the legal system of some polity, judges at this level must rely on normative construals of the law. As Meron explains,

> Elementary considerations of humanity reflect basic community values whether already crystallized as binding norms of international law or not. Professor Brownlie has observed that "considerations of humanity may depend on the subjective appreciation of the judge, but more objectively, they may be related to human values already protected by positive legal principles which, taken together, reveal certain criteria of public policy ..." The fact that the content of a norm reflects important considerations of humanity should promote its acceptance as customary law. Thus, in explaining why the Geneva Conventions can be regarded as approaching "international legislation," Hersch Lauterpacht stated that, among other reasons, "many of the provisions of these Conventions, following as they do from compelling considerations of humanity, are declaratory of universally binding international custom."

The authority of international law thus does not presuppose the authority of a lawgiver, even on a theoretical or notional level. It reflects the authority of humanity as articulated and expressed through an ongoing history, reaching into (what we hope) is an open-ended future. What is more, like every other authoritative decree, this communal consent expresses a shared judgement that these norms express rational and natural principles of action in a defensible way. And just as customary law and natural rights claims can be vindicated through judicial processes, even apart from formal enactments, so the authoritative judgements of humanity can be vindicated through courts of all kinds, whose authority is recognized—again—through contingent yet rational determinations of recognition. This situation is not so anomalous as it may seem—after all, throughout the early medieval period, European legal systems functioned without formal legislators, sustaining the rule of law through the judgements of courts. Even though there is no such thing as a generally acknowledged, comprehensive legislative authority governing the peoples of the world, legal authority is properly expressed at this level nonetheless, through customary practices as (partially) expressed through treaties and other instruments, as adjudicated by generally acknowledged courts.

C.G. Weeramantry, Universalising International Law
pp. 197–205 (2004)

6.   Necessary Extensions of Some Primary Concepts

(i) *Widening of the category of peremptory norms*

There are certain principles of international law which are so deeply entrenched that no state is free to disregard them. No treaty arrangements, no amount of acquiescence by another state, no excuses or justifications can override them.

This category is based upon the principle, first clearly formulated by the International Court in the *Barcelona Traction* case (Second Phase) that such obligations are due to the international community as a whole. They cannot therefore be derogated from.

A need of the future will be to expand this category of peremptory norms so as to include conduct which is violative of global peace either directly or potentially. The limitation of such peremptory prohibition to acts such as genocide is not enough. Genocide does not suddenly erupt but is the result of a variety of factors that promote it such as the propagation of hate literature and indoctrination in schools. The acts may not be as clear cut as genocide itself but they are often identifiable and can be prevented. A general norm of international law can be evolved outlawing such conduct so that gross and identifiable perpetrations of it can be located and prevented.

In fact it may not be too fanciful to think in terms of a court or tribunal of eminent persons before whom such complaints can be brought, whose findings will carry great persuasive authority in the international community.

The same applies to major environmental hazards. It is not merely when the hazard actually occurs which endangers a million lives that the principle should come into play, but when preparations are afoot for the action which has the potential of causing this disaster.

Peremptory or *jus cogens* norms need to be applicable on a more extensive scale to such matters as health hazards and biological experimentation that carries possible global hazards such as the spread of epidemics. For example, xenotransplantation, (i.e. the transplantation of animal organs into human beings) is thought to carry risks of a pandemic of AIDS type proportions which could endanger human health globally, and there could conceivably be an extension to such experimentation of the *jus cogens* principle. This may be especially important because there is not in place as yet an international mechanism for monitoring or controlling such experimentation.

Xenotransplantation is just one small area of scientific activity used here only for purposes of illustrating a much larger category of possible irreversible dangers to the global public, which can result if international law is slow in bringing such areas within the domain of peremptory norms.

Such considerations bring into play also the precautionary principle which modem environmental law is now raising to the status of a norm of customary international law. The precautionary principle in cases of such grave danger to the human condition can well be elevated to the level of *jus cogens*. It will be remembered that Principle 15 of the Rio Declaration on

Environment and Development, one of the outcomes of the Earth Summit held in Rio De Janeiro in June 1992, stated that:

> "In order to protect the environment, the precautionary approach shall be widely applied by states according to their capabilities. Where there are threats of serious or irreversible damage, lack of scientific certainty shall not be used as a reason for postponing cost-effective measures to prevent environmental degradation."

International law needs to be far-sighted enough to consider bringing such principles within the ambit of peremptory norms where there is a credible threat of a danger that can affect the global population or a considerable segment of it. Tardiness in according recognition to such a principle, may be likened to closing the stable door after the horse has bolted.

The urgency and universality of this need were emphasised also in the Cartagena Protocol on Bio-safety to the Convention on Biological Diversity signed in New Zealand on 25 May 2000. The Protocol dealt specifically with the safe transfer, handling and use of living modified organisms resulting from modern biotechnology that may have adverse effects on the conservation and sustainable use of biological diversity.

A principal reason supporting the extension of the *jus cogens* principles to situations such as this is the irreversibility of the damage that may ensue. Once such an item of damage is inflicted on the environment, humanity would have to live with it for the rest of time and effects can well escalate over the generations. This is as powerful an argument as can be found for elevating any particular form of activity to the level of attracting *jus cogens* principles.

Whether in the field of nuclear experimentation, mining technology, cross species breeding, bio-medical technology, chemical and biological weapons experimentation or any of its multifarious fields of new development, modern technology has the ability to impair and undermine some of the most basic legal protections offered by legal systems both domestic and international. These are often of absolutely fundamental importance and legal protections are sought to be set up too late in the day, when the technology is already well on its way.

Widening the category of peremptory norms and an increased vigilance in guarding against possible sources of denigration will be required of international law in the future.

(ii) *Widening the concept of common amenities*

Cooperation in the use of earth resources will be an imperative of the future, and international law will need to reflect this need.

The necessary recognition of this concept of international law lags far behind the needs of the age. In this area, in which perhaps international law needs to strike out on a path of its own, it is excessively dependent on the concepts and practices of municipal law. Yet municipal law itself has lagged far behind contemporary need. Consequently international law is several steps behind the level of concern and competence required of it on the world scene today.

To quote a well-known text, Brownlie, writing on common amenities and cooperation in the use of resources, observes "International law has tended so far to ape the individualistic manners of municipal law. Apart from the concepts of *res communis* as applied to the high seas and outer space, and 'the common heritage of mankind', international law depends to a large extent on voluntarist devices, in the form of concessions by private law methods, treaties and various types of international agencies and organisations, in order to provide access to resources outside national territory."

Brownlie's observations deftly pinpoint a principal source of this inadequacy—namely the individualistic orientation of domestic legal systems which have still not attuned themselves to thinking in terms of the larger communal interest rather than the narrow, rights oriented individualistic framework.

When earth resources are fast running out and even such methods for the exploitation of such resources as are available can cause much public harm, a cooperative and communitarian approach is required for husbanding, both for ourselves and for future generations, such slender stocks as now exist. Moreover, the technology to reach these stocks is largely in the hands of the affluent world with scarcely a prospect of such resources becoming available to the poor world before those resources run out. The result will be their exploitation by the industrialized world before the non-industrialised world can lay its hands upon them. What is undeniably a common resource of all humanity would then be denied to the bulk of humanity, who are all equal co-sharers of these planetary benefits.

Common resources regimes need to be set up and common resources principles and practices worked out. International law has before it the necessary principles for handling this problem if only it were prepared to draw upon global wisdom and experience as displayed in various cultures and civilisations over the last two or three millennia. Rights of future generations, the precautionary principle, obligations *erga omnes,* communal rules in regard to the preservation of common amenities, principles of trusteeship, principles of conservation and the like are richly available in the human heritage. International law needs to widen its conceptual framework to draw from them the guidance and wisdom which can be derived from them.

Areas where these principles become specially applicable are international rivers, the high seas, outer space, the polar regions and even within national boundaries there will need to be a custody under international trusteeship of particular types of scarce resources and of fauna and flora.

Some incipient effort in this direction may offer a prototype for emulation in other areas and reference may be made in this connection to the Helsinki Rules on the Uses of Waters of International Rivers, adopted by the International Law Association in 1966. Its various articles dealt with such matters as equitable and reasonable utilisation and participation (Art. 5) the obligation not to cause significant harm (Art. 6) the general obligation to co-operate (Art. 8) and the regular exchange of data or information. (Art. 9).

In outer space as well the framework is being laid for such a cooperative regime. The areas of operation of such efforts need to be vastly extended, and the conceptual and procedural work vastly intensified.

(iii) *Scope of Legitimacy of State Conduct*

The international law of the future needs to re-evaluate its concepts in regard to what state conduct is permitted and what is not.

There is a spurious doctrine coming down from the past, completely outmoded in the inter-dependent global world of today, that a state is free to indulge in any conduct save that which is expressly prohibited by some rule of international law or by its treaty arrangements with other states. Support is sought for this view from the *Lotus case* where the Court, in the absence of a principle or specific rule to which Turkey had expressly consented, held that the authority of the Turkish State should not be limited.

Even if the Permanent Court intended to propound such a general principle—and these are weighty arguments that can be urged against such a construction—such a negative view is entirely inconsistent with the needs of the future. In an age of inter-state cooperation rather than mere state co-existence, what international law is in search of is not a negative doctrine of abstention from prohibited conduct but a positive principle encouraging states towards active assistance in the cause of global peace and harmony.

This can be likened to the contrast between the principle of the common law that a person can with impunity pass by a scene where another is in dire trouble, e.g. a child drowning in a puddle of water, without giving assistance which could have saved that individual without any damage to the passer by. In most civil law systems an active duty of assistance would be imposed in such situations. Indeed in Islamic law there is the principle of bidding unto good, which requires a person to go to the assistance of a neighbour in distress.

International law in the future needs to shake off this attitude of apathy resulting from individualistic principles which find a place in some legal systems, at the expense of the general interest. The world order of the future will abound in situations of failed states or urgent environmental hazards or hyper destructive damage scenarios in which it will be the duty of all states that can help, to cooperate in rendering assistance for the communal welfare of the world community.

In disaster situations the goodwill of the world community often becomes evident, but the resulting acts of assistance are treated as examples of generosity rather than fulfilment of legal duty. International law thinking needs to be so restructured as to introduce an element of duty into such conduct rather than to leave it to the spirit of altruism of the states concerned.

The view that all state conduct is permissible which is not expressly prohibited tends also to blunt the application of a vast range of principles of international law which in effect prescribe norms of conduct. To take a telling example, reliance was placed on such a line of argument in the case of *Threat or Use of Nuclear Weapons,* in which an opinion was sought by the General Assembly from the International Court on the legality of such threat or use. The lack of express prohibition of the use of nuclear weapons was relied on as an argument against illegality. A vast range of principles of humanitarian law, human rights law and environmental law tend to be glossed over when such an approach is adopted. These principles were more than sufficient to render any use of nuclear weapons illegal despite the absence of any rule or treaty obligation specifically banning the use of nuclear weapons.

There are so many developing areas of state activity ranging from information technology, space exploration, environmental pollution, chemical and bacteriological weapons, to nuclear technology which are so new and sometimes so unimaginable that it is idle to look for specific prohibitions. What we are seeking is the relevant broader applicable principle which can take within its orbit the particular activity in question. Thus alone can such activities be effectively handled, leading thereby to the progressive development of international law.

(iv) *Extending the concept of legitimate interests*

International law gives recognition to the principle of legitimate interests in determining what claims are entitled to protection and what are not. Its determinations in doing so can lead to the progressive development of international law, for new interests may receive recognition in this way.

There are various categories of interests, which will need to receive recognition in the future, such as economic interests, environmental interests, cultural interests and historical and archaeological interests. The recognition of such interests is based on such considerations as fairness, reasonableness, equity, equality, good faith, acquiescence, recognition and the like but what is important is that through the operation of these principles, legitimate interests not traditionally accorded recognition may receive increasing recognition and lead to the progressive development of international law as an instrument sensitive to the various needs of different regions, peoples and cultures.

In the *Anglo-Norwegian Fisheries Case* the International Court in considering the rules applicable to the Norwegian coastline took into consideration "certain economic interests peculiar to a region, the reality and importance of which are evidenced by long usage." It is interesting also that the Court referred to the fact that "in these barren regions the inhabitants of the coastal zone derive their livelihood essentially from fishing" (p. 128). In the *Jan Mayen* case likewise, considerations of equity played an important role in the Court's decision and in evolving a nuanced application of the law of the sea to a particular situation.

There is an important pointer here to considerations of vital importance to large sections of the global community some of whose essential interests have traditionally been left out of the purview of international law. It is only reasonable to expect that just as such considerations can be taken into account and woven into the principles of the law of the sea, there could be other major areas of international law where such principles, which are of such cardinal importance to the very existence of vast numbers of people, can be taken into account in appropriate cases—always fitting them within accepted principles of international law and, as stated before, leading to the progressive development of the latter.

Considerations of the ways in which people derive their livelihood, the extreme difficulties and privations they endure if deprived of their traditional means and the like are relevant not merely to the law of the sea but to the broader canvas of international law and need to be taken account of in appropriate circumstances. If international law is to widen its conceptual framework, this is an area which cannot be neglected.

Given the vital importance of economic interests in so many departments of international activity, it is important to the evolution of equitable regimes in regard not only to the law of the sea, but also to land usage, environmental protection, employment regimes, global commons, common amenities, intellectual property, the uses of space, international communications technology and the like that the principle of legitimate interests be taken into account in moulding the law of the future—be those interests economic, cultural, historical, regional, or any other.

(v) *The Outlawing of War*

The UN Charter has achieved a great advance over anything known before in international law for, with certain well defined exceptions, it outlaws force or the use of force. War, but for those exceptions, is therefore a thing of the past so far as international law is concerned.

The prohibition contained in Art. 2(4) of the Charter against the threat or use of force applies not merely to their use against the territorial integrity or political independence of any State, but also to their use in any manner inconsistent with the Purposes of the United Nations. Those Purposes include maintenance of international peace and security, development of friendly relations among nations, strengthening universal peace, achieving international cooperation and harmonizing the actions of nations in the attainment of these common ends.

The tightly framed provisions in Chapter VII in relation to the circumstances in which action may be taken with respect to threats to the peace, breaches of the peace and aggression serve, if at all, to accentuate the extremely limited nature of these exceptions. All of these need to be read in the light of the Purposes and Principles of the United Nations and also in the light of the Preamble to the Charter, the very first clause of which expresses the determination of the Peoples of the United Nations "to save succeeding generations from the scourge of war which twice in our lifetime has brought untold sorrow to mankind."

It is vitally important that all readings of the exceptions set out in Chapter VII should be in the context of the conceptual framework of the Charter: This conceptual framework is set out not merely in preambular recitals but in a substantive part of the Charter itself, for they could not be more clearly formulated than they are in Article I. Any action or interpretation in respect of any article of the Charter which does not conform to Article I would be invalid in terms of the Charter.

In other words the Purposes of the Charter need to loom large in any discussions of the application of Chapter VII, thereby whittling down the occasions for the use of force to a narrow rather than a broad interpretation.

Moreover all of these provisions are set in the context of the overriding importance of the peaceful settlement of disputes for which a variety of methodologies and instrumentalities are provided in the Charter.

There is all too often a lingering on into the post-Charter era of habits of thought associated with the international law of the pre-Charter era when war was a normal and accepted method of settling disputes. The concept of peace needs to be strengthened to its widest and strongest proportions, with constant reference to the seminal fact that war is outlawed in the post-Charter world, except for the narrowest of exceptions allowed by the Charter in the most restrictive language.

International law would lack its fundamental orientation if it does not constantly remind the global public that after three millennia of conflict caused by the legality of war, the world community has been able to achieve its illegality through the immense suffering and tribulation of two World Wars. What has been achieved at such great sacrifice cannot be jeopardised by loose interpretations which lose sight of the fundamental framework of the Charter, or an inadequate consciousness that the Charter constitutes one of the most important watersheds in the history of civilisation.

(vi) *Equity*

A much more free ranging inquiry into the sources of equitable principles and the methodology for their application is required. Drawing on equitable concepts and procedures is a powerful method of rendering international law more responsive to the demands of the age and of sensitising the international legal system to the various moral overtones and nuances attendant on its application.

These have been referred to at some length in Chapter 9 below and are hence not expanded on here.

(vii) *New attitudes to sovereignty*

The entire concept of sovereignty needs careful reappraisal in the context of the future needs of international law. The subject is vast and complex, but some attempt to address this question has been made in Chapter 4 above, which it is unnecessary to duplicate here.

(viii) *Increasing Control over the Armaments Industry*

The international legal system has a blind spot in regard to the armaments industry. The trade in weapons of death is permitted to flourish with few and minor restraints upon it although it contravenes every known principle of ethics, human rights and humanitarian conduct. Arms fairs are major events at which the latest and most sophisticated weaponry is proudly displayed. They are patronized by the privileged and the powerful and every subterfuge and loophole which legal ingenuity can devise is placed at the service of arms dealers who wish to evade such regulations as there are in relation to the sale of arms.

Across the world, death and destruction ensue as a result of this trade. At a September 1998 United Nations meeting, US Secretary of State, Madeline Albright said that arms exporting states bear some responsibility for a trade which "fuels conflict, fortifies extremism and destabilises entire regimes." She was saying this in regard to a trade which runs to over a hundred billion dollars annually of which in 1994–96 the US commanded 55 percent.

This trade involves not only multi-million dollar missile systems but also massive stocks of "small arms", and also millions of land mines which have maimed unnumbered thousands of innocent civilians.

One of the arguments of the arms suppliers is that if they do not supply the aims others will. They argue that they make their supplies within the guidelines laid down by their respective governments. The governments argue that the arms are required by the purchasing countries for their security. There is a passing of responsibility at every turn and international law seems quite unable to handle this problem which attacks the very vitals of world peace.

NOTES AND QUESTIONS

1. Which "vision" is most convincing to you? Or are there elements of both that make most sense? What is the single greatest weakness of international law in your view? What is its single greatest strength?

2. Weeramantry argues that international law is certainly not sufficiently universal today but could become so:

> When international law commenced its modern career in the 16th and 17th centuries, it was cast largely in a Graeco–Judaeo–Christian mould. Since then it has moved towards greater universalization. Many more universal perspectives drawn from all the world's cultural traditions can and must be fed into it as it develops to suit the needs of the 21st century. Its success in that century will depend heavily on the extent to which it can be further universalized by harnessing the strength available in the world's rich inheritance of cultural and ideological traditions.

> International law cannot afford to remain set in a narrowly monocultural mould and hope in that form to address problems which are truly

global, multi-cultural and multi-traditional, which cry out for a universal solution.

Compare Weeramantry's perspective with that of Addis Adeno included in Chapter 1 that the very definition of the international community is a community of diversity: "[O]ne aspect of the international community that is imagined through the provision of universal jurisdiction is a community of diverse peoples and diverse ways of being. This diversity defines not only the international community (the community of communities) but the constituent communities (nation-states) as well." Can they both be right?

3.   Some argue for going in a different direction entirely. They are not content with the current structure of international law or to simply critique that structure. They are interested in developing something new. For example:

- Philip Allott argues that what the world needs is a global constitution. See THE HEALTH OF NATIONS, SOCIETY AND LAW BEYOND THE STATE (2002) and EUNOMIA, NEW ORDER FOR A NEW WORLD (2001).

- Richard Falk and Andrew Strauss argue for a global parliament in *Toward Global Parliament*, FOREIGN AFFAIRS, Jan./Feb. 2001.

- Jackie Smith sees social forums as the answer to global challenges. See SOCIAL MOVEMENTS FOR GLOBAL DEMOCRACY (2008) and THE WORLD SOCIAL FORUM AND THE CHALLENGES OF GLOBAL DEMOCRACY (2004).

Do you share the view that we need a radical replacement for international law? If not, what do you see as the greatest need for the system? Acceptance? Structural improvement? New methodology? Common values? A central enforcement agency?

4.   Note that those calling for radical change do not demand a supreme court for the world. Yet, Alec Stone Sweet argues that the existence of the European Court of Justice has been essential in the creation of a European community. See ALEC STONE SWEET, THE JUDICIAL CONSTRUCTION OF EUROPE (2004). Note, too, the emphasis placed by Porter on courts for a community united by law. The international system does not have a similar court, should it develop one? It does have a growing body of international courts (around 300 in 2009). Do you think this large number of courts might have something of the impact of one court of general, compulsory jurisdiction?

5.   For further reading, see, ADDA BOZEMAN, THE FUTURE OF LAW IN A MULTI-CULTURAL WORLD (1970): Richard Falk, LAW IN AN EMERGING GLOBAL VILLAGE: A POST-WESTPHALIAN PERSPECTIVE (1998); INEQUALITY, GLOBALIZATION AND WORLD POLITICS (A. Hurrell and N. Woods eds., 1999); HILARY CHARLESWORTH AND CHRISTINE CHINKIN THE BOUNDARIES OF INTERNATIONAL LAW (2000); MARTTI KOSKENNIEMI, THE GENTLE CIVILIZER OF NATIONS: THE RISE AND FALL OF INTERNATIONAL LAW, 1870–1960 (2002); UNITED STATES HEGEMONY AND THE FOUNDATIONS OF INTERNATIONAL LAW (Michael Byers and Georg Nolte eds., 2003); SHABTAI ROSENNE THE PERPLEXITIES OF MODERN INTERNATIONAL LAW (2004); ANTONY ANGHIE, IMPERIALISM, SOVEREIGNTY AND THE MAKING OF INTERNATIONAL LAW (2005); JOOST PAUWELYN, OPTIMAL PROTECTION OF INTERNATIONAL LAW: NAVIGATING BETWEEN EUROPEAN ABSOLUTISM AND AMERICAN VOLUNTARISM (2008).

TOPICAL INDEX

†